A-Z SH

C000227921

CON

Key to Map Pages	2-
Large Scale City Centre	4-5
Map Pages	6-177
Index to Hospitals etc.	271-272

REFERENCE

Motorway	**M1**
A Road	A629
B Road	B6150
Dual Carriageway	
One-way Street Traffic flow on A Roads is also indicated by a heavy line on the driver's left.	
Road Under Construction Opening dates are correct at time of publication	
Proposed Road	
Restricted Access	
Pedestrianized Road	
Track / Footpath	
Residential Walkway	
Railway	Level Crossing / Station / Heritage Sta. / Tunnel
Supertram The boarding of Supertrams at stops may be limited to a single direction, indicated by the arrow.	Stop
Built-up Area	BURGESS ST.
Local Authority Boundary	
National Park Boundary	
Posttown Boundary	
Postcode Boundary (within Posttown)	
Map Continuation	**86** / Large Scale City Centre **4**

Airport	✈
Car Park (selected)	🅿
Church or Chapel	†
Cycleway (selected)	●●●●●●
Fire Station	■
Hospital	Ⓗ
House Numbers (A & B Roads only)	13 ⋯ 8
Information Centre	🖪
National Grid Reference	⁴45
Park & Ride (Bus or Tram)	Abbeydale **P+R**
Police Station	▲
Post Office	★
Safety Camera with Speed Limit Fixed and long term road works cameras Symbols do not indicate camera direction	(30)
Toilet: without facilities for the Disabled	▽
with facilities for the Disabled	▽
Disabled use only	▽
Viewpoint	🌟 ☀
Educational Establishment	▬
Hospital or Healthcare Building	▬
Industrial Building	▬
Leisure or Recreational Facility	▬
Place of Interest	▬
Public Building	▬
Shopping Centre or Market	▬
Other Selected Buildings	▬

SCALE

Map Pages 6-177 1:18,103

0	¼	½ Mile
0	250	500	750 Metres

3½ inches (8.89 cm) to 1 mile   5.52 cm to 1 km

Map Pages 4-5 1:9,051

0	⅛	¼ Mile
0	100	200	300 Metres

7 inches (17.78 cm) to 1 mile   11.05 cm to 1 km

Copyright of Geographers' A-Z Map Company Limited

Fairfield Road, Borough Green, Sevenoaks, Kent TN15 8PP
Telephone: 01732 781000 (Enquiries & Trade Sales)
01732 783422 (Retail Sales)

www.az.co.uk

Copyright © Geographers' A-Z Map Co. Ltd.
Edition 6 2012

Ordnance Survey® This product includes mapping data licensed from Ordnance Survey® with the permission of the Controller of Her Majesty's Stationery Office.
© Crown Copyright 2011. All rights reserved. Licence number 100017302
Safety camera information supplied by www.PocketGPSWorld.com
Speed Camera Location Database Copyright 2012 © PocketGPSWorld.com

KEY TO MAP PAGES

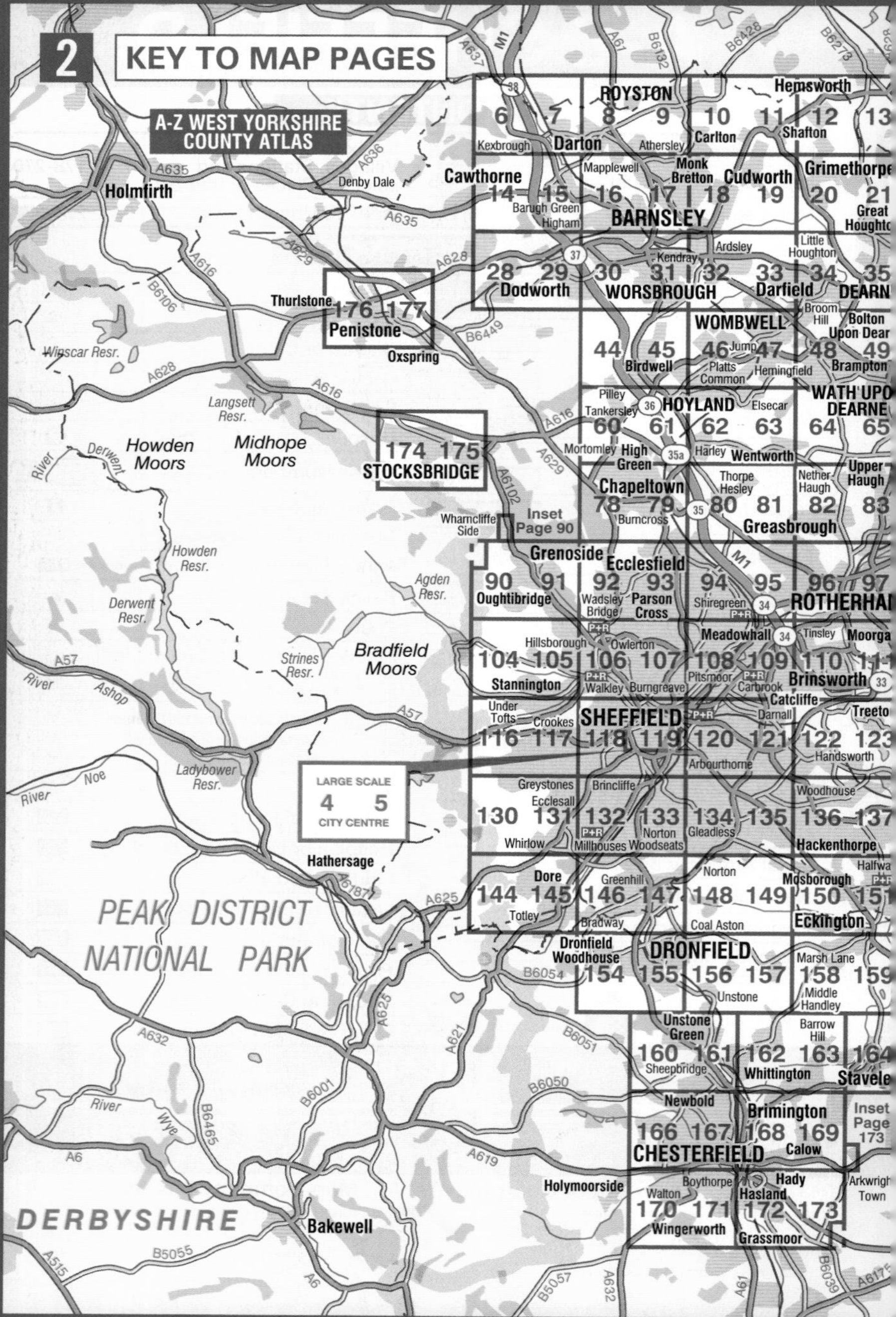

A-Z WEST YORKSHIRE COUNTY ATLAS

Holmfirth

Denby Dale

Holmfirth

ROYSTON   Hemsworth
6 7 8 9 10 11 12 13
Kexbrough Darton Athersley Carlton Shafton
Cawthorne Mapplewell Monk Bretton Cudworth Grimethorpe
14 15 16 17 18 19 20 21
Barugh Green Higham BARNSLEY Great Houghton
Thurlstone 176 177 Kendray Ardsley Little Houghton
Penistone 28 29 30 31 32 33 34 35
Oxspring Dodworth WORSBROUGH Darfield DEARN
Winscar Resr. Broom Hill Bolton Upon Dear
WOMBWELL
44 45 46 47 48 49
Birdwell Jump Platts Common Hemingfield Brampton
Langsett Resr. WATH UPO DEARNE
Howden Moors Midhope Moors Pilley Tankersley HOYLAND Elsecar 64 65
174 175 60 61 62 63
STOCKSBRIDGE Mortomley High Green Harley Wentworth Nether Haugh Upper Haugh
Chapeltown Thorpe Hesley 82 83
Wharncliffe Side 78 79 80 81
Howden Resr. Inset Page 90 Burncross Greasbrough
Derwent Resr. Grenoside Ecclesfield
Agden Resr. 90 91 92 93 94 95 96 97
Strines Resr. Oughtibridge Wadsley Bridge Parson Cross Shiregreen ROTHERHA
Bradfield Moors Hillsborough Owlerton Meadowhall Tinsley Moorga
104 105 106 107 108 109 110 111
Stannington Walkley Burngreave Pitsmoor Carbrook Brinsworth
Ladybower Resr. Under Tofts Crookes SHEFFIELD Darnall Catcliffe Treeto
116 117 118 119 120 121 122 123
LARGE SCALE Arbourthorne Handsworth
4 5 Greystones Brincliffe Woodhouse
CITY CENTRE Ecclesall 130 131 132 133 134 135 136 137
Hathersage Whirlow Millhouses Woodseats Gleadless Hackenthorpe
PEAK DISTRICT Dore Greenhill Norton Mosborough Halfwa
144 145 146 147 148 149 150 151
NATIONAL PARK Totley Bradway Coal Aston Eckington
Dronfield Woodhouse DRONFIELD Marsh Lane 158 159
154 155 156 157 Middle Handley
Unstone
Unstone Green Barrow Hill
160 161 162 163 164
Sheepbridge Whittington Stavele
Newbold Brimington Inset Page 173
166 167 168 169
CHESTERFIELD Calow Arkwrig Town
Holymoorside Walton Boythorpe Hady Hasland 172 173
170 171 Wingerworth Grassmoor

DERBYSHIRE

Bakewell

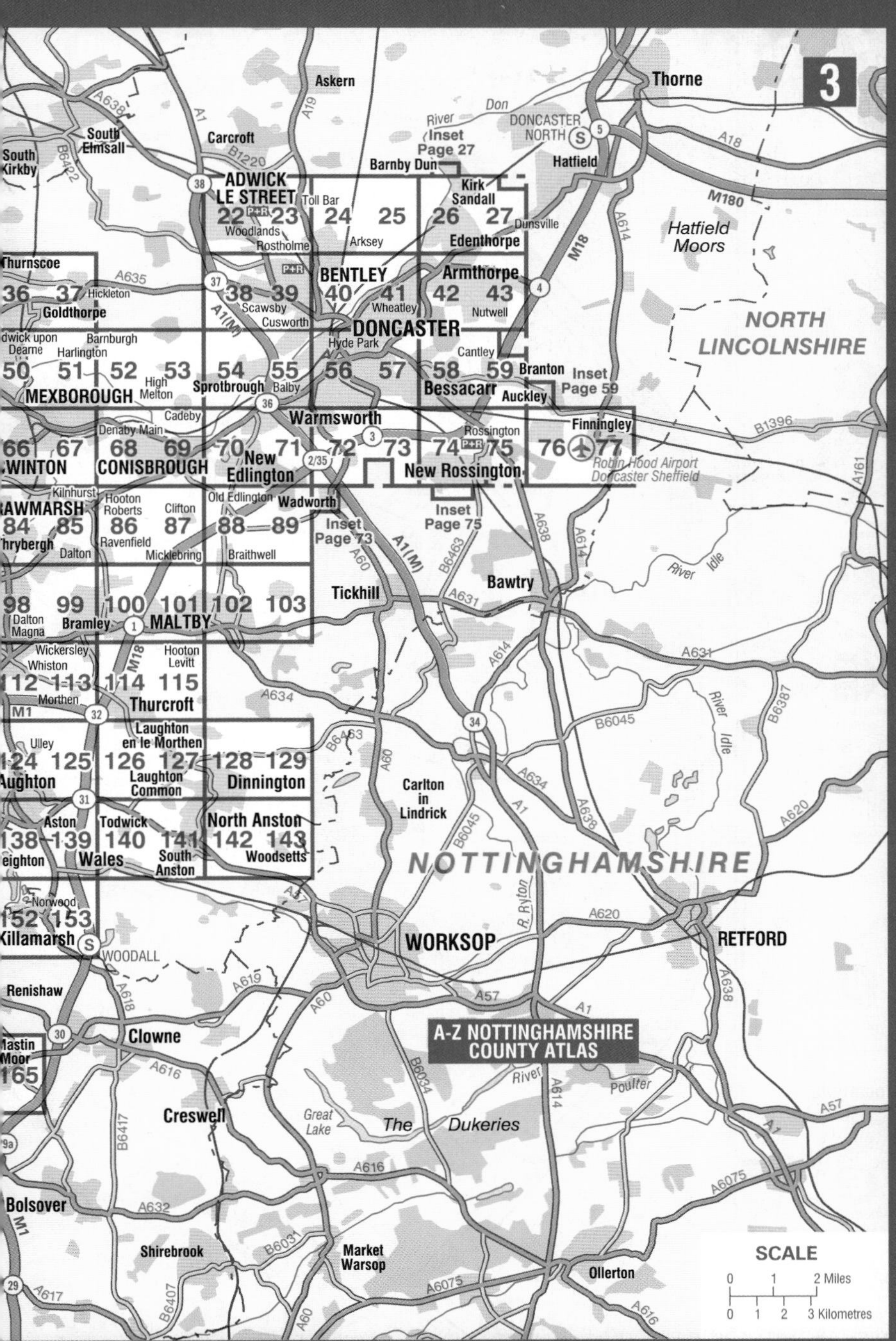

3

Askern

Thorne

River *Don*

DONCASTER NORTH (S)

Carcroft

B1220

Barnby Dun

Hatfield

Kirk Sandall

Dunsville

A18

M180

Hatfield Moors

South Elmsall

A638

South Kirkby

B6422

A1

A19

ADWICK LE STREET

38

22 P+R **23** Toll Bar **24** **25**

Woodlands

Rostholme

Arksey

26 **27**

Edenthorpe

A614

Thurnscoe

A635

Hickleton

37

P+R

38 **39** Scawsby

Cusworth

BENTLEY

40 **41**

Wheatley

DONCASTER

Hyde Park

42 **43**

Armthorpe

Nutwell

4

M18

NORTH LINCOLNSHIRE

36 **37**

Goldthorpe

A1(M)

dwick upon Dearne

Barnburgh

Harlington

50 **51** **52** **53** High Melton

MEXBOROUGH

Sprotbrough

54 **55** Balby

56 **57**

Cantley

58 **59** Branton

Bessacarr Auckley

Inset Page 59

B1396

Cadeby

Warmsworth

3

Denaby Main

66 **67**

WINTON

68 **69** **70** New Edlington

71 **72** **73**

2/35

Rossington

74 P+R **75** **76** + **77**

Finningley

Robin Hood Airport Doncaster Sheffield

A161

CONISBROUGH

New Rossington

A638

A614

River *Idle*

Kilnhurst

Hooton Roberts

Clifton

Old Edlington **Wadworth**

AWMARSH

84 **85**

hrybergh

Dalton

86 **87**

Ravenfield

Micklebring

88 = **89**

Inset Page 73

A1(M)

A60

B6463

Inset Page 75

A638

Tickhill

B6387

98 **99** **100** **101**

Dalton Magna

Bramley

1

MALTBY

102 **103**

Bawtry

A631

A614

River *Idle*

Braithwell

A634

Wickersley

Whiston

M18

Hooton Levitt

112 113 114 **115**

Morthen

M1

32

Thurcroft

A634

B6045

34

Laughton en le Morthen

Ulley

124 125 **126 127** **128 129**

Laughton Common

Dinnington

Carlton in Lindrick

A60

B6045

A634

A1

A638

A620

Aston

31

Todwick

North Anston

138 139 140 141 142 143

eighton

Wales

South Anston

Woodsetts

NOTTINGHAMSHIRE

R. Ryton

Norwood

152 153

Killamarsh (S)

WOODALL

A619

A618

A57

A1

WORKSOP

RETFORD

A638

Renishaw

lastin Moor

30

Clowne

A616

A60

A620

A-Z NOTTINGHAMSHIRE COUNTY ATLAS

165

9a

M1

Creswell

B6417

Great Lake

The *Dukeries*

River *Poulter*

A614

A57

A1

A6075

Bolsover

A632

A616

A616

A57

29

A617

B6407

Shirebrook

B6031

Market Warsop

A60

A6075

Ollerton

A614

A616

A6075

SCALE

0   1   2 Miles

0   1   2   3 Kilometres

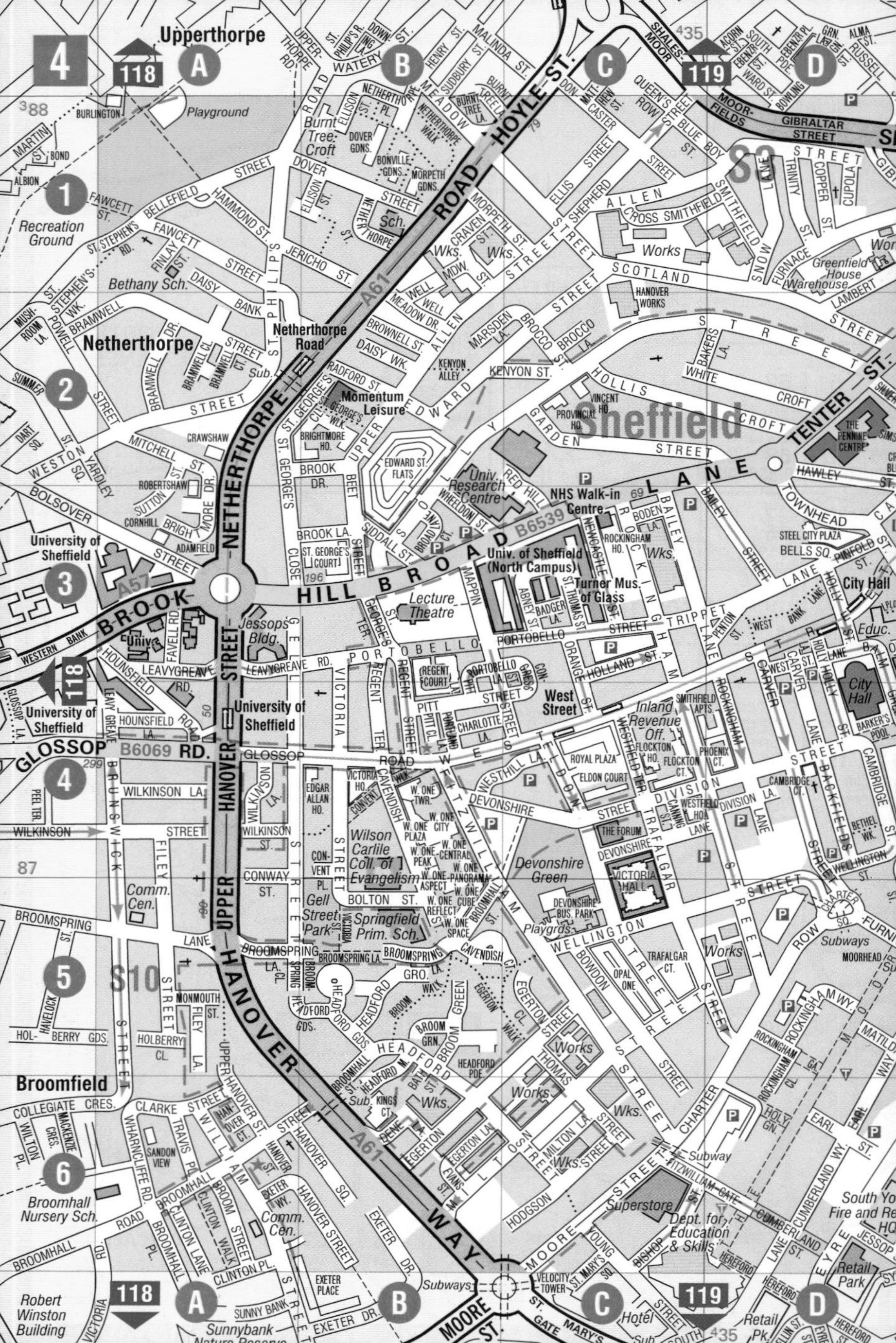

4
118
Upperthorpe
A
B
C
119
D
Playground
Burlington
Martin St.
Bond
Albion
Fawcett St.
Recreation Ground
Bellefield St.
Hammond St.
Dover Street
Burnt Tree Croft
Netherthorpe Walk
Upper Thorpe Rd.
Watery St.
Henry St.
Sudbury St.
Malinda St.
Meadow St.
Hoyle St.
Road
Shalesmoor
Moorfields
Gibraltar Street
Queen's Row
Blue Boy St.
Ellis Street
Shepherd Street
Allen Street
Cross Smithfield
Smithfield
Snow Lane
Trinity St.
Copper St.
Cupola
Works
Scotland Street
Hanover Works
Furnace
Greenfield House Warehouse
Lambert St.
S3
Jericho St.
Bethany Sch.
Daisy Bank
Bramwell Street
Netherthorpe
Netherthorpe Road
A61
Brownell St.
Daisy Wk.
Marsden La.
Brocco St.
Brocco La.
White Croft
Hollis Croft
Kenyon St.
Kenyon Alley
Momentum Leisure
Edward St.
Upper Allen St.
Garden Street
Vincent Ho.
Provincial Ho.
Sheffield
Tenter St.
The Pennine Centre
Hawley St.
Townhead
Mitchell St.
Weston St.
Yardley Sq.
Crawshaw
Robertshaw
Sutton
Cornhill
Adamfield
Bolsover Street
University of Sheffield
A57
Brook Hill
Broad Lane
B6539
Edward St. Flats
Brook Dr.
Brook La.
St. George's Court
St. George's Close
Univ. Research Centre
Red Hill
NHS Walk-in Centre
Newcastle St.
Rockingham
Bailey St.
Steel City Plaza
Bells Sq.
Pinfold St.
City Hall
Netherthorpe
Upper Hanover Street
Jessops Bldg.
Lecture Theatre
Mappin
Univ. of Sheffield (North Campus)
Turner Mus. of Glass
Western Bank
Univ.
Leavygreave Rd.
Hounsfield Rd.
Portobello
Regent Court
Pitt St.
Trippet Lane
West Bank Lane
Holland St.
West Street
Educ.
Glossop Rd.
B6069
Victoria St.
Regent Ter.
Charlotte La.
Royal Plaza
Eldon Court
Inland Revenue Off.
Smithfield Apts.
Flockton Ho.
Phoenix Ct.
Carver St.
Cambridge St.
Backfields
Barker's Pool
Brunswick Street
Wilkinson La.
Wilkinson Street
Filey Street
Conway St.
Edgar Allan Ho.
Wilson Carlile Coll. of Evangelism
Fitzwilliam St.
Devonshire St.
Division Street
The Forum
Devonshire Green
Victoria Hall
Trafalgar St.
Devonshire Bus. Park
Playgrds.
Wellington St.
Bethel Wk.
Comm. Cen.
Broomspring La.
Bolton St.
Gell Street Park
Springfield Prim. Sch.
Cavendish Ct.
Headford Gro.
Egerton Cl.
Trafalgar Ct.
Opal One
Works
Charter Row
Charter Sq.
Subways
Moorhead
S10
Monmouth St.
Holberry Gds.
Holberry Cl.
Broomfield
Collegiate Cres.
Clarke Street
Hanover Ct.
Travis Pl.
Headford St.
Broom Grn.
Broom Green
Headford Pde.
Thomas St.
Milton St.
Earl St.
Rockingham Wy.
Matilda Way
Holy Gn.
Wilton Pl.
Mackenzie Cres.
Sandon View
Broomhall Road
Broomhall Nursery Sch.
Hanover Sq.
Hanover Way
Hodgson St.
Moore Street
Superstore
Fitzwilliam Gate
Dept. for Education & Skills
Cumberland St.
Cumberland Way
South Yorks Fire and Rescue HQ
Retail Park
Robert Winston Building
Victoria Rd.
Clinton Pl.
Sunny Bank
Sunnybank Nature Reserve
Exeter Place
Exeter Dr.
Subways
Velocity Tower
St. Mary's Gate
Hotel
Sub.
Retail Pk.
Eyre St.
Hereford St.
435

5
E
F
G
H
119
DEREK DOOLEY WAY
WICKER
A61
Law Courts
Castle Market
Ponds Forge International Sports Centre
Ponds Forge/ Fitzalan Sq.
St. Peter & St. Paul's Cathedral
Cathedral
Castle Sq.
St. Marie's RC Cathedral
The Crucible Theatre
Lyceum Theatre
Library & Gall.
Town Hall
Peace Garden
Winter Garden
Millennium Gallery
Mecca Bingo
Odeon Cinema
Bus Station
Sheffield Hallam University (City Campus)
Sheffield Station/ Sheffield Hallam University
SHEFFIELD
Sheaf Valley Park
Amphitheatre
Monument Grounds
Clay Wood
The Sheffield College (Castle Centre)
Granville Rd./ The Sheffield Coll.
GRANVILLE ROAD
A6135
SHREWSBURY ROAD
B6071
TALBOT STREET
DUKE STREET
B6070
SHEAF STREET
SUFFOLK ROAD
ST. MARY'S ROAD
SHOREHAM STREET
ARUNDEL STREET
LivingWell Health Club
VICTORIA QUAYS
S1
S2
S4
Electric Works
Sheffield Science Pk.
Site Gallery
Freeman Coll.
Stoddart Building
Cutlers Hall
Montgomery Thtre.
Foundry Ho.
Vulcan Ho.
Riverside East
Blonk Bridge
Lady's Bri.
S. Yorks. Police HQ
Mag. Ct.
1
2
3
4
5
6
36
88
87

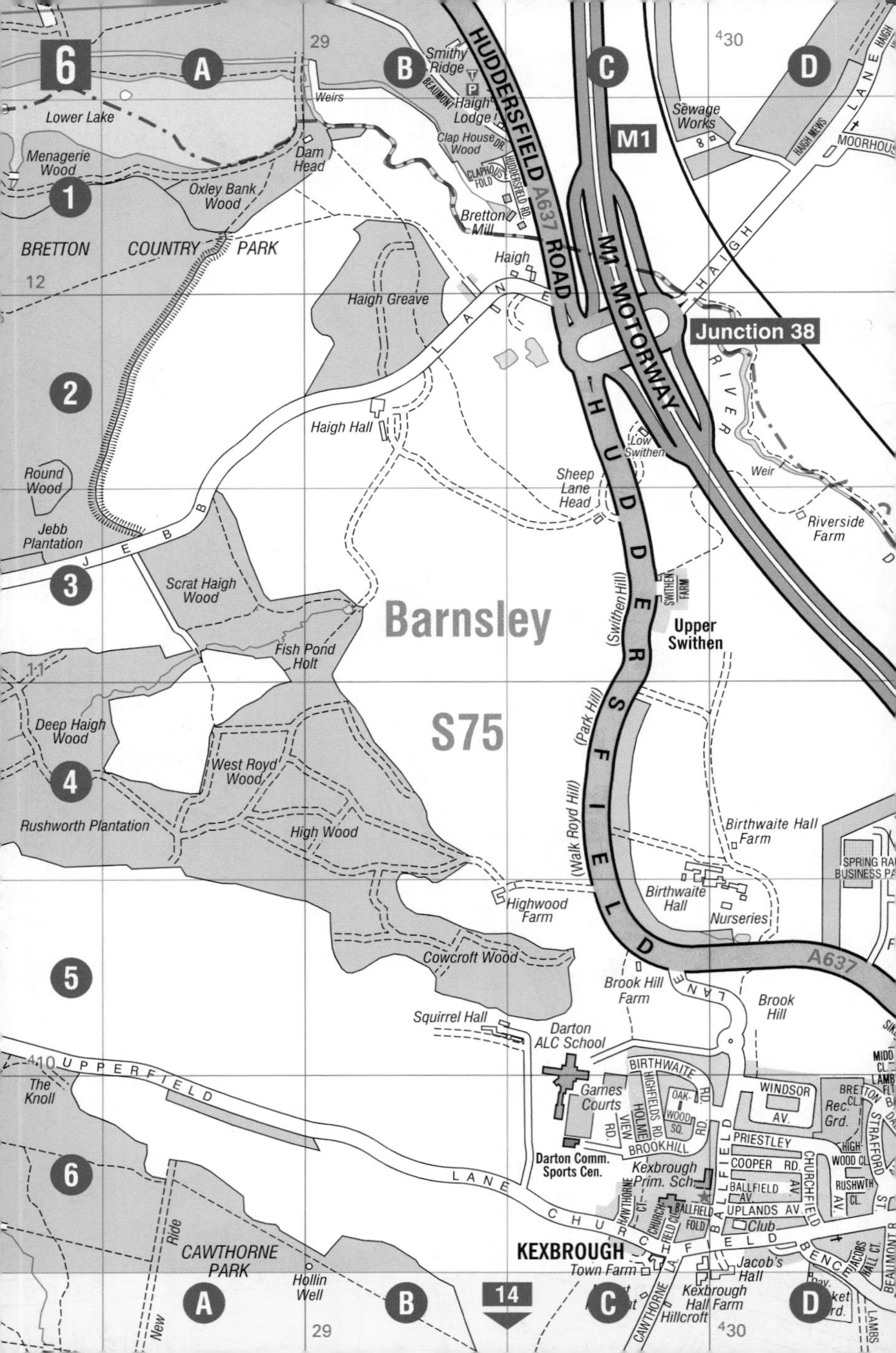

A
B
C
D
29
4 30
Smithy Ridge
Weirs
Haigh Lodge
Clap House Wood
Lower Lake
Menagerie Wood
Dam Head
Oxley Bank Wood
M1
Sewage Works
HIGH MEWS
MOORHOUSE
HUDDERSFIELD A637 ROAD
M1 MOTORWAY
Bretton Mill
BRETTON COUNTRY PARK
Haigh
12
Haigh Greave
HAIGH
LANE
Junction 38
RIVER
Haigh Hall
Low Swithen
Sheep Lane Head
Weir
Riverside Farm
Round Wood
Jebb Plantation
JEBB
Scrat Haigh Wood
Barnsley
Upper Swithen
SWITHEN FARM
(Swithen Hill)
Fish Pond Holt
11
Deep Haigh Wood
S75
(Park Hill)
HUDDERSFIELD
West Royd Wood
Rushworth Plantation
High Wood
(Walk Royd Hill)
Birthwaite Hall Farm
SPRING RA BUSINESS PA
Highwood Farm
Birthwaite Hall
Nurseries
Cowcroft Wood
A637
Brook Hill Farm
Brook Hill
Squirrel Hall
Darton ALC School
410
UPPERFIELD LANE
The Knoll
BIRTHWAITE RD.
Games Courts
WINDSOR AV.
Rec. Grd.
BRETTON CL.
STRAFFORD
HIGHFIELDS RD.
HOLME VIEW RD.
OAKWOOD SQ.
PRIESTLEY
BROOKHILL
Darton Comm. Sports Cen.
Kexbrough Prim. Sch.
COOPER RD.
CHURCHFIELD
BALLFIELD AV.
HIGH WOOD CL.
RUSHWTH CL.
HAWTHORNE CT.
UPLANDS AV.
Club
CHURCHFIELD
KEXBROUGH
Town Farm
Jacob's Hall
BENCE
JACOBS HALL CT.
BEAUMONT R
CAWTHORNE PARK
Ride
New
Hollin Well
Kexbrough Hall Farm
Hillcroft
CAWTHORNE LA.
LAMBS
1
2
3
4
5
6

14

7
Wakefield
WF4
Haw Top
Wheatley Wood
Woolley Grange
Windhill Wood
Windhill Gate Fm.
Husband Wood
Woolley Rabbit Warren
Coniston Farm
Sewage Works
Pye Wood
Sports Grd.
Football Grd.
Miners Welfare Institute
Bloomhouse
Cricket Grd.
M1 MOTORWAY
Darton
DARTON
Sports Pitch
Oaks Plantation
MAPPLEWELL
DEARNE MILLS DARTON BUSINESS PARK
Rec. Grd.
BARNSLEY RD.
DARTON RD.
STATION RD.
WAKEFIELD
BARNSLEY
15
8

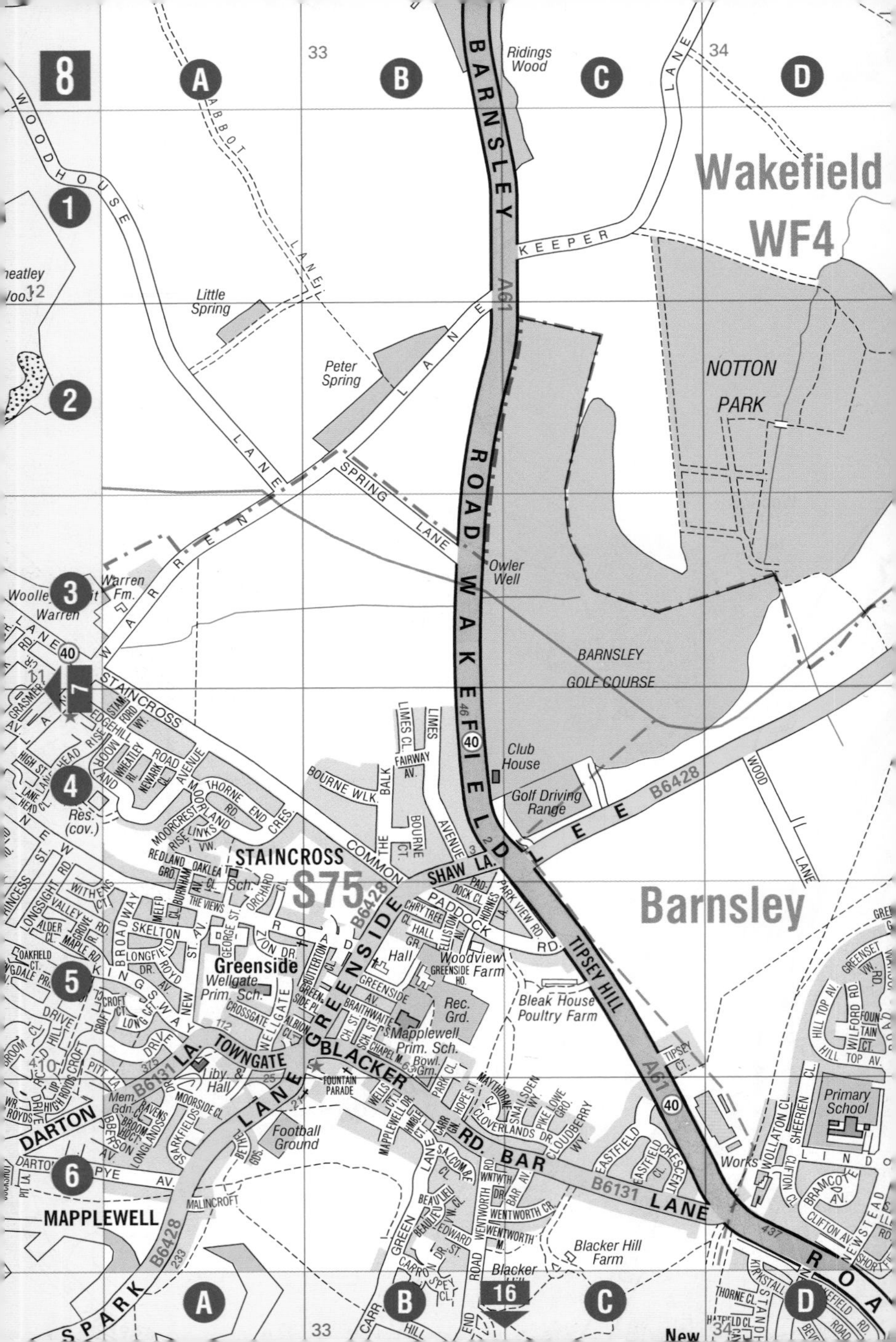
Wakefield
WF4
Barnsley
S75
NOTTON PARK
BARNSLEY GOLF COURSE
Ridings Wood
Little Spring
Peter Spring
Owler Well
Club House
Golf Driving Range
Warren Fm.
Woolley Edge Warren
STAINCROSS
Greenside
Wellgate Prim. Sch.
Mapplewell Prim. Sch.
Bleak House Poultry Farm
Woodview Farm
Rec. Grd.
Football Ground
Blacker Hill Farm
Primary School
Works
MAPPLEWELL
DARTON
BARNSLEY ROAD
WAKEFIELD ROAD
TIPSEY HILL
A61
B6428
B6131
BLACKER LANE
BAR LANE
STAINCROSS COMMON
WOODHOUSE LANE
ABBOT LANE
WARREN LANE
SPRING LANE
KEEPER LANE
LEE LANE
SHAW LA.
TOWNGATE
SPARK LANE
NEW ROAD
KINGSWAY
33
34
A
B
C
D
1
2
3
4
5
6
7
16

9
10
17
E
F
G
H
1
2
3
4
5
6
435
36
Applehaigh Wood
Applehaigh Clough
APPLEHAIGH CT.
GREEN LANE
BLEAKLEY LA.
BLEAKLEY TER.
BLEAKLEY AV.
WAKEFIELD
BARNSLEY
Windmill Hill
Low Common
Playing Fields
STATION ROAD
B6132
B6428
SUMMER LANE
HIGH STREET
MIDLAND ROAD
CHURCH ST.
COMMON LA.
WARREN
Play. Fld.
Civic Hall
Coun. Offs.
Leisure Centre
Sports Pitches
Prim. Sch.
Chapel Hill
Lib.
Sch.
Bandstand
Bowl. Grns.
Tennis Courts
Pav.
Royston Welfare Park
VICARAGE LANE
Cemy.
CHURCH HILL
Hall
Factory
Lee Lane Farm
Muscle Hill
LANE
SYCAMORE DR.
GRANGE ROAD
Play-ground
Play. Flds.
ROYSTON
ROYSTON LA.
KIRK CROSS CR.
WOOD LANE
S71
CARLTON
Carlton Green
Manor Ho.
Carlton Jun. Sch.
ATHERSLEY NORTH
Athersley Memorial Park
Playing Field
Athersley Leisure Cen.
Sports Ground
WHARNCLIFFE BUSINESS PARK
Works
Depot
Willow Cott.
CARLTON ROAD
CARLTON INDUSTRIAL ESTATE
LAITHES LANE
B6132
Tennis Cts.
Liby.
Club
ALLERTON ROAD
RADCLIFFE ROAD
MANSFIELD ROAD
FOREST RD.
SUTTON AV.
ARNOLD AV.
CROOKES LANE
SPRING LA.

A
B
C
D
1
2
3
4
5
6
37
38
Barnsley Canal (disused)
Common Lane Farm
Playing Fields
Low Common
Playgrd.
Active Workings
Works
LUND HILL LANE
B6428
Lund Hill
Barnsley
MIDLAND ROAD
LUND ROAD
WHINCOVER VW.
Bowl. Grns.
Tennis Courts
Pav.
Royston Welfare Park
Bandstand
Lib.
VICARAGE LANE
Prim. Sch.
Church Hill
CHURCH HILL
POOLS LA.
Hall
Royston Bridge
Pools Lane Bridge
ROYSTON
Scot Bridge
Sports Ground
Rabbit Ings
Sandybridge Dike
Gander Hill
Pools Ings
Pools Dike
North Field
S71
Cronk Hill
Pools Bridge
BOULDER BRIDGE LANE
Boulder Bridge
Boulder Bri. Dike
LOW CRONKHILL LA.
Barnsley Canal (Disused)
Carlton Community College
Games Courts
CARLTON
Recreation Ground
Shaw Bridge
Shaw Viaduct
Shaw Dike Bri.
Carlton Picnic Site
Shaw Dike
SHAW LANE
WEET LANE
ROYSTON
SIDCOP
Sewage Wks.
Works
Warehouse
Carlton Marsh Nature Reserve
Carlton Green
Manor Ho.
Carlton Prim. Sch.
Bakery
Cudworth Dike
ROYSTON LA.
B6132
CARLTON RD.
Cemy.
CARLTON INDUSTRIAL ESTATE
ALBION
FISH DAM LANE
30
369
410
9
18

11
SOUTH HIENDLEY
Felkirk
High Common
Recreation Ground
Chestnut Farm
South Hiendley Common
Low Common
School Farm
Wester Cliff
Old Musgrave Farm
Old Colliery Farm
Hemp Dike
Sandy Bridge
Frickley Station
The Bank
S72
SHAFTON
Red House
Sewage Wks.
Miners' Welfare Rec. Grd.
Shafton Prim. Sch.
Depot
Playing Field
Three Nooks
Works
Shafton ALC
SHAFTON TWO GATES
Hazeldene Farm
Brick Yard Farm
Cemetery
Upper Cudworth
Sewage Works
Home Farm
Tipside Farm
PARKWAY
BARNSLEY ROAD
A628
A6195
ENGINE LANE
WAKEFIELD
BARNSLEY
19
12
1
2
3
4
5
6
E
F
G
H

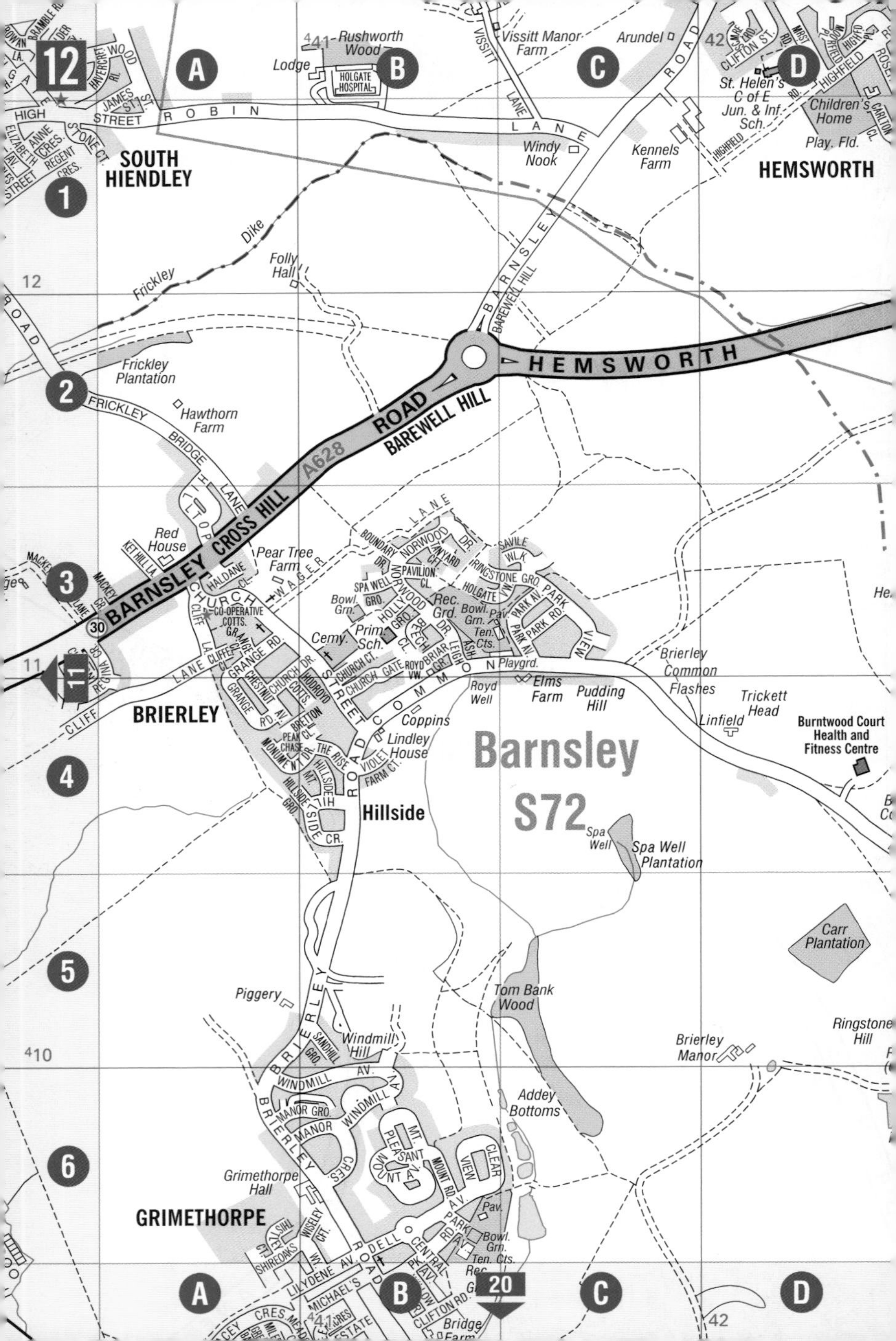
SOUTH HIENDLEY
HEMSWORTH
BRIERLEY
Barnsley
S72
Hillside
GRIMETHORPE
HEMSWORTH
BARNSLEY CROSS HILL
BAREWELL HILL
ROBIN LANE
Rushworth Wood
HOLGATE HOSPITAL
Vissitt Manor Farm
Arundel
Windy Nook
Kennels Farm
St. Helen's C of E Jun. & Inf. Sch.
Children's Home
Play. Fld.
Frickley Dike
Folly Hall
Frickley Plantation
Hawthorn Farm
Red House
Pear Tree Farm
Brierley Common Flashes
Trickett Head
Linfield
Burntwood Court Health and Fitness Centre
Elms Farm
Pudding Hill
Royd Well
Coppins
Lindley House
Spa Well
Spa Well Plantation
Carr Plantation
Tom Bank Wood
Piggery
Windmill Hill
Ringstone Hill
Brierley Manor
Addey Bottoms
Grimethorpe Hall
Bridge Farm

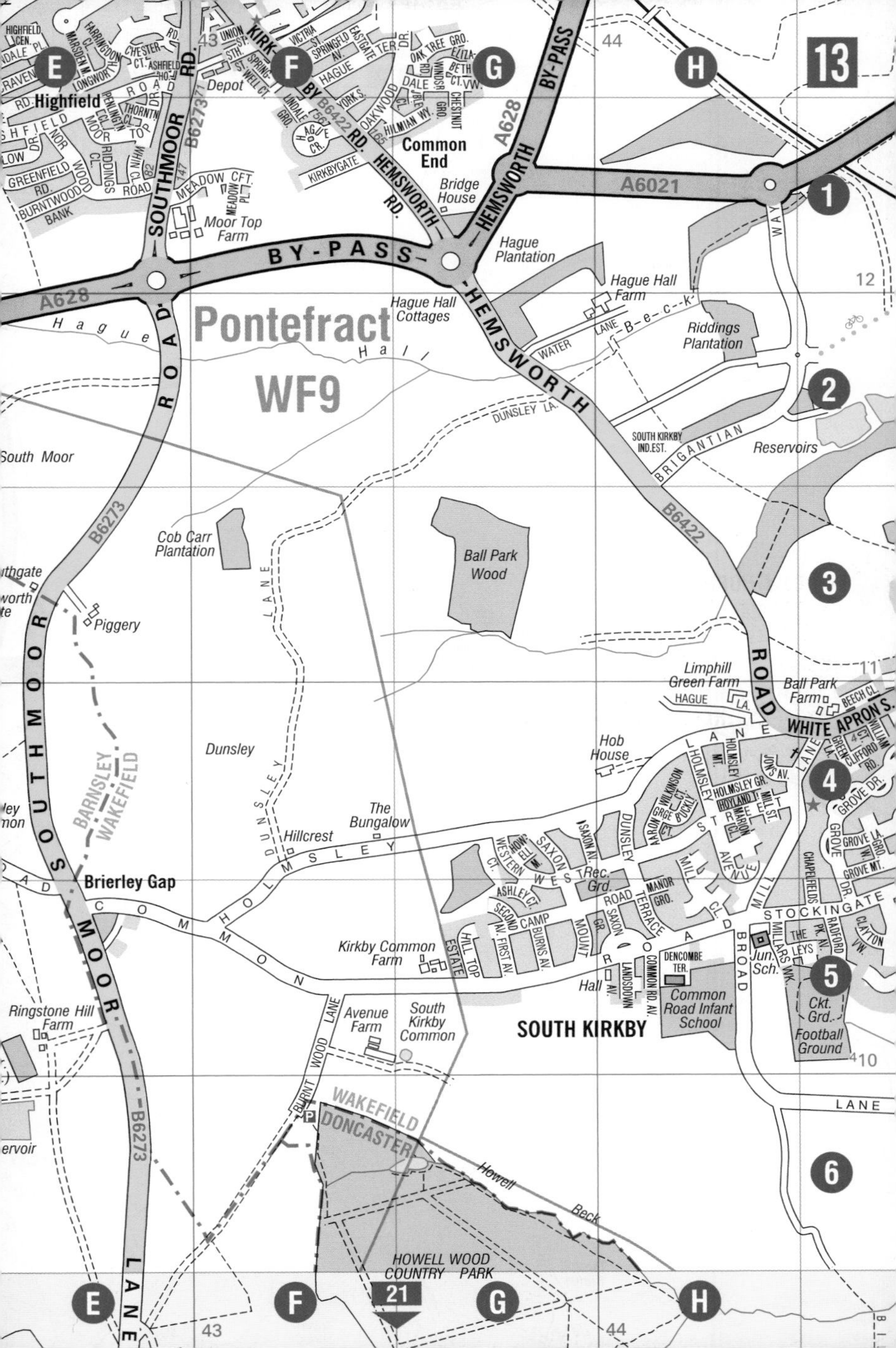
Highfield
Pontefract
WF9
Common End
Bridge House
Moor Top Farm
Hague Plantation
Hague Hall Farm
Hague Hall Cottages
Riddings Plantation
SOUTH KIRKBY IND.EST.
Reservoirs
South Moor
Cob Carr Plantation
Ball Park Wood
Piggery
Limphill Green Farm
Ball Park Farm
Hob House
Dunsley
The Bungalow
Hillcrest
Brierley Gap
BARNSLEY
WAKEFIELD
Kirkby Common Farm
Ringstone Hill Farm
Avenue Farm
South Kirkby Common
SOUTH KIRKBY
Common Road Infant School
Jun. Sch.
Ckt. Grd.
Football Ground
Rec. Grd.
DONCASTER
HOWELL WOOD COUNTRY PARK
Howell Beck
A628
A6021
B6422
B6273
BY-PASS
HEMSWORTH RD.
SOUTHMOOR RD.
SOUTHMOOR ROAD
SOUTHMOOR LANE
HOLMSLEY LANE
COMMON ROAD
BRIGANTIAN WAY
WHITE APRON S.
STOCKINGATE
BROAD LANE
MILL LANE
Depot
21
43
44
12
11
10

A
B
C
D
1
2
3
4
5
6
29
4 30
09
08
4 07
6
28
CAWTHORNE PARK
New Ride
Hollin Well
Prim. Sch.
BALLFIELD AV.
RUSHWTH CL.
CHURCHFIELD
Club
Town Farm
Jacob's Hall
Mount Pleasant
Kexbrough Hall Farm
Hillcroft
KEXBROUGH
Pav.
Cricket Grd.
LAMBS FLAT LANE
Cawthorne Dike
Cinder Hill
Cinder Farm
Weir
Cinder Hill Bridge
Mill House
Cawthorne
Clay Hall
Tennis Court
CAWTHORNE ROAD
Silkstone Beck
CAWTHORNE
Cliff Hill Bri.
DARTON
FIVE ACRES
STANHOPE AV.
STANHOPE MDWS.
ORCHARD TER.
TAYLOR HILL
HILL TOP
CHURCH
Mus.
Cemy.
Sch.
TIVY DALE
Barnby Hall
Barnby Bridge
HEAD ROAD
LANE
A635
CAWTHORNE ROAD
Barnby Green Farm
BARNBY FURNACE
Windmill Hill
SILKSTONE LANE
NORTH LANE
Weir
Furnace Bridge
ROYD
Hill Ho. Fm.
Nursery
Nursery
NORCROFT LANE
Upper Norcroft
ADAM LANE
Adam Lathe
Lower Norcroft Farm
Low Mill Farm
HUGSET WOOD
Sewage Works
Norcroft Bridge
Banks Bottom
Tanyard Spring

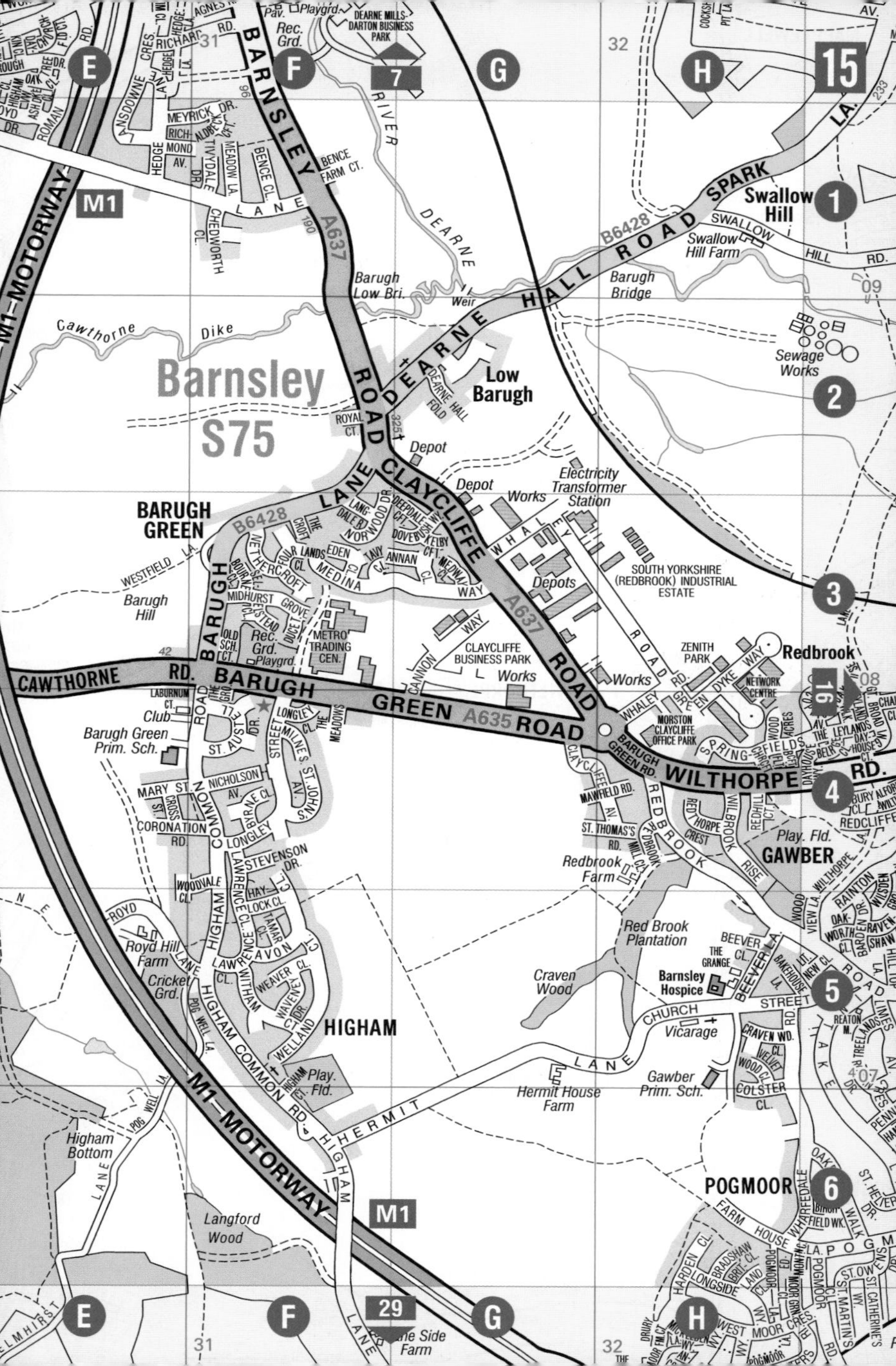

Barnsley
S75
BARUGH GREEN
Low Barugh
Swallow Hill
GAWBER
HIGHAM
POGMOOR
Redbrook
SOUTH YORKSHIRE (REDBROOK) INDUSTRIAL ESTATE
CLAYCLIFFE BUSINESS PARK
METRO TRADING CEN.
MORSTON CLAYCLIFFE OFFICE PARK
ZENITH PARK
NETWORK CENTRE
DEARNE MILLS-DARTON BUSINESS PARK
Barugh Green Prim. Sch.
Barnsley Hospice
Gawber Prim. Sch.
Sewage Works
Electricity Transformer Station
Red Brook Plantation
Craven Wood
Langford Wood
Higham Bottom
Hermit House Farm
Redbrook Farm
Royd Hill Farm
Swallow Hill Farm
Barugh Bridge
Barugh Low Bri.
Cawthorne Dike
M1-MOTORWAY
BARNSLEY ROAD
CLAYCLIFFE ROAD
DEARNE HALL ROAD
SPARK LA.
CAWTHORNE RD.
BARUGH GREEN ROAD
WILTHORPE RD.
HERMIT LANE
CHURCH STREET
HIGHAM COMMON RD.
BARUGH COMMON ROAD

MAPPLEWELL
16
A
B
C
D
33
34
8
SPARK LANE
B6428
MALINCROFT
Swallow Hill
SWALLOW HILL
CARR GRN.
HILL END ROAD
Blacker Hill
Hill End Farm
New Lodge
WAKEFIELD RD.
STANDHILL
NEW LODGE
Stand Hill
Standhill Wood
Sewage Works
Weir
Barnsley Canal (Dis.)
Barnsley
S75
Smithy Green
Croft Farm
Redbrook
REDBROOK BUSINESS PARK
15
WILTHORPE
Play. Fld.
Wilthorpe Jun. Sch.
Wilthorpe Inf. Sch.
Tennis Courts
GREENFOOT LA.
WILTHORPE RD.
HUDDERSFIELD RD.
A635
BARNSLEY BUS. & INNOVATION CENTRE
GAWBER
REDBROOK RISE
DEVONSHIRE DR.
WILLOW BANK
Bleachcroft BANK
SMITHIES LA.
Play. Field
Barnsley Coll.
Old Town
BARNSLEY DISTRICT GENERAL HOSP.
Nursing Sch.
GAWBER ROAD
SUMMER LANE
St. Mary's Prim. Sch.
Sugden's Rec. Grd.
Works
Industrial Estate
Recreation Ground
Playing Field
POGMOOR LA.
POGMOOR
GROSVENOR DR.
SPRINGFIELD
30
VICTORIA RD.
S70
WESTGATE
CHURCHFIELD
OLD ROAD
1
2
3
4
5
6
09
08
407
437

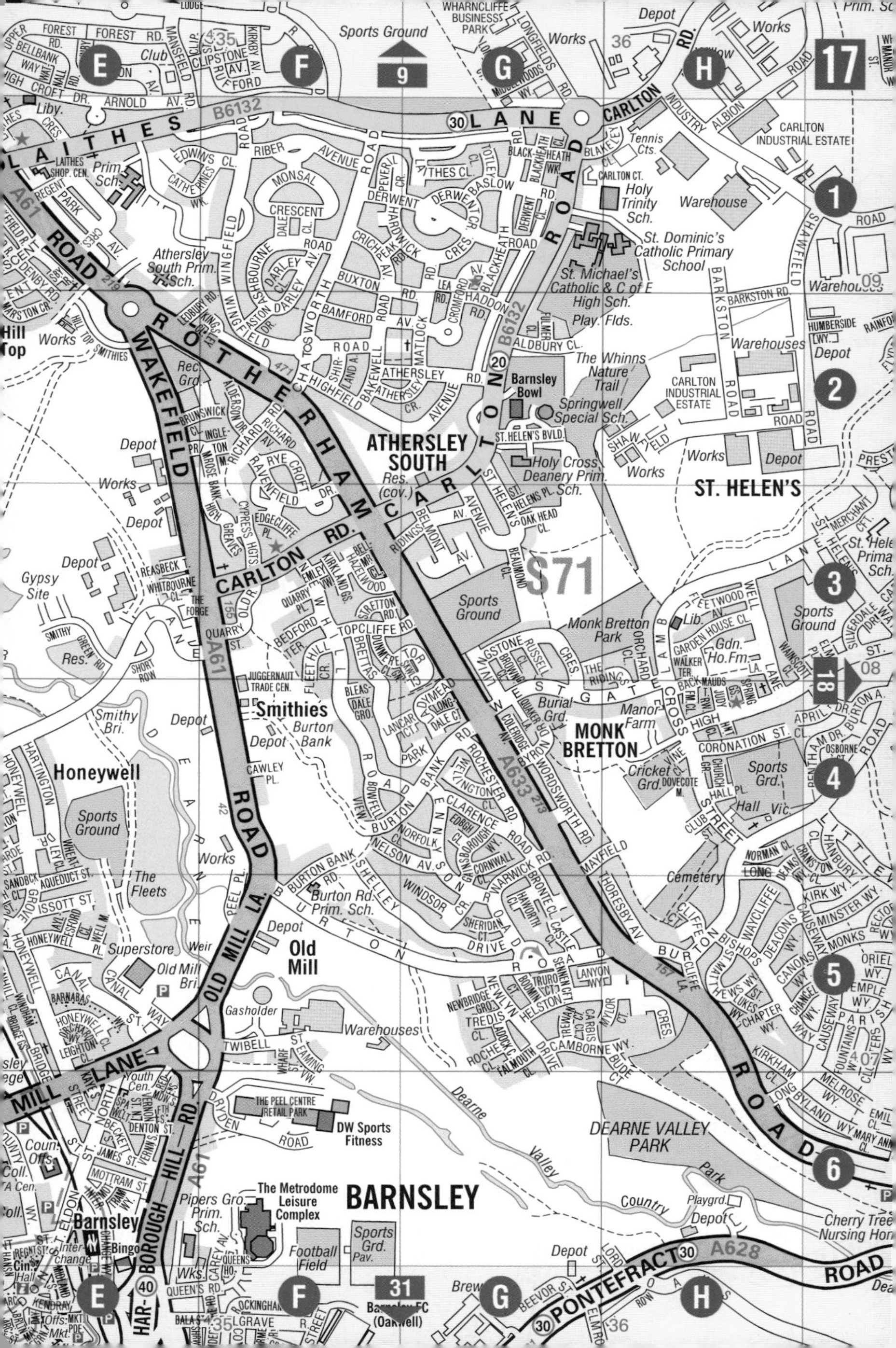
Sports Ground
9
WHARNCLIFFE BUSINESS PARK
Depot
Works
E
F
G
H
1
2
3
4
5
6
LAITHES LANE
CARLTON ROAD
CARLTON INDUSTRIAL ESTATE
Holy Trinity Sch.
St. Dominic's Catholic Primary School
St. Michael's Catholic & C of E High Sch.
Play. Flds.
Warehouse
Warehouses
Athersley South Prim. Sch.
Laithes Shop. Cen.
Hill Top
ROTHERHAM ROAD
WAKEFIELD ROAD
Barnsley Bowl
The Whinns Nature Trail
Springwell Special Sch.
ATHERSLEY SOUTH
Holy Cross Deanery Prim. Sch.
ST. HELEN'S
S71
Sports Ground
Monk Bretton Park
Gypsy Site
Smithies
Burton Bank
MONK BRETTON
Manor Farm
Burial Grd.
Cricket Grd.
Sports Grd.
Honeywell
Sports Ground
The Fleets
Old Mill
Superstore
Burton Rd. Prim. Sch.
Cemetery
Gasholder
Warehouses
The Peel Centre Retail Park
DW Sports Fitness
DEARNE VALLEY PARK
Dearne Valley Country Park
BARNSLEY
The Metrodome Leisure Complex
Pipers Gro. Prim. Sch.
Football Field
Sports Grd.
Barnsley Interchange
Bingo
Cherry Tree Nursing Home
PONTEFRACT ROAD
A628
A61
A633
B6132
18
31
Barnsley FC (Oakwell)
MILL LANE
OLD MILL LA.
HARBOROUGH HILL RD.

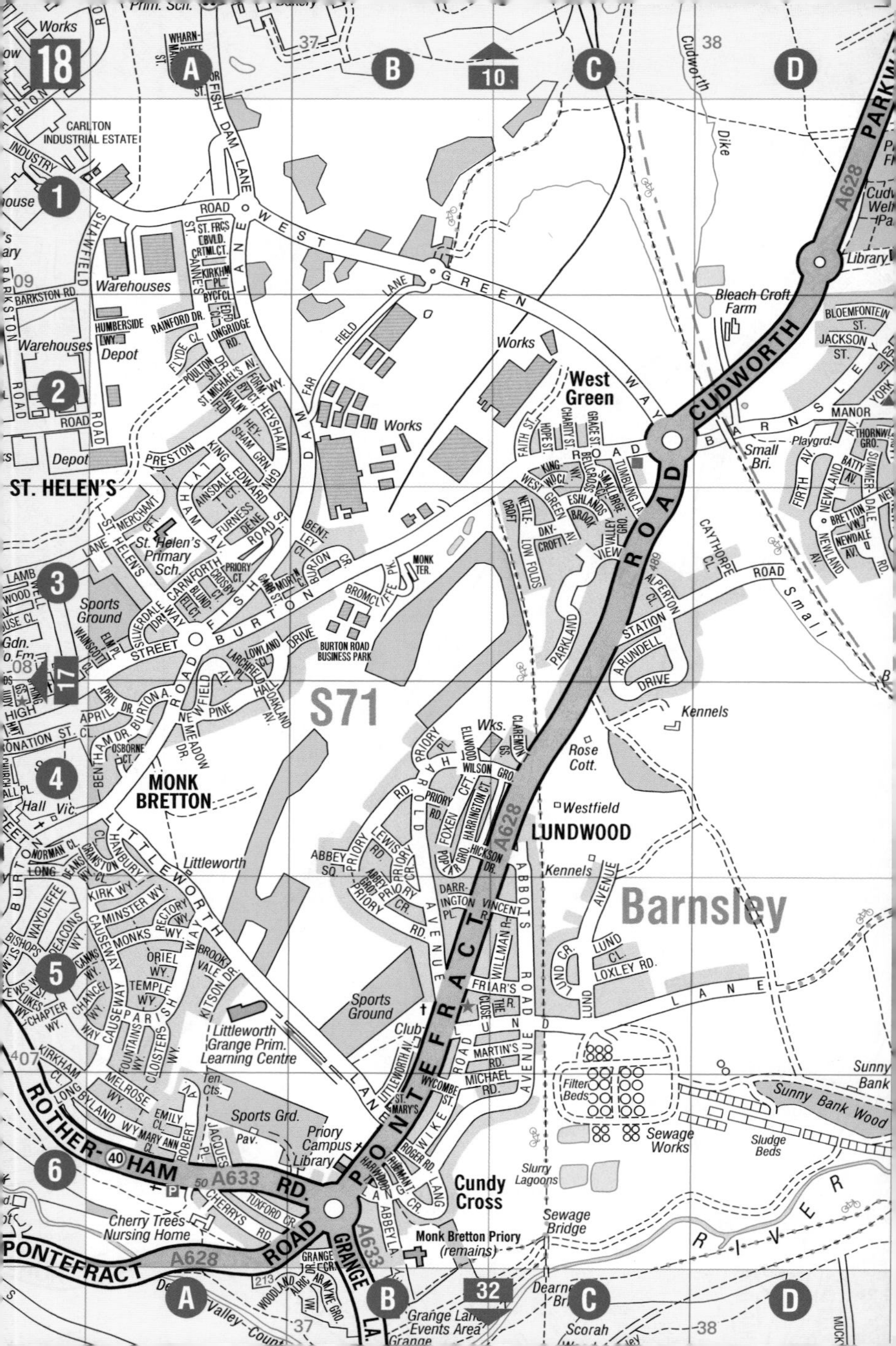
A
B
C
D
10
37
38
1
2
3
4
5
6
17
32
Works
CARLTON INDUSTRIAL ESTATE
INDUSTRY
ALBION
FISH DAM LANE
WEST GREEN WAY
Cudworth Dike
PARKWAY
A628
Library
Bleach Croft Farm
BLOEMFONTEIN ST.
JACKSON ST.
CUDWORTH ROAD
BARNSLEY ROAD
MANOR
THORNWELL GRO.
Playgrd.
Small Bri.
SHAWFIELD ROAD
BARKSTON RD.
BARKSTON ROAD
Warehouses
Depot
HUMBERSIDE WY.
RAINFORD DR.
LONGRIDGE RD.
FLYDE CL.
POULTON ST.
ST. MICHAEL'S AV.
FORMBY WY.
HEYSHAM GRN.
FAR FIELD LANE
DAM
Works
West Green
FAITH ST.
HOPE ST.
CHARITY ST.
GRACE ST.
ST. HELEN'S
PRESTON
KING EDWARD RD.
LYTHAM AV.
AINSDALE CT.
FURNESS DENE
St. Helen's Primary Sch.
ST. HELEN'S LANE
MERCHANT CFT.
CARNFORTH
PRIORY CT.
CROSBY CT.
BURTON ROAD
BENTLEY CL.
BURTON CR.
BROMCLIFFE PK.
MONK TER.
BURTON ROAD BUSINESS PARK
WEST GREEN CROFT
NETTLE CROFT
DAYCROFT
LOW FOLDS
ESHLANDS
TUMBLING LA.
VALLEY VIEW
CAYTHORPE CL.
ROAD
ALPERTON CL.
STATION
ARUNDELL DRIVE
PARKLAND
FIRTH AV.
NEWLAND AV.
BATTY AV.
SUMMERDALE
BRETTON VW.
NEWDALE AV.
Small
Sports Ground
SILVERDALE DR.
BURTON STREET
ELM PL.
LOWLAND CL.
DRIVE
LARCHFIELD PL.
NEWFIELD AV.
PINE
HALL
OAKLAND AV.
S71
APRIL DR.
BURTON A.
NEW MEADOW DR.
HIGH
CORONATION ST.
BENTHAM DR.
OSBORNE CT.
MONK BRETTON
Hall
Vic.
Kennels
Rose Cott.
Westfield
LUNDWOOD
Wks.
CLAREMONT GS.
ELLWOOD
WILSON GRO.
PRIORY PL.
HAROLD AVENUE
PRIORY RD.
FOXEN CFT.
HARRINGTON CT.
HICKSON DR.
POPLAR GRO.
ABBOTS ROAD
ABBEY SQ.
LEWIS RD.
PRIORY CR.
ABBEY GRO.
DARRINGTON PL.
VINCENT R.
WILLMAN R.
Littleworth
LITTLEWORTH LANE
NORMAN CL.
CRANSTON
HANBURY CL.
LONG
KIRK WY.
MINSTER WY.
RECTORY WY.
WAYCLIFFE
DEACONS WY.
CAUSEWAY
MONKS WY.
ORIEL WY.
TEMPLE WY.
BROOK VALE DR.
KITSON DR.
BISHOPS
CHAPTER WY.
CHANCEL WY.
PARISH
FOUNTAINS WY.
CLOISTERS WY.
Littleworth Grange Prim. Learning Centre
Barnsley
AVENUE
LUND CL.
LUND CR.
LOXLEY RD.
LANE
FRIAR'S CLOSE
THE R.
LUND AVENUE
Club
Sports Ground
Sunny Bank
Sunny Bank Wood
PONTEFRACT ROAD
LITTLEWORTH AV.
ST. MARY'S
MARTIN'S RD.
MICHAEL RD.
WYCOMBE ST.
WIKE
Filter Beds
Sewage Works
Sludge Beds
407
KIRKHAM CL.
LONG BYLAND WY.
MELROSE WY.
EMILY CL.
MARY ANN CL.
ROBERT
JACQUES
Ten. Cts.
Sports Grd.
Pav.
Priory Campus
Library
ROTHERHAM RD.
A633
40
50
CHERRYS RD.
TUXFORD CR.
ROGER RD.
LANG
Cundy Cross
Slurry Lagoons
Sewage Bridge
RIVER
Cherry Trees Nursing Home
PONTEFRACT ROAD
A628
GRANGE LA.
GRANGE CR.
ABBEY LA.
Monk Bretton Priory (remains)
213
WOODLAND
ALRIC DR.
ARTHUR
WYNNE GRO.
Dearne Valley Country
Dearne Bri.
Grange Lane Events Area
Scorah

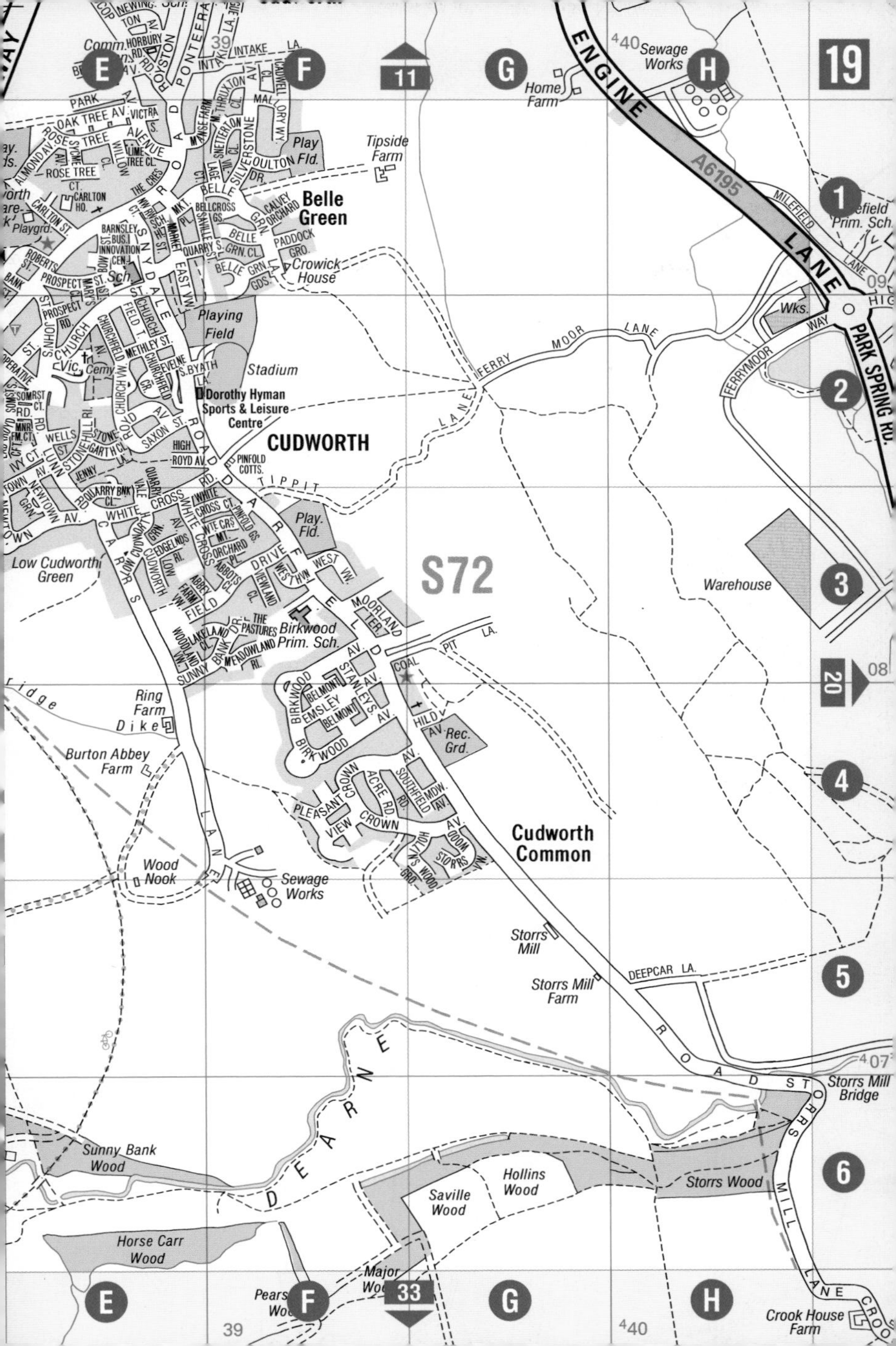
CUDWORTH
Belle Green
Cudworth Common
S72
ENGINE LANE
A6195
PARK SPRING RD.
FERRY MOOR LANE
Warehouse
Playing Field
Stadium
Dorothy Hyman Sports & Leisure Centre
Birkwood Prim. Sch.
Low Cudworth Green
Ring Farm
Burton Abbey Farm
Wood Nook
Sewage Works
Storrs Mill
Storrs Mill Farm
Storrs Mill Bridge
DEEPCAR LA.
RIVER DEARNE
Sunny Bank Wood
Horse Carr Wood
Saville Wood
Hollins Wood
Storrs Wood
Major Wood
Pears Wood
Crook House Farm
Tipside Farm
Home Farm
Crowick House
Rec. Grd.
Play Fld.
Milefield Prim. Sch.
Wks.
11
20
33
E F G H
1 2 3 4 5 6
39
440

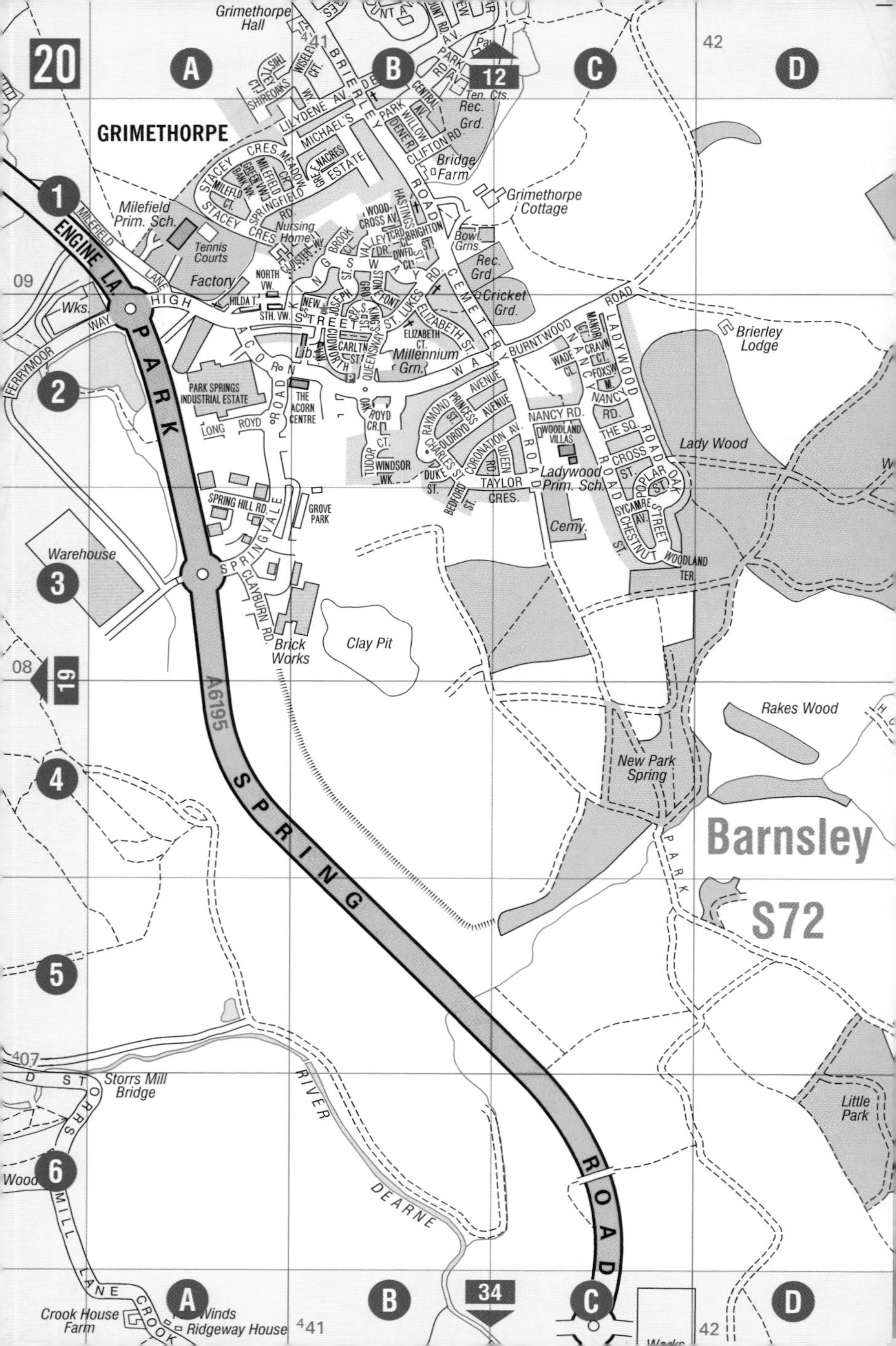
GRIMETHORPE
Grimethorpe Hall
Milefield Prim. Sch.
Tennis Courts
Factory
Nursing Home
Wks.
Warehouse
PARK SPRINGS INDUSTRIAL ESTATE
THE ACORN CENTRE
GROVE PARK
Brick Works
Clay Pit
Millennium Grn.
Bridge Farm
Grimethorpe Cottage
Rec. Grd.
Ten. Cts.
Bowl. Grns.
Cricket Grd.
Brierley Lodge
Lady Wood
Ladywood Prim. Sch.
WOODLAND VILLAS
Cemy.
Rakes Wood
New Park Spring
Barnsley
S72
Little Park
Storrs Mill Bridge
Crook House Farm
Ridgeway House
ENGINE LA.
PARK SPRING ROAD
A6195
HIGH STREET
BURNTWOOD ROAD
LADYWOOD ROAD
CEMETERY ROAD
BRIERLEY ROAD
STORRS MILL LANE
RIVER DEARNE

12
19
34

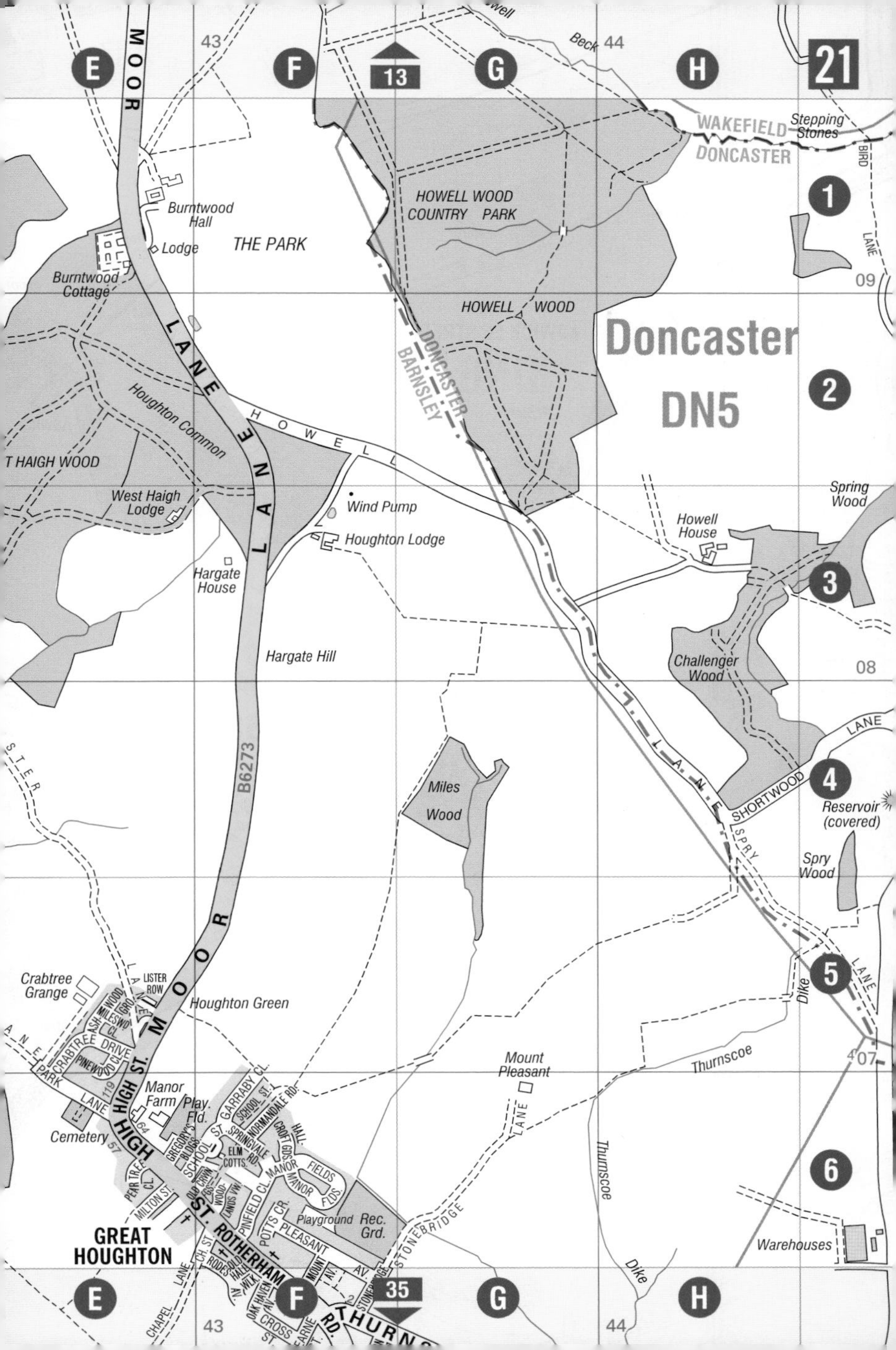

MOOR LANE
13
Beck
WAKEFIELD
DONCASTER
Stepping Stones
Burntwood Hall
Lodge
THE PARK
HOWELL WOOD COUNTRY PARK
Burntwood Cottage
HOWELL WOOD
Doncaster DN5
DONCASTER
BARNSLEY
HOWELL
Houghton Common
T HAIGH WOOD
West Haigh Lodge
Wind Pump
Houghton Lodge
Hargate House
Spring Wood
Howell House
Hargate Hill
Challenger Wood
B6273
LANE
SHORTWOOD
Miles Wood
Reservoir (covered)
SPRY
Spry Wood
Dike
Crabtree Grange
LISTER ROW
Houghton Green
Thurnscoe
Mount Pleasant
Manor Farm
Play. Fld.
Cemetery
Thurnscoe
Dike
Warehouses
GREAT HOUGHTON
HIGH ST.
ROTHERHAM RD.
STONEBRIDGE
Playground
Rec. Grd.
PLEASANT
POTTS CR.
MANOR FIELDS
35
THURNSCOE

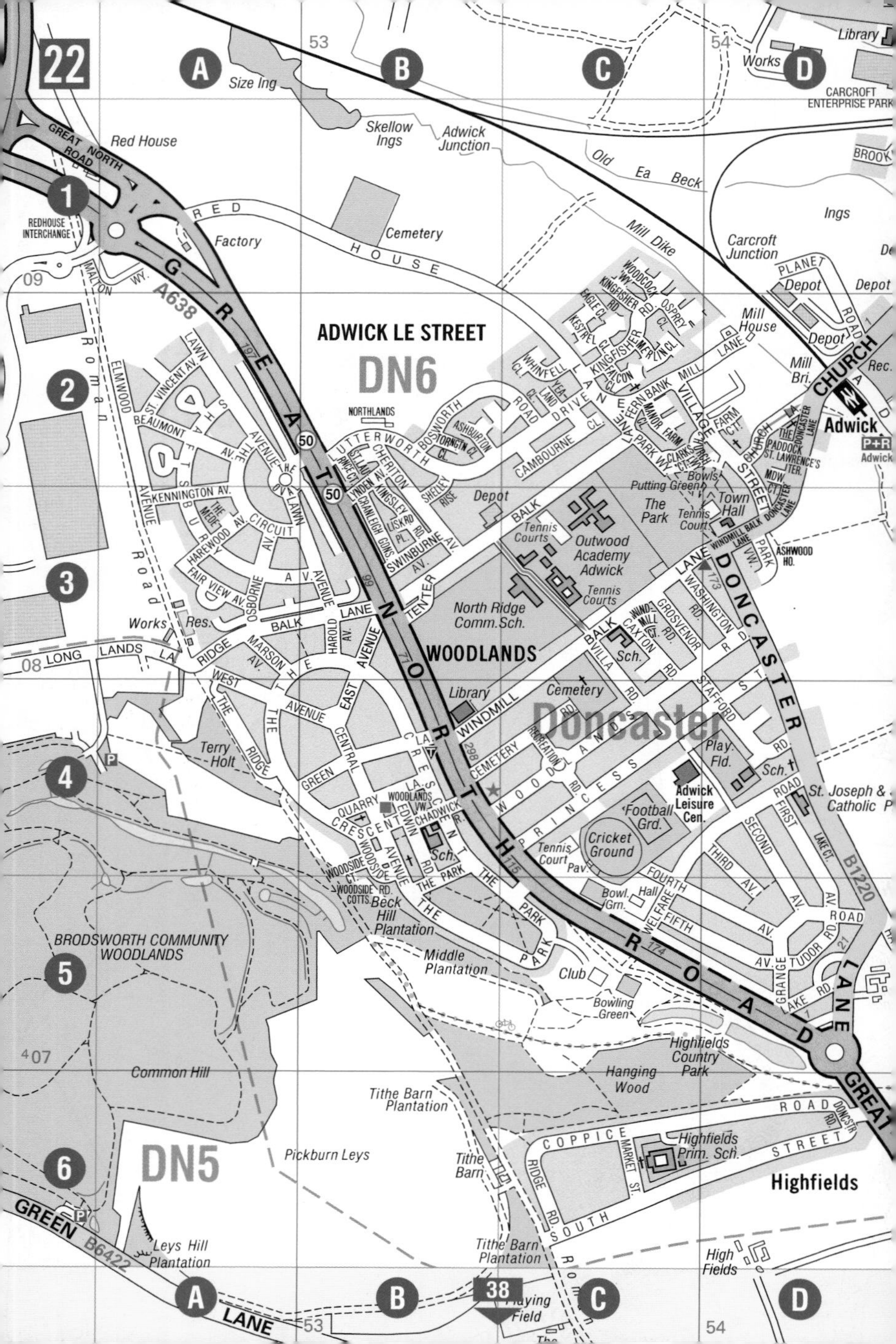
A
B
C
D
53
54
Size Ing
Library
Works
CARCROFT ENTERPRISE PARK
Red House
Skellow Ings
Adwick Junction
GREAT NORTH ROAD
BROOK
Old Ea Beck
1
REDHOUSE INTERCHANGE
RED HOUSE
Cemetery
Factory
Ings
Mill Dike
Carcroft Junction
09
MALTON WY.
A638
PLANET
Depot
Depot
Depot
ROAD
ADWICK LE STREET
DN6
Roman Road
WOODCOCK WY.
KINGFISHER RD.
OSPREY CL.
EAGLE CL.
KESTREL CL.
MERLIN CL.
KINGFISHER
FALCON CL.
Mill House
Mill Bri.
CHURCH LA.
Rec.
2
ELMWOOD AVENUE
LAWN
ST. VINCENT AV.
BEAUMONT
AVENUE
SHAFTSBURY AV.
THE OVAL
LAWN
NORTHLANDS
WHINFELL CL.
YEA-LAND CL.
ROAD
DRIVE
FERNBANK
MILL LANE
VILLAGE STREET
MANOR CL.
MANOR FARM
CLARKS CT.
CHURCH VW.
FARM CT.
PARK WY.
BOSWORTH
ASHBURTON CL.
TORNGTN CL.
LUTTERWORTH
CHERITON
CAMBOURNE CL.
THE PADDOCK
ST. LAWRENCE'S TER.
DONCASTER LANE
Adwick
P+R
Adwick
MDW. CT.
50
50
KENNINGTON AV.
THE MEDE
HAREWOOD AV.
CIRCUIT
LYNDEN AV.
KINGSLEY
CRANLEIGH GDNS.
LISK RD. PL.
SWINBURNE AV.
SHELLEY RISE
Depot
BALK
Tennis Courts
Outwood Academy Adwick
Putting Green
The Park
Bowls
Tennis Court
Town Hall
WINDMILL BALK LANE
DONCASTER LANE
PARK VW.
ASHWOOD HO.
3
FAIR VIEW AV.
OSBORNE AV.
AVENUE
TENTER
Tennis Courts
North Ridge Comm.Sch.
LANE
WASHINGTON RD.
GROSVENOR RD.
WINDMILL
CAXTON RD.
Sch.
DONCASTER
Works
Res.
BALK LANE
HAROLD AV.
EAST AVENUE
WOODLANDS
BALK
VILLA RD.
08 LONG LANDS LA.
RIDGE
MARSON AV.
WEST
THE AVENUE
THE RIDGE
GREAT NORTH ROAD
Library
WINDMILL
Cemetery
Doncaster
STAFFORD
ST.
RD.
Terry Holt
CENTRAL
CRESCENT
CEMETERY
RECREATION RD.
WOODLANDS
PRINCESS
Play. Fld.
Sch.
ROAD
FIRST
St. Joseph & Catholic P
4
P
GREEN
QUARRY
WOODLANDS VW.
EDWIN
CHADWICK
Adwick Leisure Cen.
Football Grd.
Cricket Ground
Tennis Court
Pav.
SECOND
THIRD AV.
LAKE CT.
B1220
WOODSIDE CT.
WOODSIDE RD.
WOODSIDE COTTS.
AVENUE
RD.
THE PARK
Sch.
Beck Hill Plantation
FOURTH
Bowl. Grn.
Hall
WELFARE
FIFTH
AV.
ROAD
RD.
BROADSWORTH COMMUNITY WOODLANDS
5
Middle Plantation
PARK
Club
GRANGE
TUDOR RD.
LAKE RD.
LANE
Bowling Green
Highfields Country Park
Hanging Wood
07
Common Hill
Tithe Barn Plantation
COPPICE
RIDGE RD.
MARKET ST.
ROAD
DONCSTR RD.
Highfields Prim. Sch.
STREET
6
DN5
Pickburn Leys
Tithe Barn
SOUTH
Highfields
GREEN
B6422
P
Leys Hill Plantation
Tithe Barn Plantation
Roman
High Fields
LANE
38
Playing Field

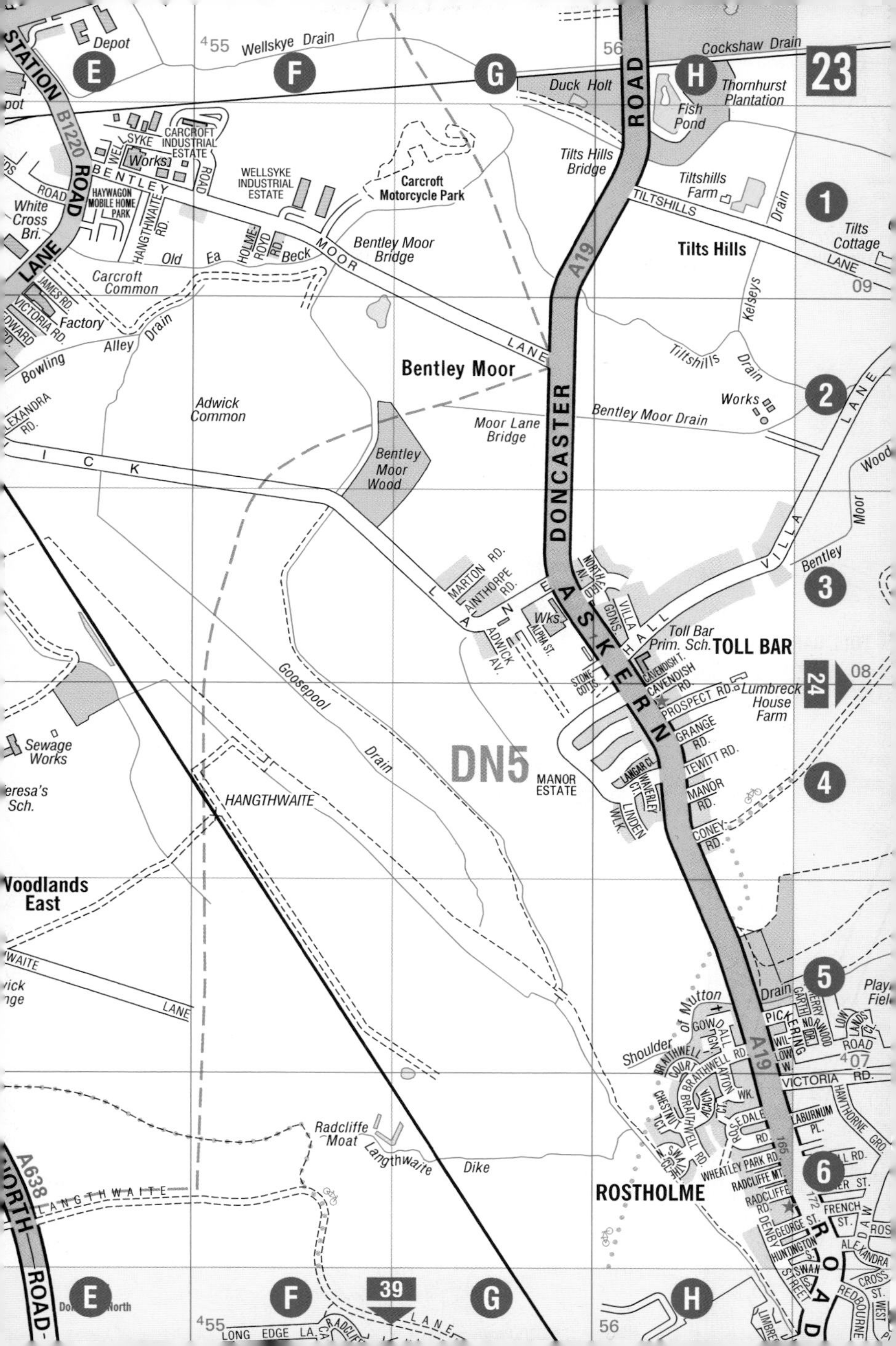
Depot
Wellskye Drain
Cockshaw Drain
Duck Holt
Thornhurst Plantation
Fish Pond
STATION ROAD
B1220
DONCASTER ROAD
A19
CARCROFT INDUSTRIAL ESTATE
WELLSYKE INDUSTRIAL ESTATE
Works
HAYWAGON MOBILE HOME PARK
HANGTHWAITE RD.
BENTLEY MOOR LANE
Carcroft Motorcycle Park
Tilts Hills Bridge
Tiltshills Farm
TILTSHILLS LANE
Drain
Tilts Cottage
Tilts Hills
White Cross Bri.
Old Ea Beck
HOLME-ROYD RD.
Bentley Moor Bridge
Carcroft Common
JAMES RD.
VICTORIA RD.
Factory
Bowling Alley Drain
Kelseys
Tiltshills Drain
Bentley Moor
ALEXANDRA RD.
Adwick Common
Works
Bentley Moor Drain
Moor Lane Bridge
Bentley Moor Wood
ADWICK LANE
Bentley Moor Wood
MARTON RD.
AINTHORPE RD.
NORTHFIELD AV.
VILLA GDNS.
VILLA HALL
Wks.
ALPHA ST.
ADWICK AV.
ASKERN
Toll Bar Prim. Sch.
TOLL BAR
CAVENDISH T.
CAVENDISH RD.
STONE COTTS.
PROSPECT RD.
Lumbreck House Farm
GRANGE RD.
TEWITT RD.
MANOR RD.
CONEY RD.
LANGAR CL.
WAVERLEY CT.
LINDEN WLK.
Goosepool Drain
DN5
MANOR ESTATE
Sewage Works
Teresa's Sch.
HANGTHWAITE
Woodlands East
HANGTHWAITE LANE
Shoulder of Mutton
Drain
GOWDALL GR.
BRATHWELL RD.
COURT
LAYTON
WK.
CHESTNUT CT.
ACACIA CT.
ROSEDALE RD.
PICKERING
WILLOW
NORWOOD DR.
CHERRY GARTH
LOW LANDS CL.
LOW ROAD
Play Field
VICTORIA RD.
LABURNUM PL.
HAWTHORNE GRO.
WHEATLEY PARK RD.
RADCLIFFE MT.
RADCLIFFE RD.
FRENCH ST.
DENBY
GEORGE ST.
HUNTINGTON ST.
SWAN STREET
ALEXANDRA
REDBOURNE
CROSS ST.
WEST ST.
ROSTHOLME
Radcliffe Moat
Langthwaite Dike
LANGTHWAITE
NORTH ROAD
A638
LONG EDGE LA.
Doncaster North
E F G H
1 2 3 4 5 6
455 56 09 08 407
24
39

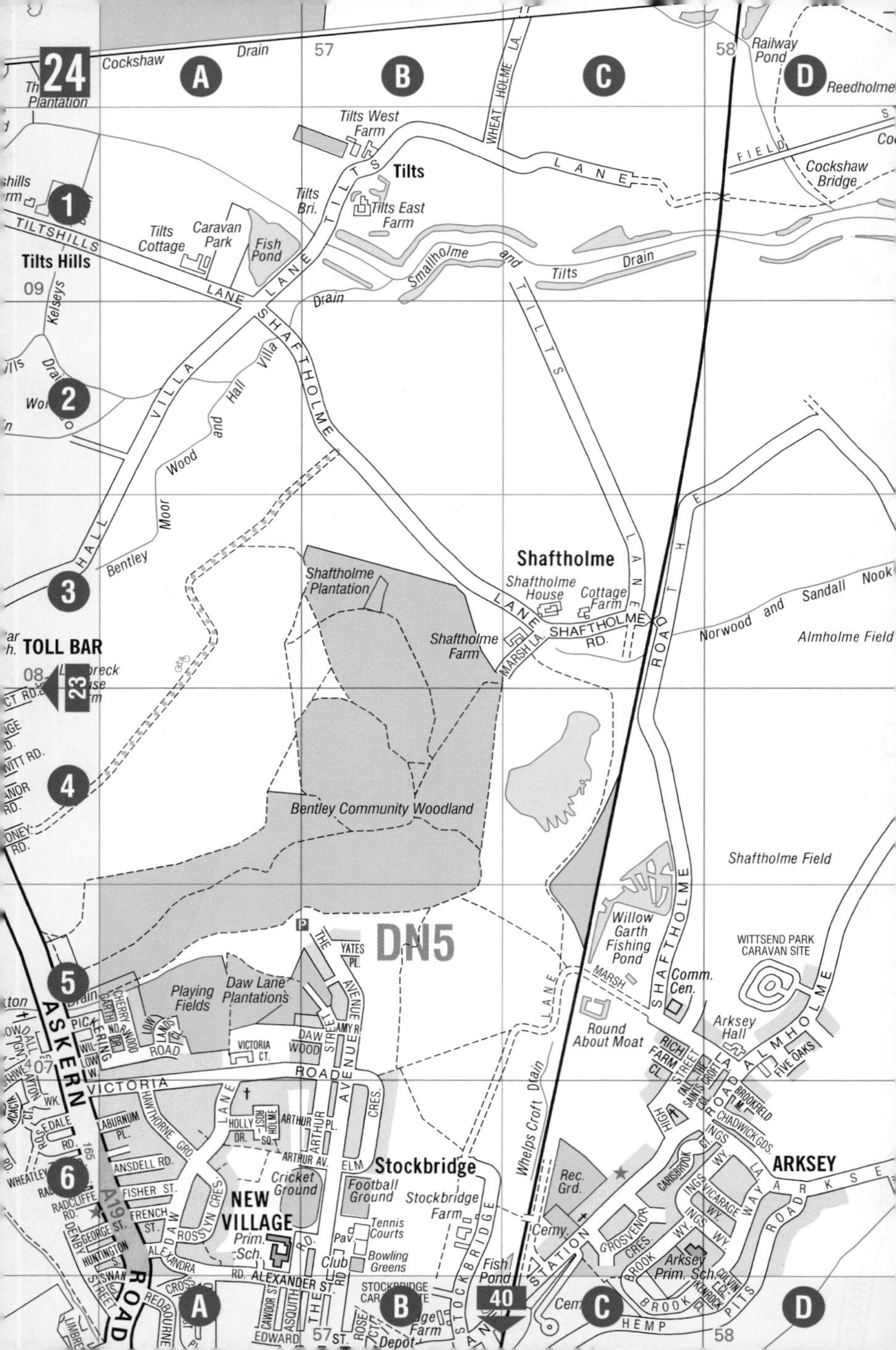

Cockshaw Drain
Tilts West Farm
Tilts
Tilts Bri.
Tilts East Farm
Wheat Holme La.
Lane
Field
Railway Pond
Reedholme
Cockshaw Bridge
Tiltshills Lane
Tilts Hills
Tilts Cottage
Caravan Park
Fish Pond
Tilts Lane
Smallholme and Tilts Drain
Drain
Shaftholme Lane
Villa Hall Lane
Moor Wood and Hall Villa
Bentley
Kelseys
Tilts Lane
The Road
Shaftholme
Shaftholme House
Cottage Farm
Shaftholme Farm
Shaftholme Rd.
Marsh La.
Norwood and Sandall Nook
Almholme Field
Shaftholme Plantation
TOLL BAR
Bentley Community Woodland
Shaftholme Field
Willow Garth Fishing Pond
DN5
The Yates Pl.
Avenue
Shaftholme
Comm. Cen.
Wittsend Park Caravan Site
Marsh Lane
Round About Moat
Arksey Hall
Almholme
Five Oaks
Playing Fields
Daw Lane Plantations
Victoria Ct.
Daw Wood
Amy R.
Street
Rich Farm Cl.
Askern Road
Victoria Road
Pickering
Cherry Garth
Norwood Dr.
Low Lands
Hawthorne Gro.
Holly Dr.
Rosemore Sq.
Arthur Pl.
Arthur Av.
Cres.
Elm
Laburnum Pl.
Ansdell Rd.
Fisher St.
French St.
Rosslyn Cres.
Daw Lane
Alexandra Rd.
Cricket Ground
NEW VILLAGE
Prim. Sch.
Stockbridge
Football Ground
Stockbridge Farm
Tennis Courts
Bowling Greens
Club
Pav.
Whelps Croft Drain
Rec. Grd.
Cemy.
Station
High Street
Saints Croft
Brookfield
Chadwick Gds.
Ings Wy.
Carisbrook Ct.
Vicarage Wy.
Grosvenor Cres.
Brook Wy.
Arksey Prim. Sch.
Colvin Cl.
Kenrock Cl.
Pits Road
Arksey Lane
ARKSEY
Hemp
Alexander St.
Stockbridge Car Park
Stockbridge
Fish Pond
Edward St.
Cawdor St.
Asquith St.
The Rd.
Rose Ct.
Depot
Cross
Redbourne
Huntington
George St.
Swan
Denby Rd.
Radcliffe Rd.
Wheatley
A19
Acacia
Rosedale Rd.
Wk.
A
B
C
D
1
2
3
4
5
6
57
58
09
08
407
165
23
40

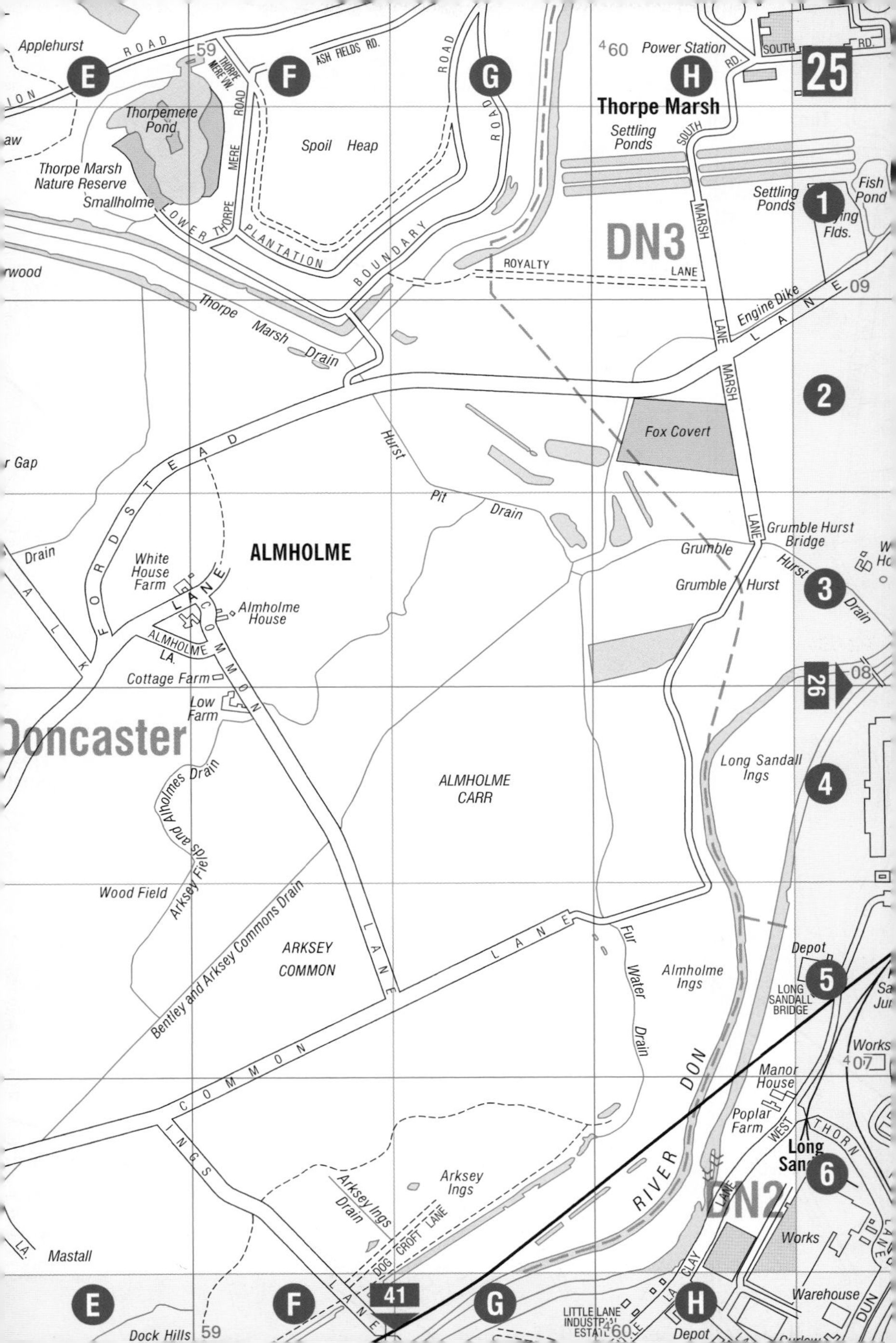
Applehurst
ROAD
Thorpemere Pond
Thorpe Marsh Nature Reserve
Smallholme
THORPE MERE VW.
ASH FIELDS RD.
Spoil Heap
MERE ROAD
LOWER THORPE
PLANTATION
BOUNDARY
ROAD
Power Station
SOUTH RD.
Thorpe Marsh
Settling Ponds
SOUTH
MARSH
Fish Pond
DN3
ROYALTY
LANE
Engine Dike
LANE
09
Thorpe Marsh Drain
MARSH
Fox Covert
Hurst
FORDSTEAD
Pit
Drain
LANE
Grumble Hurst Bridge
Grumble
Grumble
Hurst
Hurst Drain
ALMHOLME
White House Farm
Almholme House
ALMHOLME LA.
Drain
Cottage Farm
COMMON
Low Farm
Doncaster
26
08
Long Sandall Ings
Alholmes Drain
Arksey Fields and
ALMHOLME CARR
Wood Field
Bentley and Arksey Commons Drain
LANE
ARKSEY COMMON
LANE
Fur Water Drain
Almholme Ings
Depot
LONG SANDALL BRIDGE
COMMON
Works
407
Manor House
Poplar Farm
RIVER DON
WEST
THORN
Long Sand
INGS
Arksey Ings
Arksey Ings Drain
DOG CROFT LANE
DN2
LANE
CLAY
LA.
Works
LA.
Mastall
Warehouse
LANE
41
LITTLE LANE INDUSTRIAL ESTATE
460
Depot
Dock Hills
59
E
F
G
H
1
2
3
4
5
6

Thorpe Marsh
Playing Flds.
Fish Pond
Thorpe Marsh Bridge
Barnby Dun Bridge
INSET
Barnby Dun Fields
BARNBY DUN
Engine Dike
RIVER DON
RIVER DUN NAVIGATION
Croft Ings
Town End Drain
Grumble Hurst Bridge
Grumble Hurst Drain
Waite House
Glass Park Millennium Green
Moor Lane Rec. Grd.
Rugby & Football Ground
Old Kirk Sandall
Grove Farm
The Poplars
Long Sandall Ings
KIRK SANDALL INDUSTRIAL ESTATE
Works
Kirk Sandall
DN3
KIRK SANDALL
Brecks Plantation
Waste Treatment Plant
Kirk Sandall Junction
GUILDHALL INDUSTRIAL ESTATE
Factory
Warehouses
Sunnyside
Playing Field
Kirk Sandall Inf. & Jun. Schs.
Canon Popham C of E Prim. Sch.
Superstore
Hungerhill School
Edenthorpe Hall Primary School
GURTH AVENUE CARAVAN SITE
Long Sandall
DN2
Manor House
Poplar Farm
Dodge Dike
A18
THORNE ROAD
DONCASTER RD.
STATION ROAD
HATFIELD ROAD
ARMTHORPE ROAD
42

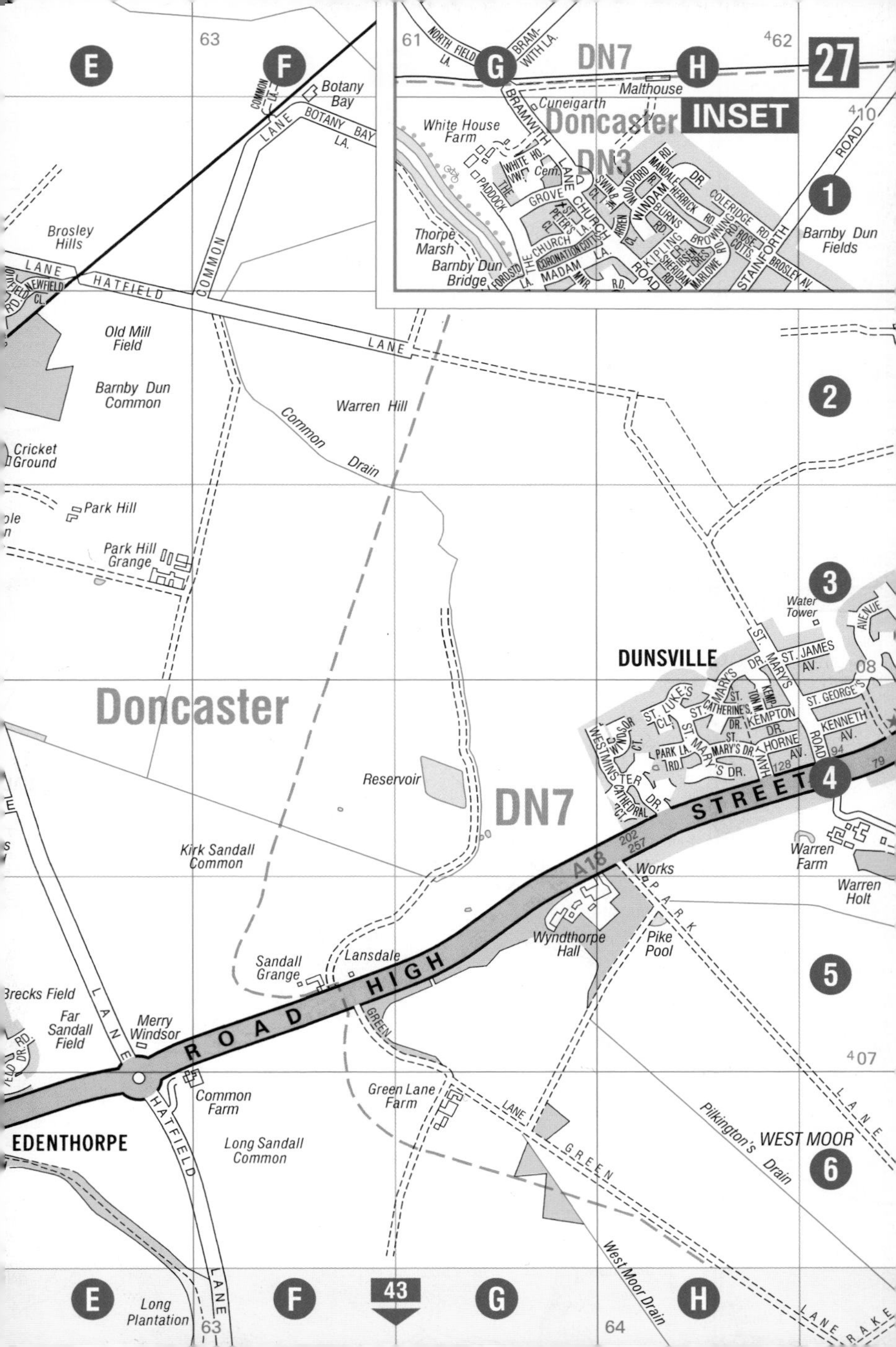

E 63 F

Botany
Bay

COMMON LANE

BOTANY BAY
LA.

Brosley
Hills

LANE

HATFIELD

NEWFIELD
CL.

Old Mill
Field

COMMON LANE

LANE

Barnby Dun
Common

Warren Hill

Common Drain

Cricket
Ground

Park Hill

Park Hill
Grange

Doncaster

Reservoir

DUNSVILLE

ST. MARY'S DR.

ST. MARY'S DR.

ST. JAMES
AV.

ST. LUKE'S
CL.

ST. CATHERINE'S
DR.

TOM
WINDAM

KEMPTON

ST. GEORGE'S

WESTMINSTER RD.

PARK LA.

ST. MARY'S DR.

CARDINAL RD.

S. DR.

HORNE

KENNETH
AV.

94

08

DN7

Reservoir

A18

STREET

Warren
Farm

Warren
Holt

4

79

Kirk Sandall
Common

Works

Wyndthorpe
Hall

Pike
Pool

202
257

PARK

5

Brecks Field

Far
Sandall
Field

Merry
Windsor

ROAD HIGH

Sandall
Grange

Lansdale

GREEN LANE

Green Lane
Farm

LANE

Common
Farm

HATFIELD LANE

Long Sandall
Common

GREEN

Pilkington's Drain

WEST MOOR

407

LANE

6

EDENTHORPE

E Long
Plantation
63

F 43 G

West Moor Drain

H

LANE RAKE

64

61 North Field La. G BRAM. WITH LA. DN7 H 462 27

Malthouse

Cuneigarth

Doncaster INSET

DN3

White House
Farm

WHITE HO
PW CEM

PADDOCK

GROVE

CHURCH

CHURCH LA.

Thorpe
Marsh

Barnby Dun
Bridge

CORONATION COTTS.

MADAM

LONDON

LA.

ISEL

MANDALE

HERRICK

ADAM

OSFORD

WINDOM

BURNS

RD.

KIPLING

COLERIDGE RD.

BROWNING

ST.

MILTON

STAINFORTH

MARLOW

BROSLEY AV.

ROAD

Barnby Dun
Fields

1

2

3 Water
Tower

AVENUE

4 10

28
A
B
C
D
14
1
2
3
4
5
6
WOOD
Norcroft Bridge
Banks Bottom
Banks Bottom Dike
Tanyard Spring
Fall Head Farmhouse
Fall Head Farm
Lees Hall Farm
Field Head
Field Head Manor
Club House
Glebe Farm
Pot Ho. Bri.
Pot Ho. Mill Farm
Weir
SILKSTONE
Roggins
ROAD
BARNSLEY ROAD
A628
NOBLETHORPE PARK
Noblethorpe
Red Lodge
White Lodge
Silkstone Primary Sch.
Silkstone Cross
Bank Ho. Farm
Hollow Spring
Silverwood Camp
SILKSTONE FALL
Tanyard Wood
Club
Cemetery
Rec. Grd.
Cricket Ground
Woolley Manor Farm
Hill Top Wood
Reservoir (covered)
Works
Champany Hill
Champany Hill Farm
Hill Top
The Villas
Blacker Green Play. Fld.
Blacker Wood
Blacker Dam
Hall Royd Farm
BEN BANK
Ben Bank
Garage
Hall Royd Wood
Silkstone Common
SILKSTONE COMMON
Lakeside View
Royd Hill
Rec. Grd.
Sewage Works
Moor End Wood
Throstle Nest Farm (Equestrian Centre)
Moor End
Moor End Houses
Silkstone Common Jun. & Inf. Sch.
Lower Coates
Icicle Wood
Nether Royd Wood
Moor End Cotts.
Knabbe's Hall Farm
Nabs Wood Nature Reserve
Dodworth Moor End
KNABBS LANE
B6449
Stubbin Wood
The Hollies
Roydcroft
Thornhill
Berry Moor House
Hadley House
Spring Wood
Hollin
Falthwaite Wood
House Carr Bridge
HOUSE CARR LANE
Dike

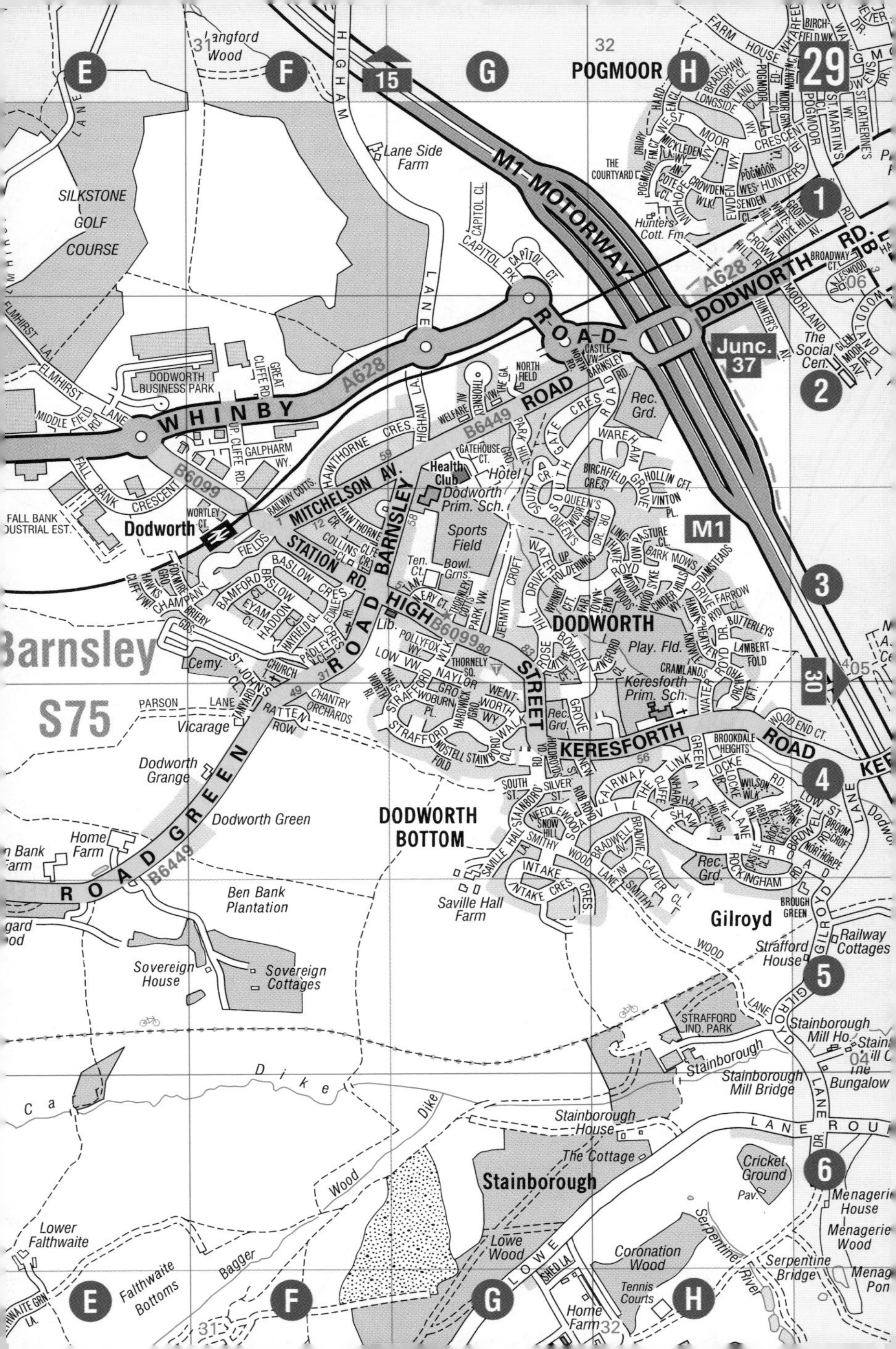

29
15
30
E
F
G
H
1
2
3
4
5
6
31
32
Langford Wood
POGMOOR
SILKSTONE GOLF COURSE
Lane Side Farm
M1 MOTORWAY
A628
DODWORTH RD.
Junc. 37
M1
The Social Cen.
DODWORTH BUSINESS PARK
WHINBY ROAD
B6099
B6449
Dodworth
MITCHELSON AV.
BARNSLEY ROAD
STATION RD.
HIGH STREET
Health Club
Hotel
Dodworth Prim. Sch.
Sports Field
DODWORTH
Play. Fld.
Keresforth Prim. Sch.
KERESFORTH ROAD
Barnsley
S75
Cemy.
Vicarage
Dodworth Grange
Dodworth Green
ROAD GREEN
Home Farm
DODWORTH BOTTOM
Gilroyd
Saville Hall Farm
Ben Bank Plantation
Sovereign House
Sovereign Cottages
Strafford House
Railway Cottages
STRAFFORD IND. PARK
Stainborough Mill Ho.
Stainborough Mill Bridge
The Bungalow
Stainborough House
The Cottage
Stainborough
Cricket Ground
Menagerie House
Menagerie Wood
Lower Falthwaite
Falthwaite Bottoms
Lowe Wood
Coronation Wood
Serpentine River
Serpentine Bridge
Tennis Courts
Home Farm

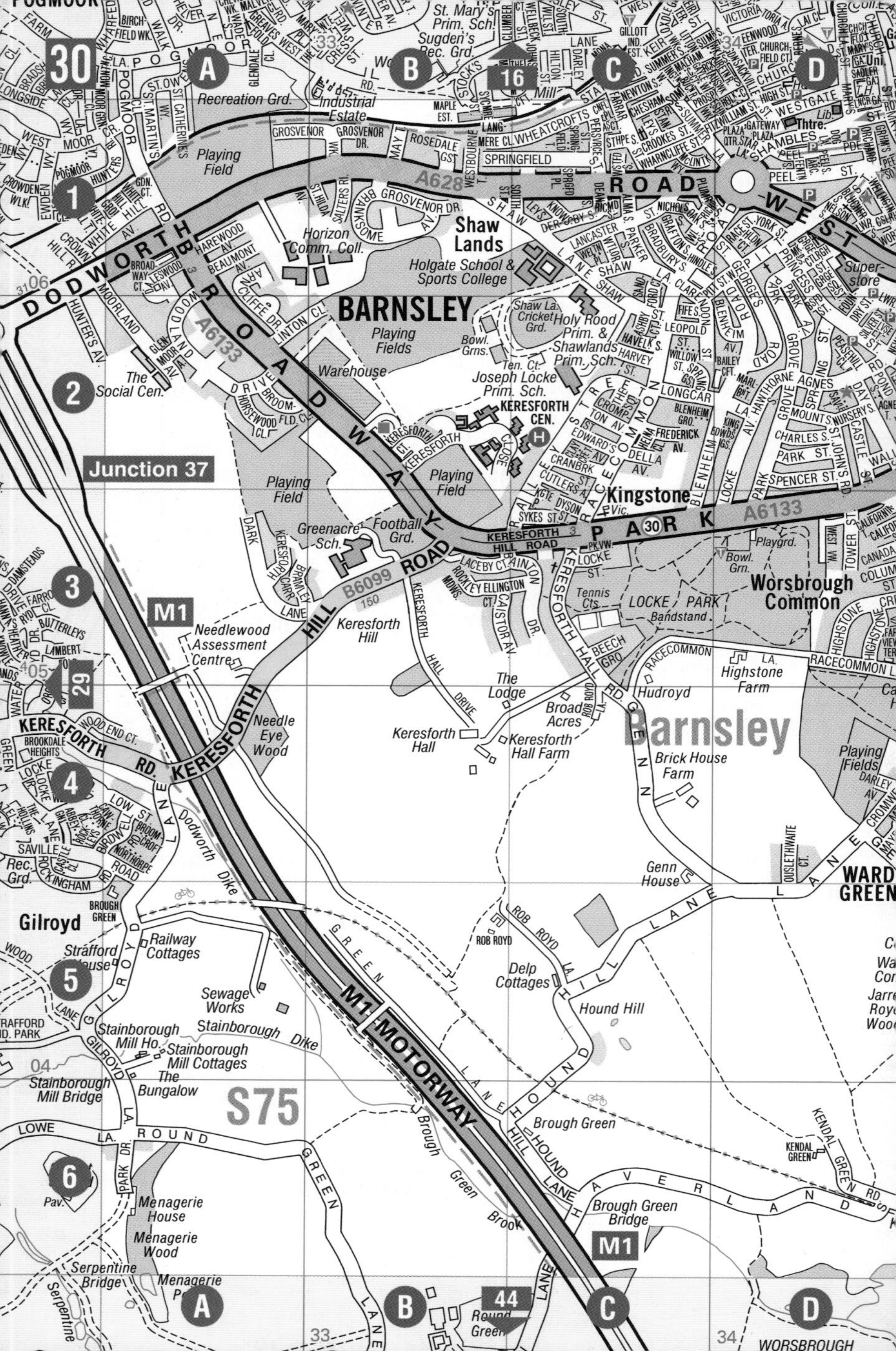

POGMOOR
A
B
C
D
16
1
2
3
4
5
6
St. Mary's Prim. Sch.
Sugden's Rec. Grd.
Recreation Grd.
Industrial Estate
Playing Field
A628
ROAD WEST
DODWORTH
BROADWAY
A6133
Horizon Comm. Coll.
Shaw Lands
Holgate School & Sports College
BARNSLEY
Playing Fields
Shaw La. Cricket Grd.
Holy Rood Prim. & Shawlands Prim. Sch.
Warehouse
Joseph Locke Prim. Sch.
KERESFORTH CEN.
The Social Cen.
Junction 37
Playing Field
Kingstone
PARK ROAD
Greenacre Sch.
Football Grd.
B6099
KERESFORTH HILL ROAD
Worsbrough Common
LOCKE PARK
Bandstand
Tennis Cts.
M1
Needlewood Assessment Centre
Keresforth Hill
29
The Lodge
Broad Acres
Keresforth Hall
Keresforth Hall Farm
Needle Eye Wood
Highstone Farm
Hudroyd
Barnsley
Brick House Farm
Playing Fields
Gilroyd
Railway Cottages
Strafford House
Genn House
WARD GREEN
ROB ROYD
Delp Cottages
Hound Hill
Sewage Works
Stainborough Mill Ho.
Stainborough Mill Cottages
Stainborough Dike
Stainborough Mill Bridge
The Bungalow
S75
M1 MOTORWAY
Brough Green
Kendal Green
HAVERLANDS
Brough Green Bridge
Brough Green Brook
Menagerie House
Menagerie Wood
Serpentine Bridge
Menagerie Pond
44
Round Green
WORSBROUGH
33
34

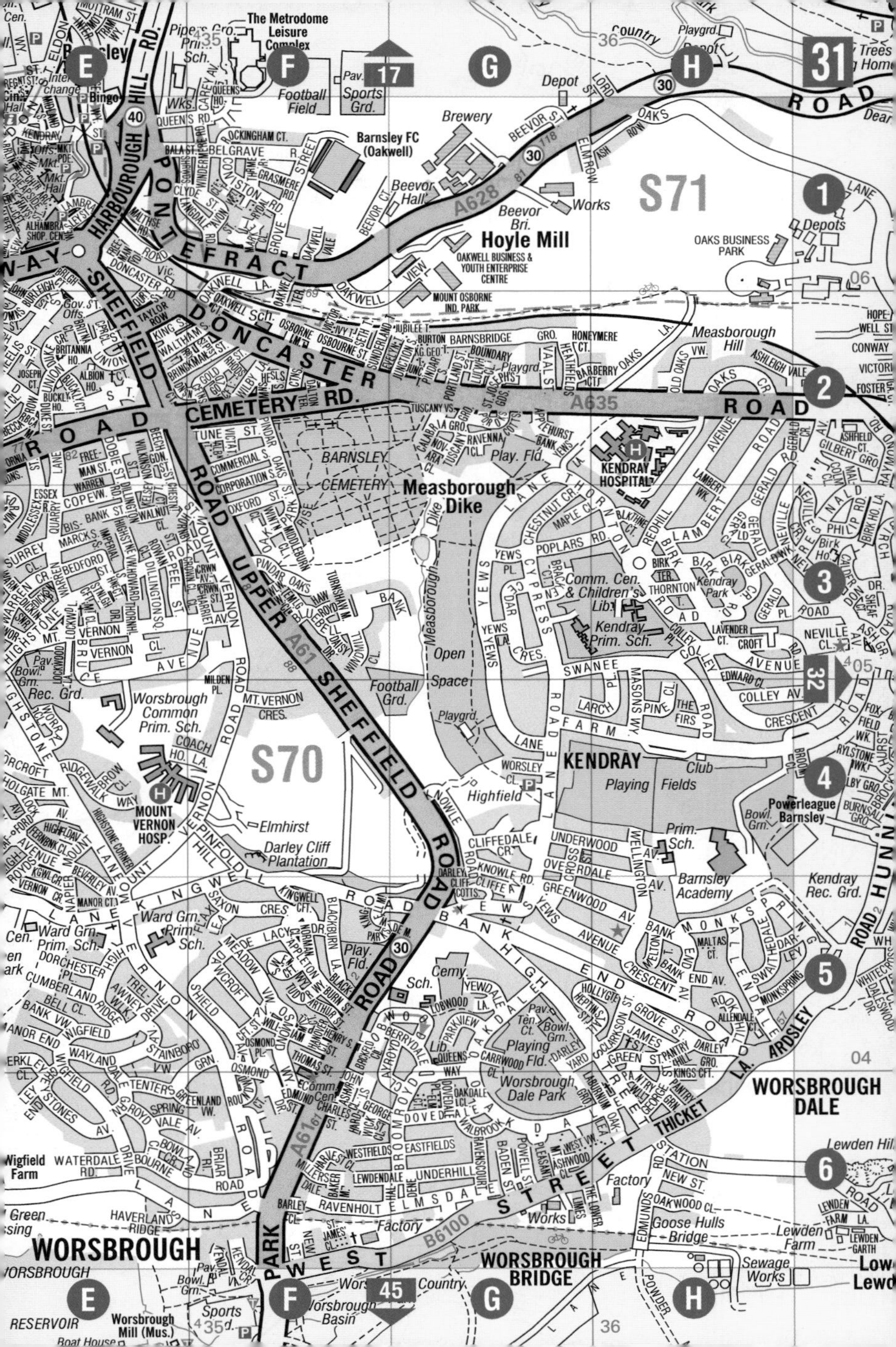
31
E
F
G
H
17
45
32
1
2
3
4
5
6
S71
S70
The Metrodome Leisure Complex
Football Field
Sports Grd.
Pav.
Barnsley FC (Oakwell)
Brewery
Depot
Playgrd.
Country
ROAD
PONTEFRACT
A628
Beevor Hall
Beevor Bri.
Works
Hoyle Mill
OAKWELL BUSINESS & YOUTH ENTERPRISE CENTRE
MOUNT OSBORNE IND. PARK
OAKS BUSINESS PARK
Depots
HARBOUROUGH HILL RD.
SHEFFIELD ROAD
DONCASTER ROAD
CEMETERY RD.
A635
Measborough Hill
BARNSLEY CEMETERY
Measborough Dike
KENDRAY HOSPITAL
Comm. Cen. & Children's Lib.
Kendray Prim. Sch.
Kendray Park
UPPER SHEFFIELD ROAD
A61
Football Grd.
Open Space
Worsbrough Common Prim. Sch.
MOUNT VERNON HOSP.
Elmhirst
Darley Cliff Plantation
Highfield
KENDRAY
Playing Fields
Club
Prim. Sch.
Barnsley Academy
Powerleague Barnsley
Kendray Rec. Grd.
Bowl. Grn.
Ward Grn. Prim. Sch.
KINGWELL ROAD
Play. Fld.
Sch.
Cemy.
Lib.
Playing Fld.
Worsbrough Dale Park
WORSBROUGH DALE
Lewden Hill
Factory
Works
Goose Hulls Bridge
Lewden Farm
Sewage Works
WEST STREET
B6100
THICKET
ARDSLEY
STATION
WORSBROUGH
WORSBROUGH BRIDGE
Wigfield Farm
Worsbrough Mill (Mus.)
RESERVOIR
Worsbrough Basin
PARK ROAD
Sports
04
05
06
35
36

32
A
B
C
D
18
46
31
1
2
3
4
5
6
Barnsley
S71
S70
STAIRFOOT
Cundy Cross
WORSBROUGH DALE
Swaithe
Lower Lewden
PONTEFRACT ROAD
A628
A633
A635
B6100
DONCASTER RD.
DONCASTER
GRANGE LANE
WOMBWELL LANE
HUNNINGLEY ROAD
ARDSLEY ROAD
Monk Bretton Priory (remains)
Grange Lane Events Area
Dearne Valley Country Park
DEARNE VALLEY PARK
Scorah Wood
Ardsley Tunnel
River Dearne
Dearne Bri.
Sewage Bridge
Lagoons
Cherry Tree Nursing Home
OAKS BUSINESS PARK
Depots
Warehouse
GRANGE LANE INDUSTRIAL ESTATE
Works
Grasmere Sch.
Measborough Hill
Comm. Cen.
Oakhill Prim. Sch.
Rec. Grd.
Superstore
STAIRFOOT BUSINESS PARK
BARNSLEY RETAIL PARK
Hunningley Primary School
Ardsley Cemy.
Kendray Park
Powerleague Barnsley
Kendray Rec. Grd.
Cork Bridge
Weir
Swaithe Hall
Swaithe Hall Farm
Swaithe Wood
Swaithe Bri.
Dob Sike
Lewden Hill
Lewden Kennels
Lewden Bridge
Lewden Spring
Lewden Farm
Sewage Works
River Dove
Yew Plantation
Hotel
MUCKY LANE
TANK ROW
CAULK LANE
WHITE CROSS LANE
STATION ROAD
ALDHAM
ALBANY CL.

Storrs Wood
Saville Wood
Hollins Wood
Horse Carr Wood
Major Wood
Pearson Wood
Horse Carr Wood
Crook House Farm
STORRS MILL LA.
CROOK
Tyers Hall Farm
Tyers Hall
The Bungalow
Tyers Hill
Tyers Hill
Tyers Hill Cotts.
WATERING LANE
Lees Hill
Wood Laithes Farm
758
THE STACKYARD
HEATHCROFT CHASE
PRIEST CROFT LANE
NEW HALL LANE
Cranford Hall
New Hall Farm
A635 ROAD
BROOKFIELD
BARNSLEY RD.
Barnsley Crematorium
LOW LAITHES VILLAGE
Low Laithes
FARM LANE
OLD
Aldham Bridge
Industrial Estate
NETHERWOOD COUNTRY PARK
S73
Low Valley Farm
NETHERWOOD ROAD
PITT STREET
ST. MATTHEW'S CT.
ALDHAM INDUSTRIAL ESTATE
ALDHAM COTTS.
MITCHELLS ENTERPRISE CENTRE
MITCHELL RD.
BARNSLEY RD.
LANE
Works
BRADBERRY BALK LA
Football Ground
Bradberry Balk Bridge
Playing Fields
Playing Fields
Bowl. Grn.
MITCHELLS A633
VALLEY WAY
WOMBWELL
Wombwell Race Circuit Go-Kart Track
STATION ROAD INDUSTRIAL ESTATE
VALLEY RD.
STATION B6096 RD.
Playing Field
Prim. Sch.
GEORGE ST.
STONYFORD RD.
Research Cen.
High View Primary Learning Cen.
RIMINGTON ROAD
Sports Ground
GENOA CL.
CORTINA RI.
LUGANO GRO.
UPPERWOOD
MODENA CT.
FERRARA CL.
SALERNO WY.
CAPRI CT.
BARI CL.
ALBA CL.
LOMBARD CRESCENT
RIMINI RI.
MARINA RI.
PARMA RI.
ANCONA RI.
FLORENCE RD.
VENETIAN CR.
ROUNDWOOD WY.
DARTREE WK.
MARSALA WK.
Prim. Sch.
HOLGATE CRESCENT
WORTLEY AV.
MOORBANK VW.
MOORBANK CL.
HOUSE
ROY KILNER RD.
ROSE GROVE
ROSE PL.
STREET
WILSON
WAINWRIGHT AV.
YVONNE
39
440
E F G H
19
47
34
1 2 3 4 5 6
06
04
405

A
B
C
D
1
2
3
4
5
6
20
33
48
441
42
06
405
04
S71
S73
Crook House Farm
Fair Winds
Ridgeway House
STORRS MILL LA.
CROOK HOUSE LANE
NORTH CARR LANE
PRIEST CROFT LANE
LOW FARM CT.
MIDDLE FARM CT.
EDDERTHORPE
EDDERTHORPE LANE
RIVER DEARNE
Works
PARK SPRING
A6195
MIDDLE LA.
Mill House
INGS LANE
Little Houghton Bridge
LITTLE HOUGHTON LANE
Open Space
SALTERSBROOK ROAD
A635
BARNSLEY ROAD
Playing Field
Cemetery
Highfield
HIGH VIEW CL.
Barnsley
Middlewood Hall
Lodge
Middlewood Park
Parklands
DONCASTER ROAD
Darfield Bridge
Upperwood Hall
Prim. Sch.
Rec. Grd.
DARFIELD
B6096
NANNY MARR RD.
Welfare Park
Council Offs.
CHURCH STREET
Lib. Mus. & Heritage Cen.
SPRINGBANK
Snape Hill
Play. Fld.
SNAPE HILL ROAD
Club
PITT STREET
GEORGE ST.
Low Valley
River Dove
WOMBWELL INGS
Caravan Park
Towns Lands
Sewage Works
Council Depot
STATION ROAD INDUSTRIAL ESTATE
STATION RD.
STONYFORD RD.
Billing Dike ROAD
FIRTH INGS
BRIDGE INGS
CLIFF ROAD
CAT HILL
Quarry Hill
BROOMHILL LA.
ST. MATTHEW'S CT.
Low Valley Farm

35
21
49
36
E
F
G
H
1
2
3
4
5
6
43
44
06
05
04
GREAT HOUGHTON
LITTLE HOUGHTON
SANDHILL
MIDDLECLIFFE
BILLINGLEY
Millhouses
Rotherham S63
S72
ROTHERHAM ROAD
THURNSCOE LANE
HOUGHTON ROAD
BILLINGLEY LANE
WEST ROAD
KIRK LANE
MIDDLECLIFF LA.
HIGH STREET
BACK LANE
CHAPEL LANE
STOCKS LANE
FLAT LANE
BILLINGLEY GREEN LA.
DEARNE VALLEY PARKWAY
DEARNE ROAD
KING'S ROAD
PASTURE LANE
NEW LANE
CATHILL ROUNDABOUT
A6195
A635
B6273
B6411
A664
Sandhill Prim. Sch.
Sewage Works
Thurnscoe Dike
SANDHILL GOLF COURSE
Golf Driving Range
Club Ho.
Club
Sports Ground
Rec. Grd.
Play-grd.
Holmes
Hall Farm
War Mem.
Primrose Hill
Billingley Green
Billingley Bridge
Rose Valley
Woodbine Cottage
Carr Dike
Carr Head
RECTORY CL.
BARN OWL CL.
WELL CT.
LES MOND CR.
SEALANDS CL.
MIDDLECLIFF COTTS.
WINDSOR CRES.
QUEEN'S CRES.
GEORGE ST.
JOHN ST.
ALBERT CR.
BELMONT
CHARLES ST.
MARY ST.
EDWARD ST.
NEW ST.
TURNER ST.
WESCOE AV.
NORFOLK
SANDHILL CT.
BYRON ST.
JOHN
EBENEZER ST.
CROSS ST.
DEARNE ST.
OAK HAVEN AV.
MOUNT AV.
PLEASANT AV.
STONEBRIDGE LA.
POTTS CR.
PINFIELD CL.
CHURCH ST.
MILTON ST.
Playground
Rec. Grd.
Colliery Farm
Warehou

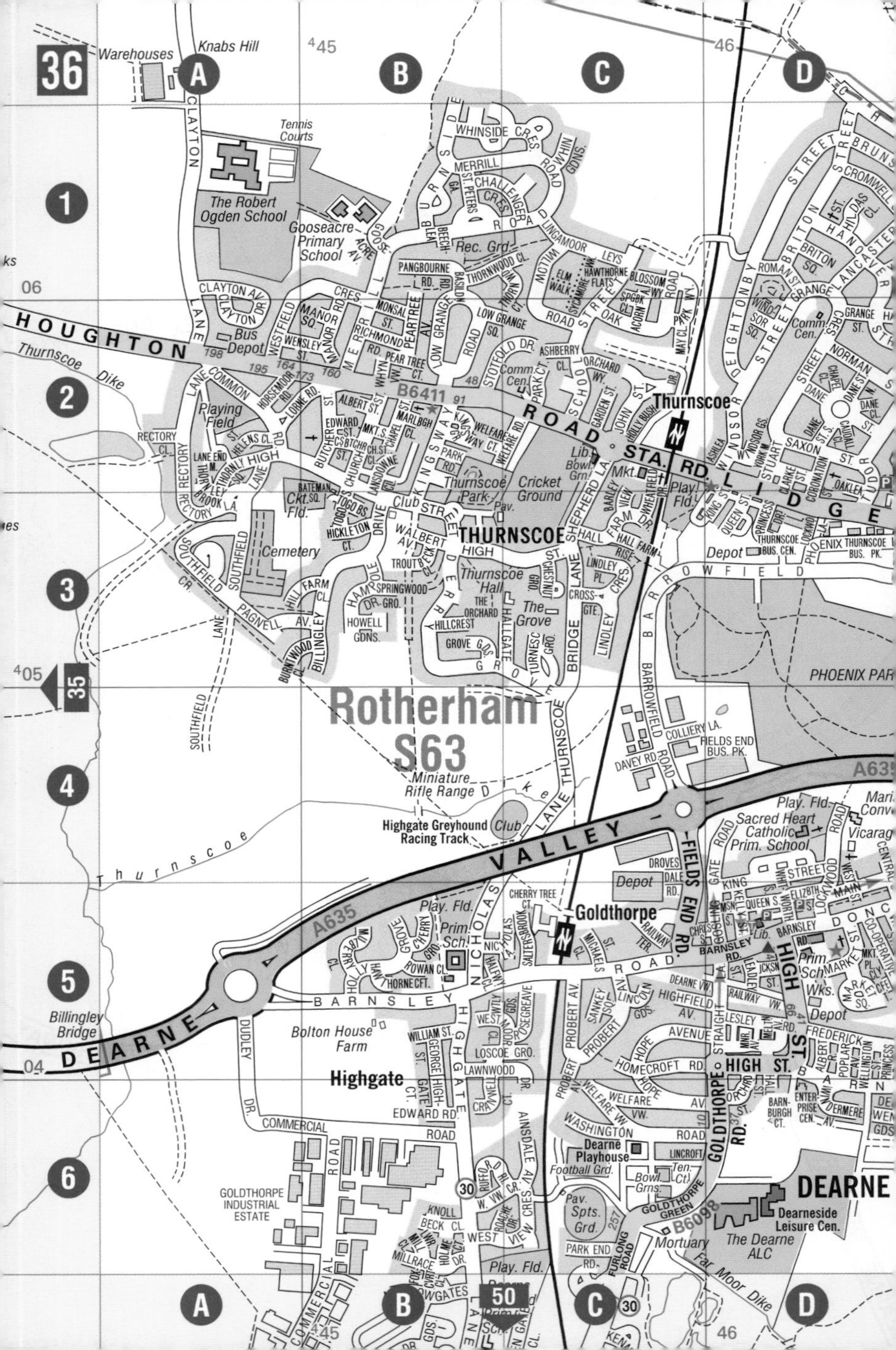
36
Warehouses
Knabs Hill
The Robert Ogden School
Gooseacre Primary School
Tennis Courts
Rec. Grd.
HOUGHTON ROAD
Thurnscoe Dike
Bus Depot
B6411
Playing Field
Ckt. Fld.
Cemetery
Thurnscoe Park
Cricket Ground
THURNSCOE
Thurnscoe Hall
The Grove
Thurnscoe
STA. RD.
LIDGET
Depot
THURNSCOE BUS. CEN.
PHOENIX THURNSCOE BUS. PK.
PHOENIX PAR
Rotherham
S63
Miniature Rifle Range
Highgate Greyhound Racing Track
Club
FIELDS END BUS. PK.
A635
DEARNE VALLEY
Sacred Heart Catholic Prim. School
Vicarag
Goldthorpe
Depot
Prim. Sch.
Play. Fld.
Billingley Bridge
Bolton House Farm
Highgate
GOLDTHORPE INDUSTRIAL ESTATE
Dearne Playhouse
Football Grd.
Spts. Grd.
Bowl. Grns.
Mortuary
B6098
DEARNE
Dearneside Leisure Cen.
The Dearne ALC
Far Moor Dike
Thurnscoe
50
35

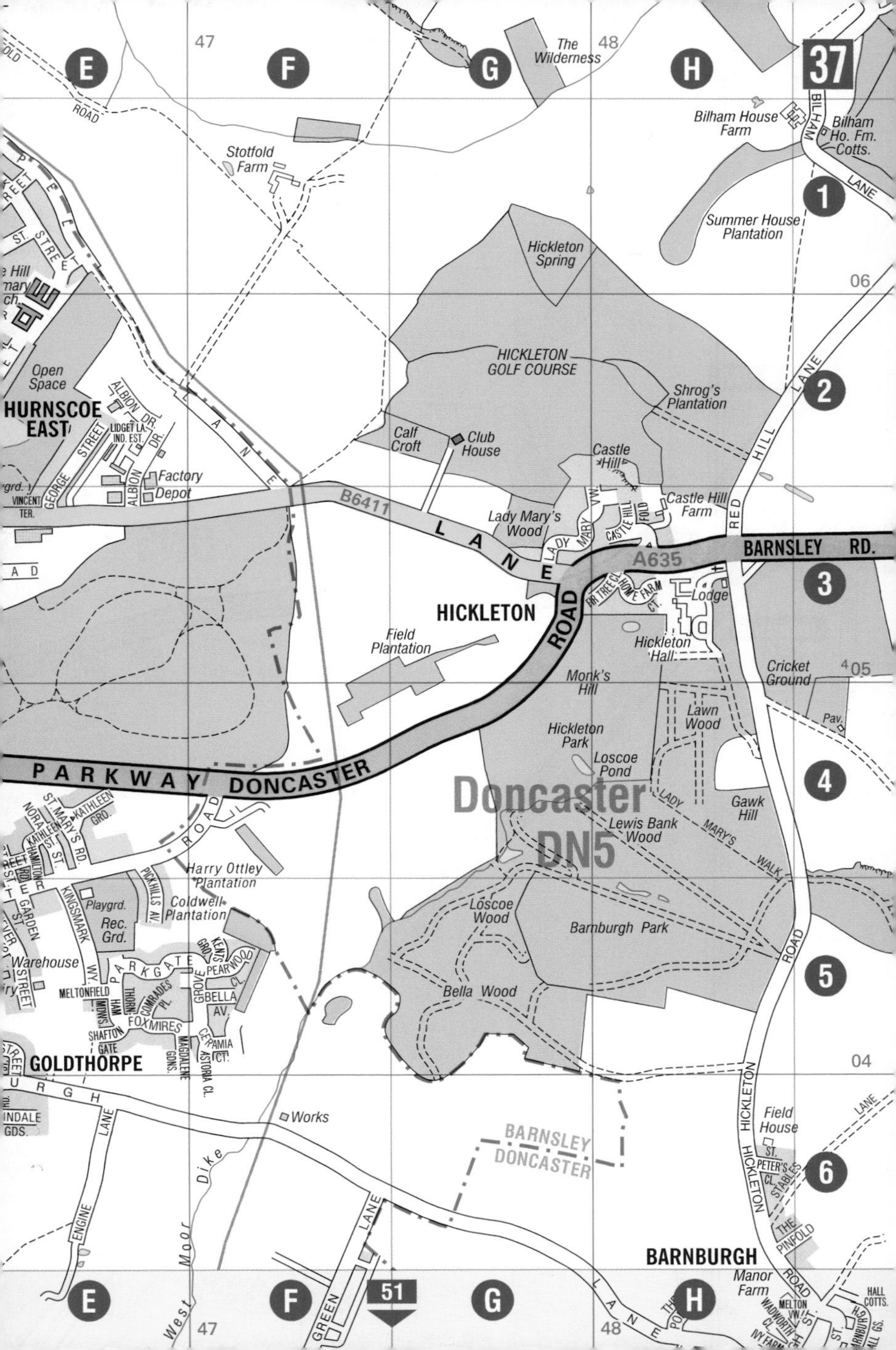

E
F
G
H
47
48
The Wilderness
Bilham House Farm
Bilham Ho. Fm. Cotts.
BILHAM LANE
Stotfold Farm
ROAD
Summer House Plantation
Hickleton Spring
06
HICKLETON GOLF COURSE
Shrog's Plantation
Open Space
THURNSCOE EAST
ALBION DR.
LIDGET LA. IND. EST.
GEORGE STREET
ALBION DR.
Factory
Depot
VINCENT TER.
LANE
Calf Croft
Club House
Castle Hill
Castle Hill Farm
RED HILL LANE
B6411
LANE
Lady Mary's Wood
LADY MARY VW.
CASTLE HILL FOLD
A635
BARNSLEY RD.
HICKLETON
ROAD
FIR TREE CL.
HOME FARM CT.
Lodge
Field Plantation
Hickleton Hall
Monk's Hill
Cricket Ground
05
Pav.
Lawn Wood
Hickleton Park
Loscoe Pond
Gawk Hill
PARKWAY DONCASTER
Doncaster DN5
LADY MARY'S WALK
Lewis Bank Wood
NORA
ST. MARY'S RD.
KATHLEEN GRO.
KATHLEEN ST.
HAMILTON RD.
Harry Ottley Plantation
Coldwell Plantation
KINGSMARK WY.
PICKHILLS AV.
Playgrd.
Rec. Grd.
Loscoe Wood
Barnburgh Park
Warehouse
PARKGATE
GROVE
KENT'S GRO.
PEARWOOD CL.
BELLA AV.
MELTONFIELD
HAM MDWS.
THORN
COMRADES PL.
FOXMIRES
SHAFTON GATE
MAGDALENE GDNS.
CERAMIA CT.
ASTORIA CL.
Bella Wood
GOLDTHORPE
04
Works
BARNSLEY
DONCASTER
HICKLETON ROAD
Field House
ST. PETER'S CL.
STABLES
THE PINFOLD
LANE
ENGINE LANE
West Moor Dike
GREEN LANE
51
BARNBURGH
Manor Farm
MELTON VW.
WADWORTH CL.
HALL COTTS.
BARNBURGH HALL GS.
LANE

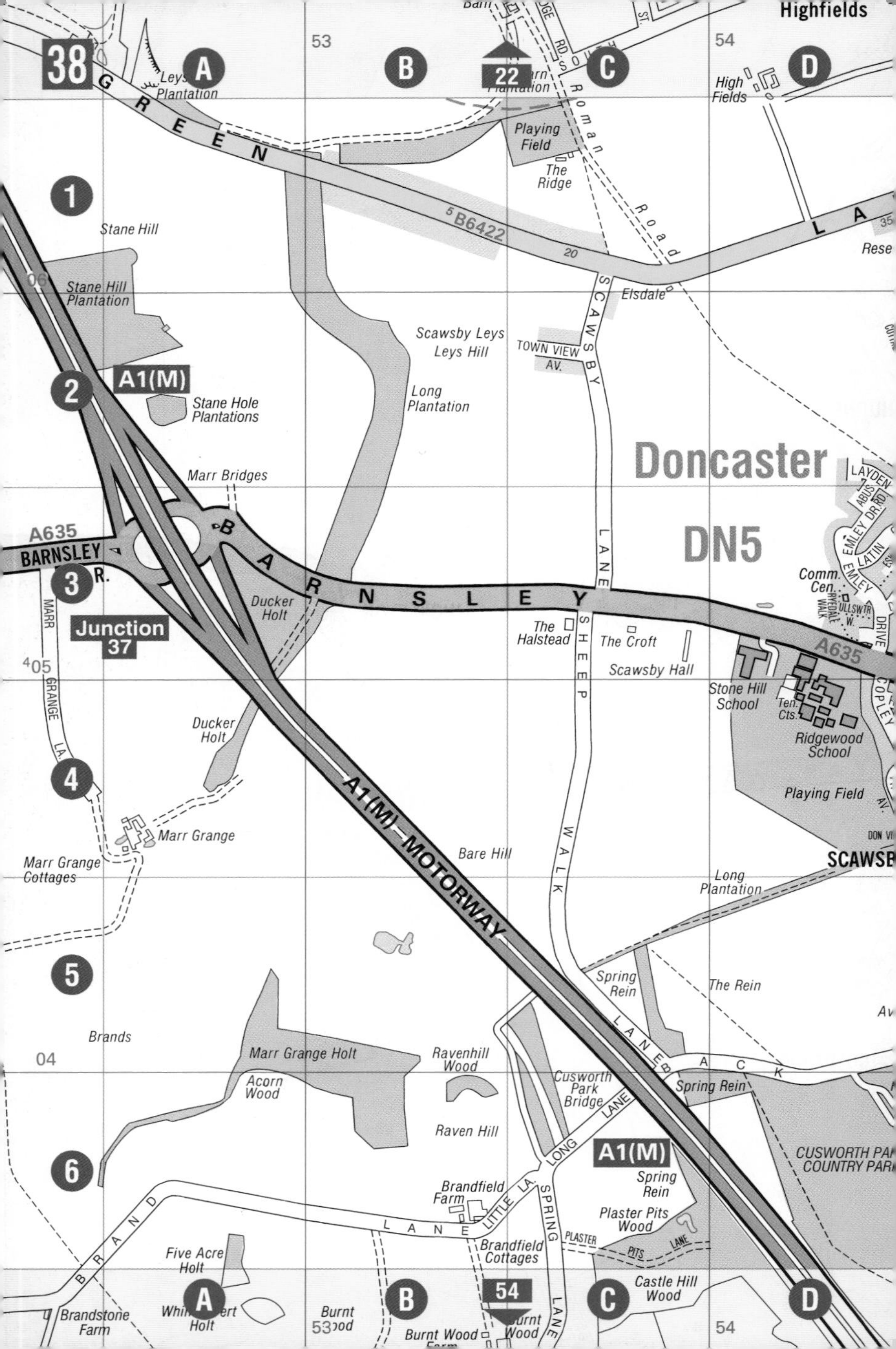

38
Highfields
22
54
Doncaster
DN5
A1(M)
Junction 37
A635
BARNSLEY RD.
GREEN LANE
B6422
Roman Road
A1(M) MOTORWAY
BARNSLEY
SCAWSBY LANE
SHEEP WALK LANE
BACK LANE
LONG LANE
LITTLE LA.
SPRING LANE
BRAND LANE
PLASTER PITS LANE
MARR GRANGE LA.
TOWN VIEW AV.
Leys Plantation
Playing Field
The Ridge
High Fields
Stane Hill
Stane Hill Plantation
Stane Hole Plantations
Marr Bridges
Scawsby Leys
Leys Hill
Long Plantation
Elsdale
Ducker Holt
The Halstead
The Croft
Scawsby Hall
Stone Hill School
Ridgewood School
Playing Field
Comm. Cen.
Marr Grange
Marr Grange Cottages
Bare Hill
SCAWSBY
Spring Rein
The Rein
Brands
Marr Grange Holt
Acorn Wood
Ravenhill Wood
Raven Hill
Cusworth Park Bridge
CUSWORTH PARK COUNTRY PARK
Spring Rein
Brandfield Farm
Brandfield Cottages
Plaster Pits Wood
Five Acre Holt
Castle Hill Wood
Brandstone Farm
Burnt Wood
Burnt Wood Farm
53
54
06
05
04

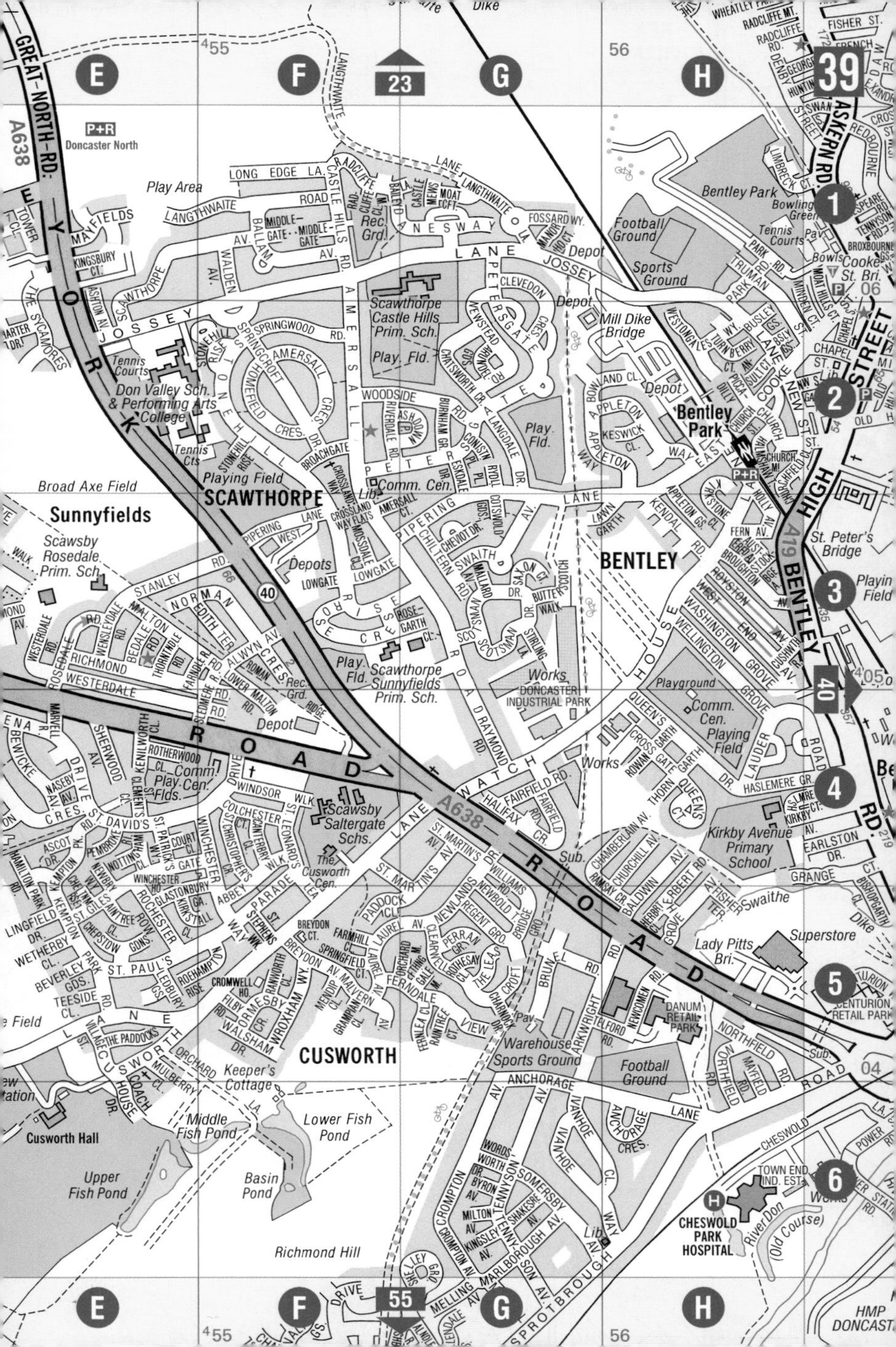
GREAT NORTH RD.
A638
YORK ROAD
P+R
Doncaster North
Play Area
LONG EDGE LA.
LANGTHWAITE ROAD
JOSSEY LANE
SCAWTHORPE
Scawthorpe Castle Hills Prim. Sch.
Play. Fld.
Don Valley Sch. & Performing Arts College
Tennis Courts
Playing Field
Broad Axe Field
Sunnyfields
Scawsby Rosedale Prim. Sch.
AMERSALL RD.
PETERSGATE
Mill Dike Bridge
Depot
Football Ground
Sports Ground
Bentley Park
Bowling Green
Tennis Courts
Bentley Park
BENTLEY
A19 BENTLEY RD.
HIGH STREET
ASKERN RD.
St. Peter's Bridge
Playing Field
Depots
Works
DONCASTER INDUSTRIAL PARK
Scawthorpe Sunnyfields Prim. Sch.
Comm. Cen.
Playing Field
Playground
Comm. Play. Flds.
Scawsby Saltergate Schs.
The Cusworth Cen.
Kirkby Avenue Primary School
Superstore
Lady Pitts Bri.
CENTURION RETAIL PARK
DANUM RETAIL PARK
Warehouse Sports Ground
Football Ground
CUSWORTH
Keeper's Cottage
Middle Fish Pond
Lower Fish Pond
Basin Pond
Upper Fish Pond
Cusworth Hall
Richmond Hill
CHESWOLD PARK HOSPITAL
TOWN END IND. EST.
River Don (Old Course)
HMP DONCAST
NORTHFIELD ROAD
ANCHORAGE LANE
SPROTBROUGH
23
40
55
E F G H
1 2 3 4 5 6
455
56

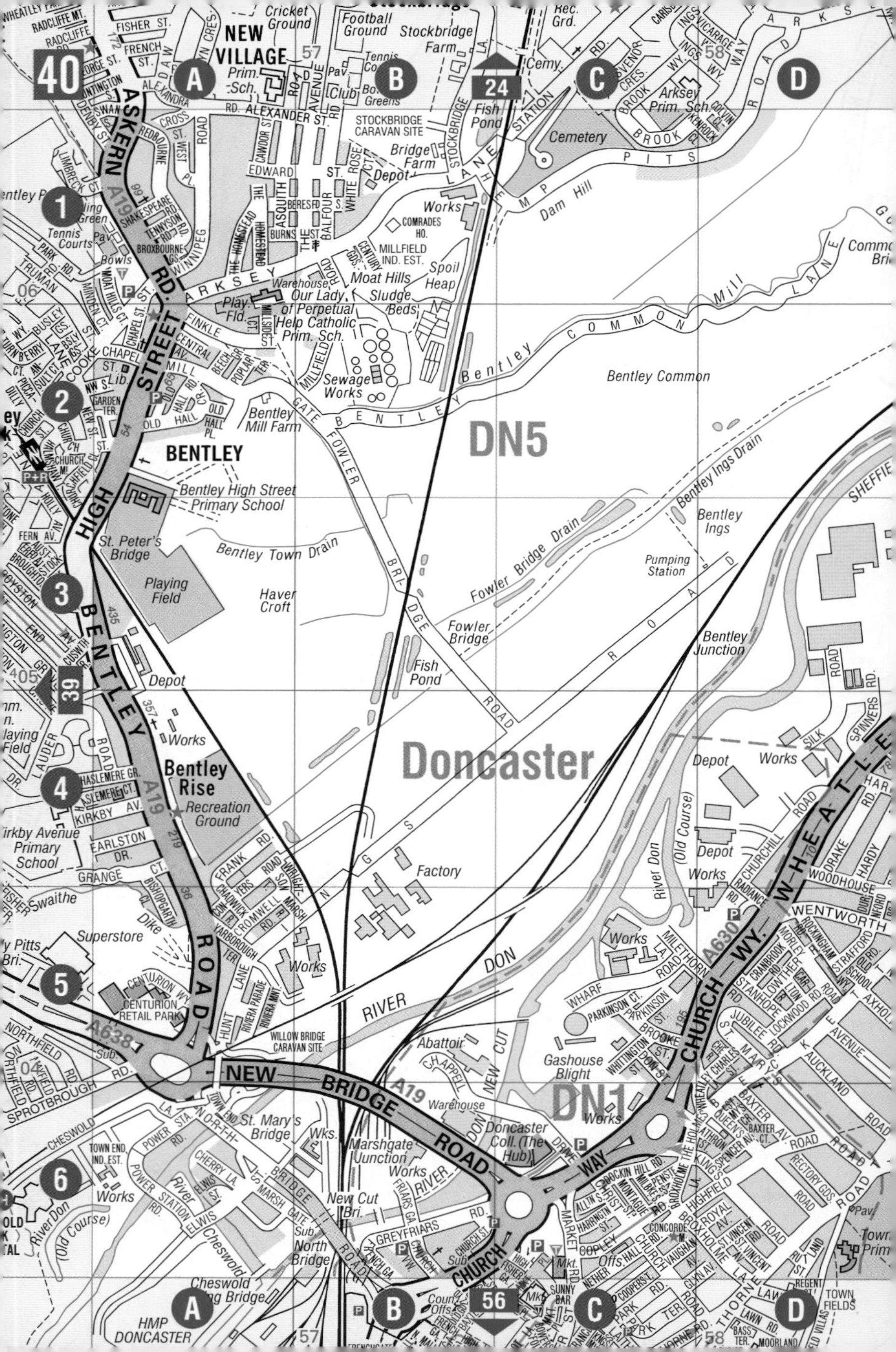
NEW VILLAGE
BENTLEY
DN5
Doncaster
DN1
Bentley Common
Bentley High Street Primary School
Bentley Rise
Recreation Ground
Playing Field
St. Peter's Bridge
Bentley Town Drain
Fowler Bridge Drain
Bentley Ings Drain
Bentley Ings
Pumping Station
Bentley Junction
Fowler Bridge
Haver Croft
Fish Pond
Depot
Works
Factory
Superstore
CENTURION RETAIL PARK
WILLOW BRIDGE CARAVAN SITE
St. Mary's Bridge
Marshgate Junction
New Cut Bri.
North Bridge
Cheswold
HMP DONCASTER
Abattoir
Gashouse Blight
Doncaster Coll. (The Hub)
Warehouse
Cemetery
Dam Hill
Spoil Heap
Sludge Beds
Sewage Works
Moat Hills
MILLFIELD IND. EST.
COMRADES HO.
Our Lady of Perpetual Help Catholic Prim. Sch.
Bentley Mill Farm
STOCKBRIDGE CARAVAN SITE
Bridge Farm
Stockbridge Farm
Football Ground
Cricket Ground
Arksey Prim. Sch.
Kirkby Avenue Primary School
TOWN END IND. EST.
RIVER DON
River Don (Old Course)
ASKERN RD.
HIGH STREET
BENTLEY ROAD
NEW BRIDGE ROAD
CHURCH WY.
WHEATLEY HALL RD.
A19
A630
A638
24
39
56
57
58
04
06
405
1
2
3
4
5
6
A
B
C
D

41
25
57
42
E
F
G
H
1
2
3
4
5
6
DN2
Wheatley Park
WHEATLEY
WHEATLEY HILLS
INTAKE
RIVER DON
& SOUTH YORKSHIRE NAVIGATION
HALL ROAD
LEGER WAY
A630
A18
DONCASTER ROYAL INFIRMARY
PARK HILL PRIVATE HOSP.
Sewage Works
Sludge Beds
Miniature Golf Course
Sandall Park
Playing Fields
Dock Hills
Wheatley Cut
Gala Bingo Club
WHEATLEY RETAIL PARK
LITTLE LANE INDUSTRIAL ESTATE
Kingfisher Prim. Sch.
Park Prim. Sch.
Sandringham Prim. Sch.
Intake Prim. Sch.
Plover Prim. Sch.
Race Course

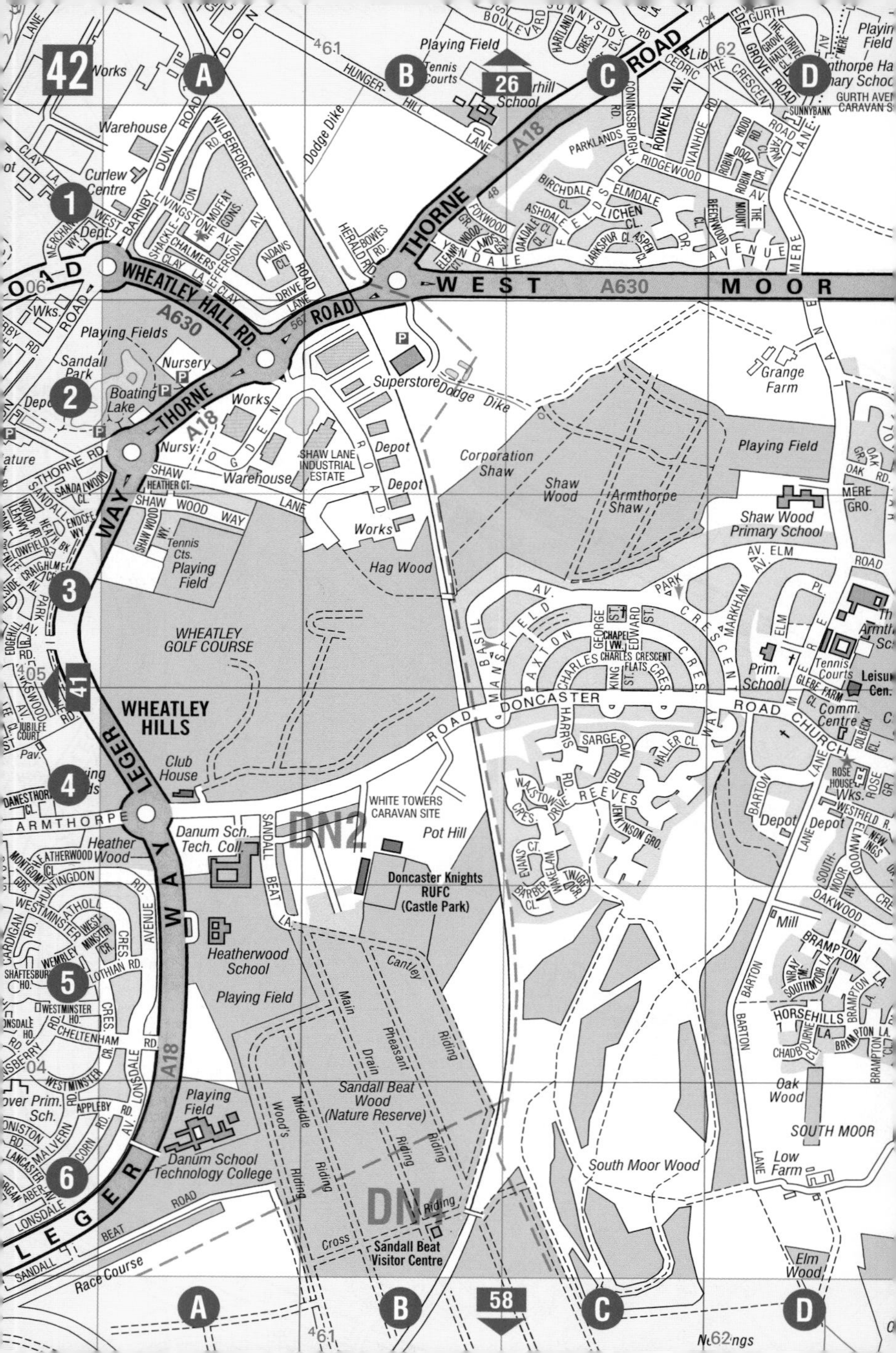

THORNE ROAD
WEST MOOR
A630
WHEATLEY HALL RD.
A18
LEGER WAY
WHEATLEY HILLS
WHEATLEY GOLF COURSE
DN2
DN4
DONCASTER ROAD
ARMTHORPE
Playing Field
Corporation Shaw
Shaw Wood
Armthorpe Shaw
Hag Wood
Shaw Wood Primary School
Superstore
SHAW LANE INDUSTRIAL ESTATE
Doncaster Knights RUFC (Castle Park)
WHITE TOWERS CARAVAN SITE
Pot Hill
Danum Sch. Tech. Coll.
Heatherwood School
Sandall Beat Wood (Nature Reserve)
Sandall Beat Visitor Centre
South Moor Wood
SOUTH MOOR
Oak Wood
Elm Wood
Low Farm
Grange Farm
Sandall Park
Boating Lake
Curlew Centre
Danum School Technology College
Race Course

26
41
58

E
F
G
H
27
59
63
64
06
05
04
1
2
3
4
5
6
Doncaster
ARMTHORPE
DN3
Nutwell
LINK
HATFIELD LANE
Long Plantation
Cozen Croft Wood
Cozen Croft
West Moor Drain
GREEN LANE
RAKE BRI. RD.
West Moor Farm
WEST MOOR LANE
The Lings
A630
Distribution Centre
Industrial Estate
Depot
Depots
WEST MOOR PARK
WEST MOOR LA.
DERBYSHIRE CT.
YORKSHIRE
LINCOLNSHIRE WY.
NOTTINGHAMSHIRE WAY
DURHAM LA.
RANDS LANE INDUSTRIAL ESTATE
GUNHILLS LA. IND. EST.
ARMTHORPE ENT. CEN.
HOLME WOOD LANE
Playing Field
Play. Fld.
Playgrd.
Works
Comm. Cen.
COW LANE RESIDENTIAL PARK
Rec. Grd.
Sewage Works
New Close Wood
Whiphills
WHIPHILL LANE
M18 MOTORWAY
M18
Subway
West Field Farm
Tranmoor
Park Closes
Tranmoor Wood
Carr
FERNBANK DRIVE
DENE
PINEWOOD
HAWTHORN
AVENUE
LAUREL ROAD
MERCEL AVENUE
HARROW RD.
SYCAMORE AV.
THE WOODLANDS
PALM DRIVE
LILAC RD.
HAZEL GR.
LABURNUM
WILLOW RD.
ASH GRO.
CEDAR RD.
RANDS LANE
GUNHILLS LA.
NOOKING CL.
MEWS CT.
CLEVELAND RD.
UPLANDS RD.
ST. MARY'S DR.
CHESTNUT
MAPLE
LIME TREE AV.
GROVE
HAWKSLEY CL.
ALMOND AV.
BEECH ROAD
POPLAR PLACE
WOODLEA
CHERRY TREE RD.
LARCH DR.
FRITH CL.
OLD SCH.
ARCH DR.
STREET
MILL STREET
Club
Bowling Greens
Pav.
Football Ground
Tennis Courts
WINHOLME
PITTAM CL.
TENNYSON AV.
MILTON GRO.
SHELLEY DR.
MACAULAY
KINGSLEY CRES.
RUSKIN DR.
COW LANE
NUTWELL LANE
MEADOW CT.
WALBANK
HANDSWORTH GDNS.
HALDYNBY GS.
WICKETT HERN RD.
WICKETT
HERN
THE LINGS
HOUSE
Armthorpe Tranmoor Prim. Sch.
Southfield Prim. Sch.
THORNHAM CL.
GREEN COMMON
TOFTSHEAD
DEANSFIELD CL.
MELTON FIELD CL.
THE CRESCENT
HORNSBY ROAD
LOCKING DR.
REGENT AV.
KIRKHILL CL.
LEYFIELD CT.
SPRING FIELD CL.
AMBASSADOR GDNS.
DICKAN GS.
BUTTERILL DR.
WHIPHILL
HARDEN M.
EASTFIELD
TRANMOOR
BROOKFIELD CT.
MOORFIELD
GREENFIELD DR.
WOODFIELD
HOLMEFIELD CL.
FENTON CL.
RAMSKER DR.
CRANFIELD
LINDRICK DR.
RAVENFIELD
ASHFIELD CL.
FORE'S RD.
SHAW CT.
PARKWAY
LADYCROFT
MILLHILL CL.
HALLCROFT DR.
MELWOOD CT.
ALDER
GRANBY CT.
HOLT CL.
FAIR HOLME VIEW
FAIR HOLME VW.
FIDDLERS DRIVE
BELLROPE
ACRE
ACER CFT.
FERRY WY.
MULB
SEVEN YARDS ROAD

44
30
60
A
B
C
D
1
2
3
4
5
6
33
34
03
02
M1
M1-MOTORWAY
MOTORWAY
S75
S35
STAINBOROUGH PARK
WORSBROUGH COUNTRY PARK
BIRDWELL
PILLEY
Pilley Hills
Menagerie House
Menagerie Wood
Menagerie Pond
Serpentine Bridge
Serpentine River
Sewage Works
Brough Green Bridge
Round Green
Strafford's House
Walker's Pond
ROUND GREEN LANE
ROCKLEY LANE
Queen Anne's Obelisk
Queen Anne's Lodge
Round Green Lodge
OLD HALL ROAD
DOE
Shed Plantation
The Temple
Ivas Wood
Stampers Hill
Rockley Pit Cottages
Rockley Old Hall
Duke of Argyle's Monument
Raven Holt
Wallside Plantation
Moor Leys Wood
Hyland House
Rockley Dike
Broom Royd Wood
Wigfield Wood
Engine Ho.
Miller Hill
Rockley Abbey Farm
Rockley Dam
Greensprings Holiday Park
Dike
Warren Dike
The Old Park Wood
Parkinson's Spring
Springs
Green
Green Springs
Beech House Fm.
Birdwell Bridge
Pilley Lane End Farm
PILLEY LA. END
CHAPEL ROAD
Hermit Hill Farm
HERMIT HILL
Bruce Lodge
Athersley Wood Cottage
Broad Ing Plantation
Playing Field
Playgrd.
Bowl. Grn.
Pilley Bri.
Fan Drift
Greenfield Cottage
Brialey Cottage
Bennette
Bottom Dike
Dike Bottom
Parks Plantation
Athersley House
Croft Head Plantation
Ivy House Farm
Pilley Sewage Works
STAINBOROUGH VW.
ROCKLEY VW.
THE AVENUE
WHARNCLIFFE CT.
LIDGETT LANE
Knoll Cotts.
Knoll Drill
Pilley Green
Birdwell Dike
THORNLEY VILLAS
THE LANE
WHARNCLIFFE COTTS.
401

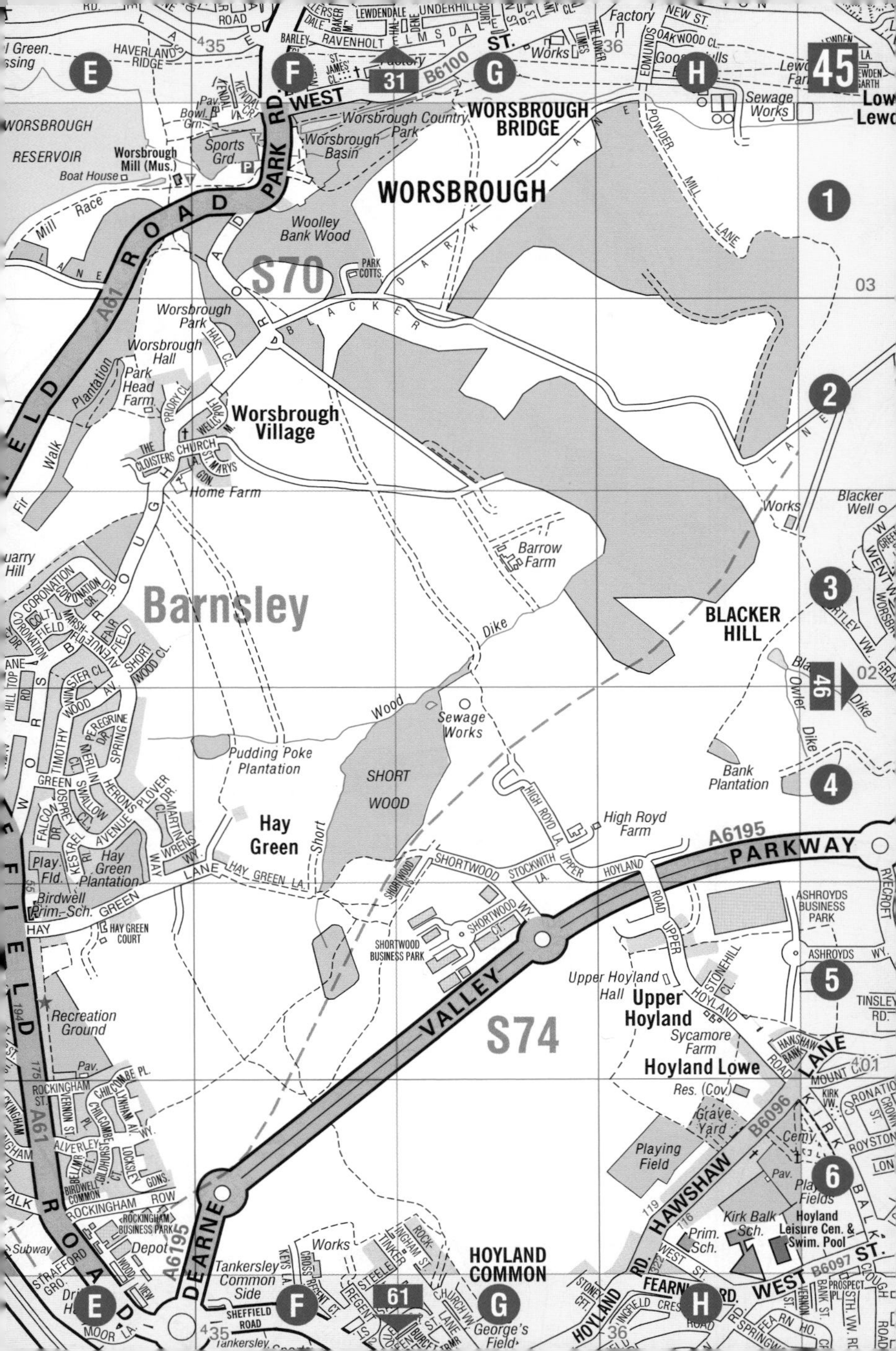
WORSBROUGH
WORSBROUGH BRIDGE
Worsbrough Village
Barnsley
BLACKER HILL
Hay Green
Upper Hoyland
Hoyland Lowe
HOYLAND COMMON
WORSBROUGH RESERVOIR
Worsbrough Mill (Mus.)
Boat House
Worsbrough Country Park
Worsbrough Basin
Woolley Bank Wood
Worsbrough Park
Worsbrough Hall
Park Head Farm
Home Farm
Barrow Farm
Pudding Poke Plantation
SHORT WOOD
Sewage Works
High Royd Farm
Bank Plantation
Blacker Well
Upper Hoyland Hall
Sycamore Farm
Hay Green Plantation
Birdwell Prim. Sch.
Recreation Ground
SHORTWOOD BUSINESS PARK
ASHROYDS BUSINESS PARK
ROCKINGHAM BUSINESS PARK
Kirk Balk Sch.
Hoyland Leisure Cen. & Swim. Pool
Playing Field
Tankersley Common Side
George's Field
S70
S74
A61
A6195
B6100
B6096
B6097
PARKWAY
DEARNE VALLEY
SHEFFIELD ROAD
PARK RD.
WEST ST.
BLACKER LANE
DARK LANE
POWDER MILL LANE
HAWSHAW LANE
HAY GREEN LANE
UPPER HOYLAND ROAD
31
46
61

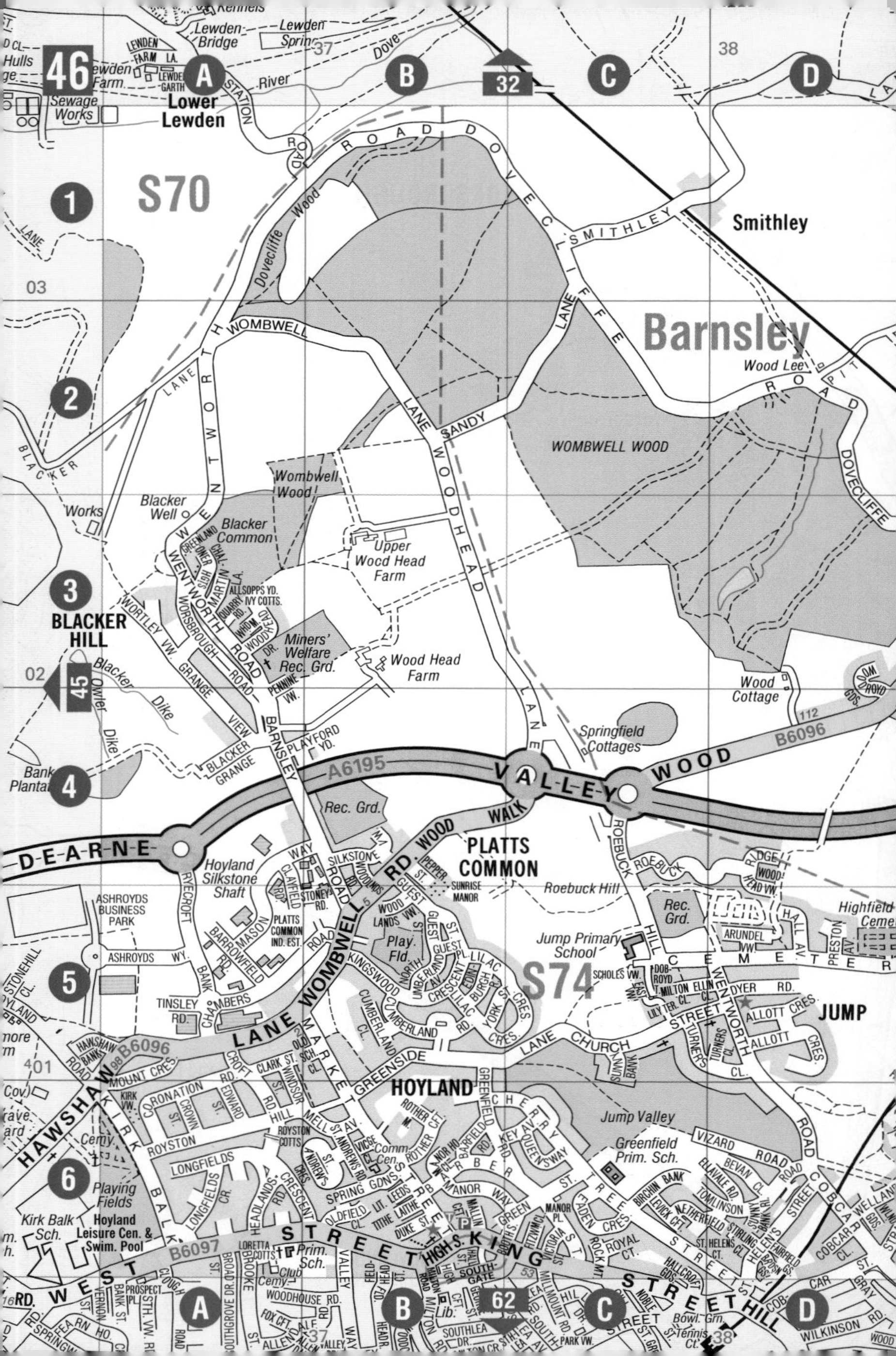
46
Lower Lewden
Lewden Bridge
Lewden Spring
Sewage Works
River Dove
S70
Smithley
Barnsley
Wood Lee
WOMBWELL WOOD
Dovecliffe Wood
Wombwell Wood
Blacker Well
Blacker Common
Upper Wood Head Farm
Wood Head Farm
Miners' Welfare Rec. Grd.
BLACKER HILL
Wood Cottage
Springfield Cottages
VALLEY WOOD
DEARNE VALLEY
A6195
B6096
PLATTS COMMON
Hoyland Silkstone Shaft
ASHROYDS BUSINESS PARK
Roebuck Hill
Jump Primary School
S74
JUMP
Highfield Cemetery
HOYLAND
Jump Valley
Greenfield Prim. Sch.
Hoyland Leisure Cen. & Swim. Pool
Playing Fields
Kirk Balk Sch.
B6097
WEST STREET
KING STREET
HIGH ST.
Prim. Sch.
Lib.
Comm. Cen.
Bowl. Grn.
Tennis Ct.
32
45
62

47
33
63
48
E
F
G
H
1
2
3
4
5
6
39
440
401
WOMBWELL
HEMINGFIELD
S73
S63
S62
Rotherham
Wombwell
Wombwell Race Circuit
Go-Kart Track
Station Road Industrial Estate
Sports Ground
Research Cen.
High View Primary Learning Cen.
Playing Field
Cemetery
Comm. Cen.
Learning Cen.
Sports Grd.
Tennis Cts.
Bowl Grn.
Pavs.
Wombwell Park
Club Ho.
WOMBWELL HILLIES GOLF COURSE
Lund Hill
Playing Fields
Wombwell Park St. Prim. Sch.
WOMBWELL WOOD
Factory
Rec. Grd.
Prim. Sch.
Lundhill Farm
Birk's Lock
Dearne & Dove Canal
Smithy Bridge
Superstore
Hemingfield Farm
Hemingfield Halt (proposed)
Tingle Bri.
Sewage Works
Elsecar Heritage Railway
Royds Farm
Weir
Rainborough Lodge
(Proposed Railway Extention)
BARNSLEY
ROTHERHAM
MITCHELLS WAY
A633
STATION ROAD
B6096
VALLEY WY.
SUMMER LANE
HOUGH LANE
WALK
DEARNE VALLEY PARKWAY
A6195
NEW ROAD
B6097
SMITHY BRIDGE LA.
WATH ROAD
LUNDHILL RD.
HOUSE
ROYDS LANE

A
B
C
D
1
2
3
4
5
6
34
47
64
WOMBWELL
BROOMHILL
Barnsley
S73
BRAMPTON
Brampton
Bierlow
Westfield
Stonyford
Bri.
STONYFORD RD.
Prim. Sch.
Caravan Park
Towns Lands
Sewage Works
Council Depot
Playing Field
WOMBWELL INGS
INGS RD.
Billing
ROAD
INGS
Sewage Works
STATION RD.
B6096
VALLEY RD.
Works
Brickworks Cottage
Park Hill
Broomhill Flash
Nature Reserve
Rec. Grd.
Dike
Marle's Bridge
BROOMHILL LANE
Gorse Pits Bridge
DEARNE INGS
Broomhill Park Old Moor
Playground
VALLEY WAY
A633
WATERSIDE PARK
Park Farm
EVERILL GATE LANE
Depot
Everill Gate Bri.
HIGHGATE
THE SIDINGS
DEARNE VALLEY
A6195
VALLEY PARK IND. EST.
MEADOW GATE
WATH RD.
PARKWAY
Old Moor House
Old Moor Nature Reserve Visitor Centre
OLD MOOR LANE
Old Moor Bri.
CENTURY PARK NETWORK CEN.
CENTURY PK.
CENTURY BUS. CEN.
WATH WEST IND. EST.
Wks.
Factory
DERWENT WAY
Works
HOLLOWGATE AV.
MOORLAND
BARNSLEY ROAD
Playing Field
Knoll Beck Bri.
KINGFISHER
BITTERN CFT.
BRAMPTON BECK
Play. Fld.
MOORBRIDGE CRES.
BRAMPTON RD.
KNOLLBECK LANE
B6089
Sch.
PONTEFRACT ROAD
Bowl. Grn.
Ten. Cts.
Hall
Playgrd.
Intake Bri.
DEARNE
CORTON WOOD BUSINESS PARK
Dearne Ho.
CORTONWOOD DRIVE
Superstore
Superstore
Playing Field
Brampton Leisure Centre
BRAMPTON ELLIS ENTERPRISE CENTRE
THE BRAMPTON CEN.
Brampton The Ellis C of E Jun. Sch.
PACKMAN RD.
MILKING LA.
WESTFIELD LANE
SMITHY BRIDGE LANE
B6097
Rainborough Lodge
The Counting Houses
ELSECAR ROAD
Westfield Farm
Bleak House Stables
QUARRY BANK
FIRTH RD.
MELTON
B6097
ROTHERHAM RD.
West Melton Jun. & Inf. Sch.
Environmental Studies Cen.
Brook
MELTON GREEN
Sch.
GROVE RD.
MASEFIELD
BYRON
DRYDEN
BURNS
TENNYSON
STOKEWELL RD.
CHRISTCHURCH RD.
COLERIDGE RD.
HOOBER VW.
DOVE
CONWAY
OVERDALE
GYPSY LANE
LUND HILL
MEADOW GATE
LEEWOOD CT.
GORSE CL.
401
441
42
03
02

PARKWAY
43
44
35
E
F
G
H
Carr Dike
Carr Head
CARR HEAD LANE
BILLINGLEY INGS
INGSFIELD LANE
Old Moor
Nature Reserve
BOLTON INGS
DEARNE
BARNSLEY
ROTHERHAM
Weir
WATERFRONT GOLF COURSE
Club Ho.
Waterfront
Driving
Range
50
Manvers
Waterfront
Boat Club
Sch.
Ings Lane
Sports
Rec.
MAORI AVENUE
INGSFIELD ROAD
WATER
BROOKFIELDS
PARK
MEADOWS
DEARNE ROAD
STATION RD.
A6023
ROTARY
HANK RD.
REED WK.
HARRIS
HAWK
FENLAKE
ONYX
RETAIL
PARK
CAMBGE
CHASE
Superstore
WREN GDS.
STARLING
RED
JACKDAW
FIRCREST
STONE CHAT
MEAD
BRAMBLING
COLLIERY AV.
Hotel
NIGHTINGALES
Football
Grd.
JOHNSON
GDS.
WHITWORTH LA.
SKYLARK
ROEBUCK
SONGTHRUSH
GOLDFINCH
A633
AVENUE
HUMMINGBIRD
CAWOOD
Bowling
Greens
Pav.
Cricket
Ground
Depot
ROAD
Sewage
Works
GREEN INGS LA.
Brook Dike
RECREATION RD.
Recreation
Ground
PARK VW. CT.
Rotherham
S63
WET MOOR LA.
NORTON RD.
VICAR
Play. Field
Vic.
Sch.
SHAKESPEARE R.
PRINCESS
HIGH ST.
BARNSLEY RD.
ORCHARD PL.
BROOK DR.
FLATS LA.
WEST
MELTON
BREWERY RD.
WHITWORTH
Super-
store
Dpt.
WEST ST.
BISCAY WAY
B6097
STATION ROAD
WATH ROUNDABOUT
DEARNE WY.
SANDYGATE
DONCASTER ROAD
Coll.
Lib.
HIGH ST.
MONTY SQ.
FITZWILLIAM CT.
OLD CROSS
Youth Cen.
ALL SAINTS' CL.
Our Lady
& St. Joseph's
Catholic
Prim. Sch.
Play. Fld.
WOODSIDE AV.
CHURCH
VALLEY DRIVE
PINFOLD
DENMAN
KEBLE MARTIN WAY
MICHAEL CROFT
BUSHFIELD RD.
SAVILLE
MATTHEWS AV.
NEWHILL
GAWTRESS RW.
CEMETERY
PARK ROAD
CHAPEL
CROSS ST.
OAKLANDS PL.
WILLOW CT.
FITZWILLIAM
65
Wath Central
Primary Sch.
FESTIVAL ROAD
STUMP CROSS
CUTTS
STRATHMORE GRO.
HIGHFIELD
WILLIAM ST.
GWENDOLINE M.
HENRY RD.
CHARLES RD.
BURMAN
OAK ROAD
CARR ROAD
CORONATION RD.
BEECH
AVENUE
SANDYMOUNT
CADMAN ST.
JAMES CL.
DUNFORD CT.
GOREHILL CL.
Wath Victoria
Prim. Sch.
WATH UPON
DEARNE
COMMON
1
2
3
4
5
6

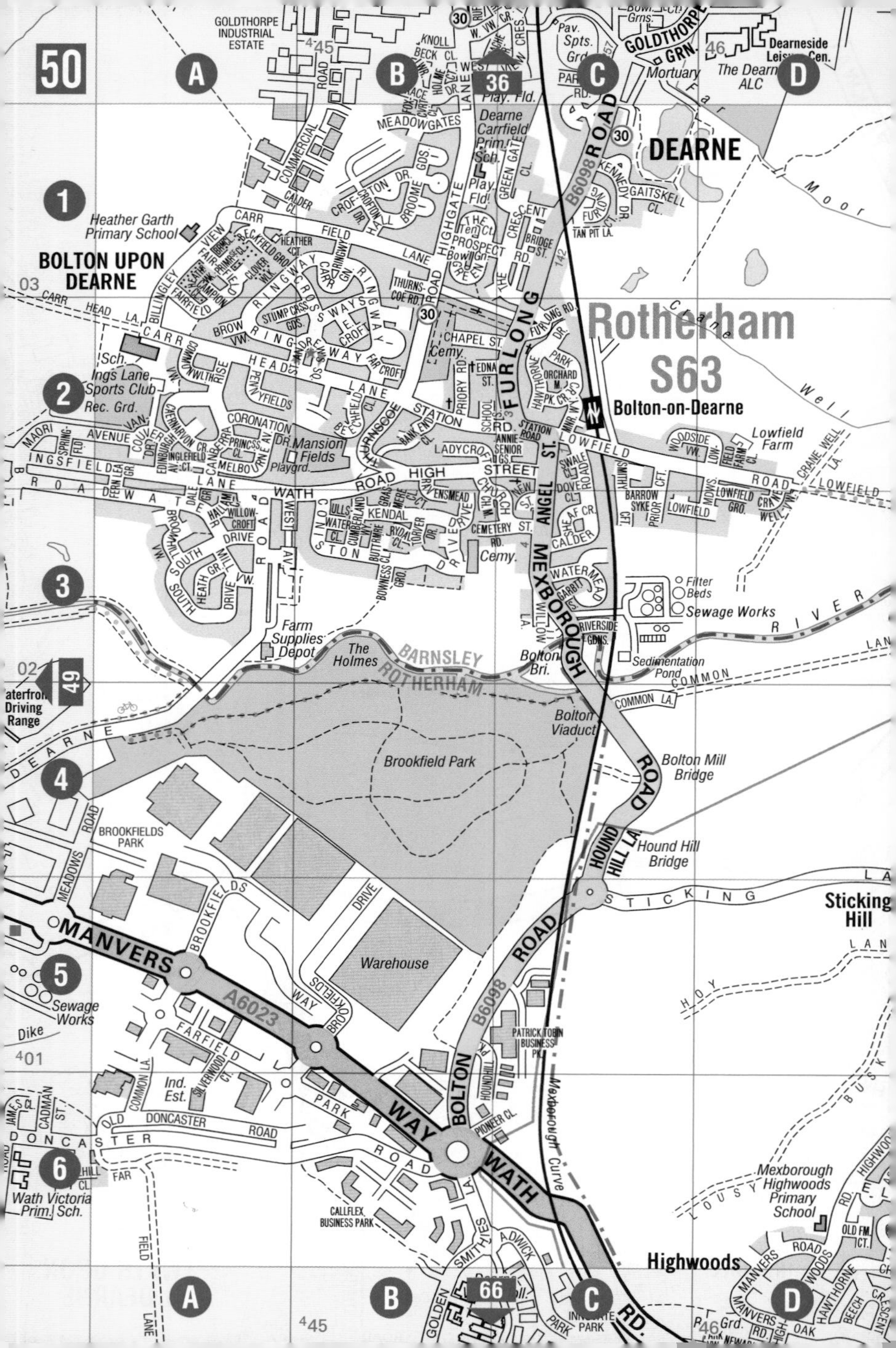
A
B
C
D
1
2
3
4
5
6
36
49
66
GOLDTHORPE INDUSTRIAL ESTATE
Dearneside Leisure Cen.
The Dearne ALC
Mortuary
DEARNE
Heather Garth Primary School
BOLTON UPON DEARNE
Dearne Carrfield Prim. Sch.
Play. Fld.
Rotherham
S63
Bolton-on-Dearne
Sch.
Ings Lane Sports Club
Rec. Grd.
Mansion Fields
Playgrd.
Lowfield Farm
Cemy.
Filter Beds
Sewage Works
Farm Supplies Depot
The Holmes
BARNSLEY
ROTHERHAM
Bolton Bri.
Sedimentation Pond
Bolton Viaduct
Brookfield Park
Bolton Mill Bridge
Hound Hill Bridge
BROOKFIELDS PARK
Warehouse
Sticking Hill
MANVERS WAY
A6023
B6098
PATRICK TOBIN BUSINESS PK.
Mexborough Curve
Ind. Est.
CALLFLEX BUSINESS PARK
Sewage Works
Wath Victoria Prim. Sch.
Mexborough Highwoods Primary School
Highwoods
CARR HEAD LA.
HIGH STREET
STATION RD.
FURLONG ROAD
MEXBOROUGH ROAD
BOLTON ROAD
STICKING LA.
OLD DONCASTER ROAD
DONCASTER ROAD
WATH ROAD
LOWFIELD ROAD
COMMON LA.
HOUND HILL LA.
RIVER DEARNE
Crane Well
Moor
Far

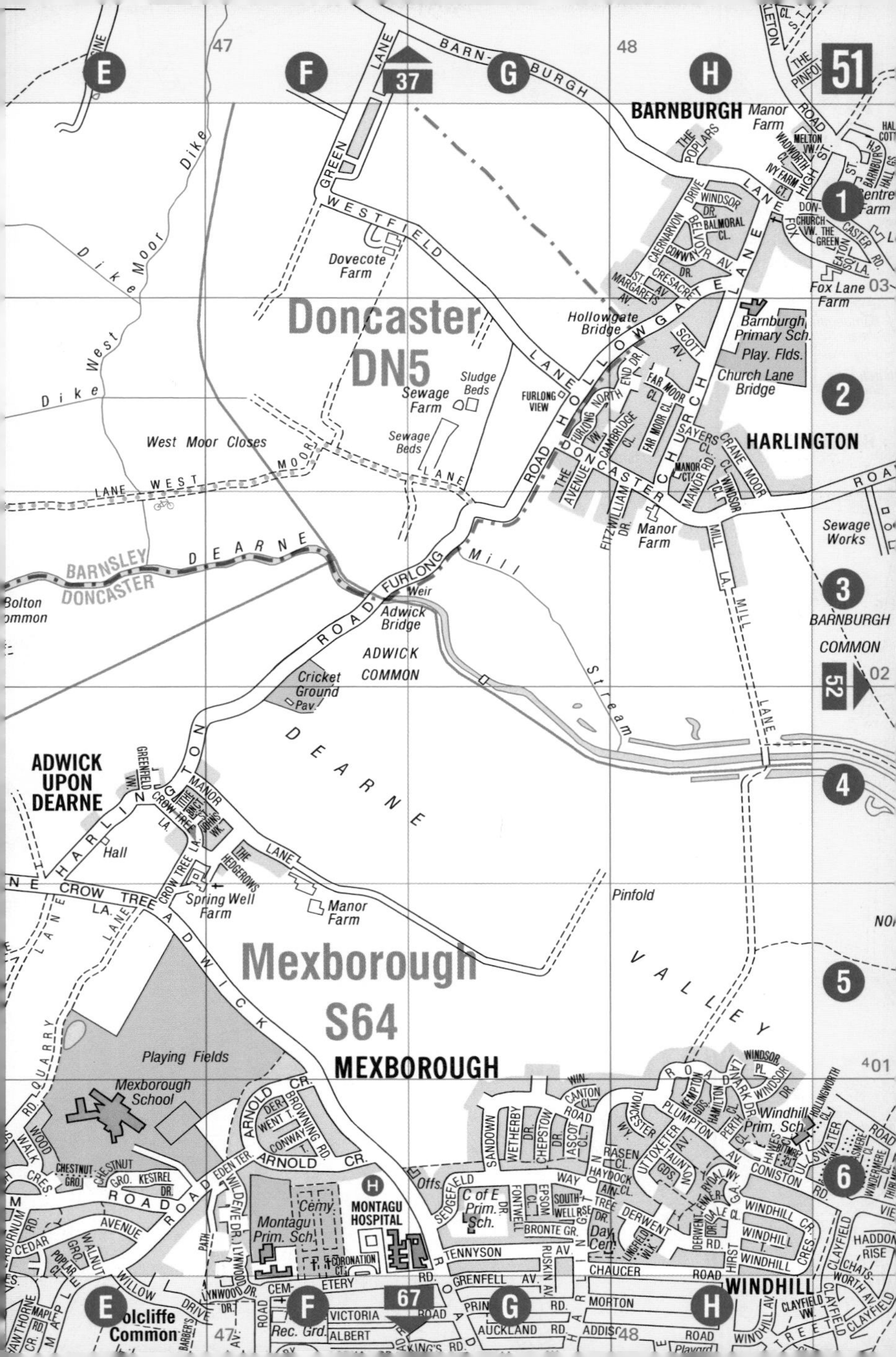

BARNBURGH
HARLINGTON
ADWICK UPON DEARNE
MEXBOROUGH
WINDHILL
Doncaster DN5
Mexborough S64
BARNBURGH COMMON
ADWICK COMMON
Dovecote Farm
Sewage Farm
Sludge Beds
Sewage Beds
West Moor Closes
Hollowgate Bridge
Barnburgh Primary Sch.
Play. Flds.
Church Lane Bridge
Manor Farm
Fox Lane Farm
Sewage Works
Adwick Bridge
Weir
Cricket Ground
Pav.
Hall
Spring Well Farm
Pinfold
Playing Fields
Mexborough School
MONTAGU HOSPITAL
Montagu Prim. Sch.
C of E Prim. Sch.
Windhill Prim. Sch.
Day Cen.
Cemy.
Rec. Grd.
Bolton Common
Bolcliffe Common
DEARNE VALLEY
BARNSLEY
DONCASTER
37
52
67

BARNBURGH
HARLINGTON
Manor Farm
Centre Farm
Low Farm
Fox Lane Farm
Barnburgh Primary Sch.
Play. Flds.
Fish Pond
St. Helen's Spring
Springfield Spring
Ludwell Spring
Melton Warren
The Temple
Barnburgh Grange
The Ripple
Bath House Farm
Bath Pond
Bath House Plantation
Sewage Works
Filter Beds
Sludge Beds
BARNBURGH COMMON
OWLER CARR
NORTH INGS
River Dearne (old course)
RIVER DEARNE
DEARNE VALLEY
Dearne Bridge
Mexborough Low Pasture
Denaby Ings Nature Reserve
Mexborough
S64
DN12
WINDHILL
Windhill Prim. Sch.
The Ings
DONCASTER ROAD
LUDWELL ROAD
ST. HELEN'S LANE
GRANGE LANE
STONE ROAD
HANGMAN HILL
MELTON MILL LANE
PASTURE ROAD
LUDWELL CL.

51
68

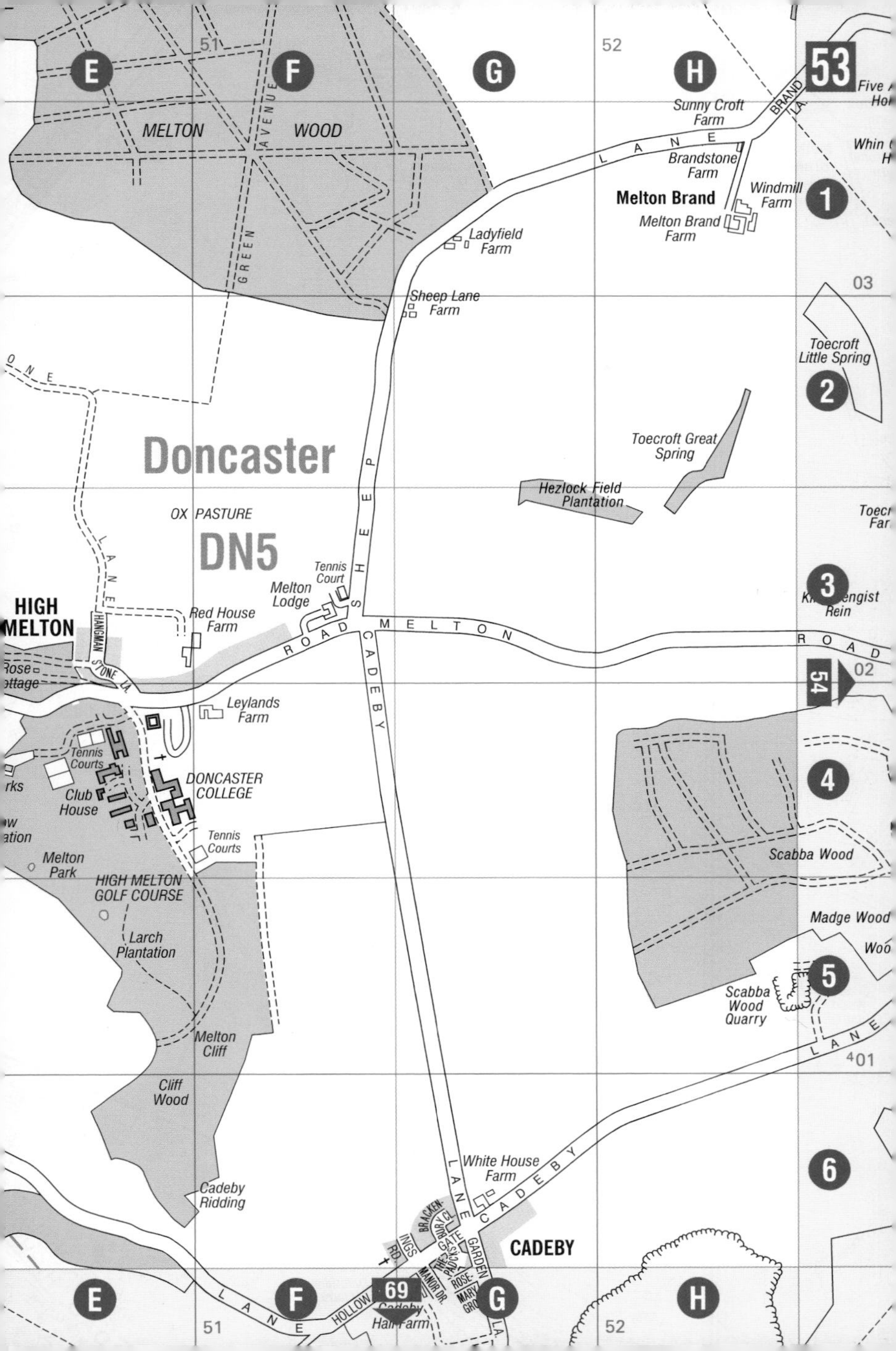

E
F
G
H
51
52
MELTON
WOOD
GREEN AVENUE
Sunny Croft Farm
BRAND LA.
LANE
Brandstone Farm
Melton Brand
Windmill Farm
Melton Brand Farm
Ladyfield Farm
Sheep Lane Farm
03
Toecroft Little Spring
Toecroft Great Spring
Hezlock Field Plantation
Doncaster
OX PASTURE
DN5
Tennis Court
Melton Lodge
SHEEP
HIGH MELTON
HANGMAN STONE LA.
Red House Farm
ROAD
MELTON
ROAD
Rose Cottage
CADEBY
54
02
Leylands Farm
Tennis Courts
Club House
DONCASTER COLLEGE
Tennis Courts
Melton Park
HIGH MELTON GOLF COURSE
Larch Plantation
Melton Cliff
Cliff Wood
Scabba Wood
Madge Wood
Scabba Wood Quarry
LANE
401
White House Farm
CADEBY
Cadeby Ridding
BRACKENBURY CL.
INGS RD.
THE GATE
PADDOCKS
GARDEN LA.
CADEBY
MANOR DR.
ROSE
MARY GRO.
HOLLOW
LANE
69
Cadeby Hall Farm
1
2
3
4
5
6

SPROTBROUGH
Sprotbrough Park
WARMSWORTH
DN5
Melton Brand
Brandfield Farm
Spring Rein
Plaster Pits Wood
Castle Hill Wood
A1(M)
A1(M) - MOTORWAY
Five Acre Holt
Whin Covert Holt
Burnt Wood
Burnt Wood Farm
Burntwood Grange
Whin Covert
Staghill Plantation
Stag Hill
Toecroft Little Spring
Fox Flat Plantation
Manor Farm House
Green Roofs
Toecroft Farm
King Hengist Rein
MELTON ROAD
School Lane Bridge
Playing Field
Scabba Wood Cottage
Wetlands Wood
Scabba Wood
Copley Junior School
Cooke's Bower
THE CARAVAN SITE
Sprotbrough Quarries
Madge Wood
Glen Villa
Woodside
Nursery Lane Bridge
Depot
Tower Cottages
Quarry
Sprotbrough Plantation
Lower Sprotbrough
Scabba Wood Quarry
CADEBY LANE
NURSERY LANE
Engine Wood
Cave
Snow's Wood
Sprotbrough Lock
Sprotbrough Cut
Sprotbrough Bridge
Weir
Sprotbrough Boat
Levitthagg Wood
SHEFFIELD & SOUTH YORKSHIRE NAVIGATION
RIVER DON
Sprotbrough Flash Nature Reserve
Levitt Hagg
Station House
Station Bridge
Pot Ridings Wood
Tunnels
Works
Dolomite Quarry
Grey Stones
Warmsworth Prim. Sch.
A630
38
53
70
A B C D
1 2 3 4 5 6
03 02 01 53 54

Upper Fish Pond
Basin Pond
CUSWORTH PARK COUNTRY PARK
Richmond Hill
39
CHESWOLD
River Don (Old Course)
HMP DONCASTER
Crimpsall
Newton Ings
Long Plantation
SPROTBROUGH ROAD
Comm. Cen.
Hall
Newton Lane Bridge
Newton Farm
Sprotbrough Road Bri.
Richmond Hill Primary School
Newton
RIVER DON
Depot
Albert Bridge
Hexthorpe Ings
HEXTHORPE
Hexthorpe Reach
Albert Plantation
Works
HEXTHORPE BUSINESS PARK
Central Prim. Sch.
Manor House
The Dell
Bowling Greens
Hexthorpe Prim. Sch.
Putting Green
Tennis Courts
Playing Flds.
Hexthorpe Flatts
Depot
56
Doncaster
A1(M)
Miniature Golf Course
Sprotbrough Ings
Fitness First
Sprotbrough Ings
Church Rein
Viaducts
Play. Fld.
Mt. Lib.
Warmsworth Burial Ground
Hexthorpe Junc.
Subway
Junc. 36
A1(M) MOTORWAY
HIGH ROAD
BALBY RD.
TA Cen.
A60
Play. Fld.
Comm. Cen.
DN4
A630
Waverley Prim. Sch.
WARMSWORTH RD.
The Cedar Adult Centre
Rosemead Children's Home
SANDFORD RD.
TICKHILL RD.
Nursing Home
BALBY
Depot
St. John's Hospice
Nexus Cen.
Mallard Prim. Sch.
Recreation Ground
Depot
TICKHILL ROAD HOSPITAL
Comm. Cen.
71
E
F
G
H
1
2
3
4
5
6

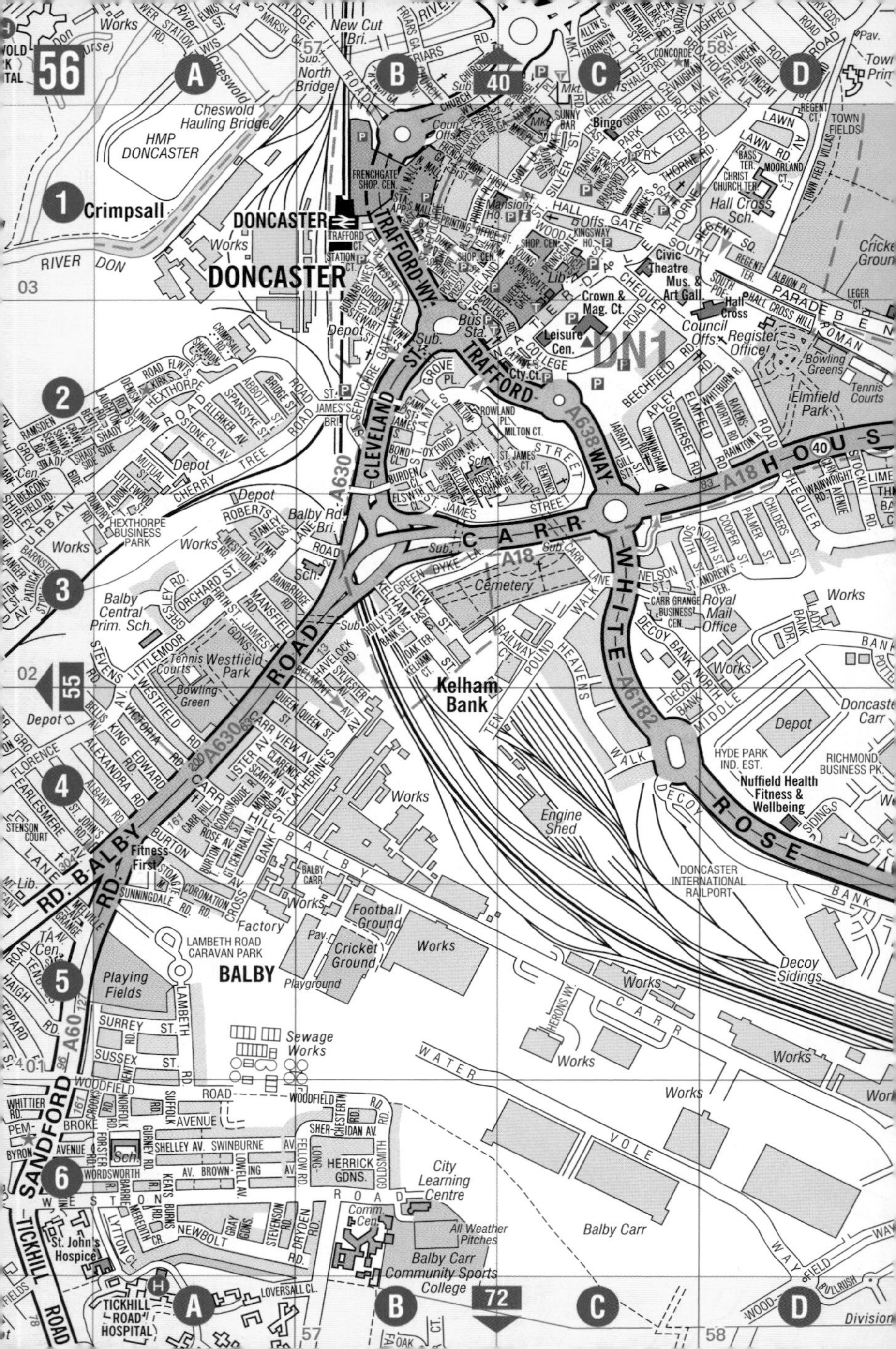

56
A
B
C
D
1
2
3
4
5
6
40
72
55
57
58
03
02
01
Crimpsall
HMP DONCASTER
Cheswold Hauling Bridge
New Cut Bri.
North Bridge
DONCASTER
Frenchgate Shop. Cen.
River Don
Works
Depot
Hexthorpe Business Park
Balby Central Prim. Sch.
Westfield Park
Tennis Courts
Bowling Green
Kelham Bank
Cemetery
Royal Mail Office
Carr Grange Business Cen.
Civic Theatre
Mus. & Art Gall.
Hall Cross
Council Offs.
Register Office
Crown & Mag. Ct.
Leisure Cen.
DN1
Hall Cross Sch.
Town Fields
Cricket Ground
Bowling Greens
Tennis Courts
Elmfield Park
Mansion Ho.
Bingo
Doncaster Carr
Hyde Park Ind. Est.
Richmond Business Pk.
Nuffield Health Fitness & Wellbeing
Engine Shed
Doncaster International Railport
Decoy Sidings
Football Ground
Cricket Ground
Lambeth Road Caravan Park
BALBY
Playing Fields
Playground
Sewage Works
Fitness First
Factory
Herrick Gdns.
City Learning Centre
All Weather Pitches
Balby Carr Community Sports College
Balby Carr
St. John's Hospice
Tickhill Road Hospital
Trafford Wy.
Cleveland St.
Carr Lane
White Rose Way
Balby Road
Carr Hill
Sandford Road
Tickhill Road
Water Vole Way
Carr Road
A630
A18
A638
A6182
A60

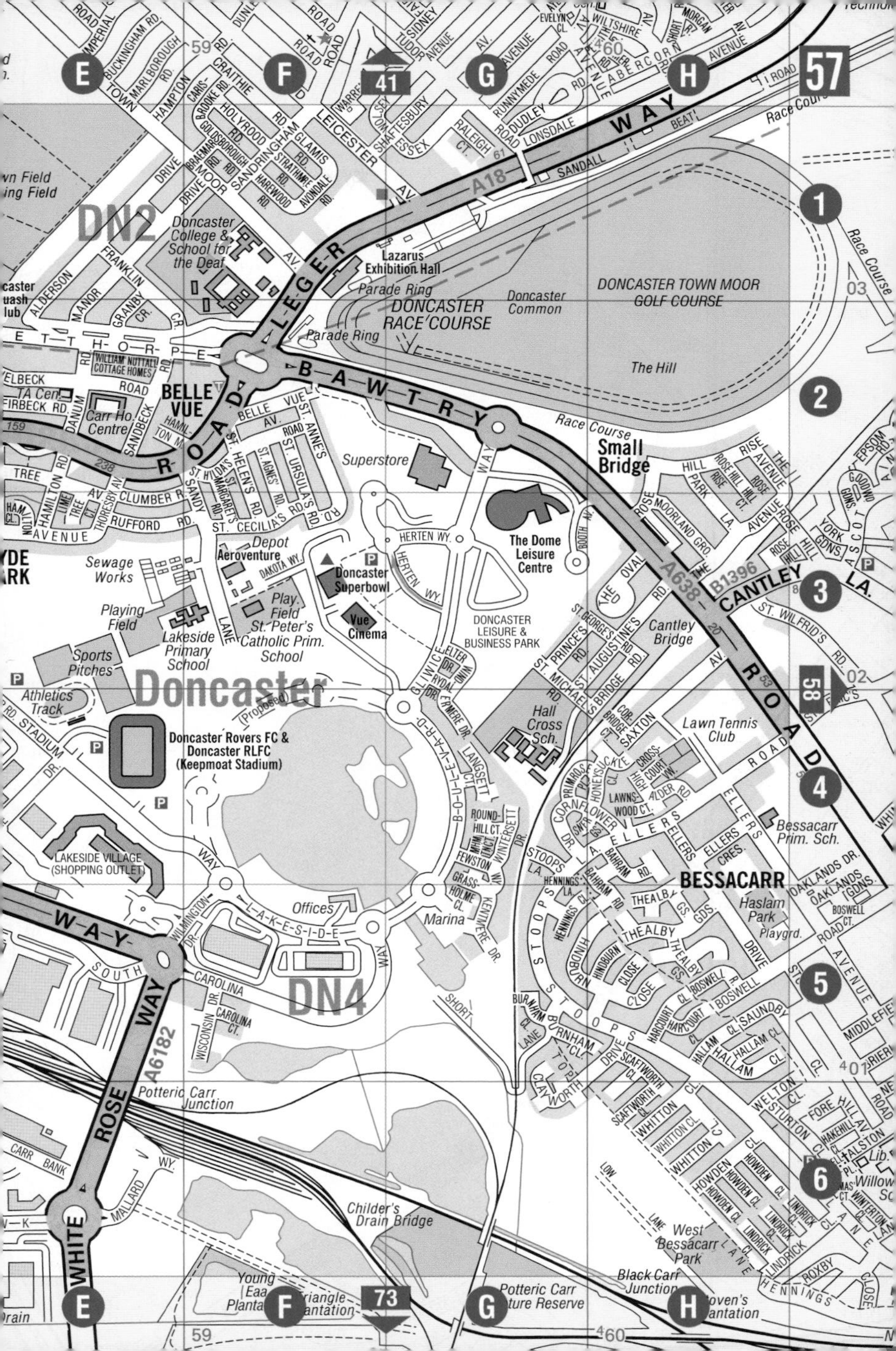
DN2
DN4
Doncaster
Doncaster College & School for the Deaf
Lazarus Exhibition Hall
Parade Ring
DONCASTER RACE COURSE
Doncaster Common
DONCASTER TOWN MOOR GOLF COURSE
The Hill
Race Course
BELLE VUE
Carr Ho. Centre
TA Cen.
Small Bridge
Superstore
The Dome Leisure Centre
DONCASTER LEISURE & BUSINESS PARK
Aeroventure
Depot
Doncaster Superbowl
Vue Cinema
Sewage Works
Playing Field
Play. Field
Lakeside Primary School
St. Peter's Catholic Prim. School
Sports Pitches
Athletics Track
Doncaster Rovers FC & Doncaster RLFC (Keepmoat Stadium)
LAKESIDE VILLAGE (SHOPPING OUTLET)
Offices
Marina
Hall Cross Sch.
Cantley Bridge
Lawn Tennis Club
Bessacarr Prim. Sch.
BESSACARR
Haslam Park
Playgrd.
Potteric Carr Junction
Childer's Drain Bridge
West Bessacarr Park
Black Carr Junction
Potteric Carr Nature Reserve
A18
A638
A6182
B1396
LEGER WAY
BAWTRY ROAD
LAKESIDE BOULEVARD
ROSE WAY
WHITE ROSE WAY
CANTLEY LA.
STOOPS LA.
41
58
73

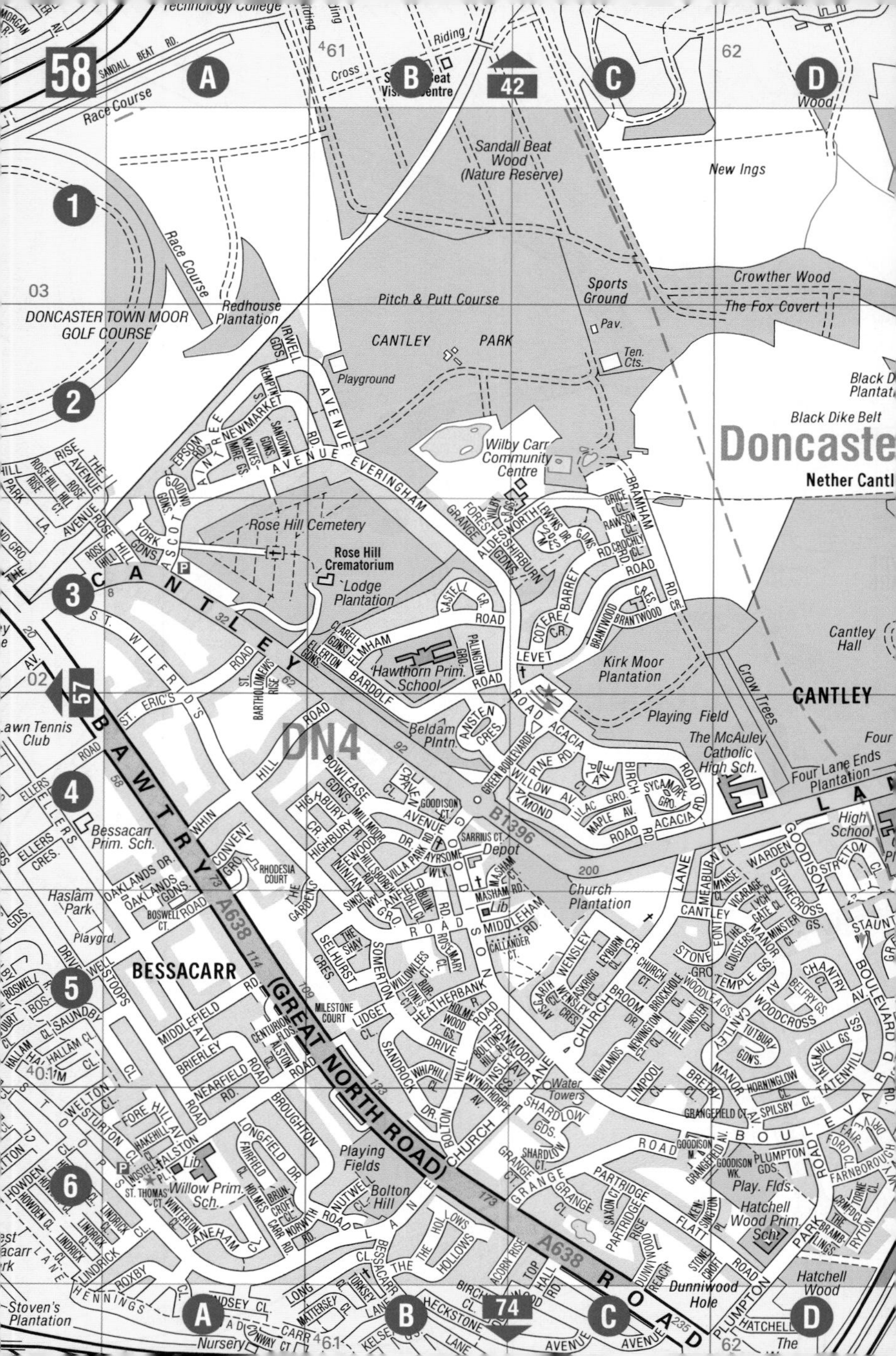

Technology College
Sandall Beat Rd.
Race Course
Sandall Beat Visitor Centre
42
Sandall Beat Wood (Nature Reserve)
New Ings
Doncaster Town Moor Golf Course
Redhouse Plantation
Pitch & Putt Course
Sports Ground
Crowther Wood
The Fox Covert
Cantley Park
Pav.
Ten. Cts.
Playground
Black Dike Belt
Doncaste
Nether Cantl
Wilby Carr Community Centre
Rose Hill Cemetery
Rose Hill Crematorium
Lodge Plantation
Everingham Avenue
Cantley Lane
Hawthorn Prim. School
Kirk Moor Plantation
Cantley Hall
Crow Trees
Cantley
Playing Field
The McAuley Catholic High Sch.
Four Lane Ends Plantation
High School
Beldam Plntn.
DN4
57
Lawn Tennis Club
Bessacarr Prim. Sch.
Haslam Park
Playgrd.
Rhodesia Court
Depot
Lib.
Church Plantation
B1396
Bawtry Road
A638
(Great North Road)
Bessacarr
Milestone Court
Water Towers
Playing Fields
Bolton Hill
Willow Prim. Sch.
Play. Flds.
Hatchell Wood Prim. Sch.
Dunniwood Hole
Hatchell Wood
Stoven's Plantation
Nursery
74
Boulevard

INSET
AUCKLEY
Dam End
Lidget
Doncaster
DN3
DN9
MAIN STREET
B1396
COMMON LANE
SCHOOL LANE
BELL BUTTS LANE
EASTFIELD LANE
Auckley School
Brooke Farm
Sports Ground
White Stoops Bridge
Old Mill Dike
RIVER TORNE
Mosham Farm
Works
BRANTON
St. Wilfrid's C of E Prim. Sch.
DONCASTER ROAD
DONCASTER RD.
NEW RD.
MOOR GAP
B1396
B3196
M18
M18-MOTORWAY
Moor Plantation
Brackens Plantation
Great Hakehill Field
Folly Plantation
Black Carr Plantation
Short Plats Plantation
Black Carr
Old Springs Wood
Yorkshire Wildlife Park
Sewage Works
Crow Hall Plantation
Insley Plantation
Round Plantation
The Carrs
Millhouse Farm
Auckley Bri.
Fiddlers Corner
Cocking Ings
Fore's Bridge
Pearsons Farm
Home Farm
Pumping Sta.
GATEWOOD LA.
NUTWELL LANE
KILHAM LANE
BRANTON GATE ROAD or WHIPHILL TOP LA.
WHIPHILL TOP LANE
TONGUE LANE
Playing Fields
Hatchell Wood
Park Closes

43
75
INSET

PILLEY
Lower Pilley
Pilley Green
Upper Tankersley
Bromley
Howbrook
Westwood
HIGH GREEN
Sheffield
S75
S35
SOUTH YORKSHIRE INDUSTRIAL PARK
WENTWORTH INDUSTRIAL PARK
WESTWOOD COUNTRY PARK
Hollins Plantation
Buck Park
Clay Royd Plantation
Potter Holes Plantation
Playing Field
Westwood Lodge
Park House
Winterbottom Busks
Low Bromley
Bromley Farm
Bromley Carr
Owler Lane
Askilona
Carr Head Farm
West Side
Howbrook Farm
Berry Fold
Holly House Farm
Hollin Berry Farm
High Green Bridge
Wheel Bank Hill
Howbrook Reservoir
Town End Spring
Storrs Bottom
West Wood
Storrs Dike
Sowell Bridge
Reservoir
Twelve Lands Plantation
Tankersley Farm
Tankersley Plantation
New Biggin Plantation
Westwood Bridge
Westwood Bottom
Blackburn Brook
Mark Brook
How Brook
Foster Ground Plantation
St. Mary's Catholic Prim. Sch.
Training Cen.
Rose Cottages
Depot
Knoll Cotts.
Knoll Drill
Greenfield Cottage
Brialey Cottage
Athersley House
Croft Head Plantation
Ivy House Farm
Parks Plant.
Fan Drift
Sewage Works
Hotel
Weir
A616
A61
60
44
78
BARNSLEY
SHEFFIELD
WESTWOOD NEW ROAD
NEW ROAD
CARR LANE
LIDGETT LANE
CHURCH LANE
WENTWORTH WAY
MAPLE ROAD
GREAVES LANE
STORRS LANE
CROSS LANE
BROMLEY CARR ROAD
CARR HEAD RD.
HOLLINBERRY LANE
HOWBROOK LA.
BERRY LANE
WORTLEY ROAD
WESTWOOD LANE
MORTOMLEY LANE
33
34
99
398
400

61
45
79
62
HOYLAND COMMON
Barnsley
S74
Junction 36
Junction 35a
M1
M1 MOTORWAY
SHEFFIELD ROAD
HOYLAND ROAD
FEARNLEY RD. WEST
B6096
A6135
A616
B6086
TANKERSLEY
Tankersley Common Side
Tankersley Common
Sports Grd.
Athletic Track
Prim. Sch.
King George's Field
Depot
Recreation Ground
Glebe Farm
Bull Wood
Bullwood
BELL GROUND
Bell Ground House
Park Side
Park Bottom
Old Hall Farm
Subway
TANKERSLEY PARK GOLF COURSE
Lower New Biggin
Club House
Tankersley Park
WENTWORTH STATION
LIDGETT GRANGE
LONGLEY SPRING
Longley Farm
Springwood Farm
Hood Hill Plantation
Hood Hill Lodge
Hood Hill
Hood Hill Farm
Tunnel
Delf Hills
Tanks
Warren
TOP WARREN
Thorncliffe Wood
THORNCLIFFE INDUSTRIAL ESTATE
Blackburn Brook
Chemical Works
Rec. Grd.
ROTUNDA BUS. CEN.
Kirk Balk Sch.
Playing Fields
Tankersley
Bowl Grn.
Playgrd.
Works
Drill Hall
ROCKINGHAM BUSINESS PARK
BIRDWELL COMMON

62
A
B
C
D
1
2
3
4
5
6
46
61
80
37
38
HOYLAND
Hoyland Leisure Cen. & Swim. Pool
Playing Fields
WEST STREET
STREET
KING STREET
HIGH S.
STREET HILL
FITZWILLIAM ST.
COBCAR
WILKINSON RD.
Elsecar
ELSECAR
Foundry
Recreation Ground
Hoyland Springwood Prim. Sch.
Milton
MILTON ROAD
ARMROYD LANE
Milton House
Barnsley
S74
Skiers Hall
Alderthwaite
Springwood Farm
Skier's Spring Wood
FOOTRILL COTTS.
Spring Cotts.
Spring Lodge
Weir
BURYING LANE
BARNSLEY
ROTHERHAM
BROADCARR ROAD
Sports Ground
Elsecar Park
Reservoir House
ELSECAR RESERVOIR
Low Wood
Barrow Field
BARROWFIELD LANE
WATER LANE
Sewage Works
Wentworth Mill
Barrowfield Gate
ALMSHOUSES
Longley Farm
LONGLEY SPRING
SHEFFIELD RD.
A6135
HARLEY RD.
DIKE HILL
B6090
BARROW HILL
THE BARROW
Low Harley
HARLEY
Sports Ground
Sewage Works
ROSEHILL COTTAGES
Barrow
Barrow Cottage
Barrow Farm
WEST HALL FOLD
Wentworth C of E Jun. Inf. Sch.
WENTWORTH
Ashes Farm
ASHES LA.
CHURCH FIELD
CHURCH FIELD ROAD
Ashcroft House
Ashcroft
COACH ROAD
Hood Hill Lodge
HOOD HILL
Hood Hill
Hood Hill Farm
KIRBY LANE
B6086
S35
Derricroft
Oak Tree Cottage
Barley Hole Springs
Barley Hall

Rotherham
S62
RAINBOROUGH PARK
Fox Covert
Rockingham
Reservoir
Simon Wood
Football Grd.
Linthwaite
KING'S WOOD
Royds Farm
LINTHWAITE LANE
GILES WOOD
Old Fox Cottages
Fox Farm
Gorrell Spring
Lea Brook
Stump Cross
Needle's Eye
Lee Wood
Street
COLEY LANE
CLAY FIELD
Saw Mill
Nursery
GLASS HOUSE GREEN
Cortworth House
Freeman's Spring
Luke Spring
Cortworth
CORTWORTH
North Lodge
Students' Hostel
Tennis Courts
Deer Shed
Lousy Bush
DEER PARK
Wentworth Woodhouse
Wentworth Woodhouse Gardens
Garden Centre
Works
Craft Workshops
Doric Lodge
WENTWORTH PARK
WINDMILL FIELD
Cortworth Field Plantation
Hoober Plantation
HOOBER HALL LANE
Coley Lane Farm
Elsecar C of E Prim. Sch.
Elsecar Heritage Cen.
Fish Pond
Temple Hill Plantation
B6097
B6090
47
81
64

Westfield Farm
ELSECAR
B6097
ROAD
48
ROTHERHAM RD.
BROOKSIDE CRES.
MELTON
The Counting Houses
Gorse Wood
Stacey Mill House
MILL
PACKMAN
Coley Lane Farm
LANE
COLEY
Dike
Brook
Reservoir
GILES
WOOD
Weir
Reservoir
Hoober Hall
HALL
HOOBER
B6089
ROAD
Hoober Hill Cottages
AMERICA
LANE
99
63
Lea Brook
LEA
Bank
Hoober
Reservoir (covered)
Rotherham
FIELD
ROAD
Birchcliff Bank
Roman Ridge
Dyke
Stand Cottage
BROOK
Hoober Plantation
Hoober Stand
STREET
LANE
Hoober Hill
HOOBER
Luke Spring
Hoober Cottage
LANE
HOOBER
B6090
LANE
PACKMAN
WENTWORTH
ROAD
Hoober House
Hoober
LA.
ANGEL
398
CORTWORTH
B6090
Cortworth Field
GOWER
Low Stubbin
B6089
Field Plantation
B6091
Fox Covert
HAUGH
UPPER HAUGH
STUBBIN
82
High Stubbin
LANE
Dropping Well
441
42

WATH UPON
DEARNE
NEWHILL
Newhill
Park
Wath
Cemetery
Wath Central
Primary School
Wath Comp.
School
Our Lady
St. Joseph's
Catholic
Prim. Sch.
Wath Victoria
Prim. Sch.
Whincover
Farm
The Oaks
Cen.
Saint Pius X Cath.
High Sch.
Playing
Field
Quarry
Hill
Wath Wood
Houses
Wath Wood
WATHWOOD
HOSPITAL
Boyd
Royd Wood
Wath Wood
Cottages
WATH
GOLF COURSE
Abdy
Farm
Club Ho.
ABDY
Mexborough
S64
S63
S62
Three
Cornered
Plantation
Keeper's
Cottage
Creighton
Woods
LAWN
PLANTATION
Blackamoor
Inn
Plantation
SWINTON
COMMON
Piccadilly
Wood
Warren House
Farm
Warren House
Cotts.
Ckt.
Grd.
Roman Ridge Dyke
Chain Bar
Plant.
Dyson's
Plantation
Birch
Wood
Warren
Vale
Works
The Bungalow
Tennis
Courts
SANDYGATE
WATH WOOD RD.
A633
WARREN VALE RD.
RACECOURSE ROAD
BLACKAMOOR ROAD
B6092
WORTH ROAD
B6090
WENTWORTH RD.
HARDING AVENUE
WARREN VALE
FESTIVAL ROAD
STUMP CROSS
QUARRY HILL ROAD
BUCKLEIGH ROAD
GREEN ROAD
ABDY ROAD
E
F
G
H
1
2
3
4
5
6
49
83
99
43
44
400
398

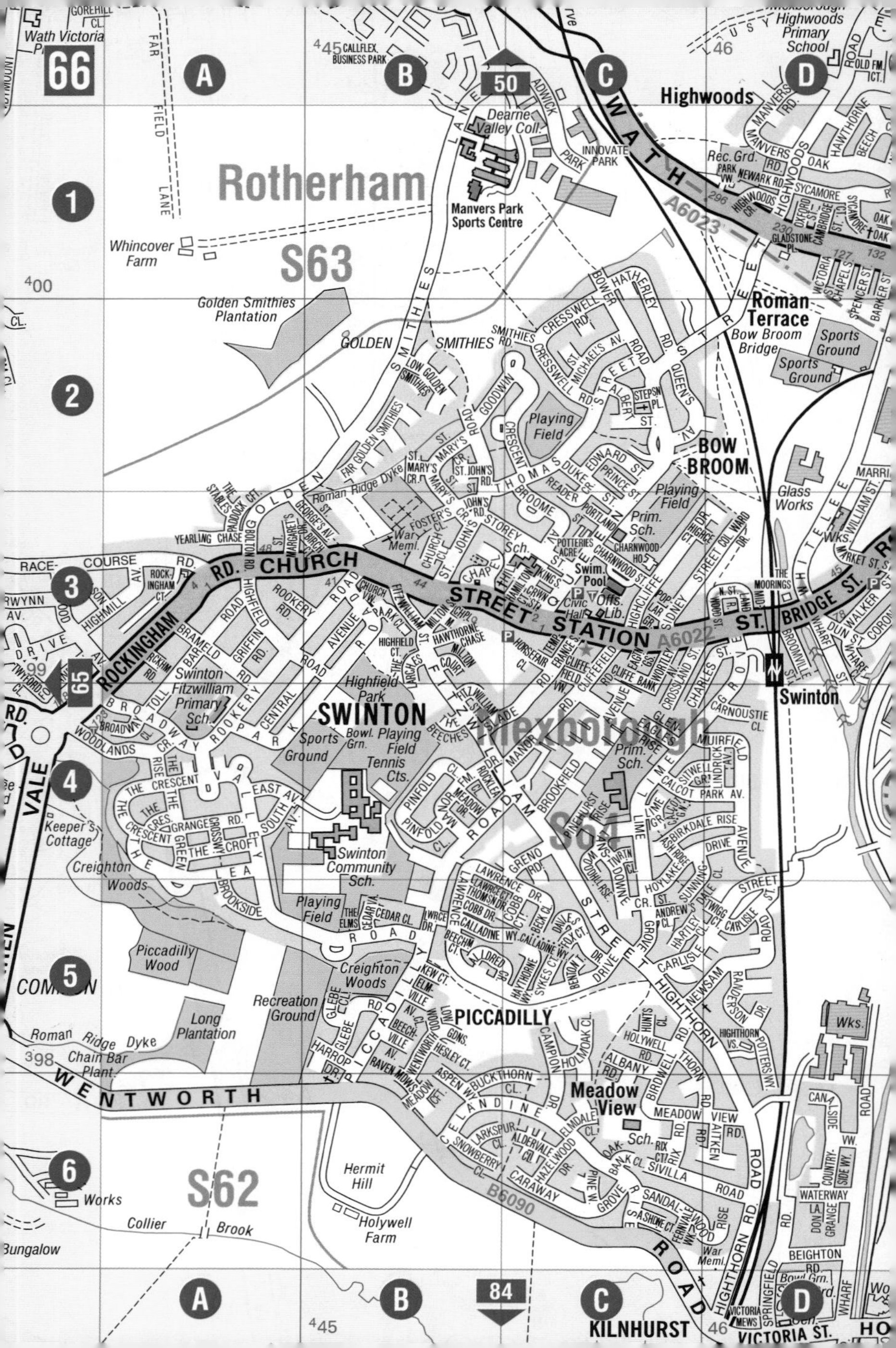

Rotherham
S63
S64
S62
Wath Victoria Pr.
Callflex Business Park
Highwoods
Mexborough Highwoods Primary School
Dearne Valley Coll.
Innovate Park
Manvers Park Sports Centre
Whincover Farm
Golden Smithies Plantation
Roman Terrace
Bow Broom Bridge
Sports Ground
Bow Broom
Glass Works
Playing Field
Prim. Sch.
War Meml.
Swim. Pool
Civic Hall
Offs. Lib.
Swinton
Swinton Fitzwilliam Primary Sch.
Highfield Park
Sports Ground
Bowl. Grn.
Tennis Cts.
Swinton Community Sch.
Mexborough
Keeper's Cottage
Creighton Woods
Piccadilly Wood
Long Plantation
Recreation Ground
Chain Bar Plant.
Piccadilly
Meadow View
Hermit Hill
Holywell Farm
Works
Collier Brook
Bungalow
Wks.
Kilnhurst
Roman Ridge Dyke
Rockingham Rd.
Church Street
Station Street
Bridge St.
Wath Road
Wentworth Road
Golden Smithies Lane
Highthorn Road
A6022
A6023
B6090
Swinton
50
84
65

MEXBOROUGH
Doncaster
DN12
OLD DENABY
SWINTON BRIDGE
WINDHILL
Dolcliffe Common
DONCASTER ROAD
A6023
DENABY COMMON
HOOTON COMMON
RIVER DON
Mexborough
Peas Hill Plantation
Hanging Wood
Old Denaby Wetlands Nature Reserve
Manor Farm
Engine House Farm
Grange Farm
Fox Well
Little Wood
Kilnhurst Bridge
Elm Tree Farm
KILNHURST RD.
Montagu Prim.
MONTAGU HOSPITAL
Ivy House Farm
Vicarage
Sewage Works
LOW MEADOW
SWINTON MEADOWS INDUSTRIAL ESTATE
DONCASTER
ROTHERHAM
51
68
85

A
B
C
D
1
2
3
4
5
6
49
450
400
99
398
52
67
86
WINDHILL
Mexborough
S64
DN12
Sewage Works
Refuse Tip
Hotel
The Ings
Water Works
Playing Field
PASTURES
NAVIGATION
Pasture Bri.
Grey's Bridge
RIVER
DON
Mexborough Low Lock
Works
DONCASTER
A6023
Dearne Valley Leisure Centre
Castle Hill Pk.
Sch.
CHURCH
SHEFFIELD & SOUTH YORKSHIRE
Mill Plantation
Wks.
Offs.
DONCASTER ROAD
Play. Field
DENABY LANE IND. ESTATE
PITMAN RD
COALPIT
DAVY RD
ELAND RD
ELAND ROAD
Works
Ivy House Farm
Old Denaby Wetlands Nature Reserve
IVY COURT
THE GREEN
THE COURTYARD
DENABY WOOD
HILL TOP ROAD
Play. Fld.
CLIFF VIEW
RAVENFIELD ST.
SHEPHARD'S CL.
HICKLETON ST.
TICKHILL
WADWORTH
Meml. Park
SCHOOL
Prim. Sch.
Play Fld.
Ckt. Grd. Pav.
Football Grd.
Convent
DENABY MAIN
Fullerton House Sch.
Cemy.
Conisbrough Crags Rec. Area
HARROGATE
TODMORDEN CL.
REDCAR CL.
TADCASTER CL.
THIRSK CL.
CATTERICK CL.
DRIVE
BOLTON
NORTHUMBERLAND LA.
WESTMORLAND LA.
WILTSHIRE AV.
SUSSEX GDS.
DEVON
SUFFOLK VW.
DONCASTER ROTHERHAM
Denaby Thicks
FITZWILLIAM AV.
FULLERTON AV.
POPE AV.
WASHINGTON AV.
CHAMBERS
PARKGATE AV.
THE CRESCENT
AVENUE
Playing Field
Pennine View Sch.
Ivanhoe Jun. & Inf. Sch.
Youth & Welfare Cen.
MAPLE GRO.
CYPRESS GRO.
CHERRY GRO.
LARCH GRO.
CEDAR GRO.
ACACIA GRO.
MICKLEBRING GRO.
PINE GRO.
SHEFFIELD ROAD
A630
CROOKED LANE
LANE
PARK
Hill Top

Doncaster
CADEBY
DN5
CONISBROUGH
Conisbrough
Burcroft
Dolomite Quarry
Cadeby Rattles
Rattles Hill Plantation
Kingswood Dearne Valley Outdoor Educational & Activity Centres
Cadeby Hall Farm
Conisbrough Tunnel
Conisbrough Viaduct
Rainbow Bridge
Conisbrough Lock
Sewage Works
Windgate Cotts.
Conisbrough Crags Rec. Area
Playing Field
De Warenne Academy
Miners' Welfare Rec. Grd.
Windmill Estate
Hollyhead Farm
Common Road Bridge
Snake Lane Bridge
CONISBROUGH COMMON
Carr Grange
Clifton Hill Bridge
Pigotts Park (Rec.Grd.)
Manor Farm
Kearsley Glen
The Bungalow
Spring Bank
Spring Bank Bungalow
Crookhill Plantations
Fish Pond
CROOKHILL PARK GOLF COURSE
LOW ROAD
DONCASTER ROAD
CLIFTON HILL
CARR LANE
A630
A6023
B6094
RIVER DON
53
70
87

DN5
DN12
Grey Stones
RIVER DON
Farcliff Wood
Far Cliff
Dolomite Quarry
Tunnels
Works
Warmsworth Prim. Sch.
DONCASTER ROAD SHEFFIELD ROAD
A630
Rainbow Bridge
Butterbusk
Butterbusk Green
Conisbrough Viaduct
Nearcliff Wood
Doncaster Road Bridge
Cliff Fields
Limestone Plantation
HEAD LANE
WARMSWORTH HALT
WARMSWORTH HALT INDUSTRIAL ESTATE
Factory
Cycling Track Ckt Grd.
Howbecks
Victoria Prim. Sch.
Playing Field
Recreation Ground
EDLINGTON LANE
B6376
HIGH ROAD
Doncaster
Sch.
The Martinwell Cen.
Comm. Cen.
Hill Top Primary Sch.
Playing Field
Edlington Leisure Cen.
Sir Thomas Wharton Comm. College
NEW EDLINGTON
Hollyhead Farm
Eden Lea
Common Road Bridge
Poultry Houses
CONISBROUGH COMMON
Havelock House
CARR LANE
B6094
COMMON ROAD
CROOKHILL PARK GOLF COURSE
Manor Farm
OLD EDLINGTON

54
88
69

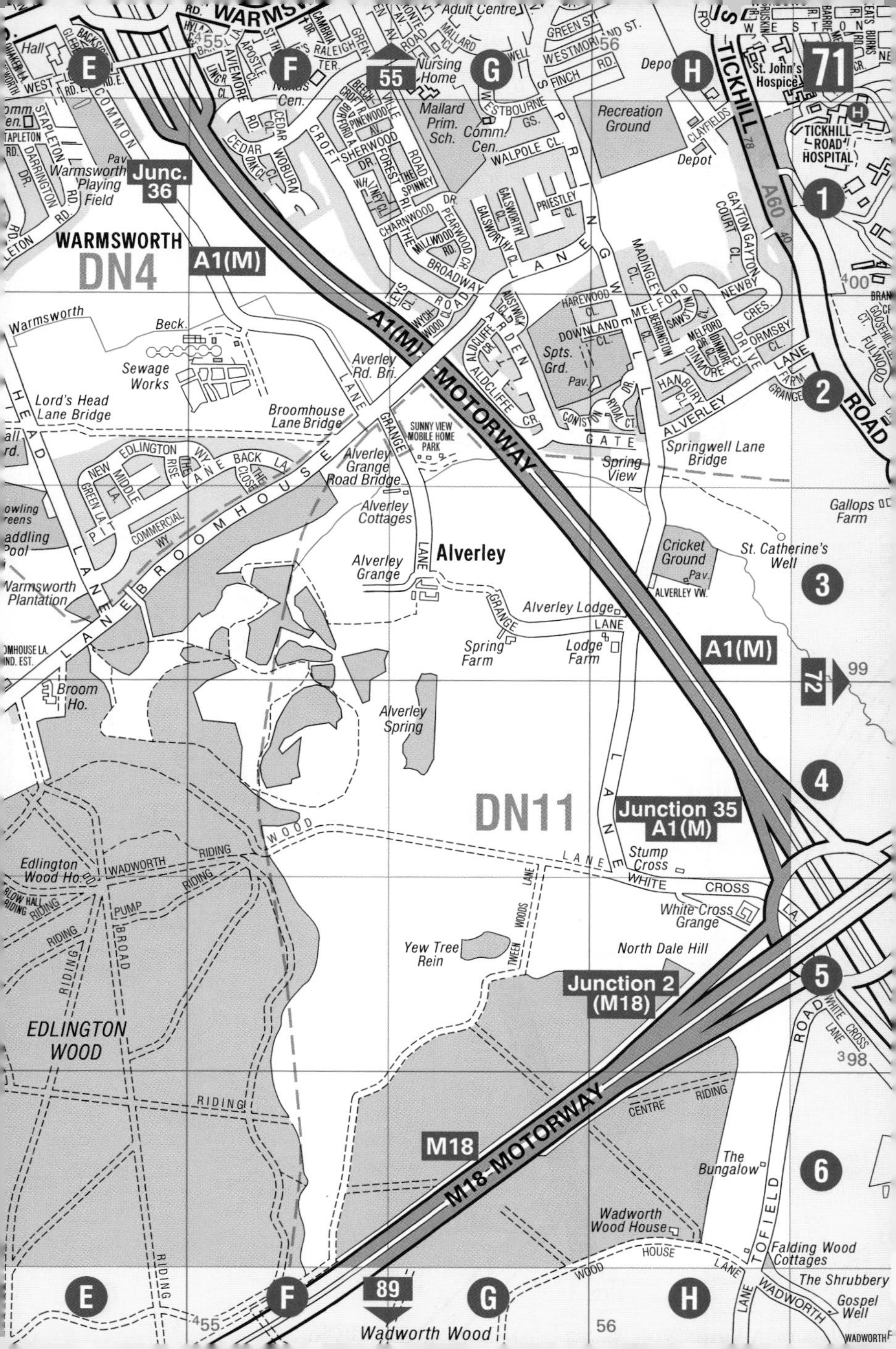
71
E
F
G
H
55
Junc. 36
A1(M)
WARMSWORTH
DN4
Warmsworth Playing Field
Nursing Home
Mallard Prim. Sch.
Comm. Cen.
Recreation Ground
Depot
St. John's Hospice
TICKHILL ROAD HOSPITAL
TICKHILL
A60
ROAD
WESTBOURNE GS.
WALPOLE CL.
WESTMORLAND ST.
FINCH RD.
GREEN ST.
CLAYFIELDS
SPRINGWELL LANE
BROADWAY
SHERWOOD
FOREST RI.
CHARNWOOD DR.
PEARWOOD CR.
MILLWOOD RD.
GALSWORTHY CL.
PRIESTLEY CL.
MADINGLEY CL.
MELFORD
HAREWOOD CL.
DOWNLAND CL.
BERRINGTON CL.
SAWSTON CL.
NEWBY CRES.
GAYTON COURT
DINMORE CL.
ORMSBY CL.
HANBURY CL.
ALDCLIFFE CR.
ARDEN GATE
CONISTON
RYDAL CT.
ALVERLEY LANE
Spts. Grd.
Pav.
1
2
3
4
5
6
Warmsworth Beck
Sewage Works
Lord's Head Lane Bridge
Broomhouse Lane Bridge
Averley Rd. Bri.
MOTORWAY
SUNNY VIEW MOBILE HOME PARK
Alverley Grange Road Bridge
Alverley Cottages
Alverley
Alverley Grange
Springwell Lane Bridge
Spring View
Cricket Ground
ALVERLEY VW.
Gallops Farm
St. Catherine's Well
NEW EDLINGTON
MIDDLE LA.
GREEN LA.
COMMERCIAL WY.
BACK LA.
THE CLOSE
BROOMHOUSE LANE
HEAD LANE
Bowling Greens
Paddling Pool
Warmsworth Plantation
Alverley Lodge
Spring Farm
Lodge Farm
GRANGE LANE
A1(M)
72
99
Broom Ho.
Alverley Spring
DN11
Junction 35 A1(M)
Stump Cross
WHITE CROSS LA.
White Cross Grange
WOOD LANE
Edlington Wood Ho.
WADWORTH RIDING
PUMP RIDING
BROAD RIDING
Yew Tree Rein
TWEEN WOODS LANE
North Dale Hill
Junction 2 (M18)
EDLINGTON WOOD
RIDING
CENTRE RIDING
M18
M18-MOTORWAY
The Bungalow
TOFIELD ROAD
WHITE CROSS LANE
398
Wadworth Wood House
HOUSE LANE
WOOD
Falding Wood Cottages
The Shrubbery
Gospel Well
WADWORTH LANE
89
455
56
Wadworth Wood
WADWORTH

72
56
71
A
B
C
D
1
2
3
4
5
6
57
58
99
400
398
TICKHILL ROAD HOSPITAL
ST. CATHERINE'S HOSPITAL
Balby Carr Community Sports College
Learning Centre
Comm. Cen.
Balby Carr
DN4
DN11
Doncaster
LOVERSALL
Loversall Farm
Loversall Hall
Lily Pond
Carr Lodge Cottages
Carr Lodge
Littlewood Plantation
Woodfield Plantation
Superstore
Huxter Well Plantation
Long Walk Plantation
Hall Balk Plantation
Gallops Farm
Balby Road Bridge
St. Catherine's Well
Quarry Farm
M18
M18 MOTORWAY
Junction 35 A1(M)
Junction 2 (M18)
A1(M) MOTORWAY
A1(M)
A60
TICKHILL
WADWORTH HILL ROAD
Pond Plantation
Robin's Gap
Lockwell Ings
Garden Cottage
Low Farm
Bubup Bri.
Mill Bri.
Washing Dike Plantation
St. Catherine's Well Stream
Little Carr
Mill Farm
New Ings
Crow Wood
Wadworth Hill Bridge
Falding Wood Cottages
The Shrubbery
Gospel Well
Sewage Works
Burr Hill
INSET
WOODFIELD WAY
BALK LANE
HALL BALK
RAKE'S LANE
DAW LANE
CROSS LANE
TOFIELD
WHITE
Division

73
57
74
E
F
G
H
1
2
3
4
5
6
Childer's Drain Bridge
Young Eaa Plantation
Triangle Plantation
Potteric Carr Nature Reserve
Black Carr Junction
Stoven's Plantation
Black Carr
POTTERIC CARR
Beeston Plantation
WHITE ROSE WAY
A6182
Cottage Plantation
M18 MOTORWAY
M18
Junction 3
Potteric Carr Farm
RAKE'S LA.
LANE
Whin Covert
LOVERSALL CARR
Pheasant Bank
BANKWOOD CR.
WEST END LA.
HOLMES
LITTLE MOOR
Holmes Carr Great Wood
Wadworth Bri.
CARR BANK
GRANGE LANE
Rossington Grange Farm
Cemetery
BALBY CARR BANK
MALLARD
Drain
HENNINGS RD.
LINDRICK CL.
HOWDEN CL.
ST. THOMAS' CT.
The Shrubbery
Gospel Well
WADWORTH
WADWORTH HALL
ROCKCLIFFE DR.
REDHILL CT.
WHITBECK CL.
HIGH ST.
VICARAGE DR.
Hall Farm
Church Farm
Ckt. Grd.
OLD SCH. LA.
CHURCH RD.
NEWTREE DR.
CHURCH LA.
CHURCH B6094 RD
MANOR WK.
WINDMILL DR.
CHURCH VW.
ST. JOHN'S CFT.
Windmill Hill
WADWORTH HILL
MAIN ST.
A60
Lidgets
OSBERTON'S
SWEET
WALNUT TREE HILL
WELL
RATTEN ROW
BEANCROFT CL.
CARR LA.
MANOR RISE
MEADOW RISE
CROSSGATES
Wadworth Primary Sch.
A1(M)
DAW LA.
Carrgate Cottage
LANE
NEW ROAD
Long Farm
Doncaster DN11
INSET
457
459
460
400
398
397

DN4
M18 MOTORWAY
Doncaster
ROSSINGTON
NEW ROSSINGTON
DN11
DONCASTER GOLF COURSE
West End Wood
Park Wood
Holmes Carr Great Wood
Bessacarr Junction
Bessacarr Crossing
Seven Arches Bridge
INSET

DN3
DN9
Doncaster DN11
NEW ROSSINGTON
INSET
Crow Hall Plantation
Insley Plantation
Round Plantation
Hatchell Wood
Twelve Months Carr
Hay Field
Hayfield Lodge Farm
Rossington Bridge
Rossington Bridge Farm
HAYFIELD LANE
GREAT NORTH ROAD
A638
BRIDGE LANE
B6463
Doncaster South
Brooks Wood
Marr Flats
Hurst Plantation
Savage Wood
Savage Wood End
HURST LANE
Hanging Carr Farm
Poultry Farm
Poplar Farm
Torne Valley Farm
Gelster Wood
Sheep Bridge
Gelster Lane Holt
Pithill
Littleworth
BACK ROW COTTAGES
Warren House Farm
Gipsy Plantation
Hag Plantation
Cadman's Plantation
Church Field
Rossington All Saints Academy
Rossington Community Sports Village
All Weather Pitches
Stone Hills
Playing Field
Hunster Grange
STRIPE ROAD
COMMON LA.
HUNSTER FLAT LA.
WILDFLOWER
BISHOPSGATE
SPITAL GRO.
HALL VIEW RD.
HADRIANS CL.
KEPPLE CL.
BOND ROAD
RADBURN WAY
CORONACH WY.
TROUTBECK WY.
CHAMOSSAIRE
MEMOIR GROVE
WHITCOMB DR.
WHITAKER CL.
PORTLAND RD.
SEATON GDNS.
FARRINGDON DR.
KINGSWAY CL.
LUDGATE CL.
HIGHGATE CL.
ALDGATE
STREET
LITTLEWORTH
LITTLEWORTH MEWS
LINDHOLME
DARFIELD CL.
SHARLSTON GDNS.
WADWORTH DRIVE
BIRCOTES WK.
CANON CL.
MEADOW
CHURCH
CHATSWORTH
BRODSWORTH WY.
FOUNTAIN CT.
TURHAM CT.
MEADOWS CT.
PLANTATION AV.
BIRCHWOOD DRIVE
BIRCHWOOD DELL
OAKLANDS
OAK CREST
TONGUE LANE
HOLLYWELL DR.
TORNE
HATCHELLWOOD
POOL DR.
LETWELL CT.
KIRKSTEAD CT.
WARNING
MUIRFIELD
GLENEAGLES
BIRKDALE
ST. ANDREWS CL.
E F G H
1 2 3 4 5 6
59
76
63 64 61 462 397 400

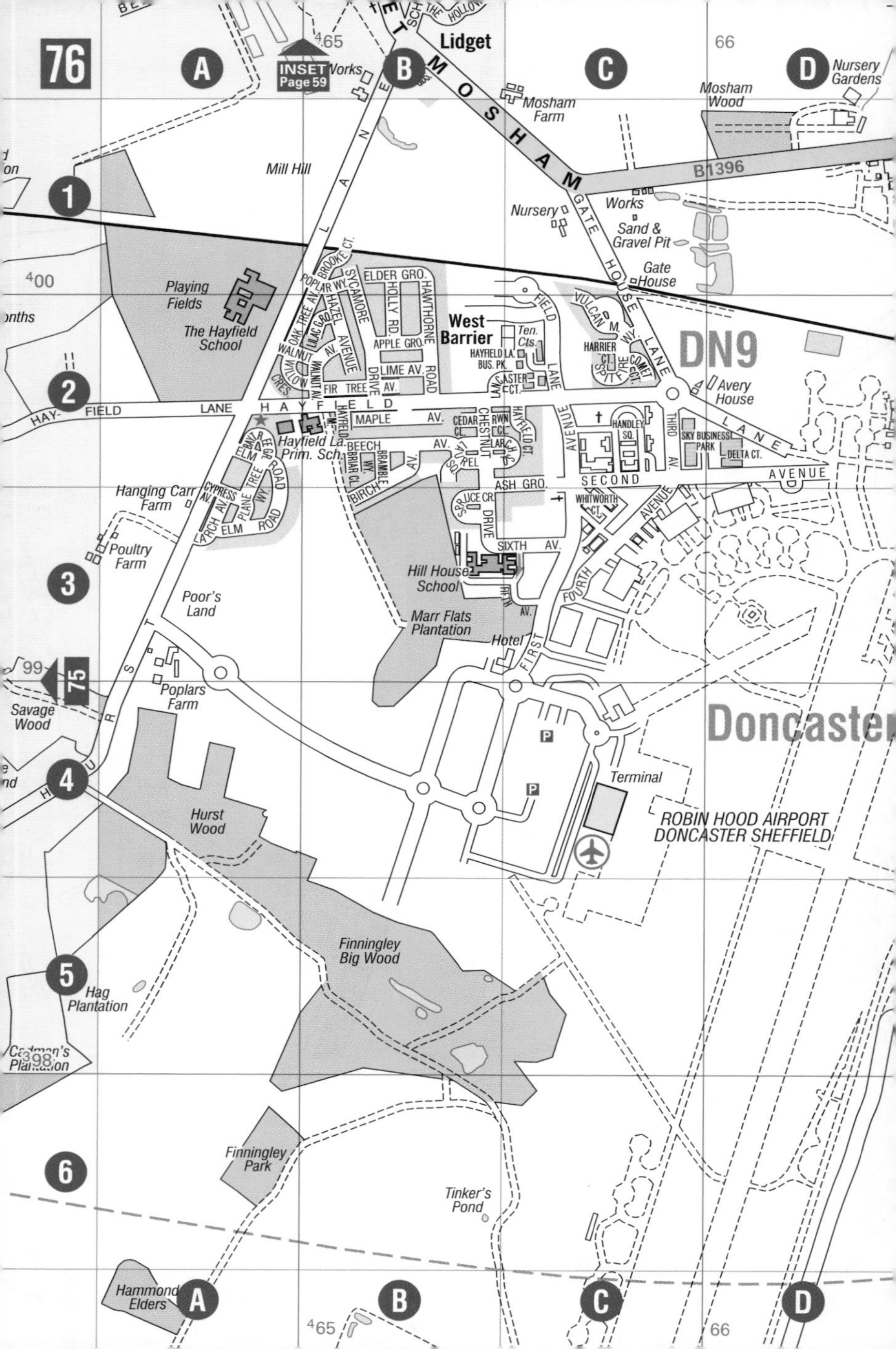

76

A · B · C · D

Lidget

INSET Page 59

Works

66

Nursery Gardens

Mosham Farm

Mosham Wood

Mill Hill

B1396

Nursery

Works

Sand & Gravel Pit

Gate House

Avery House

DN9

Playing Fields

The Hayfield School

ELDER GRO.

POPLAR WY.

LIME TREE AV.

BROKE CT.

SYCAMORE

HAZEL AV.

LILAC GRO.

HOLLY RD

HAWTHORNE

APPLE GRO.

WALNUT

WILLOW CRES.

AVENUE

FIR TREE AV.

LIME AV.

West Barrier

Ten. Cts.

HAYFIELD LA. BUS. PK.

CASTER CT.

VULCAN M.

HARRIER

HARRIER CT.

THE COMET

FIELD LANE

HAYFIELD RD

MAPLE AV.

CEDAR AV.

CHESTNUT

LARCH

HAYFIELD RD

RWN

AVENUE

HANDLEY SQ.

THIRD AV.

SKY BUSINESS PARK

DELTA CT.

LANE

AVENUE

HAY- FIELD LANE

Hayfield La. Prim. Sch.

ELM AV.

CYPRESS AV.

PLANE TREE

HAYFIELD ROAD

LARCH AV.

ELM

BEECH WY.

BRAMBLE CL.

BIRCH

CHAPEL AV.

ASH GRO.

SPRUCE CRT.

DRIVE

WHITWORTH

SECOND

AVENUE

AVENUE

Hanging Carr Farm

Poultry Farm

Poor's Land

Hill House School

Marr Flats Plantation

SIXTH AV.

FOURTH AV.

FIFTH AV.

FIRST AV.

SECOND

Hotel

99

75

Savage Wood

Poplars Farm

P

P

Terminal

Doncaster

ROBIN HOOD AIRPORT DONCASTER SHEFFIELD

Hurst Wood

Finningley Big Wood

Hag Plantation

Cadman's Plantation

398

Finningley Park

Tinker's Pond

Hammond Elders

A · B · C · D

66

465

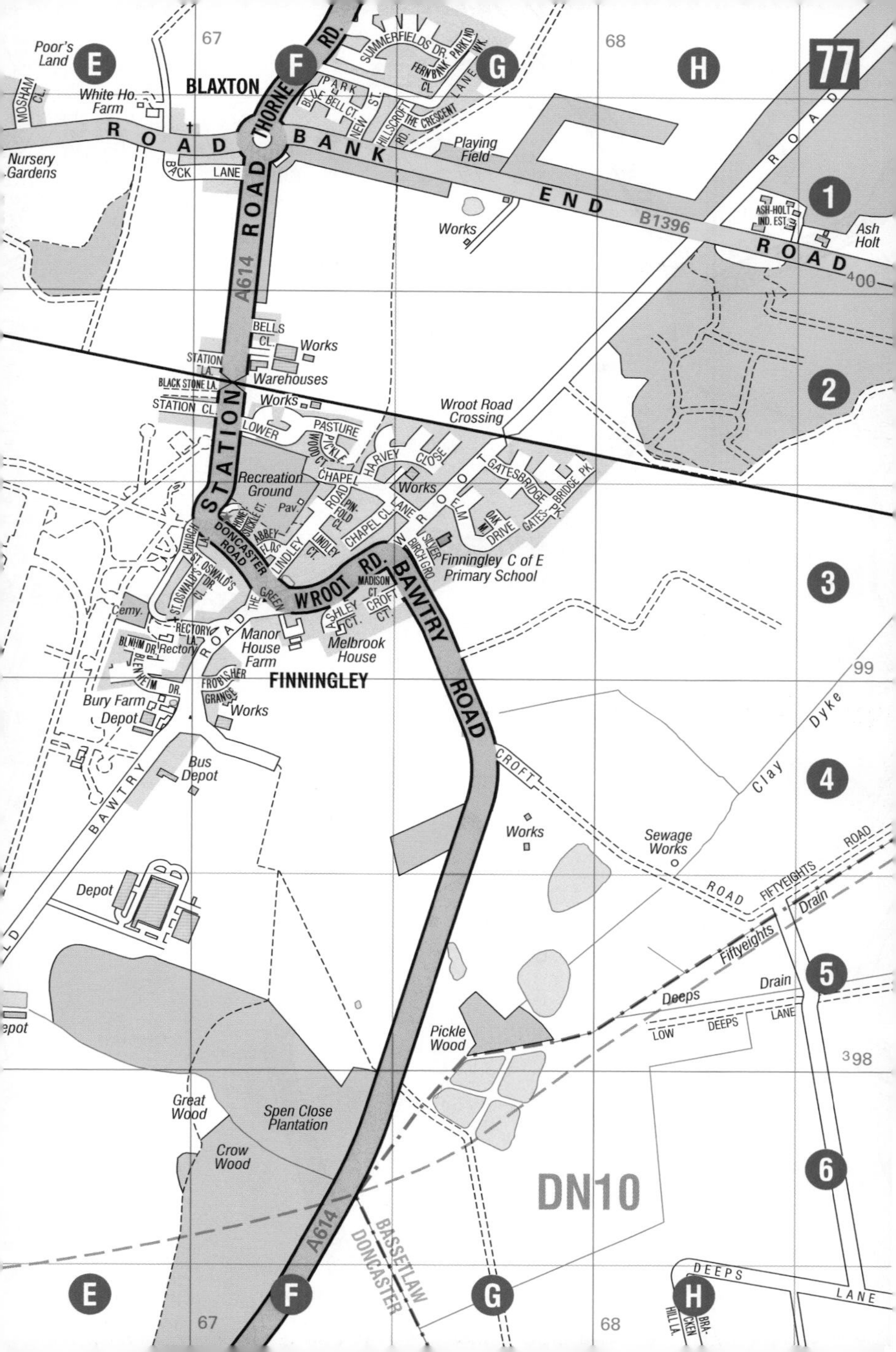

Poor's Land
BLAXTON
White Ho. Farm
MOSHAM CL.
Nursery Gardens
ROAD
BACK LANE
THORNE RD.
SUMMERFIELDS DR.
PARK WK.
FERN BANK CL.
PARK
BLUE BELL CT.
NEW ST.
HILLSCROFT RD.
THE CRESCENT
LANE
BANK END ROAD
B1396
Playing Field
Works
ASH-HOLT IND. EST.
Ash Holt
ROAD
A614 ROAD
BELLS CL.
Works
STATION LA.
Warehouses
BLACK STONE LA.
Works
STATION CL.
STATION ROAD
LOWER PASTURE
WOOD CT.
PICKLE
HARVEY CLOSE
CHAPEL ROAD
Recreation Ground
Pav.
PIN-FOLD CL.
Works
CHAPEL CL.
LANE
WROOT RD.
Wroot Road Crossing
GATESBRIDGE PK.
ELM
OAK M.
DRIVE
GATES-BRIDGE PK.
HONEY SUCKLE CT.
ABBEY FLDS.
LINDLEY
LINDLEY CT.
SILVER BIRCH GRO.
Finningley C of E Primary School
CHURCH LA.
DOCASTER ROAD
ST. OSWALD'S DR.
ST. OSWALD'S CL.
THE GREEN
MADISON CT.
BAWTRY ROAD
ASHLEY CT.
CROFT CT.
Cemy.
RECTORY LA.
Rectory
BLNHM DR.
BLENHEIM DR.
ROAD
Manor House Farm
Melbrook House
FINNINGLEY
FROBISHER GRANGE
Works
Bury Farm
Depot
Bus Depot
BAWTRY
CROFT
Works
Clay Dyke
Sewage Works
ROAD
FIFTYEIGHTS ROAD
Drain
Fiftyeights
Deeps
Drain
LOW DEEPS LANE
Depot
Pickle Wood
Great Wood
Spen Close Plantation
Crow Wood
DN10
A614
BASSETLAW
DONCASTER
DEEPS LANE
HILL LA.
BRA-CKEN
67
68
400
99
398
E F G H
1 2 3 4 5 6

Howbrook Reservoir
Town End Spring
SHEFFIELD ROAD
A629
WESTWOOD NEW RD.
A61
Oak Lodge Farm
Reservoir (covered)
Potter Hill
Sunny Bank
Hall Wood
Hall Wood
BARNSLEY
SHEFFIELD
Hallwood House
Low Hall Wood
Robin Hood Well
PENISTONE
HALLWOOD ROAD
HALL WOOD
Little Hall Wood
Low Spring
Harrison Spring
HIGH GREEN
Playing Field
Angram Bank Prim. Sch.
Charltonbrook
CHARLTON CLOUGH
BURNCROSS
Rec. Grd
Playing Field
Foxfield Spring
Horbury Common
Barnes Hall Farm
Barnes Hall
Sheffield
The Horbury
S35
Barnes Green Farm
ELLIOTT
Woodseats Farm
Wood Seats
Holt House
GRENO WOOD
Greno Knoll
WOODHEAD ROAD
Green Lane
Green Lane Spring
WOOD END
WHITLEY CARR
PEGGY LANE
The Woods
PENISTONE ROAD
WHITLEY
Mortomley Park
Catholic Prim. Sch.
Sport Grd.
Club
Bowls
Hostel
Old People's Ho.
SANDY LANE
BRACKEN HILL
SPRINGWOOD
Dike

60

92

61
Mortomley
Chemical Works
Tankersley Tunnel
Parkin Wood
WHITE LANE
A6135
M1-MOTORWAY
ROTHERHAM
SHEFFIELD
Cricket Ground
Warden's Lodge
M1
Activity Centre
HESLEY WOOD
Lane End
Warehouse
Mount Pleasant
Charlton Brook
STATION ROAD
Chapeltown
Slurry Pond
Tip (Disused)
Park
Playground
Bandstand
CHAPELTOWN
A629
ROAD
Baths
COWLEY LANE
ECCLESFIELD
80
Caravan Park
HILL
Cowley Manor
Windmill Hill Prim. Sch.
Coit Prim. Sch.
Playing Field
Ecclesfield Sch.
Smithy Wood
SMITHY WOOD BUSINESS PARK
CHAPELTOWN RD.
Hoyle House
WHITLEY LANE
Whitley Hall
Whitley Lane Farm
The Red House
Sports & Social Club
Sycamore Farm
Whitley
Steel Works
Sports Ground
Works
ECCLESFIELD
Ecclesfield Common
93
Loicher Bridge
Steel Wks.

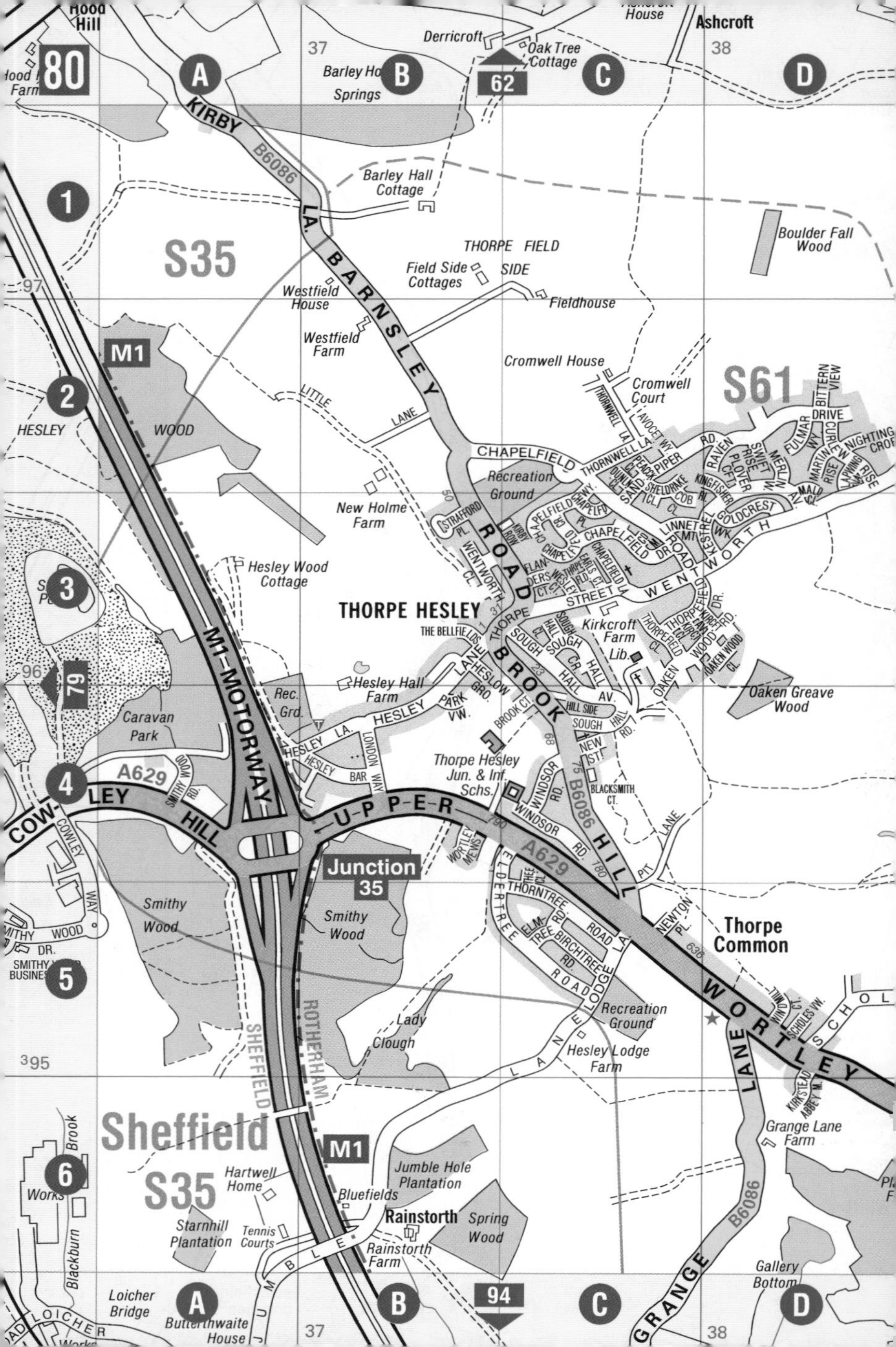

Hood Hill
Derricroft
Oak Tree Cottage
Ashcroft
Barley Hall Springs
62
KIRBY LA.
B6086
Barley Hall Cottage
S35
BARNSLEY ROAD
THORPE FIELD SIDE
Field Side Cottages
Westfield House
Fieldhouse
Westfield Farm
Boulder Fall Wood
Cromwell House
Cromwell Court
S61
M1
HESLEY
WOOD
LITTLE LANE
CHAPELFIELD
Recreation Ground
New Holme Farm
Hesley Wood Cottage
THORPE HESLEY
WENTWORTH
STREET
Kirkcroft Farm
Lib.
Hesley Hall Farm
Rec. Grd.
Oaken Greave Wood
Caravan Park
M1-MOTORWAY
A629
Thorpe Hesley Jun. & Inf. Schs.
COWLEY HILL
UPPER
Junction 35
Smithy Wood
Smithy Wood
THORNTREE ROAD
BIRCHTREE RD.
Thorpe Common
WORTLEY
Lady Clough
Recreation Ground
Hesley Lodge Farm
SHEFFIELD
ROTHERHAM
Sheffield
S35
Grange Lane Farm
Hartwell Home
Jumble Hole Plantation
Bluefields
Rainstorth
Spring Wood
Starnhill Plantation
Tennis Courts
Rainstorth Farm
Works
Blackburn Brook
GRANGE LANE
Gallery Bottom
Loicher Bridge
Butterthwaite House
JUMBLE

79
94

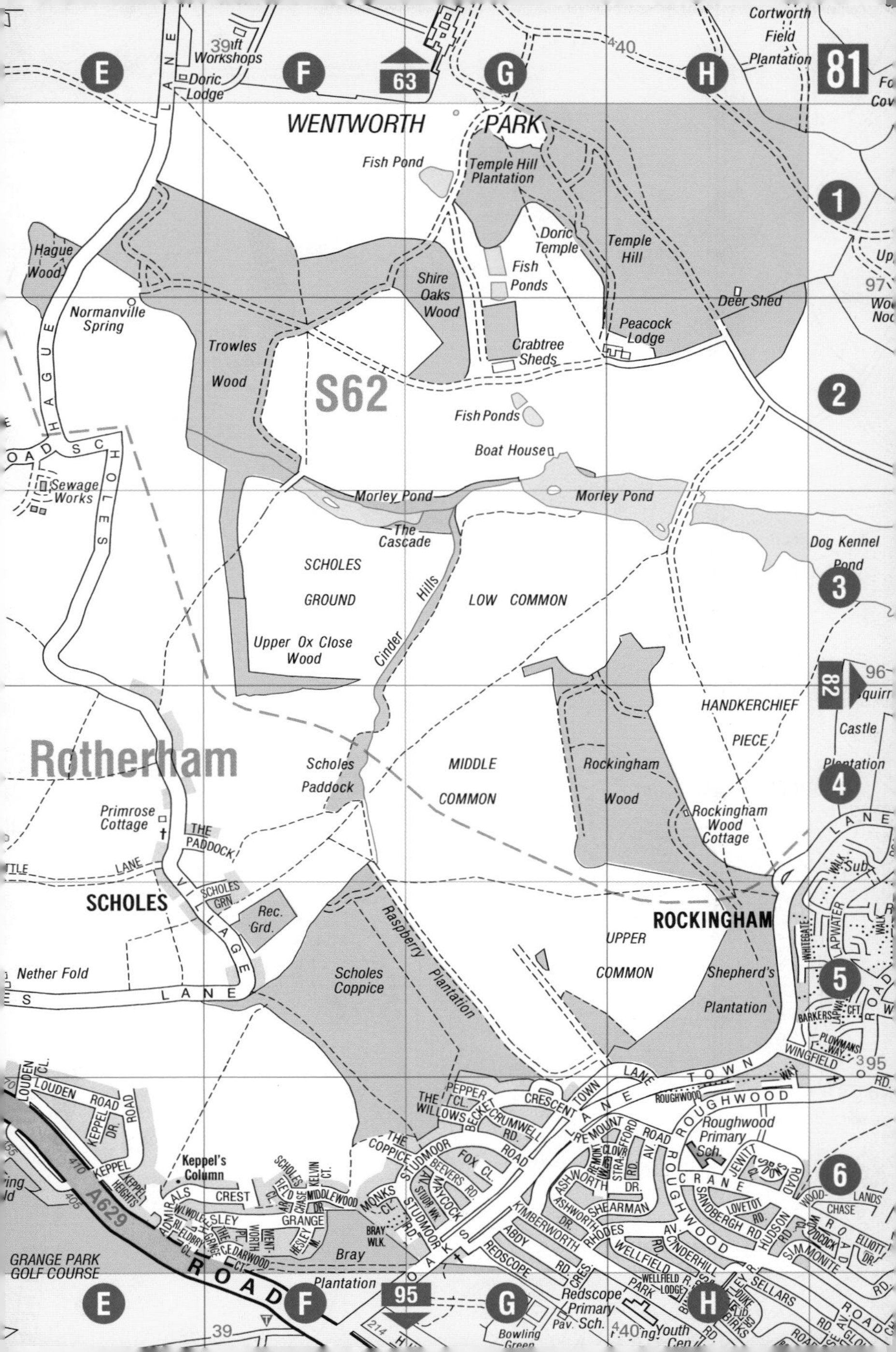
81
63
95
82
WENTWORTH PARK
S62
Rotherham
SCHOLES
ROCKINGHAM
Workshops
Doric Lodge
Cortworth Field Plantation
Fish Pond
Temple Hill Plantation
Doric Temple
Temple Hill
Fish Ponds
Hague Wood
Normanville Spring
Shire Oaks Wood
Trowles Wood
Deer Shed
Peacock Lodge
Crabtree Sheds
Boat House
Morley Pond
Sewage Works
The Cascade
Dog Kennel Pond
SCHOLES GROUND
LOW COMMON
Upper Ox Close Wood
Cinder Hills
HANDKERCHIEF PIECE
Castle Plantation
Scholes Paddock
MIDDLE COMMON
Rockingham Wood
Rockingham Wood Cottage
Primrose Cottage
THE PADDOCK
SCHOLES GRN.
Rec. Grd.
Raspberry Plantation
UPPER COMMON
Shepherd's Plantation
Nether Fold
Scholes Coppice
HAGUE LANE
SCHOLES LANE
SCHOLES VILLAGE
Keppel's Column
Bray Plantation
GRANGE PARK GOLF COURSE
A629
Roughwood Primary Sch.
Redscope Primary Sch.
Bowling Green
Youth Cen.
TOWN LANE
ROUGHWOOD ROAD
OAKS LANE
WINGFIELD RD.

Cortworth Field
Higher Stubbin
Dropping Well
Mausoleum Plantation
Mausoleum Lodge
Upper Swallow Wood
Mausoleum Park
Rockingham Mausoleum
Wood Nook
Hollin Hall
Nether Haugh
UPPER HAUGH
MANOR FARM ESTATE
Old Sough
Nether Haugh Ho.
Works
Clay Hill
Brookshank Wood
Dog Kennel Pond
Morley Lodge
Morley Plantation
Morley Bridge
Weir
Mill Dam
CINDER BRIDGE
Cinderbridge Plantation
DAM HEAD
Squirrel Castle Plantation
Wilcox's Plantation
Cinderbridge Plantation
Manor Ho.
Cinder Bridge
ROCKINGHAM
GREASBROUGH
Ochre Dike
Rec. Grd.
Comm. Cen.
Rockingham Jun. & Inf. Sch.
LIBRARY CL.
Lib.
Greasbrough Prim. Sch.
Ckt. Grd.
Nursy.
Subway
Comm. Cen.
WINGFIELD
Wingfield College
Playing Field
Tennis Courts
Hudsons Rough
KIMBERWORTH PARK
Bassingthorpe Spring
Depot
BARBOT FARM M.
CORTWORTH LANE
B6091
STUBBIN ROAD
B6089
STUBBIN LANE
STUBBIN RD.
BACK LANE
THE WHINS
CINDER BRI. RD.
MAIN ST.
POTTER HILL
CARR HILL
CHURCH LANE
COACH ROAD
COACH RD.
STREET
WINGFIELD ROAD
ROUGHWOOD ROAD
MUNSBROUGH LANE
MUNSBROUGH RISE
BARBOT HILL RD.
FENTON ROAD
WAGON ROAD
SCROOBY STREET
GREASBROUGH
S61

64
81
96

E
F
G
H
65
43
44
Vale
Works
The Bungalow
1
2
3
4
5
6
S62
S65
Rotherham
RAWMARSH
PARKGATE
A633
A6123
B6375
VALE
WARREN
ROAD
DALE
BLYTH AV.
HIGH
ST.
RAWMARSH
HILL
STREET
BROAD
RD.
ROTHERHAM
GREAT EASTERN
WAY
ALDWARKE
LA.
ALDWARKE ROAD
THOROGATE
KILNHURST
ROAD
ROSEHILL
Monkwood Prim. Sch.
Reservoir (covered)
Rawmarsh School
Cemy.
Playing Field
Cemetery
Tennis Courts
Park Hall
Rosehill Victoria Park
Play grd.
Bus Depot
Depot
Spts. Grd.
Football Grd.
Hall
School
Sports Ground
Club Ho.
Bowl. Grns.
Rawmarsh Leisure Centre
ROUNDWOOD GOLF COURSE
Aldwarke Junction
Holly House
Pav.
Spts. Grd.
Lodge
Mangham House
Works
Depot
Wks.
Nursy.
Fitness First Health Club
RETAIL WORLD
South Yorkshire Transport Museum
THE GATEWAY INDUSTRIAL ESTATE
BARBOT HALL IND. EST.
BARBOT HALL INDUSTRIAL ESTATE
Warehouse
The Bungalow
Parkfield Cottage
Barbot Hall
ALEXANDRA CEN.
PARKGATE BUS. PK.
MANGHAM
GREASBROUGH
ROAD
SCROOBY
LANE
TOPS
THE TOPS
STADIUM CT.
WADDINGTON
WATERSIDE COTTS
STADIUM
LITTLE BRIDGE
97
96
83
30
Lib.
Coun. Offs.
ASH MOUNT
RAWMARSH SHOP CEN.
ROUNDWOOD
CLAYPIT
LANE
ASH GRO.
HAWTHORNE AV.
AVENUE
INGSHEAD
PEASHILL ST.
GREEN LANE
BARBERS AVENUE
ROCKCLIFFE ROAD
WENTWORTH DR.
BOUNDARY GRN.
VICTORIA RD.
INFIRMARY RD.
HOLLYBUSH ST.
FRANCE ST.
LARK
CRAVEN ST.
LLOYD ST.
COLEMAN ST.
FOUNDRY ST.
TAYLOR'S LA.
CORNISH WAY
ROTHER CT.
BEALE WAY
MILL
RAIL
MIDLAND
STODDART WY.
ALDWARKE TERRACE
DURHAM WY.
NETHER FIELD LANE
SPALTON R.
ST. GOOSEBUTT
GOOSEBUTT
CHURCH
CHURCH CFT.
OCCUPATION RD.
WESTFIELD CRAFT PK.
NEWBIGGIN
WESTFIELD
HOLM FLATT ST.
ASHWOOD
BEAR TREE RD.
TERRACE R.
PROSPECT CT.
SCHOOL LANE
KNAPTON AV.
WEST AVENUE
MAHON AV.
MIDDLE AVENUE EAST
JOCKELL DR.
GOODWIN AV.
BIRCHWOOD
REDMARSH AV.
KENT AVENUE
WARREN AV.
MONKWOOD
HAGUE AV.
JACKSON CR.
WILSON AV.
MALLORY AV.
ROMAN CRES.
THE BUNGALOWS
KIRKLANDS DR.
UPLANDS WY.
GREEN RISE
HARDING AV.
STUBBIN LA.
MEADOW
CHAPEL WY.
THE STABLES WK.
HAUGH GREEN
LANE
MEADOWS
BUSHEY CL.
LISTER AV.
MORRIS AV.
PIPE HOUSE LA.
SCHOOLFIELD DR.
HOMESTEAD DR.
PARK GRO.
HOLLAND CL.
RIPPON CT.
ALDERSON
BRADLEA RISE
HALLAM DALE CT.
QUEEN ST.
ARTHUR ST.
ROSE HILL AV.
GRANGE
NORTH ST.
CHARLES ST.
BERNARD S.
TINKER
BANK
MAIN ST.
SOUTH
MARRION
HEATONS
ROCKINGHAM R.
ROCKINGHAM HO.
ARCON PL.
ST. NICOLAS
STEWARTS
WILLOW GARTH
WILLOW AV.
ELM PL.
MANOR PL.
GEORGE
DALE ST.
QUARRY ST.
PARK ST.
ROSEDALE
LANE HEAD
HUTCHINSON
BISBY
GALWAY
RICHARDS WY.
HARDIE PL.
BRAM
LENGDALE CT.
MUNEEB CT.
HAWLEY LA.
STOCK'S LANE
NEW ST.
CHAPEL S.
OATES
GREENFIELD
WEDGEWOOD
POTTERY CL.
BARBER'S CR.
THE GROVE
MAPLE CT.
GREEN ACRES
CARDEW CT.
ST. MARY'S
HILLTOPS
RECTORY ST.
VESEY ST.
FITZWILLIAM CT.
RYAN PL.
GOOSEBUTT HO.
ALBERT RD.
CARLTON R.
DERWENT DR.
HADLEIGH CL.
LANE
WILLIAMS ST.
TURNER CL.
MARSHALL CL.
ALBERT R.
NAYLOR
MAURICE
HENRY CT.
LINCROFT
MULBERRY
ALDWARKE
CROSS ST.
WANNOP ST.
DUDLEY
AMI CT.
BROOKSIDE CT.
HILLSIDE CT.
QUINTEC CT.
CALLUM CT.
GATEWAY CT.
SAN
ROAD
EVELY
OSBER
WHEATCROFT RD.
SOUTHWELL RD.
WALKER ST.
SWALLOW CR.
FARM
POTTERY LA.
CREIGHTON AV.
Aldw

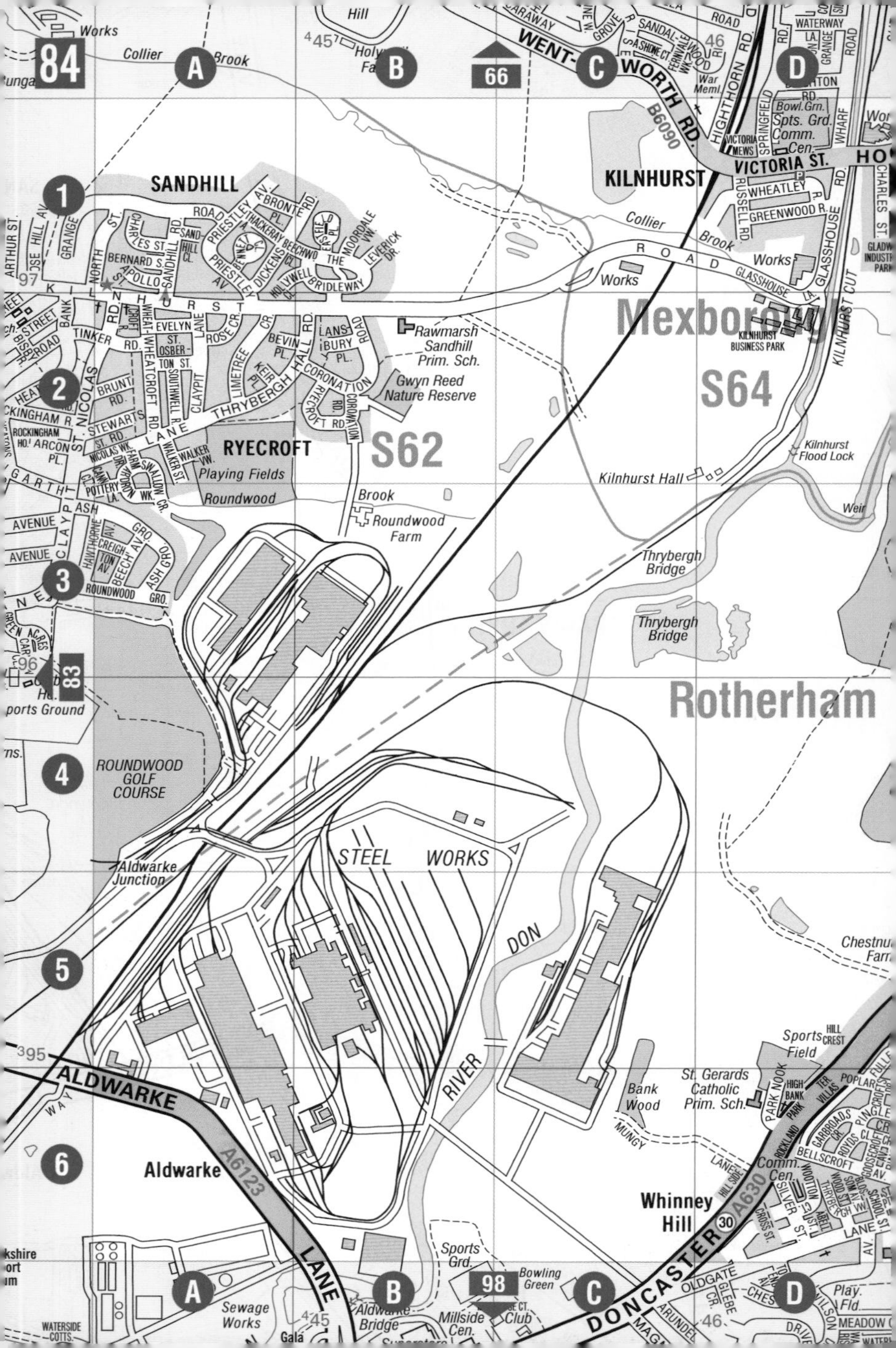

SANDHILL
KILNHURST
RYECROFT
Mexborough
S64
S62
Rotherham
Aldwarke
Whinney Hill
STEEL WORKS
RIVER DON
ROUNDWOOD GOLF COURSE
Collier Brook
Rawmarsh Sandhill Prim. Sch.
Gwyn Reed Nature Reserve
Playing Fields
Roundwood
Roundwood Farm
Kilnhurst Hall
Kilnhurst Flood Lock
KILNHURST BUSINESS PARK
Thrybergh Bridge
Aldwarke Junction
ALDWARKE LANE
A6123
DONCASTER RD.
A630
WENTWORTH RD.
B6090
VICTORIA ST.
GLASSHOUSE LA.
KILNHURST CUT
Bank Wood
St. Gerards Catholic Prim. Sch.
Sports Field
Sewage Works
Aldwarke Bridge
Millside Cen.
Bowling Green
Sports Grd.
Chestnut Farm
Weir
Works
66
83
98

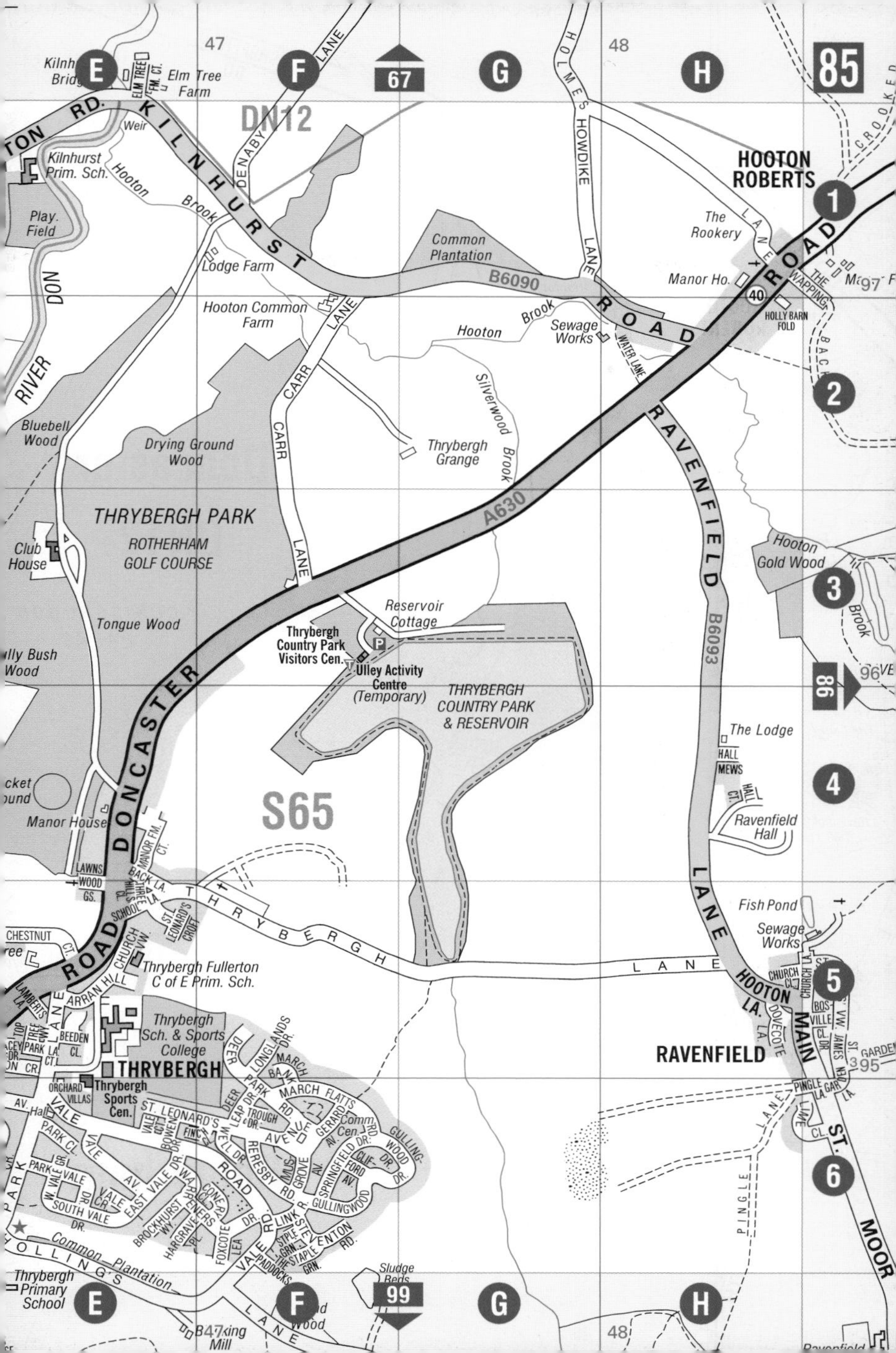

DN12
HOOTON ROBERTS
Kilnhurst Prim. Sch.
Elm Tree Farm
KILNHURST ROAD
Hooton Brook
Lodge Farm
Common Plantation
B6090
Manor Ho.
The Rookery
Hooton Common Farm
CARR LANE
Sewage Works
WATER LANE
HOLLY BARN FOLD
Silverwood Brook
Thrybergh Grange
Drying Ground Wood
Bluebell Wood
RIVER DON
Play. Field
THRYBERGH PARK
ROTHERHAM GOLF COURSE
Club House
Tongue Wood
A630
RAVENFIELD LANE
B6093
Hooton Gold Wood
Reservoir Cottage
Thrybergh Country Park Visitors Cen.
Ulley Activity Centre (Temporary)
THRYBERGH COUNTRY PARK & RESERVOIR
DONCASTER ROAD
The Lodge
HALL MEWS
Ravenfield Hall
S65
Manor House
THRYBERGH LANE
Fish Pond
Sewage Works
HOOTON LA.
MAIN ST.
RAVENFIELD
Thrybergh Fullerton C of E Prim. Sch.
Thrybergh Sch. & Sports College
THRYBERGH
Thrybergh Sports Cen.
PINGLE LANE
MOOR
Thrybergh Primary School
Common Plantation
Sludge Beds

67
98
99

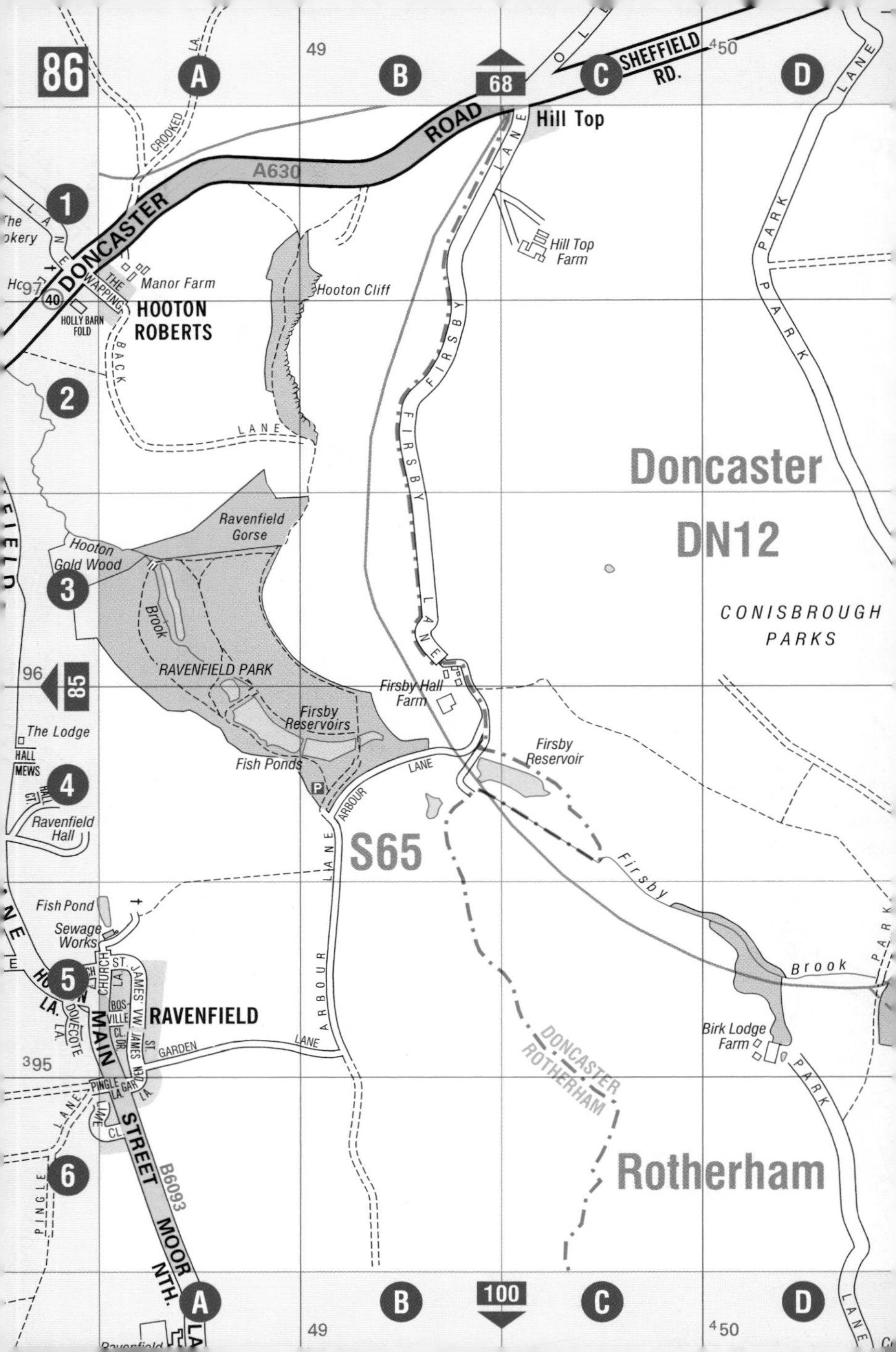

SHEFFIELD RD.
DONCASTER ROAD
A630
Hill Top
Hill Top Farm
Manor Farm
HOOTON ROBERTS
HOLLY BARN FOLD
THE WAPPING
CROOKED LA.
BACK LANE
Hooton Cliff
FIRSBY LANE
PARK LANE
Doncaster
DN12
CONISBROUGH PARKS
Ravenfield Gorse
Hooton Gold Wood
Brook
RAVENFIELD PARK
Firsby Reservoirs
Fish Ponds
Firsby Hall Farm
Firsby Reservoir
ARBOUR LANE
S65
The Lodge
HALL MEWS
HALL CT.
Ravenfield Hall
Fish Pond
Sewage Works
RAVENFIELD
CHURCH LA.
ST. JAMES' VW.
BOSVILLE CL.
JAMES ST.
GARDEN LANE
DOVECOTE LA.
HOOTON LA.
MAIN STREET
PINGLE LA.
PINGLE LANE
LIME CL.
MOOR NTH. LA.
B6093
Firsby Brook
Birk Lodge Farm
DONCASTER ROTHERHAM
Rotherham

68
85
100

Spring
Bank
Spring Bank
Spring Bank
Bungalow

E

Kearsley

51

The Bungalow

F

Kearsley
Glen

69

Manor
Farm

Crookhill
Plantations
Den

52

G

Whiteford

Denbrook

Clifton
Common
Hazeldene

DENBROOK LA.

COMMON

Fish Pond

Crookhill
Plantations

H

CARR

COMMON

LA.

B6094

87

CROOKHILL PARK
GOLF COURSE

1

Club House

97

Parks Farm
Cotts.

Brook

Clifton
Gorse

Conisbrough Parks
Farm

The

Pearson
Holt

LANE

Conisbrough
Lodge

Lidgets
Hill

2

WELL LA.

BEECH PACK LA.

CLIFTON

CLIFTON LA.

BYRES

CHURCH
LA.

BEACON
SQ.

BALK

3

BEACON
LANE

Hall

BEACON LA.

SHIPMAN

LANE

BEACON

LANE

Clifton
Beacon

Beacon
Hill

Reservoir
(covered)

88

96

RUDDLE

4

LANE

S66

The Beck

M18

M18—MOTORWAY

Subway

Prospect
Cottage

Mount
Pleasant

NEW

LANE

5

395

icklebring
Gorse

MICKLEBRING

RUDDLE

The
Gables

MICKLEBRING

ROAD

Ma
C

LANE

6

LANE

COAL PIT
LA.

SIKE

LANE

Well
Farm

ALDERNS
CL.

Manor
High Fm.
Farm

BACK
LANE

Malt
Kiln Farm

GREAVES

CROWN

LANE

101

BACK

LANE

52

Cragdon
House

H

E

F

G

brough

51

A
B
C
D
53
54
70
CARR
CROOKHILL PARK GOLF COURSE
Club House
B6094
Edlington Plantation
Manor Farm
RECTORY GS.
SCHOOL WLK.
B6376
LANE
OLD EDLINGTON
Leisure Cen.
Sir Thomas Wharton Comm. College
BACK
LANE WOOD
LANE
Manor Farm
LITTLE COCKHILL LANE
EDLINGTON
White Cross
DN12
97
COCKHILL
LEYS
B6094
SHIPMAN BALK
GREEN BALK
LONG
M18 MOTORWAY
96
87
RUDDLE LANE
M18
Newlands Farm
COCKHILL
RAKES LANE
Rotherham
S66
FIELD LANE
COCKHILL LANE
CHAPEL HOLE LANE
Ridgewood Farm
395
ROAD
Play. Fld.
Bowl. Grn.
Manor Farm Cottages
BIRCHWOOD GDS.
DONCASTER RD.
MICKLEBRING
LANE
Manor House
CHURCH GRO.
AUSTWOOD
MALTKILN FM. CT.
CARDWELL CT.
WILLOW CRES.
WILLOW PL.
HIGH ST.
BRAITHWELL
Sewage Works
Orchard Ho. Fm.
Cedar Farm
Austwood Closes
The Ruddle Mill
RUDDLE MILL LA.
Cragdon House
Hillcroft
Elmfield Farm
Old Hall Fm.
102
Moat Hall
POGGY LANE
Dike
Ruddle Mill
Quarry (Limestone)

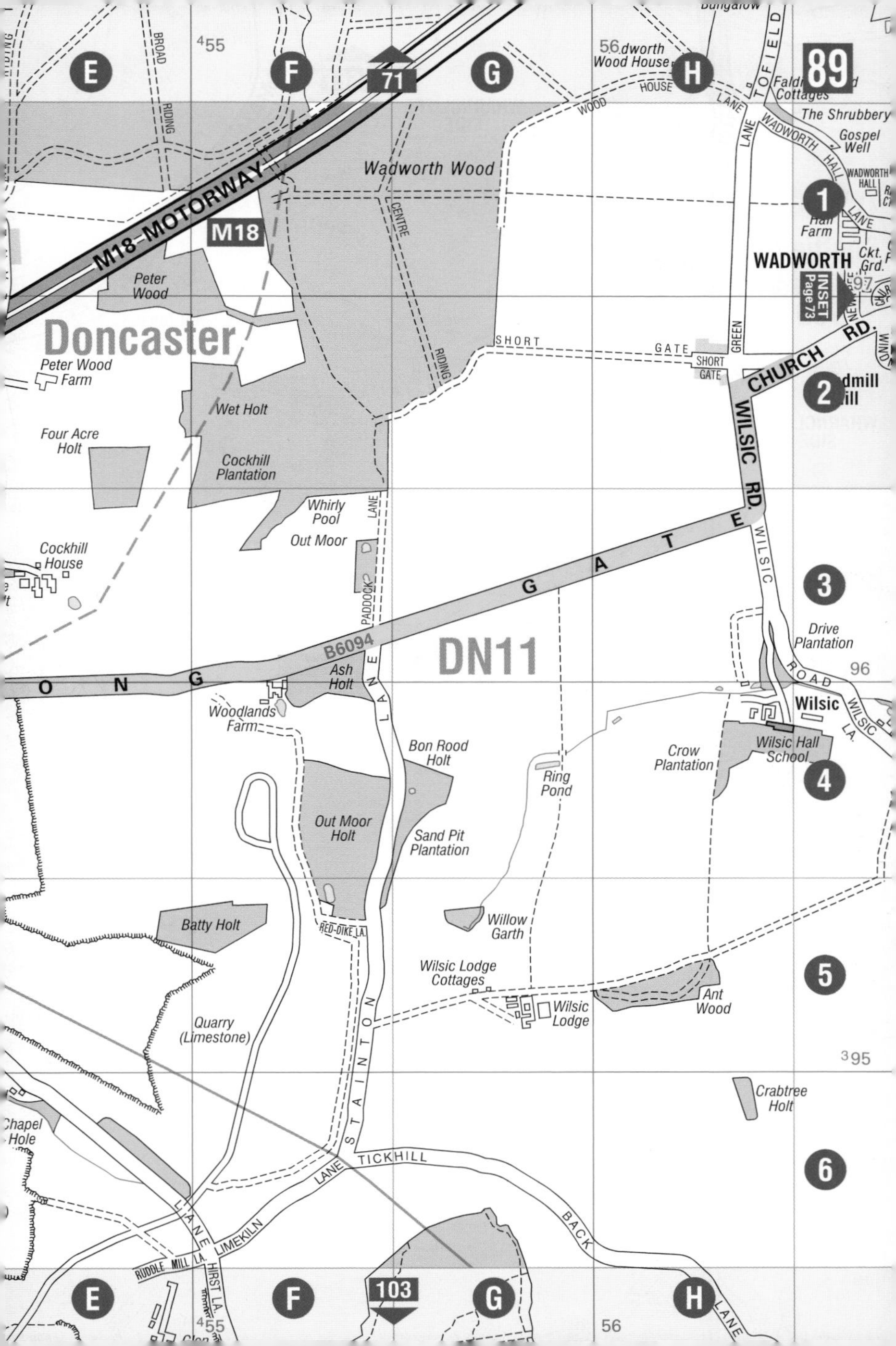

E **F** **71** **G** **H**

455

BROAD

RIDING

56.dworth
Wood House

WOOD

HOUSE

LANE

TOFIELD

Faldin
Cottages

The Shrubbery

Gospel
Well

WADWORTH HALL

WADWORTH
HALL

R.C

Wadworth Wood

CENTRE

M18—MOTORWAY

M18

Peter
Wood

1

Hall
Farm

WADWORTH
INSET
Page 73

Ckt.
Grd.

97

NEW

Doncaster

Peter Wood
Farm

Wet Holt

Four Acre
Holt

Cockhill
Plantation

RIDING

SHORT

GATE

SHORT
GATE

GREEN

CHURCH RD.

WILSIC RD.

2

dmill
ill

Whirly
Pool

Out Moor

LANE

PADDOCK

L O N G

G A T E

WILSIC

3

Drive
Plantation

96

Cockhill
House

B6094

Ash
Holt

DN11

ROAD

WILSIC

Wilsic

WILSIC LA.

Woodlands
Farm

LANE

Bon Rood
Holt

Ring
Pond

Crow
Plantation

Wilsic Hall
School

4

Out Moor
Holt

Sand Pit
Plantation

RED-DIKE LA.

Batty Holt

Willow
Garth

Wilsic Lodge
Cottages

Wilsic
Lodge

Ant
Wood

5

3 95

Quarry
(Limestone)

STAINTON

LANE

Crabtree
Holt

Chapel
Hole

TICKHILL

LANE

BACK

6

RUDDLE MILL LA.

LIMEKILN

HIRST LA.

E **F** **103** **G** **H**

455

56

LANE

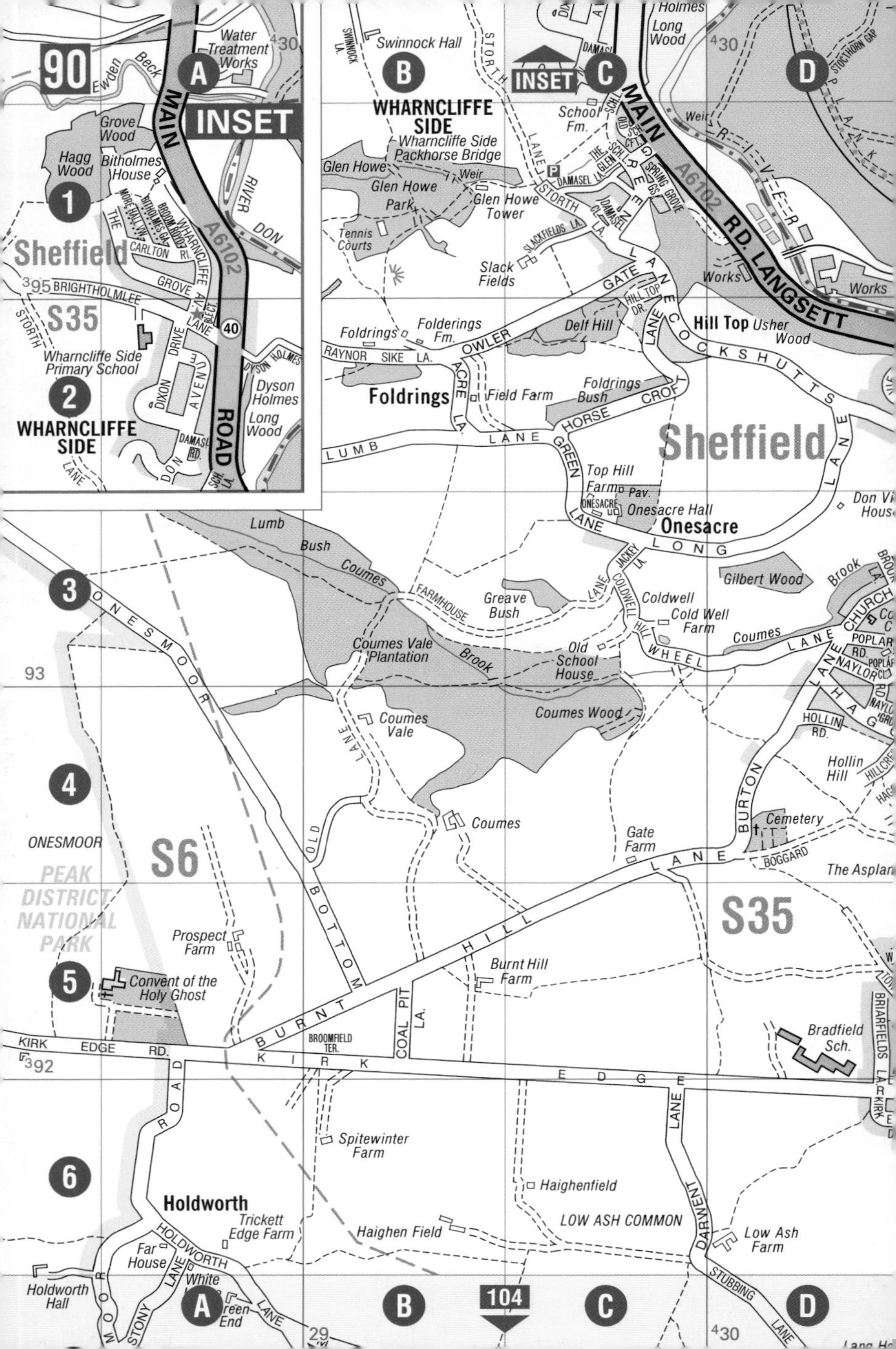

INSET
Water Treatment Works
Ewden Beck
Grove Wood
Hagg Wood
Bitholmes House
MAIN ROAD
A6102
RIVER DON
Sheffield
BRIGHTHOLMLEE
S35
Wharncliffe Side Primary School
WHARNCLIFFE SIDE
Dyson Holmes
Long Wood
Swinnock Hall
WHARNCLIFFE SIDE
Wharncliffe Side Packhorse Bridge
Glen Howe
Glen Howe Park
Weir
Glen Howe Tower
Tennis Courts
Slack Fields
School Fm.
Holmes
Long Wood
Works
Hill Top
Usher Wood
Foldrings
Folderings Fm.
Foldrings
Field Farm
Delf Hill
Foldrings Bush
Sheffield
Top Hill Farm
Onesacre Hall
Onesacre
Don View House
Lumb Bush
Coumes
Greave Bush
Coldwell
Cold Well Farm
Gilbert Wood
Coumes Vale Plantation
Brook
Old School House
Coumes Wood
Coumes Vale
Coumes
Gate Farm
Cemetery
Hollin Hill
The Asplands
ONESMOOR
S6
PEAK DISTRICT NATIONAL PARK
Prospect Farm
Convent of the Holy Ghost
Burnt Hill Farm
Bradfield Sch.
S35
KIRK EDGE RD.
BURNT HILL LANE
Spitewinter Farm
Haighenfield
Holdworth
Trickett Edge Farm
Haighen Field
LOW ASH COMMON
Low Ash Farm
Far House
White Lee
Green End
Holdworth Hall
STUBBING LANE
DARWENT LANE
104

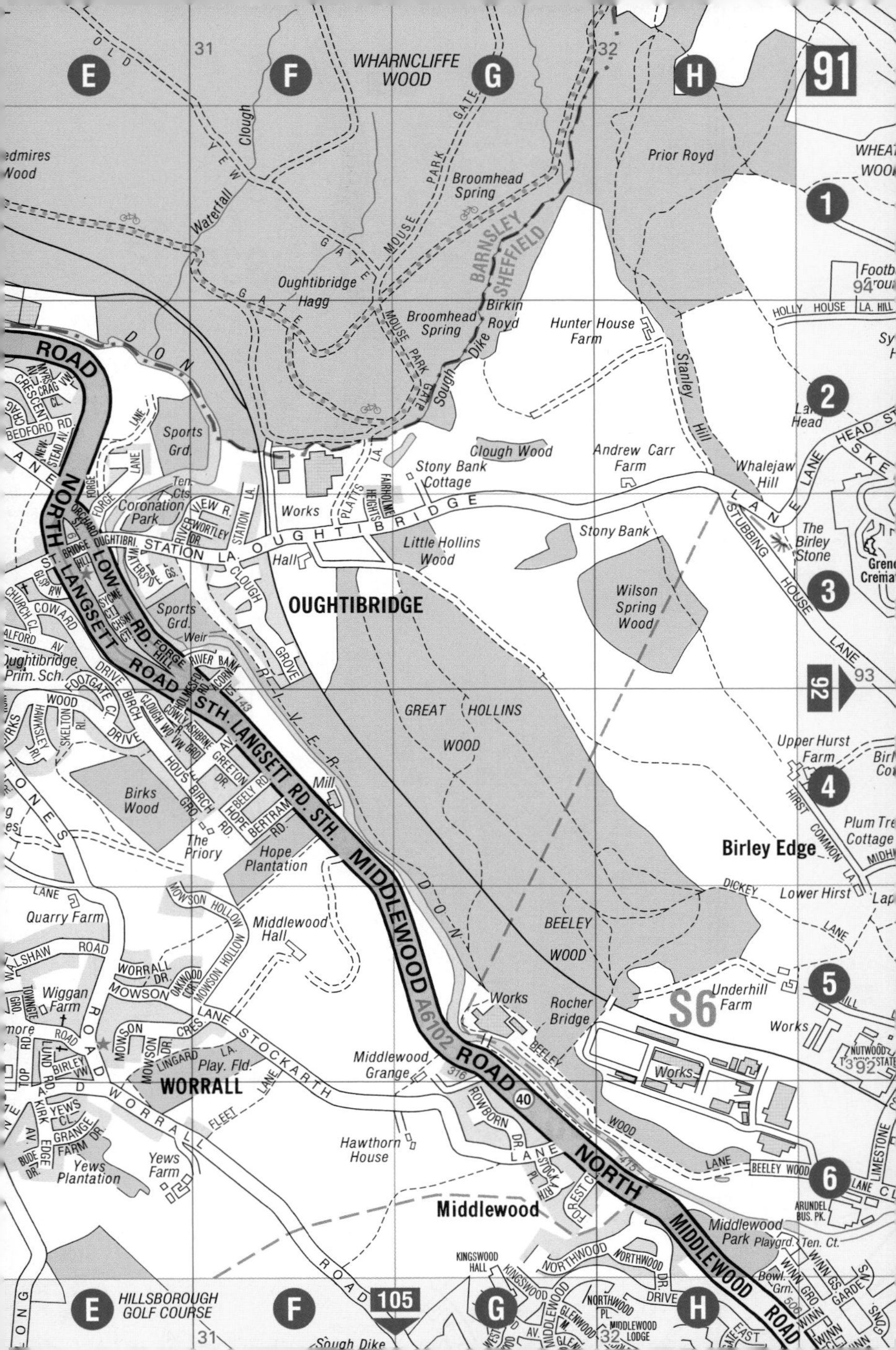
WHARNCLIFFE WOOD
Prior Royd
Broomhead Spring
Oughtibridge Hagg
BARNSLEY
SHEFFIELD
Birkin Royd
Hunter House Farm
Clough Wood
Andrew Carr Farm
Stony Bank Cottage
Whalejaw Hill
The Birley Stone
Stony Bank
Little Hollins Wood
Wilson Spring Wood
OUGHTIBRIDGE
Coronation Park
Sports Grd.
Works
GREAT HOLLINS WOOD
Upper Hurst Farm
Birley Edge
Plum Tree Cottage
Lower Hirst
BEELEY WOOD
Underhill Farm
Rocher Bridge
S6
Birks Wood
The Priory
Hope Plantation
Middlewood Hall
Quarry Farm
Wiggan Farm
WORRALL
Play. Fld.
Middlewood Grange
Hawthorn House
Yews Farm
Yews Plantation
Middlewood
Middlewood Park
HILLSBOROUGH GOLF COURSE
KINGSWOOD HALL
MIDDLEWOOD LODGE
Sough Dike
ARUNDEL BUS. PK.
MIDDLEWOOD ROAD
A6102
NORTH LANGSETT ROAD
LANGSETT RD. STH.
OUGHTIBRIDGE LANE
STUBBING HOUSE LANE
STOCKARTH LANE
WORRALL ROAD
92
105
93

A
B
C
D
78
1
2
3
4
5
6
91
106
The Woods
WOODHEAD ROAD
PENISTONE ROAD
WOOD END
WHITLEY CARR
PEGGY LANE
WHEATA WOOD
ROUGH LANE
Greno Wood House
MAIN STREET
GRENO GATE
THE LUMP
WOOD NOOK
FROSTINGS CL.
WOODSIDE LA.
WHITLEY LANE
Middleton Green
S35
Football Ground
HOLLY HOUSE LA.
HILL TOP LA.
TOP SIDE
BOWER LANE
NORFOLK HILL
WEAVERS CL.
Prim. Sch.
BROOK CL.
SCHOOL LANE
GRENO HOUSE
NETHER CR.
CINDER HILL LANE
Cinder Hill
Sycamore House
WALKER CL.
CROSS HO. RD.
VICARAGE CL.
Comm. Cen.
Rec. Grd.
Bowls
Tennis Cts.
PARK CT.
GRENOBANK RD.
NIGHTINGALE RD.
SWIFT RD.
MIDDLETON LA.
Reservoir (covered)
Lane Head
HEAD STEPHEN LANE
GRENOSIDE
VICARAGE CRES.
BLACKSMITH LANE
GRENO MORTON
GRENOSIDE PL.
A61
HALIFAX RD.
CRESWICK LANE
LAVINIA RD.
HILL TOP RISE
Whalejaw Hill
OUGHTIBRIDGE LA.
SKEW HILL LANE
SALT BOX LA.
St. Thomas More Catholic Prim. Sch.
The Birley Stone
STUBBING HOUSE LANE
Grenoside Crematorium
Skew Hill
The Chevin
GRENOSIDE GRANGE HOSP.
Holme Lane Farm
HOLME LA.
Play. Flds.
Yewlands Technology College
ROCHER AV.
CRESWICK GREEN
YEW LANE
GRIMSELL DR.
Mansel Prim. Sch.
MANSEL CRESCENT
KNUTTON RD.
COWPER AVENUE
ROAD
Upper Hurst Farm
Birley Cott.
Edge Well
Birley Hall Farm
Shaw Hill Farm
EDGE LANE
EDGE WELL RISE
Birley Edge
Plum Tree Cottage
MIDHURST
HIRST COMMON LA.
Back Lane
EDGE WELL CRESCENT
Rec. Grd.
Fox Hill Prim. Sch.
KEATS RD.
CARRILL DR.
COWPER CRESCENT
DEERLANDS AVENUE
CHAUCER CL.
FULMERE CRES.
B6087
WORDSWORTH
Royds Row
DICKEY LANE
Lower Hirst
Lapwater
FOX HILL RD.
WILCOX ROAD
CHAUCER ROAD
Chaucer Business & Enterprise Coll.
Tennis Courts
BUCHANAN
Lapwater Farm
Edge
FOX HILL CL.
BULLEN RD.
POWLEY
WOLFE RD.
WILCOX CL.
BROWNING CL.
Under Farm
UNDERHILL LANE
HAGG HILL
MIDHURST RD.
FOX HILL CRES.
CAMBORNE
LYMINSTER RD.
DOE ROYD CRES.
Works
NUTWOOD TRADING ESTATE
Reservoir (covered)
BIGNOR PL.
DOE ROYD LANE
LYTTON
92
ASH MOUNT
AYSGARTH RD.
Birley Carr
S6
Meynell Prim. Sch.
Limestone Hall Farm
LIMESTONE COTTAGE LA.
BIRLEY RI. CR.
Birley Mt.
BAXTER DRIVE
CARRVILLE RD.
GILLOTT RD.
LANE
BEELEY WOOD LA.
Brewery
CLAYWHEELS LANE
CROSS
Sch.
MEYNELL CR.
PALGRAVE CR.
ARUNDEL BUSINESS PARK
Middlewood Park
Playgrd.
Ten. Ct.
RIVER DON
Sports Fld.
Club
MAIDSTONE RD.
HEATH RD.
TRAFALGAR RD.
BAXTER RD.
SOUTHEY
AVISFORD
COOKSON CL.
HALLIWELL CRES.
Southey Green
Weir
Niagra Forge
Wadsley Bridge
Sports Fld.
WINN GDNS.
MIDDLEWOOD ROAD
33
Works
Warehouses
BINSTED
WORDSWORTH AVENUE
SOUTHEY GREEN
34
POLLARD

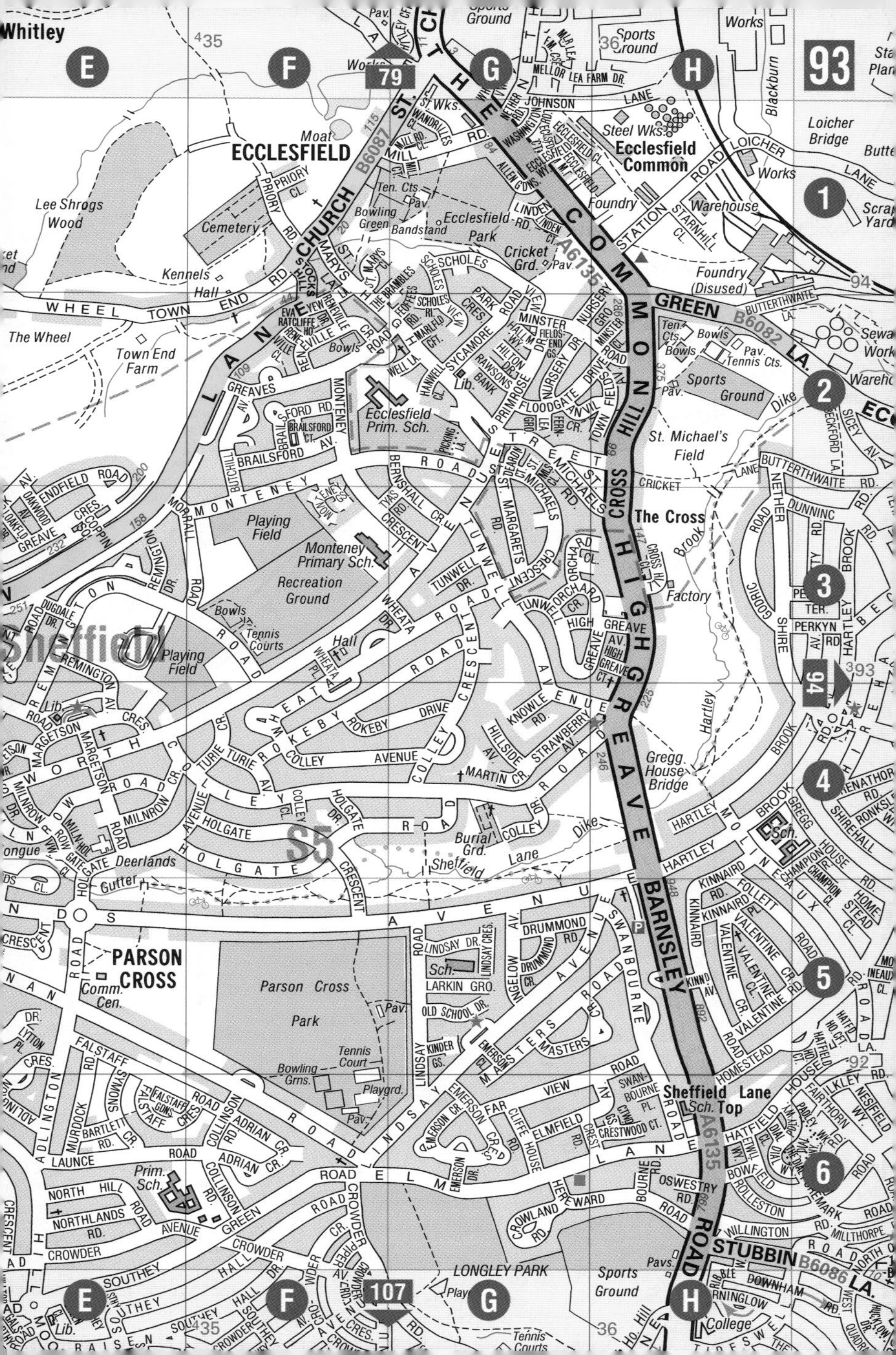
Whitley
ECCLESFIELD
Ecclesfield Common
Lee Shrogs Wood
Cemetery
Ecclesfield Park
Cricket Grd.
The Wheel
Town End Farm
Ecclesfield Prim. Sch.
Monteney Primary Sch.
Playing Field
Recreation Ground
St. Michael's Field
The Cross
Sheffield
S5
Deerlands
PARSON CROSS
Parson Cross Park
Sheffield Lane Top
LONGLEY PARK
Sports Ground
STUBBIN
CHURCH LANE
HIGH GREAVE
BARNSLEY ROAD
COMMON
A6135
B6087
B6082
B6086

79
94
107

94
A
B
C
D
1
2
3
4
5
6
80
93
108
M1
M1-MOTORWAY
S35
S5
S9
Rainstorth
Rainstorth Farm
Spring Wood
Bluefields
Home
Tennis Courts
Works
Loicher Bridge
LOICHER LANE
Butterthwaite House
JUMBLE LANE
Scrap Yard
Butterthwaite
BUTTERTHWAITE LA.
Butterthwaite Farm
The Hall
Foundry (Disused)
Sewage Works
Warehouse
PEGGY LANE
Rainstorth House
Gallery Bottom
GRANGE LANE
B6086
Kennel Wood
Club House
Grange Farm
GRANGE PARK GOLF COURSE
Grange Lane
Thundercliffe Grange
GREEN LANE
ECCLESFIELD ROAD
B6082
Blackburn Brook
Tennis Cts.
Pav.
Bowls
Sports Ground
Dike
BECKFORD LA.
SICEY AV.
BUTTERTHWAITE LANE
NETHER SHIRE
DUNNING ROAD
GATTY RD.
PERKYN TER.
PERKYN RD.
WESTNALL TER.
DUNNING TER.
PAPER MILL ROAD
BUTTERTHWAITE CRES.
BECK CL.
BECK ROAD
Beck Prim. Sch.
Sheffield
BROOKBECK ROAD
DEEP LANE
THE RAVINE
WOOLLEY ROAD
WOOLLEY WOOD ROAD
GRANGE MILL LANE
Barber Wood
Works
Sub
ECCLESFIELD ROAD
SHIREHALL ROAD
HESLEY RD.
HESLEY TER.
IVY HALL ROAD
LOWHOUSE RD.
CRESCENT
RONKSLEY ROAD
DICKINSON RD.
SHIRE AVENUE
SYCAMORE HO.
KEPPEL ROAD
CONCORD
LANE
BROOK LANE
NETHERSHIRE LANE
SHIRE
PEAR TREE
RENATHORPE RD.
RONKSLEY RD.
WHEATFIELD CR.
SICEY LA.
FIRCROFT ROAD
OAKS FOLD
MASON LATHE ROAD
KEPPEL HOUSE ROAD
Sch.
SYCAMORE
SHIREGREEN
Woolley Wood
Miniature Golf Course
CONCORD PARK
HARTLEY
HARTLEY BROOK
GREGG HOUSE CR.
GREGG HOUSE ROAD
CHAMPION CL.
KINNAIRD RD.
FOLLETT
VALENTINE
MOLINEAUX
HOMESTEAD ROAD
HOME STEAD CL.
Comm Cen.
SHIRE GREEN TER.
Arts Coll.
BELLHOUSE
Pav.
Cricket Grd.
Hatfield Prim. Sch.
OAKS LANE
Tennis Courts
Bowling Greens
Driving Range
CONCORD PARK GOLF COURSE
Low Wincobank
STANDON
WOODBURY CLOSE
STANDON DR.
STANDON CRES.
HATFIELD HOUSE LANE
ILKLEY RD.
NESFIELD WY.
TORKSEY ROAD
Football Pitch
Club House
Concord Sports Cen.
Playgrd.
Five a Side Pitches
Cemetery
Lodge
High Wincobank
Hinde House Sch.
Concord Jun. Sch.
Playground
Play. Fld.
FIFE
STANWELL
JEDBURGH DR.
Lane Top
Fairthorn
PAVILION WAY
FIELDER M.
SHIREGREEN LANE
Sports Grd.
Pav.
Bowl. Grns.
PRIMROSE AV.
FOXGLOVE RD.
BRACKEN RD.
JACOBS CL.
Pismire Hill
ROLLESTON
FOREMARK
WILLINGTON
MILLTHORPE RD.
NORTH QUADRANT
STUBBIN LA.
B6086
DOWNHAM
HORNINGLOW
College
BELLHOUSE ROAD
PATMORE
WINDMILL
LILAC RD.
JESSAMINE
HEATH
FIRTH PARK
WINCOBANK
LEEDHAM CL.
LEEDHAM RD.
JENSON
NEWMAN ROAD
NEWMAN DRIVE
MONCKTON RD.
MAPLE CROFT
MAPLE CRES.
Wincobank Inf. Sch.
WINCOBANK

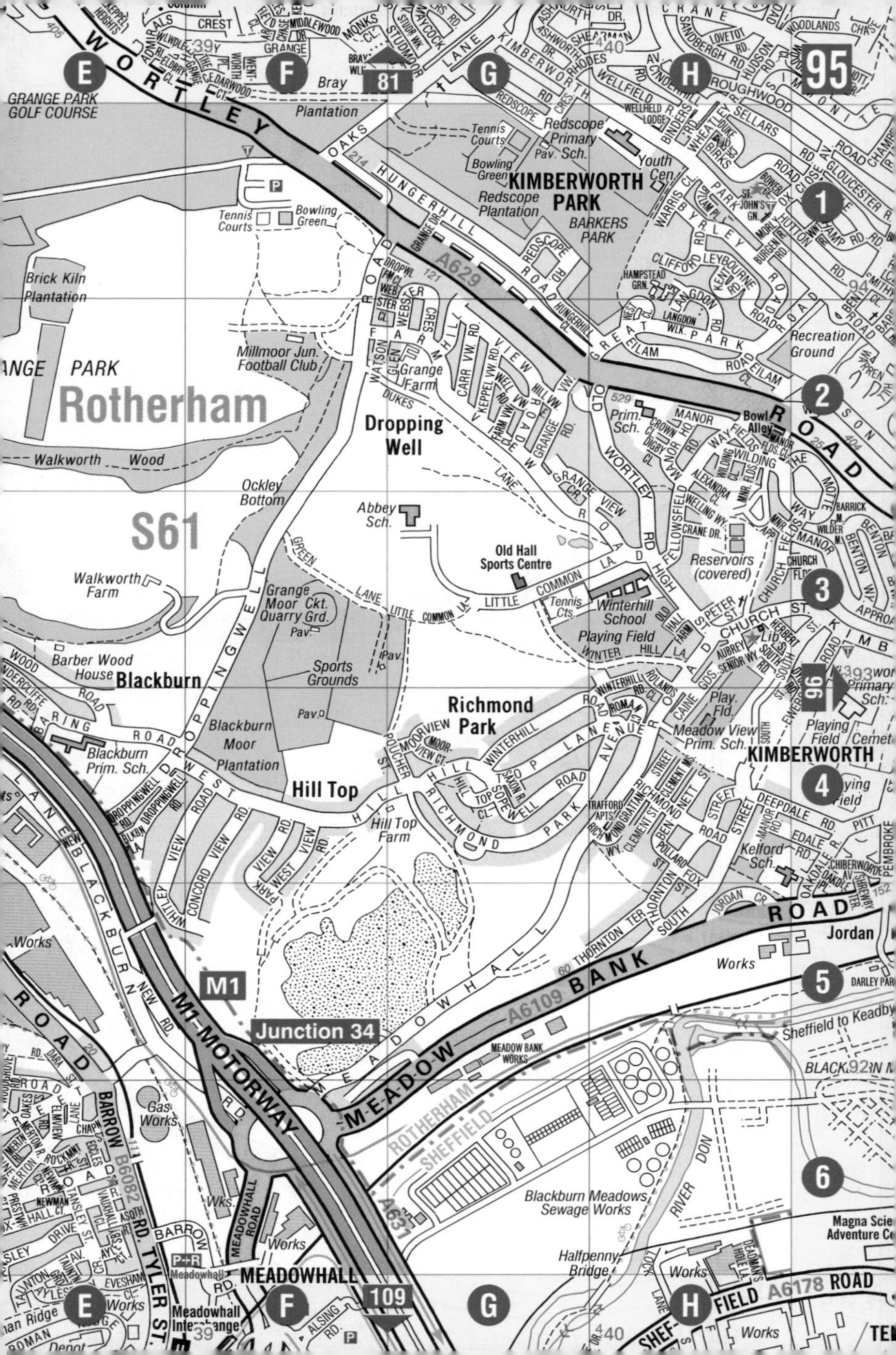
95
81
109
E
F
G
H
1
2
3
4
5
6
96
GRANGE PARK GOLF COURSE
WORTLEY ROAD
A629
Bray Plantation
OAKS LANE
HUNGERHILL RD.
Tennis Courts
Bowling Green
KIMBERWORTH PARK
Redscope Plantation
Redscope Primary Sch.
Youth Cen.
BARKERS PARK
Brick Kiln Plantation
GRANGE PARK
Rotherham
Millmoor Jun. Football Club
Grange Farm
Dropping Well
Walkworth Wood
Ockley Bottom
Abbey Sch.
S61
Old Hall Sports Centre
Walkworth Farm
Grange Moor Ckt. Grd.
Quarry
Sports Grounds
Winterhill School
Playing Field
Reservoirs (covered)
Recreation Ground
Bowl. Alley
Prim. Sch.
Barber Wood House
Blackburn
Richmond Park
Blackburn Moor Plantation
Blackburn Prim. Sch.
Hill Top
Hill Top Farm
Meadow View Prim. Sch.
KIMBERWORTH
Kelford Sch.
Jordan
Works
MEADOW BANK ROAD
A6109
M1
Junction 34
M1 MOTORWAY
MEADOW HALL ROAD
MEADOW BANK WORKS
ROTHERHAM
SHEFFIELD
Sheffield to Keadby Canal
Blackburn Meadows Sewage Works
RIVER DON
Gas Works
Wks.
Works
MEADOWHALL ROAD
BARROW RD.
TYLER ST.
B6082
MEADOWHALL
Meadowhall Interchange
P+R Meadowhall
Halfpenny Bridge
Magna Science Adventure Ce
SHEFFIELD ROAD
A6178
A6631
Depot
Playing Field
Cemet
Primary Sch.

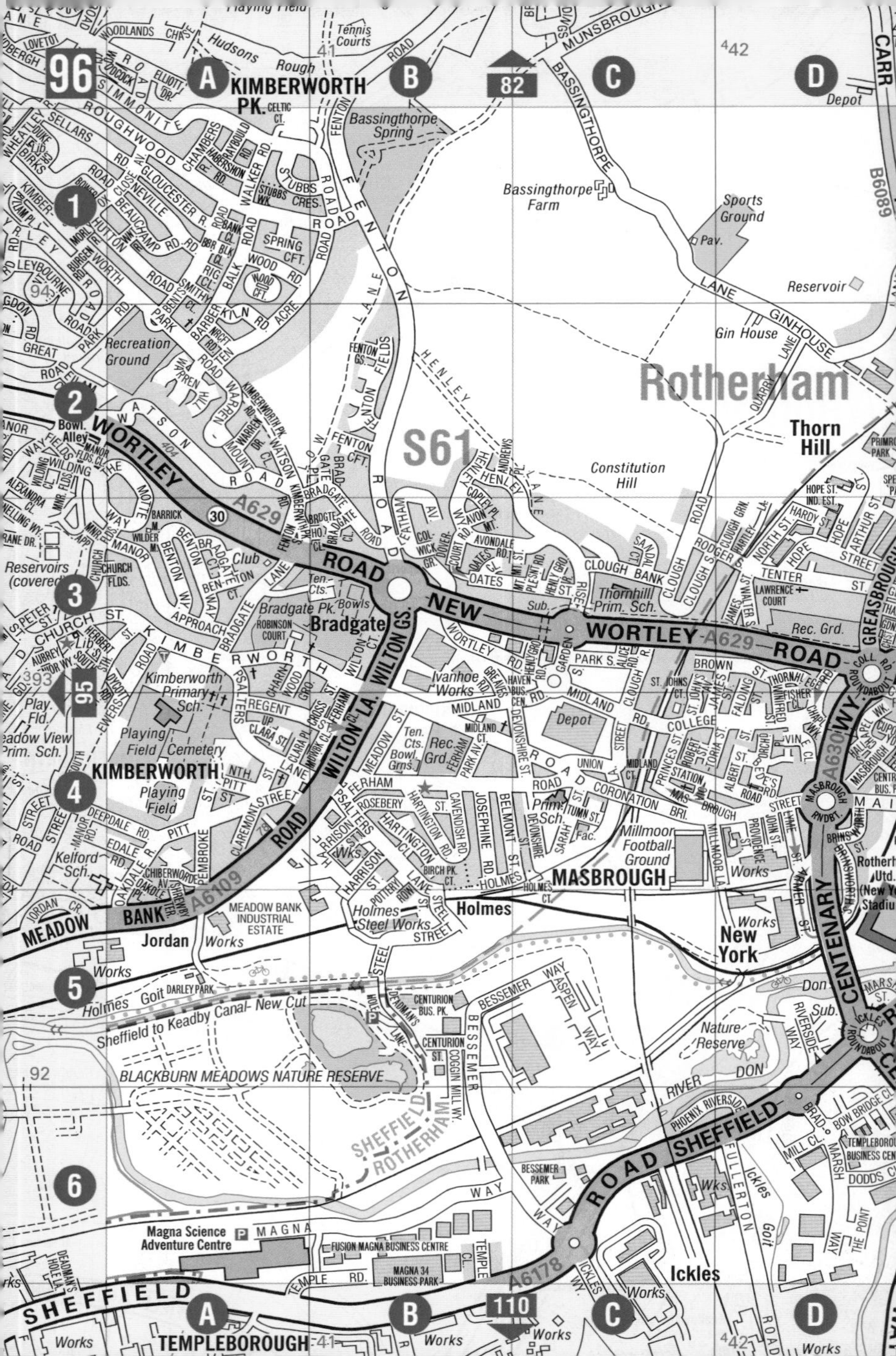
96
82
110
95
A
B
C
D
1
2
3
4
5
6
KIMBERWORTH PK.
Hudsons Rough
Tennis Courts
Bassingthorpe Spring
Bassingthorpe Farm
Sports Ground
Pav.
Reservoir
Depot
Gin House
Rotherham
Thorn Hill
Constitution Hill
S61
Recreation Ground
Bowl. Alley
Reservoirs (covered)
Kimberworth Primary Sch.
Playing Field
Cemetery
KIMBERWORTH
Kelford Sch.
Meadow View Prim. Sch.
Play. Fld.
Bradgate
Bradgate Pk.
Bowls
ROBINSON COURT
Club
Ivanhoe Works
Thornhill Prim. Sch.
LAWRENCE COURT
Rec. Grd.
Millmoor Football Ground
MASBROUGH
Holmes
Holmes Steel Works
Jordan
Works
MEADOW BANK INDUSTRIAL ESTATE
New York
Nature Reserve
RIVER DON
Holmes Goit
Sheffield to Keadby Canal- New Cut
BLACKBURN MEADOWS NATURE RESERVE
CENTURION BUS. PK.
BESSEMER PARK
Magna Science Adventure Centre
FUSION MAGNA BUSINESS CENTRE
MAGNA 34 BUSINESS PARK
TEMPLEBOROUGH BUSINESS CENTRE
Ickles
TEMPLEBOROUGH
SHEFFIELD ROTHERHAM
WORTLEY ROAD
NEW WORTLEY ROAD
A629
A6109
A6178
A630
B6089
CENTENARY WY.
SHEFFIELD ROAD
WILTON LA.
MEADOW BANK
FENTON ROAD
BASSINGTHORPE LANE
GINHOUSE LANE
HENLEY LANE
KIMBERWORTH RD.
MIDLAND RD.
CORONATION BRI.
MASBROUGH ST.
GREASBROUGH RD.
CLOUGH RD.
FULLERTON ROAD
BESSEMER WAY
MAGNA WAY
TEMPLE RD.
WATSON ROAD
ROUGHWOOD ROAD
MUNSBROUGH
CARR

97
83
111
98
E
F
G
H
1
2
3
4
5
6
43
44
The Bungalow
Parkfield Cottage
Barbot
BARBOT HALL IND. EST.
THE GATEWAY INDUSTRIAL ESTATE
STADIUM CT.
Warehouse
Aldwa
South Yorkshire Transport Museum
WADDINGTON WAY
RETAIL WORLD
STADIUM WAY
WATERSIDE COTTS.
RIVER DON
Adult Train. Cen.
SHEFFIELD & STH. YORKSHIRE NAVIGATION
SHEFFIELD & STH. YORKSHIRE NAVIGATION (Rotherham Cut)
EASTWOOD TRADING ESTATE
Earl Fitzwilliam's Canal
Superstore
MANGHAM
B6375
Depot
Works
Playing Field
Northfield
NORTHFIELD IND. EST.
A633
RAWMARSH RD.
ROTHERHAM RD.
ST. ANN'S RD.
St. Ann's
Leisure Cen.
CHESTERTON ROAD
TA Cen.
A630
EASTWOOD
Coleridge Prim. Sch.
FITZ-WILLIAM
COLERIDGE ROAD
St. Ann's Jun. & Inf.
St. Stephen's Sch.
East Dene Prim. Sch.
NHS Walk-In Cen.
CENTENARY WAY
S65
DONCASTER RD.
ROTHERHAM
Bandstand
CLIFTON PARK
Clifton Park Mus.
CLIFTON
Bowling Greens
Clifton Comm. Arts Sch.
EAST DENE
A6021
CLIFTON LA.
Rotherham Central
Club
Superstore
Thtre.
Council Off.
HOSP.
LISTER ST.
MOOR
MIDDLE LANE
WELLGATE
WELL-GATE
Rotherham Titans RUFC
PLAYING FIELD
HERRINGTHORPE
Pav.
Rudston Prep. School
ROTHERHAM HOSPICE
Herringthorpe Stadium
Tennis Courts
Spts. Grd.
Leisure Cen.
WICKERSLEY RD.
ALMA RD.
MOORGATE
S60
Broom Valley Jun. & Inf. Schs.
BROOM ROAD
BROOM
Ten. Cts.
Cemetery
Boston Castle
Thomas Rotherham Coll.
BOSTON PARK
Playing Fields
Boston Reservoirs
Bowling Green
A618
B6410
Mill

Aldwarke
A
B
C
D
84
Whinney Hill
Sewage Works
Gala Bingo
Superstore
RIVER DON
Aldwarke Bridge
Millside Cen.
Sports Grd.
Bowling Green
DONCASTER ROAD
FITZWILLIAM ROAD
A630
A6123
ALDWARKE LA.
HERRINGTHORPE VALLEY ROAD
DALTON
Dalton Parva
S65
EAST HERRINGTHORPE
Under Greave Wood
Dalton Foljambe Prim. Sch.
Playing Field
Rec. Grd.
Cricket Ground
Rotherham Crematorium
Rotherham Cemetery
Brecks Lane Farm
Rotherham
DEAN PLANTATION
Valley Park
Miniature Golf Course
Bowling Greens
Tennis Courts
HERRINGTHORPE
GIBBING GREAVE WOOD
Herringthorpe Wood
Cricket Ground
BRECKS
BRECKS LANE
St. Bernard's Cath. High Sch.
Playing Fields
Herringthorpe Inf. & Jun. Schs.
Herringthorpe Stadium
Leisure Cen.
WICKERSLEY ROAD
A6021
BAWTRY RD.
A631
S60
Sports Ground Club
EAST DENE
97
112
1
2
3
4
5
6

99
85
113
100
E
F
G
H
1
2
3
4
5
6
47
48
94
93
92
Thrybergh Primary School
Sludge Beds
Round Wood
Blacking Mill
War Mem.
GULLING WOOD
RAVENFIELD COMMON
Silver Wood
Ravenfield
Moorside Farm
Odd Hill
The Close
Spencer Wood
Sunnyside
Woodlaithes
Hill Top
Flanderwell
Black Carr
BRECKS PLANTATION
LISTERDALE
WICKERSLEY
BRAMLEY
S66
Primary Sch.
Bramley Sunnyside Schs.
Wickersley Sch. & Sports Coll.
Reservoir (cov.)
Church Field
WICKERSLEY WOOD
A631
B6060
HOLLING'S LANE
HILL TOP LANE
NORTHFIELD LANE
MORTHEN RD.
Playing Field
Tennis Cts.
Club
Comm. Cen.
Liby.
Sch.
Pav. Ckt. Grd.

A
B
C
D
49
4 50
86
94
93
92
99
114
1
2
3
4
5
6
Ravenfield Prim. Sch.
Springfield House Farm
Moorside Farm
NORTH MOOR LANE
RAVENFIELD COMMON
BRAITHWELL COMMON
Ravenfield Grange
Silverthorpe
Cattery
ROAD COMMON
ELLALINE COTTS.
The Bungalows
Nursery
Sewage Works
Priests Bridge
BRAMLEY LANE
BRAITHWELL LANE
HOLLING'S LANE
FIELDSIDE CT.
SANDINGHAM PL.
GREENACRES VW.
THE PADDOCKS
BELLWOOD CT.
RADFORD CL.
HOLLY'S HO. RD.
CEDAR DR.
GORSE CL.
TURTON RD.
KINGSLEY DR.
PARKIN CT.
WESTBY CL.
OBORNE CL.
CAYTON CL.
HOWSON CL.
POPLAR GRO.
MEADOW VW. DR.
BRIDGEWATER WAY
BLACKTHORN RISE
FIRE-THORN RISE
BARBERRY
RANFIELD CT.
HAZEL CT.
SMEATON CL.
LONGFIELD DR.
GRAYSON CL.
COMMON FARM CL.
Hellaby
Brook
S65
BIRCH WOOD DR.
ALLOTT CL.
Tennis Cts.
REASBY AV.
SPENCER DR.
SILVERMOOR DR.
STONE CL.
GREEN BANK DR.
HOLLING'S WOOD WAY
Playing Field
SANDEBY DR.
VINCENT RD.
Club
Hellaby Park Farm
LANE LIDGET
Spenwood Farm
Bramley Grange Farm
LACEBY CL.
BIGBY WY.
GRASBY CT.
SEARBY RD.
MOORFIELD GRO.
MOORFIELD AV.
MOORFIELD CL.
ELSHAM CL.
BLENHEIM CL.
HOLYROOD
HELLABY
HOLYROOD RISE
WINDSOR CL.
HAREWOOD GRO.
RAVEN VW.
EDGE
SOUTH LANE B6093
STONELY BROOK
THE COPSE
BROOK LA.
LIDGET
BELFORD
WELLCLIFFE CL.
THORNDALE CL.
BALMORAL WY.
FROGMORE CL.
COPPINS RISE
BELVEDERE DR.
FLANDERWELL
FLANDERWELL LANE
Bramley Sunnyside Schs.
GAUNT DR.
GAUNT CL.
ASKAM CT.
ASKAM RD.
Sch.
MILNER CL.
WAYFORD AV.
BRAMLEY GRANGE VW.
OULTON AV.
COLTISHALL AV.
BRAMLEY AV.
WROXHAM WY.
BRAMLEY GRANGE WY.
BRAMLEY GRANGE DR.
BRAMLEY GRANGE CR.
CRAIG WK.
NORSTEAD CR.
REEDHAM DR.
BECCLES CR.
ORMESBY WY.
RANWORTH ROAD
WARREN HO. CL.
HOWARD
BALK LA.
Hall
MAIN
CROSS ST.
MAIN ST. SHOP. CEN.
BARNES IND. EST.
Junction 1
M18 MOTORWAY
M18
BAWTRY ROAD
A631
OAK M.
PEAR TREE AV.
LAUREL AV.
ROWAN DR.
THE CENTRE
ACACIA
PEAR TREE
CHURCH LANE
Bramley Park
AUSTEN DRIVE
CROSBY AV.
FIELDING DR.
BENTLEY
PROGRESS
Dairy
PROSPECT CL.
BRAMLEY
Play. Fld.
Supermarket
Hotel
Health Club
Works
Reservoir (cov.)
Wickersley Sch. & Sports Coll.
Depot
LINGS COMMON
Playing Field
WOOD LANE
LONG MDWS.
COQUET AV.
WADSWORTH ROAD
HEATHER CT.
SEDGE CL.
THE LINGS
HOLMES
MARLOWE CL.
TEMPLE CR.
Yth. Cen.
BROOKHAVEN WY.
EYRE CT.
HUTTON BANK
BROADLANDS
VIEWLANDS CL.
STRATFORD
WESTMNSTR CL.
LINGFIELD CL.
SHERBOURNE AV.
WESTERTON DR.
FIELDS
SANDY LANE
BLAKE
Bramley Lings
Cemetery
WICKERSLEY WOOD
ORCHARD WELLS
THE ORCHARD
DENE CL.
BRAITHWELL WAY
Works
HELLABY INDUSTRIAL
ROTHER WY.
Elsworth Ho. Sch.
LOWTON WY.
LOWTON WAY
SANDBECK WY.
DENBY
BATEMAN RD.
BATEMAN CL.
BATEMAN
Hall
Playing Field
CUMWELL FIELDS
CUMWELL LANE
Newhall
Dike
Sandy Lane

E F 87 G H

51 52

M18 MOTORWAY

Cragdon House
LANE
Depot
Field Houses
Depot
Hoyle
CROFT
1
94
MALTBY

2
BIRCHWOOD HILL

Well Farm
Malt Kiln
High Fm.
Farm
CROWNHILL LANE
BACK
ALDENS LANE

brough Farm

MOOR LANE MARSH HILL ASHTON
Fordoles Farm

GREAVES LANE
SIKE LANE
LANE

Rotherham

DONCASTER ROTHERHAM

Mere Flats Holt

Amory's Holt

HAIDS
HAIDS CL.
CLOSE
3
393

Warehouse

Hellaby

Lilly Hall Farm Cottage
Lilly Hall Farm

Park Hill Lodge

Hilltop
Sch.

Playing Fields

4

Pav.

Works

CLAY PIT

Maltby Redwood Junior & Infant School

S66

Lilly Hall (Maltby) Jun. Sch.

Larch Plantation
Cave Plantation

MALTBY

Maltby Hall Inf. Sch.

Maltby Academy
257

5

East of the Pennines Assembly Hall
EAST VIEW

Play. Fld.

Dr. Training Cen.
Depot

Cliff Hills Rec. Grd.

Youth Cen.

BRAI...

Hellaby Hall

Works

390 454

HELLABY

Newhall

Hellaby Bridge

ROAD ROTHERHAM ROAD

15 98 131 140 **A631**

PARKSTONE CR.
GREENHILL
GROVE KEV...

Dike

ROAD
92

6

Kingsforth LANE

115

HOOTON LEVITT

HOOTON LA.
CHESTNUT WK.
LANE
Mansfield Farm
Spivvy

E F G H

BACK LANE CARR LA.
CARR

51 52

BRAITHWELL
MALTBY
Manor House
Orchard Ho. Fm.
Cragdon House
Hillcroft
Elmfield Farm
Croft End
Field Houses
Cedar Farm
Old Hall Fm.
The Old Rectory
Streetly House
Moat Hall Cottage
Birkwood Terrace
Pumping Station
Springdale Cottage
Holywell Cottages
The Hawthornes
Lambcote Grange
Lambcote Grange Cott.
Sewage Works
Austwood Closes
The Ruddle Mill
Ruddle Mill Holt
Ruddle Dike
MALTBY DALE HILL
Toneids Bungalow
BIRCHWOOD HILL
HAIDS CLOSES
BIRCHWOOD CLOSES
DONCASTER
ROTHERHAM
Grange Quarter
Rec. Grd.
Maltby Manor Primary Sch.
Playing Field
Playing Fields
Maltby Service Cen.
Leisure Cen.
Lib.
Youth Cen.
Maltby Hall Inf. Sch.
Maltby Academy
Coronation Park
Pav.
Cemy.
Hall
Depot
Crags Sch.
St. Mary's Cath. Prim. Sch.
War Mem.
Wood Lee Common
Football Grd.
Sports Grd.
Mansfield Farm
AUSTWOOD LANE
HIGH ST.
HOLYWELL LANE
MALTBY LA.
ASHTON LANE
HOYLE CROFT LANE
POGGY LANE
TOP LANE
RUDDLE MILL LA.
FISH POND LA.
GRANGE LANE
STAINTON LANE
BIRCHWOOD LANE
HAIDS LANE
BRAITHWELL ROAD
SALISBURY AV.
GREENLAND AVENUE
ROSSTON ROAD
HIGHFIELD
DUNNS DALE
HIGH ST.
TICKHILL
ROTHERHAM RD.
BLYTH ROAD
MUGLET LANE
LILLY HALL RD.
B6376
B6427
A631
A634
A
B
C
D
1
2
3
4
5
6
53
54
88
101

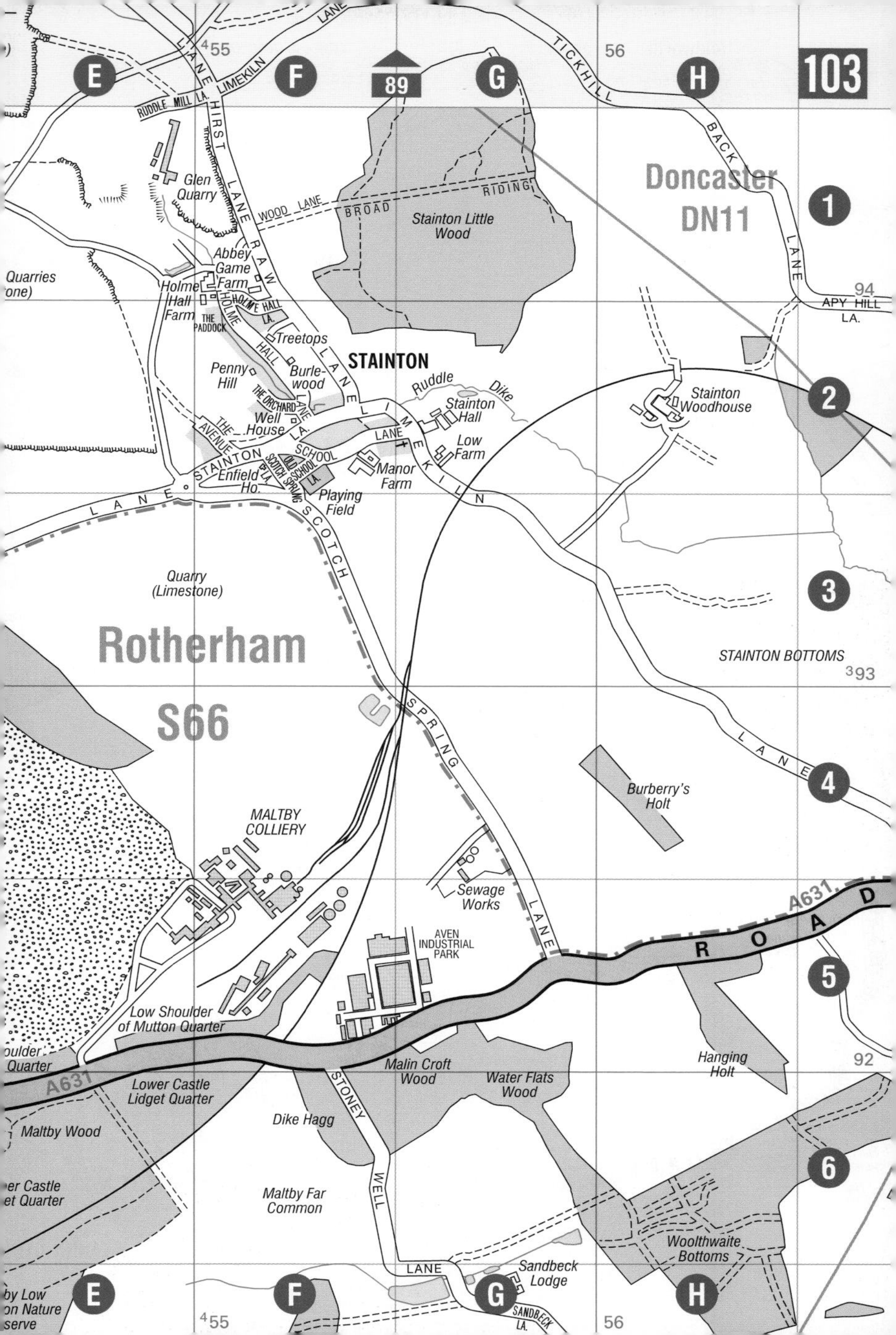

E **F** **G** **H**

455
56
89

LIMEKILN LA.
RUDDLE MILL LA.
HIRST LANE
WOOD LANE
BROAD
RIDING
TICKHILL
BACK
LANE

Doncaster
DN11

1

94
APY HILL LA.

Glen
Quarry

Stainton Little
Wood

Abbey
Game
Farm

Holme
Hall
Farm
THE PADDOCK
HOME HALL LA.

Treetops

HALL LANE

STAINTON

Penny
Hill

Burle-
wood
THE ORCHARD
Well
House
THE AVENUE
STAINTON
Enfield
Ho.
SCHOOL LA.
SUTTON SPRING LA.

SCHOOL

Playing
Field

Manor
Farm

Ruddle
LIMEKILN
LANE

Dike

Stainton
Hall

Low
Farm

Stainton
Woodhouse

2

**Quarries
(tone)**

Quarry
(Limestone)

Rotherham

S66

SCOTCH LANE

SPRING LANE

STAINTON BOTTOMS
393

LANE

3

4

Burberry's
Holt

MALTBY
COLLIERY

Sewage
Works

AVEN
INDUSTRIAL
PARK

A631
ROAD

5

92

Low Shoulder
of Mutton Quarter

oulder
Quarter

A631

Lower Castle
Lidget Quarter

Maltby Wood

Dike Hagg

STONEY

Malin Croft
Wood

Water Flats
Wood

Hanging
Holt

6

er Castle
et Quarter

Maltby Far
Common

WELL LANE

Sandbeck
Lodge

SANDBECK LA.

Woolthwaite
Bottoms

y Low
on Nature
serve

E **F** **G** **H**

455
56

Holdworth
Trickett Edge Fm.
Far House
White House
Green End
Holdworth Hall
Haighenfield
LOW ASH COMMON
Low Ash Farm
90
S35
Stubbing
Stubbing House
Lang House Farm
MYERS LANE
HOLDWORTH LANE
STONY LANE
MOOR BACK LANE
DALROYD LA.
Thorn House
WEST LANE
HOLLIN HOUSE LANE
Ben Greave
Holdworth House Farm
Bodkin Cottage
Hollin House
Low Holdworth
LOXLEY RD.
LOXLEY ROAD
LOXLEY CHASE
Loxley House
Sheffield
Golf Driving Range
Club
STACEY LA.
STACEY BANK
Stacey Bank Farm
Stacey Bridge
B6077
Lee Bank
Manor House
Claremont House
Storrs Bridge
BRIDGE LANE
STORRS
Weir
Works
Old Wheel
Old Wheel Farm
Green Fold Wood
Roe Gate
Brook
Sykehouse
DUNGWORTH GREEN
Syke
STORRS CARR
Storrs Grange
Throstle Nest
Bowling Green
ROWELL LANE
Loxley Grange
S6
Recreation Ground
PUDDING POKE
Beacon Wood
Rowel Bridge
Smeltersbank Packhorse Bri.
River
Olive House
CLIFFE HILL
RYE LA.
Cliffe House Farm
Nether Cliffe
Hill Top
STORRS GREEN
STORRS
Storrs Hall
Storrs Farm
Storrs House
STORRS LANE
Storrs Wood
SPOUT LA.
SPOUT LANE
LEE MOOR LANE
Hazelhurst Farm
Woodside Cottage
SPOON
Brook
Storrs
BROOKSIDE
BROOKSIDE BANK RD.
Brookside Bank
Hill Bank
Brookside Bridge
Hill Farm
STOPES ROAD
B6076
Broad Oak
Underbank Farm
STANNINGTON
Works
Griffs House
Griffs
Wiggin Hall
LOW ROAD
Underbank
The Griffs
RIGGS LANE
LOW
116
Townhead Farm
Upper Gate
UPPER GATE ROAD
Pav. Cricket Ground
STANNINGTON
Playing Fields
Lib. Pav.
Sch.
HIGHFIELD RISE
BANKFIELD
ACORN RD.
ALBANUS RIDGE
Jun. Sch.
SPOON OAK LEA
HOLME OAK WY.
GOLD OAK
RED OAK LA.
ROBIN
SCARLETT OAK
KNOWLE CL.
Know Top
HANMOOR RD.
GREAVES CL.
29
30
91
390
89
1 2 3 4 5 6
A B C D

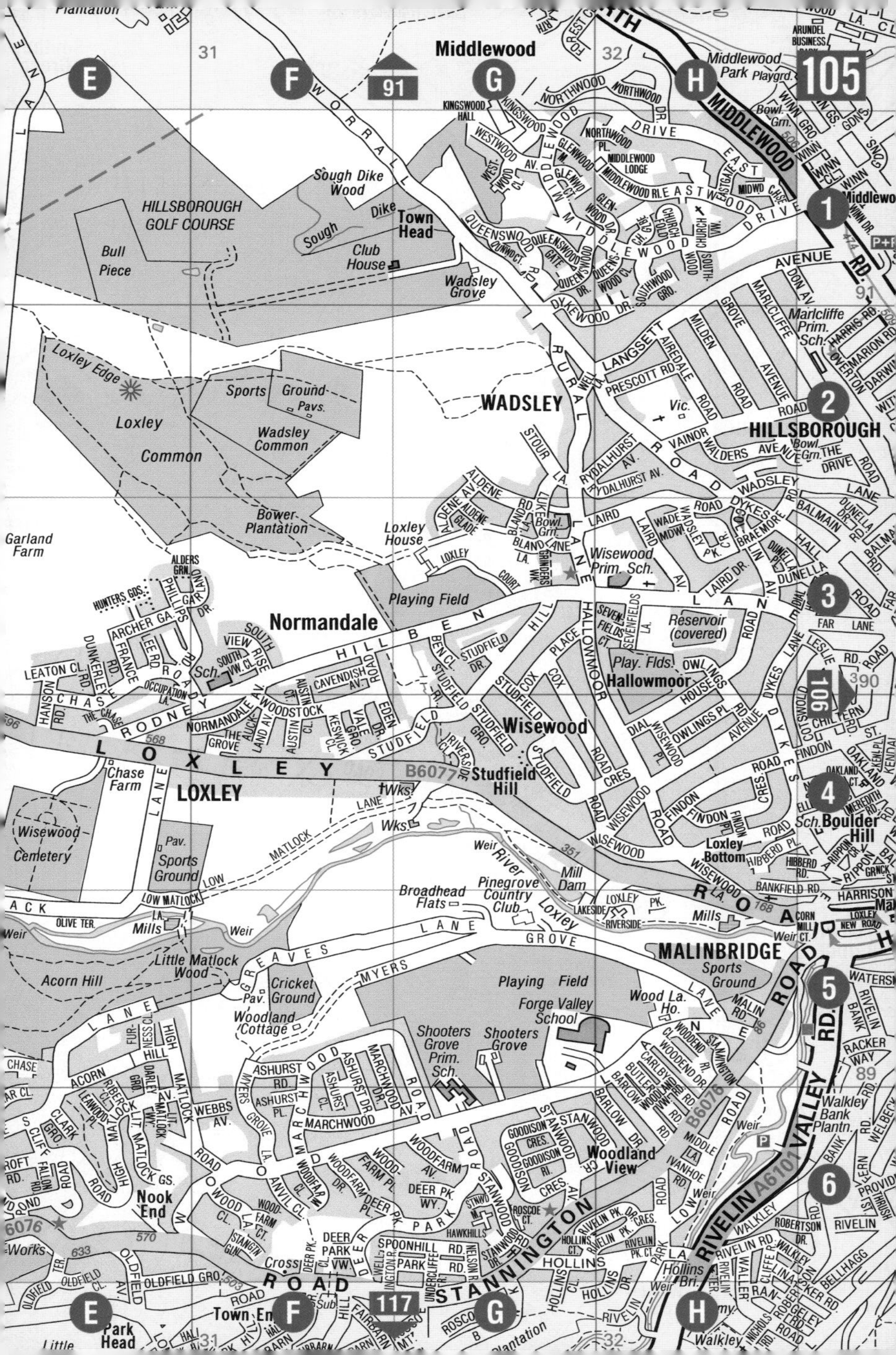
105
Middlewood
91
Middlewood Park
HILLSBOROUGH GOLF COURSE
Bull Piece
Sough Dike Wood
Town Head
Club House
Wadsley Grove
Loxley Edge
Loxley Common
Sports Ground
Wadsley Common
Bower Plantation
Garland Farm
WADSLEY
HILLSBOROUGH
Marlcliffe Prim. Sch.
Loxley House
Playing Field
Wisewood Prim. Sch.
Normandale
Reservoir (covered)
Hallowmoor
Wisewood
Studfield Hill
106
LOXLEY
Chase Farm
Wisewood Cemetery
Sports Ground
Boulder Hill
Loxley Bottom
Broadhead Flats
Pinegrove Country Club
Mill Dam
Mills
MALINBRIDGE
Acorn Hill
Little Matlock Wood
Cricket Ground
Woodland Cottage
Playing Field
Forge Valley School
Shooters Grove Prim. Sch.
Shooters Grove
Walkley Bank Plantn.
Woodland View
Nook End
Hollins Bri.
Park Head
Town End
117
B6077
B6076
A6101
LOXLEY ROAD
STANNINGTON ROAD
RIVELIN VALLEY RD.
MIDDLEWOOD RD.

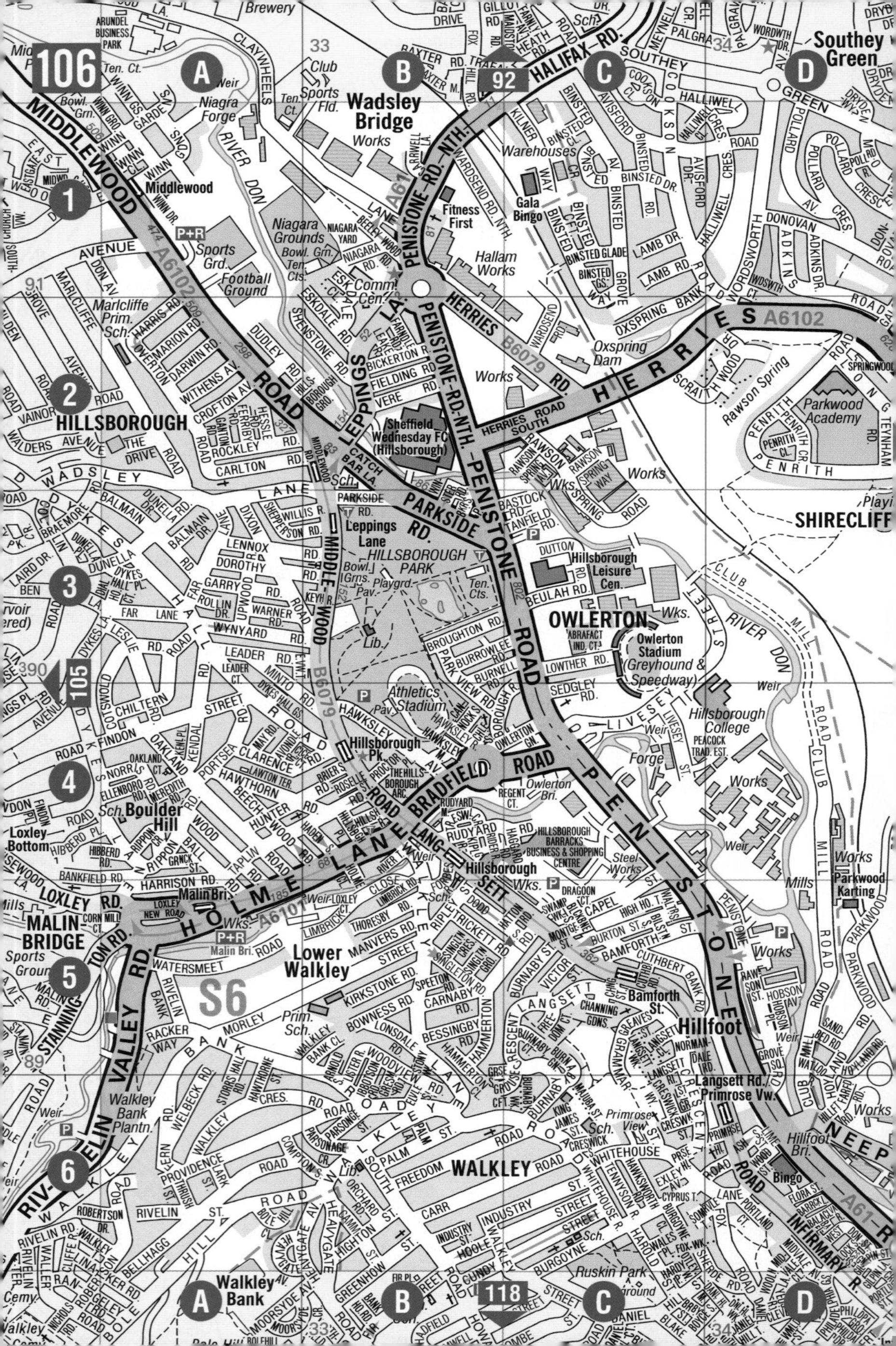
106
A
B
C
D
1
2
3
4
5
6
92
105
118
S6
Wadsley Bridge
Works
Middlewood
Niagra Forge
Niagara Grounds
Sports Grd.
Football Ground
Marlcliffe Prim. Sch.
HILLSBOROUGH
Sheffield Wednesday FC (Hillsborough)
Leppings Lane
HILLSBOROUGH PARK
Athletics Stadium
Hillsborough Pk.
Fitness First
Gala Bingo
Hallam Works
Warehouses
Comm. Cen.
Oxspring Dam
Rawson Spring
Parkwood Academy
Southey Green
SHIRECLIFF
Hillsborough Leisure Cen.
OWLERTON
Owlerton Stadium (Greyhound & Speedway)
Hillsborough College
PEACOCK TRAD. EST.
RIVER DON
Boulder Hill
Loxley Bottom
LOXLEY
MALIN BRIDGE
Malin Bri.
Lower Walkley
Hillsborough
HILLSBOROUGH BARRACKS BUSINESS & SHOPPING CENTRE
Steel Works
Bamforth St.
Hillfoot
Langsett Rd./ Primrose Vw.
Parkwood Karting
Hillfoot Bri.
Bingo
WALKLEY
Walkley Bank Plantn.
Walkley Bank
Ruskin Park
MIDDLEWOOD ROAD
PENISTONE ROAD
HERRIES ROAD
HALIFAX RD.
BRADFIELD ROAD
HOLME LANE
RIVELIN VALLEY RD.
PARKSIDE RD.
LEPPINGS LA.
MIDDLEWOOD
A6102
A61
A6101
B6079
NEEP
INFIRMARY R.

107
93
108
119
Sheffield
S3
S4
S5
E
F
G
H
1
2
3
4
5
6
Longley Park
Playground
Sports Ground
Tennis Courts
Bowling Greens
Longley Bri.
College
Hucklow Prim. Sch.
Moonshine Tank (Resr.)
Blood Transfusion Service
Northern General Hospital
Fir Vale
Upper Crabtree
Lower Crabtree
Fir Vale School
Roe Wood
Busk Meadow
Comm. Cen.
Sports Ground
Football Pitch
Sheffield United FC Academy
Little Roe Wood
Roe Wood Ho.
Firs Hill Primary Sch.
Nat. Res. Norbury
Earl Marshal Recreation Ground
Little Pear Tree Nature Reserve
Playing Field
Sheffield Ski Village
Artifical Ski Slopes
Parkwood Springs
Depot
Training Centre
Woodside
Woodside Works
Parkwood Industrial Estate
Neepsend
Gas Works
Philadelphia
Pitsmoor
War Memorial
Abbeyfield Park
Burngreave Cemetery
Byron Wood Prim. Sch.
Burngreave
Atlas
Herries Road
Barnsley Road
Burngreave Road
Rutland Road
Spital Hill
Abbeyfield Road
Pitsmoor Road
Shirecliffe Road
Firshill Crescent
Crabtree Road
Longley Lane
Southey Green Road
Herries Avenue
Piper Drive
Moonshine Lane
Cooks Wood Rd.
Mowbray
Gower St.
Carlisle
A6102
A6135
B6070
B6074
B6080
B6086

108
Pismire Hill
FIRTH PARK
S5
WINCOBANK
Playing Field
Wincobank Wood
Sports Ground
Sheffield
BRIGHTSIDE
Limpsfield Jun. Sch.
NORTHERN GENERAL HOSPITAL
FIR VALE
Fir Vale School
GRIMESTHORPE
Earl Marshal Recreation Ground
Whiteways Jun. Sch.
S4
Wood Hill
NEWHALL
Newhall Bridge Steel Works
Attercliffe Cemetery
ATTERCLIFFE
Sandersons Weir
Mill Race
Don Valley Stadium
Institute of Sports
ATLAS
BURNGREAVE
SHEFFIELD TECHNOLOGY PARK
OWLER LA.
UPWELL
A6102 STREET
HOLYWELL
HAWKE-JANSON
NEWHALL
BRIGHTSIDE LANE
SAVILE ST. EAST
CARLISLE STREET
WORKSOP RD.
ATTERCLIFFE RD.
A6135
B6086
A6109
B6082
B6083
B6080
94
107
120

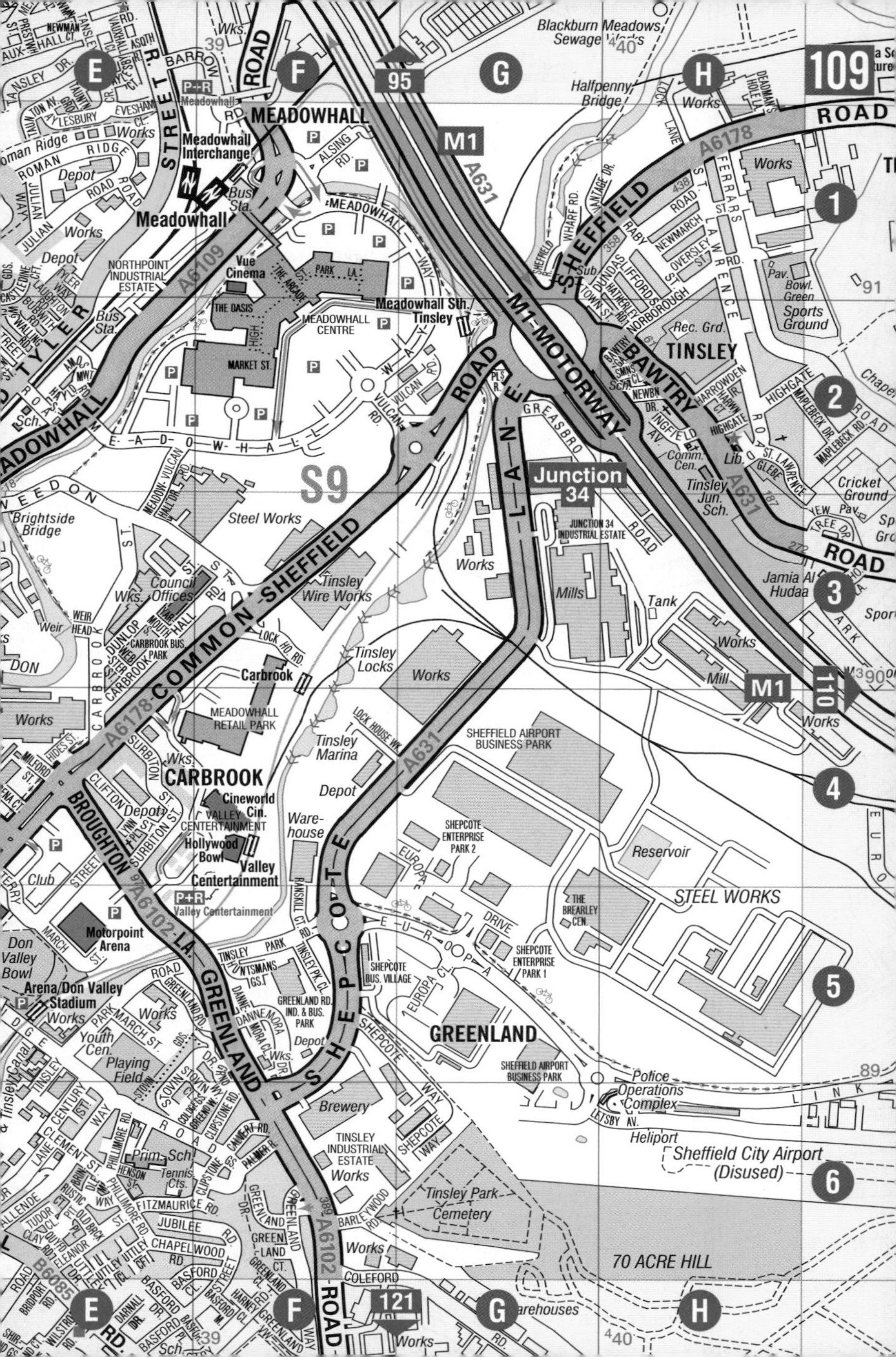
E
F
G
H
95
Blackburn Meadows Sewage Works
Halfpenny Bridge
ROAD
A6178
MEADOWHALL
Meadowhall Interchange
Meadowhall
Bus Sta.
M1
A631
Works
Depot
ROMAN RIDGE ROAD
JULIAN WAY
NORTHPOINT INDUSTRIAL ESTATE
A6109
Vue Cinema
THE ARCADE
PARK LA.
THE OASIS
HIGH ST.
MARKET ST.
MEADOWHALL CENTRE
MEADOWHALL WAY
Meadowhall Sth./Tinsley
VULCAN RD.
SHEFFIELD ROAD
M1 MOTORWAY
TINSLEY
Rec. Grd.
Sports Ground
Bowl. Green
BAWTRY ROAD
HIGHGATE
Lib.
Comm. Cen.
Tinsley Jun. Sch.
Cricket Ground
Jamia Al Hudaa
TYLER ST.
MEADOWHALL RD.
MEADOWHALL RD.
S9
WEEDON ST.
Brightside Bridge
Steel Works
Junction 34
JUNCTION 34 INDUSTRIAL ESTATE
GREASBRO ROAD
Mills
Tank
Council Offices
Weir
DON
SHEFFIELD ROAD
COMMON
Tinsley Wire Works
Tinsley Locks
Works
Mill
110
CARBROOK BUS PARK
Carbrook
MEADOWHALL RETAIL PARK
A6178
Tinsley Marina
SHEFFIELD AIRPORT BUSINESS PARK
CARBROOK
Cineworld Cin.
VALLEY CENTERTAINMENT
Hollywood Bowl
Valley Centertainment
P+R Valley Centertainment
Depot
Ware-house
SHEPCOTE ENTERPRISE PARK 2
Reservoir
STEEL WORKS
THE BREARLEY CEN.
BROUGHTON LA.
A6102
Club
Motorpoint Arena
Don Valley Bowl
Arena/Don Valley Stadium
EUROPA DRIVE
SHEPCOTE ENTERPRISE PARK 1
SHEPCOTE BUS. VILLAGE
GREENLAND RD. IND. & BUS. PARK
SHEPCOTE LANE
GREENLAND
Youth Cen.
Playing Field
GREENLAND RD.
SHEFFIELD AIRPORT BUSINESS PARK
Police Operations Complex
LINK
Brewery
LETSBY AV.
Heliport
Sheffield City Airport (Disused)
Prim. Sch.
Tennis Cts.
TINSLEY INDUSTRIAL ESTATE
Works
Tinsley Park Cemetery
70 ACRE HILL
FITZMAURICE RD.
JUBILEE RD.
CHAPELWOOD RD.
B6085
COLEFORD
121
Warehouses
1
2
3
4
5
6
39
40
89
90
91

110
Magna Science Adventure Centre
Fusion Magna Business Centre
Magna 34 Business Park
96
Ickles
Templeborough
Sheffield Road
A6178
Works
Phoenix Golf Course
Water Filtration Works
Bowling Green
Tennis Courts
Club House
Sports Ground
Warehouse
Chapel Flat Dike
Tinsley
Cricket Ground
Bawtry Road
A631
Bonet Lane
B6067
Brinsworth Road
Brinsworth Manor Jun. & Inf. Schs.
Recreation Ground
Brinsworth
Brinsworth Comprehensive School
Canklow Bri.
Running Track
Warehouses
109
M1
M1 Motorway
Europa Link
Freight Terminals
Steel Works
Sheffield
S9
Sheffield Airport Business Park
Sheffield City Airport (Disused)
70 Acre Hill
Tinsley Park Golf Course
Rotherham Road
A630
Nursery Farm
Nursery Bungalow
Hotel
Prim. Sch.
Brinsworth Howarth Prim. Sc
Superstore
122
41
42
89
A B C D
1 2 3 4 5 6

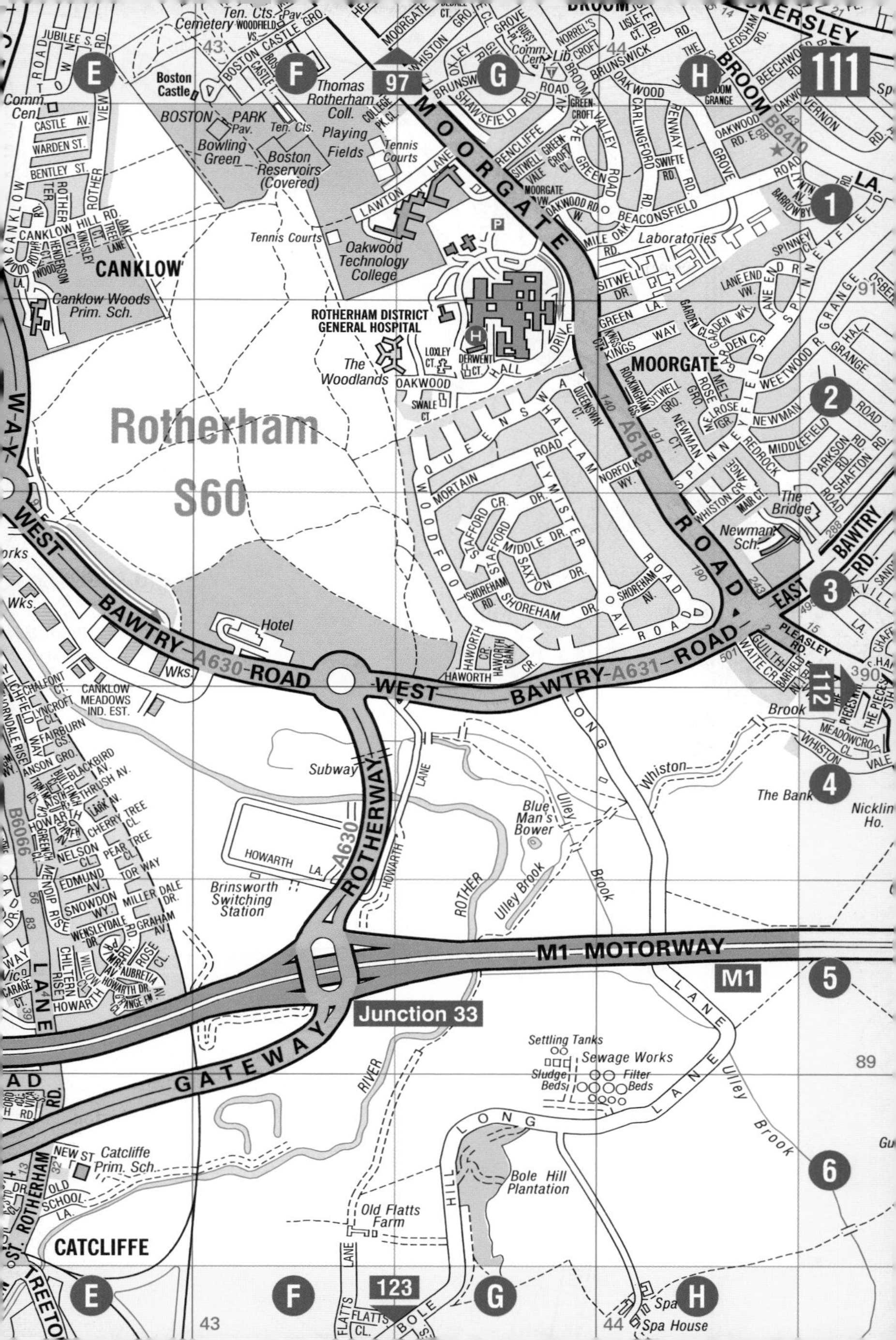

Rotherham
S60
CANKLOW
MOORGATE
CATCLIFFE
ROTHERHAM DISTRICT GENERAL HOSPITAL
Oakwood Technology College
Thomas Rotherham Coll.
Boston Castle
BOSTON PARK
Boston Reservoirs (Covered)
Bowling Green
Canklow Woods Prim. Sch.
The Woodlands
Laboratories
Hotel
CANKLOW MEADOWS IND. EST.
Brinsworth Switching Station
Subway
Blue Man's Bower
Settling Tanks
Sewage Works
Sludge Beds
Filter Beds
Bole Hill Plantation
Old Flatts Farm
Catcliffe Prim. Sch.
Newman Sch.
The Bridge
The Bank
Spa House
MOORGATE ROAD
A618
WEST BAWTRY ROAD
A630
A631
ROTHERWAY
M1 MOTORWAY
M1
Junction 33
GATEWAY
LONG LANE
B6410
B6066
97
112
123
E
F
G
H
1
2
3
4
5
6
43
44
89

WICKERSLEY ROAD
BROOM ROAD
EAST BAWTRY ROAD
A631
A6021
A6123
HERRINGTHORPE VALLEY RD.
B6410
A618
WORRY GOOSE LANE
LITTLE COMMON LA.
MOORHOUSE LANE
PLEASLEY
WHISTON
S60
Sitwell Inf. & Jun. Schs.
Whiston Jun & Inf. Sch.
Jun. & Inf. Sch.
Newman Sch.
The Bridge
Cricket Ground
Rectory
SITWELL PARK GOLF COURSE
Shrogs Wood
Club House
GREAT ROYD'S MOOR
Royds Moor
Royds Moor Bridge
Royds Moor Farm
DOLES LANE
Revel Wood
Nicklin Ho.
Garnes
M1 MOTORWAY
M1
UPPER WHISTON LANE
Fourways
Guilthwaite
Nursery
Guilthwaite Grange
Guilthwaite Hall Farm
ROAD (GUILTHWAITE HILL)
The Heights
Five Acres
Upper Whiston Farm
The Poplars
Upper Whiston
MORTHEN LANE
COMMON LANE
GUILTHWAITE
Ulley Brook
Bank
Brook
98
111
124

WICKERSLEY
Rotherham
Church Field
Playing Field
Pav.
BAWTRY RD.
MORTHEN
WICKERSLEY WOOD
LINGS COMMON
Sewage Farm
NETHERMOOR DR.
NEW HALL AV.
B6060
Millstone Farm
Parkcliff Farm
MOAT LANE
MOATLANDS
S66
Pinchmill
Pinch Mill Farm
LINER WOOD
Pinch Mill Brook
SANDY LANE
MILL LANE
FLAT LANE
The White House
Springvale Farm
MOORHILL
MORTHEN LANE
B6410
MORTHEN ROAD
MORTHEN RD.
Morthen Lodge
NINE TREES TRADING ESTATE
Works
White Mires
HALL COTTS.
Morthen Hall
Vale Fm
MORTHEN HALL LANE
SHEEP DIKE LANE
Grange Farm
MORTHEN COTTS.
Lawns Farm
MORTHEN
YORK LANE
Wildfell
Old Wildfell
Manor Farm
Pea Carr Wood
STOW BRIDGE FIELD
M1 MOTORWAY
M18 MOTORWAY
M1
M18
Junction 32
Morthen Brook
Wood Quarry
Swallow Mills Pond
S26
Wood Piece
Nursery
GRANGE CL.
Holme
99
114
125
E
F
G
H
1
2
3
4
5
6
47
48
89
90
91

LINGS COMMON
Playing Fd.
Bramley Lings
Cemetery
WICKERSLEY WOOD
Sandy Cottage
CUMWELL FIELDS
Newhall Dike
Newhall Cottage
NEWHALL GRANGE
Sewage Farm
Slacks Farm
King's Pond Plantation
Kingsforth Brook
Kingsforth Field
Moat Farm
Moat Wood
Transformer Station
Nether Moor Field
NINE TREES TRADING ESTATE
Works
Morthen Lodge
M18 MOTORWAY
MORTHEN ROAD B6060
Rotherham S66
Depot
THURCROFT IND. EST.
Factory
Wks.
The Villas
Sports Ground
Blackhill Farm
Recreation Ground Sch. & Lib.
The Willows School
Play Field
Copeland Lodge
THURCROFT
Sawn Moor
Park Lodge
Nursery
Holme Farm
Wood Quarry
Rec. Grd.

E   51   F   Brook   101   G   52   JOTON LA   CHESTNUT WK   H   LANE

LANE BACK

HOOTON COPSE

BEECH CR

Home Farm

Mansfield Farm

Spivvy

HOOTON LEVITT

Kingsforth

CARR LANE

PEAK

The Rookery

Manor House

1

91

Cliff Plantation

Carr Wood

2

BEACON HILL

COMMON HILL

ROAD

LANE

RAMPER

CARR

THE AVENUE

W O C A R R

Manor Farm

Low Farm

East Fm

TUNWELL

ABBEY GLEN

Tunwell

ROAD

Carr Hill

GREEN LANE

3

390

HOOTON

Carr Windmill (Ruin)

HOWE

LANE

HIGH

4

The Terrace

L A N E

Manor Farm

Sheffield S25

Thurcroft Hall

Brook House

ABBEY

Hall

5

Brookhouse Farm

Brookhouse

Coldwell Grn.

SLADE VW.

SLADE HOOTON

89

use   Dike

LANE

Cricket Ground

Thurcroft Lodge

Brookfield Bungalow

B ROSE LANE

BROOKHOUSE

MILL

Weir

Tinkerhole Dike

Hooton

Dike

Hooton Bridge

Sewage Works

6

E   ROAD   F   ROTHERHAM   127   G   H

ROSE ROAD

51

LANE

Tinkerhole Dike

52

Laughton All Saints

HOOTON

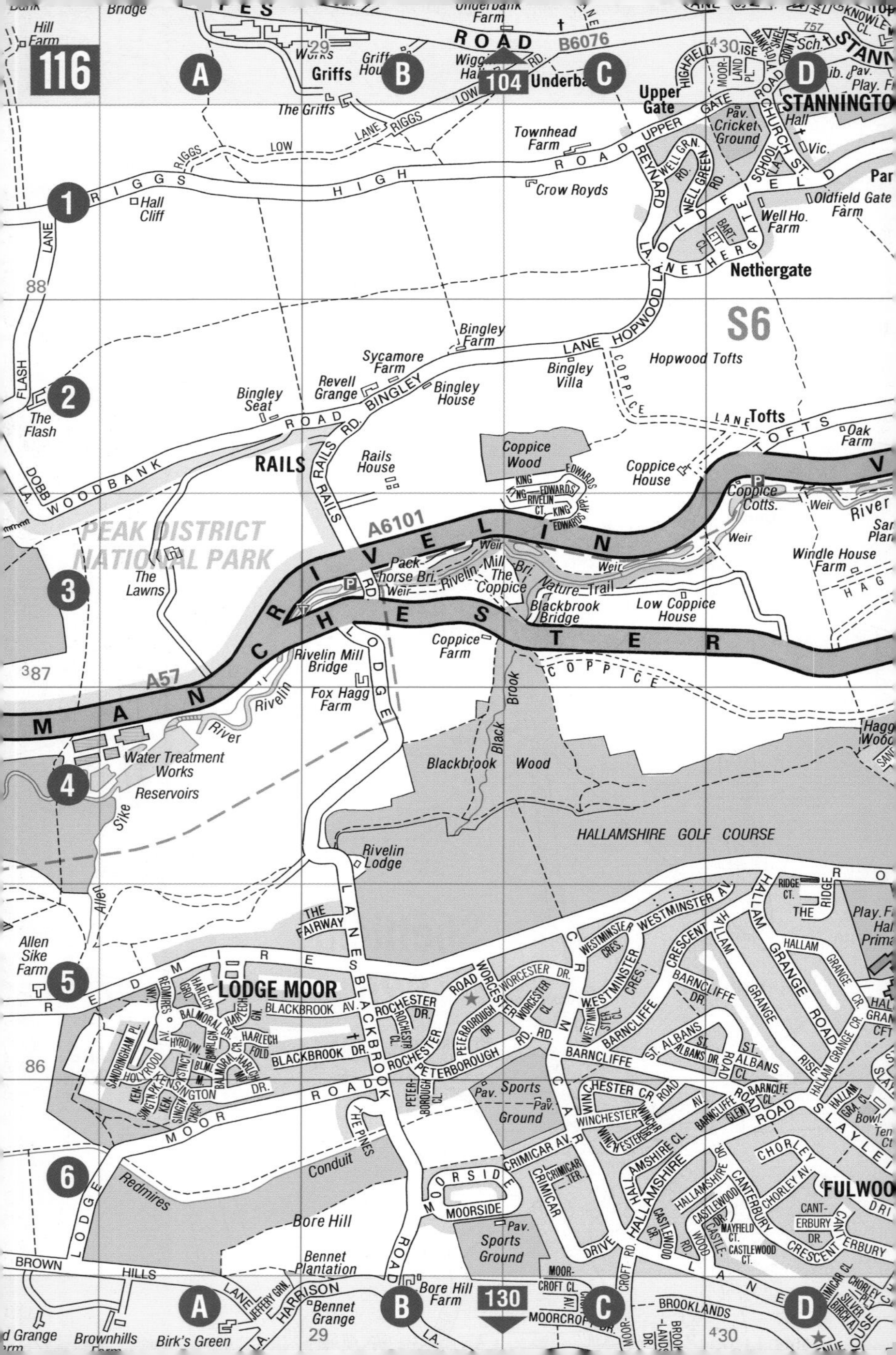
A
B
C
D
1
2
3
4
5
6
104
130
Griffs
The Griffs
Upper Gate
STANNINGTON
Nethergate
S6
Hopwood Tofts
Tofts
RAILS
PEAK DISTRICT NATIONAL PARK
A6101
A57
MANCHESTER
RIVELIN
Coppice Wood
Blackbrook Wood
HALLAMSHIRE GOLF COURSE
LODGE MOOR
FULWOOD
Water Treatment Works
Reservoirs
Bore Hill
Redmires Conduit
Sports Ground
Rivelin Mill Bridge
Fox Hagg Farm
Rivelin Lodge
Bingley Seat
Revell Grange
Sycamore Farm
Bingley Farm
Bingley House
Bingley Villa
Rails House
The Lawns
The Flash
Hall Cliff
Crow Royds
Townhead Farm
Oldfield Gate Farm
Well Ho. Farm
Coppice House
Oak Farm
Windle House Farm
Low Coppice House
Coppice Farm
Blackbrook Bridge
Allen Sike Farm
Bennet Plantation
Bennet Grange
Bore Hill Farm
Birk's Green
Brownhills
B6076

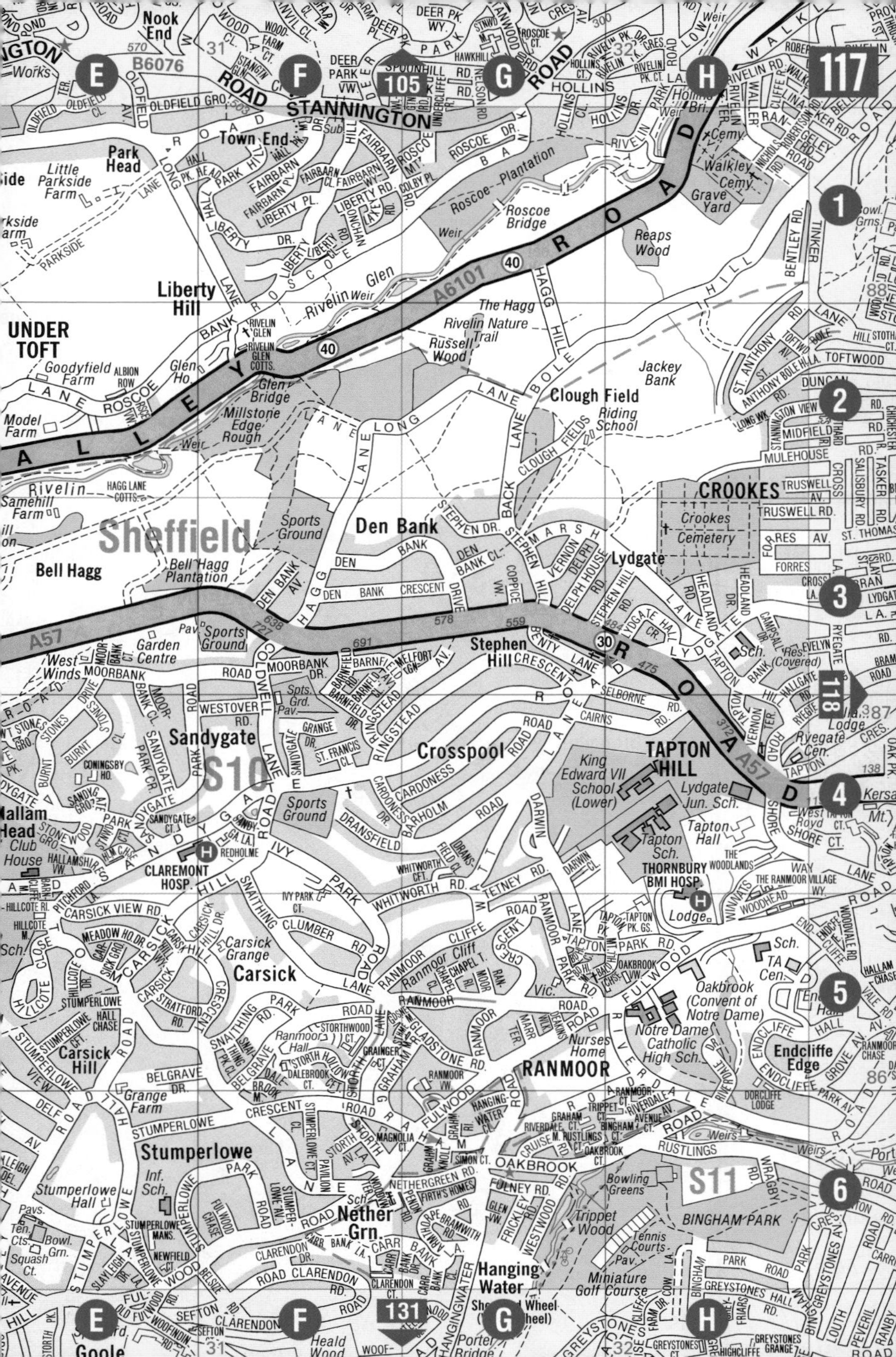
117
105
118
131
E
F
G
H
1
2
3
4
5
6
Nook End
B6076
Works
ROAD
STANNINGTON
OLDFIELD AV.
OLDFIELD GRO.
OLDFIELD CL.
DEER PARK VW.
DEER PK. WY.
SPOONHILL RD.
HAWKHILLS
HOLLINS
HOLLINS DR.
HOLLINS CL.
RIVELIN RD.
Holme Bri.
Town End
Park Head
LONG LANE
HALL PK. HEAD
PARK HILL
FAIRBARN CL.
FAIRBARN PL.
FAIRBARN WY.
LIBERTY PL.
LIBERTY RD.
LIBERTY DR.
ROSCOE DR.
ROSCOE BANK
Roscoe Plantation
Roscoe Bridge
Rivelin Glen
Weir
Cemy.
Walkley Cemy.
Grave Yard
Reaps Wood
BENTLEY RD.
TINKER LANE
Little Parkside Farm
PARKSIDE
Liberty Hill
UNDER TOFT
A6101
40
RIVELIN VALLEY ROAD
HAGG HILL
The Hagg
Rivelin Nature Trail
Russell Wood
RIVELIN GLEN
RIVELIN GLEN COTTS.
Glen Ho.
Goodyfield Farm
ALBION ROW
ROSCOE LANE
Model Farm
Glen Bridge
Millstone Edge Rough
BOLE HILL
BOLE LANE
Jackey Bank
Clough Field
Riding School
ST. ANTHONY RD.
TOFTWOOD
DUNCAN RD.
STANNINGTON VIEW
MIDFIELD RD.
MULEHOUSE
LONG LANE
CLOUGH FIELDS RD.
BACK LANE
Rivelin
HAGG LANE COTTS.
Samehill Farm
Sheffield
Bell Hagg
Bell Hagg Plantation
Sports Ground
Den Bank
DEN BANK
DEN BANK AV.
DEN BANK CL.
DEN BANK CRESCENT
DEN BANK DRIVE
HAGG LANE
STEPHEN DR.
STEPHEN HILL
MARSH
VERNON
DELPH HOUSE RD.
COPPICE VW.
CROOKES
TRUSWELL AV.
TRUSWELL RD.
Crookes Cemetery
Lydgate
HEADLAND DR.
LYDGATE LANE
LYDGATE HALL CR.
SALISBURY RD.
TASKER RD.
FORRES AV.
FORRES
ST. THOMAS
A57
638
727
578
559
691
484
475
312
30
Garden Centre
West Winds
MOORBANK
MOORBANK DR.
COLDWELL LANE
BARNFIELD
MELFORT GN.
RINGSTEAD
Stephen Hill
CRESCENT
BENTY LANE
SELBORNE RD.
CAIRNS RD.
TAPTON BANK
TAPTON HILL RD.
Res. (Covered)
Sch.
RYEGATE
EVELYN RD.
WESTOVER RD.
Sandygate
S10
Crosspool
CARDONESS
BARHOLM ROAD
DRANSFIELD
GRANGE
ST. FRANCIS CL.
CONINGSBY HO.
SANDYGATE PARK CR.
SANDYGATE ROAD
Sports Ground
King Edward VII School (Lower)
TAPTON HILL
Lydgate Jun. Sch.
Tapton Hall
Tapton Sch.
THE WOODLANDS
THORNBURY BMI HOSP.
Lodge
Ryegate Cen.
TAPTON CRES.
West Royd
SHORE LANE
TAPTON CT.
SHORE CT.
Kersal Mt.
THE RANMOOR VILLAGE WY.
WOODHEAD
WINNATS
Hallam Head
Club House
HALLAMSHIRE VW.
STONEWOOD GRO.
CLAREMONT HOSP.
REDHOLME
IVY PARK
IVY PARK CT.
WHITWORTH RD.
WHITWORTH CFT.
TETNEY RD.
DARWIN
DARWIN CL.
WATT LANE
SNAITHING LANE
CARSICK VIEW RD.
CARSICK HILL
PITCHFORD LA.
HILLCOTE CL.
Sch.
MEADOW HO. DR.
Carsick Grange
Carsick
CLUMBER RD.
RANMOOR CLIFFE ROAD
Ranmoor Cliff
RANMOOR
RANMOOR PARK RD.
TAPTON PARK RD.
TAPTON PK. GS.
OAKBROOK VW.
FULWOOD ROAD
Oakbrook (Convent of Notre Dame)
Sch.
TA Cen.
WOODVALE RD.
HALLAM CHASE
ENDCLIFFE
Vic.
Nurses Home
Notre Dame Catholic High Sch.
RIVERDALE DR.
Endcliffe Edge
ENDCLIFFE HALL AV.
ENDCLIFFE GROVE AV.
ENDCLIFFE PARK AV.
DORCLIFFE LODGE
RANMOOR CHASE
86
STUMPERLOWE
STUMPERLOWE HALL CHASE
Carsick Hill
STRATFORD RD.
BELGRAVE DR.
Grange Farm
SNAITHING PARK ROAD
Ranmoor Hall
STORTHWOOD CT.
GLADSTONE RD.
GRAHAM RD.
RANMOOR
RANMOOR
RANMOOR
TRIPPET CT.
RIVERDALE CT.
GRAHAM CT.
M. RUSTLINGS
BINGHAM CT.
AVENUE CT.
RUSTLINGS ROAD
Weirs
DELF
HALL ROAD
STUMPERLOWE CRESCENT ROAD
Stumperlowe
Inf. Sch.
Stumperlowe Hall
STUMPERLOWE PARK ROAD
MAGNOLIA CT.
OAKBROOK
NETHERGREEN RD.
FIRTH'S HOMES
FULNEY RD.
GLEN VW.
FRICKLEY RD.
WESTWOOD RD.
Bowling Greens
S11
WRAGBY
Trippet Wood
Tennis Courts
BINGHAM PARK
Nether Grn.
Pavs.
Ten. Cts.
Bowl. Grn.
Squash Ct.
STUMPERLOWE MANS.
NEWFIELD CT.
CLARENDON DR.
CARR BANK LA.
CLARENDON ROAD
CLARENDON RD.
Hanging Water
Miniature Golf Course
PARK ROAD
GREYSTONES HALL RD.
FRIARS RD.
GREYSTONES AV.
PEVERIL
LOUTH
HANGINGWATER
FULWOOD
SEFTON
Goole
Heald Wood
Porter Bridge
GREYSTONES ROAD
GREYSTONES GRANGE
HIGHCLIFFE
CLIFFE FARM DR.
31
32
88
387
138

106
132
117
4
A
B
C
D
1
2
3
4
5
6
Walkley Bank
Bole Hill Recreation Ground
Ruskin Park
Playground
Birkendale
Howard Hill
Steel Bank
S6
Upperthorpe
Netherthorpe
Recreation Ground
Netherthorpe Rd.
CROOKESMOOR
Crookes Valley Park
CROOKES
Sports Ground
Univ. of Sheffield
Gymnasium
Goodwin Sports Centre
Weston Park
Weston Park Mus.
University of Sheffield
S10
Hockey Pitches
WESTERN BANK
ROYAL HALLAMSHIRE HOSPITAL
Broomhill
Hallam Lodge
Ryegate Cen.
TAPTON HALL OF RES.
CHESTER ROAD
FULWOOD RD.
WHITHAM RD.
GLOSSOP RD.
A57
B6069
B6547
Summerfield
Broomfield
Robert Winston Bldg.
Sunnybank Nature Reserve
Sheffield Botanical Gardens
Sheffield Hallam University
CLARKEHOUSE
Endcliffe Crescent
Endcliffe Hall
Endcliffe Edge
Endcliffe Wood
ENDCLIFFE PARK
Porter Brook
Sharrow Vale
S11
A625
ECCLESALL
BROCCO BANK
HUNTERS BAR
Cemetery
Sharrow Head
Lantern Theatre
Bingo
Infirmary Rd.
WALKLEY
CROOKES
88
87
86
33
34

119
107
133
120
5
E
F
G
H
1
2
3
4
5
6
Philadelphia
Works
NEEPSEND
ROAD
RUTLAND
ROAD
Training Centre
S3
Playground
BURNGREAVE
CARLISLE
B6082
S4
Superstore
A6109
ATTERCLIFFE ROAD
TWELVE O'CLOCK CT.
Kelham Island
Climb. Cen.
Mus.
MOWBRAY
B6074
LANE
Shalesmoor
DEREK
SAVILE
SPITAL
HILL
DOOLEY
B6073
EFFINGHAM
Gas Wks.
Weir
WAY
A61
CUTLERS GATE
PARKWAY
SHEFFIELD
Hyde Pk.
CRICKET INN RD.
Law Courts
WEST BAR
Mag. Ct.
Castle Mkt.
THE QUAYSIDE
VICTORIA QUAYS
MERCHANTS CR.
HOYLE
ST.
BROAD
LA.
B6539
Univ.
Cath.
Ponds Forge Int. Sports Cen.
City Hall
RC Cath.
O2
Winter Gdn.
Lib.
Thtre.
Cin.
Bus Sta.
Univ.
ARUNDEL
S1
SHEAF
ST.
SHEFFIELD
Cinema
BERNARD
DUKE
B6070
B6071
TALBOT
SHREWSBURY
CITY
ROAD
SHEFFIELD
A6135
Playing Field
Monument Grounds
SHREWSBURY ALMSHOUSES
GRANVILLE
ROAD
ST. MARY'S
GATE
RD.
Granville Rd./ Sheffield District College
Goals
All Saints Catholic Sch.
Sheffield City Coll.
Skate Central
NORFOLK PARK STUDENTS' RESIDENCE
Hostel
Heritage Park School
Superstore
BRAMALL
LA.
A621
LONDON
RD.
B6388
Sheffield United FC (Bramall Lane)
HIGHFIELD
Little Sheffield
Park Grange Croft
Norfolk Park Sch.
Seven Hills Sch.
Bowling Greens
NORFOLK
86
S2
Works
QUEENS RETAIL PARK
QUEENS
ROAD
ALPHA HOSP.
Bus Depot
Park Grange Rd.
Depots
LOWFIELD
Sheaf
Comm. Cen.
Sports Ground
Factory
ABBEYDALE
RD.
S7
Adventure Playgrd.
Black Bank

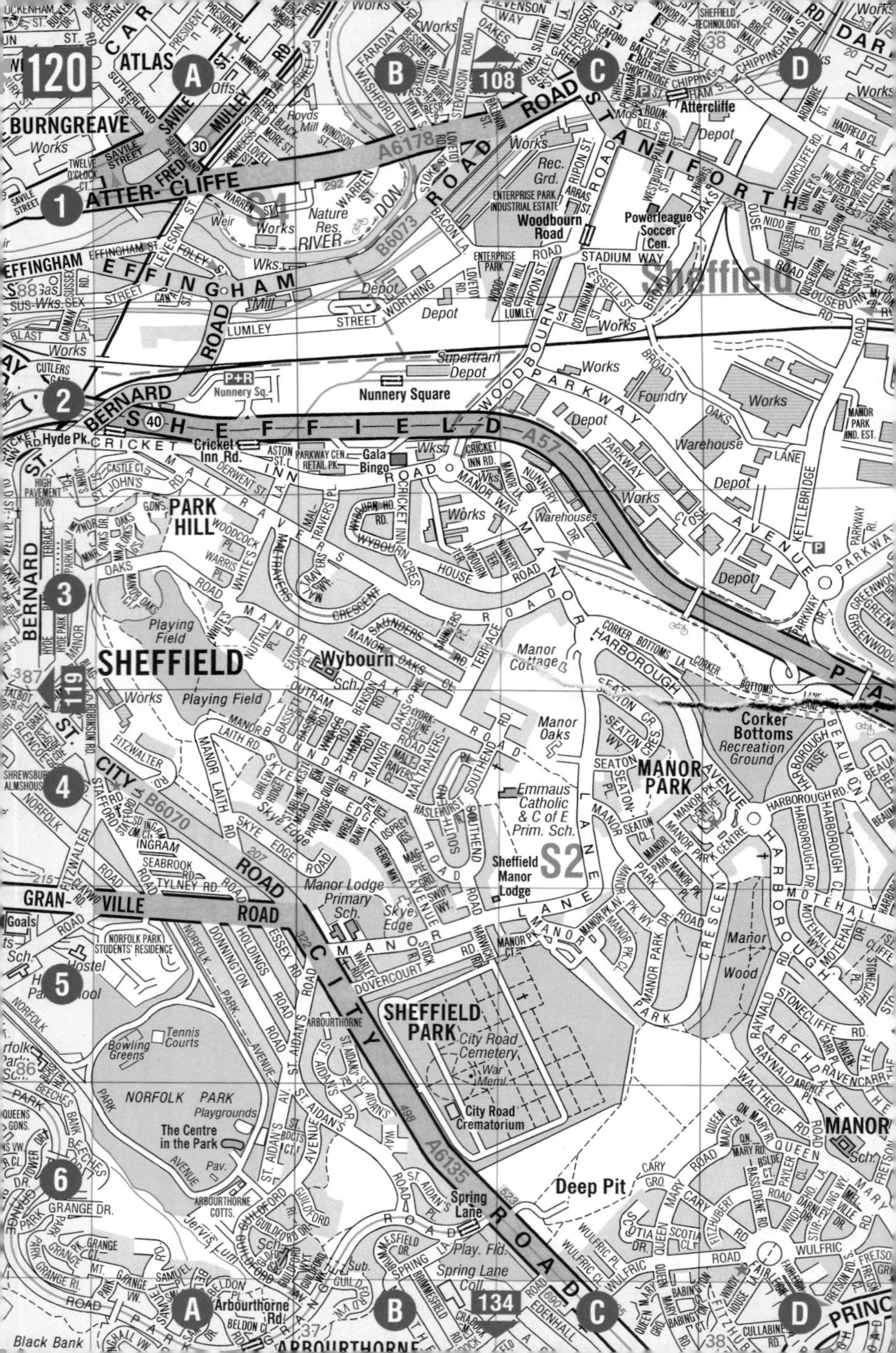
BURNGREAVE
ATLAS
ATTERCLIFFE ROAD
A6178
B6073
RIVER DON
Nature Res.
Royds Mill
EFFINGHAM ROAD
EFFINGHAM STREET
LUMLEY STREET
WORTHING
Supertram Depot
Nunnery Square
Nunnery Sq.
SHEFFIELD PARKWAY
A57
BERNARD ROAD
Hyde Pk.
CRICKET INN RD.
Cricket Inn Rd.
Gala Bingo
PARKWAY CEN. RETAIL PK.
PARK HILL
Woodbourn Road
ENTERPRISE PARK INDUSTRIAL ESTATE
Powerleague Soccer Cen.
STADIUM WAY
STANIFORTH ROAD
Attercliffe
Sheffield
WOODBOURN RD.
Foundry
Warehouse
MANOR PARK IND. EST.
KETTLEBRIDGE
MANOR OAKS RD.
MANOR LANE
Manor Cottage
Wybourn
SHEFFIELD
Playing Field
Works
Corker Bottoms Recreation Ground
HARBOROUGH
MANOR PARK
MANOR AVENUE
Manor Oaks
Emmaus Catholic & C of E Prim. Sch.
Sheffield Manor Lodge
S2
Skye Edge
CITY ROAD
B6070
GRANVILLE ROAD
NORFOLK PARK STUDENTS' RESIDENCE
Manor Lodge Primary Sch.
SHEFFIELD PARK
City Road Cemetery
War Meml.
City Road Crematorium
A6135
NORFOLK PARK
Playgrounds
Tennis Courts
Bowling Greens
The Centre in the Park
Pav.
Manor Wood
Deep Pit
MANOR
Spring Lane
Spring Lane Coll.
Play. Fld.
Arbourthorne Rd.
ARBOURTHORNE
Black Bank
108
119
134
A B C D
1 2 3 4 5 6

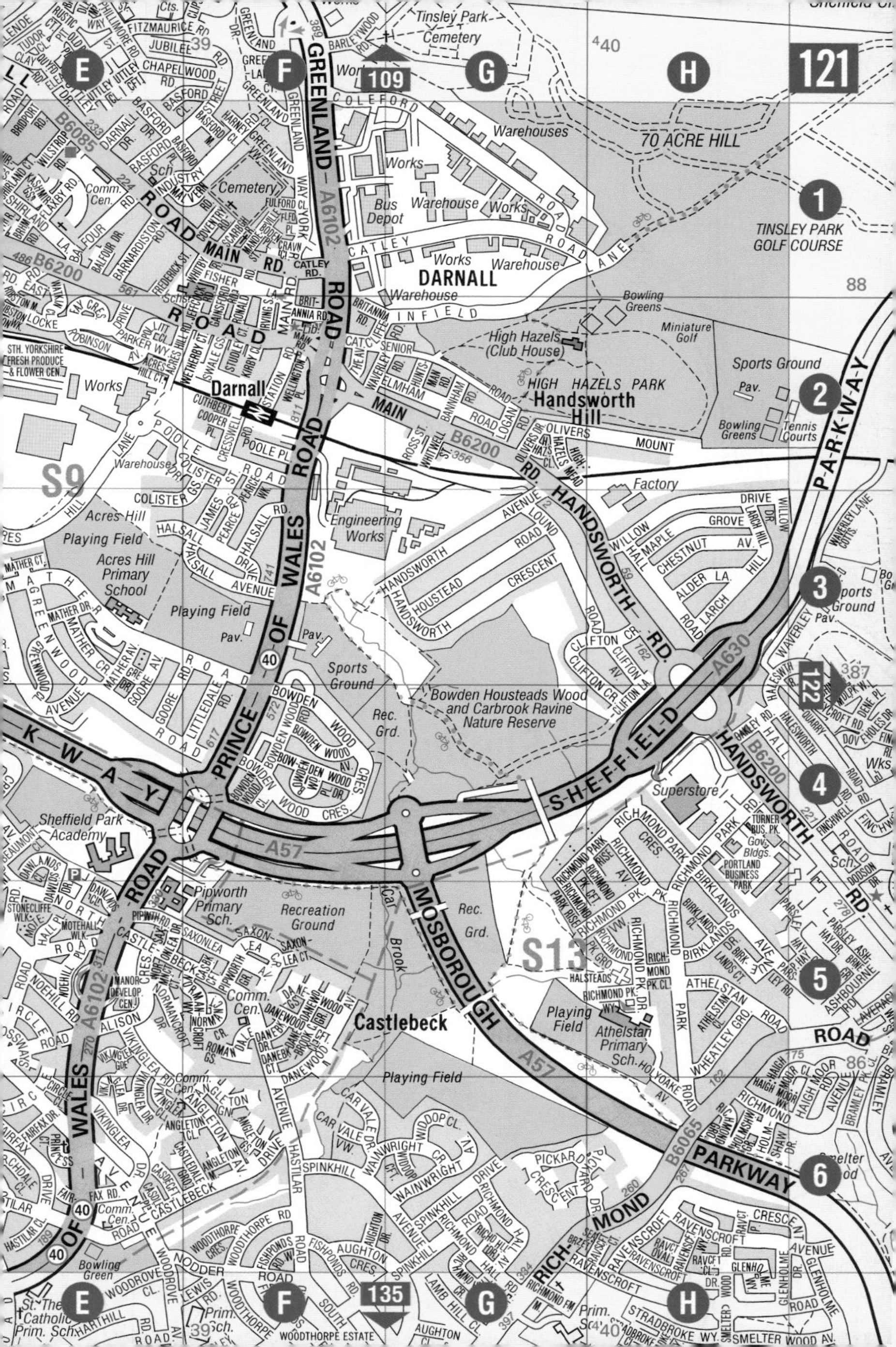
121
109
135
122
E
F
G
H
1
2
3
4
5
6
39
40
88
86
DARNALL
Darnall
Handsworth Hill
Castlebeck
S9
S13
Tinsley Park Cemetery
70 ACRE HILL
TINSLEY PARK GOLF COURSE
Warehouses
Works
Bus Depot
Warehouse
Cemetery
Comm. Cen.
HIGH HAZELS PARK
High Hazels (Club House)
Bowling Greens
Miniature Golf
Sports Ground
Tennis Courts
Factory
Engineering Works
Acres Hill Playing Field
Acres Hill Primary School
Playing Field
Sports Ground
Rec. Grd.
Bowden Housteads Wood and Carbrook Ravine Nature Reserve
Superstore
PORTLAND BUSINESS PARK
Sheffield Park Academy
Pipworth Primary Sch.
Recreation Ground
Athelstan Primary Sch.
Bowling Green
STH. YORKSHIRE FRESH PRODUCE & FLOWER CEN.
GREENLAND ROAD
A6102
PRINCE OF WALES ROAD
MAIN ROAD
B6200
B6085
A57
A630
B6065
SHEFFIELD PARKWAY
PARKWAY
HANDSWORTH RD.
MOSBOROUGH
RICHMOND PARK
ATHELSTAN ROAD
CATLEY ROAD
COLEFORD ROAD
INFIELD
POOLE ROAD
HANDSWORTH AVENUE
HANDSWORTH CRESCENT
RAVENSCROFT
CASTLEBECK AVENUE
WOODTHORPE ESTATE
SMELTER WOOD AV.

Sheffield City Airport (Disused)
110
PARKWAY
ROTHERHAM
GATEWAY
A630
POPLAR
B6533
WAY
Superstore
TWI TECHNOLOGY CENTRE
THE POPLARS INDUSTRIAL ESTATE
Recreation Ground
TINSLEY PARK GOLF COURSE
S9
Sports Ground
Bowling Greens
Tennis Courts
WAVERLEY BUSINESS PARK
WHITTLE
BRUNEL
MORSE WY.
HIGH
FIELD
SPRING
Opencast Workings
ROTHERHAM
SHEFFIELD
B6066
HIGH FIELD SPRING
Sewage Works
LA.
ORGREAVE
Sheffield
S13
Garage
ORGREAVE LA.
Warehouses
Orgreave Common
HIGHFIELD
ROTHERHAM RD.
Cemetery
Sports Ground
Bowling Green
121
MARSDEN IND. EST.
Recreation Ground
HANDSWORTH
B6200
ORGREAVE LA.
ROAD
RETFORD
KIRKDALE CRES.
BALLIFIELD
HANDSWORTH
Cemy.
Sports Field
Ballifield Primary Sch.
Handsworth Grange Sports Coll.
Play. Field
RICHMOND
Smelter Wood
Myrtle Bank
GRANGE
LANE
BEAVER HILL ROAD
Beaver Hill
South Yorkshire Fire Service Training Ce
MOSBOROUGH PARKWAY
A57
RAVENSCROFT
SMELTER WOOD AV.
Works
DORE HO. IND. EST.
136

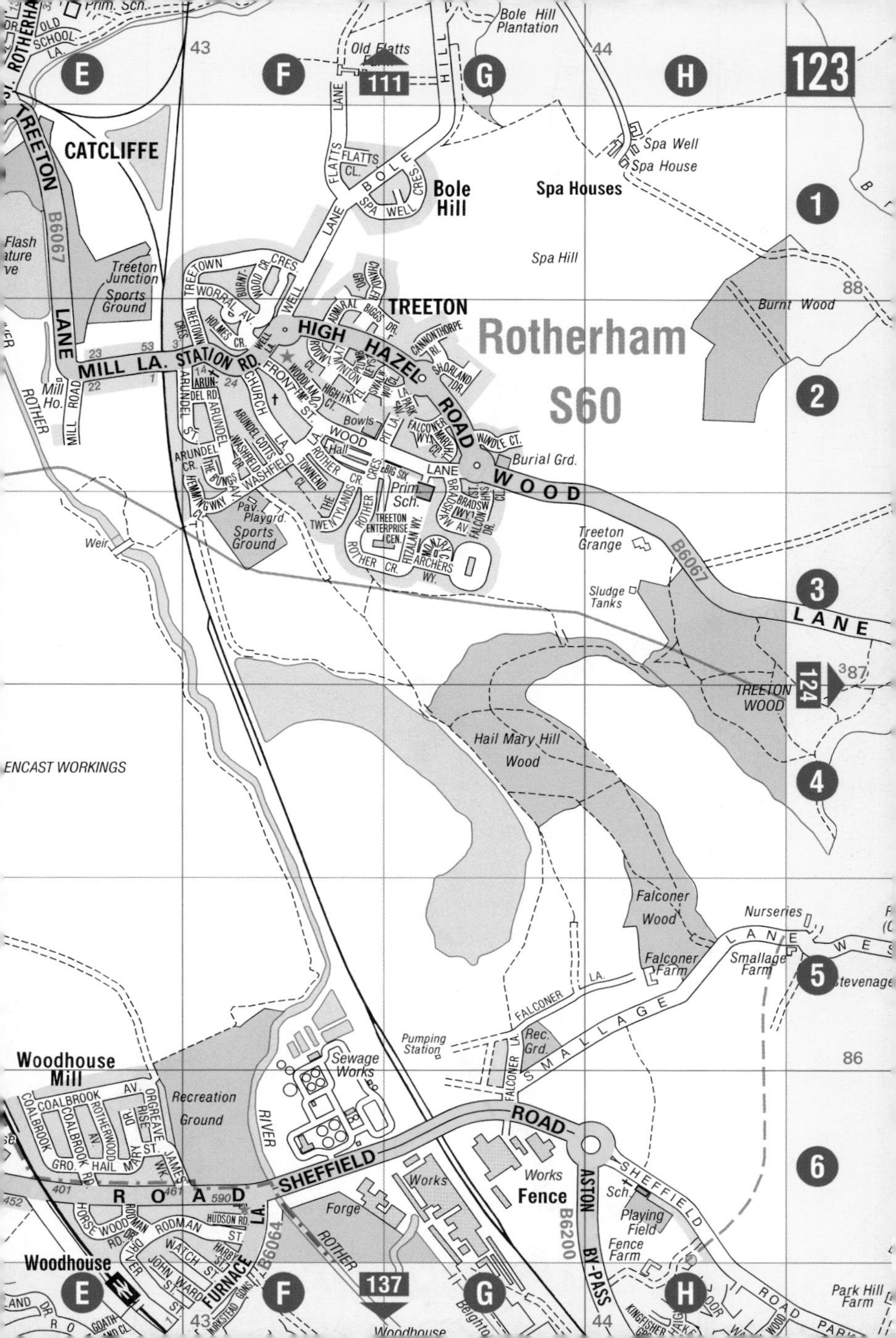
CATCLIFFE
Bole Hill
Spa Houses
Spa Well
Spa House
Bole Hill Plantation
Old Flatts Farm
111
Spa Hill
TREETON
Rotherham
S60
Burnt Wood
Treeton Junction Sports Ground
TREETON LANE
B6067
MILL LA.
STATION RD.
HIGH HAZEL ROAD
WOOD LANE
Mill Ho.
Flash
Weir
ROTHER
Burial Grd.
Treeton Grange
Sludge Tanks
Sports Ground
Pav.
Playgrd.
TREETON ENTERPRISE CEN.
Prim. Sch.
Bowls
Hall
124
TREETON WOOD
Hail Mary Hill Wood
ENCAST WORKINGS
Falconer Wood
Falconer Farm
Nurseries
Smallage Farm
Stevenage
FALCONER LA.
SMALLAGE LANE
Pumping Station
Rec. Grd.
Woodhouse Mill
Recreation Ground
Sewage Works
RIVER ROTHER
SHEFFIELD ROAD
Works
Forge
Fence
ASTON BY-PASS
B6200
B6064
Playing Field
Fence Farm
Sch.
Park Hill Farm
Woodhouse
137
Woodhouse
E
F
G
H
1
2
3
4
5
6
43
44
88
87
86

Rotherham
S60
Sheffield
S26
PLEASLEY
(GUILTHWAITE HILL)
GUILTHWAITE COMMON LANE
Depot
Ulley Brook
Burnt Wood
Packman's Bridge
Gas Valve Compound
Guilthwaite Common
Sluice
RESERVOIR ROAD
Weir
Ulley Reservoir
Sandstone Quarry
GREEN LANE
West End Farm
Ulley Country Park Visitor Centre
ULLEY COUNTRY PARK
POYNTON AV.
MAIN LANE
Ulley Holt
WOOD LA.
B6067
TREETON LA.
TREETON WOOD
ROAD
A618
ULLEY Weirs
Turnshaw Plantation
Turnshaw Common
NASCOT GDNS.
HALL FARM CL.
ASTON LANE
Sunnyside
AUGHTON
CORAL DRIVE
CORAL CL.
CORAL WY.
CORAL PL.
WELL LA.
Play. Fld.
Sch.
MARTIN CL.
RISE
MANOR FM.
ULLEY VIEW
RICKNALD CL.
DANIELS DR.
AMBLER
Kenville
Nurseries
Reservoir (Covered)
SMALLAGE LA.
Smallage
WEST LANE
Stevenage
MAIN ST.
MAIN RD.
HALL ROAD
WESTFIELD AV.
WINDY RIDGE
Aughton Prim. Sch.
GRAY AV.
GRANGE
SPRINGWOOD AV.
HALLAM CL.
TURNSHAW AV.
HEIGHTON VW.
WHARTON AV.
ASTON CL.
WOS CL.
ALDERSON CL.
WALPOLE GR.
AUGHTON AV.
WESTCOTT M.
MASON DR.
MASON AVENUE
SPRGWD CT.
VERELST AV.
DRIVE
AUGHTON LANE
Lib.
SWALLOWNEST COURT
Playgrd.
Cemetery
HOLLY WAY
AYSGARTH RI.
CHESTNUT
OAK
BEECH
LEYBURN DR.
AUGHTON ROAD
ALEXANDRA
LOVETOT
CANTILUPE CR.
CONYRS DR.
TOWN END AV.
Prim. Sch.
WESLEY ROAD
ARCUBUS
DARCY CL.
AMBY DR.
PAGENALL
ESTONE DR.
HOLDERNESS DRIVE
RD Hall
ROSEDALE CL.
ROSEGARTH
CHELMSFORD DR.
ROSSLYN AV.
MELBOURNE AV.
AVENUE OSBORNE
SWALLOWNEST
KING ST.
Bowl. Green
IVANHOE
ROSE MEWS
MEAD
NURSERY RD.
HIGH ST
Tennis Cts.
ROTHERHAM RD.
JASMINE GDNS.
MANVERS RD.
EDEN GROVE
EDEN GLADE
ARTHUR ST.
AVENUE
MILLSTONE
ST. STEPHENS DR.
BRAMLEY
CHRISTCHURCH AV.
WHARNCLIFFE AV.
Park Farm
Comm. Cen.
Sch. SCH. ST.
PARK
ALPINA
CAMELIA WY.
WORKSOP
Comm.
Mill Stone Hill
Sch.
MALTON
SUDBURY DR.
ULLEY LANE

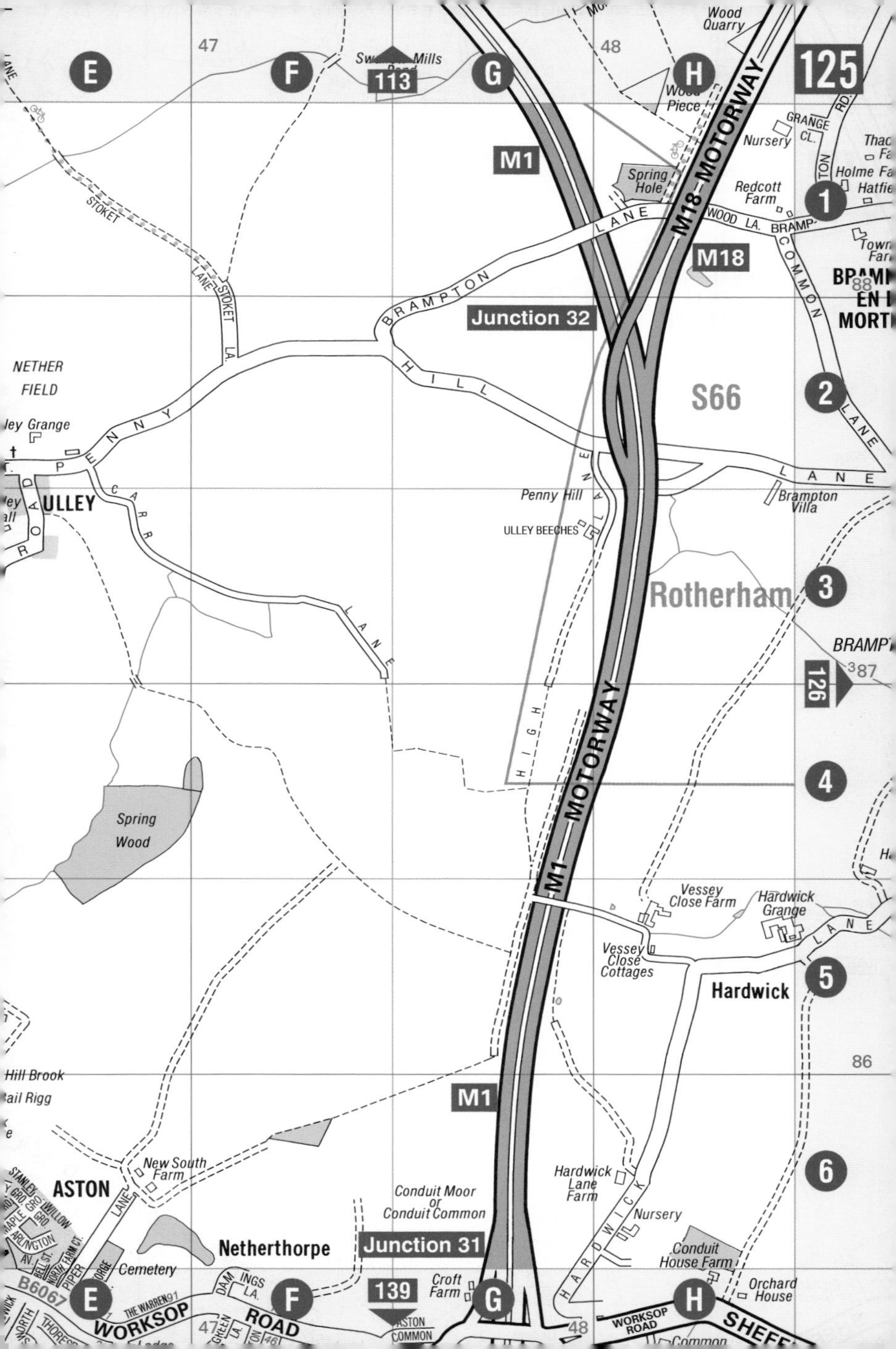
E
F
G
H
113
Swinston Mills
Wood Quarry
Wood Piece
M1
M18 MOTORWAY
M18
Junction 32
Spring Hole
Redcott Farm
Nursery
GRANGE CL.
Holme Farm
WOOD LA.
BRAMPTON LANE
STOKET LANE
STOKET LA.
PENNY HILL
NETHER FIELD
Ulley Grange
ULLEY
CARR LANE
S66
BRAMPTON EN LE MORTHEN
COMMON LANE
Penny Hill
ULLEY BEECHES
Brampton Villa
Rotherham
126
HIGH LANE
M1 MOTORWAY
Spring Wood
Vessey Close Farm
Hardwick Grange
Vessey Close Cottages
Hardwick
Hill Brook
Rail Rigg
New South Farm
ASTON
Hardwick Lane Farm
Conduit Moor or Conduit Common
Nursery
HARDWICK LANE
Netherthorpe
Junction 31
Conduit House Farm
Orchard House
Cemetery
Croft Farm
139
B6067
WORKSOP ROAD
ASTON COMMON
SHEFFIELD
1
2
3
4
5
6
47
48
88
87
86

126
Wood Quarry
M1
Grange Cl.
Nursery
Thackeray Farm
Holme Farm
Hatfield Fm.
Wood La.
Brampton Road
Townend Farm
BRAMPTON EN LE MORTHEN
Brampton Common Lane
Rotherham
S66
Brampton Mdws.
Brampton Pl.
Abbots Ford
Elgitha Drive
The Willows School
Sch. & Lib.
School Road
St. Withold
Rotherwood Cr.
Munds Rd.
Ulrica Dr.
Ivanhoe Road
Aymer Dr.
St. Ed.
Play. Fld.
Copeland Lodge
Zamor
Athelstane Dr.
Gurth Dr.
Crescent
Guilbert Av.
Rec. Grd.
Grn. Arbour Ct.
Green Arbour Road
Limetree Av.
Sawn Moor Road
Sawn Moor Rd.
Sawn Moor
Park Lodge
THURCROFT
Moor Av.
Arbour Dr.
Arbour Cr.
Laughton Road
Clarke Av.
Howards Cl.
Steadfolds Cl.
114
B6060
Green Arbour Farm
Lane
Cemetery
Side Farm
Laughton
Wiltshire
Faimaglo
Kennels
Hawk Hill Lane
Penny Hill Lane
Brampton Villa
Laughton Common
Brampton Gorse
Brampton Common
Eel
Long Road
125
Hardwick Hall Farm
Hardwick Lane
Hardwick Grange
Hardwick
Strait Mile Fishery
Sheffield
S26
Common Road
Pocket Handkerchief Lane
Aston Brook
Todwick Rd.
B6463
Dinnington Rd.
Sunny
Rosedale
Four Acres
Brookfield
Greendale
Grange Farm
Gospel Hill
Res.
Grange Gdns.
Todwick Grange
Orchard House
Poplar
Sheffield Rd.
140
1 2 3 4 5 6
A B C D
88
87
86
49
50

E
F
G
H
115
141
1
2
3
4
5
6
51
52
88
LAUGHTON
EN LE MORTHEN
LAUGHTON
COMMON
S25
DINNINGTON
ROTHERHAM LANE
ROSE LA.
COMMON LANE
BROOK-HOUSE
HIGH LANE
HOOTON LANE
Tinkerhole Dike
Laughton All Saints
C of E Prim. Sch.
Castle Hill
CHURCH CORNER
RECTORY CT.
ABBEY CL.
FIELDS
MELLOW
CROFT
OLD HALL CL.
CASTLE GRN.
STREET
FIRBECK
EASTFIELD CR.
ORCHARD CL.
ST. JOHN'S CT.
NEW ST.
GRANGEWOOD RD.
LONGTHWTE CL.
DOLESWOOD DR.
LINGODELL CL.
Rec. Grd.
KINGSWOOD AV.
KIRK CFT. RD.
Manor Farm
Laughton Inf. & Jun. School
SCHOOL LANE
Sandall House
St. John's Farm
St. John's
ST. JOHN'S ROAD
Holmlea Farm
Poultry Farm
Laughton Common Farm
The Double 'H'
B6060
ROAD
STATION RD.
OUTGANG
Recreation Ground
Playgrd
SANDALL
ALL SAINTS MDWS.
GLAISDALE CL.
GLAISDALE CT.
Hall
RIVERSIDE CT.
CLARKE AV.
ST. PAULS CL.
POPLARS
FINSBURY
WATERLOO CT.
KENSINGTON
LAUGHTON MDWS.
BAKER
ASCOT
HAYDOCK
ST. LEGER CL.
FRANKHAM CL.
SANDERS
CARSON AV.
DETTORI
MONK'S BRIDGE TRADING ESTATE
ST. PANCRAS CL.
PADDINGTON
WATERSIDE ENTERPRISE PARK
REDWALL CL.
ROTHERHAM RD.
MEADOW ST.
KIERAN CL.
PRINCESS ST.
PARK LA.
Monk's Bridge
Depot
Dike
Wks.
Mires
COMMON ROAD
B6463
Throapham Common
Sports Ground
Timber Yard
DINNINGTON BUS. CEN.
EDEN PL.
COLLIERY CL.
LANE
CLOCK CT.
REDWOOD CT.
WAY
CAMPBELL
NOBEL WY.
EVANS BUS. CEN.
CARRERA CT.
DINNINGTON BUSINESS INCUBATION CENTRE
BENTLEY BUSINESS PARK 2
CAXTON WY.
Industrial Estate
MONKSBRIDGE ROAD
CHURCH
Works
BOOKERS LA.
BOOKERS
BOOKERS WY.
TODWICK ROAD INDUSTRIAL ESTATE
BROOKLANDS PARK
HAIGH MOOR DR.
BROOKLANDS WAY
WEST CARR RD.
LOW COMMON RD.
BENTLEY BUS. PARK 1
BROOKLANDS HOUSE
ABBEY WAY
UNIVERSAL CL.
NORTH ANSTON TRADING ESTATE
HOUGHTON ROAD
Bluebell Wood
Children's Hospice
Sewage Works
Brook
Cramfit
NORTH ANSTON BUSINESS CENTRE
RODDIS CT.
RODDIS CL.
CRAMFIT CRES.
MARBECK CL.
DONSTONE VW.
WASHINGTON CL.
LIMELANDS
WHITEHEAD
BROADOAKS
ATHORPE RD.
ATHORPE GR.
PARKLANDS
MEADOW CFT.
BURGHLEY CL.
BLENHEIM CL.
Alcove Plantation
MIDDLETON AV.
CARVER DR.
FALCON
Dinnington Park
NURSERY RD.
DEVONSHIRE
PORTLAND
Aston Greenlands
Playing Fld.
MANOR DR.
UNDERGATE ROAD
LITTLEFIELD RD.
TIERCEL M.
CHURCH LA.
CONSTABLE LA.
MKT. PL.
Club
DAVIES CT.
CHINDIT CT.
CORONATION AV.
PLANTATION CT.
PLANTATION AV.
SOUTH ST.
LAUGHTON RD.
CHARLES ST.
DUKE ST.
QUEEN ST.
CHESTNUT GRO.
ANNE
HUNTER
128
Little Moor
Wks.
HALL CT.
BARLEY CROFT
FALCON CT.
HALL FM. CFT.
NEW RD.
WALNUT DR.
Burial Grd.

A B C D

53 54

1

SCAMMING LANE
LANE E A S T F I E L D L A N E
FIRBECK LA.
LDHOUGHTON CR.
'88
Doles Wood

LAUGHTON EN LE MORTHEN

FIRBECK AV.
GRANGEWOOD RD.
LONGTHWTE
LINGODELL CL.
Rec. Grd.
WOOD AV.
KINGS

2

KIRK CROFT ROAD
St. John's Farm
St John's
ST. JOHN'S ROAD
Little bor

Sheffield

S25

Lo

3

Throapham
OLDCOTES ROAD L A   LA
COMMON RD.
387
127
5 23
Sports Ground
BRECK LANE
HUNTERS PK
HUNTRS TWY
HUNTSCR
ANNE
HUNTERS CL.
CHEST
NUT
REAVILL
CLARKE CT.
LEGER WY
MANOR ROAD
QUEEN ST.
HUNTS PK
HUNTERS
ST.
OLDCOTES
CHASE
JESSOP
CL.
Lime Kiln Close Plantation
B6463

4

Timber Yard
CHARLES ST.
DUKE ST.
Wks
Rotherham Coll. of Arts and Tech.
White Gates
Tennis Courts
Dinnington Comprehensive School
LANE
MANOR DR.
GANG
DAVIES CT.
CHINDIT CT.
CORONATION AV.
PLANTATION AV.
LAUGHTON ROAD
GATEWAY
SCH
DOE QUARRY LANE
EAST ST.
QUARRY TER.
DINNINGTON
LEYS
LODGE LANE

5

THORPE RD.
Superstore
Cemy.
CONSTABLE LA.
NEW
Council Offices
Sch
Lib.
Football Grn. J.Grd.
Prim. Sch.
Spts. Grd.
EAST STREET
SCARSDALE
HOWARD
DOE QUARS.
VICTORIA ST.
ARRAS
HILL ST.
THE CRESCENT
PATERSON RD.
Bowl. Grn.
Tennis Cts.
Miners' Welfare Institute
Ty Newydd
Barto Wood
LITTLEFIELD RD.
86
KINGSWAY COMPLEX
LORDENS
LEICESTER RD.
Recreation Ground
Dinnington Lodge

6

ATHORPE RD.
CHURCH ST.
BURGH
BLENHEIM
NEW RD.
CARVER DR.
MIDDLETON AV.
NURSERY
Dinnington Park
B6060 RD.
TROON WLK.
ANDREWS ST.
EAGLE'S
BIRKDALE AV.
WENTWORTH WY.
TURNBERRY WAY
SUNNINGDALE
BARLEY CROFT LA.
THE CL.
FALCON CL.
HALL FM. CL.
LIDGATE
SWINSTON
EASTERN
CENTRAL
WESTERN AV.
SILVERDALES
SHAKESPEARE DR.
BYRON
BURNS ROAD
NOOK
SWINSTON HILL
KEATS DR.
SHELLEY RD.
Lodge Plantation
Lodge Farm
142
ROWERNFIL

A B C D

53 54

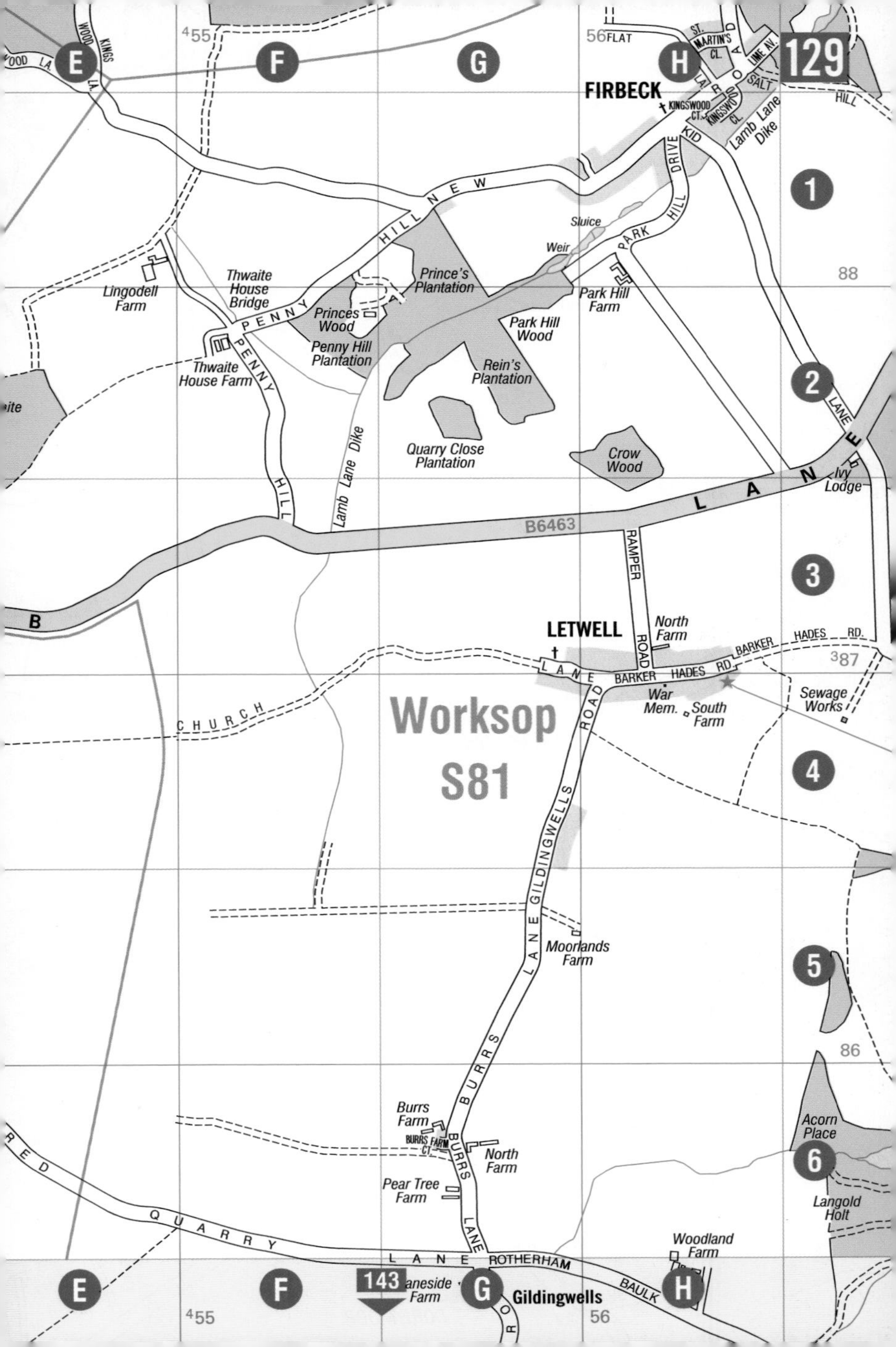
FIRBECK
ST. MARTIN'S CL.
LIME AV.
SALT HILL
KINGSWOOD CT.
Lamb Lane Dike
KID DRIVE
PARK HILL
NEW HILL
PENNY HILL
Sluice
Weir
Thwaite House Bridge
Lingodell Farm
Prince's Plantation
Princes Wood
Penny Hill Plantation
Park Hill Farm
Park Hill Wood
Rein's Plantation
Thwaite House Farm
Quarry Close Plantation
Crow Wood
Lamb Lane Dike
Ivy Lodge
LANE
B6463
RAMPER ROAD
North Farm
LETWELL
BARKER HADES RD.
CHURCH LANE
War Mem.
South Farm
Sewage Works
Worksop
S81
GILDINGWELLS ROAD
GILDINGWELLS LANE
Moorlands Farm
BURRS LANE
Burrs Farm
BURRS FARM CT.
North Farm
Pear Tree Farm
RED QUARRY LANE
ROTHERHAM BAULK
Woodland Farm
Acorn Place
Langold Holt
Gildingwells
Laneside Farm
143
455
56
88
387
86

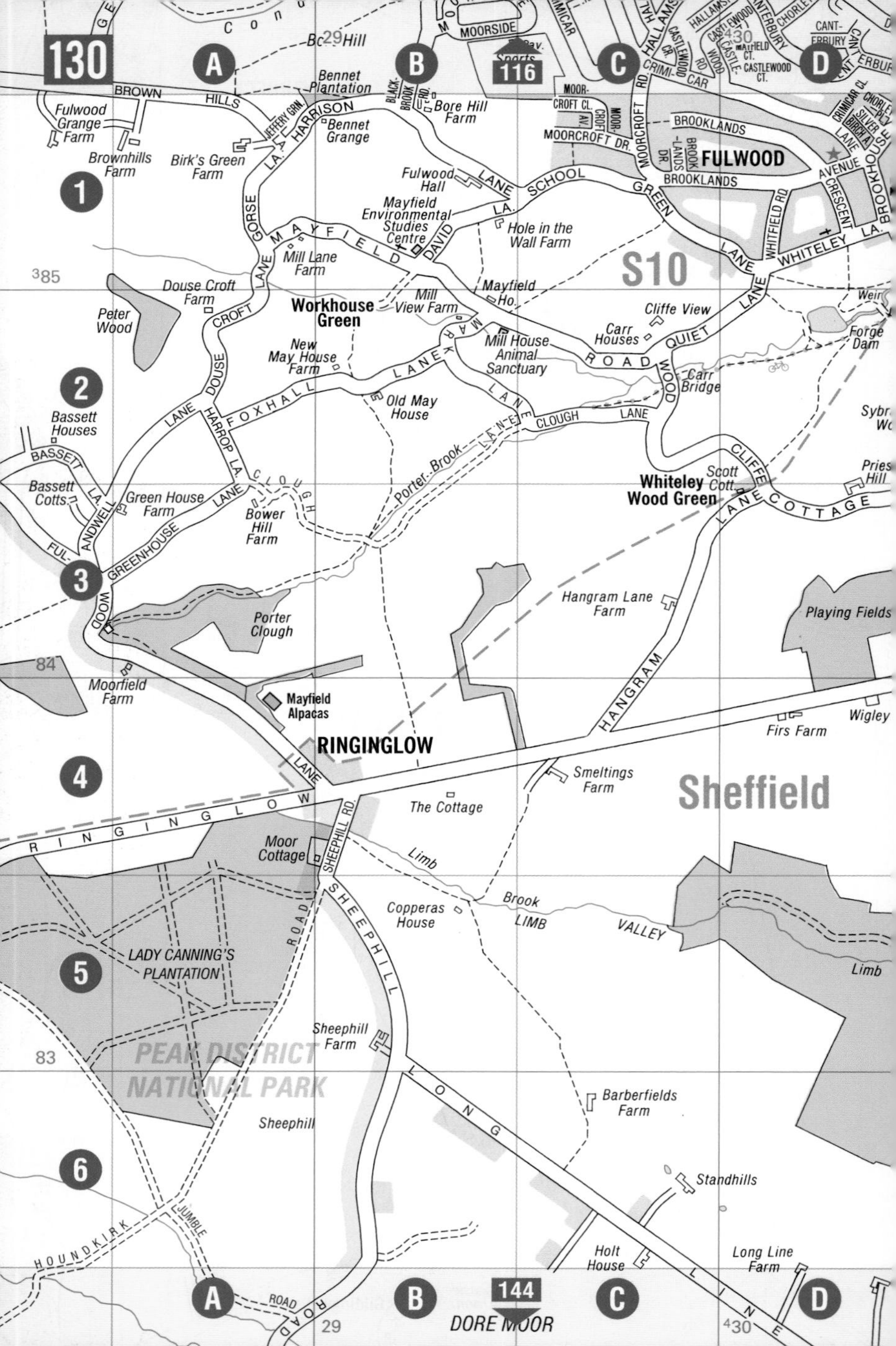

A
B
C
D
1
2
3
4
5
6
116
144
DORE MOOR
Bore Hill
Bennet Plantation
BROWN HILLS
Fulwood Grange Farm
Brownhills Farm
Birk's Green Farm
HARRISON LA.
Bennet Grange
Bore Hill Farm
MOORSIDE
Sports
FULWOOD
BROOKLANDS
MOORCROFT DR.
MOORCROFT RD
SCHOOL GREEN LANE
Fulwood Hall
Mayfield Environmental Studies Centre
DAVID LA.
Hole in the Wall Farm
S10
WHITELEY LA.
WHITFIELD RD
AVENUE
CRESCENT
BROOKHOUSE
GORSE LANE
MAYFIELD
Mill Lane Farm
Douse Croft Farm
Peter Wood
Workhouse Green
Mill View Farm
Mayfield Ho.
Cliffe View
Carr Houses
QUIET LANE
ROAD
Weir
Forge Dam
CROFT
DOUSE LANE
New May House Farm
MARK LANE
Mill House Animal Sanctuary
WOOD
Carr Bridge
Bassett Houses
BASSETT LA.
FOXHALL LANE
Old May House
CLOUGH LANE
Porter Brook
HARROP LA.
CLOUGH
Bassett Cotts.
Green House Farm
GREENHOUSE LANE
Bower Hill Farm
ANDWELL
FUL-
Whiteley Wood Green
Scott Cott.
CLIFFE
COTTAGE LANE
Priest Hill
Sybr Wo
WOOD
Porter Clough
Hangram Lane Farm
Playing Fields
84
Moorfield Farm
Mayfield Alpacas
RINGINGLOW
LANE
HANGRAM
Firs Farm
Wigley
Smeltings Farm
Sheffield
RINGINGLOW
The Cottage
Moor Cottage
SHEEPHILL RD.
Limb
Brook
Copperas House
LIMB VALLEY
Limb
LADY CANNING'S PLANTATION
ROAD
SHEEPHILL
PEAK DISTRICT NATIONAL PARK
Sheephill Farm
83
Sheephill
LONG LINE
Barberfields Farm
Standhills
HOUNDKIRK
JUMBLE
ROAD
Holt House
Long Line Farm
385
29
430

Nether Grn.
117
Hanging Water
BINGHAM PARK
Goole Green
Fulwood House
Whiteley Woods
Porter Bridge
Shepherd Wheel (Water Wheel)
Heald Wood
Bluebell Wood
Wire Mill Dam
Greystones Cliffe
GREYSTONES
Sports Ground
High Storrs School
Playing Field
Ecclesall Inf. Sch.
Ecclesall C of E Jun. Sch.
ECCLESALL
Hill Top
Bents Green School
Bents Green
Whiteley Wood Cottage
Meadow Farm
Silverdale School
Castle Dyke
Thryft Ho.
S11
Tennis Courts
Playing Fields
Manor Ho.
Holmwood Ho.
PARKHEAD
Little Common
Cricket Ground
Parkhead House
Clifford House
Hospice
Whirlow Farm
Whirlow Hall
Whirlow House
Whirlow Grange
Whirlow Court
WHIRLOW BROOK PARK
Whirlow Bridge
Whirlow Wheel (disused)
WHIRLOW
ECCLESALL WOOD
ECCLESALL ROAD
WHIRLOWDALE ROAD
ABBEY LANE
HATHERSAGE RD.
A625
B6375
B6068
132
145

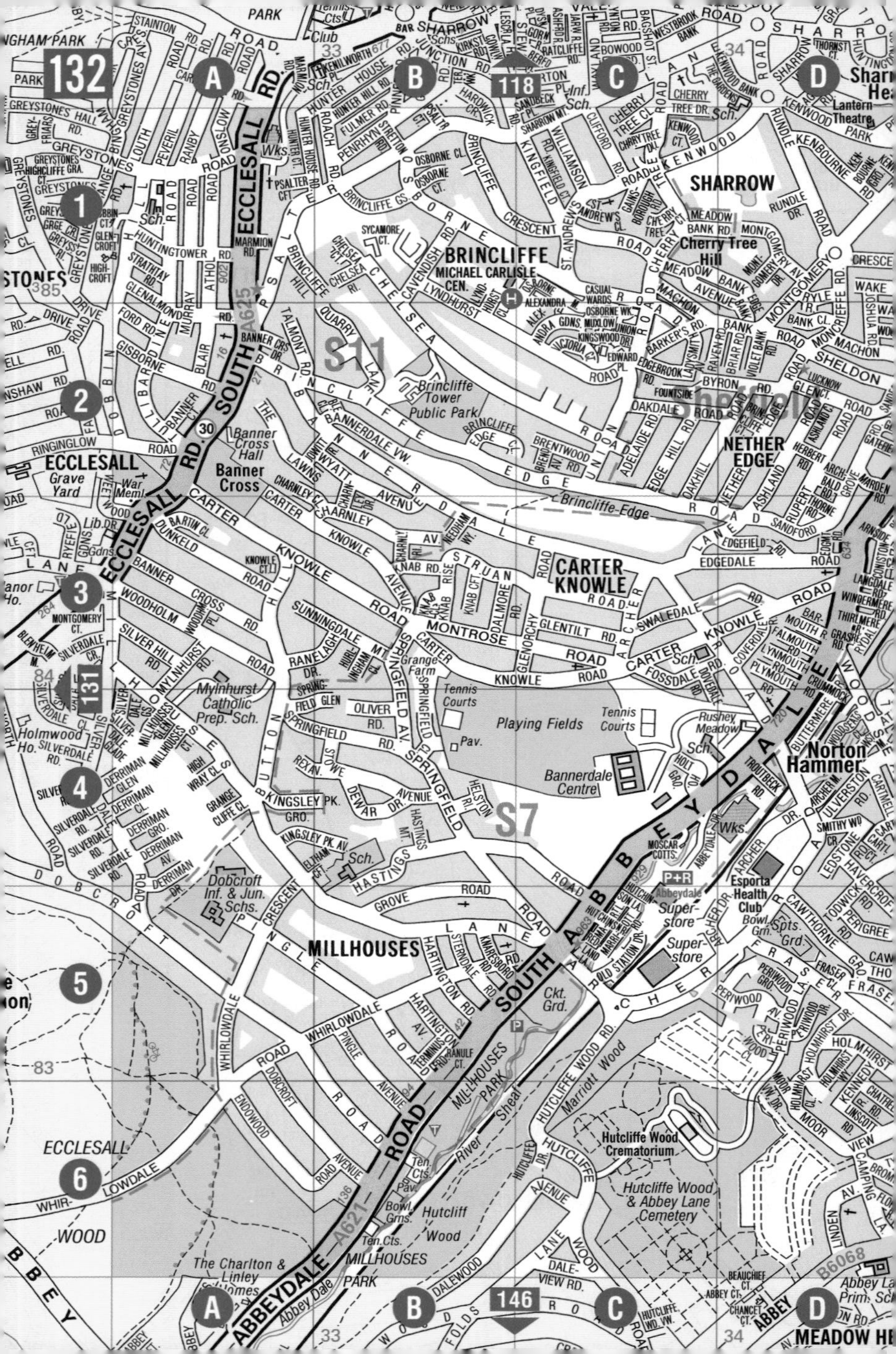
132
118
146
131
A
B
C
D
1
2
3
4
5
6
33
34
SHARROW
Cherry Tree Hill
BRINCLIFFE
MICHAEL CARLISLE CEN.
S11
Brincliffe Tower Public Park
NETHER EDGE
ECCLESALL
Grave Yard
War Meml.
Banner Cross Hall
Banner Cross
CARTER KNOWLE
Brincliffe Edge
Mylnhurst Catholic Prep. Sch.
Grange Farm
Tennis Courts
Playing Fields
Bannerdale Centre
Rushey Meadow
S7
Norton Hammer
Holmwood Ho.
Dobcroft Inf. & Jun. Schs.
MILLHOUSES
Abbeydale Superstore
Esporta Health Club
Ckt. Grd.
MILLHOUSES PARK
River Sheaf
Marriott Wood
Hutcliffe Wood Crematorium
Hutcliffe Wood & Abbey Lane Cemetery
Hutcliff Wood
ECCLESALL WOOD
The Charlton & Linley Sch. Homes
Abbey Dale
Lantern Theatre
ECCLESALL RD. SOUTH
A625
ABBEYDALE ROAD SOUTH
A621
ABBEYDALE RD.
B6068
GREYSTONES RD.
RINGINGLOW ROAD
CARTER KNOWLE ROAD
BANNERDALE RD.
BRINCLIFFE EDGE ROAD
KENWOOD ROAD
MONTGOMERY ROAD
SHELDON ROAD
SPRINGFIELD RD.
MILLHOUSES LANE
WHIRLOWDALE ROAD
DOBCROFT ROAD
HUTCLIFFE WOOD RD.
MEADOW HEAD
Abbey Lane Prim. Sch.

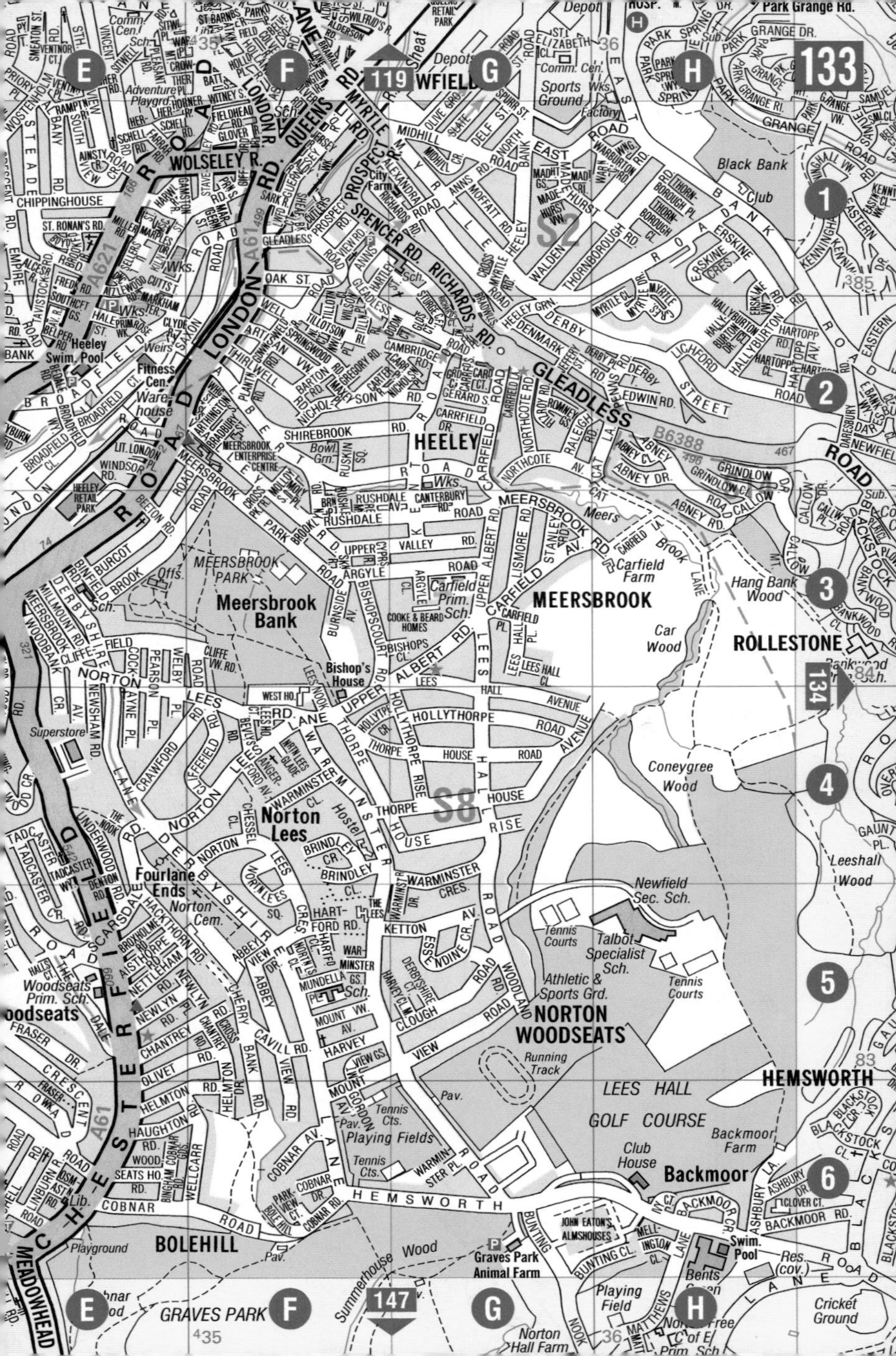
119
147
134
E
F
G
H
1
2
3
4
5
6
435
36
385
84
83
S2
S8
WOLSELEY R.
LONDON RD.
QUEENS RD.
A621
A61
B6388
CHIPPINGHOUSE
ST. RONAN'S RD.
Heeley Swim. Pool
Fitness Cen.
Warehouse
HEELEY RETAIL PARK
BROADFIELD RD.
MEERSBROOK PARK
Meersbrook Bank
Bishop's House
HEELEY
GLEADLESS ROAD
SPENCER RD.
RICHARDS RD.
PROSPECT RD.
MYRTLE RD.
City Farm
Sports Ground
Black Bank
Club
EAST BANK ROAD
DERBY STREET
LICHFORD
HARTOPP RD.
Carfield Farm
MEERSBROOK
Carfield Prim. Sch.
COOKE & BEARD HOMES
Car Wood
Hang Bank Wood
ROLLESTONE
Coneygree Wood
Leeshall Wood
HOLLYTHORPE ROAD
UPPER ALBERT RD.
NORTON LEES RD.
Norton Lees
Superstore
Fourlane Ends
Norton Cem.
DERBYSHIRE LANE
Woodseats Prim. Sch.
Woodseats
CHESTERFIELD ROAD
MEADOWHEAD
Newfield Sec. Sch.
Talbot Specialist Sch.
Tennis Courts
Athletic & Sports Grd.
NORTON WOODSEATS
Running Track
LEES HALL GOLF COURSE
Club House
Backmoor Farm
Backmoor
HEMSWORTH
HEMSWORTH ROAD
COBNAR ROAD
BOLEHILL
Playground
Playing Fields
Summerhouse Wood
Graves Park Animal Farm
GRAVES PARK
JOHN EATON'S ALMSHOUSES
Playing Field
Swim. Pool
Bents Green
Res. (cov.)
Cricket Ground
Norton Hall Farm
Norton Free C of E Prim. Sch.
BLACKSTOCK ROAD
Park Grange Rd.

134
A
B
C
D
1
2
3
4
5
6
120
133
148
Park Grange Rd.
Deep Pit
Spring Lane
Spring Lane Coll.
ARBOURTHORNE
Arbourthorne Sports Ground
Arbourthorne Rd.
Arbourthorne Prim. Sch.
Black Bank
Fairleigh
PRINCE OF WALES ROAD
CITY ROAD
A6135
Manor Top
Elm Tree
Elm Tree Hill
TA Centre
RIDGEWAY ROAD
A6102
S2
S14
S8
Springs Leisure Cen.
Sheffield Springs Academy
ARBOURTHORNE ESTATE
Pav.
GLEADLESS ROAD
B6388
Newfield Green
Comm. Cen.
Lib.
Paddock Hill
Buck Wood
Hurl Field
Common Side
Playing Field
Bankwood Prim. Sch.
ROLLESTONE
GLEADLESS
Meers Brook
Leeshall Wood
GLEADLESS VALLEY
Rollestone Wood
Herdings Wood
Gleadless Townend
Herdings
Herdings Park
Herdings/Leighton Rd.
Bowling Green
Tennis Cts.
HEMSWORTH
Backmoor Farm
Swim. Pool
Res. (cov.)
Cricket Ground
Depot
Skid Pans
Traffic Training Ground
Lightwood Ho.
Stoneley Wood
NORTON AVENUE
Hollins
37
38
83
84
85

135
E
F
G
H
121
39
40
1
2
3
4
5
6
RICHMOND
S13
Sports Ground
Pav.
Bowling Green
Tennis Courts
RICHMOND PARK
The City School
Field
Normanton Spring
NORMANTON SPRING RD.
NORMANTON HILL
B6064
WOODHOUSE RD.
RICHMOND ROAD
B6065
Four Lane Ends
Nature Reserve
Wickfield
Plantation
Intake Prim. Sch.
Playing Field
Cemy.
HOLLYBANK RD.
B6063
BIRLEY MOOR ROAD
A6135
HOLLINS END
Gleadless Prim. Sch.
Rec. Grd.
Sports Ground
Depot
Works
Factory
S12
Tennis Courts
Playing Field
Comm. Cen.
Lib.
Sports Ground
FRECHEVILLE
Birley Prim. School
Birley Nursy. Sch.
Birley Estate
Birley Comm. Coll.
Ten. Cts.
Playing Fields
Base Green
White La.
Charnock Hall Prim. Sch.
CHARNOCK HALL
Recreation Ground
B6388
Whitelane End
Eckington Leys
NORTH EAST DERBYSHIRE
SHEFFIELD
Sunny Bank
Birdfield
BIRLEY LANE
Birley Lane
Club House
BIRLEY WOOD GOLF COURSE
Birley Wood
136
149
St. Theresa's Catholic Prim. Sch.
Richmond Prim. Sch.
Prim. Sch.

A
B
C
D
122
150
135
1
2
3
4
5
6
41
42
385
84
83
Myrtle Bank
Beaver Hill
South Yorkshire Fire Station Training Centre
MOSBOROUGH PARKWAY
A57
B6066
HILL
Shirtcliff
Shirtcliff Wood
Shubert Bridge
Brook
WOODHOUSE
Grave Yard
Cemetery
RADBROKE ROAD
SHEFFIELD ROAD
B6064
Rec. Grd.
Playing Field
The City School
Woodhouse West Prim. Sch.
NORMANTON SPRING RD.
Normanton Spring
Plantation
COISLEY HILL
Coisley Hill
Shire Brook Valley
Nature Reserve
Shire Brook Visitors Centre
Works
Shire Brook
S13
S12
Sub.
Silkstone Nature Reserve
FRECHEVILLE
Birleyspa Wood
Birley Spa Prim. Sch.
Birley Spa
Cotleigh
Prim Sch.
HACKENTHORPE
Hackenthorpe
Rec. Grd.
Birley Moor Rd.
BIRLEY MOOR RD.
MOOR VALLEY
A6135
Rainbow Forge Prim. Sch.
Play. Fld.
BEIGHTON ROAD
Donetsk Way
OWLTHORPE
Ochre Dike
Medical Centre
BIRLEY WOOD GOLF COURSE
Birley Wood
Moorhole Farm

SWALLOWNEST
Fence
Woodhouse
Woodhouse Washlands Nature Reserve
Woodhouse Junction
Meadow Bank Farm
Playing Field
Sheffield
S26
Nature Reserve
Linleybank Meadow
MOSBOROUGH PARKWAY
A57
Starbuck Farm
Works
BEIGHTON
Beighton Sports and Leisure Club
Reignhead Prim. Sch.
S20
Drakehouse
DRAKE HOUSE RETAIL PARK
BECTON CENTRE
Sports Ground
Crystal Peaks
CRYSTAL PEAKS SHOPPING CENTRE
Beighton/ Drake Ho. La.
WATERTHORPE
Westfield Sports College
Sports Centre
SOTHALL
Brook House Jun. Sch.
Beighton Inf. Sch.
Park Hill Farm
B6200
B6064
B6053
ECKINGTON WAY
123
138
151

138
SWALLOWNEST
Park Hill Farm
Tennis Cts.
Comm. Cen.
ASTON BY-PASS
B6200
B6053
ROTHERHAM RD.
CHESTERFIELD RD.
HIGH ST.
MANSFIELD ROAD
A618
A57
ASTON
Aston Common
Great Bri.
Mill Stone Hill
Aston Lodge Prim. Sch.
Recreation Ground
Prim. Sch.
Works
Sewage Works
MOSBOROUGH PARKWAY
Sheffield
WALESWOOD
RIVER ROTHER
ROAD
Delves House
THE GREEN
Rose Cottage
Waleswood
DELVES
Boating Lake
ROTHER VALLEY LAKE
ROTHER VALLEY COUNTRY PARK
Bedgreave New Mill & Rother Valley Country Pk. Visitors Centre
ROTHER VALLEY GOLF COURSE
WALES COMM
Tennis Courts
Bowl. Grn.
Beighton Sports and Leisure Club
Brook House Jun. Sch.
Beighton Inf. Sch.
Play. Fld.
Cemy.
S20
SOTHALL
SHEFFIELD
ROTHERHAM
124
137
152

Conduit Moor or Conduit Common
125
Hardwick Lane Farm
Nursery
Netherthorpe
Cemetery
WORKSOP ROADS
B6067
THE WARREN
DAM INGS LA.
Croft Farm
Conduit House Farm
Orchard House
HARDWICK LA.
WORKSOP RD.
SHEFFIELD RD.
A57
ASTON COMMON
Lodge
GREEN LA.
MELTON CT.
Parklands
Common Farm Aston
GOOSECARR
Bleak Ho.
Farm Bungalow
Mona Terrace
ASTON
Hotel
Cricket Ground
Park Plantation
Junction 31
ASTON PARK
BY-PASS
Nicker Wood
M1
Aston Hall Jun. & Inf. Sch.
Engine House Plantation
Sewage Works
LANE
Fiddle Neck Pond
Upper Common Farm
FIDDLE NECK LANE
Union Plantation
M1 MOTORWAY
Hepworth Pond
Nickerwood Farm
NECK LANE
Bridge
Brook
Rookery Bottom
S26
Sewage Works
140
Low Laithes Farm
WALESWOOD RD.
WALESWOOD INDUSTRIAL ESTATE
WALES COURT
ORCHARD CFT.
ROAD
Playing Field
A618
MANSFIELD ROAD
WALESWOOD WY.
CRICKET FIELD LA.
Cricket Ground
WALESWOOD VILLAS
Pav.
Warehouses
Wales Bar
Works
HORSESHOE GDNS.
HORSE SHOE CL.
FORGE RD.
Kiveton Park Meadows Jun. Sch.
STORTH LA.
Wales High Sch.
BROOKLANDS CFT.
STORTH LANE
CYPRESS GRO.
OLD QUARRY AV.
POPLAR NOOK
LIMETREE
ASH GRO.
MAPLE RD.
CHESTNUT AV.
Play. Fld.
MANOR
BEECHES
HILL DR.
ROOKERY
CEDAR NOOK
MYRTLE GRO.
SCHOOL CL.
Club
LANE
SCHOOL ROAD
B6059
WALES ROAD
CHAPEL
FIR TREE DR.
GREEN OAK DR.
CHERRY TREE
ORCHARD LA.
SYCAMORE AV.
Lib.
Tens. Cts.
Wales Prim. Sch.
Play. Fld.
Wood Hill
M1
WALES
STREET
Grave Yard
CHURCH CL.
Wales Hall Farm
ROTHER-MOOR AV.
LITTLEMOOR AV.
HIGHMOOR AV.
FESTIVAL CL.
Tennis Courts
Rec. Grd.
GREENWAY
WALES MOOR
Sewage Works
High House Farm
CARLTON GA. DR.
LONGLANDS AV.
LAMBRELL AV.
NORWOOD CRESCENT
McLOUGHLIN WY.
CHURCH
HIGH HOUSE FM. CT.
STOCKWELL AV.
LAMB GRN.
153
Cemetery
Driving
E F G H
1 2 3 4 5 6
47 48

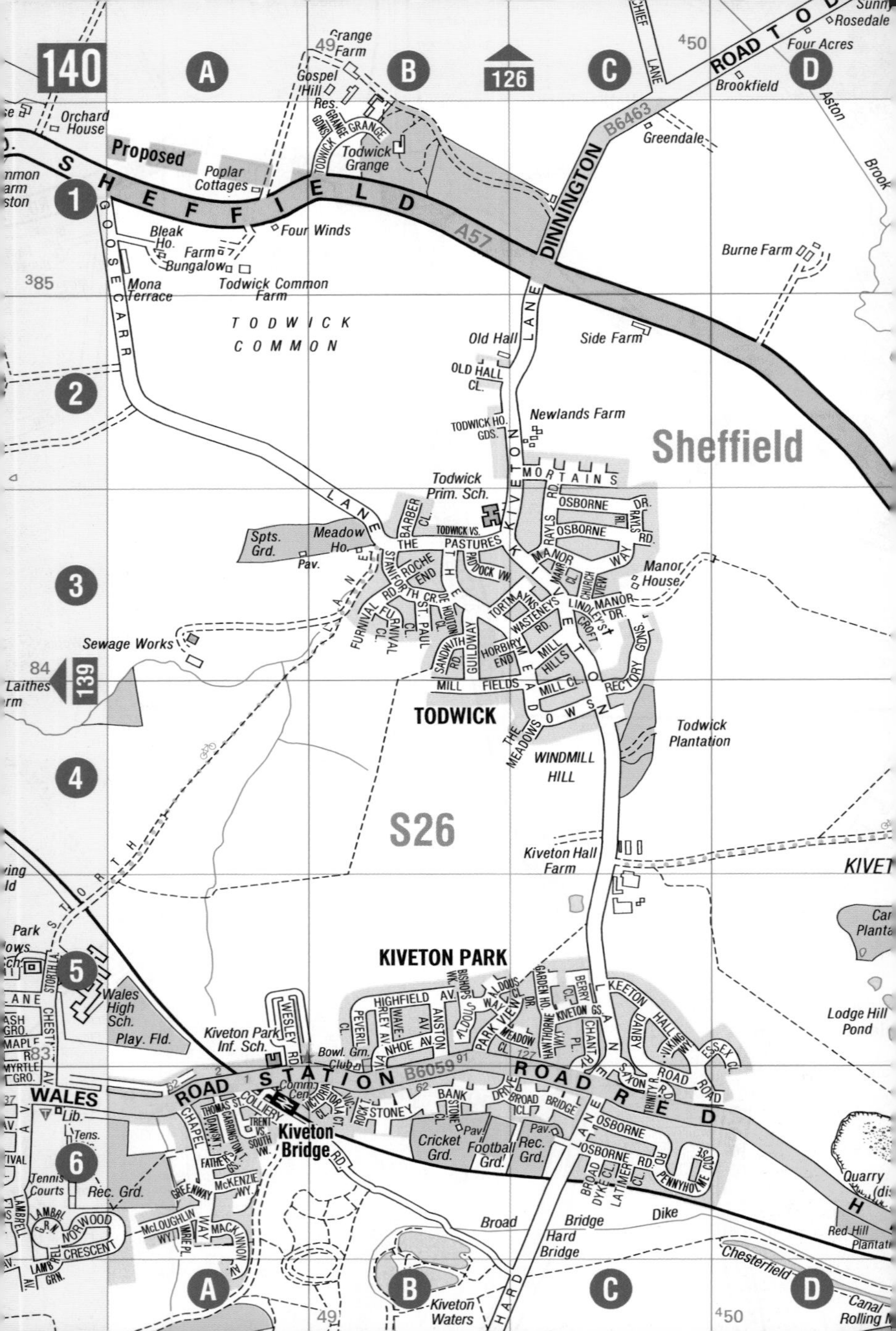
A
B
C
D
126
Grange Farm
Gospel Hill Res.
Todwick Grange
Orchard House
Proposed
Poplar Cottages
SHEFFIELD
A57
Four Winds
Bleak Ho.
Farm Bungalow
Mona Terrace
Todwick Common Farm
TODWICK COMMON
GOOSECARR
DINNINGTON
B6463
ROAD TO
Greendale
Brookfield
Four Acres
Rosedale
Aston
Brook
Burne Farm
Side Farm
Old Hall
OLD HALL CL.
Newlands Farm
TODWICK HO. GDS.
Sheffield
MORTAINS
OSBORNE DR.
RAYLS RD.
Todwick Prim. Sch.
LANE
Spts. Grd.
Meadow Ho.
Pav.
THE PASTURES
BARBER CL.
Manor House
MANOR DR.
ROCHE END
STANIFORTH RD.
Sewage Works
139
Laithes
MILL FIELDS
TODWICK
THE MEADOWS
WINDMILL HILL
Todwick Plantation
S26
Kiveton Hall Farm
KIVETON PARK
STORTH
Wales High Sch.
Play. Fld.
Kiveton Park Inf. Sch.
WESLEY RD.
Bowl. Grn. Club
STATION ROAD
B6059
ROAD
WALES
Lib.
Tens.
Tennis Courts
Rec. Grd.
Kiveton Bridge
Cricket Grd.
Football Grd.
Rec. Grd.
Broad Bridge Dike
Hard Bridge
Kiveton Waters
Chesterfield Canal
Quarry
Red Hill Plantation
Lodge Hill Pond
KIVET

127
142
NORTH ANSTON
SOUTH ANSTON
S25
Kiveton Park
Alcove Plantation
Cramfit Bridge
Caravan Park
Anston Greenlands Jun. & Inf. Schs.
Playing Fld.
Greenlands Park
The Bungalow
Anston Park Inf. & Jun. Schs.
Anston Hall
Works
Anston Bridge
Youth Club
Hall
Sch.
Sewage Works
Church Bridge
Rec. Grd.
Bowl. Grn.
Tennis Courts
Pav.
Cricket Grd.
Sykes Plantation
Anston Brook
Aston Brook
Crow Gate Hill
Prim. Sch.
Council Offices
Cemy.
Lodge Hill
Whin Covert
Quarry (disused)
Smarson Hills
Smarson Hills Plantation
WORKSOP ROAD
SHEFFIELD ROAD
NURSERY ROAD
RYTON ROAD
CROWGATE LANE
KENNELS LANE
DOG KENNELS
NEW ROAD
CRAMFIT ROAD
COMMON ROAD
WOODSETTS LANE
WINDMILL ROAD
MAIN STREET
HIGH ST.
WEST ST.
BANK
FIRST LANE
SECOND LANE
BRIDLE
THORPE
AXLE LANE

142

A   **B**   **C**   **D**

Plantation   54   Lodge Farm

ROAD

NURSERY

Anston Park Inf. & Jun Schs.

Burial Grd.

ROWERNFIELDS

White Walls Farm

Bradshaw Wood

Swinston Hill Farm

BRANDS HILL ROAD

Windmill Plantation

Tropical Butterfly House, Wildlife and Falconry Centre

Sheffield

S25

The Clump

WOODSETTS ROAD

84   141

Sykes Plantation

RACKFORD ROAD

Works

Rackford Farm

Little Stones

LANE   CRACKFORD

Dewidales Wood

Dew

Anston

ANSTON STONES WOOD

Cemy.

WORKSOP ROAD   A57

83

Brook

Lindrick Hill Farm

Hill Farm Cottage

LANE

Lindrick Bridge

Willow Green

LINDRICK GOLF COURSE

Lindrick Dale

Smarson Hills Plantation

FIRST   LANE   SECOND LANE

A HARRY CROFTS   53   **B** Anston Grange   **C**   54   **D**

Farm
Pear Tree Farm
129
RED QUARRY LANE
ROTHERHAM
Woodland Farm
Laneside Farm
Gildingwells
Sunny Bank Farm
Home Farm
BAULK
Brand's Woods
Wellswood Farm
WALLINGWELLS
LANE
WOODSETTS ROAD
Stone Heads Plantation
LANE
Brand's Farm
Owlands Wood Dike
Acorn Lodge
OAKLAND CL.
BRANDSMERE DR.
BASSETLAW
ROTHERHAM
WALLINGWELLS PARK
BRANDS CL.
Hoades Farm
AVENUE
DRIVE
Owlands Wood
Worksop
S81
NORTHFIELD
HOADES
SPRINGFIELD CL.
GILDINGWELLS
ROAD
LANE
BERNE SQ.
WHITFIELD
Pav.
Rec. Grd.
WORK
Woodsetts House
WOODSETTS
APPLE TREE CL.
Woodsetts Prim. Sch.
Manor Farm
PEAR TREE CL.
WARREN CL.
CROSS
MANOR FARM CFT.
LANE
CROSS LA.
LINDRICK CT.
CROSSFIELD DR.
Sewage Works
The Bottoms
Grange Farm
WELLFIELD CR.
SCHOLEY AVENUE
ROCKFIELD DR.
LIMESTONE CL.
CROSS
GRANGE FARM CT.
STAMBERS CL.
SCHOLEY
Owlands Wood Dike
AVENUE
Lofties Plantation
GRANGE AV.
TAYLOR CR.
TAYLOR DR.
Lindrick Lodge
LINDRICK
Socheage Hill
Cotterhill Woods High Farm
Orchard Cottage
Orchard House
Lofties
Woodside
BLACK
Cotterhill Woods LA.
Cotterhill Woods Farm
Lindrick Common Side
Quarry (Disused)
Birkett House
LINDRICK GOLF COURSE
Birket Wood
The Homestead
A57
ROAD
Quarry (Disused)
Deep Carr Farm
DEEP CARRS LA.
Deep Carrs
Rough Piece
LANE
OWDAY
Club House
Stubbings
455
56
385
84
83
E F G H
1 2 3 4 5 6

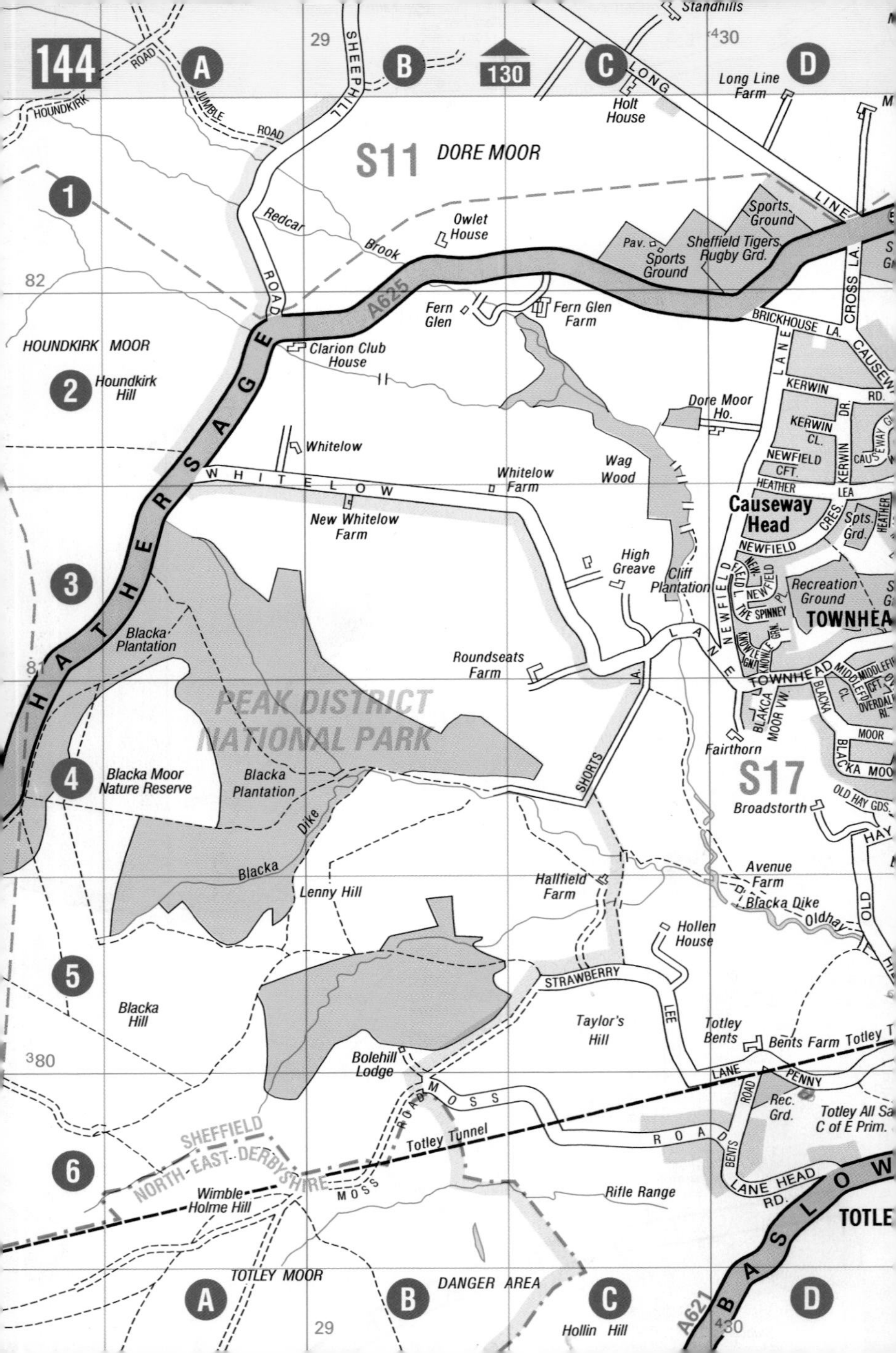
130
S11
DORE MOOR
S17
PEAK DISTRICT NATIONAL PARK
HATHERSAGE
A625
Standhills
Long Line Farm
Holt House
LONG LINE
SHEEPHILL ROAD
JUMBLE ROAD
HOUNDKIRK ROAD
Redcar Brook
Owlet House
Sports Ground
Sheffield Tigers Rugby Grd.
Pav.
Sports Ground
CROSS LA.
BRICKHOUSE LA.
Fern Glen
Fern Glen Farm
Clarion Club House
HOUNDKIRK MOOR
Houndkirk Hill
Dore Moor Ho.
KERWIN RD.
KERWIN CL.
KERWIN DR.
NEWFIELD CFT.
HEATHER LEA
Causeway Head
NEWFIELD CRES.
Spts. Grd.
Whitelow
WHITELOW
Whitelow Farm
New Whitelow Farm
Wag Wood
High Greave
Cliff Plantation
Recreation Ground
TOWNHEAD
THE SPINNEY
NEWFIELD LANE
Roundseats Farm
Blacka Plantation
LANE
TOWNHEAD
SHORTS LA.
BLACKA MOOR VW.
MIDDLEFIELD
OVERDALE RI.
Fairthorn
Blacka Moor Nature Reserve
Blacka Plantation
Blacka Dike
Broadstorth
OLD HAY GDS.
Lenny Hill
Hallfield Farm
Avenue Farm
Blacka Dike
Oldhay
Hollen House
STRAWBERRY LEE
Blacka Hill
Taylor's Hill
Totley Bents
Bents Farm
Bolehill Lodge
LANE
PENNY
Rec. Grd.
Totley All Saints C of E Prim.
MOSS ROAD
Totley Tunnel
BENTS ROAD
SHEFFIELD
NORTH EAST DERBYSHIRE
Wimble Holme Hill
Rifle Range
LANE HEAD RD.
BASLOW
A621
TOTLEY MOOR
DANGER AREA
Hollin Hill
29
430
82
81
380

WHIRLOWDALE ROAD
WHIRLOW
Whirlow Bridge
Whirlow Wheel (disused)
Ryecroft Glen
Sports Ground
131
WHIRLOW PARK
ABBEY LA B6068
1
ABBEYDALE
Tennis Courts
Sports Ground
The Moss
Square Plantation
Aldine House
Bird Sanctuary
ASH HOUSE LA.
Sports Ground
Ran Wood
S7
Ecclesall Woods Forest Walks
ECCLESALL WOOD
Abbeydale Industrial Hamlet (Museum)
Mill Pond
BRICK HOUSES
Pav.
Spts. Grd.
Limb Hill
Sheffield
Ryecroft Farm
Brook
Ryecroft Glen
SMEE Model Railway
2
Beauchief Garden
PARKERS LA.
RUSHLEY AV.
RUSHLEY
Ryecroft Glen Rd.
Limb Bridge
LADIES SPRING WOOD
DRIVE
HIGH STORES
LEYFIELD RD.
Road
LANE
FURNISS
CHURCH
OLD HAY
HAY BROOK
KINGS COPPICE
KINGS WD.
DORE
GREEN PASTURES
DORE LODGE
THORNSETT GNS.
VICTOR RD.
CAVENDISH
AVENUE
WATER
WOODLAND VIEW LANE
Dore & Totley
3
Club House
Nether Wood
81
146
MOOR
WINSTON CT.
SOUTH CT.
DORE HALL CROFT
BURLINGTON GRO.
DEVON-SHIRE DR.
BURLINGTON RD.
ASHFURLONG
CL.
ASHFURLONG RD.
Air Hall
(Abbeydale Park Cricket Grd.)
Bowl. Grn.
Abbeydale Park Sports Club
Tennis Cts.
Hockey Pitch
Rackets Club
TWENTYWELL
Dore Tunnel
Bradway Bank
4
King's Croft
Dore Prim. Sch.
GILLEYFIELD AVENUE
BUSHEY WOOD
Bushey Wood
DEVONSHIRE
ABBEYDALE PARK
DEVONSHIRE GRO.
DEVONSHIRE CT.
ABBEYDALE PARK
Devonshire Ct.
BRINKBURN VALE RD.
Brinkburn
RISE
PINE TREES WY.
PINE TREES
FIVE TREES
Poynton Wood
Poynton Wood
CASTLEROW VW.
Castlerow
CASTLE-ROW
CASTLEROW CL.
CASTLEROW DR.
Playing Field
DURVALE CT.
The Rowan Sch.
VERN GDNS.
VERNON
CHATSWORTH
WOOD ROAD
ABBEYDALE
BRINKBURN
POYNTON WOOD GLADE
ROSAMOND DR.
ROSAMOND
ROSAMOND GRO.
ROSAMOND GLADE
ROSAMOND PL.
ROSAMOND AV.
EVERARD DR.
AVENUE
TWENTYWELL VIEW
TWENTYWELL
King Ecgbert Sch.
MERCIA DR.
ECGBERT RD.
SHERWOOD CHASE
NAT. BANK
MILL LANE
VICTORIA
PROSPECT
ROAD
TOTLEY RISE
WOLLATON AV.
LONG FORD CL.
MOORWOOD
5
TOTLEY BROOK
BROOK GRO.
WESSEX CL.
BROOK
GROVE
CRESCENT
STONECROFT RD.
GROVE RD.
MILLDALE
WOODLAND RD.
LADYBOWER DR.
LONG FORD GRO.
PROSPECT RD.
Totley Grove
Aqueduct
QUARRY RD.
TERREY RD.
THE QUADRANT
GROVE
134
MAIN AVENUE
AVENDENE
QUEEN
ROAD
WOLLATON RD.
LONGFORD RD.
LONGFORD CR.
OX CLOSE AV.
A 380
Upper Bradway
Hillfoot
SHREWSBURY GRGE.
A621
175
LEMONT RD.
LAVEDE
LAVE
LAVENDER
GLOVER
MICKLEY LA.
Mickley Hall
SHEFFIELD
6
Mickley Farm
Totley Prim. Sch.
SUNNYVALE
MEADOW
GREEN OAKS
GREEN OAK
NEW TOTLEY
OAK
ALDAM RD.
ALDAM WY.
Brook
Cherry Tree
NORTH EAST DERBYSHIRE
S18
Works
TOTLEY HALL
HAVEN GRN.
GRN. OAK GRO.
St. George's Farm
Nursery
Totley Dell

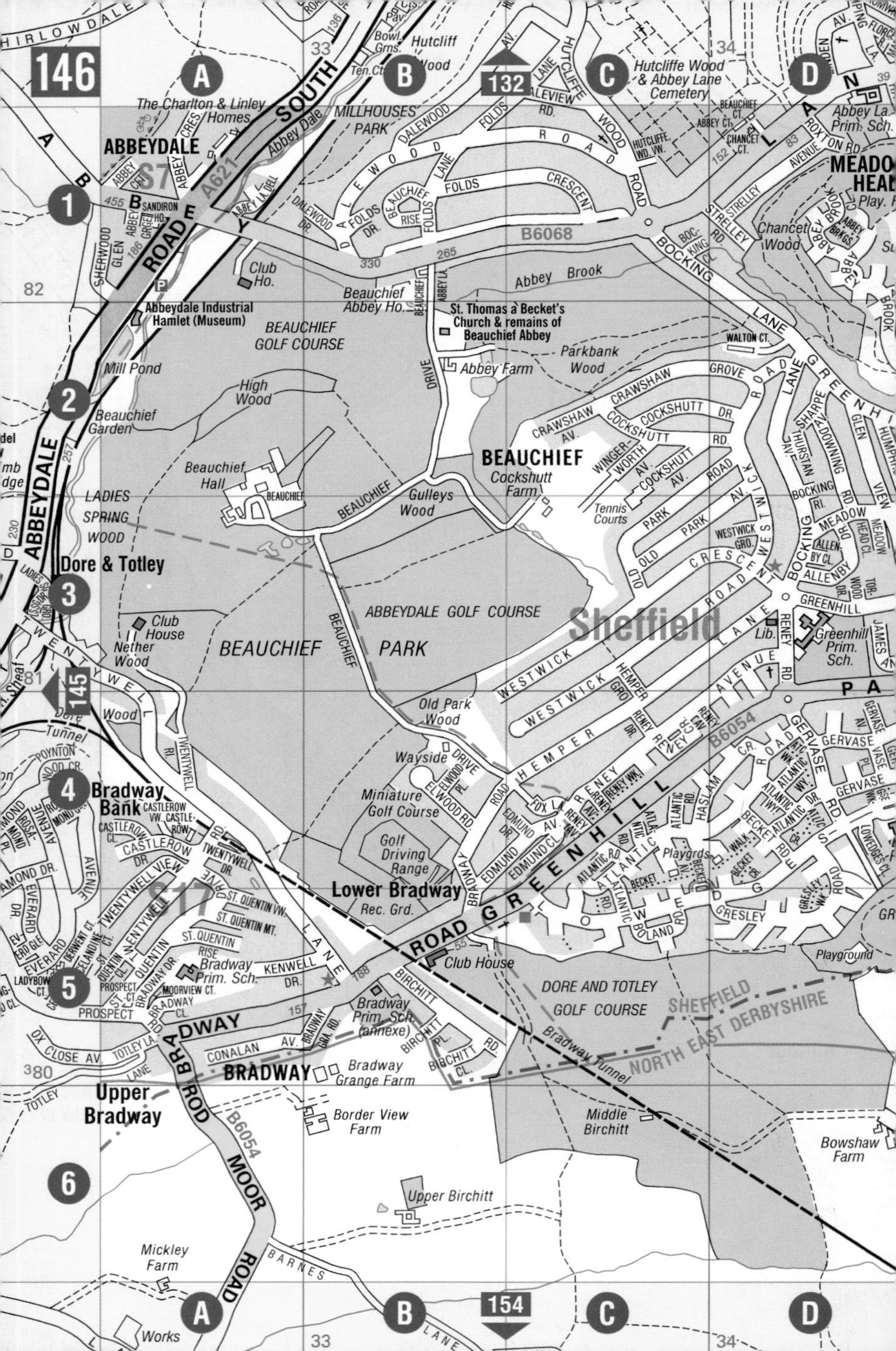

146
A
B
C
D
132
154
145
1
2
3
4
5
6
33
34
82
81
380
The Charlton & Linley Homes
ABBEYDALE
ABBEYDALE ROAD SOUTH
A621
Abbey Dale
MILLHOUSES PARK
Hutcliff Wood
Bowl. Grns.
Ten. Ct.
Hutcliffe Wood & Abbey Lane Cemetery
DALEWOOD RD.
DALEWOOD AV.
DALEWOOD DR.
FOLDS LANE
FOLDS CRESCENT
FOLDS DR.
BEAUCHIEF RISE
HUTCLIFFE WOOD ROAD
HUTCLIFFE WD. VW.
VALEVIEW RD.
ABBEY CT.
BEAUCHIEF CT.
CHANCET CT.
Abbey La. Prim. Sch.
ROXTON RD.
STRELLEY AVENUE
STRELLEY RD.
MEADOWHEAD
Chancet Wood
ABBEY BROOK
BOCKING LANE
BOCKING CL.
B6068
Abbey Brook
SHERWOOD GLEN
ABBEY CFT.
ABBEY CRES.
ABBEY GRGE.
ABBEY LA. DELL
SANDIRON HO.
S7
Club Ho.
Beauchief Abbey Ho.
ABBEY LA.
St. Thomas a Becket's Church & remains of Beauchief Abbey
Abbeydale Industrial Hamlet (Museum)
BEAUCHIEF GOLF COURSE
Mill Pond
High Wood
Abbey Farm
Parkbank Wood
WALTON CT.
Beauchief Garden
CRAWSHAW GROVE
CRAWSHAW AV.
COCKSHUTT DR.
COCKSHUTT RD.
COCKSHUTT AV.
WINGERWORTH AV.
BEAUCHIEF
Cockshutt Farm
Tennis Courts
Beauchief Hall
BEAUCHIEF DRIVE
Gulleys Wood
LADIES SPRING WOOD
OLD PARK ROAD
OLD PARK AV.
WESTWICK GRO.
WESTWICK CRESCENT
WESTWICK ROAD
GREENHILL LANE
THURSTAN AV.
SHARPE AV.
DOWNING RD.
BOCKING RI.
BOCKING HILL
MEADOW HEAD DR.
MEADOW HEAD CL.
ALLENBY CL.
ALLENBY DR.
GREENHILL
Dore & Totley
ABBEYDALE GOLF COURSE
Sheffield
Club House
Nether Wood
BEAUCHIEF PARK
Lib.
RENEY RD.
Greenhill Prim. Sch.
JAMES AV.
TWENTYWELL LANE
HEMPER GRO.
HEMPER LANE
AVENUE
PARK
Dore Tunnel
Wood
Old Park Wood
WESTWICK GRO.
HEMPER DR.
RENEY DR.
RENEY CR.
RENEY AV.
RENEY WK.
B6054
GERVASE AV.
GERVASE RD.
GERVASE DR.
TWENTYWELL RI.
POYNTON WOOD CR.
Wayside
ELWOOD PL.
ELWOOD RD.
HEMPER ROAD
FOX LA.
EDMUND DR.
EDMUND AV.
EDMUND CL.
HASLAM CR.
ATLANTIC RD.
ATLANTIC DR.
ATLANTIC WAY
Bradway Bank
CASTLEROW VW.
CASTLEROW CL.
CASTLEROW DR.
Miniature Golf Course
Golf Driving Range
Playgrds.
BECKET RD.
BECKET WALK
BECKET CR.
LOWEDGES RD.
TWENTYWELL VIEW
TWENTYWELL DR.
ST. QUENTIN VW.
ST. QUENTIN MT.
ST. QUENTIN RISE
S17
Lower Bradway
Rec. Grd.
GREENHILL ROAD
GRESLEY RD.
BOLAND RD.
Playground
EVERARD AVENUE
EVERARD DR.
LADYBOWER
KENWELL DR.
Bradway Prim. Sch.
MOORVIEW CT.
PROSPECT
Club House
BIRCHITT RD.
BIRCHITT PL.
BIRCHITT CL.
DORE AND TOTLEY GOLF COURSE
SHEFFIELD
NORTH EAST DERBYSHIRE
Bradway Prim. Sch. (annexe)
BRADWAY
BRADWAY RD.
CONALAN AV.
TOTLEY LA.
Bradway Tunnel
Bradway Grange Farm
BRADWAY
Upper Bradway
Border View Farm
Middle Birchitt
Bowshaw Farm
MOOR ROAD
Upper Birchitt
Mickley Farm
BARNES LANE
Works

BOLEHILL
GRAVES PARK
Cobnar Wood
Summerhouse Wood
Waterfall Wood
Miniature Golf Course
Boating Lake
Norton Hall Farm
Norton Hall Yard
NORTON
Little Norton
OAKS PARK
Cricket Ground
Norton Green
GREENHILL
Graves Tennis & Leisure Cen.
The Sheffield College (Norton Cen.)
Meadowhead School
Mossbrook School
Jordanthorpe Plantation
JORDANTHORPE
Coalpit Wood
Sheffield Trans. Dept. Golf Course
Sports Ground
BATEMOOR
LOWEDGES
New Leaf Nurseries
Ockley Farm
Dronfield
S8
S18
Upper Birchett Farm
Henpepper Farm
Holmefield Farm
West View Poultry Farm
Little Holme Farm
COAL ASTON
HOLMLEY COMMON
Bowshaw
MEADOWHEAD
CHESTERFIELD RD.
DRONFIELD BY-PASS
JORDANTHORPE PARKWAY
BOCHUM PARKWAY
(SHEFFIELD OUTER RING ROAD)
ECKINGTON RD.
A61
A6102
B6057
B6158
B6056
133
148
155

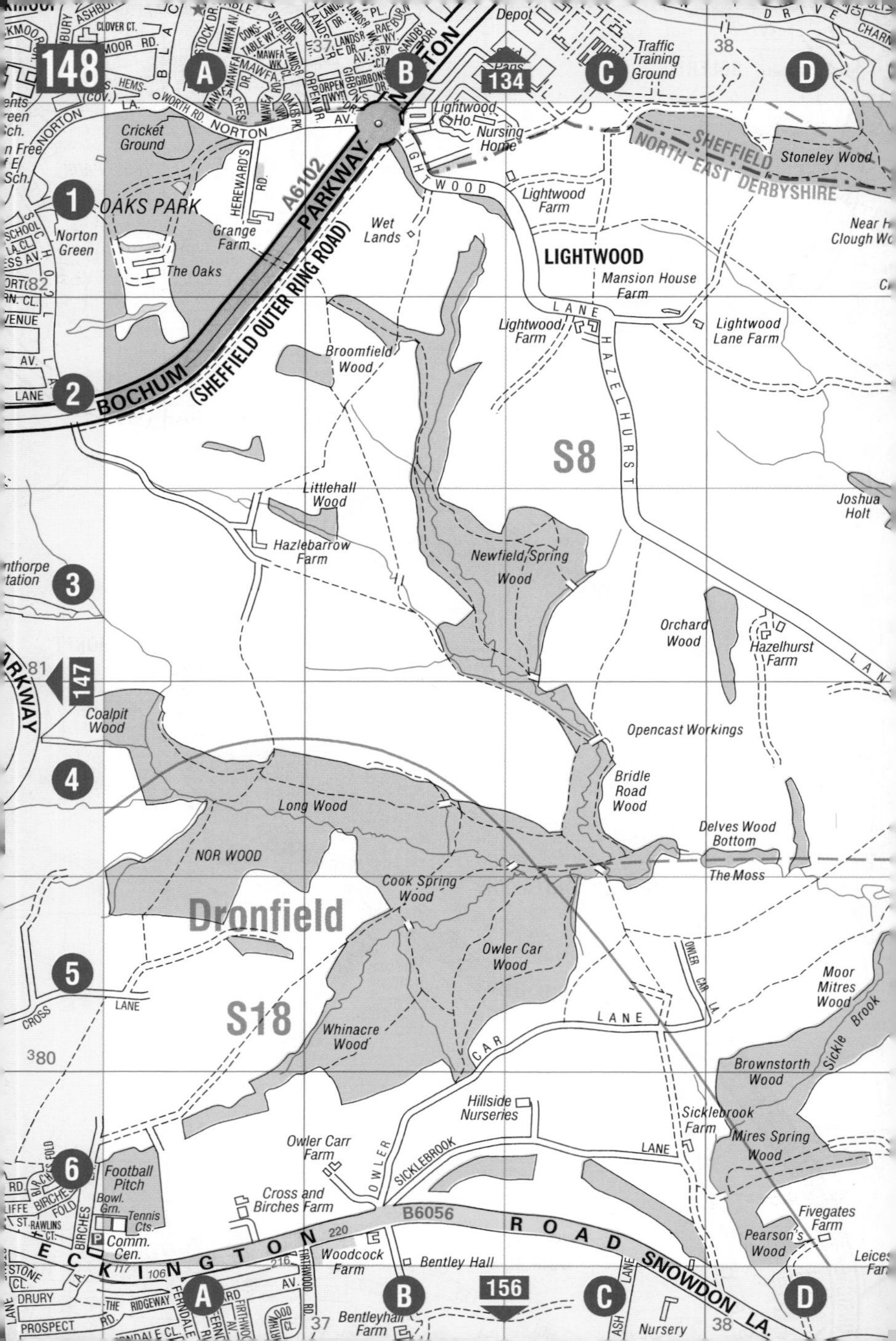
A
B
C
D
1
2
3
4
5
6
134
147
156
Depot
Traffic Training Ground
Cricket Ground
OAKS PARK
Norton Green
Grange Farm
The Oaks
Lightwood Ho.
Nursing Home
SHEFFIELD
NORTH EAST DERBYSHIRE
Stoneley Wood
Lightwood Farm
LIGHTWOOD
Mansion House Farm
Lightwood Lane Farm
Near H Clough Wo
Wet Lands
A6102
PARKWAY
BOCHUM
(SHEFFIELD OUTER RING ROAD)
NORTON
NORTON AV.
HEREWARD'S RD.
LIGHTWOOD LANE
HAZELHURST LANE
Broomfield Wood
S8
Littlehall Wood
Hazlebarrow Farm
Newfield Spring Wood
Joshua Holt
Orchard Wood
Hazelhurst Farm
Opencast Workings
Coalpit Wood
Bridle Road Wood
Long Wood
NOR WOOD
Delves Wood Bottom
The Moss
Cook Spring Wood
Dronfield
Owler Car Wood
S18
Whinacre Wood
OWLER CAR LA.
CAR LANE
CROSS LANE
Moor Mitres Wood
Sickle Brook
Brownstorth Wood
Hillside Nurseries
Sicklebrook Farm
Mires Spring Wood
Owler Carr Farm
OWLER
SICKLEBROOK LANE
Cross and Birches Farm
Football Pitch
Bowl. Grn.
Tennis Cts.
Comm. Cen.
B6056
ECKINGTON ROAD
SNOWDON LA.
Woodcock Farm
Bentley Hall
Fivegates Farm
Pearson's Wood
Bentleyhall Farm
Nursery
ASH LANE
FIRTHWOOD RD.
THE RIDGEWAY
FERNDALE RD.
PROSPECT RD.
DRURY LANE
BIRCHES FOLD
RAWLINS CT.
37
38
380
381
382

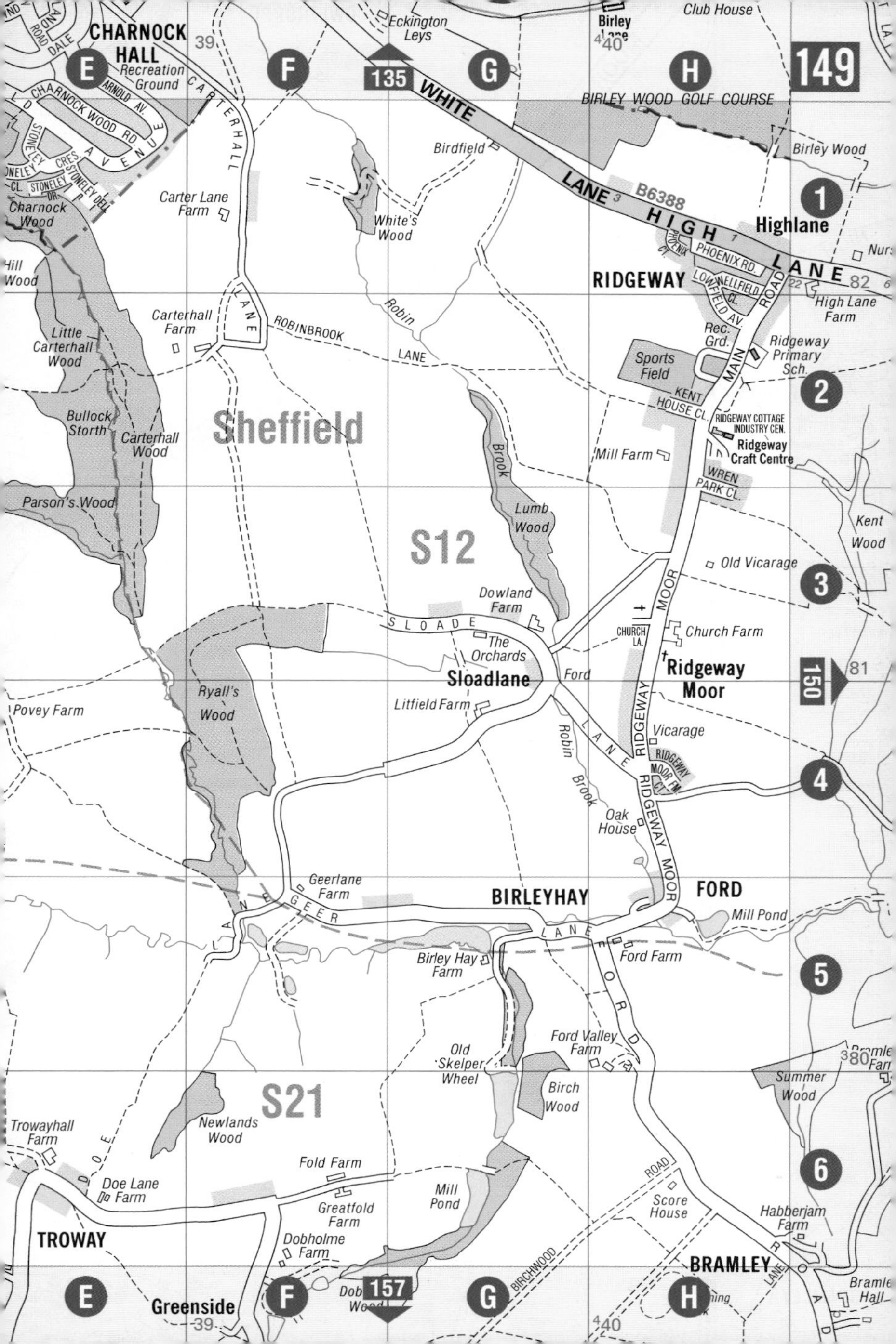
CHARNOCK HALL
Recreation Ground
Eckington Leys
Birley Lane
Club House
135
WHITE LANE
BIRLEY WOOD GOLF COURSE
Birley Wood
Birdfield
B6388
HIGH LANE
Highlane
RIDGEWAY
High Lane Farm
Carter Lane Farm
White's Wood
Charnock Wood
Hill Wood
Carterhall Farm
ROBINBROOK LANE
Little Carterhall Wood
Bullock Storth
Carterhall Wood
Sheffield
Sports Field
Rec. Grd.
Ridgeway Primary Sch.
RIDGEWAY COTTAGE INDUSTRY CEN.
Ridgeway Craft Centre
Mill Farm
Parson's Wood
Lumb Wood
S12
Kent Wood
Old Vicarage
Dowland Farm
SLOADE
The Orchards
Sloadlane
Church Farm
Ridgeway Moor
150
Ford
Litfield Farm
Ryall's Wood
Povey Farm
Vicarage
Oak House
Geerlane Farm
BIRLEYHAY
FORD
Mill Pond
GEER LANE
Birley Hay Farm
Ford Farm
Ford Valley Farm
Old Skelper Wheel
Birch Wood
Summer Wood
S21
Newlands Wood
Trowayhall Farm
Doe Lane Farm
Fold Farm
Mill Pond
Greatfold Farm
Score House
Habberjam Farm
TROWAY
Dobholme Farm
BRAMLEY
Greenside
157
Bramley Hall

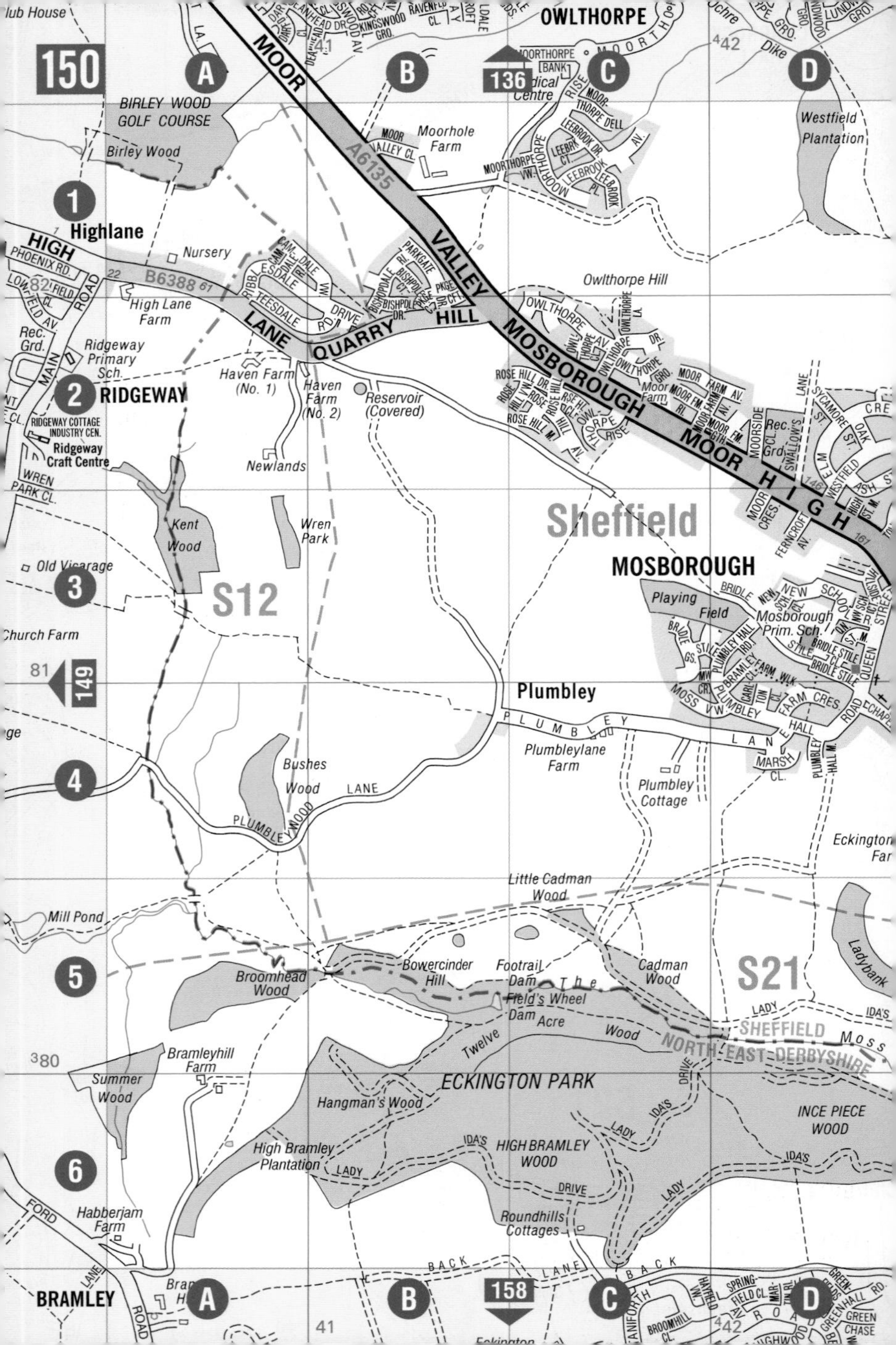
OWLTHORPE
136
Moorhole Farm
BIRLEY WOOD GOLF COURSE
Birley Wood
Westfield Plantation
Highlane
Nursery
B6388
High Lane Farm
Ridgeway Primary Sch.
RIDGEWAY
Ridgeway Craft Centre
Haven Farm (No. 1)
Haven Farm (No. 2)
Reservoir (Covered)
Newlands
Owlthorpe Hill
MOOR VALLEY
A6135
MOSBOROUGH MOOR HIGH
QUARRY HILL
Kent Wood
Wren Park
Old Vicarage
S12
Sheffield
MOSBOROUGH
Playing Field
Mosborough Prim. Sch.
Church Farm
149
Plumbley
PLUMBLEY LANE
Plumbleylane Farm
Plumbley Cottage
Bushes Wood
PLUMBLEY WOOD LANE
Eckington Far
Little Cadman Wood
Mill Pond
Bowercinder Hill
Footrail Dam
Cadman Wood
S21
Ladybank
Broomhead Wood
The Field's Wheel Dam
Twelve Acre Wood
SHEFFIELD
NORTH EAST DERBYSHIRE
Bramleyhill Farm
Summer Wood
ECKINGTON PARK
Hangman's Wood
INCE PIECE WOOD
High Bramley Plantation
HIGH BRAMLEY WOOD
LADY IDA'S DRIVE
Roundhills Cottages
Habberjam Farm
BACK LANE
BRAMLEY
158

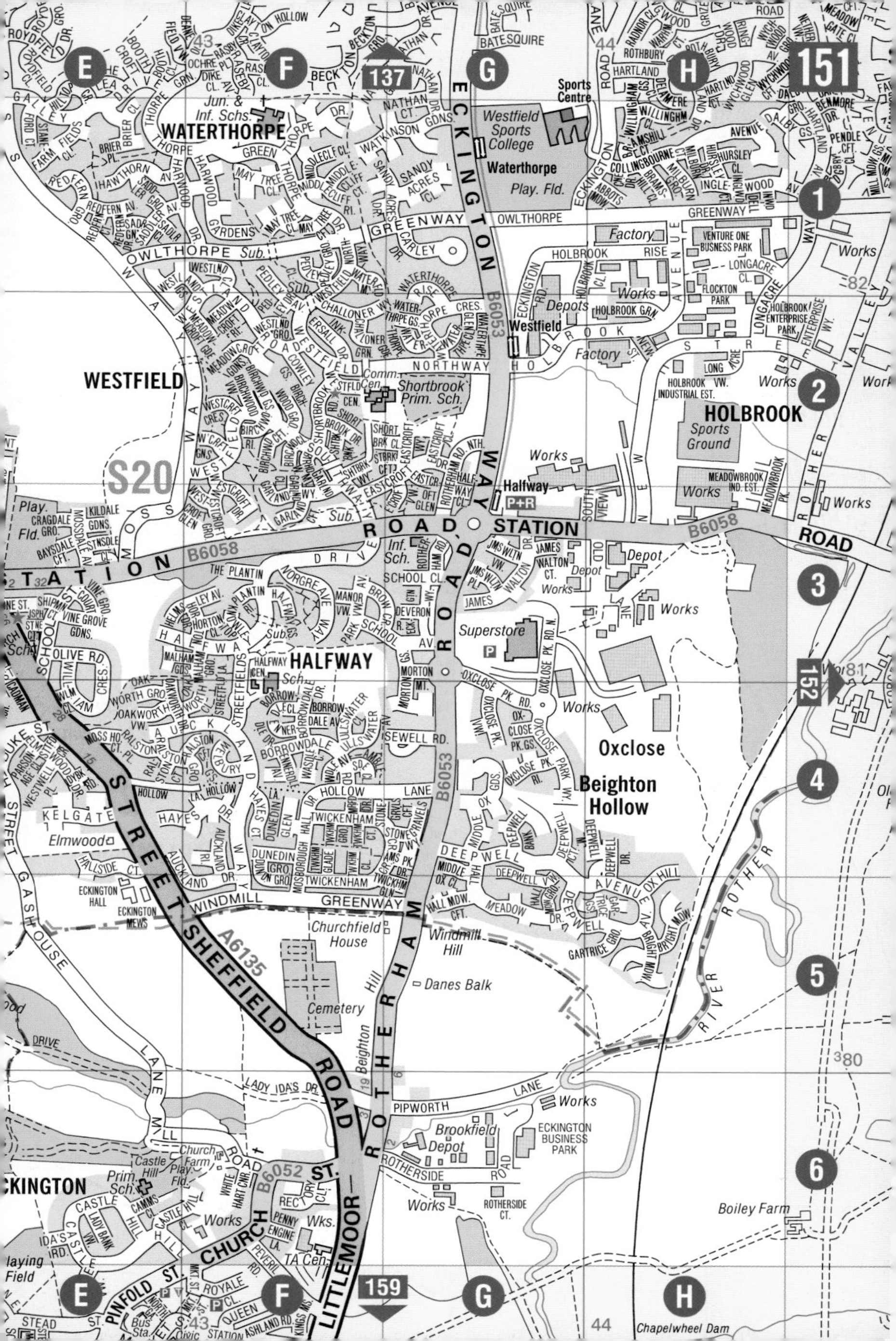

E
F
G
H
137
WATERTHORPE
Jun. & Inf. Schs.
Westfield Sports College
Sports Centre
Waterthorpe Play. Fld.
ECKINGTON WAY
GREENWAY
OWLTHORPE
Factory
VENTURE ONE BUSINESS PARK
Works
HOLBROOK RISE
LONGACRE
FLOCKTON PARK
HOLBROOK ENTERPRISE PARK
Depots
Westfield
HOLBROOK GRN
NORTHWAY
WESTFIELD
Comm. Cen.
Shortbrook Prim. Sch.
HOLBROOK INDUSTRIAL EST.
HOLBROOK
Sports Ground
MEADOWBROOK IND. EST.
S20
Halfway
P+R
STATION ROAD
B6058
B6053
ROTHER VALLEY WAY
Play. Fld.
Inf. Sch.
Superstore
HALFWAY
Oxclose
Beighton Hollow
152
ROTHERHAM ROAD
SHEFFIELD STREET
A6135
GASHOUSE LANE
Elmwood
ECKINGTON HALL
ECKINGTON MEWS
WINDMILL GREENWAY
Churchfield House
Windmill Hill
Danes Balk
Cemetery
Beighton Hill
RIVER ROTHER
PIPWORTH LANE
LADY IDA'S DR.
Brookfield Depot
ECKINGTON BUSINESS PARK
ROTHERSIDE ROAD
ROTHERSIDE CT.
Boiley Farm
ECKINGTON
Castle Hill Prim. Sch.
Church Farm
Play. Fld.
B6052
CHURCH ST.
LITTLEMOOR
TA Cen.
Wks.
159
Chapelwheel Dam
1
2
3
4
5
6

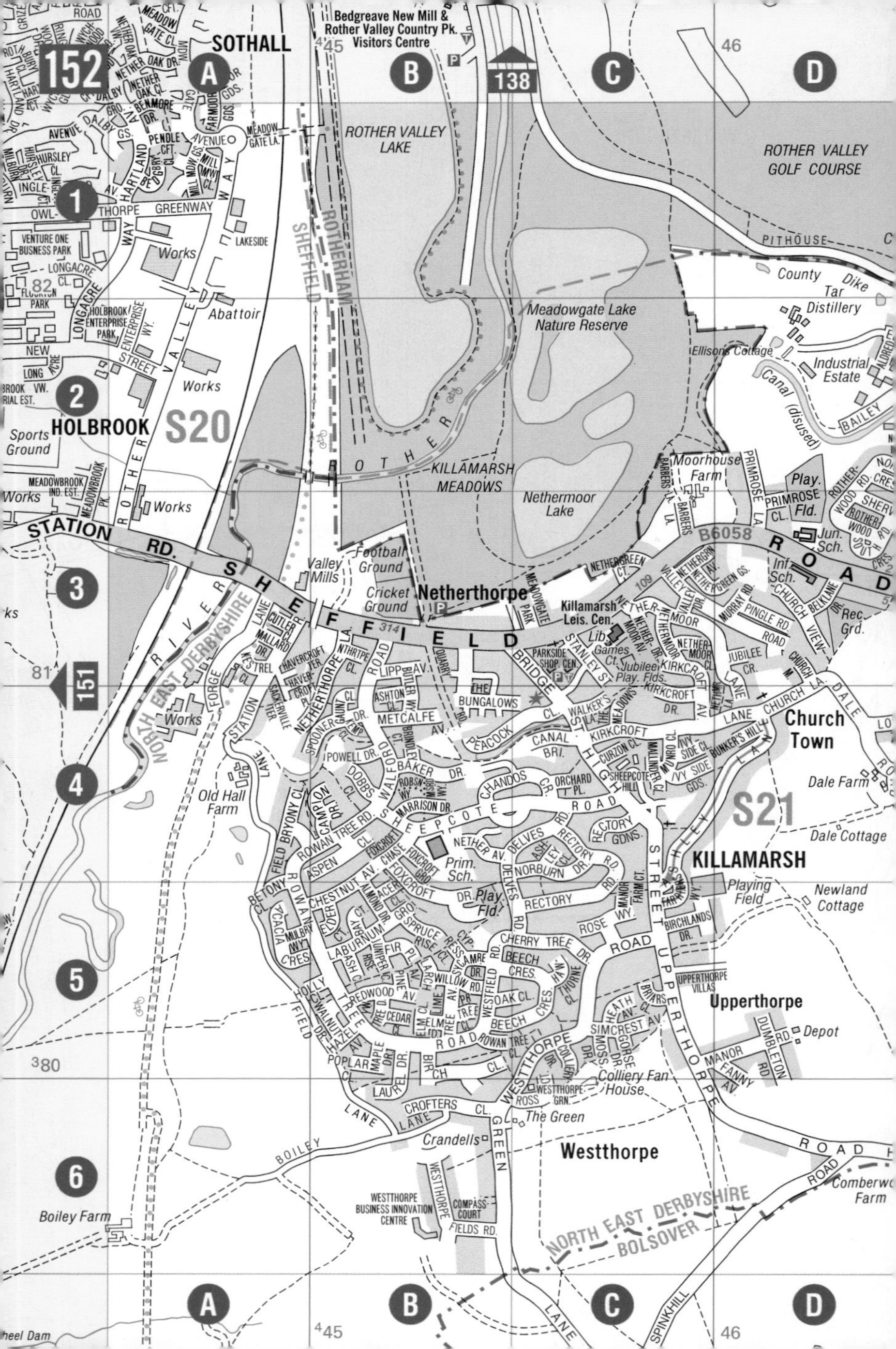
152
SOTHALL
Bedgreave New Mill & Rother Valley Country Pk. Visitors Centre
138
A
B
C
D
45
46
ROTHER VALLEY LAKE
ROTHER VALLEY GOLF COURSE
PITHOUSE
County Dike
Tar Distillery
Ellisons Cottage
Industrial Estate
Canal (disused)
BAILEY
Meadowgate Lake Nature Reserve
ROTHERHAM
SHEFFIELD
Works
Lakeside
Abattoir
VENTURE ONE BUSINESS PARK
LONGACRE
FLOURTON PARK
HOLBROOK ENTERPRISE PARK
ENTERPRISE WY.
NEW STREET
LONG ACRE
HOLBROOK
Sports Ground
S20
MEADOWBROOK IND. EST.
ROTHER VALLEY WAY
OWLTHORPE GREENWAY
STATION RD.
SHEFFIELD ROAD
B6058
RIVER ROTHER
KILLAMARSH MEADOWS
Nethermoor Lake
Moorhouse Farm
PRIMROSE LA.
Play. Fld.
Jun. Sch.
Inf. Sch.
Rec. Grd.
Valley Mills
Football Ground
Cricket Ground
Netherthorpe
Killamarsh Leis. Cen.
Lib.
Games Ct.
Jubilee Play. Flds.
PARKSIDE SHOP. CEN.
NORTH EAST DERBYSHIRE
Old Hall Farm
Church Town
Dale Farm
Dale Cottage
S21
KILLAMARSH
Playing Field
Newland Cottage
Prim. Sch.
Play. Fld.
Upperthorpe
Depot
UPPERTHORPE
Colliery Fan House
The Green
Crandells
Westthorpe
WESTTHORPE BUSINESS INNOVATION CENTRE
COMPASS COURT
FIELDS RD.
Boiley Farm
BOILEY LANE
Comberwood Farm
NORTH EAST DERBYSHIRE
BOLSOVER
SPINKHILL LANE
151
81
82
380
Wheel Dam
1
2
3
4
5
6

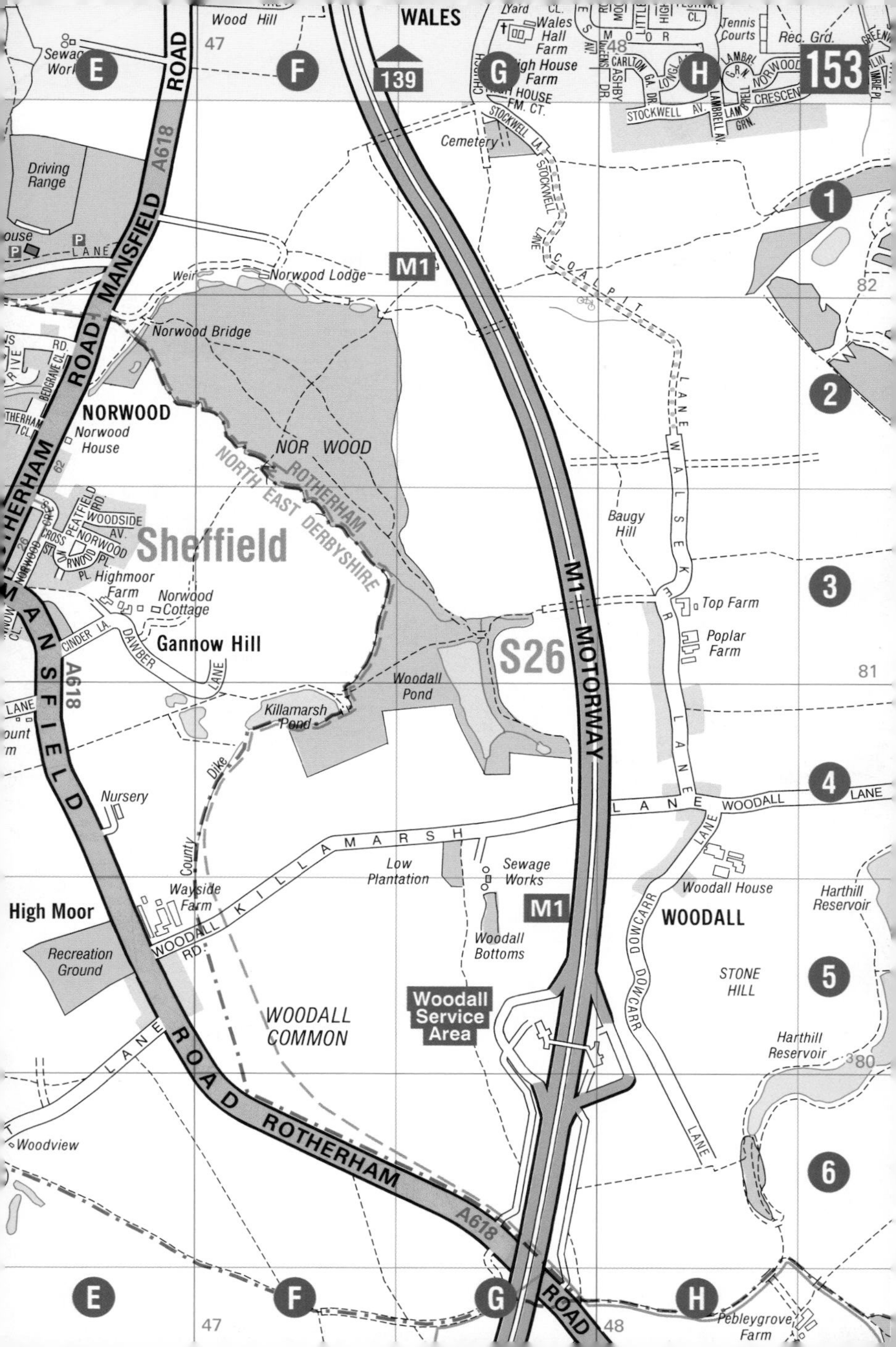
WALES
139
Wood Hill
Sewage Works
Driving Range
Norwood Lodge
Weir
Norwood Bridge
NORWOOD
Norwood House
NOR WOOD
ROTHERHAM
NORTH EAST DERBYSHIRE
Sheffield
Highmoor Farm
Norwood Cottage
Gannow Hill
Killamarsh Pond
Woodall Pond
S26
Baugy Hill
Top Farm
Poplar Farm
Cemetery
Wales Hall Farm
High House Farm
Tennis Courts
Rec. Grd.
M1 MOTORWAY
Nursery
High Moor
Wayside Farm
Recreation Ground
Low Plantation
Sewage Works
Woodall Bottoms
Woodall Service Area
WOODALL COMMON
WOODALL
Woodall House
STONE HILL
Harthill Reservoir
Woodview
Pebleygrove Farm
MANSFIELD ROAD
ROTHERHAM ROAD
KILLAMARSH LANE
WOODALL LANE
WOODALL RD.
DOWCARR LANE
WALSEKER LANE
COALPIT LANE
STOCKWELL LANE
County Dike
A618

146
Upper Birchitt
Mickley Farm
Works
Mickley
Dunston Farm
Rod Moor
Northern Common Farm
Moorview Farm
Barnes Farm
Hall Farm
Birchin Lee Farm
William Levick Prim. Sch.
Sports Grd.
Club
Playing Field
DRONFIELD WOODHOUSE
Gorseybrigg Prim. Sch.
Sch.
Sindelfingen Park
Stubley Riding
Marwell Ho.
East Hollow
Holmesfield
Sewage Works
Ravenswood
Four Acres
Kitchen Wood
Wood End Farm
Hills Farm
Spring Wood
Springwood Farm
Dronfield
The Tradewinds
S18
Cartledge
Cowley Hall
Green Paddocks
Green Wood
Greenfield Farm
Cowley
Spa House Farm
Grange Farm
Active Workings
Westwood
Lees Wood
Black Carr Lumb
Great Brind Wood
Cartledge Wood
Little Brind Wood
Peakley Hill
Peakley Hill Farm
Youth Hostel
Barlow Lees
Barlow Lees Farm
Lees Brid
ROD MOOR RD.
NORTHERN COMMON RD.
MICKLEY LANE
BARNES LANE
STUBLEY LANE
CARR LANE
HOLMESFIELD ROAD
MAIN ROAD
COWLEY LANE
GOSFORTH ROAD
CROFT ROAD
BARNES AVENUE
STUBLEY DRIVE
DOBBIN LANE
BARLOW LEES LANE
KITCHEN WOOD LANE
B6054
B6056

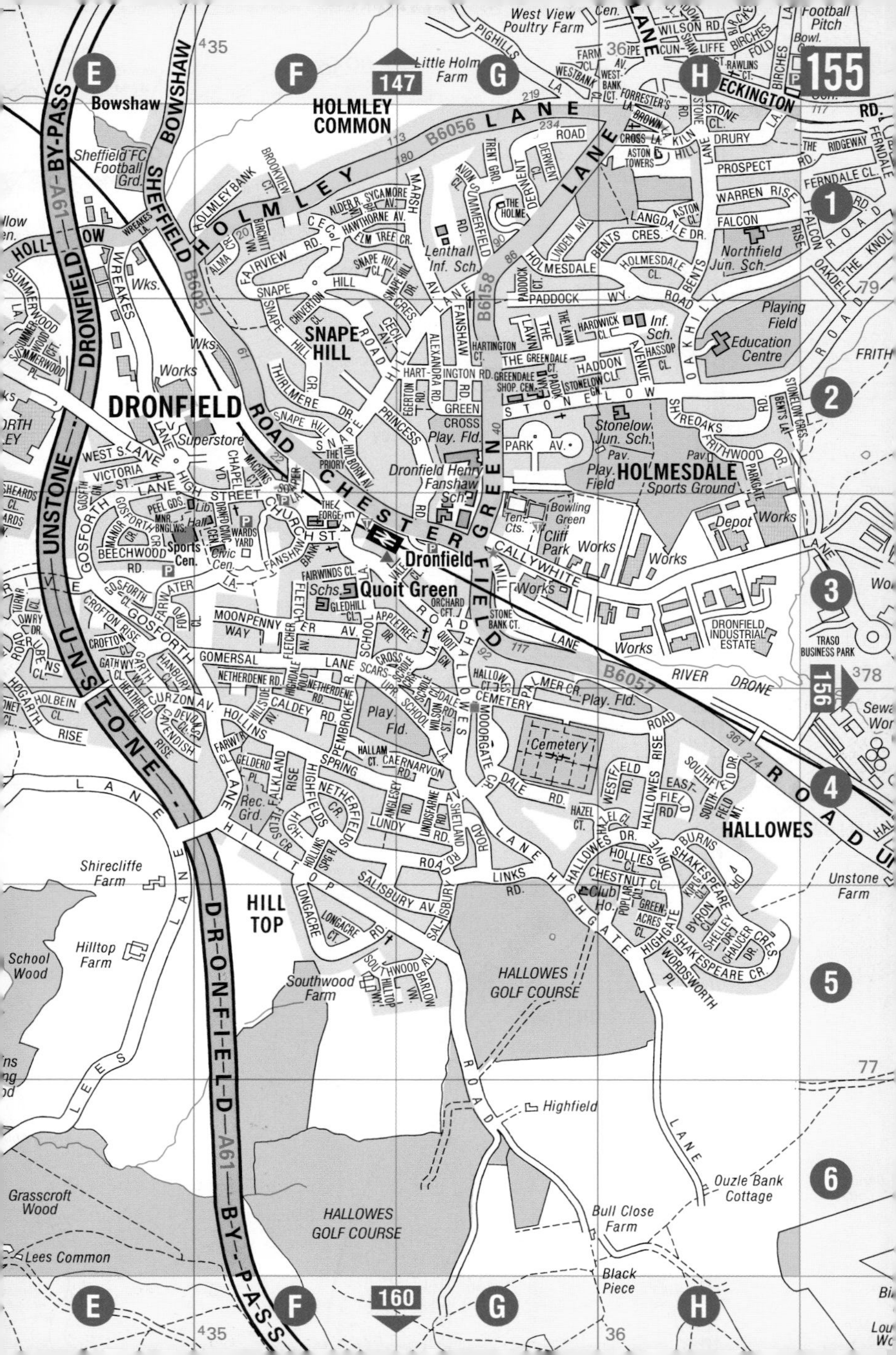

155
147
160
156
E
F
G
H
1
2
3
4
5
6
DRONFIELD
HOLMLEY COMMON
SNAPE HILL
HOLMESDALE
Quoit Green
HALLOWES
HILL TOP
Bowshaw
DRONFIELD BY-PASS
UNSTONE-DRONFIELD BY-PASS
SHEFFIELD ROAD
CHESTERFIELD ROAD
HOLMLEY LANE
GREEN LANE
HALLOWES GOLF COURSE
Little Holm Farm
West View Poultry Farm
Sheffield FC Football Grd.
Lenthall Inf. Sch.
Northfield Jun. Sch.
Education Centre
Stonelow Jun. Sch.
Holmesdale Sports Ground
Dronfield Henry Fanshaw Sch.
Dronfield
Cemetery
DRONFIELD INDUSTRIAL ESTATE
TRASO BUSINESS PARK
RIVER DRONE
Shirecliffe Farm
Hilltop Farm
School Wood
Southwood Farm
Highfield
Ouzle Bank Cottage
Bull Close Farm
Black Piece
Grasscroft Wood
Lees Common
Unstone Farm

Dronfield
S18
ECKINGTON ROAD
SNOWDEN LANE
B6056
B6057
Summerley
HOLMESDALE
APPERKNOWLE
HALLOWES
UNSTONE
Unstone Green
Hardhurst
CHESTERFIELD RD.
UNSTONE HILL MAIN RD.
SHEFFIELD ROAD
FRITH WOOD
Bridgefield Wood
Hanger Wood
Ramshaw Wood
Hollin Wood
BIRCH HALL GOLF COURSE
DRONFIELD INDUSTRIAL ESTATE
TRASO BUSINESS PARK
Summerley Hall
Summerley Farm
Summerley House
Summerley Green Farm
Elm Tree Farm
Woodcock Farm
Bentley Hall
Bentleyhall Farm
Nursery
Rushfield Farm
Top Farm
Bentley Farm
Air Strip
Red House
Grange Farm
Unstone Grange
St. Mary's Inf. Sch.
Unstone Junior Sch.
Woodsmithies Farm
Siscar Cottage
Pear Tree Cottage
Valley View Farm
Ramshaw Farm
Manor Farm
Unstone Farm
Hounscliffe Hall
Sewage Works
Cricket Ground
Northfield Jun. Sch.
Education Centre
Playing Field
Cross and Birches F.
Fivegates Farm
Mast
148
155
161

TROWAY
Greenside
Doe Lane Farm
Greatfold Farm
Dobholme Wood
Mill Pond
Score House
BRAMLEY
Running Track
MARSH LANE
Marsh La. Prim. Sch.
Playing Field
Shady Hall
Vale Cottages
Snowdon Farm
Troway Hill Farm
Wallace Farm
Leak's Plantation
QUARRY HILL
BIRCHWOOD ROAD
Bramley Moor
Warren House Farm
MAIN LANE
B6056
Lightwood
The Brushes
Whiteacres Farm
Light Wood
Moortop Farm
MOORTOP ROAD
MORTON LANE
LONG LANE
Heatherlee Farm
Sheffield
S21
BRAMLEYMOOR LANE
LIGHTWOOD LANE
LIGHTWOOD ROAD
Nursery
Rose Dene
MIDDLE HANDLEY
Butchersick Farm
Ash Lane Farm
ASH LANE
WESTFIELD
CAVENDISH TER.
CAVENDISH SQ.
WEST HANDLEY
Manor Farm
Stubbing Wood
Tapton Poultry Farm
HUNDALL
CHAPEL COTTAGES
Sewage Works
POOL'S LANE
Spring Wood
Binkley Wood
Binkley Cottages
Springwell House
SPRINGWELL HILL
B6052
Workhouse Wood
South View Farm
NORTH EAST DERBYSHIRE
CHESTERFIELD
HANDLEY LANE
SLAG LANE
Works
Opencast Workings
S41
S43
ECKINGTON ROAD
PARKGATE LA.
Parkgate Fa.
Grasscroft Wood
GLASSHOUSE COMMON
E F G H
1 2 3 4 5 6
39 40
79 78 77
30
149
158
162

158

A B 150 C 442 D

Rotherjam Farm

LADY

DRIVE

LADY

Roundhills Cottages

BACK

LANE

BACK

LANE

Bramley Hall

FORD

SCHOOL LA

1 30 B6056 31 Bramley Park Mobile Home Site

Marsh La. Prim. Sch.

ROAD

Ravencar Farm

Eckington School

SPRING HELD CL MARTIN CT GREEN HILLS RD GREEN CHASE

HATFIELD BROOMHILL CL HIGHWOOD ROAD BERRY

STANIFORTH SPENCER FERN WAY HINDERSON OSMUND CT Playgrd. WULFRIC RD

Marsh Lane Farm

Low Farm

MAIN

79

SCHOOL LA

30

30

MARSH LA

DRONFIELD

WEST

FERN PARTRIDGE CURFEW Play Fld. DARCY ROAD

MAPLE HAWKSWAY OSMUND BILTAM MOSS RISE PL STREET HIGH

SANDOWN SITWELL VW WATER 194 EAST MOSS BECK ST. ST

Depot † 30 FANSHAW AV

12 WEST HORNTHORPE FANSHAW CLUB

RD. VW. AV VLT VW FANSHAW THE BUNGALOWS

RD. 9 EAST VW. FANSHAW Football Grd.

2 BOLEHILL Lightwood Farm

Lightwood

Top Farm

Bolehill

Bolehill

BOLEHILL LA. 80

LANE

LIGHTWOOD

CRES. WARREN HALL WORTH VW

RIDGE BR AMLEY RD.

Light Wood

Bolehill Farm

FENTON RANDALL CEDAR PITT SETCUP

Inf. Sch. ELM RD LAUREL CL

CHESTNUT CR ASH CRAB ROAD

MULBERRY AV POPLAR

LIME RD. LARCH CL HAWTHORN RD

ASPEN BECK JUNIPER SCH

MAPLE ASHLEY

Wade Wood

CHESTERFIELD

MARSH QUARRY

Eckington Marsh

Turner Spring Wood

Depot

3

Rose Dene

nsery

378

157

Handley Farm

Rose Cottage

Marsh Farm

Whinnybank Wood

Red Lodge Cottages

MIDDLE HANDLEY

WEST- FIELD

4

GREEN LA.

Southgate Lodge

Red Lodge Farm

Foxstone Wood

Little Foxstone Wood

Fox D

LANE

STA VELEY

5

Nether Handley

77

B6052

Dale Farm

Belle Vue Farm

South View Farm

Eyries Farm

LANE

BRECK

White Lodge

SPRINGWELL

Workhouse Wood

6

Ironstone Cottage

Opencast Workings

Hopewell Wood

Hagge Farm

A 41 B 163 C 442 D

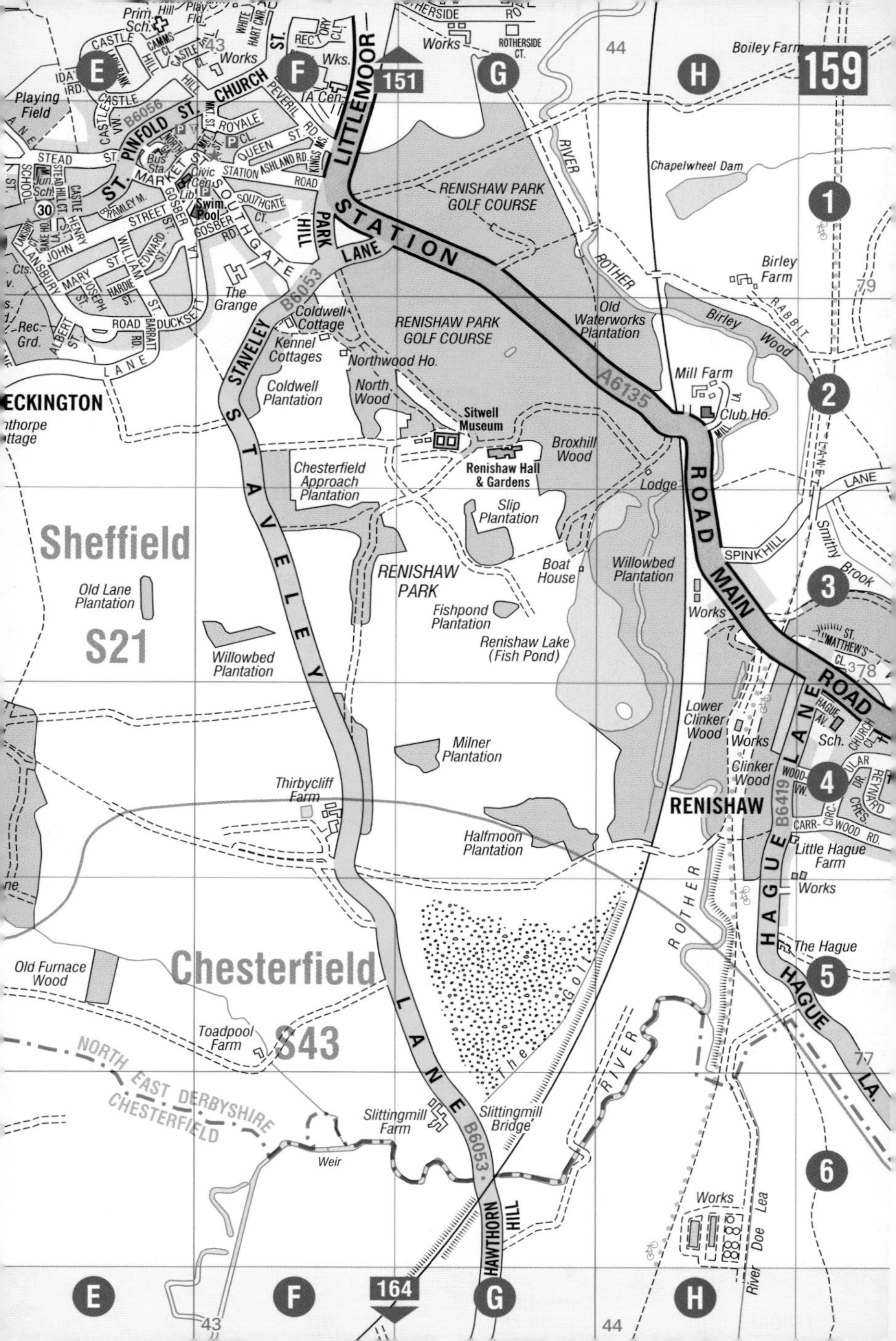
ECKINGTON
Sheffield
S21
Chesterfield
S43
RENISHAW
RENISHAW PARK
RENISHAW PARK GOLF COURSE
Renishaw Hall & Gardens
Sitwell Museum
Renishaw Lake (Fish Pond)
Willowbed Plantation
Broxhill Wood
Slip Plantation
Fishpond Plantation
Milner Plantation
Halfmoon Plantation
Chesterfield Approach Plantation
Coldwell Plantation
North Wood
Northwood Ho.
Kennel Cottages
Coldwell Cottage
The Grange
Old Waterworks Plantation
Mill Farm
Club Ho.
Lodge
Boat House
Lower Clinker Wood
Clinker Wood
Little Hague Farm
The Hague
Birley Farm
Birley Wood
Chapelwheel Dam
Boiley Farm
Thirbycliff Farm
Old Lane Plantation
Old Furnace Wood
Toadpool Farm
Slittingmill Farm
Slittingmill Bridge
Weir
Works
STAVELEY LANE
STATION LANE
LITTLEMOOR
MAIN ROAD
SPINKHILL LANE
HAGUE LANE
HAGUE LA.
HAWTHORN HILL
A6135
B6053
B6056
B6419
RIVER ROTHER
River Doe Lea
Smithy Brook
The Golf
NORTH EAST DERBYSHIRE
CHESTERFIELD
151
164

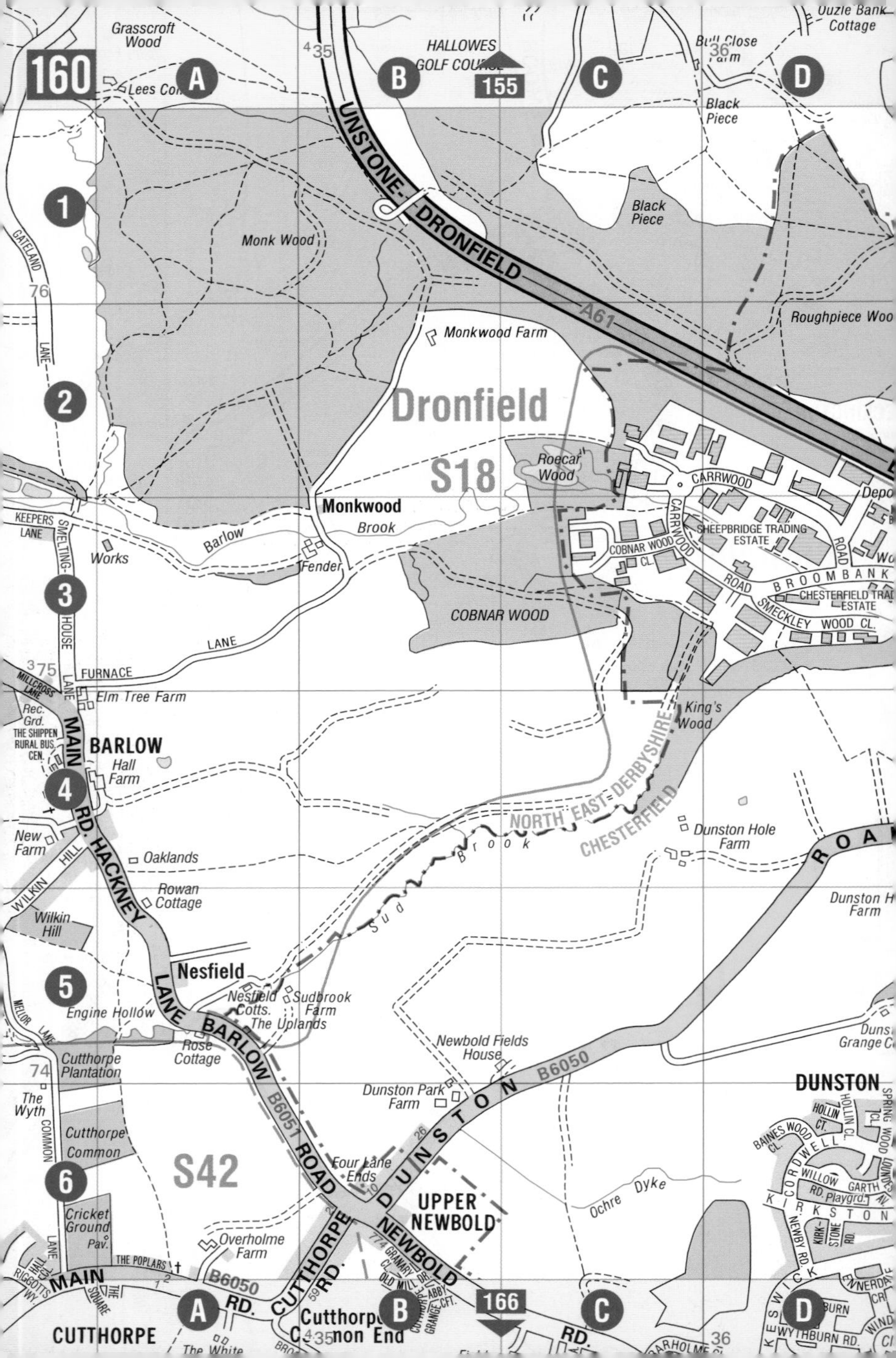
Grasscroft Wood
Lees Common
HALLOWES GOLF COURSE
155
Bull Close Farm
Ouzle Bank Cottage
Black Piece
Black Piece
UNSTONE-DRONFIELD
A61
Monk Wood
GATELAND LANE
Monkwood Farm
Roughpiece Wood
Dronfield
S18
Roecar Wood
CARRWOOD
Monkwood
Brook
Barlow
KEEPERS LANE
SMELTING-HOUSE LANE
Works
Fender
SHEEPBRIDGE TRADING ESTATE
COBNAR WOOD CL.
CARRWOOD ROAD
BROOMBANK
CHESTERFIELD TRADING ESTATE
SMECKLEY WOOD CL.
COBNAR WOOD
LANE
FURNACE
MILLCROSS LANE
Elm Tree Farm
Rec. Grd.
THE SHIPPEN RURAL BUS. CEN.
BARLOW
Hall Farm
King's Wood
NORTH EAST DERBYSHIRE
CHESTERFIELD
New Farm
WILKIN HILL
Oaklands
Dunston Hole Farm
Rowan Cottage
Sud Brook
Wilkin Hill
MAIN RD. HACKNEY LANE
Nesfield
Engine Hollow
MELLOR LANE
Nesfield Cotts.
Sudbrook Farm
The Uplands
Newbold Fields House
Rose Cottage
Cutthorpe Plantation
BARLOW B6051 ROAD
B6050
DUNSTON
DUNSTON
Dunston Park Farm
The Wyth
COMMON LANE
Cutthorpe Common
S42
Four Lane Ends
UPPER NEWBOLD
Ochre Dyke
HOLLIN CT.
HOLLIN CL.
SPRING WOOD
BAINES WOOD CL.
CORDWELL
WILLOW GARTH
KIRKSTONE
RD. Playgrd.
Cricket Ground Pav.
Overholme Farm
GRANARY CL.
OLD MILL DR.
NEWBOLD RD.
CUTTHORPE RD.
NEWBY RD.
KIRK-STONE RD.
THE POPLARS
B6050
MAIN RD.
HALL CL.
RIGGOTTS WY.
THE SQUARE
KESWICK
ENNERDALE CR.
WYTHBURN RD.
166
CUTTHORPE
Cutthorpe Common End
The White
Dunston Hall Farm
Dunston Grange

Unstone Green
Sewage Works
Birch Hall Farm
Loundes Wood
Brierley Wood
Club House
BIRCH HALL GOLF COURSE
Ramshaw Wood
Ramshaw Farm
Hardwick House Farm
Mast
SHEFFIELD ROAD
UNSTONE LANE
HUNDALL LANE
WINDMILL LANE
The Quest
Thorpe Spring Wood
Four Acres
River Drone
The Brushes
S41
Manor Syck Farm
Holly House Sch.
Mary Swanwick Prim. Sch.
Revolution Ho. (Museum)
Broomhill Farm
OLD WHITTINGTON
SHEEPBRIDGE BUSINESS CENTRE
Works
Sheepbridge
DUNSTON TRADING ESTATE
SHEEPBRIDGE WORKS
BRIDGE BUS. PARK
CHESTERFIELD ROAD
INNER RELIEF ROAD
DUNSTON ROAD
Dunston Hall
Dunston Lodge
Chesterfield
Dunston Farm
Dunston Grange
Chesterfield Panthers RUFC
DUNSTON INNOVATION CENTRE
DUNSTON TECH. PARK
The Jungle
FOXWOOD IND. PK.
ARMYTAGE INDUSTRIAL ESTATE
WHITTINGTON MOOR
STATION ROAD
BRIMINGTON ROAD
Newbold Moor
Rec. Grd.
Play Fld.
Dunston Prim.Sch.
ST. JOHN'S ROAD
Ridding Brook
Whitting
156
162
167

Hardwick House Farm
Grasscroft Wood
GLASSHOUSE COMMON
Top Mouse Park Wood
Poultry Farm
Parkgate Farm
Springwell House
Glasshouse Farm
Rookery Plantation
Fish Pond
Poultry Houses
NEW WHITTINGTON
HIGH ST.
HANDLEY ROAD
B6052
Whittington Grange
Green Farm
Manor Syck Farm
S41
Brearley Park
The Meadows Comm. Sch.
Playing Field
Brearley Wetlands
Merrians Farm
WHITTINGTON INDUSTRIAL ESTATE
RIVER
OLD WHITTINGTON
Revolution Ho.
Bluebank Lock
Chesterfield
Bluebank Wood
Sewage Works
Playing Field
Brimington Jun. Sch.
Wheeldonmill Lock
WHITTINGTON MOOR
ARMYTAGE INDUSTRIAL ESTATE
PEARSON TRADING ESTATE
Works
Wks.
ARMYTAGE IND. EST.
STATION ROAD
BRIMINGTON ROAD NORTH
B6050
Sunnybank
Ryecroft Bungalow
Wheeldonmill Plantation
Factory
Rec. Grd.
Playgrd.
CHURCH HALL

157
161
168

Grid references (top): E, F, G, H, 163, 41, 42, 158

Place names and features:
- White Lodge
- Hopewell Wood
- Hagge Farm
- **Dronfield**
- S21
- Breck Farm
- Monument
- Claypit
- Breck Farm Cottages
- Foxlowe Junc.
- **BARROW HILL**
- HILL GROVE
- BROOKS ROAD
- ROAD
- LANE
- HALL
- Campbell Cottages
- SOUTHGATE, WOODFORD, CHELMSFORD WAY
- MIDLAND
- TRAFFIC TER.
- ALLPORT
- Recreation Ground
- Playground
- Rec. Grd.
- Handleywood Golf Driving Range
- Barrow Hill Roundhouse Railway Centre
- CHIGWELL WAY
- ROMFORD WAY
- WESTLANDS
- DUEWELL CT.
- AVONSIDE CL.
- Barrow Hill Primary Sch.
- STATION
- CAMPBELL ROAD
- CAVENDISH PL.
- Handleywood Farm
- ROTHER
- WORKS
- Rec. Grd.
- Summit Sidings
- 164
- 375
- Chemical Works
- THE CLOCK TOWER BUSINESS CENTRE
- S43
- Nature Trail
- Canal
- Victoria Farm
- Hounsfield Bridge
- Sports Grd.
- Ringwood Centre
- Club
- **New Brimington**
- KING ST.
- HOLLINGWOOD ROAD
- TURNOAKS, HORNBEAM LA.
- LIBERTY CT.
- BEECHS LA.
- ALDERGATE GDNS.
- BIRCH LA.
- CHESTNUT LA.
- SYCAMORE
- Hollingwood Estate
- CRESCENT
- LABURNUM
- LILAC ST.
- FIR ST.
- **HOLLINGWOOD**
- Opencast Workings
- **MIDDLECROFT**
- A6192
- A619 ROAD
- 5
- Pondhouse Farm
- Troughbrook Wood
- ST. JOHN'S
- DIVISION
- BOND
- Comm. Cen. Playgrd.
- Playground
- THE BUNGALOWS
- KENTMERE, RYDALE
- WESTWOOD
- CAVENDISH
- AVENUE
- MAULIN AV.
- ELM, OAK, SYCAMORE, CEDAR, MYRTLE, LAUREL GRO., PINE, PEAR TREE
- QUEEN ST.
- VICTORIA ST.
- STATION ROAD
- DORSET, SOMERSET ST.
- HERE., CAMBGE.
- CHURCH HOUSES
- Prim. Sch.
- ALPINE GR., REDWD.CL., LILAC
- MAPLE STREET
- Troughbrook Hill
- 27
- INNERSALL ROAD
- Prim. Sch.
- DEVON, CORNWALL
- OXFORD, WESSEX
- KING ST., QUEEN ST., PRINCESS ST.
- BROCKHILL
- Rec. Grd.
- CHAPEL ST., BURNELL
- ELMWOOD DR.
- PRIVATE DRIVE
- **CHESTERFIELD** ROAD
- 30
- Playground
- Ringwood Park
- Weir
- Ringwood Lake
- Ringwood Hall
- DALE CL.
- CROMFORD DR.
- HUNTLEY CL.
- GREEN
- TURNER DRIVE
- ATTLEE
- DORMANT
- EDWARD, EDENSOR CT., LUMSDALE WAY, WENSLEY WAY
- WINSTER CT.
- BURBAGE RD.
- MIDDLECROFT
- CHURCH CL.
- 6
- **RING-WOOD** A619 ROAD
- 30
- 60
- **BRIMINGTON**
- 169
- MANOR AV.
- Ringwood

Grid references (bottom): E, F, G, H, 41, 42

164

A   B   **159**   C   D

Works

River Doe Lea

1

Breck Farm

76

RIVER ROTHER

HAWTHORN ROAD

Hawthorne Hill Farm

Foxlowe Plantation

B6053

2

Foxlowe Junction

Works

HARTINGTON INDUSTRIAL ESTATE

Hartington House

Recreation Ground

Playground

FARNDALE ROAD

DEEPDALE CL

Works

FRANKLYN

HILLCREST RD

WOBURN

HARTINGTON RD

3

Summit Sidings

Hall Lane Junction

STAVELEY

ECKINGTON

NORTHERN LOOP RD

Works

Library

Playgrd GRATTON CL HAYFIELD CL OVERTON RD WEDEN RD ASTON CL

BELLHOUSE

RIVERDALE PARK

Spts. Gr

S43

375

163

Chemical Works

STAVELEY

CHURCH ST

DUKE ST

MILL HO

Superstore

BARNFIELD WK

MILL CL

DEVONSHIRE ST

DEVON CL

HUNTSMAN SPEEDWELL RD IND. EST.

COMPTON ST BRINDLEY

WATER LA

MALLARD

LEANDER CT

PULLMAN

WHASH LA

VICTORIA AV

WHITE RD

MOOR VIEW RD

RALPH RD

LOW GATES

A619

Playing Field Netherthorpe School

4

RIVER ROTHER

PORTER ST

MEADOW ST

L D CL

MARKET STREET

IRELAND ST WHITEHEAD BIRD CL

NETHERTHORPE RD BARROW

LEY WY

Wks

Playground

NETHERTHORPE RD

Rec Grd

NETHERTHORPE

MARSHFIELD GR

HELDS

Netherthorpe

5

CHESTERFIELD

Chesterfield Canal

A6192

A619

ROAD

DARLEY CL

LIME AVENUE

30

CHADWICK CT

IMMINGHAM GRO

JOHNS RD

WEST TW

COLLEGE ST

FRECHEVILLE ST

MUSARD PL

ROW RD

Speedwell Inf. Sch.

Staveley Jun. Sch

Pav.

Football Ground

Pav.

Playgrd

Bowl. Grn

CEMETERY

STEPHENSON RD

HAYFORD

Ten. Cts

SPEEDWELL INDUSTRIAL ESTATE

FAN ROAD INDUSTRIAL ESTATE

LANE

Factory

COLLIERY

FAN RD

IRELAND BUS. PK

PROSPECT RD

River Doe Lea

A6192

Seyn Ju

6

MIDDLECROFT

Playground

MOLINEUX AV

CAVENDISH ST

QUEEN ST

SILVER WELL DR

HADDON

CRESSWELL

ELTON CL

LINDSAY

CALVER

St. Joseph's RC Prim. Sch.

Playing Field

IRELAND INDUSTRIAL ESTATE

ADELPHI WY

ADELPHI WY

PAVILION

MEADOWS

DRIVE

ERIN

Pav.

Weir

Poolsbrook Farm

STAVELEY ROAD

POOLSBROOK VW

POOLSBROOK CRES

POOLSBROOK SQ

Bowl. Grn

COTTAGE

A6192 R

THE BUNGALOWS

WESTNALL WAY

MANIFOLD AV

LADYCROFT

WINSTER RD

EDENSOR

LUMSDALE

WENSLEY WAY

BURBAGE RD

Comm. Cen Playgrd

MIDDLECROFT

CHURCH CL Springwell Comm. Sch.

A

43

Poolsbrook CARAVAN CLUB

B

POOLSBROOK COUNTRY PARK

C

P

POOLSBROOK

Playground

Poolsbrook Prim. Sch.

D

Play Fld

CO-OPERAT COTTS

44

74

HAGUE LANE
S21
Huggester Farm
Happy Valley
Pond Farm
Holbrook Farm
RENISHAW ROAD
B6419
WOODHOUSE LANE
BOLSOVER
CHESTERFIELD
Grange Farm
Woodhouse Lane Farm
Robinson's Lumb
A619
ROAD
MASTIN MOOR
WORKSOP ROAD
BOLSOVER ROAD
ROYAL OAK CT.
Mastin Moor Community Garden
Community Centre
M1
Playing Field
Staveley Bri.
Norbriggs
NORBRIGGS ROAD
THE PADDOCKS
Norbriggs Prim. Sch.
Play. Fld.
Norbriggs Cottages
Woodthorpe Hall
Netherthorpe Flash Nature Reserve
WOODTHORPE
Jubilee Farm
Wellsholme Farm
Bank House Farm
WOODTHORPE ROAD
St. John's Farm
Play. Fld.
Woodthorpe C of E Primary School
BRIDLE
Woodthorpe Grange
Mineral Railway
Oxcroft Junction
CHESTERFIELD
BOLSOVER
M1 MOTORWAY
WOODTHORPE ROAD
Chesterfield
MILL LANE
S44
Lodge Farm
Opencast Workings
SHUTTLEWOOD
BENTINCK RD.
Woodside
Freestan

166
A
B
C
D
1
2
3
4
5
6
160
170
UPPER NEWBOLD
CUTTHORPE
Cutthorpe Common End
MAIN ROAD
B6050
CUTTHORPE RD.
NEWBOLD RD.
Overholme Farm
THE POPLARS
The White House
Cutthorpe Green
Hall
Hall Farm
The Dower House
GREEN LANE
BROCKWELL LA.
Fields Farm
Over Newbold Farm
Ochre Dyke
HOLMEBROOK VALLEY PARK
Pav.
Holme Farm Cottages
Linacre Brook
Reservoir
Linacre Woods
Woodnook Cottage
Woodnook Farm
Sims Wood
Woodnook
WOODNOOK LANE
S42
Ashgate Hospice
THE GRANGE
Moor Lea
ASHGATE PLANTATION
MAIN RD.
ASHGATE ROAD
Caushouse Farm
Ashgate Cottage
Ash Green (Learning Disability Service)
Oak Tree Cottage
NORTH EAST DERBYSHIRE
CHESTERFIELD
Oxclose Plantation
Threenook Plantation
Treeneuk
OLD ROAD
SLACK LA.
LOUNDSLEY GREEN RD.
Holme Hall Prim. School & Community Centre
Nursing Home
Playgrd.
Sub.
LOUNDSLEY GREEN
Shop.Cen.
Hostel
Ashgate Croft Sch.
S40
ASHGATE
Playing Field
Play. Fld.
MANOR AVENUE
Manor Offices
Fitness Club
BRAMPTON
Sports Ground
Tennis Courts
Running Track
Brookfield Comm. Sch.
Westfield Infant Sch.
STORRS RD.
B6150
A619
CHATSWORTH RD.
BASLOW RD.
BROOKSIDE
Belmont Cott.
Brookside Nurseries
Weirs
Leadhill Farm
PIPER LA.
St.Mary's Catholic High Sch.
Play. Fld.
NEWBOLD
HOLME PARK AVENUE
Playgrounds
B6051
WYTHBURN RD.
KESWICK DR.
BARHOLME CL.
WATER MDW. LA.
A632
Sports

161
171
168
Newbold Moor
Newbold Village
Brockwell Hill
Brockwell
Chesterfield
STONEGRAVELS
CHESTERFIELD
S41
ST. JOHN'S ROAD
NEWBOLD ROAD
SHEFFIELD ROAD
CHESTERFIELD - INNER - RELIEF - ROAD
MARKHAM RD.
CHATSWORTH RD.
WHEATBRIDGE RD.
A61
A619
B6150
B6057
B6051
Dunston Prim. Sch.
Chesterfield FC (b2net Stadium)
Stand Road Rec. Grd.
Fitness First Health Club
Newbold Community School
Highfield Recreation Ground
Highfield Hall Prim. Sch.
Christ Church C of E Prim. Sch.
The Barnett Observatory
Brockwell Inf. & Jun. Schs.
Chesterfield Lawn Ten. Club
St. Mary's Sch.
Chesterfield College
Arts Cen.
Winding Wheel
Queen's Park Sports Centre
QUEEN'S PARK
Chesterfield Cricket Grd.
Rowland Hill House
Ravenside Retail Park
Retail Park
Parkside Com.Sch.
William Rhodes Prim. Sch.
Queen's Park Annexe
Recreation Ground
Youth Centre
Superstore
Works
Depot
Playing Field
E
F
G
H
1
2
3
4
5
6
37
38

Chesterfield
CHESTERFIELD
TAPTON
HADY
S41
CHESTERFIELD INNER RELIEF ROAD
A61
ROTHER WAY
A619
CHESTERFIELD ROAD
BRIMINGTON ROAD NORTH
STATION RD.
CHURCH HALL ROAD
BRIMINGTON ROAD
B6543
TAPTON LANE
BALMOAK LANE
PAXTON ROAD
PETTYCLOSE LANE
WHEATHILL LA.
DARK LANE
WETLANDS LANE
GREEN LANE
CROW LANE
HADY HILL
A632
HASLAND-BY-PASS
DERBY RD.
SHEFFIELD ROAD
LOCKOFORD LA.
LOCKOFORD RD.
Chesterfield Canal
River Rother
Chesterfield FC (b2net Stadium)
Superstore
Warehouse
Ryecroft Bungalow
Ryecroft Farm
Wheeldon Plantation
BRIMINGTON CEMETERY
Chesterfield & District Crematorium
Ivy House Farm
Tapton Hall Farm
Fish Pond
TAPTON PARK
Innovation Cen.
Chesterfield College (Tapton House Campus)
Castle Hill
TAPTON PARK MUNICIPAL GOLF COURSE
Fish Ponds
Court House
The Lodge
Club House
Rose Cottage
Ingman Well
Dobbin Clough Farm
CHESTERFIELD ROYAL HOSPITAL
Dryhurst
Hady Wood
Frank Merrifield Youth & Comm. Cen.
St. Peter & St. Paul School
Hady Hill Farm
Rose Cottages
Hady Prim. School
Recreation Ground
Playground
Playing Field
Pavilion
Spital Cemetery
Spital
Chesterfield
Winding Wheel
Chesterfield College
Retail Park
Nuffield Fitness Cen.
Works
Depot
Factory
162
167
172
A B C D
1 2 3 4 5 6

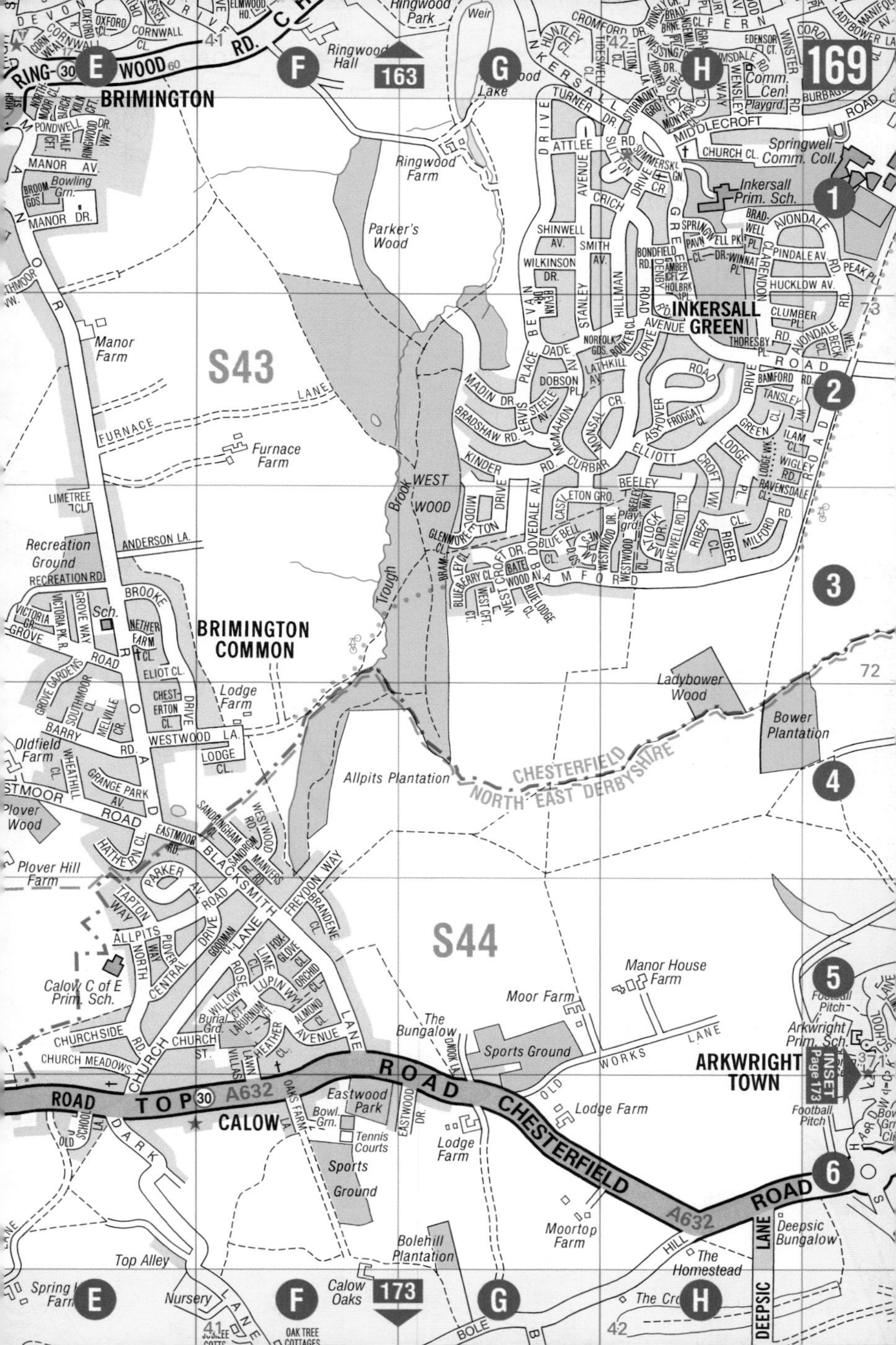

169
163
173
BRIMINGTON
BRIMINGTON COMMON
INKERSALL GREEN
ARKWRIGHT TOWN
CALOW
S43
S44
CHESTERFIELD
NORTH EAST DERBYSHIRE
Ringwood Park
Ringwood Hall
Ringwood Farm
Parker's Wood
Manor Farm
Furnace Farm
WEST WOOD
Lodge Farm
Allpits Plantation
Ladybower Wood
Bower Plantation
Recreation Ground
Oldfield Farm
Plover Wood
Plover Hill Farm
Calow C of E Prim. Sch.
Manor House Farm
Moor Farm
The Bungalow
Sports Ground
Eastwood Park
Tennis Courts
Lodge Farm
Moortop Farm
Bolehill Plantation
The Homestead
Deepsic Bungalow
Top Alley
Nursery
Calow Oaks
Springwell Comm. Coll.
Inkersall Prim. Sch.
Arkwright Prim. Sch.
Football Pitch
INSET Page 173
CHESTERFIELD ROAD
TOP ROAD
A632
RINGWOOD RD.
MANOR RD.
FURNACE LANE
WESTWOOD LA.
BLACKSMITH LANE
DEEPSIC LANE
OLD WORKS LANE
DARK LANE
BAMFORD RD.

CHATSWORTH
ROAD
BASLOW
RD.
A613
BROOKSIDE
Belmont Cott.
Belmont Park
Brookside Nurseries
Somersall Willows
Weirs
Weir
Somersall Farm
Somersall Hall
Somersall Playing Fields
Playground
Pav
WALTON
Walton Dam
Sports Ground
Walton Plantation
Horse Wood
Walton Holymoorside Primary Sch.
Tin Wood
Pine Lodge
Albion Farm
Old Spring Wood
Walton Hilltop
Rose Farm
Spring House Farm
Springfield
Branksome
Pk. Hall
Playgrd.
Cherry Tree Farm
Allison Farm
Walton House
Chesterfield
Walton Lodge
The Croft
Highfield Farm
Walton-lodge Farm
Pond
Boat Ho.
Hillside
High Beeches
Walton Wood
Walton Cottage
Lodge Cotts.
A632
High House Farm
Broadgorse Farm
Well Close Wood
Robincroft & Windsor Woods
High Lane Farm
Slatepit Dale
The Poplars
Clayton Upper Wood
Harper Hill House
Fox Hole Farm
Res. (cov.)
Harperhill Farm
Wellclose Cottage
Ivy Farm
MATLOCK ROAD
SWATHWICK LANE
Slate Pit Dale Farm
Simpson's Plantation
Hillside Farm
Harper Hill
Harperhill Plantation
Clayton Nether Wood
Green Wood
Pear Tree Farm
Pearcehill Plantation
The Great Pond of Stubbing
Harehill Plantation
MALTHOUSE LANE
STEEP LANE
STONEYCROFT LANE
WATSON LANE
S45
166

171
167
172
E
F
G
H
1
2
3
4
5
6
37
38
70
69
68
S40
S42
BOYTHORPE
BIRDHOLME
WINGERWORTH
Swathwick
St. Augustines
Walton Hospital
Boythorpe Cemetery
Chesterfield Golf Course
The Chesterfield Golf Club
Club House
Riggott's Plantation
Green View
Brook
Widdowson Spring Wood
Playing Field
Nether Speighthill Wood
Upper Speighthill Wood
Longedge Plantation
Wren Park Wood
Bradbury Wood
Birdholme Farm
Birdholme Bridge
Recreation Ground
Chesterfield Bowl
Turnoaks Business Park
Depot
River
Warehouse
Retail Park
Bus Depot
Cricket Grd.
Works
Waltonfields Farm
Superstore
William Rhodes Prim. Sch.
Parkside Com. Sch.
Queen's Park Annexe
Whitecotes Prim. Sch.
Comm. Cen.
Spire Jun. Sch.
Nrsy. & Inf. Sch.
Hunloke Comm. Gdn.
Rec. Grd.
Hunloke Pk. Prim. Sch.
Boythorpe Playing Fld.
Playground
CHESTERFIELD
NORTH EAST DERBYSHIRE
A632
A61
DERBY ROAD
WHITECOTES LANE
ST. AUGUSTINES ROAD
BOYTHORPE AV.
BOYTHORPE ROAD
HUNLOKE AVENUE
WALTON ROAD
CHURCH STREET SOUTH
STORFORTH LANE
TURNOAKS LA.
WINGERWORTH WAY
HAREHILL ROAD
LANGER LA.
LONGEDGE LANE
LONGEDGE LA.
LODGE DRIVE
CHARTWELL AVENUE
WRENPARK ROAD
RECTORY ROAD
SWATHWICK LANE
ST. DAVIDS
WINDSOR DRIVE
LANGER DRIVE
NOTTINGHAM DR.
HALL BUNGALOWS
Hall Fm.

172
168
171
A
B
C
D
1
2
3
4
5
6
Spital
Spital Brook
HASLAND ROAD
B6039
A617
A61
B6038
DERBY ROAD
St. Augustines
Recreation Ground
Chesterfield Bowl
Cineworld
Nuffield Fitness Cen.
ALMA LEISURE PARK
Pav. Sports Ground
Bank Close
STORFORTH LANE TRADING EST.
STORFORTH LANE
Hasland Green
EASTWOOD PK. APARTMENTS
HASLAND
Hasland Hall Community School
EASTWOOD PARK
Hady Plantation
Playground
Playing Field
Brook
HEATHCOTE DRIVE
CALOW LA. IND. EST.
S40
S41
S42
VANGUARD TRADING ESTATE
TURNOAKS BUSINESS PARK
BIRDHOLME
Birdholme Farm
River Rother
CHESTERFIELD
NORTH EAST DERBYSHIRE
Manor House Farm
THE GREEN
CHURCHSIDE
Cemetery
Winsick
Winsick Park
Birch Lodge
HILLOCK
FURNACE
NORTH WINGFIELD ROAD
Golf Driving Range
Club Ho.
Grasshill Farm
Grasshill
Avenue Farm
Hunloke Farm
Avenue Coking Works (Disused)
WINGERWORTH
Cottagehill Farm
LONGEDGE LA.
MEADOWSIDE
Hunloke Pk. Prim. Sch.
Hall Fm.
HALL BUNGALOWS
NOTTINGHAM
Depot
Works
Ware-house

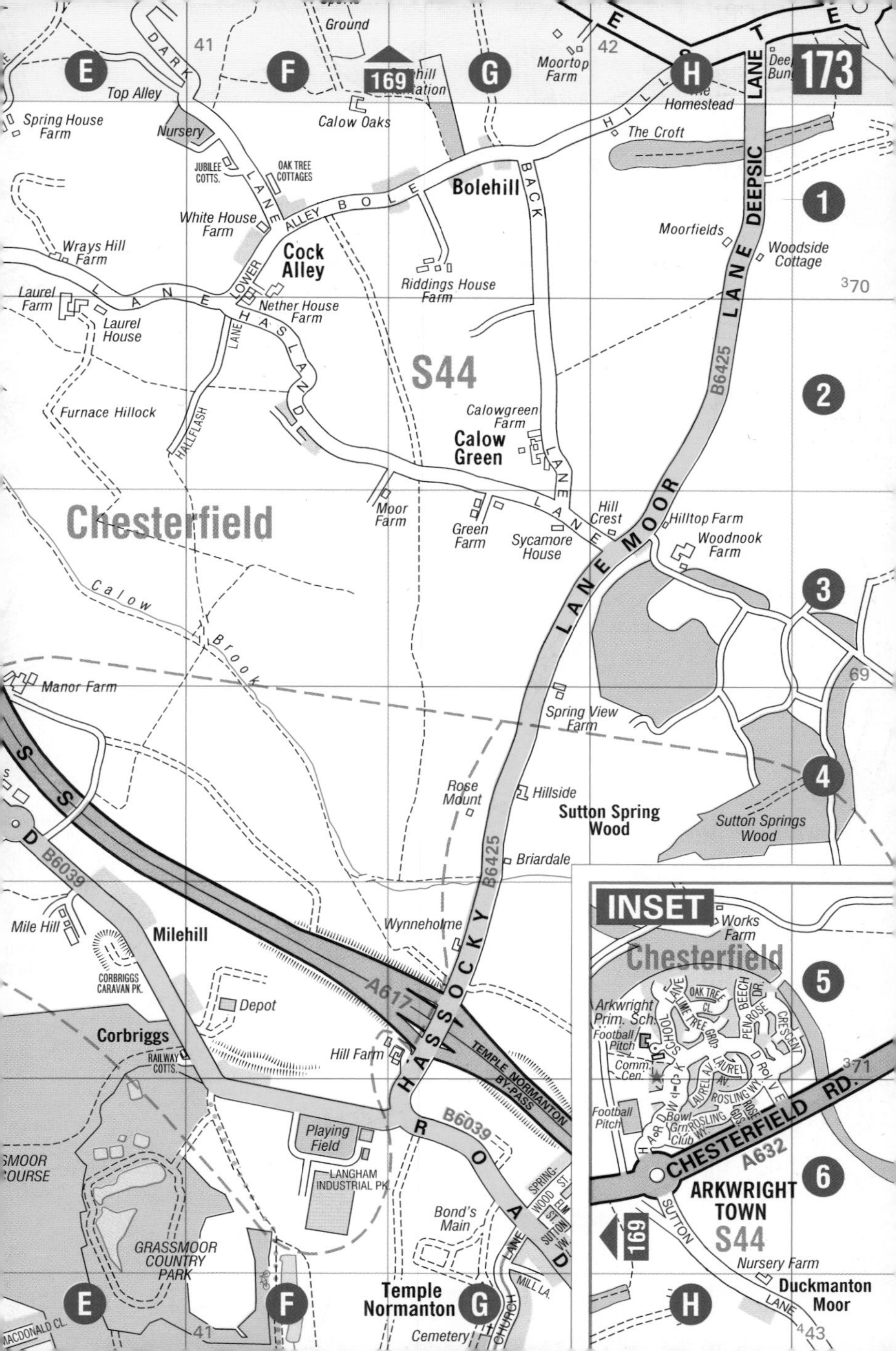
Ground
Top Alley
Spring House Farm
Nursery
Calow Oaks
Moortop Farm
The Homestead
The Croft
JUBILEE COTTS.
OAK TREE COTTAGES
Bolehill
White House Farm
Wrays Hill Farm
Cock Alley
Riddings House Farm
Moorfields
Woodside Cottage
Laurel Farm
Laurel House
Nether House Farm
S44
Furnace Hillock
Calowgreen Farm
Calow Green
Chesterfield
Moor Farm
Green Farm
Sycamore House
Hill Crest
Hilltop Farm
Woodnook Farm
Calow Brook
Manor Farm
Spring View Farm
Rose Mount
Hillside
Sutton Spring Wood
Sutton Springs Wood
Briardale
Mile Hill
Milehill
Wynneholme
CORBRIGGS CARAVAN PK.
Depot
Corbriggs
RAILWAY COTTS.
Hill Farm
TEMPLE NORMANTON BY-PASS
Playing Field
LANGHAM INDUSTRIAL PK.
GRASSMOOR COUNTRY PARK
Bond's Main
Temple Normanton
Cemetery
MACDONALD CL.
INSET
Works Farm
Chesterfield
Arkwright Prim. Sch.
Football Pitch
Comm. Cen.
Football Pitch
Bowl. Grn. Club
CHESTERFIELD RD.
A632
ARKWRIGHT TOWN
S44
Nursery Farm
Duckmanton Moor
DARK LANE
LOWER LANE
BOLE HILL
ALLEY
BACK LANE
DEEPSIC LANE
LANE
HASLAND LANE
HALLFLASH LANE
MOOR LANE
HASSOCKY ROAD
B6425
B6039
A617
SPRING-WOOD ST.
ELM ST.
SUTTON WY.
CHURCH LANE
MILL LA.
SUTTON LANE
OAK TREE CL.
LIME TREE GRO.
PENROSE CRESCENT
BEECH DR.
LAUREL AV.
ROSLING WY.
SCHOOL LANE
DEVONSHIRE DRIVE
169
169
E F G H
1 2 3 4 5 6
41 42 43 370 371 69

Hollin Bank
Underbank Hall
Rookery
HUNSHELF LA.
MUCKY LA.
Horsley House
Briery Busk Farm
Hunshelf Bank
Avice Royd
ROAD
Crimbles Farm
UNDERBANK RESERVOIR
MANCHESTER
A616
Cote House
Unsliven Bridge
BRAMALL LANE
Weirs
UNSLIVEN ROAD
White Row
SMITHY MOOR LA.
SMITHY CROSS
MOOR AVENUE
B6088
Works
CLAY PITS LA.
BACK LA.
OAKS LA.
CHURCHILL RD.
NEWTON AV.
ALRICH M.
Machin Spout
Machin Wood
HAWTHORNE AV.
COPPICE CL.
PATERSON CL.
ROAD
Smithy Moor
RIDAL CFT.
RIDAL CL.
New Hall Wood
Garden Village
AVENUE
MELBOURNE
WOOLLEY RD.
Moor House Farm
Green Farm
GREEN FARM HAMLET
MOORLAND
HOUSE LA.
EDWARD
CORONATION
LANCASTER RD.
Oxley Park
Pav.
Stockbridge Leisure Centre
TENNIS Courts
FOLLY
NEW HALL LANE
ALPINE RD.
LINDEN CR.
STOCKSBRIDGE
Pot House Wood
Stocksbridge Inf. Sch.
New Hall
Greave House Farm
The Clough
St. Ann's Sch.
Stocksbridge High Sch.
LONG LANE
Sheffield
BEECH
LABURNUM GRO.
LIME GRO.
LILAC AV.
CHESTNUT AV.
RED FERN GRO.
Stocksbridge Jun. Sch.
The Poplars
Whitwell Farm
WHITWELL MOOR
Lee House
LEE HOUSE LA.
STONE
East Whitwell
Whitwell Spring
Nursy.
Allen Croft
Allen Croft Brook
MUCKY LANE
The Height
The Cross
COAL
STONE MOOR
MOOR
Salt Springs Cott.
Salter Hills
HEADS
Hunger Hill Farm
Church
CALF CARR
Low Flat Farm
Vicarage
Waldershaigh
EWDEN BROWS
PEAK DISTRICT NATIONAL PARK
Ewden Cote
Broomhead Bridge
Wood Brook
Yew Trees Wood
Yew Trees
YEWTREES

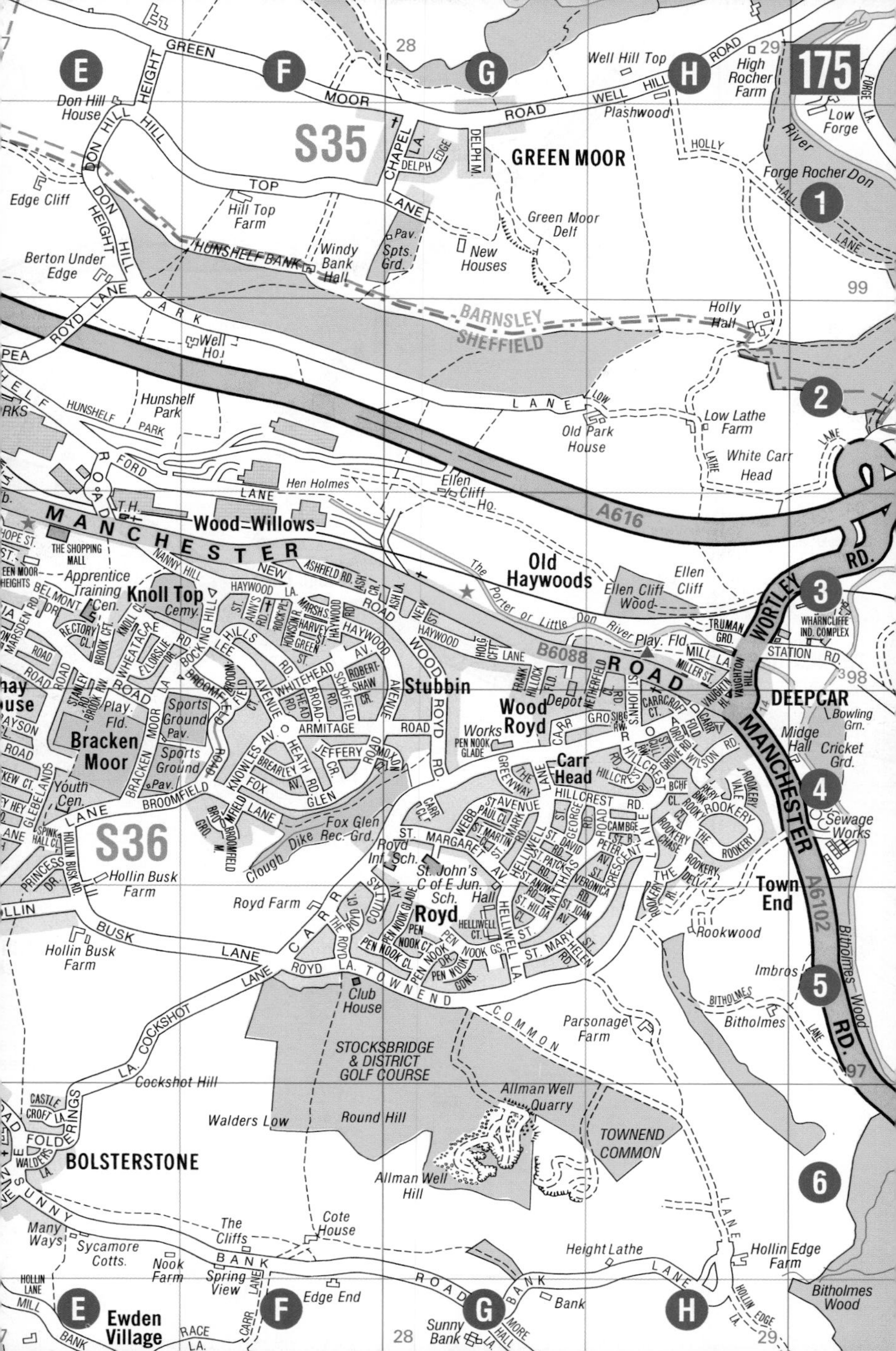

GREEN MOOR
S35
S36
Wood Willows
Knoll Top
Old Haywoods
Stubbin
Wood Royd
Carr Head
DEEPCAR
Bracken Moor
Royd
Town End
BOLSTERSTONE
Ewden Village
STOCKSBRIDGE & DISTRICT GOLF COURSE
TOWNEND COMMON
BARNSLEY
SHEFFIELD
A616
A6102
B6088
MANCHESTER ROAD
Well Hill Top
High Rocher Farm
Low Forge
Forge Rocher
Plashwood
Don Hill House
Edge Cliff
Hill Top Farm
Berton Under Edge
Windy Bank Hall
Green Moor Delf
New Houses
Holly Hall
Hunshelf Park
Well Ho
Low Lathe Farm
White Carr Head
Old Park House
Hen Holmes
Ellen Cliff Ho.
Ellen Cliff Wood
Ellen Cliff
The Porter or Little Don River
THE SHOPPING MALL
Apprentice Training Cen.
Cemy.
Sports Ground
Youth Cen.
Fox Glen Rec. Grd.
Clough Dike
Hollin Busk Farm
Royd Farm
Royd Inf. Sch.
St. John's C of E Jun. Sch.
Club House
Midge Hall
Cricket Grd.
Bowling Grn.
Sewage Works
WHARNCLIFFE IND. COMPLEX
Rookwood
Imbros
Bitholmes
Bitholmes Wood
Parsonage Farm
Allman Well Quarry
Allman Well Hill
Round Hill
Cockshot Hill
Walders Low
Cote House
The Cliffs
Many Ways
Sycamore Cotts.
Nook Farm
Spring View
Edge End
Height Lathe
Hollin Edge Farm
Bank
Sunny Bank
E
F
G
H
1
2
3
4
5
6
28
29
99
98
97

Scout Dike
Scout Dike Reservoir
Huddersfield Rd.
Halifax Road
A629
Carr Lodge Farm
Hoyland Moor Plantation
Kingswood Peak Venture Centre
Hoyland Moor
Walker Ing Wood
Malling Carr Wood
Far Westhorpe Farm
Westhorpe
Westhorpe House
Well House Tunnel
Bell Royd
Weir
Water Treatment Works
Well Ho. La.
Works
Scout Bridge Farm
Scout Bridge
Scout Dam Plantation
Well House
Norwood Lane
Folly Lane
Meadow Croft
Folly Lane Farm
Broad Hill
Weirs
Penistone Grammar Sch.
Tennis Courts
Long Lane
Playing Fields
Anna Lane
B6462
Tolson Ct.
Netherfields Annexe
Nether Mill Ho.
Depot
Barnsley Road
Royd Moor Road
Westfield Farm
Top o' th' Town
Woodland Villa
Bank Lane
Netherfield Farm
Bridge End
Penistone Bri.
Water Hall
Water Hall Bridge
Prim. Sch.
Thurlstone
Towngate
Red Ridge
Towngate Fm.
A628
Thurlstone Road
Mills
High Bank La.
Manchester Rd.
Thurlstone Bri.
Stottercliff Wood
Cemy.
Stottercliffe Road
Bridge St.
Church St.
Shrewsbury Rd.
Penistone
Superstore
Rec. Grd.
Bowl. Grns.
Playgrd.
T.H.
Cin.
Lib.
Rockside Road
Hornthwaite Bridge
Thorpe Royd
Hornthwaite Hill
Leapings Fm.
Bank Ho. La.
Hill Side La.
Cross Royd Head
Cross Lane
Hornthwaite Hill Rd.
Victoria St.
St. Mary's St.
Jun. Sch.
Play. Fld.
Inf. Sch.
Clarel Street
Schole Hill
Schole Hill Lane
Gravels
Sike House
Sike Lane
Chapel Lane
New Chapel
Rose Hill
The Green
Mortimer Road
Cubley Wood
Quakers Hill
Lumb Royd
Woodend
Gledhill Avenue
Wood End Bri.
Westfield House
Hartcliff Road
Brockholes Lane
Cubley
Hacking Hill
Royd Field
Old Cubley
Cubley Hall Farm
Joan Royd Lane
Coal Pit Dike
A B C D
1 2 3 4 5 6
23 24

25 26 27

Renald La.Ho. LANE The Cottage

E F G H

Hill
Tree
se

Renald
Crab Tree Hill La.
RENALD

Hunger Hill

Little Royd

Hoyland Swaine
Height

Crab Tree
Hill
Pleasant Rise

Bleak
House

Mast

Briar
Cliffe

The
Cliffe

HIGHFIELD

CHAPPELL

Pinfold
Farm

HOYLANDSWAINE

THE NOOK

HAIGH HEAD RD.
CH. HEIGHTS CH. LE.
WD. HIGH
HAIGH

Nook

New
Hall

Green Bottom
Farm

Play.
Fld.

War.
Mem. SYCAMORE
Hall La.
Top

The Hollies

405

1

ROAD
A4628
BARNSLEY

Green Top
Farm

Bray
Wood

Delf
House

Delf
Wood

High
Cliffe

ROAD HIGH

BARNSLEY
HIGH ROYD

High Royd
Cottages

High Royd
Farm

Cliff
Plantation

2

Vicar
Wood

ROAD

High Lee
Farm

Shrogg
Wood

High Lea
Farm

LEE LANE

Royd Wood

Upper
Storrs

04

3

Sheffield
S36

STEEP LANE

Spring Wood

White Field
Farm

LANE OXSPRING
A629

Rose
Cottage

High
Oxspring
Farm

Oxspring Tunnel

Clays Green

Jockey
House

4

03

RIVER
Denison Viaduct

Pav.
Cricket
Ground

Depot
Wks

Works

Boulder
Bridge

DON

Tom Hill

LANE

JOCKEY RD.
Jockey
Hill

Penistone

Spring
Vale

Foundry

GREEN
WEST ACRE

SHEFFIELD

Springvale
Prim. Sch.

Kirkwood Beck

Kirk Wood

Walk Mill
Bank

Works

Wood Bank
House

Willow La.
Top

Willow Bridge
Cottages

Willow

5

Castle
Green

Fairfield
Bungalow

Shepherd's Castle
Farm

Castle Green

PENNINE CT.

Works

Wks.

Mills
Kirkwood
Bridge

KIRKWOOD CL. ONGLEY INGS

B6462

Oxspring
Viaduct

Willow
Bridge

Manor Ho.
(remains of)

Oxspring
Rocher

WEST CRES.
SOUTHCROFT

Willow Lane
Bungalow

Oxspring
Croft

MANOR
LA.

New House
Farm

Castle Hill
House

NOOK LANE

CASTLE LONG LANE

Castle Dam

THE WILLOWS

MILLSTONES

6

New
House

THICKETT LA.

OXSPRING

Oxspring Prim. Sch.

Roughbirchworth
Lodge

Sycamore
Farm

ROUGH END

Playgrd.

ROAD

MAYFIELD

BIRCHWORTH

VALE VW.

TOLLBAR

BANK

Playing
Field

E F G H

25 26 27

INDEX

Including Streets, Places & Areas, Industrial Estates,
Selected Flats & Walkways, Service Areas, Stations and Selected Places of Interest.

HOW TO USE THIS INDEX

1. Each street name is followed by its Postcode District, then by its Locality abbreviation(s) and then by its map reference;
e.g. **Abbey Brook Dr.** S8: Shef . . . .1D **146** is in the S8 Postcode District and the Sheffield Locality and is to be found in square 1D on the page **146**. The page number is shown in bold type.

2. A strict alphabetical order is followed in which Av., Rd., St., etc. (though abbreviated) are read in full and as part of the street name;
e.g. **Abbeyfield Rd.** appears after **Abbey Farm Vw.** but before **Abbey Flds.**

3. Streets and a selection of flats and walkways that cannot be shown on the mapping, appear in the index with the thoroughfare to which they are connected shown in brackets; e.g. **Abbeydale Ct.** S17: Dore . . . .3H **145** (off Ladies Spring Dr.)

4. Addresses that are in more than one part are referred to as not continuous.

5. Places and areas are shown in the index in BLUE TYPE and the map reference is to the actual map square in which the town centre or area is located and not to the place name shown on the map; e.g. ARMTHORPE 4D **42**

6. An example of a selected place of interest is Abbeydale Industrial Hamlet (Museum) 2A **146**

7. An example of a station is **Adwick Station (Rail)** . . . .2D **22**. Included are Rail **(Rail)**, Supertram **(ST)**, Park & Tram and Park & Ride.
e.g. **Abbeydale (Park & Ride)** 4C **132**

8. Service Areas are shown in the index in **BOLD CAPITAL TYPE**; e.g. **WOODALL SERVICE AREA** 5G **153**

9. Map references for entries that appear on large scale pages **4** & **5** are shown first, with small scale map references shown in brackets;
e.g. **Allen St.** S3: Shef 1C **4** (2E **119**)

GENERAL ABBREVIATIONS

All. : Alley	**Flds.** : Fields	**Pde.** : Parade
App. : Approach	**Gdn.** : Garden	**Pk.** : Park
Arc. : Arcade	**Gdns.** : Gardens	**Pl.** : Place
Av. : Avenue	**Gth.** : Garth	**Pct.** : Precinct
Bk. : Back	**Ga.** : Gate	**Quad.** : Quadrant
Blvd. : Boulevard	**Gt.** : Great	**Res.** : Residential
Bri. : Bridge	**Grn.** : Green	**Ri.** : Rise
Bldgs. : Buildings	**Gro.** : Grove	**Rd.** : Road
Bungs. : Bungalows	**Hgts.** : Heights	**Rdbt.** : Roundabout
Bus. : Business	**Ho.** : House	**Shop.** : Shopping
Cen. : Centre	**Ho's.** : Houses	**Sth.** : South
Chu. : Church	**Ind.** : Industrial	**Sq.** : Square
Circ. : Circle	**Info.** : Information	**Sta.** : Station
Cl. : Close	**Intl.** : International	**St.** : Street
Comn. : Common	**La.** : Lane	**Ter.** : Terrace
Cnr. : Corner	**Lit.** : Little	**Twr.** : Tower
Cott. : Cottage	**Lwr.** : Lower	**Trad.** : Trading
Cotts. : Cottages	**Mnr.** : Manor	**Up.** : Upper
Ct. : Court	**Mans.** : Mansions	**Va.** : Vale
Cres. : Crescent	**Mkt.** : Market	**Vw.** : View
Cft. : Croft	**Mdw.** : Meadow	**Vs.** : Villas
Dr. : Drive	**Mdws.** : Meadows	**Vis.** : Visitors
E. : East	**M.** : Mews	**Wlk.** : Walk
Ent. : Enterprise	**Mt.** : Mount	**W.** : West
Est. : Estate	**Mus.** : Museum	**Yd.** : Yard
Fld. : Field	**Nth.** : North	

LOCALITY ABBREVIATIONS

Abdy : **Abdy**	Ben : **Bentley**	Brook : **Brookhouse**
Adw S : **Adwick le Street**	Bess : **Bessacarr**	Burn : **Burncross**
Ald : **Aldwarke**	Bill : **Billingley**	Cade : **Cadeby**
Alm : **Almholme**	Birdh : **Birdholme**	Cal : **Calow**
A'ley : **Alverley**	Birdw : **Birdwell**	Cant : **Cantley**
App : **Apperknowle**	Black H : **Blacker Hill**	Carc : **Carcroft**
Ard : **Ardsley**	Blax : **Blaxton**	Carl : **Carlton**
Ark : **Arksey**	Bolst : **Bolsterstone**	Carr : **Carr**
Ark T : **Arkwright Town**	Bolt D : **Bolton upon Dearne**	Cat : **Catcliffe**
Arm : **Armthorpe**	Bradf : **Bradfield**	Cawt : **Cawthorne**
Ash : **Ashgate**	Bradw : **Bradway**	Chap : **Chapeltown**
Ast : **Aston**	B'well : **Braithwell**	Ches : **Chesterfield**
Ath : **Athersley**	Braml : **Bramley**	Clay : **Clayton**
Auck : **Auckley**	Bramp : **Brampton**	Clift : **Clifton**
Augh : **Aughton**	Bramp B : **Brampton Bierlow**	Coal A : **Coal Aston**
Balb : **Balby**	Bramp M : **Brampton en le Morthen**	Con : **Conisbrough**
Barl : **Barlborough**	Brant : **Branton**	Cor : **Corbriggs**
B'low : **Barlow**	Brier : **Brierley**	Cub : **Cubley**
Barnb : **Barnburgh**	Bright : **Brightholmlee**	Cud : **Cudworth**
Barn D : **Barnby Dun**	Brim : **Brimington**	Cus : **Cusworth**
Barn : **Barnsley**	Brim C : **Brimington Common**	Cut : **Cutthorpe**
Bar H : **Barrow Hill**	Brins : **Brinsworth**	Dalt : **Dalton**
Bar G : **Barugh Green**	Brod : **Brodsworth**	Dalt M : **Dalton Magna**
Beig : **Beighton**	Brom : **Bromley**	D'fld : **Darfield**

Dart : **Darton**
Den M : **Denaby Main**
Dinn : **Dinnington**
Dod : **Dodworth**
Don : **Doncaster**
Dore : **Dore**
Dron : **Dronfield**
Dron W : **Dronfield Woodhouse**
Duck : **Duckmanton**
Dung : **Dungworth**
Dunsv : **Dunsville**
Eccl : **Ecclesfield**
Ecki : **Eckington**
Eden : **Edenthorpe**
Els : **Elsecar**
Finn : **Finningley**
Fir : **Firbeck**
Flan : **Flanderwell**
Gild : **Gildingwells**
Gol : **Goldthorpe**
Gras : **Grassmoor**
Grea : **Greasbrough**
Gt H : **Great Houghton**
Green M : **Green Moor**
Gren : **Grenoside**
Grim : **Grimethorpe**
Hai : **Haigh**
Half : **Halfway**
Ham : **Hampole**
H'ley : **Harley**
H'ton : **Harlington**
Hart : **Harthill**
Has : **Hasland**
Hatf : **Hatfield**
Hel : **Hellaby**
Hem : **Hemingfield**
Hems : **Hemsworth**
Hex : **Hexthorpe**
Hick : **Hickleton**
H'ham : **Higham**
Highf : **Highfields**
High G : **High Green**
High H : **High Hoyland**
High M : **High Melton**
Holb : **Holbrook**
Hol : **Hollingwood**
Holm : **Holme**
Holme : **Holmesfield**
Holy : **Holymoorside**
Hood G : **Hood Green**
Hoot L : **Hooton Levitt**
Hoot P : **Hooton Pagnell**
Hoot R : **Hooton Roberts**
Howb : **Howbrook**
Hoyl : **Hoyland**
H'swne : **Hoylandswaine**
Hun : **Hundall**
Ingb : **Ingbirchworth**
Ink : **Inkersall**
Jum : **Jump**
Kexb : **Kexborough**
Killa : **Killamarsh**
Kiln : **Kilnhurst**
Kimb : **Kimberworth**

Kimb P : **Kimberworth Park**
Kirk Sa : **Kirk Sandall**
Kiv P : **Kiveton Park**
Kiv S : **Kiveton Park Station**
Laugh C : **Laughton Common**
Laugh M : **Laughton en le Morthen**
Letw : **Letwell**
Lit H : **Little Houghton**
Long S : **Long Sandall**
Lov : **Loversall**
Low L : **Low Laithes**
Lox : **Loxley**
Lund : **Lundwood**
Malt : **Maltby**
Mapp : **Mapplewell**
Marr : **Marr**
Mar L : **Marsh Lane**
Mas M : **Mastin Moor**
Mexb : **Mexborough**
Mick : **Micklebring**
Midd : **Middlecliffe**
Midd H : **Middle Handley**
Midh : **Midhopestones**
Miss : **Misson**
Monk B : **Monk Bretton**
Mort : **Morthen**
Mosb : **Mosborough**
Neth Han : **Nether Handley**
Neth Hau : **Nether Haugh**
New E : **New Edlington**
New R : **New Rossington**
New W : **New Whittington**
Nth A : **North Anston**
Nott : **Notton**
Old B : **Old Brampton**
Old D : **Old Denaby**
Old E : **Old Edlington**
Old W : **Old Whittington**
Ough : **Oughtibridge**
Oxs : **Oxspring**
Parkg : **Parkgate**
Pen : **Penistone**
Pill : **Pilley**
Pool : **Poolsbrook**
Rav : **Ravenfield**
Rawm : **Rawmarsh**
Reni : **Renishaw**
Ridg : **Ridgeway**
Ross : **Rossington**
Roth : **Rotherham**
Rough : **Roughbirchworth**
Roy : **Royston**
Scaws : **Scawsby**
Scawt : **Scawthorpe**
Scho : **Scholes**
Shaft : **Shafton**
Shef : **Sheffield**
Shut : **Shuttlewood**
Silk : **Silkstone**
Silk C : **Silkstone Common**
Skell : **Skellow**
Slade H : **Slade Hooton**
Smi : **Smithies**
Sot : **Sothall**

Sth A : **South Anston**
Sth B : **South Bramwith**
Sth H : **South Hiendley**
Sth K : **South Kirkby**
Spink : **Spinkhill**
Sprot : **Sprotbrough**
Stainb : **Stainborough**
Stain : **Staincross**
Staint : **Stainton**
Stair : **Stairfoot**
Stan : **Stanfree**
Stann : **Stannington**
Stav : **Staveley**
Stoc : **Stocksbridge**
Ston E : **Stone Edge**
Sunn : **Sunnyside**
Sut S : **Sutton Scarsdale**
Swai : **Swaithe**
Swal : **Swallownest**
Swint : **Swinton**
Tank : **Tankersley**
Tem N : **Temple Normanton**
Thorpe H : **Thorpe Hesley**
Thry : **Thrybergh**
Thurc : **Thurcroft**
Thurl : **Thurlstone**
Thurn : **Thurnscoe**
Tick : **Tickhill**
Tins : **Tinsley**
Tod : **Todwick**
Tot : **Totley**
Tree : **Treeton**
Trow : **Troway**
Ull : **Ulley**
Uns : **Unstone**
Up N : **Upper Newbold**
Up W : **Upper Whiston**
Wad : **Wadworth**
Wales : **Wales**
Wales B : **Wales Bar**
Walt : **Walton**
Warm : **Warmsworth**
Water : **Waterthorpe**
Wath D : **Wath upon Dearne**
Wentw : **Wentworth**
West H : **West Handley**
Westf : **Westfield**
Wharn S : **Wharncliffe Side**
Whist : **Whiston**
Whit M : **Whittington Moor**
Wick : **Wickersley**
Wils : **Wilsic**
W'orth : **Wingerworth**
Wing : **Wingfield**
Womb : **Wombwell**
Wooda : **Woodall**
Woodl : **Woodlands**
Woods : **Woodsetts**
Woodt : **Woodthorpe**
Wool : **Woolley**
Wool G : **Woolley Grange**
Work : **Worksop**
Wors : **Worsbrough**
Wort : **Wortley**

1st Bowl
Sheffield 6A **94**

<h2>A</h2>

Aaron Wilkinson Ct.
WF9: Sth K 4H **13**
Abbey Brook Cl. S8: Shef . . .1D **146**
Abbey Brook Ct. S8: Shef . . .1D **146**
Abbey Brook Dr. S8: Shef . . .1D **146**
Abbey Brook Gdns. S8: Shef . . .1D **146**
Abbey Cl. S25: Laugh M 1G **127**
Abbey Ct. S8: Shef 1D **146**
Abbey Cres. S7: Shef 1A **146**
Abbey Ct. S7: Shef 1A **146**
S41: Up N 1B **166**
ABBEYDALE 1A **146**
Abbeydale (Park & Ride) 4C **132**

Abbeydale Ct. *S17: Dore* 3H **145**
(off Ladies Spring Dr.)
Abbeydale Dr. S7: Shef 4C **132**
Abbeydale Golf Course 3A **146**
Abbeydale Industrial Hamlet (Museum)
. . . . .2A **146**
ABBEYDALE PARK 4G **145**
Abbeydale Pk. Cres.
S17: Dore 4G **145**
Abbeydale Park Rackets & Fitness Club
. . . . .3H **145**
Abbeydale Pk. Ri. S17: Dore . . .3F **145**
Abbeydale Park Sports Club 3G **145**
Abbeydale Rd. S7: Shef 5C **132**
Abbeydale Rd. Sth.
S7: Shef 4G **145**
S17: Dore, Tot 4G **145**
Abbey Farm Vw. S72: Cud 3E **19**
Abbeyfield Rd. S4: Shef 5G **107**
Abbey Flds. DN9: Finn 3F **77**
Abbey Glen S66: Carr 3E **115**
Abbey Grange S7: Shef 1A **146**

Abbey Grn. S75: Dod 4H **29**
Abbey Gro. S71: Lund 5B **18**
Abbeyhill Cl. S42: Ash 4A **166**
Abbey La. S7: Shef 6H **131**
S8: Shef 6H **131**
S11: Shef 5G **131**
S25: Slade H 5H **115**
S71: Lund 6B **18**
(not continuous)
Abbey La. Dell S8: Shef 1A **146**
Abbey Sq. S71: Lund 4B **18**
Abbey Vw. Dr. S8: Shef 5F **133**
Abbey Vw. Rd. S8: Shef 5F **133**
Abbey Wlk. DN5: Scaws 5F **39**
Abbey Way S25: Nth A 5E **127**
Abbot La. WF4: Wool 1A **8**
Abbots Cl. S72: Cud 3F **19**
Abbots Ford Dr. S66: Thurc 6B **114**
Abbots Mdw. S20: Sot 1H **151**
Abbots Rd. S71: Lund 5C **18**
Abbott St. DN4: Hex 2A **56**
ABDY 4E **65**

Abdy La. S62: Abdy 4F 65
    S64: Swint 4F 65
Abdy Rd. S61: Kimb P 6G 81
    S62: Abdy 5D 64
Abell St. S65: Thry 6D 84
Aberconway Cres. DN11: New R 6B 74
Abercorn Rd. DN2: Don 6H 41
Abercrombie St. S41: Ches 4H 167
Aberford Gro. S74: Els 6E 47
Abingdon Gdns. S61: Grea 5C 82
Abingdon Rd. DN2: Don 5G 41
Abney Cl. S14: Shef 2H 133
    S40: Ches 2D 166
Abney Dr. S14: Shef 2H 133
Abney Rd. S14: Shef 2H 133
Abney St. S1: Shef 3C 4 (3E 119)
Abrafact Ind. Ct. S6: Shef 3C 106
Abus Rd. DN5: Scaws 3D 38
Acacia Av. S35: Chap 4F 79
    S43: Hol 6F 163
    S66: Braml 5H 99
    S66: Malt 5G 101
Acacia Ct. DN5: Ben 6H 23
Acacia Cres. S21: Killa 5A 152
Acacia Gro. DN12: Con 6D 68
    S72: Shaft 4F 11
Acacia Rd. DN4: Cant 4C 58
    S5: Shef 6B 94
Ace Bus. Cen. S3: Shef 1G 5 (1G 119)
Acer Cl. S21: Killa 5B 152
    S25: Sth A 5G 141
Acer Cft. DN3: Arm 5E 43
Ackworth Dr. S9: Tins 3A 110
Acorn Av. S63: Thurn 2C 36
Acorn Bus. Pk. *S8: Shef 4D 132*
    (off Woodseats Cl.)
Acorn Cen., The S72: Grim 2B 20
Acorn Cl. S35: Ough 3F 91
Acorn Cft. S61: Grea 6C 82
Acorn Dr. S6: Stann 6D 104
Acorn Hill S6: Stann 5E 105
Acorn Pl. S63: Wath D 2H 65
Acorn Ridge S42: Walt 3C 170
Acorn Rd. S6: Stann 6C 104
Acorn St. S3: Shef 1D 4 (1F 119)
Acorn Way S66: Sunn 3H 99
    S72: Grim 2A 20
Acre Cl. DN3: Eden 6C 26
    S66: Malt 3H 101
    S66: Thurc 5C 114
Acre Ga. S35: High G 2C 78
Acre La. S35: Ough 2B 90
    S36: H'swne 1D 176
Acre Rd. S72: Cud 4F 19
Acres Hill Cl. S9: Shef 2E 121
Acres Hill La. S9: Shef 3E 121
Acres Hill Rd. S9: Shef 2E 121
Acres Vw. S60: Roth 1A 112
Acres Vw. Cl. S41: Ches 1G 167
Acrewood Dr. S66: Sunn 2G 99
Adamfield S3: Shef 3A 4
Adam La. S75: Cawt 6B 14
Adastral Av. S12: Shef 6D 134
Addison Rd. S5: Shef 2A 108
    S64: Mexb 1G 67
    S66: Malt 5G 101
Addison Sq. S25: Dinn 5A 128
Addy Cl. DN4: Balb 1B 72
    S6: Shef 1D 118
Addy Dr. S6: Shef 1D 118
Addy St. S6: Shef 1D 118
Adelaide La. S3: Shef 1E 119
Adelaide Rd. S7: Shef 2C 132
Adelaide St. S66: Malt 6C 102
Adelphi St. S6: Shef 1D 118
Adelphi Way S43: Stav 6B 164
Adkin Royd S75: Silk 2A 28
Adkins Dr. S5: Shef 1D 106
Adkins Rd. S5: Shef 1D 106
Adlard Rd. DN2: Don 4G 41
Adlington Cres. S5: Shef 6E 93
Adlington Rd. S5: Shef 6E 93
Admiral Biggs Dr. S60: Tree 2F 123
Admirals Crest S61: Scho 6E 81
Adrian Cres. S5: Shef 6F 93
Adsetts St. S4: Shef 3B 108
Adwick (Park & Ride) 2D 22
Adwick Av. DN5: Ben 3G 23

Adwick Ct. S64: Mexb 2G 67
Adwick La. DN5: Ben 2D 22
    DN6: Adw S 2D 22
Adwick Leisure Cen. 4C 22
ADWICK LE STREET 2C 22
Adwick Pk. S63: Wath D 6C 50
Adwick Rd. S64: Mexb 5E 51
Adwick Station (Rail) 2D 22
ADWICK UPON DEARNE 4E 51
Aeroventure .3F 57
Agden Rd. S7: Shef 6D 118
Agnes Rd. S70: Barn 2D 30
Agnes Ter. S70: Barn 2D 30
Aidans Cl. DN2: Don 1A 42
Ainsdale Av. S63: Gol 6C 36
Ainsdale Cl. S71: Roy 1G 9
Ainsdale Ct. S71: Monk B 3A 18
    S21: Ecki 1C 158
Ainsley Cl. DN9: Auck 1H 59
Ainsley Rd. S10: Shef 2B 118
Ainsty Rd. S7: Shef 1E 133
Aintree Av. DN4: Cant 2A 58
Aintree Cl. DN5: Scaws 5E 39
Aintree Dr. DN4: Balb 1B 72
    S64: Mexb 6G 51
Aire Cl. S35: Chap 2E 79
Airedale Rd. S6: Shef 2H 105
    S75: Kexb 6D 6
Aireton Cl. S66: Wick 5F 99
Aireton Rd. S70: Barn 6D 16
Air Mount Cl. S66: Wick 6F 99
Aisby Dr. DN11: Hous 4D 74
Aisthorpe Rd. S8: Shef 5E 133
Aitken Rd. S64: Kiln 6D 66
Aizlewood Rd. S8: Shef 1E 133
Akley Bank Cl. S17: Tot 5G 145
Alan Rd. S75: Dart 6E 7
Alba Cl. S73: D'fld 4D 32
Albanus Cft. S6: Stann 6D 104
Albanus Ridge S6: Stann 6D 104
Albany Av. S35: Chap 4G 79
Albany Cl. S73: Womb 4D 32
Albany La. DN11: New R 5B 74
Albany Rd. DN4: Balb 4H 55
    S7: Shef 1E 133
    S36: Stoc 3D 174
    S64: Kiln 5C 66
Albany St. S65: Roth 4F 97
Albert Av. S43: New W 3C 162
Albert Cres. S72: Midd 3E 35
Albert Rd. S8: Shef 2F 133
    S12: Shef 5D 136
    S43: New W 3C 162
    S62: Parkg 4G 83
    S63: Gol 5D 36
    S63: Wath D 5E 49
    S66: Wick 1F 67
Albert St. S21: Ecki 2E 159
    S60: Roth 4D 96
    S63: Thurn 2B 36
    S64: Swint 2C 66
    S66: Malt 6C 102
    S70: Barn 1E 31
    S72: Cud 5F 11
Albert St. E. S70: Barn 1E 31
Albert St. Nth. S41: Whit M 5G 161
Albert Ter. Rd. S6: Shef 1D 118
Albion S6: Shef 1A 4 (2D 118)
Albion Dr. S63: Thurn 2E 37
Albion Ho. S70: Barn 2D 30
Albion Pl. DN1: Don 1D 56
    S60: Roth 4F 97
    S71: Carl 1H 17
Albion Row S66: Wick 2E 117
Albion St. S40: Ches 5G 167
    S60: Roth 4F 97
Albion Ter. DN4: Hex 3A 56
    S70: Barn 2F 31
Alcester Rd. S7: Shef 1E 133
Aldam Cl. S17: Tot 6F 145
    S65: Roth 3C 98
    S66: Wick 6G 99
Aldam Cft. S17: Tot 6F 145
Aldam Rd. DN4: Balb 6G 55
    S17: Tot 6G 145

Aldam Way S17: Tot 6F 145
Aldbeck Cft. S75: Dart 1F 15
Aldbury Cl. S71: Ath 2G 17
Aldcliffe Cres. DN4: Balb 2G 71
Aldene Av. S6: Shef 3G 105
Aldene Glade S6: Shef 3G 105
Aldene Rd. S6: Shef 2G 105
Alder Chase S61: Scho 6F 81
Alder Cl. S75: Mapp 5H 7
Alderford Dr. DN4: Balb 1A 72
Alder Gdns. S43: Hol 5F 163
Alder Gro. DN4: Balb 5H 55
    S73: D'fld 6A 34
Alder Holt Cl. DN3: Arm 5F 43
Alder La. S9: Shef 3H 121
Alder M. S74: Hoyl 1B 62
Alderney Rd. S2: Shef 1F 133
Alder Rd. S18: Dron 1F 155
Aldersgate Cl.
    DN11: New R . . . . .6D 74 & 6H 75
Aldersgate Ct. S66: Malt 5D 102
Alders Grn. S6: Lox 3E 105
Alderson Av. S62: Rawm 1G 83
Alderson Cl. S26: Swal 5C 124
Alderson Dr. DN2: Don 2E 57
    S71: Smi 2F 17
Alderson Pl. S2: Shef 6F 119
Alderson Rd. S2: Shef 6E 119
    (not continuous)
Alderson Rd. Nth. S2: Shef 6F 119
Aldervale Cl. S64: Swint 6C 66
Alderwood Cl. S66: Sunn 3G 99
Aldesworth Rd. DN4: Cant 3B 58
Aldfield Way S5: Shef 3G 107
Aldham Cotts. S73: Womb 5F 33
Aldham Cres. S73: Womb 4D 32
Aldham Ho. La. S73: Womb 6E 33
Aldham Ind. Est. S73: Womb 5F 33
Aldham Vw. S73: Womb 6E 33
Aldine Cl. S1: Shef 3F 5
Aldous Cl. S26: Kiv P 5B 140
Aldous Way S26: Kiv P 5B 140
Aldred Cl. S21: Killa 2D 152
    S66: Wick 5G 99
Aldred Ct. S65: Roth 5F 97
Aldred Rd. S10: Shef 1B 118
Aldred St. S65: Roth 5F 97
Aldrens Cl. S66: Mick 6G 87
Aldrin Way S66: Malt 4H 101
ALDWARKE 6A 84
Aldwarke La. S65: Ald 5H 83
Aldwarke Rd. S62: Parkg 5G 83
Aldwarke Ter. S62: Parkg 5H 83
Aleem Ct. *S66: Malt 5B 102*
    (off High St.)
Alexander St. DN5: Ben 1A 40
Alexandra Cen. S62: Parkg 6G 83
Alexandra Cl. S61: Kimb 2H 95
Alexandra Gdns. S11: Shef 2C 132
Alexandra Rd. DN4: Balb 4A 56
    DN5: Ben 6A 24
    DN6: Adw S 2E 23
    S2: Shef 1G 133
    S18: Dron 2G 155
    S26: Swal 6B 124
    S64: Mexb 1G 67
Alexandra Rd. E. S41: Ches 6B 168
Alexandra Rd. W. S40: Ches 5G 167
Alexandra St. S66: Malt 6C 102
Alexandra Ter. S71: Ard 2C 32
Alford Av. S35: Ough 3E 91
Alford Cl. S40: Ash 5D 166
    S75: Barn 4A 16
Alfred Rd. S9: Shef 5C 108
    (not continuous)
Alfred St. S71: Roy 2B 10
Algar Cl. S2: Shef 1B 134
Algar Cres. S2: Shef 1C 134
Algar Dr. S2: Shef 1B 134
Algar Pl. S2: Shef 1B 134
Algar Rd. S2: Shef 1B 134
Alhambra Shop. Cen. S70: Barn 1E 31
Alice Rd. S61: Roth 3C 96
Alice Way S18: Uns 6B 156
Alison Cl. S26: Swal 1C 138
Alison Cres. S26: Swal 5E 121
Alison Dr. S26: Swal 1C 138
Allan St. S65: Roth 4F 97

Allatt Cl.—Argyll Av.

Allatt Cl. S70: Barn 2E **31**
Alldred Cres. S64: Swint 5B **66**
Allenby Cl. S8: Shef 3D **146**
Allenby Cres. DN11: New R 6B **74**
Allenby Dr. S8: Shef 3D **146**
Allendale S70: Wors 5H **31**
Allendale Ct. S70: Wors 5H **31**
Allendale Dr. S74: Hoyl 1B **62**
Allendale Gdns. DN5: Don 1G **55**
Allendale Rd. DN5: Don 1G **55**
S42: W'orth 6G **171**
S65: Roth 6B **98**
S74: Hoyl 1A **62**
S75: Barn 4D **16**
S75: Kexb 6E **7**
Allende Way S9: Shef 6E **109**
Allen Gdns. S35: Eccl 1G **93**
Allen Rd. S20: Beig 6G **137**
Allen St. S3: Shef 1C **4** (2E **119**)
Allerton St. DN1: Don 6C **40**
Allestree Dr. S18: Dron W 3B **154**
All Hallows Dr. S66: Malt 6H **101**
Alliance St. S4: Shef 5A **108**
Alliss Rd. DN3: Brant 4H **59**
Allott Cl. S65: Rav 2A **100**
Allott Cres. S74: Jum 5D **46**
Allotts Ct. S70: Birdw 5D **44**
Allott St. S74: Els 1D **62**
S74: Hoyl 1G **61**
Allpits Rd. S44: Cal 5E **169**
Allport Ter. S43: Bar H 2G **163**
All Saints Cl. DN5: Ark 6C **24**
S63: Wath D 6F **49**
S75: Silk 1B **28**
All Saints Mdws.
S25: Laugh C 3F **127**
All Saints Sq. DN12: Den M 2D **68**
S60: Roth 4E **97**
All Saints Way S26: Ast 1D **138**
Allsopps Yd. S74: Black H 3A **46**
Allsops Pl. S41: Ches 6G **161**
Allt St. S62: Parkg 4G **83**
Alma Cres. S18: Dron 1F **155**
Alma Leisure Pk. S40: Ches 1A **172**
Alma Rd. S35: High G 1C **78**
S60: Roth 5E **97**
Alma Row S60: Whist 3B **112**
Alma St. S3: Shef 1D **4** (1F **119**) & 1E **5**
S70: Barn 1C **30**
S73: Womb 2G **47**
Alma St. W. S40: Ches 6F **167**
ALMHOLME 3E **25**
Almholme La. DN5: Alm, Ark 5D **24**
Almond Av. DN3: Arm 3E **43**
S72: Cud 1E **19**
Almond Cl. S44: Cal 5F **169**
S66: Malt 5H **101**
Almond Cres. S43: Mas M 2F **165**
Almond Cft. S73: Womb 3F **47**
Almond Dr. S21: Killa 5B **152**
Almond Glade S66: Wick 1H **113**
Almond Pl. S43: Brim 1D **168**
S63: Wath D 1G **65**
Almond Rd. DN4: Cant 4C **58**
Almond Tree Rd. S26: Wales 6F **139**
Alms Hill Cres. S11: Shef 5G **131**
Alms Hill Dr. S11: Shef 5G **131**
Alms Hill Glade S11: Shef 5G **131**
Alms Hill Rd. S11: Shef 5G **131**
Alms Houses S60: Roth 5G **97**
Almshouses S62: Wentw 4D **62**
Alney Pl. S6: Shef 6C **92**
Alnwick Dr. S12: Shef 3E **135**
Alnwick Rd. S12: Shef 3D **134**
Alperton Cl. S71: Lund 3C **18**
Alpha Rd. S65: Roth 3A **98**
Alpha St. DN5: Ben 3G **23**
Alpina Way S26: Swal 1B **138**
Alpine Cl. S36: Stoc 3C **174**
Alpine Cft. S36: Stoc 3C **174**
Alpine Gro. S43: Hol 6F **163**
Alpine Rd. S6: Shef 1C **118**
S36: Stoc 3C **174**
Alport Av. S12: Shef 3H **135**
Alport Dr. S12: Shef 3H **135**
Alport Gro. S12: Shef 3H **135**
Alport Pl. S12: Shef 4H **135**
Alport Ri. S18: Dron W 2C **154**
Alport Rd. S12: Shef 3H **135**
Alric Dr. S60: Brins 3C **110**
S71: Barn 1B **32**
Alrich M. S36: Stoc 2B **174**
Alsing Rd. S9: Shef 1F **109**
Alston Cl. DN4: Bess 5A **58**
S75: Silk 2A **28**
Alston Rd. DN4: Bess 6A **58**
Alton Cl. S11: Shef 6H **131**
S18: Dron W 4C **154**
S42: Walt 2C **170**
Alton Way S75: Mapp 5H **7**
Alum Chine Cl. S41: Has 2B **172**
Alvaston Wlk. DN12: Den M 3D **68**
ALVERLEY 3G **71**
Alverley Gdns. S43: Stav 6A **164**
Alverley La. DN4: Balb 2H **71**
Alverley Vw. DN11: A'ley 3H **71**
Alverley Way S70: Birdw 6E **45**
Alwyn Av. DN5: Scaws 3F **39**
Amalfi Cl. S73: D'fld 5A **34**
Ambassador Gdns. DN3: Arm 5F **43**
Amber Cres. S40: Walt 1D **170**
Amber Cft. S43: Ink 1H **169**
Amberley Ct. S9: Shef 5D **108**
Amberley St. S9: Shef 4D **108**
Ambler Ri. S26: Augh 5B **124**
Ambleside Cl. S20: Half 4F **151**
S41: Ches 1D **166**
S60: Brins 4B **110**
Ambleside Cres. DN5: Sprot 3B **54**
Ambleside Gro. S71: Ard 2D **32**
Ambleside Wlk. S25: Nth A 2A **142**
Amen Corner S60: Roth 3D **96**
(not continuous)
America La. S62: Wentw 5C **64**
S63: Wath D 3D **64**
Amersall Ct. DN5: Scawt 3F **39**
Amersall Cres. DN5: Scawt 2F **39**
Amersall Rd. DN5: Scawt 2F **39**
Amesbury Cl. S41: Ches 1F **167**
Ami Ct. S62: Parkg 6F **83**
Amory's Holt Cl. S66: Malt 3H **101**
Amory's Holt Dr. S66: Malt 3H **101**
Amory's Holt Rd. S66: Malt 3H **101**
Amory's Holt Way S66: Malt 4G **101**
Amos Rd. S9: Shef 2E **109**
Amy Rd. DN5: Ben 5B **24**
Anchorage Cres. DN5: Don 6H **39**
Anchorage La. DN5: Don 5G **39**
Ancona Ri. S73: D'fld 4A **34**
Ancote Cl. S75: Barn 1H **29**
Anderson Cl. S43: New W 3D **162**
Anderson Dr. S62: Rawm 6E **65**
Anderson La. S43: Brim C 3E **169**
Andover Dr. S3: Shef 6F **107**
Andover St. S3: Shef 6F **107**
Andrew La. S3: Shef 1G **5**
Andrews Pl. S61: Roth 2B **96**
Andwell La. S10: Shef 3A **130**
Anelay Rd. DN4: Balb 5G **55**
Anfield Rd. DN4: Cant 5B **58**
Angel La. S62: Wentw 6A **64**
Angel St. S3: Shef 2F **5** (2G **119**)
S63: Bolt D 3C **50**
Angel Yd. S40: Ches 5H **167**
Angerford Av. S8: Shef 4F **133**
Anglesey Rd. S18: Dron 4F **155**
Angleton Av. S2: Shef 6F **121**
Angleton Cl. S2: Shef 6F **121**
Angleton Gdns. S2: Shef 6F **121**
Angleton Grn. S2: Shef 6F **121**
Angleton M. S2: Shef 6F **121**
Angram Rd. S35: High G 6C **60**
Angram Vw. S35: High G 1C **78**
Annan Cl. S75: Bar G 3G **15**
Annat Pl. S35: High G 1B **78**
Anne Cres. S72: Sth H 1H **11**
Annesley Cl. S8: Shef 3E **147**
S41: Has 2B **172**
Annesley Rd. S8: Shef 2E **147**
Anne St. S25: Dinn 3A **128**
Annie Senior Gdns. S63: Bolt D 2C **50**
Anns Rd. S2: Shef 1F **133**
Anns Rd. Nth. S2: Shef 1G **133**
Ann St. S62: Parkg 5G **83**
Ansdell Rd. DN5: Ben 6A **24**
Ansell Rd. S11: Shef 2H **131**
Anson Gro. S60: Brins 4E **111**
Anson St. S2: Shef 3H **5** (3H **119**)
Ansten Cres. DN4: Cant 4B **58**
Anston Av. S26: Kiv P 5B **140**
Anston Cl. S25: Nth A 2G **141**
Ansult Ct. DN5: Ben 2H **39**
Antrim Av. S10: Shef 4C **118**
Anvil Cl. S6: Shef 6F **105**
Anvil Cres. S35: Eccl 2G **93**
Apley Rd. DN1: Don 2C **56**
Apollo St. S62: Rawm 1A **84**
Apostle Cl. DN4: Balb 6F **55**
APPERKNOWLE 3D **156**
Appleby Cl. S75: Dart 5G **7**
Appleby Rd. DN2: Don 6H **41**
Appleby Wlk. S25: Nth A 1A **142**
Applegarth Cl. S12: Shef 2D **134**
Applegarth Dr. S12: Shef 2D **134**
Apple Gro. DN9: Auck 2B **76**
Applehaigh Ct. WF4: Nott 1F **9**
Applehaigh Dr. DN3: Kirk Sa 3B **26**
Applehaigh Gro. S71: Roy 2F **9**
Applehaigh La. WF4: Nott 1F **9**
Applehaigh Vw. S71: Roy 3F **9**
Applehurst Bank S70: Barn 2G **31**
Appleton Cl. S65: Dalt 1C **98**
Appleton Gdns. DN5: Scawt 3H **39**
Appleton Way DN5: Scawt 2G **39**
S70: Wors 5F **31**
Apple Tree Cl. S81: Woods 4F **143**
Appletree Cl. DN4: Bess 1D **74**
Appletree Dr. S18: Dron 3F **155**
Appletree Wlk. *S18: Dron* *3G 155*
(off Appletree Dr.)
April Cl. S71: Monk B 4A **18**
April Dr. S71: Monk B 4A **18**
Apy Hill La. DN11: Tick, Wils 2H **103**
Aqueduct St. S71: Barn 5E **17**
Arbour Cl. S41: Has 4C **172**
Arbour Cres. S66: Thurc 6C **114**
Arbour Dr. S66: Thurc 6C **114**
Arbour La. S65: Rav 5B **86**
ARBOURTHORNE 1A **134**
Arbourthorne S2: Shef 5B **120**
Arbourthorne Cotts. S2: Shef 6A **120**
Arbourthorne Est. S2: Shef 2B **134**
Arbourthorne Rd. S2: Shef 1A **134**
Arbourthorne Road Stop (ST) 1A **134**
Arcade, The S9: Shef 1F **109**
S70: Barn 1E **31**
Archdale Cl. S2: Shef 6E **121**
S40: Ches 1H **171**
Archdale Pl. S2: Shef 6D **120**
Archdale Rd. S2: Shef 5D **120**
Archer Dr. S8: Shef 5C **132**
(not continuous)
Archer Ga. S6: Lox 3E **105**
Archer Ho. *S65: Roth* *3F 97*
(off Wharncliffe Hill)
Archer La. S7: Shef 3C **132**
Archer M. S8: Shef 4D **132**
Archer Rd. S8: Shef 5C **132**
Archers Way DN12: Con 4H **69**
S60: Tree 3G **123**
Archery Cl. S66: Wick 1G **113**
Archibald Rd. S7: Shef 2D **132**
Archway Cen. S1: Shef 4G **5** (3G **119**)
Archways S1: Shef 6F **5**
Arcon Pl. S62: Rawm 2H **83**
Arcubus Av. S26: Swal 6C **124**
Ardeen Rd. DN2: Don 6F **41**
Arden Cl. S40: Ches 4D **166**
Arden Ga. DN4: Balb 2G **71**
Ardmore St. S9: Shef 1D **120**
Ardron Wlk. S62: Rawm 2A **84**
ARDSLEY 2D **32**
Ardsley Av. S26: Ast 1D **138**
Ardsley Cl. S20: Mosb 6A **136**
Ardsley Dr. S20: Mosb 6A **136**
Ardsley Gro. S20: Mosb 6A **136**
Ardsley M. S71: Ard 2D **32**
Ardsley Rd. S40: Ash 5C **166**
S70: Wors 5H **31**
Arena Ct. S9: Shef 4E **109**
Arena / Don Valley Stadium Stop (ST)
5E **109**
Argyle Cl. S8: Shef 3G **133**
Argyle La. DN11: New R 5B **74**
Argyle Rd. S8: Shef 3F **133**
Argyle St. S64: Mexb 1F **67**
Argyll Av. DN2: Don 5G **41**

Arklow Cl. S41: Has 2A 172
Arklow Rd. DN2: Don 6F 41
ARKSEY 6C 24
Arksey Comn. La. DN5: Alm, Ark ...6D 24
Arksey La. DN5: Ben 1A 40
Arkwright Rd. DN5: Don 5G 39
ARKWRIGHT TOWN 5H 173
Arley St. S2: Shef 5F 119
(not continuous)
Arlington Av. S26: Ast 6E 125
Arlott Way DN12: New E 3D 70
Armer St. S60: Roth 4D 96
Armitage Bldgs. *S36: Shef* *4C 176*
(off Stottercliffe Rd.)
Armitage Rd. DN4: Balb 5G 55
S36: Spink 4F 175
Armroyd La. S74: Els, Hoyl 2B 62
Arms Pk. Dr. S20: Half 4G 151
Armstead Rd. S20: Beig 5H 137
Armstrong Wlk. S66: Malt 4H 101
ARMTHORPE 4D 42
Armthorpe Ent. Cen. DN3: Arm 3G 43
Armthorpe La. DN2: Don 5F 41
DN3: Barn D, Kirk Sa 3D 26
Armthorpe Leisure Cen. *3D 42*
Armthorpe Rd. DN2: Don 5F 41
S11: Shef 6G 117
Armyne Gro. S71: Barn 1B 32
Army Row S71: Roy 2A 10
Armytage Ind. Est.
S41: Whit M 5H 161
(not continuous)
Arncliffe Dr. S35: Chap 2E 79
S70: Barn 1A 30
Arndale Pct. S66: Malt 5B 102
Arnold Av. S12: Shef 6D 134
S71: Ath 1E 171
Arnold Cres. S64: Mexb 6F 51
Arnold Rd. S65: Roth 4A 98
Arnold St. S6: Shef 5B 106
Arnside Cl. S41: Ches 5E 161
Arnside Rd. S8: Shef 3D 132
S66: Malt 4B 102
Arnside Ter. S8: Shef 3D 132
Arran Hill S65: Thry 5E 85
Arran Rd. S10: Shef 3A 118
Arras St. S9: Shef 1C 120
Arren Cl. DN3: Barn D 1H 27
Arrowsmith Ho. *S65: Roth* *3F 97*
(off Wharncliffe Hill)
Arthington St. S8: Shef 2F 133
Arthur Av. DN5: Ben 6A 24
Arthur Pl. DN5: Ben 6A 24
Arthur Rd. S36: Stoc 3C 174
Arthur St. DN5: Ben 6B 24
S26: Swal 1C 138
S60: Roth 3D 96
S62: Rawm 1H 83
S70: Wors 5F 31
Artisan Vw. S8: Shef 2F 133
Arts Centre, The
Rotherham *3F 97*
(in York & Lancaster Regiment Mus.)
Arundel Av. S26: Tree 2F 123
S65: Dalt 1C 98
Arundel Bus. Pk. S6: Shef 6A 92
Arundel Cl. S18: Dron W 3C 154
S41: Ches 6G 161
Arundel Cotts. S60: Tree 2F 123
Arundel Ct. S11: Shef 4G 131
S43: Stav *4B 164*
(off Porter St.)
Arundel Cres. S60: Tree 2F 123
Arundel Gdns. DN5: Scawt 2G 39
S71: Roy 2H 9
Arundel Gate S1: Shef 5E 5 (4F 119)
Arundel La. S1: Shef 5F 5 (4G 119)
Arundell Dr. S71: Lund 3C 18
Arundel Rd. S35: Chap 2F 79
S60: Tree 2F 123
S65: Roth 5G 97
Arundel St. S1: Shef 6E 5 (4F 119)
S60: Tree 2F 123
Arundel Vw. S74: Jum 5D 46
Ascension S66: Malt 6C 102
Ascension M. *S66: Malt* *6B 102*
(off Firth Cres.)
Ascot Av. DN4: Cant 3A 58
Ascot Cl. S64: Mexb 6G 51

Ascot Dr. DN5: Scaws 4E 39
S25: Laugh C 4F 127
Ascot St. S2: Shef 5F 119
Ashberry Cl. S63: Thurn 2C 36
Ashberry Gdns. S6: Shef 1C 118
Ashberry Rd. S6: Shef 1C 118
Ashbourne Gro. S13: Shef 5A 122
S35: Ough 4F 91
Ashbourne Rd. S13: Shef 5A 122
S71: Ath 1F 17
Ashburnham Gdns. DN5: Don 1F 55
Ashburton Cl. DN6: Adw S 2B 22
Ashbury Dr. S8: Shef 6H 133
Ashby La. S8: Shef 6H 133
Ashby Dr. S26: Kiv P 6H 133
Ash Cl. S21: Killa 5B 152
S65: Roth 6C 98
Ash Cotts. S73: Womb 4E 33
Ash Ct. DN5: Sprot 3E 55
S66: Malt 4G 101
Ashcourt Dr. DN4: Balb 2A 72
Ash Cres. S21: Ecki 2C 158
S36: Spink 2F 175
S64: Mexb 6E 51
ASHCROFT 6C 62
Ashcroft Cl. DN12: New E 5B 70
Ashcroft Ct. S41: Old W 3A 162
Ashcroft Dr. S41: Old W 3A 162
Ashdale Cl. DN3: Eden 1C 42
Ash Dale Rd. DN4: Warm 2C 70
Ashdell S10: Shef 4B 118
Ashdell La. S10: Shef 4B 118
Ashdell Rd. S10: Shef 4B 118
Ashdene Ct. S64: Swint 6C 66
Ashdown Dr. S40: Walt 1E 171
Ashdown Gdns. S20: Sot 5H 137
Ashdown Pl. DN5: Scawt 2G 39
Ash Dyke Cl. S75: Kexb 1E 15
Asher Rd. S7: Shef 6E 119
Ashes La. S62: Wentw 6C 62
Ashfield Cl. DN3: Arm 5F 43
S12: Shef 4C 134
S36: Pen 5D 176
S75: Barn 5B 16
Ashfield Ct. S70: Barn 2A 32
Ashfield Dr. S12: Shef 4C 134
Ashfield Ho. WF9: Hems 1E 13
Ashfield Rd. DN4: Balb 6H 55
S36: Spink 3F 175
S41: Has 2C 172
WF9: Hems 1E 13
Ash Flds. Rd. DN5: Ben 1F 25
Ashfield Way S66: Sunn 3G 99
Ashford Cl. S18: Dron W 4C 154
Ashford Ct. S41: Ches 3H 167
S71: Roy 1H 9
Ashford Rd. S11: Shef 6C 118
S18: Dron W 4C 154
Ashfurlong Cl. S17: Dore 3G 145
Ashfurlong Dr. S17: Dore 3G 145
Ashfurlong Pk. S17: Dore 3G 145
Ashfurlong Rd. S17: Dore 3F 145
ASHGATE 4D 166
Ashgate Av. S40: Ash 5D 166
Ashgate Ct. S10: Shef 4B 118
Ashgate Ct. M. S40: Ches 5G 167
Ashgate La. S10: Shef 4B 118
Ashgate Rd. S10: Shef 4B 118
S40: Ash, Ches 4C 166
S42: Ash 4A 166
Ashgate Valley Rd.
S40: Ches 4E 167
Ash Gro. DN3: Arm 3F 43
DN9: Auck 2C 76
DN12: Con 5D 68
S10: Shef 4C 118
S26: Kiv P 5H 139
S43: Mas M 2E 165
S62: Rawm 3H 83
S66: Malt 4C 102
S66: Wick 5H 99
S70: Barn 3A 32
Ash-Holt Ind. Est. DN9: Finn 1H 77
Ash Ho. La. S17: Dore 1E 145
Ashland Cl. S7: Shef 2D 132
Ashland Rd. S7: Shef 2D 132
S21: Ecki 1F 159

Ash La. S18: App, Coal A 1C 156
S21: West H 4F 157
S36: Spink 3G 175
Ashlea S63: Thurn 2D 36
Ashleigh S72: Brier 3B 12
Ashleigh Av. S12: Shef 3C 134
Ashleigh Cl. S41: Old W 3A 162
Ashleigh Ct. S21: Ecki 3D 158
Ashleigh Cft. S12: Shef 3C 134
Ashleigh Dr. S12: Shef 3C 134
Ashleigh Gdns. S61: Grea 6C 82
Ashleigh Pl. S12: Shef 3C 134
Ashleigh Va. S70: Barn 2H 31
Ashley Cl. S21: Killa 4C 152
Ashley Ct. DN9: Finn 3F 77
WF9: Sth K 5G 13
Ashley Cft. S71: Roy 2G 9
Ashley Gro. S26: Ast 1C 138
Ashley Ind. Est. S60: Roth 3E 97
Ashley La. S21: Killa 4C 152
Ashmore Av. S21: Ecki 2C 158
Ash Mt. S62: Rawm 3G 83
S65: Roth *4F 97*
(off Doncaster Gate)
Ashmount S6: Shef 5B 92
Ashopton Rd. S41: Ches 2D 166
Ashover Cl. S70: Wors 6F 31
Ashover Rd. S43: Ink 2H 169
Ashpool Cl. S13: Shef 2B 136
Ashpool Fold S13: Shef 2B 136
Ash Ridge S64: Swint 4C 66
Ash Rd. S63: Wath D 1H 65
S72: Shaft 4G 11
Ash Row S71: Barn 1H 31
Ashroyds Bus. Pk.
S74: Hoyl 5A 46
Ashroyds Way S74: Hoyl 5A 46
Ash St. S6: Shef 6D 106
S20: Mosb 2D 150
S73: Womb 4D 32
Ashton Av. DN5: Scawt 1E 39
Ashton Cl. S21: Killa 4B 152
S40: Walt 2D 170
Ashton Dr. DN3: Kirk Sa 4B 26
Ashton La. S66: B'well 1H 101
Ash Tree Cl. S40: Ash 5D 166
Ash Tree Ct. *S9: Shef* *6E 95*
(off Eccles St.)
Ashurst Cl. S6: Shef 6F 105
S40: Ches 3A 166
Ashurst Dr. S6: Shef 5F 105
Ashurst Pl. S6: Shef 5F 105
Ashurst Rd. S6: Shef 5F 105
Ash Va. S40: Bramp 5C 166
Ash Vw. S35: Chap 4E 79
S61: Grea 5D 82
Ashville DN11: New R ....6D 74 & 6H 75
Ashville Ct. S70: Stair 2A 32
Ashwell Cl. S72: Shaft 3F 11
Ashwell Gro. S65: Roth 2A 98
Ashwell Rd. S13: Shef 2B 136
Ashwood Cl. DN3: Brant 4F 59
S35: High G 6B 60
S70: Wors 6G 31
Ashwood Gro. S72: Gt H 5E 21
Ashwood Ho. DN6: Adw S 3D 22
Ashwood Rd. S35: High G 1B 78
S62: Parkg 4G 83
Ashworth Dr. S61: Kimb P 6G 81
Askam Cl. S66: Braml 4A 100
Askam Rd. S66: Braml 4A 100
Askern Ho. *DN1: Don* *2B 56*
(off Oxford Pl.)
Askern Rd. DN5: Ben 3G 23
Askew Ct. S36: Stoc 4E 175
Askew Way S40: Ches 1H 171
Askrigg Cl. DN4: Cant 5C 58
Asline Rd. S2: Shef 6F 119
Aspen Cl. DN3: Eden 1C 42
S21: Killa 4B 152
Aspen Gdns. *S70: Wors* *4G 31*
(off Underwood Av.)
Aspen Gro. S73: D'fld 6B 34
Aspen Pl. S21: Ecki 3C 158
Aspen Wlk. S66: Malt 5F 101
Aspen Way S60: Roth 5C 96
S64: Swint 6B 66
Aspley Cl. S40: Ches 3F 167

Asquith Rd. DN5: Ben 1A **40**
S9: Shef 6E **95**
Astcote Ct. DN3: Kirk Sa 4B **26**
Aster Cl. S20: Beig 5G **137**
S25: Sth A 4G **141**
ASTON 1E **139**
Aston By-Pass S13: Shef 6H **123**
S26: Ast, Swal 2B **138**
Aston Cl. S18: Dron 1H **155**
S26: Swal 5C **124**
ASTON COMMON 2C **138**
Aston Comn. S26: Ast 1G **139**
Aston Ct. S43: Stav 4C **164**
Aston Dr. S71: Ath 2F **17**
Aston Forge Ct. S26: Ast 1E **139**
Aston Ho. S40: Ches 1H **171**
Aston La. S26: Augh 4C **124**
Aston St. S2: Shef 2A **120**
Aston Towers S18: Coal A 1H **155**
Astoria Cl. S63: Gol 5F **37**
Astrams Ct. S70: Barn 1C **30**
Astwell Gdns. S35: Chap 2D **78**
Atebanks Ct. DN4: Balb 2A **72**
Athelstan Cl. S13: Shef 5H **121**
Athelstane Cres.
DN3: Eden 5C **26**
Athelstane Dr. S66: Thurc 1B **126**
Athelstane Rd. DN12: Con 4E **69**
Athelstan Rd. S13: Shef 5H **121**
Athersley Cres. S71: Ath 2F **17**
Athersley Gdns.
S20: Mosb 6B **136**
ATHERSLEY NORTH 6E **9**
Athersley Rd. S71: Ath 2F **17**
ATHERSLEY SOUTH 2F **17**
Atherton Cl. S2: Shef 2C **134**
Atherton Rd. S2: Shef 2C **134**
Atholl Cl. S42: Walt 2C **170**
Atholl Cres. DN2: Don 5H **41**
Athol Rd. S8: Shef 4D **132**
Athorpe Gro. S25: Dinn 5H **127**
Athorpe Rd. S25: Dinn 5H **127**
Athron Dr. S65: Roth 6B **98**
Athron Ind. Est. *DN1: Don* *6D* ***40***
(off Athron St.)
Athron St. DN1: Don 6D **40**
Atkin Pl. S2: Shef 6F **119**
Atkinson Ct. S40: Ches 1H **171**
Atlantic Cres. S8: Shef 4D **146**
Atlantic Dr. S8: Shef 4D **146**
Atlantic Rd. S8: Shef 4C **146**
Atlantic Wlk. S8: Shef 4D **146**
Atlantic Way S8: Shef 4D **146**
ATLAS 6A **108**
Atlas St. S4: Shef 6A **108**
S60: Brins 3D **110**
Atlas Way S4: Shef 5B **108**
Atlee Cl. S66: Malt 6C **102**
Atlow Cl. S40: Ches 3C **166**
Atrium S20: Water 6F **137**
Atterby Dr. DN11: Ross 4D **74**
ATTERCLIFFE 6C **108**
Attercliffe Comn. S9: Shef 5D **108**
Attercliffe Rd. S4: Shef 1H **119**
S9: Shef 1A **120**
Attercliffe Stop (ST) 6C **108**
Attlee Av. DN11: New R 5A **74**
Attlee Cres. S73: D'fld 5D **34**
Attlee Rd. S43: Ink 1G **169**
Aubretia Av. S60: Brins 5E **111**
Aubrey Senior Way S61: Kimb 3H **95**
Auburn Rd. DN12: New E 4C **70**
Auckland Av. S6: Lox 4F **105**
Auckland Dr. S20: Half 4E **151**
Auckland Ri. S20: Half 4F **151**
Auckland Rd. DN2: Don 5D **40**
S64: Mexb 1G **67**
Auckland's Pl. S40: Ches 6H **167**
Auckland Way S20: Half 4F **151**
AUCKLEY 1H **59**
Audrey Rd. S13: Shef 1F **135**
AUGHTON 5B **124**
Aughton Av. S26: Augh 5B **124**
Aughton Cl. S13: Shef 1G **135**
Aughton Cres. S13: Shef 6F **121**
Aughton Dr. S13: Shef 6F **121**
Aughton La. S26: Ast 6D **124**
Aughton Rd. S26: Augh, Swal 6B **124**
Augustus Rd. S60: Brins 2D **110**
Aukley Rd. S8: Shef 3E **133**
Aunby Dr. S26: Swal 6C **124**
Austen Av. DN4: Balb 6F **55**
Austen Dr. S66: Braml 5B **100**
Austerfield Av. DN5: Don 3H **39**
Austin Cl. S6: Lox 4F **105**
Austin Ct. S6: Lox 3F **105**
Austwick Cl. DN4: Balb 2G **71**
S75: Mapp 4H **7**
Austwick Wlk. S70: Barn 6C **16**
Austwood La. S66: B'well 6B **88**
Autumn Cl. S66: Thurc 6D **114**
S71: Roy 3G **9**
Autumn Dr. S66: Malt 4B **102**
Aven Ind. Pk. S66: Malt 5G **103**
Avenue, The DN4: Bess 2H **57**
DN5: Ben 1B **40**
DN5: H'ton 2G **51**
S9: Shef 2F **121**
S18: Dron 2G **155**
S20: Beig 4G **137**
S66: Carr 3F **115**
S66: Staint 2F **103**
S71: Roy 2B **10**
S75: Pill 6C **44**
Avenue 1 S41: Has 2A **172**
Avenue 2 S41: Has 2A **172**
Avenue 3 S41: Has 2A **172**
Avenue 4 S41: Has 2A **172**
Avenue 5 S41: Has 2A **172**
Avenue 6 S41: Has 2A **172**
Avenue 7 S41: Has 2A **172**
Avenue 8 S41: Has 2A **172**
Avenue Ct. S10: Shef 6H **117**
Avenue Rd. DN2: Don 5D **40**
S7: Shef 2E **133**
S41: Whit M 6H **161**
S63: Wath D 1H **65**
Aviemore Cl. S43: New W 2D **162**
Aviemore Rd. DN4: Balb 6F **55**
Avill Way S66: Wick 1G **113**
Avisford Dr. S5: Shef 1C **106**
Avisford Rd. S5: Shef 6C **92**
Avoca Av. DN2: Don 6F **41**
Avocet Way
S61: Thorpe H 2C **80**
Avon Cl. S18: Dron 1G **155**
S66: Malt 4A **102**
S73: Womb 3A **48**
S75: H'ham 5F **15**
Avon Ct. DN9: Auck 1H **59**
Avondale Dr. S71: Carl 5H **9**
Avondale Rd. DN2: Don 1F **57**
S6: Shef 4A **106**
S40: Ches 4G **167**
S43: Ink 1H **169**
S61: Roth 3B **96**
Avon Gro. S35: Chap 2D **78**
Avon Mt. S61: Roth 3B **96**
Avonside Cl. S43: Bar H 3G **163**
Avon St. S71: Barn 1F **31**
Axholme Ct. DN2: Don 5E **41**
Axholme Rd. DN2: Don 5D **40**
Axle La. S25: Sth A 4E **141**
Aylesbury Ct. S9: Shef 6E **95**
Aylesbury Cres. S9: Shef 1E **109**
Aylesbury Rd. DN2: Don 6G **41**
Aylesford Cl. S71: Barn 5E **17**
Aylsham Dr. S26: Ast 1D **138**
Aylward Cl. S2: Shef 1C **134**
Aylward Rd. S2: Shef 1C **134**
Aymer Dr. S66: Thurc 6B **114**
Ayrsome Wlk. DN4: Cant 4B **58**
Aysgarth Av. S71: Ard 2E **33**
Aysgarth Cl. DN4: Cant 5C **58**
Aysgarth Ri. S26: Swal 6B **124**
Aysgarth Rd. S6: Shef 6B **92**
Ayton Wlk. DN5: Ben 6H **23**
Azalea Cl. S25: Sth A 5G **141**

B

b2net Stadium 1H **167**
Babington Cl. S2: Shef 1C **134**
Babington Ct. S2: Shef 1C **134**
Babur Rd. S4: Shef 6A **108**
Backfield Ri. S35: Chap 2F **79**
Backfields S1: Shef 4D **4** (3F **119**)
Back La. DN4: Warm 2F **71**
DN5: Cus 5C **38**
DN9: Blax 1E **77**
DN12: Old E 1B **88**
S6: Bradf 1A **104**
S10: Shef 2G **117**
S13: Shef 2D **136**
S17: Tot 5G **145**
S18: App 3C **156**
S21: Ecki 6B **150**
S25: Nth A 2H **141**
S36: Midh 2A **174**
S36: Oxs, Rough 6G **177**
S36: Pen 4D **176**
S44: Cal 1G **173**
S62: Neth Hau 2D **82**
S65: Hoot R 2A **86**
S65: Thry 4E **85**
S66: Clift 3H **87**
S66: Hoot L 1D **114**
S66: Mick 1F **101**
S71: Monk B 4H **17**
S72: Bill 3G **35**
Back La. W. S71: Roy 2F **9**
BACKMOOR 6H **133**
Backmoor Cres. S8: Shef 6H **133**
Backmoor Rd. S8: Shef 6H **133**
Bk. Poplar Ter. S71: Roy 2B **10**
Back Rd. S18: App 3C **156**
Back Row DN3: Cant 3E **59**
Back Row Cotts. DN11: Ross 5E **75**
Backside La. DN4: Warm 6E **55**
Bk. South St. S43: New W 3C **162**
(not continuous)
Bacon La. S9: Shef 1B **120**
Bacons La. S40: Birdh 2G **171**
Baden Powell Av. S40: Ches 1G **171**
Baden Powell Rd. S40: Ches 6H **167**
Baden St. S60: Roth 3D **96**
S70: Wors 6G **31**
Badger Cl. S13: Shef 1D **136**
S42: Walt 2C **170**
Badger Dr. S13: Shef 1D **136**
Badger La. S1: Shef 3C **4**
Badger Pl. S13: Shef 1D **136**
Badger Ri. S13: Shef 1D **136**
Badger Rd. S13: Shef 1D **136**
Badgers Holt DN3: Brant 4G **59**
Badsley Ct. S65: Roth 4H **97**
Badsley Moor La. S65: Roth 5G **97**
Badsley St. S65: Roth 4G **97**
Badsley St. Sth. S65: Roth 5G **97**
Badsworth Cl. S66: Braml 5B **100**
S73: Womb 2A **48**
Badsworth Pl. S66: Braml 5B **100**
Badsworth Rd. DN4: Warm 1D **70**
Badsworth Way S66: Braml 5B **100**
Bage Hill S42: Walt 4A **170**
Bagley Rd. S4: Shef 3A **108**
Bagshaw's Rd. S12: Shef 2E **135**
Bagshot St. S11: Shef 6C **118**
Bahram Gro. DN11: New R 6B **74**
Bahram Rd. DN4: Bess 4H **57**
Bailey Cft. S70: Barn 2D **30**
Bailey Dr. S21: Killa 2D **152**
Bailey La. S1: Shef 3C **4** (3E **119**)
Bailey M. DN5: Scawt 1F **39**
Bailey St. S1: Shef 3D **4** (3F **119**)
Bainbridge Rd. DN4: Balb 3A **56**
Baines Av. DN12: New E 5B **70**
Baines Wood Cl. S41: Ches 6D **160**
Bainton Dr. S70: Barn 3C **30**
Bakehouse La. S21: Ecki 1E **159**
S75: Barn 5H **15**
Baker Dr. S21: Killa 4B **152**
Bakers Field Ct. S65: Roth 5A **98**
Bakers Hill S1: Shef 3G **5** (3G **119**)
Bakers La. S1: Shef 2C **4** (2F **119**)
Baker St. S9: Shef 6C **108**
S25: Laugh C 4F **127**
Bakewell Rd. S43: Ink 3H **169**
S71: Ath 2F **17**
Balaclava La. S6: Shef 6D **106**
Balaclava Rd. S6: Shef 6D **106**
Bala St. S71: Barn 1E **31**
BALBY 6H **55**
Balby Carr DN4: Balb 4B **56**
Balby Carr Bank DN4: Balb 4B **56**
Balby Rd. DN4: Balb 4A **56**

Balby St. DN12: Den M 3E **69**
Balcarres Rd.
DN11: New R 5C **74**
Baldwin Av. DN5: Don 5H **39**
Baldwin St. S9: Shef 1B **120**
Balfour Dr. S9: Shef 1E **121**
Balfour Rd. DN5: Ben 1B **40**
S9: Shef 1E **121**
Balk, The DN5: Ark 3C **24**
S61: Grea 4C **82**
S75: Stain 4B **8**
Balk Farm Ct. S70: Birdw 3D **44**
Balk La. S60: Brins 2B **110**
S66: Braml 5A **100**
S70: Birdw 3D **44**
Balkley La. S73: D'fld 5D **34**
Ballam Av. DN5: Scawt 1F **39**
Ballard Hall Chase S10: Shef 5H **117**
Ballard Hall Ct. S10: Shef 5G **117**
Ballard Hall M. S10: Shef 5G **117**
Ballfield Av. S75: Kexb 6D **6**
Ballfield Fold S75: Kexb 6C **6**
Ballfield La. S75: Kexb 6D **6**
Ballidon Cl. S40: Ches 2D **166**
Ballifield Av. S13: Shef 5B **122**
Ballifield Cl. S13: Shef 5B **122**
Ballifield Cres. S13: Shef 5C **122**
Ballifield Dr. S13: Shef 5C **122**
Ballifield Pl. S13: Shef 5B **122**
Ballifield Ri. S13: Shef 5C **122**
Ballifield Rd. S13: Shef 5B **122**
Ballifield Way S13: Shef 5B **122**
Ball Rd. S6: Shef 4A **106**
Ball St. S3: Shef 1E **119**
Balmain Dr. S6: Shef 3A **106**
Balmain Rd. S6: Shef 3A **106**
Balmer Ri. S66: Braml 6B **100**
Balm Grn. S1: Shef 3D **4** (3F **119**)
Balmoak La. S41: Ches 2B **168**
Balmoral Cl. DN5: Barnb 1H **51**
S36: Thurl 3A **176**
Balmoral Ct. S11: Shef 4G **131**
Balmoral Cres. S10: Shef 5A **116**
S18: Dron W 2C **154**
Balmoral Glen S10: Shef 5A **116**
Balmoral M. S10: Shef 5A **116**
Balmoral Rd. DN2: Don 6E **41**
S13: Shef 2D **136**
Balmoral Way S43: New W 2D **162**
S66: Braml 4A **100**
Baltic La. *S9: Shef* *6C 108*
(off Baltic Rd.)
Baltic Rd. S9: Shef 6C **108**
Baltic Way S9: Shef 6C **108**
Bamford Av. S71: Ath 2F **17**
Bamford Cl. S75: Dod 3F **29**
Bamford Rd. S43: Ink 3G **169**
Bamford St. S43: New W 2C **162**
Bamforth St. S6: Shef 5C **106**
Bamforth Street Stop (ST) 5C **106**
Banbury Cl. *DN12: Den M* *3E 69*
(off Crags Rd.)
Bank Cl. S7: Shef 2D **132**
S61: Kimb P 1A **96**
Bank Ct. S43: Brim 6C **162**
Bank End Av. S70: Wors 5H **31**
Bank End Cl. S63: Bolt D 2B **50**
Bank End Rd. DN9: Blax, Finn 1F **77**
S70: Wors 5G **31**
Bankfield La. S6: Stann 6D **104**
Bankfield Rd. S6: Shef 4H **105**
Bank Ho. La. S36: Thurl 4A **176**
Bank Ho. Rd. S6: Shef 1B **118**
Bank La. S36: Bolst 6G **175**
Bank Rd. S41: Ches 2H **167**
Bank Sq. DN11: New R 6B **74**
Bank St. DN1: Don 3B **56**
S1: Shef 2E **5** (2G **119**)
S25: Sth A 3G **141**
S40: Ches 5F **167**
S43: Brim 6C **162**
S64: Mexb 2F **67**
S70: Barn 3E **31**
S71: Stair 2B **32**
S72: Cud 1E **19**
S74: Hoyl 1A **62**
Bank Ter. *S10: Shef* *3B 118*
(off Parker's La.)
Bank Top Rd. S65: Roth 6C **98**
Bank Vw. S12: Shef 5D **136**
S36: Oxs 6H **177**
S60: Whist 3A **112**
Bank Wood Cl. S41: Ches 1C **166**
Bankwood Cl. S14: Shef 3A **134**
Bankwood Cres.
DN11: New R 4A **74**
Bankwood La. DN11: New R 3A **74**
Bankwood Rd. S14: Shef 3A **134**
Bannatyne's Health Club
Barnsley 2G **29**
Bramley 6C **100**
Banner Ct. S11: Shef 2A **132**
BANNER CROSS 2A **132**
Banner Cross Dr. S11: Shef 2A **132**
Banner Cross Rd. S11: Shef 3A **132**
Bannerdale Cl. S11: Shef 2B **132**
Bannerdale Rd. S7: Shef 2B **132**
S11: Shef 2B **132**
Bannerdale Vw. S11: Shef 2B **132**
Bannham Rd. S9: Shef 2G **121**
Bannister Ho. DN2: Don 4F **41**
Bar Av. S75: Mapp 6C **8**
Barbados Way S66: Hel 4D **100**
Barber Balk Cl. S61: Kimb P 1A **96**
Barber Balk Rd. S61: Kimb P 2A **96**
Barber Cl. DN3: Arm 5C **42**
S26: Tod 3B **140**
Barber Cres. S10: Shef 2C **118**
Barber Pl. S10: Shef 2C **118**
Barber Rd. S10: Shef 2C **118**
Barberry Ct. S70: Barn 2G **31**
Barberry Way S65: Rav 2B **100**
Barber's Av. S62: Parkg, Rawm 3G **83**
Barber's Cres. S62: Rawm 3H **83**
Barbers La. S21: Killa 2C **152**
Barber's Path S64: Mexb 1E **67**
Barber St. S74: Hoyl 6B **46**
Barber Wood Rd. S61: Kimb 3D **94**
Barbon Cl. S40: Ches 3F **167**
Barbot Farm M. S61: Grea 6D **82**
Barbot Hall Dr. S61: Grea 6D **82**
Barbot Hall Ind. Est. S62: Parkg 6E **83**
Barbot Hill Rd. S61: Grea 6D **82**
Barclay Grange S41: Ches 5A **168**
Bar Cft. S40: Ches 2E **167**
Barcroft Flatt S75: Barn 4H **15**
Barden Cres. S60: Brins 4D **110**
Barden Dr. S75: Barn 5A **16**
Bardolf Rd. DN4: Cant 3B **58**
Bardon Rd. DN3: Eden 5C **26**
Bard St. S2: Shef 2H **5** (3H **119**)
Bardwell Rd. S3: Shef 6E **107**
Barewell Hill S72: Brier, Hems 2B **12**
(not continuous)
Barfield Av. S60: Whist 3H **111**
Barfield Rd. S74: Hoyl 6B **46**
Barholme Cl. S41: Ches 1C **166**
Barholm Rd. S10: Shef 4G **117**
Bari Cl. S73: D'fld 4H **33**
Baring Rd. S61: Kimb 4E **95**
Barkby Rd. S9: Shef 6D **94**
Barker Fold S40: Ches 5E **167**
Barker Hades Rd. S81: Letw 4H **129**
Barker La. S40: Ches 5E **167**
Barkers Cft. S61: Wing 5A **82**
Barkers La. DN12: Con 5A **70**
Barker's Pl. S6: Shef 3B **106**
Barker's Pool S1: Shef 4D **4** (3F **119**)
Barker's Rd. S7: Shef 2C **132**
Barker St. S64: Mexb 2D **66**
Bark Mdws. S75: Dod 3H **29**
Barkston Rd. S71: Carl 1H **17**
Bar La. S75: Mapp, Stain 6C **8**
Barlborough Rd.
S73: Womb 3H **47**
Barlby Gro. S12: Shef 5D **136**
Barley Cl. S70: Wors 6F **31**
Barley Cft. La. S25: Dinn 6A **128**
Barley Ho. *S11: Shef* *5D 118*
(off Napier St.)
Barley La. S42: Ash 3B **166**
Barley M. S18: Dron W 2B **154**
Barley Vw. S63: Thurn 3C **36**
Barleywood Rd. S9: Shef 6F **109**
BARLOW 4A **160**
Barlow Dr. S6: Shef 6H **105**
BARLOW LEES 6C **154**
Barlow Lees La. S18: Dron 6D **154**
Barlow Rd. S6: Shef 6H **105**
S41: Up N 5A **160**
S43: Stav 5B **164**
Barlow Vw. S18: Dron 5G **155**
Barmouth Rd. S7: Shef 3D **132**
Barnabas Wlk. S71: Barn 5E **17**
Barnard Av. S18: Coal A 1A **156**
Barnardiston Rd. S9: Shef 1E **121**
BARNBURGH 1A **52**
Barnburgh Ct. S63: Gol 6D **36**
Barnburgh Hall Gdns.
DN5: Barnb 1A **52**
Barnburgh Ho. DN12: New E 3D **70**
Barnburgh La. DN5: Barnb 6D **36**
S63: Gol 6D **36**
BARNBY DUN 1C **26**
Barnby Dun Rd. DN2: Don 3G **41**
Barnby Furnace S75: Silk 4C **14**
Barncliffe Cl. S10: Shef 6D **116**
Barncliffe Cres. S10: Shef 5C **116**
Barncliffe Dr. S10: Shef 5C **116**
Barncliffe Glen S10: Shef 6D **116**
Barncliffe M. S10: Shef 4E **117**
Barncliffe Rd. S10: Shef 5C **116**
Barn Cl. S41: Ches 2E **167**
Barnes Av. S18: Dron W 2C **154**
Barnes Ct. S2: Shef 6G **5** (4G **119**)
Barnes Grn. S35: Gren 5C **78**
Barnes Hall Rd. S35: Burn 3C **78**
Barnes Ind. Est. S66: Braml 5B **100**
Barnes La. S18: Dron W 6A **146**
Barnes Rd. S41: Ches 1D **172**
Barnet Av. S11: Shef 3F **131**
Barnet Rd. S11: Shef 3F **131**
Barnfield Av. S10: Shef 3F **117**
Barnfield Cl. S10: Shef 3F **117**
S43: Stav 4B **164**
Barnfield Dr. S10: Shef 4F **117**
Barnfield Rd. S10: Shef 3F **117**
Barnfield Wlk. S43: Stav 4B **164**
Barnfold Pl. S72: Shaft 4F **11**
Barnham Cl. S40: Walt 2C **170**
Barn Owl Cl. S72: Bill 4G **35**
Barnsbridge Gro. S70: Barn 2G **31**
Barnsdale Av. S20: Mosb 6B **136**
Barnside Cl. S36: Cub 5D **176**
BARNSLEY 6D **16**
Barnsley Av. DN12: Con 4D **68**
Barnsley Bowl 2G **17**
Barnsley Business & Innovation Cen.
S75: Barn 4A **16**
Barnsley Business Innovation Cen.
S72: Cud 1E **19**
Barnsley Crematorium S71: Ard 3E **33**
Barnsley FC 1F **31**
Barnsley Golf Course 4B **8**
Barnsley Retail Pk. S70: Stair 4C **32**
Barnsley Rd.
DN5: Marr, Scaws 3H **37** & 3A **38**
S4: Shef 4G **107**
S5: Shef 5H **93**
S36: H'swne, Pen 3C **176**
S61: Thorpe H 1B **80**
S63: Gol 5B **36**
S63: Wath D 4C **48**
S72: Brier, Shaft 4G **11**
S72: Cud, Lund 2D **18**
S73: D'fld 3A **34**
S73: Womb 5E **33**
(not continuous)
S74: Hoyl 4A **46**
S75: Bar G, Dart 6F **7**
S75: Dod 3F **29**
S75: Silk 3A **28**
WF4: Nott 1B **8**
WF9: Hems 2B **12**
Barnsley Station (Rail) 6E **17**
Barnstone St. DN4: Hex 3H **55**
Barnwell Cres. S73: Womb 5E **33**
Baron St. S1: Shef 5F **119**
Barrack La. S6: Shef 6D **106**
Barrack Rd. S18: App 3D **156**
Barracks Fld. Ter. S74: Els 1D **62**
Barrack Vw. S18: App 3D **156**
Barratt Rd. S21: Ecki 2E **159**
Barrel La. DN4: Warm 6F **55**
Barret Rd. DN4: Cant 3C **58**
Barretta St. S4: Shef 3A **108**
Barrick M. S61: Kimb 3A **96**

Barrie Cres. S5: Shef .1E **107**
Barrie Dr. S5: Shef .1E **107**
Barrie Gro. S66: Hel .6E **101**
Barrie Rd. DN4: Balb .6A **56**
S5: Shef .1E **107**
BARROW .5C **62**
Barrow, The S62: Wentw .5C **62**
Barrowby Rd. S60: Roth .1H **111**
BARROWFIELD GATE .4D **62**
Barrowfield La. S62: Wentw .4D **62**
Barrowfield Rd. S63: Gol, Thurn .3C **36**
S74: Hoyl .5A **46**
BARROW HILL .3G **163**
Barrow Hill S62: Wentw .5B **62**
Barrow Hill Roundhouse Railway Cen. .3F **163**
Barrow Rd. S9: Shef .6E **95**
Barrow St. S43: Stav .4C **164**
Barrow Syke S63: Bolt D .3C **50**
Barry Rd. S43: Brim C .4E **169**
Bartholomew Cl. S60: Whist .2C **112**
Bartholomew St. S73: Womb .1F **47**
Bartin Cl. S11: Shef .3A **132**
Bartle Av. S12: Shef .4C **134**
Bartle Dr. S12: Shef .4C **134**
Bartle Rd. S12: Shef .4C **134**
Bartlett Cl. S6: Stann .1D **116**
Bartlett Rd. S5: Shef .6E **93**
Bartle Way S12: Shef .4C **134**
Barton Cres. S40: Ches .2B **166**
Barton La. DN3: Arm .4D **42**
(not continuous)
Barton Pl. DN12: Con .5E **69**
Barton Rd. S8: Shef .2F **133**
BARUGH GREEN .4F **15**
Barugh Grn. Rd.
S75: Barn, Bar G .3F **15**
Barugh La. S75: Bar G .3F **15**
BASE GREEN .5F **135**
Basegreen Av. S12: Shef .5E **135**
Basegreen Cl. S12: Shef .5F **135**
Basegreen Cres. S12: Shef .5E **135**
Basegreen Dr. S12: Shef .5E **135**
Basegreen Pl. S12: Shef .5E **135**
Basegreen Rd. S12: Shef .5E **135**
Basegreen Way S12: Shef .5F **135**
Basford Cl. S9: Shef .1E **121**
Basford Dr. S9: Shef .1E **121**
Basford M. S9: Shef .1F **121**
Basford Pl. S9: Shef .1E **121**
Basford St. S9: Shef .1E **121**
Basil Av. DN3: Arm .3B **42**
Basil Cl. S41: Ches .5H **167**
Basildon Rd. S63: Thurn .1B **36**
Basil Griffith Ct. *S3: Shef* .*4G* ***107***
(off Orphanage Rd)
Baslow Cres. S75: Dod .3F **29**
Baslow Rd. S17: Tot .6D **144**
S42: Holy .1A **170**
S71: Ath .1G **17**
Bassett La. S10: Shef .2A **130**
Bassett Pl. S2: Shef .4A **120**
Bassett Rd. S2: Shef .4B **120**
Bassey Rd. DN3: Brant .4H **59**
Bassingthorpe La. S61: Grea .6C **82**
Bassledene Ct. S2: Shef .6D **120**
Bassledene Rd. S2: Shef .6D **120**
Bass Ter. DN1: Don .1D **56**
Bastock Rd. S6: Shef .3C **106**
Bateman Cl. S43: New W .2C **162**
S72: Cud .4E **11**
Bateman Rd. S66: Hel .6D **100**
(not continuous)
Bateman Sq. S63: Thurn .2B **36**
BATEMOOR .4F **147**
Batemoor Cl. S8: Shef .4F **147**
Batemoor Dr. S8: Shef .4F **147**
Batemoor Pl. S8: Shef .4F **147**
Batemoor Rd. S8: Shef .4F **147**
Batemoor Wlk. *S8: Shef* .*4F* ***147***
(off Batemoor Rd.)
Batesquire S20: Beig .6G **137**
Bates St. S10: Shef .1B **118**
Bate Wood Av. S43: Ink .3G **169**
Bath St. S1: Shef .6B **4** **(4E 119)**
Battison La. S63: Wath D .2E **65**
Batt St. S8: Shef .6F **119**
Batty Av. S72: Cud .2D **18**
Batworth Dr. S5: Shef .4F **107**
Batworth Rd. S5: Shef .4F **107**
Baulk Farm Cl. S61: Grea .4C **82**
Bawtry Ga. S9: Tins .2H **109**
Bawtry Rd. DN4: Bess, Don .2F **57**
DN9: Finn .3G **77**
S9: Tins .2H **109**
S60: Brins .2H **109**
S65: Roth .6D **98**
S66: Braml, Wick, Hel .6D **98**
Baxter Av. DN1: Don .6D **40**
Baxter Cl. S6: Shef .6B **92**
S26: Swal .1H **137**
Baxter Ct. DN1: Don .6D **40**
Baxter Dr. S6: Shef .6B **92**
Baxter Ga. DN1: Don .1B **56**
Baxter M. S6: Shef .6B **92**
Baxter Rd. S6: Shef .6B **92**
Bayardo Wlk. DN11: New R .6G **75**
Baycliff Cl. S71: Monk B .2A **18**
Baycliff Dr. S40: Ash .5D **166**
Bay Ct. S21: Killa .5B **152**
Bayford Way S73: Womb .1A **48**
Baysdale Cft. S20: Mosb .3E **151**
Bay Tree Av. S66: Flan .4G **99**
Baytree Gro. DN9: Auck .2A **76**
Bazley Rd. S2: Shef .2C **134**
Beacon Cl. S9: Shef .2C **108**
S75: Silk C .4B **28**
Beacon Ct. S75: Silk C .5B **28**
Beacon Cft. S9: Shef .2C **108**
Beacon Hill S75: Silk C .4B **28**
Beacon La. S66: Clift .3G **87**
Beacon Rd. S9: Shef .2C **108**
Beaconsfield Rd. DN4: Hex .3H **55**
S60: Roth .1H **111**
Beaconsfield St. S64: Mexb .1E **67**
S70: Barn .2D **30**
Beacon Sq. S66: Clift .3H **87**
Beacon Vw. S74: Els .1D **62**
Beacon Way S9: Shef .2C **108**
Beale Way S62: Parkg .6G **83**
Beancroft Cl. DN11: Wad .5F **73**
Bear Tree Cl. S62: Parkg .4G **83**
Bear Tree Rd. S62: Parkg .4G **83**
Bear Tree St. S62: Parkg .5G **83**
Beauchamp Rd. S61: Kimb P .1A **96**
BEAUCHIEF .2B **146**
Beauchief S8: Shef .2A **146**
Beauchief Abbey La. S8: Shef .1B **146**
Beauchief Abbey (remains of) .2B **146**
Beauchief Cl. S36: Spink .4H **175**
Beauchief Ct. S8: Shef .6D **132**
Beauchief Dr. S8: Shef .3B **146**
S17: Bradw .3B **146**
Beauchief Golf Course .1A **146**
Beauchief Ri. S8: Shef .1B **146**
Beaufort Rd. DN2: Don .6G **41**
S10: Shef .3C **118**
Beaulieu Cl. S75: Mapp .6B **8**
Beaulieu Vw. S75: Mapp .6B **8**
Beaumond Cl. S71: Smi .3G **17**
Beaumont Av. DN6: Woodl .2A **22**
S2: Shef .4D **120**
S70: Barn .1A **30**
Beaumont Cl. S2: Shef .4E **121**
Beaumont Cres. S2: Shef .4D **120**
Beaumont Dr. S65: Roth .5A **98**
S75: Hai .1B **6**
Beaumont M. S2: Shef .5E **121**
Beaumont Rd. S75: Kexb .1D **14**
Beaumont Rd. Nth. S2: Shef .4D **120**
Beaumont St. S74: Hoyl .1G **61**
Beaumont Way S2: Shef .4D **120**
Beaver Av. S13: Shef .6C **122**
Beaver Cl. S13: Shef .6C **122**
Beaver Dr. S13: Shef .6C **122**
BEAVER HILL .6C **122**
Beaver Hill Rd. S13: Shef .6C **122**
Beccles Way S66: Braml .5B **100**
Beck Cl. S5: Shef .3B **94**
S64: Swint .5C **66**
Beck Cft. S74: Hoyl .2H **61**
Becket Av. S8: Shef .4C **146**
Becket Cres. S8: Shef .4D **146**
S61: Kimb P .6G **81**
Becket Rd. S8: Shef .4D **146**
Beckett Hospital Ter. *S70: Barn* .*2E* ***31***
(off Dobie St.)
Beckett Rd. DN2: Don .5D **40**
Beckett St. S71: Barn .6E **17**
Becket Wlk. S8: Shef .4C **146**
Beckfield Gro. S63: Bolt D .1A **50**
Beckford La. S5: Shef .2A **94**
Beckingham Way S40: Ches .6H **167**
Becknoll Rd. S73: Bramp .4B **48**
Beck Rd. S5: Shef .3A **94**
Beckton Av. S20: Water .6F **137**
Beckton Ct. S20: Water .6G **137**
Beckton Gro. S20: Water .6F **137**
Beckwith Rd. S65: Roth .3C **98**
Bedale Cl. S26: Swal .1B **138**
Bedale Ct. S60: Roth .6G **97**
Bedale Rd. DN5: Scaws .3E **39**
S7: Shef .2E **133**
Bedale Wlk. S72: Shaft .3F **11**
Bedford Cl. S25: Nth A .1G **141**
Bedford Rd. S35: Ough .2E **91**
Bedford St. S6: Shef .1E **119**
S66: Malt .6C **102**
S70: Barn .3E **31**
S72: Grim .3B **20**
Bedford Ter. S71: Monk B .3F **17**
Bedgebury Cl. S20: Sot .1A **152**
Bedgrave Cl. S21: Killa .2E **153**
Bedgreave New Mill .6B **138**
Beecham Ct. S64: Swint .5B **66**
Beech Av. DN9: Auck .2B **76**
S62: Rawm .3A **84**
S65: Roth .6D **98**
S72: Cud .6E **11**
S75: Silk C .5B **28**
Beech Cl. S66: Malt .5G **101**
S72: Brier .3B **12**
S73: Hem .4F **47**
WF9: Sth K .4H **13**
Beech Ct. S73: D'fld .5B **34**
Beech Cres. S21: Ecki .3C **158**
S21: Killa .5C **152**
S64: Mexb .1D **66**
Beechcroft Rd. DN4: Balb .6F **55**
Beechdale Cl. S40: Ches .4E **167**
Beech Dr. DN3: Brant .3H **59**
S44: Ark T .5H **173**
Beech en Hurst *S60: Roth* .*6F* ***97***
(off Reneville Cl.)
Beeches, The DN3: Kirk Sa .4C **26**
S26: Swal .1C **138**
S64: Swint .4B **66**
S73: Hem .5G **47**
Beeches Bank S2: Shef .6H **119**
Beeches Dr. S2: Shef .6H **119**
Beeches Gro. S20: Beig .5H **137**
Beeches Hollow S2: Shef .5H **119**
Beeches Rd. S26: Wales .5G **139**
Beechfern Cl. S35: High G .6C **60**
Beechfield Cl. S63: Bolt D .2B **50**
Beechfield Rd. DN1: Don .2C **56**
Beech Gro. DN4: Warm .6D **54**
DN5: Ben .2A **40**
DN12: Con .5E **69**
S25: Dinn .1A **142**
S66: Wick .5H **99**
S70: Barn .3C **30**
Beech Hill DN12: Con .4F **69**
Beech Hill Rd. S10: Shef .4B **118**
Beech Ho. Cft. S66: Clift .2G **87**
Beech Ho. Rd. S73: Hem .4G **47**
Beechlea S63: Thurn .1B **36**
Beech Rd. DN3: Arm .4E **43**
DN11: New R .6D **74**
S63: Wath D .6H **49**
S66: Malt .5G **101**
S72: Shaft .4G **11**
Beech St. S43: Hol .5F **163**
S70: Barn .2E **31**
Beech Tree Cl. DN3: Cant .3E **59**
Beech Vs. S65: Roth .2H **97**
Beechville Av. S64: Swint .5B **66**
Beech Way S18: Dron .1F **155**
S26: Swal .6A **124**
Beechwood Cl. DN3: Eden .1D **42**
S62: Rawm .1A **84**
S63: Wath D .3G **65**
Beechwood Lodge Flats
S65: Roth .3G **97**
Beechwood Rd. S6: Shef .4A **106**
S18: Dron .3E **155**
S35: High G .2D **78**

Beechwood Rd.—Bilby La.

Beechwood Rd. S36: Stoc 4D **174**
S60: Roth .6H **97**
Beechwood Wlk. *DN12: New E 5B 70*
(off Grainger Cl.)
Beeden Cl. S65: Thry 5E **85**
Beehive Rd. S10: Shef 2C **118**
S40: Ches 6E **167**
Beehive Yd. S40: Ches 6E **167**
Beeley Cl. S43: Ink 2H **169**
Beeley St. S2: Shef 5E **119**
Beeley Vw. S42: Walt 3C **170**
Beeley Way S43: Ink 3H **169**
Beeley Wood La. S6: Shef 5G **91**
Beeley Wood Rd. S6: Shef 1B **106**
Beely Rd. S35: Ough 4F **91**
Beeston Cl. S18: Dron W 2B **154**
Beeston Sq. S71: Ath 6E **9**
Beeton Rd. S8: Shef 3E **133**
Beet St. S3: Shef 2B **4** (3E **119**)
Beetwell St. S40: Ches 6H **167**
Beever Cl. S75: Barn 5H **15**
Beever La. S75: Barn 5H **15**
Beeversleigh *S65: Roth 4F 97*
(off Allan St.)
Beevers Rd. S61: Kimb P 6G **81**
Beever St. S63: Gol 5E **37**
Beevor Ct. S71: Barn 1F **31**
Beevor St. S71: Barn 1G **31**
Begonia Cl. S25: Sth A 4F **141**
BEIGHTON 4H **137**
Beighton / Drake House Lane Stop (ST)
. . . . .6G **137**
BEIGHTON HOLLOW 4H **151**
Beighton Rd. S12: Shef 5C **136**
S13: Shef 2D **136**
S20: Beig 2D **136**
S64: Kiln .6D **66**
Beighton Rd. E. S20: Water 5E **137**
Beighton Sports and Leisure Club
. . . . .4H **137**
Belcourt Rd. S65: Roth 6C **98**
Beldon Cl. S2: Shef 1A **134**
Beldon Ct. S2: Shef 1A **134**
Beldon Pl. S2: Shef 1A **134**
Beldon Rd. S2: Shef 1A **134**
Belford Cl. S66: Sunn 4H **99**
Belford Dr. S66: Braml 4H **99**
Belfry Gdns. DN4: Cant 5D **58**
Belfry Way S25: Dinn 1B **142**
Belgrave Dr. S10: Shef 5E **117**
Belgrave Pl. S26: Swal 1B **138**
Belgrave Rd. S10: Shef 5F **117**
S71: Barn 1F **31**
Belgrave Sq. S2: Shef 6F **119**
Belklane Dr. S21: Killa 3D **152**
Bella Av. S63: Gol 5F **37**
Bellamy Cl. S65: Roth 5A **98**
Bell Bank Vw. S70: Wors 5E **31**
Bellbank Way S71: Ath 6E **9**
Bellbrooke Av. S73: D'fld 3A **34**
Bellbrooke Cl. S73: D'fld 3B **34**
Bellbrooke Pl. S73: D'fld 3A **34**
Bell Butts La. DN9: Auck 2G **59**
Bellcross Gdns. S72: Cud 1F **19**
Bellcross Way S71: Monk B 2C **18**
Bellefield St. S3: Shef 1A **4** (2D **118**)
BELLE GREEN 1F **19**
Belle Grn. Cl. S72: Cud 1F **19**
Belle Grn. Gdns. S72: Cud 1F **19**
Belle Grn. La. S72: Cud 1F **19**
BELLE VUE 2F **57**
Belle Vue Av. DN4: Don 2F **57**
Belle Vue Cl. S43: Brim 6C **162**
Belle Vue Rd. S64: Mexb 1F **67**
Bellfields, The S61: Thorpe H 3B **80**
BELL HAGG 3E **117**
Bellhagg Rd. S6: Shef 6A **106**
Bellhouse La. S43: Stav 3C **164**
Bellhouse M. S5: Shef 5B **94**
Bellhouse Rd. S5: Shef 1A **108**
Bellhouse Vw. S43: Stav 3C **164**
Bellis Av. DN4: Balb 4H **55**
Bellmer Cl. S71: Monk B 3F **17**
Bellmer Cft. S70: Birdw 6E **45**
Bellows Cl. S62: Rawm 3G **83**
Bellows Rd. S62: Rawm 3G **83**
Bellrope Acre DN3: Arm 5E **43**
Bells Cl. DN9: Blax 2F **77**
Bellscroft S73: Womb 3E **47**
Bellscroft Av. S65: Thry 6D **84**
Bells Sq. S1: Shef 3D **4** (3F **119**)
Bell St. S26: Ast 1E **139**
Bellwood Ct. S65: Rav 2B **100**
Bellwood Cres. S74: Hoyl 1H **61**
Belmont S72: Cud 4F **19**
Belmont Av. DN4: Balb 3B **56**
S35: Chap 3F **79**
S71: Smi .3G **17**
Belmont Cl. DN3: Brant 4H **59**
Belmont Cres. S72: Midd 3F **35**
Belmont Dr. S36: Pen 5E **177**
S36: Stoc 3E **175**
S43: Stav 4C **164**
Belmonte Gdns.
S2: Shef 6H **5** (4H **119**)
Belmont Pk. S42: Holy 1A **170**
Belmont St. S41: Whit M 6H **161**
S61: Roth 4B **96**
S64: Mexb 2E **67**
Belper Rd. S7: Shef 2E **133**
Belridge Cl. S75: Barn 4A **16**
Belsize Rd. S10: Shef 6F **117**
Beltoft Way DN12: Con 3H **69**
Belton Cl. S18: Dron W 3B **154**
Belvedere DN4: Balb 6G **55**
Belvedere Av. S40: Walt 2F **171**
Belvedere Cl. S25: Nth A 3A **142**
S40: Bramp 2B **170**
S72: Shaft 4F **11**
Belvedere Dr. S73: D'fld 3A **34**
Belvedere Pde. S66: Braml 3H **99**
Belvoir Av. DN5: Barnb 1H **51**
Ben Bank Rd.
S75: Dod, Silk C 5B **28**
Bence Cl. S75: Dart 1F **15**
Bence Farm Ct. S75: Dart 1F **15**
Bence La. S75: Dart, Kexb 6D **6**
Ben Cl. S6: Shef 3G **105**
Benita Av. S64: Mexb 2H **67**
Ben La. S6: Shef 3G **105**
Benmore Dr. S20: Sot 1A **152**
Bennett Cl. S62: Rawm 1A **84**
Bennett Cft. S25: Nth A 3H **141**
Bennetthorpe DN2: Don 2D **56**
Bennett St. S2: Shef 6E **119**
S61: Kimb 4H **95**
Bennimoor Way S40: Walt 2F **171**
Benson Rd. S2: Shef 4B **120**
Bentfield Av. S60: Roth 1B **112**
Bentham Dr. S71: Monk B 4A **18**
Bentham Rd. S40: Ches 3F **167**
Bentham Way S75: Mapp 4H **7**
Bentinck Cl. DN1: Don 2C **56**
Bentinck Rd. S44: Shut 6H **165**
Bentinck St. DN12: Con 4G **69**
Bent La. S43: Stav 3D **164**
Bent Lathes Av. S60: Roth 1B **112**
BENTLEY 2A **40**
Bentley Av. DN4: Hex 2H **55**
Bentley Business Park 1
S25: Dinn 5G **127**
Bentley Business Park 2
S25: Dinn 5G **127**
Bentley Cl. S71: Monk B 3B **18**
Bentley Comn. La. DN5: Ben 2B **40**
BENTLEY MOOR 2G **23**
Bentley Moor La.
DN6: Adw S 1E **23**
Bentley Park (Park & Ride) 2H **39**
Bentley Park Station (Rail) 2H **39**
BENTLEY RISE 4A **40**
Bentley Rd. DN5: Don 3H **39**
S6: Shef .1H **117**
S35: Chap 5G **79**
S66: Braml 6B **100**
Bentley St. S60: Roth 1E **111**
Benton Ct. S61: Kimb 3A **96**
Benton Ter. S64: Swint 5C **66**
Benton Way S61: Kimb 3A **96**
Bents Cl. S11: Shef 3F **131**
S35: Chap 3F **79**
Bents Cres. S11: Shef 4G **131**
S18: Dron 1H **155**
Bents Dr. S11: Shef 3F **131**
BENTS GREEN 3G **131**
Bents Grn. Av. S11: Shef 2F **131**
Bents Grn. Pl. S11: Shef 3F **131**
Bents Grn. Rd. S11: Shef 2G **131**
Bents La. S18: Dron 1H **155**
(Holmesdale Cl.)
S18: Dron 2H **155**
(Stonelow Cres.)
Bents Rd. S11: Shef 3G **131**
S17: Tot .6D **144**
S61: Kimb P 2A **96**
Bents St. S36: Pen 3C **176**
Bents Vw. S11: Shef 3F **131**
Benty La. S10: Shef 3G **117**
Beresford Rd. S66: Malt 6C **102**
Beresford St. DN5: Ben 1B **40**
Beresford Way S41: Ches 4E **161**
Berkeley Cft. S71: Roy 2G **9**
Berkeley Pct. S11: Shef 6C **118**
Berkley Cl. S70: Wors 5E **31**
Bernard Cl. S43: Brim 6E **163**
Bernard Gdns. *S2: Shef 3H 119*
(off Hyde Pk. Ter.)
Bernard Rd. DN12: New E 5C **70**
S2: Shef .2A **120**
S4: Shef .2A **120**
Bernard St. S2: Shef 2H **5** (3H **119**)
S60: Roth 5F **97**
S62: Rawm 1A **84**
Berners Cl. S2: Shef 3B **134**
Berners Dr. S2: Shef 2B **134**
Berners Pl. S2: Shef 2B **134**
Berners Rd. S2: Shef 2B **134**
Berneslai Cl. S70: Barn 6D **16**
Berne Sq. S81: Woods 4E **143**
Bernshall Cres. S5: Shef 2G **93**
Berresford Rd. S11: Shef 6C **118**
Berrington Cl. DN4: Balb 2H **71**
Berry Av. S21: Ecki 1D **158**
Berrydale S70: Wors 5G **31**
Berry Dr. S26: Kiv P 5C **140**
Berry Edge Cl. DN12: Con 5H **69**
Berry Holme Cl. S35: Chap 3F **79**
Berry Holme Ct. S35: Chap 3F **79**
Berry Holme Dr. S35: Chap 3F **79**
Berry La. S35: Howb 6A **60**
Berrywell Av. S36: Pen 5E **177**
Bertram Rd. S35: Ough 4F **91**
Berwick Av. S40: Walt 3D **170**
Berwick Cl. S40: Walt 3D **170**
Berwick Ct. S40: Walt 3D **170**
Berwick Way DN2: Don 5H **41**
Berwyn Cl. S40: Ches 3D **166**
BESSACARR 6A **58**
Bessacarr La. DN4: Bess 6B **58**
Bessemer Pk. S60: Roth 6C **96**
Bessemer Pl. S9: Shef 1B **120**
Bessemer Rd. S9: Shef 6B **108**
Bessemer Ter. S36: Stoc 2D **174**
Bessemer Way S60: Roth 5B **96**
Bessingby Rd. S6: Shef 5B **106**
Bethel Gdns. S75: Mapp 6A **8**
Bethel Rd. S65: Roth 2G **97**
Bethel Wlk. S1: Shef 4D **4**
Betjeman Gdns. S10: Shef 5B **118**
Betony Cl. S21: Killa 5A **152**
Beulah Rd. S6: Shef 3C **106**
Bevan Av. DN11: New R 5C **74**
Bevan Cl. S74: Els 6D **46**
Bevan Cres. S66: Malt 4A **102**
Bevan Dr. S43: Ink 2G **169**
Bevan Way S35: Chap 3E **79**
Bevercotes Rd. S5: Shef 1A **108**
Beverley Av. S70: Wors 4E **31**
Beverley Cl. S26: Swal 1C **138**
S71: Smi .1D **16**
Beverley Gdns. DN5: Scaws 5E **39**
Beverley Rd. DN2: Don 4F **41**
Beverleys Rd. S8: Shef 4F **133**
Beverley St. S9: Shef 6D **108**
Bevin Pl. S62: Rawm 2A **84**
Bevre Rd. DN3: Arm 2E **43**
Bewdley Ct. S71: Roy 2A **10**
Bewicke Av. DN5: Scaws 4E **39**
Bhatia Cl. S64: Mexb 1F **67**
Bib La. S25: Brook 5F **115**
Bickerton Rd. S6: Shef 2B **106**
Bierlow Cl. S73: Bramp 4B **48**
Bigby Way S66: Braml 3A **100**
Bignor Pl. S6: Shef 5C **92**
Bignor Rd. S6: Shef 5C **92**
Big Six S60: Tree 2G **123**
Bilby La. S43: Brim 5D **162**

Bilham La. DN5: Hoot P 1H 37
Billam Pl. S61: Kimb P 1H 95
Billam St. S21: Ecki 1C 158
BILLINGLEY 4G 35
Billingley Dr. S63: Thurn 3B 36
Billingley Grn. La. S72: Bill 4G 35
Billingley La. S63: Thurn 3G 35
Billingley Vw. S63: Bolt D 2A 50
Bilston St. S6: Shef 5C 106
Binders Rd. S61: Kimb P 1H 95
Binfield Rd. S8: Shef 3E 133
Bingham Ct. S10: Shef 6H 117
Bingham Pk. Cres. S11: Shef 1A 132
Bingham Pk. Rd. S11: Shef 1H 131
Bingham Rd. S8: Shef 6E 133
Bingley Ct. S75: Barn 6C 16
Bingley La. S6: Stann 2B 116
Bingley St. S75: Barn 6C 16
Binsted Av. S5: Shef 6C 92
Binsted Cl. S5: Shef 1C 106
Binsted Cres. S5: Shef 1C 106
Binsted Cft. S5: Shef 1C 106
Binsted Dr. S5: Shef 1C 106
Binsted Gdns. S5: Shef 1C 106
Binsted Glade S5: Shef 1C 106
Binsted Gro. S5: Shef 1C 106
Binsted Rd. S5: Shef 1C 106
Binsted Way S5: Shef 1C 106
Biram Wlk. *S74: Els* *2E 63*
(off Wath Rd.)
Birchall Av. S60: Whist 3A 112
Birch Av. DN9: Auck 3B 76
S35: Chap 4F 79
Birch Cl. DN5: Sprot 3E 55
S21: Killa 5B 152
Birch Ct. S64: Swint 3B 66
Birch Cres. S66: Wick 5H 99
Birchdale Cl. DN3: Eden 1C 42
Birchen Cl. DN4: Bess 1B 74
S18: Dron W 3C 154
S40: Ches 3E 167
Birches Fold S18: Coal A 6H 147
Birches La. S18: Coal A 6H 147
Birch Farm Av. S8: Shef 2F 147
Birchfield Cres. S75: Dod 2H 29
Birchfield Rd. S66: Malt 5C 102
Birchfield Wlk. S75: Barn 6A 16
Birch Grn. S66: Malt 4G 101
Birch Gro. DN12: Con 4G 69
S35: Ough 4F 91
Birch Hall Golf Course *1F 161*
Birch Holt Gro. S18: Uns 1F 161
Birch Ho. Av. S35: Ough 4E 91
Birchin Bank S74: Els 6C 46
Birchitt Cl. S17: Bradw 5B 146
Birchitt Pl. S17: Bradw 5B 146
Birchitt Rd. S17: Bradw 5B 146
Birchitt Vw. S18: Dron 1F 155
Birch Kiln Cft. S43: Brim 1E 169
Birchlands Dr. S21: Killa 5C 152
Birch La. S43: Hol 5F 163
Birch Pk. Ct. S61: Roth 4B 96
Birch Rd. DN4: Cant 4C 58
S9: Shef 6B 108
S70: Barn 3A 32
Birch Tree Cl. DN3: Barn D 1D 26
Birch Tree Rd. S36: Stoc 4D 174
Birchtree Rd. S61: Thorpe H 5C 80
Birchvale Rd. S12: Shef 5G 135
Birchwood Av. S62: Rawm 2G 83
Birchwood Cl. S20: Westf 2F 151
S66: Malt 4G 101
Birchwood Ct. DN4: Bess 1E 75
S40: Birdh 3G 171
Birchwood Cres. S40: Birdh 3G 171
Birchwood Cft. S20: Westf 2F 151
Birchwood Dell DN4: Bess 1E 75
Birchwood Dr. S65: Rav 2A 100
Birchwood Gdns. S20: Westf 2F 151
S66: B'well 6B 88
Birchwood Gro. S20: Westf 2F 151
Birchwood La. S66: Malt 3B 102
Birchwood Ri. S20: Westf 2F 151
Birchwood Rd. S21: Mar L, Trow 1G 157
Birchwood Vw. S20: Westf 2F 151
Birchwood Way S20: Westf 2F 151
Bircotes Wlk. DN11: Ross 5E 75
Bird Av. S73: Womb 2F 47
BIRDHOLME 3H 171

Birdholme Cres. S40: Birdh 2H 171
Bird Cl. DN5: Clay 1H 21
Bird St. S43: Stav 4C 164
BIRDWELL 4E 45
Birdwell Comn. S70: Birdw 6E 45
Birdwell Rd. S4: Shef 3C 108
S64: Kiln 6C 66
S75: Dod 4A 30
Birk Av. S70: Barn 3H 31
Birkbeck Ct. S35: High G 6C 60
Birk Cres. S70: Barn 3H 31
Birkdale Av. S25: Dinn 6A 128
Birkdale Cl. DN4: Cant 6E 59
S72: Cud 6F 11
Birkdale Dr. S40: Walt 2D 170
Birkdale Ri. S64: Swint 4C 66
Birkdale Rd. S71: Roy 1G 9
BIRKENDALE 1C 118
Birkendale S6: Shef 1C 118
Birkendale Rd. S6: Shef 1C 118
Birkendale Vw. S6: Shef 1C 118
Birk Grn. S70: Barn 3A 32
Birk Ho. La. S70: Barn 3A 32
Birklands Av. S13: Shef 5H 121
Birklands Cl. S13: Shef 5H 121
Birklands Dr. S13: Shef 5H 121
Birk Rd. S70: Barn 3H 31
Birks Av. S13: Shef 2C 136
Birks Holt Dr. S66: Malt 6D 102
Birks Rd. S61: Kimb P 1H 95
Birks Wood Dr. S35: Ough 4E 91
Birk Ter. S70: Barn 3H 31
Birkwood Av. S72: Cud 4F 19
Birkwood Ter. S66: B'well 1C 102
Birley Brook Dr. S41: Ches 1C 166
BIRLEY CARR 5B 92
Birley Cft. S41: Ches 1C 166
BIRLEY EDGE 4A 92
BIRLEY ESTATE 5H 135
BIRLEYHAY 5G 149
Birley La. S12: Shef 6F 135
Birley Lane Stop (ST) 6H 135
Birley Moor Av. S12: Shef 5H 135
Birley Moor Cl. S12: Shef 5H 135
Birley Moor Cres. S12: Shef 5H 135
Birley Moor Dr. S12: Shef 6H 135
Birley Moor Pl. S12: Shef 5H 135
Birley Moor Rd. S12: Shef 3G 135
Birley Moor Road Stop (ST) 6A 136
Birley Moor Way S12: Shef 6H 135
Birley Ri. Cres. S6: Shef 6B 92
Birley Ri. Rd. S6: Shef 6B 92
Birley Spa 4A 136
Birley Spa Cl. S12: Shef 4C 136
Birley Spa Dr. S12: Shef 4C 136
Birley Spa La. S12: Shef 5A 136
Birley Spa Wlk. *S12: Shef* *4C 136*
(off Carter Lodge Dr.)
Birley Va. Av. S12: Shef 4F 135
Birley Va. Cl. S12: Shef 4F 135
Birley Vw. S35: Ough 5E 91
Birley Wood Cres. S12: Shef 6A 136
Birley Wood Golf Course 6H 135
Birstall Cl. S41: Ches 1D 166
Birthwaite Rd. S75: Kexb 5C 6
Birtley St. S66: Malt 5G 101
Bisby Rd. S62: Rawm 2H 83
Biscay La. S63: Wath D 5F 49
Biscay Way S63: Wath D 6G 49
Bishopdale Dr. S20: Mosb 1B 150
Bishopdale Dr. S20: Mosb 2B 150
Bishopdale Ri. S20: Mosb 2B 150
Bishop Gdns. S13: Shef 2B 136
Bishopgarth Cl. DN5: Don 4A 40
Bishop Hill S13: Shef 2B 136
Bishops Cl. S8: Shef 3G 133
Bishopscourt Rd. S8: Shef 3F 133
Bishopsgate La. DN11: New R 6H 75
Bishopsholme Cl. S5: Shef 2F 107
Bishopsholme Rd. S5: Shef 2F 107
Bishop's House *3F 133*
Bishopstoke Ct. S65: Roth 3H 97
Bishopston Wlk. S66: Malt 4H 101
Bishop St. S1: Shef 6C 4 (4E 119)
Bishops Wlk. S26: Kiv P 5B 140
Bishops Way S40: Ches 2H 171
S71: Monk B 5H 17
Bisley Cl. S71: Roy 3B 10
Bismarck St. S70: Barn 3E 31

Bitholmes Ga. S35: Wharn S 1A 90
Bitholmes La. S36: Spink 5H 175
Bittern Cft. S73: Bramp 3B 48
Bitterne Cft. S73: Bramp 3C 48
Bittern Vw. S61: Thorpe H 2D 80
Blackamoor S64: Swint 5F 65
Blacka Moor Cres. S17: Dore 4D 144
Blacka Moor Nature Reserve *4A 144*
Blacka Moor Rd. S17: Dore 4D 144
Blackamoor Rd. S64: Swint 5F 65
Blacka Moor Vw. S17: Dore 4D 144
Blackberry Flats *S20: Half* *3F 151*
(off Halfway Dr.)
Blackbird Av. S60: Brins 4E 111
Blackbrook Av. S10: Shef 5A 116
Blackbrook Dr. S10: Shef 5A 116
Blackbrook Rd. S10: Shef 5B 116
BLACKBURN 4E 95
Blackburn Cres. S35: Chap 2D 78
Blackburn Cft. S35: Chap 2E 79
Blackburn Dr. S35: Chap 3D 78
Blackburne St. S6: Shef 5C 106
Blackburn La. S61: Kimb 4E 95
S70: Wors 5F 31
S75: Barn 6C 16
Blackburn Meadows Nature Reserve
 ....5A 96
Blackburn Rd. S61: Kimb 4E 95
Blackburn St. S70: Wors 5F 31
Black Carr Rd. S66: Wick 5F 99
Blackdown Av. S20: Water 6E 137
S40: Ches 3C 166
Blackdown Cl. S20: Water 6E 137
Blacker Grange S74: Black H 4A 46
Blackergreen La. S75: Silk, Silk C 3A 28
BLACKER HILL 3A 46
Blacker La. S70: Wors 2F 45
S72: Shaft 3F 11
S74: Black H 2F 45
Blacker Rd. S75: Mapp, Stain 5B 8
Blackheath Cl. S71: Ath 1G 17
Blackheath Rd. S71: Ath 1G 17
Blackheath Wlk. S71: Ath 1G 17
Black Hill Rd. S65: Roth 6C 98
Black Horse Cl. S75: Silk C 5B 28
Black Horse Dr. S75: Silk C 5B 28
Black La. S6: Lox 5E 105
S74: Hoyl 2E 61
S81: Woods 5G 143
Blackmoor Cres. S60: Brins 3C 110
Blackmore St. S4: Shef 1A 120
Blacksmith Ct. S61: Thorpe H 4C 80
Blacksmith La. S35: Gren 2B 92
S44: Cal 4F 169
Blacksmith Sq. *S74: Els* *2E 63*
(off Wath Rd.)
Blackstock Cl. S14: Shef 6A 134
Blackstock Cres. S14: Shef 6A 134
Blackstock Dr. S14: Shef 6A 134
Blackstock Rd. S14: Shef 3A 134
Black Stone La. DN9: Blax 2E 77
Black Swan Wlk. S1: Shef 3E 5
Blackthorn Av. S66: Braml 5H 99
Blackthorn Cl. S35: High G 6C 60
S41: Has 2C 172
Blackthorne Cl. DN12: New E 5B 70
Blackthorne Ct. S70: Barn 3H 31
Blackthorn Ri. S65: Rav 2E 98
Blackwell Cl.
 S2: Shef 3H 5 (3H 119)
Blackwell Ct. S2: Shef 3H 5 (3H 119)
Blackwell Pl.
 S2: Shef 3H 5 (3H 119)
Blackwood Av. DN4: Balb 6G 55
Blagden St. S2: Shef 3H 119
Blair Athol Rd. S11: Shef 2A 132
Blake Av. DN2: Don 4E 41
S63: Wath D 5D 48
Blake Cl. S66: Braml 1B 114
Blake Gro. Rd. S6: Shef 1D 118
Blakeley Cl. S71: Ath 1G 17
Blakeney M. *S25: Laugh C* *4F 127*
(off Mountfield Way)
Blakeney Rd. S10: Shef 3B 118
Blake St. S6: Shef 1C 118
Blandford Dr. S41: Ches 1F 167
Bland La. S6: Shef 3G 105
(not continuous)
Bland St. S4: Shef 4B 108

Blast La.—Bracken Moor La.

Blast La. S2: Shef 2H 119
(Broad St.)
S2: Shef 2H 5 (2H 119)
(Sheffield Parkway)
S4: Shef 1H 5 (2H 119)
BLAXTON 1F 77
Blaxton Cl. S20: Mosb 6B 136
Blay Ct. *S43: New W 2C 162*
(off High St.)
Blayton Rd. S4: Shef 4H 107
Bleachcroft Way S70: Stair 3B 32
Bleak Av. S72: Shaft 4F 11
Bleakley Av. WF4: Nott 1G 9
Bleakley Cl. S72: Shaft 4F 11
Bleakley La. WF4: Nott 1G 9
Bleakley Ter. WF4: Nott 1G 9
Bleasdale Gro. S71: Monk B 4F 17
Blenheim Av. S70: Barn 2D 30
Blenheim Cl. S25: Dinn 6H 127
S66: Braml 3H 99
Blenheim Ct. S66: Flan 4G 99
Blenheim Cres. S64: Mexb 1E 67
Blenheim Dr. DN9: Finn 3E 77
Blenheim Gro. S70: Barn 2C 30
Blenheim M. S11: Shef 3H 131
Blenheim Rd. S70: Barn 2C 30
Bloemfontein St. S72: Cud 2D 18
Blonk St. S1: Shef 1G 5 (2G 119)
Bloomfield Ho. S75: Silk C 5B 28
Bloomfield Ri. S75: Dart 5H 7
Bloomfield Rd. S75: Dart 5G 7
BLOOMHOUSE 4H 7
Bloomhouse La. S75: Dart 4F 7
Bloomingdale Ct.
S75: Wool G 3F 7
Blossom Av. S65: Thry 6D 84
Blossom Cres. S12: Shef 5E 135
Blossoms, The S75: Barn 6C 16
Blossom Way S63: Thurn 1C 36
Blow Hall Cres. DN12: New E 4D 70
Blow Hall Riding DN12: New E 5E 71
Blucher St. S70: Barn 1D 30
Bluebank Vw. S43: New W 3C 162
Bluebell Av. S36: Pen 4C 176
Bluebell Bank S70: Barn 3F 31
Blue Bell Cl. S43: Ink 3G 169
Bluebell Cl. S5: Shef 1B 108
S74: Hoyl 2H 61
Blue Bell Ct. DN9: Blax 1F 77
Bluebell Rd. S5: Shef 1C 108
S75: Dart 3F 7
Bluebell Wood La. S66: Sunn 3G 99
Blueberry Cl. S43: Ink 3G 169
Blueberry Ct. S66: Sunn 3G 99
Bluebird Hill S26: Ast 2D 138
Blue Boy St. S3: Shef 1C 4 (2E 119)
Blue Lodge Cl. S43: Ink 3G 169
Blue Mans Way S60: Cat 1D 122
Blue Ridge Cl. S17: Dore 3F 145
Blundell Cl. DN4: Cant 5B 58
Blundell Ct. S71: Monk B 3A 18
Blunt Av. S43: Mas M 2F 165
Blyde Rd. S5: Shef 3H 107
Bly Rd. S73: D'fld 4A 34
Blyth Av. S62: Rawm 3G 83
Blyth Cl. S40: Walt 2C 170
S60: Whist 3C 112
Blythe St. S73: Womb 1F 47
Blyth Rd. S66: Malt 6A 102
Boardman Av. S62: Rawm 6D 64
Boat La. DN5: Sprot 4C 54
Bobbin Mill La. S40: Ches 6E 167
Bochum Parkway S8: Shef 3F 147
Bocking Cl. S8: Shef 1C 146
Bocking Hill S36: Stoc 3F 175
Bocking La. S8: Shef 1C 146
Bocking Ri. S8: Shef 2D 146
Boden La. S1: Shef 3C 4 (3E 119)
Boden Pl. S9: Shef 1F 121
Bodmin Ct. S71: Monk B 5G 17
Bodmin St. S9: Shef 6C 108
Bodmin Way S40: Ches 3D 166
Boggard La. S35: Ough 4D 90
S36: Pen 5C 176
Boiley La. S21: Killa 6A 152
Boland Rd. S8: Shef 5C 146
Bold St. S9: Shef 5D 108
Bole Cl. S73: Womb 6A 34
BOLE HILL 1G 123
BOLEHILL
S8 . . . . 6F 133
S44 . . . . 1G 173
Bole Hill S8: Shef 6F 133
S44: Cal 1F 173
S60: Tree 1F 123
Bole Hill Cl. S6: Shef 6A 106
Bole Hill La. S10: Shef 2H 117
Bolehill La. S21: Ecki, Mar L 2A 158
Bole Hill Rd. S6: Shef 2G 117
Bolehill Vw. S10: Shef 1A 118
Bolsover Rd. S5: Shef 2A 108
S43: Mas M, Woodt 2G 165
Bolsover Rd. E. S5: Shef 3A 108
Bolsover St. S3: Shef 3A 4 (3D 118)
BOLSTERSTONE 6E 175
Bolton Hill Rd. DN4: Bess 6B 58
(not continuous)
Bolton-on-Dearne Station (Rail) 2C 50
Bolton Rd. S63: Wath D 6B 50
S64: Swint 3A 66
Bolton St. DN12: Den M 2C 68
S3: Shef 5B 4 (4E 119)
BOLTON UPON DEARNE 2B 50
Bond S6: Shef 1A 4 (2D 118)
Bond Cl. DN1: Don 2B 56
Bondfield Av. DN11: New R 6D 74
Bondfield Cl. S73: Womb 2G 47
Bondfield Cres. S73: Womb 2F 47
Bondfield Cres. Flats S73: Womb 2F 47
(not continuous)
Bondfield Rd. S43: Ink 1H 169
Bond Rd. S75: Barn 5C 16
Bond St. DN11: New R 6G 75
S43: Stav 6H 163
S73: Womb 1G 47
Bonet La. S60: Brins 3B 110
Bonington Ri. S66: Malt 4H 101
Bonsall Ct. *S41: Ches 1E 167*
(off Newbold Rd.)
Bonville Gdns. S3: Shef 1B 4
Booker Cl. S43: Ink 2H 169
Booker Rd. S8: Shef 6D 132
Bookers La. S25: Dinn 4E 127
(not continuous)
Bookers Way S25: Dinn 5E 127
Booth Av. DN4: Don 3G 57
Booth Cl. S20: Water 6E 137
S66: Thurc 6D 114
Booth Cft. S20: Water 6E 137
Booth Pl. S62: Rawm 1F 83
Booth Rd. S35: High G 1B 78
Booth St. S61: Grea 4C 82
S74: Hoyl 6C 46
Bootle St. S9: Shef 6D 108
Borough M. *S6: Shef 1E 119*
(off Bedford St.)
Borough Rd. S6: Shef 4B 106
Borrowdale Av. S20: Half 4F 151
Borrowdale Cl. S20: Half 4F 151
S71: Ard 2D 32
Borrowdale Cres.
S25: Dinn, Nth A 1A 142
Borrowdale Dr. S20: Half 4F 151
Borrowdale Rd. S20: Half 4F 151
Boston Castle 6E 97
Boston Castle Gro. S60: Roth 6F 97
Boston Castle Ter. S60: Roth 6F 97
Boston St. S2: Shef 5E 119
Bosville Cl. S65: Rav 5A 86
Bosville Rd. S10: Shef 3A 118
Bosville St. S36: Pen 5E 177
S65: Roth 2C 98
Boswell Cl. DN11: New R 6B 74
S35: High G 6B 60
S71: Roy 2G 9
Boswell Ct. DN4: Bess 5A 58
Boswell Rd. DN4: Bess 5H 57
S63: Wath D 2G 65
Boswell St. S65: Roth 5G 97
Bosworth Rd. DN6: Adw S 2B 22
Bosworth St. S10: Shef 2A 118
Botanical Rd. S11: Shef 5B 118
Botany Bay La. DN3: Barn D 1F 27
Botham St. S4: Shef 4B 108
Botsford St. S3: Shef 6F 107
Boulder Bri. La. S71: Carl 4C 10
BOULDER HILL 4A 106
Boulevard, The DN3: Eden 6B 26
Boulton Cl. S40: Ches 3B 166
Boulton Dr. DN3: Cant 3E 59
Boundary Av. DN2: Don 3H 41
Boundary Cl. DN12: New E 3D 70
S43: Stav 3D 164
Boundary Dr. S72: Brier 3B 12
Boundary Grn. S62: Rawm 4H 83
Boundary Rd. S2: Shef 4A 120
Boundary St. S70: Barn 2G 31
Boundary Wlk. S60: Brins 4B 110
Bourne Cl. S43: Brim 5D 162
Bourne Ct. S75: Stain 4B 8
Bourne Rd. S5: Shef 6H 93
S70: Wors 6E 31
Bourne Wlk. S75: Stain 4B 8
Bow Bri. Cl. S60: Roth 6D 96
BOW BROOM 2C 66
Bowden Gro. S75: Dod 3G 29
Bowden Housteads Wood and
Carbrook Ravine Nature Reserve
. . . . 4G 121
Bowden Wood Av. S9: Shef 4F 121
Bowden Wood Cl. S9: Shef 4F 121
Bowden Wood Cres. S9: Shef 4F 121
Bowden Wood Dr. S9: Shef 4F 121
Bowden Wood Pl. S9: Shef 4F 121
Bowden Wood Rd. S9: Shef 4F 121
Bowdon St.
S1: Shef 5C 4 (4E 119)
Bowen Dr. S65: Thry 6E 85
Bowen Rd. S65: Roth 2G 97
Bower Cl. S61: Kimb P 1H 95
Bower Farm Rd. S41: Old W 4A 162
Bower Hill S36: Oxs 6H 177
Bower Ho. S35: Gren 1B 92
Bower La. S35: Gren 1A 92
Bower Rd. S10: Shef 2C 118
S64: Swint 1C 66
Bowers Fold DN1: Don 1C 56
Bower Spring S3: Shef 1E 5
Bower Va. DN12: New E 5B 70
Bowes Rd. DN3: Eden 1B 42
Bowfell Vw. S71: Monk B 4F 17
Bowfield Ct. *S5: Shef 6H 93*
(off Etwall Way)
Bowfield Rd. S5: Shef 6H 93
Bowland Cl. DN5: Scawt 2G 39
Bowland Cres. S70: Wors 6E 31
Bowland Dr. S35: Chap 3D 78
S42: Walt 3C 170
Bowlease Gdns. DN4: Cant 4B 58
Bowling Grn. St. S3: Shef 1D 4 (1F 119)
Bowman Cl. S12: Shef 6C 134
Bowman Dr. S12: Shef 6C 134
S66: Malt 3H 101
Bowness Cl. S18: Dron W 3D 154
S41: Ches 1E 167
Bowness Gro. S63: Bolt D 3B 50
Bowness Rd. S6: Shef 5B 106
S41: Ches 1E 167
Bowood Rd. S11: Shef 6C 118
BOWSHAW 6E 147
Bowshaw S18: Dron 1E 155
Bowshaw Av. S8: Shef 5F 147
Bowshaw Cl. S8: Shef 5F 147
Bowshaw Vw. S8: Shef 5F 147
Bow St. S72: Cud 1E 19
Boyce St. S6: Shef 1C 118
Boyd Rd. S63: Wath D 3G 65
Boyland St. S3: Shef 6E 107
Boynton Cres. S5: Shef 2F 107
Boynton Rd. S5: Shef 3E 107
(not continuous)
BOYTHORPE 1G 171
Boythorpe Av. S40: Ches 6F 167
Boythorpe Cres. S40: Ches 1G 171
Boythorpe Mt. S40: Ches 6G 167
Boythorpe Ri. S40: Ches 6F 167
Boythorpe Rd. S40: Ches 6G 167
Brackenbury Cl. DN5: Cade 6G 53
Bracken Cl. DN3: Brant 3H 59
Bracken Ct. S66: Wick 1G 113
S70: Barn 3G 31
Brackendale Cl. S43: Brim 1C 168
Brackenfield Gro. S12: Shef 4G 135
Bracken Hill S35: Burn 4C 78
Bracken Hill La. DN10: Miss 6H 77
BRACKEN MOOR 4E 175
Bracken Moor La. S36: Stoc 4E 175

188 A-Z Sheffield

Bracken Rd. S5: Shef 6B **94**
(not continuous)
Brackley St. S3: Shef 6G **107**
Bradberry Balk La. S73: Womb 6F **33**
Bradbourne Cl. S43: Stav 6H **163**
Bradbury Cl. S40: Ches 5F **167**
Bradbury Dr. S42: W'orth 6F **171**
Bradbury Hall *S40: Ches 5F* ***167***
(off Chatsworth Rd.)
Bradbury's Cl. S62: Parkg 5G **83**
Bradbury St. S8: Shef 2F **133**
S70: Barn 1C **30**
Bradfield Rd. S6: Shef 4B **106**
Bradford Rd. DN2: Don 2H **41**
Bradford Row DN1: Don 1C **56**
BRADGATE .3B 96
Bradgate Cl. S61: Kimb 3B **96**
Bradgate Ct. S61: Kimb 3A **96**
Bradgate Cft. S41: Has 3B **172**
Bradgate Ho. Cl. S61: Kimb 3B **96**
Bradgate La. S61: Kimb 3A **96**
Bradgate Pl. S61: Kimb 2B **96**
Bradgate Rd. S61: Kimb 2B **96**
Bradlea Ri. S62: Rawm 1H **83**
Bradley Av. S73: Womb 1F **47**
Bradley Cl. S43: Brim 1D **168**
Bradley St. S10: Shef 1A **118**
Bradley Way S43: Brim 6D **162**
Bradman Wlk. S62: Rawm 6D **64**
Bradmarsh Way S60: Roth 6D **96**
Bradshaw Av. S60: Tree 3G **123**
Bradshaw Cl. S75: Barn 6H **15**
Bradshaw Rd. S43: Ink 2G **169**
Bradshaw Way S60: Tree 3G **123**
Bradstone Rd. S65: Roth 3B **98**
BRADWAY .5A 146
BRADWAY BANK 4A 146
Bradway Cl. S17: Bradw 5A **146**
Bradway Dr. S17: Bradw 5A **146**
Bradway Grange Rd. S17: Bradw 5B **146**
Bradway Rd. S17: Bradw 5A **146**
Bradwell Av. S75: Dod 4H **29**
Bradwell Cl. S18: Dron W 3B **154**
Bradwell Pl. S43: Ink 1H **169**
Bradwell St. S2: Shef 2G **133**
Braeburn Cl. S66: Malt 3G **101**
Braemar Cl. S43: New W 2C **162**
Braemar Rd. DN2: Don 1F **57**
Braemore Rd. S6: Shef 3H **105**
Braidwood Way S40: Ches 6H **167**
Brailsford Av. S5: Shef 2F **93**
Brailsford Ct. S5: Shef 2F **93**
Brailsford Rd. S5: Shef 2F **93**
Braithwaite M. *S75: Mapp 5B* ***8***
(off Braithwaite St.)
Braithwaite St. S75: Stain 5B **8**
BRAITHWELL 6B 88
Braithwell Ct. DN5: Ben 5H **23**
Braithwell Rd. DN5: Ben 6H **23**
S65: Rav 2A **100**
S66: Malt 5A **102**
Braithwell Wlk. DN12: Den M 2C **68**
Braithwell Way S66: Hel 3D **100**
Bramah St. S71: Carl 5H **9**
Bramall Ct. S2: Shef 6F **119**
Bramall Lane 5F 119
Bramall La. S2: Shef 5F **119**
S36: Stoc 1B **174**
Bramble Cl. S66: Wick 1G **113**
Bramble Rd. S72: Sth H 1H **11**
Brambles, The S35: Eccl 2F **93**
S71: Roy .2F **9**
Bramble Way DN9: Auck 2B **76**
S63: Wath D 6C **48**
Brambling Ct. S41: Ches 5B **168**
Brambling La. S63: Wath D 4F **49**
Bramblings, The DN4: Cant 6D **58**
Bramcote Av. S71: Ath 6D **8**
Brameld Rd. S62: Rawm 3G **83**
S64: Swint 3A **66**
Bramhall Cl. S73: Womb 3E **47**
Bramham Ct. *S9: Shef 1E* ***121***
(off Bramham Rd.)
Bramham Cft. S73: Womb 6A **34**
Bramham Rd. DN4: Cant 2C **58**
S9: Shef 1E **121**
BRAMLEY
S21 .6H 149
S66 .5A 100
Bramley Av. S13: Shef 6A **122**
S26: Ast 6D **124**
Bramley Carr S70: Barn 3A **30**
Bramley Cl. S20: Mosb 3D **150**
S43: Ink 3G **169**
Bramley Ct. DN12: Den M 3C **68**
S10: Shef 3A **118**
Bramley Dr. S13: Shef 5A **122**
Bramley Grange Cres. S66: Braml . . .5B **100**
Bramley Grange Dr. S66: Braml 5B **100**
Bramley Grange Ri. S66: Braml 5B **100**
Bramley Grange Vw. S66: Braml 4B **100**
Bramley Grange Way S66: Braml 5C **100**
Bramley Hall Rd. S13: Shef 6A **122**
Bramley La. S13: Shef 5A **122**
S65: Rav 2D **100**
BRAMLEY LINGS 1A 114
Bramley M. S21: Ecki 1E **159**
BRAMLEY MOOR 1G 157
Bramleymoor La. S21: Mar L 4G **157**
Bramley Pk. Cl. S13: Shef 6A **122**
Bramley Pk. Mobile Home Site
S21: Mar L 1A **158**
Bramley Pk. Rd. S13: Shef 5A **122**
Bramley Rd. S21: Mar L 3H **157**
Bramley Way S66: Hel 4D **100**
BRAMPTON
S40 .6C 166
S63 .5A 48
Brampton Av. S66: Thurc 6A **114**
Brampton Beck S73: Bramp 3B **48**
BRAMPTON BIERLOW 5B 48
Brampton Centre, The
S63: Wath D 5C **48**
Brampton Cl. DN3: Arm 5D **42**
Brampton Ct. S20: Mosb 6B **136**
S40: Bramp 5D **166**
Brampton Cres. S73: Womb 3A **48**
Brampton Ellis Ent. Cen.
S63: Wath D 5C **48**
BRAMPTON EN LE MORTHEN 1A 126
Brampton La. DN3: Arm 5D **42**
S26: Ull 2G **125**
Brampton Leisure Cen. 5C 48
Brampton Manor Health & Fitness Club
. . . . .5D 166
Brampton Mdws. S66: Thurc 6A **114**
Brampton Rd. S63: Wath D 5C **48**
S66: Bramp M, Thurc 1A **126**
S73: Bramp 5C **48**
S73: Womb 3A **48**
Brampton St. S73: Bramp 4C **48**
Brampton Vw. S73: Womb 3A **48**
Bramshill Cl. S20: Sot 1H **151**
Bramshill Ct. S20: Sot 1H **151**
Bramshill Ri. S40: Walt 1E **171**
Bramwell Cl. S3: Shef 2A **4** (2D **118**)
Bramwell Ct. S3: Shef 2A **4** (2D **118**)
Bramwell Dr. S3: Shef 2A **4** (2D **118**)
Bramwell St. S3: Shef 2A **4** (2D **118**)
S65: Roth 3F **97**
Bramwith La. DN3: Barn D 1G **27**
DN7: Sth B 1G **27**
Bramwith Rd. S11: Shef 6G **117**
Bramworth Rd. DN4: Hex 3G **55**
Branchcroft Dr. DN4: Balb 2A **72**
Brandene Cl. S44: Cal 5F **169**
Brander Cl. DN4: Balb 1B **72**
Brand La.
DN5: High M, Sprot . . . .1H **53** & 6A **38**
Brandon St. S3: Shef 5G **107**
Brandreth Cl. S6: Shef 1D **118**
Brandreth Rd. S6: Shef 1D **118**
Brands Cl. S81: Woods 3F **143**
Brand's La. S25: Dinn 1C **142**
S81: Gild 1C **142**
Brandsmere Dr. S81: Woods 3F **143**
Branksome Av. S70: Barn 1B **30**
Branksome Chine Av. S41: Has 3B **172**
Bransby St. S6: Shef 1C **118**
Branstone Rd. DN5: Sprot 2C **54**
BRANTON .4G 59
Branton Cl. S40: Ches 1G **171**
Branton Ga. Rd. DN3: Brant 3H **59**
Branton Ter. DN3: Brant 4G **59**
Brantwood Cres. DN4: Cant 3C **58**
Brathay Cl. S4: Shef 3C **108**
Brathay Rd. S4: Shef 3C **108**
Brayford Rd. DN4: Balb 2A **72**
Bray St. S9: Shef 1D **120**
Brayton Dr. DN4: Balb 2A **72**
Bray Wlk. S61: Kimb P 6F **81**
Brearley Av. S36: Spink 4F **175**
S43: New W 3C **162**
Brearley Centre, The S9: Tins 5G **109**
Brearley Hall S41: Old W 2B **162**
Brearley St. S41: Old W 3B **162**
Breckland Rd. S40: Walt 2C **170**
Brecklands S60: Roth 6B **98**
S66: Wick 6F **99**
Breck La. S25: Dinn 4A **128**
S43: Bar H 2H **163**
BRECKS 6D 98
Brecks Cres. S65: Roth 5D **98**
Brecks La. DN3: Kirk Sa 4C **26**
S65: Roth 3C **98**
Brecon Cl. S20: Sot 6H **137**
S40: Ches 3D **166**
Brendon Av. S40: Ches 4D **166**
Brendon Cl. S73: Womb 4A **48**
Brent Cl. S40: Ches 3E **167**
Brentwood Av. S11: Shef 2C **132**
Brentwood Cl. S74: Hoyl 2H **61**
Brentwood Rd. S11: Shef 2C **132**
Brentwood Vs. S65: Roth 3F **97**
Bressingham Cl. S4: Shef 6H **107**
Bressingham Rd. S4: Shef 6H **107**
Bressingham Rd. Nth. S4: Shef 6G **107**
Bretby Cl. DN4: Cant 5C **58**
Bretby Rd. S40: Ches 2B **166**
Brettas Pk. S71: Monk B 3F **17**
Brett Cl. S62: Rawm 6D **64**
Bretton Cl. S40: Ash 3B **166**
S72: Brier 4B **12**
S75: Kexb 6D **6**
Bretton Country Pk. 1A 6
Bretton Gro. S12: Shef 5G **135**
Bretton Ho. *DN1: Don 2B* ***56***
(off St James St.)
Bretton Rd. S75: Kexb 6D **6**
Bretton Vw. S72: Cud 3D **18**
Brewery Rd. S63: Wath D 5G **49**
Brewery St. S41: Ches 5A **168**
Brew House, The *S11: Shef 5E* ***119***
(off Napier St.)
Breydon Av. DN5: Cus 5F **39**
Breydon Ct. DN5: Cus 5F **39**
Briar Cl. DN9: Auck 2B **76**
S41: Ches 3F **167**
Briar Ct. S66: Wick 1G **113**
Briar Cft. DN4: Balb 4H **55**
Briardene Cl. S40: Ches 3A **166**
Briarfield Av. S12: Shef 5D **134**
Briarfield Cres. S12: Shef 5D **134**
Briarfield Rd. S12: Shef 5D **134**
Briarfields La. S35: Ough 5D **90**
Briar Gro. S36: Cub 5D **176**
S72: Brier 3B **12**
Briar Ri. S70: Wors 6F **31**
Briar Rd. DN3: Arm 2D **42**
S7: Shef 2D **132**
Briars Cl. S21: Killa 5C **152**
Briar Vw. S43: Brim 1D **168**
Briarwood Gdns. S66: Sunn 2G **99**
Briary Av. S35: High G 1C **78**
Briary Cl. S60: Brins 5D **110**
Brick Dr. S10: Shef 2A **118**
Brickhouse La. S17: Dore 2D **144**
BRICK HOUSES 2D 144
Brickhouse Yd. S40: Ches 5F **167**
Brick St. S10: Shef 2A **118**
Brickyard, The S72: Shaft 5F **11**
Brickyard Wlk. S40: Ches 5H **167**
Bridby St. S13: Shef 2E **137**
Bridge Bank Cl. S40: Ches 2D **166**
Bridge Bus. Pk. S41: Ches 4E **161**
BRIDGE END 3C 176
Bridge End La. S63: Wath D 4E **49**
Bridge Gdns. S71: Barn 5E **17**
Bridgegate S60: Roth 3E **97**
Bridge Gro. DN5: Cus 5G **39**
Bridge Hill S35: Ough 3E **91**
Bridgehouses S3: Shef 1F **119**
Bridgehouses Rdbt.
S3: Shef 1F **119**
Bridge Inn Rd. S35: Chap 2F **79**
Bridgelake Dr. DN4: Balb 2A **72**
Bridge Rd. DN4: Bess 4H **57**

Bridge St. DN4: Hex 2A 56
S3: Shef 1E 5 (1F 119)
S21: Killa 3C 152
S36: Pen 3C 176
S40: Ches 1H 171
S60: Roth 3E 97
S63: Bolt D 1C 50
S64: Swint 3D 66
S71: Barn 5E 17
S75: Dart 5F 7
Bridgewater Way S65: Rav 2C 100
Bridge Way S41: Ches 3E 161
Bridle Cl. S35: Chap 2F 79
Bridle Cres. S35: Chap 2F 79
Bridle La. S18: App 2E 157
Bridle Rd. S43: Woodt 5E 165
Bridle Stile S20: Mosb 3D 150
Bridle Stile Cl. S20: Mosb 3D 150
Bridle Stile Gdns. S20: Mosb 3C 150
Bridleway, The S62: Rawm 1B 84
Bridport Rd. S9: Shef 1E 121
Bridstone Gdns. S74: Els 6D 46
Brier Cl. S20: Water 1E 151
Brierey Cl. S75: Dart 6H 7
Brierfield Cl. S75: Barn 6B 16
BRIERLEY 3A 12
Brierley Cl. S43: Stav 5B 164
BRIERLEY GAP 5E 13
Brierley Rd. DN4: Bess 5A 58
S18: Uns 6B 156
S65: Dalt 1D 98
S72: Brier, Grim 5A 12
S72: Shaft 4G 11
S72: Sth H 1G 11
Brier St. S6: Shef 4B 106
Briery Gdns. S75: Dod 3F 29
Briery Mdws. S73: Hem 4F 47
Briery Wlk. S61: Grea 5C 82
Brigadier Hargreaves Ct.
S13: Shef 2B 136
Brigantian Way WF9: Hems, Sth K 2H 13
Briggs St. S71: Carl 5H 9
Brightholmlee Ct. S35: Wharn S 2A 90
Brightholmlee La.
S35: Wharn S 1A 90
Bright Meadow S20: Half 5H 151
Brightmore Dr. S3: Shef 3A 4 (3D 118)
Brightmore Ho. S3: Shef 2B 4
Brighton St. S72: Grim 1B 20
Brighton Ter. Rd. S10: Shef 2B 118
BRIGHTSIDE 2D 108
Brightside La. S9: Shef 5B 108
Brightside Way S9: Shef 4C 108
Brimham Cl. *DN3: Kirk Sa 4B 26*
(off Sandall La.)
BRIMINGTON 6E 163
BRIMINGTON COMMON 3E 169
Brimington Rd. S41: Ches 4A 168
Brimington Rd. Nth. S41: Whit M 5H 161
(not continuous)
Brimmesfield Cl. S2: Shef 1B 134
Brimmesfield Dr. S2: Shef 6B 120
Brimmesfield Rd. S2: Shef 1B 134
Brinckman St. S70: Barn 2E 31
BRINCLIFFE 1B 132
Brincliffe Cl. S40: Walt 1C 170
Brincliffe Ct. S7: Shef 2D 132
Brincliffe Cres. S11: Shef 1B 132
Brincliffe Edge Cl. S11: Shef 2B 132
Brincliffe Edge Rd. S11: Shef 2A 132
Brincliffe Gdns. S11: Shef 1B 132
Brincliffe Hill S11: Shef 1A 132
Brindle M. S9: Shef 6E 109
Brindley Cl. S8: Shef 4F 133
Brindley Ct. S21: Killa 4B 152
Brindley Cres. S8: Shef 4F 133
Brindley Ho. S41: Ches 2A 168
Brindley Rd. S41: Ches 2H 167
Brindley Way S43: Stav 4C 164
Brinkburn Cl. S17: Dore 4G 145
Brinkburn Ct. S17: Dore 4G 145
Brinkburn Dr. S17: Dore 4G 145
Brinkburn Va. Rd. S17: Dore 4G 145
Brinsford Rd. S60: Brins 3C 110
BRINSWORTH 4C 110
Brinsworth Grange S60: Brins 3B 110
Brinsworth Hall Av. S60: Brins 4C 110
Brinsworth Hall Cres. S60: Brins 4C 110
Brinsworth Hall Dr. S60: Brins 4C 110
Brinsworth Hall Gro. S60: Brins 5C 110
Brinsworth La. S60: Brins 4C 110
Brinsworth Rd. S60: Brins, Cat 5B 110
(not continuous)
Brinsworth St. S9: Shef 6C 108
S60: Roth 4D 96
Bristol Gro. DN2: Don 4F 41
Bristol Rd. S11: Shef 5B 118
Britain St. S64: Mexb 2E 67
Britannia Cl. S70: Barn 2E 31
Britannia Ho. S70: Barn 2E 31
Britannia Rd. S9: Shef 2F 121
(not continuous)
S40: Birdh 3A 172
Britannia Wlk. S60: Cat 6C 110
Britland Cl. S75: Barn 6H 15
Britnall St. S9: Shef 6D 108
(not continuous)
Briton Sq. S63: Thurn 1D 36
Briton St. S63: Thurn 1D 36
Brittain St. S1: Shef 6F 5 (4G 119)
Britten Ho. DN2: Don 4F 41
Broachgate DN5: Scawt 2F 39
Broad Bri. Cl. S26: Kiv P 6C 140
Broadcarr Rd. S74: Hoyl 4A 62
Broadcroft Cl. S20: Beig 4A 138
Broad Dyke Cl. S26: Kiv P 6C 140
Broad Elms Cl. S11: Shef 4G 131
Broad Elms La. S11: Shef 5F 131
Broadfield Cl. S8: Shef 2E 133
Broadfield Ct. S8: Shef 2E 133
Broadfield Rd. S8: Shef 2E 133
Broadfield Way S8: Shef 2E 133
Broad Gates S75: Silk 2A 28
Broadgates *DN9: Finn 3F 77*
(off Station Rd.)
Broadgorse Cl. S40: Birdh 3G 171
Broadhead Rd. S36: Spink 4F 175
Broad Inge Cres. S35: Chap 3D 78
Broadlands S66: Braml 6B 100
Broadlands Av. S20: Mosb 6B 136
Broadlands Cl. S20: Mosb 6C 136
Broadlands Cres. S66: Braml 6B 100
Broadlands Cft. S20: Mosb 6C 136
Broadlands Ri. S20: Mosb 6C 136
Broad La. S1: Shef 3B 4 (3E 119)
S3: Shef 3E 119
WF9: Sth K 5H 13
Broad La. Ct. S1: Shef 3B 4 (3E 119)
Broadley Rd. S13: Shef 1F 135
Broad Oaks S9: Shef 2C 120
Broadoaks Cl. S25: Dinn 6H 127
S41: Ches 5A 168
Broad Oaks La. S9: Shef 2C 120
Broadoaks Rd. S25: Dinn 5H 127
Broad Pavement S40: Ches 5H 167
Broad Riding DN12: New E 5E 71
S66: Staint 1F 103
Broad St. S2: Shef 2H 5 (2H 119)
S62: Parkg 5G 83
S74: Hoyl 6A 46
Broad St. W. S1: Shef 2G 5 (2G 119)
Broadwater S63: Bolt D 2H 49
Broadway S60: Brins 5C 110
S64: Swint 4A 66
S65: Roth 3A 98
S70: Barn 1A 30
S75: Mapp 5A 8
Broadway, The DN4: Balb 1G 71
Broadway Av. S35: Chap 4G 79
Broadway Cl. S64: Swint 4A 66
Broadway Ct. S70: Barn 1A 30
Broadway E. S65: Roth 3A 98
Brocco Bank S11: Shef 6B 118
Brocco La. S3: Shef 2C 4 (2E 119)
Brocco St. S3: Shef 2C 4 (2E 119)
Brockfield Cl. S70: Wors 5F 31
Brockhill Ct. S43: Brim 6E 163
Brockhole Cl. DN4: Cant 5C 58
Brockholes La. DN3: Brant 5G 59
S36: Cub, Pen 6A 176
Brockhurst Way S65: Thry 6E 85
Brocklehurst Av. S8: Shef 2H 147
S70: Stair 4A 32
Brocklehurst Ct. S40: Ches 5E 167
S70: Stair 4A 32
(off Brocklehurst Av.)
Brocklehurst Piece S40: Ches 6E 167
BROCKWELL 4E 167
BROCKWELL HILL 3E 167
Brockwell La. S40: Ches 3D 166
(Hambledon Cl.)
S40: Ches 2C 166
(Oldridge Cl.)
S40: Ches 2E 167
(Skiddaw Cl.)
S40: Up N 1A 166
S42: Up N 1A 166
Brockwell Pl. S40: Ches 4F 167
Brockwell Ter. S40: Ches 4F 167
Brockwell Wlk. S40: Ches 3E 167
Brockwood Cl. S13: Shef 1D 136
Brodsworth Community Woodlands 5A 22
Brodsworth Ho. *DN1: Don 2B 56*
(off Bond Cl.)
Brodsworth Way DN11: Ross 5D 74
Bromcliffe Pk.
S71: Monk B 3B 18
Bromehead Way S41: Ches 1E 167
Bromfield Ct. S71: Roy 2A 10
BROMLEY 4A 60
Bromley Carr Rd. S35: Brom 5A 60
Brompton Rd. DN5: Sprot 3D 54
S9: Shef 5D 108
Bromwich Rd. S8: Shef 6D 132
Bronte Av. DN4: Balb 6G 55
Bronte Cl. S71: Monk B 5G 17
Bronte Gro. S64: Mexb 6G 51
Bronte Pl. S62: Rawm 1A 84
Brookbank Av. S40: Ches 4E 167
Brook Cl. S26: Ast 1D 138
S35: Gren 1B 92
S72: Grim 1B 20
Brook Ct. S61: Thorpe H 4C 80
Brook Cft. S25: Nth A 3G 141
S36: Stoc 3E 175
Brookdale Ct. S35: Chap 6F 61
Brookdale Hgts. S75: Dod 4H 29
Brookdale Rd. S35: Chap 5F 61
Brook Dr. S3: Shef 2B 4 (2E 119)
S63: Wath D 6E 49
Brooke Ct. DN9: Auck 1B 76
Brooke Dr. S43: Brim C 3E 169
Brooke St. DN1: Don 5C 40
S74: Hoyl 6A 46
Brook Farm M. S63: Wath D 5F 49
Brookfield S71: Ard 3H 33
Brookfield Av. S40: Bramp 6B 166
S64: Swint 4C 66
Brookfield Cl. DN3: Arm 5E 43
S65: Dalt 1C 98
Brookfield M. DN5: Ark 6D 24
Brookfield Rd. S7: Shef 1E 133
Brookfields Dr. S63: Wath D 5B 50
Brookfields Pk. S63: Wath D 4A 50
Brookfields Way S63: Wath D 5A 50
Brookfield Ter. S71: Carl 6H 9
Brookfield Yd. S7: Shef 1E 133
Brook Grn. S12: Shef 5C 136
Brookhaven Way
S66: Braml 6B 100
Brook Hill S3: Shef 3A 4 (3D 118)
S61: Thorpe H 3C 80
Brookhill Rd. S75: Kexb 6C 6
BROOKHOUSE 6F 115
Brookhouse Cl. S12: Shef 5C 136
Brookhouse Ct. *S12: Shef 5C 136*
(off Sheffield Rd.)
Brookhouse Dell S66: Thurc 5D 114
Brookhouse Dr. S12: Shef 5C 136
Brookhouse Hill S10: Shef 1D 130
Brookhouse La.
S25: Brook, Laugh M 6F 115
Brookhouse Rd. S26: Ast 2C 138
Brooklands S25: Nth A 3H 141
S66: Malt 6G 101
Brooklands Av. S10: Shef 1C 130
Brooklands Bus. Pk. *S9: Shef 5D 108*
(off Brompton Rd.)
Brooklands Cres. S10: Shef 1C 130
Brooklands Cft. S26: Wales 5G 139
Brooklands Dr. S10: Shef 1C 130
Brooklands Ho. S25: Dinn 5F 127
Brooklands Pk.
S25: Dinn 5F 127
Brooklands Rd. DN6: Adw S 1D 22
Brooklands Way S25: Dinn 5G 127

Brook La. S3: Shef 3B **4** (3E **119**)
S12: Shef 5C **136**
S35: Gren 2B **92**
S35: Ough 3D **90**
S66: Braml 4A **100**
Brooklyn Dr. S40: Ches 4E **167**
Brooklyn Pl. S8: Shef 3F **133**
Brooklyn Rd. S8: Shef 3F **133**
Brooklyn Works S3: Shef 1F **119**
Brook M. S25: Nth A 3G **141**
Brook Rd. DN12: Con 4G **69**
S8: Shef 3E **133**
S35: High G 2D **78**
S65: Roth 2A **98**
Brook Row S36: Stoc 4E **175**
BROOKSIDE 6B 166
Brookside DN12: Con 5F **69**
S6: Stann 6A **104**
S64: Swint 5A **66**
S65: Roth 5B **98**
Brookside Bank Rd.
S6: Stann 6A **104**
Brookside Bar S40: Bramp 6A **166**
Brookside Cl. S12: Shef 5C **136**
Brookside Ct. S62: Parkg 6E **83**
Brookside Cres. S63: Wath D 1C **64**
Brookside Dr. S70: Stair 4A **32**
Brookside Glen S40: Bramp 6A **166**
Brookside La. S6: Stann 6A **104**
Brook Sq. DN12: Con 5F **69**
Brooks Rd. S43: Bar H 2G **163**
Brook St. S60: Whist 3A **112**
Brook Va. S40: Ches 6F **167**
Brookvale S71: Monk B 5A **18**
Brookview Ct. S18: Dron 1F **155**
Brook Way DN5: Ark 6C **24**
Brook Yd. S40: Ches 5F **167**
BROOM 5G 97
Broom Av. S60: Roth 6A **98**
Broombank Pk. S41: Ches 3E **161**
Broombank Pk. Ind. Est.
S41: Ches 3E **161**
Broombank Rd. S41: Ches 3D **160**
Broom Bus. Pk. S41: Ches 3D **160**
Broom Chase S60: Roth 6G **97**
Broomcliffe Gdns. S72: Shaft 4F **11**
Broom Cl. S2: Shef 5E **119**
S41: Ches 1E **167**
S63: Bolt D 1A **50**
S63: Wath D 2H **65**
S66: Sunn 3H **99**
S70: Barn 4A **32**
S75: Dart .5H **7**
Broom Ct. S60: Roth 6H **97**
Broom Cres. S60: Roth 6G **97**
Broomcroft S75: Dod 4A **30**
Broomcroft Pk. S11: Shef 5G **131**
Broom Dr. S60: Roth 1A **112**
Broome Av. S64: Swint 3C **66**
BROOMFIELD 6A 4 (4C 118)
Broomfield Av. S41: Has 3C **172**
Broomfield Cl. S70: Barn 2A **30**
Broomfield Ct. S36: Stoc 3F **175**
Broomfield Gro. S36: Stoc 4F **175**
S60: Roth 6G **97**
Broomfield La. S36: Stoc 4E **175**
Broomfield M. S71: Roy 3A **10**
Broomfield Rd. S10: Shef 4C **118**
S36: Stoc 3F **175**
Broomfield Ter. S35: Ough 5B **90**
Broomfield Wlk. S36: Pen 5C **176**
Broom Gdns. S43: Brim 1E **169**
Broom Grange S60: Roth 6H **97**
Broom Grn. S3: Shef 5B **4** (4E **119**)
Broom Gro. S25: Sth A 5G **141**
S60: Roth 5G **97**
Broomgrove Cres. S10: Shef 4C **118**
Broomgrove Hall S10: Shef 4C **118**
Broomgrove La. S10: Shef 4C **118**
Broomgrove Rd. S10: Shef 4C **118**
Broomhall Pl. S10: Shef 6A **4** (4D **118**)
Broomhall Rd. S10: Shef 6A **4** (5C **118**)
Broomhall St. S3: Shef 6A **4** (4D **118**)
(Broomhall Pl., not continuous)
S3: Shef 5B **4** (4E **119**)
(Cavendish Ct.)
Broomhead Ct. S75: Mapp 6A **8**
Broomhead Gdns. S73: Womb 3A **48**
Broomhead Rd. S73: Womb 3A **48**
BROOMHILL
S10 . . . . .4B 118
S73 . . . . .2C 48
Broomhill DN12: Den M 2C **68**
Broomhill Cl. S21: Ecki 1C **158**
Broom Hill Dr. DN4: Cant 5C **58**
Broomhill Flash Nature Reserve 2B 48
Broomhill La. S63: Bolt D 1D **48**
Broomhill Rd. S41: Old W 4G **161**
Broomhill Vw. S63: Bolt D 3A **50**
Broomhouse La. DN4: Balb, Warm 3E **71**
DN12: New E 5C **70**
Broomhouse La. Ind. Est.
DN12: New E 3E **71**
Broom La. S60: Roth 6H **97**
Broom Riddings S61: Grea 6C **82**
Broom Rd. S60: Roth 5G **97**
Broom Royd S35: Wharn S 1A **90**
Broomroyd S70: Wors 6G **31**
Broomspring Cl. S3: Shef 5B **4** (4E **119**)
Broomspring La. S10: Shef . . .5A **4** (4D **118**)
(not continuous)
Broom St. S10: Shef 6A **4** (4D **118**)
Broom Ter. S60: Roth 5G **97**
Broomvale Wlk. DN12: New E 5B **70**
Broom Valley Rd. S60: Roth 5F **97**
Broomville St. S64: Swint 3D **66**
Broom Wlk. S3: Shef 5B **4**
Broomwood Cl. S20: Beig 5H **137**
Broomwood Gdns. S20: Beig 5H **137**
Brosley Av. DN3: Barn D 1H **27**
Brotherton St. S3: Shef 6G **107**
Brough Grn. S75: Dod 5H **29**
Broughton Av. DN5: Don 3H **39**
Broughton La. S9: Shef 4E **109**
Broughton Rd. DN4: Bess 6A **58**
S6: Shef .3B **106**
S41: Ches 1E **167**
Brow, The S65: Roth 6D **98**
Brow Cl. S70: Wors 4E **31**
Brow Cres. S20: Half 3F **151**
Brow Hill Rd. S66: Malt 4H **101**
Brownell St. S3: Shef 2B **4** (2E **119**)
Brown Hills La. S10: Shef 6A **116**
Browning Av. DN4: Balb 6A **56**
(not continuous)
Browning Cl. S6: Shef 5C **92**
S71: Monk B 3G **17**
Browning Ct. S40: Bramp 5C **166**
S65: Roth 5A **98**
Browning Dr. S6: Shef 5C **92**
S65: Roth 4A **98**
Browning Rd. DN3: Barn D 1H **27**
S6: Shef .5B **92**
S63: Wath D 5D **48**
S64: Mexb 6F **51**
S65: Roth 4A **98**
Brown La. S1: Shef 5E **5** (4F **119**)
(not continuous)
S18: Coal A 1H **155**
Brownroyd Av. S71: Roy 4H **9**
Browns Sq. S73: Hem 5E **47**
Brown St. S1: Shef 5F **5** (4G **119**)
S60: Roth 3C **96**
Brow Vw. S63: Bolt D 2A **50**
Broxbourne Gdns. DN5: Ben 1A **40**
Broxholme La. DN1: Don 6C **40**
Broxholme Rd. S8: Shef 5E **133**
Bruce Av. S70: Barn 3E **31**
Bruce Cres. DN2: Don 5G **41**
Bruce Rd. S11: Shef 6C **118**
Bruncroft Cl. DN4: Bess 6A **58**
Brunel Rd. DN5: Don 5G **39**
Brunel Way S60: Cat, Shef 2B **122**
Bruni Way DN11: New R 6G **75**
Brunswick Cl. S71: Smi 2E **17**
Brunswick Dr. S66: Sunn 3G **99**
Brunswick Gdns. S13: Shef 1E **137**
Brunswick Gdns. Village
S13: Shef 1E **137**
Brunswick Rd. S3: Shef 1G **119**
S60: Roth 6G **97**
Brunswick St. S10: Shef 4A **4** (3D **118**)
S41: Ches 4H **167**
S63: Thurn 1D **36**
Brunt Rd. S62: Rawm 2A **84**
BRUSHES, THE 3F 161
Brushfield Gro. S12: Shef 4G **135**
Brushfield Rd. S40: Ches 3A **166**
Bryn Lea S41: Ches 5B **168**
Bryony Cl. S21: Killa 4A **152**
Bubnell Rd. S18: Dron W 2D **154**
Bubup Hill DN11: Lov 4B **72**
Bubwith Rd. S9: Shef 2E **109**
Buchanan Cres. S5: Shef 5D **92**
Buchanan Dr. S5: Shef 5D **92**
Buchanan Rd. S5: Shef 5D **92**
Buckden Cl. S40: Ches 4E **167**
Buckden Rd. S70: Barn 6C **16**
Buckenham Dr. S4: Shef 6H **107**
Buckenham St. S4: Shef 6H **107**
Buckingham Cl. S18: Dron W 2C **154**
Buckingham Ct. S71: Roy 2G **9**
Buckingham Rd. DN2: Don 6E **41**
DN12: Con 3E **69**
Buckingham Way S60: Brins 4D **110**
S66: Malt 4B **102**
S71: Roy 2G **9**
Buckleigh Rd. S63: Wath D 2F **65**
Buckley Ct. S70: Barn 2E **31**
Buckley Ho. S70: Barn 2E **31**
Buckthorn Cl. S64: Swint 6B **66**
Buck Wood Vw. S14: Shef 3A **134**
Bude Ct. S71: Monk B 5H **17**
Bude Rd. DN4: Balb 4A **56**
Bullen Rd. S6: Shef 5B **92**
Bullfinch Cl. S60: Brins 4E **111**
Bull Haw La. S75: Silk 2A **28**
Bullrush Gro. DN4: Balb 1D **72**
Bungalow Rd. DN12: New E 4C **70**
Bungalows, The *S21: Ecki 1D 158*
(off Pipeyard La.)
S21: Ecki 2D **158**
(Pitt St.)
S21: Killa 4B **152**
S40: Ches 5E **167**
S41: Ches 6A 168
(off Piccadilly Rd.)
S41: Ches 1F **167**
(Ringwood Av.)
S41: Whit M 5H **161**
S43: Stav 6H **163**
S60: Tree 2F **123**
S62: Rawm 1F **83**
Bunker's Hill S21: Killa 4D **152**
Bunting Cl. S8: Shef 6G **133**
S42: Walt 1C **170**
Bunting Ho. S41: Old W 3A **162**
Bunting Nook S8: Shef 6G **133**
Burbage Cl. S18: Dron W 2C **154**
Burbage Gro. S12: Shef 3G **135**
Burbage Rd. S43: Stav 6A **164**
Burcot Rd. S8: Shef 3E **133**
BURCROFT .3G 69
Burcroft Cl. S74: Hoyl 1G **61**
Burcroft Hill DN12: Con 3G **69**
Burden Cl. DN1: Don 2B **56**
Burford Av. DN4: Balb 1F **71**
Burford Cres. S26: Ast 1D **138**
Burgen Rd. S61: Kimb P 1H **95**
Burgess Cl. S41: Has 3C **172**
Burgess Rd. S9: Shef 6C **108**
Burgess St. S1: Shef 4E **5** (3F **119**)
Burghley Cl. S25: Dinn 6H **127**
Burgoyne Cl. S6: Shef 6C **106**
Burgoyne Rd. S6: Shef 6C **106**
Burkinshaw Av. S62: Rawm 6G **65**
Burkitt Dr. S43: Woodt 4E **165**
Burleigh Ct. S70: Barn 1E **31**
Burleigh St. S70: Barn 2E **31**
Burley Cl. S40: Birdh 3H **171**
Burlington S6: Shef 1A **4** (2D **118**)
Burlington Arc. S70: Barn 1E **31**
Burlington Cl. S17: Dore 3F **145**
Burlington Ct. S6: Shef 1D **118**
Burlington Glen S17: Dore 3F **145**
Burlington Gro. S17: Dore 3F **145**
Burlington Ho. *S40: Ches 5H 167*
(off Burlington St.)
Burlington Rd. S17: Dore 3F **145**
Burlington St. S6: Shef 1D **118**
S40: Ches 5H **167**
Burman Rd. S63: Wath D 1G **65**
Burnaby Ct. S6: Shef 5C **106**
Burnaby Cres. S6: Shef 6C **106**
Burnaby Grn. S6: Shef 5C **106**
Burnaby St. DN1: Don 2B **56**
S6: Shef .5C **106**

Burnaby Wlk. S6: Shef 6C 106
Burnaston Cl. S18: Dron W 3B 154
Burnaston Wlk. DN12: Den M 3D 68
Burnbridge Rd. S41: Old W 3B 162
BURNCROSS 3D 78
Burncross Dr. S35: Chap 3E 79
Burncross Gro. S35: Burn 3D 78
Burncross Rd. S35: Burn, Chap 3C 78
Burnell Rd. S6: Shef 3B 106
Burnell St. S43: Brim 6E 163
Burnett Cl. S36: Pen 5E 177
BURNGREAVE 6H 107
Burngreave Bank S4: Shef 5G 107
Burngreave Rd. S3: Shef 5G 107
Burngreave St. S3: Shef 6G 107
Burn Gro. S35: Chap 4H 79
Burngrove Pl. S3: Shef 5G 107
Burnham Av. S75: Mapp 5A 8
Burnham Cl. DN4: Bess 5G 57
Burnham Gro. DN5: Scawt 2G 39
Burnham Way S73: D'fld 5A 34
Burn Pl. S71: Smi 1D 16
Burnsall Cres. S60: Brins 5C 83
Burnsall Gro. S70: Stair 4A 32
Burns Av. WF9: Shth K 5G 13
Burns Cl. S40: Birdh 3G 171
Burns Ct. S35: Chap 3E 79
Burns Dr. S18: Dron 4H 155
  S35: Chap 3E 79
  S65: Roth 4A 98
Burnside S63: Thurn 1B 36
Burnside Av. S8: Shef 3F 133
Burns Rd. DN3: Barn D 1H 27
  DN4: Balb 6A 56
  S6: Shef 2C 118
  S25: Dinn 6B 128
  S65: Roth 4H 97
  S66: Malt 6B 102
Burns St. DN5: Ben 1A 40
Burns Way DN4: Balb 4H 55
  S63: Wath D 5D 48
Burnt Hill La. S35: Ough 5A 90
Burnt Stones Cl. S10: Shef 4E 117
Burnt Stones Dr. S10: Shef 4E 117
Burnt Stones Gro. S10: Shef 4E 117
Burnt Tree La. S3: Shef 1B 4 (2E 119)
Burntwood Bank WF9: Hems 1E 13
Burntwood Cl. S63: Thurn 3A 36
Burntwood Court Health & Fitness Cen.
  . . . . .4D 12
Burntwood Cres. S60: Tree 1F 123
Burnt Wood La. S72: Brier 6F 13
Burntwood Rd. S72: Grim 2C 20
Burrell St. S60: Roth 4E 97
Burrowlee Pk. Sq. S6: Shef 3B 106
  (off Burrowlee Rd.)
Burrowlee Rd. S6: Shef 3B 106
Burrows Dr. S5: Shef 2F 107
Burrows Gro. S73: Womb 1E 47
Burrs Farm Ct. S81: Gild 6G 129
Burrs La. S81: Gild 6G 129
Burrs Wood Cft. S41: Ches 1C 166
Bursden Cl. S41: Old W 5H 161
Burton Av. DN4: Balb 4A 56
  S71: Monk B 4A 18
Burton Bank Rd. S71: Monk B 5F 17
  (not continuous)
Burton Cres. S71: Monk B 3B 18
Burton La. S35: Ough 4D 90
Burtonlees Ct. DN4: Bess 5B 58
Burton Rd. S3: Shef 6E 107
  S71: Monk B 5F 17
Burton Rd. Bus. Pk. S71: Monk B . . .3B 18
Burton St. S6: Shef 5C 106
  S71: Barn 5D 16
Burton Ter. DN4: Balb 4A 56
  S70: Barn 2G 31
Burtop Cft. S73: Hem 5F 47
Burying La. S74: Hoyl 3B 62
Bushey Wood Gro. S17: Dore 3E 145
Bushey Wood Rd. S17: Dore 4F 145
Bushfield Rd. S63: Wath D 6E 49
Busk Knoll S5: Shef 2F 107
Busk Mdw. S5: Shef 2F 107
Busk Pk. S5: Shef 2F 107
Busley Gdns. DN5: Ben 2H 39
  (not continuous)
Butcher St. S63: Thurn 2B 36
Butchill Av. S5: Shef 2F 93

Bute St. S10: Shef 3A 118
Butler Rd. S6: Shef 5H 105
Butler Way S21: Killa 3B 152
Butterbusk DN12: Con 4H 69
BUTTERBUSK GREEN 2B 70
Buttercross Dr. S72: Lit H 2D 34
Butterfield Ct. S73: Bramp 4B 48
Butterill Dr. DN3: Arm 5G 43
Butterley Dr. S70: Stair 4A 32
Butterleys S75: Dod 3H 29
Buttermere Cl. S25: Nth A 1H 141
  S41: Ches 1E 167
  S63: Bolt D 3B 50
  S64: Mexb 6H 51
Buttermere Dr. S18: Dron W 3D 154
Buttermere Rd. S7: Shef 4D 132
Buttermere Way S71: Ard 2E 33
Butterscotch Wlk.
  DN5: Scawt 3G 39
BUTTERTHWAITE 1A 94
Butterthwaite Cres. S5: Shef 3B 94
Butterthwaite La. S35: Eccl 1A 94
Butterthwaite Rd. S5: Shef 2H 93
Butterton Cl. S75: Mapp 5B 8
Butterton Dr. S40: Ches 3B 166
Button Hill S11: Shef 4A 132
Button Row S36: Stoc 3D 174
Butts Hill S17: Tot 6E 145
Buxton Rd. S71: Ath 1F 17
Byath La. S72: Cud 2E 19
Byford Rd. S66: Malt 5F 101
Byland Way S71: Monk B 6A 18
Byram Ct. DN4: Balb 1B 72
Byrley Rd. S61: Kimb P 1H 95
Byrne Cl. S75: Bar G 4F 15
Byron Av. DN4: Balb 6H 55
  (not continuous)
  DN5: Don 6G 39
  S35: Chap 4E 79
Byron Cl. S18: Dron 5H 155
Byron Cres. S63: Wath D 5D 48
Byron Dr. S65: Roth 4H 97
  S71: Monk B 4G 17
Byron Rd. S7: Shef 2C 132
  S20: Beig 6H 137
  S25: Dinn 6B 128
  (not continuous)
  S40: Birdh 2H 171
  S64: Mexb 1G 67
  S66: Malt 6B 102
Byron St. S40: Ches 1A 172
  S72: Gt H 1F 35

C

CADEBY 6G 53
Cadeby Av. DN12: Con 4D 68
Cadeby Ho. DN1: Don 2B 56
  (off St James St.)
Cadeby La. DN5: Cade, Sprot 3F 53
  DN12: Den M 2D 68
Cadeby Rd. DN5: Sprot 4B 54
Cadman Cl. S20: Mosb 4E 151
Cadman La. S1: Shef 4F 5 (3F 119)
Cadman Rd. S12: Shef 3F 135
Cadman St. S4: Shef 2H 119
  S20: Mosb 4D 150
  S63: Wath D 6H 49
Cadwell Cl. S72: Cud 6F 11
Caernarvon Cl. S40: Walt 1D 170
Caernarvon Cres. S63: Bolt D 2A 50
Caernarvon Dr. DN5: Barnb 1H 51
Caernarvon Rd. S18: Dron 4G 155
Caine Gdns. S61: Kimb 4H 95
Cairn Dr. S43: New W 2C 162
Cairngorm Cl. S43: New W 2C 162
Cairns Rd. S10: Shef 4G 117
  S20: Beig 4G 137
Caister Av. S35: Chap 3E 79
Caistor Av. S70: Barn 3B 30
Calabria Gro. S70: Barn 2G 31
Calcot Grn. S64: Swint 4C 66
Calcot Pk. Av. S64: Swint 4C 66
Caldbeck Gro. S35: High G 6C 60
Caldbeck Pl. S25: Nth A 1A 142
Calder Av. S71: Roy 3B 10
Calder Cl. S71: Roy 3B 10
Calder Cres. S70: Barn 3A 32

Calder Rd. S61: Wing 6A 82
  S63: Bolt D 3C 50
Calder Ter. DN12: Con 3F 69
Caldervale S71: Roy 2B 10
Caldew Way S5: Shef 2H 107
Caldey Rd. S18: Dron 4F 155
California Cres. S70: Barn 3E 31
California Dr. S35: Chap 4F 79
  S60: Cat 1D 122
California Gdns. S70: Barn 2E 31
California St. S70: Barn 3D 30
California Ter. S70: Barn 3D 30
Calladine Way S64: Swint 5B 66
  (not continuous)
Callander Ct. DN4: Cant 5B 58
Callflex Bus. Pk. S63: Wath D 6B 50
Callis La. S36: Pen 5E 177
Callis Way S36: Cub 5D 176
Callow Dr. S14: Shef 3A 134
Callow Mt. S14: Shef 3H 133
Callow Pl. S14: Shef 3A 134
Callow Rd. S14: Shef 3H 133
Callum Ct. S62: Parkg 6F 83
Callywhite La. S18: Dron 3G 155
Calner Cft. S20: Sot 6A 138
CALOW 5E 169
Calow Brook Dr. S41: Has 2D 172
CALOW GREEN 2G 173
Calow La. S41: Has 2C 172
  S44: Cal .2C 172
Calow La. Ind. Est. S41: Has 2D 172
Calstock Cl. S40: Ash 4B 166
Calver Cl. S75: Dod 4H 29
Calver Cres. S43: Stav 4A 164
Calverley Gdns. S73: Womb 1H 47
Calvert Rd. S9: Shef 6F 109
Calvert St. S74: Hoyl 1G 61
Calvey Orchard S72: Cud 1F 19
Camborne Cl. S6: Shef 5B 92
Camborne Rd. S6: Shef 5B 92
Camborne Way S71: Monk B 5G 17
Cambourne Cl. DN6: Adw S 2C 22
Cambria Dr. DN4: Balb 6F 55
Cambrian Cl. DN5: Sprot 3B 54
  S40: Ches 2E 167
Cambridge Cl. DN5: H'ton 2G 51
Cambridge Ct. S1: Shef 4D 4
  (off Backfields)
Cambridge Cres. S65: Roth 3H 97
Cambridge M. S63: Wath D 4E 49
Cambridge Pl. S65: Roth 3H 97
Cambridge Rd. S8: Shef 2G 133
  S36: Spink 4H 175
  S43: Brim 6E 163
Cambridge St. DN11: New R 4B 74
  S1: Shef 4D 4 (3F 119)
  (not continuous)
  S64: Mexb 1D 66
  S65: Roth 4H 97
Cambron Gdns. S66: Braml 5A 100
Camdale Ri. S12: Ridg 1A 150
Camdale Vw. S12: Ridg 1A 150
Camden Gro. S66: Malt 4A 102
Camden Pl. DN1: Don 2B 56
Camelia M. S26: Swal 1B 138
Camellia Cl. DN12: Con 5G 69
Camellia Dr. DN3: Kirk Sa 5C 26
Camerory Way S43: New W 1C 162
Camlough Wlk. S41: Ches 6A 168
Cammell Rd. S5: Shef 2A 108
Camms Cl. S21: Ecki 6E 151
Camm St. S6: Shef 6B 106
Campbell Ct. S43: New W 2C 162
  (off Church Wlk.)
Campbell Dr. S43: Bar H 3F 163
  S65: Roth 5A 98
Campbell St. S61: Grea 4D 82
Camping La. S8: Shef 6D 132
Campion Cl. S63: Bolt D 1A 50
Campion Dr. S21: Killa 4B 152
  S64: Swint 5C 66
Campo La. S1: Shef 3D 4 (3F 119)
Camp Rd. WF9: Sth K 5G 13
Campsall Dr. S10: Shef 3H 117
Campsall Fld. Cl. S63: Wath D 2F 65
Campsall Fld. Rd. S63: Wath D 1F 65
Canada St. S4: Shef 5A 108
  S70: Barn 3D 30

Canal Bri. S21: Killa 4C **152**
Canal M. S41: Ches 3H **167**
Canalside Vw. S64: Kiln 6D **66**
Canal St. S4: Shef 1A **120**
S71: Barn 5E **17**
Canal Way S71: Barn 5E **17**
Canal Wharf S41: Ches 4A **168**
Canal Wharfe S64: Mexb 2H **67**
Canary Ct. S66: Sunn 3G **99**
Canberra Ri. S63: Bolt D 2A **50**
CANKLOW 1E **111**
Canklow Hill Rd. S60: Roth 1E **111**
Canklow Meadows Ind. Est.
S60: Roth 4E **111**
Canklow Rd. S60: Roth 1E **111**
Canning St. S1: Shef 4C **4** (3E **119**)
Cannock St. S6: Shef 4B **106**
Cannon Cl. S62: Rawm 2A **84**
Cannon Hall Rd. S5: Shef 3H **107**
Cannonthorpe Ri. S60: Tree 2G **123**
Cannon Way S75: Bar G 3G **15**
Canon Cl. DN11: Ross 5E **75**
Canons Way S71: Monk B 5H **17**
Cantelo Ct. DN11: New R 6F **75**
Canterbury Av. S10: Shef 6D **116**
Canterbury Cl. DN5: Scaws 4F **39**
S40: Ches 2H **171**
S65: Roth 5A **98**
Canterbury Cres. S10: Shef 6D **116**
Canterbury Dr. S10: Shef 6D **116**
Canterbury Rd. DN2: Don 4E **41**
S8: Shef 3G **133**
Cantilupe Cres. S26: Ast 6C **124**
CANTLEY 3E **59**
Cantley La. DN3: Cant 3H **57**
DN4: Bess, Cant 3H **57**
Cantley Mnr. Av. DN4: Cant 5C **58**
Cantrell Cl. S43: Brim 6C **162**
Capel Ri. S43: Brim 6C **162**
Capel St. S6: Shef 5C **106**
(not continuous)
Caperns Rd. S25: Nth A 3A **142**
Capitol Cl. S75: H'ham 1G **29**
Capitol Ct. S75: H'ham 1G **29**
Capitol Pk. S75: H'ham 1G **29**
Capri Ct. S73: D'fld 4H **33**
Capthorne Cl. S40: Ches 3A **166**
Caravan Site, The DN5: Sprot 4B **54**
Caraway Gro. S64: Swint 6C **66**
Carbis Cl. S71: Monk B 5G **17**
CARBROOK 3E **109**
Carbrook Business Pk. S9: Shef 3E **109**
Carbrook Hall Rd. S9: Shef 4E **109**
Carbrook Stop (ST) 3F **109**
Carbrook St. S9: Shef 4E **109**
Carcroft Ent. Pk. DN6: Carc 1D **22**
Carcroft Ind. Est. DN6: Adw S 1E **23**
Carcroft Motorcycle Pk. 1G **23**
Cardew Cl. S62: Rawm 3H **83**
Cardigan Rd. DN2: Don 5H **41**
Cardinal Cl. DN11: Ross 5E **75**
Cardoness Dr. S10: Shef 4F **117**
Cardoness Rd. S10: Shef 4G **117**
Cardwell Av. S13: Shef 1A **136**
Cardwell Ct. S66: B'well 6A **88**
Cardwell Dr. S13: Shef 1A **136**
Carey Av. S71: Barn 6F **17**
Carfield Av. S8: Shef 3G **133**
Carfield La. S8: Shef 3H **133**
Carfield Pl. S8: Shef 3G **133**
Carisbrook Ct. DN5: Ark 6C **24**
Carisbrooke Rd. DN2: Don 6F **41**
Carlby Rd. S6: Shef 5H **105**
Carley Dr. S20: Westf 1G **151**
Carlingford Rd. S60: Roth 1H **111**
Carlin St. S13: Shef 2H **135**
Carlisle Bus. Pk. S4: Shef 3C **108**
Carlisle Cl. S41: Old W 3F **161**
Carlisle Ct. S4: Shef 5B **108**
Carlisle Pl. *S65: Roth* *3F* ***97***
(off Wharncliffe Hill)
Carlisle Rd. DN2: Don 3G **41**
S4: Shef 4B **108**
Carlisle St. S4: Shef 1H **119**
S64: Kiln 5C **66**
(not continuous)
S65: Roth 3F **97**
Carlisle St. E. S4: Shef 6A **108**
Carlisle Ter. S25: Dinn 5A **128**
Carlthorpe Gro. S35: High G 1B **78**
CARLTON 5A **10**
Carlton Av. S65: Roth 4G **97**
Carlton Cl. DN3: Brant 4H **59**
S20: Mosb 4D **150**
WF9: Hems 1D **12**
Carlton Ct. S71: Ath 1H **17**
Carlton Ga. Dr. S26: Kiv P 6H **139**
CARLTON GREEN 6A **10**
Carlton Grn. S71: Carl 6H **9**
Carlton Ho. *DN1: Don* *2B* ***56***
(off Bond Cl.)
S72: Cud 1E **19**
Carlton Ind. Est. S71: Carl 1H **17**
(not continuous)
Carlton Marsh Nature Reserve 6C **10**
Carlton M. S2: Shef 1B **134**
S71: Carl 5H **9**
Carlton Ri. S35: Wharn S 1A **90**
Carlton Rd. DN1: Don 5D **40**
S6: Shef 2A **106**
S40: Birdh 4G **171**
S62: Rawm 4G **83**
S71: Ath, Carl, Smi 3F **17**
Carlton St. S71: Barn 4D **16**
S72: Cud 1E **19**
S72: Grim 2B **20**
Carlyle Ct. S66: Malt 6B **102**
Carlyle Rd. S66: Malt 6B **102**
Carlyle St. S64: Mexb 1F **67**
Carlyon Gdns. S40: Birdh 2G **171**
Carnaby Rd. S6: Shef 5B **106**
Carnarvon St. S6: Shef 1D **118**
Carnforth Rd.
S71: Monk B 3A **18**
Carnley St. S63: Wath D 5C **48**
Carnoustie Av. S40: Walt 2D **170**
Carnoustie Cl. S64: Swint 4D **66**
Carolina Ct. DN4: Don 5F **57**
Carolina Way DN4: Don 5F **57**
Carpenter Av. S43: Mas M 3E **165**
Carpenter Cft. S12: Shef 2F **135**
Carpenter Gdns. S12: Shef 2F **135**
Carpenter M. S12: Shef 2F **135**
CARR 3F **115**
Carr Bank DN11: Wad 6G **73**
Carr Bank Cl. S11: Shef 6G **117**
Carr Bank Dr. S11: Shef 6F **117**
Carr Bank La. S11: Shef 6F **117**
Carr Cl. S36: Spink 4G **175**
S60: Brins 4B **110**
Carrcroft Ct. S36: Spink 4H **175**
Carrera Ct. S25: Dinn 5G **127**
Carrfield Cl. S75: Kexb 6E **7**
Carrfield Ct. S8: Shef 2G **133**
Carrfield Dr. S8: Shef 2G **133**
Carr Fld. La. S63: Bolt D 1A **50**
Carrfield La. S2: Shef 2G **133**
Carrfield Rd. S8: Shef 2G **133**
Carrfield St. S8: Shef 2G **133**
Carr Fold S36: Spink 4H **175**
Carr Forge Cl. S12: Shef 4B **136**
Carr Forge La. S12: Shef 4B **136**
Carr Forge Mt. S12: Shef 4B **136**
Carr Forge Pl. S12: Shef 4C **136**
Carr Forge Rd. S12: Shef 4B **136**
Carr Forge Ter. S12: Shef 4B **136**
Carr Forge Vw. S12: Shef 4C **136**
Carr Forge Wlk. *S12: Shef* *4C* ***136***
(off Carter Lodge Dr.)
Carr Furlong S71: Ath 5E **9**
Carr Grange Bus. Cen.
DN4: Don 3C **56**
Carr Grn. S63: Bolt D 1B **50**
S75: Mapp 6B **8**
Carr Grn. La. S75: Mapp 1B **16**
Carr Gro. S36: Spink 4G **175**
CARR HEAD 4G **175**
Carr Head La. S36: Pen 1B **176**
S63: Bolt D 1F **49**
Carr Head Rd. S35: Howb 5A **60**
Carr Hill DN4: Balb 4A **56**
S61: Grea 6D **82**
Carr Hill Ct. DN4: Balb 4A **56**
Carr Ho. *S63: Gol* *5D* ***36***
(off Doncaster Rd.)
Carr Ho. Ct. S35: Brom 4A **60**
Carr Ho. Rd. DN1: Don 3C **56**
DN4: Don 3C **56**
Carriage Dr. DN4: Don 4D **56**
Carriage Way, The
DN11: Ross 5E **75**
Carrill Dr. S6: Shef 4B **92**
Carrill Rd. S6: Shef 4B **92**
Carrington Av. S75: Barn 4D **16**
Carrington Rd. S11: Shef 6A **118**
Carrington St. S65: Roth 5G **97**
S75: Barn 5C **16**
Carrington Ter. S26: Kiv P 6A **140**
Carr La. DN4: Bess 1A **74**
DN4: Don 3C **56**
DN11: Wad 5F **73**
DN12: Con 6G **69**
S18: Dron W 2B **154**
S25: Slade H 3F **115**
S26: Ull 3E **125**
S36: Bolst 6F **175**
S65: Thry 2F **85**
S66: Carr 3F **115**
S66: Hoot L 1G **115**
S75: Pill 2A **60**
Carr La. M. S18: Dron W 2C **154**
Carron Dr. S75: Mapp 6B **8**
Carr Rd. DN12: New E 5B **70**
S6: Shef 6B **106**
S36: Spink 5F **175**
S63: Wath D 6H **49**
Carrs La. S72: Cud 3E **19**
Carr St. S71: Monk B 3A **18**
Carr Vw. Av. DN4: Balb 4A **56**
Carr Vw. Rd. S61: Kimb 2G **95**
Carrville Dr. S6: Shef 6C **92**
Carrville Rd. S6: Shef 6C **92**
Carrville Rd. W. S6: Shef 6B **92**
Carrwell La. S6: Shef 1B **106**
Carrwood Cl. S70: Wors 5G **31**
Carrwood Rd. S21: Reni 4H **159**
S41: Ches 2D **160**
S71: Stair 1B **32**
CARSICK 5F **117**
Carsick Gro. S10: Shef 5E **117**
CARSICK HILL 5E **117**
Carsick Hill Cres. S10: Shef 5E **117**
Carsick Hill Dr. S10: Shef 5F **117**
Carsick Hill Rd. S10: Shef 5E **117**
Carsick Hill Way S10: Shef 5E **117**
Carsick Vw. Rd. S10: Shef 5E **117**
Carsington Cl. S40: Ches 3C **166**
Carson Av. S25: Laugh C 4F **127**
Carson Mt. S12: Shef 5E **135**
Carson Rd. S10: Shef 3A **118**
Carterhall La. S12: Shef 6F **135**
Carter Hall Rd. S12: Shef 6E **135**
CARTER KNOWLE 3C **132**
Carter Knowle Av. S11: Shef 3A **132**
Carter Knowle Rd. S7: Shef 3B **132**
S11: Shef 3A **132**
Carter Lodge Av. S12: Shef 4B **136**
Carter Lodge Dr. S12: Shef 4C **136**
Carter Lodge Pl. S12: Shef 4C **136**
Carter Lodge Ri. S12: Shef 4C **136**
Carter Lodge Wlk. *S12: Shef* *4C* ***136***
(off Carter Lodge Dr.)
Carter Pl. S8: Shef 2G **133**
Carter Rd. S8: Shef 2F **133**
CARTLEDGE 5A **154**
Cartledge La. S18: Holme 5A **154**
Cartmel Cl. S18: Dron W 3D **154**
S66: Malt 4B **102**
Cartmel Ct. S71: Monk B 1A **18**
Cartmel Cres. S41: Ches 6E **161**
Cartmell Ct. S8: Shef 4D **132**
Cartmell Cres. S8: Shef 5E **133**
Cartmell Hill S8: Shef 4D **132**
Cartmell Rd. S8: Shef 4D **132**
Cartmel Wlk. S25: Dinn 1A **142**
Cart Rd. S35: Chap 1F **79**
Car Vale Dr. S13: Shef 6F **121**
Car Vale Vw. S13: Shef 6F **121**
Carver Dr. S25: Dinn 6H **127**
Carver La. S1: Shef 3D **4** (3F **119**)
Carver St. S1: Shef 3D **4** (3F **119**)
Carwood Cl. S4: Shef 5A **108**
Carwood Grn. S4: Shef 5A **108**
Carwood Gro. S4: Shef 5A **108**
Carwood La. S4: Shef 5A **108**
Carwood Pk. Ind. Units S4: Shef 5A **108**
Carwood Rd. S4: Shef 5A **108**

Carwood Way S4: Shef 5A **108**
Cary Gro. S2: Shef 6C **120**
Cary Rd. S2: Shef 6C **120**
S21: Ecki 1C **158**
Castell Cres. DN4: Cant 3B **58**
Castle Av. DN11: Ross 6E **75**
DN12: Con 4F **69**
S60: Roth 1E **111**
CASTLEBECK 5E 121
Castlebeck Av. S2: Shef 5E **121**
Castlebeck Ct. *S2: Shef* *5F* ***121***
(off Castlebeck Av.)
Castlebeck Cft. S2: Shef 5F **121**
Castlebeck Dr. S2: Shef 6E **121**
Castle Cl. DN5: Sprot 2F **55**
S36: Pen 5E **177**
S71: Monk B 5G **17**
S75: Dod 4H **29**
Castle Ct. S2: Shef 2A **120**
Castle Cres. DN12: Con 3F **69**
Castle Cft. La. S36: Bolst 6E **175**
Castledale Cft. S2: Shef 6E **121**
Castledale Gro. S2: Shef 6F **121**
Castledale Pl. S2: Shef 6E **121**
Castledine Ct. DN4: Balb 2A **72**
Castledine Cft. S9: Shef 1E **109**
Castledine Gdns. S9: Shef 2D **108**
Castlegate S3: Shef 2G **5** (2G **119**)
CASTLE GREEN 5E 177
Castle Grn. S3: Shef 2F **5** (2G **119**)
S25: Laugh M 2G **127**
Castle Gro. DN5: Sprot 3C **54**
Castle Gro. Ter. DN12: Con 3G **69**
Castle Hill DN12: Con 4F **69**
S21: Ecki 6E **151**
Castle Hill Av. S64: Mexb 2A **68**
Castle Hill Cl. S21: Ecki 6E **151**
Castle Hill Ct. S21: Ecki 1E **159**
Castle Hill Fold DN5: Hick 3H **37**
Castle Hills Rd. DN5: Scawt 1F **39**
Castle Ho. S3: Shef 2F **5**
Castle La. S36: Pen 5E **177**
Castle M. DN5: Scawt 1G **39**
Castle Park 5B 42
Castlereagh St. S70: Barn 1D **30**
Castlerigg Way S18: Dron W 3D **154**
Castle Row S17: Bradw 4A **146**
Castlerow Cl. S17: Bradw 4A **146**
Castlerow Dr. S17: Bradw 4A **146**
Castlerow Vw. S17: Bradw 4A **146**
Castle Sq. S1: Shef 3F **5**
Castle Square Stop (ST) 3F 5 (3G 119)
Castle St. DN12: Con 4F **69**
S3: Shef 2F **5** (2G **119**)
S36: Pen 5E **177**
S70: Barn 2D **30**
Castle Ter. DN12: Con 4F **69**
Castleton Gro. S43: Ink 3G **169**
Castle Vw. DN12: New E 5C **70**
S21: Ecki 1E **159**
S70: Birdw 4D **44**
S75: Dod 2H **29**
Castle Wlk. *S2: Shef* *2A* ***120***
(off Castle Ct.)
Castlewell DN12: Con 4F **69**
Castlewood Ct. S10: Shef 6D **116**
Castlewood Cres. S10: Shef 6C **116**
Castlewood Dr. S10: Shef 6D **116**
Castlewood Rd. S10: Shef 6D **116**
Castor Rd. S9: Shef 5C **108**
Casual Wards S11: Shef 1C **132**
Catania Ri. S73: D'fld 4H **33**
Catch Bar La. S6: Shef 2B **106**
Catchford Vw. S41: Ches 1C **166**
CATCLIFFE 6E 111
Catcliffe Flash Local Nature Reserve 1D 122
Catcliffe Rd. S9: Shef 2F **121**
Cathedral Ct. DN7: Dunsv 4H **27**
Cathedral Stop (ST) 3E 5 (3F 119)
Catherine Av. S26: Swal 1C **138**
Catherine Ct. S40: Ches 5F **167**
Catherine Rd. S4: Shef 6G **107**
Catherine St. DN1: Don 2C **56**
S3: Shef 6G **107**
S40: Ches 5F **167**
S64: Mexb 1E **67**
S65: Roth 4F **97**
Catherines Wlk. S71: Ath 1E **17**
Cathill Rd. S63: Bolt D 6D **34**
Cathill Rdbt. S72: Midd 5E **35**
Cat La. S2: Shef 2H **133**
S8: Shef 3H **133**
Catley Rd. S9: Shef 1F **121**
Catling La. DN3: Barn D 1C **26**
Cattal St. S9: Shef 1D **120**
Catterick Cl. DN12: Den M 4B **68**
Catterick Ho. S65: Roth 3G **97**
Caudall Cl. S63: Thurn 2D **36**
Cauldon Dr. S40: Ches 3B **166**
Caulk La. S70: Swai 5B **32**
Causeway, The S17: Dore 3E **145**
Causeway Gdns. S17: Dore 2D **144**
Causeway Glade S17: Dore 2D **144**
CAUSEWAY HEAD 3D 144
Causeway Head Rd.
S17: Dore 2D **144**
Cavalier Ct. DN4: Balb 1B **72**
Cavendish Av. S6: Lox 3F **105**
S17: Dore 3G **145**
Cavendish Cl. S65: Roth 6C **98**
Cavendish Ct. S3: Shef 5B **4** (4E **119**)
S41: Ches 3H **167**
Cavendish Pl. S43: Bar H 3G **163**
S66: Malt 4B **102**
Cavendish Ri. S18: Dron 4E **155**
Cavendish Rd. DN5: Ben 4H **23**
S11: Shef 1B **132**
S61: Roth 4B **96**
S75: Barn 5D **16**
Cavendish Sq. S21: West H 4G **157**
Cavendish St. S3: Shef 4B **4** (3E **119**)
S40: Ches 5H **167**
S43: Stav 6H **163**
Cavendish St. Nth.
S41: Old W 4H **161**
Cavendish Ter. DN5: Ben 3H **23**
S21: West H 4G **157**
Cavill Rd. S8: Shef 5F **133**
Cawdor Rd. S2: Shef 2B **134**
Cawdor St. DN5: Ben 1A **40**
Cawdron Cl. S65: Dalt 1C **98**
Cawdron Ri. S60: Brins 5D **110**
Cawley Pl. S71: Smi 4F **17**
Cawood Dr. S63: Wath D 5G **49**
Cawston Rd. S4: Shef 4H **107**
CAWTHORNE 3A 14
Cawthorne Cl. S8: Shef 5D **132**
S65: Roth 3B **98**
S75: Dod 4H **29**
Cawthorne Gro. S8: Shef 5D **132**
Cawthorne La. S75: Cawt, Kexb 3A **14**
Cawthorne Rd. S65: Roth 3B **98**
S75: Bar G 3D **14**
Cawthorne Vw. S36: H'swne 1F **177**
Caxton Cl. S43: New W 3C **162**
Caxton La. S10: Shef 4A **118**
Caxton Rd. DN6: Woodl 3C **22**
S10: Shef 4B **118**
Caxton St. S70: Barn 6D **16**
Caxton Way S25: Dinn 5G **127**
Caythorpe Cl. S71: Lund 3D **18**
Cayton Cl. S65: Rav 2B **100**
S71: Smi 1D **16**
Cecil Av. DN4: Warm 1D **70**
S18: Dron 2F **155**
Cecil Rd. S18: Dron 1F **155**
Cecil Sq. S2: Shef 6E **119**
Cedar Av. S40: Ches 3E **167**
S64: Mexb 6E **51**
S66: Wick 5H **99**
Cedar Cl. DN4: Balb 1F **71**
DN9: Auck 2B **76**
S21: Ecki 2C **158**
S21: Killa 5B **152**
S36: Stoc 4D **174**
S64: Swint 5B **66**
S71: Roy 2F **9**
Cedar Cres. S70: Barn 3G **31**
Cedar Dr. S65: Rav 2C **100**
S66: Malt 5G **101**
Cedar Gro. DN12: Con 6D **68**
Cedar Nook S26: Kiv P 6H **139**
Cedar Rd. DN3: Arm 3F **43**
DN4: Balb 1F **71**
S36: Stoc 4D **174**
Cedars, The S10: Shef 4A **118**
Cedar St. S43: Hol 5F **163**
Cedar Va. S64: Swint 5B **66**
Cedar Way S35: Chap 4E **79**
Cedarwood Ct. S61: Scho 6F **81**
Cedric Av. DN12: Con 5D **68**
Cedric Ct. S66: Thurc 6B **114**
Cedric Cres. S66: Thurc 6B **114**
Cedric Rd. DN3: Eden 6C **26**
Celandine Ct. S17: Bradw 5H **145**
Celandine Gdns. S17: Bradw 5H **145**
Celandine Gro. S73: D'fld 5B **34**
Celandine Ri. S64: Swint 6B **66**
Celtic Ct. S61: Kimb P 6A **82**
Cemetery Av. S11: Shef 5C **118**
Cemetery La. S43: Stav 5B **164**
Cemetery Rd. DN6: Woodl 4B **22**
S11: Shef 6D **118**
S18: Dron 4G **155**
S41: Ches 6B **168**
S63: Bolt D 3B **50**
S63: Wath D 2F **65**
S64: Mexb 1F **67**
S70: Barn 2F **31**
S72: Grim 1B **20**
S73: Hem 5D **46**
Cemetery Rd. S73: Womb 1G **47**
S74: Hem, Jum 5D **46**
Cemetery Ter. S43: Brim 1D **168**
Centenary Mkt. Hall S65: Roth 3F **97**
Centenary Way S60: Roth 5D **96**
S65: Roth 5D **96**
Centenary Works *S60: Roth* *4D* ***96***
(off Masbrough St.)
Central Av. DN5: Ben 2A **40**
DN6: Woodl 4B **22**
S25: Dinn 6A **128**
S40: Ches 6F **167**
S64: Swint 4A **66**
S65: Roth 3A **98**
S66: Sunn 3G **99**
S72: Grim 6B **12**
Central Blvd. DN2: Don 4G **41**
Central Bus. Pk. S60: Roth 4D **96**
Central Cl. S18: Uns 6B **156**
Central Dr. DN11: New R 6B **74**
S41: Has 1B **172**
S44: Cal 5E **169**
S62: Rawm 6D **64**
S66: Thurc 6B **114**
S71: Roy 3H **9**
Central M. S25: Dinn 6B **128**
Central Pde. S65: Roth 4A **98**
Central Pavement S40: Ches 5H **167**
Central Rd. S60: Roth 4E **97**
Central St. S41: Has 1B **172**
S63: Gol 4D **36**
S74: Hoyl 1G **61**
Central Ter. DN12: New E 4C **70**
Central Wlk. S43: Brim 1C **168**
Centre, The S66: Braml 5A **100**
Centre in the Park, The 6A 120
Centre Riding DN11: Wad, Wils 1G **89**
Centurion Bus. Pk. S60: Roth 5B **96**
Centurion Flds. DN4: Bess 5A **58**
Centurion Retail Pk. DN5: Don 5A **40**
Centurion St. S60: Roth 5B **96**
Centurion Way DN5: Don 5A **40**
Century Bus. Cen. S63: Wath D 3D **48**
Century Cl. DN3: Kirk Sa 6A **26**
Century Ct. DN12: New E 3D **70**
Century Gdns. DN5: Ben 1B **40**
Century Pk. S63: Wath D 3D **48**
Century Pk. Network Cen.
S63: Wath D 3D **48**
Century St. S9: Shef 6E **109**
Century Vw. S60: Brins 4B **110**
Ceramia Ct. S63: Gol 5F **37**
Chadbourne Cl. DN3: Arm 5D **42**
Chaddesden Cl. S18: Dron W 3B **154**
Chaddesdon Wlk. DN12: Den M 2E **69**
Chadwell Cl. S41: Has 3B **172**
Chadwick Ct. S43: Stav 5A **164**
Chadwick Dr. S66: Malt 4A **102**
Chadwick Gdns. DN5: Ark 6D **24**
Chadwick Rd. DN5: Don 5A **40**
DN6: Woodl 4B **22**
S13: Shef 1F **135**
Chaff Cl. S60: Whist 3A **112**
Chaffinch Av. S60: Brins 4E **111**
Chaff La. S60: Whist 3A **112**

Chalbury Cl.—Cherry Brook

Chalbury Cl. S75: Barn . . . 4A **16**
Chalfont Ct. S60: Brins . . . 4E **111**
Challands Cl. S41: Has . . . 2B **172**
Challands Way S41: Has . . . 2B **172**
Challenger Cres. S63: Thurn . . . 1B **36**
Challenger Dr. DN5: Sprot . . . 1F **55**
Challiner M. S60: Cat . . . 6D **110**
Challoner Grn. S20: Westf . . . 2F **151**
Challoner Way S20: Westf . . . 2F **151**
Chalmers Dr. DN2: Don . . . 1A **42**
Chaloner Hgts. S74: Black H . . . 3A **46**
Chamberlain Av. DN5: Don . . . 4H **39**
Chamberlain Ct. S35: Chap . . . 2E **79**
Chambers Av. DN12: Con . . . 4D **68**
Chambers Dr. S35: Chap . . . 1F **79**
Chambers Gro. S35: Chap . . . 1F **79**
Chambers La. S4: Shef . . . 3C **108**
Chambers Rd. S61: Kimb P . . . 1A **96**
S74: Hoyl . . . 5A **46**
Chambers Valley Rd.
S35: Chap . . . 1F **79**
Chambers Vw. S35: Chap . . . 1F **79**
Chambers Way S35: Chap . . . 6E **61**
Chamossaire DN11: New R . . . 6F **75**
Champany Flds. S75: Dod . . . 3E **29**
Champion Cl. S5: Shef . . . 4A **94**
Champion Rd. S5: Shef . . . 4A **94**
Chancel Way S71: Monk B . . . 5H **17**
Chancery Pl. DN1: Don . . . 1B **56**
Chancet Ct. S8: Shef . . . 1D **146**
Chancet Wood S8: Shef . . . 2E **147**
Chancet Wood Cl. S8: Shef . . . 2E **147**
Chancet Wood Dr. S8: Shef . . . 2E **147**
Chancet Wood Ri. S8: Shef . . . 2E **147**
Chancet Wood Rd. S8: Shef . . . 1E **147**
Chancet Wood Vw. S8: Shef . . . 2E **147**
Chandler Gro. S60: Tree . . . 1F **123**
Chandos Cres. S21: Killa . . . 4B **152**
Chandos St. S10: Shef . . . 4B **118**
Chaneyfield Way S41: Ches . . . 1C **166**
Channing Gdns. S6: Shef . . . 5C **106**
Channing St. S6: Shef . . . 5C **106**
Chantrey Av. S41: Ches . . . 2G **167**
Chantrey Rd. S8: Shef . . . 5E **133**
Chantry Bri. S60: Roth . . . 3E **97**
Chantry Cl. DN4: Cant . . . 5D **58**
Chantry Gro. S71: Roy . . . 3H **9**
Chantry Orchards S75: Dod . . . 4F **29**
Chantry Pl. S26: Kiv P . . . 5C **140**
Chapel Av. S73: Bramp . . . 4B **48**
Chapel Cl. DN9: Finn . . . 3F **77**
S10: Shef . . . 5G **117**
S35: Burn . . . 3D **78**
S61: Wing . . . 4B **82**
S63: Thurn . . . 2D **36**
S66: Thurc . . . 5B **114**
S70: Birdw . . . 5D **44**
S72: Shaft . . . 3F **11**
Chapel Cotts. S21: West H . . . 5G **157**
Chapel Ct. S63: Wath D . . . 1F **65**
S70: Birdw . . . 5D **44**
S71: Ard . . . 2C **32**
Chapel Cft. S73: Hem . . . 5F **47**
Chapelfield Cres.
S61: Thorpe H . . . 3C **80**
Chapelfield Dr. S61: Thorpe H . . . 3C **80**
Chapel Fld. La. S36: Pen . . . 5C **176**
Chapelfield La. S61: Thorpe H . . . 3C **80**
Chapelfield Mt. S61: Thorpe H . . . 3C **80**
Chapelfield Pl. S61: Thorpe H . . . 3C **80**
Chapelfield Rd. S61: Thorpe H . . . 2C **80**
Chapelfields WF9: Sth K . . . 4H **13**
Chapel Fld. Wlk. S36: Pen . . . 5C **176**
Chapelfield Way S61: Thorpe H . . . 3C **80**
Chapel Hill S60: Whist . . . 3A **112**
S64: Swint . . . 3B **66**
*S74: Black H . . . 3A **46***
(off Wentworth Rd.)
Chapel Hole La. S66: Staint . . . 5D **88**
Chapel La. DN3: Brant . . . 4H **59**
DN9: Finn . . . 2F **77**
DN12: Con . . . 5F **69**
S9: Shef . . . 6D **108**
S17: Tot . . . 6E **145**
S18: App . . . 3D **156**
S35: Green M . . . 1G **175**
S36: Pen . . . 5C **176**
S60: Roth . . . 5E **97**
S63: Thurn . . . 1E **37**
Chapel La. S71: Carl . . . 6H **9**
S72: Bill . . . 4G **35**
S72: Gt H, Lit H . . . 2D **34**
Chapel La. E. S41: Has . . . 3C **172**
Chapel La. W. S40: Bramp . . . 6D **166**
Chapel M. S64: Swint . . . 3B **66**
S75: Stain . . . 5B **8**
Chapel Pl. S71: Ard . . . 2C **32**
Chapel Ri. S25: Nth A . . . 3G **141**
Chapel Rd. S35: Burn, Chap . . . 3D **78**
S35: High G . . . 6D **60**
S75: Pill . . . 6B **44**
Chapel St. DN5: Ben . . . 2A **40**
S13: Shef . . . 2C **136**
S20: Mosb . . . 4D **150**
*S41: Whit M . . . 6H **161***
(off Station Rd.)
S43: Brim . . . 6E **163**
S61: Grea . . . 4C **82**
S62: Rawm . . . 3G **83**
S63: Bolt D . . . 2B **50**
S63: Thurn . . . 2B **36**
S63: Wath D . . . 1F **65**
S64: Mexb . . . 1D **66**
S70: Birdw . . . 5D **44**
S71: Ard . . . 2C **32**
Chapel St. S72: Grim . . . 2B **20**
S72: Shaft . . . 3F **11**
S74: Hoyl . . . 1G **61**
Chapel Ter. S10: Shef . . . 5G **117**
CHAPELTOWN . . . 3F **79**
Chapeltown Baths . . . 3F **79**
Chapeltown Rd. S35: Eccl . . . 6G **79**
Chapeltown Station (Rail) . . . 3F **79**
Chapel Vw. DN3: Arm . . . 3C **42**
*S36: Thurl . . . 3A **176***
(off Matthew Gap)
Chapel Wlk. S1: Shef . . . 3E **5** (3F **119**)
S25: Sth A . . . 4G **141**
S60: Cat . . . 1D **122**
S60: Roth . . . 4D **96**
(not continuous)
S62: Rawm . . . 1E **83**
S64: Mexb . . . 2F **67**
Chapel Way S26: Kiv P . . . 6A **140**
S62: Rawm . . . 1E **83**
Chapelwood Rd. S9: Shef . . . 6E **109**
Chapel Yd. S18: Dron . . . 2F **155**
Chapman St. S9: Shef . . . 6E **95**
Chappell Cl. S36: H'swne . . . 1F **177**
Chappell Dr. DN1: Don . . . 5B **40**
Chappell Rd. S36: H'swne . . . 1F **177**
Chapter Way S71: Monk B . . . 5H **17**
S75: Silk . . . 1B **28**
Charity St. S71: Monk B . . . 2C **18**
Charles Ashmore Rd. S8: Shef . . . 2E **147**
Charles Cres. DN3: Arm . . . 3C **42**
Charles Cres. Flats DN3: Arm . . . 3C **42**
Charles Rd. S63: Wath D . . . 1H **65**
Charles Sq. S35: High G . . . 1C **78**
Charles St. DN1: Don . . . 5D **40**
S1: Shef . . . 4E **5** (3F **119**)
S25: Dinn . . . 4A **128**
S40: Ches . . . 5F **167**
S62: Rawm . . . 1A **84**
S63: Gol . . . 5C **36**
S64: Kiln . . . 1D **84**
S64: Swint . . . 4C **66**
S66: Thurc . . . 5B **114**
S70: Barn . . . 2D **30**
S70: Wors . . . 6F **31**
S72: Cud . . . 6F **11**
S72: Grim . . . 2B **20**
S72: Midd . . . 3F **35**
S72: Sth H . . . 1H **11**
Charlotte Ct. S2: Shef . . . 6G **119**
Charlotte La. S1: Shef . . . 4B **4**
Charlotte Rd. S1: Shef . . . 5F **119**
S2: Shef . . . 5F **119**
CHARLTONBROOK . . . 2D **78**
Charlton Brook Cres. S35: Chap . . . 2D **78**
Charlton Clough S35: Chap . . . 3C **78**
Charlton Dr. S35: High G . . . 2D **78**
Charlton Hill Ri. S35: Chap . . . 3C **78**
Charnell Av. S66: Malt . . . 5B **102**
Charnley Av. S11: Shef . . . 3B **132**
Charnley Cl. S11: Shef . . . 2A **132**
Charnley Dr. S11: Shef . . . 3B **132**
Charnley Ri. S11: Shef . . . 3B **132**
Charnock Av. S12: Shef . . . 6E **135**
Charnock Cres. S12: Shef . . . 5D **134**
Charnock Dale Rd. S12: Shef . . . 6D **134**
Charnock Dr. DN5: Cus . . . 5G **39**
S12: Shef . . . 5E **135**
Charnock Gro. S12: Shef . . . 6E **135**
CHARNOCK HALL . . . 6E **135**
Charnock Hall Rd. S12: Shef . . . 6D **134**
Charnock Vw. Rd. S12: Shef . . . 6D **134**
Charnock Wood Rd. S12: Shef . . . 6E **135**
Charnwood Ct. S20: Sot . . . 6H **137**
Charnwood Dr. DN4: Balb . . . 1G **71**
Charnwood Gro. S61: Kimb . . . 3A **96**
Charnwood Ho. S64: Swint . . . 3C **66**
Charnwood St. S64: Swint . . . 3C **66**
Charter Arc. S70: Barn . . . 1E **31**
Charter Dr. DN5: Scawt . . . 2E **39**
Charter Row S1: Shef . . . 6C **4** (4E **119**)
Charter Sq. S1: Shef . . . 5D **4** (4F **119**)
Chartwell Av. S42: W'orth . . . 5E **171**
Chartwell Ri. S42: W'orth . . . 5F **171**
Chase, The S6: Lox . . . 4E **105**
*S10: Shef . . . 5C **118***
(off Clarke Dell)
S26: Ast . . . 1D **138**
Chasecliff Cl. S40: Ches . . . 3E **167**
Chase Rd. S6: Lox . . . 4E **105**
Chatfield Rd. S8: Shef . . . 6D **132**
Chatham Ho. *S65: Roth . . . 4F **97***
(off Chatham St.)
Chatham St. S3: Shef . . . 1F **119**
S65: Roth . . . 4F **97**
Chatsworth Av. S40: Bramp . . . 6C **166**
S64: Mexb . . . 6A **52**
Chatsworth Bus. Pk. S40: Ches . . . 6F **167**
Chatsworth Cl. S26: Ast . . . 1E **139**
Chatsworth Ct. S11: Shef . . . 4G **131**
S43: Stav . . . 6A **164**
Chatsworth Cres. DN5: Scawt . . . 2G **39**
Chatsworth Dr. DN11: Ross . . . 6E **75**
Chatsworth Pk. Av. S12: Shef . . . 3D **134**
Chatsworth Pk. Dr. S12: Shef . . . 3D **134**
Chatsworth Pk. Gro. S12: Shef . . . 3D **134**
Chatsworth Pk. Ri. S12: Shef . . . 3D **134**
Chatsworth Pk. Rd. S12: Shef . . . 3D **134**
Chatsworth Pl. S18: Dron W . . . 2C **154**
Chatsworth Ri. S60: Brins . . . 4E **111**
S75: Dod . . . 3F **29**
Chatsworth Rd. S17: Dore . . . 4F **145**
S40: Bramp, Ches . . . 6A **166**
S71: Ath . . . 2F **17**
Chatterton Dr. S65: Roth . . . 6A **98**
Chaucer Cl. S5: Shef . . . 4C **92**
Chaucer Dr. S18: Dron . . . 5H **155**
Chaucer Ho. S65: Roth . . . 5A **98**
Chaucer Rd. S5: Shef . . . 5C **92**
S41: Ches . . . 6G **161**
S64: Mexb . . . 6G **51**
S65: Roth . . . 6A **98**
Chauntry Av. S36: Pen . . . 5E **177**
Cheadle St. S6: Shef . . . 4B **106**
Cheapside S70: Barn . . . 1E **31**
Checkstone Av. DN4: Bess . . . 1B **74**
Chedworth Cl. S75: Dart . . . 1F **15**
Cheedale Av. S40: Ches . . . 3D **166**
Cheedale Cl. S40: Ches . . . 2E **167**
Cheedale Wlk. S40: Ches . . . 3E **167**
Cheetham Av. S18: Uns . . . 1F **161**
Cheetham Dr. S66: Malt . . . 4B **102**
Chelmsford Av. S26: Ast . . . 6D **124**
Chelmsford Dr. DN2: Don . . . 4E **41**
Chelmsford Way S43: Bar H . . . 2G **163**
Chelsea Ct. S11: Shef . . . 1B **132**
Chelsea Ri. S11: Shef . . . 1B **132**
Chelsea Rd. S11: Shef . . . 1B **132**
Cheltenham Ri. DN5: Scaws . . . 5E **39**
Cheltenham Rd. DN2: Don . . . 5H **41**
Chelwood Ct. DN4: Balb . . . 1B **72**
Chemist La. S60: Roth . . . 3D **96**
Cheney Row S1: Shef . . . 4E **5**
Chepstow Cl. S40: Birdh . . . 2G **171**
Chepstow Dr. S64: Mexb . . . 6G **51**
Chepstow Gdns. DN5: Scaws . . . 5E **39**
S40: Birdh . . . 3G **171**
Chequer Av. DN4: Don . . . 2D **56**
Chequer Rd. DN1: Don . . . 1C **56**
Cheriton Av. DN6: Adw S . . . 2B **22**
Cherry Bank Rd. S8: Shef . . . 5F **133**
Cherry Brook S65: Roth . . . 2A **98**

Cherry Cl. S71: Roy 2F 9
  S72: Cud 6E 11
Cherry Gth. DN5: Ben 5A 24
Cherry Gro. DN11: New R 6D 74
  DN12: Con .6C 68
  S63: Gol 5B 36
Cherry Hills S75: Dart 5H 7
Cherry La. DN5: Don 6A 40
Cherrys Rd. S71: Barn 6A 18
Cherry St. S2: Shef 6F 119
Cherry St. Sth. S2: Shef 6F 119
Cherry Tree Cl. S11: Shef 1C 132
  S60: Brins .4E 111
  S75: Stain 5B 8
Cherry Tree Ct. S11: Shef 1C 132
  S63: Gol 5C 36
Cherry Tree Cres. S66: Wick 5H 99
Cherry Tree Dell S11: Shef 1C 132
Cherry Tree Dr. S11: Shef 6C 118
  S21: Killa 5C 152
Cherry Tree Gro. S43: Mas M 3F 165
CHERRY TREE HILL 1C 132
Cherry Tree Pl. S63: Wath D 1G 65
Cherry Tree Rd. DN3: Arm 4E 43
  DN4: Hex 2C 62
  S11: Shef 1C 132
Cherry Tree Rd. S26: Wales 6F 139
  S66: Malt 5G 101
Cherry Tree St. S74: Els, Hoyl 6C 46
Cherry Wlk. S35: Chap 3F 79
Chertsey Cl. S40: Birdh 2G 171
Cherwell Cl. S43: Brim 5D 162
Chesham Rd. S70: Barn 1C 30
Cheshire Rd. DN1: Don 5D 40
Chessel Cl. S8: Shef 4F 133
  WF9: Hems .1E 13
Chester Ct. S21: Ecki 2C 158
  WF9: Hems .1E 13
CHESTERFIELD 5H 167
Chesterfield and District Crematorium
  S43: Brim 2C 168
Chesterfield Av. S43: New W 3D 162
Chesterfield Bowl 3A 172
Chesterfield College
  Infirmary Rd. 4H 167
  Tapton House Campus 3B 168
Chesterfield Cricket Ground 6G 167
Chesterfield FC 1H 167
Chesterfield Golf Course 3E 171
Chesterfield Inner Relief Rd.
  S41: Ches, Whit M 4F 161
Chesterfield Lawn Tennis Club 4F 167
Chesterfield Museum & Art Gallery
  . . . . .5A 168
Chesterfield Rd. S8: Shef 6E 133
  S18: Dron 3F 155
  S21: Ecki 3B 158
  S26: Swal 2A 138
                        (not continuous)
  S43: Brim 2B 168
  S43: Hol, Stav 6F 163
  S44: Ark T, Cal, Duck 6G 169
  S44: Cal 6D 168
Chesterfield Rd. Sth. S8: Shef 5F 147
Chesterfield Small Bus. Cen.
  S41: Whit M 1H 167
                        (off Pottery La. W.)
Chesterfield Station (Rail) 5A 168
Chesterfield Trad. Est.
  S41: Ches 3D 160
Chesterhill Av. S65: Dalt 1D 98
Chester Ho. S40: Ches 5F 167
Chester Rd. DN2: Don 4E 41
Chester St. S40: Ches 5F 167
Chesterton Cl. S43: Brim C 4E 169
Chesterton Ct. S65: Roth 1H 97
Chesterton Rd. DN4: Balb 6B 56
  S65: Roth 2G 97
Chesterton Way S65: Roth 1A 98
Chesterwood Dr. S10: Shef 4A 118
Chestnut Av. DN2: Don 3G 41
  DN3: Arm 3E 43
  DN11: New R 6D 74
  S9: Shef 3H 121
  S20: Beig 3G 137
  S21: Ecki 2C 158
  S21: Killa 5B 152
  S26: Kiv P 5H 139
  S36: Stoc 4D 174
  S63: Wath D 2G 65

Chestnut Av. S65: Roth 3A 98
  S72: Brier 4A 12
Chestnut Cl. S18: Dron 4H 155
  S66: Flan 4G 99
Chestnut Ct. DN5: Ben 6H 23
  S35: Ough 3E 91
  S65: Thry 5E 85
  S70: Barn 3E 31
Chestnut Cres. S70: Barn 3G 31
Chestnut Dr. DN9: Auck 2B 76
  S35: Chap 4D 78
  S43: Hol 5F 163
  S72: Sth H .1G 11
Chestnut Gro. DN5: Sprot 4C 54
  DN12: Con .5D 68
  S25: Dinn 4A 128
  S63: Thurn .3C 36
  S64: Mexb .6E 51
                        (not continuous)
  S66: Malt 4G 101
  WF9: Hems 1G 13
Chestnut M. S72: Sth H 1G 11
Chestnut Rd. S26: Swal 6A 124
Chestnut St. S72: Grim 3C 20
Chestnut Wlk. S66: Hoot L 6H 101
Cheswold La. DN5: Don 6H 39
Chevet Ho. DN1: Don 2B 56
                        (off Grove Pl.)
Chevet Ri. S71: Roy 2G 9
Chevet Vw. S71: Roy 2F 9
Cheviot Dr. DN5: Scawt 3G 39
Cheviot Wlk. S75: Barn 6A 16
Cheviot Way S40: Ches 3D 166
Chevril Cl. S66: Wick 6F 99
Chiberworde Rd. S61: Kimb 4A 96
Chichester Rd. S10: Shef 2A 118
Chigwell Way S43: Bar H 3G 163
Chilcombe Pl. S70: Birdw 6E 45
Childers Dr. DN9: Auck 1H 59
Childers St. DN4: Don 3D 56
Chiltern Cl. S40: Ash 4D 166
Chiltern Ct. S40: Ches 4D 166
                        (off Cuttholme Rd.)
Chiltern Cres. DN5: Sprot 3B 54
Chiltern Ri. S60: Brins 5E 111
Chiltern Rd. DN5: Scawt 3G 39
  S6: Shef 4A 106
Chiltern Wlk. S75: Barn 6A 16
Chilton St. S70: Barn 2F 31
Chilwell Cl. S71: Ath 5E 9
Chilwell Gdns. S71: Ath 5E 9
Chilwell M. S71: Ath 5E 9
Chindit Ct. S25: Dinn 4A 128
Chinley St. S9: Shef 1D 120
Chippingham Pl. S9: Shef 6C 108
Chippingham St. S9: Shef 6C 108
                        (not continuous)
Chippinghouse Rd. S7: Shef 1E 133
  S8: Shef 1E 133
Chiverton Cl. S18: Dron 2F 155
Chorley Av. S10: Shef 6D 116
Chorley Dr. S10: Shef 6D 116
Chorley Pl. S10: Shef 1D 130
Chorley Rd. S10: Shef 1D 130
Christchurch Av. S26: Ast 6D 124
Christchurch Flats
  S63: Wath D 5D 48
                        (off Masefield Rd.)
Christ Chu. Rd. DN1: Don 6C 40
  S3: Shef 5G 107
Christchurch Rd. S63: Wath D 5D 48
Christ Chu. Ter. DN1: Don 1D 56
Christian Ho. S75: Barn 5C 16
Church Av. S62: Rawm 4F 83
Church Balk DN3: Eden 5B 26
Church Balk Gdns. DN3: Eden 5C 26
Church Balk La. DN3: Eden 6C 26
Church Cl. DN9: Auck 2H 59
  S21: Reni 4H 159
  S26: Kiv P 6G 139
  S35: Ough 3E 91
  S42: W'orth .6H 171
  S43: Stav 1H 169
  S64: Swint .3B 66
  S65: Rav 5H 85
  S66: Malt 6A 102
  S75: Dart 6F 7
Church Cnr. S25: Laugh M 1G 127
Church Cott. M. DN4: Balb 5F 55

Church Ct. DN4: Cant 5C 58
  S25: Sth A .4H 141
  S72: Brier 3B 12
Church Cft. DN3: Eden 5B 26
  S62: Rawm .4F 83
Churchdale M. S12: Shef 4G 135
Churchdale Rd. S12: Shef 4G 135
Church Dr. S62: Wentw 5D 62
  S72: Brier 4A 12
Church Farm Ct. S25: Sth A 4G 141
Churchfield S70: Barn 6D 16
Churchfield Av. S72: Cud 2E 19
  S75: Kexb 6D 6
Churchfield Cl. DN5: Ben 2H 39
  S75: Kexb 6C 6
Churchfield Ct. S70: Barn 6D 16
  S75: Kexb 6E 7
Churchfield Cres. S72: Cud 2E 19
Church Fld. Dr. S66: Wick 6G 99
Churchfield Gdns. S71: Carl 5A 10
Church Fld. La. S62: Wentw 6C 62
Churchfield La. S75: Dart, Kexb 6C 6
Church Flds. S61: Kimb 3H 95
Churchfields S66: Wick 1G 113
Churchfields Caravan Site DN5: Ben . .2H 39
                        (off Church St.)
Churchfields Cl. S70: Barn 6D 16
Church Flds. Rd. DN11: Ross 4E 75
Churchfield Ter. S72: Cud 2E 19
Church Fld. Vw. DN4: Warm 5F 55
Church Fold S6: Shef 1H 105
  S70: Barn 6D 16
Church Ga. S72: Brier 4B 12
Church Glebe S6: Shef 1H 105
Church Grn. DN5: Sprot 4C 54
  S63: Wath D 6F 49
Church Gro. S66: B'well 6B 88
  S71: Monk B 4H 17
Church Hgts. S66: H'swne 1F 177
Church Hill S60: Whist 3B 112
  S71: Roy 3A 10
Church Ho. M. S74: Jum 5C 46
                        (off Church St.)
Church Ho's. S43: Hol 5F 163
Churchill Av. DN5: Don 4H 39
  S66: Malt 4B 102
Churchill Rd. DN1: Don 4D 40
  S10: Shef 3B 118
  S36: Stoc 2B 174
Churchill Way S35: Chap 6E 61
Church La. DN3: Barn D 1G 27
  DN4: Bess, Cant 6B 58
  DN4: Warm .5E 55
                        (not continuous)
  DN5: Barnb, H'ton 2H 51
  DN6: Adw S 2D 22
  DN9: Finn 3E 77
  DN11: Wad .5E 73
                        (not continuous)
  S9: Shef 6C 108
  S12: Ridg 3H 149
  S12: Shef 5D 136
  S13: Shef 2C 136
  S17: Dore 4E 145
  S20: Beig 5H 137
  S21: Killa 4D 152
  S25: Dinn 5G 127
  S26: Ast 2E 139
  S36: H'swne 1F 177
  S40: Ches 5H 167
  S42: Tem N .6G 173
  S44: Cal 6E 169
  S60: Cat 6D 110
  S60: Tree 2F 123
  S63: Wath D 6F 49
  S65: Rav 5A 86
  S66: Braml .5A 100
  S66: Clift 3G 87
  S66: Malt 4A 102
  S66: Wick 6G 99
  S70: Barn 6D 16
  S70: Wors 2E 45
  S72: Sth H .1E 11
  S75: Cawt 4A 14
  S75: Tank 3D 60
  S81: Letw 4F 129
Church La. Ct. S25: Dinn 6H 127
Church La. M. S66: Braml 5A 100
Church La. Nth. S41: Old W 3H 161

Church Lea S74: Hoyl 2B **62**
Church Mdw. Rd. DN11: Ross 5E **76**
Church Mdws. S25: Dinn 6H **127**
  S44: Cal .5E **169**
Church M. DN5: Ben 2H **39**
  S20: Mosb 3E **151**
  S21: Killa 3D **152**
  S63: Bolt D 3B **50**
  S64: Mexb 2H **67**
Church Rein Cl. DN4: Warm 6D **54**
Church Rd. DN3: Barn D 1G **27**
  DN3: Kirk Sa 4C **26**
  DN11: Wad 2H **89**
  DN12: Den M 2D **68**
  DN12: New E 3C **70**
  S75: Cawt 4A **14**
Churchside S41: Has 4C **172**
  S42: Gras 4C **172**
  S44: Cal 5E **169**
Churchside La. S41: Has 4C **172**
Church St. DN1: Don 6B **40**
  DN3: Arm 4D **42**
  DN5: Ben 2H **39**
  DN12: Con 4F **69**
  S1: Shef 3E **5** (3F **119**)
  S6: Stann 1D **116**
  S18: Dron 3F **155**
  S18: Uns 5B **156**
  S21: Ecki 6F **151**
  S26: Wales 6G **139**
  S35: Eccl 1F **93**
  S35: Ough 3D **90**
  S36: Pen 4D **176**
  S43: Brim 6D **162**
  S43: Stav 4B **164**
  S44: Cal 5E **169**
  S60: Roth 4E **97**
  S61: Grea 4B **82**
  S61: Kimb 3H **95**
  S62: Rawm 4F **83**
  S63: Bolt D 2B **50**
  S63: Thurn 2B **36**
  S63: Wath D 6F **49**
  S64: Mexb 2G **67**
  S64: Swint 3A **66**
  S66: Thurc 6C **114**
  S70: Barn 6D **16**
  S71: Carl 5A **10**
  S71: Roy .3H **9**
  S72: Brier 3A **12**
  S72: Cud 2E **19**
  S72: Gt H 6F **21**
  S73: D'fld 5C **34**
  S73: Womb 2G **47**
  S74: Els .1D **62**
  S74: Jum 5C **46**
  S75: Barn 5H **15**
  S75: Cawt 3A **14**
  S75: Dart .6F **7**
  S75: Stain 5B **8**
Church St. Cl. S63: Thurn 2B **36**
Church St. Nth. S41: Old W 3H **161**
Church St. Sth. S40: Birdh 3G **171**
  (not continuous)
Church Ter. S75: Dod 3F **29**
CHURCH TOWN 4D **152**
Church Vw. DN1: Don 6B **40**
  DN5: Barnb 1H **51**
  DN11: Wad 6E **73**
  DN12: New E 5B **70**
  S6: Shef 1H **105**
  S13: Shef 2D **136**
  S21: Killa 3D **152**
  S26: Ast 1E **139**
  S26: Tod 3C **140**
  S40: Bramp 6D **166**
  S64: Swint 3B **66**
  S65: Thry 5E **85**
  S66: Wick 6G **99**
  S72: Cud 2E **19**
  S73: D'fld 5D **34**
  S74: Hoyl 1G **61**
  S75: Dod 3F **29**
Church Vw. Apartments
  S61: Grea 5C **82**
  (off Fitzwilliam Wlk.)
Church Vw. Cres. S36: Pen 4D **176**
Church Vw. Rd. S36: Pen 4D **176**

Church Wlk. DN12: Den M 2D **68**
  S40: Ches 5H **167**
  (off Stephenson Pl.)
  S43: New W 2C **162**
  S63: Thurn 2B **36**
  (off Church St.)
Church Way DN1: Don 6B **40**
  DN6: Adw S 2C **22**
  S40: Ches 5H **167**
Churcroft S75: Barn 4H **15**
Churston Rd. S40: Ash 5E **167**
Cinder Bri. Rd. S61: Grea 4D **82**
Cinder Hill La. S35: Gren 2C **92**
Cinderhill La. S8: Shef 2G **147**
Cinderhill Rd. S61: Kimb P 6H **81**
Cinder Hills Way S75: Dod 3H **29**
Cinder La. S21: Killa 3E **153**
Cineworld Cinema
  Chesterfield 1A **172**
  Sheffield 4F **109**
Circle, The DN11: New R 5B **74**
  S2: Shef 5D **120**
  S35: High G 1D **78**
Circle Cl. S2: Shef 6E **121**
Circuit, The DN6: Woodl 2A **22**
Circular Dr. S21: Reni 4H **159**
Circular Rd. S41: Has 2A **172**
  S43: Stav 6A **164**
City Hall Stop (ST) 3D **4** (3F **119**)
City Rd. S2: Shef 4A **120**
  S12: Shef 2D **134**
City Road Crematorium S2: Shef . . .6B **120**
City Vw. S4: Shef 2D **108**
City Wharfe S3: Shef 1F **5** (2G **119**)
Civic Theatre
  Doncaster 1C **56**
  Rotherham 4F **97**
Clanricarde St. S71: Barn 4D **16**
Claphouse Fold S75: Hai 1B **6**
Clara Pl. S61: Kimb 4A **96**
Clare Ct. S60: Roth 3E **97**
Clarehurst Rd. S73: D'fld 4B **34**
Clarel Cl. S36: Pen 5C **176**
Clarell Gdns. DN4: Cant 3B **58**
Clarel St. S36: Pen 5C **176**
Claremont Cres. S10: Shef 3C **118**
Claremont Gdns. S71: Lund 4C **18**
Claremont Pl. S10: Shef 3C **118**
Claremont St. S61: Kimb 4A **96**
Clarence Av. DN4: Balb 4A **56**
Clarence Ct. S6: Shef 4A **106**
Clarence La. S3: Shef 5E **119**
Clarence Pl. S66: Malt 4B **102**
Clarence Rd. S6: Shef 4A **106**
  S40: Ches 5G **167**
  S71: Monk B 4G **17**
Clarence Sq. S25: Dinn 5B **128**
Clarence St. S25: Dinn 5B **128**
  S40: Ches 5G **167**
  S63: Wath D 5D **48**
Clarendon Ct. S11: Shef 6F **117**
Clarendon Dr. S10: Shef 6F **117**
Clarendon Rd. S10: Shef 6F **117**
  S43: Ink 1H **169**
  S65: Roth 3G **97**
Clarendon St. S70: Barn 1C **30**
Clark Av. DN4: Don 2D **56**
  DN12: New E 6C **70**
Clarke Av. S25: Laugh C 3F **127**
  S66: Thurc 6D **114**
Clarke Ct. S25: Dinn 4A **128**
Clarke Dell S10: Shef 5C **118**
Clarke Dr. S10: Shef 5C **118**
Clarkegrove Rd. S10: Shef 5C **118**
Clarkehouse Rd. S10: Shef 5B **118**
Clarkes Cft. S73: Womb 1G **47**
Clarke Sq. S2: Shef 6E **119**
Clarke St. S10: Shef 6A **4** (4D **118**)
  S63: Thurn 2D **36**
  S75: Barn 5C **16**
Clark Gro. S6: Stann 6E **105**
Clarks Ct. DN6: Adw S 2C **22**
Clarkson Av. S40: Ches 2G **171**
Clarkson St. S10: Shef 3D **118**
  S70: Wors 5H **31**
Clark St. S74: Hoyl 5A **46**
Clarney Av. S73: D'fld 4A **34**
Clarney Pl. S73: D'fld 4B **34**
Clayburn Rd. S72: Grim 3A **20**

Claycliffe Av. S75: Barn 4G **15**
Claycliffe Bus. Pk. S75: Bar G 3G **15**
Claycliffe Rd.
  S75: Barn, Bar G, Birdw 2G **15**
Claycliffe Ter. S63: Gol 5D **36**
  S70: Barn 2C **30**
Clayfield Av. S64: Mexb 1A **68**
Clayfield Cl. S64: Mexb 1A **68**
Clayfield Ct. S64: Mexb 1A **68**
Clayfield La. S62: Wentw 5E **63**
Clayfield Rd. S64: Mexb 1A **68**
  S74: Hoyl 4A **46**
Clayfields DN4: Balb 1H **71**
Clayfield Vw. S64: Mexb 6A **52**
Clay Flat La. DN11: New R 6C **74**
Clay La. DN2: Don 1A **42**
  S1: Shef .5E **5**
  (not continuous)
Clay La. W. DN2: Don, Long S 6H **25**
Claypit La. S62: Rawm 3H **83**
Clay Pits La. S36: Stoc 2A **174**
Clay Pit Way S9: Shef 6E **109**
Clayroyd S70: Wors 6G **31**
Clay St. S9: Shef 5C **108**
  (not continuous)
Clayton Av. S63: Thurn 1A **36**
Clayton Cres. S20: Water 6F **137**
Clayton Dr. S63: Thurn 2A **36**
Clayton Hollow S20: Water 6F **137**
Clayton La. S63: Thurn 1A **36**
Clayton St. S41: Ches 6A **168**
Claywheels La. S6: Shef 6A **92**
Claywood Dr. S2: Shef 6H **5** (4H **119**)
Claywood Rd. S2: Shef 5H **5** (4H **119**)
  (Claywood Dr.)
  S2: Shef 5H **119**
  (Fitzwalter Rd.)
Clayworth Dr. DN4: Bess 6G **57**
Clear Vw. S72: Grim 6B **12**
Clearwell Cft. DN5: Cus 5G **39**
Cleeve Hill Gdns. S20: Water 6E **137**
Clement M. S61: Kimb 4H **95**
Clementson Rd. S10: Shef 2B **118**
Clement St. S9: Shef 6E **109**
  S61: Kimb 4H **95**
Cleveden Way S71: Roy 2G **9**
Clevedon Cres. DN5: Scawt 1G **39**
Clevedon Way S66: Malt 3C **102**
Cleveland Rd. DN3: Arm 4F **43**
Cleveland St. DN1: Don 2B **56**
  S6: Shef 1D **118**
Cleveland Way S40: Ches 4C **166**
Cliff Ct. DN12: Den M 3C **68**
Cliff Cres. DN4: Warm 6D **54**
Cliff Dr. S73: D'fld 5D **34**
Cliffe Av. S70: Wors 5G **31**
Cliffe Bank S64: Swint 3A **12**
Cliffe Cl. S72: Brier 3A **12**
Cliffe Ct. S71: Monk B 5H **17**
Cliffe Cres. S75: Dod 3F **29**
Cliffedale Cres. S70: Wors 4G **31**
Cliffe Farm Dr. S11: Shef 1H **131**
Cliffefield Rd. S8: Shef 3E **133**
  (not continuous)
  S64: Swint 3C **66**
Cliffefield Vw. S64: Swint 3C **66**
Cliffe Hill S6: Dung, Stann 5A **104**
  S75: Cawt 3A **14**
Cliffe Ho. Rd. S6: Shef 6G **93**
Cliffe La. S71: Monk B 5H **17**
Cliffe Rd. S6: Shef 6H **105**
  S73: Bramp 4B **48**
Cliffe Vw. Rd. S8: Shef 3F **133**
Cliff Hill S66: Malt 5G **101**
Cliff Hills Cl. S66: Malt 5H **101**
Cliff La. S72: Brier 3A **12**
Clifford Av. S65: Thry 6F **85**
Clifford Cl. S40: Bramp 6C **166**
Clifford Lister Bus. Cen., The
  S66: Wick 6F **99**
Clifford Rd. S11: Shef 1C **132**
  S61: Kimb P 1H **95**
  S66: Hel .6D **100**
  WF9: Sth K 4H **13**
Clifford St. S72: Cud 5F **11**
Clifford Wlk. DN12: Den M 3B **68**
Cliff Rd. S6: Stann 6E **105**
  S73: D'fld 5D **34**

Cliff St. S11: Shef .5E 119
S64: Mexb .2F 67
Cliff Ter. S71: Barn .1F 31
Cliff Vw. DN12: Den M .2C 68
CLIFTON
S65 .4G 97
S66 .3G 87
Clifton Av. S9: Shef .3H 121
S65: Roth .4H 97
S71: Ath .6D 8
Clifton Bank S60: Roth .4F 97
Clifton Byres S66: Clift .3G 87
Clifton Cl. S71: Ath .6D 8
Clifton Cres. DN2: Don .4G 41
S9: Shef .3G 121
Clifton Cres. Nth. S65: Roth .4G 97
Clifton Cres. Sth. S65: Roth .4G 97
Clifton Dr. DN5: Sprot .2F 55
Clifton Gdns. S72: Brier .3H 11
Clifton Gro. S65: Roth .4G 97
Clifton Hill DN12: Con .5F 69
Clifton La. DN12: Con .6G 69
S9: Shef .4H 121
S65: Roth .4F 97
Clifton Mt. S65: Roth .4F 97
Clifton Park Mus. .4G 97
Clifton Ri. S66: Malt .4H 101
Clifton Rd. S72: Grim .1B 20
Clifton St. S9: Shef .4E 109
S40: Ches .5F 167
S70: Barn .2F 31
WF9: Hems .1D 12
Clifton Ter. DN12: Con .4G 69
S65: Roth .4F 97
Clinton La. S10: Shef .6A 4 (4D 118)
Clinton Pl. S10: Shef .6A 4 (5D 118)
Clinton Wlk. S10: Shef .6A 4 (4D 118)
Clipstone Av. S71: Ath .6F 9
Clipstone Gdns. S9: Shef .6F 109
Clipstone Rd. S9: Shef .6F 109
Clock Ct. S25: Dinn .4G 127
Clock Tower Bus. Cen., The
S43: Hol .4G 163
Cloisters, The DN4: Cant .5D 58
S70: Wors .2E 45
Cloisters Way S71: Monk B .5A 18
Cloister Way S72: Grim .1B 20
Cloonmore Cft. S8: Shef .1H 147
Cloonmore Dr. S8: Shef .1H 147
Close, The DN3: Brant .4G 59
DN4: Warm .2F 71
S25: Dinn .6A 128
S71: Carl .5H 9
S71: Lund .5B 18
Cloudberry Way S75: Stain .6C 8
Clough, The S41: Ches .1D 172
Clough Bank S2: Shef .6G 119
S61: Roth .3C 96
CLOUGH FIELD .2G 117
Clough Flds. S10: Shef .2G 117
Clough Flds. Rd. S74: Hoyl .1H 61
Clough Grn. S61: Roth .3D 96
Clough Gro. S35: Ough .3F 91
Clough Head S36: Cub .6D 176
Clough La. S10: Shef .2A 130
Clough Rd. S1: Shef .5F 119
S2: Shef .5F 119
S61: Roth .4C 96
(not continuous)
S74: Hoyl .1A 62
Clough St. S61: Roth .3C 96
Clough Wood Vw. S35: Ough .4E 91
Clovelly Rd. DN3: Eden .6C 26
Clover Ct. S8: Shef .6A 134
Clover Gdns. S5: Shef .1B 108
Clover Grn. S61: Kimb P .6H 81
Cloverlands Dr. S75: Stain .6B 8
Clover Wlk. S63: Bolt D .1A 50
Club Gdn. Rd. S11: Shef .6E 119
Club Gdn. Wlk. *S11: Shef* .*5E 119*
(off London Rd.)
Club Grn. Rd. S11: Shef .5E 119
Club Mill Rd. S6: Shef .3D 106
Clubmill Ter. S40: Ches .4F 167
Club St. S11: Shef .6E 119
S71: Monk B .4H 17
S74: Hoyl .1G 61
Clumber Pl. S43: Ink .2H 169
Clumber Ri. S26: Ast .2D 138
Clumber Rd. DN4: Don .3E 57
S10: Shef .5F 117
Clumber St. S75: Barn .6B 16
Clun Rd. S4: Shef .6H 107
Clun St. S4: Shef .6H 107
Clyde Rd. S8: Shef .2E 133
Clyde St. S71: Barn .1E 31
Coach Ho. Dr. DN5: Cus .6E 39
Coach Ho. La. S70: Barn .4E 31
Coach Houses, The *S10: Shef* .*2C 118*
(off Moorgate Av.)
Coach Rd. S61: Grea .4C 82
S62: H'ley, Wentw .5A 62
COAL ASTON .6H 147
Coalbrook Av. S13: Shef .6E 123
Coalbrook Gro. S13: Shef .6E 123
Coalbrook Rd. S13: Shef .6E 123
Coalby Wlk. *S70: Barn* .*6D 16*
(off Fitzwilliam St.)
Coal Pit La. S35: Ough .5B 90
S36: Stoc .5D 174
S66: Mick .6F 87
S72: Cud .3G 19
S72: Shaft .4G 11
Coalpit La. S26: Wales .1G 153
Coalpit Rd. DN12: Den M .3B 68
Coal Riding La. S65: Dalt M .4E 99
Coates La. S75: Silk C .6B 28
Coates St. S2: Shef .4H 119
Cobb Ct. S64: Swint .5C 66
Cobb Dr. S64: Swint .5B 66
Cobcar Av. S74: Els .1E 63
Cobcar Cl. S74: Els .6D 46
Cobcar La. S74: Els .6D 46
Cobcar St. S74: Els .1D 62
Cobden Av. S64: Mexb .1G 67
Cobden Pl. S10: Shef .2B 118
Cobden Rd. S40: Ches .4G 167
Cobden Ter. S10: Shef .2B 118
Cobden Vw. Rd. S10: Shef .2A 118
Cobnar Av. S8: Shef .6F 133
Cobnar Dr. S8: Shef .6F 133
S41: Ches .6E 161
Cobnar Gdns. S8: Shef .6E 133
Cobnar Rd. S8: Shef .6E 133
Cobnar Wood Cl. S41: Ches .3C 160
COCK ALLEY .1F 173
Cockayne Pl. S8: Shef .3E 133
Cockerham Av. S75: Barn .5D 16
Cockerham La. S75: Barn .5D 16
Cockhill Fld. La. S66: B'well .6B 88
Cockhill La. S66: B'well, Staint .2B 88
Cockpit La. S36: Pen .4D 176
Cockshot La. S36: Bolst .5E 175
Cockshot Pit La. S75: Mapp .6H 7
Cockshutt Av. S8: Shef .2C 146
Cockshutt Dr. S8: Shef .2C 146
Cockshutt Rd. S8: Shef .2C 146
Cockshutts La. S35: Ough .2C 90
Coggin Mill Way S60: Roth .5B 96
COISLEY HILL .2A 136
Coisley Hill S13: Shef .2A 136
Coisley Rd. S13: Shef .3B 136
Coit La. S11: Shef .5E 131
Coke Hill S60: Roth .5E 97
Coke La. S60: Roth .5E 97
Colbeck Cl. DN3: Arm .4D 42
Colby Pl. S6: Shef .1G 117
Colchester Ct. DN5: Scaws .4F 39
Colchester Rd. S10: Shef .2A 118
Coldstream Av. DN4: Warm .6E 55
Coldwell Hill S35: Ough .3C 90
Coldwell La. S10: Shef .3F 117
Coldwell's Fold S36: Thurl .3A 176
Coleford Rd. S9: Shef .6F 109
Coleman St. S62: Parkg .5G 83
Coleridge Av. S71: Monk B .4G 17
Coleridge Gdns. S9: Shef .6E 109
Coleridge Rd. DN3: Barn D .1H 27
S9: Shef .5D 108
S63: Wath D .5D 48
S65: Roth .3G 97
S66: Malt .6B 102
Colewell Cl. S73: Womb .6F 33
Coley La. S62: Wentw .5G 63
Colister Dr. S9: Shef .2F 121
Colister Gdns. S9: Shef .3E 121
College Av. S43: Stav .5A 164
College Cl. S4: Shef .4H 107
College Ct. S4: Shef .4H 107
S64: Mexb .1G 67
College Ho. S75: Barn .4C 16
College La. *S65: Roth* .*4E 97*
(off Howard St.)
College Pk. Cl. S60: Roth .1F 111
College Rd. DN1: Don .2B 56
(not continuous)
S60: Roth .4C 96
(not continuous)
S64: Mexb .1G 67
College Rd. Rdbt. S60: Roth .3D 96
College St. S10: Shef .4C 118
S65: Roth .4E 97
College Ter. S73: D'fld .5B 34
College Wlk. *S60: Roth* .*3E 97*
(off Frederick St.)
College Wlk. Shop. Cen. *S60: Roth* .*3E 97*
(off Frederick St.)
Collegiate Cres. S10: Shef .6A 4 (5C 118)
Colley Av. S5: Shef .4F 93
S70: Barn .4H 31
Colley Cl. S5: Shef .4F 93
Colley Cres. S5: Shef .4G 93
S70: Barn .3H 31
Colley Dr. S5: Shef .4G 93
Colley Pl. S70: Barn .3H 31
Colley Rd. S5: Shef .4F 93
Collier Ct. S63: Bramp B .5A 48
Collier Rd. S72: Shaft .5F 11
Colliers Cl. S13: Shef .2C 136
Colliery Av. S63: Wath D .4F 49
Colliery Cl. S25: Dinn .4H 127
S43: Stav .5C 164
Colliery Dr. S21: Killa .5C 152
Colliery La. S63: Gol .4C 36
Colliery Rd. S4: Shef .3D 108
S26: Kiv P .6A 140
Colliery Vs. S66: Thurc .4C 114
Colliery Yd. S75: Pill .2C 60
Collin Av. S6: Shef .3H 105
Collindridge Rd. S73: Womb .2G 47
Collingbourne Av. S20: Sot .1H 151
Collingbourne Dr. S20: Sot .1H 151
Collingham Rd. S26: Swal .2B 138
Collins Cl. S75: Dod .3F 29
Collinson Rd. S5: Shef .6F 93
Collins Yd. *S18: Dron* .*3G 155*
(off Mill La.)
Collishaw Cl. S41: Has .2B 172
Colonel Ward Dr. S64: Swint .3D 66
Colonnades Shop. Cen. DN1: Don .1B 56
Colster Cl. S75: Barn .6H 15
Coltfield S70: Birdw .3E 45
Coltishall Av. S66: Braml .4B 100
Colton Cl. S41: Ches .5F 161
Columbia Pl. S2: Shef .6F 5
Columbia St. S70: Barn .3D 30
Columbus Way S66: Malt .4H 101
Colver Rd. S2: Shef .6F 119
(not continuous)
Colvin Cl. DN5: Ark .1D 40
Colwall St. S9: Shef .6C 108
Colwick Gro. S61: Roth .3B 96
Comelybank Dr. DN12: Den M .2A 68
Comet Ct. DN9: Auck .2C 76
Commerce St. S35: Chap .2G 79
Commercial Rd. S63: Gol .6A 36
Commercial St. S1: Shef .3G 5 (3G 119)
S70: Barn .2F 31
Commercial Way DN4: Warm .3E 71
Common, The S35: Eccl .6G 79
S72: Sth H .1H 11
COMMON END .1G 13
Common Farm Cl. S65: Rav .2A 100
Common La. DN3: Barn D .1F 27
DN4: Warm .6E 55
DN5: Alm .3F 25
DN9: Auck .1H 59
DN11: New R .6H 75
DN12: Con .1G 87
S11: Shef .2E 131
S36: Spink .5G 175
S42: Cut .6A 160
S63: Bolt D .4C 50
(not continuous)
S63: Wath D .6A 50
S65: Rav .1C 100
S66: Bramp M .1H 125

Common La. S66: Clift 1G **87**
S66: Thurc 1E **127**
S71: Roy .2H **9**
(not continuous)
Common Rd. DN12: Con 5H **69**
S25: Dinn 4G **127**
S25: Nth A 5C **126**
S63: Thurn 2A **36**
S72: Brier 4B **12**
WF9: Sth K 5E **13**
Common Rd. Av. WF9: Sth K 5H **13**
COMMON SIDE 3C 134
Commonside S10: Shef 2B **118**
Common Side Cft. S12: Shef 3C **134**
Commonwealth Vw. S63: Bolt D 2A **50**
Companions Cl. S66: Wick 6G **99**
Compass Ct. S21: Killa 6B **152**
Compass Cres. S41: Old W 3B **162**
Compton St. S6: Shef 6A **106**
S40: Ches 5G **167**
Comrades Ho. DN5: Ben 1B **40**
Comrades Pl. S63: Gol 5E **37**
Conalan Av. S17: Bradw 5A **146**
CONANBY .4E 69
Conan Rd. DN12: Con 4E **69**
Concept Ct. S63: Wath D 4D **48**
Concorde M. DN1: Don 6C **40**
Concord Park Golf Course 5B 94
Concord Rd. S5: Shef 4B **94**
Concord Sports Cen. 6B 94
Concord Vw. Rd. S61: Kimb 5F **95**
Conduit La. S10: Shef 2B **118**
Conduit Rd. S10: Shef 2B **118**
Cone La. S75: Silk, Silk C 3B **28**
Conery Cl. S65: Thry 6F **85**
Coney Rd. DN5: Ben 4H **23**
Congress St. S1: Shef 3C **4** (3E **119**)
Coningsburgh Rd. DN3: Eden 6C **26**
Coningsby Ho. S10: Shef 4E **117**
Coningsby Rd. S5: Shef 3H **107**
CONISBROUGH 4F 69
Conisbrough Castle 4F 69
Conisbrough Castle Vis. Cen. 4F 69
Conisbrough Station (Rail) 3E 69
Coniston Av. S75: Stain 4H **7**
Coniston Cl. S25: Nth A 2A **142**
S36: Pen 3D **176**
Coniston Ct. S64: Mexb 6A **52**
Coniston Dr. DN4: Balb 2G **71**
S63: Bolt D 3B **50**
Coniston Ho. *S40: Ches 1A 172*
(off Spinners Cft.)
Coniston Pl. DN5: Scawt 2G **39**
Coniston Rd. DN2: Don 6H **41**
DN3: Kirk Sa 4C **26**
S8: Shef .3D **132**
S18: Dron W 4C **154**
S41: Ches 6E **161**
S64: Mexb 6H **51**
S71: Barn 1F **31**
Coniston Ter. S8: Shef 3D **132**
Coniston Way S41: Ches 6E **161**
Connaught Dr. DN3: Kirk Sa 4C **26**
Connelly Ct. S40: Ches 5F **167**
Conrad Dr. S66: Malt 4H **101**
Constable Cl. S14: Shef 6A **134**
S18: Dron 3D **154**
S66: Flan 4G **99**
Constable Dr. S14: Shef 6A **134**
Constable La. S25: Dinn 5A **128**
Constable Pl. S14: Shef 6B **134**
S63: Wath D 6F **49**
Constable Rd. S14: Shef 6A **134**
Constable Way S14: Shef 6A **134**
S65: Dalt 1B **98**
Constitution Hill DN5: Cade 2G **69**
Convent Gro. DN4: Bess 4A **58**
Convent Pl. S3: Shef 4B **4** (3E **119**)
Convent Wlk. S3: Shef 4B **4** (3E **119**)
Conway Ct. DN4: Bess 1A **74**
Conway Cres. S65: Roth 2B **98**
Conway Dr. DN3: Brant 4G **59**
DN5: Barnb 1H **51**
Conway Pl. S73: Womb 3A **48**
Conway St. S3: Shef 4A **4** (3D **118**)
S70: Stair 2A **32**
Conway Ter. S64: Mexb 6F **51**
Conyers Dr. S26: Ast 6C **124**
Conyers Rd. DN5: Don 5A **40**
Coode S3: Shef 1F **5** (2G **119**)
Coo Hill S13: Shef 2D **136**
Cook Av. S66: Malt 4H **101**
Cooke & Beard Homes S8: Shef 3G **133**
Cooke St. DN5: Ben 2H **39**
Cookson Cl. S5: Shef 6C **92**
Cookson Rd. S5: Shef 6C **92**
Cookson St. DN4: Balb 4A **56**
Cooks Rd. S20: Beig 6H **137**
Cooks Wood Rd. S3: Shef 5F **107**
Coole Well Cl. S43: Stav 6A **164**
Coombe Pl. S10: Shef 3B **118**
Coombe Rd. S10: Shef 3B **118**
Co-operative Cotts.
S43: Pool 6D **164**
S72: Brier 3A **12**
Co-operative St. S63: Gol 5D **36**
S63: Wath D 5E **49**
S72: Cud 2D **18**
Cooper Cl. S63: Bramp B 6B **48**
Cooper Gallery 6D 16
Cooper Rd. S75: Kexb 6D **6**
Cooper Row *S75: Dod 4G 29*
(off Stainborough Rd.)
Coopers Ho. *S11: Shef 5D 118*
(off Napier St.)
Coopers Ter. DN1: Don 1C **56**
Cooper St. DN4: Don 3D **56**
Copeland Rd. S73: Womb 2F **47**
Cope St. S70: Barn 3E **31**
Copley Av. DN12: Con 4D **68**
Copley Cres. DN5: Scaws 4D **38**
Copley Gdns. DN5: Sprot 4C **54**
Copley Pl. S61: Roth 2B **96**
Copley Rd. DN1: Don 6C **40**
Copper Beech Cl. S20: Beig 5H **137**
Copper Beech Cres.
S66: Hoot L 1H **115**
Copper Cl. S70: Barn 2E **31**
Copper St. S3: Shef 1D **4** (2F **119**)
Coppice, The S61: Kimb P 6F **81**
Coppice Av. S75: Barn 4A **16**
Coppice Cl. S36: Stoc 2B **174**
S41: Has 4C **172**
Coppice Gdns. S61: Grea 6C **82**
Coppice La. S6: Stann 2C **116**
S62: H'ley 5A **62**
Coppice Ri. S35: Chap 2G **79**
Coppice Rd. DN6: Highf 6C **22**
S10: Shef 3C **116**
Coppice Vw. S10: Shef 3G **117**
Coppicewood Ct.
DN4: Balb 2B **72**
Coppins Cl. S66: Braml 4A **100**
Coppin Sq. S5: Shef 3E **93**
Copse, The S66: Braml 4A **100**
Coquet Av. S66: Braml 6A **100**
Coral Cl. S26: Augh 4B **124**
Coral Dr. S26: Augh 4B **124**
Coral Pl. S26: Augh 4B **124**
Coral Way S26: Augh 4B **124**
Corbridge Ct. DN4: Bess 4H **57**
CORBRIGGS 5E 173
Corbriggs Caravan Pk. S41: Cor 5E **173**
Corby Rd. S4: Shef 3C **108**
Cordwell Av. S41: Ches 6D **160**
Cordwell Cl. S43: Stav 6A **164**
CORKER BOTTOMS 4D 120
Corker Bottoms La. S2: Shef 3C **120**
Corker Rd. S12: Shef 3D **134**
Corner Pin Cl. S43: Stav 4C **164**
Cornfall Pl. S70: Barn 1C **30**
Cornfield Cl. S42: Ash 3B **166**
Cornflower Dr. DN4: Bess 4G **57**
Corn Hill DN12: Con 5G **69**
Cornhill S3: Shef 3A **4**
Cornish Ho. *S3: Shef 1E 119*
(off Adelaide La.)
Cornish St. S6: Shef 1E **119**
(not continuous)
Cornish Way S62: Parkg 6F **83**
Corn Mill Ct. S6: Shef 5A **106**
Cornwall Av. S43: Brim 6E **163**
Cornwall Cl. S43: Brim 6E **163**
S71: Monk B 4G **17**
Cornwall Dr. S43: Brim 6E **163**
Cornwall Rd. DN2: Don 5G **41**
Cornwall Works S3: Shef 1D **4**
Cornwell Cl. S62: Rawm 6D **64**
Coronach Way
DN11: New R . . . . .6B **74** & 6F **75**
Coronation Av. S25: Dinn 4A **128**
S71: Roy .2B **10**
S72: Grim 2B **20**
S72: Shaft 3E **11**
Coronation Bri. S60: Roth 4C **96**
S61: Roth 4C **96**
Coronation Cotts.
DN3: Barn D 1G **27**
Coronation Ct. S64: Mexb 6F **51**
Coronation Cres. S70: Birdw 3E **45**
Coronation Dr. S63: Bolt D 2A **50**
S70: Birdw 3E **45**
Coronation Gdns. DN4: Warm 6D **54**
Coronation Rd. DN4: Balb 5A **56**
S36: Stoc 3D **174**
S43: Brim 6D **162**
S62: Rawm 2B **84**
S63: Wath D 6H **49**
S64: Swint 3D **66**
S74: Hoyl 6A **46**
S75: Bar G 4E **15**
Coronation St. S63: Thurn 2D **36**
S71: Monk B 4H **17**
S73: D'fld 4C **34**
Coronation Ter. S71: Ard 2C **32**
S73: Hem 4F **47**
Corporation Bldgs. S3: Shef 2F **5**
Corporation St. S3: Shef 1E **5** (2F **119**)
S41: Ches 5A **168**
(not continuous)
S60: Roth 4E **97**
S70: Barn 3F **31**
Cortina Ri. S73: D'fld 4H **33**
Corton Wood S73: Bramp 4A **48**
Corton Wood Bus. Pk. S73: Bramp . . .4A **48**
Cortonwood Dr. S73: Bramp 4A **48**
Cortonwood Ho. *DN1: Don 2B 56*
(off Bond Cl.)
CORTWORTH 5H 63
Cortworth La. S62: Wentw 5G **63**
Cortworth Pl. S74: Els 6E **47**
Cortworth Rd. S11: Shef 4H **131**
Corunna Vw. S36: Pen 5E **177**
Corve Way S40: Ches 3A **166**
Corwen Pl. S13: Shef 2B **136**
Cosgrove Ct. DN3: Eden 6D **26**
Cossey Rd. S4: Shef 6A **108**
Cotefield Pl. S36: Pen 4D **176**
Coterel Cres. DN4: Cant 3C **58**
Cotleigh Av. S12: Shef 5B **136**
Cotleigh Cl. S12: Shef 5B **136**
Cotleigh Cres. S12: Shef 5B **136**
Cotleigh Dr. S12: Shef 5B **136**
Cotleigh Gdns. S12: Shef 5B **136**
Cotleigh Pl. S12: Shef 5B **136**
Cotleigh Rd. S12: Shef 5B **136**
Cotleigh Way S12: Shef 5B **136**
Cotswold Av. S35: Chap 3D **78**
Cotswold Cl. S40: Ches 3D **166**
S75: Barn 6A **16**
Cotswold Cres. S60: Whist 3B **112**
Cotswold Dr. DN5: Sprot 3B **54**
S26: Ast .1D **138**
S42: Gras 6D **172**
Cotswold Gdns. DN5: Scawt 3G **39**
Cotswold Rd. S6: Shef 4A **106**
Cottage Cl. S43: Pool 6D **164**
Cottage Gro. S66: B'well 1B **102**
Cottage La. S11: Shef 3D **130**
Cottam Cl. S60: Whist 3B **112**
Cottam Rd. S35: High G 1B **78**
Cottenham Rd. S65: Roth 3G **97**
Cotterdale Gdns. S73: Womb 1A **48**
Cotterhill La. S43: Brim 1D **168**
Cottesmore Cl. S75: Barn 5B **16**
Cottingham St. S9: Shef 2C **120**
Cotton Mill Row S3: Shef 1E **5** (1F **119**)
Cotton Mill Wlk. S3: Shef 1F **119**
Cotton St. S3: Shef 1E **5** (1F **119**)
Coultas Av. S36: Spink 5F **175**
Countess Rd. S1: Shef 5F **119**
Countryside Way S64: Kiln 6D **66**
County Court
Chesterfield 5A 168
Doncaster 2C 56
Rotherham 4E 97
County Way S70: Barn 6E **17**

Coupe Rd. S3: Shef .6G **107**
Coupland Cl. S41: Old W .2B **162**
Coupland Rd. S65: Roth .2B **98**
Court Cl. DN5: Scaws .4E **39**
Court Pl. S43: Stav .6H **163**
Courtyard, The DN12: Old D .3H **67**
S75: Barn .1H **29**
Coventry Gro. DN2: Don .3G **41**
Coventry Rd. S9: Shef .1F **121**
Cover Cl. S62: H'ley .5A **62**
Coverdale Rd. S7: Shef .3D **132**
Cover Dr. S73: D'fld .4C **34**
Coverleigh Rd. S63: Wath D .2G **65**
Coward Dr. S35: Ough .3E **91**
Cow Ho. La. DN3: Arm .4F **43**
Cow La. S11: Shef .6H **117**
S43: Brim .5D **162**
Cow La. Residential Pk. DN3: Arm .4F **43**
COWLEY .5C **154**
Cowley Cl. S41: Ches .5A **168**
Cowley Dr. S35: Chap .4H **79**
Cowley Gdns. S20: Westf .2F **151**
Cowley Grn. S73: Womb .2E **47**
Cowley Hill S35: Eccl .4H **79**
S61: Thorpe H .4H **79**
Cowley La. S18: Dron, Holme .4A **154**
S35: Chap .3G **79**
Cowley Pl. DN3: Kirk Sa .4C **26**
Cowley Rd. S35: Ough .4E **91**
Cowley Vw. Cl. S35: Chap .4F **79**
Cowley Vw. Rd. S35: Chap .5G **79**
Cowley Way S35: Eccl .4H **79**
Cowlishaw Rd. S11: Shef .6B **118**
Cowood St. S64: Mexb .2E **67**
Cowper Av. S6: Shef .4C **92**
Cowper Cres. S6: Shef .4C **92**
Cowper Dr. S6: Shef .4C **92**
S65: Roth .6A **98**
Cowper Rd. S64: Mexb .1G **67**
Cowpingle La. S43: Brim .5D **162**
Cowrakes Cl. S60: Whist .3B **112**
Cow Rakes La. S60: Whist .3B **112**
Coxley Ct. DN11: Ross .6E **75**
Coxley Mt. DN11: Ross .5F **75**
Cox Pl. S6: Shef .3G **105**
Cox Rd. S6: Shef .3G **105**
Crabtree Av. S5: Shef .4H **107**
Crabtree Cl. S5: Shef .3H **107**
Crabtree Ct. S71: Ard .2C **32**
Crabtree Cres. S5: Shef .3G **107**
Crabtree Dr. S5: Shef .3H **107**
S72: Gt H .5E **21**
Crab Tree Hill La. S36: H'swne .1E **177**
Crabtree La. S5: Shef .3H **107**
Crabtree Pl. S5: Shef .3H **107**
Crabtree Ponds Local Nature Reserve .4H **107**
Crabtree Rd. S5: Shef .3G **107**
Cracknell S3: Shef .1F **5** (1G **119**)
Cradley Dr. S26: Ast .1D **138**
Cradock M. S2: Shef .1B **134**
Cradock Rd. S2: Shef .1B **134**
Craganour Pl. *DN12: Den M .3C 68*
(off Stainton St.)
Cragdale Gro. S20: Mosb .3E **151**
Craggon Dr. S43: New W .2C **162**
Craglands Gro. S40: Ches .3B **166**
Cragside Cl. S41: Ches .5B **168**
Crags Rd. DN12: Den M .3E **69**
Crag Vw. Cl. S35: Ough .2E **91**
Crag Vw. Cres. S35: Ough .2E **91**
Craigholme Cres. DN2: Don .3H **41**
Craig Wlk. S66: Braml .5B **100**
Craithie Rd. DN2: Don .6E **41**
Crakehall Rd. S35: Eccl .5G **79**
Cramfit Cl. S25: Nth A .2G **141**
Cramfit Cres. S25: Dinn .5G **127**
Cramfit Rd. S25: Nth A .1F **141**
Cramlands S75: Dod .3H **29**
Cranborne Dr. S75: Dart .5G **7**
Cranborne Rd. S41: Ches .1F **167**
Cranbrook Rd. DN1: Don .5D **40**
Cranbrook St. S70: Barn .2C **30**
Crane Dr. S61: Kimb .3H **95**
Crane Moor Cl. DN5: H'ton .2H **51**
Crane Rd. S61: Kimb P .6H **81**
Crane Well La. S63: Bolt D .2D **50**
Crane Well Vw. S63: Bolt D .3D **50**
Cranfield Cl. DN3: Arm .5E **43**
Cranford Ct. S20: Mosb .6B **136**
Cranford Dr. S20: Mosb .5B **136**
Cranford Gdns. S71: Roy .2G **9**
Cranleigh Gdns. DN6: Adw S .3B **22**
Cranleigh Rd. S43: Woodt .4E **165**
Cranston Cl. S71: Monk B .4A **18**
Cranswick Way *DN12: Con .4H 69*
(off Milner Ga.)
Cranwell Ct. S63: Gol .6B **36**
Cranwell Rd. DN4: Cant .5E **59**
Cranworth Cl. S65: Roth .3H **97**
Cranworth Pl. S3: Shef .6G **107**
S65: Roth .2G **97**
Cranworth Rd. S3: Shef .6G **107**
S65: Roth .2G **97**
Craven Cl. DN4: Cant .4B **58**
S9: Shef .1F **121**
S71: Roy .2G **9**
Craven Ct. S72: Grim .2C **20**
Craven Rd. S41: Ches .3G **167**
WF9: Hems .1E **13**
Craven St. S3: Shef .1B **4** (2E **119**)
S62: Parkg .5G **83**
Craven Wood Cl. S75: Barn .5H **15**
Crawford Rd. S8: Shef .4E **133**
Crawshaw S3: Shef .2A **4** (2D **118**)
Crawshaw Av. S8: Shef .2C **146**
Crawshaw Gro. S8: Shef .2C **146**
Crawshaw M. S18: Dron W .3B **154**
Crawshaw Rd. DN4: Hex .2H **55**
Cream St. S2: Shef .5G **119**
Crecy Av. DN2: Don .6H **41**
Creighton Av. S62: Rawm .3A **84**
Cresacre Av. DN5: Barnb .1H **51**
Crescent, The DN3: Arm .5F **43**
DN3: Eden .6D **26**
DN6: Woodl .4A **22**
DN9: Blax .1G **77**
DN12: Con .4D **68**
DN12: New E .3C **70**
S17: Tot .5F **145**
S18: Holme .4A **154**
S25: Dinn .5B **128**
S43: Brim .1B **168**
S63: Bolt D .1C **50**
S64: Swint .4A **66**
S65: Roth .3F **97**
S66: Thurc .6C **114**
S72: Cud .1E **19**
S75: Barn .4A **16**
Crescent East, The S66: Sunn .3H **99**
Crescent End S66: Thurc .6C **114**
Crescent Rd. S7: Shef .1D **132**
Crescent West, The S66: Sunn .3G **99**
Cresswell Rd. S9: Shef .2F **121**
S64: Swint .2C **66**
Cresswell St. S75: Barn .6B **16**
Crest Rd. S5: Shef .6G **93**
Crestwood Ct. S5: Shef .6H **93**
Crestwood Gdns. S5: Shef .6H **93**
Creswell St. S64: Mexb .2E **67**
Creswick Av. S5: Shef .3D **92**
Creswick Cl. S40: Walt .2C **170**
S65: Roth .2C **98**
Creswick Greave S35: Gren .3D **92**
Creswick Greave Cl. S5: Shef .2D **92**
Creswick La. S35: Gren .2D **92**
Creswick Rd. S65: Roth .2C **98**
Creswick St. S6: Shef .6C **106**
(not continuous)
Creswick Way S6: Shef .6C **106**
Crewe Hall S10: Shef .5B **118**
Crich Av. S71: Ath .1F **17**
Crich Rd. S43: Ink .1H **169**
Cricketers Wlk. *S2: Shef .2A 120*
(off Castle Ct.)
Cricket Fld. La. S26: Wales B .5E **139**
Cricket Inn Cres. S2: Shef .3B **120**
Cricket Inn Rd. S2: Shef .2H **5** (2H **119**)
Cricket Inn Road Stop (ST) .2A **120**
Cricket La. S35: Eccl .2H **93**
Cricket Vw. Rd. S62: H'ley .5A **62**
Crimicar Av. S10: Shef .6C **116**
Crimicar Cl. S10: Shef .1D **130**
Crimicar Dr. S10: Shef .6C **116**
Crimicar La. S10: Shef .5C **116**
CRIMPSALL .1H **55**
Crimpsall Rd. DN4: Hex .2A **56**
Cripps Av. DN11: New R .5D **74**
Cripps Cl. S66: Malt .6C **102**
Crispin Cl. S12: Shef .4D **134**
Crispin Dr. S12: Shef .4D **134**
Crispin Gdns. S12: Shef .4D **134**
Crispin Rd. S12: Shef .4D **134**
Crochley Cl. DN4: Cant .3C **58**
Croft, The DN5: Ark .5D **24**
DN12: Con .5F **69**
S36: H'swne .1F **177**
S60: Cat .1D **122**
S64: Swint .4A **66**
S74: Els .2D **62**
S75: Bar G .3F **15**
Croft Av. S71: Roy .3G **9**
Croft Bldgs. S1: Shef .2D **4**
Croft Cl. S11: Shef .5G **131**
S25: Laugh M .1G **127**
S73: Womb .3A **48**
S75: Mapp .5A **8**
Croft Ct. DN3: Eden .5C **26**
DN9: Finn .3F **77**
Croft Dr. S75: Mapp .5H **7**
Crofters Cl. S21: Killa .6B **152**
Crofters Ct. DN4: Balb .1B **72**
Croft La. S11: Shef .5G **131**
Croft Lea S18: Dron W .2B **154**
Crofton Av. S6: Shef .2A **106**
Crofton Cl. S18: Dron .3E **155**
Crofton Dr. S63: Bolt D .1B **50**
Crofton Ri. S18: Dron .3E **155**
S35: High G .2C **78**
Croft Rd. DN4: Balb .1F **71**
DN9: Finn .4G **77**
S6: Stann .6E **105**
S12: Shef .3E **135**
S60: Brins .3C **110**
S70: Barn .3H **31**
(not continuous)
S74: Hoyl .5A **46**
Crofts, The S60: Roth .4E **97**
S66: Wick .1G **113**
Crofts Dr. S65: Thry .6D **84**
Croft St. S61: Grea .5C **82**
S70: Wors .5F **31**
Croft Vw. S43: Ink .2H **169**
Cromarty Ri. S18: Dron W .2C **154**
Cromdale Av. S43: New W .2C **162**
Cromer Cl. S62: Rawm .2G **83**
Cromer Rd. DN2: Don .6H **41**
Cromford Av. S71: Ath .2G **17**
Cromford Cl. DN4: Cant .6D **58**
Cromford Ct. *S41: Ches .1E 167*
(off Newbold Rd.)
Cromford Dr. S43: Stav .6G **163**
Cromford St. S2: Shef .5G **119**
Crompton Av. DN5: Don .6G **39**
S70: Barn .2C **30**
Crompton Bus. Pk. DN2: Don .2G **41**
Crompton Rd. DN2: Don .2G **41**
S43: Stav .4B **164**
Cromwell Dr. DN5: Don .2F **55**
Cromwell Ho. DN5: Cus .5F **39**
Cromwell Mt. S70: Wors .4D **30**
Cromwell Rd. DN5: Don .5A **40**
S40: Ches .4G **167**
S64: Mexb .1F **67**
Cromwell St. S6: Shef .1B **118**
S63: Thurn .1D **36**
Cronkhill La. S71: Carl .5A **10**
S71: Carl, Roy .4B **10**
Crooked La. DN12: Old D .1A **86**
Crooked Spire
St Mary & All Saints Church .5A **168**
CROOKES .3A **118**
Crookes S10: Shef .2A **118**
Crookes La. S71: Carl .5G **9**
CROOKESMOOR .2C **118**
Crookesmoor Dr. S6: Shef .2C **118**
Crookesmoor Rd. S6: Shef .3B **118**
S10: Shef .3B **118**
Crookes Rd. DN4: Balb .6H **55**
S10: Shef .3B **118**
Crookes St. S70: Barn .1C **30**
Crookes Valley Rd. S10: Shef .2C **118**
Crookhill Cl. DN12: New E .5B **70**
Crookhill Park Golf Course .1A **88**
Crookhill Rd. DN12: Con .4G **69**
Crook Ho. La. S71: D'fld .1A **34**

Cropston Cl. S41: Has 3B 172
Cropton Rd. S71: Roy 3G 9
Crosby Av. S66: Braml 5B 100
Crosby Ct. S71: Monk B 3A 18
Crosby Rd. S8: Shef 5E 133
Crosby St. S72: Cud 6E 11
CROSS, THE 3H 93
Cross, The S75: Silk 3A 28
Cross Allen Rd. S20: Beig 6G 137
Cross Bank DN4: Balb 5A 56
Cross Bedford St. S1: Shef 1D 118
Cross Burgess St. S1: Shef . . .4E 5 (3F 119)
Cross Butcher St. S63: Thurn 2B 36
Cross Chantrey Rd. S8: Shef 5F 133
Crosscourt Vw. DN4: Bess 5A 56
Cross Dr. S13: Shef 2C 136
Cross Field Dr. S81: Woods 5G 143
Crossfield Dr. S63: Wath D 1F 65
Crossfield Gdns. S35: High G 6C 60
Cross Ga. DN5: Don 4H 39
Crossgate S63: Thurn 3C 36
    S64: Mexb 2H 67
    S75: Mapp 5A 8
Crossgates DN11: Wad 6F 73
Cross Gilpin St. S6: Shef 6D 106
Cross Hill S35: Eccl 3H 93
    S72: Brier 3A 12
Cross Hill Cl. S35: Eccl 3H 93
Cross Ho. Cl. S35: Gren 2A 92
Cross Ho. Rd. S35: Gren 2B 92
Cross Keys La. S74: Hoyl 1F 61
Crossland Dr. S12: Shef 5D 134
Crossland Pl. S12: Shef 4H 57
Crossland St. S64: Swint 4C 66
Crossland Way DN5: Scawt 2F 39
Crossland Way Flats DN5: Scawt 3F 39
Cross La. S10: Shef 2A 118
    S17: Dore 2D 144
    . . . . .1H 155
    S18: Coal A 5H 147
                               (Aston Towers)
    S18: Coal A 5H 147
                                   (Dyche La.)
    S18: Dron 3F 155
    S35: Brom 4A 60
    S36: Cub, Thurl 5A 176
    S36: Stoc 2A 174
    S71: Roy 3B 10
    S81: Woods 4E 143
                                   (Berne Sq.)
    S81: Woods 5G 143
                               (Cross Field Dr.)
Cross La. Cl. S81: Woods 4G 143
Cross La. M. S10: Shef 3A 118
Crossley Cl. S66: Malt 4H 101
Cross London St. S43: New W 3C 162
Cross Myrtle Rd. S2: Shef 1G 133
Cross Pk. Rd. S8: Shef 3F 133
CROSSPOOL 4G 117
Cross Rd. S66: Thurc 5B 114
Cross Smithfield S3: Shef 1C 4 (2E 119)
Cross Sth. St. S61: Grea 5D 82
Cross St. DN4: Balb 5H 55
    DN5: Ben 1A 40
    DN11: New R 6C 74
    DN12: New E 4C 70
    S13: Shef 2C 136
    S21: Killa 3E 153
    S40: Ches 4G 167
    S42: Gras 6D 172
    S43: Brim 6D 162
    S61: Grea 5D 82
    S61: Kimb 4B 96
    S62: Parkg 5G 83
    S63: Gol 5E 37
    S63: Wath D 6F 49
    S65: Thry 6D 84
    S66: Braml 5A 100
    S66: Malt 5B 102
    S70: Wors 4G 31
    S71: Monk B 4H 17
    S72: Grim 2C 20
    S72: Gt H 1F 35
    S73: Womb 2F 47
    S74: Hoyl 1G 61
    S75: Bar G 4E 15
    S75: Barn 5C 8
Cross Turner St. S2: Shef . . .5G 5 (4G 119)
Cross Wlk. S11: Shef 5E 119
                              (off London Rd.)

Crossway S64: Swint 4A 66
Crossways DN2: Don 3G 41
    S63: Bolt D 2B 50
Crossways, The S2: Shef 5D 120
Crossways Nth. DN2: Don 3G 41
Crossways Sth. DN2: Don 4G 41
Cross Wellington St. S43: New W . . .3C 162
Crowden Wlk. S75: Barn 1H 29
Crowder Av. S5: Shef 6E 93
Crowder Cl. S5: Shef 1F 107
Crowder Cres. S5: Shef 1F 107
Crowder Rd. S5: Shef 6F 93
Crowgate S25: Sth A 5F 141
Crowland Rd. S5: Shef 6G 93
Crow La. S18: Uns 5B 156
    S41: Ches 5A 168
Crowley Dr. S63: Wath D 2F 65
Crown Av. S70: Barn 3F 31
    S72: Cud 4F 19
Crown Cl. S43: New W 3C 162
    S61: Kimb 2H 95
    S70: Barn 3F 31
Crown Court
    Doncaster 1C 56
Crownhill La. S66: Mick 1F 101
Crown Hill Rd. S70: Barn 1H 29
Crownhill Rd. S60: Brins 3B 112
Crown Pl. S2: Shef 3H 5 (3H 119)
Crown Rd. S41: Ches 3H 167
Crown St. S64: Swint 3C 66
    S70: Barn 3F 31
    S74: Hoyl 6A 46
Crown Well Ct. S71: Ard 2C 32
                            (off Crown Well Hill)
Crown Well Hill S71: Ard 2C 32
Crowther Pl. S7: Shef 6E 119
Crow Tree La. S64: Mexb 4E 51
                              (not continuous)
Croydon St. S11: Shef 6E 119
Crucible Theatre, The 3F 5 (3G 119)
Cruck Cl. S18: Dron W 2D 154
Cruise Rd. S11: Shef 6G 117
Crummock Rd. S7: Shef 3D 132
Crummock Way S71: Ard 2E 33
Crumpsall Dr. S5: Shef 3E 107
Crumpsall Rd. S5: Shef 3E 107
Crumwell Rd. S61: Kimb P 6G 81
Crusader Dr. DN5: Sprot 1F 55
Crystal Peaks Shop. Cen.
    S20: Water 6F 137
Crystal Peaks Stop (ST) 6E 137
CUBLEY 6C 176
Cubley Brook Ct. S36: Cub 5C 176
Cubley Ri. Rd. S36: Cub 6C 176
CUDWORTH 1E 19
CUDWORTH COMMON 3F 19
Cudworth Parkway S72: Cud 2D 18
Cudworth Vw. S72: Grim 2B 20
Cullabine Rd. S2: Shef 1D 134
Cull Row S36: Spink 4H 175
Cumberland Av. DN2: Don 6G 41
Cumberland Cl. S70: Wors 5E 31
    S74: Hoyl 5B 46
Cumberland Cres. S35: Chap 4G 79
Cumberland Dr. S71: Ard 2C 32
Cumberland Pl. DN12: Den M 3C 68
Cumberland St. S74: Hoyl 5B 46
Cumberland St. S1: Shef 6D 4 (4F 119)
    S63: Bolt D 3B 50
Cumbrian Wlk. S75: Barn 6A 16
                              (off Warner Rd.)
Cumwell La. S66: Hel 1C 114
CUNDY CROSS 1B 32
Cundy St. S6: Shef 1B 118
Cunliffe St. S18: Coal A 6H 147
Cunningham Rd. DN1: Don 2C 56
Cupola S3: Shef 1D 4 (4F 119)
Cupola Yd. S60: Roth 4D 96
Curbar Curve S43: Ink 2G 169
Curlew Av. S21: Ecki 1C 158
Curlew Ct. DN11: Ross 5D 74
Curlew Ridge S2: Shef 4A 120
Curlew Ri. S61: Thorpe H 2D 80
Curzen Cres. DN3: Kirk Sa 4D 26
Curzon Av. S18: Dron 4E 155
Curzon Cl. S21: Killa 4C 152
CUSWORTH 5F 39

Cusworth Gro. DN11: Ross 6E 75
Cusworth Hall 6E 39
Cusworth Ho. DN1: Don 2B 56
                               (off Camden Pl.)
Cusworth La. DN5: Cus 5E 39
Cusworth Park Country Pk. 6D 38
Cusworth Rd. DN5: Don 3H 39
Cuthbert Bank Rd. S6: Shef 5C 106
Cuthbert Cooper Pl. S9: Shef 2F 121
Cuthbert Rd. S6: Shef 5C 106
Cutler Cl. S21: Killa 3A 152
Cutlers Av. S70: Barn 2C 30
Cutlers Gate S4: Shef 2H 119
Cutlers Wlk. S2: Shef 1F 133
Cuttholme Cl. S40: Ash 4C 166
Cuttholme Rd. S40: Ash 4C 166
Cuttholme Way S40: Ches 4C 166
CUTTHORPE 1A 166
CUTTHORPE COMMON END 1A 166
Cutthorpe Grange S41: Up N 1B 166
Cutthorpe Rd. S42: Up N 1A 166
Cutts Av. S63: Wath D 1E 65
Cutts Fld. Vw. S71: Roy 1G 9
Cutts Ter. S8: Shef 1E 133
Cutty La. S75: Barn 5C 16
Cyclops St. S4: Shef 4B 108
Cygnet Cl. S63: Bramp B 5A 48
Cypress Av. DN9: Auck 3A 76
    S8: Shef 1H 147
Cypress Cl. S21: Killa 5B 152
Cypress Ga. S35: Chap 4E 79
Cypress Gro. DN12: Con 6C 68
    S26: Wales 5G 139
Cypress Hgts. S71: Smi 3F 17
Cypress Rd. S70: Barn 3G 31
Cyprus Rd. S8: Shef 3F 133
Cyprus Ter. S6: Shef 6C 106

D

Dade Av. S43: Ink 2G 169
Daffodil Rd. S5: Shef 1C 108
Dagnam Cl. S2: Shef 1C 134
Dagnam Cres. S2: Shef 1C 134
Dagnam Dr. S2: Shef 1C 134
Dagnam Pl. S2: Shef 2D 134
Dagnam Rd. S2: Shef 1C 134
Daisy Bank S3: Shef 1A 4 (2D 118)
Daisy Dr. S70: Barn 3F 31
Daisy Gro. S5: Shef 1C 108
Daisy Wlk. S3: Shef 2B 4 (2E 119)
    S20: Beig 5G 137
Dakota Way DN4: Don 3F 57
Dalbury Rd. S18: Dron W 3A 154
Dalby Cft. S36: Pen 4E 177
Dalby Gdns. S20: Shef 1H 151
Dalby Gro. S20: Sot 6A 138
Dale, The S8: Shef 5E 133
Dale Av. S65: Roth 5B 98
Dale Bank Cres. S43: New W 3C 162
Dalebrook Ct. S10: Shef 5F 117
Dalebrook M. S10: Shef 5F 117
Dale Cl. S43: Stav 6H 163
    S71: Ath 1F 17
Dale Grn. Rd. S70: Wors 6E 31
Dale Gro. S63: Bolt D 3A 50
Dale Hill Cl. S66: Malt 4A 102
Dale Hill Rd. S66: Malt 4G 101
Dale Rd. DN12: Con 4F 69
    S18: Dron 4G 155
    S21: Killa 4D 152
    S62: Rawm 3G 83
    S65: Roth 6B 98
    S66: Wick 6F 99
Dale Side S10: Shef 5A 118
Dale St. S62: Rawm 2G 83
Daleswood Av. S70: Barn 1A 30
Daleswood Dr. S70: Wors 5A 32
Dale Vw. WF9: Hems 1G 13
Daleview Rd. S8: Shef 6C 132
Dalewood Av. S8: Shef 1B 146
Dalewood Cl. S41: Ches 1D 172
Dalewood Dr. S8: Shef 1B 146
Dalewood Ri. S8: Shef 1B 146
Dalmore Rd. S7: Shef 3B 132
Dalroyd La. S6: Bradf 1A 104
DALTON .2B 98

Dalton Ct. DN12: Den M 3C 68
S8: Shef 1E 133
Dalton La. S65: Dalt, Roth 1C 98
DALTON MAGNA 3E 99
DALTON PARVA 2C 98
Dalton Ter. S70: Barn 2F 31
Dalvey Way S43: New W 1C 162
Damasel Cl. S35: Wharn S 1C 90
Damasel La. S35: Wharn S 1C 90
Damasel Rd. S35: Wharn S 2A 90
DAM END .1G 59
Damer St. S10: Shef 3C 118
Dam Head S61: Grea 3C 82
Dam Ings La. S26: Ast 1F 139
Damon Dr. S43: Brim 6E 163
Damson Cft. S43: Hol 5F 163
Damsteads S75: Dod 3H 29
Danbury Cl. S42: Gras 6D 172
Danby Av. S41: Old W 4A 162
Danby Rd. S26: Kiv P 5C 140
Danebrook Cl. S2: Shef 5F 121
Danebrook Ct. S2: Shef 5F 121
Danebrook Dr. S2: Shef 5F 121
Dane Cl. S63: Thurn 2D 36
Danesthorpe Cl. DN2: Don 4H 41
Dane St. S63: Thurn 2D 36
Dane St. Nth. S63: Thurn 2D 36
Dane St. Sth. S63: Thurn 2D 36
Danesway DN5: Scawt 1G 39
Danethorpe Way DN12: Con 6D 68
Danewood Av. S2: Shef 5F 121
Danewood Cft. S2: Shef 5F 121
Danewood Gdns. S2: Shef 5F 121
Danewood Gro. S2: Shef 5F 121
Daniel Hill S6: Shef 1D 118
Daniel Hill Ct. S6: Shef 1C 118
Daniel Hill M. S6: Shef 1D 118
Daniel Hill St. S6: Shef 1C 118
Daniel Hill Ter. S6: Shef 1D 118
Daniel Hill Wlk. S6: Shef 1D 118
Daniel La. S62: Neth Hau 2C 82
Daniels Dr. S26: Augh 5B 124
Dannemora Cl. S9: Shef 5F 109
Dannemora Dr. S9: Shef 5F 109
Danum Ct. DN12: Den M 3C 68
Danum Dr. S65: Rota 3G 97
Danum Retail Pk. DN5: Don 5H 39
Danum Rd. DN4: Don 2E 57
Dara St. S9: Shef 5E 95
Darcy Cl. S26: Swal 6C 124
Darcy Rd. S21: Ecki 1D 158
Daresbury Cl. S2: Shef 2A 134
Daresbury Dr. S2: Shef 2A 134
Daresbury Pl. S2: Shef 2A 134
Daresbury Rd. S2: Shef 2A 134
Daresbury Vw. S2: Shef 2A 134
DARFIELD 5B 34
Darfield Av. S20: Mosb 6A 136
Darfield Cl. DN11: Ross 5E 75
S20: Mosb 6A 136
Darfield Ho. DN1: Don 2B 56
(off Oxford Pl.)
Darfield Rd. S72: Cud 3F 19
Dargle Av. DN2: Don 5F 41
Darhaven S73: D'fld 4B 34
Dark La. S43: Brim C 4D 168
S44: Cal 6E 169
S70: Barn 3A 30
S70: Wors 1G 45
Darley S70: Wors 5H 31
Darley Av. S70: Wors 4D 30
S71: Ath 2F 17
Darley Cliff Cotts. S70: Wors 4G 31
Darley Cl. S43: Stav 5B 164
S71: Ath 1F 17
Darley Gro. S6: Stann 5E 105
S70: Wors 5H 31
Darley Pk. S61: Kimb 5A 96
Darley Ter. S75: Barn 6C 16
Darley Yd. S70: Wors 5G 31
DARNALL 2F 121
Darnall Dr. S9: Shef 1E 121
Darnall Rd. S9: Shef 6D 108
Darnall Station (Rail) 2F 121
Darnley Dr. S2: Shef 6D 120
Darrington Dr. DN4: Warm 1E 71
Darrington Pl. S71: Lund 5B 18
Dart Gro. DN9: Auck 1H 59
Dartmouth Rd. DN4: Cant 6E 59

DARTON 5F 7
Darton Bus. Pk. S75: Dart 6F 7
Darton Common Sports Cen. 6C 6
Darton Hall Cl. S75: Dart 5G 7
Darton Hall Dr. S75: Dart 5G 7
Darton La.
S75: Dart, Mapp 6G 7
Darton Rd. S75: Cawt 3A 14
Darton Station (Rail) 5F 7
Darton St. S70: Stair 2A 32
Dartree Cl. S73: D'fld 4A 34
Dartree Wlk. S73: D'fld 4A 34
Dart Sq. S3: Shef 2A 4 (2D 118)
Darwall Cl. S35: High G 6C 60
Darwent La. S35: Ough 6C 90
Darwent Rd. S41: Ches 2B 168
Darwin Av. S40: Ches 3F 167
Darwin Cl. S10: Shef 4G 117
Darwin La. S10: Shef 4G 117
Darwin Rd. S6: Shef 2A 106
S40: Ches 4G 167
Darwin Yd. S74: Els 2E 63
(off Wath Rd.)
Darwynn Av. S64: Swint 3H 65
Davey Rd. S63: Gol 4C 36
Davian Way S40: Walt 2F 171
David Cl. S13: Shef 1E 137
David La. S10: Shef 1B 130
Davids Dr. S42: W'orth 6F 171
Davies Cl. S25: Dinn 4A 128
Davies Dr. S64: Swint 5C 66
Davis Cl. S65: Dalt 1C 98
Davis St. S65: Roth 3H 97
Davy Dr. S66: Malt 4A 102
S66: Sunn 3G 99
Davy Rd.
DN12: Den M 3B 68
Dawber La. S21: Killa 3E 153
Dawcroft Av. S70: Wors 5F 31
Dawlands Cl. S2: Shef 4E 121
(not continuous)
Dawlands Dr. S2: Shef 5E 121
Daw La. DN5: Ben 6A 24
DN11: Wad 6B 72
Dawson Av. S62: Rawm 6D 64
Dawson Cft. S61: Grea 4B 82
Dawson La. S63: Wath D 2F 65
Dawson Ter. S26: Kiv P 6A 140
Daw Wood DN5: Ben 5B 24
Daycroft S71: Monk B 3C 18
Dayhouse Ct. S75: Barn 4A 16
Dayhouse La. S75: Barn 3A 16
Dayhouse Way S75: Barn 4A 16
Daykin Cl. S75: Kexb 6E 7
Daylands Av. DN12: Con 5D 68
Day St. S70: Barn 2D 30
Deacon Cl. DN11: Ross 5E 75
Deacon Cres. DN11: New R 5B 74
S66: Malt 6B 102
Deacons Way S71: Monk B 5H 17
Deadman's Hole La.
S9: Tins 6H 95
S60: Roth 5B 96
Deakins Wlk. S10: Shef 5G 117
DN11: Ross 5E 75
Dean Cl. DN5: Sprot 2E 55
DN11: Ross 5E 75
Deane Fld. Vw. S20: Water 6E 137
Deanhead Ct. S20: Mosb 6B 136
Deanhead Dr. S20: Mosb 6A 136
Dean La. S65: Dalt M 4D 98
Deans Cl. S43: Brim 1C 168
Deansfield Cl. DN3: Arm 5E 43
Dean St. S70: Barn 1C 30
Deans Way S71: Monk B 4H 17
Dearden Ct. S35: Eccl 2G 93
DEARNE 5D 36
Dearne Cl. S73: Womb 3A 48
Dearne Ct. S9: Shef 2D 108
S75: Wool G 3F 7
Dearne Hall Fold S75: Bar G 2G 15
Dearne Hall Rd. S75: Bar G 2G 15
Dearne La. S63: Wath D 4D 48
Dearne Mills S75: Dart 6F 7
Dearne Playhouse 6C 36
Dearne Rd. S63: Bolt D, Wath D 4H 49
S73: Bramp 4B 48
Dearne Rd. Flatlets S63: Bolt D 3A 50
(off Dearne Rd.)
Dearneside Leisure Cen. 6D 36

Dearne St. DN12: Con 3G 69
S9: Shef 2D 108
S72: Gt H 1F 35
S75: Dart 5G 7
Dearne Valley Leisure Cen. 2B 68
Dearne Valley Parkway
S63: Bolt D, Wath D 2D 48
S63: Gol 5F 35
S72: Bill 5F 35
S73: Bramp, Womb 1E 61
S74: Hoyl 1E 61
Dearne Vw. S63: Gol 5C 36
Dearneway S63: Wath D 6G 49
Dearnley Vw. S75: Barn 4C 16
Deben Cl. S40: Walt 2D 170
Decoy Bank DN4: Don 4C 56
Decoy Bank Nth. DN4: Don 3C 56
Decoy Bank Sth.
DN4: Don 4C 56
DEEPCAR 3H 175
Deepcar La. S72: Cud 5H 19
Deep Carrs La. S81: Work 6F 143
Deepdale Cl. S43: Stav 3B 164
Deepdale Cft. S75: Bar G 3G 15
Deepdale Rd. S61: Kimb 4H 95
Deep La. S5: Shef 3B 94
(not continuous)
DEEP PIT 6C 120
Deepsic La. S44: Ark T 1H 173
Deeps La. DN10: Miss 6H 77
Deepwell Av. S20: Half 4G 151
Deepwell Bank S20: Half 4G 151
Deepwell Ct. S20: Half 4G 151
Deepwell Dr. S20: Half 4H 151
Deepwell M. S20: Half 4H 151
Deepwell Vw. S20: Half 4G 151
Deerlands Av. S5: Shef 4D 92
Deerlands Cl. S5: Shef 4D 92
Deerlands Mt. S5: Shef 4C 92
Deerlands Rd. S40: Ash 5C 166
Deer Leap Dr. S65: Thry 6F 85
Deer Pk. Cl. S6: Shef 6F 105
Deer Pk. Pl. S6: Shef 6F 105
Deer Pk. Rd. S6: Shef 6F 105
S65: Thry 5F 85
Deer Pk. Vw. S6: Shef 6F 105
Deer Pk. Way S6: Shef 6G 105
De Houton Cl. S26: Tod 3B 140
Deightonby St. S63: Thurn 2D 36
De Lacy Dr. S70: Wors 5F 31
Delamere Cl. S20: Sot 6H 137
De La Salle Dr. S4: Shef 5H 107
Delf St. S2: Shef 1G 133
Dell, The S40: Ash 5C 166
S66: Sunn 2H 99
Della Av. S70: Barn 2C 30
Dell Av. S72: Grim 6B 12
Dell Cres. DN4: Hex 3G 55
Delmar Way S66: Flan 4G 99
Delph Bank S40: Walt 2F 171
Delph Cl. S75: Silk 1B 28
Delph Edge S35: Green M 1G 175
Delph Ho. Rd. S10: Shef 3G 117
Delph M. S35: Green M 1G 175
Delta Cl. DN9: Finn 2D 76
Delta Pl. S65: Roth 3A 98
Delta Way S66: Malt 4C 102
Delves Av. S12: Shef 4D 136
Delves Cl. S12: Shef 4D 136
S40: Walt 1E 171
Delves Dr. S12: Shef 5D 136
Delves La. S26: Wales B 5C 138
Delves Pl. S12: Shef 5C 136
Delves Rd. S12: Shef 5C 136
S21: Killa 4C 152
Delves Ter. S12: Shef 5D 136
Denaby Av. DN12: Con 5C 68
Denaby Ings Nature Reserve 6D 52
Denaby La. DN12: Old D, Den M 1F 85
Denaby La. Ind. Est. DN12: Den M . . .3B 68
(not continuous)
DENABY MAIN 2D 68
DEN BANK 3F 117
Den Bank Av. S10: Shef 3F 117
Den Bank Cl. S10: Shef 3G 117
Den Bank Cres. S10: Shef 3F 117
Den Bank Dr. S10: Shef 3F 117
Denbrook La. DN12: Con 6G 69

Denby Rd. S43: Ink 1H **169**
S71: Smi .1E **17**
Denby St. DN5: Ben 6H **23**
S2: Shef .5E **119**
Denby Way S66: Hel 5D **100**
Dencombe Ter. WF9: Sth K 5H **13**
Dene Cl. S66: Wick 6H **99**
Dene Cres. S65: Roth 2A **98**
Denehall Rd. DN3: Kirk Sa 5D **26**
Dene La. S1: Shef 6B **4** (4E **119**)
Dene Pl. S13: Shef 4A **122**
Dene Rd. S65: Roth 2A **98**
Denham Rd. S11: Shef 5D **118**
Denholme Cl. S3: Shef 1G **119**
Denison Ct. S70: Barn 2E **31**
Denison Rd. DN4: Hex 2A **56**
Denman Rd. S63: Wath D 6E **49**
Denman St. S65: Roth 2F **97**
Denmark Rd. S2: Shef 2G **133**
Denson Cl. S2: Shef 2G **133**
Dent La. S12: Shef 6A **136**
Denton Rd. S8: Shef 4E **133**
Dentons Grn. La. DN3: Kirk Sa 4C **26**
Denton St. S71: Barn 6E **17**
Derby Pl. S2: Shef 2H **133**
Derby Rd. DN2: Don 2H **41**
S40: Birdh, Ches 3H **171**
S42: W'orth 4H **171**
Derbyshire Ct. DN3: Arm 3G **43**
S8: Shef 5G **133**
Derbyshire La. S8: Shef 3E **133**
Derby St. S2: Shef 2G **133**
S70: Barn 1C **30**
Derby Ter. S2: Shef 2H **133**
Derek Dooley Way
S3: Shef 1G **5** (1G **119**)
S4: Shef 1G **5** (1G **119**)
Derriman Av. S11: Shef 4A **132**
Derriman Cl. S11: Shef 4A **132**
Derriman Dr. S11: Shef 4A **132**
Derriman Glen S11: Shef 4A **132**
Derriman Gro. S11: Shef 4A **132**
Derry Gro. S63: Thurn 3B **36**
Derwent Cl. S18: Dron 1G **155**
S25: Nth A 1A **142**
S71: Ath .1G **17**
Derwent Ct. S17: Bradw 5H **145**
S60: Roth 2G **111**
Derwent Cres. S41: Ches 1E **167**
S60: Brins 5C **110**
S71: Ath .1G **17**
Derwent Dr. DN3: Kirk Sa 5C **26**
S35: Chap 3D **78**
S62: Rawm 4G **83**
S64: Mexb 6H **51**
Derwent Gdns. S63: Gol 6D **36**
Derwent Ho. *S41: Ches 1E 167*
(off Ulverston Rd.)
Derwent Pl. DN5: Sprot 3C **54**
S73: Womb 3A **48**
Derwent Rd. S18: Dron 1G **155**
S61: Wing 5B **82**
S64: Mexb 6H **51**
S71: Ath .1F **17**
Derwent St. S2: Shef 2A **120**
Derwent Ter. S64: Mexb 6F **51**
Derwent Vw. S43: Mas M 3F **165**
Derwent Way S63: Wath D 4C **48**
Dettori M. S25: Laugh C 4F **127**
Deveron Rd. S20: Half 3G **151**
Devizes Cl. S40: Birdh 2G **171**
Devon Ct. DN12: Den M 4C **68**
Devon Dr. S43: Brim 6E **163**
Devon Pk. Vw. S43: Brim 6E **163**
Devon Rd. S4: Shef 4H **107**
Devonshire Av. E. S41: Has 2B **172**
Devonshire Av. Nth.
S43: New W 2C **162**
Devonshire Bus. Pk. S1: Shef 5C **4**
Devonshire Cl. S17: Dore 4G **145**
S18: Dron 4E **155**
S41: Ches 6G **161**
S43: Stav 4B **164**
Devonshire Ct. S17: Dore 4G **145**
S43: Brim 1C **168**
Devonshire Dr. S17: Dore 3F **145**
S25: Nth A 6H **127**
S75: Barn 4C **16**
Devonshire Glen S17: Dore 4G **145**
Devonshire Gro. S17: Dore 4F **145**
Devonshire La. S1: Shef 4C **4** (3E **119**)
Devonshire Pk. S43: Brim 6D **162**
Devonshire Rd. DN2: Don 5G **41**
S17: Dore 3F **145**
S66: Malt 4B **102**
Devonshire Rd. E. S41: Has 2B **172**
Devonshire Rd. Nth. S43: New W . . .3C **162**
Devonshire St. S3: Shef 4B **4** (3E **119**)
S41: Ches 5H **167**
S43: Brim 6D **162**
S43: Stav 4B **164**
S61: Roth 4C **96**
(not continuous)
Devonshire Ter. Rd. S17: Dore 3E **145**
Devonshire Vs. *S41: Ches 6G 161*
(off Occupation Rd.)
Dewar Dr. S7: Shef 4B **132**
Dewfield Cl. S72: Grim 1B **20**
Dewhill Av. S60: Whist 3A **112**
Dial, The S5: Shef 6A **94**
Dial Cl. S5: Shef 6H **93**
Dial Ho. Ct. S6: Shef 3A **106**
Dial Ho. Rd. S6: Shef 4H **105**
Dial Way S5: Shef 6H **93**
Diamond St. S73: Womb 1G **47**
Dickan Gdns. DN3: Arm 5G **43**
Dickens Cl. S60: Cat 6C **110**
Dickenson Ct. S35: Chap 3E **79**
Dickenson Rd. S41: Ches 1A **172**
Dickens Rd. S62: Rawm 1A **84**
Dickey La. S6: Shef 5H **91**
Dickinson Pl. S70: Barn 3E **31**
Dickinson Rd. S5: Shef 3A **94**
S70: Barn 3E **31**
Didcot Cl. S40: Birdh 2G **171**
Digby Cl. S61: Kimb 2H **95**
Dike Hill S62: H'ley 5B **62**
Dikelands Mt. S35: High G 2C **78**
Dillington Rd. S70: Barn 3E **31**
Dillington Sq. S70: Barn 3E **31**
Dillington Ter. *S70: Barn 3E 31*
(off Walnut Cl.)
Dingle Bank S44: Cal 1D **172**
Dingle La. S44: Cal 1D **172**
Dinmore Cl. DN4: Balb 2H **71**
DINNINGTON 5A **128**
Dinnington Bus. Cen. S25: Dinn 4G **127**
Dinnington Business Incubation Cen.
S25: Dinn 4G **127**
Dinnington Rd. S8: Shef 4E **133**
S26: Tod .1C **140**
S81: Woods 4D **142**
Dirleton Dr. DN4: Warm 6E **55**
Discovery Way S41: Whit M 5H **161**
S66: Malt 4G **101**
Disraeli Gro. S66: Malt 4H **101**
Distillery M. S74: Els 2E **63**
Distillery Side S74: Els 2E **63**
Ditchingham St. S4: Shef 6H **107**
Division La. S1: Shef 4D **4** (3F **119**)
Division St. S1: Shef 4C **4** (3E **119**)
S43: Stav 6H **163**
Dixon Cres. DN4: Balb 5G **55**
Dixon Cft. S43: New W 2C **162**
Dixon Dr. S35: Wharn S 2A **90**
Dixon La. S1: Shef 2G **5** (2G **119**)
Dixon Rd. DN12: New E 4B **70**
S6: Shef .3A **106**
S41: Ches 6A **168**
Dixon St. S6: Shef 1E **119**
S65: Roth 3F **97**
Dobbin Ct. S11: Shef 1H **131**
Dobbin Hill S11: Shef 2H **131**
Dobbin La. S18: B'low 6B **154**
Dobb La. S6: Stann 2A **116**
Dobbs Cl. S21: Killa 4B **152**
Dobcroft Av. S7: Shef 5A **132**
Dobcroft Cl. S11: Shef 4H **131**
Dobcroft Rd. S7: Shef 4H **131**
S11: Shef 4H **131**
Dobie St. S70: Barn 2E **31**
Dobroyd Ter. S74: Jum 5C **46**
Dobson Pl. S43: Ink 2G **169**
Dobsyke Cl. S70: Wors 5A **32**
Dockin Hill Rd. DN1: Don 6C **40**
Dock Wlk. S40: Ches 6F **167**
Doctor La. S9: Shef 6D **108**
Dodds Cl. S60: Roth 6D **96**
Dodd St. S6: Shef 5B **106**
Dodson Dr. S13: Shef 4A **122**
Dodsworth St. S64: Mexb 2E **67**
DODWORTH 3G **29**
DODWORTH BOTTOM 4G **29**
Dodworth Bus. Pk. S75: Dod 2E **29**
Dodworth Rd. S70: Barn 2H **29**
Dodworth Station (Rail) 3F **29**
Doe La. S21: Trow 6E **149**
S70: Wors 1D **44**
Doe Quarry La. S25: Dinn 4A **128**
Doe Quarry Pl. S25: Dinn 5B **128**
Doe Quarry Ter. S25: Dinn 5A **128**
Doe Royd Cres. S5: Shef 5C **92**
Doe Royd Dr. S5: Shef 5D **92**
Doe Royd La. S5: Shef 5C **92**
Dog Cft. La. DN5: Ark 1F **41**
Dog Hill S72: Shaft 3E **11**
Dog Hill Dr. S72: Shaft 3F **11**
Dog Kennel Hill S26: Kiv S 6E **141**
Dog Kennels La. S25: Sth A 6E **141**
S26: Kiv S 6E **141**
Dog La. S70: Barn 1D **30**
Dolcliffe Cl. S64: Mexb 1E **67**
DOLCLIFFE COMMON 2F **67**
Dolcliffe Rd. S64: Mexb 1F **67**
Doles Av. S71: Roy 3G **9**
Doles Cres. S71: Roy 3G **9**
Doles La. S60: Up W, Whist 4B **112**
Doleswood Dr. S25: Laugh M 2H **127**
Dome Leisure Centre, The 3G **57**
Domine La. S60: Roth 4E **97**
Dominoe Gro. S12: Shef 3G **135**
Don Av. S6: Shef 1H **105**
S35: Wharn S 2A **90**
DONCASTER 1B **56**
Doncaster Gate S65: Roth 4F **97**
Doncaster Golf Course 1D **74**
Doncaster Ind. Pk. DN5: Scawt 4G **39**
Doncaster Intl. Railport DN4: Don . . .4C **56**
Doncaster Knights RUFC 4B **42**
Doncaster La. DN6: Adw S, Woodl . . .3D **22**
(not continuous)
Doncaster Leisure & Business Pk.
DN4: Don 3G **57**
Doncaster Museum & Art Gallery 1C **56**
Doncaster North (Park & Ride) 1E **39**
Doncaster Pl. S65: Roth 3H **97**
Doncaster Race Course 2G **57**
Doncaster RLFC 4F **57**
Doncaster Rd. DN3: Arm 4C **42**
DN3: Barn D, Eden, Kirk Sa 6A **26**
DN3: Brant 4E **59**
(not continuous)
DN5: Barnb 1A **52**
(not continuous)
DN5: Ben, Holm 3G **23**
DN5: Hick 4F **37**
DN5: High M 3D **52**
(not continuous)
DN5: H'ton 2G **51**
DN6: Highf 6D **22**
DN9: Finn 3F **77**
DN12: Con 4G **69**
DN12: Con, Den M 1B **68**
S63: Gol 5D **36**
S63: Wath D 6H **49**
S64: Mexb 2G **67**
S65: Dalt, Thry 1B **98**
S65: Hoot R, Thry 4E **85**
S65: Roth 4F **97**
S66: B'well 6B **88**
S70: Barn, Stair 1E **31**
S71: Ard, Stair 2B **32**
S73: D'fld 4C **34**
Doncaster Rovers FC 4F **57**
Doncaster South (Park & Ride) 3E **75**
Doncaster Squash Club 1E **57**
Doncaster Station (Rail) 1B **56**
Doncaster St.
S3: Shef 1C **4** (2E **119**)
Doncaster Superbowl 3F **57**
Doncaster Town Moor Golf Course . . .1H **57**
Don Dr. S70: Barn 3A **32**
Donetsk Way S12: Shef 5B **136**
Donetsk Way Stop (ST) 6D **136**
Don Grange S64: Kiln 6D **66**
Don Hill Height S35: Green M 1E **175**
S36: Stoc 1E **175**

Donnington Rd. S2: Shef 5A **120**
  S64: Mexb 6A **52**
Donovan Cl. S5: Shef 1D **106**
Donovan Rd. S5: Shef 1D **106**
Don Pottery Yd. S64: Swint 3E **67**
Don Rd. S9: Shef 5C **108**
Donstone Vw. S25: Dinn 6G **127**
Don St. DN1: Don 5C **40**
  DN12: Con 3G **69**
  S36: Pen 5F **177**
  S60: Roth 4E **97**
Don Ter. S36: Thurl 3B **176**
Don Valley Stadium 5D **108**
Don Vw. DN5: Scaws 4D **38**
  S64: Mexb 1A **68**
Dorchester Pl. S70: Wors 5E **31**
Dorcliffe Lodge S10: Shef 6H **117**
DORE 3E **145**
Dore and Totley Golf Course 5B **146**
Dore Cl. S17: Dore 3H **145**
Dore Ct. *S17: Dore* *3H* **145**
       (off Ladies Spring Dr.)
Dore Hall Cft. S17: Dore 3E **145**
Dore Ho. Ind. Est. S13: Shef 6D **122**
Dore Lodge Gdns. S17: Dore 3G **145**
Dore Rd. S17: Dore 3E **145**
Dore & Totley Station (Rail) 3H **145**
Dorking St. S4: Shef 1H **119**
Dorothy Hyman Sports & Leisure Cen.
  . . . . .2F **19**
Dorothy Rd. S6: Shef 3A **106**
Dorothy Va. S40: Ash 4D **166**
Dorset Av. S43: Brim 6E **163**
Dorset Cl. S43: Brim 6E **163**
Dorset Cres. DN2: Don 5H **41**
Dorset Dr. S43: Brim 6E **163**
Dorset St. S10: Shef 4D **118**
Douglas Rd. DN4: Balb 5F **55**
  S3: Shef 6E **107**
  S41: Ches 2B **168**
Douglas St. S60: Roth 4F **97**
Douse Cft. La. S10: Shef 2A **130**
Dovebush Way S75: Bar G 3G **15**
Dovecliffe Rd. S73: Womb 1B **46**
Dovecliffe Vw. *S70: Wors* *5H* **31**
       (off Allendale)
Dove Cl. S63: Bolt D 2C **50**
  S73: Womb 3A **48**
Dovecote S73: Womb 3F **47**
Dovecote M. S71: Monk B 4H **17**
Dovecott Lea S20: Sot 5A **138**
Dovedale S70: Wors 6G **31**
Dovedale Av. S43: Ink 3G **169**
Dovedale Ct. S41: Ches 1E **167**
Dovedale Pl. S70: Wors 6G **31**
Dovedale Rd. S7: Shef 3C **132**
  S65: Roth 6B **98**
Dove Hill S71: Roy 2A **10**
Doveholes Dr. S13: Shef 4A **122**
Dove La. S26: Ast 2D **138**
Dovercourt Rd. S2: Shef 5B **120**
  S61: Roth 3B **96**
Dover Gdns. S3: Shef 1B **4** (2E **119**)
Doveridge Cl. S41: Old W 4H **161**
Dove Rd. S73: Womb 3A **48**
Dover Rd. S11: Shef 5B **118**
Dover St. S3: Shef 1B **4** (2E **119**)
Doveside Dr. S73: D'fld 5B **34**
Dove Valley Way S73: Womb 6G **33**
Dove Vw. S73: Womb 6E **33**
Dowcarr La. S26: Wooda 5H **153**
Dowdeswell St. S41: Ches 4H **167**
Dowfin S35: High G 1C **78**
Dowland Av. S35: High G 6C **60**
Dowland Cl. S35: High G 6D **60**
Dowland Ct. S35: High G 6C **60**
Dowland Gdns. S35: High G 6D **60**
Downgate Dr. S4: Shef 4C **108**
Downham Rd. S5: Shef 1H **107**
Downing La. S3: Shef 1B **4** (1E **119**)
Downing Rd. S8: Shef 2D **146**
Downing Sq. S36: Pen 5D **176**
Downland Cl. DN4: Balb 2G **71**
Downlands S43: Brim 1C **168**
Downs Cres. S75: Barn 5A **16**
Downs Ho. Cl. S72: Sth H 1G **11**
Down's Row S60: Roth 4E **97**
Dragoon Ct. S5: Shef 5C **106**

Drake Cl. S35: Burn 3D **78**
Drake Head La. DN12: Con 4H **69**
DRAKEHOUSE 5E **137**
Drake Ho. Cres. S20: Water 5E **137**
Drakehouse La. S20: Beig 5G **137**
Drake Ho. La. West S20: Beig 5G **137**
Drake Ho. Retail Pk. S20: Water 5E **137**
Drake Ho. Way S20: Water 5F **137**
Drake Rd. DN2: Don 4D **40**
  S66: Malt 6C **102**
       (off Fisher Rd.)
Drake Ter. S43: Brim 6B **162**
Drake Vw. S63: Bramp B 6A **48**
Dransfield Av. S36: Pen 5D **176**
Dransfield Cl. S10: Shef 4G **117**
Dransfield Rd. S10: Shef 4F **117**
Draycott Pl. S18: Dron W 4C **154**
Draymans Ct. *S11: Shef* *5E* **119**
       (off Napier St.)
Drive, The DN3: Eden 6D **26**
  S6: Shef 2A **106**
Driver St. S13: Shef 6E **123**
DRONFIELD 3F **155**
Dronfield Civic Cen. S18: Dron 3F **155**
Dronfield Ind. Est. S18: Dron 3H **155**
Dronfield Rd. S21: Ecki 1B **158**
Dronfield Sports Cen. 3E **155**
Dronfield Station (Rail) 3F **155**
DRONFIELD WOODHOUSE 3C **154**
DROPPING WELL 2G **95**
Droppingwell Farm Cl. S61: Kimb . . .1G **95**
Droppingwell Rd. S61: Kimb 4E **95**
Drover Cl. S35: High G 2D **78**
Droves Dale Rd. S63: Gol 4C **36**
Drummond Av. DN5: Scaws 3D **38**
Drummond Cres. S5: Shef 5G **93**
Drummond Rd. S5: Shef 5G **93**
Drummond St. S60: Roth 3E **97**
  S65: Roth 3F **97**
Drury Farm Ct. S75: Barn 1H **29**
Drury La. S17: Dore 3E **145**
  S18: Coal A 1H **155**
Dryden Av. S5: Shef 6D **92**
  S40: Birdh 2H **171**
Dryden Dr. S5: Shef 6D **92**
Dryden Rd. DN4: Balb 6B **56**
  S5: Shef 6D **92**
  S63: Wath D 5D **48**
  S64: Mexb 1G **67**
  S65: Roth 6A **98**
  S71: Barn 6F **17**
Dryden Way S5: Shef 1D **106**
Dublin Rd. DN2: Don 5F **41**
Duchess Rd. S2: Shef 6F **5** (5G **119**)
Duckham Dr. S26: Ast 2D **138**
DUCKMANTON MOOR 6H **173**
Ducksett La. S21: Ecki 2E **159**
Dudley Dr. S63: Gol 5A **36**
Dudley Rd. DN2: Don 1G **57**
  S6: Shef 2A **106**
Dudley St. S62: Parkg 5G **83**
Duewell Ct. S43: Bar H 3G **163**
Duftons Cl. DN12: Con 3G **69**
Dugdale Dr. S5: Shef 3E **93**
Dugdale Rd. S5: Shef 3D **92**
Duke Av. DN11: New R 5B **74**
  S66: Malt 6C **102**
Duke Cres. S61: Kimb P 1H **95**
  S70: Barn 2E **31**
Duke La. S1: Shef 6E **5** (4F **119**)
Duke of Norfolk La. S66: Wick 6D **98**
Dukeries Dr. S25: Nth A 1H **141**
Duke's Cres. DN12: New E 3C **70**
Dukes Dr. S41: Ches 2F **167**
Dukes La. S61: Kimb 2G **95**
Dukes Pl. S65: Roth 6A **98**
Duke St. DN1: Don 1B **56**
  S2: Shef 3H **5** (3H **119**)
  S20: Mosb 4E **151**
  S25: Dinn 4A **128**
  S41: Whit M 6H **161**
  S43: Stav 4B **164**
  S64: Swint 2C **66**
  S70: Barn 2E **31**
  S72: Grim 2B **20**
  S74: Hoyl 6B **46**
Dumbleton Rd. S21: Killa 5D **152**
Dumble Wood Grange S41: Ches . . .1D **166**
Duncan Rd. S10: Shef 2A **118**

Duncan St. S60: Brins 3D **110**
Duncombe St. S6: Shef 1B **118**
Dundas Rd. DN2: Don 4D **40**
  S9: Tins 1H **109**
Dundonald Rd. S40: Ches 1H **171**
Dunedin Glen S20: Half 4F **151**
Dunedin Gro. S20: Half 4F **151**
Dunella Dr. S6: Shef 3A **106**
Dunella Pl. S6: Shef 3H **105**
Dunella Rd. S6: Shef 3A **106**
Dunfields S3: Shef 1E **119**
Dunford Ct. S63: Wath D 6H **49**
Dungworth Grn. S6: Dung 4A **104**
Dunkeld Rd. S11: Shef 3A **132**
Dunkerley Rd. S6: Lox 3E **105**
Dun La. S3: Shef 1E **119**
Dunleary Rd. DN2: Don 6F **41**
Dunlin Cl. S61: Thorpe H 2C **80**
Dunlop St. S9: Shef 3E **109**
Dunmere Cl. S71: Monk B 3F **17**
Dunmow Rd. S4: Shef 3B **108**
Dunninc Rd. S5: Shef 3A **94**
Dunninc Ter. S5: Shef 3A **94**
Dunniwood Av. DN4: Bess 1B **74**
Dunniwood Reach DN4: Bess 6C **58**
Dunns Dale S66: Malt 5C **102**
Dunscroft Gro. DN11: Ross 5E **75**
Dunsley La. S72: Brier 4F **13**
  WF9: Hems 2G **13**
Dunsley Ter. WF9: Sth K 4H **13**
Dunstan Rd. S66: Malt 6H **101**
DUNSTON 6E **161**
Dunston Ct. S41: Whit M 5G **161**
Dunstone Hgts. S36: Pen 5E **177**
Dunston Innovation Cen.
  S41: Whit M 5G **161**
Dunston La. S41: Ches 5E **161**
Dunston Pl. S41: Whit M 5G **161**
Dunston Rd.
  S41: Up N, Ches, Whit M 6B **160**
Dunston Technology Pk.
  S41: Whit M 5G **161**
Dunston Trad. Est. S41: Ches 4F **161**
Dunston Way S41: Ches 5F **161**
Dun St. S3: Shef 1E **119**
  S64: Swint 3D **66**
DUNSVILLE 4H **27**
Durham Av. S43: New W 3C **162**
Durham Cl. S43: New W 3C **162**
Durham La. DN3: Arm 3G **43**
  S10: Shef 3D **118**
Durham Pl. S65: Roth 6A **98**
Durham Rd. DN2: Don 3E **41**
  S10: Shef 3D **118**
Durham St. S66: Malt 6C **102**
Durham Way S62: Parkg 5H **83**
Durley Chine Dr. S41: Has 2B **172**
Durlstone Cl. S12: Shef 3D **134**
Durlstone Cres. S12: Shef 3D **134**
Durlstone Dr. S12: Shef 3D **134**
Durlstone Gro. S12: Shef 3D **134**
Durmast Gro. S6: Stann 6D **104**
Durnan Gro. S62: Rawm 6D **64**
Durnford Rd. DN2: Don 5D **40**
Durrant Rd. S41: Ches 5H **167**
Dursley Ct. DN9: Auck 1G **59**
Durvale Ct. S17: Dore 4F **145**
Dutton Rd. S6: Shef 3C **106**
Duxford Ct. DN4: Cant 6D **58**
DW Sports Fitness
  Barnsley 6F **17**
Dyche Cl. S8: Shef 4G **147**
Dyche Dr. S8: Shef 4G **147**
Dyche La. S8: Shef 3F **147**
  S18: Coal A 5G **147**
Dyche Pl. S8: Shef 4G **147**
Dyche Rd. S8: Shef 4G **147**
Dycott Rd. S61: Kimb 3A **96**
Dyer Rd. S74: Jum 5D **46**
Dykes Hall Gdns. S6: Shef 4A **106**
Dykes Hall Pl. S6: Shef 3A **106**
Dykes Hall Rd. S6: Shef 3H **105**
Dykes La. S6: Shef 3H **105**
Dyke Vale Av. S12: Shef 4B **136**
Dyke Vale Cl. S12: Shef 4B **136**
Dyke Vale Pl. S12: Shef 4B **136**
Dyke Va. Rd. S12: Shef 3A **136**
Dyke Vale Way S12: Shef 4B **136**
Dykewood Dr. S6: Shef 1G **105**

Dynne Ct. S25: Dinn .6A **128**
Dyson Holmes La. S35: Wharn S .2A **90**
Dyson Pl. S11: Shef .6C **118**
Dyson St. S70: Barn .3C **30**

E

Eaden Cres. S74: Hoyl .6C **46**
Eagleton Dr. S35: High G .6D **60**
Eagleton Gdns. S64: Swint .3C **66**
Eagleton Ri. S35: High G .6D **60**
Eagle Vw. S26: Ast .2D **138**
Ealands Cl. S72: Midd .3F **35**
Ealand Way DN12: Con .3H **69**
Eaming Vw. S71: Barn .5F **17**
Earl Av. DN11: New R .5A **74**
S66: Malt .6B **102**
Earldom Cl. S4: Shef .6H **107**
Earldom Dr. S4: Shef .6H **107**
Earldom Rd. S4: Shef .5H **107**
Earldom St. S4: Shef .6H **107**
Earlesmere Av. DN4: Balb .4H **55**
Earl Marshal Cl. S4: Shef .3A **108**
Earl Marshal Dr. S4: Shef .3H **107**
Earl Marshal Rd. S4: Shef .4H **107**
Earl Marshal Vw. S4: Shef .3H **107**
Earls Ct. S61: Thorpe H .3C **80**
Earlsmere Dr. S71: Ard .2D **32**
Earlston Dr. DN5: Don .4A **40**
Earl St. S1: Shef .6D **4** (4F **119**)
(not continuous)
Earlswood Ct. DN3: Barn D .2D **26**
Earl Way S1: Shef .6D **4** (4F **119**)
Earnshaw Hall S10: Shef .5A **118**
Earnshaw Ter. S75: Barn .5C **16**
Earsham St. S4: Shef .6H **107**
Easedale Cl. S40: Ches .3A **166**
East Av. DN6: Woodl .4B **22**
S62: Rawm .2G **83**
S64: Swint .4A **66**
S73: Womb .1E **47**
East Bank Cl. S2: Shef .2A **134**
East Bank Pl. S2: Shef .2A **134**
East Bank Rd. S2: Shef .5G **119**
East Bank Vw. S2: Shef .2A **134**
East Bank Way S2: Shef .2A **134**
E. Bawtry Rd. S60: Roth .3H **111**
East Cl. S36: Oxs .6G **177**
E. Coast Rd. S9: Shef .6B **108**
East Cres. S36: Stoc .3C **174**
S65: Roth .3A **98**
East Cft. S63: Bolt D .2B **50**
Eastcroft Cl. S20: Westf .2G **151**
Eastcroft Dr. S20: Westf .3F **151**
Eastcroft Glen S20: Westf .2G **151**
Eastcroft Vw. S20: Westf .3G **151**
Eastcroft Way S20: Westf .2G **151**
EAST DENE .3H **97**
East Earsham St. S4: Shef .6A **108**
East End Cres. S71: Roy .3B **10**
Eastern Av. S2: Shef .2A **134**
S25: Dinn .5B **128**
Eastern Cl. S25: Dinn .6B **128**
Eastern Cres. S2: Shef .2A **134**
Eastern Dr. S2: Shef .1A **134**
Eastern Wlk. S2: Shef .1A **134**
Eastfield Av. S36: Pen .4D **176**
Eastfield Cl. S75: Stain .6C **8**
Eastfield Cres. S25: Laugh M .1H **127**
S75: Stain .6C **8**
East Field La. S25: Laugh M .1A **128**
Eastfield La. DN9: Auck .2H **59**
Eastfield Pl. S62: Rawm .1B **84**
Eastfield Rd. DN3: Arm .5E **43**
S10: Shef .1B **118**
S18: Dron .4H **155**
Eastfields S70: Wors .6G **31**
Eastgate S6: Shef .1H **105**
S70: Barn .6D **16**
WF9: Hems .1F **13**
Eastgate Ct. S65: Roth .4A **98**
E. Glade Av. S12: Shef .5H **135**
E. Glade Cl. S12: Shef .5H **135**
E. Glade Cres. S12: Shef .5H **135**
E. Glade Dell S12: Shef .4H **135**
E. Glade Pl. S12: Shef .5H **135**
E. Glade Rd. S12: Shef .4H **135**
E. Glade Sq. S12: Shef .5H **135**
E. Glade Way S12: Shef .4H **135**
Eastgrove Rd. S10: Shef .5C **118**
EAST HERRINGTHORPE .3B **98**
E. Laith Ga. DN1: Don .1C **56**
Eastleigh S65: Roth .3H **97**
Eastleigh Ct. S41: Has .2C **172**
E. Lodge La. S61: Grea .4D **82**
East Mall S20: Water .5F **137**
Eastmoor Gro. S71: Carl .4H **9**
Eastmoor Rd.
S43: Brim C .4E **169**
East Pde. S1: Shef .3E **5** (3F **119**)
East Pinfold S71: Roy .3H **9**
East Rd. S2: Shef .1G **133**
S36: Oxs .6G **177**
S65: Roth .3A **98**
Eastside Cl. S41: Whit M .6A **162**
Eastside Rd. S41: Whit M .6A **162**
East St. DN1: Don .3B **56**
S25: Dinn .5A **128**
S63: Gol .4E **37**
S72: Sth H .1H **11**
S73: D'fld .4B **34**
East Ter. S26: Wales B .5E **139**
East Vale Dr. S65: Thry .6E **85**
East Vw. S40: Ches .6H **167**
S66: Hel .5E **101**
S72: Cud .1E **19**
S74: Jum .5C **46**
East Vw. Av. S21: Ecki .2D **158**
East Vw. Ter. S6: Shef .3A **106**
Eastwell Gro. S73: Womb .3A **48**
EAST WHITWELL .4D **174**
EASTWOOD .2H **97**
Eastwood S6: Shef .1H **105**
Eastwood Av. S25: Nth A .3H **141**
Eastwood Cl. S41: Has .2B **172**
Eastwood Ct. S65: Roth .2H **97**
Eastwood Dr. S44: Cal .6G **169**
Eastwood Ho. *S65: Roth .3G **97***
(off Doncaster Rd.)
Eastwood La. S65: Roth .3F **97**
Eastwood Mt. S65: Roth .4H **97**
Eastwood Pk. Apartments
S41: Has .3B **172**
Eastwood Pk. Dr. S41: Has .2C **172**
Eastwood Rd. S11: Shef .6C **118**
Eastwood Trad. Est. S65: Roth .1H **97**
Eastwood Va. S65: Roth .2H **97**
Eastwood Vw. S65: Roth .2A **98**
Eaton Pl. S2: Shef .3A **120**
Eaton Sq. DN5: Barnb .1A **52**
Ebenezer Pl. S3: Shef .1D **4** (1F **119**)
S74: Els .1D **62**
Ebenezer St. S3: Shef .1D **4** (1F **119**)
S72: Gt H .1G **35**
Eben St. S9: Shef .2D **108**
Ebor Cl. S73: Womb .2H **47**
ECCLESALL .3A **132**
Ecclesall Rd. S11: Shef .1A **132**
Ecclesall Rd. Sth. S11: Shef .6F **131**
Eccles Dr. DN12: New E .6C **70**
ECCLESFIELD .1F **93**
Ecclesfield Cl. S35: Eccl .1G **93**
ECCLESFIELD COMMON .1G **93**
Ecclesfield Ct. S35: Eccl .1G **93**
Ecclesfield M. S35: Eccl .1G **93**
Ecclesfield Rd. S5: Shef .2A **94**
S9: Shef .2A **94**
S35: Chap .3G **79**
Ecclesfield Way S35: Eccl .1G **93**
Eccles St. S9: Shef .6E **95**
Eccleston Rd. DN3: Kirk Sa .3D **26**
ECKINGTON .1F **159**
Eckington Bus. Pk.
S21: Ecki .6G **151**
Eckington Hall S20: Mosb .5E **151**
Eckington M. S20: Mosb .5E **151**
Eckington Pool .1F **159**
Eckington Rd. S18: Coal A .6H **147**
S20: Beig, Holb .2G **151**
(not continuous)
S43: New W .1C **162**
S43: Stav .3C **164**
Eckington Way S20: Half .3G **151**
S20: Holb, Water .4E **137**
Ecton Ct. DN3: Kirk Sa .3B **26**
Edale Ct. S41: Ches .1F **167**
Edale Ri. S75: Dod .3F **29**
Edale Rd. S11: Shef .1H **131**
S43: Mas M .3F **165**
S61: Kimb .4A **96**
EDDERTHORPE .2B **34**
Edderthorpe La. S71: D'fld .2B **34**
S73: D'fld .2B **34**
Eddyfield Rd. S36: Oxs .5G **177**
Eden Cl. S66: Hel .5E **101**
S75: Bar G .3F **15**
Edencroft Dr. DN3: Eden .5D **26**
Eden Dr. S6: Lox .4F **105**
Edenfield Cl. S71: Monk B .2A **18**
Eden Fld. Rd. DN3: Eden .6D **26**
Eden Glade S26: Swal .6C **124**
Eden Gro. DN4: Hex .2H **55**
S26: Swal .6C **124**
Eden Gro. Rd. DN3: Eden .6D **26**
Edenhall Rd. S2: Shef .1C **134**
Eden Pl. S25: Dinn .4H **127**
Edensor Ct. S43: Stav .6H **163**
Edensor Rd. S5: Shef .2G **107**
Eden St. S42: W'orth .6F **171**
Eden Ter. S64: Mexb .6F **51**
EDENTHORPE .6D **26**
Edenthorpe Dell S20: Mosb .6C **136**
Edenthorpe Gro. S20: Mosb .6D **136**
Edenthorpe Wlk. *S20: Mosb .6D **136***
(off Edenthrope Gro.)
Edgar Allan Ho. S3: Shef .4B **4**
Edgar La. DN11: New R .5A **74**
Edgbaston Way DN12: New E .3D **70**
Edge Bank S7: Shef .2D **132**
Edgebrook Rd. S7: Shef .2C **132**
Edgecliffe Pl. S71: Smi .3F **17**
Edge Climbing Centre, The .5F **119**
Edge Cl. S6: Shef .4B **92**
Edgedale Rd. S7: Shef .3C **132**
Edgefield Rd. S7: Shef .3D **132**
Edge Grn. DN3: Kirk Sa .4C **26**
Edge Hill Rd. S7: Shef .2C **132**
Edgehill Rd. DN2: Don .3H **41**
S75: Stain .4H **7**
Edgelands Ri. S72: Cud .3E **19**
Edge La. S6: Shef .4B **92**
Edgemount Rd. S7: Shef .3D **132**
Edge Well Cl. S6: Shef .4B **92**
Edge Well Cres. S6: Shef .4B **92**
Edge Well Dr. S6: Shef .5B **92**
Edge Well La. S6: Shef .4A **92**
Edge Well Pl. S6: Shef .4A **92**
Edge Well Ri. S6: Shef .4A **92**
Edge Well Way S6: Shef .4B **92**
Edinburgh Av. S63: Bolt D .2A **50**
Edinburgh Cl. S71: Monk B .4G **17**
Edinburgh Ct. S42: W'orth .6F **171**
Edinburgh Dr. S25: Nth A .1G **141**
Edinburgh M. S41: Ches .4G **167**
Edinburgh Rd. S41: Ches .3G **167**
S42: W'orth .6F **171**
S74: Hoyl .5B **46**
Edith Ter. DN5: Scaws .3F **39**
Edlington La. DN4: Warm .3D **70**
DN12: New E .3D **70**
DN12: New E, Old E .1B **88**
Edlington Leisure Cen. .6C **70**
Edlington Riding DN12: New E .5D **70**
Edmonton Cl. S75: Barn .6H **15**
Edmund Av. S17: Bradw .4B **146**
S60: Brins .5E **111**
Edmund Cl. S17: Bradw .4C **146**
Edmund Ct. S2: Shef .5G **119**
Edmund Dr. S17: Bradw .4C **146**
Edmund Rd. S2: Shef .6G **119**
Edmunds Rd. S70: Wors .6H **31**
Edmund St. S41: Ches .6G **161**
S70: Wors .6F **31**
Edna St. S63: Bolt D .2B **50**
Edward Cl. S70: Barn .3H **31**
Edward Pl. S11: Shef .2C **132**
Edward Rd. DN6: Adw S .2E **23**
S63: Gol .6B **36**
S63: Wath D .4D **48**
Edward St. DN3: Arm .3C **42**
DN5: Ben .1A **40**
DN11: New R .5A **74**
S3: Shef .2B **4** (2E **119**)
S21: Ecki .1E **159**
S25: Dinn .5A **128**
S36: Stoc .3D **174**

Edward St. S43: Stav 6H **163**
S63: Thurn 2B **36**
S64: Swint 2C **66**
S72: Gt H 1F **35**
S73: D'fld 5B **34**
S73: Womb 1H **47**
S74: Hoyl 6A **46**
S75: Mapp 6B **8**
Edward St. Flats S3: Shef 2B **4** (2E **119**)
Edwin Av. S40: Walt 2E **171**
Edwin Rd. DN6: Woodl 4B **22**
S2: Shef 2H **133**
Edwins Cl. S71: Ath 1E **17**
Effingham La. S4: Shef 1H **5** (2H **119**)
Effingham Rd. S4: Shef 1A **120**
S9: Shef 1A **120**
Effingham Sq. *S65: Roth 3E 97*
(off Water St.)
Effingham St. S4: Shef 1H **5** (1H **119**)
S65: Roth 4E **97**
(College St.)
S65: Roth 3F **97**
(Kenneth St.)
Egerton Cl. S3: Shef 5C **4** (4E **119**)
Egerton La. S1: Shef 6B **4** (4E **119**)
Egerton Rd. S18: Dron 2G **155**
S26: Swal 1C **138**
Egerton St. S1: Shef 6B **4** (4E **119**)
Egerton Wlk. S3: Shef 5B **4**
Eggington Cl. DN4: Cant 5E **59**
Egmanton Rd. S71: Ath 5E **9**
Egremont Ct. S66: Malt 3G **101**
Egremont Ri. S66: Malt 3G **101**
Eilam Cl. S61: Kimb P 2H **95**
Eilam Rd. S61: Kimb P 2H **95**
Eland Cl. DN11: Ross 4C **74**
Eland Rd. DN12: Den M 3A **68**
Elcroft Gdns. S20: Beig 6G **137**
Elder Av. S25: Nth A 3A **142**
Elderberry Cl. S61: Scho 6E **81**
Elder Ct. S21: Killa 5B **152**
Elder Dr. S66: Sunn 4G **99**
Elder Gro. DN9: Auck 1B **76**
DN12: Con 5D **68**
Eldertree Rd. S61: Thorpe H 4C **80**
Elder Way S40: Ches 5H **167**
S72: Sth H 1H **11**
Eldon Arc. *S70: Barn 1E 31*
(off Midland St.)
Eldon Ct. S1: Shef 4C **4** (3E **119**)
Eldon Rd. S65: Roth 2G **97**
Eldon St. S1: Shef 4C **4** (3E **119**)
S70: Barn 1E **31**
Eldon St. Nth. S71: Barn 6E **17**
Eleanor Ct. DN3: Eden 1B **42**
Eleanor St. S9: Shef 6E **109**
Elgar Dr. S66: Malt 6D **102**
Elgin Cl. S40: Walt 3D **170**
Elgin St. S10: Shef 3A **118**
Elgitha Dr. S66: Thurc 6B **114**
Eliot Cl. S43: Brim C 3E **169**
Elizabeth Av. DN3: Kirk Sa 4D **26**
S72: Sth H 1H **11**
Elizabeth Ct. S72: Grim 2B **20**
WF9: Hems 1G **13**
Elizabeth Rd. S26: Ast 2C **138**
Elizabeth St. S63: Gol 5D **36**
S72: Grim 2B **20**
Elizabeth Way *S60: Roth 4D 96*
(off Vine Cl.)
Elkstone Rd. S40: Ches 3B **166**
Ellaline Cotts. S65: Rav 2D **100**
Elland Cl. S71: Smi 1D **16**
Ella Rd. S4: Shef 5H **107**
Ellavale Rd. S74: Els 6D **46**
Ellenboro Rd. S6: Shef 4A **106**
Ellen Tree Cl. S60: Brins 3C **110**
Ellerker Av. DN4: Hex 2A **56**
Ellers Av. DN4: Bess 4H **57**
Ellers Cres. DN4: Bess 4H **57**
Ellers Dr. DN4: Bess 4H **57**
Ellershaw La. DN12: Con 5D **68**
Ellershaw Rd. DN12: Con 5E **69**
Ellers La. DN9: Auck 1H **59**
Ellers Rd. DN4: Bess 4H **57**
Ellerton Gdns. DN4: Cant 3B **58**
Ellerton Rd. S5: Shef 2A **108**
Ellesmere Rd. S4: Shef 6H **107**
(not continuous)
Ellesmere Rd. Nth.
S4: Shef 5H **107**
Ellesmere Ter. S65: Roth 4G **97**
Ellesmere Wlk. S4: Shef 6H **107**
Ellin Cl. S74: Jum 5C **46**
Ellington Ct. S70: Barn 3B **30**
Ellin St. S1: Shef 6D **4** (5F **119**)
Elliott Av. S73: Womb 3G **47**
Elliott Cl. S63: Wath D 5D **48**
Elliott Ct. S65: Roth 3F **97**
Elliott Dr. S43: Ink 2H **169**
S61: Kimb P 6A **82**
Elliott La. S35: Gren 4C **78**
Elliott M. *S61: Kimb 3A 96*
(off Benton Way)
Elliott Rd. S6: Shef 2C **118**
Elliottville St. S6: Shef 6B **106**
Ellis Av. S63: Wath D 2E **65**
Ellis Ct. S73: Hem 4F **47**
Ellis Cres. DN11: New R 5B **74**
S73: Bramp 5B **48**
Ellisons Rd. S21: Killa 2D **152**
Ellison St. S3: Shef 1B **4** (2E **119**)
(not continuous)
Ellis St. S3: Shef 1C **4** (2E **119**)
S60: Brins 3D **110**
Elliston Av. S75: Stain 5B **8**
Ellorslie Dr. S36: Stoc 3E **175**
Ellwood S71: Lund 4B **18**
Elmbridge Cl. S71: Roy 3B **10**
Elm Cl. DN3: Barn D 1C **26**
DN11: Ross 6E **75**
S21: Killa 5B **152**
S41: Ches 1G **167**
Elm Cotts. S72: Gt H 6F **21**
Elm Ct. S70: Wors 6G **31**
Elm Cres. DN5: Ben 6B **24**
S20: Mosb 2D **150**
Elmdale Cl. S64: Swint 6C **66**
Elmdale Dr. DN3: Eden 1C **42**
Elm Dr. DN9: Finn 3G **77**
S21: Killa 5B **152**
Elmfield Av. S5: Shef 6G **93**
Elmfield Rd. DN1: Don 2C **56**
DN11: New R 6C **74**
Elm Grn. La. DN12: Con 4F **69**
Elm Gro. S61: Grea 5C **82**
Elmham Rd. DN4: Cant 3B **58**
S9: Shef 2G **121**
Elmhirst Dr. S65: Roth 6C **98**
Elmhirst La. S75: Silk 2E **29**
(not continuous)
Elm La. S5: Shef 6G **93**
Elm Lodge Farm Cl. S41: Ches 1G **167**
Elm M. *S70: Barn 1D 30*
(off Nelson St.)
Elmore Rd. S10: Shef 3B **118**
Elm Pl. DN3: Arm 3D **42**
S40: Ches 6F **167**
S62: Rawm 3H **83**
S71: Monk B 3A **18**
Elm Ri. S35: Chap 4E **79**
Elm Rd. DN3: Arm 3D **42**
DN9: Auck 2A **76**
S20: Beig 4H **137**
S21: Ecki 2D **158**
S64: Mexb 6D **50**
Elm Row S71: Barn 1G **31**
Elmroyd Ct. S36: Pen 5E **177**
Elms, The S64: Swint 5B **66**
Elmsdale S70: Wors 6G **31**
Elm St. S42: Tem N 6G **173**
S43: Hol 5E **163**
S74: Hoyl 1G **61**
Elm Tree Cl. S25: Nth A 3A **142**
Elm Tree Cres. S18: Dron 1F **155**
Elm Tree Dr. S42: W'orth 6G **171**
Elm Tree Farm Ct. S65: Hoot R 6E **67**
ELM TREE HILL 2D **134**
Elm Tree Rd. S66: Malt 5G **101**
Elmtree Rd. S61: Thorpe H 5C **80**
Elmview Rd. S9: Shef 6E **95**
Elmville Av. S64: Swint 5B **66**
Elm Wlk. S63: Thurn 1C **36**
Elm Way S63: Wath D 2H **65**
Elmwood Av. DN6: Woodl 2A **22**
Elmwood Cres. DN3: Arm 4D **42**
Elmwood Dr. S20: Mosb 4E **151**
Elmwood Ho. S43: Hol 6F **163**
Elmwood Way S75: Barn 4C **16**
ELSECAR .1D **62**
Elsecar Heritage Cen. 2E **63**
Elsecar Heritage Railway
Rockingham Station 2E **63**
Elsecar Ho. *DN1: Don 2B 56*
(off Bond Cl.)
Elsecar Rd. S63: Bramp B, Wath D . . .6B **48**
Elsecar Station (Rail) 1D **62**
Elsham Cl. S66: Braml 3A **100**
Elstead Cl. S75: Bar G 3F **15**
Elstree Dr. S12: Shef 4E **135**
Elstree Rd. S12: Shef 4E **135**
Elsworth Cl. DN1: Don 3B **56**
Elter Dr. DN4: Don 3G **57**
Eltham Cft. S7: Shef 4A **132**
Elton La. S66: Sunn 3G **99**
Elton St. S40: Ches 6H **167**
Elton Vw. S43: Stav 6A **164**
Elvaston Cl. S18: Dron W 3A **154**
Elwin Ct. DN4: Balb 2A **72**
Elwis St. DN5: Don 6A **40**
Elwood Rd. S17: Bradw 4B **146**
Ely Rd. DN2: Don 3E **41**
Ely St. DN11: New R 4B **74**
Embankment Rd. S10: Shef 3B **118**
Emerson Cl. S5: Shef 5G **93**
Emerson Cres. S5: Shef 6G **93**
Emerson Dr. S5: Shef 6G **93**
Emily Cl. S71: Barn 6A **18**
Emily Rd. S7: Shef 2D **132**
Emley Dr. DN5: Scaws 3D **38**
Emley Ho. *DN1: Don 2B 56*
(off St James St.)
Emley Vw. S71: Monk B 3F **17**
Emmet Fld. Cl. S40: Birdh 2G **171**
Empire Dr. S66: Malt 3G **101**
Empire Rd. S7: Shef 1E **133**
Empire Ter. S71: Roy 2A **10**
Emsley Av. S72: Cud 4F **19**
Endcliffe Av. S10: Shef 5B **118**
ENDCLIFFE CRESCENT 5A **118**
Endcliffe Cres. S10: Shef 4A **118**
ENDCLIFFE EDGE 5H **117**
Endcliffe Edge S10: Shef 5A **118**
Endcliffe Glen Rd. S11: Shef 5B **118**
Endcliffe Gro. Av. S10: Shef 5H **117**
Endcliffe Hall Av. S10: Shef 5H **117**
Endcliffe Ri. Rd. S11: Shef 5B **118**
Endcliffe Ter. Rd. S11: Shef 5B **118**
Endcliffe Va. Av. S11: Shef 6B **118**
Endcliffe Va. Rd. S10: Shef 5A **118**
Endcliffe Way DN2: Don 3H **41**
Endfield Rd. S5: Shef 3E **93**
Endowood Rd. S7: Shef 6A **132**
S40: Bramp 2B **170**
Enfield Pl. S13: Shef 4A **122**
Enfield Rd. S41: Ches 3G **167**
Engine La. S63: Gol 6E **37**
S72: Shaft 5G **11**
Engine La. Cl. S72: Shaft 5G **11**
Ennerdale Av. S20: Half 4F **151**
Ennerdale Cl. S18: Dron W 3D **154**
S25: Nth A 1H **141**
S64: Mexb 6H **51**
Ennerdale Cres. S41: Ches 1D **166**
Ennerdale Dr. S20: Half 4F **151**
Ennerdale Rd. DN2: Don 4H **41**
S71: Ard 2E **33**
Ennis Cres. DN2: Don 5F **41**
Enterprise Cen. S63: Gol 6D **36**
Enterprise Pk. S9: Shef 1B **120**
Enterprise Park Ind. Est. S9: Shef . . .1C **120**
Enterprise Way S20: Holb 2A **152**
Entwhistle Rd. S35: High G 1D **78**
Epping Gdns. S20: Sot 6H **137**
Epping Gro. S20: Sot 6H **137**
Epsom Cl. S64: Mexb 6G **51**
Epsom Rd. DN4: Cant 2A **58**
Epworth Ct. *DN5: Ben 2A 40*
(off Chapel St.)
Erin Rd. S43: Pool, Stav 6C **164**
Ernest Copley Ho. S35: High G 2E **79**
Errington Av. S2: Shef 2B **134**
Errington Cl. S2: Shef 2B **134**
Errington Cres. S2: Shef 2B **134**
Errington Rd. S2: Shef 1B **134**
S40: Walt 2E **171**
Errington Way S2: Shef 1B **134**

Erskine Cres. S2: Shef 1H **133**
Erskine Rd. S2: Shef 1H **133**
S65: Roth 2F **97**
Erskine Vw. S2: Shef 2H **133**
Eshlands Brook
S71: Monk B 3C **18**
Eshton Ct. S75: Mapp 4H **7**
Eshton Wlk. S70: Barn 1D **30**
Eskdale Cl. S6: Shef 1B **106**
S18: Dron W 3D **154**
Eskdale Dr. DN5: Scawt 2G **39**
Eskdale Rd. S6: Shef 2B **106**
S61: Wing 5A **82**
S71: Ard 2D **32**
Eskdale Wlk. DN5: Scaws 3D **38**
Eslaforde Ter. *S65: Roth 2A **98***
(off Doncaster Rd.)
Esperanto Pl. S1: Shef 3F **5**
Esporta Health & Fitness
Sheffield 4D 132
Essendine Cres. S8: Shef 5G **133**
Essex Av. DN2: Don 1G **57**
Essex Cl. S26: Kiv P 5D **140**
Essex Rd. S2: Shef 5A **120**
S70: Barn 3E **31**
Essoldo Chambers *S60: Roth 4E **97***
(off High St.)
Estate Rd. S62: Rawm 1F **83**
Estone Dr. S26: Swal 6C **124**
Ettrick Cl. S40: Ches 3D **166**
Etwall Cl. S40: Ches 2B **166**
Etwall Way S5: Shef 6H **93**
Europa Cl. S9: Shef 5G **109**
Europa Ct. S9: Shef 6B **110**
Europa Dr. S9: Shef 4G **109**
Europa Link S9: Shef 5G **109**
S60: Shef 6B **110**
Europa Vw. S9: Shef 6A **110**
Europa Way S9: Tins 4A **110**
Euston Way S25: Laugh C 4F **127**
Evans Bus. Cen. S25: Dinn 4G **127**
Evans Ct. DN3: Arm 4C **42**
Evans St. S3: Shef 6B **4**
Evanston Gdns. DN4: Balb 4H **55**
Eva Ratcliffe Ho. S5: Shef 2F **93**
Eveline St. S72: Cud 2E **19**
Evelyn Av. DN2: Don 6G **41**
Evelyn Cl. DN2: Don 6G **41**
Evelyn Rd. S10: Shef 3A **118**
Evelyn St. S62: Rawm 2A **84**
Evelyn Ter. S70: Barn 2F **31**
Everard Av. S17: Bradw 5H **145**
Everard Dr. S17: Bradw 5H **145**
Everard Glade S17: Bradw 5H **145**
Everett Cl. S43: Brim 1D **168**
Everill Cl. S73: Womb 3A **48**
Everill Ga. La. S73: Womb 2A **48**
(not continuous)
Everingham Cl. S5: Shef 1F **107**
Everingham Cres. S5: Shef 1E **107**
Everingham Pl. S5: Shef 2F **107**
Everingham Rd. DN4: Cant 2B **58**
S5: Shef 1F **107**
Everson Cl. S66: Malt 3H **101**
Everton Rd. S11: Shef 6B **118**
Evesham Cl. S9: Shef 1E **109**
Ewden Ho. *S10: Shef 5A **116***
(off Holyrood Av.)
Ewden Rd. S73: Womb 3A **48**
EWDEN VILLAGE 6E **175**
Ewden Way S75: Barn 1H **29**
Ewers Rd. S61: Kimb 4A **96**
Ewood Dr. DN4: Cant 4B **58**
Excalibur Way S41: Ches 5A **168**
Excelsior Ct. DN12: Con 4F **69**
Exchange Gateway S1: Shef 3E **5**
Exchange Pl. S2: Shef 2G **5** (2G **119**)
Exchange St. DN1: Don 2B **56**
S2: Shef 2G **5** (2G **119**)
Exchange Works S1: Shef 6E **5**
Exeter Dr. S3: Shef 6B **4** (5E **119**)
Exeter Pl. S3: Shef 6B **4** (5E **119**)
Exeter Rd. DN2: Don 4F **41**
Exeter Way S3: Shef 6A **4** (4D **118**)
Exley Av. S6: Shef 6C **106**
Eyam Cl. S75: Dod 3F **29**
Eyam Rd. S10: Shef 3A **118**
Eyncourt Rd. S5: Shef 1A **108**
Eyre Ct. S66: Braml 6B **100**
Eyre Gdns. S35: High G 2C **78**
S41: Ches 4G **167**
Eyre La. S1: Shef 6E **5** (4F **119**)
Eyre St. S1: Shef 6D **4** (4F **119**)
Eyre St. E. S41: Has 3B **172**

F

Fabian Way S66: Braml 6B **100**
Factory St. S40: Ches 6E **167**
Faheem Ct. S65: Roth 1A **98**
Fairbank Rd. S5: Shef 2F **107**
Fairbank Vw. S60: Whist 3B **112**
Fairbarn Cl. S6: Shef 1F **117**
Fairbarn Dr. S6: Shef 1F **117**
Fairbarn Pl. S6: Shef 1F **117**
Fairbarn Rd. S6: Shef 1F **117**
Fairbarn Way S6: Shef 1F **117**
Fairburn Gdns. S60: Brins 4E **111**
Fairburn Gro. S74: Els 6E **47**
Fair Cl. S40: Ches 4F **167**
Fairfax Dr. S2: Shef 6E **121**
Fairfax Rd. DN2: Don 6G **41**
S2: Shef 6E **121**
Fairfield S63: Bolt D 1A **50**
S70: Birdw 3E **45**
Fairfield Cl. DN4: Bess 6A **58**
S43: Brim 6C **162**
S66: Braml 3H **99**
Fairfield Ct. DN3: Arm 5E **43**
S42: Ash 4A **166**
S73: Womb 6A **34**
Fairfield Dr. S42: Ash 4A **166**
Fairfield Gdns. S74: Els 6D **46**
Fairfield Hgts. S10: Shef 4A **118**
Fairfield Rd. DN5: Don 4G **39**
S40: Ches 4G **167**
Fairford Cl. DN4: Cant 6D **58**
S40: Birdh 3G **171**
Fairholme Hgts. S35: Ough 2F **91**
Fair Holme Vw. DN3: Arm 6F **43**
FAIRLEIGH 6D **120**
Fairleigh S2: Shef 6D **120**
Fairleigh Dr. S60: Roth 6F **97**
Fairmount Gdns. S12: Shef 5B **136**
Fairthorn Rd. S5: Shef 6A **94**
Fair Vw. S40: Ches 4F **167**
Fair Vw. Av. DN6: Woodl 3A **22**
Fairview Cl. DN3: Brant 5G **59**
S74: Hoyl 1H **61**
Fairview Ct. DN3: Barn D 2C **26**
Fair Vw. Dr. S26: Ast 1D **138**
Fairview Rd. S18: Dron 1F **155**
Fairview Ter. DN3: Barn D 2C **26**
Fairview Vs. DN3: Barn D 2D **26**
Fairway S75: Dod 4H **29**
Fairway, The S10: Shef 5B **116**
Fairway Av. S75: Stain 4B **8**
Fairways S66: Wick 6G **99**
Fairwinds Cl. S18: Dron 3F **155**
Faith St. S71: Monk B 2C **18**
Falcon Cl. DN6: Adw S 2C **22**
Falcon Ct. DN11: Ross 5D **74**
S25: Dinn 6A **128**
Falcon Dr. S60: Tree 3G **123**
S70: Birdw 4E **45**
Falconer Cl. S75: Kexb 5E **7**
Falconer La. S13: Shef 6G **123**
Falconer Way S60: Tree 2G **123**
Falcon Knowle Ing S75: Kexb 5D **6**
Falcon Ri. S18: Dron 1A **156**
Falcon Rd. S18: Dron 1H **155**
Falcon St. S70: Barn 6D **16**
Falcon Way S25: Dinn 1H **141**
Falcon Yd. *S40: Ches 5H **167***
(off Low Pavement)
Falding St. S35: Chap 3G **79**
S60: Roth 4D **96**
Falkland Ri. S18: Dron 4F **155**
Falkland Rd. S11: Shef 2H **131**
Fall Bank Cres. S75: Dod 2E **29**
Fall Bank Ind. Est. S75: Dod 3E **29**
Fall Head La. S75: Silk 1C **28**
Fallon Cl. S25: Laugh C 4F **127**
Fallon Rd. S6: Stann 6E **105**
Fallowfield Rd. S43: New W 3C **162**
Fall Vw. S75: Silk 2B **28**
Falmouth Cl. S71: Monk B 5G **17**
Falmouth Rd. S7: Shef 3D **132**
Falstaff Cres. S5: Shef 6E **93**
Falstaff Gdns. S5: Shef 6E **93**
Falstaff Rd. S5: Shef 5E **93**
Falthwaite Grn. La. S75: Hood G 6E **29**
Fane Cres. S26: Swal 6C **124**
Fanny Av. S21: Killa 5D **152**
Fan Rd. S43: Stav 5C **164**
Fan Rd. Ind. Est. S43: Stav 5B **164**
Fanshaw Av. S21: Ecki 2D **158**
Fanshaw Bank S18: Dron 3F **155**
Fanshaw Cl. S21: Ecki 2D **158**
Fanshaw Dr. S21: Ecki 2D **158**
Fanshaw Rd. S18: Dron 2G **155**
S21: Ecki 2D **158**
Fanshaw Way S21: Ecki 2D **158**
Faraday Rd. S9: Shef 6B **108**
Faranden Rd. S9: Shef 1D **120**
Farcliff DN5: Sprot 3C **54**
Far Cres. S65: Roth 3A **98**
Far Cft. S63: Bolt D 2B **50**
Farcroft Gro. S4: Shef 3C **108**
Far Dalton La. S65: Dalt M 1D **98**
Fardell Gdns. S66: Braml 6A **100**
Far Field Cl. DN3: Eden 5D **26**
Far Field La. S63: Wath D 6A **50**
S71: Monk B 2B **18**
Farfield Pk. S63: Wath D 5A **50**
Far Field Rd. DN3: Eden 5D **26**
S65: Roth 5B **98**
Farfield Rd. S3: Shef 6D **106**
Fargate S1: Shef 3E **5** (3F **119**)
Far Golden Smithies S64: Swint 2B **66**
Farish Pl. S2: Shef 2G **133**
Far La. S6: Shef 3A **106**
S65: Roth 2A **98**
Far Lawns S71: Carl 5A **10**
Farlawns Ct. DN4: Balb 2A **72**
Farlow Cft. S35: High G 6B **60**
Farlow Rd. S18: Dron W 2D **154**
Farm Bank Rd. S2: Shef 6H **5** (4H **119**)
Farm Cl. DN3: Eden 1D **42**
S12: Shef 6E **135**
S18: Coal A 6G **147**
S40: Birdh 4G **171**
S60: Brins 5C **110**
S71: Monk B 4H **17**
Farm Ct. DN6: Adw S 2D **22**
Farm Cres. S20: Mosb 4D **150**
Farm Dr. S62: Rawm 2A **84**
Farm Flds. Cl. S20: Water 1E **151**
Farm Grange DN4: Balb 2H **71**
Farmhill Cl. DN5: Cus 5F **39**
Farm Ho. La. S75: Barn 6H **15**
Farmhouse La. S35: Ough 3B **90**
Farm La. S21: Ecki 1D **158**
Far Moor Cl. DN5: H'ton 2H **51**
Farmoor Gdns. S20: Sot 6A **138**
Farm Rd. S2: Shef 5G **119**
S70: Barn 4G **31**
Farmstead Cl. S14: Shef 3A **134**
Farm Vw. Cl. S12: Shef 5C **136**
S61: Kimb 2G **95**
Farm Vw. Dr. S12: Shef 5C **136**
Farm Vw. Gdns. S12: Shef 5C **136**
Farm Vw. Rd. S61: Kimb 2G **95**
Farm Wlk. S20: Mosb 3D **150**
Farm Way S73: D'fld 4B **34**
Farnaby Dr. S35: High G 6C **60**
Farnaby Gdns. S35: High G 6C **60**
Farnborough Dr. DN4: Cant 6D **58**
Farndale Av. S42: Walt 2C **170**
Farndale Rd. DN5: Scaws 3E **39**
S6: Shef 2B **106**
S43: Stav 2B **164**
Farnham Way S25: Laugh C 3F **127**
Farnley Av. S6: Shef 6C **92**
Farnley Rd. DN4: Balb 1B **72**
Farnon Cl. S40: Ches 1A **172**
Farnsworth Ct. S41: Has 2C **172**
Farnsworth Rd. S65: Roth 3B **98**
Farnsworth St. S41: Has 2B **172**
Far Pl. S65: Roth 3A **98**
Farquhar Rd. S66: Malt 5C **102**
(not continuous)
Farrand St. S70: Birdw 5D **44**
Farrar Rd. S7: Shef 1E **133**
Farrar St. S70: Barn 1C **30**
Farrier Ga. S35: High G 2D **78**

Farriers Way S21: Killa 5C 152
Farringdon Cl. WF9: Hems 1E 13
Farringdon Dr. DN11: New R 6H 75
Farrington Ct. S66: Wick 6H 99
Farrow Cl. S75: Dod 3H 29
Farthing Gale M. DN5: Cus 5G 39
Far Townend S75: Dod 3G 29
Far Vw. Rd. S3: Shef 6G 93
Far Vw. Ter. S70: Barn 3D 30
Farwater Cl. S18: Dron 4F 155
Farwater La. S18: Dron 3E 155
Fathers Gdns. S26: Kiv P 6A 140
Favell Rd. S3: Shef 3A 4 (3D 118)
        S65: Roth 3C 98
Fawcett St. S3: Shef 1A 4 (2D 118)
                                          (not continuous)
Fawn Cl. S42: W'orth 6G 171
Fay Cres. S9: Shef 2E 121
Fearnehough St. S9: Shef 1C 120
Fearnley Rd. S74: Hoyl 1H 61
Fearn Ho. Cres. S74: Hoyl 1H 61
Fearn's Bldgs. S36: Pen 4C 176
                                       (off Stottercliffe Rd.)
Fearnville Gro. S71: Roy 3H 9
Felkin St. S41: Ches 5A 168
FELKIRK 1E 11
Felkirk Cotts. S72: Sth H 1E 11
Felkirk Vw. S72: Shaft 3E 11
Fellbrigg Rd. S2: Shef 1A 134
Fellowsfield Way S61: Kimb 3H 95
Fellows Wlk. S73: Womb 6E 33
Fell Rd. S9: Shef 5D 108
Fell St. S9: Shef 4C 108
FENCE 6G 123
Fen Cl. DN3: Eden 6D 26
Fenlake Wlk. S63: Wath D 4E 49
Fenland Way S40: Walt 2F 171
Fenney La. S11: Shef 6F 131
Fenn Rd. S75: Tank 1E 61
Fensome Way S73: D'fld 4B 34
Fenton Cl. DN3: Arm 5E 43
Fenton Cft. S61: Roth 2B 96
Fenton Dr. S12: Shef 4A 136
Fenton Rd. S61: Grea, Roth, Wing . . .1B 96
Fenton St. S21: Ecki 2C 158
        S61: Kimb 3A 96
        S70: Barn 1D 30
Fentonville St. S11: Shef 6D 118
Fenton Way S61: Grea 6C 82
Feoffees Rd. S61: Eccl 2G 93
Ferguson St. S9: Shef 6C 108
Ferham Cl. S61: Roth 4B 96
Ferham Pk. Av. S61: Roth 4B 96
Ferham Rd. S61: Roth 4B 96
Fern Av. DN5: Don 3H 39
        S20: Beig 4G 137
        S43: Stav 6H 163
Fern Bank DN6: Adw S 2C 22
Fernbank Cl. DN9: Blax 1G 77
        S70: Wors 4E 31
Fernbank Dr. DN3: Arm 2E 43
        S21: Ecki 1C 158
Fern Cl. DN2: Don 4H 41
        S21: Ecki 1C 158
        S73: D'fld 6B 34
Fern Ct. S66: Sunn 3H 99
Ferncroft Av. S20: Mosb 3D 150
Ferndale Cl. S18: Coal A 1A 156
Ferndale Dr. S66: Braml 4H 99
Ferndale Pl. WF9: Hems 1E 13
Ferndale Ri. S18: Coal A 1A 156
Ferndale DN12: Con 4E 69
        S18: Coal A 1A 156
Ferndale Vw. DN5: Cus 5G 39
Fernhall Cl. DN3: Kirk Sa 5D 26
Fernhall Cft. S73: Womb 1H 47
Fern Hollow S66: Wick 1H 113
Fernhurst Rd. DN2: Don 4H 41
Fernlea Cl. DN5: Cus 5G 39
Fern Lea Gro. S63: Bolt D 2A 50
Fernlea Gro. S35: Eccl 2G 93
Fernleigh Dr. S60: Brins 2C 110
Fern Rd. S6: Shef 6A 106
Fernvale Wlk. S64: Swint 6C 66
Fern Vw. S12: Shef 5A 136
Fern Vw. Gro. S12: Shef 5A 136
Fern Way S21: Ecki 1C 158
Fernwood Cl. S41: Has 3D 172

Ferrara Cl. S73: D'fld 4H 33
Ferrars Cl. S9: Tins 2A 110
Ferrars Dr. S9: Tins 3A 110
Ferrars Rd. S9: Tins 1H 109
Ferrars Way S9: Tins 3A 110
Ferrers Rd. DN2: Don 5E 41
Ferriby Rd. S6: Shef 2A 106
Ferry Boat La. DN12: Old D 3H 67
        S64: Mexb 2H 67
Ferry La. DN12: Con 3F 69
Ferry Moor La. S72: Grim 2G 19
Ferrymoor Way S72: Grim 2H 19
Ferrymore Ho. DN1: Don 2B 56
                                          (off Oxford Pl.)
Ferry Ter. DN12: Con 3F 69
Fersfield St. S4: Shef 1A 120
Festival Cl. S26: Kiv P 6H 139
Festival Rd. S63: Wath D 1G 65
Fewston Way DN4: Don 4G 57
Fiddle Neck La. S26: Ast 3F 139
Fiddler's Dr. DN3: Arm 6F 43
Field Cl. S18: Dron W 2B 154
        S73: D'fld 4B 34
Fielder M. S5: Shef 6A 94
Fielders Way DN12: New E 3D 70
Fieldfare Ho. S41: Old W 3A 162
Field Ga. DN11: Ross 4D 74
Field Head Ct. S74: Hoyl 6B 46
Field Head Rd. S74: Hoyl 1B 62
Fieldhead Rd. S8: Shef 1F 133
Fieldhead Way S41: Ches 2D 166
Field Ho. Rd. DN5: Sprot 4C 54
Fieldhouse Way S4: Shef 5A 108
Fielding Dr. S66: Braml 5A 100
Fielding Gro. S62: Rawm 1G 83
Fielding Way S60: Shef 2B 106
Field La. DN9: Auck 2C 76
        S21: Killa 3A 110
                                             (Bryony Cl.)
        S21: Killa 5A 152
                                             (Holly Cl.)
        S60: Up W 6D 112
        S66: Mort 6D 112
        S70: Stair 3B 32
Fields End S36: Oxs 6H 177
Fields End Bus. Pk. S63: Gol 4D 36
Fieldsend Gdns. S35: Eccl 2G 93
Fields End Rd. S63: Gol 4C 36
Fieldside DN3: Eden 1C 42
Fieldside Ct. S65: Rav 1A 100
Field Sta. Rd. DN5: Ben 1D 24
Field Vw. S40: Birdh 3H 171
        S40: Ches 5F 167
                                         (off Chatsworth Rd.)
        S60: Brins 3D 110
        S71: Roy 3H 9
Fieldview DN12: New E 5B 70
                                         (off Sunningdale Dr.)
Fieldview Pl. S41: Ches 2D 166
Field Way S60: Roth 2E 97
Fife Gdns. S9: Shef 6D 94
Fife St. S9: Shef 6D 94
        S70: Barn 2C 30
Fife Way S9: Shef 6D 94
Fifth Av. DN6: Woodl 5C 22
        DN9: Finn 3C 76
Fiftyeights Rd. DN9: Finn 5H 77
Figtree La. S1: Shef 2E 5 (2F 119)
Filby Rd. DN5: Cus 5F 39
Filey Av. S71: Roy 2A 10
Filey La. S3: Shef 5A 4 (4D 118)
Filey St. S10: Shef 4A 4 (3D 118)
Finch Cl. S65: Thry 6E 85
Finch Gdns. S66: Braml 6B 100
Finch Ri. S26: Ast 2D 138
Finch Rd. DN4: Balb 6G 55
Finchwell Cl. S13: Shef 4A 122
Finchwell Cres. S13: Shef 4A 122
Finchwell Ri. S13: Shef 4A 122
Finchwell Rd. S13: Shef 4A 122
Findon Cres. S6: Shef 4H 105
Findon Pl. S6: Shef 4H 105
Findon Rd. S6: Shef 4H 105
Findon St. S6: Shef 4A 106
Finkle St. DN5: Ben 2A 40
Finlay Rd. S65: Roth 2H 97
Finlay St. S3: Shef 1A 4 (2D 118)

FINNINGLEY 3F 77
Finningley Lodge S26: Kiv P 6A 140
                                          (off Victoria Cl.)
Finsbury Cl. S25: Laugh C 3F 127
FIRBECK 1H 129
Firbeck Av. S25: Laugh M 1H 127
Firbeck Ho. DN1: Don 2B 56
                                             (off Grove Pl.)
Firbeck La. S25: Laugh M 1H 127
Firbeck Rd. DN4: Don 2E 57
        S8: Shef 5D 132
Firbeck Way DN11: Ross 4E 75
Fircroft Av. S5: Shef 5A 94
Fircroft Rd. S5: Shef 5B 94
Fircrest Way S63: Wath D 4F 49
Fire, Police Mus. 1E 5 (2F 119)
Firethorn Ri. S65: Rav 2B 100
Firham Cl. S71: Roy 2F 9
Fir Pl. S6: Shef 1B 118
        S21: Killa 5B 152
Fir Rd. S21: Ecki 2D 158
Firs, The S70: Barn 4H 31
        S71: Roy 2F 9
Firsby La. DN12: Con 2B 86
Firshill Av. S4: Shef 4G 107
Firshill Cl. S4: Shef 4G 107
Firshill Cres. S4: Shef 4F 107
Firshill Cft. S4: Shef 4F 107
Firshill Gdns. S4: Shef 4F 107
Firshill Glade S4: Shef 4F 107
Firshill M. S3: Shef 4G 107
                                         (off Pitsmoor Rd.)
Firshill Ri. S4: Shef 4F 107
Firshill Wlk. S4: Shef 4F 107
Firshill Way S4: Shef 4F 107
Firs La. S36: H'swne 1D 176
First Av. DN6: Woodl 4D 22
        DN9: Finn 3C 76
        S65: Roth 3H 97
        S71: Roy 2A 10
        WF9: Sth K 5G 13
First La. S25: Sth A 5H 141
        S66: Wick 1H 113
Fir St. S6: Shef 1B 118
        S63: Hol 5G 163
Firth Av. S72: Cud 3D 18
Firth Ct. S43: New W 2C 162
Firth Cres. DN11: New R 5B 74
        S66: Malt 6B 102
Firth Dr. S4: Shef 6A 108
FIRTH PARK 1A 108
Firth Pk. Av. S5: Shef 1B 108
Firth Pk. Cres. S5: Shef 1A 108
Firth Pk. Rd. S5: Shef 1A 108
Firth Rd. S63: Wath D 6C 48
Firth's Homes S11: Shef 6G 117
Firth St. DN4: Balb 3A 56
        S61: Grea 5D 82
        S71: Barn 6E 17
Firthwood Av. S18: Coal A 1A 156
Firthwood Cl.
        S18: Coal A 1A 156
Firthwood Rd. S18: Coal A 1A 156
Fir Tree Av. DN9: Auck 2B 76
Fir Tree Cl. DN5: Hick 3H 37
Fir Tree Dr. S26: Wales 6F 139
Fir Tree Gdns. S70: Birdw 6D 44
Firtree Ri. S35: Chap 4F 79
FIR VALE 3H 107
Fir Vale Pl. S5: Shef 3H 107
Fir Vale Rd. S5: Shef 3H 107
Firvale Rd. S42: Walt 2C 170
Fir Vw. Gdns. S4: Shef 4A 108
Fir Wlk. S66: Malt 5F 101
Fish Dam La.
        S71: Carl, Monk B 6A 10
Fisher Cl. S40: Birdh 3G 171
        S60: Roth 4D 96
Fisher La. S9: Shef 1F 121
Fisher Rd. S66: Malt 6C 102
Fisher St. S5: Ben 6A 24
Fisher Ter. DN5: Don 5H 39
Fish Pond La. S66: B'well 2B 102
Fishponds Rd. S13: Shef 6F 121
Fishponds Rd. W.
        S13: Shef 6F 121
Fishponds Vw. S13: Shef 1G 135

Fitness First
  Chesterfield 1H 167
  Doncaster 4A 56
  Rotherham 5H 83
  Sheffield Hillsborough 1B 106
Fitzalan Rd. S13: Shef 5A 122
Fitzalan Sq. S1: Shef 3F 5 (3G 119)
Fitzalan Way S60: Shef 3G 123
Fitzgerald Rd. S10: Shef 2A 118
Fitzhubert Rd. S2: Shef 6D 120
           (not continuous)
Fitzmaurice Rd. S9: Shef 6E 109
Fitzroy Rd. S2: Shef 2G 133
Fitzwalter Rd. S2: Shef 4A 120
           (not continuous)
Fitzwilliam Av. DN12: Con 4C 68
Fitzwilliam Cl. S74: Hoyl 6C 46
Fitzwilliam Ct. S62: Rawm 4G 83
  S63: Wath D 6F 49
  S74: Hoyl *6C 46*
          (off Fitzwilliam Cl.)
Fitzwilliam Dr. DN5: H'ton 3H 51
Fitzwilliam Gate S1: Shef . . .6C 4 (4F 119)
Fitzwilliam Rd. S65: Roth 3F 97
  S73: D'fld 4D 34
Fitzwilliam Sq. S61: Grea 4C 82
  S74: Els *2E 63*
           (off Wath Rd.)
Fitzwilliam St. S1: Shef 4B 4 (3E 119)
  S62: Parkg 5G 83
  S63: Wath D 1F 65
  S64: Swint 3B 66
           (not continuous)
  S70: Barn 1D 30
  S73: Hem 5E 47
  S74: Els 1D 62
  S74: Hoyl 1G 61
Fitzwilliam Wlk. S61: Grea 5C 82
Five Acres S75: Cawt 3A 14
Five Oaks DN5: Ark 5D 24
Five Trees Av. S17: Dore 4H 145
Five Trees Cl. S17: Dore 4H 145
Five Trees Dr. S17: Dore 4H 145
Five Weirs Wlk. S9: Shef 6C 108
Fixby Ho. DN1: Don 2B 56
           (off Grove Pl.)
Flamsteed Cres. S41: Ches 2H 167
Flanders Ct. S61: Thorpe H 3C 80
FLANDERWELL 4G 99
Flanderwell Av. S66: Braml 5H 99
Flanderwell Ct. S66: Sunn 4H 99
Flanderwell Gdns. S66: Sunn 4H 99
Flanderwell La. S66: Braml, Sunn . . .3G 99
Flash La. S60: Stann 2A 116
  S66: Braml 6B 100
Flask Vw. S6: Stann 5D 104
Flat La. S60: Whist 3A 112
  S72: Bill 5F 35
  S81: Fir 1H 129
Flat St. S1: Shef 3F 5 (3G 119)
Flatts Cl. S60: Tree 1F 123
Flatts La. S60: Tree 1F 123
  S63: Wath D 6E 49
Flaxby Rd. S9: Shef 1E 121
Flax Lea S70: Wors 5F 31
Fleet Cl. S63: Bramp B 5C 48
Fleet Hill Cres. S71: Monk B 3F 17
Fleet La. S35: Ough 6F 91
Fleetwood Av. S71: Monk B 3H 17
Fleming Gdns. S66: Flan 4G 99
Fleming Pl. S70: Barn 2D 30
Fleming Sq. S63: Wath D 6F 49
Fleming Way S66: Flan 5F 99
Fletcher Av. S18: Dron 3F 155
Fletcher Ho. *S65: Roth* *3F 97*
       (off Wharncliffe Hill)
Fleury Cl. S14: Shef 4B 134
Fleury Cres. S14: Shef 4B 134
Fleury Pl. S14: Shef 4B 134
Fleury Ri. S14: Shef 4B 134
Fleury Rd. S14: Shef 4B 134
Flint Rd. DN2: Don 4H 41
Flintson Av. S43: New W 2C 162
Flintway S63: Wath D 3G 65
Flockton Av. S13: Shef 6D 122
Flockton Ct. S1: Shef 4C 4 (3E 119)
Flockton Cres. S13: Shef 6C 122
Flockton Dr. S13: Shef 6D 122

Flockton Ho. S1: Shef 4C 4
Flockton Pk. S20: Holb 1H 151
Flockton Rd. S13: Shef 6C 122
Flodden St. S10: Shef 2A 118
Floodgate Dr. S35: Eccl 2G 93
Flora St. S6: Shef 6D 106
Florence Av. DN4: Balb 4H 55
  S26: Swal 1C 138
Florence Cl. S40: Birdh 4G 171
Florence Ri. S73: D'fld 5A 34
Florence St. S8: Shef 6D 132
  S42: W'orth 6F 171
Flower St. S63: Gol 5E 37
Flowitt St. DN4: Hex 2A 56
  S64: Mexb 1E 67
Fold, The S65: Roth 2C 98
Folderings La. S36: Bolst 6E 175
Folder La. DN5: Sprot 3B 54
FOLDRINGS 2B 90
Folds Cres. S8: Shef 1B 146
Folds Dr. S8: Shef 1B 146
Folds La. S8: Shef 1B 146
Foley Av. S73: Womb 2F 47
Foley St. S4: Shef 1A 120
Foljambe Av. S40: Walt 2E 171
Foljambe Cres. DN11: New R 5A 74
Foljambe Dr. S65: Dalt 1D 98
Foljambe Rd. S40: Ches 5G 167
  S43: Brim 6D 162
  S65: Roth 2A 98
Foljambe St. S62: Parkg 4G 83
Folkwood Gro. S11: Shef 3F 131
Follett Rd. S5: Shef 5H 93
Folly La. S36: Thurl 2A 176
Fonteyn Ho. DN2: Don 4E 41
Fontwell Dr. S64: Mexb 6G 51
Foolow Av. S40: Ches 1G 171
Footgate Cl. S35: Ough 3E 91
Footrill Cotts. S74: Hoyl 2B 62
Forbes Rd. S6: Shef 5B 106
FORD .5H 149
Ford Cl. S18: Dron 3E 155
Ford La. S36: Stoc 2E 175
Fordoles Head La.
  S66: Malt, Mick 2F 101
Ford Rd. S11: Shef 2A 132
  S21: Mar L 4H 145
Fordstead La.
  DN3: Barn D . . . . . . .3E 25 & 1G 27
  DN5: Alm 3E 25
Foremark Rd. DN4: Bess 6A 58
Foremark St. S5: Shef 6A 94
Fore's Rd. DN3: Arm 5F 43
Forest Cl. S35: Ough 6G 91
Forest Edge S11: Shef 1H 145
Forest Grange DN4: Cant 3B 58
Forest Ri. DN4: Balb 1F 71
Forest Rd. S71: Ath 6E 9
Forge, The S2: Shef 5E 119
  S18: Dron 3F 155
  S71: Smi 3E 17
Forge Dr. S40: Ches 1H 171
Forge Hill S35: Ough 3E 91
Forge La. S21: Killa 4A 152
  S35: Ough 3E 91
  S35: Wort 1H 175
  S60: Roth *2C 98*
           (off Bridge St.)
  S74: Els 2E 63
Forge Rd. S26: Wales 5G 139
Forge Way S60: Roth 1F 97
Formby Cl. S71: Monk B 2A 18
Forncett St. S4: Shef 6A 108
Fornham St. S2: Shef 6F 5 (4G 119)
           (not continuous)
Forres Av. S10: Shef 3H 117
Forres Rd. S10: Shef 3H 117
Forrester Cl. S66: Flan 4G 99
Forrester's La. S18: Coal A 6H 147
Forster Rd. DN4: Balb 6A 56
Forth Av. S18: Dron W 2C 154
Fort Hill Rd. S9: Shef 1C 108
Fortway Rd. S60: Brins 2D 110
Forum, The S1: Shef 4C 4
Fossard Cl. DN2: Don 3F 41
Fossard Way DN5: Scawt 1G 39
Fossdale Rd. S7: Shef 3C 132
Foster Ct. S3: Shef 1F 5
Foster Rd. S66: Wick 5G 99

Foster's Cl. S64: Swint 3B 66
Foster St. S70: Stair 2A 32
Foster Way S35: High G 6C 60
Foston Dr. S40: Ches 3C 166
Fothergill Dr. DN3: Eden 5D 26
Foulstone Row S73: Womb 2H 47
Foundry, The S41: Ches 6A 168
Foundry Climbing Centre, The . .1F 119
Foundry Cl. S3: Shef 5G 107
Foundry Ga. S73: Womb 3E 47
Foundry Rd. DN4: Hex 3A 56
Foundry St. S41: Whit M 6H 161
  S62: Parkg 5G 83
  S70: Barn 2D 30
           (not continuous)
  S74: Els 2E 63
Foundry St. Ind. Est. *S41: Whit M* . .*6H 161*
         (off Foundry St.)
Fountain Cl. S75: Dart 5F 7
Fountain Ct. DN11: Ross 6E 75
  S71: Ath 5D 8
Fountain Pde. S75: Mapp 6B 8
Fountain Pct. S1: Shef 3E 5
Fountains Cl. DN3: Kirk Sa 4B 26
Fountain Sq. S75: Dart 5F 7
Fountains Way S71: Monk B 5A 18
Four Lands Cl. S75: Bar G 3F 15
Fountside S7: Shef 2C 132
FOUR LANE ENDS 3G 135
FOURLANE ENDS 4E 133
Fourth Av. DN6: Woodl 5C 22
  DN9: Finn 3C 76
Four Wells Dr. S12: Shef 4B 136
Fowler Bri. Rd. DN5: Ben 2B 40
Fowler Cres. DN11: New R 5B 74
Fowler St. S41: Old W 4G 161
Foxbrook Cl. S42: Ash 3A 166
Foxbrook Ct. S40: Walt 2C 170
Foxbrook Dr. S40: Walt 1C 170
Fox Cl. S61: Kimb P 6G 81
Foxcote Lea S65: Thry 6F 85
Foxcote Way S42: Walt 2C 170
Fox Ct. S64: Swint 5C 66
Foxcovert Cl. S63: Gol 1B 50
Fox Croft S8: Shef 3E 147
  S74: Hoyl 1A 62
Foxcroft Chase S21: Killa 4B 152
Foxcroft Dr. S21: Killa 4B 152
Foxcroft Gro. S21: Killa 4B 152
Foxcroft Mdws. S66: Malt 6A 102
Foxdale Av. S12: Shef 3E 135
Foxen Cft. S71: Lund 4B 18
Fox Farm Ct. S63: Bramp B 5B 48
Foxfield Cl. S12: Shef 6A 136
Fox Flds. S36: Oxs 6G 177
Foxfield Wlk. S70: Stair 4A 32
Fox Glen Rd. S36: Spink 4F 175
Foxglove Cl. S44: Cal 5F 169
Foxglove Rd. S5: Shef 6B 94
Fox Gro. DN4: Warm 6D 54
Foxhall La. S10: Shef 2A 130
Fox Hill S3: Shef 6G 107
Fox Hill Cl. S6: Shef 5B 92
Fox Hill Cres. S6: Shef 5B 92
           (not continuous)
Fox Hill Dr. S6: Shef 5B 92
Fox Hill Pl. S6: Shef 4B 92
Fox Hill Rd. S6: Shef 6B 92
Fox Hill Way S6: Shef 4B 92
Foxland Av. S64: Swint 4H 65
Fox La. DN5: Barnb 1H 51
  S12: Shef 6F 135
  S17: Bradw 4C 146
Fox La. Ct. S12: Shef 4F 135
Fox La. Vw. S12: Shef 4F 135
Foxley Oaks S41: Old W 5A 162
Foxmire Gro. S75: Dod 3E 29
Foxmires Gro. S63: Gol 5E 37
Fox Rd. S6: Shef 6D 106
Foxroyd Cl. S71: Ard 2C 32
Foxshaw M. S72: Grim 2C 20
Fox's Pl. S40: Ches 6E 167
Foxstone Cl. S43: Stav 6A 164
Fox St. S3: Shef 6F 107
  S61: Kimb 4H 95
Fox Wlk. S6: Shef 6C 106
Foxwood Av. S12: Shef 2E 135
Foxwood Cl. S41: Ches 5F 161
  S41: Has 4C 172

Foxwood Dr. S12: Shef 2E 135
Foxwood Gro. DN3: Eden 1B 42
S12: Shef 3E 135
Foxwood Ind. Pk.
S41: Ches 5G 161
Foxwood Rd. S12: Shef 2E 135
S41: Ches 4F 161
Foxwood Way S41: Ches 4F 161
Foyers Way S41: Ches 5A 168
Framlingham Cl. S41: Stav 1A 134
Framlingham Rd. S2: Shef 1A 134
France Rd. S6: Lox 3E 105
Frances Dr. S42: W'orth 6F 171
Frances St. DN1: Don 1C 56
France St. S62: Parkg 5G 83
Francis Cl. S43: Brim 1C 168
Francis Cres. Nth. S60: Roth 1C 112
Francis Cres. Sth. S60: Roth 1C 112
Francis Dr. S60: Roth 6C 98
Francis Gro. S35: High G 1C 78
Francis St. S60: Roth 5F 97
Francus Royd S71: Carl 5H 9
Frankham Cl. S25: Laugh C 4F 127
Franklin Cres. DN2: Don 1E 57
Franklyn Dr. S43: Stav 3C 164
Franklyn Rd. S40: Ches 4F 167
Frank Pl. S9: Shef 5D 108
Frank Rd. DN5: Don 4A 40
Fraser Cl. S8: Shef 5D 132
Fraser Cres. S8: Shef 5D 132
Fraser Dr. S8: Shef 5E 133
Fraser Rd. S8: Shef 5D 132
S60: Roth 5G 97
Fraser Wlk. S8: Shef 6E 133
FRECHEVILLE 4G 135
Frecheville St. S43: Stav 5A 164
Frederick Av. S70: Barn 2C 30
Frederick Dr. S35: Gren 1A 92
Frederick Rd. S7: Shef 1E 133
Frederick St. S9: Shef 1E 121
S60: Cat 1D 122
S60: Roth 3E 97
S63: Gol 5D 36
S63: Wath D 5E 49
S64: Mexb 2E 67
S65: Roth 3E 97
S73: Womb 1F 47
Fred Mulley Rd. S4: Shef 1A 120
Freebirch Vw. S41: Ches 1C 166
Freedom Ct. S6: Shef 5C 106
Freedom Rd. S6: Shef 6B 106
Freeman Gdns. S35: High G 2C 78
Freeman Rd. S66: Wick 5G 99
Freeman St. S70: Barn 2E 31
Freemans Yd. S70: Barn 1E 31
Freesia Cl. S25: Sth A 4F 141
Freeston Pl. S9: Shef 5D 108
French Ga. DN1: Don 6B 40
(not continuous)
Frenchgate Shop. Cen. DN1: Don 1B 56
French St. DN5: Ben 6A 24
Fretson Cl. S2: Shef 6D 120
Fretson Grn. S2: Shef 6D 120
Fretson Rd. S2: Shef 6D 120
Fretson Rd. Sth. S2: Shef 1D 134
Fretwell Cl. S66: Malt 4H 101
Fretwell Rd. S65: Roth 2B 98
S66: Hel 5E 101
Freydon Way S44: Cal 5F 169
Friar Cl. S6: Stann 6E 105
Friars Ga. DN1: Don 6B 40
Friar's Rd. S71: Lund 5B 18
Frickley Bri. La. S72: Brier 2H 11
Frickley Rd. S11: Shef 6G 117
Friers Cft. S62: Wentw 5E 63
Frinton Cl. S40: Birdh 3G 171
Frithbeck Cl. S3: Arm 4E 43
Frith Cl. S12: Shef 3E 135
Frith Rd. S12: Shef 3E 135
Frithwood Dr. S18: Dron 2H 155
Frobisher Grange DN9: Finn 4F 77
Frobisher Gro. S66: Malt 4H 101
Froggatt Cl. S43: Ink 1B 60
Froggatt La. S1: Shef 5E 5 (4F 119)
Frogmore Cl. S66: Braml 4A 100
Frog Wlk. S11: Shef 6D 118
Front St. S60: Tree 2F 123
Frostings, The S35: Gren 1B 92

Frostings Cl. S35: Gren 1B 92
(not continuous)
Fulford Cl. S9: Shef 1F 121
S40: Walt 2D 170
S75: Dart .5H 7
Fulford Pl. S9: Shef 1F 121
Fulford Way DN12: Con 3H 69
Fuller Dr. S41: Ches 2B 168
Fullerton Av. DN12: Con 4C 68
Fullerton Cres. S65: Thry 5A 86
Fullerton Dr. S60: Brins 4C 110
Fullshaw Bank S36: Pen 5E 177
Fulmar Way S61: Thorpe H 2D 80
Fulmer Cl. S71: Ath 2G 17
Fulmere Cres. S5: Shef 4D 92
Fulmere Rd. S5: Shef 4D 92
Fulmer Rd. S11: Shef 1B 132
Fulney Rd. S11: Shef 6G 117
Fulton Rd. S6: Shef 1B 118
FULWOOD 1D 130
Fulwood Chase S10: Shef 6F 117
Fulwood Dr. DN4: Balb 2A 72
Fulwood La. S10: Shef 3A 130
S11: Shef 3A 130
Fulwood Rd. S10: Shef 1E 131
Furlong Ct. S63: Gol 1C 50
Furlong Mdws. S63: Bramp B 6A 48
Furlong Rd. DN5: H'ton 3F 51
S63: Bolt D, Gol 2C 50
Furlong Vw. DN5: H'ton 2G 51
(not continuous)
Furnace Hill S3: Shef 1D 4 (2F 119)
S40: Ches 6F 167
Furnace Hillock Way S41: Has 5D 172
S42: Gras 5D 172
Furnace La. S13: Shef 1E 137
S18: B'low 3A 160
S43: Brim C 2E 169
Furnace Yd. S74: Els 2E 63
Furness Cl. S6: Stann 5E 105
S25: Dinn 1A 142
Furness Dene S31: Monk B 3A 18
Furness Rd. S35: High G 1B 78
Furniss Av. S17: Dore 4E 145
Furniss M. S17: Dore 4F 145
Furnival Cl. S26: Tod 3B 140
Furnival Gate S1: Shef 5D 4 (4F 119)
Furnival Ho. S1: Shef 5F 5
Furnivall Rd. DN4: Balb 4H 55
Furnival Rd. S4: Shef 2G 5 (2G 119)
S26: Tod 3B 140
Furnival Sq. S1: Shef 5E 5 (4F 119)
Furnival St. S1: Shef 5E 5 (4F 119)
Furnival Way S60: Whist 3C 112
Fusion Magna Bus. Cen. S60: Roth . . .6B 96
Future Wlk. S40: Ches 5G 167
Fylde Cl. S71: Monk B 2A 18

G

Gainsborough Cl. S66: Flan 5G 99
Gainsborough Rd. S11: Shef 1C 132
S18: Dron 4D 154
Gainsborough Way S71: Monk B 4G 17
Gainsford Rd. S9: Shef 2F 121
Gaitskell Cl. S63: Gol 1C 50
S66: Malt 6C 102
Gala Bingo
Barnsley 6E 17
Doncaster 3G 41
Rotherham 1A 98
Sheffield 2B 120
Sheffield Hillsborough 1C 106
Gala Cres. S66: Malt 4G 101
Gallery, The S1: Shef 2G 5 (2G 119)
Galley Dr. S20: Water 1E 151
Gallow Tree Rd. S65: Roth 6B 98
Galpharm Way S75: Dod 2F 29
Galsworthy Av. S5: Shef 1E 107
Galsworthy Cl. DN4: Balb 1G 71
(not continuous)
Galsworthy Rd. S5: Shef 2D 106
Galway Cl. S62: Rawm 2H 83
S71: Roy 5D 14
Gamston Rd. S8: Shef 1E 133
Gannow Cl. S21: Killa 3E 153
GANNOW HILL 3E 153

Ganton Pl. S71: Smi 1D 16
Ganton Rd. S6: Shef 2A 106
Garbroads Cres. S65: Thry 6D 84
Garbutt St. S63: Bolt D 3C 50
Garden Cl. S43: New W 3C 162
S60: Roth 2H 111
Garden Cres. S60: Roth 2H 111
Garden Dr. S73: Bramp 4B 48
Gardener Cl. S36: Pen 5E 177
Garden Gro. S73: Hem 4F 47
Garden Ho. Cl. S71: Monk B 3H 17
Garden Ho. Dr. S26: Kiv P 5C 140
Gardenia Rd. DN3: Kirk Sa 5B 26
Garden La. DN4: Hex 3G 55
DN5: Cade 6G 53
S60: Roth 3D 96
S65: Rav 6A 86
Gardens, The DN4: Bess 5A 58
S7: Shef 6D 118
Gardens La. DN12: Con 4E 69
Garden St. S1: Shef 2C 4 (2E 119)
S61: Roth 3C 96
S63: Gol 5E 37
S63: Thurn 2C 36
S63: Wath D 5E 49
S64: Mexb 1F 67
S70: Barn 2E 31
S73: D'fld 5B 34
Garden Ter. DN5: Ben 2A 40
GARDEN VILLAGE 3C 174
Garden Wlk. S20: Beig 5H 137
S60: Roth 2H 111
Gardom Cl. S18: Dron W 3C 154
Garfield Mt. S65: Roth 4F 97
Garland Cl. S20: Westf 2F 151
Garland Cft. S20: Westf 3F 151
Garland Dr. S6: Lox 3F 105
Garland Mt. S20: Westf 3F 151
Garland Way S20: Westf 3F 151
Garraby Cl. S72: Gt H 6F 21
Garry Rd. S6: Shef 3A 106
Garside's Bldgs. S36: Pen 4C 176
(off Stottercliffe Rd.)
Garter St. S4: Shef 5A 108
Garth Cl. S9: Shef 1D 120
Garth Rd. S9: Shef 3E 155
Garth Way S18: Dron 3E 155
Garth Way Cl. S18: Dron 3E 155
Gartrice Gdns. S20: Half 5H 151
Gartrice Gro. S20: Half 5H 151
Gashouse La. S20: Mosb 5E 151
S21: Ecki 5E 151
Gate, The S75: Dod 2G 29
Gate Cres. S75: Dod 2G 29
Gatefield Cl. S41: Ches 2D 166
Gatefield Rd. S7: Shef 2D 132
Gatehouse Ct. S75: Dod 2G 29
Gate Ho. La. DN9: Auck 1C 76
Gateland La.
S18: B'low . . . . .6D 154 & 1A 160
Gatesbridge Pk. DN9: Finn 2G 77
Gateway, The S2: Shef 2H 5
S25: Dinn 4A 128
S62: Parkg 6F 83
Gateway Cl. S62: Parkg 1F 97
Gateway Ct. S62: Parkg 6F 83
Gateway Ind. Est., The S62: Parkg . . .6F 83
Gateway Pl. S62: Parkg 1F 97
Gateway Plaza S70: Barn 1D 30
Gatewood La. DN3: Brant, Cant 2F 59
Gattison La. DN11: New R 6C 74
Gatty Rd. S5: Shef 3A 94
Gaunt Cl. S14: Shef 5A 134
S21: Killa 4B 152
S66: Braml 4A 100
Gaunt Dr. S14: Shef 5A 134
S66: Braml 4A 100
Gaunt Pl. S14: Shef 5A 134
Gaunt Rd. S14: Shef 5A 134
S66: Braml 4A 100
Gaunt Way S14: Shef 5A 134
GAWBER 4H 15
Gawber Rd. S75: Barn 5B 16
Gawtress Row S63: Wath D 6F 49
Gayle Cl. S70: Barn 6C 16
Gayton Cl. DN4: Balb 1H 71
Gayton Ct. DN4: Balb 1H 71
Gayton Rd. S4: Shef 4H 107
Geer La. S12: Ridg 5F 149

Gelderd Pl.—Goosebutt Ho.

Gelderd Pl. S18: Dron 4F **155**
Gell St. S3: Shef 3A **4** (3D **118**)
Genn La. S70: Barn, Wors 4C **30**
Genoa Cl. S73: D'fld 3H **33**
Genoa St. S64: Mexb 1G **67**
George Buckley Ct. WF9: Sth K 4H **13**
George Pl. S62: Rawm 3H **83**
S64: Mexb 1H **67**
George Sq. S70: Barn 1D **30**
George St. DN3: Arm 3C **42**
DN5: Ben 6H **23**
S1: Shef 3F **5** (3G **119**)
S41: Old W 4G **161**
S43: Brim 6D **162**
S60: Roth 3E **97**
S63: Gol 5B **36**
S63: Thurn 3E **37**
S70: Barn 1D **30**
S70: Wors 6F **31**
(John St.)
S70: Wors 6H **31**
(Pantry Grn.)
S72: Cud 6F **11**
S72: Midd 3E **35**
S73: Womb 2G **47**
(Hoyland St.)
S73: Womb 6A **34**
(Stonyford Rd.)
S74: Hoyl 1B **62**
S75: Mapp 5A **8**
George Woofindin Almshouses
S11: Shef 6B **118**
George Yd. S70: Barn 1D **30**
Georgian M. S60: Cat 6D **110**
Gerald Cl. S70: Barn 3H **31**
Gerald Cres. S70: Barn 2H **31**
Gerald Pl. S70: Barn 3H **31**
Gerald Rd. S70: Barn 3H **31**
Gerald St. S9: Shef 5D **108**
Gerald Wlk. S70: Barn 3H **31**
Gerard Av. S65: Thry 6F **85**
Gerard Cl. S8: Shef 2G **133**
S40: Walt 1D **170**
Gerard Rd. S60: Roth 5F **97**
Gerard St. S8: Shef 2G **133**
Gervase Av. S8: Shef 4D **146**
Gervase Dr. S8: Shef 4D **146**
Gervase Pl. S8: Shef 4D **146**
Gervase Rd. S8: Shef 4D **146**
Gervase Wlk. S8: Shef 4D **146**
Gibb Ct. *S43: New W 2C 162*
(off Handley Rd.)
Gibbing Greaves Rd. S65: Roth 6D **98**
Gibbons Dr. S14: Shef 6B **134**
Gibbons Wlk. *S14: Shef 6B 134*
(off Gibbons Dr.)
Gibraltar St. S3: Shef 1D **4** (2F **119**)
Gibson La. S36: Stoc 2E **175**
Gifford Dr. DN4: Warm 6E **55**
Gifford Rd. S8: Shef 1F **133**
Gilbert Av. S40: Walt 2E **171**
Gilbert Ct. S2: Shef 5H **5**
Gilbert Gro. S70: Barn 2A **32**
Gilberthorpe Ct. S65: Roth 4G **97**
Gilberthorpe Dr. S65: Roth 4H **97**
Gilberthorpe Rd. DN4: Balb 5G **55**
Gilberthorpe St. S65: Roth 4G **97**
Gilbert Row S2: Shef 3H **5** (3H **119**)
Gilder Way S72: Shaft 4F **11**
Gildhurst Ct. S70: Birdw 6E **45**
GILDINGWELLS 1G **143**
Gildingwells Rd. S81: Letw 5G **129**
S81: Woods 4F **143**
Giles Av. S63: Wath D 6D **48**
Gileswood Cres. S63: Bramp B 5B **48**
Gill Cl. S66: Wick 1H **113**
Gill Cft. S6: Stann 6D **104**
Gilleyfield Av. S17: Dore 3F **145**
Gill Mdws. S6: Stann 6D **104**
Gillott Dell S66: Wick 1G **113**
Gillott Ind. Est. S75: Barn 6C **16**
Gillott La. S66: Wick 1G **113**
Gillott Rd. S6: Shef 6B **92**
Gill St. DN1: Don 2C **56**
S74: Hoyl 1C **62**
Gilpin La. S6: Shef 1D **118**
Gilpin St. S6: Shef 6D **106**
GILROYD 5H **29**
Gilroyd La. S75: Dod, Stainb 5H **29**
Ginhouse La. S61: Grea 2D **96**
Gipsy Grn. La. S63: Wath D 2G **65**
Gipsy La. S18: App 3D **156**
S41: Old W 5A **162**
Gisborne Cl. S43: Stav 5C **164**
Gisborne Rd. S11: Shef 2A **132**
Glade, The S10: Shef 5A **118**
S40: Ches 5E **167**
Glade Cl. S40: Ches 3F **167**
Glade Cft. S12: Shef 4D **134**
Glade Lea S12: Shef 4D **134**
Glade Vw. DN3: Kirk Sa 4C **26**
Gladstone M. S10: Shef 5F **117**
Gladstone Pl. S64: Mexb 1D **66**
Gladstone Rd. DN4: Hex 3H **55**
S10: Shef 5G **117**
S40: Ches 4G **167**
S66: Malt 4H **101**
Gladwin Gdns. S40: Walt 2E **171**
Gladwin Ind. Pk. S64: Kiln 1D **84**
Gladys St. S65: Roth 4H **97**
Glaisdale Cl. S25: Laugh C 3F **127**
Glaisdale Ct. S25: Laugh C 3F **127**
Glamis Rd. DN2: Don 1F **57**
Glass House Grn. S62: Wentw 4G **63**
Glasshouse La. S43: New W 1C **162**
S64: Kiln 1D **84**
Glasshouse Rd. S64: Kiln 1D **84**
Glasshouse St. S60: Roth 3D **96**
Glastonbury Ga. DN5: Scaws 5E **39**
GLEADLESS 5D **134**
Gleadless Av. S12: Shef 4C **134**
Gleadless Bank S12: Shef 4C **134**
Gleadless Comn. S12: Shef 2C **134**
Gleadless Ct. S2: Shef 2G **133**
Gleadless Dr. S12: Shef 4C **134**
Gleadless Mt. S12: Shef 5D **134**
Gleadless Ri. S12: Shef 3C **134**
Gleadless Rd. S2: Shef 1F **133**
(not continuous)
S12: Shef 3B **134**
S14: Shef 3B **134**
GLEADLESS TOWNEND 5C **134**
Gleadless Townend Stop (ST) 5D **134**
GLEADLESS VALLEY 4B **134**
Gleadless Vw. S12: Shef 3C **134**
Glebe, The S41: Old W 4H **161**
Glebe Cl. *S64: Mexb 2G 67*
(off Doncaster Rd.)
S64: Swint 5B **66**
Glebe Ct. S41: Old W 4H **161**
S75: Tank 1D **60**
Glebe Cres. S65: Thry 1D **98**
Glebe Farm Cl. DN3: Arm 3D **42**
Glebeland Cl. S62: Rawm 1F **83**
Glebelands Rd. S36: Stoc 4E **175**
Glebe Rd. S10: Shef 2B **118**
S64: Swint 5B **66**
Glebe St. DN4: Warm 6E **55**
Glebe Way, The S41: Old W 4H **161**
Gledhill Av. S36: Cub 6C **176**
Gledhill Cl. S18: Dron 3F **155**
Glen, The S10: Shef 5A **118**
S35: Wharn S 1C **90**
Glenalmond Rd. S11: Shef 1A **132**
Glenavon Cl. S43: New W 1C **162**
Glencairn Cl. *S66: Malt 5D 102*
(off Woodside Cl.)
Glencoe Dr. S2: Shef 4H **119**
Glencoe Pl. S2: Shef 4H **119**
Glencoe Rd. S2: Shef 5H **5** (4H **119**)
Glencoe Way S40: Ash 4C **166**
Glencroft S11: Shef 1H **131**
Glendale Cl. S75: Barn 6A **16**
Glendale Rd. DN5: Sprot 3C **54**
Gleneagles Cl. S40: Walt 2D **170**
Gleneagles Dr. DN4: Cant 6E **59**
Gleneagles Ri. S64: Swint 4C **66**
Gleneagles Rd. S25: Dinn 6A **128**
Glen Fld. Av. DN4: Hex 3H **55**
Glenfield Cres. S41: Ches 1G **167**
Glen Head S17: Dore 1E **145**
Glenholme Dr. S13: Shef 1H **135**
Glenholme Pl. S13: Shef 1A **136**
Glenholme Rd. S13: Shef 1A **136**
Glenholme Way S13: Shef 6H **121**
Glenmoor Av. S70: Barn 2A **30**
Glenmore Cl. S43: Ink 3G **169**
Glenmore Cft. S12: Shef 2E **135**
Glenmore Ri. S73: Womb 3H **47**
Glenorchy Rd. S7: Shef 3C **132**
Glen Rd. DN3: Brant 4H **59**
S7: Shef 2D **132**
(not continuous)
Glenthorne Cl. S40: Bramp 6D **166**
Glentilt Rd. S7: Shef 3C **132**
Glen Va. S18: Dron W 3C **154**
Glen Vw. S11: Shef 6G **117**
S64: Mexb 1G **67**
Glen Vw. M. S64: Mexb 2G **67**
Glen Vw. Rd. S8: Shef 2D **146**
Glenville Cl. S74: Hoyl 1A **62**
Glenwood Ct. S6: Shef 1G **105**
Glenwood Cres. S35: Chap 3G **79**
Glenwood Dr. S6: Shef 1G **105**
Glenwood M. S6: Shef 1G **105**
Gliwice Way DN4: Don 3G **57**
Glossop La. S10: Shef 4A **4** (3D **118**)
Glossop Rd. S10: Shef 4A **4** (4B **118**)
Glossop Row S35: Ough 3E **91**
Glossop's Cft. S41: Old W 4A **162**
Gloucester Av. S41: Ches 2G **167**
Gloucester Cres. S10: Shef 4D **118**
Gloucester Rd. DN2: Don 5F **41**
S41: Ches 3G **167**
S61: Kimb P 1A **96**
Gloucester St. S10: Shef 4D **118**
Glover Rd. S8: Shef 1F **133**
S17: Tot 6G **145**
Glumangate S40: Ches 5H **167**
Glyn Av. DN1: Don 6D **40**
Goals Soccer Cen.
Sheffield 6H **5** (5H **119**)
Goathland Cl. S13: Shef 1E **137**
Goathland Dr. S13: Shef 1E **137**
Goathland Pl. S13: Shef 1E **137**
Goathland Rd. S13: Shef 1E **137**
Goddard Av. S36: Stoc 2B **174**
Goddard Hall Rd. S5: Shef 3H **107**
Godley Cl. S71: Roy 2A **10**
Godley St. S71: Roy 2A **10**
Godric Dr. S60: Brins 3C **110**
Godric Grn. S60: Brins 3C **110**
Godric Rd. S5: Shef 3H **93**
Godstone Rd. S60: Roth 5F **97**
Goldcrest Ho. S41: Old W 3A **162**
Goldcrest Wlk. S61: Thorpe H 3D **80**
Gold Cft. S70: Barn 2F **31**
Golden Oak Dell S6: Stann 5D **104**
Golden Smithies La. S63: Wath D 3A **66**
S64: Swint 3A **66**
Goldfinch Ct. S63: Wath D 5E **49**
Goldsborough Rd. DN2: Don 1F **57**
Goldsmith Dr. S65: Roth 4A **98**
Goldsmith Rd. DN4: Balb 6B **56**
S65: Roth 4A **98**
Gold St. S70: Barn 2F **31**
Goldsworthy Way S75: Wool G 3E **7**
GOLDTHORPE 5D **36**
Goldthorpe Grn. S63: Gol 6C **36**
Goldthorpe Ind. Est. S63: Gol 6A **36**
Goldthorpe Rd. S63: Gol 6D **36**
Goldthorpe Station (Rail) 5C **36**
Gomersal La. S18: Dron 3F **155**
Gomersall Av. DN12: Con 4C **68**
Gooder Av. S71: Roy 3H **9**
Goodison Blvd. DN4: Cant 4B **58**
Goodison Ct. DN4: Cant 4B **58**
Goodison Cres. S6: Shef 6G **105**
Goodison M. DN4: Cant 6C **58**
Goodison Ri. S6: Shef 6G **105**
Goodison Wlk. DN4: Cant 6D **58**
Goodman Ct. S44: Cal 5F **169**
Goodwin Av. S62: Rawm 2G **83**
Goodwin Cres. S64: Swint 2B **66**
Goodwin Rd. S8: Shef 2F **133**
S61: Wing 4B **82**
Goodwin Sports Cen. 3C **118**
Goodwin Way S61: Wing 4B **82**
Goodwood Gdns. DN4: Cant 2A **58**
Goodyear Cres. S73: Womb 2G **47**
GOOLE GREEN 1E **131**
Goore Av. S9: Shef 4E **121**
Goore Dr. S9: Shef 3E **121**
Goore Rd. S9: Shef 4E **121**
Gooseacre Av. S63: Thurn 1B **36**
Goosebutt Ct. S62: Parkg 4G **83**
Goosebutt Ho. S62: Parkg 4G **83**

A-Z Sheffield 211

Goosebutt St. S62: Parkg 4G **83**
Goosecarr La. S26: Tod 1H **139**
Goose Ct. S66: Wick 6H **99**
Goosecroft Av. S65: Thry 6D **84**
Goosehill Ct. DN4: Balb 2A **72**
Goose La. S66: Wick 6H **99**
Gordon Av. S8: Shef 6F **133**
Gordon Rd. DN12: New E 4C **70**
S11: Shef 6C **118**
Gordon Rd. Flats DN12: New E 4C **70**
Gordon St. DN1: Don 1B **56**
S70: Stair 2B **32**
Gordon Ter. S65: Roth 4G **97**
Gorehill Cl. S63: Wath D 6H **49**
Gorman Cl. S41: Ches 6F **161**
Gorse, The S65: Roth 5B **98**
S66: Wick 1G **113**
Gorse Cl. S63: Bramp B 6A **48**
S65: Rav 2C **100**
Gorse Dr. S21: Killa 5C **152**
Gorseland Ct. S66: Wick 6F **99**
Gorse La. S10: Shef 1A **130**
Gorse Valley Rd. S41: Has 3D **172**
Gorse Valley Way S41: Has 3D **172**
Gorsey Brigg S18: Dron W 3C **154**
Gosber Rd. S21: Ecki 1F **159**
Gosber St. S21: Ecki 1E **159**
Gosforth Cl. S18: Dron 3E **155**
Gosforth Cres. S18: Dron 3E **155**
Gosforth Dr.
S18: Dron, Dron W 3C **154**
Gosforth Grn. S18: Dron 3E **155**
Gosforth La. S18: Dron 3E **155**
Gosling Ga. Rd. S63: Gol 5D **36**
Gotham Rd. S60: Brins 2D **110**
Gough Cl. S65: Roth 6B **98**
Goulding St. S64: Mexb 2E **67**
Gowdall Grn. DN5: Ben 5H **23**
Gower Cres. S40: Ches 3D **166**
Gower St. S4: Shef 6H **107**
S73: Womb 2H **47**
Gower Way S62: Rawm 6D **64**
Goyt Side Rd. S40: Ches 6E **167**
Goyt Ter. S40: Ches 6F **167**
Grace Rd. DN12: New E 3D **70**
Grace St. S71: Monk B 2C **18**
Grady Dr. DN4: Balb 1B **72**
Graftdyke Cl. DN11: Ross 5E **75**
Grafton St. S2: Shef 5H **5** (4H **119**)
S70: Barn 1C **30**
Grafton Way S65: Roth 3F **97**
Graham Av. S60: Brins 5E **111**
Graham Ct. S10: Shef 6G **117**
Graham Knoll S10: Shef 6G **117**
Graham Ri. S10: Shef 6G **117**
Graham Rd. DN3: Kirk Sa 5C **26**
S10: Shef 5F **117**
Graham's Orchard
S70: Barn 1D **30**
Grainger Cl. DN12: New E 5B **70**
Grainger Ct. S10: Shef 5F **117**
Grammar St. S6: Shef 5C **106**
(not continuous)
Grampian Cl. DN5: Cus 5F **39**
S75: Barn 6A **16**
Grampian Cres. S40: Ches 4C **166**
Granary, The *S11: Shef 5E* ***119***
(off Napier St.)
Granary Cl. S41: Up N 6B **160**
Granary Ct. *S25: Nth A 2G* ***141***
(off The Green)
Granby Ct. DN3: Arm 5F **43**
Granby Cres. DN2: Don 2E **57**
Granby La. DN11: New R 4A **74**
Granby Rd. DN12: New E 4D **70**
S5: Shef .2A **108**
Grange, The S42: Ash 4A **166**
S43: Brim 6B **162**
S61: Scho 6F **81**
S75: Barn 5H **15**
S75: Wool G 3F **7**
Grange Av. DN4: Balb 5H **55**
S18: Dron W 3D **154**
S26: Augh 5B **124**
S81: Woods 5F **143**
Grange Cliffe Cl. S11: Shef 4A **132**
Grange Cl. DN4: Bess 6C **58**
S66: Bramp M 1A **126**
S72: Brier 3A **12**
Grange Ct. DN4: Bess 6C **58**
DN5: Don 4A **40**
S66: Wick 1G **113**
S72: Brier 3A ***12***
(off Grange Cl.)
S73: Womb 2H **47**
Grange Cres. S11: Shef 6D **118**
S63: Thurn 1D **36**
S71: Barn 6B **18**
Grange Cres. Rd. S11: Shef 6D **118**
Grange Dr. S61: Kimb 1G **95**
S66: Hel 6E **101**
Grange Farm Cl. S60: Brins 5E **111**
Grange Farm Ct. *S63: Bolt D 2B* ***50***
(off High St.)
S81: Woods 5F **143**
Grange Farm Dr. S26: Ast 2D **138**
S35: Ough 6E **91**
Grangefield Av. DN4: Cant 6C **58**
DN11: New R 5C **74**
Grangefield Cres.
DN11: New R 5C **74**
Grangefield Ter. DN11: New R 5C **74**
Grange Gdns. S26: Tod 1B **140**
GRANGE LANE 2C 94
Grange La. DN4: A'ley 2F **71**
DN5: H'ton 2A **52**
DN11: A'ley 3G **71**
DN11: New R 6H **73**
S5: Shef .2C **94**
S13: Shef 6B **122**
S60: Brins, Roth 1B **110**
S61: Thorpe H 2C **94**
S66: Malt 5B **102**
S70: Stair 6B **18**
S71: Barn, Stair 6B **18**
Grange La. Ind. Est. S71: Stair 1B **32**
Grange M. S66: Wick 6G **99**
Grange Mill La. S5: Shef 2C **94**
S9: Shef .2C **94**
Grangemill Pl. S43: Stav 6H **163**
Grange Pk. DN3: Kirk Sa 3D **26**
Grange Pk. Av. S43: Brim C 4E **169**
Grange Park Golf Course 1D 94
Grange Rd. DN4: Bess, Cant 6C **58**
DN5: Ben 4H **23**
DN6: Woodl 5D **22**
DN11: New R 6B **74**
S11: Shef 6D **118**
S20: Beig 5G **137**
S60: Roth 2A **112**
S62: Rawm 1H **83**
S63: Wath D 1E **65**
S64: Swint 4A **66**
S71: Roy .3F **9**
S72: Brier 3A **12**
Grange St. S63: Thurn 2D **36**
Grange Vw. DN4: Balb 4H **55**
S74: Black H 3A **46**
Grange Vw. Cres. S61: Kimb 2G **95**
Grange Vw. Rd. S61: Kimb 2G **95**
Grange Way DN12: Den M 3C **68**
Grangewood Rd. S25: Laugh M 2H **127**
S40: Birdh 3G **171**
Granham Acre S72: Shaft 4F **11**
Gransden Way S40: Walt 2D **170**
Grantham St. DN11: New R 5B **74**
Grantley Cl. S73: Womb 4A **48**
Granville Cl. S41: Has 2C **172**
Granville Rd. S2: Shef 6G **5** (4G **119**)
Granville Road / The Sheffield College Stop (ST) 6G 5 (5G 119)
Granville Sq. S2: Shef 6G **5** (4G **119**)
Granville St. S2: Shef 6G **5** (4G **119**)
S75: Barn 5C **16**
Granville Ter. S65: Roth 4G **97**
Grasby Ct. S66: Braml 3A **100**
Grasmere Av. DN2: Don 6H **41**
Grasmere Cl. S25: Nth A 2A **142**
S36: Pen 3D **176**
S41: Ches 1E **167**
S63: Bolt D 3B **50**
S64: Mexb 6A **52**
Grasmere Cres. S75: Stain 4H **7**
Grasmere Rd. DN12: Con 4E **69**
S8: Shef .3D **132**
S18: Dron W 3C **154**
S71: Barn 1F **31**
Grasscroft Cl. S40: Ches 2E **167**
Grasscroft Ho. *S40: Ches 1H* ***171***
(off Archdale Cl.)
Grasscroft Mobile Home Pk.
S43: New W 1C **162**
Grassdale Vw. S12: Shef 5A **136**
GRASSHILL 6D 172
Grassholme Cl. DN4: Don 4G **57**
Grassington Cl. S12: Shef 5C **136**
Grassington Dr. S12: Shef 5C **136**
Grassington Way
S35: Chap 2E **79**
Grassmoor Cl. S12: Shef 3C **134**
Grassmoor Country Pk. 6E 173
Grassmoor Golf Course 6D 172
Grassthorpe Rd. S12: Shef 4E **135**
Grattan St. S61: Kimb 4H **95**
Gratton Ct. S43: Stav 3C **164**
Graven Cl. S35: Gren 2A **92**
Graves Art Gallery 4F 5
Graves Park Animal Farm 6G 133
Graves Tennis & Leisure Cen. 3G 147
Graves Trust Homes
S8: Shef .2E **147**
(Meadow Vw. Rd.)
S8: Shef .2F **147**
(Serpentine Wlk.)
S12: Shef 3D **134**
Gray Av. S26: Swal 5C **124**
Gray Cl. S65: Roth 2F **97**
Gray Gdns. DN4: Balb 6A **56**
Grays Ct. DN12: Den M 2D **68**
Grayshott Wlk. S40: Birdh 2G **171**
Grayson Cl. S36: Stoc 4E **175**
S65: Rav 2A **100**
Grayson Rd. S61: Wing 4B **82**
Gray's Rd. S71: Carl 5H **9**
Gray St. S3: Shef 6G **107**
S20: Mosb 3D **150**
S74: Els .1D **62**
Greasbro Rd. S9: Tins 2G **109**
GREASBROUGH 5D 82
Greasbrough La. S62: Rawm 4D **82**
Greasbrough Rd. S60: Roth 6D **82**
(not continuous)
S61: Grea 1E **97**
S62: Parkg 5E **83**
Greasbrough St. S60: Roth 3D **96**
Gt. Bank Rd. S65: Roth 6B **98**
Gt. Broad Ing S75: Barn 4A **16**
Gt. Central Av. DN4: Balb 4A **56**
Gt. Cliffe Rd. S75: Dod 2F **29**
Great Cft. S18: Dron W 2C **154**
Gt. Eastern Way S62: Parkg 6G **83**
GREAT HOUGHTON 1F 35
Great Nth. Rd. DN4: Bess 5A **58**
DN5: Scawt 6D **22**
DN6: Woodl, Adw S 1A **22**
DN6: Highf 6D **22**
DN11: Ross 3F **75**
Great Pk. Rd. S61: Kimb P 2H **95**
Great Stubbing S73: Womb 1E **47**
Greaves Cl. S6: Stann 6D **104**
Greaves Fold S75: Barn 6A **16**
Greaves La. S6: Shef, Stann 6D **104**
S35: High G 4C **60**
Greaves Rd. S5: Shef 2F **93**
S61: Roth 3B **96**
Greaves Sike La. S66: Mick 1E **101**
Greaves St. S6: Shef 5C **106**
Greave Way S43: Brim 6B **162**
Grebe Ct. S73: Bramp 3B **48**
GREEN, THE 5D 176
Green, The DN5: Barnb 1A **52**
DN9: Auck 1H **59**
DN9: Finn 3F **77**
DN12: Old D 3H **67**
S9: Shef .2F ***121***
(off The Avenue)
S17: Tot .6E **145**
S25: Nth A 2G **141**
S26: Wales B 5C **138**
S36: Pen 5C **176**
S36: Thurl 3A **176**
S41: Has 4B **172**
S60: Roth 1G **111**
S60: Whist 4A **112**
S63: Bolt D 1B **50**
S64: Swint 4A **66**
S66: Sunn 3H **99**

Green, The S71: Roy 3H **9**
(not continuous)
S72: Shaft 3E **11**
S73: Hem 5F **47**
Greenacre Cl. S12: Shef 4C **134**
Green Acres S36: Pen 4E **177**
S62: Rawm 3H **83**
S72: Grim 1B **20**
S74: Hoyl 1B **62**
Greenacres Cl. S18: Dron 5H **155**
S74: Hoyl 1C **62**
Greenacres Vw. S65: Rav 2A **100**
Greenacre Way S12: Shef 4C **134**
Green Arbour Ct. S66: Thurc 1B **126**
Green Arbour Rd. S66: Thurc 5B **114**
Green Av. DN5: High M, Marr 1F **53**
Green Balk S66: Clift 3A **88**
Greenbank S71: Ath 5E **9**
Green Bank Dr. S66: Sunn 2H **99**
Greenbank Dr. S40: Ash 4D **166**
Greenbank Wlk. S72: Grim 1A **20**
Green Blvd. DN4: Cant 4B **58**
Green Brook Pl. S36: Pen 5D **176**
Green Chase S71: Ecki 1D **158**
Green Cl. S18: Uns 6B **156**
S43: Ink 2H **169**
Green Comn. DN3: Arm 5E **43**
Green Ct. S66: Sunn 3H **99**
Greencroft S60: Roth 1G **111**
Greencroft Cl. S60: Roth 1G **111**
Green Cross S18: Dron 2G **155**
Greendale Av. S42: Holy 2A **170**
Greendale Ct. S18: Dron 2G **155**
Greendale Shop. Cen. S18: Dron ..2G **155**
Green Dyke La. DN1: Don 3B **56**
Green Dyke Way S75: Barn 4H **15**
Green Farm Cl. S40: Ches 2D **166**
Green Farm Hamlet S36: Stoc ...3A **174**
Greenfield S62: Rawm 3G **83**
Greenfield Cl. DN3: Arm 5F **43**
DN3: Barn D 2D **26**
S8: Shef 3E **147**
S65: Roth 2C **98**
Greenfield Cotts. S71: Carl 6H **9**
Greenfield Ct. DN4: Balb 4H **55**
S66: Flan 4G **99**
Greenfield Dr. S8: Shef 3E **147**
S66: Flan 4G **99**
S71: Ath 5D **8**
Greenfield La. DN4: Balb, Hex ...3H **55**
Greenfield M. S63: Wath D 6E **49**
Greenfield Rd. S8: Shef 3E **147**
S65: Roth 2C **98**
S74: Hoyl 6B **46**
WF9: Hems 1E **13**
Greenfields S21: Ecki 1D **158**
Greenfield Vw. S64: Mexb 4E **51**
Greenfinch Cl. S60: Brins 4E **111**
Greenfoot Cl. S75: Barn 5C **16**
Greenfoot La. S75: Barn 4C **16**
(not continuous)
Green Gables S64: Mexb 1E **67**
Green Gate Cl. S63: Bolt D 1C **50**
Greengate Cl. S13: Shef 2E **137**
S40: Bramp 6D **166**
Greengate Ct. S35: High G 1D **78**
Greengate La. S13: Shef 2D **136**
S35: High G 2C **78**
Greengate Rd. S13: Shef 2E **137**
Glen Glen S40: Bramp 6D **166**
Greenhall Rd. S21: Ecki 1D **158**
Greenhead Gdns. S35: Chap 3F **79**
Greenhead La. S35: Chap 3F **79**
GREENHILL 3D **146**
Greenhill Av. S8: Shef 2D **146**
S66: Hel 6E **101**
S71: Barn 5E **17**
Green Hill Gro. S36: H'swne 1G **177**
Greenhill Main Rd. S8: Shef 3D **146**
Greenhill Parkway S8: Shef 4C **146**
Greenhill Rd. S8: Shef 6E **133**
Greenhouse Ct. DN2: Don 5F **41**
Greenhouse La. S10: Shef 3A **130**
Green Ho. Rd. DN2: Don 4G **41**
Greenhow St. S6: Shef 1B **118**
Green Ings La. S63: Wath D 5H **49**
GREENLAND 5F **109**
Greenland S74: Black H 3A **46**

Green St. DN4: Balb 6G **55**
S36: Spink 3F **175**
S41: Old W 4H **161**
S61: Grea 4C **82**
S70: Wors 5H **31**
S74: Hoyl 6C **46**
Green Vw., The S72: Shaft 2E **11**
Greenway S26: Kiv P 6A **140**
Greenway, The S24: Shef 2E **147**
S36: Spink 4G **175**
Greenways S40: Walt 2D **170**
Greenway Vw. S73: Shef 5G **47**
Greenwood Av. DN4: Balb 4G **55**
S9: Shef 3D **120**
S70: Wors 5G **31**
Greenwood Cl. S9: Shef 3E **121**
Greenwood Cres. S9: Shef 3D **120**
S66: Wick 5H **99**
S71: Roy 2G **9**
Greenwood Dr. S9: Shef 3D **120**
Greenwood La. S13: Shef 1E **137**
Greenwood Rd. S9: Shef 3E **121**
S35: High G 1E **79**
S64: Kiln 1D **84**
Greenwood Ter. S70: Wors 6D **16**
Greenwood Way S9: Shef 3D **120**
Greeton Dr. S35: Ough 4F **91**
Gregg Ho. Cres. S5: Shef 5A **94**
Gregg Ho. Rd. S5: Shef 4A **94**
Greggs Ct. S70: Stair 3A **32**
Gregory Cl. S43: Brim 6C **162**
Gregory La. S43: Brim 5C **162**
Gregory Rd. S8: Shef 2F **133**
Gregory's Bldgs. S72: Gt H 6E **21**
Grendon Vs. S65: Roth 3H **97**
Grenfell Av. S64: Mexb 1G **67**
Grenfolds Rd. S35: Green 2C **92**
Grenfore Cres. S35: Green 2C **92**
Grenobank Rd. S35: Green 2C **92**
Greno Cres. S35: Green 2C **92**
Greno Ga. S35: Green 1B **92**
Grenomoor Cl. S35: Green 2B **92**
Greno Rd. S64: Swint 4C **66**
GRENOSIDE 1B **92**
Grenoside Crematorium S35: Gren ..3A **92**
Grenoside Grange Cl. S35: Green ..2C **92**
Grenoside Mt. S35: Green 3C **92**
Greno Vw. S74: Hoyl 1H **61**
Greno Vw. Rd. S35: High G 1D **78**
Greno Wood Ct. S35: Gren 1B **92**
Grenville Pl. S75: Barn 5B **16**
Grenville Rd. DN4: Balb 6F **55**
Gresford Cl. S75: Wool G 3E **7**
Gresham Av. S60: Brins 3D **110**
Gresham Rd. S6: Shef 6B **106**
Gresley Rd. DN4: Balb 3A **56**
S8: Shef 5D **146**
Gresley Wlk. S8: Shef 5D **146**
Greyfriars Rd. DN1: Don 1H **131**
Greyfriars Rd. DN1: Don 6B **40**
Greystock St. S4: Shef 6B **108**
GREYSTONES 1H **131**
Greystones Av. S11: Shef 1A **132**
S70: Wors 6E **31**
GREYSTONES CLIFFE 1G **131**
Greystones Cl. S11: Shef 1H **131**
Greystones Cres. S11: Shef 1H **131**
Greystones Dr. S11: Shef 1H **131**
Greystones Grange S11: Shef 1H **131**
Greystones Grange Cres.
S11: Shef 1H **131**
Greystones Grange Rd. S11: Shef ..1H **131**
Greystones Hall Rd. S11: Shef ...6H **117**
Greystones Ri. S11: Shef 1H **131**
Greystones Rd. S11: Shef 1G **131**
Greywood Cl. DN2: Don 2G **41**
Grice Cl. DN4: Cant 2C **58**
Griffen Cl. S43: Stav 6B **164**
Griffin Rd. S64: Swint 3A **66**
Griffiths Cl. S62: Parkg 4G **83**
Griffiths Rd. S35: High G 2D **78**
GRIFFS 6B **104**
GRIMESTHORPE 3C **108**
Grimesthorpe Rd. S4: Shef 5H **107**
(Ellesmere Rd., not continuous)
S4: Shef 6H **107**
(Grimesthorpe Rd. Sth.)

Greenland Av. S66: Malt 3B **102**
Greenland Av. Sth.
S66: Malt 4B **102**
Greenland Cl. S9: Shef 6F **109**
S25: Nth A 2G **141**
Greenland Ct. S9: Shef 6F **109**
Greenland Dr. S9: Shef 6F **109**
Greenland Rd. S9: Shef 6F **109**
Greenland Rd. Industrial & Business Pk.
S9: Shef 5F **109**
Greenlands Av. DN11: Ross 4D **74**
Greenland Vw. S9: Shef 1F **121**
S70: Wors 6E **31**
Greenland Wlk. S9: Shef 6F **109**
Greenland Way S9: Shef 6F **109**
(Greenland Dr.)
S9: Shef 5F **109**
(Greenland Rd.)
S66: Malt 3B **102**
Green La. DN3: Cant 3E **59**
DN4: Warm 3E **71**
DN5: Barnb 1F **51**
DN5: Scawt 6A **22**
DN6: Woodl 4B **22**
DN7: Dunsv, Hatf 5F **27**
DN11: Wad 2H **89**
S3: Shef 1D **4** (1E **119**)
S6: Shef 1E **119**
S18: Coal A, Dron 3G **155**
S21: Killa 6B **152**
S21: Midd H 4A **158**
S26: Ast 1F **139**
S26: Ull 2C **124**
S35: Eccl 2H **93**
S35: Ough 2C **90**
S35: Wharn S 1C **90**
S36: Stoc 2A **174**
S42: Cut 1A **166**
S43: Brim C 4C **168**
S60: Cat 5C **110**
S60: Roth 2H **111**
S61: Kimb 3F **95**
S62: Rawm 3G **83**
S63: Wath D 3E **65**
S66: Carr 4F **115**
S66: Thurc, Wick 3A **114**
S66: Wick 5F **99**
S70: Wors 5B **30**
S74: Hoyl 1F **61**
S75: Dod 4H **29**
WF4: Nott 1F **9**
WF9: Sth K 4H **13**
Green Lea S18: Dron W 2B **154**
Greenleafe Av. DN2: Don 3H **41**
GREEN MOOR 1G **175**
Green Moor Hgts. S36: Stoc 3E **175**
Green Moor Rd.
S35: Green M 1F **175**
Green Oak Av. S17: Tot 6F **145**
Green Oak Cres. S17: Tot 6F **145**
Green Oak Dr. S17: Tot 6F **145**
S26: Wales 6F **139**
Green Oak Gro. S17: Tot 6F **145**
Green Oak Rd. S17: Tot 6F **145**
Green Oak Vw. S17: Tot 6F **145**
Greenock St. S6: Shef 4A **106**
Green Pastures S17: Dore 3F **145**
Green Ri. S62: Rawm 1E **83**
Green Rd. S36: Pen 5D **176**
S75: Dod 4F **29**
Greenset Vw. S71: Ath 5D **8**
Greens Health & Fitness Club
Sheffield 5E **119**
GREENSIDE ....
S21 ....1E **157**
S75 ....5B **8**
Greenside S36: H'swne 1G **177**
S61: Grea 5C **82**
S72: Shaft 2E **11**
S75: Mapp, Stain 5B **8**
Greenside Av. S41: Ches 1G **167**
S75: Stain 5B **8**
Greenside Gdns. S36: H'swne 1G **177**
Greenside Ho. S75: Stain 5B **8**
Greenside La. S74: Hoyl 5B **46**
Greenside M. S12: Shef 5C **136**
Greenside Pl. S75: Mapp 5B **8**
Green Spring Av. S70: Birdw 4E **45**
Greens Rd. S65: Roth 4A **98**

Grimesthorpe Rd. Sth. S4: Shef 6H **107**
GRIMETHORPE 2B **20**
Grimsell Cl. S6: Shef 3C **92**
Grimsell Cres. S6: Shef 3C **92**
Grimsell Dr. S6: Shef 3C **92**
Grimsell Wlk. S6: Shef 4C **92**
Grinders Hill S1: Shef 5F **5**
Grinders Wlk. S6: Shef 3G **105**
Grindlow Av. S40: Ches 1G **171**
Grindlow Cl. S14: Shef 2H **133**
Grindlow Dr. S14: Shef 2H **133**
Grindon Cl. S40: Ches 3D **166**
Grinton Wlk. S40: Ches 2G **171**
Grisedale Wlk. S18: Dron W 3D **154**
Grizedale Av. S20: Sot 6H **137**
Grizedale Cl. S20: Sot 6H **137**
Grosvenor Cres. DN4: Warm 6E **55**
DN5: Ark .6C **24**
Grosvenor Dr. S70: Barn 1B **30**
(not continuous)
Grosvenor Rd. DN6: Woodl 3C **22**
S65: Roth 2G **97**
Grosvenor Sq. S2: Shef 6E **119**
Grosvenor Ter. DN4: Warm 6E **55**
Grosvenor Wlk. S70: Barn 1A **30**
Grouse Cft. S6: Shef 6C **106**
Grouse St. S6: Shef 5B **106**
Grove, The DN2: Don 5F **41**
(not continuous)
DN3: Barn D 1G **27**
S6: Lox .4F **105**
S17: Tot 6E **145**
S35: Wharn S 1A **90**
S43: Pool 6D **164**
S62: Rawm 3H **83**
S65: Roth 3A **98**
S66: Wick 5G **99**
S72: Cud .5E **11**
S75: Bar G 4F **15**
Grove Av. DN5: Don 5H **39**
S6: Shef 2H **105**
S17: Tot 6E **145**
Grove Cl. S36: Cub 6D **176**
S63: Wath D 4D **48**
Grove Cotts. *S40: Ches 6E 167*
(off Walton Rd.)
Grove Ct. S66: Malt 5G **101**
Grove Dr. WF9: Sth K 4H **13**
Grove Farm Cl. S43: Brim 1D **168**
Grove Gdns. S43: Brim C 4E **169**
S63: Thurn 3B **36**
Grove Hall Cl. DN3: Eden 6D **26**
Grove Hill Rd. DN2: Don 3H **41**
Grove Ho. Ct. S17: Tot 5F **145**
Grove La. WF9: Sth K 4H **13**
Grove Mt. WF9: Sth K 4H **13**
Grove Pk. S72: Grim 3B **20**
Grove Pl. DN1: Don 2B **56**
Grove Rd. DN3: Kirk Sa 4A **26**
S7: Shef 5B **132**
S17: Tot .5F **145**
S36: Spink 4H **175**
S41: Whit M 1H **167**
S43: Brim C 3D **168**
S60: Roth 5E **97**
S63: Wath D 4D **48**
S75: Mapp 5H **7**
Grove Sq. S6: Shef 5D **106**
Grove St. S41: Has 2B **172**
S70: Wors 5H **31**
S71: Barn 1F **31**
Grove Va. DN2: Don 3H **41**
Grove Way S43: Brim C 3E **169**
WF9: Sth K 4H **13**
Guardian Cen. S65: Roth 3F **97**
Guernsey Rd. S2: Shef 1F **133**
Guest La. DN4: Warm 5E **55**
S75: Silk .1B **28**
Guest Pl. S60: Roth 6G **97**
S74: Hoyl 5B **46**
Guest Rd. S11: Shef 6B **118**
S60: Roth 6G **97**
S75: Barn 5C **16**
Guest St. S74: Hoyl 5B **46**
Guilbert Av. S66: Thurc 1B **126**
Guildford Av. S2: Shef 6A **120**
S40: Walt 2E **171**
Guildford Cl. S2: Shef 6A **120**
Guildford Dr. S2: Shef 6A **120**
Guildford Ri. S2: Shef 6B **120**
Guildford Rd. DN2: Don 3G **41**
S71: Roy 1G **9**
Guildford Vw. S2: Shef 1B **134**
Guildford Wlk. S2: Shef 6B **120**
Guildford Way S2: Shef 6A **120**
Guildhall Ind. Est. DN3: Kirk Sa 5B **26**
Guild Rd. S65: Roth 4A **98**
Guildway S26: Tod 3B **140**
GUILTHWAITE 5B **112**
Guilthwaite Comn. La. S60: Up W . . .1B **124**
Guilthwaite Cres. S60: Whist 3H **111**
Guilthwaite Hill S60: Whist 6B **112**
Gullane Dr. DN4: Warm 6E **55**
Gullingwood Dr. S65: Thry 6F **85**
Gunhills La. DN3: Arm 3F **43**
Gunhills La. Ind. Est. DN3: Arm 3F **43**
Gun La. S3: Shef 1G **5**
Gurney Rd. DN4: Balb 6A **56**
Gurth Av. DN3: Eden 6D **26**
Gurth Av. Caravan Site DN3: Eden 6D **26**
Gurth Dr. S66: Thurc 1B **126**
Gwendoline M. S63: Wath D 1G **65**
Gwyn Reed Nature Reserve 2B **84**
Gypsy La. S73: Womb 3H **47**
WF4: Wool 1F **7**

H

Habershon Dr. S35: Chap 2E **79**
Habershon Rd. S61: Kimb P 1A **96**
HACKENTHORPE 5A **136**
Hackenthorpe Stop (ST) 5B **136**
Hackings Av. S36: Cub 6C **176**
Hackness La. S60: Brins 3C **110**
Hackney La. S18: B'low 4A **160**
Hackthorn Rd. S8: Shef 5E **133**
Haddon Cl. S18: Dron 2G **155**
S40: Bramp 6D **166**
S75: Dod .3F **29**
Haddon Pl. S43: Stav 6A **164**
Haddon Ri. S64: Mexb 6A **52**
Haddon Rd. S71: Ath 2G **17**
Haddon St. S3: Shef 6E **107**
Haddon Way S26: Ast 1E **139**
Haden St. S6: Shef 4B **106**
Hadfield Cl. S9: Shef 1D **120**
Hadfield St. S6: Shef 1B **118**
S73: Womb 3G **47**
Hadleigh Cl. S62: Rawm 4G **83**
Hadrian Rd. S60: Brins 2D **110**
Hadrians Cl. DN11: New R 6H **75**
HADY 6C **168**
Hady Cres. S41: Ches 6B **168**
Hady Hill S41: Ches 6A **168**
Hady La. S41: Ches 6C **168**
Haggard Rd. S6: Shef 4C **106**
Hagg Hill S6: Shef 1G **117**
Hagg Hill La. S6: Shef 5A **92**
Hagg La. S10: Shef 3D **116**
Hagg La. Cotts. S10: Shef 2E **117**
Haggstones Dr. S35: Ough 4D **90**
Haggstones Rd. S35: Ough 4D **90**
Hague Av. S21: Reni 4H **159**
S62: Rawm 1F **83**
Hague Cres. WF9: Hems 1F **13**
Hague La. S21: Reni . . . . .5H **159** & 1E **165**
S35: High G 1B **78**
S62: Wentw 2E **81**
WF9: Sth K 4H **13**
Hague Row S2: Shef 3H **5** (3H **119**)
(not continuous)
Hague Ter. WF9: Hems 1F **13**
Haids Cl. S66: Malt 3A **102**
Haids La. S66: Malt 3A **102**
Haids Rd. S66: Malt 3H **101**
Haig Cres. DN11: New R 6B **74**
Haigh Cl. S36: H'swne 1F **177**
Haigh Ct. S63: Bramp B 6A **48**
Haigh Cft. S71: Roy 2G **9**
Haigh Head Rd. S36: H'swne 1F **177**
Haigh Hill S75: Hai 1D **6**
Haigh La. S36: H'swne 1G **177**
S75: Hai 1D **6**
Haigh Memorial Homes *S8: Shef 3F 147*
(off Meadowhead)
Haigh M. S75: Hai 1D **6**
Haigh Moor Cl. S13: Shef 5H **121**
Haigh Moor Dr. S25: Dinn 5F **127**
Haigh Moor Rd. S13: Shef 6A **122**
Haigh Moor Wlk. S13: Shef 6H **121**
Haigh Moor Way S26: Swal 1H **137**
S71: Roy .1H **9**
Haigh Rd. DN4: Balb 5H **55**
Hail Mary Dr. S13: Shef 6E **123**
Haise Mt. S75: Dart 5H **7**
Hakehill Cl. DN4: Bess 6A **58**
Halcyon Cl. S12: Shef 5A **136**
Haldane Cl. S72: Brier 3A **12**
Haldane Rd. S65: Roth 2H **97**
Haldene S70: Wors 6G **31**
Haldynby Gdns. DN3: Arm 4F **43**
Hale St. S8: Shef 2E **133**
Halesworth Cl. S40: Walt 2C **170**
Halesworth Rd. S13: Shef 4H **121**
Halfacre La. S18: Dron 4A **156**
Half Cft. S43: Brim 1E **169**
HALFWAY 3F **151**
Halfway (Park & Tram) 3G **151**
Halfway Cen. S20: Half 3F **151**
Halfway Cl. S20: Westf 3G **151**
S63: Gol .5B **36**
Halfway Dr. S20: Half 3F **151**
Halfway Gdns. S20: Half 3F **151**
Halfway Stop (ST) 3G **151**
Halifax Av. DN12: Con 4D **68**
Halifax Cres. DN5: Don 4G **39**
Halifax Hall of Residence
S10: Shef 5A **118**
Halifax Rd. S6: Gren, Shef 6C **92**
S35: Gren 3C **92**
S36: Pen 1C **176**
Halifax St. S71: Barn 4D **16**
Hallam Chase S10: Shef 5A **118**
(Endcliffe Va. Rd.)
S10: Shef 4E **117**
(Sandygate Rd.)
Hallam Cl. DN4: Bess 5H **57**
S26: Augh 5B **124**
S73: Womb 2H **47**
Hallam Ct. *S10: Shef 5C 118*
(off Clarke Dell)
S18: Dron 4F **155**
S63: Bolt D 3A **50**
Hallam Dale Ct. S62: Rawm 1H **83**
Hallamgate Rd. S10: Shef 4A **118**
Hallam Grange Cl. S10: Shef 6D **116**
Hallam Grange Cres. S10: Shef 5D **116**
Hallam Grange Cft. S10: Shef 5D **116**
Hallam Grange Ri. S10: Shef 5D **116**
Hallam Grange Rd. S10: Shef 5D **116**
HALLAM HEAD 4E **117**
Hallam La. S1: Shef 6E **5** (4F **119**)
Hallam Pl. S62: Rawm 3H **83**
Hallam Rd. S60: Roth 2G **111**
Hallam Rock S5: Shef 3G **107**
Hallamshire Cl. S10: Shef 6C **116**
Hallamshire Dr. S10: Shef 6C **116**
Hallamshire Golf Course 4E **117**
Hallamshire Rd. S10: Shef 6C **116**
Hallamshire Vw. S10: Shef 4E **117**
Hallam Way S35: Eccl 2G **93**
Hall Av. S64: Mexb 1G **67**
S74: Jum .5D **46**
Hall Balk La. DN11: Lov 4B **72**
S75: Barn 5C **16**
Hall Bank S75: Barn 4C **16**
Hall Broome Gdns. S63: Bolt D 1B **50**
Hall Bungs. S42: W'orth 6H **171**
Hallcar St. S4: Shef 1H **119**
Hall Cl. S18: Dron W 2B **154**
S25: Nth A 2G **141**
S42: Cut .6A **160**
S63: Bramp B 5C **48**
S70: Wors 2F **45**
Hall Cl. Av. S60: Whist 3B **112**
Hall Cotts. DN5: Barnb 1A **52**
S66: Mort 4G **113**
Hall Ct. S25: Dinn 6H **127**
S65: Rav .4H **85**
Hall Cres. S60: Roth 2A **112**
Hall Cft. S66: Wick 6H **99**
Hallcroft Dr. DN3: Arm 6F **43**
Hallcroft Gdns. S72: Gt H 6F **21**
S74: Hoyl 6C **46**
Hallcroft Ri. S71: Roy 3G **9**
Hall Cross 2D **56**

Hall Cross Av. S73: Womb 3A **48**
Hall Cross Hill DN1: Don 2D **56**
Hall Dr. S63: Wath D 1E **65**
Haller Cl. DN3: Arm 4C **42**
Hall Farm Cl. S26: Augh 4B **124**
S41: Has 3C **172**
Hall Farm Cft. S25: Dinn 6A **128**
Hall Farm Dr. S63: Thurn 3C **36**
Hall Farm Gro. S36: H'swne 1G **177**
Hall Farm Ri. S63: Thurn 3C **36**
Hallfield Cl. S42: W'orth 6A **172**
Hallflash La. S44: Cal 2F **173**
Hall Flat La. DN4: Balb 5H **55**
Hall Ga. DN1: Don 1C **56**
S36: Pen 3D **176**
S64: Mexb 2H **67**
Hallgate S63: Thurn 3C **36**
Hallgate Rd. S10: Shef 3H **117**
Hall Gro. S60: Roth 5F **97**
S75: Stain 5B **8**
Halliwell Cl. S5: Shef 1C **106**
Halliwell Cres. S5: Shef 6C **92**
Hall La. S36: H'swne 1G **177**
S43: Stav 2H **163**
Hall Meadow Cft. S20: Half 5G **151**
Hall Meadow Dr. S20: Half 4G **151**
Hall Meadow Gro. S20: Half 5G **151**
Hall Mews S65: Rav 4H **85**
HALLOWES 4H **155**
Hallowes Ct. S18: Dron 3G **155**
Hallowes Dr. S18: Dron 4G **155**
Hallowes Golf Course 5G **155**
Hallowes La. S18: Dron 3G **155**
Hallowes Ri. S18: Dron 4H **155**
HALLOWMOOR 3H **105**
Hallowmoor Rd. S6: Shef 3G **105**
Hall Pk. Head S6: Shef 1E **117**
Hall Pk. Hill S6: Shef 1F **117**
Hall Pk. Mt. S6: Shef 1F **117**
Hall Pl. S71: Monk B 4H **17**
Hall Rd. S9: Shef 3H **121**
S13: Shef 4H **121**
S26: Augh 5B **124**
S43: Brim 1D **168**
S60: Roth 5F **97**
S66: Malt 5F **101**
Hall Royd La. S75: Silk C 4B **28**
Hall Royd Wlk. S75: Silk C 5B **28**
Halls Ct. S8: Shef 5E **133**
Hallside Ct. DN3: Cant 3E **59**
S20: Mosb 4E **151**
Hall's Row S40: Ches 6E **167**
Hall St. DN5: Barnb 1A **52**
S60: Roth 4D **96**
S63: Gol 6D **36**
S73: Womb 2H **47**
S74: Hoyl 6B **46**
Hallsworth Av. S73: Hem 5E **47**
Hall Vw. S35: Chap 2F **79**
S40: Ches 5F 167
(off Chatsworth Rd.)
S41: Ches 2F **167**
Hall Vw. Rd. DN11: New R 6H **75**
Hall Villa La. DN5: Ben 3H **23**
Hallwood Ri. S35: Chap 3C **78**
Hallwood Rd. S35: Chap 3B **78**
Hallworth Wlk. S21: Mar L 2H **157**
Hallyburton Cl. S2: Shef 2H **133**
Hallyburton Dr. S2: Shef 2H **133**
Hallyburton Rd. S2: Shef 2H **133**
Halmshaw Ter. DN5: Ben 2H **39**
Halsall Av. S9: Shef 3F **121**
Halsall Dr. S9: Shef 3E **121**
Halsall Rd. S9: Shef 3F **121**
Halsbury Rd. S65: Roth 2H **97**
Halstead Gro. S75: Mapp 4H **7**
Halsteads S13: Shef 5G **121**
Halton Cl. S41: Ches 5F **161**
Halton Ct. S12: Shef 5D **136**
Hamble Ct. S75: Mapp 6B **8**
Hambledon Cl. S40: Ches 3D **166**
Hambleton Cl. S74: Els 6E **47**
S75: Barn 6A **16**
Hameline Rd. DN12: Con 4E **69**
Hamer Wlk. S65: Roth 3B **98**
Hamilton Cl. DN4: Don 3E **57**
S64: Mexb 6H **51**
Hamilton Ct. DN12: Con 4F **69**
S64: Swint 3C **66**
Hamilton M. DN4: Don 2E **57**
Hamilton Pk. Rd. DN5: Scaws 4E **39**
Hamilton Rd. DN4: Don 3E **57**
S5: Shef 2A **108**
S63: Gol 4E **37**
S66: Malt 6C **102**
Hammerton Cl. S6: Shef 5B **106**
Hammerton Rd. S6: Shef 5B **106**
Hammond St. S3: Shef 1A **4** (2D **118**)
Hampden Rd. S64: Mexb 1F **67**
Hamper La. S36: H'swne, Pen 1F **177**
Hampole Dr. S63: Thurn 3B **36**
Hampson Gdns. DN3: Eden 5D **26**
Hampstead Grn. S61: Kimb P 1H **95**
Hampton Ct. S73: D'fld 5A **34**
Hampton Rd. DN2: Don 1E **57**
S5: Shef 3H **107**
Hampton St. S41: Has 3C **172**
Hanbury Cl. DN4: Balb 2H **71**
S18: Dron 3E **155**
S40: Ches 3B **166**
S71: Monk B 4A **18**
Handby St. S41: Has 2C **172**
Handley Ct. S43: New W 2C **162**
Handley Rd. S43: New W 5G **157**
Handley Sq. DN9: Finn 2C **76**
Handley St. S3: Shef 1G **119**
Handleywood Golf Driving Range . . . 2E **163**
Hands Rd. S10: Shef 2B **118**
HANDSWORTH 5A **122**
Handsworth Av. S9: Shef 3G **121**
Handsworth Cres. S9: Shef 3G **121**
Handsworth Gdns. DN3: Arm 4F **43**
Handsworth Grange Cl. S13: Shef . . 6B **122**
Handsworth Grange Cres.
S13: Shef 5B **122**
Handsworth Grange Dr. S13: Shef . . 5C **122**
Handsworth Grange Rd.
S13: Shef 5B **122**
Handsworth Grange Way
S13: Shef 5C **122**
HANDSWORTH HILL 2G **121**
Handsworth Rd. S9: Shef 3G **121**
S13: Shef 4H **121**
Hanging Bank Ct. S25: Nth A 3H **141**
HANGING WATER 6G **117**
Hangingwater Cl. S11: Shef 6G **117**
Hangingwater Cotts. *S11: Shef 1G 131*
(off Hangingwater Rd.)
Hangingwater Rd. S11: Shef 1G **131**
Hangman Stone La.
DN5: High M, Marr 1D **52**
Hangman Stone Rd.
DN5: Barnb, Marr 3C **52**
Hangram La. S11: Shef 4C **130**
Hangsman La.
S25: Laugh C, Laugh M 3F **127**
Hangthwaite La. DN6: Woodl 5D **22**
Hangthwaite Rd. DN6: Adw S 1E **23**
Hanley Cl. S12: Shef 4C **136**
Hanmoor Rd. S6: Stann 6D **104**
Hannah Rd. S13: Shef 1E **137**
Hannas Royd S75: Dod 3H **29**
Hanover Ct. S3: Shef 6A **4** (4D **118**)
S70: Wors 5F **31**
Hanover Sq. S3: Shef 6B **4** (4E **119**)
S63: Thurn 2D **36**
Hanover St. S3: Shef 6A **4** (4E **119**)
(not continuous)
S63: Thurn 1D **36**
Hanover Way S3: Shef 5A **4** (4D **118**)
Hanover Works S3: Shef 1C **4**
Hanslope Vw. DN3: Kirk Sa 3B **26**
Hanson Rd. S6: Lox 4E **105**
Hanson St. S70: Barn 6E **17**
Hanston Ct. *S43: New W 2C 162*
(off Handley Rd.)
Hanwell Cl. S35: Eccl 2G **93**
Harbord Rd. S8: Shef 6D **132**
Harborough Av. S2: Shef 3C **120**
Harborough Cl. S2: Shef 4D **120**
Harborough Dr. S2: Shef 4D **120**
Harborough Hill Rd. S71: Barn 1E **31**
Harborough Ri. S2: Shef 4D **120**
Harborough Rd. S2: Shef 4D **120**
Harborough Way S2: Shef 5D **120**
Harbury St. S13: Shef 6F **123**
Harcourt Cl. DN4: Bess 5H **57**
S41: Has 3B **172**
Harcourt Cres. S10: Shef 2C **118**
Harcourt Ri. S35: Chap 4G **79**
Harcourt Rd. S10: Shef 3C **118**
Harcourt Ter. S65: Roth 4G **97**
Hardcastle Dr. S13: Shef 1B **136**
Hardcastle Gdns. S13: Shef 1B **136**
Hardcastle Rd. S13: Shef 2B **136**
Harden Cl. S36: Cub 5D **176**
S75: Barn 6H **15**
Harden M. DN3: Arm 5F **43**
HARDHURST 6B **156**
Hardhurst Rd. S18: Uns 1F **161**
Hardie Cl. S66: Malt 6C **102**
Hardie Pl. S43: Stav 6A **164**
S62: Rawm 2G **83**
Hardie St. S21: Ecki 1E **159**
Harding Av. S62: Rawm 6E **65**
Harding Cl. S62: Rawm 1E **83**
Harding Ct. S62: Rawm 6E **65**
Hard La. S26: Kiv P 6B **140**
HARDWICK 5H **125**
Hardwick Av. S43: New W 3C **162**
Hardwick Cl. S18: Dron 2G **155**
S26: Ast 1E **139**
S70: Wors 6F **31**
S71: Roy 2A **10**
Hardwick Ct. *S43: Stav 4B 164*
(off Porter St.)
Hardwick Cres. S11: Shef 6B **118**
S71: Ath 1F **17**
Hardwick Dr. S44: Ark T 6H **173**
Hardwicke Rd. S65: Roth 2F **97**
Hardwick Gro. S75: Dod 4G **29**
Hardwick La. S26: Ast 1G **139**
Hardwick St. S41: Ches 4H **167**
S65: Roth 2C **98**
Hardwicks Yd. S40: Ches 6F **167**
Hardy Pl. S6: Shef 6C **106**
Hardy Rd. DN2: Don 4D **40**
Hardy St. S60: Roth 3D **96**
Haredon Cl. S75: Mapp 4H **7**
Harefield Rd. S11: Shef 6C **118**
Harehill Cres. S42: W'orth 6E **171**
Harehill Rd. S40: Birdh 3G **171**
Harehills Rd. S60: Roth 5F **97**
Harewood Av. DN3: Kirk Sa 4C **26**
DN6: Woodl 3A **22**
S70: Barn 1A **30**
Harewood Cl. DN4: Balb 2G **71**
Harewood Ct. DN11: Ross 6E **75**
Harewood Gro. S66: Braml 4A **100**
Harewood Rd. DN2: Don 1F **57**
Harewood Way S11: Shef 6H **131**
Hargrave Pl. S65: Thry 6E **85**
Harland Rd. S11: Shef 5D **118**
Harlech Cl. S35: Chap 2E **79**
Harlech Fold S10: Shef 5A **116**
Harlech Grn. S10: Shef 5A **116**
Harlech Gro. S10: Shef 5A **116**
Harlech Mead S10: Shef 5A **116**
Harleston St. S4: Shef 6A **108**
(not continuous)
HARLEY 5A **62**
Harley Rd. S11: Shef 3G **131**
S62: H'ley 5A **62**
HARLINGTON 2H **51**
Harlington DN5: H'ton 2A **52**
Harlington Ct. DN12: Den M 3D **68**
Harlington Rd. S64: Mexb 4E **51**
(Crow Tree La.)
S64: Mexb 1G **67**
(Herbert St., not continuous)
Harmer La. S1: Shef 4F **5** (3G **119**)
Harmony Way S60: Cat 6D **110**
Harney Cl. S9: Shef 1F **121**
Harold Av. DN6: Woodl 3B **22**
S71: Lund 4B **18**
Harold Cft. S61: Grea 4D **82**
Harold St. S6: Shef 6C **106**
HARPER HILL 6B **170**
Harperhill Cl. S40: Birdh 3G **171**
Harrier Ct. DN9: Auck 2C **76**
Harriet Cl. S70: Barn 3F **31**
Harrington Ct. S71: Lund 4B **18**
Harrington Rd. S2: Shef 6F **119**
Harrington St. DN1: Don 6C **40**
Harris Hawk Way S63: Wath D 4E **49**
Harrison La. S10: Shef 1A **130**
Harrison Rd. S6: Shef 5A **106**

Harrison St. S61: Roth 4B **96**
Harris Rd. DN3: Arm 4C **42**
S6: Shef 2A **106**
Harrogate Dr. DN12: Den M 3B **68**
Harrogate Rd. S26: Swal 2B **138**
Harrop Dr. S64: Swint 5B **66**
Harrop Gdn. Flats *S64: Swint* *3C 66*
(off Queen St.)
Harrop La. S10: Shef 2A **130**
Harrowden Ct. S9: Tins 2H **109**
Harrowden Rd. DN2: Don 4D **40**
S9: Tins 2H **109**
Harrow Rd. DN3: Arm 3F **43**
Harrow St. S11: Shef 5E **119**
Harry Firth Cl. S9: Shef 1D **120**
Harry Rd. S75: Barn 5A **16**
Hartcliff Av. S36: Pen 4C **176**
Hartcliff Hill Rd. S36: Pen 6A **176**
Hartfield Cl. S41: Has 3A **172**
Hartfield Ct. S41: Has 3A **172**
Hartford Cl. S8: Shef 5F **133**
Hartford Rd. S8: Shef 5F **133**
Hart Hill S62: Rawm 6E **65**
Harthill Rd. DN12: Con 5D **68**
S13: Shef 1E **135**
Hart Hills S73: Hem 5E **47**
Hartington Av. S7: Shef 5B **132**
Hartington Cl. S61: Roth 4B **96**
Hartington Ct. S18: Dron 2G **155**
Hartington Dr. S71: Barn 4E **17**
Hartington Ind. Est. S43: Stav 2B **164**
Hartington Rd. S7: Shef 5B **132**
S18: Dron 2G **155**
S41: Ches 6B **168**
S61: Roth 4B **96**
Hartington Vw. S43: Stav 2C **164**
Hartland Av. S20: Sot 6H **137**
Hartland Ct. S20: Sot 6H **137**
Hartland Cres. DN3: Eden 6C **26**
Hartland Dr. S20: Sot 6H **137**
Hartland Way S41: Old W 5H **161**
Hartley Brook Av. S5: Shef 4H **93**
Hartley Brook Rd. S5: Shef 4H **93**
Hartley Cl. S64: Kiln 5C **66**
Hartley La. S61: Roth 3D **96**
Hartley St. S2: Shef 1F **133**
S64: Mexb 2E **67**
Hartopp Av. S2: Shef 2H **133**
Hartopp Cl. S2: Shef 2H **133**
Hartopp Dr. S2: Shef 2A **134**
Hartopp Rd. S2: Shef 2H **133**
Hartshaw *S60: Roth* *5F 97*
(off Moorgate Rd.)
Hartshead S1: Shef 2E **5** (2G **119**)
Hartshead Sq. S1: Shef 2F **5**
Hartside Cl. S40: Ches 3E **167**
Harvest Cl. DN3: Eden 5D **26**
DN4: Balb 4G **55**
S66: Malt 6F **101**
S70: Wors 6F **31**
Harvest La. S3: Shef 1F **119**
Harvest Rd. S66: Wick 5G **99**
Harvest Way S42: Ash 3B **166**
Harvey Cl. DN9: Finn 2F **77**
Harvey Clough M. S8: Shef 5G **133**
Harvey Clough Rd. S8: Shef 5F **133**
Harvey Rd. S35: Chap 3F **79**
S41: Ches 6D **168**
Harvey St. S36: Spink 3F **175**
S70: Barn 2C **30**
Harwell Rd. S8: Shef 1E **133**
Harwich Rd. S2: Shef 5B **120**
Harwood Cl. S2: Shef 6F **119**
Harwood Dr. S20: Water 1E **151**
Harwood Gdns. S20: Water 1F **151**
Harwood St. S2: Shef 6F **119**
Harwood Ter. S71: Lund 6B **18**
Haslam Ct. S41: Ches 4H **167**
Haslam Cres. S8: Shef 4C **146**
Haslam Pl. S66: Malt 4C **102**
Haslam Rd. DN11: New R 5C **74**
HASLAND 3C **172**
Hasland By-Pass S41: Ches, Has 1B **172**
HASLAND GREEN 3B **172**
Hasland La. S44: Cal 2F **173**
Hasland Rd. S41: Ches, Has 1A **172**
(not continuous)
Haslehurst Rd. S2: Shef 4B **120**
Haslemere Ct. DN5: Don 4H **39**
Haslemere Gro. DN5: Don 4H **39**
Hassocky La. S42: Tem N 5G **173**
S44: Cal 5G **173**
Hassop Cl. S18: Dron 2H **155**
S40: Ches 2D **166**
Hassop Rd. S43: Stav 3C **164**
Hastilar Cl. S2: Shef 6E **121**
Hastilar Rd. S2: Shef 6E **121**
Hastilar Rd. Sth. S13: Shef 6F **121**
Hastings Cl. S41: Ches 2E **167**
Hastings Mt. S7: Shef 4B **132**
Hastings Rd. S7: Shef 4B **132**
Hastings St. S72: Grim 1B **20**
Hatchell Dr. DN4: Bess 1D **74**
Hatchellwood Vw. DN4: Bess 1E **75**
Hatfield Cl. S71: Smi 1D **16**
Hatfield Gdns. S71: Roy 2G **9**
Hatfield Ho. *DN1: Don* *2B 56*
(off Grove Pl.)
Hatfield Ho. Ct. S5: Shef 5A **94**
Hatfield Ho. Cft. S5: Shef 5A **94**
Hatfield Ho. La. S5: Shef 6H **93**
Hatfield La. DN3: Arm, Eden 6E **27**
DN3: Barn D 1C **26**
Hathaway Ct. S26: Wales 6G **139**
Hatherley Rd. S9: Tins 1H **109**
S64: Swint 1C **66**
S65: Roth 3F **97**
Hathern Cl. S43: Brim C 4E **169**
Hathersage Rd. S17: Dore 3A **144**
Hatter Dr. DN12: New E 6C **70**
Hatton Cl. S18: Dron W 4C **154**
Hatton Dr. S40: Ches 3C **166**
Hatton Rd. S6: Shef 5C **106**
Haugh Grn. S62: Rawm 6E **65**
Haugh La. S11: Shef 4G **131**
Haugh Rd. S62: Rawm 6D **64**
Haughton Rd. S8: Shef 6E **133**
Havelock Rd. DN4: Balb 3B **56**
Havelock St. S10: Shef 5A **4** (4D **118**)
S70: Barn 2C **30**
S73: D'fld 5B **34**
Haven, The S26: Kiv S 6E **141**
Haven Bus. Cen. S61: Roth 3C **96**
Havenfield S73: D'fld 4B **34**
Havens, The S40: Ash 4E **167**
Havercroft Pl. S21: Killa 3A **152**
Havercroft Ri. S72: Sth H 1H **11**
Havercroft Rd. S8: Shef 4D **132**
S60: Roth 1B **112**
Havercroft Ter. S21: Killa 3A **152**
Haverdale Ri. S75: Barn 5C **16**
Haverhill Gro. S73: Womb 1H **47**
Haverlands La. S70: Wors 6C **30**
Haverlands Ridge S70: Wors 6E **31**
Haw Ct. S75: Silk 1A **28**
Hawes Cl. S64: Mexb 6H **51**
Hawfield Cl. DN4: Hex 3H **55**
Hawke Cl. S62: Rawm 1D **82**
Hawke Rd. DN2: Don 4E **41**
Hawke St. S9: Shef 4D **108**
Hawk Hill La. S66: Bramp M 2A **126**
Hawkhills S6: Shef 6G **105**
Hawking Ho's. S40: Ches 3E **167**
Hawkins Av. S35: Burn 3D **78**
Hawks Cliff Vw. S75: Dod 3E **29**
Hawkshead Av. S18: Dron W 3C **154**
Hawkshead Cres. S25: Nth A 2A **142**
Hawkshead Rd. S4: Shef 3C **108**
Hawksley Av. S6: Shef 4B **106**
S40: Ches 3F **167**
Hawksley Cl. DN3: Arm 4E **43**
Hawksley Ct. DN3: Arm 3E **43**
Hawksley M. S6: Shef 4B **106**
Hawksley Ri. S35: Ough 4E **91**
Hawksley Rd. S6: Shef 4B **106**
Hawksway S21: Ecki 1C **158**
Hawksworth Cl. S65: Roth 3B **98**
Hawksworth Rd. S6: Shef 6C **106**
S65: Roth 3B **98**
Hawkwell Bank S71: Ard 2D **32**
Hawley St. S1: Shef 2D **4** (2F **119**)
S18: App 3D **156**
S62: Rawm 3G **83**
Haworth Bank S60: Roth 3G **111**
Haworth Cl. S71: Monk B 5G **17**
Haworth Cres. S60: Roth 3G **111**
Haw Royd S70: Barn 3F **31**
Hawshaw Bank S74: Hoyl 5H **45**
Hawshaw La. S74: Hoyl 6H **45**
Hawthorn Av. DN3: Arm 2E **43**
S20: Water 1E **151**
S66: Malt 5G **101**
Hawthorne Av. DN7: Dunsv 4H **27**
S18: Dron 1F **155**
S25: Sth A 5G **141**
S36: Stoc 2B **174**
S43: Mas M 2F **165**
S62: Rawm 3H **83**
Hawthorne Chase S64: Swint 3B **66**
Hawthorne Cl. S21: Killa 5C **152**
Hawthorne Ct. S65: Roth 3A **98**
S75: Kexb 6C **6**
Hawthorne Cres. S64: Mexb 1D **66**
S75: Dod 2F **29**
Hawthorne Cft. S63: Gol 5B **36**
Hawthorne Dr. S63: Bolt D 2C **50**
Hawthorne Farm Ct.
S63: Bolt D *2C 50*
(off Station Rd.)
Hawthorne Flats S63: Thurn 1C **36**
Hawthorne Gro. DN5: Ben 6A **24**
Hawthorne Pl. S26: Swal 1D **138**
Hawthorne Rd. DN9: Auck 2B **76**
S63: Wath D 1H **65**
Hawthornes, The S20: Beig 4G **137**
S66: B'well 2B **102**
Hawthorne St. S6: Shef 6A **106**
S40: Ches 1A **172**
S70: Barn 2D **30**
S72: Shaft 3F **11**
Hawthorne Way S26: Kiv P 5C **140**
S72: Shaft 3F **11**
Hawthorn Gro. DN12: Con 6D **68**
S75: Silk 1A **28**
Hawthorn Hill S43: Stav 1C **164**
Hawthorn M. S35: High G 6C **60**
Hawthorn Rd. S6: Shef 4A **106**
S21: Ecki 2C **158**
S35: High G 1D **78**
Hawthorn Ter. *S10: Shef* *3B 118*
(off Parker's La.)
Hawthorn Way S42: Ash 3A **166**
Hawtop La. WF4: Wool 1G **7**
Haxby Cl. S13: Shef 2H **135**
Haxby Pl. S13: Shef 2H **135**
Haxby St. S13: Shef 2H **135**
Haybrook Ct. S17: Tot 5F **145**
Haycroft Gdns. S43: Mas M 2E **165**
Haydn Rd. S66: Malt 6C **102**
Haydock Av. S25: Laugh C 4F **127**
Haydock Chase S25: Laugh C 4F **127**
Haydock Cl. S64: Mexb 6G **51**
Haydon Gro. S66: Flan 4G **99**
Hayes Ct. S20: Half 4F **151**
Hayes Cft. S70: Barn 1E **31**
Hayes Dr. S20: Half 4E **151**
Hayfield Cl. DN3: Barn D 1D **26**
S18: Dron W 3C **154**
S42: W'orth 6G **171**
S43: Stav 3C **164**
S75: Dod 3F **29**
Hayfield Ct. DN9: Auck 2C **76**
Hayfield Cres. S12: Shef 5G **135**
Hayfield Dr. S12: Shef 5G **135**
Hayfield La. DN9: Auck, Finn 3F **75**
Hayfield La. Bus. Pk. DN9: Auck 2C **76**
Hayfield M. DN9: Auck 2B **76**
Hayfield Pl. S12: Shef 5G **135**
Hayfield Vw. S21: Ecki 1C **158**
Hayfield Wlk. *S61: Kimb P* *1H 95*
(off Byrley Rd.)
Hayford Way S43: Stav 5B **164**
HAY GREEN 5E **45**
Hay Grn. Ct. S70: Birdw 5E **45**
Hay Grn. La. S70: Birdw 5E **45**
Hayhurst Cres. S66: Malt 6B **102**
Hayland St. S9: Shef 2E **109**
Haylock Cl. S75: H'ham 5F **15**
Haymarket S1: Shef 2F **5** (2G **119**)
Haythorne Way S64: Swint 5C **66**
Haywagon Mobile Home Pk.
DN6: Adw S 1E **23**
Haywood Av. S36: Spink 3F **175**
Haywood Cl. S65: Roth 3B **98**
Haywood La. S36: Spink 3F **175**
(not continuous)
Haywood Rd. S36: Spink 3F **175**

Hazel Av. DN9: Auck 2B **76**
  S21: Killa 5B **152**
Hazelbadge Cres. S12: Shef 5H **135**
Hazel Cl. S18: Dron 4H **155**
Hazel Ct. S18: Dron 4G **155**
  S65: Rav 2B **100**
Hazel Dr. S40: Walt 2E **171**
  S42: W'orth 6A **172**
Hazel Gdns. *S70: Wors* 4G *31*
             (off Overdale Av.)
Hazel Gro. DN3: Arm 3F **43**
  DN11: New R 6C **74**
  DN12: Con 5E **69**
  S35: Chap 4F **79**
  S43: Mas M 2F **165**
  S66: Wick 5H **99**
Hazel Ho. *S8: Shef* 4D *132*
              (off Archer Rd.)
Hazelhurst S41: Has 4C **172**
Hazelhurst Cl. S65: Dalt 1C **98**
Hazelhurst La. S8: Shef 2C **148**
Hazelmeres, The S40: Walt 2E **171**
Hazel Rd. DN12: New E 4C **70**
  S21: Ecki 2D **158**
  S66: Malt 5G **101**
Hazelshaw S75: Dod 4H **29**
Hazelshaw Gdns. S35: High G 1C **78**
Hazelwood S71: Monk B 3F **17**
Hazelwood Cl. S18: Dron W 3B **154**
Hazelwood Dr. S64: Swint 6C **66**
Hazlebarrow Cl. S8: Shef 4G **147**
Hazlebarrow Ct. S8: Shef 3G **147**
Hazlebarrow Cres. S8: Shef 4G **147**
Hazlebarrow Dr. S8: Shef 3G **147**
Hazlebarrow Gro. S8: Shef 3H **147**
Hazlebarrow Rd. S8: Shef 4G **147**
Hazledene Cres. S72: Shaft 5G **11**
Hazledene Rd. S72: Shaft 5F **11**
Hazlehurst Av. S41: Ches 3H **167**
Hazlehurst La. S41: Ches 3H **167**
Headford Gdns. S3: Shef . . .5B **4** (4E **119**)
Headford Gro. S3: Shef 5B **4** (4E **119**)
Headford M. S3: Shef 6B **4** (4E **119**)
Headford Pde. S3: Shef 5B **4**
Headford St. S3: Shef 5B **4** (4E **119**)
Headingley Cl. DN3: Kirk Sa 3C **26**
Headingley Way
  DN12: New E 3D **70**
Headland Cl. S43: Brim 1D **168**
Headland Dr. S10: Shef 3H **117**
Headland Rd. S10: Shef 3H **117**
  S43: Brim 1D **168**
Headlands Rd. S74: Hoyl 6A **46**
Heads La. S36: Bolst 6B **174**
Healaugh Way S40: Ches 2A **172**
Healthy Living Cen.
  Staveley 5B **164**
  Upperthorpe 1D **118**
Heath Av. S21: Killa 5C **152**
Heath Bank Rd. DN2: Don 3H **41**
Heathcote Cl. S75: Wool G 3F **7**
Heathcote Dr. S41: Has 2D **172**
Heathcote Rd. *S41: Ches* 2A *168*
            (off Tapton Lock Hill)
Heathcote St. S4: Shef 3A **108**
Heath Ct. DN4: Warm 5E **55**
  S40: Ches 2H **171**
Heathcroft Chase S71: Ard 2E **33**
Heatherbank Rd. DN4: Bess 5B **58**
Heathercliff Way S36: Pen 4E **177**
Heather Cl. S44: Cal 5F **169**
  S60: Roth 6F **97**
Heather Ct. DN2: Don 2A **42**
  S63: Bolt D 1A **50**
  S66: Braml 6A **100**
Heatherdale Rd. S66: Malt 5C **102**
Heather Gdns. S41: Has 3D **172**
Heather Knowle S75: Dod 3H **29**
Heather Lea Av. S17: Dore 3D **144**
Heather Lea Pl. S17: Dore 3D **144**
Heather Rd. S5: Shef 1B **108**
Heather Va. Cl. S41: Has 3D **172**
Heather Va. Rd. S41: Has 3C **172**
Heather Wlk. S63: Bolt D 1A **50**
Heatherwood Cl. DN2: Don 4H **41**
Heathfield Av. S40: Ches 5E **167**
Heathfield Cl. DN3: Barn D 2D **26**
  S18: Dron 4E **155**
  S42: W'orth 6A **172**

Heathfield Rd. S12: Shef 4G **135**
Heathfields S70: Barn 2G **31**
Heath Gro. S63: Bolt D 3A **50**
Heath Ho. *DN1: Don* 2B *56*
              (off Grove Pl.)
Heath Rd. S6: Shef 6C **92**
  S36: Spink 4F **175**
Heaton Cl. S18: Dron W 3C **154**
Heaton Gdns. DN12: New E 4D **70**
Heatons Bank S62: Rawm 2H **83**
Heaton St. S40: Bramp 6D **166**
Heavens Wlk. DN4: Don 3C **56**
Heavygate Av. S10: Shef 6A **106**
Heavygate Rd. S10: Shef 6B **106**
Hedge Hill Rd. S36: Thurl 4A **176**
Hedge La. S75: Dart 1E **15**
            (not continuous)
Hedgerows, The S64: Mexb 4F **51**
Hedley Dr. S43: Brim 6C **162**
HEELEY 2G **133**
Heeley Bank Rd. S2: Shef 1G **133**
Heeley City Farm 1F **133**
Heeley Grn. S2: Shef 2G **133**
Heeley Retail Pk.
  S8: Shef 2E **133**
Heeley Swimming Pool 2E **133**
Heelis St. S70: Barn 2E **31**
Heighton Vw. S26: Augh 5C **124**
Helena Cl. S70: Barn 2C **30**
Helena St. S64: Mexb 1F **67**
HELLABY 6E **101**
Hellaby (Euroway) Ind. Est.
  S66: Hel 4D **100**
Hellaby Hall Rd. S66: Hel 6E **101**
Hellaby La. S66: Hel 5E **101**
Hellaby Rd. S66: Rav 3A **100**
Helliwell Cl. S36: Spink 5G **175**
Helliwell Cft. *S36: Spink* 4G *175*
            (off Helliwell La.)
Helliwell La. S36: Spink 4G **175**
Helmsley Av. S20: Half 3E **151**
Helmsley Cl. S26: Swal 2B **138**
  S41: Ches 1D **166**
Helmton Dr. S8: Shef 6F **133**
Helmton Rd. S8: Shef 6E **133**
Helston Cl. S41: Has 2A **172**
Helston Cres. S71: Monk B 5G **17**
Helston Ri. S7: Shef 4B **132**
HEMINGFIELD 5F **47**
Hemmingfield Rd.
  S73: Hem, Womb 3E **47**
Hemmingway Cl. S60: Tree 2F **123**
Hemper Gro. S8: Shef 3C **146**
Hemper La. S8: Shef 4C **146**
Hemp Pits Rd. DN5: Ark 1C **40**
HEMSWORTH
  S14 . . . . .6A **134**
  WF9 . . . . .1D **12**
Hemsworth By-Pass S72: Brier 2C **12**
  WF9: Hems 1G **13**
Hemsworth Rd. S8: Shef 6F **133**
  WF9: Hems, Sth K 1F **13**
Henderson Cl. S60: Roth 1E **111**
Henderson Glen S71: Roy 3F **9**
Hendon St. S13: Shef 5A **122**
Hengist Rd. DN5: Don 2G **55**
Henley Av. S8: Shef 2G **147**
Henley Gro. Rd. S61: Roth 3C **96**
            (not continuous)
Henley La. S61: Roth 2B **96**
Henley Ri. S61: Roth 2B **96**
Henley Rd. DN2: Don 5H **41**
Henley Way S61: Roth 2B **96**
Hennings Cl. DN4: Bess 5G **57**
Hennings La. DN4: Bess 4G **57**
Hennings Rd. DN4: Bess 1H **73**
Henry Cl. S72: Shaft 3F **11**
Henry Ct. S62: Parkg 5G **83**
  S65: Roth 3E **97**
Henry La. DN11: New R 4A **74**
Henry Moore Ct. S75: Wool G 3E **7**
Henry Pl. S64: Mexb 1H **67**
Henry Rd. S63: Wath D 6A **48**
Henry St. S3: Shef 1B **4** (1E **119**)
  S21: Ecki 1E **159**
  S35: High G 1B **78**
  S41: Whit M 6A **162**
  S65: Roth 3E **97**
            (not continuous)

Henry St. S70: Wors 5F **31**
  S73: Womb 6A **34**
Henshall Ho. *S41: Ches* 2A *168*
            (off Tapton Lock Hill)
Henshall St. S70: Barn 2F **31**
Henson St. S9: Shef 6E **109**
Heppenstall La. S9: Shef 6C **108**
Heptinstall St. S70: Wors 5G **31**
Hepworth Cl. S75: Wool G 3F **7**
Hepworth Dr. S26: Ast, Swal 1C **138**
Hepworth Rd. DN4: Balb 5G **55**
Herald Rd. DN3: Eden 1B **42**
Herbert Cl. DN5: Don 5H **39**
Herbert Rd. DN5: Don 5H **39**
  S7: Shef 2D **132**
Herbert St. S61: Kimb 3H **95**
  S64: Mexb 1G **67**
HERDINGS 5B **134**
Herdings Ct. S12: Shef 5D **134**
Herdings / Leighton Road Stop (ST)
              . . . . .5C **134**
Herdings Park Stop (ST) 6B **134**
Herdings Rd. S12: Shef 5D **134**
Herdings Vw. S12: Shef 5C **134**
Hereford Dr. S43: Brim 6E **163**
Hereford Rd. DN2: Don 3G **41**
Hereford St. S1: Shef 6D **4** (5F **119**)
            (not continuous)
Hereward Ct. DN12: Con 4H **69**
Hereward Rd. S5: Shef 6G **93**
Hereward's Rd. S8: Shef 1A **148**
Heritage Ct. *S73: Hem* 4G *47*
            (off Beech Ho. Rd.)
Heritage M. S74: Els 2D **62**
Hermitage St. S2: Shef 5E **119**
Hermit Hill S35: Wort 6A **44**
Hermit La. S75: Barn, H'ham 6F **15**
Heron Cl. DN2: Don 3F **41**
  DN12: Con 4A **70**
Heron Dr. S63: Bramp B 5A **48**
Heron Hill S26: Ast 2D **138**
Heron Mt. S2: Shef 4B **120**
Herons Way DN4: Balb 5C **56**
  S70: Birdw 4E **45**
Herrick Gdns. DN4: Balb 6B **56**
Herrick Rd. DN3: Barn D 1H **27**
Herries Av. S5: Shef 2F **107**
Herries Dr. S5: Shef 2F **107**
Herries Pl. S5: Shef 2F **107**
Herries Rd. S5: Shef 2C **106**
  S6: Shef 2B **106**
Herries Rd. Sth. S6: Shef 2B **106**
HERRINGTHORPE 5A **98**
Herringthorpe Av. S65: Roth 6A **98**
Herringthorpe Cl. S65: Roth 5A **98**
Herringthorpe Gro. S65: Roth 6B **98**
Herringthorpe La. S65: Roth 5B **98**
Herringthorpe Leisure Cen. 6H **97**
Herringthorpe Stadium 5H **97**
Herringthorpe Valley Rd.
  S60: Roth 2B **98**
  S65: Roth 2B **98**
Herriot Dr. S40: Ches 1A **172**
Herschell Rd. S7: Shef 1E **133**
            (not continuous)
Herten Way DN4: Don 3G **57**
Hesketh Dr. DN3: Kirk Sa 4D **26**
Hesley Bar S61: Thorpe H 4B **80**
Hesley Ct. DN12: Den M 3C **68**
  S64: Swint 5B **66**
Hesley Grange S61: Scho 6F **81**
Hesley Gro. S35: Chap 4H **79**
Hesley La. S61: Thorpe H 4B **80**
Hesley M. S61: Scho 6F **81**
Hesley Rd. DN11: New R 6C **74**
  S5: Shef 3A **94**
Hesley Ter. S5: Shef 3A **94**
Heslow Gro. S61: Thorpe H 3B **80**
Hessey St. S13: Shef 2A **136**
Hessle Rd. S6: Shef 2A **106**
Hethersett Way DN11: New R 6F **75**
Hewitt St. S64: Mexb 1H **67**
HEXTHORPE .2A **56**
Hexthorpe Bus. Pk. DN4: Hex 3A **56**
Hexthorpe Rd. DN4: Hex 2A **56**
Heyhouse Dr. S35: Chap 1E **79**
Heyhouse Way S35: Chap 1E **79**
Heysham Grn. S71: Monk B 2A **18**
Heywood St. S43: Brim 6D **162**

Hibberd Pl. S6: Shef 4H **105**
Hibberd Rd. S6: Shef 4H **105**
Hibbert Ter. *S70: Barn 3E 31*
(off Walnut Cl.)
HICKLETON 3H **37**
Hickleton Ct. S63: Thurn 3B **36**
Hickleton Golf Course 2G **37**
Hickleton Rd. DN5: Barnb 6H **37**
Hickleton St. DN12: Den M 3C **68**
Hickleton Ter. *S63: Thurn 3D 36*
(off Lidget La.)
Hickmott Rd. S11: Shef 6C **118**
Hickson Dr. S71: Lund 4B **18**
Hicks St. S3: Shef 6F **107**
Hides St. S9: Shef 4E **109**
High Alder Rd. DN4: Bess 4H **57**
HIGHAM 5F **15**
Higham Comn. Rd.
S75: Bar G, H'ham 5F **15**
Higham Ct. S75: H'ham 5F **15**
Higham La. S75: H'ham 6F **15**
(not continuous)
Higham Vw. S75: Kexb 1E **15**
High Ash Dr. S25: Sth A 5G **141**
High Balk S75: Barn 4C **16**
High Bank S36: Thurl 3A **176**
S65: Thry 6D **84**
High Bank La. S36: Thurl 4A **176**
Highbury Av. DN4: Cant 4B **58**
Highbury Cres. DN4: Cant 4B **58**
Highbury Gro. S41: Ches 3G **167**
Highbury Rd. S41: Ches 3G **167**
Highbury Va. DN12: New E 5B **70**
Highcliffe Ct. S11: Shef 1H **131**
S64: Swint 3C **66**
Highcliffe Dr. S11: Shef 2G **131**
S35: Ough 4E **91**
S64: Swint 3C **66**
Highcliffe Pl. S11: Shef 2G **131**
Highcliffe Rd. S11: Shef 1G **131**
High Cl. S75: Kexb 5E **7**
High Ct. S1: Shef 2F **5** (2G **119**)
High Cft. S74: Hoyl 6B **46**
Highcroft S11: Shef 1H **131**
High Cft. Dr. S71: Ath 6E **9**
Highdale Fold S18: Dron 3F **155**
Higher Albert St. S41: Ches 4H **167**
HIGHER STUBBIN 1C **82**
HIGHFIELD
S1 5F **119**
WF9 1E **13**
Highfield S63: Wath D 6G **49**
Highfield Av. S26: Kiv P 5B **140**
S41: Ches 2F **167**
S63: Gol 5C **36**
S70: Wors 4E **31**
S71: Ath 2F **17**
Highfield Cen. WF9: Hems 1E **13**
Highfield Cl. DN3: Barn D 1D **26**
Highfield Cotts. S75: Silk 1B **28**
Highfield Ct. S64: Swint 3B **66**
S73: Womb 1F **47**
Highfield Gro. S63: Wath D 5B **48**
High Fld. Knoll S36: Pen 5E **177**
Highfield La. S13: Shef 4C **122**
S41: Ches 2F **167**
Highfield Pk. S66: Malt 4C **102**
(not continuous)
Highfield Pl. S2: Shef 6F **119**
WF9: Hems 1D **12**
Highfield Range S73: D'fld 3B **34**
Highfield Ri. S6: Stann 6C **104**
Highfield Rd. DN1: Don 6D **40**
DN12: Con 4G **69**
S41: Ches 3G **167**
S61: Grea 6D **82**
S64: Swint 3A **66**
S73: D'fld 4B **34**
WF9: Hems 1D **12**
HIGHFIELDS 6D **22**
Highfields S36: H'swne 1F **177**
Highfields Country Pk. 5C **22**
Highfields Cres. S18: Dron 4F **155**
High Field Spring S13: Shef 2B **122**
S60: Cat 2B **122**
Highfields Rd. S18: Dron 4F **155**
S75: Kexb 6C **6**
Highfield Ter. S41: Ches 3G **167**
Highfield Vw. S60: Cat 6D **110**
Highfield Vw. Rd. S41: Ches 3G **167**
(not continuous)
High Fisher Ga. DN1: Don 6C **40**
HIGHGATE 5B **36**
Highgate S9: Tins 2H **109**
(not continuous)
S73: Womb 2C **48**
Highgate Cl.
DN11: New R 6D **74** & 6H **75**
S43: New W 3C **162**
High Gate Ct. S70: Stair 2A **32**
Highgate Ct. S63: Gol 6B **36**
Highgate Dr. S18: Dron 5H **155**
Highgate Greyhound Racing Track 4B **36**
Highgate La. S18: Dron 5G **155**
S63: Bolt D, Gol 1B **50**
High Gate Way S72: Shaft 4F **11**
Highgreave S5: Shef 3H **93**
High Greave Av. S5: Shef 3G **93**
High Greave Ct. S5: Shef 3H **93**
High Greave Pl. S65: Roth 3B **98**
High Greave Rd. S65: Roth 2B **98**
High Greaves S71: Smi 3F **17**
HIGH GREEN 6C **60**
High Gro. DN4: Bess 1D **74**
Highgrove Cl. S41: Whit M 6H **161**
Highgrove Ct. DN4: Cant 6D **58**
High Hazel Ct. S60: Tree 2F **123**
High Hazel Cres. S60: Cat 6D **110**
High Hazel Rd. S60: Tree 2F **123**
High Hazels 2G **121**
High Hazels Cl. S9: Shef 2G **121**
High Hazels Mead S9: Shef 2G **121**
High Hooton Rd. S25: Slade H 4H **115**
S66: Hoot L 4H **115**
High Ho. Farm Ct. S26: Wales 6G **139**
High Ho. Ter. S6: Shef 5C **106**
Highland Rd. S43: New W 1C **162**
HIGHLANE 1H **149**
High La. S12: Ridg 1H **149**
S42: Walt 5A **170**
S66: Bramp M 4G **125**
High Lee La. S36: H'swne 2F **177**
Highlow Cl. S40: Ches 3D **166**
Highlow Vw. S60: Brins 3D **110**
High Matlock Av. S6: Stann 6E **105**
High Matlock Rd. S6: Stann 5E **105**
HIGH MELTON 3E **53**
High Melton Golf Course 4E **53**
Highmill Av. S64: Swint 3H **65**
HIGH MOOR 5E **153**
Highmoor Av. S26: Kiv P 6H **139**
Highnam Cres. Rd. S10: Shef 3B **118**
High Nook Rd. S25: Dinn 6B **128**
High Pavement Row S2: Shef 2H **119**
High Ridge S70: Wors 5E **31**
Highridge Cl. DN12: Con 5G **69**
High Rd. DN4: Balb 5H **55**
DN4: Warm 6D **54**
DN12: New E 5C **70**
High Royd Av. S72: Cud 2E **19**
High Royd La. S36: H'swne 2G **177**
S74: Hoyl 4G **45**
Highroyds S70: Wors 4E **31**
Highstone Av. S70: Barn 3D **30**
Highstone Cnr. S70: Wors 4E **31**
Highstone Ct. S70: Barn 3E **31**
Highstone Cres. S70: Barn 3D **30**
Highstone La. S70: Wors 4E **31**
Highstone Rd. S70: Barn 3E **31**
Highstone Va. S70: Barn 3D **30**
Highstone Vw. S70: Barn 3E **31**
High Storrs Cl. S11: Shef 2G **131**
High Storrs Cres. S11: Shef 1H **131**
High Storrs Dr. S11: Shef 2G **131**
High Storrs Ri. S11: Shef 1H **131**
High Storrs Rd. S11: Shef 2G **131**
High St. DN1: Don 1B **56**
DN3: Barn D 1B **26**
DN5: Ark 6C **24**
DN5: Barnb 1H **51**
DN5: Ben 3A **40**
DN7: Dunsv 5G **27**
DN11: Wad 5E **73**
DN12: Con 4F **69**
S1: Shef 3E **5** (3G **119**)
S9: Shef 2F **109**
S17: Dore 3E **145**
S18: App 3D **156**
High St. S18: Dron 2E **155**
S20: Beig 4H **137**
S20: Mosb 3D **150**
S21: Ecki 1D **158**
S21: Killa 4C **152**
S25: Laugh M 1G **127**
S25: Sth A 4G **141**
S26: Swal 1B **138**
S35: Eccl 2F **93**
S36: Pen 4D **176**
S40: Ches 5H **167**
S41: Old W 4H **161**
(not continuous)
S43: Brim 1E **169**
(not continuous)
S43: New W 3B **162**
S43: Stav 4B **164**
S60: Roth 4E **97**
S60: Whist 3A **112**
S61: Kimb 3H **95**
S62: Rawm 4G **83**
S63: Bolt D 2B **50**
S63: Gol 5D **36**
S63: Thurn 2A **36**
S63: Wath D 6G **49**
S64: Mexb 2F **67**
S66: B'well 6B **88**
S66: Malt 5B **102**
S70: Barn 6D **16**
S70: Wors 5G **31**
S71: Monk B 4H **17**
S71: Roy 3F **9**
S72: Bill 3G **35**
S72: Grim 2A **20**
S72: Gt H 6E **21**
S72: Shaft 3F **11**
S72: Sth H 1H **11**
S73: Womb 1G **47**
S74: Hoyl 6B **46**
S75: Dod 3G **29**
S75: Silk 3A **28**
S75: Stain 4H **7**
High St. La. S2: Shef 3H **5** (3H **119**)
High St. Mews S20: Mosb 3D **150**
Highthorn Rd. S64: Kiln 5C **66**
High Thorns S75: Silk 2A **28**
Highthorn Vs. S64: Kiln 5D **66**
Highton St. S6: Shef 6B **106**
High Trees S17: Dore 3E **145**
S60: Roth 1A **112**
High Vw. S5: Shef 4F **107**
S71: Roy 3G **9**
High Vw. Cl. S41: Ches 6C **168**
S73: D'fld 4C **34**
HIGH WINCOBANK 6D **94**
Highwood Cl. S75: Kexb 6D **6**
Highwood Pl. S21: Ecki 1D **158**
HIGHWOODS 1D **66**
Highwoods Cres.
S64: Mexb 1D **66**
Highwoods Rd. S64: Mexb 1D **66**
High Wray Cl. S11: Shef 4A **132**
Hilary Way S26: Swal 1C **138**
Hilda Ter. S72: Grim 2A **20**
Hild Av. S72: Cud 4G **19**
Hillary Ho. DN2: Don 4E **41**
Hillberry Ri. S40: Birdh 4G **171**
Hill Cl. S6: Stann 6D **104**
S65: Roth 6D **98**
Hillcote Cl. S10: Shef 5E **117**
Hillcote Dr. S10: Shef 5E **117**
Hillcote M. S10: Shef 5E **117**
Hillcote Ri. S10: Shef 5E **117**
Hill Crest S65: Thry 5D **84**
S74: Hoyl 1H **61**
Hillcrest S63: Thurn 3B **36**
Hillcrest Dr. S25: Sth A 5G **141**
S35: Ough 4D **90**
Hillcrest Gro. S43: Stav 2C **164**
Hillcrest Ri. S36: Spink 4H **175**
Hill Crest Rd. S35: Chap 3E **79**
S65: Roth 3A **98**
Hillcrest Rd. DN2: Don 4F **41**
S36: Spink 4G **175**
S41: Has 3C **172**
Hillcrest Way S66: Sunn 2G **99**
Hilldrecks Vw. S65: Rav 1A **100**
Hill End Rd. S75: Mapp 1B **16**
Hill Farm Cl. S63: Thurn 3A **36**

HILLFOOT
S6 .5C 106
S17 .6E 145
Hillfoot Ct. S17: Tot 6E 145
Hillfoot Rd. S3: Shef 6D 106
S17: Tot 5D 144
Hill Gro. S43: Bar H 2G 163
Hillman Dr. S43: Ink 2H 169
Hill Rise Cl. S66: Sunn 4H 99
HILLSBOROUGH 4B 106
Hillsborough 2B 106
Hillsborough Arcade, The S6: Shef . .4B 106
Hillsborough Barracks Business &
Shopping Cen. S6: Shef 4C 106
Hillsborough Golf Course 1G 105
Hillsborough Gro. S6: Shef 2C 106
Hillsborough Leisure Cen. 3C 106
Hillsborough Park Stop (ST) 4B 106
Hillsborough Pl. S6: Shef 4B 106
S6: Shef 4B 106
Hillsborough Stop (ST) 4B 106
Hills Cl. DN5: Sprot 2F 55
S64: Mexb 1F 67
Hillscroft Rd. DN9: Blax 1F 77
HILLSIDE 4B 12
Hill Side S60: Whist 3A 112
S61: Thorpe H 4C 80
S65: Thry 6D 84
Hillside S20: Mosb 3D 150
S25: Nth A 2G 141
S71: Ard 2D 32
Hillside Av. S5: Shef 4G 93
S18: Dron 4F 155
Hillside Cl. S36: H'swne 1F 177
Hillside Ct. DN5: Sprot 4C 54
S61: Grea 1E 97
Hillside Cres. S72: Brier 4B 12
Hillside Dr. DN12: New E 5B 70
S40: Walt 6E 167
S43: Mas M 3F 165
S74: Hoyl 1C 62
Hillside Gro. S72: Brier 4A 12
Hill Side La. S36: Thurl 5A 176
Hillside Mt. S72: Brier 4B 12
Hillside Rd. DN2: Don 3H 41
Hills Rd. S36: Spink 3F 175
Hill St. S2: Shef 5E 119
S71: Stair 2B 32
S73: D'fld 5B 34
S74: Els 1D 62
HILL TOP
DN12 . . . . .1C 86
S6 . . . . .5A 104
S11 .3F 131
S18 .5F 155
S35 . . . . .2C 90
S61 . . . . .4F 95
S71 . . . . .1E 17
Hill Top S75: Cawt 3A 14
Hilltop S72: Brier 3A 12
Hill Top Av. S71: Ath 5D 8
Hill Top Cl. S60: Brins 3C 110
S61: Kimb 4G 95
S66: Malt 4G 101
Hill Top Cres. DN2: Don 3H 41
DN12: New E 6C 70
S20: Water 1E 151
Hill Top Dr. S35: Wharn S 2C 90
Hill Top Est. WF9: Sth K 5G 13
Hilltop Gdns. DN12: Den M 4C 68
Hilltop Grn. S5: Shef 1E 107
Hill Top La. S35: Green M 1E 175
S35: Gren 2A 92
S61: Kimb 4G 95
S65: Dalt M 3E 99
S66: Dalt M 3E 99
S75: Barn 5A 16
Hill Top Ri. S35: Gren 3C 92
Hill Top Rd. DN12: Con, Den M 2C 68
S35: Gren 3C 92
S70: Birdw 4E 45
Hilltop Rd. S18: Dron 4F 155
S41: Old W 4H 161
S42: W'orth 6E 171
Hilltops S62: Rawm 4G 83
Hill Top Smithies S71: Smi 2E 17
Hilltop Way S18: Dron 5F 155
Hill Turrets Cl. S11: Shef 4G 131

Hill Vw. E. S61: Kimb 2G 95
Hill Vw. Rd. S43: Brim 6D 162
S61: Kimb 2G 95
Hilmian Way WF9: Hems 1G 13
Hilton Dr. S35: Eccl 2G 93
Hilton St. S75: Barn 6C 16
Hindburn Cl. DN4: Bess 5G 57
Hinde Ho. Cres. S4: Shef 2B 108
Hinde Ho. Cft. S4: Shef 2B 108
Hinde Ho. La. S4: Shef 3A 108
Hinde St. S4: Shef 3B 108
Hindewood Cl. S4: Shef 2B 108
Hindle St. S70: Barn 1C 30
Hind Rd. S60: Whist 2B 112
Hipley Cl. S40: Ches 2C 166
Hipper St. S40: Ches 6H 167
Hipper St. Sth. S40: Ches 6H 167
Hipper St. W. S40: Ches 6F 167
Hirst Comn. La. S6: Shef 4A 92
Hirst Dr. S65: Roth 3C 98
Hirst Ga. S64: Mexb 1H 67
Hirst La. S66: Staint 1F 103
HMP Doncaster DN5: Don 1A 56
Hoades Av. S81: Woods 4F 143
Hobart St. S11: Shef 6E 119
Hobner La. S43: Stav 6H 163
Hobson Av. S6: Shef 5D 106
Hobson Pl. S6: Shef 5D 106
Hockley La. S42: W'orth 6H 171
Hodder Ct. S35: Chap 2E 79
Hodgkinson Av. S36: Pen 4D 176
Hodgson St. S3: Shef 6C 4 (4E 119)
Hodroyd Cl. S72: Shaft 5G 11
Hodroyd Cotts. S72: Brier 4B 12
Hodroyd La. S72: Shaft 5G 11
Hodster La. S72: Gt H 4D 20
Hogarth Ri. S18: Dron 4E 155
Holbeach Dr. S40: Walt 2F 171
Holbeck Cl. S41: Ches 4A 168
Holbein Cl. S18: Dron 4E 155
Holberry Cl. S10: Shef 5A 4 (4D 118)
Holberry Gdns. S10: Shef . .5A 4 (4D 118)
Holborn Av. S18: Dron 2F 155
Holbourne Gro. S35: High G 5C 60
HOLBROOK 2H 151
Holbrook Av. S20: Holb 2G 151
Holbrook Cl. S20: Holb 1G 151
S40: Walt 2D 170
Holbrook Dr. S13: Shef 2E 135
Holbrook Ent. Pk. S20: Holb 2H 151
Holbrook Grn. S20: Holb 2H 151
Holbrook Ind. Est. S20: Holb 2H 151
Holbrook Pl. S43: Ink 1H 169
Holbrook Ri. S20: Holb 1G 151
Holbrook Rd. S13: Shef 1E 135
Holden Ct. S70: Barn 1D 30
Holderness Dr. S26: Ast, Swal 6C 124
Holdings Rd. S2: Shef 5A 120
Holdroyds Yd. S75: Dod 4G 29
HOLDWORTH 6A 90
Holdworth La. S6: Bradf 6A 90
Hole Ho. La. S36: Stoc 3D 174
Holgate S73: Womb 5E 33
Holgate Cl. S5: Shef 5E 93
Holgate Ct. S5: Shef 4E 93
Holgate Cres. S5: Shef 4F 93
Holgate Dr. S5: Shef 4F 93
Holgate Hospital WF9: Hems 1B 12
Holgate Mt. S70: Wors 4E 31
Holgate Rd. S5: Shef 4F 93
(not continuous)
Holgate Vw. S72: Brier 3B 12
Holiwell Cl. S66: Malt 4C 102
Holkham Ri. S11: Shef 6G 131
Holland Cl. S62: Rawm 1G 83
Holland Pl. S2: Shef 6F 119
Holland Rd. S2: Shef 6F 119
S35: High G 1C 78
S41: Old W 4G 161
Holland St. S1: Shef 3C 4 (3E 119)
Hollens Way S40: Ches 3A 166
Hollies Cl. S18: Dron 4H 155
Hollinberry La. S35: Howb 5A 60
HOLLIN BUSK 5D 174
Hollin Busk La. S36: Spink 5E 175
Hollin Busk Rd. S36: Spink 4E 175
Hollin Cl. DN11: Ross 4E 75
S41: Ches 6D 160
Hollin Cft. S75: Dod 2H 29

Hollindale Dr. S12: Shef 3F 135
Hollin Edge La. S36: Bolst 6H 175
Holling Cft. S36: Spink 3G 175
Holling Hill La. S66: Wick 6E 99
Holling Moor La. S66: Wick 6F 99
Holling's La. S65: Rav, Thry 6E 85
Hollingswood Way S66: Sunn 3H 99
HOLLINGWOOD 5F 163
Hollingwood Cres. S43: Hol 4F 163
Hollingwood Est. S43: Hol 5F 163
Hollingworth Cl. S64: Mexb 6A 52
Hollin Ho. La. S6: Lox 1A 104
Hollin La. S36: Bolst 6E 175
S75: Cawt 3A 14
Hollin Rd. S35: Ough 4D 90
Hollins, The S75: Dod 4H 29
Hollins Cl. S6: Shef 1G 117
Hollins Dr. S6: Shef 6G 105
Hollins Dr. S6: Shef 1H 117
HOLLINS END 3F 135
Hollinsend Av. S12: Shef 3F 135
Hollinsend Pl. S12: Shef 3F 135
Hollinsend Rd. S12: Shef 4D 134
Hollinsend Stop (ST) 3D 134
Hollins La. S6: Shef 6G 105
Hollins Spring Av. S18: Dron 3F 155
Hollins Spring Rd. S18: Dron 4F 155
Hollins Wood Gro. S72: Cud 4G 19
Hollis Cl. S62: Rawm 6E 65
Hollis Cft. S1: Shef 2C 4 (2E 119)
S13: Shef 2B 136
Hollis La. S41: Ches 6A 168
(not continuous)
Hollowdene S75: Barn 5A 16
Hollow Ga. DN5: Cade 1F 69
S35: Chap 3C 78
S60: Whist 3A 112
Hollowgate DN5: H'ton, Barnb 2G 51
S60: Roth 5F 97
Hollowgate Av. S63: Wath D 4D 48
Hollow La. S20: Half 4E 151
Hollows, The DN4: Bess 6B 58
DN9: Auck 2H 59
Holly Av. DN5: Don 3H 39
Hollybank Av. S12: Shef 2F 135
Hollybank Cl. S12: Shef 2G 135
Hollybank Cres. S12: Shef 2F 135
Hollybank Dr. S12: Shef 2G 135
Hollybank Rd. S12: Shef 2F 135
Hollybank Way S12: Shef 2G 135
Holly Barn Fold S65: Hoot R 2H 85
Holly Bush Dr. S63: Thurn 2C 36
Holly Bush La. DN3: Kirk Sa 5C 26
Hollybush St. S62: Parkg 5G 83
Holly Cl. S21: Killa 5B 152
S35: Chap 4E 79
S41: Old W 3A 161
Holly Ct. S10: Shef 5A 118
S70: Barn 3E 31
(off Hornby St.)
Holly Cres. S66: Sunn 4H 99
Hollycroft Av. S71: Roy 3G 9
Holly Dene DN3: Arm 2D 42
Holly Dr. DN5: Ben 6A 24
Holly Farm S72: Shaft 3F 11
Holly Gdns. S12: Shef 2F 135
Hollygate S70: Wors 5H 31
Holly Gro. DN11: Ross 4D 74
S12: Shef 2F 135
S63: Gol 5B 36
S63: Wath D 2G 65
S72: Brier 3B 12
S73: D'fld 5B 34
(off Snape Hill Rd.)
Holly Hall La. S35: Green M 1H 175
Holly Ho. La. S35: Gren 2H 91
Holly La. S1: Shef 3D 4 (3H 119)
Holly Mt. S66: Wick 6H 99
Holly Rd. DN9: Auck 2B 76
Holly's Ho. Rd. S65: Rav 1B 100
Holly St. DN1: Don 3B 56
S1: Shef 3D 4 (3H 119)
(not continuous)
Holly Ter. DN4: Balb 5G 55
S26: Swal 6B 124
Hollythorpe Cl. S41: Has 2C 172
Hollythorpe Cres. S8: Shef 4F 133
Hollythorpe Ri. S8: Shef 4G 133
Hollythorpe Rd. S8: Shef 4G 133

Hollytree Av.—Hoyland Leisure Centre & Swimming Pool

Hollytree Av. S66: Malt 4G **101**
Hollywell Cl. S62: Rawm 1A **84**
Hollywell Dr. DN4: Bess 1E **75**
Hollywood Bowl
Sheffield 4F **109**
Holmbrook Wlk. S40: Ches 3D **166**
Holm Cl. S18: Dron W 2C **154**
Holme, The S18: Dron 1G **155**
Holmebank Cl. S40: Ches 4F **167**
Holmebank E. S40: Ches 4F **167**
Holmebank Vw. S40: Ches 4F **167**
Holmebank W. S40: Ches 4F **167**
Holmebrook Vw. S40: Ches 2D **166**
Holme Cl. S6: Shef 4B **106**
Holme Ct. S63: Gol 6B **36**
Holmefield Cl. DN3: Arm 5F **43**
Holme Hall Cres. S40: Ches 2C **166**
Holme Hall La. S66: Staint 2F **103**
Holme La. S6: Shef 5A **106**
S35: Gren 3C **92**
Holme Oak Way S6: Stann 5D **104**
Holme Pk. Av. S41: Ches 1C **166**
Holme Rd. S41: Ches 2H **167**
Holmeroyd Rd. DN6: Adw S 1F **23**
HOLMES 5B **96**
Holmes, The DN1: Don 6C **40**
Holmes Carr Cres.
DN11: New R 5A **74**
Holmes Carr Rd. DN4: Bess 6A **58**
DN11: New R 5A **74**
Holmes Ct. S61: Roth 4C **96**
Holmes Cres. S60: Tree 2F **123**
HOLMESDALE 1H **155**
Holmesdale Cl. S18: Dron 1H **155**
Holmesdale Rd. S18: Dron 1G **155**
HOLMESFIELD 4A **154**
Holmesfield *S61: Roth* *4B* ***96***
(off Rosebery St.)
Holmes Fld. Cl. S26: Kiv S 6F **141**
Holmesfield Rd. S18: Dron W 3A **154**
S35: Ough 4E **91**
Holmes La. DN12: Old D 6G **67**
S61: Roth 4B **96**
S65: Hoot R 6G **67**
Holmes Mkt., The *DN1: Don* *6D* ***40***
(off Kings Rd.)
Holmes Rd. S66: Braml 6A **100**
Holme Vw. Rd. S75: Kexb 6C **6**
Holme Wood Ct. DN3: Eden 6D **26**
Holme Wood Gdns. DN4: Bess 5B **58**
Holme Wood La. DN3: Arm 4G **43**
(not continuous)
Holm Flatt St. S62: Parkg 5F **83**
Holmhirst Cl. S8: Shef 6D **132**
Holmhirst Dr. S8: Shef 5D **132**
Holmhirst Rd. S8: Shef 5D **132**
Holmhirst Way S8: Shef 5D **132**
Holmley Bank S18: Dron 1F **155**
HOLMLEY COMMON 1F **155**
Holmley La. S18: Coal A, Dron 1F **155**
Holmoak Cl. S64: Swint 5C **66**
Holmshaw Cl. DN3: Eden 5D **26**
Holmshaw Dr. S13: Shef 6H **121**
Holmshaw Gro. S13: Shef 6H **121**
Holmsley Av. WF9: Sth K 4H **13**
Holmsley Gro. WF9: Sth K 4H **13**
Holmsley La. S72: Brier 5F **13**
WF9: Sth K 5F **13**
Holmsley Mt. WF9: Sth K 4H **13**
Holt Ho. Gro. S7: Shef 4C **132**
Holtwood Rd. S4: Shef 5G **107**
Holwick Cl. S75: Silk 2A **28**
Holwick Ct. S70: Barn 1D **30**
Holy Grn. S1: Shef 6D **4** (4F **119**)
Holymoor Rd. S42: Holy 1A **170**
Holyoake Av. S13: Shef 5H **121**
Holyrood Av. S10: Shef 5A **116**
Holyrood Ri. S66: Braml 3A **100**
Holyrood Rd. DN2: Don 1F **57**
Holyrood Vw. S10: Shef 5A **116**
Holywell Cotts. S66: B'well 2B **102**
Holywell Ct. S4: Shef 2D **108**
Holywell Cres. S66: B'well 1B **102**
Holywell Ga. S4: Shef 2D **108**
Holywell Hgts. S4: Shef 2D **108**
Holywell La. DN12: Con 5F **69**
S66: B'well 1B **102**
Holywell Pl. *S65: Roth* *3F* ***97***
(off Wharncliffe Hill)
Holywell Rd. S4: Shef 3C **108**
S9: Shef 3C **108**
S64: Kiln 5C **66**
Holywell St. S41: Ches 4H **167**
Homecroft Rd. S63: Gol 5C **36**
Home Farm Ct. DN5: Hick 3H **37**
Homefield Cres. DN5: Scawt 2F **39**
Homeport M. S41: Ches 4H **167**
Homestead, The DN5: Ben 1A **40**
Homestead Cl. S5: Shef 5A **94**
Homestead Dr. S60: Brins 3C **110**
S62: Rawm 1G **83**
Homestead Rd. S5: Shef 5H **93**
Honeymere Ct. S70: Barn 2G **31**
Honeysuckle Cl. DN4: Bess 4H **57**
S73: D'fld 6B **34**
Honeysuckle Ct. DN9: Finn 3F **77**
Honeysuckle Rd. S5: Shef 1C **108**
S41: Has 3D **172**
HONEYWELL 5E **17**
Honeywell Cl. S71: Barn 5E **17**
Honeywell Gro. S71: Barn 4E **17**
Honeywell La. S71: Barn 5D **16**
S75: Barn 5D **16**
Honeywell Pl. S71: Barn 5E **17**
Honeywell St. S71: Barn 5E **17**
Honister Cl. S63: Bramp B 5B **48**
HOOBER 5B **64**
Hoober Av. S11: Shef 3G **131**
Hoober Ct. S62: Rawm 6E **65**
Hoober Fld. Rd. S62: Wentw 5B **64**
S63: Wath D 5B **64**
Hoober Hall La. S62: Wentw 3H **63**
S63: Wath D 3H **63**
Hoober La. S62: Wentw 5B **64**
Hoober Rd. S11: Shef 3H **131**
Hoober Stand 4A **64**
Hoober St. S63: Wath D 5C **48**
Hoober Vw. S62: Rawm 6E **65**
S73: Womb 3A **48**
Hoodhill Rd. S62: H'ley 6A **62**
Hoole La. S10: Shef 4B **118**
Hoole Rd. S10: Shef 3B **118**
Hoole St. S6: Shef 6B **106**
S41: Has 2C **172**
Hooley Rd. S13: Shef 2E **137**
Hooton Cl. S25: Laugh M 1H **127**
Hooton La.
S25: Laugh M, Slade H 1H **127**
S65: Rav 5H **85**
S66: Hoot L 6H **101**
HOOTON LEVITT 6H **101**
Hooton Rd. S64: Kiln 1D **84**
HOOTON ROBERTS 2A **86**
Hope Av. S63: Gol 5C **36**
Hopedale Rd. S12: Shef 4G **135**
Hopefield Av. S12: Shef 4G **135**
Hope Rd. S35: Ough 4F **91**
Hope St. S36: Stoc 3E **175**
S40: Ches 5F **167**
S60: Roth 3D **96**
S64: Mexb 2F **67**
S71: Monk B 2C **18**
S73: Womb 2H **47**
(Gower St.)
S73: Womb 6A **34**
(Providence St.)
S75: Barn 6C **16**
S75: Stain 6B **8**
Hope St. Ind. Est. S60: Roth 2D **96**
Hopewell St. S70: Stair 2A **32**
Hopwood La. S6: Stann 2C **116**
Hopwood St. S70: Barn 6D **16**
Horace St. S60: Roth 5F **97**
Horbiry End S26: Tod 3B **140**
Horbury La. S35: Burn 4D **78**
Horbury Rd. S72: Cud 6E **11**
Hornbeam Cl. S35: Chap 4E **79**
S43: Hol 4F **163**
Hornbeam Rd. S66: Flan 4G **99**
Hornby Ct. S11: Shef 1H **131**
Hornby M. *S70: Barn* *3F* ***31***
(off Hornby St.)
Hornby St. S70: Barn 3E **31**
(not continuous)
Horncroft S75: Cawt 3A **14**
Horndean Rd. S5: Shef 3A **108**
Horner Cl. S36: Stoc 3D **174**
Horner Rd. S7: Shef 1E **133**
Hornes La. S75: Stain 5B **8**
Horninglow Cl. DN4: Cant 5D **58**
S5: Shef 1H **107**
Horninglow Mt. S5: Shef 1H **107**
Horninglow Rd. S5: Shef 1H **107**
Hornsby Rd. DN3: Arm 5F **43**
Hornthorpe Rd. S21: Ecki 2C **158**
Hornthwaite Cl. S36: Thurl 4A **176**
Hornthwaite Hill Rd.
S36: Thurl 5A **176**
Horse Carr Av. S71: Ard 2D **32**
Horsechestnut Cl. S40: Ches 1H **171**
Horse Cft. La. S35: Wharn S 2C **90**
Horsefair Cl. S64: Swint 3C **66**
Horsehills La. DN3: Arm 5D **42**
Horsemoor Rd. S63: Thurn 2A **36**
Horseshoe Cl. S26: Wales 5H **139**
Horse Shoe Ct. DN4: Balb 5G **55**
Horseshoe Gdns. S26: Wales 5G **139**
Horsewood Cl. S70: Barn 2A **30**
Horsewood Rd. S13: Shef 6E **123**
S42: Walt 2C **170**
Horsley Cl. S40: Ches 3B **166**
Horton Cl. S20: Half 3F **151**
Horton Dr. S20: Half 3F **151**
Horton Vw. DN3: Kirk Sa 3B **26**
Hough Cl. S40: Ches 1H **171**
Hough La. S73: Womb 3E **47**
Houghton Rd. S25: Nth A 5E **127**
S63: Thurn 2H **35**
Houldsworth Dr. S41: Ches 6C **168**
Hound Hill La. S64: Mexb 4C **50**
S70: Wors 6C **30**
Houndhill Pk. S63: Wath D 6B **50**
Houndkirk Rd. S11: Shef 1A **144**
Hounsfield Cres. S65: Roth 3C **98**
Hounsfield La. S3: Shef 4A **4**
Hounsfield Rd. S3: Shef 3A **4** (3D **118**)
S65: Roth 3C **98**
House Carr La. S75: Hood G 6C **28**
Housley La. S35: Chap 3E **79**
Housley Pk. S35: Chap 2E **79**
Houstead Rd. S9: Shef 3G **121**
Hoveringham Ct. S26: Swal 2B **138**
Howard Dr. S41: Old W 4H **161**
HOWARD HILL 1B **118**
Howard La. S1: Shef 5F **5** (4G **119**)
Howard Rd. S6: Shef 1B **118**
S66: Braml 5A **100**
S66: Malt 6C **102**
Howards Cl. S66: Thurc 6D **114**
Howard St. S1: Shef 5F **5** (4G **119**)
S25: Dinn 5B **128**
S60: Roth 3E **97**
S65: Roth 4F **97**
S70: Barn 3E **31**
S73: D'fld 5D **34**
Howarth Dr. S60: Brins 5E **111**
Howarth La. S60: Brins 4F **111**
(not continuous)
Howarth Rd. S60: Brins 4E **111**
Howbeck Cl. DN12: New E 5B **70**
Howbeck Dr. DN12: New E 5B **70**
HOWBROOK 5A **60**
Howbrook Cl. S35: High G 6B **60**
Howbrook La. S35: Wort, Howb 5A **60**
Howden Cl. DN4: Bess 6H **57**
S43: Stav 3C **164**
S75: Dart 5G **7**
Howden Rd. S9: Shef 5D **108**
Howdike La. S65: Hoot R 1G **85**
Howe La. S25: Slade H 4H **115**
Howell Gdns. S63: Thurn 3B **36**
Howell La. DN5: Clay 2F **21**
S72: Brier 2F **21**
Howell M. WF9: Sth K 4G **13**
Howells Pl. S43: Mas M 2E **165**
Howell Wood Country Pk. 1G **21**
Howlett Cl. S60: Whist 3C **112**
Howlett Dr. S60: Brins 5D **110**
Howse St. S74: Els 6E **47**
Howson Cl. S65: Rav 2B **100**
Howson Rd. S36: Spink 3F **175**
Hoylake Av. S40: Walt 3D **170**
Hoylake Dr. S64: Swint 5C **66**
HOYLAND 6B **46**
HOYLAND COMMON 1G **61**
Hoyland Leisure Centre & Swimming Pool
. . . . 6A **46**

220 A-Z Sheffield

HOYLAND LOWE 6A 46
Hoyland Rd. S3: Shef 6D 106
S74: Hoyl .1G 61
Hoyland St. S66: Malt 5C 102
S73: Womb 2G 47
HOYLANDSWAINE 1G 177
Hoyland Ter. WF9: Sth K 4H 13
Hoy La. S64: Mexb 5D 50
Hoyle Cft. La. S66: B'well 1H 101
HOYLE MILL 1G 31
Hoyle Mill La. S36: Thurl 3B 176
Hoyle Mill Rd. S70: Stair 2A 32
Hoyle St. S3: Shef 1C 4 (1E 119)
HUBS, The .5F 5
Hucklow Av. S40: Ches 2G 171
S43: Ink .1H 169
Hucklow Dr. S5: Shef 1A 108
Hucklow Rd. S5: Shef 2A 108
Hucknall Av. S40: Ash 4D 166
Huddersfield Rd. S36: Pen 1A 176
S70: Barn 4B 16
S75: Barn 4B 16
S75: Barn 1B 16
S75: Dart, Hai, Kexb 2C 6
S75: Hai .1B 6
Hudson Haven S73: Womb 6E 33
(off Upton Cl.)
Hudson Rd. S13: Shef 6F 123
S61: Kimb P 6H 81
Hudson's M. DN1: Don 1B 56
Humberside Way S71: Carl 2A 18
Hummingbird Wlk. S63: Wath D 5G 49
Humphrey Rd. S8: Shef 2D 146
Humphries Av. S62: Rawm 1E 83
HUNDALL .5E 157
Hundall La. S18: Uns 5C 156
S41: Old W 2H 161
Hungerhill Cl. S61: Kimb P 2G 95
Hunger Hill La. S60: Whist 3B 112
Hungerhill La. DN3: Eden 6A 26
Hunger Hill Rd. S60: Whist 2A 112
Hungerhill Rd. S61: Kimb 1G 95
Hunloke Av. S40: Ches, Walt 1E 171
Hunloke Cres. S40: Ches 1F 171
Hunloke Vw. S42: W'orth 6A 172
Hunningley Cl. S70: Stair 3A 32
Hunningley La. S70: Stair 4A 32
(Burnsall Gro.)
S70: Stair 2A 32
(Greggs Ct.)
Hunsdon Rd. S21: Ecki 1D 158
HUNSHELF BANK 1D 174
Hunshelf La. S35: Eccl 6G 79
Hunshelf Pk. S30: Stoc 2E 175
Hunshelf Rd. S35: Chap 3E 79
S36: Stoc 2D 174
(Pea Royd La.)
S36: Stoc 1B 174
(Underbank La.)
Hunsley St. S4: Shef 4B 108
Hunster Cl. DN4: Cant 5C 58
Hunster Flat La. DN11: New R 6G 75
Hunster Gro. DN11: New R 6C 74
Hunstone Av. S8: Shef 3F 147
Hunt Cl. S71: Monk B 4H 17
Hunter Ct. S11: Shef 1A 132
Hunter Hill Rd. S11: Shef 6B 118
Hunter Ho. Rd. S11: Shef 6B 118
Hunter Rd. S6: Shef 4A 106
Hunter's Av. S70: Barn 2H 29
Hunters Bar S11: Shef 6B 118
Hunters Chase S25: Dinn 3A 128
Hunters Cl. S25: Dinn 3A 128
Hunters Ct. S25: Dinn 3A 128
Hunters Dr. S25: Dinn 3A 128
Hunters Gdns. S6: Lox 3E 105
S25: Dinn 3A 128
Hunters Grn. S25: Dinn 3A 128
Hunters La. S13: Shef 2F 135
Hunters Pk. S25: Dinn 3A 128
Hunters Ri. S75: Barn 1H 29
Hunters Way S25: Dinn 3A 128
Huntingdon Cres. S11: Shef 6D 118
Huntingdon Rd. DN2: Don 5H 41
Huntington St. S65: Ben 6H 23
Huntington Way S66: Malt 3H 101
Huntingtower Rd. S11: Shef 1A 132
Hunt La. DN5: Don 5A 40
Huntley Cl. S43: Ink 6G 163
Huntley Gro. S11: Shef 2G 131

Huntley Rd. S11: Shef 2H 131
Huntsman Rd. S9: Shef 2G 121
S43: Stav 4B 164
Huntsmans Gdns. S9: Shef 5F 109
Hunt St. S74: Hoyl 1G 61
Hurl Dr. S12: Shef 3C 134
Hurley Cft. S63: Bramp B 5B 48
(not continuous)
HURL FIELD 3B 134
Hurlfield Av. S12: Shef 3C 134
Hurlfield Ct. S12: Shef 2D 134
Hurlfield Dr. S12: Shef 2C 134
S65: Rav 3A 100
Hurlfield Rd. S12: Shef 3B 134
Hurlfield Vw. S12: Shef 2C 134
Hurlingham Cl. S11: Shef 3B 132
Hurlstone Cl. DN3: Eden 5D 26
Hursley Cl. S20: Sot 1H 151
Hursley Dr. S20: Sot 1H 151
Hurst Grn. S35: High G 1C 78
Hurst La. DN9: Auck . . . . . .5G 75 & 2H 59
Huskar Cl. S75: Silk 2A 28
Hutchinson Cl. S60: Roth 5F 97
Hutchinson La. S7: Shef 5C 132
Hutchinson Rd. S7: Shef 5C 132
S62: Rawm 2H 83
Hutcliffe Dr. S8: Shef 6C 132
Hutcliffe Wood Crematorium
S8: Shef 6C 132
Hutcliffe Wood Rd. S8: Shef 6C 132
Hutcliffe Wood Vw. S8: Shef 1C 146
Hut La. S21: Killa 6D 152
Hutton Bank S66: Braml 6B 100
Hutton Cft. S12: Shef 5C 136
Hutton Rd. S61: Kimb P 1H 95
Hut Yd. DN11: Lov 4B 72
Huxterwell Dr. DN4: Balb 2A 72
Hyacinth Cl. S5: Shef 1C 108
Hyacinth Rd. S5: Shef 1C 108
HYDE PARK 3C 56
Hyde Pk. Ind. Est. DN4: Don 4D 56
Hyde Park Stop (ST) 2A 120
Hyde Pk. Ter. S2: Shef 3H 119
Hyde Pk. Wlk. S2: Shef 3H 119
(not continuous)
Hyland Cres. DN4: Balb 6F 55
Hyman Cl. DN4: Warm 5E 55
Hyperion Way DN11: New R 6B 74

I

Ians Way S40: Ash 4D 166
Ibberson Av. S75: Mapp 6A 8
Ibbotson Rd. S6: Shef 6B 106
Ibsen Cres. DN3: Barn D 1H 27
iceSheffield 5D 108
ICKLES 6C 96
Ickles Rdbt. S60: Roth 5D 96
Ickles Way S60: Roth 6C 96
Icknield Way S60: Brins 4D 110
Ida Gro. S66: Malt 4G 101
Ida's Rd. S21: Ecki 6E 151
Idsworth Rd. S5: Shef 2A 108
Iford Cl. S43: New W 2C 162
(off Bamford St.)
Ilam Cl. S43: Ink 2H 169
Ilkley Cres. S26: Swal 2B 138
Ilkley Rd. S5: Shef 6A 94
Illsley Rd. S73: D'fld 4B 34
Immingham Gro. S43: Stav 5A 164
Imperial Bldgs. S60: Roth 4E 97
Imperial Cres. DN2: Don 6E 41
Imperial M. S70: Birdw 4D 44
Imperial St. S70: Barn 3E 31
Imrie Pl. S26: Kiv P 6A 140
Inchburn Cres. S36: Pen 4E 177
Industry Rd. S9: Shef 1E 121
S71: Carl 1H 17
Industry St. S6: Shef 6B 106
(not continuous)
Infield La. S9: Shef 2G 121
Infirmary Rd. S6: Shef 6D 106
S41: Ches 4H 167
S62: Parkg 5H 83
Infirmary Road Stop (ST) 1D 118
Ingbirchworth Rd. S36: Thurl 3A 176
Ingelow Av. S5: Shef 5G 93
Ingfield Av. S9: Tins 2H 109

Ingleborough Cft. S35: Chap 2E 79
Ingleborough Dr. DN5: Don 2F 55
Ingleby Cl. S18: Dron W 3B 154
Ingledene M. DN3: Barn D 1C 26
Inglefield Cl. S63: Bolt D 2A 50
Ingle Gro. DN5: Don 2F 55
Inglenook Ct. S66: Malt 6D 102
(off Sousa St.)
Ingleton M. S71: Smi 2F 17
Ingleton Rd. S41: Has 3A 172
Ingleton Wlk. S70: Barn 6C 16
Inglewood S75: Dart 5H 7
Inglewood Av. S20: Sot 1H 151
Inglewood Ct. S20: Sot 1H 151
Inglewood Dell S20: Sot 1H 151
Ingram Ct. S2: Shef 4A 120
Ingram Rd. S2: Shef 4A 120
Ingsfield La. S63: Bolt D 2F 49
(not continuous)
Ingshead Av. S62: Rawm 3G 83
Ings La. DN5: Ark 6E 25
DN5: Sprot 2F 55
S72: Lit H 3C 34
Ings Rd. DN5: Ben, Don 5A 40
DN5: Cade 6G 53
S73: Womb 6A 34
(not continuous)
Ings Way DN5: Ark 6C 24
Inkerman Cotts. S40: Ash 4D 166
Inkerman Rd. S73: D'fld 5B 34
Inkersall Dr. S20: Westf 2F 151
INKERSALL GREEN 1H 169
Inkersall Grn. Rd. S43: Ink 6G 163
Inkersall Rd. S43: Stav 8B 164
Innovate Pk. S63: Wath D 1C 66
Innovation Way S75: Barn 4B 16
Insley Gdns. DN4: Bess 5B 58
Institute of Sports 5D 108
INTAKE
DN2 . . . . .6F 41
S12 . . . . .3D 134
Intake Cres. S75: Dod 4G 29
Intake Gdns. S75: Barn 6A 16
(off Wade St.)
Intake La. S72: Cud 6F 11
S75: Barn 5A 16
Interchange Way S70: Barn 6E 17
S71: Barn 6E 17
Iquarter S3: Shef 2G 119
(off Blonk St.)
Ireland Bus. Pk. S43: Stav 5C 164
Ireland Cl. S43: Stav 5C 164
Ireland Ind. Est. S43: Stav 6B 164
Ireland St. S43: Stav 4C 164
Irongate S40: Ches 5H 167
(off High St.)
Ironside Cl. S14: Shef 6A 134
Ironside Pl. S14: Shef 5B 134
Ironside Rd. S14: Shef 6A 134
Ironside Wlk. S14: Shef 6A 134
Ironstone Cres. S35: Chap 1E 79
Ironstone Dr. S35: Chap 1E 79
Ironworks Pl. S74: Els 2E 63
(off Wath Rd.)
Ironworks Row S74: Els 2E 63
(off Wath Rd.)
Irving St. S9: Shef 2F 121
Irwell Gdns. DN4: Cant 2A 58
Island Cl. S60: Roth 1B 112
Islay St. S10: Shef 3A 118
Issott St. S71: Barn 5E 17
Ivanbrook Cl. S18: Dron W 3B 154
Ivanhoe Av. S26: Kiv P 5B 140
Ivanhoe Cl. DN5: Don 6G 39
Ivanhoe M. S26: Swal 6B 124
Ivanhoe Rd. DN3: Eden 1C 42
DN4: Balb 6F 55
DN12: Con 4E 69
DN12: New E 5C 70
S6: Shef 6H 105
S66: Thurc 6B 104
Ivanhoe Way DN5: Don 6G 39
Ivor Gro. DN4: Balb 4H 55
Ivy Cl. DN11: Ross 5D 74
S41: Old W 4H 161
Ivy Cott. La. S11: Shef 2E 131
Ivy Cotts. S11: Shef 1F 131
S71: Roy 2A 10
S74: Black H 3A 46

Ivy Ct. DN12: Old D . . . 3A **68**
S8: Shef . . . 6H **133**
S72: Cud . . . 2E **19**
Ivy Dr. S10: Shef . . . 2C **118**
Ivy Farm Cl. S71: Carl . . . 5A **10**
Ivy Farm Ct. DN5: Barnb . . . 1H **51**
Ivy Farm Cft. S65: Dalt . . . 1C **98**
Ivy Gro. *S10: Shef . . . 2C* ***118***
(off Ivy Dr.)
Ivy Hall Rd. S5: Shef . . . 4B **94**
Ivy Ho. Ct. DN9: Auck . . . 1G **59**
Ivy Ho. Farm La. S43: Brim . . . 1D **168**
Ivy La. S20: Beig . . . 4H **137**
Ivy Pk. Ct. S10: Shef . . . 5F **117**
Ivy Pk. Rd. S10: Shef . . . 4F **117**
Ivy Side Cl. S21: Killa . . . 4C **152**
Ivy Side Gdns. S21: Killa . . . 4C **152**
Ivy Spring Cl. S42: W'orth . . . 6A **172**
Ivy Ter. S70: Barn . . . 2F **31**

J

Jack Cl. Orchard S71: Roy . . . 2H **9**
Jackdaw Dr. S63: Wath D . . . 4F **49**
Jackey La. S35: Ough . . . 3C **90**
Jackson Cres. S62: Rawm . . . 1F **83**
Jackson St. S63: Gol . . . 5D **36**
S72: Cud . . . 2D **18**
Jackson Way S61: Grea . . . 5D **82**
Jacobs Cl. S5: Shef . . . 6B **94**
Jacobs Dr. S5: Shef . . . 6B **94**
Jacobs Hall Ct. S75: Kexb . . . 6D **6**
Jacques Pl. S71: Barn . . . 6A **18**
Jamaica St. S4: Shef . . . 5A **108**
James Andrew Cl. S8: Shef . . . 3E **147**
James Andrew Cres. S8: Shef . . . 3D **146**
James Andrew Cft. S8: Shef . . . 3E **147**
James Rd. DN6: Adw S . . . 1E **23**
James St. S9: Shef . . . 3F **121**
S41: Ches . . . 2H **167**
S60: Roth . . . 3D **96**
(not continuous)
S64: Mexb . . . 1A **68**
S70: Wors . . . 5H **31**
S71: Barn . . . 6E **17**
S72: Sth H . . . 1A **12**
James Walton Ct. S20: Half . . . 3G **151**
James Walton Dr. S20: Half . . . 3G **151**
James Walton Pl. S20: Half . . . 3G **151**
James Walton Vw. S20: Half . . . 3G **151**
Janet's Wlk. S73: Womb . . . 6D **32**
Janson St. S9: Shef . . . 4D **108**
Jardine Cl. S9: Shef . . . 6D **94**
Jardine St. S9: Shef . . . 6E **95**
S73: Womb . . . 2G **47**
Jarratt St. DN1: Don . . . 2C **56**
Jarrow Rd. S11: Shef . . . 6C **118**
Jasmine Av. S20: Beig . . . 5G **137**
Jasmine Cl. DN12: Con . . . 5G **69**
Jasmine Gdns. S26: Swal . . . 6B **124**
Jaunty Av. S12: Shef . . . 5E **135**
Jaunty Cl. S12: Shef . . . 5E **135**
Jaunty Cres. S12: Shef . . . 4E **135**
Jaunty Dr. S12: Shef . . . 5E **135**
Jaunty La. S12: Shef . . . 4E **135**
Jaunty Mt. S12: Shef . . . 5F **135**
Jaunty Pl. S12: Shef . . . 5E **135**
Jaunty Rd. S12: Shef . . . 5F **135**
Jaunty Vw. S12: Shef . . . 5F **135**
Jaunty Way S12: Shef . . . 4E **135**
Jaw Bones Hill S40: Ches . . . 2H **171**
Jay La. S26: Ast . . . 2D **138**
Jebb Gdns. S40: Bramp . . . 6D **166**
Jebb La. S75: Hai . . . 3A **6**
Jedburgh Dr. S9: Shef . . . 6D **94**
Jedburgh St. S9: Shef . . . 6D **94**
Jeffcock Pl. S35: High G . . . 1D **78**
Jeffcock Rd. S9: Shef . . . 2F **121**
S35: High G . . . 1D **78**
Jefferson Av. DN2: Don . . . 1A **42**
Jeffery Cres. S36: Spink . . . 4F **175**
Jeffery Grn. S10: Shef . . . 1A **130**
Jeffery St. S2: Shef . . . 2G **133**
Jenkin Av. S9: Shef . . . 2D **108**
Jenkin Cl. S9: Shef . . . 1D **108**
Jenkin Dr. S9: Shef . . . 2D **108**
Jenkin Rd. S5: Shef . . . 1C **108**
S9: Shef . . . 1D **108**
Jenkinson Gro. DN3: Arm . . . 4C **42**
Jenkin Wood Cl. S66: Sunn . . . 3H **99**
Jennings Cl. S65: Roth . . . 2F **97**
Jenny La. S72: Cud . . . 2E **19**
Jepson Rd. S5: Shef . . . 6C **94**
S41: Has . . . 3B **172**
Jericho St. S3: Shef . . . 1A **4** (2E **119**)
Jermyn Av. S12: Shef . . . 4H **135**
Jermyn Cl. S12: Shef . . . 5A **136**
Jermyn Cres. S12: Shef . . . 5A **136**
Jermyn Cft. S75: Dod . . . 3G **29**
Jermyn Dr. S12: Shef . . . 5A **136**
Jermyn Sq. S12: Shef . . . 5A **136**
Jermyn Way S12: Shef . . . 5A **136**
Jersey Rd. S2: Shef . . . 1F **133**
Jervis Pl. S43: Ink . . . 2G **169**
Jesmond Av. S71: Roy . . . 3G **9**
Jessamine Rd. S5: Shef . . . 6B **94**
Jessell St. S9: Shef . . . 1C **120**
Jessop Ct. S25: Dinn . . . 4A **128**
Jessop St. S1: Shef . . . 6D **4** (4F **119**)
Jewitt Rd. S61: Kimb P . . . 6H **81**
Jew La. S1: Shef . . . 3G **5**
Joan La. S66: Hoot L . . . 6H **101**
Joan Royd La. S36: Cub . . . 6B **176**
Jockell Dr. S62: Rawm . . . 3G **83**
Jockey Rd. S36: Oxs . . . 5H **177**
John Calvert Rd. S13: Shef . . . 2E **137**
John Eaton's Almshouses
S8: Shef . . . 6G **133**
John Hartop Pl. *S74: Els . . . 2E* ***63***
(off Wath Rd.)
John Hibbard Av. S13: Shef . . . 1F **137**
John Hibbard Cl. S13: Shef . . . 1F **137**
John Hibbard Cres. S13: Shef . . . 1F **137**
John Hibbard Ri. S13: Shef . . . 1F **137**
John La. DN11: New R . . . 5B **74**
Johnson Ct. DN12: New E . . . 3D **70**
S65: Roth . . . 5G ***97***
(off Johnson St.)
Johnson Gdns. S63: Wath D . . . 4E **49**
Johnson La. S3: Shef . . . 1F **5** (2G **119**)
S35: Eccl . . . 1G **93**
Johnson St. S3: Shef . . . 1F **5** (1G **119**)
S36: Stoc . . . 3D **174**
S65: Roth . . . 5G **97**
S75: Barn . . . 6C **16**
Johnstone Cl. S40: Ches . . . 1G **171**
John St. S2: Shef . . . 5E **119**
S21: Ecki . . . 1E **159**
S40: Ches . . . 5F **167**
S43: Brim . . . 6D **162**
S60: Roth . . . 4D **96**
S63: Thurn . . . 2C **36**
S64: Mexb . . . 2F **67**
S66: Thurc . . . 5B **114**
S70: Barn . . . 2E **31**
S70: Wors . . . 6F **31**
S72: Gt H . . . 1F **35**
S72: Midd . . . 3F **35**
S73: Womb . . . 1F **47**
John Trickett Ho. *S35: Chap . . . 3E* ***79***
(off Bevan Way)
John Ward St. S13: Shef . . . 1E **137**
John West St. S36: Stoc . . . 4D **174**
Joiner St. S3: Shef . . . 1F **5** (2G **119**)
Jones Av. S73: Womb . . . 1E **47**
Jons Av. WF9: Sth K . . . 4H **13**
JORDAN . . . **5A 96**
Jordan Cres. S61: Kimb . . . 5H **95**
Jordan Hill S75: Barn . . . 5C **16**
JORDANTHORPE . . . **4G 147**
Jordanthorpe Cen. S8: Shef . . . 4G **147**
Jordanthorpe Grn. S8: Shef . . . 4H **147**
Jordanthorpe Parkway S8: Shef . . . 3G **147**
Jordanthorpe Vw. S8: Shef . . . 3H **147**
Joseph Ct. S70: Barn . . . 2E **31**
Josephine Rd. S61: Roth . . . 4B **96**
Joseph Rd. S6: Shef . . . 1B **118**
Joseph Stone Ct. S20: Mosb . . . 3E **151**
Joseph St. S21: Ecki . . . 1E **159**
S70: Barn . . . 2E **31**
S72: Grim . . . 2B **20**
Joshua Rd. S7: Shef . . . 2D **132**
Josselin Ct. S35: Chap . . . 3E **79**
Jossey La. DN5: Ben, Scawt . . . 2E **39**
Jowitt Cl. S66: Malt . . . 6C **102**
Jowitt Rd. S11: Shef . . . 2A **132**
Jubb Cl. S65: Roth . . . 6C **98**
Jubilee Cl. WF9: Hems . . . 1G **13**
Jubilee Cotts. S44: Cal . . . 1F **173**
S60: Brins . . . 3C **110**
S74: Hoyl . . . 1F ***61***
(off Sheffield Rd.)
Jubilee Ct. DN2: Don . . . 4H **41**
Jubilee Cres. S21: Killa . . . 3D **152**
Jubilee Gdns. S71: Roy . . . 2A **10**
Jubilee Rd. DN1: Don . . . 5D **40**
S9: Shef . . . 6E **109**
Jubilee St. S60: Roth . . . 6E **97**
Jubilee Ter. S70: Barn . . . 2G **31**
Judith Rd. S26: Ast . . . 2C **138**
Judy Row S71: Monk B . . . 4H **17**
Juggernaut Trade Cen. S71: Smi . . . 3F **17**
Julian Rd. S9: Shef . . . 1E **109**
Julian Way S9: Shef . . . 1E **109**
Jumble La. S35: Eccl . . . 1A **94**
Jumble Rd. S11: Shef . . . 6A **130**
JUMP . . . **5D 46**
Junction 34 Ind. Est. S9: Tins . . . 3G **109**
Junction Cl. S73: Womb . . . 3B **48**
Junction Rd. DN11: New R . . . 6B **74**
S11: Shef . . . 6B **118**
S13: Shef . . . 1E **137**
Junction St. S70: Barn . . . 2G **31**
S73: Womb . . . 3A **48**
Junction Ter. S70: Barn . . . 2G **31**
June Rd. S13: Shef . . . 1E **137**
Jungle, The . . . **5G 161**
Juniper Cl. S43: Hol . . . 4F **163**
Juniper Ri. S21: Killa . . . 5B **152**

K

Kaldo Ct. S60: Roth . . . 1F **97**
Kariba Cl. S41: Ches . . . 5A **168**
Kashmir Gdns. S9: Shef . . . 1E **121**
Katherine Ct. S66: Thurc . . . 6B **114**
Katherine Rd. S66: Thurc . . . 5B **114**
Katherine St. S66: Thurc . . . 6C **114**
Kathleen Gro. S63: Gol . . . 4E **37**
Kathleen St. S63: Gol . . . 4E **37**
Kay Cres. S62: Rawm . . . 6D **64**
Kaye Pl. S10: Shef . . . 2C **118**
Kaye St. S71: Barn . . . 6E **17**
Kay's Ter. S70: Stair . . . 3B **32**
Kay St. S74: Hoyl . . . 1G **61**
Kea Pk. Cl. S66: Hel . . . 5D **100**
Kearsley La. DN12: Con . . . 6E **69**
Kearsley Rd. S2: Shef . . . 6F **119**
Keats Dr. S25: Dinn . . . 6C **128**
Keats Gro. S36: Pen . . . 3D **176**
Keats Rd. DN4: Balb . . . 6A **56**
S6: Shef . . . 4C **92**
S41: Ches . . . 6G **161**
Keats Way S42: Gras . . . 6D **172**
Keble Martin Way S63: Wath D . . . 6E **49**
Kedleston Cl. S41: Ches . . . 1D **166**
Kedleston Ct. *S43: Stav . . . 4B* ***164***
(off Porter St.)
Keeper La. WF4: Nott . . . 1C **8**
Keepers Cl. DN11: Ross . . . 4E **75**
S5: Shef . . . 6A **94**
Keepers La. S18: B'low . . . 3A **160**
Keepmoat Stadium . . . **4F 57**
Keeton Hall Rd. S26: Kiv P . . . 5C **140**
Keeton's Hill S2: Shef . . . 6E **119**
Keighley Wlk. DN12: Con . . . 5C **68**
Keilder Ct. S40: Walt . . . 1E **171**
Keir Pl. S62: Rawm . . . 2A **84**
Keir St. S70: Barn . . . 6C **16**
Keir Ter. S70: Barn . . . 6C **16**
Kelburn Av. S40: Walt . . . 1D **170**
Kelby Cft. S75: Bar G . . . 3G **15**
Kelgate S20: Mosb . . . 4E **151**
KELHAM BANK . . . **3B 56**
Kelham Ct. DN1: Don . . . 3B **56**
KELHAM ISLAND . . . **1F 119**
Kelham Island S3: Shef . . . 1F **119**
Kelham Island Mus. . . . **1F 119**
Kelham Sq. S3: Shef . . . 1F **119**
Kelham St. DN1: Don . . . 3B **56**
Kelly St. S63: Gol . . . 5D **36**
Kelsey Gdns. DN4: Bess . . . 1B **74**
Kelsey Ter. S70: Barn . . . 3E **31**
Kelso Dr. DN4: Warm . . . 5E **55**
Kelvin Ct. S61: Scho . . . 6F **81**

Kelvin Gro. S73: Womb 2H **47**
Kelvin St. S64: Mexb 1F **67**
Kemp Cl. S21: Killa 4B **152**
Kempton Dr. DN7: Dunsv 4H **27**
Kempton Gdns. S64: Mexb 6H **51**
Kempton Pk. Rd. DN5: Scaws 4E **39**
Kempton Dr. DN4: Cant 2A **58**
Kempwell Dr. S62: Rawm 6G **65**
Kenbourne Gro. S7: Shef 1D **132**
Kenbourne Rd. S7: Shef 1D **132**
Kendal Av. S25: Nth A 2A **142**
Kendal Cl. DN5: Sprot 3B **54**
Kendal Cres. DN12: Con 4G **69**
  S70: Wors 6F **31**
Kendal Dr. S18: Dron W 3C **154**
  S63: Bolt D 3B **50**
Kendal Grn. S70: Wors 6D **30**
Kendal Grn. Rd. S70: Wors 6D **30**
Kendal Gro. S71: Ard 2D **32**
Kendal Pl. S6: Shef 4A **106**
Kendal Rd. DN5: Scawt 3H **39**
  S6: Shef 4A **106**
  S41: Ches 6F **161**
Kendal Va. S70: Wors 6F **31**
KENDRAY .3A **32**
Kendray St. S70: Barn 1E **31**
Kenilworth Cl. DN5: Scaws 4E **39**
Kenilworth Ct. S11: Shef 4G **131**
Kenilworth Pl. S11: Shef 6B **118**
Kenilworth Rd. DN4: Balb 5F **55**
Kenmare Cres. DN2: Don 5F **41**
Kennedy Ct. S10: Shef 3A **118**
Kennedy Dr. S63: Gol 1C **50**
Kennedy Rd. S8: Shef 6D **132**
Kennels, The S62: Wentw 5F **63**
Kenneth Av. DN7: Dunsv 4H **27**
Kenneth St. S65: Roth 3F **97**
Kennet Va. S40: Ches 3E **167**
Kenninghall Cl. S2: Shef 1A **134**
Kenninghall Dr. S2: Shef 1A **134**
Kenninghall Rd. S2: Shef 1A **134**
Kenninghall Vw. S2: Shef 1A **134**
Kennington Av. DN6: Woodl 3A **22**
Kennington Gro. DN12: New E 3D **70**
Kenrock Cl. DN5: Ark 1D **40**
Kensington Av. S36: Thurl 3A **176**
Kensington Chase S10: Shef 4A **116**
Kensington Ct. S25: Laugh C 4F **127**
Kensington Ct. S10: Shef 5A **116**
Kensington Dr. S10: Shef 5A **116**
Kensington Pk. S10: Shef 5A **116**
Kensington Pl. DN4: Bess 6C **58**
Kensington Rd. S75: Barn 5C **16**
Kent Av. S62: Rawm 1F **83**
Kent Cl. S41: Ches 3G **167**
  S71: Roy 2H **9**
Kent Ho. Cl. S12: Ridg 2H **149**
Kentmere Cl. S18: Dron W 3D **154**
Kentmere Dr. DN4: Don 5G **57**
Kentmere Way S43: Stav 4H **163**
Kent Rd. DN4: Balb 5A **56**
  S8: Shef 2G **133**
  S61: Kimb P 1H **95**
Kents Gro. S63: Gol 5F **37**
Kent St. S41: Has 2B **172**
Kenwell Dr. S17: Bradw 5A **146**
Kenwood Av. S7: Shef 1D **132**
Kenwood Bank S7: Shef 6D **118**
Kenwood Chase S7: Shef 6E **119**
  (off Wostenholm Rd.)
Kenwood Cl. S70: Stair 2A **32**
Kenwood Ct. S7: Shef 1C **132**
Kenwood Pk. Rd. S7: Shef 1D **132**
Kenwood Ri. S66: Braml 4H **99**
Kenwood Rd. S7: Shef 1C **132**
Kenworthy Rd. S36: Stoc 4D **174**
  S70: Barn 3E **31**
Kenyon All. S3: Shef 2B **4**
Kenyon Rd. S41: Ches 1D **172**
Kenyon St. S1: Shef 2B **4** (2E **119**)
Keppel Dr. S61: Scho 6E **81**
Keppel Hgts. S61: Scho 6E **81**
Keppel Pl. S5: Shef 4B **94**
Keppel Rd. S5: Shef 4C **94**
  S61: Scho 6E **81**
Keppel's Column 6E **81**
Keppel Vw. Rd. S61: Kimb 2G **95**
Keppel Wharf S60: Roth 4E **97**
Kepple Cl. DN11: New R 6G **75**

Keresforth S70: Barn 3A **30**
Keresforth Cl. S70: Barn 2B **30**
Keresforth Ct. S70: Barn 2B **30**
Keresforth Hall Dr. S70: Barn 3B **30**
Keresforth Hall Rd. S70: Barn 4A **30**
Keresforth Hill Rd. S70: Barn 4G **29**
Keresforth Rd. S75: Dod 4G **29**
Kerwin Cl. S17: Dore 2D **144**
Kerwin Dr. S17: Dore 2D **144**
Kerwin Rd. S17: Dore 2D **144**
Kestrel Av. S61: Thorpe H 3D **80**
Kestrel Cl. S21: Killa 3A **152**
Kestrel Dr. DN6: Adw S 2C **22**
  DN11: Ross 5D **74**
  S21: Ecki 1C **158**
  S64: Mexb 6E **51**
Kestrel Grn. S2: Shef 4B **120**
Kestrel Ri. S26: Swal 1H **137**
  S70: Birdw 4E **45**
Keswick Cl. DN5: Scawt 2H **39**
  S6: Lox .4F **105**
Keswick Cres. S60: Brins 5C **110**
Keswick Dr. S41: Ches 1D **166**
Keswick Pl. S18: Dron W 3C **154**
Keswick Rd. S75: Stain 3H **7**
Keswick Wlk. S71: Ard 2D **32**
Keswick Way S25: Nth A 2A **142**
Ket Hill La. S72: Brier 3A **12**
Kettlebridge Rd. S9: Shef 3D **120**
Ketton Av. S8: Shef 5G **133**
Ketton Wlk. S75: Barn 5B **16**
Kevin Gro. S66: Hel 6E **101**
Kew Cl. S64: Swint 5B **66**
Kew Cres. S12: Shef 6C **134**
KEXBROUGH 6D **6**
Kexbrough Dr. S75: Kexb 6E **7**
Key Av. S74: Hoyl 6C **46**
Keyworth Pl. S13: Shef 2B **136**
Keyworth Rd. S6: Shef 3B **106**
Khartoum Rd. S11: Shef 5C **118**
Kibroyd Dr. S75: Kexb 1D **14**
Kibworth Cl. S41: Has 3B **172**
Kidd La. S81: Fir 1H **129**
Kidsley Cl. S40: Ches 3B **166**
Kieran Cl. S25: Laugh C 4F **127**
Kier Hardie Av. DN11: New R 6C **74**
Kilburn Rd. S18: Dron W 3B **154**
Kildale Gdns. S20: Mosb 3E **151**
Kildonan Gro. S12: Shef 5F **135**
Kilham La. DN3: Brant 3H **59**
KILLAMARSH 4C **152**
Killamarsh La. S26: Wooda 5F **153**
Killamarsh Leisure Cen. 3C **152**
Kiln Ct. DN3: Barn D 3C **26**
Kiln Cft. S73: Womb 3F **47**
Kilner Ct. DN12: Den M 2E **69**
Kilner Way S6: Shef 1C **106**
Kiln Hill S18: Coal A 1H **155**
KILNHURST 1D **84**
Kilnhurst Bus. Pk. S64: Kiln 2D **84**
Kilnhurst Rd. S62: Rawm 2H **83**
  S64: Kiln 2H **83**
  S65: Hoot R 1E **85**
Kiln Rd. S61: Kimb P 2A **96**
Kilnsea Wlk. S70: Barn 1D **30**
  (off Fitzwilliam St.)
Kiln St. S8: Shef 1E **133**
Kilton Hill S3: Shef 6G **107**
Kilton Pl. S3: Shef 6G **107**
Kilvington Av. S13: Shef 1E **135**
Kilvington Cres. S13: Shef 2E **135**
Kilvington Rd. S13: Shef 2E **135**
Kimberley St. S9: Shef 6C **108**
KIMBERWORTH 3H **95**
KIMBERWORTH PARK 1H **95**
Kimberworth Pk. Rd.
  S61: Kimb, Kimb P 6G **81**
  (not continuous)
Kimberworth Rd. S61: Kimb, Roth 3A **96**
Kinder Gdns. S5: Shef 5G **93**
Kinder Rd. S43: Ink 2G **169**
King Av. DN11: New R 5B **74**
  S66: Malt 4C **102**
King Ecgbert Rd. S17: Dore 5F **145**
King Edward Rd. DN4: Balb 4A **56**
King Edwards S6: Shef 2C **116**
King Edwards App. S6: Shef 3C **116**
King Edwards Gdns. S70: Barn 2D **30**
King Edwards Swimming Pool 4C **118**

King Edward St. S71: Monk B 2A **18**
Kingfield Ct. S11: Shef 1C **132**
Kingfield Rd. S11: Shef 1C **132**
Kingfisher Cl. DN2: Don 3G **41**
Kingfisher Ct. DN11: Ross 5D **74**
  DN12: Con 4A **70**
Kingfisher Dr. S73: Bramp 3B **48**
Kingfisher Gro. S26: Swal 1H **137**
Kingfisher Ho. S41: Old W 3A **162**
Kingfisher M. S73: Bramp 3C **48**
Kingfisher Ri. S61: Thorpe H 2D **80**
Kingfisher Rd. DN6: Adw S 2C **22**
King Georges Cl. DN11: New R 6A **74**
King George Sq. DN3: Kirk Sa 4C **26**
King George's Rd. DN11: New R 4A **74**
King George Ter. S70: Barn 2G **31**
King James St. S6: Shef 6C **106**
Kingsbrook Chase S63: Wath D 4E **49**
Kingsbury Ct. DN5: Scawt 1E **39**
Kingsclere Wlk. S40: Birdh 3G **171**
Kings Coppice S17: Dore 4E **145**
Kings Ct. S1: Shef 6B **4**
  S60: Roth 2H **111**
King's Cres. DN12: New E 3C **70**
Kings Cft. S70: Wors 6H **31**
Kingscroft Cl. S17: Dore 2F **145**
Kingsforth La. S66: Thurc 4B **114**
Kingsforth Rd. S66: Thurc 5B **114**
Kingsgate DN1: Don 1C **56**
Kingsgate Flats DN1: Don 1C **56**
  (off Cleveland St.)
Kingsland Cl. S71: Roy 2A **10**
Kingsley Av. DN5: Don 6G **39**
  S40: Birdh 2G **171**
  (not continuous)
Kingsley Cl. S71: Ath 2F **17**
Kingsley Ct. S60: Roth 1E **111**
Kingsley Cres. DN3: Arm 4F **43**
Kingsley Dr. S65: Rav 2C **100**
Kingsley Pk. Av. S7: Shef 4A **132**
Kingsley Pk. Gro. S11: Shef 4A **132**
Kingsley Rd. DN6: Adw S 3B **22**
Kingsmark Way S63: Gol 5E **37**
Kingsmead Dr. DN3: Brant 4G **59**
Kingsmede Av. S40: Walt 1E **171**
Kings M. DN1: Don 1C **56**
  S21: Ecki 1F **159**
Kings Rd. DN1: Don 6D **40**
  S64: Mexb 1G **67**
  S72: Cud 5F **11**
  S73: Womb 2H **47**
King's Stocks S72: Bill, Midd 4F **35**
Kings St. DN1: Don 1C **56**
  S72: Grim 2B **20**
Kingston Cl. DN3: Brant 3H **59**
KINGSTONE 3C **30**
Kingstone Pl. S70: Barn 3C **30**
Kingston Rd. DN2: Don 6G **41**
Kingston St. S4: Shef 5A **108**
King St. DN3: Arm 3C **42**
  S3: Shef 2F **5** (2G **119**)
  S26: Swal 6B **124**
  S35: Chap 2F **79**
  S43: Brim 5E **163**
  S63: Gol 5D **36**
  S63: Thurn 3D **36**
  S64: Swint 3C **66**
  S70: Barn 2E **31**
  S74: Hoyl 6B **46**
King St. Nth. S41: Whit M 1H **167**
King St. Sth. S40: Birdh 3H **171**
Kings Way S60: Roth 1H **111**
Kingsway S63: Thurn 2B **36**
  S72: Grim 1B **20**
  S73: Womb 2G **47**
  S75: Mapp 5H **7**
Kingsway Cl. DN11: New R 6H **75**
Kingsway Complex S25: Dinn 5A **128**
Kingsway Gro. S63: Thurn 2B **36**
Kingsway Ho. DN1: Don 1C **56**
Kingswood S6: Shef 6G **91**
  S11: Shef 2C **132**
Kingswood Av. S20: Mosb 6B **136**
  S25: Laugh M 2H **127**
Kingswood Cl. S20: Mosb 6B **136**
  S41: Ches 5E **161**
  S81: Fir 1H **129**
Kingswood Cres. S74: Hoyl 5B **46**

Kingswood Cft. S20: Mosb .6B **136**
Kingswood Dearne Valley
Outdoor Educational & Activity Centres .2E **69**
Kingswood Gro. S20: Mosb .6B **136**
Kingswood Hall S6: Shef .6G **91**
Kings Wood La. S25: Laugh M .1E **129**
S66: Malt .1E **129**
Kingwell Cres. S70: Wors .4E **31**
Kingwell Cft. S70: Wors .5F **31**
Kingwell M. S70: Wors .5F **31**
Kingwell Rd. S70: Wors .5E **31**
Kingwood Cl. S71: Monk B .2C **18**
Kinharvie Rd. S5: Shef .1E **107**
Kinnaird Av. S5: Shef .5H **93**
Kinnaird Pl. S5: Shef .5H **93**
Kinnaird Rd. S5: Shef .5H **93**
Kinsey Rd. S35: High G .1B **78**
Kipling Av. DN4: Balb .6G **55**
Kipling Cl. S18: Dron .5H **155**
Kipling Rd. DN3: Barn D .1H **27**
S6: Shef .4B **106**
S41: Ches .6G **161**
Kirby Cl. S9: Shef .2F **121**
S41: Has .3B **172**
Kirby La. S35: Chap .6A **62**
Kirby Row S61: Thorpe H .3C **80**
Kirby St. S64: Mexb .1F **67**
Kirk Balk S74: Hoyl .6A **46**
Kirkby Av. DN5: Don .4H **39**
S12: Shef .4D **134**
S71: Ath .6F **9**
Kirkby Dr. S12: Shef .4D **134**
Kirkbygate WF9: Hems .1F **13**
Kirkby Rd. S12: Shef .4D **134**
WF9: Hems .1F **13**
Kirkby Vw. S12: Shef .4D **134**
Kirkby Way S12: Shef .5D **134**
Kirkcroft Av. S21: Killa .3C **152**
S61: Thorpe H .3D **80**
Kirkcroft Cl. S61: Thorpe H .3C **80**
Kirkcroft Dr. S21: Killa .4C **152**
Kirkcroft La. S21: Killa .4C **152**
Kirk Cft. Rd. S25: Laugh M .2H **127**
Kirk Cross Cres. S71: Roy .4H **9**
Kirkdale Cl. S40: Ches .2A **172**
Kirkdale Cres. S13: Shef .5C **122**
Kirkdale Dr. S13: Shef .5C **122**
Kirk Edge Av. S35: Ough .6E **91**
Kirk Edge Dr. S35: Ough .6D **90**
Kirk Edge Rd. S6: Bradf .5A **90**
S35: Ough .5A **90**
Kirkfield Cl. S75: Cawt .4A **14**
Kirkfield Way S71: Roy .4H **9**
Kirkgate La. S72: Sth H .1E **11**
Kirkham Cl. S71: Monk B .5H **17**
Kirkham Pl. S71: Monk B .1A **18**
Kirkhill Bank S36: Cub .6C **176**
Kirkhill Cl. DN3: Arm .5F **43**
Kirk Ho. *S65: Roth* .*5A 98*
(off Browning Rd.)
Kirkland Gdns. S71: Monk B .3F **17**
Kirklands Dr. S62: Rawm .2F **83**
KIRK SANDALL .4C **26**
Kirk Sandall Ind. Est. DN3: Kirk Sa .4A **26**
(not continuous)
Kirk Sandall Station (Rail) .4B **26**
Kirkstall Cl. DN5: Scaws .5E **39**
S25: Sth A .5G **141**
S60: Brins .3B **110**
Kirkstall Rd. S11: Shef .6B **118**
S71: Smi .1D **16**
Kirkstead Abbey M. S61: Thorpe H .6D **80**
Kirkstead Gdns. S13: Shef .1F **137**
Kirkstead Rd. S61: Kimb .3D **94**
Kirkstone Cl. DN5: Don .2H **39**
Kirkstone Rd. S6: Shef .5B **106**
S41: Ches .6D **160**
Kirk St. DN4: Hex .2A **56**
S4: Shef .6H **107**
Kirk Vw. S74: Hoyl .6A **46**
Kirk Way S71: Monk B .5A **18**
Kirkwood Cl. S36: Pen .5F **177**
Kirstead Ct. DN4: Bess .1E **75**
Kirton Rd. S4: Shef .5H **107**
Kitchen Wood La.
S18: Dron W, Holme .4A **154**
Kitchin Rd. S73: Womb .1E **47**
Kitson Dr. S71: Monk B .5A **18**
Kiveton Bridge Station (Rail) .6A **140**
Kiveton Gdns. S26: Kiv P .5C **140**
Kiveton La. S26: Kiv P, Tod .3C **140**
KIVETON PARK .5B **140**
Kiveton Park Station (Rail) .6E **141**
Knabbs La. S75: Silk C .5A **28**
Knab Cl. S7: Shef .3B **132**
Knab Cft. S7: Shef .3B **132**
Knab Ri. S7: Shef .3B **132**
Knab Rd. S7: Shef .3B **132**
Knapton Av. S62: Rawm .2F **83**
Knaresborough Cl. S26: Swal .1B **138**
Knaresborough Rd. DN12: Con .5C **68**
S7: Shef .5B **132**
Knavesmire Av. S25: Laugh C .4F **127**
Knavesmire Gdns. DN4: Cant .2A **58**
Knifesmithgate S40: Ches .5H **167**
Knighton Cl. S41: Has .3A **172**
Knightsbridge Ct. S40: Ches .5G **167**
Knoll, The S18: Dron .1A **156**
S40: Bramp .6A **166**
Knollbeck Av. S73: Bramp .4B **48**
Knoll Beck Cl. S63: Gol .6B **36**
Knollbeck Cres. S73: Bramp .4B **48**
Knollbeck La. S73: Bramp .4B **48**
Knoll Cl. S36: Stoc .3E **175**
Knoll M. S75: Wool G .3F **7**
KNOLL TOP .3E **175**
Knowle Cl. S6: Stann .6D **104**
Knowle Ct. S11: Shef .3A **132**
Knowle Cft. S11: Shef .3H **131**
Knowle Grn. S17: Dore .3D **144**
Knowle La. S11: Shef .3G **131**
Knowle Rd. S5: Shef .4G **93**
S70: Barn, Wors .4G **31**
Knowles Av. S36: Spink .4F **175**
Knowles St. S36: Pen .5F **177**
KNOWLE TOP .6D **104**
Knowle Top S20: Half .3F **151**
Knowsley St. S70: Barn .1C **30**
Knutton Cres. S5: Shef .4D **92**
Knutton Ri. S5: Shef .3D **92**
Knutton Rd. S5: Shef .4D **92**
Kyle Cl. S5: Shef .6D **92**
Kyle Cres. S5: Shef .6D **92**
Kynance Cres. S60: Brins .5C **110**

L

Laburnum Av. S66: Sunn .4G **99**
Laburnum Cl. S25: Sth A .4G **141**
S35: Chap .4F **79**
Laburnum Ct. S44: Cal .5F **169**
S75: Bar G .4E **15**
Laburnum Dr. DN3: Arm .3F **43**
Laburnum Gro. DN12: Con .5D **68**
S21: Killa .5B **152**
S36: Stoc .4D **174**
S70: Wors .6G **31**
Laburnum Pde. S66: Malt .5G **101**
Laburnum Pl. DN5: Ben .6A **24**
Laburnum Rd. DN4: Balb .6G **55**
S64: Mexb .6E **51**
S66: Malt .5G **101**
Laburnum St. S43: Hol .5G **163**
Laceby Cl. S66: Braml .3A **100**
Laceby Ct. S70: Barn .3B **30**
Ladies Spring Ct. *S17: Dore* .*3H 145*
(off Ladies Spring Dr.)
Ladies Spring Dr. S17: Dore .3H **145**
Ladies Spring Gro. S17: Dore .3H **145**
Ladock Cl. S71: Monk B .5G **17**
Lady Bank Dr. DN4: Don .3D **56**
Ladybank Rd. S20: Mosb .4E **151**
Lady Bank Vw. S21: Ecki .6E **151**
Ladybower Ct. S17: Bradw .5H **145**
Ladybower La. S43: Stav .6A **164**
Lady Cft. S63: Wath D .6F **49**
Ladycroft S63: Bolt D .2B **50**
Lady Cft. La. S73: Hem .5F **47**
Ladycroft Rd. DN3: Arm .6E **43**
Lady Ida's Dr. S21: Ecki .6B **150**
(not continuous)
Lady Mary's Wlk. DN5: Hick .4H **37**
Lady Mary Vw. DN5: Hick .3G **37**
Ladymead S71: Monk B .4G **17**
Lady Oak Rd. S65: Roth .1B **98**
Ladyoak Way S65: Roth .1B **98**
Ladyroyd S75: Silk C .5A **28**
Ladyroyd Cft. S72: Cud .2E **19**
Lady's Bri. S3: Shef .1F **5** (2G **119**)
Ladyshaw Cres. S36: Pen .5E **177**
Ladysmith Av. S7: Shef .2C **132**
Ladywood Dr. S41: Ches .1D **166**
Ladywood Rd. S72: Grim .2C **20**
Laird Av. S6: Shef .3H **105**
Laird Dr. S6: Shef .3H **105**
Laird Rd. S6: Shef .3H **105**
Lairds Way S36: Pen .4E **177**
Laithe Cft. S75: Dod .3G **29**
Laithes Cl. S71: Ath .1G **17**
Laithes Cres. S71: Ath .1E **17**
Laithes La. S71: Ath .1E **17**
Laithes Shop. Cen. S71: Ath .1E **17**
Lake Cl. DN12: New E .5B **70**
Lake Ct. DN6: Woodl .4D **22**
Lakeen Rd. DN2: Don .6F **41**
Lakeland Cl. S72: Cud .3E **19**
Lakeland Dr. S25: Dinn, Nth A .2H **141**
Lake Rd. DN6: Woodl .5D **22**
Lakeside S6: Shef .5G **105**
S20: Holb .1A **152**
Lakeside Blvd. DN4: Don .5F **57**
Lakeside Cl. S41: Old W .2B **162**
S66: Sunn .2H **99**
Lakeside Ct. S63: Bramp B .5A **48**
Lakeside Vw. S36: Pen .1A **176**
Lakeside Village DN4: Don .4E **57**
Lake Vw. Av. S40: Walt .1D **170**
Lambcote Way S66: Malt .4C **102**
Lambcroft La. S13: Shef .2D **136**
Lambcroft Vw. S13: Shef .2D **136**
Lamb Dr. S5: Shef .1C **106**
Lambecroft S71: Carl .5H **9**
Lambe Flatt S75: Kexb .6D **6**
Lambert Fold S75: Dod .3H **29**
Lambert Rd. S70: Barn .3H **31**
Lamberts La. S65: Thry .5E **85**
Lambert St. S3: Shef .2D **4** (2F **119**)
Lambert Wlk. S63: Wath D .4D **48**
S70: Barn .2H **31**
Lambeth Rd. DN4: Balb .5A **56**
Lambeth Rd. Caravan Pk.
DN4: Balb .5A **56**
Lamb Hill Cl. S13: Shef .1G **135**
Lamb La. S71: Monk B .3H **17**
S81: Fir .3D **128**
Lambourne Ct. S41: Has .3B **172**
Lambra Rd. S70: Barn .1E **31**
Lambrell Av. S26: Kiv P .6H **139**
Lambrell Grn. S26: Kiv P .6H **139**
Lamb Rd. S5: Shef .1C **106**
Lambs Flat La. S75: Kexb .1D **14**
Lamp Room Theatre .1D **30**
Lanark Dr. S64: Mexb .5H **51**
Lanark Gdns. DN2: Don .5H **41**
Lancar Ct. S71: Monk B .4F **17**
Lancaster Av. DN2: Don .6H **41**
DN3: Kirk Sa .4C **26**
Lancaster Ga. S70: Barn .1D **30**
Lancaster Rd. S36: Stoc .3D **174**
S41: Ches .6F **161**
Lancaster St. S3: Shef .1E **119**
S63: Thurn .1D **36**
S70: Barn .1C **30**
Lancelot Cl. S40: Walt .2E **171**
Lancing Rd. S2: Shef .6F **119**
(not continuous)
Landon Cl. S42: Walt .3C **170**
Landsdown Av. WF9: Sth K .5H **13**
Landseer Cl. S14: Shef .6A **134**
S18: Dron .3D **154**
Landseer Ct. S66: Flan .4G **99**
Landseer Dr. S14: Shef .6B **134**
Landseer Pl. S14: Shef .6B **134**
Landseer Wlk. S14: Shef .6B **134**
Lane, The S71: Roy .2H **9**
Lane Cotts. S71: Roy .3H **9**
LANE END .1F **79**
Lane End S35: Chap .1E **79**
Lane End M. S63: Thurn .2A **36**
Lane End Rd. S60: Roth .2H **111**
Lane End Vw. S60: Roth .1H **111**
Laneham Cl. DN4: Bess .6A **58**
Lane Head S35: Gren .2A **92**
Lane Head Cl. S62: Rawm .2H **83**
S75: Stain .4H **7**

Lane Head Ri. S75: Stain 4H **7**
Lane Head Rd. S17: Tot 6D **144**
S75: Cawt 4A **14**
Lanes, The S65: Roth 3A **98**
Laneside Cl. DN4: Hex 3H **55**
Langar Cl. DN5: Ben 4H **23**
Lang Av. S71: Lund 6B **18**
Langcliff Cl. S75: Mapp 4H **7**
Lang Cres. S71: Lund 6B **18**
Langdale Cl. S40: Ches 3A **166**
Langdale Ct. S71: Barn 1E **31**
Langdale Dr. DN5: Scawt 2G **39**
S18: Dron 1H **155**
Langdale Rd. S8: Shef 3D **132**
S71: Barn 1F **31**
S75: Bar G 3F **15**
Langdale Sq. S43: Brim 6C **162**
Langdale Way S25: Dinn 1A **142**
Langdon Rd. S61: Kimb P 2H **95**
Langdon St. S11: Shef 6E **119**
Langdon Wlk. S61: Kimb P 2H **95**
S70: Barn 6D **16**
Langer Fld. Av. S40: Birdh 3H **171**
Langer La. S40: Birdh 6F **171**
S42: W'orth 6F **171**
Langer St. DN4: Hex 3H **55**
Langford Cl. S75: Dod 3H **29**
Langford Cft. S40: Ches 1H **171**
Langham Ind. Pk. S41: Cor 6F **173**
Langhurst Ct. S40: Ash 4E **167**
Langhurst Rd. S40: Ash 4E **167**
Langley Cl. S40: Ches 3B **166**
S65: Roth 3C **98**
Langmere Cl. S70: Barn 1B **30**
Langsett Av. S6: Shef 2H **105**
Langsett Cl. S6: Shef 5C **106**
Langsett Ct. DN4: Don 4G **57**
S71: Smi 1D **16**
Langsett Cres. S6: Shef 5C **106**
Langsett Gro. S6: Shef 6C **106**
Langsett Ri. S6: Shef 5C **106**
Langsett Rd. S6: Shef 4B **106**
S71: Smi 1D **16**
Langsett Rd. Nth. S35: Ough 1D **90**
Langsett Road / Primrose View Stop (ST) 6D 106
Langsett Rd. Sth. S35: Ough 3E **91**
Langsett Wlk. S6: Shef 5C **106**
Langthwaite La. DN5: Scawt 6E **23**
Langthwaite Rd. DN5: Scawt 1E **39**
Langton Gdns. DN3: Brant 4H **59**
Langtree Av. S41: Old W 5H **161**
Lansbury Av. DN11: New R 5D **74**
S35: Chap 3E **79**
S43: Mas M 2E **165**
S66: Malt 6C **102**
Lansbury Ct. S21: Ecki 1E **159**
Lansbury Pl. S62: Rawm 2B **84**
Lansbury Rd. S21: Ecki 1E **159**
Lansdowne Av. S41: Ches 1F **167**
Lansdowne Cl. S63: Thurn 2B **36**
Lansdowne Cres.
S64: Swint 4C **66**
S75: Dart 1E **15**
Lansdowne Rd. DN2: Don 5H **41**
S11: Shef 5E **119**
S43: Brim 1C **168**
Lantern Theatre 1D 132
Lanyon Way S71: Monk B 5G **17**
Lapwater Rd. S61: Wing 5A **82**
Lapwater Wlk. S61: Wing 5A **82**
Lapwing Va. S61: Thorpe H 2D **80**
Larch Av. DN9: Auck 3A **76**
S21: Killa 5B **152**
S66: Wick 5G **99**
Larch Cl. S73: D'fld 5B **34**
Larch Dr. DN3: Arm 4E **43**
(not continuous)
Larches, The S64: Swint 3B **66**
Larchfield Pl. S71: Monk B 3A **18**
Larchfield Rd. DN4: Balb 5G **55**
Larch Gro. DN12: Con 6D **68**
S26: Ast 6D **124**
S35: Chap 4F **79**
Larch Hill S9: Shef 3H **121**
Larch M. S65: Roth 2A **98**
Larch Pl. S70: Barn 4G **31**
Larch Rd. S21: Ecki 2C **158**
S66: Malt 4G **101**
Larch Sq. DN9: Auck 2B **76**
Larch Way S40: Ches 3E **167**
Lark Av. S60: Brins 4E **111**
Larkhill Cl. S62: Parkg 5G **83**
Larkin Gro. S5: Shef 5G **93**
Larkspur Cl. DN3: Eden 1C **42**
S64: Swint 6B **66**
Lark St. S6: Shef 6A **106**
Larwood Gro. DN12: New E 3D **70**
Latchmoor Cl. S75: Barn 4C **16**
Latham Sq. DN3: Kirk Sa 3D **26**
S11: Shef 3F **131**
Lathe Rd. S60: Roth 2B **112**
Lathkill Av. S43: Ink 2G **169**
Lathkill Cl. S13: Shef 1F **135**
Lathkill Rd. S13: Shef 1F **135**
Latimer Cl. S26: Kiv P 6C **140**
Latin Gdns. DN5: Scaws 3D **38**
Lauder Rd. DN5: Don 4H **39**
Lauder St. S4: Shef 2A **108**
Laudsdale Cl. S65: Roth 3C **98**
Laudsdale Rd. S65: Roth 2B **98**
LAUGHTON COMMON 3F 127
Laughton Comn. Rd. S66: Thurc 2C **126**
LAUGHTON EN LE MORTHEN 1G 127
Laughton Mdws. S25: Laugh C 3F **127**
Laughton Rd. DN4: Hex 2A **56**
S9: Shef 1E **109**
S25: Dinn 4A **128**
S66: Thurc 6C **114**
Launce Rd. S5: Shef 6E **93**
Laurel Av. DN5: Cus 5F **39**
S44: Ark T 5H **173**
S66: Braml 5A **100**
S70: Barn 3A **32**
Laurel Cl. S21: Ecki 2D **158**
S25: Sth A 5G **141**
Laurel Ct. S10: Shef 5A **118**
Laurel Cres. S43: Hol 5F **163**
Laurel Dr. S21: Killa 6B **152**
Laurel Gth. Cl. S41: Old W 3A **162**
Laurel Rd. DN3: Arm 3E **43**
(not continuous)
Laurel Sq. DN9: Auck 2B **76**
Laurel Ter. DN4: Balb 5H **55**
Laurence Cl. S41: Old W 4H **161**
Lavender Cl. DN12: Con 5G **69**
Lavender Ct. S70: Barn 3H **31**
Lavender Way S5: Shef 1C **108**
Laverack St. S13: Shef 5A **122**
Laverdene Av. S17: Tot 6G **145**
Laverdene Cl. S17: Tot 6F **145**
Laverdene Dr. S17: Tot 6G **145**
Laverdene Rd. S17: Tot 6F **145**
Laverdene Way S17: Tot 6G **145**
Laverock Way S5: Shef 5A **94**
Lavinia Rd. S35: Gren 2D **92**
Law Courts
Barnsley 6D 16
Sheffield 1E 5 (2F 119)
Lawn, The S18: Dron 2G **155**
(not continuous)
Lawn Av. DN1: Don 1D **56**
DN6: Woodl 2A **22**
Lawndale Fold S75: Dart 5G **7**
Lawn Gth. DN5: Scawt 3H **39**
Lawn Rd. DN1: Don 1D **56**
Lawns, The S11: Shef 2A **132**
Lawnswood Ct. DN4: Bess 4H **57**
Lawns Wood Gdns. S65: Thry 4E **85**
Lawn Vs. S44: Cal 5F **169**
Lawnwood Dr. S63: Gol 5B **36**
Lawrence Cl. S66: Flan 5G **99**
S75: H'ham 4F **15**
Lawrence Ct. S60: Roth 3D **96**
S64: Swint 5B **66**
Lawrence Dr. S64: Swint 4B **66**
Lawrence St. S9: Shef 6C **108**
Lawson Rd. S10: Shef 4A **118**
Lawton La. S60: Roth 1F **111**
Lawton Ter. S6: Shef 4A **106**
Laxey Rd. S6: Shef 1F **117**
Laxfield Cl. S40: Walt 2D **170**
Laxton Cl. S66: Malt 4G **101**
Laxton Rd. S71: Ath 6E **9**
Laycock Av. S26: Ast 1D **138**
Layden Ct. S66: Malt 6H **101**
Layden Dr. DN5: Scaws 2D **38**
Layton Dr. S41: Old W 5A **162**
Lazarus Exhibition Hall 1G 57
Lea, The S20: Water 6E **137**
S64: Swint 4A **66**
LEA BROOK 3H 63
Lea Brook La. S62: Wentw 3H **63**
Leabrook Rd. S18: Dron W 3B **154**
Leach La. S64: Mexb 2G **67**
Leadbeater Dr. S12: Shef 3D **134**
Leadbeater Rd. S12: Shef 4C **134**
Leader Ct. S6: Shef 3A **106**
Leader Rd. S6: Shef 3A **106**
Leadhill Rd. S40: Ash 4B **166**
Leadley St. S63: Gol 5D **36**
Leadmill Ct. S1: Shef 6F **5**
Leadmill Point S1: Shef 6F **5**
Leadmill Rd. S1: Shef 5F **5** (4G **119**)
S2: Shef 6F **5** (4G **119**)
Leadmill St. S1: Shef 6F **5** (4G **119**)
Leaf Cl. S66: Malt 4C **102**
Leake Rd. S6: Shef 2B **106**
Leamington Gdns. DN2: Don 5G **41**
Leamington St. S10: Shef 2B **118**
Leander Ct. S43: Stav 4C **164**
Leapings La. S36: Thurl 4A **176**
Lea Rd. S18: Dron 3F **155**
S71: Ath 1G **17**
Leas, The DN5: Cus 5G **39**
Lease Gate Rd. S60: Whist 2A **112**
Leatham Av. S61: Roth 3B **96**
Leaton Cl. S6: Lox 3E **105**
Leavy Greave S3: Shef 4A **4** (3D **118**)
Leavygreave Rd. S3: Shef 3A **4** (3D **118**)
Leawood Pl. S6: Stann 6E **105**
Ledbury Gdns. DN5: Scaws 5E **39**
Ledbury Rd. S71: Ath 2E **17**
Ledsham Ct. S74: Els 5E **47**
Ledsham Rd. S60: Roth 6H **97**
Ledstone Rd. S8: Shef 4D **132**
Lee Av. S36: Spink 3F **175**
Leebrook Av. S20: Mosb 1C **150**
Leebrook Ct. S20: Mosb 1C **150**
Leebrook Dr. S20: Mosb 1C **150**
Leebrook Pl. S20: Mosb 1C **150**
Lee Cft. S1: Shef 2E **5** (2F **119**)
S66: Malt 6C **102**
Leedham Cl. S5: Shef 6C **94**
Leedham Rd. S5: Shef 6C **94**
S65: Roth 6B **98**
Leeds Av. S25: Nth A 1H **141**
Leeds Rd. S9: Shef 6D **108**
Lee Ho. La. S36: Stoc 4B **174**
Lee La. S71: Roy, Stain 4C **8**
Lee Moor La. S6: Stann 5A **104**
Lee Rd. S6: Lox 3E **105**
S41: Ches 6D **168**
Lees, The S8: Shef 5F **133**
S71: Ard 2E **33**
Lees Av. S36: Pen 4D **176**
Lees Comn. S18: B'low 6B **154**
Lees Hall Av. S8: Shef 3G **133**
Lees Hall Golf Course 6H 133
Lees Hall Pl. S8: Shef 3G **133**
Lees Hall Rd. S8: Shef 3G **133**
Lees Ho. Ct. S8: Shef 4F **133**
Lees Nook S8: Shef 3F **133**
Leeswood Cl. S41: Ches 6E **161**
Leewood Cl. S63: Bramp B 6A **48**
Leger Ct. DN2: Don 1D **56**
Leger Way DN2: Don 2F **57**
Legion Dr. S26: Ast 1D **138**
Leicester Av. DN2: Don 1F **57**
Leicester Rd. S25: Dinn 5B **128**
Leigh St. S9: Shef 5D **108**
Leigh St. Ind. Est. S9: Shef 5D **108**
Leighton Cl. S71: Barn 5E **17**
Leighton Dr. S14: Shef 5C **134**
Leighton Pl. S14: Shef 5C **134**
Leighton Rd. S14: Shef 3B **134**
Leighton Vw. S14: Shef 3B **134**
Leinster Av. DN2: Don 5F **41**
Lemont Rd. S17: Tot 6F **145**
Lengdale Ct. S62: Rawm 3G **83**
Lennox Rd. DN2: Don 5G **41**
S6: Shef 3A **106**
Lenthall's Back Row
S40: Ash 5E **167**
Lenton St. S2: Shef 6F **5** (5G **119**)
Leonard Cl. S2: Shef 1D **134**
Leopold Av. S25: Dinn 6A **128**

Leopold Sq. S1: Shef 3D 4
Leopold St. S1: Shef 3E 5 (3F 119)
  S25: Dinn 5A 128
  S70: Barn 2C 30
Leppings La. S6: Shef 2B 106
Leppings Lane Stop (LRT)
  Middlewood Rd. (North) . . .2B 106
  Middlewood Rd. (South) 3B 106
Lepton Gdns. S70: Stair 4A 32
Lescar La. S11: Shef 6B 118
Lesley Rd. S63: Gol 5D 36
Leslie Av. DN12: Con 4D 68
  S66: Malt 5G 101
Leslie Rd. S6: Shef 3A 106
Lesmond Cres. S72: Midd 4F 35
Lestermoor Av. S26: Kiv P 6H 139
Letard Dr. S60: Brins 3D 110
Letsby Av. S9: Shef 4H 109
LETWELL 4H 129
Letwell Ct. DN4: Bess 1E 75
Levens Way S41: Ches 6F 161
Leverick Dr. S62: Rawm 1B 84
Leverton Dr. S11: Shef 5E 119
Leverton Gdns. S11: Shef 5E 119
Leverton Way S65: Dalt 1D 98
Leveson St. S4: Shef 1A 120
Levet Rd. DN4: Cant 3C 58
Levick Cft. S74: Els 6C 46
Lewdendale S70: Wors 6F 31
Lewden Farm La. S70: Wors 6A 32
Lewden Gth. S70: Wors 6A 32
Lewes Rd. DN12: Con 5E 69
Lewis Rd. S13: Shef 1F 135
  S71: Lund 4B 18
Lewyns Dr. DN4: Cant 3C 58
Leybourne Rd. S61: Kimb P 1H 95
Leyburn Cl. DN4: Cant 5C 58
  S40: Ches 3E 167
Leyburn Dr. S26: Swal 6B 124
Leyburn Gro. S35: Chap 2F 79
Leyburn Rd. S8: Shef 2E 133
Ley End S70: Wors 6E 31
Leyfield Ct. DN3: Arm 5F 43
Leyfield Pl. S73: Womb 6A 34
Leyfield Rd. S17: Dore 3E 145
Leylands, The S75: Barn 4A 16
Leyland Wlk. S75: Barn 4A 16
Leys, The WF9: Sth K 5H 13
Leys Cl. DN4: Balb 2G 71
Leys La. S25: Dinn 5C 128
Liberty Cl. S6: Shef 1F 117
Liberty Dr. S6: Shef 1F 117
LIBERTY HILL 1F 117
Liberty Hill S6: Shef 1F 117
Liberty Pl. S6: Shef 1F 117
Liberty Rd. S6: Shef 1F 117
Library Cl. S61: Wing 5B 82
Lichen Cl. DN3: Eden 1C 42
Lichfield Gdns. DN12: New E 5B 70
Lichfield Rd. DN2: Don 4E 41
  S40: Walt 2D 170
Lichfield Way S60: Brins 4E 111
Lichford Rd. S2: Shef 2H 133
Lidgate La. S72: Shaft 3E 11
LIDGET 2H 59
Lidget Cl. DN4: Bess 5B 58
  S26: Swal 2A 138
  S63: Thurn 3D 36
Lidget La. DN5: Hick 3D 36
  S63: Thurn 3D 36
  S74: Barn 4A 100
Lidget La. Ind. Est. S63: Thurn 2E 37
Lidgett Gdns. DN9: Auck 2H 59
Lidgett Grange S74: Hoyl 4H 61
Lidgett La. S25: Dinn 6A 128
  S75: Pill 1C 60
Lidgett Way S71: Roy 2H 9
Lidster La. S25: Sth A 4H 141
Lifestyle Ho. S10: Shef 4B 118
Liffey Av. DN2: Don 5F 41
Lifford Pl. S74: Els 1E 63
Lifford Rd. DN2: Don 5E 41
Lifford St. S9: Tins 1H 109
LIGHTWOOD
  S8 . . . . .1C 148
  S21 . . . . .2A 158
Lightwood La. S8: Shef 1B 148
  S21: Midd H 3H 157
Lightwood Rd. S21: Mar L 3H 157

Lilac Av. S36: Stoc 4D 174
Lilac Cl. S25: Sth A 4G 141
Lilac Cres. DN12: New E 5C 70
  S74: Hoyl 5B 46
Lilac Farm Cl. S66: Wick 6G 99
Lilac Rd. DN4: Cant 4C 58
  DN9: Auck 2B 76
  DN12: Con 5D 68
  S66: Braml 5H 99
  S66: Malt 5G 101
Lilac Rd. DN3: Arm 3F 43
  S5: Shef 1B 108
  S20: Beig 5G 137
Lilacs, The S71: Roy 2B 10
Lilac St. S43: Hol 5F 163
Lilian St. S60: Roth 5F 97
Lilian St. Sth. S60: Roth 5F 97
Lilleymede Cl. S40: Birdh 4G 171
Lillford Rd. DN3: Brant 4H 59
Lilly Hall Cl. S66: Malt 4G 101
Lilly Hall Rd. S66: Malt 4G 101
Lilydene Av. S72: Grim 1A 20
Lily Ter. S74: Jum 5C 46
Limb La. S17: Dore 2E 145
Limbreck Cl. DN5: Ben 1H 39
Limbrick Cl. S6: Shef 5B 106
Limbrick Rd. S6: Shef 5B 106
Lime Av. DN9: Auck 2B 76
  S43: Stav 5B 164
  S81: Fir 1H 129
Lime Cl. S44: Cal 5F 169
  S65: Rav 6A 86
Lime Ct. DN5: Sprot 3E 55
Limecroft Vw. S42: W'orth 6H 171
Limedale Vw. DN3: Barn D 2D 26
Lime Gro. S35: Chap 4F 79
  S36: Stoc 4D 174
  S60: Roth 6H 97
  S64: Swint 4C 66
  S66: Malt 5C 102
  S71: Carl 5H 9
Limekiln La. S66: Staint 6F 89
                 (Hirst La.)
  S66: Staint 2F 103
            (Stainton La.)
Limekilns S25: Nth A 2G 141
Limelands Rd. S25: Dinn 5H 127
Lime Rd. S21: Ecki 3C 158
Limes, The S60: Roth 6H 97
Limes Av. S75: Barn 5A 16
  S75: Stain 4B 8
Limes Cl. S75: Stain 4B 8
Limestone Cl. S81: Woods 5F 143
Limestone Cott. La. S6: Shef 6A 92
Lime St. S6: Shef 6D 106
  S20: Beig 4G 137
Limesway S66: Malt 5A 102
  S75: Barn 5A 16
Lime Tree Av. DN3: Arm 3E 43
  DN4: Don 2D 56
  S21: Killa 5B 152
Limetree Av. S26: Kiv P 5H 139
  S66: Thurc 6C 114
Lime Tree Cl. S72: Cud 1E 19
Lime Tree Ct. DN4: Don 3E 57
Lime Tree Cres. DN11: New R 6D 74
Limetree Cres. S62: Rawm 2A 84
Lime Tree Gro. S44: Ark T 5H 173
Lime Tree Wlk. DN12: Den M 2C 68
Limpool Cl. DN4: Cant 6C 58
Limpsfield Rd. S9: Shef 2D 108
Linacre Ho. S40: Ches 1H 171
            (off Archdale Cl.)
Linacre Rd. S40: Ash, Ches 4B 166
LINACRE WOODS 3B 166
Linaker Rd. S6: Shef 6H 105
Linburn Cl. S71: Roy 2F 9
Linburn Rd. S8: Shef 6E 133
Lincoln Cl. DN12: Den M 4C 68
Lincoln Gdns. S63: Gol 5C 36
Lincoln Rd. DN2: Don 4E 41
Lincolnshire Way DN3: Arm 3A 44
Lincoln St. DN11: New R 4B 74
  S9: Shef 2E 109
  S40: Birdh 2H 171
  S60: Roth 7E 97
  S66: Malt 6B 102

Lincroft S63: Gol 6C 36
Lincroft Dr. S62: Parkg 5G 83
Lindale Cl. S25: Nth A 3A 142
Lindale Gdns. S63: Gol 6E 37
Lindale Gro. WF9: Hems 1F 13
Lindale Rd. S41: Ches 5E 161
Lindales, The S75: Barn 6B 16
Linden Av. S8: Shef 6D 132
  S18: Dron 1G 155
  S40: Bramp 1C 170
  S66: Wick 4H 99
Linden Ct. S10: Shef 5A 118
  S35: Eccl 1G 93
Linden Cres. S36: Stoc 3D 174
Linden Dr. S41: Has 4C 172
Linden Gro. DN12: New E 5C 70
  S66: Malt 5G 101
Linden Pk. Gro. S40: Ches 5F 167
Linden Rd. S35: Eccl 1G 93
  S63: Warth D 6C 48
Linden Wlk. DN5: Ben 4H 23
Lindholme Rd. DN11: Ross 4E 75
Lindholme Gdns. S20: Mosb 6D 136
Lindhurst Lodge S71: Ath 6E 9
Lindhurst Rd. S71: Ath 6D 8
Lindisfarne Ct. S40: Walt 1D 170
Lindisfarne Rd. S18: Dron 4G 155
Lindley Cl. DN9: Finn 3F 77
Lindley Cres. S63: Thurn 3C 36
Lindley Rd. DN9: Finn 3F 77
  S5: Shef 2A 108
Lindley's Cft. S26: Tod 3C 140
Lindley St. S65: Roth 2F 97
Lindrick Av. S64: Swint 4D 66
Lindrick Cl. DN4: Bess 6H 57
  DN12: Con 3H 69
  S72: Cud 5F 11
Lindrick Ct. S81: Woods 5G 143
Lindrick Dr. DN3: Arm 5E 43
Lindrick Gdns. S40: Walt 2D 170
Lindrick Golf Course 6F 143
Lindrick Rd. S81: Woods 5F 143
Lindsay Av. S5: Shef 6F 93
Lindsay Cres. S5: Shef 5G 93
Lindsay Dr. S5: Shef 5G 93
Lindsay Pl. S26: Swal 1C 138
Lindsay Rd. S5: Shef 5G 93
Lindsey Cl. DN4: Bess 1A 74
Lindum Dr. S66: Wick 6H 99
Lindum St. DN4: Hex 2A 56
Lindum Ter. S65: Roth 4F 97
Lindup Rd. S18: Dron W 2D 154
Lineside S71: Roy 2B 10
Lingamoor Leys S63: Thurn 1C 36
Lingard Ct. S75: Barn 6C 16
Lingard La. S35: Ough 5E 91
Lingard St. S75: Barn 5C 16
Lingfield Cl. S66: Braml 6B 100
Lingfield Dr. DN5: Scaws 5E 39
Lingfield Wlk. S64: Mexb 6H 51
Lingfoot Av. S8: Shef 4G 147
Lingfoot Cl. S8: Shef 4G 147
Lingfoot Cres. S8: Shef 4G 147
Lingfoot Dr. S8: Shef 4G 147
Lingfoot Pl. S8: Shef 4G 147
Lingfoot Wlk. S8: Shef 4H 147
Lingmoor Cl. DN4: Balb 6F 55
Lingodell Cl. S25: Laugh M 2A 128
Ling Rd. S40: Walt 2E 171
Lings, The DN3: Arm 5G 43
  S66: Braml 6A 100
Lings La. S66: Wick 6H 99
Lingthwaite S75: Dod 3H 29
Link, The S75: Dod 4H 29
Link Rd. S65: Thry 6F 85
Link Row S2: Shef 2H 119
            (off Hyde Pk. Ter.)
Links Rd. S18: Dron 4G 155
Links Vw. S75: Stain 4A 8
Linkswood Av. DN2: Don 3H 41
Linkswood Rd. S65: Dalt 1C 98
Linkway DN2: Don 4G 41
Linley La. S12: Shef 3G 135
Linnet Ho. S41: Old W 3H 161
Linnet Mt. S61: Thorpe H 3C 80
Linscott Cl. S41: Ches 1E 167
Linscott Rd. S8: Shef 6D 132
Linthwaite La. S62: Wentw 2F 63
  S74: Els 2F 63

Linton Cl. S70: Barn 2A **30**
Linton Rd. S40: Walt 2D **170**
Lipp Av. S21: Killa 3B **152**
Liskeard Pl. DN6: Adw S 3B **22**
Lisle Rd. S60: Roth 6H **97**
Lismore Rd. S8: Shef 3G **133**
Lister Av. DN4: Balb 4A **56**
S12: Shef 4E **135**
S62: Rawm 1F **83**
Lister Cl. S12: Shef 5E **135**
S41: Ches 4H **167**
Lister Ct. DN2: Don 5F **41**
Lister Cres. S12: Shef 5D **134**
LISTERDALE **6F 99**
Listerdale Shop. Cen. S65: Roth 6D **98**
Lister Dr. S12: Shef 5E **135**
Lister Pl. S12: Shef 5E **135**
Lister Rd. S6: Shef 5B **106**
Lister Row S72: Gt H 5E **21**
Lister St. S65: Roth 4G **97**
Lister Way S12: Shef 5E **135**
Little Bri. Rd. S60: Roth 1F **97**
Lit. Brind Rd. S41: Ches 1C **166**
Lit. Cockhill La. DN12: Old E 1C **88**
LITTLE COMMON **5H 131**
Little Comn. La. S11: Shef 5G **131**
S60: Whist 3D **112**
S61: Kimb 3G **95**
Littledale Rd. S9: Shef 4F **121**
Littlefield La. S73: Womb 1G **47**
(not continuous)
Littlefield Rd. S25: Dinn 5H **127**
Lit. Haynooking La. S66: Malt 5A **102**
Littlehey Cl. S66: Malt 4G **101**
LITTLE HOUGHTON **2D 34**
Lit. Houghton La. S73: D'fld 4C **34**
Little La. DN2: Long S 1H **41**
DN5: Sprot 6B **38**
S4: Shef 3B **108**
S12: Shef 2E **135**
S61: Scho 4E **81**
S61: Thorpe H 2B **80**
Little La. Ind. Est. DN2: Long S 1G **41**
Little Leeds S74: Hoyl 6B **46**
Lit. London Pl. S8: Shef 2E **133**
Lit. London Rd. S8: Shef 4D **132**
Lit. Matlock Gdns. S6: Stann 6E **105**
Lit. Matlock Way S6: Stann 6E **105**
Littlemoor S21: Ecki 1F **159**
S41: Ches 2E **167**
Littlemoor Av. S26: Kiv P 6H **139**
Littlemoor Cen. S41: Ches 1F **167**
Littlemoor Cres. S41: Ches 1E **167**
Littlemoor La. DN4: Balb 3A **56**
Littlemoor St. DN4: Balb 3A **56**
Little New Cl. S75: Barn 5A **16**
LITTLE NORTON **2F 147**
Lit. Norton Av. S8: Shef 3F **147**
Lit. Norton Dr. S8: Shef 2F **147**
Lit. Norton La. S8: Shef 2F **147**
Lit. Norton Way S8: Shef 3F **147**
Little Pear Tree Nature Reserve **4F 107**
LITTLE SHEFFIELD **5E 119**
Little Stubbing S73: Womb 6E **33**
Little Westfields S71: Roy 2F **9**
Lit. Wood Dr. S12: Shef 5D **134**
Lit. Wood Rd. S12: Shef 5D **134**
Littlewood St. DN4: Hex 2A **56**
Littlewood Way S66: Malt 4C **102**
LITTLEWORTH **5E 75**
Littleworth Av. S71: Lund 6B **18**
Littleworth Cl. DN11: Ross 5E **75**
Littleworth La. DN11: Ross 4E **75**
S71: Lund, Monk B 4A **18**
Littleworth M. DN11: Ross 4E **75**
Litton Cl. S43: Stav 6H **163**
S72: Shaft 3F **11**
Litton Wlk. S70: Barn 6C **16**
S72: Shaft 3F **11**
Liverpool Av. DN2: Don 4E **41**
Liverpool St. S9: Shef 5C **108**
Livesey St. S6: Shef 4C **106**
Livingstone Av. DN2: Don 1A **42**
Livingstone Cres. S71: Monk B 3G **17**
Livingstone Rd. S35: Chap 3D **78**
Livingstone Ter. S70: Barn 2D **30**
Livingston Rd. S9: Shef 6B **108**
LivingWell Health Club Sheffield **2G 5**
Lloyd St. S4: Shef 3A **108**
S62: Parkg 5G **83**
Loakfield Dr. S5: Shef 3E **93**
Lobelia Ct. S25: Sth A 4G **141**
Lobelia Cres. DN3: Kirk Sa 5C **26**
Lobwood S70: Wors 5F **31**
Lobwood La. S70: Wors 5G **31**
Lock Av. S70: Wors 4E **31**
Lockeaflash Cres. S70: Stair 3A **32**
Lockeaflash Gdns. S70: Stair 3A **32**
Locke Av. S70: Barn 2D **30**
Locke Dr. S9: Shef 2E **121**
Locke Rd. S75: Dod 4H **29**
Lockesley Av. DN12: Con 4D **68**
Locke St. S70: Barn 3C **30**
Lock Ho. Rd. S9: Tins 3F **109**
Lock Ho. Wlk. S9: Tins 4F **109**
Locking Dr. DN3: Arm 5F **43**
Lock La. S9: Tins 6H **95**
Lockoford La. S41: Ches 2A **168**
(Muirfield Cl.)
S41: Ches 2H **167**
(William St., not continuous)
Lockoford Rd. S41: Ches 2H **167**
Locksley Av. DN3: Eden 6C **26**
Locksley Dr. S66: Thurc 6B **114**
Locksley Gdns. S70: Birdw 6E **45**
Lock St. S6: Shef 6D **106**
Lockton Cl. S35: High G 6B **60**
Lockton Way DN12: Con 3G **69**
Lockwood Av. S25: Sth A 4G **141**
Lockwood Cl. S65: Roth 3B **98**
Lockwood Gdns. S36: H'swne 1G **177**
Lockwood La. S63: Thurn 3D **36**
S70: Barn 3E **31**
Lockwood Rd. DN1: Don 5D **40**
S63: Gol 5D **36**
S65: Roth 3B **98**
Lodge, The S11: Shef 3H **131**
Lodge Cl. S26: Ast 1D **138**
S43: Brim C 4F **169**
Lodge Dr. S42: W'orth 6H **171**
S62: H'ley 5A **62**
Lodge Farm Cl. S25: Nth A 2G **141**
S42: Walt 3D **170**
Lodge Farm M. S25: Nth A 2G **141**
Lodge Hill Dr. S26: Wales 6G **139**
Lodge La. S6: Shef 3B **116**
S10: Shef 3B **116**
S25: Dinn 5C **128**
S26: Ast 2C **138**
S61: Thorpe H 5C **80**
LODGE MOOR **5B 116**
Lodge Moor Rd. S10: Shef 6A **116**
Lodge Pl. S43: Ink 2H **169**
Lodge Wlk. S43: Ink 2H **169**
Lodge Way S60: Brins 3D **110**
Loganberry Cl. S66: Sunn 3G **99**
Logan Rd. S9: Shef 2G **121**
Loicher La. S35: Eccl 1H **93**
Lomas Cl. S6: Stann 5D **104**
Lomas Lea S6: Stann 6C **104**
Lombard Cl. S75: Barn 5D **16**
Lombard Cres. S73: D'fld 5H **33**
London Rd. S2: Shef 5E **119**
London St. S43: New W 3C **162**
London Way S61: Thorpe H 4B **80**
Long Acre S71: Carl 5G **9**
Longacre Cl. S20: Holb 1H **151**
Longacre Ct. S18: Dron 5F **155**
Longacre Rd. S18: Dron 5F **155**
Long Acre Vw. S20: Holb 2H **151**
Longacre Way S20: Holb 2H **151**
Longcar La. S70: Barn 2C **30**
Long Causeway S71: Monk B 4H **17**
Long Cliffe Cl. S72: Shaft 4F **11**
Longcliff Wlk. S40: Ches 2E **167**
Long Cl. DN4: Bess 1A **74**
Long Cft. S75: Mapp 5A **8**
Longcroft Av. S18: Dron W 2B **154**
Longcroft Ct. S40: Birdh 3G **171**
Longcroft Cres. S18: Dron W 2B **154**
Longcroft Rd. S18: Dron W 2B **154**
Longdale Cft. S71: Monk B 4G **17**
Longedge Gro. S42: W'orth 6A **172**
Long Edge La. DN5: Scawt 1F **39**
Longedge La. S42: W'orth 6F **171**
Longedge Ri. S42: W'orth 6H **171**
Longfellow Dr. S65: Roth 5A **98**
Longfellow Fold S65: Roth 5A **98**
Longfellow Rd. DN4: Balb 6B **56**
Longfield Cl. S73: Womb 6E **33**
Longfield Dr. DN3: Eden 6D **26**
DN4: Bess 6A **58**
S65: Rav 2A **100**
S75: Mapp 5A **8**
Long Fld. Grange S41: Ches 2D **166**
Long Fld. Rd. DN3: Eden 5D **26**
Longfield Rd. S10: Shef 1A **118**
Longfields Ct. S71: Ath 6G **9**
Longfields Cres. S74: Hoyl 6A **46**
Longfields Rd. S71: Carl 6G **9**
Long Fold S63: Wath D 6D **48**
Longford Cl. S17: Bradw 5H **145**
Longford Cres. S17: Bradw 5H **145**
Longford Dr. S17: Bradw 6G **145**
Longford Rd. S17: Bradw 6G **145**
Longford Spinney S17: Bradw 6G **145**
Long Furlong S36: Pen 5E **177**
Long Gate DN11: Wils 4E **89**
Long Henry Row S2: Shef 3H **5** (3H **119**)
(not continuous)
Longlands Av. S26: Kiv P 6H **139**
Longlands Dr. S65: Thry 5F **85**
S75: Mapp 6A **8**
Long Lands La. DN5: Brod 3A **22**
Long La. DN5: Sprot 6C **38**
S6: Lox 3D **104**
S6: Stann 1E **117**
S10: Shef 2F **117**
S21: Killa 4D **152**
S21: Mar L, West H 3F **157**
S35: Ough 3C **90**
(Jackey La.)
S35: Ough 3D **104**
(Loxley Rd.)
S36: Pen 6F **177**
(Castle La.)
S36: Pen 2B **176**
(Huddersfield Rd.)
S36: Stoc 4A **174**
S60: Tree, Whist 4G **111**
Longley Av. W. S5: Shef 2D **106**
Longley Cl. S5: Shef 2G **107**
S75: Bar G 4F **15**
Longley Cres. S5: Shef 1G **107**
Longley Dr. S5: Shef 2G **107**
Longley Farm Vw. S5: Shef 2G **107**
Longley Hall Gro. S5: Shef 2H **107**
Longley Hall Ri. S5: Shef 1G **107**
Longley Hall Rd. S5: Shef 1H **107**
Longley Hall Way S5: Shef 2H **107**
Longley Ings S36: Pen 5G **177**
Longley La. S5: Shef 2G **107**
Long Leys La. S66: B'well 3B **88**
Longley Spring S74: Hoyl 4H **61**
Longley St. S75: Bar G 4F **15**
Long Line S11: Shef 6B **130**
Longman Rd. S70: Barn 5D **16**
Long Meadows S66: Braml 6A **100**
Long Plantation DN3: Eden 6D **26**
Long Pye Cl. S75: Wool G 3F **7**
Longridge Rd. S71: Monk B 2A **18**
Long Rd. S66: Bramp M 3A **126**
Long Royd S72: Grim 2A **20**
LONG SANDALL **6A 26**
Long Sandall Bri. DN2: Long S 5H **25**
Long Shambles *S40: Ches 5H 167*
(off Central Pavement)
Longshaw Cl. S43: Stav 6A **164**
Longside Way S75: Barn 6H **15**
Longsight Rd. S75: Mapp 5H **7**
Long Spring Gro. S75: Tank 1D **60**
Longstone Cres. S12: Shef 4G **135**
Longthwaite Cl. S25: Laugh M 2H **127**
Longton Rd. DN3: Kirk Sa 4D **26**
Long Wlk. S10: Shef 2H **117**
Longwood Cl. S66: Sunn 2G **99**
Longworth Rd. WF9: Hems 1E **13**
Lonsdale Av. DN2: Don 1G **57**
S71: Ard 2E **33**
Lonsdale Cl. S25: Nth A 2A **142**
Lonsdale Ho. DN2: Don 5H **41**
Lonsdale Rd. S6: Shef 5B **106**
Loosemore Dr. S12: Shef 3C **134**
Lopham Cl. S3: Shef 1G **119**
Lopham St. S3: Shef 6G **107**
(not continuous)

Lordens Hill S25: Dinn 5B **128**
Lord Roberts Rd. S40: Ches 1H **171**
Lords Cl. DN12: New E 3D **70**
Lord's Head La. DN4: Warm 1D **70**
Lordsmill Ga. S41: Ches 6A **168**
Lordsmill St. S41: Ches 6A **168**
Lord St. S65: Roth 3H **97**
S71: Barn 6H **17**
Loretta Cotts. S74: Hoyl 6A **46**
Lorna Rd. S64: Mexb 1F **67**
Lorne Cl. S18: Dron W 2C **154**
Lorne Rd. S63: Thurn 2A **36**
Loscoe Gro. S63: Gol 5B **36**
Lothian Rd. DN2: Don 5H **41**
Louden Cl. S61: Scho 6E **81**
Louden Rd. S61: Scho 6E **81**
Lounde Cl. DN5: Sprot 3D **54**
Loundes Rd. S18: Uns 6B **156**
Loundeswood Av. S41: Ches 6D **160**
Lound Rd. S9: Shef 3G **121**
Lound Side S35: Chap 2F **79**
Loundsley Ct. S42: Ash 4A **166**
LOUNDSLEY GREEN 3D **166**
Loundsley Grn. Rd. S40: Ches 4C **166**
Lousy Busk La. S64: Mexb 6D **50**
Louth Rd. S11: Shef 1A **132**
Lovell St. S4: Shef 1A **120**
LOVERSALL 4B **72**
Loversall Cl. DN4: Balb 1A **72**
Love St. S3: Shef 1E **5** (2F **119**)
Lovetot Av. S26: Ast 6C **124**
Lovetot Rd. S9: Shef 1B **120**
(Bacon La.)
S9: Shef 1B **120**
(Stoke St.)
S61: Kimb P 6H **81**
LOW BARUGH 2G **15**
Lowburn Rd. S13: Shef 1F **135**
Low Comn. Rd. S25: Dinn 5G **127**
Low Cft. S71: Roy 3A **10**
S73: Womb 1H **47**
Low Cronkhill La. S71: Carl 4B **10**
Low Cudworth S72: Cud 3E **19**
Low Cudworth Grn. S72: Cud 3E **19**
Low Deeps La. DN10: Miss 5H **77**
LOWEDGES 4E **147**
Low Edges S8: Shef 4F **147**
Lowedges Cl. S8: Shef 4D **146**
Lowedges Cres. S8: Shef 4E **147**
Lowedges Dr. S8: Shef 4E **147**
Lowedges Pl. S8: Shef 4F **147**
Lowedges Rd. S8: Shef 5C **146**
Lowe La. S75: Stainb 6G **29**
Lowell Av. DN4: Balb 6A **56**
Lower All. S44: Cal 1F **173**
Lwr. Boundary Rd. DN5: Ben 1E **25**
LOWER BRADWAY 4B **146**
Lwr. Castlereagh St. S70: Barn 1D **30**
Lwr. Collier Fold S75: Cawt 3A **14**
LOWER CRABTREE 4H **107**
Lwr. Dolcliffe Rd. S64: Mexb 1E **67**
Lower Gro. Rd. S40: Ches 5G **167**
Lwr. Haigh Head S36: H'swne 1F **177**
Lwr. High Royds S75: Dart 6H **7**
LOWER LEWDEN 6A **32**
Lwr. Limes, The S70: Wors 6G **31**
Lwr. Malton Rd. DN5: Scaws 3F **39**
Lwr. Mill Cl. S63: Gol 6B **36**
Lower Pasture DN9: Blax 2F **77**
LOWER PILLEY 1D **60**
Lwr. Thomas St. S70: Barn 2D **30**
Lwr. Unwin St. S36: Pen 5D **176**
LOWER WALKLEY 5B **106**
Lwr. York St. S73: Womb 1G **47**
Low Farm Ct. S71: D'fld 2B **34**
LOWFIELD 6F **119**
Lowfield Av. S12: Ridg 1H **149**
S61: Grea 5D **82**
Lowfield Cl. DN3: Barn D 2E **27**
Lowfield Ct. S2: Shef 1F **133**
Lowfield Farm Cl. S63: Bolt D 2D **50**
Lowfield Gro. S63: Bolt D 3D **50**
Lowfield La. S63: Bolt D 2D **50**
Lowfield Mdws. S63: Bolt D 3C **50**
Lowfield Rd. DN2: Don 3H **41**
S63: Bolt D 2C **50**
Lowfields S43: Stav 4D **164**
Lowfield Wlk. DN12: Den M 2C **68**
Low Folds S71: Monk B 3C **18**
Lowgate DN5: Scawt 3F **39**
Lowgates S43: Stav 4C **164**
Low Golden Smithies S64: Swint 2B **66**
Low Grange Rd. S63: Thurn 2B **36**
Low Grange Sq. S63: Thurn 2B **36**
Lowgreave S65: Roth 2B **98**
Lowhouse Rd. S5: Shef 3B **94**
LOW LAITHES 4E **33**
Low Laithes Vw. S73: Womb 6E **33**
Low Laithes Village S71: Low L 4F **33**
Lowland Cl. S71: Monk B 3A **18**
Low Lands Cl. DN5: Ben 5A **24**
Low La. DN4: Bess 6H **57**
S61: Kimb, Roth 2B **96**
S66: Carr, Hoot L 2F **115**
Low Lathe La. S36: Spink 2H **175**
Low Matlock La. S6: Lox 5E **105**
Low Pasture Cl. S75: Dod 3H **29**
Low Pavement S40: Ches 5H **167**
Low Riddings S66: Sunn 4G **99**
Low Rd. DN4: Balb 5H **55**
DN12: Con 3F **69**
S6: Shef 6H **105**
S35: Ough 3E **91**
Low Rd. E. DN4: Warm 6E **55**
(not continuous)
Low Rd. W. DN4: Warm 1D **70**
Low Row S75: Dart 3F **7**
Lowry Dr. S18: Dron 3E **155**
Low St. S75: Dod 4A **30**
LOW STUBBIN 6D **64**
Lowther Rd. DN1: Don 5D **40**
S6: Shef 3C **106**
Lowton Way S66: Hel 5D **100**
LOW VALLEY 6A **34**
Low Vw. S75: Dod 3G **29**
LOW WINCOBANK 5D **94**
Low Wood Cl. S64: Swint 5B **66**
Loxdale Gdns. S70: Barn 6C **16**
LOXLEY 4F **105**
Loxley Av. S73: Womb 2F **47**
LOXLEY BOTTOM 4H **105**
Loxley Cl. S40: Ash 5C **166**
Loxley Ct. S6: Shef 3G **105**
(Ben La.)
S6: Shef 5B **106**
(Limbrick Cl.)
S60: Roth 2G **111**
Loxley New Rd. S6: Shef 5A **106**
Loxley Pk. S6: Shef 5H **105**
Loxley Rd. S6: Bradf, Lox, Shef 2A **104**
S71: Lund 5C **18**
Loxley Vw. Rd. S10: Shef 1A **118**
Loy Cl. S61: Wing 5B **82**
Lucas Rd. S41: Ches 2F **167**
Lucas St. S4: Shef 5H **107**
Lucknow Ct. S7: Shef 2D **132**
Ludgate Cl. DN11: New R 6H **75**
Ludham Cl. S41: Ches 1G **167**
Ludham Gdns. S41: Ches 1G **167**
Ludwell Cl. DN5: Barnb 2B **52**
Ludwell Hill DN5: Barnb 2B **52**
Lugano Gro. S73: D'fld 4H **33**
Luke La. S6: Shef 3G **105**
Lulworth Cl. S70: Barn 2G **31**
Lumb La. S35: Ough 2B **90**
Lumley Cl. S66: Malt 5D **102**
Lumley Cres. S66: Malt 6D **102**
Lumley Dr. S66: Malt 6C **102**
Lumley St. S4: Shef 2A **120**
S9: Shef 2C **120**
Lump La. S35: Gren 1B **92**
Lumsdale Rd. S43: Stav 6H **163**
Luna Cft. S12: Shef 6C **134**
Lunbreck Rd. DN4: Warm 1D **70**
Lund Av. S71: Lund 5C **18**
Lund Cl. S71: Lund 5C **18**
Lund Cres. S71: Lund 5C **18**
Lundhill Cl. S73: Womb 3H **47**
Lundhill Farm M. S73: Hem 4G **47**
Lundhill Gro. S73: Womb 3H **47**
Lund Hill La. S71: Roy 2C **10**
Lundhill Rd. S73: Womb 4H **47**
Lund La. S71: Lund 5C **18**
Lund Rd. S35: Ough 5E **91**
LUNDWOOD 5B **18**
Lundwood Cl. S20: Mosb 6D **136**
Lundwood Dr. S20: Mosb 6D **136**
Lundwood Gro. S20: Mosb 6D **136**
Lundwood Ho. *DN1: Don* *2B* ***56***
(off Bond Cl.)
Lundy Rd. S18: Dron 4F **155**
Lunn Rd. S72: Cud 2E **19**
Lupin Way S44: Cal 5F **169**
Lupton Cres. S8: Shef 4E **147**
Lupton Dr. S8: Shef 4E **147**
Lupton Rd. S8: Shef 4E **147**
Lupton Wlk. S8: Shef 4F **147**
Luterel Dr. S26: Swal 6C **124**
Lutterworth Dr. DN6: Adw S 2B **22**
Lutyens Ct. S40: Bramp 6A **166**
Lyceum Theatre
Sheffield 4F **5** (3G **119**)
Lych Ga. Cl. DN4: Cant 5D **58**
Lydden Cl. S43: Brim 6D **162**
Lydford Av. S41: Old W 5A **162**
LYDGATE 3H **117**
Lydgate Ct. S10: Shef 3A **118**
Lydgate Dr. S42: W'orth 6F **171**
Lydgate Hall Cres. S10: Shef 3H **117**
Lydgate La. S10: Shef 3H **117**
Lymegate S63: Bramp B 6A **48**
Lyme St. S60: Roth 4D **96**
Lyminster Rd. S6: Shef 5B **92**
Lyminton La. S60: Tree 2F **123**
Lymister Av. S60: Roth 2G **111**
Lyncroft Cl. S60: Brins 4E **111**
Lyndale Av. DN3: Eden 1B **42**
Lynden Av. DN6: Adw S 3B **22**
Lyndhurst Bank S36: Pen 5D **176**
Lyndhurst Cl. S11: Shef 1B **132**
Lyndhurst Cres. DN3: Eden 5B **26**
Lyndhurst Rd. S11: Shef 1B **132**
Lynham Av. S70: Birdw 6E **45**
Lynmouth Rd. S7: Shef 3D **132**
Lynn Pl. S9: Shef 4E **109**
Lynthwaite Cl. S63: Bramp B 5A **48**
Lynton Av. S60: Roth 1H **111**
Lynton Dr. DN3: Eden 6B **26**
Lynton Pl. S75: Kexb 6E **7**
Lynton Rd. S11: Shef 6C **118**
Lynwood Cl. S18: Dron W 3C **154**
Lynwood Dr. S64: Mexb 6F **51**
S71: Carl 5H **9**
Lyons Cl. S4: Shef 5H **107**
Lyons Rd. S4: Shef 5H **107**
Lyons St. S4: Shef 5H **107**
Lytham Av. S25: Dinn 1A **142**
S71: Monk B 2A **18**
Lytham Cl. DN4: Cant 6E **59**
Lyttleton Ct. S36: Cub 6C **176**
Lyttleton Cres. S36: Cub 6C **176**
Lytton Av. S5: Shef 5D **92**
Lytton Cl. DN4: Balb 6A **56**
Lytton Cres. S5: Shef 5D **92**
Lytton Dr. S5: Shef 5D **92**
Lytton Rd. S5: Shef 5D **92**

M

Mabel St. S60: Roth 5G **97**
Macaulay Cres. DN3: Arm 4F **43**
McConnel Cres. DN11: New R 5A **74**
Macdonald Cl. S42: Gras 6E **173**
McGregor's Way S40: Birdh 3A **172**
Machin Dr. S62: Rawm 6D **64**
Machin La. S36: Stoc 2A **174**
Machins Ct. S18: Dron 2F **155**
Machon Bank S7: Shef 2D **132**
Machon Bank Rd. S7: Shef 1C **132**
McIntyre Rd. S36: Stoc 3D **174**
Mackenzie Cres. S10: Shef 6A **4** (4D **118**)
S35: Burn 4C **78**
Mackenzie St. S11: Shef 6D **118**
McKenzie Way S26: Kiv P 6A **140**
Mackey Cres. S72: Brier 3H **11**
Mackey La. S72: Brier 3H **11**
Mackinnon Av. S26: Kiv P 6A **140**
McLaren Cres. S66: Malt 6B **102**
McLintock Way S70: Barn 1C **30**
McLoughlin Way S26: Kiv P 6A **140**
McMahon Av. S43: Ink 2G **169**
McManus Av. S62: Rawm 6G **65**
Macmillan M. S40: Bramp 5C **166**
Macnaughten Rd. S75: Tank 1E **61**
Macro Rd. S73: Womb 2H **47**
Madam La. DN3: Barn D 1G **27**

Madehurst Gdns. S2: Shef 1G **133**
Madehurst Ri. S2: Shef 1G **133**
Madehurst Rd. S2: Shef 1G **133**
Madehurst Vw. S2: Shef 1G **133**
Madin Dr. S43: Ink 2G **169**
Madingley Cl. DN4: Balb 1H **71**
Madin St. S41: Ches 4H **167**
Madison Ct. DN9: Finn 3F **77**
Mafeking Pl. S35: Chap 2F **79**
Magdalene Gdns. S63: Gol 5E **37**
Magellan Rd. S66: Malt 4H **101**
Magistrates' Court
  Chesterfield 5A **168**
  Doncaster 2C **56**
  Sheffield 2F **5** (2G **119**)
Magna 34 Business Pk.
  S60: Roth 6B **96**
Magna Cl. S66: Flan 4G **99**
Magna Cres. S66: Flan 4F **99**
Magna La. S65: Dalt 1C **98**
Magna Science Adventure Cen. . . .6A **96**
Magna Way S60: Roth 6A **96**
Magnolia Cl. DN3: Kirk Sa 5C **26**
  S25: Sth A 5G **141**
  S72: Shaft 4G **11**
Magnolia Ct. S10: Shef 6F **117**
Magpie Gro. S2: Shef 4B **120**
Mahon Av. S62: Rawm 2G **83**
Maidstone Rd. S6: Shef 6C **92**
Maidwell Way DN3: Kirk Sa 4B **26**
Main Av. DN12: New E 3C **70**
  S17: Tot 6F **145**
Main Rd. S9: Shef 1F **121**
  S12: Ridg 2H **149**
  S18: B'low 4A **160**
  S18: Holme 4A **154**
  S18: Uns 5B **156**
  S21: Mar L 2H **157**
  S21: Reni 3H **159**
  S21: West H 5G **157**
  S35: Wharn S 1A **90**
  S42: Cut 1A **166**
  S42: Old B 4A **166**
Main St. DN3: Cant 3E **59**
  DN5: Sprot 4C **54**
  DN9: Auck 1G **59**
  DN11: Wad 5E **73**
  S12: Shef 4C **136**
  S25: Nth A 3G **141**
  S26: Augh 5B **124**
  S26: Swal 1B **138**
  S26: Ull 3D **124**
  S35: Gren 1B **92**
  S60: Cat 1E **123**
  S60: Roth 4D **96**
  S61: Grea 4D **82**
  S62: Rawm 2H **83**
  S62: Wentw 5D **62**
  S63: Gol 5D **36**
  S64: Mexb 1E **67**
  S65: Rav 5A **86**
  S66: Braml 5A **100**
  S72: Sth H 1G **11**
  S73: Womb 1F **47**
Main St. Shop. Cen.
  S66: Braml 5A **100**
Mair Ct. S60: Roth 3H **111**
Majestic Cl. S75: Dart 5F **7**
Majuba St. S6: Shef 6C **106**
Makin St. S64: Mexb 2H **67**
Malcolm Cl. S70: Barn 2A **32**
Malham Cl. S40: Ches 3E **167**
  S72: Shaft 3F **11**
Malham Ct. S70: Barn 6C **16**
Malham Gdns. S20: Half 3E **151**
Malham Gro. S20: Half 3F **151**
Malham Pl. S35: Chap 2E **79**
Malham Tarn Cl. DN4: Don 4G **57**
Malia Rd. S41: Ches 2B **168**
MALINBRIDGE 5A **106**
Malin Bridge (Park & Ride) 5A **106**
Malin Bridge Stop (ST) 5A **106**
Malincroft S75: Mapp 6A **8**
Malinda St. S3: Shef 1B **4** (1E **119**)
Malin Rd. S6: Shef 5H **105**
  S65: Roth 2C **98**
Malkin St. S41: Ches 5A **168**
Mallard Av. DN3: Barn D 2C **26**
  DN5: Scawt 3G **39**

Mallard Cl. DN4: Balb 6G **55**
  S61: Thorpe H 2D **80**
Mallard Ct. DN11: Ross 5D **74**
  S43: Stav 4C **164**
Mallard Dr. S21: Killa 3A **152**
Mallard Way DN4: Don 6E **57**
Mallin Cft. S74: Hoyl 6B **46**
Mallinder Cl. S21: Killa 4C **152**
Mallin Dr. DN12: New E 6C **70**
Mallory Av. S62: Rawm 2F **83**
Mallory Cl. S41: Old W 3F **161**
Mallory Dr. S42: Mexb 6A **52**
Mallory Rd. S65: Roth 2B **98**
Mallory Way S72: Cud 1F **19**
Malon Way S13: Shef 5C **122**
Malsin Gdns. S73: Womb 3F **47**
Malson Way S41: Ches 2G **167**
Maltas Ct. S70: Wors 5H **31**
MALTBY 5A **102**
Maltby Av. S75: Wool G 4F **7**
Maltby Ho. DN1: Don 2B **56**
             (off Burden Cl.)
Maltby La. S66: B'well 1B **102**
Maltby Leisure Cen. 5A **102**
Maltby Low Common Nature Reserve
  . . . . .6E **103**
Maltby St. S9: Shef 5D **108**
Malthouse Cotts. S26: Kiv S 6E **141**
Malthouse Ct. S41: Ches 4H **167**
Malthouse La. S42: W'orth 6C **170**
Malthouse Rd. S71: Barn 1E **31**
Malting La. S4: Shef 1H **5** (2H **119**)
Maltings, The S11: Shef 2E **19**
             (off Napier St.)
  S36: Cub 5C **176**
            (off Mortimer Rd.)
  S60: Roth 5E **97**
Maltings Ct. DN3: Kirk Sa 3C **26**
Maltkiln Cotts. DN3: Barn D 3C **26**
Maltkiln Farm Ct.
  S66: B'well 6A **88**
Malt Kiln Row S75: Cawt 3A **14**
            (off Hill Top)
Maltkiln St. S60: Roth 5E **97**
Malton Dr. S26: Ast 1D **138**
Malton Pl. S71: Smi 1D **16**
Malton Rd. DN2: Don 5G **41**
  DN5: Scaws 3E **39**
Malton St. S4: Shef 5H **107**
Malton Wlk. S40: Birdh 3G **171**
Malton Way DN6: Woodl 1A **22**
Maltravers Cl. S2: Shef 4B **120**
Maltravers Cres. S2: Shef 3A **120**
Maltravers Pl. S2: Shef 3B **120**
Maltravers Rd. S2: Shef 2A **120**
Maltravers Ter. S2: Shef 4B **120**
          (not continuous)
Maltravers Way S2: Shef 3B **120**
Malvern Av. DN5: Cus 5F **39**
Malvern Cl. S75: Barn 6A **16**
Malvern Dr. S66: Sunn 3G **99**
Malvern Rd. DN2: Don 6H **41**
  S9: Shef 1E **121**
  S40: Ches 4F **167**
Malvern Way S66: Sunn 3G **99**
Malwood Way S66: Malt 4C **102**
Manchester Rd. S6: Shef 4A **116**
  S10: Shef 4A **116**
  S36: Spink, Stoc 1A **174**
  S36: Thurl 4A **176**
Mandale Rd. DN3: Barn D 1H **27**
Mandeville St. S9: Shef 1F **121**
Mangham Rd. S61: Grea 1E **97**
  S62: Parkg 1E **97**
Mangham Way S61: Grea 1E **97**
Manifold Av. S43: Stav 6A **164**
Manknell Rd. S41: Whit M 6H **161**
Mannering Rd. DN4: Balb 6F **55**
Manners St. S3: Shef 6E **107**
MANOR 6D **120**
Manor App. S61: Kimb 3H **95**
Manor Av. S43: Brim 1E **169**
  S63: Gol 5D **36**
Manor Bungs. S18: Dron 3E **155**
Manor Cl. DN3: Barn D 1B **26**
  S26: Tod 3C **140**
  S62: Rawm 6D **64**
  S63: Bramp B 5C **48**
  S66: Malt 5A **102**

Manor Ct. DN5: H'ton 2H **51**
  DN12: Den M 3C **68**
  S65: Roth 2C **98**
  S70: Wors 5E **31**
  S71: Roy 3F **9**
  S72: Grim 2C **20**
Manor Cres. S18: Dron 3E **155**
  S40: Ash 5E **167**
  S60: Brins 5D **80**
  S72: Grim 6B **12**
Manor Cft. S72: Sth H 1G **11**
Manor Development Cen.
  . . . . .5E **121**
Manor Dr. DN2: Don 2E **57**
  DN5: Cade 1G **69**
  S25: Dinn 4H **127**
  S26: Tod 3C **140**
  S40: Ash 5D **166**
  S43: Brim 1E **169**
  S60: Whist 3B **112**
  S71: Roy 3G **9**
  S72: Sth H 1G **11**
Manor End S70: Wors 5E **31**
Manor Est. DN5: Ben 4G **23**
Mnr. Farm Cl. DN6: Adw S 2C **22**
  S26: Augh 4C **124**
  S71: Carl 6A **10**
Mnr. Farm Cl. S20: Beig 5H **137**
  S21: Killa 5C **152**
  S65: Thry 4E **85**
  S71: Ard 2E **33**
           (off Doncaster Rd.)
  S72: Cud 2E **19**
Mnr. Farm Cft. S81: Woods 4F **143**
Mnr. Farm Dr. S64: Swint 4B **66**
Mnr. Farm Est. S62: Rawm 1D **82**
Mnr. Farm Gdns. S25: Sth A 4G **141**
Mnr. Farm M. S20: Beig 5H **137**
Manor Flds. S61: Kimb 2H **95**
  S72: Gt H 6F **21**
Manor Fields Cl. S61: Kimb 2H **95**
Manor Gdns. DN5: Sprot 3C **54**
  S71: Ard 2E **33**
  S72: Shaft 4F **11**
Manor Gro. S71: Roy 3G **9**
  S72: Grim 6A **12**
  WF9: Sth K 5H **13**
Manor Ho. S6: Stann 6D **104**
Manor Ho. Cl. S74: Hoyl 6B **46**
Manor Ho. Cl. DN5: Scawt 1G **39**
Manor Ho. Rd. S61: Kimb 2H **95**
Manor Laith Rd. S2: Shef 4A **120**
Manor La. S2: Shef 2C **120**
  S25: Dinn 3B **128**
  S36: Oxs 6H **177**
  S64: Mexb 4E **51**
Manor Oaks Cl. S2: Shef 3B **120**
Manor Oaks Ct. S2: Shef 3A **120**
Manor Oaks Dr. S2: Shef 3A **120**
Manor Oaks Gdns. S2: Shef 3H **119**
Manor Oaks Pl. S2: Shef 4B **120**
Manor Oaks Rd. S2: Shef 3H **119**
Mnr. Occupation Rd.
  S71: Roy 2G **9**
MANOR PARK 4D **120**
Manor Pk. S75: Silk 3A **28**
Manor Pk. Av. S2: Shef 5C **120**
Manor Pk. Cen. S2: Shef 4C **120**
Manor Pk. Cl. S2: Shef 5C **120**
Manor Pk. Ct. S2: Shef 5C **120**
Manor Pk. Cres. S2: Shef 5C **120**
Manor Pk. Dr. S2: Shef 5C **120**
Manor Park Ind. Est.
  S9: Shef 2D **120**
Manor Pk. Pl. S2: Shef 4C **120**
Manor Pk. Ri. S2: Shef 4C **120**
Manor Pk. Rd. S2: Shef 4C **120**
Manor Pk. Way S2: Shef 4C **120**
Manor Pl. S62: Rawm 3H **83**
  S74: Hoyl 6C **46**
Manor Ri. DN11: Wad 6F **73**
  S73: Womb 6E **33**
Manor Rd. DN3: Barn D 1G **27**
  DN5: Ben 4H **23**
  DN5: H'ton 3H **51**
  S21: Killa 5D **152**
  S25: Dinn 3A **128**
  S26: Kiv S 6E **141**
  S26: Wales 5G **139**

Manor Rd. S40: Ash 5D 166
　　　　(Ash Tree Cl.)
　S40: Ash 5E 167
　　　　(Lenthall's Back Row)
　S43: Brim, Brim C 1E 169
　S60: Brins 4C 110
　S61: Kimb 4H 95
　S63: Bramp B 5B 48
　S63: Thurn 2B 36
　S64: Swint 4C 66
　S66: Malt 5B 102
　S72: Cud 2D 18
Manor Sq. S63: Thurn 2B 36
Manor St. S71: Carl 6A 10
Manor Top / Elm Tree Stop (ST) . . .2D 134
Manor Vw. S20: Half 3F 151
　S72: Shaft 4F 11
Manor Wlk. DN11: Wad 6E 73
Manor Way S2: Shef 2B 120
　S26: Tod 3C 140
　S63: Bolt D 2C 50
　S74: Hoyl 6B 46
Manse Cl. DN4: Cant 4D 58
Manse Farm M. S72: Cud 1E 19
Mansel Av. S5: Shef 4D 92
Mansel Ct. S5: Shef 4D 92
Mansel Cres. S5: Shef 4C 92
Mansel Rd. S5: Shef 4D 92
Mansfeldt Cres. S41: Ches 2F 167
Mansfeldt Rd. S41: Ches 2F 167
Mansfield Cres. DN3: Arm 3B 42
Mansfield Dr. S12: Shef 2E 135
Mansfield Rd. DN4: Balb 3A 56
　S12: Shef 2D 134
　S21: Killa 3E 153
　S26: Ast, Swal, Wales B 1B 138
　　　　(not continuous)
　S41: Has, Cor 3C 172
　S60: Roth 4F 97
　S71: Ath 6E 9
Mansfield Vw. S12: Shef 2E 135
Manton Ho. DN1: Don 2B 56
　　　　(off Oxford Pl.)
Manton St. S2: Shef 6F 5 (5G 119)
Manvers Cl. S25: Nth A 1H 141
　S26: Swal 1C 138
Manvers Ct. S41: Ches 4H 167
　　　　(off Nightingale Cl.)
Manvers Park Sports Cen. 1B 66
Manvers Rd. S6: Shef 5B 106
　S20: Beig 4G 137
　S26: Swal 1B 138
　S44: Cal 4F 169
　S64: Mexb 1D 66
Manvers Waterfront Boat Club 4H 49
Manvers Way S63: Wath D 3D 48
Maori Av. S63: Bolt D 2H 49
Maple Av. DN4: Cant 4C 58
　DN9: Auck 2B 76
　S66: Malt 5G 101
Maplebeck Dr. S9: Tins 2A 110
Maplebeck Rd. S9: Tins 2A 110
Maple Cl. S70: Barn 3G 31
Maple Ct. S62: Rawm 3H 83
　S75: Tank 3B 60
Maple Cft. Cres. S9: Shef 1C 108
Maple Cft. Rd. S9: Shef 1C 108
Maple Dr. DN9: Auck 1H 59
　S21: Killa 5B 152
　S66: Flan 4G 99
Maple Est. S75: Barn 1B 30
Maple Gro. DN3: Arm 3E 43
　DN12: Con 6C 68
　S9: Shef 3H 121
　S26: Ast 6E 125
　S36: Stoc 4D 174
Maple Pl. S35: Chap 4F 79
Maple Rd. S26: Kiv P 5H 139
　S64: Mexb 1E 67
　S75: Mapp 5H 7
　S75: Tank 3C 60
Maple St. S43: Hol 6G 163
Maplewood Av. S66: Sunn 2G 99
Mapperley Rd. S18: Dron W 3B 154
Mappin Ct. S1: Shef 4B 4
　　　　(off Mappin St.)
Mappin's Rd. S60: Cat 1D 122
Mappin St. S1: Shef 3B 4 (3E 119)
Mapplebeck Rd. S35: High G 1D 78

MAPPLEWELL 6H 7
Mapplewell Dr. S75: Mapp 6B 8
Maran Av. S73: D'fld 5D 34
Marbeck Cl. S25: Dinn 5G 127
Marcham Dr. S20: Beig 4H 137
March Bank S65: Thry 5F 85
March Flatts Rd. S65: Thry 6F 85
March Ga. DN12: Con 5F 69
March St. DN12: Con 4F 69
　S9: Shef 5E 109
　　　　(not continuous)
March Va. Ri. DN12: Con 5F 69
Marchwood Av. S6: Shef 6F 105
Marchwood Cl. S40: Ches 4G 167
Marchwood Dr. S6: Shef 5F 105
Marchwood Rd. S6: Shef 6F 105
Marcliff Cl. S66: Wick 6E 99
Marcliff Cres. S66: Wick 6E 99
Marcliff La. S66: Wick 6E 99
Mardale Cl. S41: Ches 5F 161
Mardale Dr. S41: Ches 5F 161
Mardale Wlk. DN2: Don 4H 41
Marden Rd. S7: Shef 2D 132
Margaret Cl. S26: Ast 2C 138
　S73: D'fld 5A 34
Margaret Ct. S73: Womb 2H 47
Margaret Rd. S73: D'fld 5A 34
　S73: Womb 2H 47
Margaret St. S1: Shef 5F 119
　S66: Malt 6C 102
Margate Dr. S4: Shef 4A 108
Margate St. S4: Shef 4B 108
Margerison St. S8: Shef 1F 133
Margetson Cres. S5: Shef 4E 93
Margetson Dr. S5: Shef 4E 93
Margetson Rd. S5: Shef 4E 93
Marian Rd. DN3: Eden 5B 26
Marigold Cl. S5: Shef 1B 108
Marina Ri. S73: D'fld 5H 33
Marine Dr. S41: Ches 5B 168
Marion Cl. WF9: Sth K 4H 13
Marion Rd. S6: Shef 2A 106
Markbrook Dr. S35: High G 6B 60
Market Cl. S71: Barn 1F 31
Market Hall S40: Ches 5H 167
Market Hill S70: Barn 1D 30
Market Pde. S70: Barn 1E 31
Market Pl. DN1: Don 1C 56
　S1: Shef 2F 5 (2G 119)
　S25: Dinn 5A 128
　S35: Chap 3G 79
　S36: Pen 4D 176
　S40: Ches 5H 167
　S43: Stav 4B 164
　S60: Roth 4E 97
　S63: Gol 5D 36
　S72: Cud 1E 19
　S73: Womb 2H 47
　S74: Els 1D 62
Market Rd. DN1: Don 6C 40
Market Sq. S13: Shef 2D 136
　S60: Roth 4E 97
　　　　(off Market Pl.)
　S63: Gol 5D 36
　S65: Roth 3F 97
Market St. DN6: Highf 6C 22
　S9: Shef 2F 109
　S13: Shef 2D 136
　S21: Ecki 1E 159
　S35: Chap 3G 79
　S36: Pen 4D 176
　S43: Stav 4B 164
　S60: Roth 4E 97
　S63: Gol 5D 36
　S63: Thurn 2B 36
　S64: Mexb 2F 67
　　　　(not continuous)
　S64: Swint 3D 66
　S70: Barn 1D 30
　S72: Cud 1E 19
　S74: Hoyl 5B 46
Markfield Dr. S66: Flan 4G 99
Mark Gro. S66: Flan 5B 98
Markham Av. DN3: Arm 3D 42
　DN12: Con 4D 68
Markham Cotts. DN12: Con 4D 68
　　　　(off Leslie Av.)
Markham Ct. DN12: Con 4D 68

Markham Cres. S43: Stav 4C 164
Markham Ho. DN1: Don 2B 56
　　　　(off Burden Cl.)
Markham Quay S41: Ches 6A 168
　　　　(off Camlough Wlk.)
Markham Rd. DN12: New E 4C 70
　S40: Ches 6G 167
Markham Sq. DN12: New E 4D 70
Markham Ter.
　DN12: New E 4C 70
　S8: Shef 2E 133
Mark La. S10: Shef 2B 130
Mark St. S70: Barn 1D 30
Marlborough Av. DN5: Don 6G 39
Marlborough Cl.
　S25: Nth A 1G 141
　S63: Thurn 2B 36
Marlborough Ri. S26: Ast 2D 138
Marlborough Rd. DN2: Don 6E 41
　S10: Shef 3B 118
Marlborough Ter. S70: Barn 2D 30
Marlcliffe Rd. S6: Shef 1H 105
Marles Cl. S73: Womb 3F 47
Marlfield Cft. S35: Eccl 2G 93
Marlow Cl. DN2: Don 5H 41
Marlowe Cl. S66: Braml 6A 100
Marlowe Dr. S65: Roth 5A 98
Marlowe Rd. DN3: Barn D 1C 26
　S65: Roth 5A 98
Marlow Rd. DN2: Don 5H 41
Marmion Rd. S11: Shef 6A 118
　　　　(Kenilworth Pl.)
　S11: Shef 1A 132
　　　　(Psalter La.)
Marples Cl. S8: Shef 1E 133
Marples Dr. S8: Shef 1E 133
Marquis Gdns. DN3: Barn D 1C 26
Marr Grange La. DN5: Marr 3A 38
Marrick Ct. S35: Chap 3E 79
Marrion Rd. S62: Rawm 2H 83
Marriott La. S7: Shef 5C 132
Marriott Pl. S62: Rawm 1E 83
Marriott Rd. S7: Shef 5C 132
　S64: Swint 2D 66
Marrison Dr. S21: Killa 4B 152
Marr Ter. S10: Shef 5G 117
Marsala Wlk. S73: D'fld 4A 34
Marsden Gdns. DN3: Kirk Sa 4B 26
　　　　(off Sandall La.)
Marsden Ind. Est. S13: Shef 4A 122
Marsden La. S3: Shef 2B 4 (2E 119)
Marsden M. WF9: Hems 1E 13
Marsden Pl. S40: Ches 6E 167
　　　　(South Pl.)
　S40: Ches 4H 167
　　　　(Spencer St.)
Marsden Rd. S36: Stoc 3E 175
Marsden St. S40: Ches 5H 167
Marshall Av. DN4: Balb 5H 55
Marshall Cl. S62: Parkg 5G 83
Marshall Gro. S63: Wath D 1G 65
Marshall Hall S10: Shef 5C 118
Marshall Rd. S8: Shef 6D 132
Marsh Av. S18: Dron 1G 155
Marsh Cl. S20: Mosb 4D 150
Marshfield S70: Birdw 3E 45
Marshfield Gro. S43: Stav 4D 164
Marsh Ga. DN5: Don 6A 40
Marsh Hill S66: Mick 1F 101
Marsh Ho. Rd. S11: Shef 3G 131
MARSH LANE 2H 157
Marsh La. DN3: Barn D 1H 25
　DN5: Ark 5C 24
　DN5: Ben 3C 24
　S10: Shef 3G 117
Marsh Quarry S21: Ecki 3B 158
Marsh Rd. DN5: Don 5B 40
Marsh St. S36: Spink 3F 175
　S60: Roth 5D 96
　S73: Womb 1H 47
Marsh Vw. S21: Ecki 2C 158
Marsh Wlk. S2: Shef 2A 120
　　　　(off Castle Ct.)
Marson Av. DN6: Woodl 3A 22
Marston Cl. S18: Dron W 4C 154
Marston Cres. S71: Smi 2E 17
Marstone Cres. S17: Tot 5F 145
Marston Rd. S10: Shef 2A 118
Martin S6: Shef 1A 4 (1D 118)

Martin Cl. S6: Shef 1D 118
  S26: Augh 4B 124
  S70: Birdw 4E 45
Martin Ct. S21: Ecki 1D 158
Martin Cres. S5: Shef 4G 93
Martin Cft. S75: Silk 2A 28
Martindale Cl. S43: Stav 6H 163
Martin La. S14: Black H 3A 46
Martin Ri. S21: Ecki 1D 158
  S61: Thorpe H 2D 80
Martin St. S6: Shef 1A 4 (2D 118)
                (not continuous)
Martin Well's Rd. DN12: New E 5D 70
Marton Rd. DN5: Ben 3G 23
Marvell Rd. DN5: Scaws 4E 39
Marvel Way S63: Wath D 5G 49
Mary Ann Ct. S71: Barn 6A 18
Mary Ann St. S41: Old W 2F 161
Maryhill Cl. S60: Tree 2G 123
Mary La. S73: D'fld 5C 34
Mary's Pl. S75: Barn 6B 16
Mary St. S1: Shef 6E 5 (5F 119)
  S21: Ecki 1E 159
  S60: Roth 3D 96
  S72: Midd 3F 35
  S75: Bar G 4E 15
Marys Wlk. S2: Shef 2A 120
                (off Castle Ct.)
Mary Tozer Ho. S10: Shef 3A 118
MASBROUGH 4B 96
Masbrough Rdbt. S60: Roth 4D 96
Masbrough St. S60: Roth 4C 96
              (not continuous)
Masefield Cl. S25: Dinn 6B 128
Masefield Flats S63: Wath D 5D 48
             (off Masefield Rd.)
Masefield Rd. DN2: Don 3H 41
  S13: Shef 1F 135
  S63: Wath D 5D 48
Masham Ct. DN4: Cant 4B 58
Masham Rd. DN4: Cant 5B 58
Mason Av. S26: Swal 5C 124
Mason Cres. S13: Shef 1G 135
Mason Dr. S26: Swal 5C 124
Mason Gro. S13: Shef 1G 135
Mason Lathe Rd. S5: Shef 5D 88
Mason St. S63: Gol 5D 36
Masons Way S70: Barn 4H 31
Mason Way S74: Hoyl 5A 46
Massey Rd. S13: Shef 3E 137
Masson Cl. S40: Ches 3E 167
Mastall La. DN5: Ark 6D 24
Masters Cres. S5: Shef 5G 93
Masters Rd. S5: Shef 5G 93
MASTIN MOOR 2F 165
Mather Av. S9: Shef 3E 121
Mather Cl. S9: Shef 3E 121
Mather Cres. S9: Shef 3E 121
Mather Dr. S9: Shef 3E 121
Mather Rd. S9: Shef 3E 121
Mather Wlk. S9: Shef 3E 121
               (off Mather Rd.)
Matilda La. S1: Shef 6F 5 (4G 119)
Matilda St. S1: Shef 5D 4 (4F 119)
              (not continuous)
Matilda Way S1: Shef 5D 4 (4F 119)
Matlock Dr. S43: Ink 3H 169
Matlock Rd. S6: Shef 1B 118
  S40: Walt 6A 170
  S42: Walt 6A 170
  S45: Ston E 6A 170
  S71: Ath 2G 17
Mattersey Cl. DN4: Bess 1B 74
Matthew Gap S36: Thurl 3A 176
Matthew Ho. S75: Barn 5C 16
Matthews Av. S63: Wath D 6E 49
Matthews Cl. S63: Wath D 1E 65
Matthews Dr. S66: Wick 1G 113
Matthews Fold S8: Shef 1H 147
Matthews La. S8: Shef 1H 147
Matthew St. S3: Shef 1C 4 (1E 119)
Maudesley Av. S40: Ches 1H 171
Mauds Ter. S71: Monk B 3H 17
Maugerhay S8: Shef 1H 147
Maulays Cl. DN11: Ross 6E 75
Mauncer Cres. S13: Shef 1C 136
Mauncer Dr. S13: Shef 1C 136
Mauncer La. S13: Shef 2C 136

Maun Way S5: Shef 1H 107
Maurice Dobson Museum &
  Heritage Centre, The 5C 34
Maurice St. S62: Parkg 5G 83
Mawfa Av. S14: Shef 6A 134
Mawfa Cres. S14: Shef 6A 134
Mawfa Dr. S14: Shef 6A 134
Mawfa La. S14: Shef 6A 134
               (Constable Rd.)
S14: Shef 6A 134
               (Ironside Cl.)
Mawfa Rd. S14: Shef 1A 148
Mawfa Wlk. S14: Shef 6A 134
Mawfield Rd. S75: Barn 4G 15
Maxey Pl. S8: Shef 2F 133
Maxfield Av. S10: Shef 3B 118
Maxwell St. S4: Shef 6H 107
Maxwell Way S4: Shef 6H 107
May Av. DN4: Balb 6H 55
  S41: Old W 3B 162
Mayberry Dr. S75: Silk 2A 28
May Cl. S63: Thurn 2C 36
Maycock Av. S61: Kimb P 6G 81
Maydal Dr. S75: Wool G 3E 7
May Day Grn. S70: Barn 1E 31
May Day Grn. Arc. S70: Barn 1E 31
               (off Cheapside)
Mayfield S36: Oxs 6H 177
  S71: Monk B 4G 17
Mayfield Alpacas 4A 130
Mayfield Ct. S10: Shef 6D 116
  S36: Oxs 6H 177
Mayfield Cres. DN11: New R 6C 74
  S70: Wors 4D 30
Mayfield Hgts. S10: Shef 1E 131
Mayfield Rd. DN5: Don 5H 39
  S10: Shef 1A 130
  S40: Bramp 6D 166
Mayfields DN5: Scawt 1E 39
Mayflower Ct. S12: Shef 2E 135
Mayflower Cres. DN4: Warm 1D 70
Mayflower Rd. DN4: Warm 1D 70
Mayflower Way S73: Womb 2H 47
Maynard Rd. S40: Ches 1G 171
  S60: Roth 1B 112
May Rd. S6: Shef 4A 106
May Ter. S70: Barn 1B 30
Maythorne Cl. S75: Stain 6B 8
May Tree Cl. S20: Water 1F 151
Maytree Cl. S73: D'fld 5B 34
May Tree Dr. S20: Water 1F 151
May Tree La. S20: Water 1F 151
Meaburn Cl. DN4: Cant 4C 58
Mead, The S41: Has 2B 172
Meadow, The DN5: Sprot 3D 54
Meadow Av. S62: Rawm 1E 83
  S72: Cud 4G 19
Meadow Bank Av. S7: Shef 1C 132
Meadowbank Cl. S61: Kimb 4B 96
Meadow Bank Ind. Est. S61: Kimb . .5A 96
Meadow Bank Rd. S11: Shef 1C 132
  S61: Kimb 6F 95
Meadow Bank Works S61: Kimb 5G 95
Meadowbrook Ind. Est. S20: Half . . .2H 151
Meadowbrook Pk. S20: Half 3H 151
Meadow Cl. S18: Coal A 6H 147
  S26: Kiv P 5C 140
  S43: New W 4C 162
  S65: Dalt 1D 98
Meadow Ct. DN3: Arm 4F 43
  DN6: Adw S 2D 22
  DN11: New R 6B 74
  S43: New W 2C 162
              (off Bamford St.)
  S71: Roy 3A 10
Meadowcourt S9: Shef 2E 109
Meadow Cres. S20: Mosb 3C 150
  S71: Roy 2A 10
  S72: Grim 1A 20
Meadow Cft. DN3: Eden 6D 26
  DN5: Sprot 4E 55
  S64: Swint 6B 66
  S72: Shaft 3F 11
  WF9: Hems 1F 13
Meadowcroft Cl. S60: Whist 4A 112
Meadowcroft Gdns. S20: Westf 2F 151
Meadowcroft Glade
  S20: Westf 2F 151
Meadowcroft Ri. S20: Westf 2F 151

Meadow Dr. S35: Chap 3D 78
  S64: Swint 4B 66
  S71: Monk B 4A 18
  S73: D'fld 5C 34
Meadowfield Dr. S74: Hoyl 2B 62
Meadow Fld. Rd. DN3: Barn D 2D 26
Meadow Ga. S73: Womb 3B 48
Meadowgate S63: Bramp B 6A 48
Meadow Gate Av. S20: Sot 5A 138
Meadow Gate Cl. S20: Sot 6A 138
Meadowgate Lake Nature Reserve
  . . . . .2C 152
Meadow Gate La. S20: Sot 1A 152
Meadowgate Pk. S21: Killa 3C 152
Meadowgates S63: Bolt D 1B 50
Meadow Gro. S17: Tot 6F 145
Meadow Gro. Rd. S17: Tot 6E 145
MEADOWHALL 1F 109
Meadowhall (Park & Ride) 6E 95
Meadowhall Cen. S9: Shef 2F 109
Meadowhall Dr. S9: Shef 3E 109
Meadowhall Interchange Stop (ST)
  . . . . .1F 109
Meadowhall Retail Pk. S9: Shef 4F 109
Meadowhall Rd. S9: Shef 2E 109
  S61: Kimb 5F 95
Meadowhall South / Tinsley Stop (ST)
  . . . . .2G 109
Meadowhall Station (Rail) 1E 109
Meadowhall Way S9: Shef 1F 109
MEADOW HEAD 6E 133
Meadowhead S8: Shef 1E 147
Meadow Head Av. S8: Shef 3D 146
Meadow Head Cl. S8: Shef 3D 146
Meadow Head Dr. S8: Shef 2E 147
Meadowhill Rd. S41: Has 2C 172
Meadow Ho. Dr. S10: Shef 5E 117
Meadowland Ri. S72: Cud 3F 19
Meadow La. DN12: Old D 3F 67
  S62: Rawm 6E 65
  S66: Malt 6B 102
  S75: Dart 1F 15
Meadowpark Cft. S25: Dinn 6H 127
Meadow Rise DN3: Barn D 1D 26
  DN11: Wad 6F 73
  S42: Ash 4A 166
Meadow Rd. S71: Roy 3A 10
Meadows, The S21: Killa 4C 152
  S26: Tod 3B 140
  S42: Ash 3A 166
  S75: Bar G 4F 15
  S75: Silk C 5A 28
Meadows Cl. DN11: Ross 4A 74
Meadows Dr. S43: Stav 5B 164
Meadowside Cl. S42: W'orth 6H 171
Meadows Rd. S63: Wath D 5H 49
Meadow St. S3: Shef 1B 4 (1E 119)
  S25: Laugh C 4F 127
               (not continuous)
  S61: Roth 4B 96
  S71: Barn 6E 17
Meadow Ter. S11: Shef 6B 118
MEADOW VIEW 6C 66
Meadow Vw. S36: H'swne 1F 177
  S40: Bramp 2B 170
  S70: Wors 5F 31
Meadow Vw. Cl. S74: Hoyl 1A 62
Meadow Vw. Dr. S65: Rav 2B 100
Meadow Vw. Rd. S8: Shef 2E 147
  S64: Kiln 6C 66
Meadow Wlk. DN3: Eden 5D 26
Meadow Way S64: Swint 3E 67
Meads, The S8: Shef 2G 147
Meadstead Dr. S71: Roy 3G 9
Meadstead Fold S71: Roy 3G 9
Meadway, The S17: Dore 3E 145
Meadway Dr. S17: Dore 3D 144
Meakin St. S41: Has 2C 172
Mears Cl. S36: Pen 4E 177
MEASBOROUGH DIKE 3G 31
Mecca Bingo
  Chesterfield 5G 167
  Doncaster 1C 56
  Rotherham 4E 97
  Sheffield, Flat St. . . .3F 5 (3G 119)
  Sheffield, Langsett Rd. 6D 106
Mede, The DN6: Woodl 3A 22
Medina Way S75: Bar G 3F 15
Medlar Cft. S75: Barn 6C 16

Medley Vw. DN12: Con 5G **69**
Medlock Cl. S13: Shef 5B **122**
S42: Walt 3C **170**
Medlock Ct. S25: Dinn 6A **128**
Medlock Cres. S13: Shef 4B **122**
Medlock Cft. S13: Shef 4B **122**
Medlock Dr. S13: Shef 5B **122**
Medlock Rd. S13: Shef 5B **122**
S40: Walt 2D **170**
Medlock Way S13: Shef 4B **122**
Medway Cl. S75: Bar G 3G **15**
Medway Pl. S73: Womb 3A **48**
MEERSBROOK 3G **133**
Meersbrook Av. S8: Shef 3E **133**
MEERSBROOK BANK 3E **133**
Meersbrook Ent. Cen.
S8: Shef 2F **133**
Meersbrook Pk. Rd. S8: Shef 2F **133**
Meersbrook Rd. S8: Shef 3G **133**
Meetinghouse Cft. S13: Shef 2D **136**
Meetinghouse La. S1: Shef . . .2F **5** (2G **119**)
S13: Shef 2D **136**
Mekyll Cl. S66: Sunn 4G **99**
Melbeck Ct. S35: Chap 3D **78**
Melbourne Av. S10: Shef 4B **118**
S18: Dron W 3A **154**
S26: Ast 6D **124**
S63: Bolt D 2A **50**
Melbourne Ct. *S43: Stav* *4B* ***164***
(off Duke St.)
Melbourne Rd. DN4: Balb 6F **55**
S36: Stoc 3C **174**
Melbourn Rd. S10: Shef 2B **118**
Melciss Rd. S66: Wick 6F **99**
Meld Cl. DN11: New R 6G **75**
Melford Cl. S75: Mapp 5A **8**
Melford Dr. DN4: Balb 2H **71**
Melfort Glen S10: Shef 3G **117**
Mell Av. S74: Hoyl 6B **46**
Melling Av. DN5: Don 1G **55**
Melling Cl. S40: Birdh 2G **171**
Melling Ct. S40: Birdh 2G **171**
Mellington Cl. S8: Shef 6H **133**
Mellor La. S18: B'low 5A **160**
Mellor Lea Farm Chase S35: Eccl 6G **79**
Mellor Lea Farm Cl. *S35: Eccl* *6G* ***79***
(off Mellor Lea Farm Dr.)
Mellor Lea Farm Dr. S35: Eccl 6G **79**
Mellor Lea Farm Gth. *S35: Eccl* *6G* ***79***
(off Mellor Lea Farm Dr.)
Mellor Rd. S73: Womb 2G **47**
Mellor Way S40: Birdh 3H **171**
Mellow Flds. Rd. S25: Laugh M 2G **127**
Mellwood Gro. S73: Hem 4F **47**
Melrose Cl. DN4: Balb 5F **55**
S40: Ash 5D **166**
S66: Thurc 6A **114**
Melrose Cotts. S60: Whist 3B **112**
Melrose Gro. S60: Roth 2H **111**
Melrose Rd. S3: Shef 5G **107**
Melrose Way S71: Monk B 6A **18**
Meltham La. S41: Ches 2A **168**
Melton Av. S63: Gol 5D **36**
S73: Bramp 4C **48**
MELTON BRAND 1H **53**
Melton Ct. DN12: Den M 2C **68**
S26: Ast 1F **139**
Meltonfield S63: Gol 5E **37**
Meltonfield Cl. DN3: Arm 5F **43**
Melton Gdns. DN5: Sprot 3C **54**
Melton Grn. S63: Wath D 6D **48**
Melton Gro. S20: Mosb 6B **136**
Melton High St. S63: Wath D 6D **48**
Melton Mill La. DN5: High M 3C **52**
Melton Rd. DN5: Sprot 3G **53**
Melton St. S64: Mexb 2H **67**
S73: Bramp 4C **48**
Melton Ter. S70: Wors 5H **31**
Melton Vw. DN5: Barnb 1H **51**
Melton Way S71: Roy 1H **9**
Melton Wood Gro. DN5: Sprot 3C **54**
Melville Av. DN4: Balb 5H **55**
Melville Cres. S43: Brim C 4E **169**
Melville Dr. S2: Shef 6D **120**
Melville St. S73: Womb 1G **47**
Melvinia Cres. S75: Barn 4C **16**
Melwood Ct. DN3: Arm 6F **43**
Memoir Gro. DN11: New R 6F **75**
Memory La. S25: Nth A 2G **141**

Mendip Cl. DN5: Cus 5F **39**
S75: Barn 6A **16**
Mendip Cres. S40: Ash 4C **166**
Mendip Ri. S60: Brins 5E **111**
Merbeck Dr. S35: High G 5D **60**
Merbeck Gro. S35: High G 6D **60**
Mercaston Cl. S40: Ches 3B **166**
Mercel Av. DN3: Arm 2F **43**
Merchant Cft. S71: Monk B 3A **18**
Merchants Cres.
S2: Shef 2G **5** (2H **119**)
Merchant Way DN2: Don 1H **41**
Mercia Dr. S17: Dore 4F **145**
Meredith Cres. DN4: Balb 6A **56**
Meredith Rd. S6: Shef 4A **106**
Mere Gro. DN3: Arm 2D **42**
Mere La. DN3: Arm, Eden 3D **42**
(not continuous)
Mere Vw. S63: Wath D 5F **49**
Merlin Cl. DN6: Adw S 2C **22**
S70: Birdw 4E **45**
Merlin Way S5: Shef 1H **107**
S61: Thorpe H 2D **80**
Merrick Cl. S40: Ches 3E **167**
Merrill Rd. S63: Thurn 2B **36**
Merton La. S9: Shef 6E **95**
Merton Ri. S9: Shef 6E **95**
Merton Rd. S9: Shef 6E **95**
Metcalfe Av. S21: Killa 4B **152**
Methley Cl. S12: Shef 2C **134**
Methley Ho. *DN1: Don* *2B* ***56***
(off Grove Pl.)
Methley St. S72: Cud 2E **19**
Metrodome Leisure Complex, The . . .6F **17**
Metro Trad. Cen. S75: Bar G 3F **15**
Mews, The *DN5: Hick* *3H* ***37***
(off Castle Hill Fold)
Mews Ct. DN3: Arm 3F **43**
MEXBOROUGH 2F **67**
Mexborough Bus. Cen. S64: Mexb . . .1G **67**
Mexborough Rd. S63: Bolt D 3C **50**
Mexborough Station (Rail) 2F **67**
Meynell Cl. S40: Bramp 6D **166**
Meynell Cres. S5: Shef 6C **92**
Meynell Rd. S5: Shef 6C **92**
Meynell Way *S21: Killa* *4B* ***152***
(off Marrison Dr.)
Meyrick Dr. S75: Dart 1E **15**
Michael Cl. S42: W'orth 5H **171**
Michael Cft. S63: Wath D 6E **49**
Michael Rd. S71: Lund 6B **18**
Michael's Est. S72: Grim 1B **20**
MICKLEBRING 6G **87**
Micklebring Gro. DN12: Con 6D **68**
Micklebring La. S66: B'well, Mick 6G **87**
Micklebring Way S66: Hel 3E **101**
Mickleden Way S75: Barn 1H **29**
MICKLEY 1A **154**
Mickley La. S17: Tot 6F **145**
S18: Dron W . . . . .6F **145** & 1A **154**
Middle Av. S62: Rawm 3G **83**
Middle Bank DN4: Don 4D **56**
Middleburn Cl. S70: Barn 3F **31**
Middlecliff Cl. S20: Water 1F **151**
Middlecliff Cotts. S72: Midd 3F **35**
Middlecliff Ct. S20: Water 1F **151**
MIDDLECLIFFE 3F **35**
Middlecliff La. S72: Lit H, Midd 2D **34**
Middlecliff Ri. S20: Water 1F **151**
Middle Cl. S75: Kexb 5D **6**
MIDDLECROFT 6H **163**
Middlecroft Rd. S43: Stav 1H **169**
Middle Dr. S60: Roth 3G **111**
Middle Farm Ct. S71: D'fld 2A **34**
Middlefield Cl. S17: Dore 3D **144**
Middlefield Cft. S17: Dore 3D **144**
Middle Fld. La. WF4: Wool 1F **7**
Middle Fld. Rd. S75: Silk 2E **29**
Middlefield Rd. DN4: Bess 5A **58**
S60: Roth 2H **111**
Middlefields Dr. S60: Whist 3B **112**
Middlegate DN5: Scawt 1F **39**
(not continuous)
Middleham Rd. DN4: Cant 5B **58**
MIDDLE HANDLEY 4A **158**
Middle Hay Cl. S14: Shef 3B **134**
Middle Hay Pl. S14: Shef 4B **134**
Middle Hay Ri. S14: Shef 4B **134**
Middle Hay Vw. S14: Shef 4B **134**

Middle La. DN4: Warm 2E **71**
S6: Shef 6H **105**
S35: Gren 1A **92**
S65: Roth 3G **97**
Middle La. Sth. S65: Roth 4H **97**
Middle Ox Cl. S20: Half 4G **151**
Middle Ox Gdns. S20: Half 4G **151**
Middle Pavement *S40: Ches* *5H* ***167***
(off Central Pavement)
Middlepeak Way S13: Shef 4A **122**
Middle Pl. S65: Roth 3A **98**
Middlesex St. S70: Barn 3E **31**
Middle Shambles *S40: Ches* *5H* ***167***
(off High St.)
Middleton Av. S25: Dinn 6H **127**
Middleton Dr. S43: Ink 3G **169**
Middleton La. S35: Gren 2C **92**
Middleton Rd. S65: Roth 4G **97**
MIDDLEWOOD 6G **91**
Middlewood (Park & Tram) 1A **106**
Middlewood Chase S6: Shef 1H **105**
Middlewood Dr. S6: Shef 1G **105**
S61: Scho 6F **81**
Middlewood Dr. E. S6: Shef 1G **105**
Middlewood Lodge S6: Shef 1H **105**
Middlewood Ri. S6: Shef 1H **105**
Middlewood Rd. S6: Shef 6H **91**
Middlewood Rd. Nth. S35: Ough 4F **91**
Middlewoods S75: Dod 3H **29**
Middlewood Stop (ST) 1A **106**
Middlewoods Way S71: Ath 6G **9**
Midfield Rd. S10: Shef 2H **117**
Midhill Cres. S2: Shef 1G **133**
Midhill Rd. S2: Shef 1G **133**
Midhope Way S75: Barn 1H **29**
Midhurst Gro. S75: Bar G 3F **15**
Midhurst Rd. S6: Shef 4A **92**
Midland Cotts. S41: Has 3A **172**
Midland Ct. S41: Has 3A **172**
S60: Roth 4C **96**
S61: Roth 4B **96**
Midland Rd. S61: Roth 4B **96**
S64: Swint 3D **66**
S71: Roy .2H **9**
Midland St. S1: Shef 5F **119**
S62: Parkg 6G **83**
S70: Barn 1E **31**
Midland Ter. S41: Has 3A **172**
S43: Bar H 2G **163**
Midvale Av. S6: Shef 6D **106**
Midvale Cl. S6: Shef 6D **106**
Milano Ri. S73: D'fld 5A **34**
Milbanke St. DN1: Don 6C **40**
Milburn Ct. S20: Sot 1H **151**
Milburn Gro. S20: Sot 1H **151**
Milden Pl. S70: Barn 3F **31**
Milden Rd. S6: Shef 2H **105**
Milefield Ct. S72: Grim 1A **20**
Milefield La. S72: Grim, Shaft 1H **19**
Milefield Vw. S72: Grim 1A **20**
MILEHILL 5E **173**
Mile Oak Rd. S60: Roth 1G **111**
Miles Cl. S5: Shef 3F **107**
Miles Rd. S5: Shef 3E **107**
S35: High G 1D **78**
Milestone Ct. DN4: Bess 5B **58**
Mileswood Cl. S72: Gt H 5E **21**
Milethorn La. DN1: Don 5C **40**
Milford Av. S74: Els 6E **47**
Milford Rd. S43: Ink 3H **169**
Milford St. S9: Shef 4E **109**
Milgate St. S71: Roy 2A **10**
Milgrove Cres. S35: High G 6C **60**
Milking La. S73: Bramp 5B **48**
Millais Ri. S66: Flan 3G **99**
Millard La. S66: Malt 5B **102**
Millars Wlk. WF9: Sth K 5H **13**
Millbank Cl. S35: High G 2C **78**
Mill Cl. S25: Brook 6G **115**
S26: Tod 4C **140**
S60: Roth 6D **96**
WF9: Sth K 4H **13**
Mill Ct. S35: Eccl 1G **93**
S70: Wors 5F **31**
Millcross La. S18: B'low 3A **160**
Milldale Cl. S40: Ches 3D **166**
Milldale Rd. S17: Tot 5G **145**
Milldyke Cl. S60: Whist 3C **112**
Millennium Gallery 4F **5** (3G **119**)

Millennium Sq. S1: Shef 4E 5 (3F 119)
Millennium Way S41: Whit M 5F 161
Miller Av. S43: Mas M 2F 165
Miller Cft. S13: Shef 2B 136
Miller Dale Dr. S60: Brins 5E 111
Miller Rd. S7: Shef 1E 133
Millers Cft. S71: Roy 2H 9
Millers Dale S70: Wors 6F 31
Miller St. S36: Spink 3H 175
Mill Fld. Ct. DN3: Barn D 2D 26
Millfield Ind. Est. DN5: Ben 1B 40
Millfield Rd. DN5: Ben 2B 40
Mill Flds. S26: Tod 4B 140
Mill Ga. DN5: Ben 2A 40
Mill Grn. S43: Stav 4B 164
Mill Haven S25: Nth A 3G 141
Mill Hill S60: Whist 3B 112
  S73: Womb 6E 33
Mill Hill Cl. DN5: Don 1G 55
Millhill Cl. DN3: Arm 6F 43
Mill Hills S26: Tod 3C 140
Millhouse Ct. S65: Dalt 1B 98
Mill Ho. M. S43: Stav 4B 164

MILLHOUSES
  S7 . . . . .5C 132
  S73 . . . . .4D 34
Millhouses Ct. S11: Shef 4A 132
Millhouses Glen S11: Shef 4A 132
Millhouses La. S7: Shef 3H 131
  S11: Shef 3H 131
Millhouses St. S74: Hoyl 1B 62
Millicent Av. S66: Malt 6B 102
Millindale S66: Malt 6B 102
Mill La. DN3: Brant 4F 59
  DN4: Warm 4C 54
  DN5: H'ton 3H 51
  DN6: Adw S 2C 22
  S17: Tot 5G 145
  S18: Dron 3G 155
  S21: Reni 2H 159
  S25: Sth A 3G 141
  S36: Spink 3H 175
  S36: Thurl 4A 176
  S40: Ches 6E 167
  S42: Tem N 6G 173
  S44: Stan 6H 165
  S60: Tree 2E 123
  S62: Wentw 4C 62
  S63: Wath D 1D 64
  S75: Dart 5F 7
  WF9: Sth K 5H 13
Mill Mdw. Cl. S20: Sot 1A 152
Mill Mdw. Gdns. S20: Sot 1A 152
Millmoor Ct. S73: Womb 6A 34
Millmoor La. S60: Roth 4C 96
Millmoor Rd. DN4: Cant 4B 58
  S73: Womb 6A 34
Millmount Rd. S8: Shef 3E 133
  S74: Hoyl .1C 62
Millrace Dr. S63: Gol 6B 36
Mill Rd. S21: Ecki 6E 151
  S35: Eccl 1G 93
  S60: Tree 2E 123
Mill Rd. Cl. S35: Eccl 1G 93
Millsands S3: Shef 1F 5 (1G 119)
Millside S72: Shaft 3F 11
Millside Ct. DN5: Ben 2A 40
Millside Wlk. S72: Shaft 3F 11
Millstone Cl. S18: Dron W 2C 154
Millstone Dr. S26: Ast 6C 124
Millstones S36: Oxs 6H 177
Mill Stream Cl. S40: Walt 1D 170
Millstream Cl. DN5: Sprot 3E 55
Mill St. DN3: Arm 4E 43
  S41: Ches 5A 168
  S60: Roth 5E 97
  S61: Grea 4C 82
  WF9: Sth K 4H 13
Millthorpe Rd. S8: Shef 6A 94
Millua S3: Shef 1F 119
          (off Kelham Island)
Mill Vw. S63: Bolt D 3A 50
Millwood Rd. DN4: Balb 1G 71
Millwood Vw. S6: Stann 5D 104
Milner Av. S36: Pen 3B 176
Milner Cl. S66: Braml 4B 100
Milner Ga. DN12: Con 3G 69
          (not continuous)
Milner Ga. Ct. DN12: Con 4H 69

Milner Ga. La. DN12: Con 4G 69
Milner Rd. DN4: Balb 5G 55
Milnes St. S70: Barn 2F 31
Milne St. S75: Bar G 4F 15
Milnrow Cres. S5: Shef 4E 93
Milnrow Dr. S5: Shef 4E 93
Milnrow Rd. S5: Shef 4E 93
Milnrow Vw. S5: Shef 4E 93
MILTON .2B 62
Milton Av. DN5: Don 6G 39
Milton Cl. S61: Grea 4C 82
  S63: Wath D 4C 48
  S74: Jum 5C 46
Milton Ct. DN1: Don 2C 56
  S64: Swint 3B 66
Milton Cres. S40: Birdh 2H 171
  S74: Hoyl 1B 62
Milton Gro. DN3: Arm 4E 43
  DN3: Eden 6C 26
  S73: Womb 6F 33
Milton La. S3: Shef 6C 4 (4E 119)
Milton Pl. S43: Stav 4C 164
Milton Rd. DN3: Brant 3H 59
  S7: Shef 1D 132
  S25: Dinn 6B 128
  S35: Burn 3C 78
  S64: Mexb 1F 67
  S65: Roth 2G 97
  S74: Hoyl 6B 46
Milton St. S1: Shef 6B 4 (4E 119)
  S1: Shef 6B 4 (4E 119)
  S60: Roth 2D 96
  S64: Swint 3B 66
  S66: Malt 6A 102
  S72: G H 6E 21
Milton Wlk. DN1: Don 2B 56
Minden Cl. S66: Wick 6G 99
Minden Ct. DN5: Ben 1H 39
Minimum Ter. S40: Ches 6F 167
Minna Rd. S3: Shef 5G 107
Minneymoor Hill DN12: Con 3G 69
Minneymoor La. DN12: Con 4G 69
Minster Cl. DN4: Cant 5D 58
  S35: Eccl 2H 93
Minster Rd. S35: Eccl 2G 93
Minster Way S71: Monk B 5A 18
Minto Rd. S6: Shef 3A 106
Miriam Av. S40: Bramp 2B 170
Mission Cl. S75: Wool G 3F 7
          (off Wooley Edge La.)
Mission Fld. S73: Bramp 4B 48
Mitchell Cl. S70: Wors 5A 32
Mitchell Rd. S8: Shef 6E 133
  S73: Womb 5F 33
Mitchells Ent. Cen. S73: Womb 5F 33
Mitchell St. S3: Shef 2A 4 (2D 118)
  S70: Swai 5B 32
Mitchells Way S73: Womb 6F 33
Mitchell Way S43: New W 3D 162
Mitchelson Av. S75: Dod 3F 29
Moat Cl. S66: Surn 3H 99
Moat Cft. DN5: Scawt 1G 39
Moat Hills Ct. DN5: Ben 1A 40
Moat Ho. Way DN12: Con 3F 69
Moatlands S66: Wick 2H 113
Moat La. S66: Wick 3H 113
Mobray Dr. S75: Wool G 3F 7
Modena Ct. S73: D'fld 4H 33
Moffat Gdns. DN2: Don 1A 42
Moffatt Rd. S2: Shef 1G 133
Molineaux Cl. S5: Shef 5A 94
Molineaux Rd. S5: Shef 4H 93
Molineux Av. S43: Stav 5A 164
Molloy Pl. S8: Shef 2F 133
Molloy St. S8: Shef 2F 133
Momentum Leisure Cen. 2B 4
Mona Av. S10: Shef 2B 118
Mona Rd. DN4: Balb 4A 56
  S10: Shef 2B 118
Mona St. S75: Barn 6C 16
Monckton St. S75: Barn 1C 108
Moncrieffe Rd. S7: Shef 2D 132
MONK BRETTON 4G 17
Monk Bretton Priory (remains) 6B 18
Monksbridge Rd. S25: Laugh C 4F 127
Monk's Bri. Trad. Est.
  S25: Laugh C 4G 127
Monks Cl. S61: Kimb P 6F 81
Monkspring S70: Wors 5H 31

Monks Way S71: Monk B 5A 18
Monk Ter. S71: Monk B 3B 18
Monkton Way S71: Roy 1H 9
MONKWOOD 3B 160
Monkwood Rd. S41: Ches 6E 161
  S62: Rawm 1E 83
Monmouth Rd. DN2: Don 4F 41
Monmouth St. S1: Shef 5A 4 (4D 118)
Monsal Cres. S43: Ink 2G 169
Monsal St. S63: Thurn 2B 36
  S31: Ath .1F 17
Montague Av. DN12: Con 4D 68
Montague St. DN1: Don 6C 40
  S6: Shef 5C 106
  S11: Shef 5D 118
  S72: Cud 6F 11
Montagu Rd. DN5: Don 2F 55
Montagu Sq. S64: Mexb 2F 67
Montagu St. S64: Mexb 2G 67
Monteney Cres. S5: Shef 2F 93
Monteney Gdns. S5: Shef 3F 93
Monteney Rd. S5: Shef 3F 93
Montfort Dr. S3: Shef 6G 107
Montgomery Av. S7: Shef 1D 132
Montgomery Cl. S60: Tree 3G 123
Montgomery Ct. S11: Shef 3H 131
Montgomery Dr. S7: Shef 1D 132
Montgomery Gdns. DN2: Don 4H 41
Montgomery M. S63: Wath D 6E 49
Montgomery Rd. S7: Shef 2D 132
  S63: Wath D 6F 49
Montgomery Sq. S63: Wath D 6G 49
Montgomery Ter. Rd. S6: Shef 1E 119
Montgomery Theatre 4E 5 (3F 119)
Montrose Av. DN2: Don 5G 41
  S75: Dart .5G 7
Montrose Ct. S11: Shef 4G 131
Montrose Pl. S18: Dron W 2C 154
Montrose Rd. S7: Shef 3B 132
Mont Wlk. S73: Womb 6D 32
Monument Dr. S72: Brier 4A 12
Monyash St. S43: Stav 1H 169
Moonpenny Way S18: Dron 3F 155
Moonshine La. S5: Shef 1E 107
Moonshine Way S5: Shef 2E 107
Moor, The S1: Shef 6D 4 (4F 119)
Moorbank Cl. S10: Shef 4E 117
  S73: Womb 6E 33
Moorbank Ct. S10: Shef 3E 117
Moorbank Dr. S10: Shef 3E 117
Moorbank Rd. S10: Shef 3E 117
  S73: Womb 5E 33
Moorbank Vw. S73: Womb 5E 33
Moorbridge Cres. S73: Bramp 3C 48
Moor Cres. S20: Mosb 3D 150
Moorcrest Ri. S75: Stain 4A 8
Moorcroft Av. S10: Shef 1C 130
Moorcroft Cl. S10: Shef 1C 130
Moorcroft Dr. S10: Shef 1C 130
Moorcroft Ho. S40: Ches 1H 171
          (off Archdale Cl.)
Moorcroft Rd. S10: Shef 1C 130
Moordale Vw. S62: Rawm 1B 84
Moor End Ho's. S75: Silk C 5C 28
Moorend La. S75: Silk C 5B 28
Moor End Rd. S10: Shef 2B 118
Moore St. S3: Shef 6B 4 (5E 119)
Moor Farm Av. S20: Mosb 2C 150
Moor Farm Gth. S20: Mosb 2C 150
Moor Farm Ri. S20: Mosb 2C 150
Moorfield Av. S65: Rav 3A 100
Moorfield Cl. S65: Rav 3A 100
Moorfield Dr. DN3: Arm 5E 43
Moorfield Gro. S65: Rav 3A 100
Moorfield Pl. WF9: Hems 1D 12
Moorfields S3: Shef 1D 4 (2F 119)
Moorfields Flats S3: Shef 1D 4
          (off Moorfields)
Moor Gap DN3: Brant 4G 59
MOORGATE 2H 111
Moorgate Av. S10: Shef 2C 118
  S60: Roth 6F 97
Moorgate Bus. Cen. S60: Roth 5F 97
          (off Moorgate Rd.)
Moorgate Chase S60: Roth 5F 97
Moorgate Cl. S60: Roth 5F 97
Moorgate Cres. S18: Dron 4G 155
Moorgate Gro. S60: Roth 6G 97

Moorgate La. S60: Roth 6F **97**
Moorgate Rd. S60: Roth 5F **97**
Moorgate St. S60: Roth 4E **97**
Moorgate Vw. S60: Roth 1G **111**
Moorgate Wlk. S60: Roth 6F **97**
Moor Grn. Cl. S75: Barn 1H **29**
Moorhay Cl. S41: Ches 1C **166**
Moorhead S1: Shef 5D **4**
Moorhead Way S66: Braml 5C **100**
Moorhouse Cl. S60: Whist 3C **112**
Moorhouse La. S60: Whist 3B **112**
S75: Hai 1D **6**
Moorings, The S64: Swint 3D **66**
Moorland Av. S70: Barn 2A **30**
S75: Stain .4A **8**
Moorland Ct. DN1: Don 1D **56**
Moorland Cres. S75: Stain 4A **8**
Moorland Dr. S36: Stoc 3C **174**
Moorland Gro. DN4: Bess 3H **57**
Moorland Pl. S6: Stann 6D **104**
S75: Silk C 5B **28**
Moorlands S66: Wick 6E **99**
Moorlands Ct. S63: Wath D 4D **48**
Moorlands Cres. S60: Whist 3B **112**
Moorland Ter. S72: Cud 3F **19**
Moorland Vw. S12: Shef 6D **134**
S18: App 3D **156**
S26: Ast 1D **138**
S63: Wath D 4D **48**
Moorland Vw. Rd. S40: Walt 2D **170**
Moor La. DN3: Kirk Sa 3A **26**
S44: Ark T, Cal 3H **173**
S66: Mick 1E **101**
S70: Birdw 1E **61**
S72: Brier, Gt H 5E **13**
Moor La. Nth. S65: Rav 6A **86**
Moor La. Sth. S65: Rav 2A **100**
Moor Ley S70: Birdw 3E **45**
Moor Oaks Rd. S10: Shef 3B **118**
Moor Pk. Av. S40: Walt 2D **170**
Moor Rd. S6: Bradf 1A **104**
S63: Wath D 6G **49**
(not continuous)
S65: Roth 4A **98**
Moorshutt Rd. WF9: Hems 1D **12**
Moorside S10: Shef 6B **116**
Moorside Av. S36: Cub 5D **176**
Moorside Cl. S20: Mosb 2D **150**
S75: Mapp 6A **8**
Moorsyde Av. S10: Shef 1A **118**
Moorsyde Cres. S10: Shef 1A **118**
Moorthorpe Bank S20: Mosb 6C **136**
Moorthorpe Dell S20: Mosb 6C **136**
Moorthorpe Gdns. S20: Mosb 6B **136**
Moorthorpe Grn. S20: Mosb 6A **136**
Moorthorpe Ri. S20: Mosb 1C **150**
Moorthorpe Vw. S20: Mosb 1B **150**
Moorthorpe Way S20: Mosb 6C **136**
(Moorthorpe Bank)
S20: Mosb 6A **136**
(Sheffield Rd.)
Moor Top Dr. WF9: Hems 1E **13**
Moortop Rd. S18: App 3E **157**
Moortown Av. S25: Dinn 1B **142**
Moor Valley S20: Mosb 6A **136**
Moor Valley Cl. S20: Mosb 1B **150**
Moor Vw. DN3: Brant 4G **59**
Moorview S61: Kimb 4G **95**
Moorview Cl. S42: W'orth 6A **172**
S43: Brim 1C **168**
Moorview Ct. S17: Bradw 5A **146**
S61: Kimb 4G **95**
Moor Vw. Dr. S8: Shef 6D **132**
Moor Vw. Rd. S8: Shef 6D **132**
S43: Stav 4D **164**
Moor Vw. Ter. S11: Shef 3F **131**
Moorwinstow Cft. S17: Dore 3F **145**
Moorwoods Av. S35: Chap 3F **79**
Moorwoods La. S35: Chap 3F **79**
Moray Pl. S18: Dron W 2C **154**
Mordaunt Rd. S2: Shef 2C **134**
More Hall La. S36: Bolst 6G **175**
More Hall Vw. S35: Wharn S 1A **90**
Morgan Av. S5: Shef 2E **107**
Morgan Cl. S5: Shef 1E **107**
Morgan Rd. DN2: Don 6H **41**
S5: Shef 2E **107**
Morland Bank S14: Shef 5B **134**
Morland Cl. S14: Shef 5C **134**
Morland Dr. S14: Shef 5C **134**
Morland Pl. S14: Shef 5C **134**
Morland Rd. S14: Shef 5B **134**
Morley Av. S40: Ash 4D **166**
Morley Cl. S18: Dron W 3B **154**
Morley Pl. DN12: Con 5E **69**
Morley Rd. DN1: Don 5D **40**
S61: Kimb P 1H **95**
Morley St. S6: Shef 5A **106**
S62: Parkg 4G **83**
Morpeth Gdns. S3: Shef 1B **4**
Morpeth St. S3: Shef 1B **4** (2E **119**)
S65: Roth 4F **97**
Morrall Rd. S5: Shef 3E **93**
Morrell St. S66: Malt 6B **102**
Morris Av. S41: Ches 3F **167**
S62: Rawm 6G **65**
Morris Dr. S41: Ches 3F **167**
Morrison Av. S66: Malt 4B **102**
Morrison Dr. DN11: New R 6D **74**
Morrison Pl. S73: D'fld 4B **34**
Morrison Rd. S73: D'fld 4A **34**
Morse Way S60: Cat, Shef 2B **122**
Morston Claycliffe Office Pk.
S75: Barn 4H **15**
Mortain Rd. S60: Roth 2G **111**
Mortains S26: Tod 2C **140**
MORTHEN .5G **113**
Morthen Cotts. S66: Mort 5F **113**
Morthen Gdns. S66: Wick 6G **99**
Morthen Hall La. S66: Mort 5G **113**
Morthen La. S60: Up W 6D **112**
S66: Mort 4F **113**
Morthen Rd.
S66: Thurc, Wick 6G **99**
Mortimer Dr. S36: Cub 6C **176**
Mortimer Hgts. S36: Cub 6C **176**
Mortimer Rd.
S36: Cub, Midh, Pen 6C **176**
S66: Malt 6D **102**
Mortimer St. S1: Shef 6F **5** (4G **119**)
Mortlake Rd. S5: Shef 2A **108**
MORTOMLEY 1D **78**
Mortomley Cl. S35: High G 1D **78**
Mortomley Cft. S35: Chap 1E **79**
Mortomley Hall Gdns. S35: High G . . .1D **78**
Mortomley La. S35: High G 6D **60**
Morton Cl. S71: Monk B 3A **18**
Morton Gdns. S20: Half 4G **151**
Morton La. S21: West H 3F **157**
Morton Mt. S20: Half 3G **151**
Morton Pl. S35: Gren 2B **92**
Morton Rd. S64: Mexb 1G **67**
MOSBOROUGH 3E **151**
Mosborough Hall Dr. S20: Half 5F **151**
Mosborough Moor S20: Mosb 2C **150**
Mosborough Parkway S12: Shef 3A **136**
S13: Shef 5G **121**
S20: Beig 3F **137**
Mosborough Rd. S13: Shef 1E **135**
Moscar Cotts. S7: Shef 4C **132**
Moscrop Cl. S13: Shef 1D **136**
Mosham Cl. DN9: Blax 1E **77**
Mosham Rd. DN9: Auck, Blax 2H **59**
Moss Beck Ct. S21: Ecki 1D **158**
Moss Cl. S66: Wick 6G **99**
Mossdale Av. S20: Mosb 3E **151**
Mossdale Cl. DN5: Scawt 3F **39**
Moss Dr. S21: Killa 5C **152**
Moss Gro. S12: Shef 5E **137**
Moss Ho. Ct. S20: Mosb 4E **151**
Mossley Pl. S36: Pen 4E **177**
Moss Ri. Pl. S21: Ecki 1D **158**
Moss Rd. S17: Tot 6B **144**
Moss Vw. S20: Mosb 4C **150**
Moss Way
S20: Water, Westf 5D **136**
Moss Way Stop (ST) 5E **137**
Moston Wlk. S40: Birdh 4F **171**
Motehall Dr. S2: Shef 5D **120**
Motehall Pl. S2: Shef 5E **121**
Motehall Rd. S2: Shef 5D **120**
Motehall Wlk. S2: Shef 5E **121**
Motehall Way S2: Shef 5D **120**
Motorpoint Arena 5E **109**
Motte, The S61: Kimb 2A **96**
Mottram St. S71: Barn 6E **17**
Mottram Way S71: Barn 6E **17**
Mound Rd. S40: Ches 1H **171**
Mount, The DN3: Eden 1D **42**
S41: Old W 3H **161**
S66: Sunn 3G **99**
Mount Av. S72: Grim 6B **12**
S72: Gt H 1F **35**
Mountbatten Dr. S35: Burn 3C **78**
Mountcastle St. S41: Ches 6G **161**
Mountcastle Wlk. S41: Ches 6G **161**
Mount Cl. S70: Barn 3E **31**
Mount Cres. S74: Hoyl 5A **46**
Mountenoy Rd. S60: Roth 5E **97**
Mountfield Way S25: Laugh C 4F **127**
Mountford Cft. S17: Tot 5F **145**
Mount Olive S36: Stoc 3D **174**
Mt. Osborne Ind. Pk. S71: Barn 2G **31**
Mt. Pleasant DN4: Balb 5H **55**
S35: Chap 2F **79**
S70: Wors 6G **31**
S72: Grim 6B **12**
Mt. Pleasant Cl. S35: Chap 2F **79**
Mt. Pleasant Rd. S7: Shef 6E **119**
S61: Roth 3C **96**
S63: Wath D 2G **65**
Mount Rd. S3: Shef 5E **107**
S35: Chap 3D **78**
S72: Grim 6B **12**
Mount St. S11: Shef 5E **119**
S61: Roth 3C **96**
S70: Barn 2D **30**
S71: Ard .2C **32**
Mount Ter. S63: Wath D 6D **48**
S73: Womb 1F **47**
Mt. Vernon Av. S70: Barn 3E **31**
Mt. Vernon Cres. S70: Barn 4F **31**
Mt. Vernon Rd. S70: Barn, Wors 3F **31**
Mount Vw. DN12: New E 5C **70**
Mount Vw. Av. S8: Shef 5F **133**
Mount Vw. Gdns. S8: Shef 5F **133**
Mount Vw. Rd. S8: Shef 6F **133**
Mousehole Cl. S65: Dalt 1D **98**
Mousehole La. S65: Dalt 1D **98**
Mouse Pk. Gate S35: Gren 1G **91**
Mowbray Gdns. S65: Roth 2B **98**
Mowbray Pl. S65: Roth 2B **98**
Mowbray St. S3: Shef 1F **119**
S65: Roth 2A **98**
Mowson Cres. S35: Ough 5E **91**
Mowson Dr. S35: Ough 5E **91**
Mowson Hollow S35: Ough 5E **91**
Mowson La. S35: Ough 5E **91**
Moxon Cl. S36: Spink 4G **175**
Mucky La. S36: Stoc 1C **174**
(Hunshelf Rd.)
S36: Stoc 5B **174**
(Lee Ho. La.)
S71: Ard .1D **32**
Muglet La. S66: Malt 5B **102**
Muirfield Av. DN4: Cant 6E **59**
S64: Swint 4D **66**
Muirfield Cl. S41: Ches 2A **168**
S72: Cud 5F **11**
Muirfields, The S75: Dart 5H **7**
Mulberry Cl. DN5: Cus 5E **39**
S42: W'orth 6H **171**
S62: Parkg 5G **83**
S63: Gol 5B **36**
S73: D'fld 5B **34**
Mulberry Ct. DN4: Warm 5E **55**
Mulberry Cft. S43: Hol 5F **163**
Mulberry Rd. S21: Ecki 2C **158**
S25: Nth A 2H **141**
Mulberry St. S1: Shef 3F **5** (3G **119**)
Mulberry Way DN3: Arm 6E **43**
S21: Killa 5A **152**
Mulehouse Rd. S10: Shef 2H **117**
Mundella Pl. S8: Shef 5F **133**
Muneeb Ct. S62: Rawm 3G **83**
Mungy La. S65: Thry 6C **84**
Munro Cl. S21: Killa 4C **152**
Munsbrough La. S61: Grea 6C **82**
(not continuous)
Munsbrough Ri. S61: Grea 5C **82**
Murdoch Pl. S71: Smi 1D **16**
Murdock Rd. S5: Shef 6E **93**
Murrayfield Dr. S20: Half 4F **151**
Murray Rd. S11: Shef 2A **132**
S21: Killa 3D **152**
S62: Rawm 2H **83**
Musard Pl. S43: Stav 5A **164**

Musard Way S21: Killa 4B 152
Musgrave Cres. S5: Shef 3F 107
Musgrave Dr. S5: Shef 3F 107
Musgrave Pl. S5: Shef 3F 107
Musgrave Rd. S5: Shef 3E 107
Musgrove Av. S65: Thry 6F 85
Mushroom La. S3: Shef 2A 4 (3C 118)
S10: Shef 3C 118
Muskoka Av. S11: Shef 3F 131
Muskoka Dr. S11: Shef 2F 131
Mutual St. DN4: Hex 2A 56
Muxlow S11: Shef 2C 132
Myers Av. S35: Ough 2E 91
Myers Gro. La. S6: Shef 5F 105
(not continuous)
Myers La. S6: Lox 1B 104
Mylnhurst Rd. S11: Shef 3A 132
Mylor Ct. S71: Monk B 5H 17
Mylor Rd. S11: Shef 2H 131
Myndon Wlk. DN12: Den M 3D 68
Myrtle Cl. S2: Shef 2H 133
Myrtle Cres. S2: Shef 1H 133
S66: Wick 5H 99
Myrtle Dr. S2: Shef 2H 133
Myrtle Gro. DN9: Auck 1H 59
S26: Kiv P 6H 139
S43: Hol 5F 163
Myrtle Rd. S2: Shef 1F 133
S73: Womb 1F 47
Myrtle Springs S12: Shef 3B 134
(not continuous)
Myrtle Springs Dr. S12: Shef 3C 134
Myrtle St. S75: Barn 6B 16
Mysten Cft. S75: Barn 4C 16
Myton Rd. S9: Shef 2D 120

N

Nabeel Ct. S60: Roth 5F 97
Nairn Dr. S18: Dron W 3C 154
Nairn St. S10: Shef 3A 118
Nancy Rd. S72: Grim 2C 20
Nanny Hill S36: Stoc 3E 175
Nanny Marr Rd. S73: D'fld 5B 34
Napier Mt. S70: Wors 5E 31
Napier St. S11: Shef 5D 118
Narrow La. S25: Nth A 3H 141
Narrow Twitchell *S60: Roth 4F 97*
(off Hollowgate)
Narrow Wlk. S10: Shef 3B 118
Nascot Cl. S66: Braml 1C 114
Nascot Gdns. S26: Augh 4B 124
Naseby Av. DN5: Scaws 4E 39
Naseby St. S9: Shef 2D 108
Nasmyth Row *S74: Els 2E 63*
(off Wath Rd.)
Nathan Ct. S20: Water 1G 151
Nathan Dr. S20: Water 6G 137
Nathan Gro. S20: Water 6F 137
Navan Rd. S2: Shef 1D 134
Navigation Way S73: Bramp 3B 48
Naylor Gro. S35: Ough 4D 90
S75: Dod 3G 29
Naylor Rd. S35: Ough 3D 90
Naylor St. S62: Parkg 5G 83
Neale Bank S43: Brim 1C 168
Neale Rd. DN2: Don 2G 41
Nearcroft Rd. S61: Kimb P 2A 96
Nearfield Rd. DN4: Bess 6A 58
Needham Way S7: Shef 3B 132
Needle's Eye 4G 63
Needlewood S75: Dod 4G 29
NEEPSEND 6E 107
Neepsend Ind. Est. S3: Shef 5D 106
Neepsend La. S3: Shef 6D 106
Neill Rd. S11: Shef 6B 118
Nelson Av. S71: Monk B 4F 17
Nelson Cl. S60: Brins 4E 111
Nelson Mandela Wlk. *S2: Shef 5E 121*
(off Castlebeck Av.)
Nelson Pl. S35: Burn 3C 78
Nelson Rd. DN11: New R 5A 74
DN12: New E 4C 70
S6: Shef 6G 105
S66: Malt 5C 102
(not continuous)
Nelson Rd. Flats *DN12: New E 4C 70*
(off Nelson Rd.)
Nelson St. DN4: Don 3C 56
S41: Ches 2H 167
S65: Roth 3F 97
S70: Barn 1D 30
S72: Sth H 1H 11
Nemesia Cl. S25: Sth A 4F 141
Nene Gro. DN9: Auck 1H 59
NESFIELD 5A 160
Nesfield Cl. S41: Ches 6E 161
Nesfield Way S5: Shef 6A 94
Nether Av. S21: Killa 4B 152
S35: Gren 1C 92
NETHER CANTLEY 2E 59
Nether Cantley La. DN3: Cant 2E 59
Nether Cres. S35: Gren 1C 92
Nethercroft S75: Bar G 3F 15
Nether Cft. Cl. S43: Brim 1D 168
Nether Cft. Rd. S43: Brim 1D 168
Netherdene Rd. S18: Dron 3F 155
(not continuous)
NETHER EDGE 2D 132
Nether Edge Rd. S7: Shef 2D 132
Nether Farm Cl. S43: Brim C 3E 169
Netherfield S74: Els 6C 46
Netherfield Cl. S36: Spink 4H 175
S43: Stav 4C 164
Netherfield Ct. S65: Roth 2F 97
Netherfield Cft. S72: Shaft 4F 11
Netherfield La. S62: Parkg 4G 83
Netherfield Rd. S10: Shef 1A 118
S40: Bramp 2B 170
Netherfields Cres. S18: Dron 4F 155
Netherfield Vw. S65: Dalt 2C 98
NETHERGATE 1D 116
Nethergate S6: Stann 1C 116
NETHER GREEN 6F 117
Nethergreen Av. S21: Killa 3C 152
Nethergreen Ct. S21: Killa 3C 152
Nethergreen Gdns. S21: Killa 3C 152
Nethergreen Rd. S11: Shef 6G 117
Nether Hall Rd. DN1: Don 1C 56
NETHER HANDLEY 5A 158
NETHER HAUGH 2C 82
Nether La. S35: Eccl 6G 79
Netherleigh Ct. S40: Bramp 5C 166
Netherleigh Rd. S40: Ash 5C 166
Nether Ley Av. S35: Chap 3F 79
Nether Ley Ct. S35: Chap 3F 79
Nether Ley Cft. S35: Chap 3F 79
Nether Ley Gdns. S35: Chap 3F 79
Nethermoor Av. S21: Killa 3C 152
Nethermoor Cl. S21: Killa 3C 152
Nethermoor Dr. S21: Killa 3C 152
S66: Wick 2H 113
Nethermoor La. S21: Killa 3C 152
Nether Oak Cl. S20: Sot 6A 138
Nether Oak Dr. S20: Sot 6A 138
Nether Oak Vw. S20: Sot 6A 138
Nether Rd. S35: Eccl 1G 93
S75: Silk 1B 28
Nether Royd Vw. S75: Silk C 5B 28
Nether Shire La. S5: Shef 3H 93
NETHERTHORPE
S3 2A 4 (2D 118)
S21 3B 152
S26 6F 125
S43 4C 164
Netherthorpe S43: Stav 4C 164
Netherthorpe Cl. S21: Killa 3B 152
S43: Stav 5C 164
Netherthorpe Flash Nature Reserve 4E 165
Netherthorpe La. S21: Killa 4A 152
Netherthorpe Pl. S3: Shef 1B 4 (1E 119)
Netherthorpe Rd. S3: Shef 3A 4 (3D 118)
S43: Stav 4C 164
Netherthorpe Road Stop (ST) 2B 4 (2E 119)
Netherthorpe St. S3: Shef 1B 4 (2E 119)
Netherthorpe Wlk. S3: Shef 1B 4 (2E 119)
Netherthorpe Way S25: Nth A 1H 141
Nether Wheel Row S13: Shef 3A 136
Netherwood Av. S12: Shef 3H 135
Netherwood Country Pk. 5F 33
Netherwood Rd. S73: Womb 5G 33
Nettlecroft S71: Monk B 3C 18
Nettleham Rd. S8: Shef 5E 133
Network Cen. S75: Barn 3H 15
Neville Av. S70: Barn 3A 32
Neville Cl. S3: Shef 1G 119
S70: Barn 3A 32
S73: Womb 6E 33
Neville Ct. S73: Womb 6E 33
Neville Cres. S70: Barn 3A 32
Neville Dr. S3: Shef 6G 107
Neville Rd. S61: Kimb P 1A 96
Neville St. S60: Roth 3E 97
Nevis Cl. S40: Ches 4E 167
Newark *S20: Westf 2F 151*
(off Shortbrook Rd.)
Newark Cl. S75: Stain 4A 8
Newark Rd. S64: Mexb 1D 66
Newark St. DN11: New R 4B 74
S9: Shef 5D 108
New Beetwell St. S40: Ches 5H 167
Newbiggin Cl. S62: Parkg 4F 83
Newbiggin Dr. S62: Parkg 4F 83
NEWBOLD 1F 167
Newbold Av. S41: Ches 2F 167
Newbold Bk. La. S40: Ches 2E 167
Newbold Ct. S41: Ches 1E 167
Newbold Dr. S41: Ches 2F 167
NEWBOLD MOOR 6G 161
Newbold Rd. S41: Up N, Ches 6B 160
Newbold Ter. DN5: Cus 5G 39
NEWBOLD VILLAGE 2E 167
Newbold Village S41: Ches 2E 167
Newbolt Rd. DN4: Balb 6A 56
Newbould Cres. S20: Beig 5H 137
Newbould La. S10: Shef 4B 118
Newbridge Ct. S41: Old W 5H 161
Newbridge Dr. S43: Brim 6C 162
Newbridge Gro. DN12: New E 4D 70
S71: Monk B 5G 17
Newbridge La. S41: Old W 4H 161
S43: Brim 4H 161
New Bridge Rd. DN1: Don 5A 40
DN5: Don 5A 40
Newbridge St. S41: Old W 5H 161
NEW BRIMINGTON 5E 163
Newburn Dr. S9: Tins 2H 109
Newburn Rd. *S9: Tins 2G 109*
(off Town St.)
Newbury Rd. S10: Shef 2A 118
Newbury Way DN5: Scaws 4E 39
Newby Cres. DN4: Balb 1H 71
Newby Rd. S41: Ches 6D 160
Newcastle Cl. S25: Nth A 1H 141
Newcastle St. S1: Shef 3C 4 (3E 119)
New Chapel Av. S36: Cub 6C 176
New Cl. S75: Silk 2A 28
Newcomen Rd. DN5: Don 5H 39
Newcroft Cl. S20: Sot 5A 138
New Cross Dr. S13: Shef 2B 136
New Cross Wlk. S13: Shef 2B 136
New Cross Way S13: Shef 2B 136
Newdale Av. S72: Cud 3D 18
New Droppingwell Rd. S61: Kimb 4E 95
NEW EDLINGTON 4C 70
New Edlington Way DN4: Warm 2E 71
Newent La. S10: Shef 2A 118
Newfield Av. S71: Monk B 4A 18
Newfield Cl. DN3: Barn D 1E 27
Newfield Ct. S10: Shef 6E 117
Newfield Cres. S17: Dore 3D 144
S63: Wath D 1E 65
Newfield Cft. S17: Dore 2D 144
Newfield Farm Cl. S14: Shef 3B 134
NEWFIELD GREEN 3A 134
Newfield Grn. Rd. S2: Shef 2A 134
Newfield La. S17: Dore 3D 144
Newfield Pl. S17: Dore 3D 144
Newgate Cl. S35: High G 1C 78
NEWHALL 4D 108
Newhall Av. S66: Wick 2H 113
New Hall Cres. S36: Stoc 2B 174
Newhall Grange S66: Carr 1D 114
New Hall La. S36: Stoc 3A 174
S71: Ard 3E 33
Newhall La. S66: Carr 1D 114
New Hall Rd. S40: Bramp 6E 167
Newhall Rd. DN3: Kirk Sa 5D 26
S9: Shef 4B 108
Newhaven Cl. S40: Walt 1C 170
New Haven Gdns. S17: Tot 6F 145
NEWHILL 1E 65
New Hill DN12: Con 4F 69
Newhill S63: Wath D 1E 65

Newhill Grange S63: Wath D 1E 65
Newhill La. S12: Shef 4A 136
Newhill Rd. S63: Wath D 1E 65
S71: Monk B 3F 17
New Houses S41: Ches 5B 168
New Image Health & Fitness Studio
. . . . .3H 9
(off High St.)
New Ings DN3: Arm 4D 42
Newington Av. S72: Cud 6E 11
Newington Cl. DN4: Cant 5C 58
Newington Dr. S26: Ast 1D 138
Newington Rd. S11: Shef 6B 118
Newland Av. S66: Malt 4A 102
S72: Cud 3D 18
Newland Dale S41: Ches 4H 167
Newland Gdns. S41: Ches 3F 167
Newland Rd. S71: Smi 1D 16
Newlands Av. S12: Shef 2D 134
S40: Ash 5D 166
Newlands Cl. DN4: Cant 5C 58
Newlands Dr. DN5: Cus 5G 39
S12: Shef 2D 134
Newlands Gro. S12: Shef 2E 135
Newlands Rd. S12: Shef 2D 134
Newlands Way S73: Womb 3B 48
New La. DN5: Sprot 3B 54
DN11: Ross 5D 74
S63: Bolt D 6E 35
(not continuous)
NEW LODGE 1E 17
New Lodge Cres. S71: Smi 1D 16
Newlyn Dr. S71: Monk B 5G 17
Newlyn Pl. S8: Shef 5E 133
Newlyn Rd. S8: Shef 5E 133
Newman Av. S71: Carl 5H 9
Newman Cl. S9: Shef 6E 95
Newman Ct. S9: Shef 6E 95
S60: Roth 2H 111
Newman Dr. S9: Shef 6D 94
Newman Rd. S9: Shef 1C 108
S60: Roth 2H 111
Newmarch St. S9: Tins 1H 109
Newmarket Rd. DN4: Cant 2A 58
New Mdws. S62: Rawm 6E 65
New Mill Bank S36: Bolst 6E 175
New Orchard La. S66: Thurc 5B 114
New Orchard Rd. S66: Thurc 5B 114
New Oxford Rd. S64: Mexb 2G 67
New Queen St. S41: Ches 4G 167
New Rd. DN3: Brant 4H 59
DN11: Wad 6F 73
S18: App 3D 156
S25: Dinn 6A 128
S25: Nth A 2F 141
S36: Spink 3F 175
S42: W'orth 6F 171
S61: Kimb 5E 95
S63: Wath D 6G 49
S66: B'well 5H 87
S73: Hem 5G 47
S75: Mapp, Stain 4H 7
S75: Pill, Tank 1C 60
S81: Fir 1G 129
NEW ROSSINGTON . . . . .5B 74 & 6F 75
New Row S72: Cud 1E 19
Newsam Rd. S64: Kiln 5C 66
New School Cl. S20: Mosb 3D 150
New School Ct. S20: Mosb 3D 150
New School Rd. S20: Mosb 3D 150
Newsham Rd. S8: Shef 4E 133
New Smithy Av. S36: Thurl 3A 176
New Smithy Dr. S36: Thurl 3A 176
Newsome Av. S73: Womb 1E 47
New Sq. S40: Ches 5H 167
New Station Rd. S64: Swint 3D 66
Newstead Av. S12: Shef 6H 135
S35: Ough 2E 91
Newstead Cl. S12: Shef 5H 135
S18: Dron W 3B 154
Newstead Dr. S12: Shef 6H 135
Newstead Gro. S12: Shef 6H 135
Newstead Pl. S12: Shef 6H 135
Newstead Rd. DN5: Scawt 2G 39
S12: Shef 5H 135
(not continuous)
S71: Ath 6D 8
Newstead Way S12: Shef 6H 135
(not continuous)

New St. DN1: Don 3B 56
DN5: Ben 2H 39
DN9: Blax 1F 77
S1: Shef 2E 5 (2F 119)
S20: Holb 3H 151
S25: Dinn 5A 128
S25: Laugh M 2H 127
S35: High G 6C 60
S36: Spink 3G 175
S40: Ches 6H 167
S60: Cat 6E 111
S61: Grea 4C 82
S61: Thorpe H 4C 80
S62: Rawm 3G 83
S63: Bolt D 3D 50
S64: Mexb 1A 68
S70: Barn 1G 23
(not continuous)
S70: Wors 6H 31
(Edmunds Rd.)
S70: Wors 6F 31
(West St.)
S71: Roy 3H 9
S71: Stair 2B 32
S72: Grim 2B 20
S72: Gt H 1F 35
S72: Sth H 1G 11
S73: D'fld 5B 34
S73: Hem 5E 47
S73: Womb 1H 47
S75: Dod 4G 29
S75: Mapp 5A 8
New St. La. S2: Shef 2H 5 (2H 119)
NEWTON 1G 55
Newton Av. S36: Stoc 2B 174
Newton Chambers Rd. S35: Chap . . .6E 61
Newton Cl. S35: Chap 1F 79
Newton Ct. S70: Barn 6C 16
(off Newton St.)
Newton Cft. S13: Shef 2C 136
Newton Dr. DN5: Don 1G 55
S65: Roth 4H 97
Newton Gdns. S35: Chap 1F 79
Newton La. DN5: Don 1G 55
S1: Shef 6E 5 (4F 119)
S36: Stoc 2B 174
Newton Pl. S61: Thorpe H 4C 80
Newton Rd. S35: High G 1D 78
Newton St. S65: Roth 4H 97
S70: Barn 6C 16
Newton Va. S35: Chap 1F 79
NEW TOTLEY 6F 145
Newtown Av. S71: Roy 2G 9
S72: Cud 3D 18
Newtown Grn. S72: Cud 3E 19
Newtree Dr. DN11: Wad 6E 73
Newven Ho. S65: Roth 2A 98
(off St Leonard's Rd.)
NEW VILLAGE 6A 24
NEW WHITTINGTON 3C 162
New Winterwell S63: Wath D 5E 49
New Wortley Rd. S60: Roth 3B 96
S61: Roth 3B 96
NEW YORK 5D 96
New York Stadium 5D 96
Niagara Rd. S6: Shef 1B 106
Niagara Yd. S6: Shef 1B 106
Nicholas La. S63: Gol 5B 36
Nicholas St. S41: Has 3C 172
S70: Barn 1C 30
Nicholson Av. S63: Wath D 1E 65
S75: Bar G 4F 15
Nicholson Pl. S8: Shef 2G 133
Nicholson Rd. DN4: Hex 3H 55
S8: Shef 2F 133
Nichols Rd. S6: Shef 1H 117
Nickerwood Dr. S26: Ast 2C 138
Nickleby Ct. S60: Cat 6C 110
Nidderdale Pl. S66: Sunn 4H 99
Nidderdale Rd. S61: Wing 5A 82
Nidd Rd. S9: Shef 1D 120
Nidd Rd. E. S9: Shef 1E 121
Nightingale Cl. S41: Ches 4H 167
S60: Roth 5E 97
Nightingale Ct. S60: Roth 5E 97
Nightingale Cft. S61: Thorpe H 2D 80
Nightingale Rd. S35: Gren 2C 92
Nightingales, The S63: Wath D 4F 49
Nile St. S10: Shef 4B 118

Nine Trees Trad. Est. S66: Thurc 4A 114
Ninian Gro. DN4: Cant 4B 58
Nobel Way S25: Dinn 4G 127
Noble St. S74: Hoyl 1C 62
Nodder Rd. S13: Shef 6F 121
Noehill Pl. S2: Shef 5E 121
Noehill Rd. S2: Shef 5E 121
Nook, The S8: Shef 4E 133
S10: Shef 2C 118
S36: H'swne 1G 177
NOOK END 6E 105
Nookery Cl. S66: Malt 4C 102
Nooking Cl. DN3: Arm 3F 43
Nook La. S8: Stann 6D 104
S36: Pen 6E 177
S44: Cal 5G 169
Nora St. S63: Gol 4E 37
Norborough Rd. DN2: Don 5E 41
S9: Tins 2H 109
Norbreck Cres. DN4: Warm 2D 70
Norbreck Rd. DN4: Warm 1D 70
NORBRIGGS 3E 165
Norbriggs Rd. S43: Woodt 3E 165
Norbrook Way S60: Whist 3C 112
Norburn Dr. S21: Killa 4C 152
Norbury Cl. S18: Dron W 3C 154
S40: Ches 3C 166
Norcroft S70: Wors 4E 31
Norcroft La. S75: Cawt 5A 14
Norcross Gdns. S73: D'fld 5C 34
Norfolk Cl. S42: Walt 2C 170
S71: Monk B 4G 17
Norfolk Ct. S65: Roth 3F 97
(off Norfolk St.)
Norfolk Dr. S25: Nth A 2H 141
Norfolk Gdns. S43: Ink 2G 169
Norfolk Hill S35: Gren 1B 92
Norfolk Hill Cft. S35: Gren 1B 92
Norfolk Park Av. S2: Shef 5H 119
Norfolk Park Dr. S2: Shef 5H 119
Norfolk Park Rd. S2: Shef 5G 119
Norfolk Park Students' Residence
S2: Shef 5A 120
Norfolk Pl. S66: Malt 5B 102
Norfolk Rd. DN4: Balb 6A 56
S2: Shef 5H 5 (4H 119)
S72: Gt H 6F 21
Norfolk Row S1: Shef 3E 5 (3F 119)
Norfolk St. S1: Shef 4E 5 (3F 119)
(not continuous)
S65: Roth 3F 97
Norfolk Way S60: Roth 2H 111
Norgreave Way S20: Half 3F 151
Norman Cl. S70: Wors 5F 31
S71: Monk B 4H 17
Norman Cres. DN5: Scaws 3E 39
DN11: New R 5B 74
Normancroft Ct. S2: Shef 5E 121
Normancroft Cres. S2: Shef 5F 121
Normancroft Dr. S2: Shef 5E 121
Normancroft Way S2: Shef 5F 121
NORMANDALE 3F 105
Normandale Av. S6: Lox 4F 105
Normandale Rd. S6: Shef 5C 106
S72: Gt H 6F 21
Norman St. S9: Shef 5C 108
S63: Thurn 2D 36
Normanton Gdns. S4: Shef 5H 107
Normanton Gro. S13: Shef 2A 136
Normanton Hill S13: Shef 2F 135
NORMANTON SPRING 2H 135
Normanton Spring Cl. S13: Shef 3A 136
Normanton Spring Ct. S13: Shef 3A 136
Normanton Spring Rd. S13: Shef 3H 135
Normanville Av. S60: Brins 3C 110
Norrel's Cft. S60: Roth 6G 97
Norrels Dr. S60: Roth 6G 97
Norris Rd. S6: Shef 4A 106
Norroy St. S4: Shef 6A 108
Norstead Cres. S66: Braml 5B 100
Northampton Rd. DN2: Don 5H 41
NORTH ANSTON 3H 141
Nth. Anston Bus. Cen. S25: Nth A 6F 127
Nth. Anston Trad. Est. S25: Nth A 6F 127
North Bank S3: Shef 1G 5 (2G 119)
North Bri. Rd. DN5: Don 6A 40
Nth. Carr La. S71: D'fld 2B 34
Nth. Church St. S1: Shef 2E 5 (2F 119)
Nth. Cliff Rd. DN12: Con 3E 69

North Cl. S18: Uns .6B **156**
S71: Roy .3H **9**
Northcote Av. S2: Shef .2G **133**
Northcote Rd. S2: Shef .2G **133**
Northcote Ter. S75: Barn .6B **16**
North Cres. S21: Killa .2D **152**
S65: Roth .3H **97**
Northcroft S72: Shaft .4F **11**
North Dr. S60: Roth .2E **97**
North End Dr. DN5: H'ton .2G **51**
Northern Av. S2: Shef .1B **134**
Northern Comn. S18: Dron W .1A **154**
Nth. Farm Ct. S26: Ast .1E **139**
NORTHFIELD .2E 97
North Fld. S75: Dod .2G **29**
S75: Silk .2A **28**
Northfield Av. DN5: Ben .3G **23**
S10: Shef .1A **118**
S62: Rawm .1G **83**
Northfield Cl. S10: Shef .1B **118**
Northfield Ct. S10: Shef .1A **118**
S66: Wick .5G **99**
Northfield Dr. S81: Woods .4F **143**
Northfield Ind. Est. S60: Roth .2E **97**
North Fld. La. DN7: Sth B .1G **27**
Northfield La. S66: Wick .5F **99**
Northfield Rd. DN5: Don .5H **39**
S10: Shef .2A **118**
S60: Roth .3E **97**
North Gate S21: Ecki .1E **159**
S64: Mexb .1H **67**
Northgate S72: Sth H .1H **11**
S75: Barn .5B **16**
North Hill Rd. S5: Shef .6E **93**
Northlands DN6: Adw S .2B **22**
S71: Roy .2H **9**
Northlands Rd. S5: Shef .6E **93**
North La. S75: Cawt, Silk .6B **14**
North Mall *DN1: Don* .*1B* ***56***
(off French Ga.)
Northmoor Cl. S43: Brim .1E **169**
Northmoor Vw. S43: Brim .1E **169**
Northorpe S75: Dod .4A **30**
Nth. Pitt St. S61: Kimb .4A **96**
North Pl. S65: Roth .3H **97**
S75: Barn .5A **16**
Northpoint Ind. Est.
S9: Shef .1E **109**
North Quad. S5: Shef .6A **94**
North Quay Dr. S2: Shef .1H **5** (2H **119**)
North Rd. S44: Cal .5E **169**
S65: Roth .3H **97**
S71: Roy .1A **10**
S75: Dod .2G **29**
Nth. Royds Wood S71: Ath .5E **9**
Northside Rd. S63: Wath D .6G **49**
North Sq. DN12: New E .4D **70**
North St. DN4: Don .3D **56**
DN12: New E .4D **70**
S60: Roth .3D **96**
S62: Rawm .1H **83**
S64: Swint .3D **66**
S73: D'fld .4B **34**
Nth. Swaithe Cl. DN5: Ben .6H **23**
North Ter. S41: Has .3A **172**
Northumberland Av. DN2: Don .5G **41**
S74: Hoyl .5B **46**
Northumberland La.
DN12: Den M .3B **68**
Northumberland Rd. S10: Shef .3C **118**
Northumberland Way S71: Ard .2C **32**
North Vw. S72: Grim .1A **20**
Nth. Wingfield Rd. S42: Gras .5C **172**
Northwood S6: Shef .6H **91**
Northwood Dr. S6: Shef .6G **91**
Northwood Pl. S6: Shef .1H **105**
NORTON .1H 147
Norton Av. S8: Shef .1A **148**
S12: Shef .6B **134**
S14: Shef .6B **134**
S40: Bramp .2B **170**
Norton Church Glebe
S8: Shef .1G **147**
Norton Chu. Rd. S8: Shef .1G **147**
Norton Grn. Cl. S8: Shef .1H **147**
NORTON HAMMER .4D 132
Norton Hammer La. S8: Shef .4D **132**
Norton La. S8: Shef .3F **147**
(not continuous)
Norton Lawns *S8: Shef* .*1H* ***147***
(off School La. Cl.)
NORTON LEES .4F 133
Norton Lees Cl. S8: Shef .5F **133**
Norton Lees Cres. S8: Shef .4F **133**
Norton Lees Glade S8: Shef .4F **133**
Norton Lees La. S8: Shef .4F **133**
Norton Lees Rd. S8: Shef .3E **133**
Norton Lees Sq. S8: Shef .4F **133**
Norton M. S8: Shef .1H **147**
Norton Pk. Av. S8: Shef .2G **147**
Norton Pk. Cres. S8: Shef .2F **147**
Norton Pk. Dr. S8: Shef .2F **147**
Norton Pk. Rd. S8: Shef .3F **147**
Norton Pk. Vw. S8: Shef .2F **147**
Norton Rd. DN2: Don .5G **41**
S63: Wath D .5E **49**
NORTON WOODSEATS .5G 133
Norville Cres. S73: D'fld .4C **34**
Norwich Rd. DN2: Don .3F **41**
Norwich Row S2: Shef .3H **5** (3H **119**)
(not continuous)
Norwith Rd. DN4: Bess .6A **58**
NORWOOD .2E 153
Norwood Av. DN9: Auck .1H **59**
S5: Shef .2G **107**
S41: Has .3C **172**
S66: Malt .4A **102**
Norwood Cl. S5: Shef .3G **107**
S41: Has .4D **172**
S66: Malt .4A **102**
Norwood Cres. S21: Killa .3E **153**
S26: Kiv P .6H **139**
Norwood Dr. DN5: Ben .5A **24**
S5: Shef .3G **107**
S72: Brier .3B **12**
S75: Bar G .3F **15**
Norwood Grange Dr.
S5: Shef .2G **107**
Norwood Ind. Est. S21: Killa .2D **152**
Norwood La. S36: Thurl .2A **176**
Norwood Pl. S21: Killa .3E **153**
Nor Wood Rd. WF9: Hems .1E **13**
Norwood Rd. DN12: Con .4E **69**
S5: Shef .3G **107**
Norwood St. S65: Dalt .1C **98**
Nostel Ho. *DN1: Don* .*2B* ***56***
(off Grove Pl.)
Nostell Fold S75: Dod .4G **29**
Nostell Pl. DN4: Bess .6A **58**
Nottingham Cliff S3: Shef .6G **107**
Nottingham Cl. DN5: Scaws .4E **39**
S25: Sth A .4G **141**
S42: W'orth .6A **172**
S71: Ard .3D **32**
Nottingham Dr. S42: W'orth .6A **172**
Nottinghamshire Way
DN3: Arm .4G **43**
Nottingham St. S3: Shef .5G **107**
S65: Roth .3F **97**
Novara Cl. S70: Barn .2G **31**
Novello St. S66: Malt .6D **102**
Nowill Ct. S8: Shef .2F **133**
Nowill Pl. S8: Shef .2F **133**
Nuffield Health Club
Chesterfield .1A 172
Doncaster .4D 56
Nunnery Cres. S60: Cat .6D **110**
Nunnery Dr. S2: Shef .2C **120**
Nunnery Square (Park & Ride) .2A 120
Nunnery Square Stop (ST) .2B 120
Nunnery Ter. S2: Shef .3C **120**
Nunnington Way
DN3: Kirk Sa .4B **26**
Nursery Cres. S25: Nth A .1G **141**
Nursery Dr. S35: Eccl .2G **93**
S60: Cat .6D **110**
Nursery Gdns. S70: Stair .3B **32**
Nursery Gro. S35: Eccl .2H **93**
Nursery La. DN5: Sprot .5B **54**
S3: Shef .1F **5** (1G **119**)
Nursery Rd. S25: Dinn, Nth A .2H **141**
(not continuous)
S26: Swal .6B **124**
Nursery St. S3: Shef .1F **5** (1G **119**)
S70: Barn .2D **30**
Nuttall Pl. S2: Shef .3A **120**
NUTWELL .6F 43
Nutwell Cl. DN4: Bess .6B **58**
Nutwell La. DN3: Arm, Cant .4F **43**
Nutwood Trad. Est. S6: Shef .5A **92**

O

O2 Academy
Sheffield .3F 5 (3G 119)
Oadby Dr. S41: Has .3B **172**
Oakamoor Cl. S40: Ches .3C **166**
Oak Apple Wlk. S6: Stann .5D **104**
Oak Av. S63: Wath D .1H **65**
Oak Bank Av. S41: Old W .3A **162**
Oakbank Cl. S64: Swint .6C **66**
Oakbank Ct. S17: Tot .5F **145**
Oakbrook Ct. S10: Shef .6G **117**
Oakbrook Rd. S11: Shef .6G **117**
Oakbrook Vw. S10: Shef .5H **117**
Oakbrook Wlk.
S65: Roth .2A **98**
Oakburn Ct. S10: Shef .5C **118**
Oak Cl. S21: Killa .5B **152**
S43: Brim .1C **168**
S63: Wath D .2H **65**
S64: Mexb .1D **66**
S66: Flan .4G **99**
S74: Hoyl .1H **61**
Oak Ct. DN4: Balb .1B **72**
DN5: Sprot .3E **55**
S64: Mexb .1D **66**
Oak Cres. S42: W'orth .6G **171**
Oak Crest DN4: Bess .2E **75**
Oakdale S70: Wors .5G **31**
Oakdale Cl. DN3: Eden .1C **42**
S70: Wors .6G **31**
Oakdale Pl. S61: Kimb .4A **96**
Oak Dale Rd. DN4: Warm .2D **70**
Oakdale Rd. S7: Shef .2C **132**
S25: Nth A .3A **142**
S61: Kimb .4A **96**
Oakdell S18: Dron .1A **156**
Oakdene DN11: New R .6C **74**
Oakenroyd Cft. S74: Els .6E **47**
Oaken Wood Cl. S61: Thorpe H .3D **80**
Oaken Wood Rd.
S61: Thorpe H .3C **80**
Oakes Grn. S9: Shef .6B **108**
Oakes Pk. Vw. S14: Shef .1A **148**
Oakes St. S9: Shef .6E **95**
Oakfern Gro. S35: High G .6C **60**
Oakfield Av. S40: Bramp .1C **170**
Oakfield Ct. S75: Mapp .5H **7**
Oakfield Wlk. S75: Barn .6A **16**
Oak Gro. DN3: Arm .2D **42**
DN12: Con .5D **68**
S66: Thurc .5C **114**
Oakham Dr. S3: Shef .6E **107**
Oakham Pl. S75: Barn .5B **16**
Oak Haven Av. S72: Gt H .1F **35**
Oak Head Cl. S71: Smi .3G **17**
Oakhill Ct. S71: Ard .2C **32**
Oakhill Rd. DN2: Don .4G **41**
S7: Shef .2C **132**
S18: Dron .2H **155**
Oakholme M. S10: Shef .5B **118**
Oakholme Rd. S10: Shef .4B **118**
Oakland Av. S71: Monk B .4A **18**
Oakland Cl. S81: Woods .3F **143**
Oakland Ct. S6: Shef .4A **106**
Oakland Rd. S6: Shef .4A **106**
Oaklands DN4: Bess .2F **75**
S66: Wick .1H **113**
Oaklands Dr. DN4: Bess .4A **58**
Oaklands Gdns. DN4: Bess .5A **58**
Oaklands Pl. S63: Wath D .1F **65**
Oakland Ter. DN12: New E .4C **70**
Oak Lea S61: Grea .5C **82**
S70: Wors .6H **31**
Oaklea S63: Thurn .2D **36**
Oak Lea Av. S63: Wath D .5D **48**
Oaklea Cl. S75: Stain .4A **8**
Oak Leigh S75: Cawt .4A **14**
Oakley Av. S40: Ches .4F **167**
Oakley Rd. S13: Shef .4H **121**
Oak Lodge Rd. S35: High G .1B **78**
Oak Mdws. S65: Roth .2A **98**
Oak M. S66: Braml .5A **100**
Oak Pk. S10: Shef .4A **118**
Oak Pk. Ri. S70: Barn .3F **31**

Oak Rd.—Orchard Cres.

Oak Rd. DN3: Arm 2D 42
S12: Shef 6D 134
S20: Beig 4G 137
S63: Thurn 2C 36
S63: Wath D 1H 65
S64: Mexb 1D 66
S66: Malt 5G 101
S72: Shaft 4G 11
Oakroyd Cres. S72: Grim 2B 20
Oaks, The S10: Shef 4A 118
Oaks Av. S36: Stoc 3C 174
Oaks Bus. Pk. S71: Stair 1H 31
Oaks Cres. S70: Barn 2H 31
Oaks Farm Cl. S75: Dart 5G 7
Oaks Farm Dr. S75: Dart 5G 7
Oaks Farm La. S44: Cal 6F 169
Oaks Fold S5: Shef 4B 94
Oaks Fold Av. S5: Shef 5B 94
Oaks Fold Rd. S5: Shef 5B 94
Oaks La. S5: Shef 5B 94
S36: Midh 2A 174
S61: Kimb P 1F 95
S70: Barn 2H 31
S71: Barn, Stair 1H 31
Oak St. S8: Shef 1F 133
S20: Mosb 2D 150
S43: Hol 5F 163
S70: Barn 1C 30
S72: Grim 2C 20
Oaks Wood Dr. S75: Dart 6G 7
Oak Ter. DN1: Don 3B 56
S26: Swal 6A 124
Oak Tree Av. DN9: Auck 2A 76
S72: Cud 1E 19
Oak Tree Cl. S44: Ark T 5H 173
S66: Wick 5H 99
S75: Kexb 6E 7
Oak Tree Cotts. S44: Cal 1F 173
Oak Tree Ct. S60: Roth 1E 111
Oak Tree Gro. WF9: Hems 1G 13
Oak Tree Rd. DN3: Brant 3H 59
Oak Vw. S17: Dore 5F 145
Oakwell 1F 31
Oakwell Business & Youth Enterprise Cen.
S71: Barn 1G 31
Oakwell Cl. S66: Malt 4B 102
Oakwell Ct. S70: Barn 2F 31
Oakwell La. S71: Barn 1F 31
Oakwell Ter. S71: Barn 2F 31
Oakwell Va. S71: Barn 1F 31
Oakwell Vw. S71: Barn 2F 31
Oakwood Av. S5: Shef 3E 93
S71: Roy 2H 9
Oakwood Cl. S70: Wors 6H 31
Oakwood Cres. S35: Ough 5E 91
S62: Rawm 1F 83
S71: Roy 2G 9
Oakwood Dr. DN3: Arm 5D 42
DN3: Brant 4G 59
S60: Roth 6H 97
WF9: Hems 1F 13
Oakwood Flats S5: Shef 3G 107
Oakwood Gro. S60: Roth 6H 97
Oakwood Hall Dr. S60: Roth 2G 111
Oakwood Rd. DN4: Balb 5G 55
S71: Roy 2G 9
Oakwood Rd. E. S60: Roth 1H 111
Oakwood Rd. W. S60: Roth 1G 111
Oakwood Sq. S75: Kexb 6C 6
Oakwood Way S43: Mas M 2E 165
Oakworth Cl. S20: Half 4F 151
S75: Barn 5A 16
Oakworth Dr. S20: Half 4E 151
Oakworth Gro. S20: Half 4E 151
Oakworth Vw. S20: Half 4E 151
Oasis, The S9: Shef 2F 109
Oates Av. S62: Rawm 3G 83
Oates Cl. S61: Roth 3B 96
Oates Orchard S20: Mosb 4E 151
Oates St. S61: Roth 3B 96
Oberon Cres. S73: D'fld 4A 34
Oborne Cl. S65: Rav 2B 100
Occupation La. S6: Lox 3E 105
S12: Shef 5H 135
Occupation Rd. S41: Ches 6G 161
S62: H'ley 5A 62
S62: Parkg 4F 83
Ochre Dike Cl. S20: Water 6F 137
Ochre Dike La. S20: Water 6E 137
Ochre Dike Wlk. S61: Wing 4A 82
Octagon Cen. *S10: Shef* *3D 118*
(off Durham Rd.)
Octavia Cl. S60: Brins 2D 110
Odeon Cinema
Barnsley 6E 17
Sheffield 3F 5 (3G 119)
Odom Ct. S2: Shef 2G 133
Ogden Pl. S8: Shef 2F 147
Ogden Rd. DN2: Don 2A 42
Oil Mill Fold S60: Roth 4E 97
Oldale Cl. S13: Shef 3D 136
Oldale Ct. S13: Shef 2D 136
Oldale Gro. S13: Shef 3D 136
Old Anna La. S36: Thurl 3A 176
Old Bakery Cl. S41: Old W 4H 161
Old Bawtry Rd. DN9: Finn 5E 77
Old Brick Pl. S9: Shef 6E 109
Old Brick Works La. S41: Ches 2H 167
Old Clifton La. S65: Roth 4G 97
Old Colliery Way S20: Swal 2A 138
Oldcotes Cl. S25: Dinn 4A 128
Oldcotes Rd. S25: Dinn 3A 128
Old Cottage Cl. S13: Shef 1E 137
Old Cross La. S63: Wath D 6G 49
Old Crown Gdns. S72: Gt H 6F 21
OLD CUBLEY 6C 176
Old Cubley S36: Cub 6D 176
OLD DENABY 3H 67
Old Denaby Wetlands Nature Reserve
3H 67
Old Doncaster Rd. S63: Wath D 6A 50
OLD EDLINGTON 1B 88
Old Farm Ct. S64: Mexb 6D 50
Old Farm La. S71: Low L 4E 33
S73: Low L, Womb 4E 33
Oldfield Av. DN12: Con 4C 68
S6: Stann 6E 105
Oldfield Cl. DN3: Barn D 1E 27
S6: Stann 6E 105
S74: Hoyl 6B 46
Oldfield Gro. S6: Stann 6E 105
Oldfield Rd. S6: Stann 1C 116
S65: Roth 3C 98
Old Field Shutt La. S65: Dalt M 2E 99
Oldfield Ter. S6: Stann 1E 117
Old Forge Bus. Pk. *S2: Shef* *1F 133*
(off Sark Rd.)
Old Fulwood Rd. S10: Shef 1E 131
Old Garden Dr. S65: Roth 3H 97
Oldgate La. S65: Thry 1C 98
Old Guildhall Yd. DN1: Don 1B 56
Old Hall Cl. DN5: Sprot 3D 54
S25: Laugh M 2G 127
S26: Tod 2B 140
S66: Braml 5A 100
Old Hall Cres. DN5: Ben 2A 40
Old Hall Dr. S66: Braml 5A 100
Old Hall Farm S61: Kimb 3H 95
Old Hall M. S8: Shef 3E 147
S66: Braml 5A 100
Old Hall Pl. DN5: Ben 2A 40
Old Hall Rd. DN5: Ben 2A 40
S9: Shef 5D 108
S40: Ches 6E 167
S70: Wors 2D 44
S75: Wors 2C 44
Old Hall Sports Cen. 3G 95
Old Hall Wlk. S72: Gt H 1F 35
Old Hay Cl. S17: Dore 4E 145
Old Hay Gdns. S17: Dore 4D 144
Old Hay La. S17: Dore 5D 144
OLD HAYWOODS 3G 175
Old Hellaby La. S66: Hel 5E 101
Old Hexthorpe DN4: Hex 3G 55
Old Hill DN12: Con 4F 69
Old Hill La. S65: Dalt M 3E 99
Old House Cl. S73: Hem 5F 47
Old House Rd. S40: Ches 2E 167
Old Houses S41: Ches 5B 168
OLD KIRK SANDALL 3B 26
Old La. S20: Half 3H 151
S35: Ough 4B 90
Old Manor Dr. S36: Oxs 6H 177
Old Market Pl. S73: Womb 2G 47
OLD MILL 5F 17
Old Mill Dr. S41: Up N 1B 166
Old Mill La. S70: Barn 6D 16
S71: Barn 6D 16
Old Mill Rd. DN12: Con 5G 69
Old Moor La. S73: Wath D 3D 48
Old Moor Nature Reserve 3E 49
Old Moor Nature Reserve Vis. Cen.
3D 48
Old Oaks Vw. S70: Barn 2H 31
Old Park Av. S8: Shef 3C 146
Old Park Rd. S8: Shef 3C 146
Old Pheasant Ct.
S40: Bramp 6B 166
Old Quarry Av. S26: Wales 5G 139
Old Retford Rd. S13: Shef 6D 122
Oldridge Cl. S40: Ches 2C 166
Old Rd. DN12: Con 6C 68
S40: Bramp, Ches 5C 166
S42: Bramp 5B 166
S71: Smi 3F 17
Old Row S74: Els 1E 63
Oldroyd Av. S72: Grim 2B 20
Oldroyd Row *S75: Dod* *4G 29*
(off Stainborough Rd.)
Old School Cl. DN3: Arm 4E 43
S61: Grea 4D 82
S74: Hoyl 5B 46
Old School Ct. S75: Bar G 3F 15
Old School Cft. S35: Wharn S 1C 90
Old School Dr. S5: Shef 5G 93
Old School Ho., The *DN5: Ben* *2A 40*
(off Chapel St.)
Old School La. DN11: Wad 5E 73
S44: Cal 6E 169
S60: Cat 6E 111
Old School Rd. DN2: Don 5D 40
Old Scotch Spring La. S66: Staint 2F 103
Old Sheffield Rd. S60: Roth 5E 97
Old Ship La. S40: Ches 6H 167
Old Stables, The S62: Rawm 1E 83
Old Station Dr. S7: Shef 5C 132
Old Station Yd. S43: Brim 6B 162
Old St. S2: Shef 2H 5 (2H 119)
OLD TOWN 5C 16
Old Town Hall *S65: Roth* *3E 97*
(off Effingham St.)
Old Warren Vale S62: Rawm 1G 83
Oldwell Cl. S17: Tot 6E 145
OLD WHEEL 3C 104
OLD WHITTINGTON 4H 161
Old Whittington La. S18: Uns 6B 156
Old Works La. S44: Cal 6G 169
Old Wortley Rd. S61: Kimb 2H 95
Old Yew Ga. S35: Ough 1E 91
Olive Cl. S26: Swal 1C 138
Olive Cres. S12: Shef 6D 134
Olive Gro. Rd. S2: Shef 1G 133
Oliver Ho. S41: Ches 5A 168
Olive Rd. S20: Mosb 3E 151
S36: Stoc 3D 174
Oliver Rd. DN4: Balb 5H 55
S7: Shef 4B 132
Olivers Dr. S9: Shef 2G 121
Olivers Mt. S9: Shef 2G 121
Oliver St. S64: Mexb 1E 67
Olivers Way S60: Cat 5C 110
Olive Ter. S6: Lox 5E 105
Olivet Rd. S8: Shef 5E 133
Ollerton Rd. S71: Ath 5E 9
Onchan Rd. S6: Shef 1F 117
ONESACRE 3C 90
Onesacre S35: Ough 3C 90
Onesmoor Bottom S6: Bradf 3A 90
S35: Bradf 3A 90
Onslow Rd. S11: Shef 1A 132
Onyx Retail Pk. S63: Wath D 4E 49
Opal One S1: Shef 5C 4 (4E 119)
Orange St. S1: Shef 3C 4 (3E 119)
Orchard, The S25: Nth A 2H 141
S63: Thurn 3B 36
S66: Staint 2F 103
S66: Wick 6H 99
Orchard Av. S25: Nth A 1H 141
Orchard Cl. DN3: Kirk Sa 4B 26
S5: Shef 3G 93
S25: Laugh M 1H 127
S60: Cat 6E 111
S64: Mexb 1F 67
S71: Monk B 3H 17
S75: Silk C 5B 28
S75: Stain 5A 8
Orchard Cres. S5: Shef 3G 93

238 A-Z Sheffield

Orchard Cft. S18: Dron 3G 155
S26: Wales 5G 139
S75: Dart 6F 7
S75: Dod 4H 29
Orchard Dr. S71: Roy 3F 9
S35: Sth H 1G 11
Orchard Flatts Cres.
S61: Wing 6B 82
Orchard Gdns. S25: Sth A 4G 141
Orchard Gro. S66: Malt 4G 101
Orchard La. DN5: Cus 5E 39
S1: Shef 3D 4 (3F 119)
S20: Beig 6G 137
S26: Wales 6G 139
Orchard Lea Dr. S26: Swal 1C 138
Orchard M. DN5: Cus 5G 39
S25: Nth A 2H 141
S63: Bolt D 2C 50
S75: Barn 5D 16
Orchard Pl. S21: Killa 4C 152
S60: Roth 4D 96
S63: Wath D 6E 49
S72: Cud 3F 19
Orchard Rd. S6: Shef 6B 106
Orchard Sq. S1: Shef 3E 5 (3F 119)
S18: Dron W 2C 154
Orchard Square Shop. Cen.
S1: Shef 3E 5 (3F 119)
Orchard St. DN4: Balb 3A 56
S1: Shef 3E 5 (3F 119)
S35: Ough 3E 91
S36: Spink 4H 175
S63: Gol 6D 36
S73: Womb 1G 47
Orchards Way S40: Walt 1D 170
Orchard Ter. S75: Cawt 4A 14
Orchard Vw. Rd. S40: Ash 4D 166
Orchard Vs. S65: Thry 6E 85
Orchard Wlk. DN9: Auck 1H 59
S71: Barn 5E 17
Orchard Way S60: Brins 5D 110
S63: Thurn 2C 36
Orchard Wells S66: Wick 6H 99
Orchid Cl. S44: Cal 5F 169
Orchid Cres. S5: Shef 1C 108
Orchid Way S25: Sth A 4F 141
Ordnance Ter. S61: Kimb 4A 96
(off Up. Clara St.)
. . . . .4C 122
ORGREAVE 4C 122
Orgreave Cl. S13: Shef 5D 122
Orgreave Cres. S13: Shef 5D 122
Orgreave Dr. S13: Shef 5D 122
Orgreave Ho. DN1: Don 2B 56
(off Burden Cl.)
Orgreave La. S13: Shef 5B 122
Orgreave Pl. S13: Shef 4C 122
Orgreave Ri. S13: Shef 6E 123
Orgreave Rd. S13: Shef 5C 122
S60: Cat 1D 122
Orgreave Way S13: Shef 6D 122
Oriel Mt. S10: Shef 1D 130
Oriel Rd. S10: Shef 1E 131
Oriel Way S71: Monk B 5A 18
Ormesby Cl. S18: Dron W 3B 154
Ormesby Cres. DN5: Cus 5F 39
Ormesby Way S66: Braml 5B 100
Ormes Mdw. S20: Mosb 6D 136
Ormond Cl. S8: Shef 4G 147
S42: Walt 3C 170
Ormond Dr. S8: Shef 4G 147
Ormonde DN11: New R 6B 74
Ormond Rd. S8: Shef 4G 147
Ormond Way S8: Shef 4G 147
Ormsby Cl. DN4: Balb 2H 71
Ormsby Rd. S41: Ches 1G 167
Orpen Dr. S14: Shef 6B 134
Orpen Way S14: Shef 6B 134
Orphanage Rd. S3: Shef 4G 107
Orwell Cl. S73: Womb 3A 48
Orwins Cl. S41: Ches 1E 167
Osbert Dr. S66: Thurc 5B 114
Osberton Pl. S11: Shef 6C 118
Osberton St. DN11: Wad 5F 73
S62: Rawm 2A 84
Osberton Way S65: Dalt 1B 98
Osbert Rd. S60: Roth 1A 112
Osborne Av. DN6: Woodl 3A 22
S26: Ast 6D 124
Osborne Cl. S11: Shef 1B 132

Osborne Ct. S11: Shef 1B 132
S71: Monk B 4A 18
Osborne Dr. S26: Tod 3C 140
Osborne M. S11: Shef 1C 132
S70: Barn 2F 31
Osborne Rd. DN2: Don 6E 41
S11: Shef 1B 132
S26: Kiv P 6C 140
S26: Tod 3C 140
Osborne St. S70: Barn 2F 31
Osgathorpe Cres. S4: Shef 4H 107
Osgathorpe Dr. S4: Shef 4H 107
Osgathorpe Rd. S4: Shef 4H 107
(not continuous)
Osmaston Rd. S8: Shef 6E 133
Osmond Dr. S70: Wors 5F 31
Osmond Pl. S70: Wors 5F 31
Osmond Way S70: Wors 5F 31
Osmund Ct. S21: Ecki 1D 158
Osmund Rd. S21: Ecki 1C 158
Osprey Av. S70: Birdw 4E 45
Osprey Cl. DN6: Adw S 2C 22
Osprey Gdns. S2: Shef 4B 120
Osprey Rd. S26: Ast 2D 138
Oswestry Rd. S5: Shef 6H 93
Oswin Av. DN4: Balb 4G 55
Otley Cl. DN12: Con 4G 69
Otley Wlk. S6: Shef 6C 106
Otter St. S9: Shef 6C 108
OUGHTIBRIDGE 3E 91
Oughtibridge S35: Ough 3E 91
Oughtibridge La. S35: Gren, Ough . . .3F 91
Oughton Way S4: Shef 5A 108
Oulton Av. S66: Braml 4B 100
Oulton Dr. S72: Cud 1F 19
Oulton Ri. S64: Mexb 6A 52
Ouseburn Cft. S9: Shef 1D 120
Ouseburn Rd. S9: Shef 2D 120
Ouseburn St. S9: Shef 1D 120
Ouse Rd. S9: Shef 1D 120
Ouse Ter. DN12: Con 3F 69
Ouslethwaite Ct. S70: Wors 4D 30
Ouson Gdns. S71: Carl 5H 9
Outgang La. S25: Dinn 4H 127
S25: Dinn, Laugh C 3F 127
S66: Malt 6C 102
Outram Rd. S2: Shef 4B 120
S41: Ches 2G 167
Oval, The DN4: Bess 3H 57
DN6: Woodl 2A 22
DN12: Con 3F 69
S5: Shef 1H 107
S25: Nth A 2H 141
Oval Rd. S65: Roth 3A 98
Overcroft Ri. S17: Tot 6E 145
Overdale Av. S70: Wors 4G 31
Overdale Gdns. S17: Dore 4D 144
Overdale Ri. S17: Dore 4D 144
Overdale Rd. S73: Womb 3H 47
Overend Cl. S14: Shef 4A 134
Overend Dr. S14: Shef 4A 134
Overend Rd. S14: Shef 4A 134
Overend Way S14: Shef 4A 134
Oversley Rd. DN2: Don 4E 41
Oversley St. S9: Tins 1H 109
Overton Cl. S43: Stav 3C 164
Overton Rd. S6: Shef 2A 106
Owday La. S81: Work 6H 143
Owen Cl. S6: Shef 4C 92
S65: Roth 2F 97
Owen Falls Av. S41: Ches 5B 168
Owen Pl. S6: Shef 4C 92
Owen Wlk. S6: Shef 4C 92
Owler Car La. S18: Coal A 6B 148
S21: Trow 5C 148
Owler Ga. S35: Wharn S 2B 90
Owler La. S4: Shef 4A 108
(Firth Pk. Rd.)
S4: Shef 3B 108
(Upwell St.)
OWLERTON 3C 106
Owlerton Grn. S6: Shef 4C 106
Owlerton Stadium
(Greyhound & Speedway) . . .3C 106
Owlet La. S4: Shef 3B 108
Owlings Pl. S6: Shef 4H 105
Owlings Rd. S6: Shef 3H 105
OWLTHORPE 6C 136

Owlthorpe Av. S20: Mosb 2C 150
Owlthorpe Cl. S20: Mosb 2C 150
Owlthorpe Dr. S20: Mosb 2C 150
Owlthorpe Greenway
S20: Holb, Water 1E 151
Owlthorpe Gro. S20: Mosb 2C 150
Owlthorpe La. S20: Mosb 2C 150
Owlthorpe Ri. S20: Mosb 2C 150
Owram St. S73: D'fld 5B 34
Ox Carr DN3: Arm 4D 42
OXCLOSE 4G 151
Ox Cl. Av. S17: Bradw 5H 145
S61: Kimb P 1H 95
Oxclose Dr. S18: Dron W 3B 154
Oxclose La. S18: Dron W 3B 154
Oxclose Pk. Gdns. S20: Half 4G 151
Oxclose Pk. Ri. S20: Half 4G 151
Oxclose Pk. Rd. S20: Half 3G 151
Oxclose Pk. Rd. Nth. S20: Half 3G 151
Oxclose Pk. Vw. S20: Half 4G 151
Oxclose Pk. Way S20: Half 4G 151
Oxford Cl. S8: Shef 2D 118
Oxford Cl. S43: Brim 6E 163
S61: Grea 5D 82
Oxford Pl. DN1: Don 2B 56
S71: Stair 2B 32
Oxford Rd. S43: Brim 6E 163
Oxford St. DN11: New R 5B 74
S6: Shef 2C 118
S64: Mexb 1D 66
S65: Roth 3H 97
S70: Barn 3F 31
S71: Stair 2B 32
Oxford Vs. S65: Roth 3H 97
(off Oxford St.)
. . . . .5H 151
Ox Hill S20: Half 5H 151
Oxley Cl. S36: Stoc 3C 174
Oxley Ct. S60: Roth 6G 97
Oxley Gro. S60: Roth 6G 97
OXSPRING 6H 177
Oxspring Bank S5: Shef 2C 106
Oxspring La. S36: Oxs 3G 177
Oxted Rd. S9: Shef 2D 108
Oxton Dr. DN4: Warm 6E 55
Oxton Rd. S71: Ath 6E 9

P

Packers Row S40: Ches 5H 167
Pack Horse Grn. S75: Silk 2A 28
Pack Horse La. S35: High G 6D 60
Packington Rd. DN4: Cant 5D 58
Packman Rd. S62: Wentw 5D 64
S63: Wath D 5D 64
(Brampton Rd.)
S63: Wath D 1D 64
(Mill La.)
Packmans Cl. S35: Gren 1B 92
Packmans Way S35: Gren 1B 92
Packman Way S63: Wath D 6C 48
Packwood Cl. S66: Malt 4C 102
Paddington Cl. S25: Laugh C 4F 127
Paddock, The DN3: Barn D 1G 27
DN6: Adw S 2D 22
S61: Scho 4E 81
S66: Staint 2F 103
S73: D'fld 4B 34
S73: Hem 4F 47
Paddock Cl. DN5: Cus 5F 39
S75: Stain 5B 8
Paddock Cres. S2: Shef 3B 134
Paddock Cft. S64: Swint 3A 66
Paddock Dr. S66: Sunn 3H 99
Paddock Gro. S72: Cud 1F 19
Paddock La. DN11: Wils 3F 89
Paddock Rd. S75: Stain 5B 8
Paddocks, The DN5: Cade 6G 53
DN5: Cus 5E 39
DN9: Auck 2H 59
S26: Ast 1D 138
S43: Woodt 3F 165
S65: Rav 2B 100
S65: Thry 6F 85
Paddock Vw. S26: Tod 3B 140
Paddock Way S18: Dron 1G 155
(Holmesdale Rd.)
S18: Dron 2G 155
(Stonelow Grn.)

Padley Cl. S75: Dod . . . 3F **29**
Padley Wlk. S5: Shef . . . 6A **94**
Padley Way S5: Shef . . . 6H **93**
Padua Ri. S73: D'fld . . . 5A **34**
Page Hall Rd. S4: Shef . . . 3A **108**
Pagenall Dr. S26: Swal . . . 6C **124**
Paget St. S9: Shef . . . 5C **108**
Pagnell Av. S63: Thurn . . . 3A **36**
Paisley Cl. S43: Stav . . . 6H **163**
Palermo Fold S73: D'fld . . . 4A **34**
Palgrave Cres. S5: Shef . . . 6D **92**
Palgrave Rd. S5: Shef . . . 6C **92**
Palington Gro. DN4: Cant . . . 3B **58**
Pall Mall S70: Barn . . . 1E **31**
Palm Av. DN3: Arm . . . 3F **43**
Palmer Cl. S36: Cub . . . 6C **176**
Palmer Cres. S18: Dron . . . 3G **155**
Palmer Rd. S9: Shef . . . 6F **109**
Palmersgate *S40: Ches . . . 5H* ***167***
(off Central Pavement)
Palmerston Av. S66: Malt . . . 4H **101**
Palmerston Rd. S10: Shef . . . 3C **118**
Palmer St. DN4: Don . . . 3D **56**
S9: Shef . . . 1C **120**
Palmers Way S66: Thurc . . . 6A **114**
Palm Gro. DN12: Con . . . 5D **68**
Palm Hollow Cl. S66: Wick . . . 6E **99**
Palm La. S6: Shef . . . 6B **106**
Palm St. S6: Shef . . . 6B **106**
S75: Barn . . . 5C **16**
Pamela Dr. DN4: Warm . . . 6D **54**
Pangbourne Rd.
S63: Thurn . . . 1B **36**
Pantry Grn. S70: Wors . . . 6H **31**
Pantry Hill S70: Wors . . . 5H **31**
Pantry Well S70: Wors . . . 6H **31**
Paper Mill Rd. S5: Shef . . . 3B **94**
Parade, The S12: Shef . . . 2D **134**
S62: Rawm . . . 1F **83**
S74: Hoyl . . . 1A **62**
Paradise La. S1: Shef . . . 2E **5**
Paradise Sq. S1: Shef . . . 2E **5** (2F **119**)
Paradise St. S1: Shef . . . 2E **5** (2F **119**)
Paramount Cinema . . . 4D **176**
Parish Way S71: Monk B . . . 5A **18**
Park, The DN6: Woodl . . . 5B **22**
Park & Ride
Abbeydale . . . 4C **132**
Adwick . . . 2D **22**
Bentley Park . . . 2H **39**
Doncaster North . . . 1E **39**
Doncaster South . . . 3E **75**
Malin Bridge . . . 5A **106**
Meadowhall . . . 6E **95**
Nunnery Square . . . 2A **120**
Valley Centertainment . . . 5E **109**
Park & Tram
Halfway . . . 3G **151**
Middlewood . . . 1A **106**
Park Av. DN3: Arm . . . 3C **42**
DN5: Sprot . . . 3D **54**
DN12: Con . . . 5F **69**
S10: Shef . . . 6A **118**
S18: Dron . . . 2G **155**
S25: Dinn, Nth A . . . 1H **141**
S35: Chap . . . 4F **79**
S36: Pen . . . 4C **176**
S60: Tree . . . 2G **123**
S60: Whist . . . 2B **112**
S64: Mexb . . . 1F **67**
S70: Barn . . . 1D **30**
S71: Ath . . . 1E **17**
S71: Roy . . . 3A **10**
S72: Brier . . . 3C **12**
S72: Cud . . . 1E **19**
S72: Grim . . . 6B **12**
Park Cl. DN3: Arm . . . 4E **43**
DN5: Sprot . . . 3D **54**
S40: Birdh . . . 3H **171**
S64: Swint . . . 3B **66**
S65: Thry . . . 6E **85**
S75: Stain . . . 6B **8**
Park Cotts. S70: Wors . . . 1F **45**
Park Ct. S35: Gren . . . 2B **92**
S63: Thurn . . . 2C **36**
Park Cres. DN4: Warm . . . 1D **70**
S10: Shef . . . 4C **118**
S35: Eccl . . . 2G **93**
Park Cres. S63: Bolt D . . . 2C **50**
S71: Roy . . . 3A **10**
Park Dr. DN5: Sprot . . . 3C **54**
S26: Swal . . . 1A **138**
S36: Stoc . . . 3D **174**
S41: Ches . . . 1A **172**
S75: Stainb . . . 6A **30**
Park Dr. Way S36: Stoc . . . 2D **174**
(not continuous)
Park End Rd. S63: Gol . . . 6C **36**
Parker Av. S44: Cal . . . 4E **169**
Parkers La. S10: Shef . . . 3B **118**
S17: Dore . . . 2E **145**
Parker's Rd. S10: Shef . . . 3B **118**
Parker's Ter. S70: Birdw . . . 5D **44**
Parker St. S70: Barn . . . 1C **30**
Parkers Yd. S41: Ches . . . 5A **168**
Parker Way S9: Shef . . . 2E **121**
Park Farm S18: Dron W . . . 2B **154**
Parkfield Ct. S62: Parkg . . . 5G **83**
Parkfield Pl. S2: Shef . . . 6F **119**
Parkfield Rd. S65: Roth . . . 4G **97**
PARKGATE . . . **5G 83**
Parkgate S18: Dron . . . 2H **155**
S63: Gol . . . 5E **37**
Parkgate Av. DN12: Con . . . 4D **68**
Parkgate Bus. Pk.
S62: Parkg . . . 6G **83**
Parkgate Cl. S20: Mosb . . . 2B **150**
Parkgate Ct. *S62: Parkg . . . 6F* ***83***
(off The Gateway)
Parkgate Cft. S20: Mosb . . . 1B **150**
Parkgate Dr. S20: Mosb . . . 1B **150**
Parkgate La. S21: Neth Han . . . 1D **162**
Park Grange Ct. S2: Shef . . . 6A **120**
Park Grange Cft. S2: Shef . . . 5H **119**
Park Grange Croft Stop (ST) . . . **5H** 119
Park Grange Dr. S2: Shef . . . 6H **119**
Park Grange Mt. S2: Shef . . . 6H **119**
Park Grange Ri. S2: Shef . . . 6H **119**
Park Grange Rd. S2: Shef . . . 5H **119**
Park Grange Road Stop (ST) . . . **6H** 119
Park Grange Vw. S2: Shef . . . 1A **134**
Park Gro. S36: Stoc . . . 2D **174**
S62: Rawm . . . 1G **83**
S66: Braml . . . 5A **100**
S70: Barn . . . 1D **30**
Park Hall Av. S42: Walt . . . 2B **170**
Park Hall Cl. S42: Walt . . . 3C **170**
Park Hall Gdns. S42: Walt . . . 2C **170**
PARK HEAD . . . **1E 117**
PARKHEAD . . . **4G 131**
Parkhead Cl. S71: Roy . . . 2F **9**
Parkhead Ct. S11: Shef . . . 4G **131**
Parkhead Cres. S11: Shef . . . 4G **131**
Parkhead Rd. S11: Shef . . . 5F **131**
PARK HILL . . . **3A 120**
Park Hill DN3: Barn D . . . 3D **26**
S21: Ecki . . . 1F **159**
S26: Swal . . . 1A **138**
S73: D'fld . . . 4C **34**
Parkhill Cres. DN3: Barn D . . . 1D **26**
Park Hill Dr. S81: Fir . . . 1H **129**
Park Hill Gdns. S26: Swal . . . 1A **138**
Park Hill Gro. S75: Dod . . . 2G **29**
Park Hill Rd. S73: Womb . . . 1H **47**
Parkhill Rd. DN3: Barn D . . . 1D **26**
Park Hollow S73: Womb . . . 2H **47**
Park Homes S64: Mexb . . . 2H **67**
Park Ho. La. S9: Tins . . . 3A **110**
Parkin Ct. S65: Rav . . . 2C **100**
Parkinson St. DN1: Don . . . 5C **40**
Parkland Cres. S12: Shef . . . 6H **135**
(not continuous)
Parkland Dr. DN11: Ross . . . 5E **75**
Parklands DN3: Eden . . . 1C **42**
Parklands Av. S25: Dinn . . . 6H **127**
Parklands Cl. DN11: Ross . . . 5D **74**
Parklands Vw. S26: Ast . . . 3D **138**
Parkland Vw. S71: Lund . . . 3C **18**
Parkland Wlk. DN9: Blax . . . 1G **77**
Park La. DN4: Bess . . . 2H **57**
DN7: Dunsv, Hatf . . . 5H **27**
DN9: Blax . . . 1F **77**
DN12: Con . . . 1D **86**
S9: Shef . . . 1F **109**
S10: Shef . . . 4C **118**
S25: Laugh C . . . 4F **127**
Park La. S35: High G . . . 5F **61**
S36: Pen . . . 4C **176**
S36: Spink, Stoc . . . 2E **175**
S41: Ches . . . 1G **167**
S65: Rav . . . 6D **86**
S65: Thry . . . 6E **85**
S72: Gt H, Grim . . . 4C **20**
Park La. Ct. S65: Thry . . . 5E **85**
Park La. Rd. DN7: Dunsv . . . 4H **27**
Park Mdws. S72: Shaft . . . 3G **11**
Park Mt. S65: Roth . . . 4F **97**
Park Nook S65: Thry . . . 6D **84**
Park Pl. S65: Roth . . . 3A **98**
Park Ri. S18: Holme . . . 4A **154**
Park Rd. DN1: Don . . . 1C **56**
DN5: Ben . . . 1H **39**
DN12: Con . . . 5E **69**
S6: Shef . . . 6G **105**
S40: Ches . . . 1G **171**
(not continuous)
S63: Thurn . . . 2B **36**
S63: Wath D . . . 1F **65**
S64: Mexb . . . 1F **67**
S64: Swint . . . 4A **66**
S65: Roth . . . 3A **98**
S70: Barn . . . 3C **30**
S70: Wors . . . 1F **45**
S72: Brier . . . 3C **12**
S72: Grim . . . 1B **20**
PARK SIDE . . . **1D 116**
Parkside S41: Ches . . . 1H **167**
S71: Carl . . . 5A **10**
Parkside Cl. S12: Shef . . . 6A **136**
Parkside La. S6: Stann . . . 1E **117**
Parkside M. S70: Wors . . . 5F **31**
Parkside Rd. S6: Shef . . . 3B **106**
S74: Hoyl . . . 2G **61**
Parkside Shop. Cen. S21: Killa . . . 3C **152**
Parkside Vw. S41: Ches . . . 2C **166**
Parkside Way S75: Kexb . . . 5E **7**
Parkson Rd. S60: Roth . . . 2A **112**
Park Spring Dr. S2: Shef . . . 6H **119**
Park Spring Rd.
S72: Grim, Lit H, Midd . . . 2A **20**
Park Springs Ind. Est. S72: Grim . . . 2A **20**
Park Spring Way S2: Shef . . . 6H **119**
Park Sq. S2: Shef . . . 2G **5** (3G **119**)
S35: Chap . . . 1F **79**
Parkstone Cres. S66: Hel . . . 6E **101**
Parkstone Delph S12: Shef . . . 6D **134**
Parkstone Way DN2: Don . . . 3H **41**
Park St. S26: Swal . . . 1B **138**
S40: Birdh . . . 3H **171**
S61: Roth . . . 3C **96**
S62: Rawm . . . 2G **83**
S70: Barn . . . 2D **30**
S73: Womb . . . 2H **47**
Park Ter. DN1: Don . . . 1C **56**
S35: Chap . . . 4G **79**
S65: Thry . . . 6D **84**
Park Vale Dr. S65: Thry . . . 6E **85**
Park Vw. DN6: Adw S . . . 3D **22**
S26: Kiv P . . . 5B **140**
S41: Has . . . 3C **172**
S61: Grea . . . 5C **82**
S61: Thorpe H . . . 4B **80**
S64: Mexb . . . 1D **66**
S66: Malt . . . 5C **102**
(not continuous)
S70: Barn . . . 3C **30**
S70: Wors . . . 5G **31**
S71: Roy . . . 2A **10**
S72: Brier . . . 3C **12**
S72: Shaft . . . 4F **11**
S74: Hoyl . . . 1C **62**
S75: Dod . . . 3G **29**
Park Vw. Av. S20: Half . . . 3F **151**
Park Vw. Ct. S63: Wath D . . . 5G **49**
Parkview Ct. S8: Shef . . . 6F **133**
Park Vw. Rd. S6: Shef . . . 3B **106**
S35: Chap . . . 4F **79**
S61: Kimb . . . 5F **95**
S75: Stain . . . 5C **8**
Park Wlk. *S2: Shef . . . 2A* ***120***
(off Castle Ct.)
Park Way DN6: Adw S . . . 2C **22**
S63: Thurn . . . 2C **36**
Parkway DN3: Arm . . . 5E **43**

Parkway Av. S9: Shef .2C **120**
Parkway Centre Retail Pk.
S2: Shef .2B **120**
Parkway Cl. S9: Shef .2C **120**
Parkway Dr. S9: Shef .3D **120**
Parkway Nth. DN2: Don .4E **41**
Parkway Ri. S9: Shef .3D **120**
Parkway Sth. DN2: Don .4E **41**
Parkwood Ind. Est. S3: Shef .6F **107**
Parkwood Karting .5D **106**
Parkwood Ri. DN3: Barn D .3D **26**
Parkwood Rd. S3: Shef .5D **106**
Parkwood Rd. Nth. S5: Shef .2E **107**
PARKWOOD SPRINGS .5E **107**
Parliament St. S11: Shef .5D **118**
Parma Ri. S73: D'fld .5H **33**
Parsley Hay Cl. S13: Shef .5A **122**
Parsley Hay Dr. S13: Shef .5A **122**
Parsley Hay Gdns. S13: Shef .5A **122**
Parsley Hay Rd. S13: Shef .5A **122**
Parsonage Cl. S20: Mosb .4E **151**
Parsonage Ct. *S6: Shef .6B **106***
(off Parsonage Cres.)
Parsonage Cres. S6: Shef .6B **106**
Parsonage St. S6: Shef .6B **106**
PARSON CROSS .4E **93**
Parson Cross Rd. S6: Shef .6B **92**
Parson La. S75: Dod .4E **29**
Partridge Cl. S21: Ecki .1C **158**
Partridge Flatt Rd. DN4: Bess .6C **58**
Partridge Pl. S26: Ast .2D **138**
Partridge Ri. DN4: Bess .6C **58**
Partridge Rd. DN3: Barn D .1C **26**
Partridge Vw. S2: Shef .4B **120**
Parwich Cl. S40: Ches .3B **166**
Pashley Cft. S73: Womb .2E **47**
Passfield Rd. DN11: New R .6D **74**
Passhouses Rd. S4: Shef .4G **107**
Pasture Cl. DN3: Arm .5D **42**
(not continuous)
Pasture Cft. S66: Thurc .5C **114**
Pasture Gro. S21: Ecki .1D **158**
Pasture La. DN5: Cade .5D **52**
S63: Bolt D .6E **35**
Pastures, The S26: Tod .3B **140**
S71: Roy .3F **9**
Pastures Ct. DN11: Ross .6E **75**
S64: Mexb .1A **68**
Pastures M. S64: Mexb .1A **68**
Pastures Rd. S64: Mexb .1A **68**
Paternoster Row S1: Shef .5F **5** (4G **119**)
Paterson Cl. S36: Stoc .2C **174**
Paterson Ct. S36: Stoc .2C **174**
Paterson Cft. S36: Stoc .2C **174**
Paterson Gdns. S36: Stoc .2C **174**
Paterson Rd. S25: Dinn .5B **128**
Patmore Rd. S5: Shef .6A **94**
Paton Gro. S43: Brim .6C **162**
Patrick Stirling Ct. DN4: Hex .3H **55**
Patrick Tobin Bus. Pk. S63: Wath D .5C **50**
Patterdale Cl. S18: Dron W .3D **154**
Patterdale Gro. S66: Wick .6E **99**
Patterdale Way S25: Nth A .2A **142**
Pavement, The S2: Shef .3H **5** (3H **119**)
Pavements Shop. Centre, The
S40: Ches .5H **167**
Pavilion Cl. S43: Ink .1H **169**
S72: Brier .3B **12**
Pavilion Ct. S10: Shef .6F **117**
Pavilion Dr. S43: Stav .6B **164**
Pavilion La. S60: Brins .2C **110**
Pavilion Way S5: Shef .6A **94**
Pavillion Cl. DN12: New E .3D **70**
Paxton Ct. S14: Shef .4C **134**
Paxton Cres. DN3: Arm .3C **42**
Paxton La. S10: Shef .4C **118**
Paxton Rd. S41: Ches .3B **168**
Payler Cl. S2: Shef .6D **120**
Payne Cres. S62: Rawm .1F **83**
Peace Garden .4E **5**
Peacehaven DN3: Barn D .1C **26**
Peacock Cl. S21: Killa .4B **152**
S61: Thorpe H .2C **80**
Peacock La. S25: Nth A .3G **141**
Peacock Trad. Est. S6: Shef .4D **106**
Peak Chase S72: Brier .4A **12**
Peak Cl. S66: Sunn .3G **99**
Peakdale Cres. S12: Shef .3H **135**
Peak District National Pk. .4A **144**
Peake Av. DN12: Con .4D **68**
Peak La. S66: Hoot L .1H **115**
PEAKLEY HILL .6B **154**
Peak Pl. S43: Ink .1H **169**
Peak Rd. S71: Ath .1F **17**
Peaks Mt. S20: Water .5F **137**
Peak Sq. S20: Water .6F **137**
Peakstone Cl. DN4: Balb .5G **55**
Peakstone M. S62: Rawm .3G **83**
Peak Vw. Rd. S40: Ches .4E **167**
Pearce Rd. S9: Shef .3F **121**
Pearce Wlk. S9: Shef .2F **121**
Pearl St. S11: Shef .6D **118**
Pearmain Dr. S66: Malt .4G **101**
Pea Royd La. S36: Stoc .2E **175**
Pearson Cres. S73: Womb .5E **33**
Pearson Cft. S41: Ches .2D **166**
Pearson Pl. S8: Shef .3E **133**
Pearson's Cl. S65: Roth .6B **98**
Pearson's Fld. S73: Womb .1G **47**
Pearson St. S36: Stoc .2D **174**
Pearson Trad. Est. S41: Old W .5A **162**
Pear St. S11: Shef .5D **118**
Pear Tree Av. S42: W'orth .6F **171**
S66: Braml .5A **100**
Peartree Av. S63: Thurn .2B **36**
Pear Tree Cl. S21: Killa .5B **152**
S43: Hol .6F **163**
S60: Brins .4E **111**
S72: Gt H .6E **21**
S81: Woods .4F **143**
Pear Tree Ct. S63: Thurn .2B **36**
Pear Tree M. DN11: Lov .4B **72**
Peartree Orchard S71: Roy .1A **10**
Pear Tree Rd. S5: Shef .4A **94**
Pearwood Cl. S63: Gol .5F **37**
Pearwood Cres. DN4: Balb .1G **71**
Peasehill Cl. S70: Barn .2D **30**
Peashill St. S62: Rawm .3G **83**
Peatfield Rd. S21: Killa .3E **153**
Peckham Rd. S35: High G .2E **79**
Pedley Av. S20: Westf .1F **151**
Pedley Cl. S20: Westf .1F **151**
Pedley Dr. S20: Westf .2F **151**
Pedley Gro. S20: Westf .1F **151**
Peel Cen. Retail Pk., The
S71: Barn .6F **17**
Peel Cl. S66: Malt .4H **101**
Peel Gdns. S18: Dron .3E **155**
Peel Pde. S70: Barn .1D **30**
Peel Pl. S71: Barn .5F **17**
Peel Sq. S70: Barn .1D **30**
Peel St. S10: Shef .4B **118**
S70: Barn .3E **31**
(Rowan Cl.)
S70: Barn .1D **30**
(West Way)
Peel St. Arc. S70: Barn .1D **30**
Peel Ter. S10: Shef .4A **4** (3D **118**)
Peg Folly S36: Stoc .3A **174**
Peggy La. S35: Eccl .1B **94**
S35: Gren .1C **92**
Pell's Cl. DN1: Don .1B **56**
Pembrey Ct. S20: Sot .6H **137**
Pembridge Ct. *S71: Roy .2H **9***
(off Strawberry Gdns.)
Pembroke Av. DN4: Balb .6H **55**
(not continuous)
Pembroke Cl. S40: Walt .1D **170**
Pembroke Ct. S41: Ches .1F **167**
Pembroke Cres. S35: High G .2C **78**
Pembroke Ri. DN5: Scaws .4E **39**
S25: Sth A .4G **141**
Pembroke Rd. S18: Dron .4F **155**
Pembroke St. S11: Shef .5D **118**
S61: Kimb .4A **96**
Pendeen Rd. S11: Shef .6G **117**
Pendlebury Gro. S74: Hoyl .1H **61**
Pendle Cft. S20: Sot .1A **152**
Pendon Ho. S36: Pen .4D **176**
Pengeston Rd. S36: Pen .4B **176**
PENISTONE .4D **176**
Penistone Ct. S36: Pen .4E **177**
Penistone Ho. *S3: Shef .1E **119***
(off Adelaide La.)
Penistone Rd. S6: Shef .2B **106**
S35: Chap, Gren .2A **78**
Penistone Rd. Nth. S6: Shef .1B **106**
Penistone Station (Rail) .4E **177**
Penistone St. DN1: Don .6C **40**
Penley St. S11: Shef .6E **119**
Penlington Cl. WF9: Hems .1E **13**
Penmore Cl. S41: Has .2B **172**
Penmore Gdns. S41: Has .1B **172**
Penmore La. S41: Has .2B **172**
Penmore St. S41: Has .2B **172**
Pennine Centre, The S1: Shef .2D **4**
Pennine Cl. S75: Dart .4H **7**
Pennine Ct. S36: Pen .5F **177**
Pennine Gdns. S66: Malt .4G **101**
Pennine Vw. S36: Stoc .5D **174**
S74: Black H .3A **46**
S75: Dart .4H **7**
Pennine Way S40: Ches .3D **166**
S75: Barn .6A **16**
Pennington Ct. S66: Malt .6H **101**
Pen Nook Cl. S36: Spink .5F **175**
Pen Nook Ct. S36: Spink .5G **175**
Pen Nook Dr. S36: Spink .5G **175**
Pen Nook Gdns. S36: Spink .5G **175**
Pen Nook Glade S36: Spink .5G **175**
(Pen Nook Ct.)
S36: Spink .4G **175**
(The Greenway)
Penns Rd. S2: Shef .2H **133**
Penny Engine La.
S21: Ecki .6F **151**
Pennyfields S63: Bolt D .2A **50**
Penny Hill S81: Fir .2F **129**
Penny Hill La. S26: Ull .2E **125**
S66: Bramp M .2E **125**
Pennyholme Cl. S26: Kiv P .6C **140**
Penny La. S17: Tot .6D **144**
Penny Piece La. S25: Nth A .2G **141**
Penny Piece Pl.
S25: Nth A .2G **141**
Penrhyn Rd. S11: Shef .1B **132**
Penrhyn Wlk. S71: Ard .2D **32**
Penrith Cl. S5: Shef .2D **106**
Penrith Cres. S5: Shef .2D **106**
Penrith Gro. S71: Ard .2C **32**
Penrith Rd. DN2: Don .6H **41**
S5: Shef .2D **106**
Penrose Cres. S44: Ark T .5H **173**
Penrose Pl. S13: Shef .2B **136**
Penthorpe Cl. S12: Shef .2E **135**
Pentland Cl. S40: Ches .3D **166**
Pentland Gdns. S20: Water .6E **137**
Pentland Rd. S18: Dron W .3C **154**
Penton St. S1: Shef .3D **4** (3F **119**)
Penwood Wlk. S66: Sunn .2G **99**
Penyghent Cl. S35: Chap .2E **79**
Pepper Cl. S61: Kimb P .6G **81**
Pepper St. S74: Hoyl .4B **46**
Percy St. S3: Shef .1E **119**
S65: Roth .4F **97**
Peregrine Dr. S70: Birdw .4E **45**
Perigree Rd. S8: Shef .5D **132**
Periwood Av. S8: Shef .5D **132**
Periwood Cl. S8: Shef .5D **132**
Periwood Dr. S8: Shef .5D **132**
Periwood Gro. S8: Shef .5D **132**
Periwood La. S8: Shef .5D **132**
Perkyn Rd. S5: Shef .3A **94**
Perkyn Ter. S5: Shef .3A **94**
Perran Gro. DN5: Cus .5G **39**
Perseverance St. S70: Barn .1C **30**
Persimmon Cl. DN11: New R .6G **75**
Perth Cl. S64: Mexb .6H **51**
Petal Cl. S66: Malt .4C **102**
Peterborough Cl. S10: Shef .6B **116**
Peterborough Dr. S10: Shef .5B **116**
Peterborough Rd. S10: Shef .5B **116**
Peterdale Cl. S43: Brim .6D **162**
Peterdale Rd. S43: Brim .6D **162**
Peterfoot Way S71: Carl .5G **9**
Petersgate DN5: Scawt .2G **39**
Peter's Rd. DN12: New E .5C **70**
Peter St. S61: Kimb .3H **95**
S66: Thurc .5B **114**
Peters Yd. *S61: Kimb .3H **95***
(off Peter St.)
Petre Dr. S4: Shef .4B **108**
Petre St. S4: Shef .5A **108**
Pettyclose La. S41: Ches .3C **168**

Petunia Rd. DN3: Kirk Sa 5C **26**
Petworth Cft. S71: Roy 2G **9**
Petworth Dr. S11: Shef 6G **131**
Pevensey Av. S41: Ches 2F **167**
Pevensey Ct. S41: Ches 1F **167**
Peveril Cl. S26: Kiv P 5B **140**
Peveril Cres. S71: Ath 1F **17**
Peveril Rd. DN4: Balb 6F **55**
S11: Shef 1A **132**
S21: Ecki 6F **151**
S41: Ches 1G **167**
Pexton Rd. S4: Shef 4H **107**
Pheasant Bank DN11: Ross 5D **74**
PHILADELPHIA 6E **107**
Philadelphia Dr. S6: Shef 1D **118**
Philadelphia Gdns. S6: Shef 1D **118**
Philadelphia Gro. S6: Shef 1D **118**
Philip La. S35: Howb 6A **60**
Philip Rd. S70: Barn 3A **32**
Phillimore Rd. S9: Shef 6E **109**
Phillips Rd. S6: Lox 3E **105**
Phoenix Ct. S1: Shef 4D **4**
S12: Ridg 1H **149**
Phoenix Golf Course 2C **110**
Phoenix Gro. S60: Brins 2C **110**
Phoenix La. S63: Thurn 3D **36**
Phoenix Riverside S60: Roth 6C **96**
Phoenix Rd. S12: Ridg 1H **149**
PICCADILLY 5C **66**
Piccadilly DN5: Ben 2H **39**
Piccadilly Hgts. *S41: Ches 6A **168***
(off Piccadilly Rd.)
Piccadilly Rd. S41: Ches 6A **168**
S64: Swint 5B **66**
Pickard Cres. S13: Shef 6G **121**
Pickard Dr. S13: Shef 6H **121**
Pickering Cres. S26: Swal 2A **138**
Pickering Rd. DN5: Ben 5H **23**
S3: Shef 5E **107**
Pickhill's Av. S63: Gol 5E **37**
Picking La. S35: Eccl 2G **93**
Pickle Wood Ct. DN9: Finn 2F **77**
Pickmere Rd. S10: Shef 2A **118**
Pickton Cl. S40: Walt 6E **167**
Pickup Cres. S73: Womb 3G **47**
Pickwick Dr. S60: Cat 6C **110**
Piece End S35: High G 1C **78**
(Alma Rd.)
S35: High G 6C **60**
(Piece End Cl.)
Piece End Cl. S35: High G 6C **60**
Pieces Nth., The S60: Whist 4A **112**
Pieces Sth., The S60: Whist 4A **112**
Pigeon Bri. Way S26: Ast 2D **138**
Pighills La. S18: Coal A 6G **147**
Pike Cl. S40: Ches 3C **166**
Pike Lowe Gro. S75: Stain 6C **8**
Pike Rd. S60: Brins 3D **110**
Pilgrim St. S3: Shef 5G **107**
Pilkingtons Yd. *S21: Ecki 1F **159***
(off Station Rd.)
PILLEY 6C **44**
PILLEY GREEN 1C **60**
Pilley Grn. S75: Pill 1C **60**
PILLEY HILLS 6B **44**
Pilley La. S75: Pill 6C **44**
Pilley La. End S75: Pill 5B **44**
Pinchfield Ct. S66: Wick 1G **113**
Pinchfield Holt S66: Wick 2G **113**
Pinchfield La. S66: Wick 1G **113**
PINCHMILL 3F **113**
Pinchmill Hollow S66: Wick 2G **113**
Pinch Mill La. S60: Whist 3D **112**
Pinchwell Vw. S66: Wick 1G **113**
Pindale Av. S43: Ink 1H **169**
Pindar Oaks S70: Barn 3F **31**
Pindar Oaks Cotts. S70: Barn 2G **31**
Pindar Oaks St. S70: Barn 2F **31**
Pindar St. S70: Barn 2G **31**
Pine Av. S25: Sth A 5G **141**
Pine Cl. S21: Killa 5B **152**
S66: Sunn 4H **99**
S70: Barn 4H **31**
S74: Hoyl 1B **62**
Pine Cft. S35: Chap 4F **79**
Pinecroft Way S35: Chap 4F **79**
Pinefield Av. DN3: Barn D 2D **26**
Pinefield Rd. DN3: Barn D 2D **26**
Pine Gro. DN12: Con 6D **68**
Pine Hall Dr. S71: Monk B 4A **18**
Pine Hall Rd. DN3: Barn D 2C **26**
Pinehurst Ri. S64: Swint 4C **66**
Pine Rd. DN4: Cant 4C **58**
Pines, The S10: Shef 6B **116**
S66: Wick 1H **113**
Pine St. S43: Hol 6F **163**
Pine Vw. S40: Ash 5C **166**
Pine Wlk. S64: Swint 6C **66**
Pinewood Av. DN3: Arm 2E **43**
DN4: Balb 1F **71**
Pinewood Cl. S65: Dalt 1C **98**
S72: Gt H 5E **21**
Pinfield Cl. S72: Gt H 6F **21**
Pinfold S63: Wath D 6F **49**
Pinfold, The DN5: Barnb 6H **37**
Pinfold Cl. DN9: Finn 3F **77**
S64: Swint 4B **66**
S71: Stair 2B **32**
Pinfold Cotts. S72: Cud 2F **19**
Pinfold Ct. DN3: Barn D 2C **26**
Pinfold Gdns. S72: Cud 3F **19**
Pinfold Hill S70: Wors 4F **31**
Pinfold Lands S64: Mexb 2G **67**
Pinfold La. S3: Shef 5F **107**
S60: Roth 5F **97**
S71: Roy 3H **9**
S73: D'fld 5C **34**
Pinfold St. S1: Shef 3D **4** (3F **119**)
S21: Ecki 1E **159**
Pingle Av. S7: Shef 5B **132**
Pingle Grange S43: Brim 1D **168**
Pingle La. S65: Rav 6H **85**
Pingle Rd. S7: Shef 5A **132**
S21: Killa 3D **152**
Pingles Cres. S65: Thry 6D **84**
Pinnacles, The S2: Shef 2H **5** (2H **119**)
Pinner Rd. S11: Shef 6B **118**
Pinsent S3: Shef 1F **5**
Pinstone St. S1: Shef 5E **5** (4F **119**)
Pioneer Cl. S63: Wath D 6B **50**
Pipe Ho. La. S62: Rawm 6G **65**
(not continuous)
Piper Cl. S5: Shef 1F **107**
Piper Ct. S5: Shef 1F **107**
Piper Cres. S5: Shef 6F **93**
Pipering La. E. DN5: Scawt 3G **39**
Pipering La. W.
DN5: Scawt 3F **39**
Piper La. S26: Ast 1E **139**
S42: Ash 5A **166**
Piper Rd. S5: Shef 1G **107**
Pipeyard La. S21: Ecki 1D **158**
Pippin Ct. S66: Malt 4G **101**
Pipworth Gro. S2: Shef 5F **121**
Pipworth La. S21: Ecki 6G **151**
Pipworth Rd. S2: Shef 5E **121**
Pisgah Ho. Rd. S10: Shef 3B **118**
PISMIRE HILL 6A **94**
Pitchford La. S10: Shef 5E **117**
Pithouse La. S26: Wales B 1D **152**
Pit La. DN4: Warm 3E **71**
S12: Shef 2D **134**
S60: Tree 2G **123**
S61: Thorpe H 4C **80**
S73: Womb 2D **46**
Pitman Rd. DN12: Den M 3B **68**
Pit Row S73: Hem 6F **47**
PITSMOOR 5G **107**
Pitsmoor Rd. S3: Shef 6F **107**
(not continuous)
Pittam Cl. DN3: Arm 4E **43**
Pitt Cl. S1: Shef 4B **4**
Pitt La. S1: Shef 4B **4**
S75: Mapp 5H **7**
Pitt St. S1: Shef 4B **4** (3E **119**)
S21: Ecki 2D **158**
S61: Kimb 4A **96**
S64: Mexb 1H **67**
S70: Barn 1D **30**
S73: Womb 5H **33**
Pitt St. W. S70: Barn 1C **30**
Plane Cl. DN4: Cant 4C **58**
Plane Dr. S66: Wick 5H **99**
Plane Tree Way DN9: Auck 3A **76**
Planet Rd. DN6: Adw S 1D **22**
Plank Gate S35: Ough 1D **90**
Plantation Av. DN4: Bess 2E **75**
S25: Dinn 5A **128**
S25: Nth A 2H **141**
S71: Roy 3A **10**
Plantation Cl. S40: Ash 3B **166**
S66: Malt 4A **102**
Plantation Ct. S25: Dinn 5A **128**
Plantation Rd. DN4: Balb 2B **72**
DN5: Ben 1F **25**
S8: Shef 2F **133**
Plantation Wlk. *S25: Dinn 5A **128***
(off Plantation Av.)
Plantin, The S20: Half 3F **151**
Plantin Ri. S20: Half 3F **151**
Plaster Pits La. DN5: Sprot 6C **38**
PLATTS COMMON 5B **46**
Platts Comn. Ind. Est.
S74: Hoyl 5A **46**
Platts Dr. S20: Beig 4H **137**
Platts La. S35: Ough 3F **91**
Platt St. S3: Shef 6F **107**
Playford Yd. S74: Hoyl 4A **46**
Plaza Quarter S70: Barn 1D **30**
Pleasance Cl. DN12: New E 6B **70**
Pleasant Av. S72: Gt H 6F **21**
Pleasant Cl. S12: Shef 2E **135**
Pleasant Pl. S40: Ches 5E **167**
Pleasant Rd. S12: Shef 2E **135**
Pleasant Vw. S72: Cud 4F **19**
Pleasant Vw. Cft. S71: Barn 4D **16**
Pleasley Rd. S26: Augh 3H **111**
S60: Whist 3A **112**
Ploughmans Cft. S63: Bramp B 5A **48**
Plover Ct. DN11: Ross 5D **74**
S2: Shef 4B **120**
Plover Cft. S61: Thorpe H 2D **80**
Plover Dr. S70: Birdw 4E **45**
Plover Way S44: Cal 5E **169**
Plowmans Way S61: Wing 5A **82**
Plowright Cl. S14: Shef 3A **134**
Plowright Dr. S14: Shef 3A **134**
Plowright Mt. S14: Shef 3A **134**
Plowright Way S14: Shef 3A **134**
Plumber St. S70: Barn 1C **30**
PLUMBLEY 4D **150**
Plumbley Hall M. S20: Mosb 4D **150**
Plumbley Hall Rd. S20: Mosb 3D **150**
Plumbley La. S20: Mosb 4C **150**
Plumb Leys S60: Tree 2F **123**
Plumbleywood La. S12: Ridg 4A **150**
S20: Mosb 4A **150**
Plum La. S3: Shef 1E **5** (2F **119**)
Plumpers Rd. S9: Tins 2G **109**
Plumpton Av. S64: Mexb 6H **51**
Plumpton Ct. S36: Thurl 4A **176**
Plumpton Gdns. DN4: Cant 6D **58**
Plumpton Pk. S72: Shaft 4F **11**
Plumpton Pk. Rd. DN4: Bess, Cant . . .1D **74**
Plum St. S3: Shef 1E **5** (2F **119**)
Plunket Rd. DN2: Don 6E **41**
Plymouth Rd. S7: Shef 3D **132**
Pocket Handkerchief La.
S26: Tod 5C **126**
Poggy La. S66: B'well 1C **102**
POGMOOR 6A **16**
Pogmoor La. S75: Barn 6H **15**
(Farm Ho. La.)
S75: Barn 1H **29**
(The Courtyard)
Pogmoor Rd. S70: Barn 6A **16**
S75: Barn 6A **16**
Pog Well La. S75: H'ham 5F **15**
(not continuous)
Point, The S60: Roth 6D **96**
Polka Ct. S3: Shef 5F **107**
Pollard Av. S5: Shef 1D **106**
Pollard Cres. S5: Shef 1D **106**
Pollard Rd. S5: Shef 1D **106**
Pollard St. S61: Kimb 4H **95**
Pollitt Cl. S9: Shef 2E **121**
Pollitt St. S75: Barn 5C **16**
Pollyfox Way S75: Dod 3G **29**
Pomegranate Theatre 5A **168**
Pomona St. S11: Shef 5D **118**
Pond Cl. S6: Stann 6E **105**
Pond Hill S1: Shef 3F **5** (3G **119**)
Pond La. S42: W'orth 6F **171**
Pond Rd. S6: Stann 6E **105**

Ponds Forge / Fitzalan Square Stop (ST)
. . . . .3G 5 (3G 119)
Ponds Forge International Sports Cen.
. . . . .3G 5 (3G 119)
Pond Sq. S1: Shef 3G 5
Pond St. S1: Shef 3F 5 (3G 119)
(not continuous)
S40: Ches 6H 167
S70: Barn 2D 30
(not continuous)
Pondwell Dr. S43: Brim 1E 169
Pontefract Rd. S70: Barn 1E 31
S71: Barn, Lund 1E 31
S72: Cud, Shaft 6E 11
S73: Bramp 5C 48
Pool Dr. DN4: Bess 1E 75
Poole Pl. S9: Shef 2F 121
Poole Rd. S9: Shef 2E 121
POOLSBROOK 6D 164
Poolsbrook Av. S43: Pool 6D 164
Poolsbrook Caravan Club
S43: Stav 6B 164
Poolsbrook Country Pk. 6B 164
Poolsbrook Cres. S43: Pool 6D 164
Poolsbrook Sq. S43: Pool 6D 164
Poolsbrook Vw. S43: Pool 6D 164
Pools La. S21: West H 5F 157
S71: Roy 3B 10
Pool Sq. S1: Shef 4E 5 (3F 119)
Pope Av. DN12: Con 4C 68
Pop La. DN12: Con 4F 69
Poplar Av. S20: Beig 3G 137
S36: Stoc 4D 174
S40: Bramp 6C 166
S63: Gol 5D 36
S65: Thry 6D 84
S72: Shaft 4F 11
Poplar Cl. DN3: Brant 3G 59
S18: Dron 5H 155
S21: Killa 5B 152
S35: Ough 3D 90
S64: Mexb 6E 51
Poplar Dr. S2: Don 4H 41
S60: Brins 4C 110
S63: Wath D 2G 65
Poplar Glade S66: Wick 6G 99
Poplar Gro. DN4: Warm 2D 70
DN12: Con 6E 69
S64: Swint 3C 66
S65: Rav 2B 100
S71: Lund 4B 18
Poplar Nook S26: Kiv P 5H 139
Poplar Pl. DN3: Arm 4E 43
S41: Ches 6G 161
Poplar Ri. S66: Malt 4G 101
Poplar Rd. S21: Ecki 2D 158
S35: Ough 3D 90
S73: Womb 2H 47
Poplars, The DN5: Barnb 1H 51
DN12: Con 5E 69
S25: Laugh C 3F 127
S42: Cut 6A 160
Poplars Ind. Est., The S60: Cat 1C 122
Poplars Rd. S70: Barn 3G 31
Poplar St. S72: Grim 2C 20
Poplar Ter. DN5: Ben 2A 40
S71: Roy 2A 10
Poplar Way DN9: Auck 1B 76
S60: Cat 1B 122
Popple St. S4: Shef 3A 108
Poppyfields Way DN3: Brant 5F 59
Poppy Pl. S5: Shef 1C 108
Porter Av. S75: Barn 6B 16
Porter Brook Vw. S11: Shef 6C 118
(not continuous)
Porter St. S43: Stav 4B 164
Porter Ter. S11: Shef 6B 118
S75: Barn 6A 16
Portland Av. S26: Ast 1D 138
Portland Bldgs. S6: Shef 1D 118
(off Portland St.)
Portland Bus. Pk. S13: Shef 4H 121
Portland Cl. S25: Nth A 6H 127
S41: Ches 4H 167
Portland Ct. S6: Shef 6D 106
Portland La. S1: Shef 4B 4 (3E 119)
Portland Pl. DN1: Don 1B 56
S66: Malt 5B 102

Portland Rd. DN11: New R 6G 75
S20: Beig 6H 137
Portland St. S6: Shef 1D 118
(Cross Bedford St.)
S6: Shef 1D 118
(Straw La.)
S64: Swint 3C 66
S70: Barn 2G 31
Portobello S1: Shef 3B 4 (3E 119)
Portobello La. S1: Shef 3B 4 (3E 119)
Portobello St. S1: Shef 3C 4 (3E 119)
Portsea Rd. S6: Shef 4A 106
Portway Cl. S12: Shef 3H 135
Pot House La. S36: Stoc 3D 174
Potterdyke Av. S62: Rawm 6G 65
POTTER HILL 1B 78
Potter Hill S61: Grea 5D 82
Potter Hill La. S35: High G 1B 78
Potteric Carr Nature Reserve 1G 73
Potteric Carr Rd. DN4: Don 3D 56
Potteries, The DN11: New R 5C 74
Potteries Acre S64: Swint 3C 66
Potters Cl. S41: Old W 4A 162
Potters Ga. S35: High G 1B 78
(not continuous)
Potters Way S64: Kiln 5D 66
Pottery Cl. S62: Rawm 3G 83
Pottery La. S62: Rawm 3A 84
Pottery La. E. S41: Whit M 1A 168
Pottery La. W. S41: Whit M 1H 167
Pottery Row S61: Roth 5B 96
Potts Cres. S72: Gt H 6F 21
Poucher St. S61: Kimb 4G 95
Poulton St. S71: Monk B 2A 18
Powder Mill La. S70: Wors 1H 45
Powell Dr. S21: Killa 4D 152
Powell St. S3: Shef 2A 4 (2D 118)
S70: Wors 6G 31
Powerhouse Sq. S74: Els 2E 63
(off Wath Rd.)
Powerleague
Barnsley 4H 31
Sheffield 1C 120
Power Sta. Rd. DN5: Don 6A 40
(not continuous)
Powley Rd. S6: Shef 5C 92
Poynton Av. S26: Ull 3D 124
Poynton Dr. S25: Dinn 4A 128
Poynton Way S26: Ull 3D 124
Poynton Wood Cres. S17: Bradw 4H 145
Poynton Wood Glade
S17: Bradw 4H 145
Prescott Rd. S6: Shef 2H 105
President Way S4: Shef 6A 108
Preston Av. S74: Jum 5D 46
Preston St. S8: Shef 1F 133
Preston Way S71: Monk B 2A 18
Prestwich St. S9: Shef 6E 95
Prestwold Way S41: Has 3B 172
Prestwood Gdns. S35: Chap 3D 78
Priest Cft. La. S71: D'fld 2A 34
Priestfield Gdns. S41: Ches 1C 166
Priestley Av. S62: Rawm 1A 84
S75: Kexb 6D 6
Priestley Cl. DN4: Balb 1G 71
Priestley St. S2: Shef 5G 119
Priest Royd S75: Dart 5H 7
Primrose Av. S5: Shef 6B 94
S60: Brins 5E 111
S73: D'fld 5A 34
Primrose Bank DN3: Smi 2F 17
Primrose Circ. DN11: New R 6D 74
Primrose Cl. S21: Killa 3D 152
S63: Bolt D 1A 50
Primrose Cres. S20: Beig 5G 137
Primrose Dr. S35: Eccl 2G 93
Primrose Hill S6: Shef 6C 106
(not continuous)
S60: Roth 2D 96
S74: Hoyl 1B 62
Primrose La. S21: Killa 2D 152
Primrose Pk. S60: Roth 2D 96
Primrose Pl. DN4: Bess 4G 57
Primrose Wlk. S8: Shef 2E 133
Primrose Way S74: Hoyl 2A 62
Primulas Cl. S25: Sth A 4F 141
Prince Arthur St. S75: Barn 6C 16
Princegate DN1: Don 1C 56

Prince of Wales Rd. S2: Shef 1D 134
S9: Shef 4F 121
Prince's Cres. DN12: New E 3C 70
Prince's Rd. DN4: Bess 3G 57
Princess Cl. S63: Bolt D 2A 50
Princess Ct. S2: Shef 6E 121
Princess Dr. S36: Spink 4E 175
S63: Thurn 3D 36
Princess Gdns. S73: Womb 2G 47
Princess Gro. S75: Pill 1B 60
Prince's Sq. DN3: Kirk Sa 4C 26
Princess Rd. S18: Dron 2F 155
S63: Gol 5D 36
S64: Mexb 1G 67
Princess St. DN6: Woodl 4C 22
S4: Shef 1A 120
S25: Laugh C 4F 127
S41: Ches 4G 167
S43: Brim 5E 163
S63: Wath D 5E 49
S70: Barn 1D 30
S72: Cud 5F 11
S72: Grim 2B 20
S73: Womb 1F 47
S74: Hoyl 1G 61
S75: Mapp 5H 7
Princes St. DN1: Don 1C 56
S60: Roth 4C 96
Prince St. S64: Swint 2C 66
Pringle La. S41: Old W 2G 161
Pringle Rd. S60: Brins 3C 110
Printing Office St. DN1: Don 1B 56
Prior Cft. S63: Bolt D 3C 50
Prior Rd. DN12: Con 5E 69
Priory, The S18: Dron 2F 155
Priory Av. S7: Shef 6E 118
Priory Cl. DN12: Con 3F 69
S35: Eccl 1F 93
S42: Walt 3C 170
S64: Mexb 4H 67
S70: Wors 2E 45
Priory Ct. S71: Monk B 3A 18
Priory Cres. S71: Lund 5B 18
Priory Pl. DN1: Don 1B 56
S7: Shef 6E 119
S71: Lund 4B 18
(not continuous)
Priory Rd. S7: Shef 1D 132
S35: Eccl 1F 93
S63: Bolt D 2B 50
S71: Lund 4B 18
(not continuous)
Priory Ter. S7: Shef 6E 119
Priory Wlk. DN1: Don 1C 56
(off High St.)
Priory Way S26: Ast 1D 138
Pritchard Cl. S12: Shef 5C 136
Private Dr. S43: Hol 6F 163
Probert Av. S63: Gol 5C 36
Proctor Pl. S6: Shef 4B 106
Progress Dr. S66: Braml 6A 100
Prominence Way S66: Sunn 2G 99
Prospect S36: Thurl 4A 176
Prospect Cl. S66: Braml 6A 100
Prospect Ct. S17: Bradw 5H 145
S62: Parkg 4G 83
Prospect Dr. S17: Bradw 5G 145
Prospect Ho. S43: Stav 5C 164
Prospect Pl. DN1: Don 2B 56
S17: Bradw 4H 145
S74: Hoyl 1A 62
Prospect Rd. DN5: Ben 4H 23
S2: Shef 1F 133
S17: Bradw 5H 145
S18: Dron 1H 155
S41: Old W 4G 161
S63: Bolt D 1B 50
S72: Cud 2E 19
Prospect St. S70: Barn 1C 30
S72: Cud 1E 19
Prospect Ter. S40: Ches 4F 167
Providence Ct. S70: Barn 2D 30
S73: Womb 6A 34
(off Providence St.)
Providence Rd. S6: Shef 6A 106
Providence St. S60: Roth 4D 96
S61: Grea 5D 82
S73: Womb 6A 34
Provincial Ho. S1: Shef 2C 4 (2E 119)

Psalter Ct. S11: Shef 1B **132**
Psalter Cft. S11: Shef 1A **132**
Psalter La. S11: Shef 1A **132**
Psalters Dr. S36: Oxs 6H **177**
Psalters La. S61: Kimb 3A **96**
Pudding Poke S6: Dung 4A **104**
Pullman Cl. S43: Stav 3C **164**
Pump Riding
DN12: New E 5E **71**
Purbeck Av. S40: Ches 4E **167**
Purbeck Ct. S20: Water 6E **137**
Purbeck Gro. S20: Water 6E **137**
Purbeck Rd. S20: Water 6E **137**
Purcell Cl. S66: Malt 6D **102**
Purslove Cl. S66: Braml 6B **100**
Pye Av. S75: Mapp 6H **7**
Pye Bank Cl. S3: Shef 6F **107**
Pye Bank Dr. S3: Shef 6F **107**
Pye Bank Rd. S3: Shef 1F **119**
Pym Rd. S64: Mexb 1F **67**
Pynot Rd. S41: Old W 4A **162**

Q

Quadrant, The S17: Tot 5F **145**
Quail Ri. S2: Shef 4B **120**
Quaker Cl. S63: Wath D 1E **65**
Quaker La. DN4: Warm 6E **55**
S71: Ard 2C **32**
(Crown Well Hill)
S71: Ard 2D **32**
(Top Fold)
S71: Monk B 4G **17**
Quantock Way S40: Ches 3C **166**
Quarry Bank S63: Wath D 6C **48**
Quarry Bank Cl. S72: Cud 3E **19**
Quarry Bank Ho.
S70: Barn 5D **16**
Quarry Bank Rd.
S41: Ches 6B **168**
Quarry Cl. S60: Brins 4B **110**
S75: Kexb 6E **7**
Quarry Field La. S66: Wick 1G **113**
(not continuous)
Quarryfield La. S66: Malt 4A **102**
Quarryfield Rd. S9: Shef 6E **109**
Quarry Flds. S66: Wick 1G **113**
Quarry Hill S20: Mosb 2B **150**
S21: Trow 1F **157**
S60: Roth 4E **97**
Quarry Hill Ct. S63: Wath D 2F **65**
Quarry Hill Rd.
S63: Wath D 2F **65**
QUARRY HILLS 5D **34**
Quarry La. DN3: Brant 4G **59**
DN6: Woodl 4B **22**
S11: Shef 2B **132**
S25: Nth A 2G **141**
S40: Bramp 6D **166**
S61: Grea 2D **96**
S64: Mexb 5E **51**
S73: D'fld 5D **34**
Quarry Pl. S71: Monk B 3F **17**
Quarry Rd. S13: Shef 4A **122**
S17: Tot 5F **145**
S18: App 3D **156**
S21: Killa 3B **152**
S74: Black H 3A **46**
Quarry St. S62: Rawm 2G **83**
S64: Mexb 2G **67**
S70: Barn 2E **31**
S71: Smi 3F **17**
S72: Cud 1E **19**
Quarry Va. S72: Cud 2E **19**
Quarry Va. Gro. S12: Shef 4F **135**
Quarry Va. Rd. S12: Shef 4F **135**
Quayside, The
S2: Shef 1H **5** (2H **119**)
Queen Av. DN11: New R 5B **74**
S66: Malt 6B **102**
Queen Mary Cl. S2: Shef 1D **134**
Queen Mary Cres.
DN3: Kirk Sa 4C **26**
S2: Shef 6D **120**
Queen Mary Gro. S2: Shef 1C **134**
Queen Mary M. S2: Shef 1D **134**
Queen Mary Ri. S2: Shef 6D **120**
Queen Mary Rd. S2: Shef 6C **120**
(not continuous)
S40: Bramp 1C **170**
Queen Mary's Rd.
DN11: New R 5B **74**
Queen Mary St. S66: Malt 6C **102**
Queen Rd. S72: Grim 2C **20**
Queens Av. S26: Kiv P 6H **139**
S64: Swint 2C **66**
S72: Midd 3E **35**
S75: Barn 6C **16**
Queensberry Rd. DN2: Don 5H **41**
Queen's Ct. DN5: Don 4H **39**
Queens Cres.
DN12: New E 3C **70**
S74: Hoyl 1F **61**
Queens Dr. DN5: Don 4H **39**
S72: Cud 5F **11**
S72: Shaft 3E **11**
S75: Barn 5B **16**
S75: Dod 3G **29**
Queens Gdns. S2: Shef 6H **119**
S73: Womb 2G **47**
S74: Hoyl 1G **61**
S75: Barn 5B **16**
Queensgate DN1: Don 1C **56**
S35: Gren 2C **92**
Queens Ho. S71: Barn 6F **17**
Queens M. S2: Shef 6H **119**
Queens Pk. DN12: New E 3C **70**
Queen's Park Miniature Railway *6G 167*
(off Boythorpe Rd.)
Queen's Park Sports Cen. 6G **167**
Queens Retail Pk.
S2: Shef 6G **119**
Queens Rd. DN1: Don 6D **40**
S2: Shef 6G **5** (1F **133**)
S20: Beig 4G **137**
S26: Swal 1B **138**
S71: Barn 1E **31**
S72: Cud 5F **11**
Queen's Row S3: Shef 1C **4** (2E **119**)
Queens Stables S2: Shef 6H **119**
Queen's Ter. S64: Mexb 1F **67**
Queen St. DN4: Balb 4A **56**
(not continuous)
S1: Shef 2E **5** (2F **119**)
S20: Mosb 3D **150**
S21: Ecki 1F **159**
S25: Dinn 4A **128**
S35: Chap 3F **79**
S36: Pen 4E **177**
S40: Ches 4G **167**
S43: Brim 5E **163**
S43: Stav 6A **164**
S62: Rawm 1H **83**
S63: Gol 5D **36**
S63: Thurn 3D **36**
S64: Swint 3C **66**
S65: Roth 3H **97**
S70: Barn 1D **30**
S73: D'fld 4C **34**
S74: Hoyl 1F **61**
Queen St. M. S20: Mosb 3D **150**
Queen St. Nth.
S41: Whit M 6H **161**
Queen St. Sth. S70: Barn 1E **31**
Queens Vw. S2: Shef 6H **119**
Queensway S60: Roth 2G **111**
S70: Wors 5G **31**
S71: Roy 2H **9**
S72: Grim 2B **20**
S74: Hoyl 6C **46**
S75: Barn 5B **16**
Queensway Ct. S60: Roth 2G **111**
Queenswood Cl. S6: Shef 1H **105**
Queenswood Ct. S6: Shef 1G **105**
Queenswood Dr. S6: Shef 1G **105**
Queenswood Ga. S6: Shef 1G **105**
Queenswood Rd. S6: Shef 1G **105**
Queen Victoria Rd.
S17: Bradw 6G **145**
Quern Way S73: D'fld 4B **34**
Quest Av. S73: Hem 4F **47**
Quiet La. S10: Shef 2C **130**
Quilter Rd. S66: Malt 6D **102**
Quintec Ct. S61: Grea 1F **97**
QUOIT GREEN 3G **155**
Quoit Grn. S18: Dron 3G **155**
Quorn Dr. S40: Ches 3B **166**

R

Rabbit La. S21: Spink 2H **159**
Raby Rd. DN2: Don 5E **41**
Raby St. S9: Tins 1H **109**
Race Comn. Av. S36: Cub 6C **176**
Racecommon La. S70: Barn 3C **30**
(not continuous)
Racecommon Rd. S70: Barn 3C **30**
Racecourse Cl. S64: Swint 3H **65**
Racecourse Mt. S41: Ches 6G **161**
Racecourse Rd.
S41: Ches, Whit M 6G **161**
S64: Swint 3H **65**
Race La. S36: Bolst 6F **175**
Race St. S70: Barn 1D **30**
Racker Way S6: Shef 5A **106**
Rackford La. S25: Nth A 4A **142**
S81: Work 4A **142**
Rackford Rd. S25: Nth A 3H **141**
Radbourne Comn.
S18: Dron W 3C **154**
Radburn Rd. DN11: New R 6B **74** & 6F **75**
Radcliffe Cl. DN5: Scawt 1F **39**
Radcliffe La. DN5: Scawt 1F **39**
Radcliffe Mt. DN5: Ben 6H **23**
Radcliffe Rd. DN5: Ben 6H **23**
S71: Ath 6E **9**
Radford Cl. S65: Rav 2B **100**
Radford Pk. Av. WF9: Sth K 5H **13**
Radford St. S3: Shef 2B **4** (2E **119**)
Radiance Rd. DN1: Don 5D **40**
Radley Av. S66: Wick 5G **99**
Radnor Cl. S20: Sot 6H **137**
Radnor Way DN2: Don 5H **41**
Raeburn Cl. S14: Shef 6B **134**
Raeburn Pl. S14: Shef 5B **134**
Raeburn Rd. S14: Shef 6B **134**
Raeburn Way S14: Shef 6B **134**
Ragusa Dr. DN11: New R 6G **75**
Raikes St. S64: Mexb 2E **67**
Rail Mill Way S62: Parkg 6G **83**
RAILS 2B **116**
Rails Rd. S6: Shef, Stann 2B **116**
Railway Av. S60: Cat 1D **122**
Railway Cotts. S41: Cor 5E **173**
S60: Cat 6D **110**
S75: Dod 3F **29**
Railway Ct. DN4: Don 3C **56**
Railway Ter. S41: Has 3A **172**
S60: Roth 4D **96**
S63: Gol 5C **36**
S71: Roy 2F 9
(off High St.)
Railway Vw. S63: Gol 5D **36**
Rainborough Ct. S63: Bramp B 6A **48**
Rainborough M. S63: Bramp B 5C **48**
Rainborough Rd. S63: Wath D 6C **48**
Rainboro Vw. S73: Hem 5F **47**
Rainbow Av. S12: Shef 4C **136**
Rainbow Cl. S12: Shef 4C **136**
Rainbow Cres. S12: Shef 4D **136**
Rainbow Dr. S12: Shef 4D **136**
Rainbow Gro. S12: Shef 4D **136**
Rainbow Pl. S12: Shef 4D **136**
Rainbow Rd. S12: Shef 4D **136**
Rainbow Wlk. *S12: Shef 4C 136*
(off Carter Lodge Dr.)
Rainbow Way S12: Shef 4C **136**
Rainford Dr. S71: Monk B 2A **18**
Rainford Sq. DN3: Kirk Sa 3C **26**
RAINSTORTH 6B **80**
Rainton Gro. S75: Barn 5A **16**
Rainton Rd. DN1: Don 2D **56**
Raintree Ct. DN5: Cus 5G **39**
Raisen Hall Pl. S5: Shef 2F **107**
Raisen Hall Rd. S5: Shef 1E **107**
Rake Bri. Rd. DN7: Hatf 1H **43**
Rakes La. DN11: Lov 4B **72**
DN12: Old E 5D **88**
Raleigh Ct. DN2: Don 1G **57**
Raleigh Dr. S35: Burn 3C **78**
Raleigh Rd. S2: Shef 2G **133**
Raleigh Ter. DN4: Balb 6F **55**

Raley St. S70: Barn 3C **30**
(not continuous)
Ralph Ellis Dr. S36: Stoc 4D **174**
Ralph Rd. S43: Stav 4D **164**
Ralston Ct. S20: Half 4E **151**
Ralston Cft. S20: Half 4F **151**
Ralston Gro. S20: Half 4E **151**
Ralston Pl. S20: Half 4E **151**
Ramper La. DN3: Barn D 1B **26**
Ramper Rd. S66: Carr 3E **115**
S81: Letw 3H **129**
Rampton Rd. S7: Shef 1E **133**
Ramsay Cres. DN5: Don 4G **39**
Ramsden Rd. DN4: Hex 2H **55**
S60: Roth 5F **97**
Ramsey Av. S40: Walt 1E **171**
Ramsey Rd. S10: Shef 2B **118**
Ramshaw Cl. S41: Ches 1D **166**
Ramshaw Rd. S18: Uns 6B **156**
Ramsker Dr. DN3: Arm 5E **43**
Ranby Rd. S11: Shef 1A **132**
Randall Pl. S2: Shef 6E **119**
Randall St. S2: Shef 5F **119**
S21: Ecki 2C **158**
Randerson Dr. S64: Kiln 5D **66**
Rands La. DN3: Arm 3F **43**
Rands La. Ind. Est. DN3: Arm 3G **43**
Ranelagh Dr. S11: Shef 3A **132**
Raneld Mt. S40: Walt 2D **170**
Ranfield Ct. S65: Rav 2B **100**
Rangeley Rd. S6: Shef 1H **117**
Range Rd. S4: Shef 3C **108**
RANMOOR **5G 117**
Ranmoor Chase S10: Shef 5A **118**
Ranmoor Cliffe Rd. S10: Shef 5F **117**
Ranmoor Cl. S41: Has 2B **172**
Ranmoor Ct. S10: Shef 6H **117**
Ranmoor Cres. S10: Shef 5G **117**
Ranmoor Pk. Rd. S10: Shef 5G **117**
Ranmoor Ri. S10: Shef 5G **117**
Ranmoor Rd. S10: Shef 5G **117**
Ranmoor Vw. S10: Shef 5G **117**
Ranmoor Village, The
S10: Shef 4H **117**
Ranskill Ct. S9: Shef 5F **109**
Ranulf Ct. S7: Shef 5B **132**
Ranworth Cl. DN5: Cus 5F **39**
Ranworth Rd. S66: Braml 5B **100**
Ranyard Rd. DN4: Balb 5G **55**
Raseby Av. S20: Water 6F **137**
Raseby Cl. S20: Water 6F **137**
Raseby Pl. S20: Water 6F **137**
Rasen Cl. S64: Mexb 6H **51**
Ratcliffe Cl. S41: Has 3B **172**
Ratcliffe Rd. S11: Shef 6C **118**
Ratten Row DN11: Wad 5F **73**
S75: Dod 4F **29**
Rattigan Ho. *DN2: Don* *4F* ***41***
(off Parkway Nth.)
Ravencar Rd. S21: Ecki 1C **158**
Ravencarr Pl. S2: Shef 5D **120**
Ravencarr Rd. S2: Shef 5D **120**
Raven Dr. S61: Thorpe H 2D **80**
Raven Edge S65: Rav 4A **100**
RAVENFIELD **5A 86**
Ravenfield Cl. S20: Mosb 6B **136**
RAVENFIELD COMMON **2A 100**
Ravenfield Ct. DN12: Con 5C **68**
Ravenfield Dr. S71: Smi 2F **17**
Ravenfield La. S65: Hoot R, Rav 2H **85**
Ravenfield Rd. DN3: Arm 5F **43**
Ravenfield St. DN12: Den M 2C **68**
Ravenholt S70: Wors 6F **31**
Raven La. S72: Sth H 1D **10**
Raven Mdws. S64: Swint 5B **66**
Ravenna Cl. S70: Barn 2G **31**
Raven Rd. S7: Shef 2C **132**
Raven Royd S71: Ath 5E **9**
Ravenscar Cl. DN12: Den M 3B **68**
Ravens Cl. S75: Mapp 6A **8**
Ravenscourt S70: Wors 6G **31**
Ravenscroft Av. S13: Shef 6H **121**
Ravenscroft Cl. S13: Shef 6H **121**
Ravenscroft Ct. S13: Shef 6H **121**
Ravenscroft Cres. S13: Shef 6H **121**
Ravenscroft Dr. S13: Shef 6H **121**
Ravenscroft Oval S13: Shef 6H **121**
Ravenscroft Pl. S13: Shef 6H **121**
Ravenscroft Rd. S13: Shef 6G **121**
Ravenscroft Way S13: Shef 6H **121**
Ravensdale Cl. S43: Ink 2H **169**
Ravensdale Rd. S18: Dron W 3B **154**
Ravenshaw Cl. S75: Barn 5A **16**
Ravenside Retail Pk. S40: Ches 6H **167**
Ravensmead Ct. S63: Bolt D 3B **50**
Ravens Wlk. DN12: Con 4H **69**
Ravenswood Dr. DN9: Auck 1H **59**
S66: Sunn 2G **99**
Ravenswood Rd. S40: Ches 3B **166**
Ravensworth Rd. DN1: Don 2D **56**
Ravine, The S5: Shef 3B **94**
Raw La. S66: Staint 1F **103**
Rawlins Ct. S18: Coal A 6H **147**
RAWMARSH **3G 83**
Rawmarsh Hill S62: Parkg 4G **83**
Rawmarsh Ho. *S62: Parkg* *4G* ***83***
(off Ryan Pl.)
Rawmarsh Leisure Cen. **4H 83**
Rawmarsh Rd. S60: Roth 3E **97**
Rawmarsh Shop. Cen.
S62: Rawm 3G **83**
Rawson Cl. DN4: Cant 3C **58**
Rawson Rd. S65: Roth 3F **97**
Rawsons Bank S35: Eccl 2G **93**
Rawson Spring Av. S6: Shef 2C **106**
Rawson Spring Rd. S6: Shef 2C **106**
Rawson Spring Way S6: Shef 2C **106**
Rawson St. S6: Shef 5D **106**
Raybould Rd. S61: Kimb P 1A **96**
Rayleigh Av. S43: Brim 6C **162**
Rayls Ri. S26: Tod 3C **140**
Rayls Rd. S26: Tod 3C **140**
Raymond Av. S72: Grim 2B **20**
Raymond Rd. DN5: Scawt 4G **39**
S70: Barn 2A **32**
Raynald Rd. S2: Shef 5D **120**
Raynor Sike La. S35: Ough 2B **90**
Reader Cres. S64: Swint 2C **66**
Reaper Cres. S35: High G 2D **78**
Reasbeck Ter. S71: Smi 3E **17**
Reasby Av. S65: Rav 2A **100**
Reaton M. S75: Barn 5A **16**
Reavill Cl. S25: Dinn 4A **128**
Rebecca M. S70: Barn 2E **31**
Rebecca Row S70: Barn 2E **31**
Recreation Av. S66: Thurc 6C **114**
Recreation La. DN11: New R 5B **74**
Recreation Rd. DN6: Woodl 4C **22**
S43: Brim C 3E **169**
S63: Wath D 5G **49**
Rectory Cl. S21: Ecki 6F **151**
S36: Stoc 3E **175**
S63: Thurn 2A **36**
S71: Carl 5A **10**
S73: Womb 2G **47**
Rectory Ct. S25: Laugh M 1G **127**
Rectory Dr. S42: W'orth 6F **171**
S60: Whist 4B **112**
Rectory Gdns. DN1: Don 6D **40**
DN12: Old E 1B **88**
S21: Killa 4C **152**
S26: Tod 4C **140**
Rectory La. DN9: Finn 3E **77**
S63: Thurn 2A **36**
Rectory M. DN5: Sprot 4C **54**
Rectory Rd. S21: Killa 4C **152**
S43: Stav 4B **164**
Rectory St. S62: Rawm 4G **83**
Rectory Way S71: Monk B 5A **18**
Redbourne Rd. DN5: Ben 1A **40**
REDBROOK **3A 16**
Redbrook Av. S41: Has 2A **172**
Redbrook Bus. Pk. S75: Barn 3A **16**
Redbrook Ct. S75: Barn 4B **16**
Redbrook Cft. S20: Mosb 5B **136**
Redbrook Gro. S20: Mosb 5B **136**
Redbrook Mill Cl. S75: Barn 4H **15**
Redbrook Rd. S75: Barn 4H **15**
Redbrook Vw. S75: Barn 4B **16**
Redbrook Wlk. S75: Barn 4B **16**
Redcar Cl. DN12: Den M 4B **68**
Redcar Rd. S10: Shef 3B **118**
Redcliffe Cl. S75: Barn 4A **16**
Red Dike La. DN11: Wils 5F **89**
Redfearn St. S71: Barn 6E **17**
Redfern Av. S20: Water 1E **151**
Redfern Ct. S20: Water 1E **151**
Redfern Dr. S20: Water 1E **151**
Red Fern Gro. S36: Stoc 4D **174**
Redfern Gro. S20: Water 1E **151**
Redgrave S3: Shef 1F **5**
Redgrave Pl. S66: Flan 4G **99**
Redgrove Way S40: Walt 2D **170**
Redhall Cl. DN3: Kirk Sa 4D **26**
Red Hill S1: Shef 2C **4** (3E **119**)
S26: Kiv P, Kiv S 6C **140**
Redhill Av. S70: Barn 3H **31**
Redhill Ct. DN11: Wad 5E **73**
S75: Barn 4H **15**
Red Hill La. DN5: Hick 3H **37**
Redholme S10: Shef 4F **117**
Red Ho. Cl. S43: New W 2C **162**
Redhouse Interchange DN6: Woodl . . .1A **22**
Red Ho. La. DN6: Adw S 1A **22**
Red Ho. Wlk. S40: Ches 3E **167**
Red Kite Av. S63: Wath D 4F **49**
Redland Gro. S75: Stain 4A **8**
Redland La. S7: Shef 5C **132**
Redland Way S66: Malt 4H **101**
Red La. S10: Shef 5B **118**
S41: Old W 5B **162**
Red Lion Yd. *S60: Roth* *4E* ***97***
(off Effingham St.)
Redmarsh Av. S62: Rawm 1F **83**
Redmires La. S10: Shef 5A **116**
Redmires Way S10: Shef 5A **116**
Rednall Cl. S40: Ches 3B **166**
Red Oak La. S6: Stann 5D **104**
Red Quarry La. S25: Dinn 6E **129**
S81: Gild 6E **129**
Redrock Rd. S60: Roth 2H **111**
Redscope Cres. S61: Kimb P 6G **81**
Redscope Rd. S61: Kimb 1G **95**
Redshank Pl. S73: Bramp 3C **48**
Redshank Rd. S63: Wath D 4E **49**
Redthorne Way S72: Shaft 3E **11**
Redthorn Rd. S13: Shef 6A **122**
Redthorpe Crest S75: Barn 4H **15**
Redvers Buller Rd. S40: Ches 1H **171**
Redwall Cl. S25: Laugh C 4F **127**
Redwood Av. S21: Killa 5B **152**
S71: Roy 3H **9**
Redwood Cl. S43: Hol 6F **163**
S74: Hoyl 1A **62**
Redwood Ct. S25: Dinn 4H **127**
Redwood Dr. S66: Malt 5F **101**
Redwood Glen S35: Chap 4E **79**
Reed Cl. S73: D'fld 5B **34**
Reedham Dr. S66: Braml 5B **100**
Reed Wlk. S63: Wath D 4E **49**
Reeves Way DN3: Arm 4C **42**
Regent Av. DN3: Arm 5F **43**
Regent Ct. DN1: Don 1D **56**
S1: Shef 3B **4**
S6: Shef 4C **106**
S74: Hoyl 1F **61**
S75: Barn 4B **16**
Regent Cres. S71: Ath 1E **17**
S72: Sth H 1H **11**
Regent Gdns. S70: Barn 5D **16**
Regent Gro. DN5: Cus 5G **39**
DN11: New R . . . . .6D **74** & 6H **75**
Regent Sq. DN1: Don 1D **56**
Regent St. DN4: Balb 5H **55**
S1: Shef 3B **4** (3E **119**)
S61: Kimb 4A **96**
S70: Barn 6D **16**
S72: Sth H 1H **11**
S74: Hoyl 1F **61**
Regent St. Sth. S70: Barn 6E **17**
Regents Way S26: Ast 1D **138**
Regent Ter. DN1: Don 1D **56**
S3: Shef 3B **4** (3E **119**)
Regina Cres. S72: Brier 4H **11**
Reginald Rd. S70: Barn 3A **32**
S73: Womb 2A **48**
Rembrandt Dr. S18: Dron 3D **154**
Remington Av. S5: Shef 3E **93**
Remington Dr. S5: Shef 3E **93**
Remington Rd. S5: Shef 4E **93**
Remount Rd. S61: Kimb P 6G **81**
Remount Way S61: Kimb P 6G **81**
Rempstone Dr. S41: Has 3A **172**
Renald La. S36: H'swne 1E **177**

Renathorpe Rd. S5: Shef 4A 94
Rencliffe Av. S60: Roth 1G 111
Reneville Cl. S5: Shef 2F 93
  S60: Roth 6F 97
Reneville Ct. S60: Roth 6E 97
Reneville Cres. S5: Shef 2F 93
Reneville Dr. S5: Shef 2F 93
Reneville Rd. S60: Roth 6E 97
Reney Av. S8: Shef 4C 146
Reney Cres. S8: Shef 4C 146
Reney Dr. S8: Shef 4C 146
Reney Pl. S8: Shef 3D 146
Reney Wlk. S8: Shef 4C 146
RENISHAW 4H 159
Renishaw Av. S60: Roth 2A 112
Renishaw Hall & Gardens 2G 159
Renishaw Park 3G 159
Renishaw Park Golf Course 2H 159
Renshaw Rd. S43: Mas M 1F 165
Renshaw Cl. S35: High G 6B 60
Renshaw Rd. S13: Shef 2H 131
Renville Cl. S62: Rawm 1F 83
Renway Rd. S60: Roth 1H 111
Repton Cl. S40: Ches 3B 166
Repton Pl. S18: Dron W 3B 154
Reresby Cres. S60: Whist 2B 112
Reresby Dr. S60: Whist 2B 112
Reresby Rd. S60: Whist 2A 112
  S65: Thry 6F 85
Reresby Wlk. DN12: Den M 2C 68
Reservoir Rd. S10: Shef 3B 118
  S26: Ull 2B 124
Reservoir Ter. S40: Ches 4F 167
Retail World S60: Roth 6G 83
Retford Dr. S13: Shef 5C 122
Retford Wlk. DN11: Ross 5E 75
Revell Cl. S65: Roth 3C 98
Revill Cl. S66: Malt 4A 102
Revill La. S13: Shef 2D 136
Revolution House (Museum) 3H 161
Rex Av. S7: Shef 4A 132
Reynard Cres. S21: Reni 4H 159
Reynard La. S6: Stann 1C 116
Reynolds Cl. S18: Dron 4D 154
  S66: Flan 4G 99
Rhodes Av. S41: Ches 3F 167
  S61: Kimb P 6G 81
Rhodes Dr. S60: Whist 2B 112
Rhodesia Ct. DN4: Bess 4A 58
Rhodesia Rd. S40: Bramp 6C 166
Rhodes St.
  S2: Shef 4H 5 (3H 119)
Rhodes Ter. S70: Barn 2F 31
Rialto S3: Shef 1F 119
   (off Kelham Island)
Ribble Cft. S35: Chap 2F 79
Ribblesdale Dr. S12: Ridg 1A 150
Ribble Way S5: Shef 1H 107
Riber Av. S71: Ath 1F 17
Riber Cl. S6: Stann 6E 105
  S43: Ink 3H 169
Riber Ter. S40: Ches 6F 167
Ribston Cl. S9: Shef 1D 120
Ribston M. S9: Shef 2E 121
Ribston Pl. S9: Shef 2E 121
Ribston Rd. S9: Shef 2D 120
Ribston Wlk. S9: Shef 2E 121
Richard Av. S71: Smi 2F 17
Richard La. DN11: New R 5B 74
Richard Rd. S60: Roth 5F 97
  S71: Smi 2F 17
  S75: Dart 6E 7
Richards Ct. S2: Shef 2G 133
Richardson Wlk. S73: Womb 6E 33
Richards Rd. S2: Shef 1F 133
   (not continuous)
Richard St. S70: Barn 1C 30
Richards Way S62: Rawm 2H 83
Rich Farm Cl. DN5: Ark 5C 24
RICHMOND 1G 135
Richmond Av. S13: Shef 6H 121
  S75: Dart 1E 15
Richmond Bus. Pk. DN4: Don 4D 56
Richmond Cl. S40: Walt 2F 171
Richmond Ct. S13: Shef 1G 135
Richmond Farm M. S13: Shef 1G 135
Richmond Gro. S13: Shef 6H 121
Richmond Hall Av. S13: Shef 6G 121

Richmond Hall Cres. S13: Shef 6G 121
Richmond Hall Dr. S13: Shef 6G 121
Richmond Hall Rd. S13: Shef 6G 121
Richmond Hall Way S13: Shef 1G 135
Richmond Hill Ho. S13: Shef 1G 135
Richmond Hill Rd. DN5: Don 2F 55
RICHMOND PARK 4G 95
Richmond Pk. Av. S13: Shef 4H 121
  S61: Kimb 4G 95
Richmond Pk. Cl. S13: Shef 5H 121
Richmond Pk. Cres. S13: Shef 4H 121
Richmond Pk. Cft. S13: Shef 5H 121
Richmond Pk. Dr. S13: Shef 5H 121
Richmond Pk. Gro. S13: Shef 5H 121
Richmond Pk. Ri.
  S13: Shef 4G 121
Richmond Pk. Rd. S13: Shef 4H 121
Richmond Pk. Vw. S13: Shef 5H 121
Richmond Pk. Way S13: Shef 5H 121
Richmond Pl. S13: Shef 1G 135
Richmond Rd. DN5: Scaws 3E 39
  S13: Shef 2F 135
  S61: Kimb 4H 95
  S63: Thurn 2B 36
Richmond Way S61: Kimb 4H 95
Richworth Rd. S13: Shef 6A 122
Ricknald Cl. S26: Augh 5C 124
Ridal Av. S36: Stoc 2C 174
Ridal Cl. S36: Stoc 2C 174
Ridal Cft. S36: Stoc 2C 174
Riddings Cl. S2: Shef 1D 134
  S66: Thurc 6C 114
  WF9: Hems 1E 13
Riddings Cft. S41: Ches 2D 166
Rider Rd. S6: Shef 4B 106
Ridge, The DN6: Woodl 4A 22
  S10: Shef 5D 116
Ridge Balk La. DN6: Woodl 3A 22
Ridge Cl. S10: Shef 4D 116
  S65: Roth 3G 97
Ridgehill Av. S12: Shef 2D 134
Ridgehill Gro. S12: Shef 3E 135
Ridge Rd. DN6: Highf 6C 22
  S21: Mar L 2H 157
  S61: Kimb 5B 80
Ridge Vw. Cl. S9: Shef 1D 108
Ridge Vw. Dr. S9: Shef 1D 108
Ridgewalk Way S70: Wors 4E 31
RIDGEWAY 2H 149
Ridgeway S65: Roth 3B 98
Ridgeway, The S18: Coal A 1A 156
Ridgeway Cl. S65: Roth 3C 98
Ridgeway Cott. Industry Cen.
  S12: Shef 2H 149
Ridgeway Craft Cen. 2H 149
Ridgeway Cres. S12: Shef 3D 134
  S71: Carl 5H 9
Ridgeway Dr. S12: Shef 2D 134
RIDGEWAY MOOR 4H 149
Ridgeway Moor S12: Ridg 4H 149
Ridgeway Moor Farm Ct.
  S12: Shef 4H 149
Ridgeway Rd. S12: Shef 2D 134
  S36: Brins 4D 110
Ridgewood Av. DN3: Eden 1C 42
Ridgway Av. S73: D'fld 4B 34
Ridgway Cl. S66: Hel 5D 100
Riding Cl. DN4: Bess 6E 59
  S66: Flan 5F 99
Ridings, The S71: Monk B 3G 17
Ridings Av. S71: Smi 3G 17
Rig Cl. S61: Kimb P 1A 96
Rig Dr. S64: Swint 3H 65
Riggotts La. S42: Walt 3E 171
Riggotts Way S42: Cut 6A 160
Riggs High Rd. S6: Stann 1A 116
Riggs Low La. S6: Stann 1A 116
Riggs Low La. S6: Stann 1B 116
Rig La. S62: Neth Hau 2D 82
Riley Av. DN4: Balb 6G 55
Riley Cl. S61: Kimb P 1A 96
Riley Rd. S63: Wath D 1G 65
Rimington Rd. S73: Womb 1G 47
Rimini Ri. S73: D'fld 5H 33
RINGINGLOW 4B 130
Ringinglow Gdns. S11: Shef 3F 131

Ringinglow Rd. S11: Shef 4A 130
Ringstead Av. S10: Shef 4F 117
Ringstead Cres. S10: Shef 4F 117
Ringstone Gro. S72: Brier 3B 12
Ringway S63: Bolt D 2A 50
Ringwood Av. S41: Ches 1F 167
  S43: Stav 6H 163
Ringwood Cres. S20: Sot 6H 137
Ringwood Dr. S20: Sot 6H 137
Ringwood Gro. S20: Sot 6H 137
Ringwood Rd. S20: Sot 6H 137
  S43: Brim 6E 163
Ringwood Vw. S43: Brim 1E 169
Ripley Gro. S75: Barn 4A 16
Ripley St. S6: Shef 5B 106
Ripon Av. DN2: Don 4E 41
Ripon St. S9: Shef 1C 120
   (not continuous)
Ripon Way S26: Swal 1B 138
Rippon Ct. S62: Rawm 1G 83
Rippon Cres. S6: Shef 4A 106
Rippon Rd. S6: Shef 4A 106
Rise, The DN4: Warm 2E 71
  S25: Nth A 3H 141
  S64: Swint 4A 66
  S72: Brier 4B 12
Risedale Rd. S63: Gol 6E 37
Rising St. S3: Shef 6G 107
Rivelin Bank S6: Shef 5A 106
Rivelin Ct. S6: Shef 3C 116
Rivelin Glen S6: Shef 2F 117
Rivelin Glen Cotts.
  S6: Shef 2F 117
Rivelin Pk. Ct. S6: Shef 6H 105
Rivelin Pk. Cres. S6: Shef 6H 105
Rivelin Pk. Dr. S6: Shef 6G 105
Rivelin Pk. Rd. S6: Shef 1H 117
Rivelin Rd. S6: Shef 6H 105
Rivelin St. S6: Shef 6A 106
Rivelin Ter. S6: Shef 6H 105
Rivelin Valley Rd. S6: Shef 3A 116
River Bank S35: Ough 3F 91
River Ct. S17: Dore 3H 145
   (off Ladies Spring Dr.)
Riverdale Av. S10: Shef 6H 117
Riverdale Dr. S10: Shef 6H 117
Riverdale M. S10: Shef 6G 117
Riverdale Pk. S43: Stav 3D 164
Riverdale Rd. DN5: Scawt 2F 39
  S10: Shef 5H 117
Riverhead DN5: Sprot 3C 54
Riverside S6: Shef 5H 105
Riverside Cl. DN4: Hex 3G 55
  DN12: Con 3F 69
  S6: Shef 4G 105
  S73: D'fld 5D 34
Riverside Ct. S9: Shef 5C 108
  S25: Laugh C 3F 127
  S64: Mexb 2H 67
Riverside Dr. DN5: Sprot 4D 54
Riverside Gdns. DN9: Auck 1G 59
  S63: Bolt D 3C 50
Riverside Ho. S60: Roth 4D 96
Riverside M. S6: Shef 4B 106
   (off off Rudyard Rd.)
Riverside Pk. S2: Shef 5G 119
Riverside Pct. S60: Roth 4E 97
   (off Corporation St.)
Riverside Way S60: Roth 5D 96
River Ter. S6: Shef 4B 106
River Vw. S75: Wool G 3F 7
River Vw. Rd. S35: Ough 3E 91
River Way DN9: Auck 1G 59
Riviera Mt. DN5: Don 5A 40
Riviera Pde. DN5: Don 5A 40
Rix Ct. S64: Kiln 6C 66
Rix Rd. S64: Kiln 6C 66
Roache Dr. S63: Gol 6B 36
Roach Rd. S11: Shef 1B 132
Robert Av. S71: Barn 6A 18
Robert Cl. S18: Uns 1F 161
Robert Rd. S8: Shef 3E 147
Roberts Av. DN12: Con 5G 69
Roberts Gro. S26: Ast 1D 138
Robertshaw S3: Shef 2A 4
Robertshaw Cres. S36: Spink 3F 175
Robertson Dr. S6: Shef 6H 105
Robertson Rd. S6: Shef 1H 117

Roberts Rd.—Rose Tree Av.

Roberts Rd. DN4: Balb . . . 3A **56**
DN12: New E . . . 5D **70**
Roberts St. S72: Cud . . . 1E **19**
S73: Womb . . . 2F **47**
Robert St. S60: Roth . . . 4C **96**
Robey St. S4: Shef . . . 3A **108**
Robinbrook La. S12: Shef . . . 2F **149**
Robin Cft. S40: Birdh . . . 3G **171**
Robincroft Rd. S42: W'orth . . . 6E **171**
Robinets Rd. S61: Wing . . . 5B **82**
ROBIN HOOD AIRPORT DONCASTER SHEFFIELD . . . 4C 76
Robin Hood Av. S71: Roy . . . 2A **10**
Robin Hood Chase S6: Stann . . . 5D **104**
Robin Hood Cres. DN3: Eden . . . 1D **42**
Robin Hood Rd. DN3: Eden . . . 1D **42**
S9: Shef . . . 6D **94**
Robin La. S20: Beig . . . 3G **137**
S71: Roy . . . 2A **10**
WF9: Hems . . . 1A **12**
Robin Pl. S26: Ast . . . 2D **138**
Robins Cl. S26: Ast . . . 1D **138**
Robinson Av. S9: Shef . . . 2E **121**
Robinson Ct. S61: Kimb . . . 3A **96**
Robinson Rd. S2: Shef . . . 4H **119**
Robinson's Sq. S70: Birdw . . . 5D **44**
Robinson St. S60: Roth . . . 6E **97**
Robinson Way S21: Killa . . . 4B **152**
Rob Royd S70: Wors . . . 5B **30**
S75: Dod . . . 4G **29**
Rob Royd La. S70: Wors . . . 5C **30**
Roche *S20: Westf* . . . *2F **151***
(off Shortbrook Dr.)
Roche Cl. S71: Monk B . . . 5G **17**
Roche End S26: Tod . . . 3B **140**
Rocher Av. S35: Gren . . . 3D **92**
Rocher Cl. S35: Gren . . . 3D **92**
Rocher Gro. S35: Gren . . . 3D **92**
Rochester Cl. S10: Shef . . . 5B **116**
Rochester Dr. S10: Shef . . . 5B **116**
Rochester Rd. S10: Shef . . . 5B **116**
S25: Sth A . . . 5G **141**
S71: Monk B . . . 4G **17**
Rochester Row DN5: Scaws . . . 5E **39**
Rockcliffe Cl. DN11: Wad . . . 5E **73**
Rockcliffe Dr. DN11: Wad . . . 5E **73**
Rockcliffe Ho's. *S62: Rawm* . . . *4G **83***
(off High St.)
Rockcliffe Rd. S62: Rawm . . . 4G **83**
Rockfield Dr. S81: Woods . . . 5F **143**
ROCKINGHAM . . . 5A 82
Rockingham *S20: Westf* . . . *2F **151***
(off Shortbrook Dr.)
Rockingham Bus. Pk. S70: Birdw . . . 6E **45**
Rockingham Cl. S1: Shef . . . 6D **4**
S18: Dron W . . . 3B **154**
S40: Ash . . . 5D **166**
S70: Birdw . . . 6E **45**
Rockingham Ct. S64: Swint . . . 3A **66**
S71: Barn . . . 1F **31**
Rockingham Gdns. S60: Roth . . . 2H **111**
Rockingham Gate S1: Shef . . . 5D **4** (4F **119**)
Rockingham Ho. *DN1: Don* . . . *2B **56***
(off Elsworth Cl.)
S1: Shef . . . 3C **4**
S62: Rawm . . . 2H **83**
Rockingham La. S1: Shef . . . 4D **4** (3F **119**)
Rockingham Mausoleum . . . 1B 82
Rockingham M. S70: Birdw . . . 6D **44**
Rockingham Rd. DN2: Don . . . 5D **40**
S62: Rawm . . . 2H **83**
S64: Swint . . . 4H **65**
S75: Dod . . . 4H **29**
Rockingham Row S70: Birdw . . . 6E **45**
Rockingham Station Elsecar Heritage Railway . . . 2E 63
Rockingham St. S1: Shef . . . 3C **4** (3E **119**)
S70: Birdw . . . 6E **45**
S71: Barn . . . 4D **16**
S74: Hoyl . . . 6G **45**
Rockingham Way S1: Shef . . . 5D **4** (4F **119**)
S61: Wing . . . 5A **82**
Rockland Dr. *S65: Thry* . . . *6D **84***
(off Poplar Av.)
Rockland Vs. S65: Thry . . . 6D **84**
Rocklea Cl. S64: Swint . . . 4B **66**
Rockley Av. S70: Birdw . . . 4D **44**
S73: Womb . . . 3E **47**
Rockley Cl. S40: Birdh . . . 3F **171**
Rockley Cres. S70: Birdw . . . 5D **44**
Rockley La. S70: Birdw . . . 4C **44**
S75: Wors . . . 1B **44**
Rockley Mdws. S70: Barn . . . 3B **30**
Rockley Nook DN2: Don . . . 3G **41**
Rockley Rd. S6: Shef . . . 2A **106**
Rockleys S75: Dod . . . 4H **29**
Rockley Vw. S75: Pill . . . 6C **44**
Rockley Vw. Ct. S70: Birdw . . . 6D **44**
Rockliffe Av. DN4: Balb . . . 6F **55**
Rock Mt. S74: Hoyl . . . 6C **46**
Rockmount Rd. S9: Shef . . . 6E **95**
Rock Pl. S36: Spink . . . 3F **175**
Rockside Rd. S36: Thurl . . . 4A **176**
Rock St. S3: Shef . . . 1F **119**
S70: Barn . . . 6C **16**
Rock Ter. DN12: Con . . . 5E **69**
Rockwood Cl. S35: Chap . . . 3D **78**
S75: Dart . . . 5G **7**
Roddis Cl. S25: Dinn . . . 5G **127**
Roden Way S62: Rawm . . . 6D **64**
Rodes Av. S72: Gt H . . . 6F **21**
Rodge Cft. S41: Old W . . . 3H **161**
Rodger Rd. S13: Shef . . . 1E **137**
Rodger St. S61: Roth . . . 3C **96**
Rodman Dr. S13: Shef . . . 6E **123**
Rodman St. S13: Shef . . . 6E **123**
Rod Moor Rd. S18: Dron W . . . 6A **146**
Rodney Hill S6: Lox . . . 4E **105**
Rodsley Cl. S40: Ches . . . 3C **166**
Rodwell Cl. S60: Tree . . . 2F **123**
Roebuck Chase S63: Wath D . . . 5E **49**
Roebuck Hill S74: Jum . . . 4C **46**
Roebuck Ridge S74: Jum . . . 4C **46**
Roebuck Rd. S6: Shef . . . 2C **118**
Roebuck St. S73: Womb . . . 2H **47**
Roeburn Cl. S75: Mapp . . . 4H **7**
Roecar Cl. S41: Old W . . . 4A **162**
Roe Cft. Cl. DN5: Sprot . . . 2C **54**
Roehampton Ri.
DN5: Scaws . . . 5E **39**
S60: Brins . . . 3B **110**
S71: Ard . . . 2C **32**
Roe La. S3: Shef . . . 4G **107**
Roewood Ct. *S3: Shef* . . . *4G **107***
(off Orphanage Rd.)
Roger Rd. S71: Lund . . . 6B **18**
Rojean Rd. S35: Gren . . . 2C **92**
Rokeby Dr. S5: Shef . . . 4F **93**
Rokeby Rd. S5: Shef . . . 4F **93**
Rolands Cl. S61: Kimb . . . 3H **95**
Rolleston Av. S66: Malt . . . 6H **101**
ROLLESTONE . . . 4A 134
Rolleston Rd. S5: Shef . . . 6H **93**
Rollin Dr. S6: Shef . . . 3A **106**
Rolling Dales Cl. S66: Malt . . . 4H **101**
Rolls Cres. S62: Rawm . . . 6D **64**
Roman Ct. S61: Kimb . . . 4H **95**
Roman Cres. S60: Brins . . . 2D **110**
S62: Rawm . . . 2F **83**
Romandale Gdns. S2: Shef . . . 5F **121**
Roman Ridge DN5: Scaws . . . 3F **39**
S5: Shef . . . 1C **108**
Roman Ridge Rd. S9: Shef . . . 1E **109**
Roman Rd. DN4: Don . . . 2D **56**
S75: Kexb . . . 1E **15**
Roman St. S63: Thurn . . . 1D **36**
ROMAN TERRACE . . . 2D 66
Romford Way S43: Bar H . . . 3G **163**
Romney Cl. S66: Flan . . . 4G **99**
Romney Dr. S18: Dron . . . 3D **154**
Romney Gdns. S2: Shef . . . 2G **133**
Romsdal Rd. S10: Shef . . . 2A **118**
Romwood Av. S64: Swint . . . 3H **65**
Ronald Rd. DN4: Balb . . . 5H **55**
S9: Shef . . . 2F **121**
Ronksley Cres. S5: Shef . . . 4A **94**
Ronksley Rd. S5: Shef . . . 3A **94**
Rookdale Cl.
S75: Barn . . . 4A **16**
Rookery, The S36: Spink . . . 4H **175**
Rookery Bank S36: Spink . . . 4H **175**
Rookery Chase S36: Spink . . . 4H **175**
Rookery Cl. S26: Wales . . . 5H **139**
S36: Spink . . . 4H **175**
Rookery Dell S36: Spink . . . 4H **175**
Rookery Ri. S36: Spink . . . 5H **175**
Rookery Rd. S64: Swint . . . 4A **66**
Rookery Vale S36: Spink . . . 4H **175**
Rook Hill S70: Wors . . . 5H **31**
Rosamond Av. S17: Bradw . . . 4H **145**
Rosamond Cl. S17: Bradw . . . 4H **145**
Rosamond Ct. S17: Bradw . . . 4H **145**
Rosamond Dr. S17: Bradw . . . 4H **145**
Rosamond Glade
S17: Bradw . . . 4H **145**
Rosamond Pl. S17: Bradw . . . 4H **145**
Rosa Rd. S10: Shef . . . 2B **118**
Roscoe Bank S6: Shef . . . 2E **117**
Roscoe Ct. S6: Shef . . . 6G **105**
Roscoe Dr. S6: Shef . . . 1G **117**
Roscoe Mt. S6: Shef . . . 1G **117**
Roscoe Rd. S3: Shef . . . 1E **119**
Roscoe Vw. S6: Shef . . . 2E **117**
Rose Av. DN4: Balb . . . 4A **56**
S20: Beig . . . 5G **137**
S44: Cal . . . 5F **169**
S73: D'fld . . . 3A **34**
Roseberry Cl. S74: Hoyl . . . 2B **62**
Rosebery St. S61: Roth . . . 4B **96**
S70: Stair . . . 2A **32**
Rosebery Ter. S70: Barn . . . 2E **31**
Rose Cl. S60: Brins . . . 5E **111**
Rose Cott. DN3: Barn D . . . 1H **27**
Rose Cotts. S41: Ches . . . 6B **168**
Rose Ct. DN4: Balb . . . 4H **55**
S66: Wick . . . 6F **99**
Rose Cres. DN5: Scawt . . . 3F **39**
S43: Mas M . . . 2F **165**
S62: Rawm . . . 2A **84**
Rosedale Av. S40: Ches . . . 2A **172**
S62: Rawm . . . 2G **83**
Rosedale Cl. S26: Ast . . . 6D **124**
Rosedale Gdns. S11: Shef . . . 6C **118**
S70: Barn . . . 1B **30**
Rosedale Rd. DN5: Ben . . . 6H **23**
DN5: Scaws . . . 3E **39**
S11: Shef . . . 6C **118**
S26: Ast . . . 6C **124**
Rosedale Vw. S42: Walt . . . 3C **170**
Rosedale Way S66: Sunn . . . 4H **99**
Rosedene Cl. S70: Stair . . . 2A **32**
Rose Dr. S66: Wick . . . 5H **99**
Rosefield Av. S75: Wool G . . . 3F **7**
Rose Gdns. S44: Ark T . . . 6H **173**
Rosegarth Av. S26: Ast . . . 6C **124**
Rose Gth. Cl. S41: Ches . . . 1B **172**
Rosegarth Cl. DN5: Scawt . . . 3G **39**
Rosegreave S63: Gol . . . 5C **36**
Rose Gro. DN3: Arm . . . 4D **42**
S73: Womb . . . 6E **33**
Rose Hill DN4: Bess . . . 3H **57**
S20: Mosb . . . 2C **150**
S40: Ches . . . 5G **167**
Rosehill S62: Rawm . . . 1G **83**
Rose Hill Av. S20: Mosb . . . 2C **150**
S62: Rawm . . . 1H **83**
Rosehill Av. WF9: Hems . . . 1D **12**
Rose Hill Cemetery & Crematorium
DN4: Cant . . . 3B **58**
Rose Hill Cl. S20: Mosb . . . 2C **150**
S36: Cub . . . 5D **176**
Rosehill Cotts. S62: H'ley . . . 5B **62**
Rose Hill Ct. DN4: Bess . . . 2H **57**
Rosehill Ct. S70: Barn . . . 6D **16**
Rose Hill Dr. S20: Mosb . . . 2C **150**
S75: Dod . . . 3G **29**
Rose Hill E. S40: Ches . . . 5H **167**
Rose Hill M. S20: Mosb . . . 2C **150**
Rose Hill Ri. DN4: Bess . . . 3H **57**
Rosehill Rd. S62: Rawm . . . 2G **83**
Rose Hill Vw. S20: Mosb . . . 2C **150**
Rose Hill W. S40: Ches . . . 5G **167**
Rose Ho. DN3: Arm . . . 4D **42**
Rose La. S25: Brook . . . 1E **127**
Roselle St. S6: Shef . . . 4B **106**
Rosemary Cl. DN4: Cant . . . 5B **58**
Rosemary Ct. *S10: Shef* . . . *1B **118***
(off Bank Ho. Rd.)
Rosemary Gro. DN5: Cade . . . 1G **69**
Rosemary Rd. S20: Beig . . . 4G **137**
S66: Wick . . . 5F **99**
Rose Mead S26: Swal . . . 6B **124**
Rose Pl. S73: Womb . . . 6F **33**
Rose Tree Av. S72: Cud . . . 1E **19**

A-Z Sheffield 247

Rose Tree Ct. S72: Cud ... 1E **19**
Rose Way S21: Killa ... 5C **152**
Rosewell Ct. S65: Roth ... 2A **98**
Rose Wood Cl. S41: Ches ... 6E **161**
Rosewood Dr. DN3: Barn D ... 1B **26**
Rosling Way S44: Ark T ... 6H **173**
Roslin Rd. S10: Shef ... 3B **118**
Ross Ct. S21: Killa ... 6C **152**
Rossendale Cl. S40: Walt ... 2F **171**
Rosser Av. S12: Shef ... 6C **134**
Rossetti Mt. S66: Flan ... 4G **99**
ROSSINGTON ... **5D 74**
Rossington Community Sports Village ... **6G 75**
Rossington Ho. *DN1: Don* ... *3B* ***56***
(off Elsworth Cl.)
Rossington Leisure Cen. ... **5C 74**
Rossington Rd. S11: Shef ... 6B **118**
Rossington St. DN12: Den M ... 2C **68**
Rossiter Rd. S61: Grea ... 4D **82**
Rosslyn Av. S26: Ast ... 6D **124**
Rosslyn Cres. DN5: Ben ... 6A **24**
Rossmoor Cl. DN9: Auck ... 1H **59**
Ross St. S9: Shef ... 2G **121**
Rosston Rd. S66: Malt ... 5C **102**
ROSTHOLME ... **6H 23**
Rostholme Sq. DN5: Ben ... 6A **24**
Roston Cl. S18: Dron W ... 3C **154**
Rotary Dr. S63: Wath D ... 4E **49**
Rothay Cl. S18: Dron W ... 4D **154**
Rothay Rd. S4: Shef ... 3C **108**
Rothbury Cl. S20: Sot ... 6H **137**
Rothbury Ct. S20: Sot ... 6H **137**
Rothbury Way S60: Brins ... 3D **110**
Rother Av. S43: Brim ... 6C **162**
Rother Cl. S40: Walt ... 2F **171**
Rother Ct. S62: Parkg ... 6F **83**
Rother Cres. S60: Tree ... 2F **123**
Rother Cft. S74: Hoyl ... 6B **46**
ROTHERHAM ... **4E 97**
Rotherham Baulk S81: Gild ... 1G **143**
Rotherham Central Station (Rail) ... **4E 97**
Rotherham Cl. S21: Killa ... 2E **153**
Rotherham College of Arts & Technology ... ***4E 97***
(off Howard St.)
Rotherham Crematorium S65: Roth ... 4B **98**
Rotherham Gateway S60: Cat ... 6C **110**
Rotherham Golf Course ... **3E 85**
Rotherham La. S25: Laugh M ... 1F **127**
Rotherham Leisure Complex ... **2F 97**
Rotherham Pl. S13: Shef ... 5C **122**
Rotherham Rd. S13: Shef ... 4C **122**
S20: Beig ... 4H **137**
S20: Half ... 6F **151**
S21: Ecki ... 6F **151**
S21: Killa ... 3E **153**
S21: Killa, Barl ... 6F **153**
S25: Laugh C ... 4F **127**
S26: Swal ... 1B **138**
S43: Barl ... 6F **153**
S60: Cat ... 6E **111**
S60: Roth ... 1F **97**
S62: Parkg ... 1F **97**
S63: Wath D ... 6C **48**
S66: Malt ... 5F **101**
S71: Ath, Barn, Monk B, Smi ... 2E **17**
S72: Gt H, Midd ... 6F **21**
Rotherham Rd. Nth. S20: Westf ... 3G **151**
Rotherham St. S9: Shef ... 5D **108**
Rotherham Titans RUFC ... **5G 97**
Rotherham United ... **4D 96**
Rotherhill Cl. S65: Roth ... 3H **97**
Rother M. S74: Hoyl ... 6B **46**
Rothermoor Av. S26: Kiv P ... 6H **139**
Rother Rd. S60: Roth ... 1E **111**
Rotherside Ct. S21: Ecki ... 6G **151**
Rotherside Rd. S21: Ecki ... 6G **151**
Rotherstoke Cl. S60: Roth ... 6F **97**
Rother St. S73: Bramp ... 4B **48**
Rother Ter. S60: Roth ... 1E **111**
Rothervale Cl. S20: Beig ... 4H **137**
Rothervale Rd. S40: Birdh ... 3H **171**
S40: Ches ... 2H **171**
Rother Valley Country Park ... **5C 138**
Rother Valley Country Park Visitors Cen. ... **6B 138**
Rother Valley Golf Course ... **1E 153**
Rother Valley Way S20: Holb ... 3A **152**
Rother Vw. Cl. S26: Swal ... 1H **137**
Rother Vw. Gdns. S26: Swal ... 1H **137**
Rother Vw. Rd. S60: Roth ... 1E **111**
Rother Way S41: Ches ... 2A **168**
S66: Hel ... 4D **100**
Rotherway S60: Roth ... 4F **111**
Rotherwood Av. S13: Shef ... 6E **123**
Rotherwood Cl. DN5: Scaws ... 4E **39**
Rotherwood Cres. S66: Thurc ... 6B **114**
Rotherwood Rd. S21: Killa ... 2D **152**
Rothesay Cl. DN5: Cus ... 5G **39**
Rothey Gro. S40: Ches ... 3A **166**
Rotunda Bus. Cen. S35: Chap ... 1F **79**
Roughbirchworth S36: Oxs ... 6H **177**
Rough La. S35: Gren ... 1A **92**
Roughwood Grn. S61: Wing ... 5B **82**
Roughwood Rd. S61: Kimb P, Wing ... 6H **81**
Roughwood Way
S61: Kimb P, Wing ... 6H **81**
Roundacre S75: Barn ... 4C **16**
Roundel St. S9: Shef ... 1C **120**
Round Grn. La. S75: Stainb, Wors ... 6A **30**
Round Hill S75: Dart ... 5H **7**
Roundhill Ct. DN4: Don ... 4G **57**
Roundwood Ct. S70: Wors ... 6F **31**
Roundwood Golf Course ... **4H 83**
Roundwood Gro. S62: Rawm ... 3H **83**
Roundwood Way S73: D'fld ... 4A **34**
Row, The DN3: Cant ... 3E **59**
Rowan Cl. DN9: Auck ... 2B **76**
S35: Chap ... 4F **79**
S63: Gol ... 5B **36**
S70: Barn ... 3E **31**
Rowan Ct. DN2: Don ... 4H **41**
Rowan Dr. S66: Braml ... 5H **99**
S75: Barn ... 5A **16**
Rowan Gth. DN5: Don ... 4H **39**
Rowan La. S72: Sth H ... 1H **11**
Rowan Mt. DN2: Don ... 4G **41**
Rowan Ri. S66: Malt ... 5G **101**
Rowan Rd. S21: Ecki ... 3D **158**
S43: Mas M ... 3F **165**
Rowan Tree Cl. S21: Killa ... 5B **152**
Rowan Tree Dell S17: Tot ... 6F **145**
Rowan Tree Rd. S21: Killa ... 4B **152**
Rowborn Dr. S35: Ough ... 6G **91**
Rowdale Cres. S12: Shef ... 3G **135**
Rowell La. S6: Lox ... 4C **104**
Rowena Av. DN3: Eden ... 1C **42**
Rowena Dr. DN5: Scaws ... 4E **39**
S66: Thurc ... 5B **114**
Rowena Rd. DN12: Con ... 4E **69**
Rowernfields S25: Dinn ... 1C **142**
Rowland Pl. DN1: Don ... 2B **56**
Rowland Rd. S2: Shef ... 6F **119**
S75: Barn ... 5B **16**
Rowland St. S3: Shef ... 1F **119**
S71: Roy ... 2A **10**
Rowley Way S66: Sunn ... 2G **99**
Rowms La. S64: Swint ... 3D **66**
Rowsley Cres. S43: Stav ... 6H **163**
Rowsley St. S2: Shef ... 5G **119**
Roxby Cl. DN4: Bess ... 6A **58**
Roxton Av. S8: Shef ... 2E **147**
Roxton Rd. S8: Shef ... 1D **146**
Royal Av. DN1: Don ... 6D **40**
Royal Ct. S41: Ches ... 4H **167**
S74: Hoyl ... 6C **46**
S75: Bar G ... 2F **15**
Royale Cl. S21: Ecki ... 1F **159**
Royal Oak Ct. S43: Mas M ... 2G **165**
Royal Plaza S1: Shef ... 4C **4**
Royal St. S70: Barn ... 1D **30**
Royalty La. DN3: Barn D ... 1G **25**
ROYD ... **5G 175**
Royd, The S36: Spink ... 5F **175**
Royd Av. S72: Cud ... 2E **19**
S75: Mapp ... 5A **8**
Royd Cl. S70: Wors ... 6E **31**
Royd Ct. S36: Spink ... 5F **175**
Roydfield Cl. S20: Water ... 6E **137**
Roydfield Dr. S20: Water ... 6E **137**
Roydfield Gro. S20: Water ... 6E **137**
Royd Fld. La. S36: Cub ... 6D **176**
Royd La. S36: Spink ... 5F **175**
S75: H'ham, Silk ... 5D **14**
Royd Moor Ct. S36: Thurl ... 3A **176**
Royd Moor Rd. S36: Thurl ... 3A **176**
Royds Av. S60: Whist ... 2B **112**
Royds Cl. Cres. S65: Thry ... 6D **84**
Royds La. S74: Els ... 1F **63**
ROYDS MOOR ... **3E 113**
Royds Moor Hill S60: Whist ... 3E **113**
Royd Vw. S72: Brier ... 3B **12**
Roy Kilner Rd. S73: Womb ... 6E **33**
(not continuous)
ROYSTON ... **3H 9**
Royston Av. DN5: Don ... 3H **39**
S20: Mosb ... 6B **136**
Royston Cl. S20: Mosb ... 6B **136**
S42: Walt ... 3C **170**
Royston Cotts. S74: Hoyl ... 6A **46**
Royston Cft. S20: Mosb ... 6B **136**
Royston Gro. *S20: Mosb* ... *6B* ***136***
(off Royston Cl.)
Royston Hill S74: Hoyl ... 6A **46**
Royston La. S71: Carl, Roy ... 4H **9**
Royston Leisure Cen. ... **2H 9**
Royston Rd. S72: Cud ... 5D **10**
Rubens Cl. S18: Dron ... 3E **155**
Rubens Row *S2: Shef* ... *2H* ***119***
(off Hyde Pk. Ter.)
Rud Broom Cl. S36: Cub ... 5B **176**
Rud Broom La. S36: Pen ... 4B **176**
Ruddle La. S66: Clift, Mick ... 6G **87**
Ruddle Mill La. S66: Staint ... 1D **102**
(not continuous)
Rudyard M. S6: Shef ... 4B **106**
Rudyard Rd. S6: Shef ... 4B **106**
Rufford Av. S71: Ath ... 6F **9**
Rufford Cl. S40: Ches ... 1F **171**
Rufford Ct. S20: Sot ... 6H **137**
Rufford Ri. S20: Sot ... 6H **137**
S63: Gol ... 6B **36**
Rufford Rd. DN4: Don ... 3E **57**
Rufus La. DN11: New R ... 5A **74**
Rugby St. S3: Shef ... 6F **107**
Rundle Dr. S7: Shef ... 1D **132**
Rundle Rd. S7: Shef ... 1D **132**
S36: Stoc ... 3D **174**
Runnymede Rd. DN2: Don ... 6G **41**
Rupert Rd. S7: Shef ... 3D **132**
Rural Cres. DN3: Brant ... 4G **59**
Rural La. S6: Shef ... 2G **105**
Ruscombe Pl. S71: Carl ... 5H **9**
Rushby St. S4: Shef ... 3A **108**
Rushdale Av. S8: Shef ... 3F **133**
Rushdale Mt. S8: Shef ... 3F **133**
Rushdale Rd. S8: Shef ... 3F **133**
Rushdale Ter. S8: Shef ... 3F **133**
Rushen Mt. S40: Birdh ... 4G **171**
Rushey Cl. S62: Rawm ... 6F **65**
Rushleigh Ct. S17: Dore ... 3E **145**
Rushley Av. S17: Dore ... 2E **145**
Rushley Cl. DN9: Auck ... 2H **59**
S17: Dore ... 2E **145**
Rushley Dr. S17: Dore ... 2E **145**
Rushley Rd. S17: Dore ... 2E **145**
Rushworth Cl. S75: Kexb ... 6D **6**
Ruskin Av. S64: Mexb ... 6G **51**
Ruskin Cl. S63: Wath D ... 5D **48**
Ruskin Dr. DN3: Arm ... 4F **43**
Ruskin Rd. DN4: Balb ... 6H **55**
Ruskin Sq. S8: Shef ... 2F **133**
Russell Cl. S26: Swal ... 1A **138**
S71: Monk B ... 3G **17**
Russell Ct. S11: Shef ... 6H **131**
Russell Ho. S25: Sth A ... 3G **141**
Russell Pl. S66: Malt ... 4B **102**
Russell Rd. S64: Kiln ... 1D **84**
Russell St. S3: Shef ... 1D **4** (1F **119**)
S65: Roth ... 2F **97**
Russett Ct. S66: Malt ... 4G **101**
Rustic Ct. S9: Shef ... 6E **109**
Rustlings Ct. S10: Shef ... 6G **117**
Rustlings Rd. S11: Shef ... 6H **117**
Ruston Cl. S40: Ches ... 2C **166**
Ruston Dr. S71: Roy ... 2H **9**
Ruthin St. S4: Shef ... 4B **108**
Ruth Sq. S10: Shef ... 4D **118**
Ruthven Dr. DN4: Warm ... 5E **55**
Rutland Av. S25: Nth A ... 1G **141**
Rutland Ho. *S3: Shef* ... *1E* ***119***
(off Adelaide La.)
Rutland La. DN11: New R ... 5A **74**

Rutland Pk. S10: Shef 4B **118**
Rutland Pl. S73: Womb 2E **47**
Rutland Rd. S3: Shef 1E **119**
S40: Ches 5G **167**
Rutland St. DN1: Don 6D **40**
S3: Shef 6F **107**
S41: Old W 4H **161**
Rutland Way S3: Shef 6E **107**
S75: Barn 5B **16**
Ryan Dr. S13: Shef 1F **137**
Ryan Pl. S62: Parkg 4G **83**
Rydal Cl. S18: Dron W 3C **154**
S25: Dinn 1A **142**
S36: Pen 3D **176**
S63: Bolt D 3B **50**
Rydal Ct. DN4: Balb 2H **71**
Rydal Cres. S41: Ches 6F **161**
Rydal Dr. DN4: Don 3G **57**
Rydalhurst Av.
S6: Shef 2H **105**
Rydall Pl. DN5: Scawt 2G **39**
Rydal Rd. S8: Shef 3D **132**
S25: Dinn 1A **142**
Rydal Ter. S71: Barn 1F **31**
Rydal Way S64: Mexb 6H **51**
Rye Bank S60: Whist 3C **112**
RYECROFT 2A **84**
Rye Cft. DN12: Con 4H **69**
S71: Smi 2F **17**
Ryecroft Bank S74: Hoyl 5A **46**
Ryecroft Glen Rd.
S17: Dore 2H **145**
Ryecroft Rd. S62: Rawm 2B **84**
Ryecroft Vw. S17: Dore 2E **145**
Ryedale Wlk. DN5: Scaws 3D **38**
Ryefield Gdns. S11: Shef 3H **131**
Rye Flatt La. S40: Bramp 6C **166**
Ryegate Cres. S10: Shef 3A **118**
Ryegate Rd. S10: Shef 4A **118**
Ryehill Av. S40: Bramp 6B **166**
Rye La. S6: Stann 5A **104**
Ryeview Gdns. S61: Grea 6C **82**
Ryhill Dr. S20: Mosb 6B **136**
Rykneld Sq. *S40: Ches 5H **167***
(off Church Way)
Ryle Rd. S7: Shef 1D **132**
Rylstone Ct. S12: Shef 5C **136**
Rylstone Gro. S12: Shef 6C **136**
Rylstone Wlk. S70: Stair 4A **32**
Ryton Av. S73: Womb 3A **48**
Ryton Cl. S66: Malt 5B **102**
Ryton Rd.
S25: Nth A, Sth A 4G **141**
Ryton Way DN4: Cant 6D **58**

S

Sackerville Ter. S21: Killa 4A **152**
Sackup La. S75: Dart, Stain 5G **7**
Sackville Cl. S42: Walt 2C **170**
Sackville Hgts. *S70: Barn 6D **16***
(off Sackville St.)
Sackville Rd. S10: Shef 2A **118**
Sackville St. S70: Barn 6C **16**
Saddler Av. S20: Water 1E **151**
Saddler Cl. S20: Water 1E **151**
Saddler Grn. S20: Water 1E **151**
Saddler Gro. S20: Water 1E **151**
Saddletree Vw.
S43: Mas M 2E **165**
Sadler Ga. S70: Barn 6D **16**
Sadler's Ga. S73: Womb 6F **33**
Saffron Ct. S73: Womb 2H **47**
St Agnes' Rd. DN4: Don 2F **57**
St Aidan's Av. S2: Shef 6A **120**
St Aidan's Dr. S2: Shef 5B **120**
St Aidan's Pl. S2: Shef 6B **120**
St Aidan's Ri. S2: Shef 5B **120**
St Aidan's Rd. S2: Shef 5A **120**
St Aidan's Way
S2: Shef 6B **120**
St Albans Cl. S10: Shef 5D **116**
St Alban's Ct. S66: Wick 6G **99**
St Albans Dr. S10: Shef 5C **116**
St Albans Rd. S10: Shef 5C **116**
St Alban's Way S66: Wick 6F **99**
St Andrew Rd. S36: Spink 4G **175**
St Andrews Cl. DN4: Cant 6E **59**
S11: Shef 1C **132**
S25: Dinn 6A **128**
S64: Swint 5C **66**
S66: Sunn 3H **99**
St Andrews Cres. S74: Hoyl 6B **46**
St Andrews Dr. S75: Dart 5H **7**
St Andrews Ri. S40: Walt 2D **170**
St Andrews Rd. DN12: Con 5E **69**
S11: Shef 1C **132**
S74: Hoyl 6B **46**
St Andrew's Sq. S63: Bolt D 2B **50**
St Andrew's Ter. DN4: Don 3C **56**
St Andrew's Wlk. S60: Brins 3B **110**
St Andrews Way DN3: Barn D 2D **26**
S71: Ard 3D **32**
St Anne's Cl. S43: Stav 6A **164**
St Anne's Dr. S71: Monk B 1A **18**
St Anne's Rd. DN4: Don 2F **57**
ST ANN'S 2F **97**
St Ann's Rd. S36: Spink 3F **175**
S65: Roth 2F **97**
St Ann's Rdbt. S65: Roth 3F **97**
St Anthony Rd. S10: Shef 2H **117**
ST AUGUSTINES 2H **171**
St Augustines Av. S40: Ches 2H **171**
St Augustines Cres. S40: Ches 2H **171**
St Augustines Dr. S40: Ches 1H **171**
St Augustines Mt. S40: Ches 2H **171**
St Augustines Ri. S40: Ches 2H **171**
St Augustines Rd. DN4: Bess 3H **57**
S40: Ches 2G **171**
St Austell Dr. S75: Bar G 4F **15**
St Barbara's Cl. S66: Hoot L 6H **101**
St Barbara's Rd. S73: D'fld 5A **34**
St Barnabas La. S2: Shef 6F **119**
St Barnabas Rd. S2: Shef 6F **119**
St Bartholomew's Cl. S66: Malt 6H **101**
St Bartholomews Ri. DN4: Bess 4A **58**
St Bart's Ter. *S70: Barn 2E **31***
(off Dobie St.)
St Bede's Rd. S60: Roth 4D **96**
St Benedicts Ct. S2: Shef 6A **120**
St Catherine's Av. DN4: Balb 4A **56**
St Catherine's Dr. DN7: Dunsv 4H **27**
St Catherine's Way S75: Barn 1A **30**
St Cecilia's Rd. DN4: Don 3F **57**
St Chad's Sq. DN12: Den M 2C **68**
St Chad's Way DN5: Sprot 3D **54**
S41: Whit M 6H **161**
St Charles St. S9: Shef 6B **108**
St Christopher's *DN4: Balb 5H **55***
(off Ashfield Rd.)
St Christophers Cl. S71: Ard 3D **32**
St Christopher's Cres.
DN5: Scaws 4F **39**
St Clements Cl. DN5: Scaws 4E **39**
S71: Ard 3D **32**
St David Rd. S36: Spink 4G **175**
St David's Dr. DN5: Scaws 4E **39**
S25: Sth A 5G **141**
S60: Brins 3B **110**
S71: Ard 2C **32**
St David's Ri. S40: Walt 2E **171**
St David's Rd. DN12: Con 4E **69**
St Dominic's Cl. DN5: Sprot 4C **54**
St Edmund's Av. S66: Thurc 1B **126**
St Edward's Av. S70: Barn 2C **30**
St Elizabeth Cl. S2: Shef 6G **119**
St Eric's Rd. DN4: Bess 4A **58**
St Francis Blvd. S71: Monk B 1A **18**
St Francis Cl. S10: Shef 4F **117**
S66: Sunn 3H **99**
St George Ga. DN1: Don 1B **56**
St George Rd. S36: Spink 4G **175**
St George's Av. DN7: Dunsv 4H **27**
S64: Swint 3A **66**
St Georges Cl.
S3: Shef 2A **4** (2D **118**)
S81: Woods 4F **143**
St George's Ct. S3: Shef 3B **4**
St George's Dr. S60: Brins 3B **110**
St George's Rd. DN4: Bess 3G **57**
S70: Barn 1D **30**
St George's Ter. S1: Shef 3B **4** (3E **119**)
St George's Wlk.
S3: Shef 2B **4** (2E **119**)
St Giles Cl. S40: Ches 2A **172**
St Giles Ga. DN5: Scaws 5E **39**
St Giles Sq. S35: Chap 3E **79**
St Helen Rd. S36: Spink 5G **175**
ST HELEN'S 3A **18**
St Helen's Av. S71: Smi 3G **17**
St Helen's Blvd. S71: Smi 2G **17**
St Helens Cl. S41: Ches 4H **167**
S60: Tree 3G **123**
S63: Thurn 2A **36**
St Helens Ct. S74: Els 6D **46**
St Helen's La. DN5: Barnb 2B **52**
St Helens Pl. S71: Smi 3G **17**
St Helen's Rd. DN4: Don 2F **57**
St Helen's Sq. DN3: Kirk Sa 4C **26**
St Helen's St. S41: Ches 4H **167**
S74: Els 6D **46**
St Helen's Way S71: Monk B 3A **18**
St Helier Dr. S75: Barn 6A **16**
St Hilda Av. S70: Barn 1B **30**
St Hilda Cl. S36: Spink 5G **175**
St Hildas Cl. S63: Thurn 1D **36**
St Hilda's Rd. DN4: Don 2F **57**
St James Av. DN7: Dunsv 3H **27**
S25: Sth A 4G **141**
St James Cl. DN3: Kirk Sa 4C **26**
S41: Has 1B **172**
S63: Wath D 6H **49**
S70: Wors 6F **31**
St James Ct. DN1: Don 2C **56**
St James Dr. S65: Rav 5A **86**
St James' Gdns. DN4: Balb 3A **56**
St James Leisure Cen. 2C **56**
St James' Row
S1: Shef 2E **5** (2F **119**)
St James's Bri. DN4: Don 2B **56**
St James Sq. *S40: Ches 5H **167***
(off Vicar La.)
*S74: Hoyl 6B **46***
(off West St.)
St James St. DN1: Don 2B **56**
S1: Shef 3E **5** (3F **119**)
St James' Vw. S65: Rav 5A **86**
St James Wlk. S13: Shef 6E **123**
St Joan Av. S36: Spink 5G **175**
St Johns S36: H'swne 1F **177**
St John's Av. S60: Roth 4C **96**
S66: Sunn 4H **99**
S75: Bar G 4F **15**
St Johns Cl. S2: Shef 2H **119**
S36: Pen 5C **176**
S42: Walt 3C **170**
S65: Roth 2H **97**
S75: Dod 3F **29**
St Johns Ct. S25: Laugh M 2H **127**
*S41: Whit M 6G **161***
(off St John's Rd.)
S60: Roth 3C **96**
S66: Sunn 4H **99**
St John's Cft. DN11: Wad 6E **73**
St Johns Grn. S61: Kimb P 1H **95**
St John's Mt. S41: Ches 6G **161**
St Johns Pl. S43: Stav 5A **164**
St Johns Rd. DN4: Balb 4H **55**
DN12: New E 4C **70**
S2: Shef 2A **120**
S18: Uns 4B **156**
S25: Laugh M 2H **127**
S36: Spink 3H **175**
S41: Ches, Whit M 1F **167**
(not continuous)
S43: Stav 5H **163**
S64: Swint 3B **66**
S65: Roth 2H **97**
S70: Barn 2D **30**
S72: Cud 2E **19**
St John's Wlk. S64: Mexb 4F **51**
S71: Roy 3A **10**
St Joseph's Ct. S25: Dinn 5A **128**
St Joseph's Gdns. S70: Barn 2G **31**
St Joseph's Rd. S13: Shef 4A **122**
St Julien's Mt. S75: Cawt 4A **14**
St Julien's Way S75: Cawt 4A **14**
St Laurence Ct. DN6: Adw S 2B **22**
St Lawrence Glebe S9: Tins 2H **109**
St Lawrence Rd. S9: Tins 1H **109**
St Lawrence's Ter. DN6: Adw S 2D **22**
St Leger Cl. S25: Laugh C 4F **127**
St Leger Way S25: Dinn 4A **128**

St Leonard's Av. S65: Thry 6E 85
St Leonard's Cl. S25: Dinn 6H 127
St Leonards Ct. S5: Shef 1G 107
St Leonards Cft. S65: Thry 5E 85
St Leonards Dr. S41: Ches 1B 172
St Leonard's La. S65: Roth 3G 97
St Leonard's Lea DN5: Scaws 4F 39
St Leonards Pl. S65: Roth 3G 97
St Leonard's Rd. S65: Roth 3F 97
St Leonards Way S71: Ard 3D 32
St Luke's Cl. DN7: Dunsv 4H 27
St Lukes Ct. S41: Ches 6G 161
St Lukes Rd. S72: Grim 2B 20
St Lukes Way S71: Monk B 5H 17
St Margaret Av. S36: Spink 4G 175
St Margaret's Av.
  DN5: Barnb 1H 51
St Margaret's Dr. S40: Ches 5G 167
  S64: Swint 3A 66
St Margarets Rd. DN4: Don 2F 57
  S35: Eccl 3G 93
St Marie's RC Cathedral 3E 5 (3F 119)
St Mark Rd. S36: Spink 4G 175
St Mark's Cres. S10: Shef 4C 118
St Mark's Rd. S40: Ches 5F 167
St Martin Cl. S36: Spink 4G 175
St Martin's Av. DN5: Cus 4F 39
St Martin's Cl. S41: Ches 2E 167
  S75: Barn 1A 30
  S81: Fir 1H 129
St Mary & All Saints Church Crooked Spire
  . . . . .5A 168
St Mary Cres. S36: Spink 5G 175
St Mary's S71: Lund 6B 18
St Marys Cl. S35: Eccl 1F 93
  S72: Cud 1E 19
St Mary's Cres. DN1: Don 6D 40
  S64: Swint 2B 66
St Mary's Dr. DN3: Arm 4F 43
  DN7: Dunsv 4H 27
  (not continuous)
  S60: Cat 6D 110
St Marys Gdn. S70: Wors 2F 45
St Mary's Ga. S2: Shef 6C 4 (5E 119)
  S41: Ches 5A 168
  S70: Barn 6D 16
St Marys La. S35: Eccl 1F 93
St Mary's Pl. S41: Ches 5A 168
  (off St Mary's Ga.)
  S70: Barn 6D 16
St Mary's Rd. DN1: Don 5D 40
  DN7: Dunsv 3H 27
  DN12: New E 5D 70
  S2: Shef 6E 5 (5F 119)
  S62: Rawm 3H 83
  S63: Gol .4E 37
  S73: D'fld 5C 34
  S73: Womb 2F 47
St Mary's Sq. S1: Shef 6C 4 (5E 119)
St Mary's St. S36: Pen 4D 176
St Mary's Ter. S36: Bolst 6E 175
  (off Heads La.)
St Mary's Vw. S61: Grea 5C 82
St Mary's Wlk. DN5: Sprot 4C 54
St Matthew's Cl. S21: Reni 3H 159
St Matthew's Ct. S73: Womb 5A 34
St Matthews Way
  S71: Monk B 5H 17
St Matthias Rd. S36: Spink 5G 175
St Michaels Av. DN11: Ross 4D 74
  S64: Swint 2C 66
  S71: Monk B 2A 18
St Michaels Cl. S35: Eccl 2G 93
  S63: Gol .5C 36
St Michaels Cres. S35: Eccl 2G 93
St Michaels Rd. DN4: Bess 3G 57
  S35: Eccl 2G 93
St Nicholas Cl. DN3: Eden 6B 26
St Nicolas Rd. S62: Rawm 2H 83
St Nicolas Wlk. S62: Rawm 2A 84
St Oswalds Cl. DN9: Finn 3E 77
St Oswald's Dr. DN3: Eden 6C 26
  DN9: Finn 3F 77
St Owens St. S75: Barn 6A 16
St Pancras Cl. S25: Laugh C 4E 127
St Patrick Rd. S36: Spink 4G 175
St Patrick's Rd. DN2: Don 5F 41
St Patrick's Way DN5: Scaws 4E 39

St Paul Cl. S26: Tod 3B 140
  S36: Spink 4G 175
St Pauls Av. S41: Has 4C 172
St Pauls Cl. S25: Laugh C 3F 127
St Paul's Pde. DN5: Scaws 5E 39
  S1: Shef .4E 5
  S71: Ard .2C 32
St Pauls Rd. S75: Barn 5B 16
St Paul's Sq. S1: Shef 4E 5
St Peter & St Paul's Cathedral
  . . . . .2E 5 (2F 119)
St Peter Av. S36: Spink 4H 175
St Peter's Cl. DN3: Barn D 1G 27
  DN5: Barnb 6H 37
  S1: Shef 2E 5 (2F 119)
  S60: Brins 4B 110
St Peter's Dr. DN12: Con 5E 69
St Peters Ga. S63: Thurn 1B 36
St Peters Hgts. DN12: New E 6C 70
St Peters Pl. S65: Thry 6D 84
St Peter's Rd. DN4: Balb 5F 55
  DN12: Con 5E 69
St Peter's Ter. S70: Barn 2F 31
St Philip's Cl. S66: Malt 6H 101
St Philip's Dr. S41: Has 2A 172
St Philip's La. S3: Shef 1E 119
St Philip's Rd. S3: Shef 2A 4 (2D 118)
  (not continuous)
St Quentin Cl. S17: Bradw 5A 146
St Quentin Dr. S17: Bradw 5A 146
St Quentin Mt. S17: Bradw 5A 146
St Quentin Ri. S17: Bradw 5A 146
St Quentin Vw. S17: Bradw 5A 146
St Ronan's Rd. S7: Shef 1E 133
St Sepulchre Ga. DN1: Don 1B 56
St Sepulchre Ga. W. DN1: Don 2B 56
  DN4: Don 2B 56
St Stephens Dr. S26: Ast 6C 124
St Stephen's Rd. S3: Shef . . .1A 4 (2D 118)
  S65: Roth 3F 97
St Stephens Wlk. DN5: Scaws 5F 39
  S3: Shef 2A 4 (2D 118)
St Thomas a Becket's Church 2B 146
St Thomas' Ct. DN4: Bess 6A 58
St Thomas Rd. S10: Shef 3A 118
St Thomas's Cl. DN4: Balb 6A 58
St Thomas's Rd. S75: Barn 4H 15
St Thomas St. S1: Shef 3C 4 (4D 118)
  S40: Bramp 6D 166
St Ursula's Rd. DN4: Don 2F 57
St Veronica Rd. S36: Spink 4H 175
St Vincent Av. DN1: Don 6D 40
  DN6: Woodl 2A 22
St Vincent Rd. DN1: Don 6D 40
St Vincent's Av. DN3: Brant 5F 59
St Wandrilles Cl. S35: Eccl 1G 93
St Wilfrid's Rd. DN4: Bess, Cant 3H 57
  S2: Shef .6F 119
St Withold Av. S66: Thurc 6B 114
St Withold Cl. S66: Thurc 6B 114
Salcey Sq. S40: Walt 1E 171
Salcombe Cl. S75: Mapp 6B 8
Sale Hill S10: Shef 4A 118
Salerno Way S73: D'fld 4H 33
Sale St. S74: Hoyl 1F 61
Salisbury Av. S18: Dron 4F 155
  S41: Ches 1F 167
Salisbury Cres. S41: Ches 1G 167
Salisbury Rd. DN4: Hex 3H 55
  S10: Shef 2A 118
  S18: Dron 5G 155
  S66: Malt 4A 102
Salisbury St. S75: Barn 5C 16
Salmon Pastures Nature Reserve . .1B 120
Salmon St. S11: Shef 6E 119
Salt Box Gro. S35: Gren 2B 92
Salt Box La. S35: Gren 3B 92
Saltergate S40: Ches 5G 167
Salter Oak Cft. S71: Carl 5H 9
Saltersbrook S63: Gol 5C 36
Saltersbrook Rd. S73: D'fld 3A 34
Salters Ri. S70: Barn 1B 30
Salters Way S36: Cub 5D 176
Salt Hill S81: Fir 1H 129
Samson St. S2: Shef 4H 119
Samuel Cl. S2: Shef 1A 134
Samuel Ct. S72: Cud 6F 11
Samuel Dr. S2: Shef 1A 134

Samuel Pl. S2: Shef 6A 120
Samuel Rd. S2: Shef 1A 134
  S75: Barn 5A 16
Samuel Sq. S75: Barn 5A 16
Samuel St. DN4: Balb 6G 55
Sanctuary Flds. S25: Nth A 1G 141
Sandal Ct. S61: Roth 3C 96
Sandall Beat La. DN2: Don 4A 42
Sandall Beat Rd. DN2: Don 1G 57
Sandall Beat Vis. Cen. 6B 42
Sandall Beat Wood (Nature Reserve)
  . . . . .6B 42
Sandall Carr Rd. DN3: Kirk Sa 5B 26
Sandall La. DN3: Kirk Sa 3A 26
  (not continuous)
Sandall Pk. Dr. DN2: Don 3H 41
Sandall Ri. DN2: Don 4G 41
Sandall Stones Rd. DN3: Kirk Sa 5A 26
Sandall Vw. S25: Laugh C 3F 127
Sandal Rd. DN12: Con 5D 68
Sandalwood Cl. DN2: Don 2H 41
Sandalwood Ri. S64: Swint 6C 66
Sandbeck Cl. S71: Barn 5E 17
Sandbeck Ct. DN11: Ross 6D 74
  DN12: Den M 3C 68
Sandbeck Ho. DN1: Don 2B 56
  (off Grove Pl.)
Sandbeck La. S66: Malt 6G 103
Sandbeck Pl. S11: Shef 6C 118
Sandbeck Rd. DN4: Don 2E 57
Sandbeck Way S66: Hel 5D 100
Sandbed Rd. S3: Shef 5D 106
Sandbergh Rd. S61: Kimb P 6H 81
Sandby Ct. S14: Shef 6B 134
Sandby Cft. S14: Shef 6B 134
Sandby Dr. S14: Shef 6B 134
Sandcliffe Rd. DN2: Don 4G 41
Sandcroft Cl. S74: Hoyl 1H 61
Sandeby Dr. S65: Rav 3A 100
Sanderson St. S9: Shef 5C 108
Sanders Way S25: Laugh C 4F 127
Sandford Ct. DN4: Balb 5H 55
  S70: Barn 1C 30
Sandford Gro. Rd. S7: Shef 3D 132
  (not continuous)
Sandford Rd. DN4: Balb 6H 55
SANDHILL
  S62 . . . . .1A 84
  S72 . . . . .1G 35
Sandhill Cl. S62: Rawm 1A 84
Sandhill Ct. S72: Gt H 1G 35
Sandhill Golf Course 2E 35
Sandhill Gro. S72: Grim 5B 12
Sandhill Ri. DN9: Auck 1G 59
Sandhill Rd. S62: Rawm 1A 84
Sandhurst Pl. S10: Shef 2B 118
Sandhurst Rd. DN4: Cant 5D 58
Sandiron Ho. S7: Shef 1A 146
Sandiway S40: Walt 2D 170
Sandon Vw. S10: Shef 6A 4
Sandown Cl. S21: Ecki 1C 158
Sandown Gdns. DN4: Cant 2A 58
Sandown Rd. S64: Mexb 6G 51
Sandpiper Rd. S61: Thorpe H 2C 80
Sandpit Hill DN3: Brant 4F 59
Sandringham Av. S60: Whist 3A 112
Sandringham Cl. S36: Thurl 3A 176
  S41: Whit M 6H 161
  S44: Cal .4F 169
Sandringham Pl. S10: Shef 5A 116
  S65: Rav .2A 100
Sandringham Rd. DN2: Don 1F 57
  S9: Shef .6D 94
  S44: Cal .4F 169
Sandrock Dr. DN4: Bess 5B 58
Sands Cl. S14: Shef 4B 134
Sandstone Av. S9: Shef 2C 108
  S42: Walt .2C 170
Sandstone Cl. S9: Shef 1D 108
Sandstone Dr. S9: Shef 2C 108
Sandstone Rd. S9: Shef 2C 108
Sandwith Rd. S26: Tod 3B 140
Sandy Acres Cl. S20: Water 1G 151
Sandy Acres Dr. S20: Water 1G 151
Sandybridge La. S72: Shaft 1D 10
Sandybridge La. Ind. Est.
  S72: Shaft 2E 11
Sandycroft Cres. DN4: Balb 5F 55

Sandy Flat La. S66: Wick 3F 113
SANDYGATE .4E 117
Sandygate S63: Wath D 6G 49
(not continuous)
Sandygate Ct. S10: Shef 4E 117
Sandygate Cres. S63: Wath D 2G 65
Sandygate Grange Dr. S10: Shef . . .4F 117
Sandygate Gro. S10: Shef 4F 117
Sandygate La. S10: Shef 4F 117
S71: Stair 2B 32
Sandygate Pk. S10: Shef 4D 116
Sandygate Pk. Cres. S10: Shef 4E 117
Sandygate Pk. Rd. S10: Shef 4E 117
Sandygate Rd. S10: Shef 4E 117
Sandy La. DN4: Don 3F 57
S35: Chap 4B 78
S66: Braml 1B 114
S66: Thurc 5C 114
S73: Womb 2B 46
Sandymount Rd. S63: Wath D 1H 65
Sanforth St. S41: Ches 2H 167
Sankey Sq. S63: Gol 5C 36
Sarah Ct. DN3: Arm 3H 43
Sarah St. S61: Roth 4C 96
S64: Mexb 2F 67
Sargeson Rd. DN3: Arm 4C 42
Sark Rd. S2: Shef 1F 133
Sarrius Ct. DN4: Cant 4B 58
Saundby Cl. DN4: Bess 5H 57
Saunderson Rd. S36: Pen 3B 176
Saunders Pl. S2: Shef 3B 120
Saunders Rd. S2: Shef 3B 120
Saunder's Row S73: Womb 2F 47
Savage La. S17: Dore 3E 145
Savile St. S3: Shef 1G 119
S4: Shef 1G 119
Savile St. E. S4: Shef 1A 120
Savile Wlk. S72: Brier 3C 12
Saville Ct. S74: Hoyl 1G 61
Saville Hall La. S75: Dod 4G 29
Saville La. S36: Thurl 4A 176
Saville Rd. S60: Whist 3A 112
S63: Wath D 6F 49
S75: Dod 4G 29
Saville St. S65: Dalt 1B 98
S72: Cud 1F 19
Saville Ter. S70: Barn 2D 30
Sawdon Rd. S11: Shef 5D 118
Sawn Moor Av. S66: Thurc 6C 114
Sawn Moor Rd. S66: Thurc 1C 126
Sawston Cl. DN4: Balb 2H 71
Saxon Av. WF9: Sth K 4G 13
Saxon Ct. DN3: Barn D 1C 26
DN3: Eden 6B 26
DN4: Bess 6C 58
DN5: Scawt 3G 39
Saxon Cres. S70: Wors 5F 31
Saxon Gro. WF9: Sth K 5H 13
Saxonlea Av. S2: Shef 5F 121
Saxonlea Cl. S2: Shef 5F 121
Saxonlea Cres. S2: Shef 5F 121
Saxonlea Dr. S2: Shef 5E 121
Saxon Mt. WF9: Sth K 4G 13
Saxon Rd. S8: Shef 2F 133
S26: Kiv P 6C 140
S61: Kimb 4G 95
Saxon Row DN12: Con 5H 69
Saxon St. S63: Thurn 2D 36
S72: Cud 2E 19
Saxton Av. DN4: Bess 4H 57
Saxton Cl. S41: Has 2B 172
S74: Els 6E 47
Saxton Dr. S60: Roth 3G 111
Sayers Cl. DN5: H'ton 2H 51
Scafell Cl. S14: Shef 2A 142
Scaftworth Cl. DN4: Bess 5H 57
Scammadine Cl. S60: Brins 4E 111
Scamming La. S25: Laugh M 1A 128
Scampton Lodge S5: Shef 2G 107
Scarborough Cl. S25: Nth A 1H 141
Scarborough La. DN11: New R 5A 74
Scarborough Rd. S9: Shef 1F 121
S66: Wick 5G 99
Scarbrough Cres. S66: Malt 6B 102
Scarbrough Farm Ct. S66: Malt 5A 102
Scarfield Cl. S71: Ard 2C 32
Scargill Cft. S1: Shef 2E 5 (2F 119)
Scar La. S71: Ard 2C 32

Scarlett Oak Mdw. S6: Stann 6D 104
Scarll Rd. DN4: Hex 3H 55
Scarsdale Cl. S18: Dron 4G 155
Scarsdale Cres. S43: Brim 1C 168
Scarsdale Cross S18: Dron 3G 155
Scarsdale Rd. S8: Shef 5E 133
S18: Dron 3F 155
S41: Whit M 6H 161
Scarsdale St. S25: Dinn 5B 128
Scarth Av. DN4: Balb 4A 56
SCAWSBY 4E 39
Scawsby La. DN5: Scaws 2C 38
SCAWTHORPE 2F 39
Scawthorpe Av. DN5: Scawt 2E 39
Scawthorpe Cotts. DN5: Scawt 2D 38
Sceptone Gro. S72: Shaft 3F 11
Sceptre Gro. DN11: New R 6F 75
Schofield Dr. S73: D'fld 4B 34
Schofield Pl. S73: D'fld 4B 34
Schofield Rd. S36: Spink 3F 175
S73: D'fld 4B 34
Schofield St. S64: Mexb 1E 67
Scholar's Ga. S72: Cud 6E 11
Schole Av. S36: Pen 4C 176
Schole Hill La. S36: Cub 5B 176
(not continuous)
SCHOLES 5F 81
Scholes Fld. Cl. S61: Scho 6F 81
Scholes Grn. S61: Scho 5F 81
Scholes La. S61: Scho 5D 80
Scholes Ri. S35: Eccl 2G 93
Scholes Vw. S35: Eccl 1G 93
S61: Thorpe H 5D 80
S74: Hoyl 1B 62
S74: Jum 5C 46
Scholes Village S61: Scho 2E 81
Scholey Av. S81: Woods 5F 143
Scholey Rd. S66: Wick 5G 99
Scholey St. S3: Shef 1G 5 (1G 119)
Scholfield Cres. S66: Malt 6C 102
School Av. S20: Half 3F 151
School Board La. S40: Ches 5F 167
School Cl. S20: Half 3G 151
S26: Wales 5G 139
School Ct. DN1: Don 6C 40
(off Dockin Hill Rd.)
Schoolfield Dr. S62: Rawm 1G 83
School Grn. La. S10: Shef 1C 130
School Gro. S26: Ast 1D 138
School Hill S60: Whist 3B 112
S72: Cud 1E 19
School La. DN3: Cant 4E 59
DN9: Auck 2H 59
S2: Shef 4H 5 (3H 119)
S6: Stann 1D 116
S8: Shef 3E 145
(James Andrew Cft.)
S8: Shef 3E 145
(School La. Cl.)
S18: Dron 3F 155
S21: Mar L 1H 157
S35: Gren 1B 92
S35: Wharn S 2A 90
(not continuous)
S44: Ark T 5H 173
S62: Parkg 5F 83
S65: Thry 5E 85
S66: Staint 2F 103
School La. Cl. S8: Shef 1H 147
School Rd. S10: Shef 3A 118
S20: Beig 5H 137
S25: Laugh M 2G 127
S26: Wales 6F 139
S35: High G 1D 78
S41: Whit M 1H 167
S66: Thurc 6C 114
School St. S20: Mosb 3E 151
S21: Ecki 1E 159
S25: Dinn 5A 128
S26: Swal 1B 138
S63: Bolt D 2B 50
S63: Thurn 2C 36
S65: Thry 6D 84
S70: Stair 2A 32
S72: Cud 6E 11
S72: Gt H 6E 21
S73: D'fld 4C 34
S73: Hem 5F 47

School St. S73: Womb 1G 47
S75: Barn 5C 16
S75: Dart 5F 7
S75: Stain 5B 8
School Ter. DN12: Con 4E 69
School Wlk. DN12: Den M 2C 68
DN12: Old E 1B 88
S66: Malt 5A 102
Scorah's La. S64: Swint 3H 65
Scotch Spring La. S66: Malt 3F 103
Scotia Cl. S2: Shef 6C 120
Scotia Dr. S2: Shef 6C 120
Scotland St. S3: Shef 1C 4 (2E 119)
Scot La. DN1: Don 1C 56
Scotsman Dr. DN5: Scawt 3G 39
Scott Av. DN5: Barnb 2H 51
DN12: Con 4D 68
Scott Cl. S42: Gras 6D 172
Scott Cres. DN3: Eden 5B 26
Scott Hill DN5: Sprot 4C 54
Scott Rd. S4: Shef 4G 107
Scott Wlk. S66: Malt 4G 101
Scott Way S35: Chap 4E 79
SCOUT DIKE .1B 176
Scovell Av. S62: Rawm 1E 83
Scovell Ho. S62: Rawm 1E 83
Scowerdons Cl. S12: Shef 3A 136
Scowerdons Dr. S12: Shef 3A 136
Scraith Wood Dr. S5: Shef 2C 106
Scrooby Dr. S61: Grea 5D 82
Scrooby La. S62: Parkg 5E 83
Scrooby Pl. S61: Grea 5D 82
Scrooby St. S61: Grea 5D 82
Sea Breeze Ter. S13: Shef 6G 121
Seabrook Rd. S2: Shef 4A 120
Seagrave Av. S12: Shef 4E 135
Seagrave Cres. S12: Shef 5D 134
Seagrave Dr. S12: Shef 4E 135
S41: Has 3B 172
Seagrave Rd. S12: Shef 4D 134
Searby Rd. S66: Braml 3A 100
Seaton Cl. S2: Shef 4C 120
Seaton Cres. S2: Shef 4C 120
Seaton Gdns. DN11: New R 6G 75
Seaton Pl. S2: Shef 4C 120
Seaton Way S2: Shef 4C 120
Sebastian Vw. S60: Brins 2D 110
Second Av. DN6: Woodl 4D 22
DN9: Finn 2C 76
WF9: Sth K 5G 13
Second La. S25: Sth A 5H 141
S66: Wick 2H 113
Sedan St. S4: Shef 5H 107
Sedbergh Cres. S41: Ches 1E 167
Sedge Cl. S66: Braml 6B 100
Sedgefield Way 6G 51
Sedgemoor Cl. S40: Ches 4C 166
Sedgley Rd. S6: Shef 4C 106
Sefton Ct. S10: Shef 1F 131
Sefton Rd. S10: Shef 1E 131
Selborne Rd. S10: Shef 4H 117
Selborne St. S65: Roth 2F 97
Selbourne Cl. S75: Bar G 3F 15
S40: Walt 2D 170
Selby Cl. S26: Swal 1B 138
Selby Rd. DN2: Don 5F 41
S4: Shef 3A 108
S71: Smi 1E 17
Selhurst Cres. DN4: Bess 5B 58
Selhurst Rd. S41: Ches 3G 167
Selig Pde. S12: Shef 6F 135
(off White La.)
Selkirk Av. DN4: Warm 6E 55
Selkirk Rd. DN2: Don 4H 41
Sellars Row S61: Kimb P 1H 95
Sellars Row S35: High G 6C 60
Sellers St. S8: Shef 1E 133
Selly Oak Gro. S8: Shef 4H 147
Selly Oak Rd. S8: Shef 4H 147
Selmer Ct. S43: Brim 6C 162
Selwood Flats S65: Roth 3G 97
Selwyn St. S65: Roth 2F 97
Senior Rd. DN4: Hex 2H 55
S9: Shef 2G 121
Seniors Pl. S35: Chap 2E 79
Sennen Cft. S71: Monk B 5G 17

Serlby Ho. *DN1: Don* *2B* **56**
(*off Grove Pl.*)
Serpentine Wlk. S8: Shef 2F **147**
Setcup La. S21: Ecki 2D **158**
Seth Ter. S70: Barn 2F **31**
Setts Way S42: W'orth 6A **172**
Sevenairs Fold S20: Beig 5F **137**
Sevenairs Rd. S20: Beig 5F **137**
Sevenairs Vw. S20: Beig 5F **137**
Sevenfields Ct. S6: Shef 3H **105**
Sevenfields La. S6: Shef 3H **105**
Seven Hills Swimming Pool 6H 133
Seven Yards Rd. DN3: Cant 6H **43**
Severn Ct. S10: Shef 3C **118**
Severn Rd. S10: Shef 3C **118**
Severnside Dr. S13: Shef 1B **136**
Severnside Gdns. S13: Shef 1B **136**
Severnside Pl. S13: Shef 1B **136**
Severnside Wlk. S13: Shef 1B **136**
Sewell Rd. S20: Half 4G **151**
Sexton Dr. S66: Braml 6A **100**
Seymore Rd. S26: Ast 2C **138**
Seymour La. S43: Woodt 5F **165**
Seymour Rd. S66: Malt 5C **102**
Shackleton Rd. DN2: Don 1A **42**
Shackleton Vw. S36: Cub 5D **176**
Shadyside DN4: Hex 3H **55**
(not continuous)
Shaftesbury Av. DN2: Don 1G **57**
S40: Ches 5E **167**
Shaftesbury Dr. S74: Hoyl 1A **62**
Shaftesbury Ho. DN2: Don 5H **41**
Shaftesbury Sq. S65: Roth 3F **97**
Shaftesbury St. S70: Stair 2B **32**
SHAFTHOLME 3C 24
Shaftholme La. DN5: Ben 2A **24**
Shaftholme Rd. DN5: Ark 5C **24**
(not continuous)
SHAFTON 3F 11
Shafton Ga. S63: Gol 5E **37**
Shafton Hall Dr. S72: Shaft 3E **11**
Shafton Rd. S60: Roth 2A **112**
SHAFTON TWO GATES 5F 11
Shaftsbury Av. DN6: Woodl 2A **22**
Shakespeare Av. DN5: Don 6G **39**
Shakespeare Cres. S18: Dron 4H **155**
Shakespeare Dr. S25: Dinn 6B **128**
Shakespeare Rd. DN5: Ben 1A **40**
S63: Wath D 5E **49**
S65: Roth 2G **97**
Shakespeare St. S42: Gras 6D **172**
Shaldon Gro. S26: Ast 1C **138**
Shalesmoor S3: Shef 1D **4** (2F **119**)
(Gibraltar St.)
S3: Shef 1C **4** (1E **119**)
(Hoyle St.)
Shalesmoor Rdbt. *S3: Shef* *1E* **119**
(*off Shalesmoor*)
Shalesmoor Stop (ST) 1E 119
Shambles, The *S40: Ches* *5H* **167**
(*off Packers Row*)
Shambles St. S70: Barn 1D **30**
Shamrock Pl. S43: Mas M 2F **165**
Shap Cl. S40: Ches 3D **166**
Shardlow Ct. DN4: Bess 6C **58**
Shardlow Gdns. DN4: Bess 6C **58**
Sharlston Gdns. DN11: Ross 5E **75**
Sharman Cl. S18: App 3D **156**
Sharman Wlk. S18: App 3D **156**
Sharpe Av. S8: Shef 2D **146**
Sharpfield Av. S62: Rawm 6F **65**
Sharrard Cl. S12: Shef 3E **135**
Sharrard Dr. S12: Shef 3E **135**
Sharrard Gro. S12: Shef 2E **135**
Sharrard Rd. S12: Shef 3E **135**
SHARROW 1C 132
SHARROW HEAD 6D 118
Sharrow La. S11: Shef 6D **118**
Sharrow Mt. S11: Shef 1C **132**
Sharrow St. S11: Shef 6E **119**
SHARROW VALE 6C 118
Sharrow Vale Rd. S11: Shef 6B **118**
Sharrow Vw. S7: Shef 6D **118**
Shaw Ct. DN3: Arm 5F **43**
Shawfield Cl. DN3: Barn D 2D **26**
Shawfield Rd. S71: Carl 1A **18**
SHAW LANDS 1B 30
Shawlands Ct. S63: Wath D 5D **48**
Shaw La. DN2: Don 2A **42**
S70: Barn 1B **30**
S71: Carl 5A **10**
S75: Stain 4B **8**
Shaw La. Ind. Est. DN2: Don 2B **42**
Shaw Rd. DN12: New E 3D **70**
S65: Roth 2H **97**
Shawsfield Rd. S60: Roth 6G **97**
Shaw's Row S40: Ches 6E **167**
Shaw St. S18: Coal A 6H **147**
S41: Whit M 6H **161**
S70: Barn 1C **30**
Shaw Wood Way DN2: Don 3A **42**
Shay, The DN4: Bess 5B **58**
SHAY HOUSE 3E 175
Shay Ho. La. S36: Stoc 4D **174**
Shay Rd. S36: Stoc 3D **174**
Sheaf Av. S7: Shef 2D **132**
Sheaf Bank S2: Shef 1F **133**
Sheaf Cl. DN12: Con 5G **69**
Sheaf Ct. S70: Barn 3A **32**
Sheaf Cres. S63: Bolt D 3C **50**
Sheaf Gdns. S2: Shef 5G **119**
Sheaf Gdns. Ter. S2: Shef 5G **119**
Sheaf Sq. S1: Shef 5G **5** (4G **119**)
Sheaf St. S1: Shef 5F **5** (4G **119**)
Sheardown St. DN4: Hex 2A **56**
Sheards Cl. S18: Dron W 2E **155**
Sheards Dr. S18: Dron W 3D **154**
Sheards Way S18: Dron W 3E **155**
Shearman Av. S61: Kimb P 6G **81**
Shearwood Rd. S10: Shef 3C **118**
Shed La. S75: Stainb 6G **29**
SHEEPBRIDGE 4F 161
Sheepbridge Bus. Cen.
S41: Old W 3G **161**
Sheep Bri. La. DN11: Ross 5D **74**
Sheepbridge La. S41: Ches 3F **161**
Sheepbridge Trad. Est.
S41: Ches 3D **160**
Sheepbridge Works S41: Ches 4F **161**
Sheepcote Hill S21: Killa 4C **152**
Sheep Cote Rd. S60: Roth 1C **112**
Sheepcote Rd. S21: Killa 4B **152**
Sheepcote Wlk. S70: Stair 2A **32**
Sheep Dike La. S66: Mort 4H **113**
Sheephill Rd. S11: Shef 4B **130**
Sheep La. DN5: High M 3F **53**
Sheep Wlk. La. DN5: Scaws 3C **38**
Sheerien Cl. S71: Ath 6D **8**
SHEFFIELD 3G 119
Sheffield Airport Bus. Pk.
S9: Shef 5G **109**
(Europa Link)
S9: Shef 6A **110**
(Europa Vw.)
S9: Tins 4G **109**
Sheffield Botanical Gdns. 5B 118
Sheffield Hallam University
City Campus 4F 5 (3G 119)
Collegiate Crescent Campus
5C 118
Sheffield La. S60: Cat 1D **122**
SHEFFIELD LANE TOP 6H 93
Sheffield Manor Lodge 4C 120
Sheffield Outer Ring Rd. S8: Shef 3G **147**
SHEFFIELD PARK 5B 120
Sheffield Parkway
S2: Shef 2H **5** (2H **119**)
S9: Shef 4G **121**
Sheffield Rd. DN4: Warm 2C **70**
DN12: Con 6C **68**
S9: Tins 3F **109**
(not continuous)
S12: Shef 6A **136**
S13: Shef 6F **123**
(Furnace La.)
S13: Shef 2B **136**
(Wolverley Rd.)
S18: Dron 1E **155**
(Bowshaw)
S18: Dron 5F **147**
(Jordanthorpe Parkway)
S18: Uns 5B **156**
S21: Ecki 5F **151**
S21: Killa 3A **152**
S25: Sth A 3G **141**
S26: Sth A, Tod 1H **139**
Sheffield Rd. S26: Swal 6F **123**
S35: Wort 1A **78**
S36: Oxs, Pen 4E **177**
S41: Ches, Whit M 6H **161**
(not continuous)
S41: Old W, Whit M 3F **161**
S60: Roth 6C **96**
S70: Barn 2E **31**
S70: Birdw, Wors 3D **44**
S74: Hoyl 1F **61**
Sheffield Ski Village 5E 107
Sheffield Station (Rail) 5G **5** (4G **119**)
Sheffield Station /
Sheffield Hallam University Stop (ST)
4G **5** (3G **119**)
Sheffield Technology Pk. S9: Shef 6D **108**
Sheffield Transport Department Golf Course
3E 147
Sheffield United FC 5F 119
Sheffield United FC Academy 4G 107
Sheffield Wednesday FC 2B 106
Sheldon Av. DN12: Con 5G **69**
Sheldon La. S6: Stann 6D **104**
Sheldon Rd. S7: Shef 2D **132**
S36: Stoc 3E **175**
S40: Ches 3C **166**
Sheldon Row S3: Shef 1G **5** (2G **119**)
Sheldon St. S2: Shef 5F **119**
Sheldrake Cl. S61: Thorpe H 2C **80**
Shelley Av. DN4: Balb 6A **56**
Shelley Cl. S36: Pen 3D **176**
Shelley Dr. DN3: Arm 4F **43**
S18: Dron 5H **155**
S25: Dinn 6C **128**
S65: Roth 5A **98**
S71: Monk B 5F **17**
Shelley Gro. DN5: Don 1G **55**
Shelley Ri. DN6: Adw S 3B **22**
Shelley Rd. S65: Roth 4A **98**
Shelley Way S63: Wath D 5D **48**
Shenstone Dr. S65: Roth 6A **98**
Shenstone Rd. S6: Shef 2B **106**
S65: Roth 6A **98**
Shepcote Business Village
S9: Shef 5F **109**
Shepcote Enterprise Park 1
S9: Shef 5G **109**
Shepcote Enterprise Park 2
S9: Tins 4G **109**
Shepcote La. S9: Shef, Tins 5F **109**
Shepcote Way S9: Shef 5F **109**
Shephard's Cl. DN12: Den M 3C **68**
Shepherd Dr. S35: Chap 2D **78**
Shepherd La. S63: Thurn 3C **36**
Shepherd St. S3: Shef 1C **4** (2E **119**)
Shepherd Wheel (Water Wheel) 1G 131
Shepley Cft. S35: High G 2D **78**
Shepley St. S40: Ches 6E **167**
Shepleys Yd. S40: Ches 5H **167**
Sheppard Rd. DN4: Balb 5H **55**
Shepperson Rd. S6: Shef 3A **106**
Sherbourne Av. S41: Ches 6F **161**
S66: Braml 1B **114**
Sherburn Ga. S35: Chap 2E **79**
Sherburn Rd. S71: Smi 1D **16**
Sherde Rd. S6: Shef 1D **118**
Sheridan Av. DN4: Balb 6B **56**
Sheridan Ct. S71: Monk B 5G **17**
Sheridan Dr. S65: Roth 4B **98**
Sheridan Rd. DN3: Barn D 1H **27**
Sheringham Cl. S35: High G 1C **78**
Sheringham Gdns. *S35: High G* *1C* **78**
(*off Sheringham Cl.*)
Sherwood Av. DN3: Eden 6C **26**
DN5: Scaws 4E **39**
DN12: Con 5D **68**
Sherwood Chase S17: Dore 5F **145**
Sherwood Cres. S60: Roth 4F **97**
Sherwood Dr. DN4: Balb 1F **71**
Sherwood Glen S7: Shef 1A **146**
Sherwood Pl. S18: Dron W 3C **154**
Sherwood Rd. DN11: New R 6D **74**
S18: Dron W 3C **154**
S21: Killa 3D **152**
Sherwood St. S40: Ches 1A **172**
S71: Barn 1E **31**
Sherwood Way S72: Cud 5D **10**
Shetland Gdns. DN2: Don 5G **41**

Shetland Rd. S18: Dron 4G **155**
Shield Av. S70: Wors 5F **31**
Shining Bank S13: Shef 4A **122**
Shinwell Av. S43: Ink 1G **169**
Shipcroft Cl. S73: Womb 2H **47**
Ship Hill S60: Roth 4E **97**
Shipman Balk S66: Clift 3H **87**
Shipman Ct. S20: Mosb 3E **151**
Shippen Rural Bus. Cen., The
S18: B'low 4A **160**
Shipton St. S6: Shef 1D **118**
Shirburn Gdns. DN4: Cant 3C **58**
Shirebrook Rd. S8: Shef 2F **133**
Shire Brook Valley Nature Reserve
. . . . 3B **136**
Shire Brook Vis. Cen. 3B **136**
SHIRECLIFFE 2F **107**
Shirecliffe Cl. S3: Shef 4G **107**
Shirecliffe La. S3: Shef 5F **107**
Shirecliffe Rd. S5: Shef 2F **107**
SHIREGREEN 4A **94**
Shiregreen La. S5: Shef 6B **94**
Shiregreen Ter. S5: Shef 5A **94**
Shirehall Cres. S5: Shef 3A **94**
Shirehall Rd. S5: Shef 4A **94**
Shire Oak Dr. S74: Els 1E **63**
Shireoaks Rd. S18: Dron 2H **155**
Shireoaks Way S72: Grim 1A **20**
Shires Cl. DN5: Sprot 3C **54**
Shirewood Cl. S63: Bramp B 6B **48**
Shirland Av. S71: Ath 2F **17**
Shirland Cl. S9: Shef 6C **108**
Shirland Ct. S9: Shef 1E **121**
Shirland La. S9: Shef 6C **108**
Shirland M. S9: Shef 1D **120**
Shirland Pl. S9: Shef 1E **121**
Shirland St. S41: Ches 4H **167**
Shirley Cl. S40: Ches 3C **166**
Shirley Rd. DN4: Hex 3H **55**
S3: Shef 5G **107**
Shooters Hill Dr. DN11: Ross 6E **75**
Shopping Mall, The S36: Stoc 3E **175**
Shore Ct. S10: Shef 4H **117**
Shoreham Av. S60: Roth 3H **111**
Shoreham Dr. S60: Roth 3G **111**
Shoreham Rd. S60: Roth 3G **111**
Shoreham St. S1: Shef 6E **5** (4G **119**)
S2: Shef 6E **5** (6F **119**)
(not continuous)
Shore La. S10: Shef 4H **117**
Shorland Dr. S60: Tree 2G **123**
Shortbrook Bank S20: Westf 2F **151**
Shortbrook Cl. S20: Westf 2F **151**
Shortbrook Cft. S20: Westf 2F **151**
Shortbrook Dr. S20: Westf 2F **151**
Shortbrook Rd. S20: Westf 2F **151**
Shortbrook Wlk. *S20: Westf* *2G* ***151***
(off Eastcroft Way)
Shortbrook Way S20: Westf 2F **151**
Shortfield Ct. S71: Ath 6D **8**
Short Ga. DN11: Wils 2G **89**
Short La. DN4: Don 5G **57**
Shortridge St. S9: Shef 6C **108**
Short Rd. DN2: Don 6H **41**
Short Row S71: Smi 3E **17**
Shorts La. S17: Dore 4C **144**
Short St. S74: Hoyl 1G **61**
Shortwood Bus. Pk. S74: Hoyl 5F **45**
Short Wood Cl. S70: Birdw 3E **45**
Shortwood Ct. S74: Hoyl 5G **45**
Shortwood La. DN5: Clay 4H **21**
Shortwood Vs. S74: Hoyl 5F **45**
Shortwood Way S74: Hoyl 4G **45**
Shotton Wlk. DN1: Don 2B **56**
Showroom Cinema, The 5F **5** (4G **119**)
Shrewsbury Almshouses
S2: Shef 5H **5** (4H **119**)
Shrewsbury Cl. S36: Pen 4D **176**
S64: Mexb 1E **67**
Shrewsbury Rd. S2: Shef 6G **5** (4G **119**)
S36: Pen 4D **176**
Shrewsbury Ter. S17: Tot 6E **145**
S61: Kimb 5A **96**
Shroggs Head Cl. S73: D'fld 4C **34**
Shrogswood Rd. S60: Roth 1C **112**
Shubert Cl. S13: Shef 6C **122**
Shude Hill S1: Shef 2G **5** (2G **119**)
Shuttle Cl. DN11: Ross 6E **75**
SHUTTLEWOOD 6H **165**
Shuttleworth Cl. DN11: Ross 6D **74**
Sibbering Row S36: Spink 4H **175**
Sicey Av. S5: Shef 2A **94**
Sicey La. S5: Shef 4A **94**
Sicklebrook La. S18: Coal A 6B **148**
Sidcop Rd. S72: Cud 5D **10**
Siddall St. S1: Shef 3B **4** (3E **119**)
Sidings, The S73: Womb 2C **48**
Sidings Ct. DN4: Don 4D **56**
Sidlaw Cl. S40: Ches 3D **166**
Sidney Rd. DN2: Don 6G **41**
Sidney St. S1: Shef 6E **5** (4F **119**)
S64: Swint 3C **66**
Sidons Cl. S61: Kimb P 6H **81**
Siemens Cl. S9: Tins 2H **109**
Siena Cl. S73: D'fld 4H **33**
Sike Cl. S75: Kexb 5D **6**
Sike La. S36: Cub 6A **176**
Sikes Rd. S25: Nth A 3G **141**
Silk Rd. DN2: Don 4D **40**
SILKSTONE 2A **28**
Silkstone Cl. S12: Shef 4H **135**
S75: Pill 1C **60**
SILKSTONE COMMON 5B **28**
Silkstone Common Station (Rail) 5A **28**
Silkstone Cres. S12: Shef 4H **135**
SILKSTONE CROSS 3A **28**
Silkstone Dr. S12: Shef 4G **135**
Silkstone Golf Course 2D **28**
Silkstone La. S75: Cawt, Silk 4A **14**
Silkstone Pl. S12: Shef 4H **135**
Silkstone Rd. S12: Shef 4G **135**
Silkstone Vw. S74: Hoyl 4B **46**
Silver Birch Av. S10: Shef 1D **130**
Silver Birch Gro. DN9: Finn 3G **77**
Silverdale Cl. DN3: Brant 4H **59**
S11: Shef 4H **131**
S41: Ches 5F **161**
Silverdale Ct. *S11: Shef* *3A* ***132***
(off Silverdale Rd.)
Silverdale Cres. S11: Shef 3H **131**
Silverdale Cft. S11: Shef 4H **131**
Silverdale Dr. S71: Monk B 3A **18**
Silverdale Gdns. S11: Shef 4A **132**
Silverdale Glade S11: Shef 4A **132**
Silverdale Rd. S11: Shef 4H **131**
Silverdales S25: Dinn 5B **128**
Silver Hill Rd. S11: Shef 3A **132**
Silver Jubilee Cl. DN2: Don 4H **41**
Silver Mill Rd. S2: Shef 6F **119**
Silvermoor Dr. S65: Rav 2A **100**
Silverstone Av. S72: Cud 1F **19**
Silver St. DN1: Don 1C **56**
S1: Shef 2E **5** (2F **119**)
S65: Thry 6D **84**
S70: Barn 2D **30**
S75: Dod 4G **29**
Silver St. Head S1: Shef 2D **4** (2F **119**)
Silver Well Dr. S43: Stav 6A **164**
Silverwood Cl. S66: Sunn 3G **99**
Silverwood Ct. S63: Wath D 6A **50**
Silverwood Ho. *DN1: Don* *3B* ***56***
(off St James St.)
Silverwood Rd. S75: Wool G 4F **7**
Silverwood Vw. DN12: Con 4E **69**
Silverwood Wlk. S66: Flan 4G **99**
Simcrest Av. S21: Killa 5C **152**
Simmonite Rd. S61: Kimb P 6H **81**
Simon Ct. S10: Shef 6G **117**
Simons Ct. S73: Womb 5E **33**
Simons Way S73: Womb 5E **33**
Simpson Pl. S64: Mexb 1E **67**
Sims Cft. S41: Old W 3B **162**
Sims St. S1: Shef 2D **4** (2F **119**)
Sincil Way DN4: Cant 5B **58**
Singleton Cres. S6: Shef 5B **106**
Singleton Gro. S6: Shef 5B **106**
Singleton Rd. S6: Shef 5B **106**
Site Gallery 5F **5** (4G **119**)
Sitka Cl. S71: Roy 4G **9**
Sitwell *S20: Westf* *2F* ***151***
(off Shortbrook Way)
Sitwell Av. S36: Stoc 3C **174**
S40: Ches 1G **171**
Sitwell Dr. S60: Roth 1H **111**
Sitwell Gro. S60: Roth 2H **111**
S64: Swint 4C **66**
Sitwell La. S66: Wick 1G **113**
Sitwell Museum 2G **159**
Sitwell Park Golf Course 1D **112**
Sitwell Pk. Rd. S60: Roth 1C **112**
Sitwell Pl. S7: Shef 6E **119**
Sitwell Rd. S7: Shef 6E **119**
(not continuous)
Sitwell St. S21: Ecki 2C **158**
Sitwell Ter. S66: Wick 1G **113**
Sitwell Va. S60: Roth 1G **111**
Sitwell Vw. S60: Whist 3C **112**
Sivilla Rd. S64: Kiln 6C **66**
Sixth Av. DN9: Finn 3C **76**
Skate Central 5G **119**
Skeldale Dr. S40: Ches 2A **172**
Skelton Av. S75: Mapp 5A **8**
Skelton Cl. S13: Shef 3C **136**
Skelton Dr. S13: Shef 2C **136**
Skelton Gro. S13: Shef 2C **136**
Skelton La. S13: Shef 2C **136**
S20: Beig 5G **137**
Skelton Ri. S35: Ough 4E **91**
Skelton Rd. S8: Shef 3F **133**
Skelton Wlk. S13: Shef 2D **136**
Skelton Way S13: Shef 2C **136**
Skelwith Cl. S4: Shef 3C **108**
S41: Ches 6E **161**
Skelwith Dr. S4: Shef 2C **108**
Skelwith Rd. S4: Shef 3C **108**
Skew Hill S35: Gren 3B **92**
Skew Hill La. S35: Gren 2A **92**
Skiddaw Cl. S40: Ches 2E **167**
Skiers Vw. Rd. S74: Hoyl 1H **61**
Skiers Way S74: Hoyl 1H **61**
Skinnerthorpe Rd. S4: Shef 3A **108**
Skinpit La. S36: H'swne 1G **177**
(not continuous)
Skipton Cl. DN12: Den M 3B **68**
Skipton Rd. S4: Shef 4H **107**
S26: Swal 1B **138**
Skipwith Cl. DN11: Lov 4B **72**
Skipwith Gdns. DN11: New R 6B **74**
Sky Bus Pk. DN9: Finn 2C **76**
Skye Cft. S71: Roy 1H **9**
Skye Edge Av. S2: Shef 4A **120**
Skye Edge Rd. S2: Shef 4A **120**
Skylark Vw. S63: Wath D 5E **49**
Slackfields La. S35: Wharn S 1C **90**
Slack La. S40: Ash 5C **166**
S72: Sth H 1E **11**
Slacks La. S66: Braml 1B **114**
SLADE HOTON 5H **115**
Slade Rd. S64: Swint 4B **66**
Slade Vw. S25: Slade H 5H **115**
Slag La. S21: Neth Han 6G **157**
Slaidburn Av. S35: Chap 2E **79**
SLATEPIT DALE 5A **170**
Slate St. S2: Shef 1G **133**
Slayleigh Av. S10: Shef 6D **116**
Slayleigh Delph S10: Shef 6E **117**
Slayleigh Dr. S10: Shef 6E **117**
Slayleigh La. S10: Shef 6D **116**
Sleaford St. S9: Shef 6C **108**
Sledgate Dr. S66: Wick 1E **113**
Sledgate La. S66: Wick 1E **113**
Sledmere Rd. DN5: Scaws 4F **39**
Slinn St. S10: Shef 2B **118**
Slitting Mill La. S9: Shef 6C **108**
Sloade La. S12: Ridg 3G **149**
SLOADLANE 3G **149**
Smallage La. S13: Shef 5G **123**
SMALL BRIDGE 3H **57**
Smallbridge Cl. S71: Monk B 2C **18**
Smalldale Rd. S12: Shef 4G **135**
Smeaton Cl. S65: Rav 2A **100**
Smeaton St. S7: Shef 6E **119**
Smeckley Wood Cl. S41: Ches 3D **160**
SMEE Model Railway 2H **145**
Smelter Wood Av. S13: Shef 1H **135**
Smelter Wood Cl. S13: Shef 1H **135**
Smelter Wood Ct. *S13: Shef* *1H* ***135***
(off Smelter Wood Way)
Smelter Wood Cres. S13: Shef 1A **136**
Smelter Wood Dr. S13: Shef 1H **135**
Smelter Wood La. S13: Shef 1H **135**
Smelter Wood Pl. S13: Shef 1A **136**
Smelter Wood Ri. S13: Shef 1A **136**
Smelter Wood Rd. S13: Shef 1H **135**

Smelter Wood Way—Spa Brook Dr.

Smelter Wood Way S13: Shef 1H **135**
Smeltinghouse La.
S18: B'low 3A **160**
Smillie Rd. DN11: New R 6D **74**
Smith Av. S43: Ink 1G **169**
Smith Cres. S41: Ches 1C **172**
Smithey Cl. S35: High G 2C **78**
Smithfield S3: Shef 1D **4** (2F **119**)
Smithfield Apartments S1: Shef 4C **4**
Smithfield Av. S41: Has 3B **172**
Smithfield Rd. S12: Shef 6D **134**
SMITHIES .3F **17**
Smithies La. S71: Barn, Smi 4D **16**
S75: Barn 4D **16**
Smithies Rd. S64: Swint 2C **66**
Smithies St. S71: Barn 4D **16**
SMITHLEY .1C **46**
Smithley La. S73: Womb 1C **46**
Smith Rd. S36: Stoc 3D **174**
Smith Sq. DN4: Balb 5G **55**
Smith St. DN4: Balb 5G **55**
S35: Chap 3F **79**
S73: Womb 1H **47**
Smithy Bri. La. S63: Bramp B 5H **47**
S73: Hem 5G **47**
(not continuous)
Smithy Carr Av. S35: Chap 3E **79**
Smithy Carr Cl. S35: Chap 3E **79**
Smithy Cl. S61: Kimb P 1A **96**
Smithy Cft. S18: Dron W 2B **154**
S63: Bolt D 2C **50**
SMITHY GREEN 3E **17**
Smithy Grn. Rd. S71: Smi 3E **17**
SMITHY MOOR 2B **174**
Smithy Moor Av. S36: Stoc 1A **174**
Smithy Moor La. S36: Stoc 2A **174**
Smithy Wood Bus. Pk. S35: Eccl 5H **79**
Smithy Wood Cres. S8: Shef 4D **132**
(not continuous)
Smithy Wood Dr. S35: Eccl 5H **79**
Smithy Wood La. S75: Dod 4G **29**
Smithy Wood Rd. S8: Shef 4D **132**
S61: Thorpe H 4A **80**
Snail Hill S60: Roth 4E **97**
Snailsden Way S75: Stain 6C **8**
Snaithing La. S10: Shef 5F **117**
Snaithing Pk. Cl. S10: Shef 5F **117**
Snaithing Pk. Rd. S10: Shef 5F **117**
Snake La. DN12: Con 5G **69**
SNAPE HILL
S18 . . . . .2F **155**
S73 . . . . .5A **34**
Snape Hill S18: Dron 2F **155**
Snape Hill Cl. S18: Dron 1F **155**
Snape Hill Cres. S18: Dron 1F **155**
Snape Hill Dr. S18: Dron 1F **155**
Snape Hill La. S18: Dron 2F **155**
Snape Hill Rd. S73: D'fld 5A **34**
Snelston Cl. S18: Dron W 3B **154**
Snetterton Cl. S72: Cud 1F **19**
Snig Hill S3: Shef 2F **5** (2G **119**)
Snowberry Cl. S41: Has 3D **172**
S64: Swint 6B **66**
Snowden Ter. S73: Womb 1G **47**
Snowdon La. S18: Coal A 1D **156**
S21: Mar L, Trow 1D **156**
Snowdon Way S60: Brins 5E **111**
Snow Hill S75: Dod 4G **29**
Snow La. S3: Shef 1D **4** (2F **119**)
Snydale Rd. S72: Cud 1E **19**
Soaper La. S18: Dron 2F **155**
Soap Ho. La. S13: Shef 1F **137**
(not continuous)
Society St. DN1: Don 1C **56**
Sokell Av. S73: Womb 2F **47**
Solario Way DN11: New R 6F **75**
Solly St. S1: Shef 3B **4** (3E **119**)
Solway Ri. S18: Dron W 2C **154**
Somercotes Rd. S12: Shef 3G **135**
Somersall Cl. S40: Bramp 1B **170**
Somersall Hall Dr. S40: Bramp 2B **170**
Somersall La. S40: Bramp 2B **170**
Somersall Pk. Rd. S40: Bramp 1B **170**
Somersall Willows S40: Bramp 1B **170**
Somersby Av. DN5: Don 6G **39**
S42: Walt 3C **170**
Somerset Ct. S72: Cud 2E **19**
Somerset Dr. S43: Brim 5E **163**
Somerset Rd. DN1: Don 2C **56**
S3: Shef 6G **107**
Somerset St. S3: Shef 6G **107**
S66: Malt 6C **102**
S70: Barn 6C **16**
S72: Cud .2E **19**
Somerton Dr. DN4: Bess 5B **58**
Somerville Ter. S6: Shef 6C **106**
Somin Ct. DN4: Balb 1B **72**
Songthrush Way
S63: Wath D 5E **49**
Sopewell Rd. S61: Kimb 4G **95**
Sorby Hall S10: Shef 5A **118**
Sorby Rd. S26: Swal 1A **138**
Sorby St. S4: Shef 1H **119**
Sorby Way S66: Wick 1F **113**
Soresby St. S40: Ches 5H **167**
Sorrel Rd. S66: Sunn 4H **99**
Sorrelsykes Cl. S60: Whist 4A **112**
Sorrento Way S73: D'fld 3A **34**
SOTHALL 6H **137**
Sothall Cl. S20: Beig 5G **137**
Sothall Ct. S20: Beig 5G **137**
Sothall Grn. S20: Beig 5G **137**
Sothall M. S20: Beig 5G **137**
Sough Hall Av. S61: Thorpe H 3C **80**
Sough Hall Cl. S61: Thorpe H 3C **80**
Sough Hall Cres.
S61: Thorpe H 3C **80**
Sough Hall Rd. S61: Thorpe H 4C **80**
Sousa St. S66: Malt 6D **102**
Southall St. S8: Shef 2F **133**
SOUTH ANSTON 4G **141**
South Av. S64: Swint 4A **66**
Southbourne Ct. S17: Dore 4E **145**
Southbourne Hall S10: Shef 4C **118**
Southbourne M. S10: Shef 5B **118**
Southbourne Rd. S10: Shef 4B **118**
South Cl. S18: Uns 6C **156**
S71: Roy .4H **9**
Southcote Dr. S18: Dron W 3C **154**
South Ct. S17: Dore 3F **145**
South Cres. S21: Killa 3D **152**
S65: Roth 3A **98**
S75: Dod 3G **29**
South Cft. S72: Shaft 3F **11**
Southcroft Gdns. S7: Shef 2E **133**
Southcroft Wlk. *S7: Shef 2E 133*
(off Southcroft Gdns.)
Southdown Av. S40: Ches 4D **166**
South Dr. S63: Bolt D 3A **50**
S71: Roy .4H **9**
Southend Pl. S2: Shef 4B **120**
Southend Rd. S2: Shef 4B **120**
Southey Av. S5: Shef 1F **107**
Southey Cl. S5: Shef 1E **107**
(not continuous)
Southey Cres. S5: Shef 1E **107**
S66: Malt 5B **102**
Southey Dr. S5: Shef 1F **107**
SOUTHEY GREEN 6D **92**
Southey Grn. Cl. S5: Shef 1E **107**
Southey Grn. Rd. S5: Shef 6C **92**
Southey Hall Dr. S5: Shef 1F **107**
Southey Hall Rd. S5: Shef 1E **107**
Southey Hill S5: Shef 6D **92**
Southey Pl. S5: Shef 1E **107**
Southey Ri. S5: Shef 1E **107**
Southey Rd. S66: Malt 5B **102**
Southey Wlk. S5: Shef 1E **107**
Southfield Av. S41: Has 4C **172**
Southfield Cotts. S71: Carl 5H **9**
Southfield Cres. S63: Thurn 3A **36**
Southfield Dr. S18: Dron 4H **155**
Southfield La. S63: Thurn 4A **36**
(not continuous)
Southfield Mt. S18: Dron 4H **155**
Southfield Rd. DN3: Arm 4D **42**
S72: Cud .4F **19**
Southgate S21: Ecki 1F **159**
S36: Pen .5E **177**
S72: Shaft 4G **11**
S72: Sth H 1H **11**
S74: Hoyl .6B **46**
S75: Barn .5B **16**
Southgate Ct. S21: Ecki 1F **159**
Southgate Way S43: Bar H 2G **163**
South Gro. S60: Roth 5E **97**
South Gro. Dr. S74: Hoyl 1A **62**
Southgrove Rd. S10: Shef 5C **118**
SOUTH HIENDLEY 1H **11**
SOUTH KIRKBY 4H **13**
Sth. Kirkby Ind. Est.
WF9: Sth K 2H **13**
Southlands Way S26: Ast 1D **138**
South La. S1: Shef 6C **4** (5E **119**)
Southlea Av. S74: Hoyl 1C **62**
Southlea Cl. S74: Hoyl 1C **62**
Southlea Dr. S74: Hoyl 1B **62**
Southlea Rd. S74: Hoyl 1C **62**
Sth. Lodge Ct. S40: Bramp 5C **166**
South Mall DN1: Don 1B **56**
Southmoor Av. DN3: Arm 4D **42**
Southmoor Cl. S43: Brim C 4E **169**
Southmoor La. DN3: Arm 5D **42**
Southmoor Rd. S72: Brier 4E **13**
WF9: Hems 1E **13**
South Pde. DN1: Don 1C **56**
S3: Shef 1D **4** (1F **119**)
South Pl. S40: Ches 6H **167**
(Beetwell St.)
S40: Ches 6E **167**
(Hall's Row)
S73: Womb 1E **47**
S75: Barn 5A **16**
Sth. Quay Dr. S2: Shef 1H **5** (2H **119**)
South Rd. DN3: Barn D 1H **25**
S6: Shef .6B **106**
S35: High G 1C **78**
S61: Kimb 3H **95**
S75: Dod .3G **29**
Southsea Rd. S13: Shef 2B **136**
South St. DN4: Don 3C **56**
DN6: Highf 6C **22**
S2: Shef 3H **5** (3H **119**)
S20: Mosb 4E **151**
S25: Dinn 5A **128**
S40: Ches 6H **167**
S61: Grea 5D **82**
S61: Kimb 5H **95**
S62: Rawm 2H **83**
S66: Thurc 5C **114**
S70: Barn 1C **30**
S73: D'fld 5B **34**
S75: Dod .4G **29**
WF9: Hems 1F **13**
South St. Nth. S43: New W 3C **162**
South Ter. S26: Wales B 5E **139**
S60: Roth 4E 97
(off Moorgate St.)
South Va. Dr. S65: Thry 6E **85**
South Vw. DN12: New E 5B **70**
S20: Holb 3H **151**
S26: Kiv P 6A **140**
S72: Grim 2A **20**
S73: D'fld 5B **34**
South Vw. Cl. S6: Lox 3F **105**
South Vw. Cres. S7: Shef 1E **133**
South Vw. Ri. S6: Lox 3F **105**
South Vw. Rd. S7: Shef 6E **119**
S74: Hoyl 1A **62**
South Vw. Ter. S60: Cat 1D **122**
Southwell Gdns. S26: Swal 1H **137**
(not continuous)
Southwell Ri. S64: Mexb 6G **51**
Southwell Rd. DN2: Don 4E **41**
S4: Shef .3C **108**
S62: Rawm 2A **84**
Southwell St. S75: Barn 6C **16**
Southwood S6: Shef 1H **105**
Southwood Av. S18: Dron 5F **155**
Southwood Gro. S6: Shef 1H **105**
Sth. Yorkshire Bldgs.
S75: Silk C 5B **28**
Sth. Yorkshire Fresh Produce & Flower Cen.
S9: Shef .2E **121**
Sth. Yorkshire Ind. Pk.
S75: Pill, Tank 2B **60**
Sth. Yorkshire (Redbrook) Ind. Est.
S75: Barn 3H **15**
South Yorkshire Transport Mus. 1H **97**
Sowters Row *S40: Ches 5H 167*
(off High St.)
Spa Brook Cl. S12: Shef 4A **136**
Spa Brook Dr. S12: Shef 3A **136**
(not continuous)

SPA HOUSES 1G **123**
Spa La. S13: Shef 3D **136**
S41: Ches 5A **168**
(not continuous)
Spa La. Cft. S13: Shef 2D **136**
Spalton Rd. S62: Parkg 4G **83**
Spansyke St. DN4: Hex 2A **56**
Sparkfields S75: Mapp 6A **8**
Spark La. S75: Mapp 1H **15**
Spartan Vw. S66: Malt 3G **101**
Spa Vw. Av. S12: Shef 5A **136**
Spa Vw. Dr. S12: Shef 5A **136**
Spa Vw. Pl. S12: Shef 5A **136**
Spa Vw. Rd. S12: Shef 5A **136**
Spa Vw. Ter. S12: Shef 5A **136**
Spa Vw. Way S12: Shef 5A **136**
Spa Well Cres. S60: Tree 1F **123**
Spa Well Gro. S72: Brier 3B **12**
Spa Well Ter. S71: Barn 6E **17**
Speedwell Ind. Est. S43: Stav 5B **164**
(Hayford Way)
S43: Stav 4C **164**
(Telford Way)
Speeton Rd. S6: Shef 5B **106**
Speighthill Cres. S42: W'orth 6F **171**
Spencer Av. DN1: Don 6D **40**
S43: Woodt 4E **165**
Spencer Ct. S60: Whist 3C **112**
Spencer Cft. S75: Cawt 3A **14**
Spencer Dr. S65: Rav 2A **100**
Spencer Grn. S60: Whist 3C **112**
Spencer Pk. S60: Roth 2D **96**
Spencer Rd. S2: Shef 1F **133**
Spencer St. S40: Ches 4H **167**
S64: Mexb 2D **66**
S70: Barn 2D **30**
Spenser Rd. S65: Roth 5A **98**
Spey Cl. S75: Mapp 1B **16**
Spey Dr. DN9: Auck 1H **59**
Spilsby Cl. DN4: Cant 6D **58**
SPINK HALL 4D **174**
Spink Hall Cl. S36: Stoc 4E **175**
Spink Hall La. S36: Stoc 4D **174**
Spinkhill Av. S13: Shef 6F **121**
Spinkhill Dr. S13: Shef 6G **121**
Spinkhill La.
S21: Reni, Spink 3H **159**
Spinkhill Rd. S13: Shef 1F **135**
S21: Killa 6C **152**
Spinner Cft. S40: Ches 1H **171**
Spinners Rd. DN2: Don 4D **40**
Spinners Wlk. S60: Roth 5F **97**
(off Warwick St.)
Spinney, The DN3: Barn D 2D **26**
DN4: Balb 1G **71**
S17: Dore 3D **144**
S43: Brim 6C **162**
Spinney Cl. S60: Roth 1H **111**
Spinneyfield S60: Roth 2H **111**
Spinney Hill DN3: Sprot 4C **54**
Spire Lodge S41: Ches 3H **167**
Spire Wlk. S40: Ches 6H **167**
Spire Wlk. Bus. Pk. S40: Ches 6A **168**
SPITAL 1B **172**
Spital Brook Cl. S41: Ches 1B **172**
Spitalfields S3: Shef 1G **119**
Spital Gdns. S41: Ches 1B **172**
Spital Gro. DN11: New R 6H **75**
Spital Hill S4: Shef 1H **119**
Spital La. S3: Shef 1H **119**
S41: Ches 6A **168**
Spital St. S3: Shef 1G **119**
Spitfire Way DN9: Auck 2C **76**
Spofforth Rd. S9: Shef 1D **120**
Spooner Dr. S21: Killa 4B **152**
Spooner Rd. S10: Shef 4B **118**
Spoon Glade S6: Stann 6D **104**
Spoonhill Rd. S6: Shef 6G **105**
Spoon La. S6: Stann 6D **104**
Spoon M. S6: Stann 6D **104**
Spoon Oak Lea S6: Stann 6D **104**
Spoon Way S6: Stann 6D **104**
Spotswood Cl. S14: Shef 4B **134**
Spotswood Dr. S14: Shef 3B **134**
Spotswood Mt. S14: Shef 4A **134**
Spotswood Pl. S14: Shef 4A **134**
Spotswood Rd. S14: Shef 4A **134**
Spout Copse S6: Stann 6C **104**

Spout La. S6: Stann 5C **104**
Spout Spinney S6: Stann 6C **104**
Spreadeagle Yd. S40: Ches 6H **167**
(off Beetwell St.)
Springbank S18: Uns 4B **156**
S73: D'fld 5C **34**
Springbank Cl. S71: Carl 6H **9**
Spring Bank Rd. DN12: Con 6E **69**
S40: Ches 5G **167**
Springbrook Cl. S63: Thurn 1C **36**
Spring Cl. S60: Whist 3B **112**
Spring Cl. S14: Shef 4C **134**
Spring Cl. Dell S14: Shef 4C **134**
Spring Cl. Dr. S14: Shef 4C **134**
Spring Cl. Mt. S14: Shef 4C **134**
Spring Cl. Vw. S14: Shef 4B **134**
Spring Cres. DN5: Sprot 3C **54**
Spring Cft. S61: Kimb P 1A **96**
Springcroft Dr.
DN5: Scawt 2F **39**
Spring Dr. S73: Bramp 4B **48**
Springfield S63: Bolt D 2H **49**
Springfield Av. S7: Shef 3B **132**
S40: Ches 5E **167**
WF9: Hems 1F **13**
Springfield Cl. DN3: Arm 5F **43**
S7: Shef 4B **132**
S21: Ecki 1D **158**
S61: Grea 1E **97**
S73: D'fld 5C **34**
S81: Woods 4F **143**
Springfield Cl. DN5: Cus 5F **39**
Springfield Cres. S73: D'fld 5C **34**
S74: Hoyl 1H **61**
Springfield Dr. S65: Thry 6F **85**
Springfield Glen S7: Shef 4A **132**
Springfield Path S64: Mexb 2F **67**
Springfield Pl. S70: Barn 1C **30**
Springfield Rd. DN12: New E 4D **70**
S7: Shef 4A **132**
S64: Kiln 1D **84**
S66: Wick 5F **99**
S72: Grim 1A **20**
S74: Hoyl 1G **61**
Springfields S75: Barn 4H **15**
Springfield St. S70: Barn 1B **30**
Springfield Ter. S25: Nth A 1F **141**
S70: Barn 1C **30**
Springfield Way S35: Burn 3C **78**
Spring Gdns. DN1: Don 1B **56**
DN3: Cant 3F **59**
S70: Barn 2C **30**
S71: Monk B 4H **17**
S74: Hoyl 6B **46**
Spring Gro. S71: Carl 5A **10**
Spring Gro. Gdns. S35: Wharn S 1C **90**
Spring Hill S10: Shef 2B **118**
S75: Wool G 3F **7**
Springhill Av. S73: Bramp 4B **48**
Spring Hill Cl. DN5: Sprot 3C **54**
Spring Hill Rd. S10: Shef 2B **118**
S72: Grim 3A **20**
Spring Ho. Rd. S10: Shef 2B **118**
Spring La. DN5: Sprot 6C **38**
S2: Shef 6B **120**
S71: Carl 6A **10**
WF4: Wool 2B **8**
Spring Lane Stop (ST) 6B **120**
Spring Pl. S40: Ches 5H **167**
Spring Ram Bus. Pk.
S75: Kexb 4D **6**
Springs Leisure Cen. 2C **134**
Spring St. S3: Shef 1E **5** (2F **119**)
S65: Roth 3F **97**
S70: Barn 2D **30**
SPRING VALE 4E **177**
Spring Vale Av. S70: Wors 6E **31**
Springvale Cl. S66: Malt 4A **102**
S66: Wick 2H **113**
Springvale Gro. S36: Pen 4E **177**
Spring Vale Rd. S43: Brim 6C **162**
Springvale Rd. S6: Shef 2C **118**
S10: Shef 2A **118**
S72: Grim 3A **20**
S72: Gt H 6F **21**
Springvale Wlk. S6: Shef 1C **118**
Spring Vw. Rd. S10: Shef 2B **118**

Spring Wlk. S65: Roth 3F **97**
(off Carlisle St.)
S73: Womb 6E **33**
Spring Water Av. S12: Shef 5B **136**
Spring Water Cl. S12: Shef 5A **136**
Spring Water Dr. S12: Shef 5B **136**
Springwell S20: Beig 4F **137**
Springwell Av. S20: Beig 4F **137**
Springwell Cl. S66: Malt 4C **102**
Springwell Ct. WF9: Hems 1F **13**
Springwell Cres. S20: Beig 4F **137**
Springwell Dr. S20: Beig 4F **137**
Springwell Gdns. DN4: Balb 6G **55**
Springwell Gro. S20: Beig 4F **137**
Springwell Hill S21: Neth Han 6H **157**
Springwell La. DN4: Balb 6G **55**
(not continuous)
DN11: A'ley 6G **55**
Springwell Pk. Dr. S43: Ink 1H **169**
Springwood S5: Shef 2D **106**
Springwood Av. S26: Augh 5B **124**
Spring Wood Cl. S41: Ches 6D **160**
Springwood Cl. DN3: Brant 5G **59**
Springwood Ct. S26: Ast 5C **124**
S43: New W 2C **162**
Springwood Gro. S63: Thurn 3B **36**
Springwood Ho. DN1: Don 2B **56**
(off Elsworth Cl.)
Springwood La. S35: High G 1B **78**
Springwood Rd. DN5: Scawt 2F **39**
S8: Shef 2F **133**
S74: Hoyl 1H **61**
Springwood St. S42: Tem N 6G **173**
Springwood Vw. S36: Pen 4F **177**
SPROTBROUGH 3C **54**
Sprotbrough Flash Nature Reserve . . .68 **54**
SPROTBROUGH PARK 3E **55**
Sprotbrough Rd. DN5: Don 1G **55**
Spruce Av. S66: Wick 5H **99**
S71: Roy 3G **9**
Spruce Cl. S40: Bramp 6C **166**
Spruce Cres. DN9: Auck 3B **76**
Spruce Ri. S21: Killa 5B **152**
Spry La. DN5: Clay 4H **21**
Spurley Hey Gro. S36: Stoc 4E **175**
Spurr St. S2: Shef 6G **119**
Square, The S26: Wales 6G **139**
S42: Cut 1A **166**
(not continuous)
S62: H'ley 5A **62**
S70: Barn 2C **30**
S72: Grim 2C **20**
Square East, The S66: Sunn 3H **99**
Square West, The S66: Sunn 3G **99**
Squirrel Cft. S61: Wing 4A **82**
Stable Gdns. DN5: Sprot 4D **54**
Stables, The S64: Swint 3A **66**
Stables La. DN5: Barnb 6H **37**
Stables Way S63: Wath D 5G **49**
Stacey Bank S6: Lox 2A **104**
Stacey Cres. S72: Grim 1A **20**
Stacey Dr. S65: Thry 5E **85**
Stacey La. S6: Lox 2A **104**
Stackyard, The S71: Ard 2E **33**
Stacye Av. S13: Shef 2E **137**
Stacye Ri. S13: Shef 2E **137**
Stadium Ct. S62: Parkg 6F **83**
Stadium Way DN4: Don 4E **57**
S9: Shef 1C **120**
S60: Roth 1G **97**
Stafford Cl. S18: Dron W 2B **154**
Stafford Cres. S60: Roth 3G **111**
Stafford Dr. S60: Roth 3G **111**
Stafford La. S2: Shef 4A **120**
Stafford M. S2: Shef 4A **120**
Stafford Pl. DN12: Den M 3C **68**
Stafford Rd. DN6: Woodl 4D **22**
S2: Shef 4A **120**
Staffordshire Cl. S66: Malt 5C **102**
Stafford St. S2: Shef 5H **5** (4H **119**)
Stafford Way S35: Chap 3E **79**
Stag Cl. S60: Roth 1B **112**
Stag Cres. S60: Roth 1B **112**
Stag La. S60: Roth 1A **112**
Stag Willow Cl. S60: Roth 1A **112**
STAINBOROUGH 6H **29**
Stainborough Cl. S75: Dod 4G **29**
Stainborough Rd. S75: Dod 4G **29**

Stainborough Vw. S70: Wors 5E 31
S75: Pill 6C 44
STAINCROSS 4A 8
Staincross Comn. S75: Stain 3A 8
Staindrop Cl. S35: Chap 2E 79
Staindrop Vw. S35: Chap 2F 79
Stainer Ct. S41: Has 3B 172
Stainforth Rd.
DN3: Barn D 1C 26 & 1H 27
Stainley Cl. S75: Barn 4A 16
Stainmore Av. S20: Sot 6H 137
Stainmore Cl. S75: Silk 2A 28
STAINTON 2F 103
Stainton Cl. S71: Smi 2D 16
Stainton La. DN11: Wils 6F 89
S66: Malt, Staint 3C 102
Stainton Rd. S11: Shef 6A 118
Stainton St. DN12: Den M 3C 68
STAIRFOOT 2B 32
Stairfoot Bus. Pk. S70: Stair 3B 32
Stairfoot Way S70: Stair 3B 32
Stair Rd. S4: Shef 4H 107
Staithes Wlk. DN12: Den M 2D 68
Stalker Lees Rd. S11: Shef 6C 118
Stalker Wlk. S11: Shef 5D 118
Stambers Cl. S81: Woods 5F 143
Stamford Rd. S66: Sunn 2G 99
Stamford St. S9: Shef 5C 108
Stamford Way S75: Stain 4A 8
Stanage Ri. S12: Shef 3H 135
Stanage Way S40: Ches 3A 166
Stanbury Cl. S75: Barn 4A 16
Standhill Cres. S71: Smi 1D 16
Standish Av. S5: Shef 4F 107
Standish Bank S5: Shef 4F 107
Standish Cl. S5: Shef 3F 107
Standish Dr. S5: Shef 3F 107
Standish Gdns. S5: Shef 3F 107
Standish Rd. S5: Shef 3F 107
Standish Way S5: Shef 4F 107
Standon Cres. S9: Shef 5D 94
Standon Dr. S9: Shef 5D 94
Standon Rd. S9: Shef 5D 94
Stand Pk. Ind. Est. S41: Ches 1H 167
Stand Rd. S41: Ches 6G 161
Staneford Ct. S20: Water 1E 151
Stanford Cl. S66: Malt 6D 102
Stanford Rd. S18: Dron W 3B 154
Stanford Way S42: Walt 2C 170
Stanhope Av. S75: Cawt 3A 14
Stanhope Gdns. S75: Barn 5B 16
Stanhope Mdws. S75: Cawt 3A 14
Stanhope Rd. DN1: Don 5D 40
S12: Shef 3F 135
Stanhope St. S70: Barn 1C 30
Staniforth Av. S21: Ecki 1C 158
Staniforth Cres. S26: Tod 3B 140
Staniforth Rd. S9: Shef 1C 120
Stanley Av. S43: Ink 2G 169
Stanley Ct. *S66: Malt 5G 101*
(off Leslie Av.)
Stanley Gdns. DN4: Balb 3A 56
Stanley Gro. S26: Ast 6D 124
(not continuous)
Stanley La. S3: Shef 1G 5 (1G 119)
Stanley Rd. DN5: Scaws 3E 39
S8: Shef 3G 133
S35: Chap 2C 78
S36: Stoc 4E 175
S70: Stair 2B 32
Stanley Sq. DN3: Kirk Sa 4C 26
Stanley St. S3: Shef 1F 5 (1G 119)
S21: Killa 3C 152
S41: Ches 6B 168
S60: Roth 4E 97
S70: Barn 1C 30
S72: Cud 3F 19
Stanley Ter. S66: Malt 5G 101
STANNINGTON 6D 104
Stannington Glen S6: Stann 6F 105
Stannington Ri. S6: Shef 5H 105
Stannington Rd. S6: Shef, Stann 6C 104
Stannington Vw. Rd. S10: Shef 2H 117
Stanton Cres. S12: Shef 4G 135
Stanwell Av. S9: Shef 6D 94
Stanwell Cl. S9: Shef 6D 94
Stanwell St. S9: Shef 6D 94
Stanwell Wlk. S9: Shef 6D 94
Stanwood Av. S6: Shef 6G 105
Stanwood Cres. S6: Shef 6G 105
Stanwood Dr. S6: Shef 6G 105
S42: Walt 2C 170
Stanwood M. S6: Shef 6G 105
Stanwood Rd. S6: Shef 6G 105
Staple Grn. S65: Thry 6F 85
Stapleton Rd. DN4: Warm 1E 71
(not continuous)
Star La. DN12: Con 4F 69
S70: Barn 1D 30
Starling Cl. S63: Wath D 4F 49
Starling Mead S2: Shef 4A 120
Starnhill Cl. S35: Eccl 1H 93
Station App. *DN1: Don 1B 56*
(off Factory La.)
Station Bk. La. S41: Ches 5A 168
Station Cl. DN9: Blax 2E 77
Station Cotts. S75: Dart 5F 7
Station Ct. DN1: Don 1B 56
S25: Sth A 3G 141
Station La. DN9: Blax 2F 77
S9: Shef 2D 108
S18: App 3D 156
S35: Ough 3E 91
S41: New W, Old W 4H 161
Station La. Ind. Est.
S41: Old W 4A 162
Station Rd. DN3: Barn D 2C 26
DN5: Ark 1C 40
DN6: Adw S, Carc 1E 23
DN9: Blax 3F 77
DN11: Ross 5D 74
DN12: Con 3F 69
S9: Shef 2F 121
S13: Shef 2D 136
S20: Half, Mosb 3E 151
S21: Ecki, Reni 1F 159
S21: Killa 4A 152
S25: Laugh C 3F 127
S26: Kiv P 6A 140
S35: Chap 3G 79
S35: Eccl 1H 93
S36: Spink 3H 175
S41: Ches 5A 168
S41: Whit M 5H 161
S43: Bar H 3G 163
S43: Brim 6B 162
S43: Hol 5E 163
S60: Cat 6D 110
S60: Roth 4C 96
S60: Tree 2F 123
S63: Bolt D 2B 50
S63: Thurn 2C 36
S63: Wath D 6G 49
S64: Mexb 2F 67
(not continuous)
S70: Barn 6C 16
S70: Wors 6H 31
S71: Lund 3C 18
S71: Roy 1G 9
S73: Womb 1H 47
(not continuous)
S75: Dart 5F 7
S75: Dod 3F 29
Station Rd. Ind. Est. S73: Womb 6H 33
Station St. S64: Swint 3C 66
Station Ter. S43: Brim 6B 162
S71: Roy 2B 10
Station Way S25: Laugh C 3F 127
Staton Av. S20: Beig 4H 137
Statutes, The S60: Roth 4E 97
Staunton Cl. S40: Birdh 4H 171
Staunton Rd. DN4: Cant 5D 58
STAVELEY 4B 164
Staveley La. S21: Ecki 2F 159
S21: Neth Han 5A 158
S43: Bar H 5A 158
S43: Stav 2F 159
Staveley Northern Loop Rd.
S43: Stav 3B 164
Staveley Rd. S8: Shef 1F 133
S43: New W 3D 162
S43: Pool 6C 164
Staveley St. DN12: New E 3C 70
Steade Rd. S7: Shef 1E 133
Steadfield Rd. S74: Hoyl 2G 61
Steadfolds Cl. S66: Thurc 6D 114
Steadfolds Gdns. S66: Thurc 6D 114
Steadfolds La. S66: Thurc 5C 114
Steadfolds Ri. S66: Thurc 6D 114
Steadlands, The S62: Rawm 6E 65
Stead La. S74: Hoyl 1G 61
Stead M. S21: Ecki 1E 159
Stead St. S21: Ecki 1E 159
STEEL BANK 1B 118
Steel City Plaza S1: Shef 3D 4 (3F 119)
Steele Av. S43: Ink 2G 169
Steele St. S74: Hoyl 1F 61
Steelhouse La. S3: Shef 1E 5
Steel Rd. S11: Shef 6B 118
Steel St. S61: Roth 5B 96
Steeping Cl. S43: Brim 6D 162
Steep La. S36: H'swne 3F 177
S42: W'orth 6B 170
Steeplegate S40: Ches 5H 167
Steeton Ct. S74: Els 6D 46
Stella Ho. S65: Dalt 1B 98
Stemp St. S11: Shef 6E 119
Stenson Ct. DN4: Balb 4H 55
Stenton Rd. S8: Shef 3E 147
Stentons Ter. S64: Mexb 2G 67
Stephen Dr. S10: Shef 3G 117
S35: Gren 2A 92
STEPHEN HILL 3G 117
Stephen Hill S10: Shef 3G 117
Stephen Hill Rd. S10: Shef 3G 117
Stephen La. S35: Gren 2A 92
Stephenson Ct. S40: Bramp 6C 166
Stephenson Hall of Residence
S10: Shef 5B 118
Stephenson Pl. S40: Ches 5H 167
S64: Swint 2C 66
Stephenson Rd. S43: Stav 5B 164
Stepney St. S2: Shef 2H 5 (2H 119)
Stepping La. S35: Gren 1A 92
Sterland St. S40: Ches 5F 167
Sterndale Rd. S7: Shef 5B 132
Steven Cl. S35: Chap 4E 79
Steven Cres. S35: Chap 3E 79
Steven Mangle Cl. S12: Shef 6H 135
Steven Pl. S35: Chap 4E 79
Stevenson Dr. S65: Roth 5A 98
S75: H'ham 4F 15
Stevenson Ho. *S41: Ches 2A 168*
(off Tapton Lock Hill)
Stevenson Rd. DN4: Balb 6A 56
S9: Shef 5C 108
(Alfred Rd.)
S9: Shef 6B 108
(St Charles St.)
Stevenson Way S9: Shef 6C 108
Stevens Rd. DN4: Balb 3A 56
Steventon Rd. S65: Thry 6F 85
Stewart Rd. S11: Shef 6C 118
Stewarts Rd. S62: Rawm 2A 84
Stewart St. DN1: Don 2B 56
STICKING HILL 5D 50
Sticking La. S64: Mexb 5C 50
Stillman Cl. S41: Has 2B 172
Stirling Cl. S74: Els 6D 46
Stirling Ct. S41: Ches 4H 167
Stirling La. DN5: Scawt 3G 39
Stirling St. DN1: Don 2B 56
Stirling Way S2: Shef 6D 120
Stockarth La. S35: Ough 5F 91
Stockarth Pl. S35: Ough 6G 91
STOCKBRIDGE 1B 40
Stockbridge Av. DN5: Don 3H 39
Stockbridge Caravan Site DN5: Ben 1B 40
Stockbridge La. DN5: Ben 1B 40
Stockil Rd. DN4: Don 2D 56
Stockingate WF9: Sth K 5H 13
Stock Rd. S2: Shef 5B 120
STOCKSBRIDGE 3E 175
Stocksbridge & District Golf Course 5F 175
Stocksbridge Leisure Cen. 3C 174
Stocks Grn. Ct. S17: Tot 6E 145
Stocks Grn. Dr. S17: Tot 6E 145
Stocks Hill S35: Eccl 1F 93
Stockshill Cl. S71: Carl 5H 9
Stock's La. S62: Rawm 3G 83
S75: Barn 6B 16
Stockton Cl. S3: Shef 1G 119
Stockwell Av. S26: Kiv P 1H 153

Stockwell Ct. S75: Wool G 3E **7**
Stockwell Grn. S71: Monk B 3G **17**
Stockwell La. S26: Wales 1G **153**
Stockwith La. S74: Hoyl 4G **45**
Stocthorn Gap S35: Ough 1D **90**
Stoddart Way S62: Parkg 6G **83**
Stoke St. S9: Shef 1B **120**
Stoket La. S26: Ull 1E **125**
Stokewell Rd. S63: Wath D 5D **48**
Stoneacre Av. S12: Shef 5C **136**
Stoneacre Cl. S12: Shef 5C **136**
Stoneacre Dr. S12: Shef 6C **136**
Stoneacre Ri. S12: Shef 5C **136**
Stone Bank Ct. S18: Dron 3G **155**
Stonebridge La. S72: Gt H 1F **35**
Stonechat Mead S63: Wath D 4F **49**
Stonecliffe Cl. S2: Shef 5D **120**
Stonecliffe Dr. S36: Stoc 5D **174**
Stonecliffe Pl. S2: Shef 5D **120**
Stonecliffe Rd. S2: Shef 5D **120**
Stonecliffe Wlk. S2: Shef 5E **121**
Stonecliff Wlk. DN12: Den M 2D **68**
Stone Cl. S18: Coal A 1H **155**
S26: Kiv P 6B **140**
S65: Rav 3A **100**
Stone Cl. Av. DN4: Hex 2A **56**
Stone Cotts. DN5: Ben 3G **23**
Stone Ct. S72: Sth H 1H **11**
Stone Cres. S66: Wick 5G **99**
Stone Cft. DN4: Bess 6C **58**
Stonecroft Ct. S75: Silk C 5A **28**
Stonecroft Rd. S17: Tot 5G **145**
Stone Cross Dr. DN5: Sprot 2C **54**
Stonecross Gdns. DN4: Cant 4D **58**
Stone Delf S10: Shef 5D **116**
Stone Font Gro. DN4: Cant 5C **58**
Stonefont Gro. S72: Grim 1B **20**
Stonegarth Cl. S72: Cud 2E **19**
Stonegate M. DN4: Balb 4A **56**
STONEGRAVELS 3H **167**
Stonegravels Cft. S20: Half 4F **151**
Stonegravels La. S41: Ches 3H **167**
Stonegravels Way S20: Half 4G **151**
Stone Gro. S10: Shef 3C **118**
Stonehill Cl. S74: Hoyl 5H **45**
Stone Hill Dr. S26: Swal 1C **138**
Stonehill Ri. DN5: Scawt 2F **39**
S36: Cub 6C **176**
S72: Cud 2E **19**
Stone La. S13: Shef 3B **136**
S43: New W 2C **162**
Stonelea Cl. S75: Silk 2A **28**
Stone Leigh S75: Pill 1C **60**
Stoneleigh Cl. S25: Dinn 1C **142**
Stoneleigh Cft. S70: Barn 3E **31**
Stoneley Cl. S12: Shef 1E **149**
Stoneley Cres. S12: Shef 1E **149**
Stoneley Dell S12: Shef 1E **149**
Stoneley Dr. S12: Shef 1E **149**
Stonelow Ct. *S18: Dron 2G* ***155***
(off Stonelow Rd.)
Stonelow Cres. S18: Dron 2H **155**
Stonelow Grn. S18: Dron 2G **155**
Stonelow Rd. S18: Dron 2G **155**
Stonely Brook S65: Rav 4A **100**
Stone Moor Rd. S36: Bolst, Stoc 4C **174**
Stone Pk. Cl. S66: Malt 5C **102**
Stone Riding DN12: New E 1E **89**
Stone Ridings DN12: New E 5B **70**
Stone Rd. S18: Coal A 6H **147**
Stone Row S40: Ches 6F **167**
Stone Row Ct. S75: Pill 2C **60**
Stonerow Way S60: Roth 1F **97**
Stonesdale Cl. S20: Mosb 3E **151**
Stones Inge S35: High G 1C **78**
Stone St. S20: Mosb 3E **151**
S71: Barn 4D **16**
Stonewood Ct. S10: Shef 4E **117**
Stonewood Gro. S10: Shef 4E **117**
S74: Hoyl 2B **62**
Stoney Bank Dr. S26: Kiv P 6B **140**
Stoney Cft. S74: Hoyl 1G **61**
Stoneycroft La. S42: W'orth 6B **170**
Stoneycroft Rd. S13: Shef 4A **122**
Stoney Ga. S35: High G 6C **60**
Stoney Royd S71: Ath 5E **9**
Stoney Well La. S66: Malt 6F **103**
Stonyford Rd. S73: Womb 6A **34**
Stony La. S6: Bradf 1A **104**
Stony Wlk. S6: Shef 5B **106**
Stoops Cl. S40: Ches 2E **167**
Stoops La. DN4: Bess 5G **57**
Stoops Rd. DN4: Bess 5A **58**
Stopes Rd. S6: Stann 6A **104**
Stoppard Row S40: Bramp 6D **166**
Store St. S2: Shef 5G **119**
Storey's Ga. S73: Womb 1E **47**
Storey St. S64: Swint 3B **66**
Storforth La. S40: Birdh, Has 3H **171**
S41: Has 3H **171**
Storforth La. Ter. S41: Has 2B **172**
Storforth La. Trad. Est.
S41: Has 2A **172**
Stormont Gro. S43: Ink 1H **169**
STORRS 5B **104**
Storrs Bri. La. S6: Lox 3B **104**
Storrs Carr S6: Stann 4A **104**
Storrs Grn. S6: Stann 4A **104**
Storrs Hall Rd. S6: Shef 6A **106**
Storrs La. S6: Stann 5B **104**
S35: Brom 4A **60**
S36: Oxs 4H **177**
Storrs Mill La. S72: Cud 6H **19**
Storrs Rd. S40: Bramp 6C **166**
Storrs Wood Vw. S72: Cud 4G **19**
Storth Av. S10: Shef 6F **117**
Storth Hollow Cft. S10: Shef 5F **117**
Storth La. S10: Shef 5F **117**
S26: Kiv P, Tod 5G **139**
S35: Wharn S . . . . 2A **90** & 1B **90**
Stortholme M. S10: Shef 5F **117**
Storth Pk. S10: Shef 1E **131**
Storthwood Ct. S10: Shef 5F **117**
Stotfold Dr. S63: Thurn 2B **36**
Stotfold Rd. DN5: Hoot P 1E **37**
Stothard Ct. S10: Shef 2A **118**
Stothard Rd. S10: Shef 2A **118**
Stottercliffe Rd.
S36: Pen, Thurl 4B **176**
Stour Cl. S43: Brim 6D **162**
Stour La. S6: Shef 2G **105**
Stovin Cl. S9: Shef 5E **109**
Stovin Dr. S9: Shef 6E **109**
Stovin Gdns. S9: Shef 6E **109**
Stow Bri. La. S60: Up W 6D **112**
Stowe Av. S7: Shef 4B **132**
Stradbroke Av. S13: Shef 1G **135**
Stradbroke Cl. S13: Shef 1H **135**
Stradbroke Cres. S13: Shef 1H **135**
Stradbroke Dr. S13: Shef 1H **135**
Stradbroke Pl. S13: Shef 1H **135**
Stradbroke Ri. S40: Walt 2D **170**
Stradbroke Rd. S13: Shef 1G **135**
Stradbroke Wlk. S13: Shef 1G **135**
Stradbroke Way S13: Shef 1H **135**
Strafford Av. S70: Wors 4E **31**
S74: Els 6D **46**
Strafford Gro. S70: Birdw 6E **45**
Strafford Ind. Pk. S75: Dod 5H **29**
Strafford Pl. S61: Thorpe H 3B **80**
Strafford Rd. DN2: Don 5D **40**
S61: Kimb P 6H **81**
Strafford St. S75: Kexb 6D **6**
Strafford Wlk. S75: Dod 4G **29**
Strafforth Ho. *DN12: Den M 3B* ***68***
(off Ravenscar Cl.)
Straight La. S63: Gol 5D **36**
Straight Riding DN12: New E 6D **70**
Strait La. S63: Wath D 6F **49**
Stratford Rd. S10: Shef 5E **117**
Stratford Way S66: Braml 6B **100**
Strathmore Gro. S63: Wath D 6G **49**
Strathmore Rd. DN2: Don 1F **57**
Strathtay Rd. S11: Shef 1A **132**
Strauss Cres. S66: Malt 6C **102**
Strawberry Av. S5: Shef 4G **93**
Strawberry Gdns. S71: Roy 2H **9**
Strawberry Lee La. S17: Tot 5C **144**
Straw La. S6: Shef 1D **118**
Streatfield Cres. DN11: New R 6B **74**
STREET 4H **63**
Streetfield Cres. S20: Mosb 4E **151**
Streetfield La. S20: Half 4F **151**
Streetfields S20: Half 4F **151**
Street La. S62: Wentw 4G **63**
Strelley Av. S8: Shef 1D **146**
Strelley Rd. S8: Shef 1D **146**
S71: Ath 6D **8**
Stretton Cl. DN4: Cant 4D **58**
Stretton Rd. S11: Shef 1B **132**
S71: Monk B 3F **17**
Stride, The S40: Birdh 3G **171**
Strines Ho. *S10: Shef 5A* ***116***
(off Holyrood Av.)
Stringers Cft. S60: Whist 3C **112**
Stripe Rd.
DN11: New R, Ross . . . . 5D **74** & 6H **75**
Struan Rd. S7: Shef 3B **132**
Strutt Rd. S3: Shef 5F **107**
Stuart Cl. S41: Ches 2B **168**
Stuart Gro. S35: Chap 4G **79**
Stuart Rd. S35: Chap 4G **79**
Stuart St. S63: Thurn 2D **36**
STUBBIN 3G **175**
Stubbin Cl. S62: Rawm 1E **83**
STUBBING 1D **104**
Stubbing Ho. La. S6: Shef 3H **91**
Stubbing La. S35: Ough 1D **104**
Stubbing Riding DN12: New E 5D **70**
Stubbing Rd. S40: Birdh 3G **171**
Stubbin La. S5: Shef 6H **93**
S62: Rawm 6D **64**
(not continuous)
Stubbin Rd. S62: Neth Hau, Rawm 1C **82**
Stubbins Hill DN12: New E 4C **70**
Stubbs Cres. S61: Kimb P 1A **96**
Stubbs Rd. S73: Womb 2F **47**
Stubbs Wlk. S61: Kimb P 1A **96**
Stubley Cl. S18: Dron W 1D **154**
Stubley Cft. S18: Dron W 2C **154**
Stubley Dr. S18: Dron W 2D **154**
Stubley Hollow S18: Dron 1D **154**
Stubley La. S18: Dron, Dron W 2C **154**
Stubley Pl. S18: Dron 2D **154**
Studfield Cres. S6: Shef 4G **105**
Studfield Dr. S6: Shef 3G **105**
Studfield Gro. S6: Shef 4G **105**
STUDFIELD HILL 4G **105**
Studfield Hill S6: Lox, Shef 4F **105**
Studfield Ri. S6: Shef 3G **105**
Studfield Rd. S6: Shef 3G **105**
Studios, The *S40: Ches 5F* ***167***
(off School Board La.)
Studley Ct. S9: Shef 2F **121**
Studley Gdns. DN3: Kirk Sa 4B **26**
Studmoor Rd. S61: Kimb P 6G **81**
Studmoor Wlk. S61: Kimb P 6G **81**
STUMP CROSS 4G **63**
Stump Cross Gdns. S63: Bolt D 2A **50**
Stump Cross Rd. S63: Wath D 1F **65**
STUMPERLOWE 6E **117**
Stumperlowe Av. S10: Shef 6F **117**
Stumperlowe Cl. S10: Shef 6F **117**
Stumperlowe Cres. Rd. S10: Shef 6E **117**
Stumperlowe Cft. S10: Shef 5E **117**
Stumperlowe Hall Chase
S10: Shef 5E **117**
Stumperlowe Hall Rd. S10: Shef 6E **117**
Stumperlowe La. S10: Shef 6E **117**
Stumperlowe Mans. S10: Shef 6E **117**
Stumperlowe Pk. Rd. S10: Shef 6E **117**
Stumperlowe Vw. S10: Shef 5E **117**
Stupton Rd. S9: Shef 2D **108**
Sturge Cft. S2: Shef 2G **133**
Sturton Cl. DN4: Bess 6H **57**
Sturton Cft. S65: Dalt 1D **98**
Sturton Rd. S4: Shef 4H **107**
Sub-Station La. *S41: Whit M 6H* ***161***
(off Sheffield Rd.)
Sudbury Cl. S40: Ches 3C **166**
Sudbury Dr. S26: Ast 1D **138**
Sudbury St. S3: Shef 1B **4** (1E **119**)
Sudhall Cl. S41: Ches 6E **161**
Sudhall Ct. S41: Ches 6E **161**
Suffolk Cl. S25: Nth A 2H **141**
Suffolk La. S2: Shef 6G **5** (4G **119**)
Suffolk Rd. DN4: Balb 6A **56**
S2: Shef 5F **5** (4G **119**)
Suffolk Vw. DN12: Den M 4C **68**
Sulby Gro. S70: Stair 4A **32**
Summerdale Rd. S72: Cud 2D **18**
SUMMERFIELD 4B **118**
Summerfield S10: Shef 4B **118**
S65: Roth 4F **97**

Summerfield Cres. S43: Brim 6C **162**
Summerfield Rd. S18: Dron 1G **155**
S40: Ches 1G **171**
Summerfields Dr. DN9: Blax 1F **77**
Summerfield St. S11: Shef 5D **118**
Summer La. S17: Tot 6E **145**
S70: Barn 6B **16**
S71: Roy .2G **9**
S73: Womb 1E **47**
S75: Barn 6B **16**
SUMMERLEY 2B 156
Summerley Lwr. Rd.
S18: App 2B **156**
Summerley Rd. S18: App 2B **156**
Summerley Wlk. S40: Ches 3E **167**
Summer Rd. S71: Roy 2G **9**
Summerskill Grn. S43: Ink 1H **169**
Summer St. S3: Shef 2A **4** (2D **118**)
S70: Barn 6C **16**
(not continuous)
Summer Vw. S71: Roy 3G **9**
Summerwood Cft. S18: Dron 2E **155**
Summerwood La. S18: Dron 1E **155**
Summerwood Pl. S18: Dron 2E **155**
Sumner Rd. S65: Roth 2G **97**
Sunbury Ct. S10: Shef 4B **118**
Sunderland St. S11: Shef 5D **118**
Sunderland Ter. S70: Barn 2F **31**
Sundew Cft. S35: High G 6C **60**
Sundew Gdns. S35: High G 6C **60**
Sundown Pl. S13: Shef 6A **122**
Sundown Rd. S13: Shef 6A **122**
Sunflower Gdns. DN4: Bess 4G **57**
Sunflower Gro. S5: Shef 1C **108**
Sunlea Flats *S65: Roth* *3G 97*
(off Ridge Rd.)
Sunningdale Av. S75: Dart 5H **7**
Sunningdale Cl. DN4: Cant 6E **59**
S40: Walt 2F **171**
S64: Swint 5C **66**
Sunningdale Dr. DN12: New E 5B **70**
S72: Cud .6F **11**
Sunningdale Mt. S11: Shef 3A **132**
Sunningdale Ri. S40: Walt 2D **170**
Sunningdale Rd. DN2: Don 5F **41**
DN4: Balb 5A **56**
S25: Dinn 6A **128**
Sunny Bank S10: Shef 6A **4** (5D **118**)
S35: High G 1C **78**
S74: Jum .5C **46**
Sunnybank DN3: Eden 1D **42**
Sunnybank Cres. S60: Brins 4D **110**
Sunny Bank Dr. S72: Cud 3E **19**
Sunnybank Nature Reserve
. . . . .6A 4 (5D 118)
Sunny Bank Ri. S74: Els 6D **46**
Sunny Bank Rd. S36: Bolst 6E **175**
S75: Silk .2A **28**
Sunny Bar DN1: Don 1C **56**
Sunnybrook Cl. S74: Hoyl 2B **62**
SUNNYFIELDS 3E 39
SUNNYSIDE
DN3 . . . . .5C 26
S66 . . . . .2G 99
Sunnyside DN3: Brant 4H **59**
DN3: Eden 5B **26**
Sunnyside Cl. S25: Nth A 2H **141**
Sunny Springs S41: Ches 4H **167**
Sunnyvale Av. S17: Tot 6E **145**
Sunnyvale Rd. S17: Tot 6E **145**
Sunny Vw. Mobile Home Pk.
DN11: A'ley 2G **71**
Sunrise Mnr. S74: Hoyl 5B **46**
Superbowl 2000
Rotherham 2H 95
Surbiton St. S9: Shef 4E **109**
Surrey Cl. S70: Barn 3E **31**
Surrey La. S1: Shef 5F **5** (4G **119**)
Surrey Pl. S1: Shef 4F **5** (3G **119**)
Surrey St. DN4: Balb 5A **56**
S1: Shef 4E **5** (3F **119**)
Surtees Cl. S66: Malt 3H **101**
Sussex Gdns. DN12: Den M 3C **68**
Sussex Rd. S4: Shef 1H **119**
S35: Chap 3F **79**
Sussex St. DN4: Balb 5A **56**
S4: Shef 1H **5** (1H **119**)
Suthard Cross Rd. S10: Shef 2A **118**
Sutherland Ho. DN2: Don 4F **41**
Sutherland Rd. S4: Shef 6H **107**
Sutherland St. S4: Shef 6A **108**
Sutton Av. S71: Ath 6E **9**
Sutton Cres. S43: Ink 1H **169**
Sutton La.
S44: Ark T, Sut S 6H **173**
Sutton Rd. DN3: Kirk Sa 3D **26**
SUTTON SPRING WOOD 4G 173
Sutton St. DN4: Hex 3H **55**
S3: Shef 3A **4** (3D **118**)
Sutton Vw. S42: Tem N 6G **173**
Swaddale Av. S41: Ches 2A **168**
Swaddale Cl. S41: Ches 2A **168**
Swaith Av. DN5: Scawt 3G **39**
SWAITHE .5B 32
Swaithedale S70: Wors 5H **31**
Swaithe Vw. S70: Wors 5A **32**
S75: Wool G 4F **7**
Swalebank Cl. S40: Ches 2A **172**
Swale Cl. S63: Bolt D 2C **50**
Swale Ct. S60: Roth 2G **111**
Swaledale Dr. S73: Womb 1H **47**
Swaledale Rd. S7: Shef 3C **132**
Swale Dr. S35: Chap 3D **78**
Swale Gdns. S9: Shef 2F **121**
Swale Rd. S61: Wing 5B **82**
Swallow Cl. S70: Birdw 4E **45**
S75: Kexb .6E **7**
Swallow Ct. DN11: Ross 5D **74**
Swallow Cres. S62: Rawm 2A **84**
SWALLOW HILL 1H 15
Swallow Hill Rd. S75: Bar G 1H **15**
Swallow La. S26: Ast 2D **138**
SWALLOWNEST 1B 138
Swallownest Ct. S26: Swal 6B **124**
Swallowood Ct.
S63: Bramp B 6A **48**
Swallow's La. S20: Mosb 2D **150**
Swallow Wood Cl. S60: Tree 2F **123**
Swallow Wood Ct. S13: Shef 2B **136**
Swallow Wood Rd.
S26: Swal 1H **137**
Swamp Wlk. S6: Shef 5C **106**
Swanbourne Cl. S41: Has 1B **172**
Swanbourne Pl. S5: Shef 6H **93**
Swanbourne Rd. S5: Shef 5H **93**
Swanee Rd. S70: Barn 3G **31**
Swangate S63: Bramp B 5A **48**
Swannington Cl. DN4: Cant 5E **59**
Swan Rd. S26: Ast 2D **138**
Swan St. DN5: Ben 1A **40**
S60: Roth .5E **97**
Swanwick St. S41: Old W 4H **161**
Swarcliffe Rd. S9: Shef 1D **120**
SWATHWICK 6F 171
Swathwick Cl. S42: W'orth 6F **171**
Swathwick La. S42: W'orth 6A **170**
Sweeney Ho. S36: Stoc 3C **174**
Sweet La. DN11: Wad 5F **73**
Sweyn Cft. S70: Wors 5F **31**
Swifte Rd. S60: Roth 1H **111**
Swift Ri. S61: Thorpe H 2D **80**
Swift Rd. S35: Gren 2C **92**
Swift St. S75: Barn 5C **16**
Swift Way S2: Shef 5B **120**
Swim School, The *2C 162*
(off Red Ho. Cl.)
Swinburne Av. DN4: Balb 6A **56**
(not continuous)
DN6: Adw S 3B **22**
Swinburne Cl. DN3: Barn D 1H **27**
Swinburne Pl. S65: Roth 5A **98**
Swinburne Rd. S65: Roth 5A **98**
Swinnock La. S35: Bright 1B **90**
Swinscoe Way S40: Ches 3B **166**
Swinston Hill Gdns. S25: Dinn 6B **128**
Swinston Hill Rd.
S25: Dinn, Nth A 6A **128**
SWINTON .3C 66
SWINTON BRIDGE 3E 67
Swinton Meadows Bus. Pk.
S64: Swint 3E **67**
Swinton Meadows Ind. Est.
S64: Swint 3E **67**
Swinton Rd. S64: Mexb 2E **67**
(not continuous)
Swinton Station (Rail) 3D 66
Swinton St. S3: Shef 1F **119**
Swinton Swimming Pool 3C 66
Swithen Farm S75: Hai 3C **6**
Swithland Cl. S41: Has 3B **172**
Sycamore Av. DN3: Arm 3F **43**
S18: Dron 1F **155**
S26: Kiv P 6G **139**
S40: Ches 1F **171**
S66: Wick .5H **99**
S72: Cud 1E **19**
S72: Grim .3C **20**
Sycamore Cen. S65: Roth 1A **98**
Sycamore Ct. S11: Shef 1B **132**
S35: Ough .3E **91**
S64: Mexb 1D **66**
S71: Roy 2F **9**
Sycamore Cres. S63: Wath D 1H **65**
Sycamore Dr. DN9: Auck 1B **76**
S21: Killa 5B **152**
S44: Cal .5C **168**
S66: Thurc 5C **114**
S71: Roy 3F **9**
Sycamore Farm Cl. S66: Wick 1G **113**
Sycamore Gro. DN4: Cant 4C **58**
DN12: Con 5D **68**
Sycamore Ho. Rd. S5: Shef 4B **94**
Sycamore La. S36: H'swne 1G **177**
S43: Hol .5F **163**
Sycamore Rd. DN3: Barn D 1C **26**
S35: Eccl .2G **93**
S36: Stoc .4C **174**
S43: Hol .5E **163**
S64: Mexb 1D **66**
S65: Roth .1A **98**
WF9: Hems 1D **12**
Sycamores, The DN5: Scawt 2E **39**
Sycamore St. S20: Beig 4G **137**
S20: Mosb 2D **150**
S75: Barn .6B **16**
Sycamore Vw. DN5: Sprot 3E **55**
Sycamore Wlk. S36: Pen 4D **176**
S63: Thurn 2C **36**
Sydney Rd. S6: Shef 2C **118**
Sydney St. S40: Ches 5F **167**
Sykes Av. S75: Barn 6C **16**
Sykes Ct. S64: Swint 5C **66**
Sykes St. S70: Barn 3C **30**
Sylvan Cl. S41: Ches 1A **172**
S66: Malt .4C **102**
Sylvester Av. DN4: Balb 3B **56**
Sylvester Gdns. S1: Shef 6E **5** (4F **119**)
Sylvester St. S1: Shef 6D **4** (4F **119**)
Sylvestria Ct. DN11: Ross 5D **74**
Sylvia Cl. S13: Shef 1E **137**
Sylvia Rd. S18: Uns 6A **156**
Symes Gdns. DN4: Cant 3C **58**
Symonds Av. S62: Rawm 6D **64**
Symons Cres. S5: Shef 6E **93**

T

Tadcaster Cl. DN12: Den M 4B **68**
Tadcaster Cres. S8: Shef 4E **133**
Tadcaster Rd. S8: Shef 4E **133**
Tadcaster Way S8: Shef 4E **133**
Taddington Rd. S40: Ches 3C **166**
Tait Av. DN12: New E 6C **70**
Talbot Av. DN3: Barn D 1C **26**
Talbot Circ. DN3: Barn D 1D **26**
Talbot Cres. S2: Shef 5H **5** (4H **119**)
S41: Has .3C **172**
Talbot Gdns. S2: Shef 5H **5** (4H **119**)
Talbot Pl. S2: Shef 5H **5** (4H **119**)
Talbot Rd. S2: Shef 5H **5** (4H **119**)
S36: Pen .3C **176**
S64: Swint 3E **67**
Talbot St. S2: Shef 5H **5** (4H **119**)
S41: Has .3C **172**
Talmont Rd. S11: Shef 2A **132**
Tamar Cl. S75: H'ham 5F **15**
Tanfield Cl. S71: Roy 2F **9**
Tanfield Rd. S6: Shef 3C **106**
Tanfield Way S66: Wick 6G **99**
Tanglewood Ct. S70: Barn 2A **32**
TANKERSLEY 2E 61
Tankersley La. S74: Hoyl 2E **61**
Tankersley Park Golf Course 5F 61

Tank Row S71: Stair 1A 32
Tannery Cl. S13: Shef 2C 136
Tannery Ct. S75: Dod 3G 29
Tannery St. S13: Shef 2C 136
Tan Pit La. S63: Gol 1C 50
Tansley Dr. S9: Shef 6E 95
S40: Ash 3B 166
Tansley St. S9: Shef 6E 95
Tansley Way S43: Ink 2H 169
Tanyard S75: Dod 4F 29
Tanyard Cft. S72: Brier 3B 12
Tap La. S40: Ches 5F 167
Taplin Rd. S6: Shef 4A 106
TAPTON 2B 168
Tapton Bank S10: Shef 4H 117
Tapton Ct. S10: Shef 4A 118
Tapton Cres. Rd. S10: Shef 4H 117
Tapton Grange S43: Brim C 3D 168
Tapton Gro. S43: Brim C 3D 168
Tapton Hall of Residence
S10: Shef 3B 118
TAPTON HILL 4H 117
Tapton Hill Rd. S10: Shef 3H 117
Tapton Ho. Rd. S10: Shef 4A 118
Tapton La. S41: Ches 5A 168
Tapton Lock Hill S41: Ches 2A 168
Tapton Lock Vis. Cen. 2A 168
Tapton M. S10: Shef 3A 118
Tapton Mt. Cl. S10: Shef 4A 118
Tapton Pk. Gdns. S10: Shef 5H 117
Tapton Pk. Mt. S10: Shef 5H 117
Tapton Park Municipal Golf Course
. . . . 4B 168
Tapton Pk. Rd. S10: Shef 5G 117
Tapton Ter. S41: Ches 4A 168
Tapton Va. S41: Ches 3B 168
Tapton Vw. Rd. S41: Ches 3F 167
Taptonville Cres. S10: Shef 4B 118
Taptonville Head S10: Shef 3B 118
Taptonville Rd. S10: Shef 3B 118
Tapton Wlk. S10: Shef 4A 118
S41: Ches 5A 168
(off Tapton La.)
Tapton Way S44: Cal 5E 169
Tarleton Cl. DN3: Kirk Sa 4D 26
Tarn Ho. *S70: Barn 2E 31*
(off Union St.)
Tasker Rd. S10: Shef 2A 118
Tasman Gro. S66: Malt 4H 101
Tatenhill Gdns. DN4: Cant 5D 58
Taunton Av. S9: Shef 1E 109
Taunton Gdns. S64: Mexb 6H 51
Taunton Gro. S9: Shef 6E 95
Taverner Cl. S35: High G 5C 60
Taverner Cft. S35: High G 6D 60
Taverner Way S35: High G 6C 60
Tavistock Rd. S7: Shef 2E 133
Tavy Cl. S75: Bar G 3F 15
Tay Cl. S18: Dron W 2C 154
S75: Mapp 1B 16
Taylor Cres. S41: Ches 1C 172
S72: Grim 2C 20
S81: Woods 5F 143
Taylor Dr. S81: Woods 5F 143
Taylor Hill S75: Cawt 4A 14
Taylor Row S63: Wath D 2E 65
S70: Barn 2E 31
Taylor's Cl. S62: Parkg 6F 83
Taylor's Ct. S62: Parkg 6G 83
Taylor's La. S62: Parkg 6F 83
Taylor St. DN12: Con 4G 69
Tay St. S6: Shef 2C 118
Teesdale Rd. S12: Ridg 2A 150
S61: Wing 5A 82
Teeside Cl. DN5: Scaws 5E 39
Telford Cres. S43: Stav 4C 164
Telford Rd. DN5: Don 5H 39
Telson Cl. S64: Swint 3H 65
Temperance St. S64: Swint 3C 66
Tempest Av. S73: D'fld 3B 34
Templar Cl. S66: Thurc 6A 114
TEMPLEBOROUGH 1B 110
Templeborough Bus. Cen.
S60: Roth 6D 96
Temple Cl. S60: Roth 6B 96
Temple Cres. S66: Braml 6A 100
Temple Gdns. DN4: Cant 5D 58
TEMPLE NORMANTON 6G 173
Temple Normanton By-Pass
S42: Tem N 5G 173
Temple Rd. S60: Roth 1A 110
Templestowe Ga. DN12: Con 4H 69
Temple Way S71: Monk B 5A 18
Templing Cl. S70: Barn 3F 31
Ten Acre Rd. S61: Kimb P 2A 96
Tenby Gdns. DN4: Balb 5H 55
Tennyson Av. DN3: Arm 4E 43
DN5: Don 6G 39
S40: Ches 5G 167
S64: Mexb 6G 51
Tennyson Cl. S25: Dinn 6B 128
S36: Pen 3D 176
Tennyson Ri. S63: Wath D 4D 48
Tennyson Rd. DN5: Ben 1A 40
S6: Shef 6C 106
S65: Roth 5H 97
S66: Malt 6B 102
S71: Monk B 4G 17
Tennyson Way S42: Gras 6D 172
Ten Pound Wlk. DN4: Don 4B 56
Tenter Balk La. DN6: Adw S 3B 22
Tenterden Rd. S5: Shef 6C 94
Tenter Hill S36: Thurl 3A 176
Tenter La. DN4: Warm 6D 54
Tenter Rd. DN4: Warm 6D 54
Tenters Grn. S70: Wors 6E 31
Tenter St. S1: Shef 2D 4 (2F 119)
S60: Roth 3D 96
Terminus Rd. S7: Shef 5B 132
Terrace, The S5: Shef 1B 108
Terrace Rd. S62: Parkg 4G 83
Terrace Wlk. S11: Shef 6B 118
Terrey Rd. S17: Tot 5F 145
Terry St. S9: Shef 4E 109
Tetney Rd. S10: Shef 4G 117
Tewitt Rd. DN5: Ben 4H 23
Teynham Dr. S5: Shef 2E 107
Teynham Rd. S5: Shef 2D 106
Thackeray Av. S62: Rawm 1A 84
Thames St. S60: Roth 3D 96
Thatch Pl. S61: Wing 5B 82
The . . . .
Names prefixed with 'The' for example 'The Acorn Cen.' are indexed under the main name such as 'Acorn Cen., The'
Thealby Gdns. DN4: Bess 5H 57
(not continuous)
Theatre La. S41: Ches 5A 168
Theatre Yd. *S40: Ches 5H 167*
(off Low Pavement)
Thellusson Av. DN5: Scaws 4D 38
Theobald Av. DN4: Don 3E 57
Theobald Cl. DN4: Don 3D 56
Thicket Dr. S66: Malt 4C 102
Thicket La. S70: Wors 6H 31
Thickett La. S36: Pen 6E 177
Third Av. DN6: Woodl 4D 22
DN9: Finn 2C 76
Thirlmere Ct. S64: Mexb 6A 52
Thirlmere Dr. S18: Dron 2F 155
S25: Nth A 2A 142
Thirlmere Gdns. DN3: Kirk Sa 5C 26
Thirlmere Rd. S8: Shef 3D 132
S41: Ches 1D 166
S71: Barn 1F 31
Thirlwall Av. DN12: Con 4D 68
Thirlwell Rd. S8: Shef 2F 133
Thirsk Cl. DN12: Den M 4B 68
Thistley Ct. S72: Grim 6A 12
Thomas St. DN12: New E 5C 70
S1: Shef 5C 4 (4E 119)
S26: Kiv P 6A 140
S64: Kiln 1E 85
S64: Swint 2C 66
S70: Barn 2E 31
S70: Wors 5F 31
S73: D'fld 5C 34
Thompson Av. DN12: New E 4C 70
Thompson Cl. S41: Whit M 6H 161
S62: Rawm 6D 64
S66: Malt 3H 101
Thompson Dr. S64: Swint 5B 66
Thompson Gdns. S35: High G 6B 60
Thompson Hill S35: High G 1B 78
Thompson Rd. S11: Shef 5C 118
S73: Womb 2G 47
Thompson St. S41: Whit M 6H 161
(not continuous)
Thomson Av. DN4: Balb 5G 55
Thomson Cl. S63: Wath D 6G 49
Thoresby Av. DN4: Don 3E 57
S71: Monk B 5H 17
Thoresby Cl. S26: Ast 1E 139
Thoresby Pl. S43: Ink 2H 169
Thoresby Rd. S6: Shef 5B 106
Thornborough Cl. S2: Shef 1H 133
Thornborough Pl. S2: Shef 1H 133
Thornborough Rd. S2: Shef 1G 133
Thornbridge Av. S12: Shef 5G 135
Thornbridge Cl. S12: Shef 5G 135
Thornbridge Cres. S12: Shef 5H 135
S40: Birdh 4G 171
Thornbridge Dr. S12: Shef 5G 135
Thornbridge Gro. S12: Shef 5G 135
Thornbridge La. S12: Shef 5H 135
Thornbridge Pl. S12: Shef 5G 135
Thornbridge Ri. S12: Shef 5H 135
Thornbridge Rd. S12: Shef 6G 135
Thornbridge Way S12: Shef 5H 135
Thornbrook Cl. S35: Chap 2G 79
Thornbrook Gdns. S35: Chap 2G 79
Thornbrook M. S35: Chap 2F 79
Thorncliffe Cl. S26: Swal 2A 138
Thorncliffe Gdns. DN9: Auck 1H 59
Thorncliffe Ind. Est. S35: Chap 6E 61
Thorncliffe La. S35: Chap 1E 79
Thorncliffe Pk. Est. S35: Chap 1F 79
Thorncliffe Rd. S35: Chap 6F 61
Thorncliffe Vw. S35: Chap 1E 79
Thorncliffe Vs. S35: Chap 1E 79
Thorncliffe Way S75: Tank 1D 60
Thorndale Ri. S60: Brins 4E 111
Thorndene Cl. S41: Ches 2G 167
Thorndon Way S40: Walt 2D 170
Thorne Cl. S42: Ash 4A 166
S71: Smi 1D 16
Thorne End Rd. S75: Stain 4A 8
Thornely Av. S75: Dod 2G 29
Thornely Sq. S75: Dod 3G 29
Thorne Rd. DN1: Don 1C 56
DN2: Don 6E 41
DN3: Eden 1B 42
DN9: Blax 1F 77
S7: Shef 3D 132
Thornfield Av. S40: Bramp 1C 170
Thornfield Ct. S41: Ches 3H 167
Thorn Gth. DN5: Don 4H 39
Thornham Cl. DN3: Arm 5E 43
Thornham Mdws. S63: Gol 5E 37
THORN HILL 2D 96
Thornhill Av. DN2: Don 4G 41
S60: Brins 5C 110
Thornhill Dr. S70: Barn 3E 31
Thornhill Edge S60: Roth 3D 96
Thornhill Pl. S63: Wath D 6F 49
Thorn La. DN2: Long S 6A 26
Thornlea Ct. DN12: New E 5B 70
Thornley Brook S63: Thurn 2A 36
Thornley Cotts. S75: Dod 3G 29
Thornley Sq. S63: Thurn 2A 36
Thornley Vs. S70: Birdw 5D 44
Thorn Rd. S64: Kiln 5C 66
Thornsett Ct. S11: Shef 6D 118
Thornsett Gdns. S17: Dore 3G 145
Thornsett Rd. S7: Shef 6D 118
Thornton Cl. WF9: Hems 1E 13
Thorntondale Rd. DN5: Scaws 3E 39
Thornton Pl. S18: Dron W 3B 154
Thornton Rd. S70: Barn 3H 31
Thornton St. S61: Kimb 5H 95
Thornton Ter. S61: Kimb 5H 95
S70: Barn 3H 31
Thorntree Cl. S61: Thorpe H 4C 80
Thorntree Ct. S40: Birdh 3G 171
Thorntree La. S75: Barn 5C 16
Thorntree Rd. S61: Thorpe H 5C 80
Thornwell Gro. S72: Cud 2D 18
Thornwell La. S61: Thorpe H 2C 80
Thornwood Cl. S63: Thurn 1B 36
Thornwood Ct. S63: Thurn 1C 36
Thorogate S62: Rawm 1F 83
Thorold Pl. DN3: Kirk Sa 3C 26
Thorp Cl. S2: Shef 6F 119
Thorpe Av. S18: Coal A 6H 147

Thorpe Bank DN3: Barn D 1A **26**
Thorpe Bridle Rd. S25: Sth A 6G **141**
Thorpe Cl. S41: Ches 6G **161**
THORPE COMMON 5C **80**
Thorpe Dr. S20: Water 1F **151**
Thorpefield Cl. S61: Thorpe H 3C **80**
Thorpefield Dr. S61: Thorpe H 3C **80**
Thorpe Field M. S61: Thorpe H 3C **80**
Thorpe Grn. S20: Water 1E **151**
Thorpehall Rd. DN3: Kirk Sa 5D **26**
(not continuous)
THORPE HESLEY 3C **80**
Thorpe Ho. Ri. S8: Shef 4G **133**
Thorpe Ho. Av. S8: Shef 4F **133**
Thorpe Ho. Rd. S8: Shef 4F **133**
Thorpe La. DN5: Sprot 3C **54**
THORPE MARSH 1H **25**
Thorpe Marsh Nature Reserve 1E **25**
Thorpe Mere Rd. DN5: Ben 1F **25**
Thorpe Mere Vw. DN5: Ben 1F **25**
Thorpe St. S61: Thorpe H 3B **80**
Thorpleigh Rd. S43: Woodt 4E **165**
Three Hills Cl. S65: Thry 5E **85**
Three Nooks La. S72: Cud 5E **11**
Threshfield Way S12: Shef 5C **136**
THROAPHAM 3A **128**
Thrush Av. S60: Brins 4E **111**
Thrush St. S6: Shef 6A **106**
Thruxton Cl. S72: Cud 6F **11**
THRYBERGH 6E **85**
Thrybergh Country Park & Reservoir
. . . . .4G **85**
Thrybergh Country Park Visitors Cen.
. . . . .3F **85**
Thrybergh Ct. DN12: Den M 3E **69**
Thrybergh Hall Rd. S62: Rawm 2A **84**
Thrybergh La. S65: Thry 5F **85**
Thrybergh Sports Cen. 6E **85**
Thrybergh Vw. S65: Thry 6D **84**
Thundercliffe Rd. S61: Kimb 3E **95**
Thurbrook Gdns. S66: Thurc 5D **114**
THURCROFT 5B **114**
Thurcroft Ho. DN1: Don 2B **56**
(off St James St.)
Thurcroft Ind. Est. S66: Thurc 4B **114**
THURLSTONE 3A **176**
Thurlstone Rd. S36: Pen 4B **176**
THURNSCOE 3B **36**
Thurnscoe Bri. La. S63: Thurn 4C **36**
Thurnscoe Bus. Cen. S63: Thurn 3D **36**
Thurnscoe Bus. Pk. S63: Thurn 3D **36**
THURNSCOE EAST 2D **36**
Thurnscoe La. S72: Gt H 1F **35**
Thurnscoe Rd. S63: Bolt D 2B **50**
Thurnscoe Station (Rail) 2C **36**
Thurstan Av. S8: Shef 2D **146**
Tiber Vw. S60: Brins 3D **110**
Tickhill Bk. La. DN11: Wils 6F **89**
Tickhill Rd. DN4: Balb 5H **55**
(not continuous)
S66: Malt 5C **102**
Tickhill Sq. DN12: Den M 3C **68**
Tickhill St. DN12: Den M 2C **68**
Tickhill Way DN11: Ross 6E **75**
Tideswell Cl. S43: Stav 6G **163**
Tideswell Ct. S5: Shef 1H **107**
Tideswell Rd. S5: Shef 1H **107**
Tiercel M. S25: Dinn 5H **127**
Tilford Rd. S13: Shef 2D **136**
Tillotson Cl. S8: Shef 2F **133**
Tillotson Ri. S8: Shef 2F **133**
Tillotson Rd. S8: Shef 2F **133**
TILTS 1B **24**
TILTS HILLS 1H **23**
Tiltshills La. DN5: Ben 1H **23**
Tilts La. DN5: Ben 1B **24**
(not continuous)
Timothy Wood Av. S70: Birdw 4E **45**
Tinglebridge S73: Hem 5F **47**
Tingle Bri. Av. S73: Hem 5F **47**
Tingle Bri. Cres. S73: Hem 5F **47**
Tingle Bri. La. S73: Hem 5F **47**
Tingle Cl. S73: Hem 5F **47**
Tinker La. S6: Shef 1A **118**
S10: Shef 1A **118**
S74: Hoyl 6F **45**
Tinker Rd. S62: Rawm 2H **83**
TINSLEY 2H **109**

Tinsley Ind. Est. S9: Shef 6F **109**
Tinsley Pk. Cl. S9: Shef 5F **109**
Tinsley Park Golf Course 2G **121**
Tinsley Pk. Rd. S9: Shef 6E **109**
(not continuous)
Tinsley Rd. S74: Hoyl 5A **46**
Tippit La. S72: Cud 2F **19**
Tipsey Ct. S75: Stain 5C **8**
Tipsey Hill S75: Stain 5C **8**
Tipton St. S9: Shef 1D **108**
Tissington Cl. S40: Ches 3C **166**
Tithe Barn Av. S13: Shef 1C **136**
Tithe Barn Cl. S13: Shef 1D **136**
Tithe Barn Ct. S64: Mexb 4E **51**
Tithe Barn La. S13: Shef 2C **136**
Tithe Barn Way S13: Shef 1C **136**
Tithe Laithe S74: Hoyl 6B **46**
Titterton Cl. S9: Shef 6D **108**
Titterton St. S9: Shef 6D **108**
Tiverton Cl. S64: Swint 4C **66**
Tivy Dale Cl. S75: Cawt 4A **14**
Tivydale Dr. S75: Dart 1F **15**
Toad Holes La. DN11: Ross 3C **74**
Toad La. S66: Bramp M 1A **126**
Toch Yd. S40: Ches 6E **167**
Tockwith Rd. S9: Shef 1E **121**
Todmorden Cl. DN12: Den M 3B **68**
TODWICK 3B **140**
Todwick Grange S26: Tod 1B **140**
Todwick Ho. Gdns. S26: Tod 2B **140**
Todwick Rd. S8: Shef 5D **132**
S25: Dinn, Nth A 6D **126**
S26: Tod 6D **126**
Todwick Rd. Ind. Est. S25: Dinn 5E **127**
Todwick Vs. S26: Tod 3B **140**
Toecroft La. DN5: Sprot 3A **54**
Tofield Rd. DN11: Wad 6H **71**
TOFTS 2D **116**
Tofts La. S6: Stann 2D **116**
Toftstead DN3: Arm 5E **43**
Toftwood Av. S10: Shef 2H **117**
Toftwood Rd. S10: Shef 2A **118**
Togo Bldgs. S63: Thurn 3B **36**
Togo St. S63: Thurn 3B **36**
TOLL BAR .4H **23**
Toll Bar Av. S12: Shef 3B **134**
Toll Bar Cl. S12: Shef 3B **134**
Tollbar Cl. S36: Oxs 6H **177**
Toll Bar Dr. S12: Shef 3C **134**
Toll Bar Rd. S12: Shef 3B **134**
S64: Swint 4A **66**
S65: Roth 5D **98**
Tollbridge Rd. S43: Woodt 4E **165**
Tollgate Cl. S72: Shaft 4G **11**
Tollgate Ct. S3: Shef 5G **107**
Toll Ho. Mead S20: Mosb 3D **150**
Tolson Wlk. S63: Wath D 5G **49**
Tom La. S10: Shef 5E **117**
Tomlinson Rd. S74: Els 6D **46**
Tontine Rd. S40: Ches 6H **167**
Tooker Rd. S60: Roth 5F **97**
Topcliffe Rd. S71: Monk B 3F **17**
Top Fld. La. S65: Roth 2C **98**
Top Fold S71: Ard 2D **32**
Top Fold Cotts. DN12: Old D 4H **67**
Top Hall Rd. DN4: Bess 6C **58**
Top La. DN4: Bess 5G **57**
S66: B'well 2D **102**
Toppham Dr. S8: Shef 4E **147**
Toppham Rd. S8: Shef 4E **147**
Toppham Way S8: Shef 4E **147**
Top Pingle Cl. S43: Brim 1D **168**
Top Rd. DN3: Barn D 1C **26**
S35: Ough 5E **91**
S44: Cal 6E **169**
Top Row S75: Dart 3F **7**
Tops, The S62: Neth Hau, Rawm 2D **82**
Top Side S35: Gren 1A **92**
Top Ter. S10: Shef 3B **118**
(off Parker's La.)
Top Tree Way S65: Thry 5E **85**
Top Vw. Cres. DN12: New E 6C **70**
Top Warren S35: Chap 6G **61**
Torbay Rd. S4: Shef 5A **108**
Tor Cl. S71: Monk B 3G **17**
Torksey Cl. DN4: Bess 1B **74**
Torksey Rd. S5: Shef 6A **94**
Torksey Rd. W. S5: Shef 6A **94**

Torne Cl. DN4: Cant 6D **58**
Torne Vw. DN9: Auck 1H **59**
Torrington Cl. DN6: Adw S 2B **22**
Torry Ct. S13: Shef 2D **136**
Tortmayns S26: Tod 3B **140**
Torver Dr. S63: Bolt D 3B **50**
Tor Way S60: Brins 4E **111**
Torwood Dr. S8: Shef 3D **146**
TOTLEY 6E **145**
TOTLEY BROOK 5F **145**
Totley Brook Cl. S17: Dore 5E **145**
Totley Brook Cft. S17: Dore 5E **145**
Totley Brook Glen S17: Dore 4E **145**
Totley Brook Gro. S17: Dore 5E **145**
Totley Brook Rd. S17: Dore 5E **145**
Totley Brook Way S17: Dore 5E **145**
Totley Cl. S17: Ath 1G **17**
Totley Grange Cl. S17: Tot 6E **145**
Totley Grange Dr. S17: Tot 6E **145**
Totley Grange Rd. S17: Tot 6E **145**
Totley Hall Cft. S17: Tot 6E **145**
Totley Hall Dr. S17: Tot 6E **145**
Totley Hall La. S17: Tot 6E **145**
Totley Hall Mead S17: Tot 6E **145**
Totley La. S17: Bradw 6H **145**
S17: Tot 6G **145**
(not continuous)
Totley M. S17: Tot 6E **145**
Totley Mt. S43: Brim 6C **162**
TOTLEY RISE 5G **145**
Tourist Info. Cen.
Barnsley 1E **31**
Chesterfield 5H **167**
Doncaster 1C **56**
Rotherham 3E **97**
Sheffield 3E **5** (3F **119**)
Towcester Way S64: Mexb 6H **51**
Tower Cl. DN5: Scawt 1E **39**
S2: Shef 6H **119**
Tower Dr. S2: Shef 6H **119**
Tower Ho. S2: Shef 6H **119**
Tower St. S70: Barn 3D **30**
TOWN END
S6 . . . . .1F **117**
S36 . . . . .4H **175**
Town End DN5: Don 6A **40**
S18: App 3C **156**
Town End Av. S26: Ast 6D **124**
Townend Av. S65: Dalt 1D **98**
Townend Cl. S60: Tree 2F **123**
Town End Ind. Est. DN5: Don 6H **39**
Townend La. S36: Spink 5G **175**
Town End Rd. S35: Eccl 2E **93**
Townend St. S10: Shef 1B **118**
Town Flds. DN1: Don 1D **56**
Town Flds. Av. S35: Eccl 2H **93**
Town Fld. Vs. DN1: Don 1D **56**
Towngate S36: Thurl 3A **176**
S75: Mapp 5A **8**
S75: Silk 2A **28**
Towngate Gro. S35: Ough 5E **91**
Towngate Rd. S35: Ough 5D **90**
TOWN HEAD 1G **105**
TOWNHEAD 3D **144**
Townhead Rd. S17: Dore 3D **144**
Townhead St. S1: Shef 3D **4** (3F **119**)
Town Lands Cl. S73: Womb 6A **34**
Town La. S61: Kimb P, Wing 6G **81**
Town Moor Av. DN2: Don 6E **41**
Town St. S9: Tins 1G **109**
S60: Roth 6E **97**
Town Vw. Av. DN5: Scaws 2C **38**
Town Wells Ct. S25: Nth A 3G **141**
Toyne St. S10: Shef 2A **118**
Traditional Heritage Museum, The
. . . . .6B **118**
Trafalgar Ct. S1: Shef 5C **4** (4E **119**)
Trafalgar Rd. S6: Shef 6B **92**
Trafalgar St. S1: Shef 4C **4** (3E **119**)
Traffic Ter. S41: Has 3A **172**
S43: Bar H 2G **163**
Trafford Apartments S61: Kimb 4H **95**
Trafford Ct. DN1: Don 1B **56**
Trafford Way DN1: Don 1B **56**
Tranmoor Av. DN4: Bess 5B **58**
Tranmoor Ct. S74: Hoyl 1G **61**
Tranmoor La. DN3: Arm 5E **43**
(not continuous)

Tranquil Wlk. DN11: New R 6A 74
Trap La. S11: Shef 2F 131
Traso Bus. Pk. S18: Dron 3A 156
Travey Rd. S2: Shef 1D 134
Travis Gdns. DN4: Hex 3G 55
(not continuous)
Travis Pl. S10: Shef 6A 4 (4D 118)
Tredis Cl. S71: Monk B 5G 17
Treecrest Ri. S75: Barn 4D 16
Treefield Cl. S61: Wing 5B 82
Treelands S75: Barn 5A 16
Treeneuk Cl. S40: Ash 5C 166
Tree Root Wlk. S10: Shef 3C 118
TREETON 2F 123
Treeton Enterprise Cen. S60: Tree . . .3G 123
Treeton Ho. DN1: Don 2B 56
(off Oxford Pl.)
Treeton La. S26: Augh 3B 124
S60: Tree 1E 123
Treetown Cres. S60: Tree 1F 123
Treherne Rd. S60: Roth 5G 97
Trelawney Wlk. S70: Wors 5E 31
Trenchard Cl. S72: Grim 1B 20
Trent Cl. DN12: New E 3D 70
Trent Gdns. DN3: Kirk Sa 3C 26
Trent Gro. S18: Dron 1G 155
Trentham Cl. S60: Brins 4E 111
Trenton Cl. S13: Shef 2E 137
Trenton Ri. S13: Shef 2E 137
Trent St. S9: Shef 6B 108
Trent Ter. DN12: Con 3F 69
Trent Vs. S26: Kiv P 6A 140
Treswell Cres. S6: Shef 4B 106
Trevorrow Cres. S40: Ches 1H 171
Trevose Cl. S40: Walt 3D 170
Trewan Ct. S71: Monk B 5G 17
Trickett Rd. S6: Shef 5B 106
S35: High G 6B 60
Trigon, The S1: Shef 6F 5
Trinity Cl. S41: Ches 4G 167
Trinity Rd. S26: Kiv P 6C 140
Trinity St. S3: Shef 1D 4 (2F 119)
Trippet Ct. S10: Shef 6G 117
Trippet La. S1: Shef 3C 4 (3E 119)
Tristford Cl. S60: Cat 6E 111
Troon Cl. S40: Walt 2D 170
Troon Wlk. S25: Dinn 6A 128
Tropical Butterfly House, Wildlife and
Falconry Cen. 2B 142
Troughbrook Hill S43: Stav 6H 163
Troughbrook Rd. S43: Hol 5G 163
Trough Dr. S65: Thry 6F 85
Troutbeck Cl. S63: Thurn 3B 36
Troutbeck Rd. S7: Shef 4D 132
Troutbeck Way DN11: New R 6F 75
TROWAY 6E 149
Trowell Way S71: Ath 6E 9
Trueman Rd. S66: Malt 4H 101
Trueman Ter. S71: Lund 6B 18
Truman Gro. S36: Spink 3H 175
Truman St. DN5: Ben 1H 39
Truro Av. DN2: Don 2G 41
Truro Ct. S71: Monk B 5G 17
Truswell Av. S10: Shef 2H 117
Truswell Rd. S10: Shef 3H 117
Tudor Cl. S9: Shef 6E 109
Tudor Ct. DN3: Barn D 2C 26
S72: Grim 2B 20
Tudor Rd. DN2: Don 6F 41
DN6: Woodl 5D 22
Tudor Sq. S1: Shef 4F 5 (3G 119)
Tudor St. DN11: New R 6C 74
S43: Stav 4C 164
S63: Thurn 2D 36
Tudor Way S70: Wors 5F 31
Tuffolds Cl. S2: Shef 1D 134
Tulip Tree Cl. S20: Beig 3H 137
Tullibardine Rd. S11: Shef 2A 132
Tulyar Cl. DN11: New R 6G 75
Tumbling La. S71: Monk B 2C 18
Tummon Rd. S2: Shef 4B 120
Tummon St. S61: Roth 4C 96
Tune St. S70: Barn 2F 31
S73: Womb 2F 47
Tunstall Cl. S73: Womb 3F 47
Tunstall Grn. S40: Walt 1E 171
Tunstall Way S40: Walt 1E 171
Tunwell Av. S5: Shef 3G 93

Tunwell Dr. S5: Shef 3G 93
Tunwell Greave S5: Shef 3G 93
Tunwell Rd. S66: Carr 3F 115
Turham Ct. DN11: Ross 6E 75
Turie Av. S5: Shef 4F 93
Turie Cres. S5: Shef 4F 93
Turnberry Cl. S40: Walt 2D 170
Turnberry Ct. DN5: Ben 2H 39
Turnberry Gro. S72: Cud 6F 11
Turnberry Way S25: Dinn 1A 142
Turnbull Cl. S40: Ches 1G 171
Turner Av. S73: Womb 1E 47
Turner Bus. Pk. S13: Shef 4H 121
Turner Cl. S18: Dron 3E 155
Turner Dr. S43: Ink 6G 163
Turner La. S60: Whist 3A 114
Turner Museum of Glass 3C 4 (3E 119)
Turners Cl. S14: Jum 5C 46
Turners La. S10: Shef 4B 118
Turner St. S2: Shef 5F 5 (4G 119)
S72: Gt H 1F 35
Turnesc Gro. S63: Thurn 3C 36
Turnoaks Bus. Pk.
S40: Birdh 3A 172
Turnoaks La. S40: Birdh 3H 171
Turnpike Cft. S35: Gren 1B 92
Turnshaw Av. S26: Augh 5B 124
Turnshaw M. S70: Barn 3F 31
Turnshaw Rd. S26: Ull 5D 124
Turquoise S41: Ches 6A 168
(off Wain Av.)
Turton Rd. S65: Rav 2C 100
Tuscany Gdns. S70: Barn 2G 31
Tuscany Vs. S70: Barn 2G 31
Tutbury Gdns. DN4: Cant 5D 58
Tuxford Cres. S71: Barn 6A 18
Tween Woods La. DN11: Wad 5G 71
Twelve Lands Cl. S75: Tank 1D 60
Twelve O'Clock Ct. S4: Shef 1H 119
Twentylands, The S60: Tree 3F 123
Twentywell Cl. S17: Dore 4A 146
(off Ladies Spring Dr.)
Twentywell Dr. S17: Bradw 4A 146
Twentywell La. S17: Dore, Bradw 3H 145
Twentywell Ri. S17: Bradw 4A 146
Twentywell Rd. S17: Bradw 5A 146
Twentywell Vw. S17: Bradw 5A 146
Twibell St. S71: Barn 5F 17
Twickenham Cl. S20: Half 4F 151
Twickenham Ct. S20: Half 4F 151
Twickenham Cres. S20: Half 4F 151
Twickenham Glade S20: Half 4F 151
Twickenham Glen S20: Half 5G 151
Twickenham Gro. S20: Half 4F 151
Twigg Cl. S4: Kiln 5D 66
Twigg Cres. DN3: Arm 4C 42
Twitchill Dr. S13: Shef 2C 136
TWI Technology Cen.
S60: Cat 1C 122
Two Gates Way S72: Shaft 4F 11
Twyford Cl. S64: Swint 3H 65
Tyas Pl. S64: Mexb 1H 67
Tyas Rd. S5: Shef 3F 93
Tye Rd. S20: Beig 5H 137
TYERS HILL .1G 33
Tyler St. S9: Shef 2E 109
Tyler Way S9: Shef 1E 109
Tylney Rd. S2: Shef 4A 120
S40: Walt 2C 170
Tynedale Ct. DN3: Kirk Sa 4D 26
Tynker Av. S20: Beig 5H 137
Tyzack Rd. S8: Shef 6D 132

U

ULLEY 3D 124
Ulley Activity Cen. 3F 85
Ulley Beeches S66: Bramp M 3G 125
Ulley Country Park 3B 124
Ulley Country Park Visitor Cen. 3B 124
Ulley Cres. S13: Shef 1E 135
Ulley La. S26: Ast 5D 124
S26: Ull .4C 124
Ulley Rd. S13: Shef 1E 135
Ulley Vw. S26: Augh 4C 124
Ullswater Av. S20: Half 4F 151

Ullswater Cl. S18: Dron W 2D 154
S20: Half 4F 151
S25: Nth A 1H 141
S63: Bolt D 3B 50
Ullswater Dr. S18: Dron W 3D 154
Ullswater Pk. S18: Dron W 2D 154
Ullswater Rd. S64: Mexb 6A 52
S71: Ard .2E 33
Ullswater Wlk. DN5: Scaws 3D 38
Ulrica Dr. S66: Thurc 6B 114
Ulverston Rd. S8: Shef 4D 132
S41: Ches 1E 167
UNDERBANK 6C 104
Underbank La. S36: Stoc 1B 174
Undercliffe Rd. S6: Shef 1G 117
Undergate Rd. S25: Dinn 4H 127
Underhill S70: Wors 6G 31
Underhill La. S6: Shef 5A 92
UNDER TOFTS 2E 117
Underwood Av. S70: Wors 4G 31
Underwood Rd. S8: Shef 4E 133
Union Ct. S70: Barn 2E 31
Union Dr. S11: Shef 2C 132
Union La. S1: Shef 5E 5 (4F 119)
DN1: Don 2C 132
Union St. DN1: Don 2B 56
S1: Shef 5E 5 (4F 119)
S61: Barn 4C 96
S70: Barn 2E 31
WF9: Hems 1F 13
Union Wlk. S40: Ches 5H 167
Unistates Bus. Pk. S41: Old W 4A 162
Unity Pl. S60: Roth 6E 97
Universal Cl. S25: Nth A 6E 127
Universal Cres. S25: Nth A 6E 127
University of Derby
Chesterfield Campus 3H 167
University off Huddersfield
Barnsley Campus 6D 16
University of Sheffield
Bolsover St. 3A 4 (3H 118)
Crookesmoor Building 3B 118
Dorset St. 4C 118
Drama Studio 3D 118
Jessops Building 3D 118
North Campus 3C 4 (3E 119)
Northumberland Rd. 3C 118
School of Nursing & Midwifery
. . . . .2D 118
Western Bank 3C 118
University of Sheffield Stop (ST)
. . . . .4A 4 (3D 118)
Unsliven Rd. S36: Stoc 1A 174
UNSTONE 5B 156
Unstone Dronfield By-Pass
S18: Dron, Uns 3E 155
UNSTONE GREEN 1F 161
Unstone Hill S18: Uns 4A 156
Unstone Rd. S41: Old W 1G 161
Unstone St. S2: Shef 5F 119
Unwin Cres. S36: Pen 5D 176
Unwin St. S36: Pen 5D 176
Upland Ri. S40: Walt 1E 171
Uplands Av. S75: Kexb 6D 6
Uplands Rd. DN3: Arm 4F 43
Uplands Way S62: Rawm 2F 83
Up. Albert Rd. S8: Shef 4F 133
Up. Allen St. S3: Shef 2B 4 (2E 119)
UPPER BRADWAY 6A 146
Upper Chambers S35: Chap 6E 61
Up. Clara St. S61: Kimb 4A 96
Up. Cliffe Rd. S75: Dod 2F 29
UPPER CRABTREE 3H 107
Up. Croft Cl. S43: Brim 1D 168
UPPER CUDWORTH 6E 11
Upperfield Cl. S66: Malt 4A 102
Upperfield La. S75: High H, Kexb 5A 6
Upperfield Rd. S66: Malt 3H 101
Upper Folderings S75: Dod 3G 29
Up. Forest Rd. S71: Ath 6E 9
UPPER GATE 6C 104
Up. Gate Rd. S6: Stann 1C 116
Up. Hanover St. S3: Shef 5A 4 (4D 118)
(not continuous)
UPPER HAUGH 1E 83
Up. High Royds S75: Dart 6H 7
UPPER HOYLAND 5H 45

Up. Hoyland Rd. S74: Hoyl 4G 45
Up. King St. S43: Brim 5E 163
Up. Ley Cl. S35: Chap 4F 79
Up. Ley Dell S35: Chap 3F 79
Up. Lum Cl. S41: Ches 6C 168
Up. Lunns Cl. S71: Roy 3B 10
Upper Millgate S60: Roth 4E 97
Up. Moor St. S40: Bramp 6C 166
UPPER NEWBOLD 6B 160
Up. Newbold Cl. S41: Ches 1C 166
Up. New St. S70: Barn 2E 31
Up. Rye Cl. S60: Whist 3C 112
Up. School La. S18: Dron 4G 155
Up. Sheffield Rd.
  S70: Barn, Wors 3F 31
UPPER SWITHEN 3C 6
UPPER TANKERSLEY 3C 60
UPPERTHORPE
  S6 . . . . .1A 4 (1D 118)
  S21 . . . . .5C 152
Upperthorpe Gien S6: Shef 1C 118
Upperthorpe Glen S6: Shef 1C 118
Upperthorpe Rd. S6: Shef 1B 4 (1D 118)
  S21: Killa 5C 152
Upperthorpe Vs. S21: Killa 5C 152
Up. Valley Rd. S8: Shef 3F 133
UPPER WHISTON 5C 112
Up. Whiston Cl. S60: Whist 5B 112
Up. Whiston La.
  S60: Up W, Whist 5B 112
Upperwood Rd. S73: D'fld 4H 33
Up. Wortley Rd.
  S61: Kimb, Scho, Thorpe H 4B 80
Upton Cl. S66: Malt 3H 101
  S73: Womb 6E 33
                    (not continuous)
Upwell Hill S4: Shef 3B 108
Upwell La. S4: Shef 3B 108
Upwell St. S4: Shef 3B 108
Upwood Cl. S60: Ches 3A 166
Upwood Rd. S6: Shef 3A 106
Urban Rd. DN4: Hex 3H 55
Urch Cl. DN12: Con 5F 69
Usker Cl. S36: Pen 5E 177
Utah Ter. S12: Shef 5D 136
Uttley Cl. S9: Shef 6E 109
Uttley Cft. S9: Shef 6E 109
Uttley Dr. S9: Shef 6E 109
Uttoxeter Av. S64: Mexb 6H 51

V

Vaal St. S70: Barn 2G 31
Vainor Rd. S6: Shef 2H 105
Vale Av. S65: Thry 6E 85
Vale Cl. S18: Dron 3G 155
Vale Ct. S65: Thry 6E 85
Vale Cres. S65: Thry 6E 85
Vale Gro. S6: Lox 4F 105
Valentine Cl. S5: Shef 5H 93
Valentine Cres. S5: Shef 5H 93
                    (not continuous)
Valentine Rd. S5: Shef 5H 93
Vale Rd. S3: Shef 5E 107
  S65: Thry 6E 85
Valetta Ho. S62: Parkg 4G 83
                    (off Allt St.)
Vale Vw. S36: Oxs 6H 177
Valiant Gdns. DN5: Sprot 1F 55
Valley Centertainment S9: Shef 4F 109
Valley Centertainment (Park & Ride)
  . . . . .5E 109
Valley Centertainment Stop (ST) 4F 109
Valley Cres. S41: Ches 6B 168
Valley Dr. DN3: Brant 4G 59
  S21: Killa 3C 152
  S63: Wath D 6E 49
  S72: Grim 1B 20
  S74: Hoyl 1B 62
Valley Gro. S71: Lund 3C 18
Valley Park Ind. Est.
  S73: Womb 3B 48
Valley Rd. S8: Shef 2F 133
  S12: Shef 5D 136
  S21: Killa 3C 152
  S35: High G 2D 78
  S41: Ches 6B 168

Valley Rd. S43: Mas M 2F 165
  S64: Swint 4A 66
  S73: Womb 6H 33
  S75: Mapp 5H 7
Valley Vw. DN12: Con 3H 69
  S36: Pen 4E 177
Valley Vw. Cl. S21: Ecki 2D 158
  S41: Has 3D 172
Valley Way S73: Womb 2H 47
  S74: Hoyl 6B 46
Vancouver Dr. S63: Bolt D 2A 50
Vanguard Trad. Est.
  S40: Birdh 3A 172
Vantage Dr. S9: Tins 1G 109
Varley Gdns. S66: Flan 4G 99
Varley Ho. S41: Ches 2A 168
                    (off Tapton Lock Hill)
Varney Rd. S63: Wath D 1F 65
Vaughan Av. DN1: Don 6C 40
Vaughan Rd. S75: Barn 5A 16
Vaughan Ter. S72: Gt H 6F 21
                    (off School St.)
Vaughton Hill S36: Spink 4H 175
Vauxhall Cl. S9: Shef 6E 95
Vauxhall Rd. S9: Shef 6E 95
Velocity Twr.
  S1: Shef 6C 4 (5E 119)
Velvet Wood Cl. S75: Barn 5H 15
Venetian Cres. S73: D'fld 5A 34
Ventnor Cl. DN4: Balb 5G 55
Ventnor Ct. S7: Shef 6E 119
Ventnor Pl. S7: Shef 6E 119
Venture One Bus. Pk.
  S20: Holb 1H 151
Venture Way S41: Whit M 5G 161
Venus Ct. S60: Brins 2D 110
Verdant Way S5: Shef 5A 94
Verdon St. S3: Shef 6G 107
Verdon Street Recreation Cen. 1G 119
Verelst Av. S26: Ast 5C 124
Vere Rd. S6: Shef 2B 106
Verger Cl. DN11: Ross 5D 74
Vernon Cl. S70: Barn 3E 31
Vernon Cres. S70: Wors 5E 31
Vernon Delph S10: Shef 3G 117
Vernon Dr. S35: Chap 3F 79
Vernon Rd. S17: Dore 4F 145
  S40: Ches 5E 167
  S60: Roth 1A 112
  S70: Wors 5E 31
Vernon St. S70: Birdw 6E 45
  S71: Barn 6E 17
  S74: Hoyl 1H 61
Vernon St. Nth. S71: Barn 6E 17
Vernon Ter. S10: Shef 4H 117
Vernon Way S66: Malt 4H 101
  S75: Barn 5A 16
Verona Ri. S73: D'fld 5B 34
Vesey St. S62: Rawm 4G 83
Vicarage Cl. DN4: Cant 5D 58
  S35: Gren 2B 92
  S64: Mexb 2H 67
  S65: Roth 2C 98
  S74: Hoyl 6B 46
Vicarage Ct. S60: Brins 5E 111
Vicarage Cres. S35: Gren 2B 92
Vicarage Dr. DN11: Wad 5E 73
Vicarage Farm Ct.
  S75: Silk 2B 28
Vicarage La. S17: Dore 3E 145
  S65: Roth 4E 97
  S71: Roy 3H 9
Vicarage Rd. S9: Shef 5C 108
  S35: Gren 2B 92
Vicarage Wlk. S36: Pen 4D 176
Vicarage Way DN5: Ark 6D 24
Vicar Cres. S73: D'fld 5C 34
Vicar La. S1: Shef 3E 5 (3F 119)
  S13: Shef 1C 136
  S40: Ches 5H 167
Vicar Rd. S63: Wath D 5E 49
  S73: D'fld 5C 34
Vickers Dr. S5: Shef 1A 108
Vickers Rd. S5: Shef 2A 108
  S35: High G 1C 78
Victoria Av. S43: Stav 3C 164
  S65: Roth 4G 97
  S70: Barn 6D 16

Victoria Cl. S26: Kiv P 6B 140
  S36: Stoc 3D 174
Victoria Ct. DN5: Ben 5A 24
  S11: Shef 2C 132
  S26: Kiv P 6B 140
Victoria Cres. S70: Birdw 5D 44
  S75: Barn 6C 16
Victoria Cres. W. S75: Barn 6C 16
Victoria Gro. S43: Brim C 3E 169
Victoria Hall S1: Shef 4C 4 (3E 119)
Victoria Ho. S3: Shef 4B 4
Victoria Jubilee Mus. 4A 14
Victoria La. DN11: New R 5B 74
Victoria M. S64: Kiln 1D 84
Victorian Cres. DN2: Don 6E 41
Victoria Pk. Rd. S43: Brim C 3E 169
Victoria Quays S2: Shef 2H 5 (2H 119)
Victoria Rd. DN4: Balb 4A 56
  DN5: Ben 6A 24
  DN6: Adw S 2E 23
  DN12: New E 3C 70
  S10: Shef 6A 4 (5D 118)
  S20: Beig 4G 137
  S36: Stoc 3D 174
  S62: Parkg 4G 83
                    (not continuous)
  S64: Mexb 1F 67
  S70: Barn 6D 16
  S71: Roy 2A 10
  S73: Womb 1G 47
Victoria Rd. E. S63: Wath D 5E 49
Victoria Rd. W. S63: Wath D 5E 49
Victoria Sta. Rd. S4: Shef . . .2G 5 (2G 119)
Victoria St. S3: Shef 4B 4 (3E 119)
  S18: Dron 2E 155
  S25: Dinn 5B 128
  S36: Pen 4D 176
  S36: Stoc 3D 174
  S41: Ches 4H 167
  S43: Brim 5E 163
  S60: Cat 6E 111
  S60: Roth 4C 96
                    (not continuous)
  S63: Gol 5D 36
  S64: Kiln 1D 84
  S64: Mexb 1D 66
  S66: Malt 6B 102
  S70: Barn 6D 16
  S70: Stair 2A 32
  S72: Cud 1E 19
  S73: D'fld 4C 34
  S74: Hoyl 6C 46
  WF9: Hems 1F 13
Victoria St. Old W 4G 161
Victoria St. W. S40: Bramp 6D 166
Victoria Ter. S70: Barn 2F 31
Victoria Vs. S6: Shef 1D 118
                    (off Upperthorpe)
  S75: Pill 1D 60
Victoria Way S66: Malt 4G 101
Victor Rd. S17: Dore 3G 145
Victor St. S6: Shef 5C 106
Victor Ter. S70: Barn 2F 31
Viewland Cl. S72: Cud 3F 19
Viewlands S75: Silk C 5B 28
Viewlands Cl. S36: Pen 2D 176
  S66: Braml 6B 100
View Rd. S2: Shef 1F 133
  S65: Roth 2H 97
Views, The S75: Mapp 5A 8
Viewtree Cl. S62: H'ley 5A 62
Vikinglea Cl. S2: Shef 6E 121
Vikinglea Dr. S2: Shef 6E 121
                    (not continuous)
Vikinglea Glade S2: Shef 5E 121
Vikinglea Rd. S2: Shef 5E 121
Viking Way S26: Kiv P 5C 140
Villa Gdns. DN5: Ben 3H 23
Village Cl. S72: Cud 1F 19
Village St. DN5: Cus 5E 39
  DN6: Adw S 2C 22
Villa Pk. Rd. DN4: Cant 4B 58
Villa Rd. DN6: Woodl 3C 22
Villiers Cl. S2: Shef 2B 134
Villiers Dr. S2: Shef 2B 134
Vincent Cres. S40: Bramp 6C 166
Vincent Ho. S1: Shef 2C 4 (2E 119)
Vincent La. S40: Bramp 6C 166

Vincent Rd.—Warren Vw.

Vincent Rd. S7: Shef .6E 119
S65: Rav .3A 100
S71: Lund .5C 18
Vincent Ter. S63: Thurn .3E 37
Vine Cl. S60: Roth .4D 96
S71: Monk B .4H 17
Vine Grove Ct. S20: Mosb .3E 151
Vine Grove Gdns. S20: Mosb .3E 151
Viola Bank S36: Stoc .3D 174
Violet Av. DN12: New E .5C 70
S20: Beig .5F 137
Violet Bank Rd. S7: Shef .2D 132
Violet Farm Ct. S72: Brier .4B 12
Virgin Active
Sheffield .2E 133
Vissitt La. WF9: Hems .1B 12
Vista S60: Roth .5E 97
Vivian Rd. S5: Shef .2A 108
Vizard Rd. S74: Els .6D 46
Vue Cinema
Doncaster .3F 57
Sheffield .1F 109
Vulcan Ho. S65: Roth .3H 97
Vulcan M. DN9: Auck .2C 76
Vulcan Rd. S9: Shef .2E 109
(Meadowhall Way)
S9: Shef .2F 109
(Sheffield Rd.)

W

Wadbrough Rd. S11: Shef .5C 118
Waddington Rd. S75: Barn .6A 16
Waddington Ter. S64: Mexb .2G 67
Waddington Way S65: Ald .1H 97
Wade Cl. S60: Roth .6G 97
S72: Grim .2C 20
Wade Mdw. S6: Shef .3H 105
Wade St. S4: Shef .3B 108
S75: Barn .6A 16
WADSLEY .3G 105
WADSLEY BRIDGE .1B 106
Wadsley La. S6: Shef .2H 105
Wadsley Pk. Cres. S6: Shef .3H 105
Wadsworth Av. S12: Shef .3F 135
Wadsworth Cl. S12: Shef .2G 135
Wadsworth Dr. S12: Shef .2G 135
S62: Rawm .6D 64
Wadsworth Rd. S12: Shef .3F 135
S66: Braml .6A 100
WADWORTH .5E 73
Wadworth Av. DN11: Ross .5E 75
Wadworth Cl. DN5: Barnb .1H 51
Wadworth Hall DN11: Wad .5E 73
Wadworth Hall La. DN11: Wad .1H 89
Wadworth Hill DN11: Wad .5E 73
Wadworth Riding DN12: New E .4E 71
Wadworth Ri. S65: Dalt .1D 98
Wadworth St. DN12: Den M .3D 68
Wager La. S72: Brier .3B 12
Wagon Rd. S61: Grea .5C 82
Wain Av. S41: Ches .5A 168
Waingate S3: Shef .2F 5 (2G 119)
Wainscott Cl. S71: Monk B .3H 17
Wainwright Av. S13: Shef .6G 121
S73: Womb .1E 47
Wainwright Cres. S13: Shef .6F 121
Wainwright Pl. S73: Womb .1E 47
Wainwright Rd. DN4: Don .2D 56
S61: Kimb P .1A 96
Wakefield Rd. S71: Ath, Smi .1D 16
(not continuous)
S75: Stain .3B 8
Wakelam Dr. DN3: Arm .4C 42
Wake Rd. S7: Shef .1D 132
Walbank Rd. DN3: Arm .4F 43
Walbert Av. S63: Thurn .3B 36
Walbrook S70: Wors .6G 31
Walden Av. DN5: Scawt .1F 39
Walden Rd. S2: Shef .1G 133
Walders Av. S6: Shef .2H 105
Walders La. S36: Bolst .6E 175
WALES .6G 139
WALES BAR .5E 139
Wales Ct. S26: Wales .4G 139
Walesmoor Av. S26: Kiv P .6G 139
Wales Pl. S6: Shef .6C 106
Wales Rd. S26: Kiv P, Wales .6G 139
WALESWOOD .5C 138
Waleswood Ind. Est.
S26: Wales B .4E 139
Waleswood Rd. S26: Wales B .3B 138
(Delves La.)
S26: Wales B .4E 139
(Waleswood Ind. Est.)
Waleswood Vw. S26: Ast .2C 138
Waleswood Vs. S26: Wales B .5E 139
Waleswood Way S26: Wales B .5E 139
Walford Rd. S21: Killa .4B 152
Walgrove Av. S40: Ches .1E 171
Walgrove Rd. S40: Walt .1E 171
Walk, The S65: Roth .3A 98
S70: Birdw .6D 44
Walker Cl. S35: Gren .2B 92
Walker La. S65: Roth .3F 97
Walker Pl. *S65: Roth .3F 97*
(off Drummond St.)
Walker Rd. S61: Kimb P .1A 96
S75: Tank .1E 61
Walker's La. S21: Killa .4C 152
Walkers Ter. S71: Monk B .3H 17
Walker St. S3: Shef .1G 5 (1G 119)
S62: Rawm .2A 84
S64: Swint .3D 66
Walker Vw. S62: Rawm .2A 84
WALKLEY .6B 106
WALKLEY BANK .1A 118
Walkley Bank Cl. S6: Shef .5B 106
Walkley Bank Rd. S6: Shef .6H 105
Walkley Cres. Rd. S6: Shef .6A 106
Walkley La. S6: Shef .4B 106
Walkley Rd. S6: Shef .6B 106
Walkley St. S6: Shef .6B 106
Walkley Ter. S6: Shef .6H 105
Wallace Rd. DN4: Balb .6F 55
S3: Shef .5E 107
Waller Rd. S6: Shef .6H 105
Walling Cl. S9: Shef .2E 109
Walling Rd. S9: Shef .2E 109
Wallingwells La. S81: Gild .2G 143
Wallis Way S60: Cat .1C 122
Wallsend Cotts. S41: Ches .3F 167
Wall St. S70: Barn .2D 30
Walney Fold S71: Monk B .2A 18
Walnut Av. DN9: Auck .2A 76
(not continuous)
Walnut Cl. S70: Barn .3E 31
Walnut Dr. S21: Killa .5B 152
S25: Dinn .6A 128
Walnut Gro. S64: Mexb .6E 51
Walnut Pl. S35: Chap .4E 79
(not continuous)
Walnut Tree Hill DN11: Wad .5F 73
Walpole Cl. DN4: Balb .1G 71
Walpole Gro. S26: Swal .5C 124
Walseker La. S26: Wooda .2H 153
Walsham Dr. DN5: Cus .5F 39
Walshaw Gro. S35: Ough .5D 90
Walshaw Rd. S35: Ough .5E 91
Walstow Cres. DN3: Arm .4C 42
Walters Rd. S66: Malt .5C 102
Walter St. S6: Shef .5C 106
S60: Roth .3D 96
Waltham Cft. S41: Has .3B 172
Waltham Gdns. S20: Sot .6H 137
Waltham St. S70: Barn .2E 31
Waltheof Rd. S2: Shef .6D 120
WALTON .2C 170
Walton Bk. La. S42: Walt .3A 170
Walton Cl. S18: Dron W .2B 154
S35: High G .6B 60
S40: Walt .2C 170
Walton Ct. S8: Shef .2D 146
Walton Cres. S40: Ches .1F 171
Walton Dr. S40: Ches .1F 171
Walton Dr. Ct. S40: Ches .1F 171
Walton Fields Rd. S40: Ches .6E 167
Walton Ho. *DN1: Don .2B 56*
(off Grove Pl.)
Walton Rd. S11: Shef .5C 118
S40: Walt .6E 167
Walton St. S75: Barn .5B 16
Walton St. Nth. S75: Barn .5B 16
Walton Wlk. S40: Ches .6F 167
Walton Way S42: W'orth .6F 171
Walton Works S40: Ches .6E 167
Wannop St. S62: Parkg .5G 83
Wansfell Rd. S4: Shef .3C 108
Wansfell Ter. S71: Barn .1F 31
Wapping, The S65: Hoot R .1A 86
Warburton Cl. S2: Shef .1H 133
Warburton Gdns. S2: Shef .1H 133
Warburton Rd. S2: Shef .1H 133
Ward Cl. S36: Pen .5D 176
Warde Aldam Cres. S66: Wick .5F 99
Warde Av. DN4: Balb .6G 55
Warden Cl. DN4: Cant .4D 58
Warden St. S60: Roth .1E 111
Wardgate Way S40: Ches .3B 166
WARD GREEN .5E 31
Wardlow Cl. S40: Ches .2G 171
Wardlow Rd. S12: Shef .3G 135
Ward Pl. S7: Shef .6E 119
Wards Ct. *S11: Shef .5E 119*
(off Napier St.)
Wardsend Rd. S6: Shef .2C 106
Wardsend Rd. Nth. S6: Shef .1B 106
Ward St. S3: Shef .1D 4 (1F 119)
S36: Pen .5D 176
Wards Yd. S18: Dron .3F 155
Wareham Ct. S20: Sot .6H 137
Wareham Gro. S75: Dod .2H 29
Warehouse La. S63: Wath D .6F 49
Warley Rd. S2: Shef .5B 120
Warminster Cl. S8: Shef .4F 133
Warminster Cres. S8: Shef .4G 133
Warminster Dr. S8: Shef .5G 133
Warminster Gdns. S8: Shef .5F 133
Warminster Pl. S8: Shef .6G 133
Warminster Rd. S8: Shef .4F 133
WARMSWORTH .1D 70
Warmsworth Ct. DN4: Warm .6E 55
Warmsworth Halt DN4: Warm .2C 70
Warmsworth Halt Ind. Est.
DN4: Warm .2D 70
Warmsworth Rd. DN4: Balb .6F 55
Warner Av. S75: Barn .6A 16
Warner Pl. S75: Barn .6B 16
Warner Rd. S6: Shef .3A 106
S75: Barn .6A 16
Warner St. S41: Ches .1A 172
Warnington Dr. DN4: Bess .1D 74
Warning Tongue La.
DN3: Cant .4E 59
DN4: Bess, Cant .4E 59
WARREN .6F 61
Warren, The DN11: Ross .4D 74
S26: Ast .1E 139
Warren Av. S62: Rawm .1F 83
Warren Cl. DN2: Don .6F 41
DN4: Warm .6D 54
S71: Roy .1A 10
S81: Woods .4F 143
Warren Cres. S21: Mar L .2H 157
S70: Barn .3E 31
Warren Dr. S61: Kimb .2A 96
Warreners Dr. S65: Thry .6E 85
Warren Gdns. S35: Chap .6G 61
Warren Hill S61: Kimb P .2A 96
Warren Ho. Cl. S66: Braml .5A 100
Warren La. DN4: Bess .1C 74
(not continuous)
DN11: Ross .1C 74
S35: Chap .5F 61
(not continuous)
S35: High G .5E 61
(not continuous)
S75: Stain .3A 8
WF4: Wool .3A 8
Warren Mt. S61: Kimb .2A 96
Warren Pl. S70: Barn .3E 31
Warren Quarry La. S70: Barn .3E 31
Warren Ri. S18: Dron .1H 155
Warren Rd. DN12: Con .5E 69
S66: Wick .5G 99
Warren St. S4: Shef .1A 120
(not continuous)
WARREN VALE .6H 65
Warren Vale S62: Rawm .1H 83
S64: Swint .1H 83
Warren Vale Rd. S64: Swint .3H 65
Warren Vw. S70: Barn .3E 31
S74: Hoyl .2H 61

A-Z Sheffield 263

Warren Wlk. S21: Mar L 2H 157
  S71: Roy 2H 9
                (Queensway)
  S71: Roy 1A 10
                (Warren Cl.)
Warrington Rd. S10: Shef 2C 118
Warris Cl. S61: Kimb P 1H 95
Warris Pl. S2: Shef 3A 120
Warsop Rd. S71: Ath 5D 8
Warwick Rd. DN2: Don 5G 41
  S66: Malt .5F 101
  S71: Monk B 5G 17
Warwick St. S10: Shef 2B 118
  S40: Birdh 3A 172
  S60: Roth .5F 97
Warwick St. Ind. Est. S40: Birdh . . .3A 172
Warwick St. Sth. S60: Roth 5F 97
Warwick Ter. S10: Shef 2B 118
Warwick Way S25: Nth A 2H 141
Wasdale Av. S20: Half 4F 151
Wasdale Cl. S20: Half 4F 151
Washfield Cres. S60: Tree 2F 123
Washfield La. S60: Tree 2F 123
Washford Rd. S9: Shef 6B 108
Wash Ho. La. S42: Bramp 6D 166
Washington Av. DN12: Con 4C 68
  S73: Womb 2E 47
Washington Cl. S25: Dinn 6G 127
Washington Gro. DN5: Don 3H 39
Washington Rd. DN6: Woodl 3C 22
  S11: Shef .6E 119
  S35: Eccl .1G 93
  S63: Gol 6C 36
Washington St. S64: Mexb 1G 67
Wasteneys Rd. S26: Tod 3C 140
Watch Ho. La. DN5: Don 4G 39
Watchley Gdns. S63: Gol 5B 36
Watch St. S13: Shef 6F 123
Waterdale DN1: Don 2C 56
Waterdale Cl. DN5: Sprot 4E 55
Waterdale Rd. S70: Wors 6E 31
Waterdale Shop. Cen. DN1: Don 1C 56
Waterfield M. S20: Westf 1F 151
Waterfield Pl. S70: Stair 2B 32
Waterfront Driving Range 4H 49
Waterfront Golf Course 4H 49
             (not continuous)
Water Hall La. S36: Pen 3D 176
Waterhall Vw. S36: Pen 3D 176
Waterhouse Cl. S65: Dalt 1D 98
Wateringbury Gro. S43: Stav 4C 164
Watering La. S71: Ard 2F 33
Watering Pl. Rd. S36: Thurl 4A 176
Water La. S17: Dore 3G 145
  S60: Roth .5E 97
  S62: Wentw 3D 62
  S65: Hoot R 2H 85
  WF9: Hems 2G 13
Waterloo Ct. S25: Laugh C 3F 127
Waterloo Rd. S3: Shef 5D 106
  S70: Barn .1C 30
Waterloo Wlk. S6: Shef 1E 119
Watermead S63: Bolt D 3C 50
Watermeade S21: Ecki 2C 158
Water Mdw. La. S41: Ches 1C 166
Water Royd Dr. S75: Dod 3G 29
Waterside Cotts. S65: Ald 1H 97
Waterside Dr. S66: Sunn 2H 99
Waterside Ent. Pk. S25: Laugh C . . .4F 127
Waterside Gdns. S35: Ough 3E 91
Waterside Pk. S73: Womb 2A 48
Waterside Vw. DN12: Con 3F 69
Water Slacks Cl. S13: Shef 2C 136
Water Slacks Dr. S13: Shef 2C 136
Water Slacks La. S13: Shef 2B 136
Water Slacks Rd. S13: Shef 2C 136
Water Slacks Wlk. S13: Shef 2C 136
Water Slacks Way S13: Shef 2C 136
Watersmeet Rd. S6: Shef 5A 106
Water St. S3: Shef 1E 5 (2F 119)
WATERTHORPE 6F 137
Waterthorpe Cl. S20: Westf 2G 151
Waterthorpe Cres. S20: Westf 2G 151
Waterthorpe Gdns. S20: Westf 2G 151
Waterthorpe Glade S20: Westf 2G 151
Waterthorpe Glen S20: Westf 2G 151
Waterthorpe Greenway
  S20: Water 5E 137

Waterthorpe Ri. S20: Westf 1G 151
Waterthorpe Stop (ST) 1G 151
Water Vole Way DN4: Balb 5B 56
Waterway La. S64: Kiln 6D 66
Watery St. S3: Shef 1B 4 (1E 119)
Wath Golf Course 4F 65
Wath Rd. S7: Shef 2D 132
  S63: Bolt D 3A 50
  S64: Mexb 4C 50
  S73: Bramp, Womb 2A 48
  S73: Hem .2E 63
  S74: Els 2E 63
Wath Rdbt. S63: Wath D 6G 49
WATH UPON DEARNE 6G 49
Wath West Ind. Est. S63: Wath D . . .4D 48
WATH WOOD 2G 65
Wath Wood Bottom S63: Wath D 3F 65
Wath Wood Dr. S64: Swint 3G 65
Wath Wood Rd. S63: Wath D 2G 65
Watkin Cl. S9: Shef 1E 121
Watkinson Gdns. S20: Water 1F 151
Watnall Rd. S71: Ath 6E 9
Watson Cl. S61: Kimb 2A 96
Watson Glen S61: Kimb 2F 95
Watson La. S42: W'orth 6D 170
Watson Rd. S10: Shef 4B 118
  S61: Kimb .2A 96
Watson St. S74: Hoyl 1G 61
Watson Wlk. S1: Shef 2F 5
Watt La. S10: Shef 4G 117
Waveney Dr. S75: H'ham 5F 15
Waverley Av. DN4: Balb 5F 55
  DN12: Con 4F 69
  S26: Kiv P .5B 140
  S66: Thurc 6C 114
Waverley Bus. Pk. S60: Shef 2B 122
Waverley Cotts. S13: Shef 3A 122
Waverley Ct. DN5: Ben 4H 23
Waverley La. S13: Shef 3A 122
Waverley Rd. S9: Shef 2F 121
Waverley Vw. S60: Cat 1D 122
Way, The S40: Walt 2C 170
Waycliffe S71: Monk B 5H 17
Wayford Av. S41: Has 1A 172
  S66: Braml 4B 100
Wayland Av. S70: Wors 5E 31
Wayland Rd. S11: Shef 6C 118
Wayside S43: Brim 6C 162
Wayside Ct. S43: Brim 6C 162
Weakland Cl. S12: Shef 6A 136
Weakland Cres. S12: Shef 5A 136
Weakland Dr. S12: Shef 5A 136
Weakland Way S12: Shef 5A 136
Weaver Cl. S75: H'ham 5F 15
Weavers Cl. S35: Gren 1B 92
Webb Av. S36: Spink 4G 175
Webbs Av. S6: Stann 6F 105
Webster Cl. S61: Kimb 2F 95
Webster Ct. S40: Ches 3F 167
         (off Newbold Bk. La.)
Webster Cres. S61: Kimb 2G 95
Webster Cft. S41: Old W 4A 162
Webster St. S9: Shef 3E 109
Wedgewood Cl. S62: Rawm 3G 83
Weedon St. S9: Shef 3E 109
Weetshaw Cl. S72: Shaft 5F 11
Weetshaw La. S72: Cud 5D 10
  S72: Shaft 4F 11
Weetwood Dr. S11: Shef 2H 131
Weetwood Rd. S60: Roth 2H 111
Weigh La. S2: Shef 4H 5 (3H 119)
Weir Cl. S74: Hoyl 2B 62
Weir Head S9: Shef 3E 109
Welbeck Cl. S18: Dron W 2B 154
  S43: Ink 2H 169
Welbeck Dr. S26: Ast 1E 139
  S42: W'orth 6F 171
Welbeck Rd. DN4: Don 2E 57
  S6: Shef 6A 106
Welbeck St. S75: Barn 6C 16
            (not continuous)
Welbury Gdns. S20: Half 4F 151
Welby Pl. S8: Shef 3E 133
Welcome Way DN1: Don 2B 56
Welfare Av. DN12: Con 4D 68
  S40: Ches 5E 167
Welfare Ct. S63: Thurn 2B 36

Welfare Rd. DN6: Woodl 5C 22
  S63: Thurn 2C 36
Welfare Vw. S63: Gol 6C 36
  S75: Dod .2G 29
Welham Dr. S60: Roth 6F 97
Welland Cl. S3: Shef 4E 107
Welland Ct. S75: H'ham 5F 15
Welland Cres. S74: Els 6D 46
Welland Gdns. S74: Els 6D 46
Wellbeck Ct. S43: Stav 4B 164
             (off Porter St.)
Wellbourne Cl. S35: Chap 4H 79
Wellcarr Rd. S8: Shef 6F 133
Wellcliffe Cl. S66: Braml 4H 99
Well Ct. S12: Shef 5C 136
Well Cft. S35: High G 1C 78
Wellcroft Cl. DN2: Don 4H 41
Wellcroft Gdns. S66: Braml 6B 100
Wellcroft Ho. S71: Roy 3H 9
           (off Church St.)
Wellcroft M. S70: Wors 2F 45
Well Dr. S65: Thry 6F 85
Wellesley Rd. S10: Shef 3C 118
Wellfield Cl. S6: Shef 2C 118
  S12: Ridg .1H 149
Wellfield Cres. S81: Woods 4F 143
Wellfield Gdns. S71: Roy 1A 10
Wellfield Gro. S36: Pen 2D 176
Wellfield Lodge S61: Kimb P 1H 95
Wellfield Rd. S6: Shef 1C 118
  S61: Kimb P 6H 81
  S75: Barn .5C 16
Wellgate DN12: Con 4F 69
  S60: Roth .4F 97
  S75: Mapp 5A 8
Wellgate Mt. S60: Roth 4F 97
Wellgate Ter. S60: Roth 4F 97
Well Grn. Rd. S6: Stann 1C 116
Wellhead Rd. S8: Shef 2F 133
Well Hill Dr. S71: Roy 2H 9
Well Hill Rd. S35: Wort 1H 175
Well Ho. La. S36: Pen 1B 176
Wellhouse La. S36: Pen 2D 176
Wellhouse Way S36: Pen 2D 176
Wellingley Rd. DN4: Balb 2B 72
Wellington Av. S25: Nth A 1G 141
Wellington Cl. S71: Monk B 4G 17
Wellington Cres. S70: Wors 4H 31
Wellington Gro. DN5: Don 3H 39
Wellington Pl. S9: Shef 2F 121
  S70: Barn .1C 30
Wellington Rd. DN12: New E 4C 70
  S6: Shef 6F 105
Wellington St.
  S1: Shef 5C 4 (4E 119)
            (not continuous)
  S43: New W 2C 162
  S63: Gol 5D 36
  S64: Mexb 1F 67
  S70: Barn .1D 30
Welling Way S61: Kimb 3H 95
Well La. DN11: Wad 5F 73
            (not continuous)
  S6: Shef 2G 105
  S12: Shef .4C 136
  S26: Augh 4B 124
  S35: Eccl .2G 93
  S35: Gren .1B 92
  S60: Tree .2F 123
  S60: Up W 5C 112
  S60: Whist 3A 112
  S66: Clift .3G 87
  S71: Monk B 3H 17
Well La. Ct. S72: Bill 4G 35
Well Meadow Dr. S3: Shef . . .2B 4 (2E 119)
Well Meadow St.
  S3: Shef 1B 4 (2E 119)
Wells, The S25: Nth A 3G 141
Wells Ct. S75: Mapp 6B 8
Wells Gdn. Wlk. S25: Nth A 3G 141
Well Spring Cl. S43: Brim 1D 168
Wellspring Cl. S42: W'orth 6A 172
Wells Rd. DN2: Don 4E 41
Wells St. S72: Cud 2E 19
  S75: Dart .6F 7
Well St. S70: Barn 1C 30
Wellsyke Ind. Est. DN6: Adw S 1F 23

Wellsyke Rd. DN6: Adw S 1E **23**
Well Vw. Rd. S61: Kimb 2G **95**
Wellway, The S66: Sunn 3G **99**
Wellwyn Ct. S12: Shef 4E **135**
Welney Pl. S6: Shef 6B **92**
Welshpool Pl. S40: Ches 5E **167**
Welshpool Yd. S40: Ches 6E **167**
Welton Cl. DN4: Bess 6H **57**
Welwyn Cl. S12: Shef 4E **135**
S40: Ches 5E **167**
Welwyn Rd. S12: Shef 4E **135**
Wembley Av. DN12: Con 4D **68**
Wembley Cl. DN2: Don 5H **41**
Wendel Gro. S74: Els 6E **47**
Wenlock Cl. S40: Ash 4E **167**
Wenlock Cres. S40: Ash 4D **166**
Wenlock St. S13: Shef 5A **122**
Wensley Cl. S4: Shef 3B **108**
Wensley Ct. S4: Shef 2B **108**
S71: Smi .1D **16**
Wensley Cres. DN4: Cant 5C **58**
Wensley Cft. S4: Shef 2B **108**
Wensleydale Dr. S60: Brins 5E **111**
Wensleydale Rd. DN5: Scaws 3E **39**
S61: Wing 5A **82**
Wensley Dr. S4: Shef 2B **108**
Wensley Gdns. S4: Shef 2B **108**
Wensley Grn. S4: Shef 2B **108**
Wensley Rd. S71: Smi 1D **16**
Wensley St. S4: Shef 2B **108**
S63: Thurn 2A **36**
Wensley Way S43: Stav 6H **163**
WENTWORTH **5D 62**
Wentworth Av. S11: Shef 6G **131**
S26: Ast 2E **139**
S40: Walt 2F **171**
Wentworth Cl. DN5: Sprot 3D **54**
S61: Thorpe H 3B **80**
Wentworth Ct. S61: Grea 4C **82**
*S70: Barn 3E **31***
(off Warren Quarry La.)
Wentworth Cres. S36: Pen 4D **176**
S75: Mapp 6C **8**
Wentworth Dr. S62: Rawm 4G **83**
S75: Mapp 6B **8**
Wentworth Gdns. S64: Swint 5B **66**
Wentworth Ho. *DN1: Don 2B **56***
(off St James St.)
Wentworth Ind. Pk. S75: Tank 2C **60**
Wentworth Mdws. S36: Pen 3D **176**
Wentworth M. S36: Pen 4D **176**
Wentworth Park **6F 63**
Wentworth Pl. S61: Scho 6F **81**
Wentworth Rd. DN2: Don 5D **40**
S18: Dron W 3B **154**
S36: Pen 3C **176**
(not continuous)
S61: Thorpe H 3C **80**
S62: Rawm 5D **64**
S64: Kiln, Swint 5H **65**
S74: Black H 3A **46**
S74: Els 2D **62**
S74: Jum 5D **46**
S75: Kexb 6E **7**
S75: Mapp 6B **8**
Wentworth Sta. S74: Hoyl 4H **61**
Wentworth St. S70: Birdw 5D **44**
S71: Barn 5D **16**
Wentworth Vw. S73: Womb 3G **47**
S74: Hoyl 1B **62**
(Millhouses St.)
S74: Hoyl 1H **61**
(Willow Cl.)
Wentworth Way S25: Dinn 1A **142**
S75: Dod 4G **29**
S75: Tank 2C **60**
Wentworth Woodhouse Gdns. **6F 63**
Wescoe Av. S72: Gt H 1F **35**
Wesley Av. S26: Ast, Swal 6C **124**
Wesley Ct. S61: Thorpe H 3C **80**
Wesley La. S10: Shef 3A **118**
Wesley Pl. S25: Sth A 4G **141**
Wesley Rd. S26: Kiv P 5A **140**
S35: High G 1B **78**
(not continuous)
Wesley St. S70: Barn 1E **31**
Wessenden Cl. S75: Barn 1H **29**
Wessex Cl. S43: Brim 6E **163**
Wessex Gdns. S17: Dore 5E **145**
Wessington Dr. S43: Stav 6H **163**
West Acre S36: Pen 4E **177**
West Av. DN4: Balb 5H **55**
DN6: Woodl 3A **22**
S62: Rawm 2G **83**
S63: Bolt D 3A **50**
S71: Roy 2A **10**
S73: Womb 1E **47**
Westbank Cl. S18: Coal A 6G **147**
Westbank Ct. S18: Coal A 6H **147**
West Bank Dr. S25: Sth A 4F **141**
W. Bank La. S1: Shef 3D **4** (3F **119**)
W. Bank Ri. S25: Sth A 4G **141**
West Bar S3: Shef 2E **5** (2F **119**)
Westbar Grn. S1: Shef 2E **5** (2F **119**)
WEST BARRIER **2A 76**
West Bars S40: Ches 5G **167**
W. Bawtry Rd. S60: Roth 3E **111**
Westbourne Gdns. DN4: Balb 1G **71**
Westbourne Gro.
S40: Bramp 5C **166**
S75: Barn 5C **16**
Westbourne Rd. S10: Shef 5B **118**
Westbourne Ter. S70: Barn 1B **30**
Westbrook Bank S11: Shef 6C **118**
Westbrook Cl. S40: Bramp 6A **166**
Westbrook Dr. S40: Bramp 6A **166**
Westbrook Rd. S35: Chap 3F **79**
Westbury Av. S35: Chap 4G **79**
Westbury Cl. S75: Barn 4A **16**
Westbury St. S9: Shef 1C **120**
Westby Cl. S65: Rav 2B **100**
Westby Cres. S60: Whist 3A **112**
Westby Wlk. S66: Braml 5B **100**
W. Carr Rd. S25: Dinn 5G **127**
West Cl. S61: Kimb P 2H **95**
Westcott M. S26: Augh 5B **124**
West Cres. S36: Oxs 5G **177**
S36: Stoc 3C **174**
West Cft. Ct. S43: Ink 3G **169**
Westcroft Cres. S20: Westf 2F **151**
West Cft. Dr. S43: Ink 3G **169**
Westcroft Dr. S20: Westf 3F **151**
Westcroft Gdns. S20: Westf 2F **151**
Westcroft Glen S20: Westf 3F **151**
Westcroft Gro. S20: Westf 3F **151**
West Don St. S6: Shef 6D **106**
West End Av. DN5: Don 3H **39**
S71: Roy 3F **9**
West End Ct. DN11: Ross 6E **75**
West End Cres. S71: Roy 3F **9**
West End La. DN11: New R 5H **73**
West End Rd. S63: Wath D 5C **48**
West End Vw. S21: Ecki 2D **158**
Westerdale Rd. DN5: Scaws 3E **39**
Western Av. S25: Dinn 6A **128**
Western Bank
S10: Shef 3A **4** (3C **118**)
Western Cl. S25: Dinn 6A **128**
Western Ct. WF9: Sth K 4G **13**
Western M. S70: Barn 6C **16**
Western Rd. S10: Shef 2A **118**
S65: Roth 3H **97**
Western St. S70: Barn 6C **16**
Western Ter. S73: Womb 1F **47**
Westerton Dr. S66: Braml 6C **100**
W. Farm La. S65: Roth 2C **98**
WESTFIELD
S20 . . . .**2F 151**
S63 . . . .**6B 48**
Westfield Av. S12: Shef 5D **136**
S26: Augh 5B **124**
S36: Thurl 3A **176**
S40: Bramp 1C **170**
Westfield Cen. S20: Westf 2F **151**
Westfield Cl. S40: Bramp 6C **166**
Westfield Craft Pk. S62: Parkg 4F **83**
Westfield Cres. S20: Mosb 2D **150**
S63: Thurn 2A **36**
Westfield Cft. S63: Bramp B 5B **48**
Westfield Gdns. S40: Bramp 6C **166**
Westfield Gro. S12: Shef 5C **136**
Westfield Ho. S1: Shef 4C **4**
Westfield La. DN5: Barnb 1F **51**
S21: Midd H 4G **157**
S36: Thurl 3A **176**
S75: Bar G 3E **15**
Westfield Northway S20: Westf 1F **151**
(not continuous)
Westfield Rd. DN3: Arm 4D **42**
DN4: Balb 4A **56**
S18: Dron 4H **155**
S21: Killa 5B **152**
S62: Parkg 5F **83**
S63: Bramp B 6B **48**
S66: Braml 5A **100**
S73: Bramp 6B **48**
Westfields S70: Wors 6F **31**
S71: Roy 2F **9**
Westfield Southway S20: Westf 2F **151**
Westfield Sports Cen. **6G 137**
Westfield Stop (ST) **2G 151**
Westfield St. S70: Barn 1C **30**
Westfield Ter. S1: Shef 4C **4** (3E **119**)
Westgarth Cl. S25: Dinn 5A **128**
West Gate S64: Mexb 1H **67**
Westgate S36: Pen 5E **177**
S60: Roth 4E **97**
S63: Bramp B 6B **48**
S70: Barn 1D **30**
S71: Monk B 4G **17**
WEST GREEN **2C 18**
West Green Av. S71: Monk B 2C **18**
West Green Dr. DN3: Kirk Sa 4B **26**
West Green Way S71: Monk B 1A **18**
West Gro. DN2: Don 5F **41**
S71: Roy 2F **9**
West Hall Fold S62: Wentw 5D **62**
WEST HANDLEY **4G 157**
Westhaven S72: Cud 3F **19**
West Hill S61: Kimb 4F **95**
Westhill La. S3: Shef 4B **4** (3E **119**)
S42: Gras 6D **172**
Westholme Rd. DN4: Balb 3A **56**
West House S8: Shef 4F **133**
W. Kirk La. S72: Bill, Midd 3F **35**
W. Laith Ga. DN1: Don 1B **56**
Westland Cl. S20: Westf 1F **151**
Westland Gdns. S20: Westf 1E **151**
Westland Gro. S20: Westf 2F **151**
Westland Rd. S20: Westf 2F **151**
Westlands S43: Bar H 3G **163**
West La. S6: Lox 2A **104**
S26: Augh 5A **124**
S66: Carr 3E **115**
West Lea S40: Bramp 6D **166**
Westleigh Ct. S40: Ches 3F **167**
West Mall DN1: Don 1B **56**
S20: Water 6F **137**
Westmeads S71: Roy 3G **9**
WEST MELTON **5E 49**
Westminster Av. S10: Shef 5C **116**
Westminster Cl. S10: Shef 5C **116**
S66: Braml 6B **100**
Westminster Cres. DN2: Don 5G **41**
S10: Shef 5C **116**
Westminster Dr. DN7: Dunsv 4H **27**
Westminster Ho. DN2: Don 5H **41**
Westmoor Cl. S63: Gol 5B **36**
W. Moor Cres. S75: Barn 1H **29**
W. Moor La. DN3: Arm 3G **43**
(not continuous)
DN5: H'ton 2E **51**
S63: Bolt D 2E **51**
W. Moor Link DN3: Eden 1B **42**
West Moor Pk. DN3: Arm 4H **43**
Westmoor Rd. S43: Brim C 4E **169**
Westmoreland St. S6: Shef 1D **118**
Westmorland La. DN12: Den M 3C **68**
Westmorland St. DN4: Balb 6G **55**
Westmorland Way DN5: Sprot 3B **54**
West Mt. Av. S63: Wath D 4D **48**
Westnall Ho. *S35: Ough 3E **91***
(off Glossop Row)
Westnall Rd. S5: Shef 3A **94**
Westnall Ter. S5: Shef 3A **94**
Weston Cl. S40: Ches 3B **166**
West One Aspect S3: Shef 4B **4**
West One Central S1: Shef 4B **4**
West One City S1: Shef 4B **4**
West One Cube S3: Shef 5B **4**
West One Panorama S1: Shef 4B **4**
West One Peak S3: Shef 4B **4**
West One Plaza S3: Shef 4B **4** (3E **119**)
West One Reflect S3: Shef 5B **4**

West One Space S3: Shef 5B 4
West One Twr. S3: Shef 4B 4
Westongales Way
  DN5: Ben .2H 39
Weston Park Mus. 3C 118
Weston Rd. DN4: Balb 6H 55
Weston St. S3: Shef 2A 4 (2D 118)
Weston Vw. S10: Shef 3B 118
Westover Rd. S10: Shef 4F 117
West Pk. Dr. S26: Swal 1A 138
West Pinfold S71: Roy 3H 9
Westpit Hill S63: Bramp B 5B 48
West Pl. DN5: Ben 1A 40
West Quadrant S5: Shef 1A 108
West Rd. S64: Mexb 1E 67
  S75: Barn .6A 16
Westside Grange DN4: Balb 4G 55
West St. DN1: Don 1B 56
  DN12: Con .4F 69
  S1: Shef 4B 4 (3E 119)
  S18: Dron .2E 155
  S20: Beig .5G 137
  S21: Ecki .2D 158
  S25: Sth A 4G 141
  S40: Ches 4G 167
  S63: Gol 4D 36
  S63: Wath D 6F 49
              (not continuous)
  S64: Mexb .2F 67
  S66: Thurc 5C 114
  S70: Wors .6F 31
  S71: Roy 2A 10
  S72: Sth K .1H 11
  S73: D'fld .5B 34
  S73: Womb 1F 47
  S74: Hoyl .6H 45
  WF9: Sth K .5G 13
West St. La. S1: Shef 3D 4 (3F 119)
West Street Stop (ST) 4C 4 (3E 119)
WESTTHORPE 5C 152
Westthorpe Bus. Innovation Cen.
  S21: Killa .6B 152
Westthorpe Flds. Rd. S21: Killa 6B 152
Westthorpe Grn. S21: Killa 6C 152
Westthorpe Rd. S21: Killa 5C 152
West Vale Gro. S65: Thry 6E 85
West Vw. S43: Stav 5A 164
  S70: Barn 3D 30
  S70: Wors .6G 31
  S72: Cud 3F 19
  S75: Silk C .4B 28
West Vw. Cl. S17: Tot 4G 145
West Vw. Cres. S63: Gol 6B 36
West Vw. La. S17: Tot 4G 145
West Vw. Rd. S41: Ches 2F 167
  S61: Kimb .4F 95
  S64: Mexb .2F 67
West Vw. Ter. S70: Wors 6G 31
              (off West St.)
Westville Rd. S75: Barn 5C 16
West Way S70: Barn 1D 30
Westwell Pl. S20: Mosb 4E 151
Westwick Cres. S8: Shef 3C 146
Westwick Gro. S8: Shef 3D 146
Westwick Rd. S8: Shef 3C 146
WESTWOOD 5C 60
Westwood S35: High G 5C 60
Westwood Av. S6: Shef 1G 105
  S43: Stav .6H 163
Westwood Cl. S6: Shef 1G 105
  S43: Ink 3H 169
Westwood Country Pk. 5C 60
Westwood Ct. S35: High G 6C 60
  S70: Barn 6D 16
Westwood Dr. S43: Ink 3H 169
Westwood Dr. Gdns. S43: Ink 3G 169
Westwood La. S35: Brom 2A 58
  S43: Brim C 4E 169
Westwood New Rd. S35: High G 1A 78
  S75: Tank 3C 60
Westwood Rd. S11: Shef 6G 117
  S35: High G 6C 60
  S44: Cal 4F 169
Wetherby Cl. DN5: Scaws 5E 39
Wetherby Ct. S9: Shef 2F 121
Wetherby Dr. S26: Swal 1B 138
  S64: Mexb .6G 51
Wetlands La. S43: Brim C 4D 168

Wet Moor La. S63: Wath D 5E 49
              (Norton Rd.)
  S63: Wath D 5G 49
              (Stables Way)
Whaley Rd. S75: Barn 3G 15
Wharf Cl. S64: Swint 3D 66
Wharfedale St. S35: Chap 3D 78
Wharfedale Rd. S75: Barn 6A 16
Wharf La. S41: Ches 4H 167
  S43: Stav .3C 164
Wharf Rd. DN1: Don 5C 40
  S9: Tins 1G 109
  S64: Kiln 1D 84
Wharf St. S2: Shef 2G 5 (2H 119)
  S64: Swint .3D 66
  S71: Barn 5F 17
Wharncliffe Av. S26: Ast 6D 124
  S35: Wharn S 1A 90
  S63: Wath D 6G 49
              (off Moor Rd.)
Wharncliffe Bus. Pk. S71: Ath 6G 9
Wharncliffe Cl. S62: Rawm 6E 65
  S74: Hoyl 2A 62
Wharncliffe Cotts. S75: Pill 1D 60
Wharncliffe Ct. S75: Pill 1B 60
Wharncliffe Hill S65: Roth 3F 97
Wharncliffe Ind. Complex
  S36: Spink .3H 175
Wharncliffe Rd. S10: Shef 6A 4 (4D 118)
  S35: High G 1C 78
WHARNCLIFFE SIDE 2A 90
Wharncliffe St. DN4: Hex 2H 55
  S65: Roth 3F 97
  S70: Barn 1C 30
  S71: Carl 6A 10
Wharton Av. S26: Swal 5C 124
Wharton Dr. S41: Ches 5A 168
Wheatacre Rd. S36: Stoc 3E 175
Wheata Dr. S5: Shef 3G 93
Wheata Pl. S5: Shef 3F 93
Wheata Rd. S5: Shef 4F 93
Wheatbridge Retail Pk.
  S40: Ches .6G 167
Wheatbridge Rd. S40: Ches 5F 167
Wheatcroft Cl. S42: W'orth 6H 171
Wheatcroft Gdns. S36: Pen 5E 177
Wheatcroft Rd. S62: Rawm 2A 84
Wheatcrofts S70: Barn 1C 30
Wheatfield Cl. DN3: Barn D 2D 26
Wheatfield Cres. S5: Shef 4A 94
Wheatfield Dr. S63: Thurn 3C 36
Wheatfield Way S42: Ash 3A 166
Wheathill Cl. S42: Ash 4A 166
  S43: Brim C 4E 169
Wheathill La. S43: Brim C 4C 168
Wheathill St. S60: Roth 5E 97
Wheat Holme La. DN5: Ben 1B 24
Wheatlands Rd. S42: W'orth 6F 171
WHEATLEY .5D 40
Wheatley Cl. S71: Barn 4E 17
Wheatley Dr. S75: Wool G 3F 7
Wheatley Golf Course 4A 42
Wheatley Gro. S13: Shef 5H 121
Wheatley Hall Retail Pk. DN2: Don . . .2G 41
Wheatley Hall Rd. DN2: Don 4D 40
Wheatley Hall Trade Pk. DN2: Don . . .2G 41
WHEATLEY HILLS 4H 41
Wheatley La. DN1: Don 6D 40
WHEATLEY PARK 3G 41
Wheatley Pk. Rd. DN5: Ben 6H 23
Wheatley Pl. DN12: Den M 3C 68
Wheatley Ri. S75: Stain 4A 8
Wheatley Rd. S61: Kimb P 1H 95
  S64: Kiln 1D 84
  S70: Stair 3B 32
Wheatley St. DN12: Den M 3C 68
Wheats La. S1: Shef 2E 5
Wheel, The S35: Eccl 2D 92
Wheeldon Cres. S43: Barn 6C 162
Wheeldon St. S1: Shef 3B 4 (3E 119)
Wheel La. S35: Gren 2C 92
  S35: Ough .3C 90
Wheldrake Rd. S5: Shef 2A 108
Whernside Av. S35: Chap 2E 79
Whinacre Cl. S8: Shef 4G 147
Whinacre Pl. S8: Shef 4F 147

Whinacre Wlk. S8: Shef 4F 147
Whinby Cft. S75: Dod 3G 29
Whinby Rd. S75: Dod, H'ham 2F 29
Whin Cl. WF9: Hems 1E 13
Whin Cnr. S72: Shaft 2E 11
Whincover Vw. S71: Roy 2B 10
Whinfell Cl. DN6: Adw S 2C 22
Whinfell Ct. S11: Shef 6F 131
Whin Gdns. S63: Thurn 1C 36
Whin Hill Rd. DN4: Bess 4A 58
Whinmoor Cl. S75: Silk 1A 28
Whinmoor Ct. S75: Silk 1A 28
Whinmoor Dr. S75: Silk 1A 28
Whinmoor Rd. S5: Shef 1C 108
  S35: High G 1B 78
Whinmoor Vw. S75: Silk 1A 28
Whinmoor Way S75: Silk 2A 28
WHINNEY HILL 6D 84
Whins, The S62: Neth Hau 2D 82
Whinside Cres. S63: Thurn 1B 36
Whiphill Cl. DN4: Bess 5B 58
Whiphill La. DN3: Arm 5F 43
Whiphill Top La. DN3: Brant 3H 59
              (not continuous)
WHIRLOW 6G 131
Whirlow Ct. Rd. S11: Shef 6G 131
Whirlow Cft. S11: Shef 5G 131
Whirlowdale Cl. S11: Shef 6F 131
Whirlowdale Cres. S7: Shef 5A 132
Whirlowdale Ri. S11: Shef 6F 131
Whirlowdale Rd. S7: Shef 6F 131
  S11: Shef .6F 131
Whirlow Elms Chase S11: Shef 4G 131
Whirlow Farm M. S11: Shef 5F 131
Whirlow Grange Av. S11: Shef 6F 131
Whirlow Grange Dr. S11: Shef 6F 131
Whirlow Grn. S11: Shef 6F 131
Whirlow Gro. S11: Shef 6G 131
Whirlow La. S11: Shef 6F 131
Whirlow M. S11: Shef 5G 131
Whirlow Pk. Rd. S11: Shef 6G 131
Whisperwood Dr. DN4: Balb 2A 72
WHISTON 3A 112
Whiston Brook Vw. S60: Whist 3B 112
Whiston Grange S60: Roth 3H 111
Whiston Grn. S60: Whist 4A 112
Whiston Gro. S60: Roth 6G 97
Whiston Va. S60: Whist 4A 112
Whitaker Cl. DN11: New R 6G 75
Whitaker Sq. DN11: New R 6B 74
Whitbeck Cl. DN11: Wad 5E 73
Whitbourne Cl. S71: Smi 3E 17
Whitburn Rd. DN1: Don 2D 56
Whitby Rd. DN11: New R 6B 74
  S9: Shef 1F 121
Whitcomb Dr. DN11: New R 6G 75
White Apron St. WF9: Sth K 4H 13
Whitebank Cl. S41: Ches 1A 172
Whitecotes Cl. S40: Walt 2F 171
Whitecotes La. S40: Ches, Walt 2E 171
Whitecotes Pk. S40: Walt 2G 171
White Cft. S1: Shef 2C 4 (2F 119)
Whitecroft Cres. S60: Brins 4D 110
White Cross Av. S72: Cud 3E 19
White Cross Ct. S72: Cud 3F 19
White Cross La. DN11: Wad 5H 71
              (not continuous)
  S70: Swai, Wors 5A 32
White Cross Mt. S72: Cud 3F 19
Whitecross Ri. S70: Wors 5A 32
White Cross Rd. S72: Cud 3E 19
White Cross Vw. S70: Wors 5A 32
White Edge Cl. S40: Ches 3E 167
White Ga. S25: Sth A 2A 142
Whitegate Wlk. S61: Wing 5H 81
Whitehall Rd. S61: Wing 4A 82
Whitehall Way S61: Wing 5B 82
White Hart Cnr. S21: Ecki 6F 151
Whitehead Av. S36: Spink 3F 175
Whitehead Cl. S25: Dinn 5H 127
Whitehead St. S43: Stav 4C 164
White Hill Av. S70: Barn 1H 29
Whitehill Av. S60: Brins 4D 110
White Hill Gro. S70: Barn 1A 30
Whitehill Dr. S60: Brins 5D 110
White Hill Gro. S70: Barn 1A 30
Whitehill La. S60: Brins 3D 110
Whitehill Rd. S60: Brins 4C 110
Whitehill Ter. S70: Barn 1H 29

Whitehill Willow S60: Brins 5D **110**
Whitehouse La. S6: Shef 6C **106**
Whitehouse Rd. S6: Shef 6C **106**
Whitehouses S41: Ches 1A **172**
White Ho. Vw. DN3: Barn D 1G **27**
White La. S12: Shef 5E **135**
S35: Chap 1G **79**
White Lane Stop (ST) 5E **135**
Whitelea Gro. S64: Mexb 2E **67**
Whitelea Grove Trad. Est.
S64: Mexb 2E **67**
White Leas S40: Ash 4C **166**
Whitelee Rd. S64: Swint 3D **66**
Whiteley La. S10: Shef 1D **130**
Whiteleys Av. S62: Rawm 1F **83**
Whiteley Wood Cl. S11: Shef 1G **131**
WHITELEY WOOD GREEN 3C **130**
Whiteley Wood Rd. S11: Shef 2E **131**
WHITELEY WOODS 1G **131**
Whitelow La. S17: Dore 2A **144**
White Rd. S43: Stav 3D **164**
White Rose Ct. DN5: Ben 1B **40**
White Rose Ho. S60: Roth 5E **97**
White Rose Way DN4: Don 3C **56**
White's La. S2: Shef 3A **120**
White Thorns Cl. S8: Shef 4G **147**
White Thorns Dr. S8: Shef 5G **147**
White Thorns Vw. S8: Shef 4G **147**
White Towers Caravan Site
DN2: Don 4B **42**
Whiteways Cl. S4: Shef 4A **108**
Whiteways Dr. S4: Shef 4A **108**
Whiteways Gro. S4: Shef 4A **108**
Whiteways Rd. S4: Shef 4A **108**
Whitewood Cl. S71: Roy 4G **9**
Whitfield Gdns. S81: Woods 4E **143**
Whitfield Rd. S10: Shef 1D **130**
S62: Rawm 1E **83**
Whitham Rd. S10: Shef 4B **118**
Whiting St. S8: Shef 2F **133**
WHITLEY 6E **79**
Whitley Carr S35: Gren 6D **78**
Whitley Cft. S35: Eccl 6G **79**
Whitley La. S35: Gren, Eccl 1C **92**
Whitley Vw. S35: Eccl 6G **79**
Whitley Vw. Rd. S61: Kimb 5E **95**
Whitney Cl. DN4: Balb 1F **71**
Whittier Rd. DN4: Balb 6H **55**
Whitting M. S41: Old W 4G **161**
Whittington Hill S41: Old W 5H **161**
Whittington Ind. Est. S43: New W 3C **162**
Whittington La. S18: Uns 6B **156**
WHITTINGTON MOOR 6H **161**
Whittington Rd.
S43: Bar H, New W 2D **162**
Whittington St. DN1: Don 5C **40**
Whittington Way S41: Whit M 5H **161**
Whitting Valley Rd. S41: Old W 5H **161**
Whittle Way S60: Shef 2A **122**
Whitton Cl. DN4: Bess 6H **57**
(not continuous)
Whitwell Cres. S36: Stoc 3D **174**
Whitwell La. S36: Stoc 4C **174**
Whitwell St. S9: Shef 2G **121**
Whitwell Vw. DN11: Ross 5E **75**
Whitworth Ct. DN9: Finn 3C **76**
Whitworth Cft. S10: Shef 4G **117**
Whitworth La. S9: Shef 5D **108**
S63: Wath D 4E **49**
Whitworth Rd. S10: Shef 5F **117**
S41: Ches 2G **167**
Whitworth's Ter. *S63: Thurn* *2D* ***36***
(off Coronation St.)
Whitworth St. S63: Gol 5D **36**
Whitworth Way S63: Wath D 5F **49**
Whybourne Gro. S60: Roth 5F **97**
Whybourne Ter. S60: Roth 4F **97**
Whyn Vw. S63: Thurn 2B **36**
Wickens Pl. S43: Mas M 2E **165**
Wicker S3: Shef 1G **5** (2G **119**)
Wicker La. S3: Shef 1F **5** (2G **119**)
(not continuous)
WICKERSLEY 6G **99**
Wickersley Ct. S66: Wick 6E **99**
Wickersley Rd. S60: Roth 6H **97**
Wickett Hern Rd. DN3: Arm 4F **43**
Wicket Way DN12: New E 3D **70**
Wickfield Cl. S12: Shef 3A **136**
Wickfield Dr. S12: Shef 3A **136**
Wickfield Gro. S12: Shef 4H **135**
Wickfield Rd. S12: Shef 4A **136**
Wicklow Rd. DN2: Don 5F **41**
Widdop Cl. S13: Shef 6G **121**
Widdop Cft. S13: Shef 6G **121**
Wigfield Dr. S70: Wors 5E **31**
Wigfield Farm 6E **31**
Wigfull Rd. S11: Shef 5B **118**
Wigley Rd. S43: Ink 2H **169**
Wignall Av. S66: Wick 6E **99**
Wikeley Way S43: Brim 6C **162**
Wike Rd. S71: Lund 6B **18**
Wilberforce Rd. DN2: Don 1A **42**
S25: Sth A 3G **141**
Wilbrook Ri. S75: Barn 4H **15**
Wilby Carr Gdns. DN4: Cant 3B **58**
Wilby La. S70: Barn 2F **31**
Wilcox Cl. S6: Shef 5C **92**
Wilcox Grn. S61: Wing 4B **82**
Wilcox Rd. S6: Shef 5B **92**
Wild Av. S62: Rawm 1D **82**
Wilden Cft. S43: Brim 6B **162**
Wildene Dr. S64: Mexb 6F **51**
Wilder M. S61: Kimb 3A **96**
Wildflower Cl. DN11: New R 6F **75**
Wilding Cl. S61: Kimb 2H **95**
Wilding Way S61: Kimb 2H **95**
Wilford Rd. S71: Ath 5D **8**
Wilfred Cl. S9: Shef 1D **120**
Wilfred Dr. S9: Shef 1D **120**
Wilfred St. S60: Roth 4E **97**
Wilfrid Rd. S9: Shef 1D **120**
Wilkin Hill S18: B'low 5A **160**
Wilkinson Av. DN11: New R 6D **74**
Wilkinson Cl. S40: Birdh 4H **171**
Wilkinson Dr. S43: Ink 1G **169**
Wilkinson La. S10: Shef 4A **4** (3D **118**)
(not continuous)
Wilkinson Rd. S74: Els 1D **62**
Wilkinson St. S10: Shef 4A **4** (3D **118**)
(not continuous)
S70: Barn 2E **31**
Willan Dr. S60: Cat 1D **122**
Willbury Dr. S12: Shef 2D **134**
Willersley Ct. *S41: Ches* *1E* ***167***
(off Newbold Rd.)
Willey St. S3: Shef 1G **5** (2G **119**)
William Brown Sq. S40: Ches 1H **171**
William Cl. S20: Mosb 4E **151**
William Ct. WF9: Sth K 4H **13**
William Cres. S20: Mosb 3E **151**
William La. DN11: New R 4A **74**
William Nuttall Cott. Homes
DN4: Don 2E **57**
Williamson Rd. S11: Shef 1C **132**
Williams Rd. DN5: Cus 4G **39**
Williams St. S62: Parkg 4H **83**
William St. S10: Shef 6A **4** (4D **118**)
S21: Ecki 1E **159**
S41: Ches 2H **167**
S60: Roth 4F **97**
S63: Gol 5B **36**
S63: Wath D 6G **49**
S64: Swint 3D **66**
S70: Wors 5F **31**
S73: Womb 1F **47**
William St. Nth. S41: Old W 4G **161**
Willingham Cl. S20: Sot 1H **151**
Willingham Gdns. S20: Sot 1H **151**
Willington Rd. S5: Shef 6H **93**
Willis Rd. S6: Shef 3A **106**
Willman Rd. S71: Lund 5C **18**
Willoughby St. S4: Shef 2B **108**
Willow Av. DN4: Cant 4C **58**
S62: Rawm 3H **83**
Willow Bank S71: Barn 3C **16**
S75: Barn 4D **16**
Willow Beck S65: Roth 2A **98**
Willow Bri. Caravan Site
DN5: Don 5A **40**
Willow Brook Cl. S75: Dart 6H **7**
Willow Chase S25: Nth A 3H **141**
Willow Cl. S25: Sth A 5G **141**
S60: Brins 5E **111**
S66: Flan 4H **99**
S72: Cud 1E **19**
S74: Hoyl 1H **61**
Willow Ct. S44: Cal 5F **169**
S62: Rawm 2H **83**
S63: Wath D 1F **65**
S66: Wick 6G **99**
S73: D'fld 5B **34**
Willow Cres. DN9: Auck 2A **76**
S35: Chap 4F **79**
S66: B'well 6B **88**
Willowcroft S63: Bolt D 3A **50**
Willowdale Cl. DN5: Sprot 4D **54**
Willowdale Ri. S61: Scho 6E **81**
Willow Dene Rd. S72: Grim 1B **20**
Willow Dr. DN12: New E 3D **70**
S9: Shef 3H **121**
S43: Mas M 2F **165**
S64: Mexb 1E **67**
S66: Flan 4H **99**
WF9: Hems 1E **13**
Willow Gdns. S73: Womb 1H **47**
Willowgarth S62: Rawm 2H **83**
Willowgarth Av. S60: Brins 4D **110**
Willow Gth. Rd. S41: Ches 6D **160**
Willow Glen DN3: Brant 4H **59**
Willow Gro. S26: Ast 6E **125**
Willow La. DN11: Ross 5D **74**
S36: Oxs 5H **177**
S63: Bolt D 3C **50**
Willowlees Ct. DN4: Bess 5B **58**
Willow Pl. S66: B'well 6B **88**
Willow Rd. DN3: Arm 3F **43**
S21: Killa 5B **152**
S36: Stoc 5D **174**
S63: Thurn 1C **36**
S63: Wath D 2H **65**
S66: Malt 5G **101**
Willows, The S36: Oxs 6H **177**
S61: Kimb P 6G **81**
S65: Roth *5G* ***97***
(off Johnson St.)
S73: D'fld 5B **34**
Willow St. DN12: Con 4G **69**
S70: Barn 2C **30**
Willow Wlk. DN5: Ben 5H **23**
S70: Barn 3F **31**
Wilmington Dr. DN4: Don 5E **57**
Wilsden Gro. S75: Barn 5A **16**
WILSIC 4H **89**
Wilsic Ho. *DN1: Don* *2B* ***56***
(off Grove Pl.)
Wilsic La. DN11: Tick, Wils 4H **89**
Wilsic Rd. DN11: Wils 2H **89**
Wilson Av. S36: Pen 5D **176**
S62: Rawm 2F **83**
Wilson Dr. S65: Dalt 1D **98**
Wilson Gro. S71: Lund 4B **18**
Wilson Pl. S8: Shef 2F **133**
Wilson Rd. S11: Shef 6B **118**
S18: Coal A 6H **147**
S36: Spink 4H **175**
Wilson St. S3: Shef 6F **107**
S18: Dron 4G **155**
S73: Womb 1E **47**
Wilson Wlk. S75: Dod 4H **29**
Wilstrop Rd. S9: Shef 1E **121**
WILTHORPE 4B **16**
Wilthorpe Av. S75: Barn 4B **16**
Wilthorpe Cres. S75: Barn 4B **16**
Wilthorpe Farm Rd. S75: Barn 4B **16**
Wilthorpe Gdns. S20: Mosb 5B **136**
Wilthorpe Grn. S75: Barn 4B **16**
Wilthorpe La. S75: Barn 4A **16**
Wilthorpe Rd. S75: Barn 4H **15**
Wilton Cl. S62: Rawm 3G **83**
Wilton Ct. S61: Kimb 3B **96**
Wilton Gdns. S61: Roth 3B **96**
Wilton La. S61: Roth 4B **96**
Wilton Pl. S10: Shef 6A **4** (4D **118**)
Wiltshire Av. DN12: Den M 3C **68**
Wiltshire Rd. DN2: Don 6H **41**
Wimborne Cres. S41: Ches 1F **167**
Winberry Av. S25: Nth A 3H **141**
Wincanton Cl. S64: Mexb 6G **51**
Winchester Av. DN2: Don 4F **41**
S10: Shef 6C **116**
Winchester Ct. *S65: Roth* *3F* ***97***
(off Nottingham St.)
Winchester Cres. S10: Shef 6C **116**
Winchester Dr. S10: Shef 6C **116**

Winchester Ho.—Woodhead Way

Winchester Ho. DN5: Scaws 4E **39**
Winchester Rd. S10: Shef 6C **116**
S41: Ches 1F **167**
Winchester Way DN5: Scaws 4F **39**
S60: Brins 3B **110**
S71: Ard 3D **32**
WINCOBANK **1C 108**
Wincobank Av. S5: Shef 1B **108**
Wincobank Cl. S5: Shef 1C **108**
Wincobank La. S4: Shef 3C **108**
Wincobank Rd. S5: Shef 1C **108**
Winco Rd. S4: Shef 3C **108**
Winco Wood La. S5: Shef 1C **108**
Windam Dr. DN3: Barn D 1H **27**
Windermere Av. DN2: Don 5H **41**
S18: Dron W 3D **154**
S63: Gol 6D **36**
Windermere Cl. S64: Mexb 6A **52**
Windermere Ct. S25: Nth A 2H **141**
Windermere Cres. DN3: Kirk Sa 4C **26**
Windermere Dr. DN4: Don 3G **57**
Windermere Grange
DN12: New E 5C **70**
Windermere Rd. S8: Shef 3D **132**
S36: Pen 3D **176**
S41: Ches 1D **166**
S71: Barn 1F **31**
Winders Pl. S73: Womb 2G **47**
Windgate Hill DN12: Con 3G **69**
Windham Cl. S71: Barn 5E **17**
WINDHILL **6H 51**
Windhill Av. S64: Mexb 1H **67**
S75: Stain 3H **7**
Windhill Cres. S64: Mexb 6H **51**
S75: Stain 3H **7**
Windhill Dr. S75: Stain 3H **7**
Windhill La. S75: Stain 3H **7**
Windhill Mt. S75: Stain 3H **7**
Windhill Ri. S75: Wool G 3F **7**
Windhill Ter. S64: Mexb 6H **51**
Windings, The S63: Thurn 3E **37**
Winding Wheel, The **5A 168**
Windle Ct. S60: Tree 2G **123**
Windle Rd. DN4: Hex 3H **55**
Windle Sq. DN3: Kirk Sa 4C **26**
Windmill Av. DN12: Con 5G **69**
S72: Grim 6A **12**
Windmill Balk La.
DN6: Adw S, Woodl 4B **22**
Windmill Cl. S70: Barn 3F **31**
Windmill Ct. DN6: Woodl 3C **22**
S61: Thorpe H 5D **80**
S73: Womb 2E **47**
Windmill Dr. DN11: Wad 6E **73**
Windmill Est. DN12: Con 5G **69**
Windmill Greenway S20: Half 5F **151**
WINDMILL HILL **6E 73**
Windmill Hill La. S35: Burn 4D **78**
Windmill La. S5: Shef 6B **94**
S18: Hun 1H **161**
S36: Thurl 4A **176**
Windmill Rd. S25: Nth A 2H **141**
S73: Womb 2E **47**
Windmill Ter. S71: Roy 1G **9**
Windmill Way S43: Brim 6B **162**
Windsor Av. S36: Thurl 3A **176**
S75: Kexb 6D **6**
Windsor Cl. DN5: H'ton 2H **51**
S40: Walt 1D **170**
S66: Braml 4A **100**
Windsor Ct. DN7: Dunsv 4H **27**
S11: Shef 4G **131**
S70: Barn 6D **16**
Windsor Cres. S71: Monk B 5G **17**
S72: Midd 3E **35**
Windsor Dr. DN5: Barnb 1H **51**
S18: Dron W 3B **154**
S42: W'orth 6F **171**
S64: Mexb 6H **51**
S75: Dod 3G **29**
Windsor Gdns. S63: Thurn 2D **36**
Windsor Ri. S26: Ast 2D **138**
Windsor Rd. DN2: Don 6E **41**
DN12: Con 3E **69**
S8: Shef 2E **133**
S61: Thorpe H 4C **80**
WF9: Hems 1G **13**
Windsor Sq. S63: Thurn 2D **36**
Windsor St. S4: Shef 6A **108**
(not continuous)
S63: Thurn 2D **36**
S74: Hoyl 5A **46**
Windsor Vw. DN11: New R 6A **74**
Windsor Wlk. DN5: Scaws 4F **39**
S25: Sth A 5F **141**
S41: Has 1B **172**
S72: Grim 2B **20**
Windy Ho. La. S2: Shef 1C **134**
Windy Ridge S26: Augh 5B **124**
Winfield Rd. S63: Wath D 1G **65**
WINGERWORTH **6H 171**
Wingerworth Av. S8: Shef 2C **146**
Wingerworth Hall Est. *S42: W'orth . . .6H 171*
(off Longedge Ri.)
Wingerworth Way S40: Birdh 4G **171**
WINGFIELD **5B 82**
Wingfield Cl. S18: Dron W 4B **154**
S61: Wing 5B **82**
Wingfield Ct. S61: Wing 6A **82**
Wingfield Cres. S12: Shef 3F **135**
Wingfield Rd. S61: Wing 5H **81**
S71: Ath 2F **17**
Winholme DN3: Arm 4E **43**
Winifred St. S60: Roth 4D **96**
Winkley Ter. S5: Shef 5B **94**
Winlea Av. S65: Roth 6D **98**
Winmarith Ct. S71: Roy 3G **9**
Winnat Pl. S43: Ink 1H **169**
Winnats Cl. S40: Ches 3D **166**
Winnats Way S10: Shef 5H **117**
Winn Cl. S6: Shef 1A **106**
Winn Dr. S6: Shef 1A **106**
Winn Gdns. S6: Shef 1A **106**
(not continuous)
Winn Gro. S6: Shef 6H **91**
Winnipeg Rd. DN5: Ben 1A **40**
Winsford Rd. S6: Shef 5B **92**
WINSICK **4D 172**
Winster Cl. S70: Birdw 4E **45**
Winster Ct. S41: Ches 4H **167**
Winster Rd. S6: Shef 3B **106**
S43: Stav 6H **163**
Winston Av. S36: Stoc 2B **174**
Winter Av. S71: Roy 1H **9**
S75: Barn 6B **16**
Winter Garden . . . .**4E 5 (3F 119)**
Winter Hill La. S61: Kimb 3H **95**
Winterhill Rd. S61: Kimb 4G **95**
Winter Rd. S75: Barn 6B **16**
Wintersett Dr. DN4: Don 4G **57**
Winter St. S3: Shef 2D **118**
Winter Ter. S75: Barn 6B **16**
Winterton Cl. DN4: Bess 6A **58**
Winterton Gdns. S12: Shef 5D **136**
Winterwell Rd. S63: Wath D 5D **48**
(not continuous)
Winton Cl. S70: Barn 3F **31**
Winton Rd. DN2: Don 6G **41**
Wisbech Cl. S40: Walt 2F **171**
Wisconsin Dr. DN4: Don 5F **57**
Wiseley Cft. S72: Grim 6B **12**
Wiseton Rd. S11: Shef 6B **118**
WISEWOOD **4G 105**
Wisewood Av. S6: Shef 4H **105**
Wisewood La. S6: Shef 4H **105**
Wisewood Pl. S6: Shef 4H **105**
Wisewood Rd. S6: Shef 4H **105**
Wishing Well Grn. S26: Swal 1A **138**
Wiston Way S41: Has 3B **172**
Witham Cl. S41: Ches 2B **168**
Witham Ct. S40: Bramp 5D **166**
S75: H'ham 5F **15**
Withens Av. S6: Shef 2A **106**
Withens Ct. S75: Mapp 5H **7**
Witney St. S8: Shef 6F **119**
Wittsend Park Caravan Site
DN5: Ark 5D **24**
Wivelsfield Rd. DN4: Balb 5F **55**
Woburn Cl. DN4: Balb 1F **71**
Woburn Pl. S11: Shef 6G **131**
S75: Dod 4G **29**
Wolfe Cl. S40: Walt 1E **171**
Wolfe Dr. S6: Shef 5C **92**
Wolfe Rd. S6: Shef 5C **92**
Wollaton Av. S17: Bradw 5H **145**
Wollaton Cl. S71: Ath 6D **8**
Wollaton Dr. S17: Bradw 5H **145**
Wollaton Rd. S17: Bradw 6G **145**
Wolseley Rd. S8: Shef 1F **133**
Wolsey Av. DN2: Don 1F **57**
Wolverley Rd. S13: Shef 2B **136**
WOMBWELL **1G 47**
Wombwell Av. S63: Wath D 1F **65**
Wombwell Hillies Golf Course **3G 47**
Wombwell La. S70: Stair 3B **32**
S73: Womb 3B **32**
S74: Black H 2A **46**
Wombwell Race Circuit Go-Kart Track
. . . .**6H 33**
Wombwell Rd. S74: Hoyl 5B **46**
Wombwell Station (Rail) **2E 47**
Wood Acres S75: Barn 4H **15**
WOODALL **5H 153**
Woodall La. S26: Hart, Wooda 4H **153**
Woodall Rd. S21: Killa 5E **153**
S65: Roth 5B **98**
Woodall Rd. Sth. S65: Roth 5B **98**
WOODALL SERVICE AREA **5G 153**
Woodbank Ct. *S17: Dore 3H 145*
(off Ladies Spring Dr.)
Woodbank Cres. S8: Shef 3E **133**
Woodbank Rd. S6: Stann 3A **116**
Woodbourne Gdns. S75: Tank 1D **60**
Woodbourn Hill S9: Shef 1C **120**
Woodbourn Rd. S9: Shef 2C **120**
Woodbourn Road Stop (ST) **1C 120**
Woodbridge Ri. S40: Walt 2C **170**
Woodburn Ct. *S61: Roth 3C 96*
(off Alice Rd.)
Woodburn Dr. S35: Chap 3G **79**
Woodbury Cl. S9: Shef 5D **94**
Woodbury Rd. S9: Shef 5D **94**
Wood Cliffe S10: Shef 2C **130**
Wood Cl. S35: Chap 4H **79**
S42: W'orth 6E **171**
S62: Rawm 1F **83**
S65: Rav 2H **99**
Woodcock Cl. S61: Kimb P 6A **82**
Woodcock Pl. S2: Shef 3A **120**
Woodcock Rd. S74: Hoyl 1B **62**
Woodcock Way DN6: Adw S 1C **22**
Wood Cft. S61: Kimb P 1A **96**
Woodcroft Vw. S73: Hem 5F **47**
Woodcross Av. DN4: Cant 5D **58**
S72: Grim 1B **20**
Wood End S35: Gren 6D **78**
Wood End Av. S36: Cub 6C **176**
Woodend Cl. S6: Shef 5H **105**
Wood End Ct. S75: Dod 4H **29**
Woodend Dr. S6: Shef 5H **105**
Woodfarm Av. S6: Shef 6G **105**
Woodfarm Cl. S6: Shef 6F **105**
Woodfarm Dr. S6: Shef 6F **105**
Woodfarm Pl. S6: Shef 6F **105**
Woodfield Av. S64: Mexb 1G **67**
Woodfield Cl. S73: D'fld 4B **34**
Woodfield Rd. DN3: Arm 5F **43**
DN4: Balb 5H **55**
(not continuous)
S10: Shef 1A **118**
S63: Wath D 6C **48**
Wood Flds. S66: Braml 6B **100**
Woodfield Vs. S60: Roth 6F **97**
Woodfield Way DN4: Balb 2A **72**
(Atebanks Ct.)
DN4: Balb 1D **72**
(Bullrush Gro.)
Wood Fold S3: Shef 5F **107**
Woodfoot Rd. S60: Roth 3G **111**
Woodford Rd. DN3: Barn D 1H **27**
Woodford Way S43: Bar H 2G **163**
Woodgrove Rd. S9: Shef 6E **95**
S65: Roth 3B **98**
Woodhall Cl. S73: D'fld 4B **34**
Woodhall Flats S73: D'fld 4B **34**
Woodhall Ri. S64: Swint 4C **66**
Woodhall Rd. S73: D'fld 4B **34**
Woodhead Dr. S74: Black H 3A **46**
Woodhead La. S74: Hoyl 2B **46**
Woodhead M. S74: Black H 3A **46**
Woodhead Rd. S2: Shef 6F **119**
S35: Gren 4A **78**
Woodhead Vw. S74: Jum 4D **46**
Woodhead Way S10: Shef 5H **117**

WOOD HILL 4A **108**
Woodholm Pl. S11: Shef 3A **132**
Woodholm Rd. S11: Shef 3A **132**
WOODHOUSE 2C **136**
Woodhouse Av. S20: Beig 4G **137**
Woodhouse Cl. S62: Rawm 6E **65**
Woodhouse Ct.
S20: Beig 4F **137**
Woodhouse Cres. S20: Beig 4G **137**
Woodhouse Gdns. S13: Shef 2D **136**
Woodhouse Grn. S66: Thurc 5B **114**
(not continuous)
Wood Ho. La. DN11: Wad 1G **89**
Woodhouse La. S20: Beig 3F **137**
(not continuous)
S43: Barl 1F **165**
WF4: Wool 1H **7**
WOODHOUSE MILL 6E **123**
Woodhouse Rd. DN2: Don 4D **40**
S12: Shef 2E **135**
S74: Hoyl 1A **62**
Woodhouse Station (Rail) 1E **137**
Woodhouse Washlands Nature Reserve
. . . . 1G **137**
Woodkirk Cl. S36: Pen 5F **177**
Woodknot M. DN4: Balb 2A **72**
WOODLAITHES 3G **99**
Woodlaithes Rd. S66: Sunn 2H **99**
Woodland Av. S25: Nth A 3H **141**
Woodland Cl. S60: Cat 1D **122**
S66: Wick 1H **113**
Woodland Ct. S35: Chap 3C **78**
Woodland Dr. S12: Shef 6E **135**
S25: Nth A 3H **141**
S70: Barn 2A **30**
Woodland Gdns. S66: Malt 5C **102**
Woodland Gro. S63: Wath D 2G **65**
Woodland Pl. S17: Bradw 5G **145**
Woodland Ri. S75: Silk C 5B **28**
Woodland Rd. S8: Shef 5G **133**
S41: Old W 2G **161**
S63: Wath D 2G **65**
WOODLANDS 3C **22**
Woodlands S43: Brim 1C **168**
S60: Roth 1B **112**
Woodlands, The DN3: Arm 3F **43**
S10: Shef 4H **117**
Woodlands Av. S20: Beig 3G **137**
Woodlands Chase
S61: Kimb P 6A **82**
Woodlands Cl. S26: Swal 5C **124**
Woodlands Ct. S75: Wool G 3F **7**
Woodlands Cres. S64: Swint 4H **65**
WOODLANDS EAST 5D **22**
Woodlands Farm S60: Tree 2F **123**
Woodlands Gdns. DN3: Eden 1B **42**
Woodlands Rd. DN6: Woodl 4C **22**
S74: Hoyl 4B **46**
Woodlands Ter. DN12: New E 5C **70**
Woodlands Vw. DN6: Woodl 4B **22**
S72: Gt H 6F **21**
S73: Womb 4D **46**
S74: Hoyl 5B **46**
Woodlands Way DN12: Den M 3C **68**
Woodland Ter. S72: Grim 3C **20**
WOODLAND VIEW 6H **105**
Woodland Vw. S12: Shef 6E **135**
S17: Dore 3H **145**
S64: Mexb 2H **67**
S71: Barn 1A **32**
S72: Cud 3E **19**
S75: Silk C 5B **28**
Woodland Vw. Rd. S6: Shef 6H **105**
Woodland Vs. S72: Grim 2C **20**
S75: Pill 1D **60**
Woodland Wlk. S40: Ches 3A **166**
Woodland Way S65: Roth 5B **98**
Wood La. DN11: Wad 4F **71**
DN12: Old E 1C **88**
S6: Shef 6F **105**
S12: Shef 5C **134**
S60: Cat 5B **110**
S60: Roth 1E **111**
(not continuous)
S60: Tree 2F **123**
S66: Braml, Wick 1H **113**
S66: Bramp M 1H **125**
S66: Staint 1F **103**
Wood La. S71: Carl 4F **9**
(Ruscombe Pl.)
S71: Carl 5H **9**
(Woodroyd Av.)
S71: Stain 4D **8**
Wood La. Cl. S6: Shef 6F **105**
Woodlea Gdns. DN4: Cant 5C **58**
Woodlea Gro. DN3: Arm 4E **43**
Woodlea Way DN2: Don 3H **41**
Woodleigh Cl. S40: Ches 3A **166**
Woodleys Av. S62: Rawm 6F **65**
Woodman Dr. S64: Swint 4H **65**
Woodmere Dr. S41: Old W 2B **162**
Woodmoor St. S71: Carl 6A **10**
WOODNOOK 4A **166**
Wood Nook S35: Gren 1B **92**
Woodnook Cl. S42: Ash 4A **166**
Woodnook Gro. S21: Mar L 2H **157**
Woodnook La. S42: Old B 3A **166**
Woodnook Way S42: Ash 4A **166**
Wood Pk. Vw. S71: Ath 5E **9**
Woodpecker Cl. S26: Ast 2D **138**
Wood Rd. S6: Shef 4A **106**
S61: Kimb P 1A **96**
Woodrove Av. S13: Shef 6E **121**
Woodrove Cl. S13: Shef 1E **135**
WOOD ROYD 4G **175**
Woodroyd Av. S71: Carl 5H **9**
Woodroyd Cl. S71: Carl 5H **9**
Woodroyd Gdns.
S73: Womb 3D **46**
Wood Royd Rd. S36: Spink 3G **175**
WOOD SEATS 5C **78**
WOODSEATS 5E **133**
Woodseats S35: Gren 5C **78**
Woodseats Cl. S8: Shef 4D **132**
Woodseats Ho. Rd.
S8: Shef 6E **133**
Woodseats M. S8: Shef 4D **132**
Woodseats Rd. S8: Shef 4D **132**
WOODSETTS 4F **143**
Woodsetts Rd. S25: Nth A 2H **141**
S81: Gild 2G **143**
Woodsett Wlk. DN12: Con 4H **69**
WOODSIDE 6F **107**
Woodside Av. S21: Killa 3E **153**
S63: Wath D 6G **49**
Woodside Cl. S40: Ash 4C **166**
S66: Malt 5C **102**
Woodside Cotts. DN6: Woodl 5B **22**
Woodside Ct. DN6: Woodl 4B **22**
S66: Malt *6D* ***102***
(off Woodside Cl.)
S66: Wick 1H **113**
Woodside La. S3: Shef 6F **107**
(not continuous)
S35: Gren 1B **92**
Woodside Rd. DN5: Scawt 2F **39**
DN6: Woodl 4B **22**
Woodside Vw. S18: Holme 4A **154**
S63: Bolt D 2C **50**
Woodside Wlk. S61: Grea 5C **82**
Woodspring Ct. S4: Shef 4B **108**
Woodstock Dr. S41: Has 2B **172**
Woodstock Gdns. S75: Barn 4C **16**
Woodstock Ri. S41: Has 2B **172**
Woodstock Rd. DN4: Balb 5F **55**
S6: Lox 4F **105**
S7: Shef 2D **132**
S75: Barn 4C **16**
Wood St. DN1: Don 1C **56**
S6: Shef 6D **106**
S64: Mexb 1E **67**
S64: Swint 3D **66**
S65: Thry 6D **84**
S70: Barn 2D **30**
S72: Sth H 1H **11**
S73: Womb 2F **47**
Wood Syke S75: Dod 3H **29**
WOODTHORPE 4F **165**
Woodthorpe Cres. S13: Shef 6F **121**
Woodthorpe Est. S13: Shef 1F **135**
Woodthorpe Rd. S13: Shef 6F **121**
(not continuous)
S43: Woodt 4F **165**
S44: Shut 5H **165**
Woodvale Cl. S40: Bramp 2B **170**
S75: H'ham 4F **15**
Woodvale Flats S10: Shef 4A **118**
Woodvale Rd. S10: Shef 5A **118**
Wood Vw. DN3: Brant 3H **59**
DN12: Con 5H **69**
DN12: New E 3D **70**
S66: Malt 5C **102**
S70: Birdw 6E **45**
S74: Els 1D **62**
(not continuous)
Woodview DN5: Sprot 3C **54**
S21: Reni 4H **159**
Woodview Ho. *S21: Ecki* *1D* ***158***
(off West St.)
Wood Vw. La. S75: Barn 5H **15**
Woodview Rd. S6: Shef 5B **106**
Wood Vw. Ter. S11: Shef 6F **117**
Woodville Hall S10: Shef 5D **118**
Wood Wlk. S64: Mexb 6E **51**
S71: Roy 1H **9**
S73: Womb 4C **46**
S74: Hoyl 4B **46**
Woodway, The S66: Sunn 3G **99**
WOOD WILLOWS 3F **175**
Woofindin Av. S11: Shef 1F **131**
Woofindin Rd. S10: Shef 1E **131**
Wooldale Cl. S20: Mosb 6B **136**
Wooldale Cft. S20: Mosb 6B **136**
Wooldale Dr. S20: Mosb 6B **136**
Wooldale Gdns. S20: Mosb 6B **136**
Wooley Av. S73: Womb 2F **47**
Wooley Edge La. S75: Wool G 3F **7**
Woollen La. S6: Shef 1D **118**
Woolley Colliery Rd. S75: Dart 5F **7**
Woolley Edge La. WF4: Wool 1F **7**
WOOLLEY GRANGE 3F **7**
Woolley Ho. *DN1: Don* *3B* ***56***
(off Elsworth Cl.)
Woolley Rd. S36: Stoc 3C **174**
Woolley Wood Rd. S5: Shef 3B **94**
Wootton Ct. S65: Thry 6D **84**
Worcester Av. DN2: Don 3E **41**
Worcester Cl. S10: Shef 5C **116**
Worcester Dr. S10: Shef 5C **116**
Worcester Rd. S10: Shef 5B **116**
Wordsworth Av. DN4: Balb 6H **55**
S5: Shef 1D **106**
S25: Dinn 6B **128**
S36: Pen 5C **176**
Wordsworth Cl. S5: Shef 4D **92**
Wordsworth Ct. S5: Shef 1D **106**
S36: Pen 3D **176**
Wordsworth Cres. S5: Shef 6D **92**
Wordsworth Dr. DN5: Don 6G **39**
S5: Shef 6D **92**
S65: Roth 4H **97**
Wordsworth Pl. S18: Dron 5H **155**
Wordsworth Rd. S41: Ches 6G **161**
S63: Wath D 5D **48**
S71: Monk B 4G **17**
Work Bank La. S36: Pen, Thurl 3A **176**
WORKHOUSE GREEN 2A **130**
Workhouse La.
S3: Shef 1E **5** (2F **119**)
Worksop Rd. S9: Shef 6D **108**
S25: Sth A 4G **141**
S26: Ast, Swal 1C **138**
S43: Mas M 3E **165**
S81: Woods 4F **143**
S81: Work 4G **141**
Works Rd. S43: Hol 3G **163**
Worral Av. S60: Tree 1F **123**
Worral Cl. S70: Wors 4E **31**
Worral Ct. DN3: Eden 6D **26**
WORRALL 5E **91**
Worrall Dr. S35: Ough 5E **91**
Worrall Rd. S6: Ough, Shef 1F **105**
S35: High G 2D **78**
S35: Ough 6E **91**
Worry Goose La. S60: Whist 2B **112**
Worsborough Vw. S75: Pill 6C **44**
WORSBROUGH 6F **31**
WORSBROUGH BRIDGE 6G **31**
WORSBROUGH COMMON 3E **31**
Worsbrough Country Pk.
Doe La. 1D **44**
Park Rd. 1F **45**
WORSBROUGH DALE 5H **31**
Worsbrough Mill (Museum) 1E **45**

Worsbrough Rd. S70: Birdw, Wors 4E 45
S74: Black H 3A 46
WORSBROUGH VILLAGE 2F 45
Worsley Cl. S70: Barn 4G 31
Worthing Cres. DN12: Con 4G 69
Worthing Rd. S9: Shef 2B 120
Wortley Av. DN12: Con 4D 68
S64: Swint 3C 66
S73: Womb 5E 33
Wortley Ct. S35: High G 6C 60
S75: Dod 3F 29
Wortley Dr. S35: Ough 3F 91
Wortley M. S61: Thorpe H 4B 80
Wortley Rd. S35: High G 6B 60
S36: Spink 3H 175
S61: Kimb 2A 96
(not continuous)
Wortley St. S70: Barn 1D 30
Wortley Vw. S74: Black H 3A 46
Wostenholm Rd. S7: Shef 1E 133
Wragby Rd. S11: Shef 6H 117
Wragg Rd. S2: Shef 4B 120
Wreakes La. S18: Dron 1E 155
Wrelton Cl. S71: Roy 3G 9
Wren Bank S2: Shef 4B 120
Wren Gdns. S63: Wath D 4F 49
Wren Pk. Cl. S12: Ridg 2H 149
S40: Birdh 3G 171
Wrenpark Rd. S42: W'orth 6E 171
Wrens Way S70: Birdw 4E 45
Wright Cres. S73: Womb 2G 47
Wright's Hill S2: Shef 6E 119
Wrightson Av. DN4: Warm 1D 70
Wrightson Ter. DN5: Don 4A 40
Wright St. S25: Nth A 2H 141
Wroot Rd. DN9: Finn 3F 77
Wroxham Cl. S66: Braml 5B 100
Wroxham Dr. S66: Braml 5B 100
Wroxham Way DN5: Cus 5F 39
S66: Braml 4B 100
Wulfric Cl. S2: Shef 6C 120
Wulfric Pl. S2: Shef 6C 120
Wulfric Rd. S2: Shef 1C 134
S21: Ecki 1D 158
Wyatt Av. S11: Shef 2B 132
WYBOURN .3B 120

Wybourn Ho. Rd. S2: Shef 3B 120
Wybourn Ter. S2: Shef 3B 120
Wychwood Cl. DN4: Balb 2G 79
Wychwood Cft. S20: Sot 6H 137
Wychwood Glen S20: Sot 6H 137
Wychwood Gro. S20: Sot 6H 137
Wycombe St. S71: Lund 6B 18
Wyedale Ct. S41: Ches 1F 167
Wyedale Cft. S20: Beig 4G 137
Wyming Ho. S10: Shef 5A 116
(off Holyrood Av.)
Wyndthorpe Av. DN4: Bess 5B 58
Wyn Gro. S73: Bramp 4B 48
Wynmoor Cres. S73: Bramp 5B 48
Wynyard Rd. S6: Shef 3A 106
Wythburn Rd. S41: Ches 1D 166
Wyvern Gdns. S17: Dore 4F 145

Y

Yarborough Ter. DN5: Don 5A 40
Yardley Sq. S3: Shef 2A 4 (2D 118)
Yarmouth St. S9: Shef 3E 109
Yarncliff Cl. S40: Ches 3E 167
Yarwell Dr. S66: Malt 4H 101
Yates Cl. S66: Wick 1G 113
Yealand Cl. DN6: Adw S 2C 22
Yearling Chase S64: Swint 3A 66
Yeldersley Cl. S40: Ches 3C 166
Yeomans Rd. S6: Shef 1D 118
Yeomans Way S25: Sth A 4G 141
Yew Greave Cres. S5: Shef 3E 93
Yew La. S5: Shef 3D 92
Yews, The S65: Roth 3G 97
Yews Av. S70: Wors 5G 31
Yews Cl. S35: Ough 6E 91
Yews La. S70: Barn, Wors 5G 31
Yews Pl. S70: Barn 3G 31
Yew Tree Av. S25: Nth A 3A 142
Yew Tree Cl. S66: Thurc 5C 114
Yew Tree Cres. DN11: Ross 4D 74
Yew Tree Dr. S9: Tins 3A 110
S21: Killa 5B 152
S40: Bramp 2A 170

Yew Tree Rd. S66: Malt 4F 101
Yewtrees La. S36: Bolst 6D 174
Yoredale Av. S35: Chap 2E 79
York & Lancaster Regiment Mus. 3F 97
York Bldgs. DN12: New E 3C 70
(off Edlington La.)
York Gdns. DN4: Cant 3A 58
S63: Wath D 5E 49
York La. S66: Mort 5G 113
York M. S63: Thurn 2D 36
York Ri. S26: Swal 1B 138
York Rd. DN5: Don, Scawt 1E 39
S9: Shef 1F 121
S36: Stoc 3D 174
S65: Roth 3F 97
Yorkshire Way DN3: Arm 3G 43
Yorkshire Wildlife Pk. 5G 59
York Sq. S64: Mexb 2F 67
Yorkstone Ct. S2: Shef 4B 120
York St. DN11: New R 4B 74
S1: Shef 2E 5 (2F 119)
S41: Has 3B 172
S63: Thurn 1D 36
S64: Mexb 1E 67
S70: Barn 1D 30
S72: Cud 2D 18
S73: Womb 1G 47
S74: Hoyl 5B 46
WF9: Hems 1F 13
York Way DN12: Con 3H 69
Youlgreave Dr. S12: Shef 3G 135
Young St. DN1: Don 1C 56
S1: Shef 6C 4 (4E 119)
Yvonne Gro. S73: Womb 1E 47

Z

Zamor Cres. S66: Thurc 1B 126
Zenith Pk. S75: Barn 3H 15
Zetland Rd. DN2: Don 5E 41
S74: Els 1E 63
Zion Dr. S75: Mapp 5A 8
Zion La. S9: Shef 6C 108
Zion Pl. S9: Shef 6C 108
Zion Ter. S70: Stair 3B 32

The representation on the maps of a road, track or footpath is no evidence of the existence of a right of way.

The Grid on this map is the National Grid taken from Ordnance Survey® mapping with the permission of the Controller of Her Majesty's Stationery Office.

SAFETY CAMERA INFORMATION

PocketGPSWorld.com's CamerAlert is a self-contained speed and red light camera warning system for SatNavs and Android or Apple iOS smartphones/tablets. Visit www.cameralert.co.uk to download.

Safety camera locations are publicised by the Safer Roads Partnership which operates them in order to encourage drivers to comply with speed limits at these sites. It is the driver's absolute responsibility to be aware of and to adhere to speed limits at all times.

By showing this safety camera information it is the intention of Geographers' A-Z Map Company Ltd., to encourage safe driving and greater awareness of speed limits and vehicle speed. Data accurate at time of printing.

Printed and bound in the United Kingdom by Polestar Wheatons Ltd., Exeter.

HOSPITALS, HOSPICES and selected HEALTHCARE FACILITIES covered by this atlas.

N.B. Where it is not possible to name these facilities on the map,
the reference given is for the road in which they are situated.

ALPHA HOSPITAL, SHEFFIELD 6H **119**
  83 East Bank Road
  SHEFFIELD
  S2 3PX
  Tel: 0114 279 3350

ASHGATE HOSPICE 4A **166**
  Ashgate Road
  Ashgate
  CHESTERFIELD
  S42 7JD
  Tel: 01246 568801

BARNSLEY DISTRICT GENERAL HOSPITAL 5B **16**
  Gawber Road
  BARNSLEY
  S75 2EP
  Tel: 01226 730000

BARNSLEY HOSPICE 5H **15**
  104 Church Street
  Gawber
  BARNSLEY
  S75 2RL
  Tel: 01226 244244

BECTON CENTRE 5F **137**
  Sevenairs Road
  Beighton
  SHEFFIELD
  S20 1NZ
  Tel: 0114 3053106

BIRKDALE CLINIC 4G **97**
  2 Clifton Lane
  ROTHERHAM
  S65 2AJ
  Tel: 01709 828928

BLUEBELL WOOD CHILDREN'S HOSPICE 6F **127**
  Cramfit Road
  North Anston
  SHEFFIELD
  S25 4AJ
  Tel: 01909 517369

CHARLES CLIFFORD DENTAL HOSPITAL 3C **118**
  76 Wellesley Road
  SHEFFIELD
  S10 2SZ
  Tel: 0114 2717800

CHESTERFIELD ROYAL HOSPITAL 5D **168**
  Chesterfield Road
  Calow
  CHESTERFIELD
  S44 5BL
  Tel: 01246 277271

CHESWOLD PARK HOSPITAL 6H **39**
  Cheswold Lane
  DONCASTER
  DN5 8AR
  Tel: 01302 762862

CLAREMONT HOSPITAL 4E **117**
  401 Sandygate Road
  SHEFFIELD
  S10 5UB
  Tel: 0114 2630330

DONCASTER ROYAL INFIRMARY 5F **41**
  Thorne Road
  DONCASTER
  DN2 5LT
  Tel: 01302 366666

GRENOSIDE GRANGE HOSPITAL 3C **92**
  Salt Box Lane, Grenoside
  SHEFFIELD
  S35 8QS
  Tel: 0114 2718445

KENDRAY HOSPITAL 2H **31**
  Doncaster Road
  BARNSLEY
  S70 3RD
  Tel: 01226 730000

KERESFORTH CENTRE 2C **30**
  Keresforth Close
  BARNSLEY
  S70 6RS
  Tel: 01226 730000

MICHAEL CARLISLE CENTRE 1B **132**
  Osborne Road
  SHEFFIELD
  S11 9BF
  Tel: 0114 2718063

MONTAGU HOSPITAL 6F **51**
  Adwick Road
  MEXBOROUGH
  S64 0AZ
  Tel: 01709 585171

MOUNT VERNON HOSPITAL 4E **31**
  Mount Vernon Road
  BARNSLEY
  S70 4DP
  Tel: 01226 730000

NHS WALK-IN CENTRE (ROTHERHAM) 3E **97**
  Greasbrough Road
  ROTHERHAM
  S60 1RY
  Tel: 01709 423000

Hospitals, Hospices and selected Healthcare Facilities

NHS WALK-IN CENTRE (SHEFFIELD) 3C **4**
    Rockingham House
    Broad Lane
    SHEFFIELD
    S1 3PB
    Tel: 0114 271 2700

NORTHERN GENERAL HOSPITAL 3H **107**
    Herries Road
    SHEFFIELD
    S5 7AU
    Tel: 0114 2434343

PARK HILL PRIVATE HOSPITAL 5E **41**
    Thorne Road
    DONCASTER
    DN2 5TH
    Tel: 01302 730300

ROTHERHAM DISTRICT GENERAL HOSPITAL 2G **111**
    Moorgate Road
    ROTHERHAM
    S60 2UD
    Tel: 01709 820000

ROTHERHAM HOSPICE 5H **97**
    Broom Road
    ROTHERHAM
    S60 2SW
    Tel: 01709 308900

ROYAL HALLAMSHIRE HOSPITAL 4C **118**
    Glossop Road
    SHEFFIELD
    S10 2JF
    Tel: 0114 2711900

ST CATHERINE'S HOSPITAL .1A **72**
    Tickhill Road
    Balby
    DONCASTER
    DN4 8QN
    Tel: 01302 796000

ST JOHN'S HOSPICE 6H **55**
    Weston Road
    DONCASTER
    DN4 8JS
    Tel: 01302 796666

ST LUKE'S HOSPICE 5G **131**
    Little Common Lane
    SHEFFIELD
    S11 9NE
    Tel: 0114 2369911

THORNBURY BMI HOSPITAL .5H **117**
    312 Fulwood Road
    SHEFFIELD
    S10 3BR
    Tel: 0114 2661133

TICKHILL ROAD HOSPITAL 1A **72**
    Weston Road
    DONCASTER
    DN4 8QL
    Tel: 01302 796000

WALTON HOSPITAL 3F **171**
    Whitecotes Lane
    CHESTERFIELD
    S40 3HW
    Tel: 01246 515151

WATHWOOD HOSPITAL 3G **65**
    Gipsy Green Lane
    Wath-Upon-Dearne
    ROTHERHAM
    S63 7TQ
    Tel: 01709 870800

WESTON PARK HOSPITAL 3C **118**
    Whitham Road
    SHEFFIELD
    S10 2SJ
    Tel: 0114 2265000